Links Across Time and Place

A WORLD HISTORY

Ross E. Dunn, *Senior Author*

Dorothy Abrahamse   Gary Davison
Edward Farmer   James J. Garvey
Denny Schillings   David Victor

William H. McNeill, *Senior Consultant*

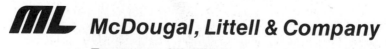
McDougal, Littell & Company

Evanston, Illinois

New York   Dallas   Sacramento   Columbia, SC

Authors

Ross E. Dunn, the author of books and articles on African, Islamic, and world history, is a Professor of History at San Diego State University. He was a founding member and first president of the World History Association.

Dorothy Abrahamse, Department Chairperson of History at California State University, Long Beach specializes in Byzantine History.

Edward L. Farmer is Chairperson of the East Asian Studies Department of the University of Minnesota at Minneapolis.

Gary Marvin Davison has taught history in the United States and Taiwan. He is a specialist in Chinese History.

Denny Schillings, author of articles and curriculum materials, teaches at Homewood-Flossmoor High School in Illinois.

James J. Garvey has taught history and other social sciences in Maine Township high schools in Illinois for over 15 years.

David Victor is the Social Studies Department Administrator and a teacher at Lake Park High School in Roselle, Illinois.

Consultants

The authors and publisher wish to thank the educators who critically reviewed this book in manuscript.

William H. McNeill, *Senior Consultant*, is a Professor of History at the University of Chicago and the author of over 20 books. He is perhaps best known for *The Rise of the West.*

Spiro Caro; Wingfield High School; Jackson, Mississippi.

Edward Korfhage; Atherton High School; Louisville, Kentucky.

Ralph Mann; Homestead High School; Cupertino, California.

Barbara Schuman; St. Cloud High School; St. Cloud, Florida.

Special Contributors

Christopher Müller-Wille, Cartographer; Cartographics Laboratory; Texas A&M University.

Nancy J. Obermeyer, Geographer.

Special thanks to Thomas F. Hadac, Gerald R. Levine, and John M. Pomatto of Lake Park High School in Roselle, Illinois for field testing the work in their classrooms.

Cover and Frontispiece
This astrolabe from 1532 was made by Georg Hartmann, vicar of Nuremberg and a student of astronomy. Now in the Musée de Cluny, Paris, it is composed of gilt brass. Thought to be of Hellenistic origin, the astrolabe can determine the time of day, the rising and setting of a star, and the appearance of the sky at any moment, past, present, or future. The Muslims perfected the device and introduced it into Spain. Astrolabes, widely used in Medieval Europe in the 10th and 11th centuries, were replaced by the sextant and other more accurate instruments. More than a thousand astrolabes are in museums throughout the world.

Acknowledgments: See page 822

ISBN 0-8123-5889-9

93 94 / 15 14 13 12 11 10 9 8 7 6

Dear Reader,

I begin teaching my world history classes with a question: What will you learn in a world history class that will be important in life? The study of world history should lead to knowledge, skills, and attitudes that you can use effectively in the real and ever-changing world of today.

KNOWLEDGE A Global Perspective. First, I would like you to discover that peoples and civilizations have always been interdependent, exchanging products, skills, and ideas. Exchanges began with early farmers, nomads, and merchants. These workers and traders linked farm villages to cities in fertile river valleys. Gradually this interacting zone grew, drawing both the civilized and barbarian cultures in Asia, Africa, and Europe into a vast exchange network. Later, the interacting zone expanded to include the peoples of the Western Hemisphere as well.

You live in a world that does not end at the edge of your neighborhood. You live in a vast interacting and interdependent global community. Knowledge about that community is a powerful tool for understanding the causes and effects of events in your world.

SKILLS Critical and Creative Thinking. Second, I hope world history will promote a way of thinking about people and change that you can use throughout your life. The stories of history teach us to understand people whose experiences are different from our own. The stories of history can be analyzed and applied to the present. The stories of history teach us to expect accelerating change. Studying world history encourages critical and creative thinking skills by considering and comparing alternative solutions.

ATTITUDES Valuing Diversity. Third, I hope world history will teach you to respect all the world's people. To be not only tolerant but curious about other peoples' ways of life is an important goal for your study of world history. In the context of world history, you will learn that the growth of democracy in the United States was a very special and unusual happening. Over the long course of world history, democracy and respect for human rights have been rare.

Above all, I hope you will realize that you are an important character in the drama of human history. You have a worthwhile part to play in the human adventure.

Ross E. Dunn

v

Links Across Time and Place

A WORLD HISTORY

McDougal, Littell's **Links Across Time and Place: A World History** vividly narrates the stories of world history. The text shows how communication and trade linked the people of the earliest civilizations to form an interacting community. Gradually, communication grew to include the peoples of Asia, Africa, and finally the Western Hemisphere.

Clear Organization

The text is made up of eight units, each of which is divided into four chapters. The units open with a picture that captures the spirit of the time. The four chapters of each unit are divided into sections based on a clear learning objective.

Exciting Stories of World History

Each chapter contains exciting stories of people. Their adventures in distant lands established links between peoples of different cultures. A Global Time Line at the beginning of each chapter provides a global perspective of history. The time line illustrates how the people of the world form an interacting human community.

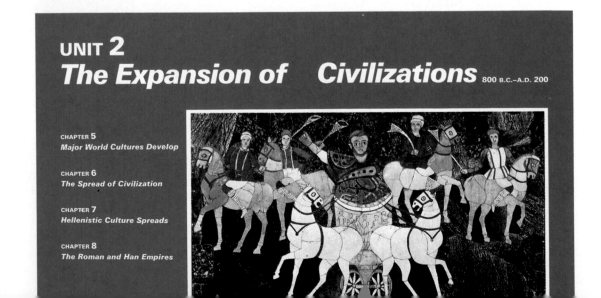

UNIT 2
The Expansion of Civilizations 800 B.C.–A.D. 200

CHAPTER **5**
Major World Cultures Develop

CHAPTER **6**
The Spread of Civilization

CHAPTER **7**
Hellenistic Culture Spreads

CHAPTER **8**
The Roman and Han Empires

Geography in History

A two-page feature in each chapter focuses on geography. Students learn map skills and basic geography concepts. The features highlight the relationship between geography and history. They illustrate the ways in which climate, vegetation, and geographical features influence people's lives and thus history.

Unique Focus Features

Each section offers you a special focus feature. Focus on People and Focus on Society help you understand people's cultures and customs. Focus on Sources contains firsthand accounts of events of the past. These features enhance your view of the world and your understanding of the cause-and-effect relationships in history.

Vocabulary Development

Difficult new words are defined in a special box at the beginning of each section. The pronunciation and origin of difficult words appear along with their definitions. A glossary at the end of the book lists these words and their definitions.

Study Questions for Review and Critical Thinking

Questions at the end of sections review vocabulary and the main ideas of the section. Chapter Reviews contain a summary and help you develop a sense of history, interpret events, and identify trends. Unit Reviews present a short summary and help you think critically.

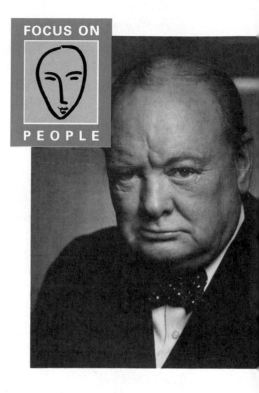

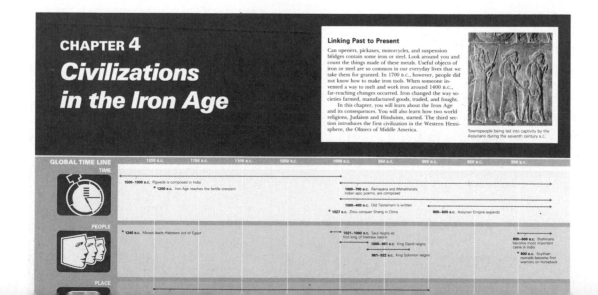

CHAPTER 4

Civilizations in the Iron Age

Linking Past to Present

Can openers, pickaxes, motorcycles, and suspension bridges contain some iron or steel. Look around you and count the things made of these metals. Useful objects of iron or steel are so common in our everyday lives that we take them for granted. In 1700 B.C., however, people did not know how to make iron tools. When someone invented a way to melt and work iron around 1400 B.C., far-reaching changes occurred. Iron changed the way societies farmed, manufactured goods, traded, and fought.

In this chapter, you will learn about the Iron Age and its consequences. You will also learn how two world religions, Judaism and Hinduism, started. The third section introduces the first civilization in the Western Hemisphere, the Olmecs of Middle America.

Townspeople being led into captivity by the Assyrians during the seventh century B.C.

GLOBAL TIME LINE

| TIME | 1200 B.C. | 1150 B.C. | 1100 B.C. | 1050 B.C. | 1000 B.C. | 950 B.C. | 900 B.C. | 850 B.C. | 800 B.C. |

1500–1000 B.C. *Rigveda* is composed in India
* 1200 B.C. Iron Age reaches the fertile crescent

1000–700 B.C. *Ramayana* and *Mahabharata*, Indian epic poems, are composed

1000–400 B.C. Old Testament is written

* 1027 B.C. Zhou conquer Shang in China   900–600 B.C. Assyrian Empire expands

PEOPLE

* 1240 B.C. Moses leads Hebrews out of Egypt

1021–1000 B.C. Saul reigns as first king of Hebrew nation

1000–961 B.C. King David reigns

961–922 B.C. King Solomon reigns

800–600 B.C. Brahmans become most important caste in India

* 800 B.C. Scythian nomads become first warriors on horseback

PLACE

Contents

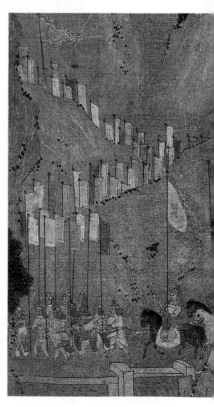

UNIT 6
Revolutions and Enlightenment 1650–1850   468

Focus Features

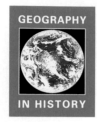

GEOGRAPHY IN HISTORY

Geography in History

FOCUS ON PEOPLE

Focus on People

Focus on Sources

Focus on Society

Maps

Charts and Graphs

Reference Section

UNIT 1
The Development

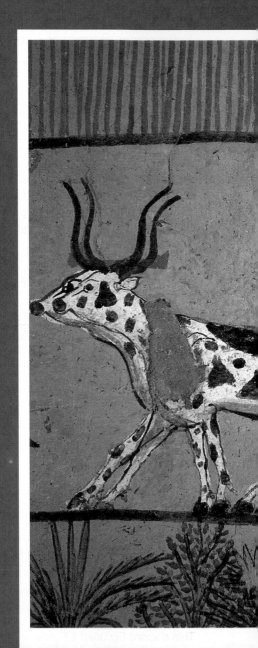

# of Civilization to 800 B.C.

This ancient Egyptian painting is from the tomb of Sennutem in Thebes.

CHAPTER 1
Civilizations Begin

GLOBAL TIME LINE

TIME

4 million–10,000 B.C. Old Stone Age

PEOPLE

4 million B.C. Earliest known hominids appear

4 million–4000 B.C. Hunting and gathering societies prevail

750,000 B.C. Humans migrate through Eurasia

250,000–70,000 B.C. Early evidence of thinking people (*homo sapiens*)

PLACE

3 million B.C. *East Africa;*[1] Earliest hominids appear

750,000–500,000 B.C. *Java and Peking;*[2] People use stone axes and fire

4,000,000 B.C.	1,000,000 B.C.	500,000 B.C.	100,000 B.C.

Linking Past to Present

The checker at the supermarket slides the cereal box over the electronic scanner, and the price flashes across the digital display. At the same time, a computer-generated voice announces, "Breakfast cereal, $2.87." In a short time, every item in a full cart is scanned.

The "electronics revolution" has transformed our lives. Thousands of amazing advances are evidence of the ever increasing pace of change in the modern world.

When humans gathered roots and hunted with spears in the grasslands of East Africa, change was slow. For over two million years, discoveries occurred thousands of years apart. This chapter introduces you to the broad geographical setting of world history and to the patterns of change that gradually led to civilization.

Stone Age humans combined art and technology in this axe.

80,000 B.C.	60,000 B.C.	40,000 B.C.	20,000 B.C.	1 B.C./A.D.

150,000–10,000 B.C. Last Ice Age; glaciers recede

10,000–8000 B.C. Middle Stone Age

8000–3000 B.C. New Stone Age

35,000 B.C. Cro-Magnons develop new tools

100,000–35,000 B.C. Neanderthals develop new customs

30,000 B.C. People migrate to Australia and the Americas across land bridges

13,000 B.C. Some people begin to farm

11,000 B.C. Some people domesticate animals

35,000 B.C. *Eurasia;*[3] Cro-Magnons use tools to make tools

150,000–70,000 B.C. *Eurasia;*[3] Neanderthals use scrapers, knives, and spears

20,000 B.C. *Europe;*[4] Cave paintings drawn

11,000 B.C. *Europe and Middle East;*[5] evidence of domesticated animals

6000 B.C. *Pan-Po;*[6] Millet is cultivated in northern China

1 *Geography Influences History*

OBJECTIVE: *To understand how geography influences historical development*

Environments Influence People

Today, as in the past, people need to understand and respond to their physical environment. This includes climate, soil, resources, and living things. People depend on the resources of the physical environment for shelter, food, and other basic needs.

Resources for life's basic necessities vary in different physical environments. The environment and resources of cold arctic regions differ greatly from those of desert, tropical, or mountainous environments. People have always responded very differently to their environments. Humans have succeeded partly because of their ability to adapt and change such contrasting environments. To understand the varied geographic settings for world history, imagine the world as an astronaut would see it from orbit in space.

An Astronaut's View. During the 1960s, humans made dramatic progress in space exploration. Circling the earth at 5 miles per second, astronauts gained a new perspective on the earth. After returning to earth, astronaut Scott Carpenter spoke in wonder of what he saw:

❝ The sight was overwhelming. There were cloud formations that any painter could be proud of. . . . I could look off for perhaps a thousand miles in any direction. . . . I could note rivers and lakes—and even a train on a track. ❞

VOCABULARY DEVELOPMENT

physical environment (FIH zih kuhl) *adj.* (ehn VY ruhn muhnt) *noun:* all the conditions, including the climate, soil, and resources, that influence living things and people.

arid (AR rihd) *adj.:* lacking water for things to grow. Excessively dry climate that supports farming only where rivers or underground water sources can be used for irrigation.

hemisphere (HEM uh sfihr) *noun:* a view of half of the globe. From the Greek word, *hemisphairion,* meaning half of a sphere.

Eastern Hemisphere (EEST uhrn) *adj.* (HEM uh sfihr) *noun:* the half of the globe that lies to the east of the Atlantic Ocean; consists of Eurasia, Africa, and Australia, their surrounding islands, and most of the Pacific Ocean.

Western Hemisphere (WEHST uhrn) *adj.* (HEM uh sfihr) *noun:* the half of the globe that lies chiefly to the west of the Atlantic Ocean and consists of North and South America and their surrounding islands, and the Atlantic Ocean.

Ice Age (IYS AYJ) *noun:* the most recent period, 70,000 to 12,000 years ago, in which the average temperature dropped 15 to 20 degrees *Fahrenheit,* and during which glaciers extended over all of present-day Canada and northern Europe.

glacier (GLAY zhur) *noun:* sheets of ice, often hundreds of feet high, that spread across the land.

geography (jee AH gruh fee) *noun:* the study of the earth's landforms, climates, resources, and life forms. From the Greek words *geo,* meaning earth, and *graphia,* meaning to write.

From space, astronauts see a huge globe covered with a patchwork of bright blues, varied greens, and rich browns and yellows. The globe appears to be mostly blue because oceans cover over 70 percent of the earth's surface. Astronauts see deserts or arid grasslands as rich brown and yellow regions. Arid lands are too dry to farm unless rivers or underground water can be used for irrigation. Astronauts also see lush greens where plants thrive in watered environments.

The Hemispheres. Astronauts, traveling hundreds of miles above the earth, see continents come into view and then disappear as they circle the globe. Only half of the earth, a hemisphere, is visible at any moment. An astronaut easily identifies the Eastern and Western hemispheres. The Eastern Hemisphere is made up of the huge land mass of Eurasia, the combined continents of Europe and Asia, and the continent of Africa. To the south and east of these land masses are hundreds of islands including Japan, Taiwan, the Philippines, and Indonesia. Southeast of these islands lies the continent of Australia.

The Western Hemisphere is made up of North and South America and the surrounding islands. North America touches the Arctic Ocean in the north. South America's tip extends toward the island continent of Antarctica.

Earth's Changing Environment

If astronauts had traveled in space 12,000 years ago, they would have seen different belts of blues, greens, yellows, and browns across the earth. Then, severe changes in climate modified environments which, in turn, influenced where the early history of people began. Scientists believe that in the last 2 million years, alternating cold and

When Apollo 17 astronaut Joe Allen moved through space in 1972, he saw the planet Earth as a sphere of patchwork colors against a black background.

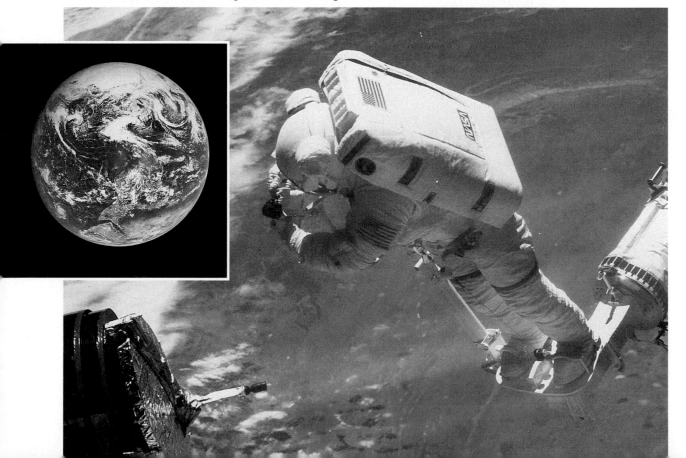

warm temperatures have influenced the earth's environments. Some 12,000 years ago, the earth was experiencing the last lengthy Ice Age. During that Ice Age, average temperatures around the world dropped 5 to 10 degrees Fahrenheit.

Ice mountains hundreds of feet high, called glaciers, extended thousands of miles beyond the polar regions. They covered the entire Great Lakes region in North America. Ice sheets buried present-day Scandinavia and parts of northern Eurasia, as well as most of Britain.

Land Bridges. Ice Age glaciers caused great changes in the earth's coastlines. Because much of the earth's water was frozen in ice sheets, the ocean levels dropped more than 300 feet. Ancient astronauts, therefore, would have seen connecting bridges of land between some areas now separated by water. The map, Early Human Migrations, on page 16, shows the land bridges.

A land bridge joined present-day Alaska and Asian Siberia. In the Ice Age, Japan was not a chain of islands off the coast of Asia. Instead, Japan was connected to mainland

Byam Martin Mountain is a modern glacier, similar to the ice mountains that shaped the earth's land masses during ancient Ice Ages.

Korea. Thousands of islands of present-day Southeast Asia were also part of the Asian mainland 12,000 years ago. Present-day Vietnam, China, the Philippines, and Borneo enclosed a huge lake. Today the Philippines and Borneo are islands. The islands of Great Britain and Ireland were once connected to western Europe. Plants, animals, and people used these land bridges to migrate to areas that have been separated by water ever since.

Early Migrations. In addition to the huge glaciers and the altered coastlines of the continents, ancient astronauts would have seen a different pattern of colors during an Ice Age space flight.

Temperatures, as well as changes in rainfall, altered the physical environment. As the Ice Age came to an end about 10,000 B.C., less rain watered many parts of the world. In some areas, the decreasing rainfall changed green grasslands to brown and yellow deserts. The Sahara, the vast desert of north Africa, was once rich in game, fish, and plants. As the Sahara and other areas dried up, some humans adopted ways more suitable to their changing environments; some migrated to different environments; and some did not survive the changes.

People Change Environments

People have lived throughout the earth for thousands of years. They have lived in all environments: in deserts, on plains, in swamplands, near lakes and oceans, next to rushing rivers, on polar ice caps, and on the tops of mountains.

People can adapt to many different environments when water resources are available. The amount of water greatly influenced how early groups of people lived. Permanent villages and the earliest cities developed in areas that received enough rainfall or had rivers or wells to supply water. In geographic terms, these areas are called well-watered zones.

Early artists left this record of a Stone Age cattle round-up. This cave painting was found in northern Africa's Tassili Mountains.

Arid zones, by contrast, led to quite different developments. In arid areas, people continually moved to new pastures. They lived by hunting and herding animals.

Physical environments influenced the ways of life developed by different people. Environmental conditions and resources affect food, shelter, and clothing. For instance, the people of southeast Asia eat rice because rice thrives in this area. Mediterranean people eat bread because wheat is easy to grow in that environment.

The environment has always played an important part in the events of people's lives. The environment, then, is the setting for the drama of the stories of history.

Geography, the study of the earth's environments and its life forms, provides an important source of information for understanding the stories of history. As you study the text, you will see how geography influences history. Remember that the physical environment influences your life every day.

SECTION 1 *Study Skills*

Developing Vocabulary Explain each of the following in a sentence: **1.** physical environment. **2.** arid. **3.** hemisphere. **4.** Eastern Hemisphere. **5.** Western Hemisphere. **6.** Ice Age. **7.** glacier. **8.** geography.

Reviewing Main Ideas 1. Explain why settlements first occurred in well-watered zones. **2.** Describe three ways people have reacted to changes in the physical environment.

Understanding Geography 1. Name the landmasses that make up the Eastern Hemisphere. **2.** What landmasses make up the Western Hemisphere? **3.** Describe the world environment 12,000 years ago. **4.** What areas were connected by land bridges 12,000 years ago?

Challenge 1. Describe three ways that the environment influences how people in the United States live today. **2.** Does the environment influence people as much today as it did 12,000 years ago? Explain.

The Drifting Continents

Earth is the stage on which the human drama, the story of history, is played. The sets of that stage mirror the tremendous variety of the earth's landmasses. Long before written history, however, natural events shaped the earth's geographical features.

The Formation of Continents

People are often surprised to learn that the diverse continents were once joined together to form one supercontinent. Evidence indicates that 200 million years ago only one giant continent existed.

The German naturalist, Alexander von Humboldt, theorized around 1800 that the continents and islands washed by the Atlantic Ocean had once been joined together. Much evidence supports this theory. First, upper South America and lower Africa look like they fit together like pieces of a jigsaw puzzle, as do upper Africa and the lower part of North America.

Second, the variety and location of plants also point to a single continent. Tropical plants once grew in Greenland. Scientists have found coal buried within rock beneath the ice of Antarctica. The presence of coal means that once Antarctica had a climate warm enough to support lush vegetation, which later compacted to form coal.

Third, paleontologists, scientists who study fossils, have also found evidence of a single supercontinent. Fossils are the remains of a living organism. These scientists discovered fossils of similar land animals in Asia, Europe, and North America. Scientists have also found fossils of the same age and type in both America and South Africa. The 200-million-year-old fossil remains of a reptile called Mesosaurus were found in only one part of South America and the part of Africa across from it. Mesosaurus could not swim well enough to cross an ocean.

Fourth, geologists, scientists who study rocks, found ancient rocks along the Brazilian coast identical to rocks in west Africa. Geologists also believe the mountains of the eastern United States were once part of the Caledonian mountain system that runs through Northern Ireland, Scotland, and Scandinavia.

Finally, the oldest rocks that make up the floor of the Atlantic Ocean, rocks about 200 million years old, are found close to the continents. The rocks near the middle of the Atlantic Ocean are much younger.

Continental Drift

In 1912, a German climate specialist, Alfred Wegener, introduced his theory of continental drift to explain how the continents developed. Wegener suggested the name Pangaea for the original supercontinent because the Greek word *pangaia* means all earth. He believed that Pangaea existed 200 million years ago. The center of the supercontinent was Africa. Few people took Wegener and his theory seriously.

About 200 million years ago, according to Wegener, Pangaea broke into two large landmasses called Laurasia and Gondwanaland. Later, other pieces split off and began to drift toward their present locations. Some of the continents moved in straight paths, while others drifted. Most of these lands drifted at a rate of about one inch a year.

Plate Tectonics

In the 1960s, United States scientists proposed a theory to explain continental drift. The continents rest on huge rigid plates.

Continents and Plates

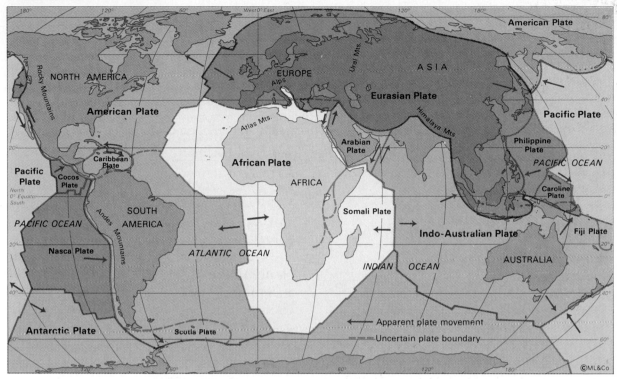

Map Skills **1.** Name the single land mass from which the continents originated. **2.** Name the northern and southern land masses into which Pangaea divided.

Each plate is about 30 to 60 miles thick. These plates float on a soft layer of magma or molten rock near the earth's core.

As new molten material bubbles up, it pushes the plates farther apart. Molten rock fills the gap between the plates and builds up the ocean floor. The molten rock also continues to push the continents apart. In some areas a moving plate bends downward forming ocean trenches. In other areas the plate crumbles and forms mountains.

In this way drifting plates shape the geographical features of the continents. For example, the highest mountains in the world, the Himalayas in southern Asia, resulted from the collision of two plates. As these plates, supporting India and Eurasia, collided the land they forced upward formed the towering Himalayas. The study of these changes in the earth's surface along its plates is called plate tectonics.

Earth scientists have used plate tectonics and the theory of continental drift to predict what the earth's surface will look like in 50 million years. They believe the California coast will separate from the mainland and drift toward Alaska. Australia, drifting north, will collide with Asia. Africa and South America will move farther apart.

Magma adds new islands to the oceans. Continents continue to drift. The map of the world slowly changes.

STUDY SKILLS Understanding Geography

1. What evidence suggests there was originally one supercontinent?
2. What causes the continents to drift?
3. Explain the theory of plate tectonics.
4. How can the shifting of plates cause mountains to develop?
5. Why do volcanoes and earthquakes occur in specific locations?

2 History Brings Slow Changes

OBJECTIVE: *To understand that human development underwent important changes from 5 million to 2 million B.C.*

Knowledge of Early History

The millions of years before people used written records is called prehistory. Our knowledge of prehistory depends on archaeology, the study of the life and activities of early humans and their ancestors. Archaeologists learn about early people by excavating and examining the remains of their campsites or settlements.

Archaeologists today rely on sophisticated scientific tools including the use of radioactive elements to advance our knowledge of prehistory. Scientists are able to assign dates to objects from the remote past.

To learn how early people lived, archaeologists use all existing evidence at an excavation. For instance, they examine, catalog, and date the bones of early people; the bones of animals found in the same area; and the weapons, tools, and other utensils located near the skeletal remains. Other techniques such as pollen analysis and aerial photography also help archaeologists unlock the secrets of the past. The archaeologist's search reveals surprising details of the ordinary lives of people who lived many thousands of years ago.

Measuring Time. Prehistory spans millions of years. For this reason, a chronology, or arrangement, of events in the order in which they occurred is a help. Students can better understand the causes and consequences of past events. The knowledge of when events occurred helps to determine

---

VOCABULARY DEVELOPMENT

archaeology (ahr kee AHL uh jee) *noun:* the scientific study of the life and activities of ancient peoples by excavation of past cities and relics.

chronology (kruh NAHL uh jee) *noun:* the arrangement of events in the order in which they occurred. From the Greek *chronikos,* meaning time.

B.C. *abbreviation:* the years before the birth of Christ, literally before Christ.

A.D. *abbreviation:* the years after the birth of Christ. From the Latin words, *anno Domini,* meaning in the year of the Lord.

age (AYJ) *noun:* a period of time characterized by a central feature, such as the age of dinosaurs.

Stone Age (STOHN AYJ) *noun:* time during which people made most of their tools from stone.

Old Stone Age (OHLD STOHN AYJ) *noun:* the time period from human beginnings to about 10,000 B.C., also called the Paleolithic Age from Greek words meaning ancient stone.

Middle Stone Age (MIHD uhl STOHN AYJ) *noun:* the time period from about 10,000 to about 8000 B.C., also called the Mesolithic Age.

New Stone Age (NOO STOHN AYJ) *noun:* the time period from about 8000 to about 4000 B.C., also called the Neolithic Age.

hominid (HAHM uh nihd) *noun:* Any of the family of recent humans, their immediate ancestors, and related forms. From the Latin word, *homo,* meaning man or person.

---

whether one event may have influenced another. It also helps to explain the relationship between developments.

Dates are sometimes arranged in a sequence called a time line. A time line places events in chronological order. The sequence and possible cause and effect relationships between events can then be seen. Time lines may use years, decades, centuries, or any other convenient division of time. Refer to the time line on pages 4-5. Decide what cause and effect relationships exist.

The study of history requires a knowledge of terms for measuring time. For example, Americans and Europeans commonly use the initials B.C. and A.D. as broad divisions of time. B.C. means before Christ. A.D., from the Latin term *anno Domini*, means in the year of the Lord. As time approaches the birth of Christ, the numbers marking the years decrease. For example, 100 B.C., or 100 years before Christ, came before 99 B.C.

Although current dates are not usually labeled A.D., the year 1986 could be written A.D. 1986. Sometimes, the initials B.P. are used to refer to time before the present.

Other terms often are used to refer to spans of time. A decade is a 10-year period, such as 1981 to 1990. A century refers to a 100-year period, such as 1901 to 2000. Certain periods, such as the Ice Age or the Stone Age, refer to periods of time so long that we call them ages.

The Stone Age. The terms years, decades, and centuries are not adequate to refer to the time from about 2 million B.C. to about 3500 B.C. now called the Stone Age. Because the Stone Age encompasses an enormous time span, the age is even further divided. The subdivisions of the Stone Age are based on advances in stone tools made by Stone Age people.

The period from the beginnings of human life to about 10,000 B.C. is called the Old Stone Age, or Paleolithic Age. The oldest stone tools used for chopping date

Richard Leakey's excavation site in South Africa shows the great care archaeologists take to preserve relics. Archaeologists' discoveries have revealed much of what we know about early humans.

back to this period. From about 10,000 B.C. to about 8000 B.C., people made finer stone tools, such as blades, arrowheads, and barbs. This period is called the Middle Stone Age, or Mesolithic Age. People who learned to polish stone tools, make pottery, and farm and raise animals lived in the New Stone Age. This period, also called the Neolithic Age, begins about 8000 B.C. and ends about 3500 B.C.

Human existence occupies only a small fraction of time when compared to the whole history of the earth. Thinking about the 4.5-billion-year history of the earth puts human history in perspective.

The Earth's 46th Birthday

Today scientists in many fields study the history of the earth and the beginnings of early people. Nigel Calder, who received his Master's degree in natural sciences from Cambridge University, has written about the history of the earth. He is currently a physicist at England's Mullard Research Laboratories. The following excerpt from his book, *The Restless Earth,* puts the history of people in perspective:

❝ Ten years is a long time in modern science and a long time in the life of a man. But to our planet ten years is almost nothing. It is scarcely long enough to add a tenth of an inch to the great thicknesses of rock that grow by the accumulation of mud on the bed of a shallow sea. It allows time for a few volcanoes to erupt and for the release of a multitude of earthquakes, but not for the continents to shift their ground by much more than a foot or so. . . .

Given time, hard rock flows like pitch. Given time, the continent where you sit could split open and allow a new ocean basin to form, as broad as the Atlantic. Or another continent might bear down upon your favorite beach and heave it above the snowline. Such events are commonplace in geological maps of the new style, but nothing of the kind will happen summarily in our lifetimes. The Earth takes about 100 million years, a megacentury, to engineer or dismantle a major ocean basin.

For instance, the Earth is so old that the huge continents of the planet have been amassed at an average rate of only ten acres a year. Had Atlas been paid a penny a day for holding the Earth for all this time, he could have bought up Fort Knox long ago.

Or we can depict Mother Earth as a lady of 46, if her 'years' are megacenturies, a million centuries. The first seven of those years are wholly lost to the biographer, but the deeds of her later childhood are to be seen in old rocks in Greenland and South Africa. Like the human memory, the surface of our planet distorts the record, emphasizing more recent events and letting the rest pass into vagueness—or at least into unimpressive joints in worn-down mountain chains.

Most of what we recognize on Earth, including all substantial animal life, is the product of the past six years of the lady's life. She flowered, literally, in her middle age. Her continents were quite bare of life until she was getting on for 42, and flowering plants did not appear until she was 45—just one year ago. At that time the great reptiles, including the dinosaurs, were her pets and the breakup of the last supercontinent was in progress.

The dinosaurs passed away eight months ago, and the upstart mammals replaced them. In the middle of last week, in Africa, some man-like apes turned into ape-like men and at the weekend Mother Earth began shivering with the latest series of ice ages. Just over four hours have elapsed since a new species calling itself *homo sapiens* started chasing the other animals, and in the last hour it has invented agriculture and settled down.

A quarter of an hour ago, Moses led his people to safety across a crack in the Earth's shell, and about five minutes later Jesus was preaching on a hill farther along the fault-line. Just one minute has passed, out of Mother Earth's 46 'years' since man began his industrial revolution, three human lifetimes ago. During that minute he has multiplied his numbers and his skills prodigiously and ransacked the planet for metal and fuel. ❞

Last weekend, according to Nigel Calder's time frame, the ancestors of humans were shivering along with Mother Earth in the latest series of ice ages. That last weekend spans a period from about 3 million B.C. to 500,000 B.C. ■

Human Beginnings

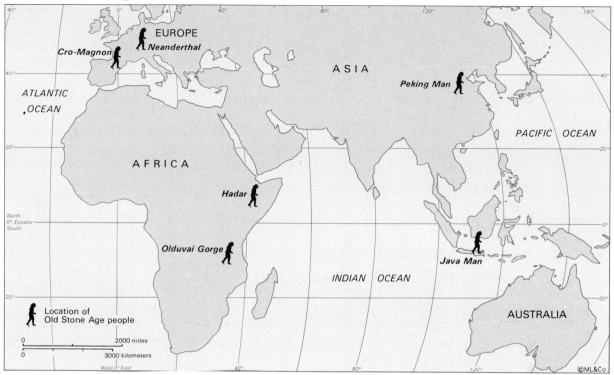

Map Skills **1.** On which continent is Olduvai Gorge located? **2.** On which continent did Neanderthal people live?

Human Beginnings

Archaeological evidence indicates that hominids, ancestors of present-day humans, have been on earth about 4 million years. Remains of early people and their tools show the slow development of the basic capabilities that distinguish humans from other animals. These unique characteristics include: (1) upright posture; (2) the use of language; (3) the ability to have and use ideas. These abilities could be realized only very gradually through the physical, social, and mental development of early hominids.

African Origins. The first hominids probably lived in the grasslands of Africa. In 1974, archaeologist Donald Johanson discovered the skeletal remains of a hominid, who lived 2.5 to 3.0 million years ago. Johanson and a fellow worker, Tom Gray, were exploring a small gully at an East African site called Hadar when they saw a bone sticking out of the ground. Johanson and Gray soon uncovered almost half of the skeletal remains of a female hominid. That night the archaeologists sat around their campfire talking of their discovery. They began referring to the ancient hominid as Lucy. She is one of the earliest hominids known today.

At another site in east Africa, the Olduvai (OHL duh way) Gorge, archaeologist Mary Leakey found campsites of hominids that lived nearly 2 million years ago. From the evidence she found at those campsites, Leakey was able to reconstruct many of the early hominids' habits. For instance, they protected themselves inside stone or brush circles, which may have been primitive shelters. They made and used stone chopping tools. The presence of bones indicates they ate a variety of large and small animals.

Early Accomplishments. Early hominids traveled in small groups of from 12 to 50 individuals. They hunted the large and small animals that roamed the grasslands, as well as gathered seeds and wild plants. By about 2 million years ago they had learned to make primitive chopping tools by chipping rocks to make a sharp cutting edge.

Early Stone Age hominids were hunters, but large animals also hunted the hominids. Hominids probably could not talk or think well, but they possessed some important skills. They knew how to change their environment by making primitive tools and how to protect themselves inside shelters. They established home base camps to which they brought food. They must have communicated in some way, since group hunting and sharing of food requires planning.

Advances during this period occurred infrequently. Primitive chopping tools like those found in Olduvai Gorge continued to be made for at least the next 1.5 million years. However, important advances can be seen when the 1.8-million-year-old remains found in Olduvai Gorge are compared with

the tools used by other hominids living some 500,000 to 750,000 years ago.

Hominid Advances. Some tropical African hominids left their homelands for reasons not clear to us and migrated to places throughout Eurasia. The human population increased and spread. Evidence of hominids living in England, Spain, France, China, and Indonesia dates from 750,000 to 500,000 years ago. Their routes from Africa can be seen on the map, Early Human Migrations. The remains of one skeleton, now called Java man, were found off the coast of southeast Asia on the island of Java. Another, called Peking man, was found in a cave near Peking, China. Locations of the remains of early people are shown on the map, Human Beginnings.

Hominids learned to use and control fire. Burned bones found in the Chinese cave show that some people cooked their food. Fire also allowed early hominids to keep warm in cold climates and to frighten away animals at night. Without the use of fire and clothes, early humans could not have sur-

Early Human Migrations

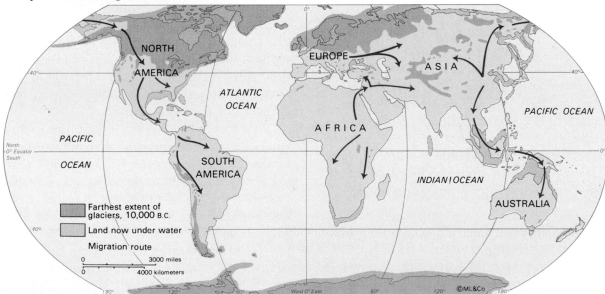

Map Skills Compare this map with the map, Human Beginnings, on page 15. Name three land areas that were covered with water when the climate warmed.

When hominids learned to make tools and use fire, they also began to live in small groups. Historians believe people then developed language to communicate.

vived outside tropical climates. Despite the controlled use of fire, the tools found at these sites were still very simple.

By 750,000 to 500,000 years ago, people had also developed new abilities. A campsite in France showed a regular pattern of migration. Roving hunters who used the campsite returned to it every spring. This practice indicates that these hominids planned where they would go at different seasons, and they knew directions and their territory very well.

These hominids sometimes built huts of saplings held up by posts. They used special areas inside the huts to make tools and prepare food. The hunters slept on animal skins and may have used a container shaped like a bowl.

In summary, between 4 million and 500,000 years ago, the ancestors of modern humans learned to make tools, adapt to drastic temperature changes, and use fire. These people also developed the ability to think and talk to one another during the last million years.

SECTION 2 *Study Skills*

Developing Vocabulary Explain the relationship between each group of words: **1.** chronology, age. **2.** archaeology, hominids. **3.** B.C., A.D., B.P. **4.** Stone Age, Old Stone Age, Middle Stone Age, New Stone Age.

Reviewing Main Ideas 1. Describe the way of life of early hominids. **2.** What advances were accomplished by early hominids? **3.** List and explain three characteristics that make people different from other animals. **4.** About when did the Stone Age begin and end?

Understanding Geography 1. Where were the earliest hominid remains found? **2.** By what routes did hominids migrate from East Africa to Eurasia? **3.** Using the map on page 15, locate the island of Java and the city of Peking. What is the land mass closest to each? What is the closest body of water?

Challenge What would a civilization from outer space learn of our culture if it investigated our cemeteries, junk yards, and, perhaps, our garbage dumps?

3 Civilizations Develop from Farming

OBJECTIVE: *To understand that the beginnings of agriculture had many causes and important consequences*

Emergence of Modern Humans

By about 100,000 B.C., hominids had acquired many new skills and more refined physical characteristics. Since then skeletal remains more closely resemble modern skeletons. For instance, brain sizes are similar. The best known example of these later hominids is a group of people called Neanderthals (nee AN duhr thawls). The name came from the Neanderthal Valley in Germany, where their remains were first found. Groups with patterns similar to those of the Neanderthal Valley people have been found throughout Eurasia.

The Neanderthal people made specialized tools, such as axes, scrapers, and knives, and developed the art of making sharp tools from thin flakes of stone. They made spears by attaching a stone tip to a wood shaft.

Evidence suggests that Neanderthals tried to explain and control their world, a giant step for early humans. First, they developed simple religious beliefs. Burial sites show that Neanderthals placed tools and food beside the body, the first sign of belief in an afterlife. One body had been covered with flowers when buried. Second, Neanderthals developed ceremonies that involved animals, especially huge bears. Neanderthals placed the skulls of these bears in chests and buried them in caves.

Neanderthals also cared for people in their group who could not work. Burial sites contain the remains of both old and handicapped people.

Cro-Magnons. Between 40,000 and 35,000 B.C., the Neanderthals disappeared. Why they disappeared is a mystery. Neanderthals may have died out as glaciers again advanced southward and covered much of Europe and North America. A new people may have introduced a disease that killed off the Neanderthal population. Finally, Neanderthals may simply have intermingled with other types of early humans.

VOCABULARY DEVELOPMENT

anthropologist (an thruh PAHL uh juhst) *noun*: a student who examines physical and cultural characteristics of people, their homes and customs, and their social relationships.

domesticate (duh MEHS tuh kayt) *verb*: to adapt a plant or animal for human use.

Middle America, *noun*: area of land that includes the southern half of Mexico, the Yucatan Peninsula, and the Central American land bridge.

agricultural revolution, *noun*: the far-reaching changes in human life resulting from the beginnings of farming. The consequences of the agricultural revolution include the creation of early civilizations.

artisans (AHR tih zuhns) *noun*: people skilled in producing a particular product.

zone of communication, *noun*: an area throughout which people exchange goods, ideas, and customs.

About 35,000 B.C., Cro-Magnon (kroh MAG nahn) people settled in southwest France. Their skeletal remains show a brain size similar to that of modern man.

With the Cro-Magnon people, the pace of change, as well as the population, increased. The tools they made were more sophisticated and specialized. They fashioned tools for making other tools and used materials other than stone.

Cro-Magnons invented sewing needles made of bone. They also used stones for striking sparks to make a fire. Because they lived during the very cold weather of the last Ice Age, these inventions were crucial to their survival.

The Cro-Magnons used many of their new tools for hunting. Hunters began to use spear throwers—long, straight sticks with a groove blocked by a hook at one end. Hunters placed the spear in the groove and used the stick to launch it like a rocket, thereby increasing their range, force, and accuracy. Spear throwing also gave hunters the advantage of remaining hidden. The numbers of animal skeletons found at campsites indicate that Cro-Magnon hunters were skillful and successful.

Cro-Magnons produced the most famous of all prehistoric remains, cave paintings. Deep in the caves in France and Spain are pictures of bison, mammoths, and other animals painted as many as 20,000 years ago. Historians do not know why the pictures were painted. Perhaps they were part of Cro-Magnon ceremonies for a successful hunt. They could be early symbols for counting or keeping track of time.

Hunting and Gathering. The ancestors of humans developed a way of life centered around hunting and gathering. In those societies, men were the hunters and women the gatherers.

Because women bore and nursed children, they probably stayed near camp and gathered seeds, nuts, and berries in nearby areas. Gathering, like hunting, was a highly

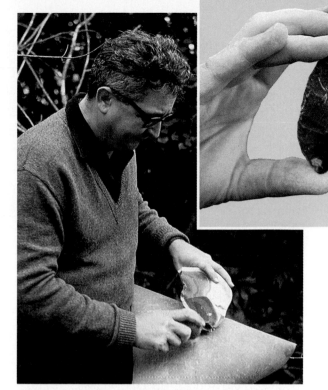

Cro-Magnon hunters relied on sophisticated flint tools that were carefully chipped and shaped. Here a professor crafts a Paleolithic tool.

specialized job. Gatherers developed special skills to learn what was safe to eat and where to find it. A result of this specialization of labor was that successful hunters and gatherers shared their food with all members of the group.

One cause for the success of hunting and gathering societies was their mobility. Bands of people could split up when their numbers grew too large. Hunters and gatherers were free to move in search of more food, often following animal migrations. Because of this mobility, hunters and gatherers did not have many possessions. They owned only what they could carry from place to place.

To understand the life of hunters and gatherers, anthropologists study existing hunting and gathering societies. Anthropologists are scientists who study groups of people to determine the patterns of their ways of life. Some hunting and gathering societies still exist. Many of the aboriginals of Australia, for example, continue to live by hunting and gathering.

David Soren—Archaeologist

Archaeologists study the material evidence of early people to discover how they lived. One of the most respected archaeologists today is David Soren. His interest in archaeology probably began at a movie theatre in New Jersey. David Soren was enthralled with a cycle of horror movies with archaeological themes. Movies about mummies and buried cities were his favorites.

Soren's Varied Background.
Soren has not always been an archaeologist. He has been a tap dancer, a performer on a children's television show, and a member of a rock group called The Sphinx.

Soren earned his Ph.D. in classics at Harvard and began his climb to the top of his field. By the age of 32, he chaired the department of art history and archaeology at the University of Missouri. At the same time, he lectured on horror movies at the university and authored two books on the subject, *Unreal Reality* and *The Rise and Fall of the Horror Film.*

David Soren's collection of French-language movie posters reflects classical and archaeological themes.

Discoveries in Cyprus.
Soren was excited when the director of antiquities on the island of Cyprus offered him a dig site at Kourion, on the southern coast. The ancient city of Kourion had been destroyed by an earthquake on July 21, A.D. 365.

Soren and a team of scientists from the University of Arizona began systematically unearthing the city. They were searching not for the remains and riches of royalty, but for the objects of common life. They studied everything from the bones of domestic animals to the remains of meals. With great care they reconstructed the lives of ordinary people. The team developed a new branch of archaeology called seismic archaeology. Archaeologists working in this specialty excavate places buried by earthquakes.

Camelia of Kourion.
In 1984, the team found the remains of a girl they named Camelia. Nearby they found a mule tethered to a stone trough. A forensic expert and a paleoosteologist determined Camelia's age, between 12 and 14, and the fact that she walked with a limp.

Soren reconstructed Camelia's last hours in these words:

❝ This isn't some dry, faraway historical event. We're talking about a thirteen-year-old girl, perhaps a cripple, and perhaps sick as well, awakened early in the morning by an awful shuddering of the earth. She goes out into the courtyard to try to calm her mule. And then, as she takes the mule's chain in her hand, the tremor suddenly grows much worse. A glass vessel full of money falls to the earth, and the column supporting the roof collapses. The bone hairpin in her hair falls to the ground, and she's buried alive by stone. **❞**

Today, at the age of 40, David Soren supports and encourages young archaeologists because he sees them as tomorrow's discoverers. ∎

An Agricultural Revolution

From the time of the Cro-Magnons, about 40,000 years ago, the human population began to increase dramatically. Eventually, this Stone Age population explosion led to a growing scarcity of food. New methods of obtaining food were invented, leading to one of the great breakthroughs of history—the agricultural revolution.

At first, hungry gatherers probably stumbled on a huge field of wild grass near their camp. As they walked, the grass seeds fell to the ground. A brave or curious gatherer tasted the seed and found it good. Later, a band of gatherers would return to the field carrying crude bags and a stick to tap the stalks and obtain precious seeds.

Gradually, the gatherers began to cut down the grasses and take the entire stalk back to camp, where they removed the seeds. Some seeds were used for food, but others were saved and put into the soil to grow, insuring a future food supply.

Early Farmers Domesticate Plants. Gatherers saved seeds from the largest and tastiest plants for replanting. Eventually, people learned how to select the strongest plants. Through generations of such selection, people domesticated plants.

As early farmers domesticated wheat and barley, they developed seeds that would not drop off when shaken by the wind. Over time, the domesticated plants became dependent on human care. Farmers had to sow the seeds or no new plants would grow. See Early Farming Communities, below.

The domestication of plants and animals, the invention of new tools, and the creation of a farm surplus caused an agricultural revolution One result of this revolution was a drastic change in human diet. The diets of hunters and gatherers consisted

Early Farming Communities

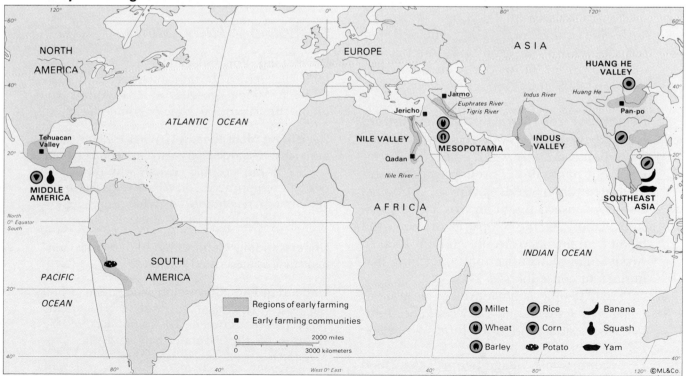

Map Skills   1. What river was important to the people of each of the early farming sites?
2. On which continents are early farming sites located?

Estimated World Population		
Chronology	Population (millions)	Growth (percent)
Old Stone Age	0.8	
Middle Stone Age	1.2	50
New Stone Age	50.0	4067
B.C./A.D.	300.0	500
1300 A.D.	400.0	33

of about 20 percent meat and 80 percent plants. The agricultural revolution reversed the proportions.

Farmers Domesticate Animals. Farmers also learned to domesticate animals. Dogs, descendants of wolves, were first used as hunting companions about 11,000 B.C. In southwest Asia, some people started to raise sheep and goats for food. Remains of domestic sheep have been found in ruins dating back to 9000 B.C.

Early agricultural life depended on domestic animals as an additional source of both energy and food. The combined patterns of improving grain and taming animals began in most parts of the world between 9000 and 5000 B.C.

Results of the Agricultural Revolution. Early farmers had to work harder to supply food than had hunters and gatherers. Farmers spent many hours preparing fields and caring for their crops. Even so, droughts, floods, or insects might destroy a whole season's labor. If the crops flourished, the farmer might harvest only enough food to survive. For all its uncertainty, farming had important consequences.

First, people could develop permanent villages or settlements. They could accumulate possessions and store food to provide for periods of scarcity.

Second, some village people performed specialized tasks other than farming. A few individuals specialized in making tools or

weaving cloth or producing clay pots. These specialists were called artisans.

Third, intervillage trade developed as a result of farm surpluses. Besides grain, traders also eventually exchanged cloth and pottery, from village to village.

Villages traded with one another, sometimes over long distances. An ever wider communicating zone developed among villages. A zone of communication is an area in which people regularly trade with one another and exchange skills, customs, ideas, or tools. Through trade, the ideas and products of the New Stone Age passed throughout expanding zones of communication.

The revolutionary changes of the New Stone Age formed a complex set of developments including the domestication of plants and animals, the invention of pottery, and the beginning of settled life in villages and towns. The stage was set for further changes in the way people lived, changes as revolutionary as those that occurred during the New Stone Age.

SECTION 3 *Study Skills*

Developing Vocabulary Define each of the following terms: **1.** anthropologist. **2.** domesticate. **3.** Middle America. **4.** agricultural revolution. **5.** artisans. **6.** zone of communication.

Reviewing Main Ideas **1.** What evidence suggests that Neanderthals tried to control their world? **2.** List possible reasons why the Neanderthals disappeared. **3.** What events led to the agricultural revolution? **4.** What were the results of the agricultural revolution?

Understanding Geography Where were animals first domesticated for food?

Understanding Chronology 1. About when did people first begin to farm? **2.** How many years passed between the beginnings of the cultures of the Neanderthals and the Cro-Magnons?

Challenge How are changes in jobs today changing other aspects of how people live?

CHAPTER 1 *Summary & Review*

Summarizing Main Ideas

The physical environment plays an important role in shaping how people live. The earth includes many different physical environments. Next to climate, the most important factor of an area's environment is the presence or absence of water.

Remains of hominids found in Africa date from 3 million B.C. Early hominids lived in small groups, hunted animals, gathered roots, seeds, and berries, and made simple tools. Around 100,000 B.C., hominids began making more sophisticated tools. By 35,000 B.C., Cro-Magnon people were making tools that made other tools. During that time period humans migrated over much of the earth.

Evidence of the earliest farming dates to about 13,000 B.C. Gradually some peoples domesticated plants and animals, adapted tools to suit their new way of life, and changed from hunters and gathers to farmers.

"Like I know you've been a hunter all your life, Dad— would it make you feel bad if I go into gathering?"

Questions for Critical Thinking

COMPREHENSION Interpreting Events

1. Explain the special knowledge necessary to develop a gathering and producing culture.
2. How did the Ice Age affect coastlines?
3. Explain why the change from hunting and gathering to farming is important for the development of civilization.

ANALYSIS Identifying Trends

1. How did the development of the use of fire affect how people lived?
2. Use examples to illustrate the gradual progress from hunting and gathering to domesticating plants and animals.

APPLICATION Comparing Past to Present

1. Use examples to illustrate how the physical environment of the earth has changed since 12,000 B.C.
2. Explain how the cartoon on this page links the past to the present.

SYNTHESIS Developing Map Skills

1. Describe the areas of the earth that were uninhabitable because of glacial expansion according to the map, Early Human Migrations, on page 16. What modern nations lie in these areas?
2. Using the map, Early Human Migrations, on page 16, locate the migration routes of early peoples to the Americas, Japan, and Australia. Describe the environmental conditions that determined these routes.

EVALUATION Weighing Consequences

1. In what ways did Cro-Magnon people differ from earlier Neanderthals?
2. Why did trade expand as a result of the development of farming?

CHALLENGE

1. Use examples to explain how the physical characteristics of a region influence history.
2. Use examples to explain how migration and trade affected the exchange of ideas.

CHAPTER 2
River Valley Civilizations

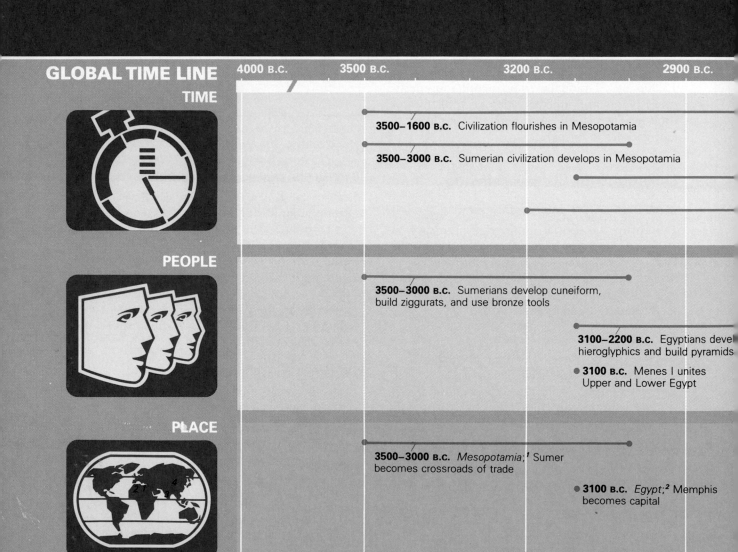

GLOBAL TIME LINE

	4000 B.C.	3500 B.C.	3200 B.C.	2900 B.C.

TIME

3500–1600 B.C. Civilization flourishes in Mesopotamia

3500–3000 B.C. Sumerian civilization develops in Mesopotamia

PEOPLE

3500–3000 B.C. Sumerians develop cuneiform, build ziggurats, and use bronze tools

3100–2200 B.C. Egyptians develop hieroglyphics and build pyramids

3100 B.C. Menes I unites Upper and Lower Egypt

PLACE

3500–3000 B.C. *Mesopotamia;*[1] Sumer becomes crossroads of trade

3100 B.C. *Egypt;*[2] Memphis becomes capital

Linking Past to Present

From the top of the Sears Tower, the tallest building in the world, a visitor has a breathtaking view of the sprawling city of Chicago. The panorama includes an array of skyscrapers, residential communities, factories, railyards, crowded traffic arteries, and shopping malls. Like other giant cities of the world, Chicago is a dynamic symbol of the modern urbanized, industrial world.

Early cities also served as centers of government, commerce, religious worship, and cultural life. The first cities were built in the river valleys between the Tigris and Euphrates rivers about 3000 B.C. Within 1,500 years, cities also appeared in river valleys in Egypt, India, and China.

As you read this chapter, think about the similarities and differences between past and present cities.

An aerial view of downtown Chicago.

2600 B.C.	2300 B.C.	2000 B.C.	1700 B.C.

2500–1720 B.C. Harappan civilization flourishes in Indus River valley

3100–2080 B.C. Period of Egyptian Old Kingdom

3200–1720 B.C. Egyptian civilization flourishes in Nile River valley

2500–1700 B.C. Harappans build planned cities and develop a writing system

1792 B.C. Hammurabi of Babylon conquers Mesopotamia

1760 B.C. Shang warriors conquer northern China; Chinese make bronze tools and vessels

2350 B.C. Sargon I of Akkad defeats Sumer and creates first Mesopotamian Empire

2500 B.C. *India;³* Harappans build cities in the Indus River valley

2100 B.C. *Egypt;²* Thebes becomes new capital

1960 B.C. *China;⁴* Panpo and nearby villages on Huang He become farming centers

1 Cultures and Civilizations

OBJECTIVE: *To understand how important social studies terms such as culture, society, and civilization promote an understanding of history*

Culture: A Society's Total Way of Life

As a social studies term, culture refers to a society's entire way of life including all the tools, customs, arts, and ideas that the group shares. In the United States today, for example, local government agencies, religious services, Christmas celebrations, and video recorders are all part of the complex American culture.

The cultures of early hominids included using stone tools, sharing food, and communicating in some way. Later, Cro-Magnon hunters and gatherers developed a culture that went beyond that of the early hominids. Cro-Magnons used finely made spear points and invented tools for making tools.

Groups of farmers developed even more complex cultures. In agrarian communities, farmers not only used simple stone tools, but they also invented sickles and hoes. These tools were more advanced than the hand axes used by some Stone Age hunters and gatherers.

A Shared Culture. The term society refers to the group of people who share a common culture. Members of a society develop and use tools, speak the same language, and share ideas. For example, the people of Jericho developed an agrarian society on the Palestinian hillsides near Jericho about 6000 B.C. They used stone sickles, built clay houses, and practiced religious ceremonies to help the barley crops grow.

VOCABULARY DEVELOPMENT

culture (KUHL chuhr) *noun:* all the tools, skills, customs, arts, and ideas of a particular group of people in a certain period of time, a way of life.

agrarian (uh GREHR ee uhn) *adj.:* **1.** relating to land; **2.** in general, referring to agriculture or farmers. From the Latin word, *ager,* meaning a field or the country.

society (suh SY uh tee) *noun:* a group of people who share the same culture. From the Latin word, *socius,* meaning companion.

civilization (SIV uh luh ZAY shun) *noun:* a society characterized by specialization of labor, organized leadership, a system of writing, common beliefs, and the existence of cities. From the Latin word, *civitas,* meaning city.

surplus (SUR pluhs) *noun:* an amount that remains after needs have been satisfied. From the Old French word *sur,* meaning above, and the Latin word, *plus,* meaning more.

Huang He (hwahng hee) *noun:* river in northern China where civilization developed; until recently, translated into English as Huang Ho.

pastoral (PAS tuh ruhl) *adj.:* a rural or nomadic way of life based on the herding of domesticated animals. From the Latin word, *pastor,* meaning a shepherd.

Civilizations: Why They Develop

As some farming cultures developed, they gradually learned to produce somewhat regular agricultural surpluses. That is, they grew more food than they needed to survive. Those surpluses led to the development of new tools, customs, and ideas. New inventions, in turn, prepared the way for a revolutionary change—the development of complex cultures, called civilizations.

Agricultural Surplus. Surplus food was the key to the growth of civilized societies. Civilization became possible only when survival no longer depended on having every adult person produce food. When ways were found to transport and store surplus food, individuals were freed to become craftspersons, traders, record keepers, religious leaders, government managers, or soldiers. Because people engaged in so many new activities and produced so many new products, cultural life became much more complex. Civilization was born.

Civilizations: Some Common Characteristics

Past, as well as present, civilizations share a number of distinct characteristics. These characteristics include (1) specialization of labor, (2) social classes, (3) cities, (4) government systems, (5) a system for writing, and (6) a world view.

Specialization of Labor. In hunting and gathering societies, everyone produced food. In civilized societies, food surplus freed some of the people from full-time food-producing activities. Some workers became skilled at making baskets and pottery in which to store grain. Other people became especially skillful at weaving cloth, keeping records, making metal tools or other objects such as jewelry, or trading goods. Gradually, skills and crafts improved because of specialization.

This Sumerian couple, carved in stone, reflects the skill and sense of beauty of that ancient civilization.

Social Classes. Some individuals, such as the priests and soldiers in early civilized societies, had more power and influence than others. Early civilizations respected priests for their influence with the gods and their explanations of events. Soldiers protected the people against those who would steal grain or invade villages and cities. Soldiers used special tools and weapons and had special influence in society. Soldiers and priests were members of special groups that enjoyed great prestige.

As civilizations developed, the specialized groups, such as priests, soldiers, craftspeople, and merchants, gained power and influence over other people. Gradually, social class divisions emerged to make up the structure of the society.

Importance of Cities. Cities became the centers of religious worship, government, and trade. Constructing grand buildings such as temples and palaces required public taxes, resources, and labor. These monuments did not serve the needs and interests of the common people. They were built to serve and glorify the people in the powerful classes.

Government Systems. The cities required government or a system of ruling. In all societies, leaders emerge to make and enforce rules. In early civilizations, for example, when farmers relied on the rituals of priests for a successful harvest, the priests often served also as rulers of the cities. They made laws, appointed tax collectors, and directed public projects. As the wealth of farmers and cities increased, soldiers were needed for protection. But the cost of their protection was more taxes.

In most early civilizations, certain cities became the ruling centers for surrounding areas. Priests ruled like kings. Government systems developed for collecting taxes, sending messages, and maintaining order.

System of Writing. Civilized societies developed a system of writing before 3000 B.C. Writing was used to communicate in government and commerce, to keep records, and to preserve the society's history, customs, and traditions.

A Common World View. The individuals in a civilization shared certain religious beliefs, moral values, and customs. These shared ideas and attitudes were the cultural glue that held society together. The particular values and preferences of a civilization are often revealed in its art or architecture. The art of Islamic civilization, for example, includes little sculpture. European civilization has both stone and wood sculptures.

Civilizations: Early Examples

The first sizable communities necessary for the development of civilization could arise only in a favorable geographic environment. The environment would have to have the water, soil, and climate required for agricultural surpluses. Fertile river valleys in the Eastern Hemisphere provided that favorable environment. The earliest river valley civilization developed between 4000 and 3000 B.C., in the fertile valley between the

Tigris and Euphrates rivers. This area was called Mesopotamia (MEHS uh puh TAY mee uh), and is in present-day Iraq.

As civilization in Mesopotamia was developing, other centers of civilization also arose in the Nile River valley of Egypt and in the Indus River valley of India. In northern China, along the Huang He River valley, civilization gradually emerged around 1600 B.C. In the Western Hemisphere, civilized society first developed around 1000 B.C. Mexico became the first center of civilization in the Americas. The map on the next page, Early Agricultural Cultures, shows the locations of the first civilizations.

Alternatives to Civilization. All societies possess a culture, but not all develop a civilization. While early civilizations were starting, many people continued to live by hunting and gathering. Others lived in small agricultural villages. They did not develop the major characteristics of civilization, such as cities, writing, or complex specialization of labor.

Another alternative to civilization was pastoralism. People developed a pastoral way of life based on raising domesticated animals. Herds of sheep and goats, for instance, ate grass. They could survive on land that was too dry for farming.

Before 3000 B.C., some people learned to raise herds of animals, moving them from one place to another in search of good pasture. These nomads also learned to drink the milk of animals and to shear sheep for their wool. The pastoral life of the nomads, therefore, became a specialized culture. The nomadic culture adapted well to the arid parts of Eurasia and Africa.

Around 3000 B.C., people who lived in the grasslands north of the Caucasus Mountains and around the Black Sea domesticated and herded the horse. At first the nomads raised horses for meat, not for riding. Their horses were small, no more than 4 feet tall, and not easy to tame. The people of the Eurasian grasslands also in-

Early Agricultural Cultures

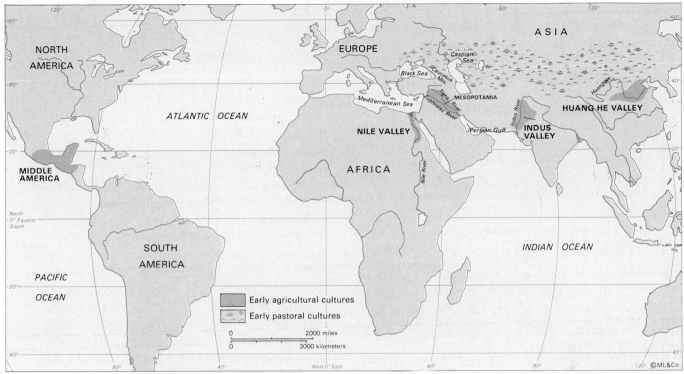

Map Skills 1. What environmental characteristics did early agricultural civilizations share?
2. Between which two rivers is Mesopotamia located?

vented horse-drawn carts to pull their goods. By 1750 B.C., these people were using light, two-wheeled carts.

About 3000 B.C., some people in Africa and the grasslands of Eurasia also developed herding. As much of northern Africa became the great desert, the Sahara, small farming communities on its fringes turned to herding to raise food. A group called the Cattle People painted rock art depicting their life tending herds of cattle.

Like farmers who lived in small villages, pastoral populations of herders and nomads also developed cultures with rich, complex traditions in religion, art, and social life. Herders and nomads, however, did not build cities or rely on specialized labor skills because they had to carry their possessions and customs with them as they searched for grazing land. In general, the pastoral culture of the nomads did not encourage the development of civilization.

SECTION 1 *Study Skills*

Developing Vocabulary Explain the relation among the following terms: **1.** culture, society, civilization. **2.** agrarian, surplus, pastoralism.

Reviewing Main Ideas 1. Briefly explain the six elements that characterize civilizations. **2.** Who controlled early societies?

Understanding Geography 1. Using the map on this page locate the four early river valley civilizations. Why would these locations attract ancient farmers? **2.** Which elements of ancient civilizations are most easily recognized? Explain your answer.

Understanding Chronology 1. Construct a time line including dates for the early hominid, Cro-Magnon, and agrarian cultures. **2.** Could pastoralists develop a civilization? Explain.

Challenge Why is developing a surplus still an important concern today?

Interpreting Maps

Geographers study why things are where they are. Maps are important in geography because they show location. Maps visually explain many aspects of the physical and human environment. This feature identifies various types of maps and explains how to read a map.

Types of Maps

One of the most common types of maps is the physical map, a map showing the location of one or more features of the earth's physical or natural environment. A basic physical map shows the location of the landforms called continents and water systems such as oceans, lakes, and rivers. A relief map is a physical map that shows the location of various landforms, including mountain ranges and valleys on the surface of the earth. Other features commonly shown on physical maps include weather, climate, vegetation, temperature, rainfall, bodies of water, and natural resources.

Geographers have also mapped many aspects of the environment made or shaped by humans. The most common map of the human environment is the political map. A political map shows the boundaries of cities, states, nations, and other political units. Other features of the human environment commonly shown on maps include roads, trade patterns, and population.

Many maps show features of both the physical and human environments. For example, see the map, Rainfall in Southwest Asia, on the following page. This map shows physical features such as rivers and seas. It also shows human environment features such as cities and countries.

Reading a Map

Most maps include clues to make them easy to read. Such clues include title, legend, scale, and direction. The title identifies the information shown and suggests the purpose of the map. The legend shows any symbols used in the map and explains what each represents. Common symbols in a legend include boundary lines, highways, railroads, mountains, and rivers.

The scale indicates the proportion—relation of size between the map and the real world. The scale can be shown in two ways. The first way is with a representative fraction (RF). The RF 1:38,016,000 means that one unit on the map equals 38,016,000 units of actual length. The bigger the number on the right side of the RF, the more the earth shown on the map has been reduced. The second way to show distance is with a line marked to show how many miles or kilo-

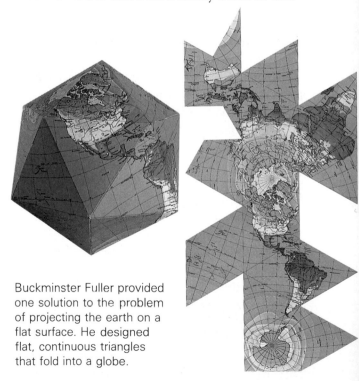

Buckminster Fuller provided one solution to the problem of projecting the earth on a flat surface. He designed flat, continuous triangles that fold into a globe.

Rainfall in Southwest Asia

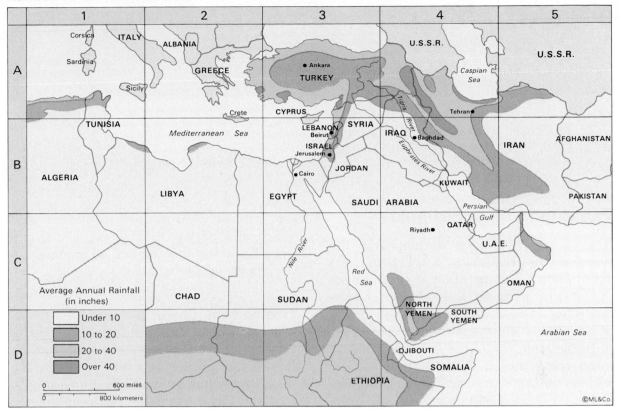

Map Skills **1.** What sea is west of Saudi Arabia? **2.** What gulf is east of Saudi Arabia? **3.** In what direction would you travel to reach Iraq from Saudi Arabia?

meters in the real world are equal to a given unit on the map.

The fourth part of a map is the direction symbol. Often, the map will include an arrow that points to the north on the map. If no direction is indicated, assume that north is at the top of the page.

Grid System. Some maps, such as road maps, are used specifically to find places. These maps often include an index. An index lists specific places on the map in alphabetical order, along with the coordinates for each place.

The coordinates refer to a grid system that uses numerals along the top and letters along the sides of the map to help locate places. A place is located across from the letter and below the numeral of its coordinates. For example, the coordinates for

Riyadh (ree YAHD), the capital of Saudi Arabia, are C-4. To find Riyadh, look across from C and below 4. Indexes, coordinates, and grid systems make unfamiliar places easier to find.

STUDY SKILLS Reading Maps

1. Name three features that can be mapped on a physical map.
2. What features can be shown on a map of the human environment?
3. List four clues that maps include to help readers interpret the maps.
4. According to the map on this page, what are the coordinates of Jerusalem?
5. What are the coordinates of the point where the Tigris and the Euphrates rivers meet?
6. Draw a map of a neighborhood. Include three types of physical information, three types of human environment information, and a grid.

2 Civilization Begins in Mesopotamia

OBJECTIVE: *To understand how civilization began, developed, and spread in Mesopotamia from about 5000 to 1750 B.C.*

Farming in Mesopotamia

The earliest civilization developed in the valley of the Tigris and Euphrates rivers about 3000 B.C. This valley is called Mesopotamia, meaning the land between the rivers. The map on page 33 shows ancient Mesopotamia. Mesopotamia is part of an arc of fertile land, the fertile crescent, that extends from the southeastern end of the Mediterranean Sea to the Persian Gulf. The fertile crescent is within a great arid zone that extends across Africa and Eurasia.

The earliest farming people in the fertile crescent grew wheat and barley on the hillsides of the Zagros Mountains, along the eastern edge of the fertile crescent. There the natural environment supported wild wheat and barley, wild sheep, goats, and pigs. Early farmers learned to domesticate the grain and the animals.

Environment Challenges Early Farmers.

The success of the hillside farmers led to increased food supplies and population. As population grew, however, some people were forced to leave the hillsides and move into the flood plain of the lower Tigris-Euphrates Valley. Little rain falls in the valley. To survive, farmers had to learn how to irrigate crops with river water. People had to cooperate to build and maintain irrigation canals and to defend the canals from

---

VOCABULARY DEVELOPMENT

irrigate *verb:* to supply arid land with water by means of ditches or channels. From the Latin word, *irrigare,* meaning to bring water.

silt (sihlt) *noun:* soil carried by flowing water such as rivers and deposited elsewhere.

polytheism (PAHL ih thee ihz uhm) *noun:* belief in, or worship of, many gods. From the Greek words *poly,* meaning many, and *theism,* meaning belief in a god or gods.

ziggurat (ZIHG oo raht) *noun:* a temple built of sun-dried bricks in the form of a terraced pyramid, in which each story is smaller than the one below it; a public building characteristic of Mesopotamian cities. From the Assyrian word, *ziggura-tu,* meaning height or pinnacle.

city-state *noun:* an independent state made up of a city and the surrounding territory.

dynasty (DY nuhs tee) *noun:* a family of rulers who pass power to their children or a relative over many years. From the Greek word, *dynasteia,* meaning lordship or rule.

secular (SEHK yuh luhr) *noun:* worldly rather than religious. From the Latin word, *saecularis,* meaning worldly or heathen.

cuneiform (kyoo NEE uh fawrm) *noun:* the Mesopotamian writing system, consisting of a series of wedge-shaped marks in soft clay made with the tip of a sharpened reed. From the Latin word, *cuneus,* meaning a wedge shape.

empire (EHM pyr) *noun:* a usually large state governing people of several different languages or nationalities. From the Latin word, *imperare,* meaning to command.

---

nomads or travelers in search of water. Together the farmers in the valley decided how to fairly distribute the supplies of water to irrigate their crops.

The farmers in the valley did not have the natural resources they were accustomed to using for constructing shelter. They found no stone for building homes or making tools. Without adequate rainfall, the valley did not produce trees the farmers could burn for fuel. Besides, the behavior of the Tigris and Euphrates rivers was never predictable. Sometimes in spring and early summer, the swollen rivers overflowed their banks, drowning crops and villages. In other years, the rivers did not rise high enough to irrigate all of the newly planted crops.

Bountiful Harvests. The major advantage farmers in Mesopotamia enjoyed was the rich soil made of silt deposited by the floods. This fertile soil was nourished by the waters of the Tigris and Euphrates when farmers coaxed water to flow into the plain by digging channels from the riverbanks. By building networks of canals and ditches farther and farther from the rivers, farmers could often grow abundant crops. They began to produce a surplus of food.

Early Sumer

The earliest cities of Mesopotamia were built in the southern stretch of the Tigris-Euphrates Valley, an area known as Sumer. The Sumerians developed religious beliefs and worshiped many gods. The worship of many gods, polytheism (PAHL ee thee ihz uhm), and the ability to organize city life, represent the development of abstract ideas. Sumerians believed that every city belonged to a god who lived in the temple and ruled the affairs of the city. Thus, the temple became the center of government as well as of religious activities.

Priests acted as intermediaries between the people and their gods. The farmers believed that the success of their crops de-

Ancient Mesopotamia, 3000–1750 B.C.

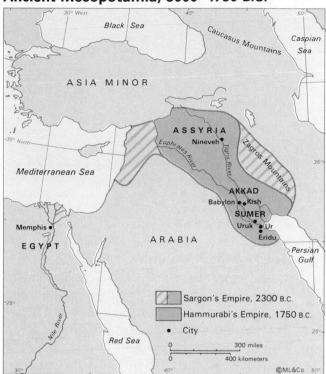

Map Skills **1.** Was Sargon's Empire larger or smaller than Hammurabi's Empire? **2.** In which direction would an Egyptian travel to reach Assyria?

pended on the blessing of these gods. Only the priests could ensure that the gods heard the farmers' prayers. The high priest, the leader of the priests, became the city's most powerful citizen.

The temple area was large, having courtyards, shrines, houses for the people who served the gods, and storerooms for supplies that belonged to the gods. Sumerians built tall, pyramid-shaped stepped towers called ziggurats (ZIHG oo rahts). These towers dedicated to the gods loomed over the Sumerian cities.

The temples were also economic centers for the rest of the city. Food and trade items were brought there to be given out to the population of the cities. Merchants traveled in and out of Sumerian cities. Pottery from Sumer has been found in northern Mesopotamia and along the eastern coast of the Arabian Peninsula.

Four-thousand years ago Mesopotamian artists honored Sargon I in this cast bronze bust. They also built the Ziggurat at Ur to worship the moon god Nanna.

The Bronze Revolution. About 3500 B.C., some people of southwest Asia learned to use a new metal that greatly expanded the possibilities for building civilization. The invention was bronze, a metal made by combining molten copper with tin that was mined in the northern hills of Mesopotamia. Molten bronze was poured into clay molds to make a variety of tools and weapons that were stronger than those made from either copper or tin alone.

By 3000 B.C., Sumerians were making bronze weapons and body armor that gave them a military advantage over their enemies. However, bronze objects, made by combining copper and tin, were expensive to produce. Farmers, therefore, continued to use stone tools long after kings and soldiers were fighting with bronze swords.

The term Bronze Age describes the period when societies were making bronze objects in addition to stone ones. This period varied from region to region throughout Eurasia and Africa. The Bronze Age extended from about 3500 to about 1000 B.C.

Kings Take Control. Around 3000 B.C., Mesopotamia underwent major cultural changes. Before that time, priests generally ruled Sumerian cities. These independent cities and their surrounding lands were city-states. During times of invasion or war, however, the priests and leaders of the com-

munity picked a military ruler. When the crisis ended, this warrior gave up authority.

After 3000 B.C., Sumerian cities seemed to be in crises. Local disputes arose over water rights and the use of irrigation works. Even worse, the rich cities were tempting targets for raids by pastoral tribes that inhabited the hills and plains around Mesopotamia. Gradually, Sumerian priests and people gave military leaders permanent control of standing armies. In time, some military leaders became kings, and passed their authority on to their heirs. As the leadership of the city was passed from heir to heir within a family, a dynasty developed. Dynasties ruled so many Sumerian city-states after 3000 B.C. that historians have called this time the Dynastic Period.

This change from priestly to dynastic rule was the result of a struggle between religious and secular, or worldly, leaders. The secular kings eventually won the struggle for power in all the Mesopotamian cities. They supervised the activities of farmers, merchants, and artisans, and collected taxes for their treasuries.

A Written Language. When archaeologists discovered the temples of the Sumerian city of Uruk in 1912, they found clay tablets that held the world's first writing. The writing system, called cuneiform (kyoo NEE uh fawrm), consisted of a series of cone-shaped marks made by the tip of a sharpened reed pressed into soft clay. The clay tablets were baked to preserve the writing.

Later cuneiform tablets contained references to two leaders—a chief administrator of a temple and the lord of the city—and an assembly of important people. Tablets written about 1800 B.C. contain long works of literature. *Enuma Elish* (eh NOO muh eh LEESH) is the Sumerian story of creation. *Gilgamesh* is a long tale containing an account of a flood like the biblical flood.

The Akkadian Empire

Farther north in the Tigris-Euphrates Valley was a region known as Akkad, meaning north, as Sumer meant south. Those northern people spoke a language different from that of Sumer, but they adopted many of Sumer's customs.

In Akkad, a great leader, Sargon, came to power. He became the first empire builder in history. According to legend, his mother put him in a reed basket in the Euphrates when he was a baby. A water-carrier rescued him and brought him up as a gardener. When Sargon grew up, he organized a mighty army and defeated the city-states of Sumer about 2350 B.C.

By taking control of both northern and southern Mesopotamia, Sargon created the first empire. This form of government unites several peoples, nations, or previously independent states under one ruler. At its height, about 2340 B.C., Sargon's empire extended from Nineveh in the north to the Persian Gulf in the south, and from Lebanon in the west to Iran in the east. The expansion of this empire also spread the ideas, customs, and art styles of Mesopotamia to neighboring regions beyond the Tigris-Euphrates Valley.

The Babylonian Empire

The empire started by Sargon lasted about 200 years. A long period of political disunity and instability followed. Then in 1792 B.C., Hammurabi, the second great empire builder, came to power. He began his career as king of the city of Babylon. Eventually, he united the cities of the Tigris-Euphrates Valley in a mighty empire.

Hammurabi called himself King of the Four Quarters of the World. He developed new ways of governing. He set up government outposts throughout his empire and appointed regional governors. The regional governors were responsible for repairing irrigation canals, caring for temple and royal lands, and gathering taxes.

Hammurabi also developed a legal system that proved to be his most enduring legacy. Hammurabi's Code consisted of legal directions to governors and local leaders.

Hammurabi's Code of Law

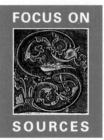

FOCUS ON SOURCES

As cities developed and trade expanded, life in the ancient world became more complex. Kings could not settle every conflict themselves. Instead, their decisions were recorded by scribes and used by government officials. Collections of the kings' decisions are known as law codes.

The most famous law code of the ancient world was the Code of Hammurabi, king of Babylon in the 1700s B.C. Many of the laws had their origins in earlier Sumerian and Akkadian practices. The purpose of Hammurabi's Code was to establish a uniform system of law throughout his kingdom.

Hammurabi's laws included those for crimes such as lying and stealing and for settling domestic and economic problems. The following selections from Hammurabi's Code indicate the duties and the harsh punishment that the code imposed.

Theft. **"** If a person has hidden a lost slave belonging to the king or any free subject of the king, that person shall be put to death.

If a person has broken into a house, that person shall be killed and buried there.

If a person has committed highway robbery and has been caught, that person shall be put to death.

If a fire breaks out in a house, and someone offers to help the owner put it out, but then steals from the house, that person shall be thrown into the fire.

Hardship. If a farmer owes interest on a debt, and the Weather God floods his field and destroys his crop or does not send enough water for the crop to grow, the farmer shall not pay interest for that year.

Family. If a man's wife spends their savings, wastes their money, and reduces her husband's wealth, the man may divorce her, send her away, and remarry.

If a son has struck his father, the son's hand shall be cut off.

Fees and Penalties of a Surgeon. If the surgeon caused the death of someone of high class, the surgeon's hand shall be cut off.

Obligations of a Builder. If a builder has constructed a house and the walls fall down, the builder shall repair the walls. If the house collapses, killing the owner, the builder shall be put to death. **"** ■

Evidence of Trade

Other evidence of the early influence and extent of trade includes recent findings of Mesopotamian trade goods outside Mesopotamia. For example, pottery made in the city of Uruk has been found west of Syria and east of Iran. In Sargon's time, ships sailed up the Persian Gulf to the riverbanks of his capital, bringing copper, beads, and ivory that may have come from India.

Civilization in Mesopotamia reached its peak of influence between 3500 and 1750 B.C. Mesopotamian ideas, customs, skills, and goods spread beyond the boundaries of Mesopotamia into the rest of southwest Asia.

This stele expressing Hammurabi's Code shows the god Shamash dictating laws to his servant, Hammurabi. It also shows how early people represented gods in human form.

SECTION 2 *Study Skills*

Developing Vocabulary Use each of the following terms in a sentence: **1.** irrigate. **2.** silt. **3.** polytheism. **4.** ziggurat. **5.** city-state. **6.** dynasty. **7.** secular. **8.** cuneiform. **9.** empire.

Reviewing Main Ideas **1.** In early Mesopotamia, what reduced the priests' power? **2.** What was the major result of Hammurabi's rule?

Understanding Geography **1.** Draw a map of the fertile crescent. Locate and label the following cities: Ur, Uruk, Akkad, Babylon. **2.** On the map on page 29, trace the route of a Mesopotamian trader to China. What present-day countries would the trader visit?

Understanding Chronology **1.** Study the time line on page 25. How many years passed between the rise of the Sumerian and the Egyptian civilizations? **2.** When was the Bronze Age?

Challenge Would Hammurabi's Code be acceptable to most people today? Explain.

3 Civilizations in Egypt, India, and China

OBJECTIVE: *To understand the variety of civilizations that developed in the Nile, Indus, and Huang He river valleys*

Egypt, the Nile River Valley

Shortly after the Sumerians began living in cities, civilization also started in Egypt. While Sumerian and Egyptian civilizations had much in common, they also differed greatly. The natural environment played a major role in shaping these differences.

The Nile River is the most important geographical feature of Egypt. The river flows north from the lakes of East Africa, tumbling down a series of six waterfalls called cataracts. The Nile then continues through the eastern Sahara Desert, through almost 600 miles of hot, dry land.

About 75 miles before reaching the Mediterranean Sea, the Nile fans out in a multitude of streams. See the map, Ancient Egypt, on page 38. Each of these streams makes its separate way to the sea, forming a delta. A delta is a triangular piece of land at a river's mouth, formed by silt deposits. The Nile Delta covers about 8,000 square miles,

an area larger than the present-day state of Connecticut in the United States.

Each year spring rains and melting mountain snow swelled the Nile River at its source in East Africa. Flowing north, this water reached Egypt, where it overflowed the river banks. In ancient times, the Nile flooded the Egyptian plain slowly and receded slowly, leaving behind wet lands and a thin layer of rich silt.

Natural Boundaries. Egyptians lived in the fertile areas within a few miles of the river on either bank. They called the southern area of the river Upper Egypt. They also lived in the northern delta region, called Lower Egypt. To the east and west of the river lay the barren wastes of the desert called Sahara. The six cataracts of the Nile and the vast swamp called the Sudd separated Egypt from regions of Africa to the south. This geographical environment tended to isolate Egypt from traders or invaders within the

---

VOCABULARY DEVELOPMENT

cataract (KAHT uh RAKT) *noun:* **1.** a large waterfall; **2.** steep rapids in a river. From the Greek word, *katarassein,* meaning to dash down.

delta (DEHL tuh) *noun:* a triangular piece of land formed by deposits of silt at a river's mouth. From the Greek word, *delta,* the fourth letter of their alphabet, which is a triangle when written.

pharaoh (FER oh) *noun:* the title of the rulers of ancient Egypt. From the Egyptian word, *pr-'o,* meaning great house.

hieroglyphics (HY uhr uh GLIHF ihks) *noun:* ancient Egyptian writings. From the Greek words *hieros,* meaning sacred, and *glyphein,* to carve.

bureaucracy (byoo RAH kruh see) *noun:* **1.** a group of officials who administer a government or other institution strictly according to established rules; **2.** governmental officialism or inflexible routine; **3.** a complex structure of administrative bureaus. From the French words *bureau,* meaning writing table or desk, and *cratie,* meaning power.

Ancient Egypt, 3000 B.C.

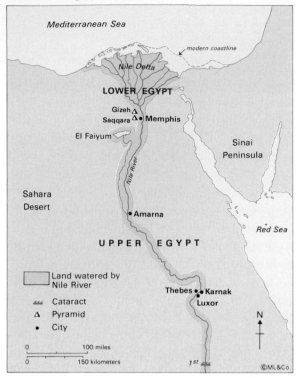

Map Skills **1.** Name the natural barriers that isolated Egypt. **2.** Near which city were most of the pyramids built? **3.** Which city is closest to the Nile delta?

interacting zone. Changes in Egypt came slowly because merchants and other strangers brought goods and new ideas to Egypt less often than to Mesopotamia.

Life in Ancient Egypt. The Egyptians did not realize that the regular flooding of the Nile was natural. They believed, like the Sumerians, that the river rose and fell according to the will of the gods. The Egyptians, however, thought of their gods as gentler and friendlier than did the Sumerians, perhaps because life in the Nile Valley was easier and more pleasant.

The Nile Valley was a fertile field in which Egyptian farmers grew wheat, barley, dates, and other fruits. Besides the fertile soil, the Egyptians had the advantage of other natural resources, limestone and granite. They used blocks of these stones to build monuments such as the great pyra-

mids and public buildings. Also, in the deserts beyond the valley, Egyptians mined copper and gold to make tools, weapons, jewelry, and other valuable items.

Union of Upper and Lower Egypt. About 3100 B.C., a strong leader named Menes (MEE neez) came to power in Upper Egypt. Known as the "smasher of skulls," he conquered the northern lower valley, thus uniting Upper and Lower Egypt. With the union of Upper and Lower Egypt, Menes started the first dynasty of kings, called pharaohs. Menes built a new capital city, Memphis, at the frontier between Upper and Lower Egypt.

The Egyptians did not consider their rulers as political leaders only. They believed the pharaohs were actually gods who ensured the prosperity of the country by making the Nile River flood each year.

The Pyramids. Egyptian pharaohs, because they were gods, were thought to enjoy life after death in another world. Egyptian pharaohs spent considerable time and resources in providing for their life after death. Egypt's greatest monuments, the pyramids, were the tombs in which the early pharaohs were buried.

The pyramids, built between 2660 and 2450 B.C., were the world's first great stone buildings. The largest, the Great Pyramid of Cheops (KEE ahps), soars over 40 stories high and covers more than 13 acres. Thousands of peasants built the pyramids from stone blocks that weighed as much as 30,000 pounds apiece. Each block was hauled up ramps and into position without the use of pulleys, cranes, or wheels.

Hieroglyphic Writing. A great achievement of the Egyptians was the invention of a writing system known as hieroglyphics (HY uhr uh GLIHF ihks), meaning "sacred carving." Hieroglyphics began as picture writing or pictographs.

The Egyptians also invented a paperlike material called papyrus (pah PY ruhs) on which to write. Papyrus was made from a reed plant. In time, the Egyptians developed a flowing script called hieratic writing. Hieratic writing resembled hieroglyphics in much the same way that cursive writing resembles printing.

Egypt's Early History

Historians divide Egyptian history into three periods: the Old, Middle, and New Kingdoms. During the Old Kingdom, 3100 to 2080 B.C., the Egyptian civilization developed, the pyramids were built, and the pharaohs' power was at its height. The pharaohs ruled through a strong bureaucracy of local government leaders and priests. Officials administered the government and performed religious ceremonies.

The Old Kingdom. Between 2250 and 2080 B.C., the government of the Old Kingdom collapsed. The authority of the pharaoh declined as various districts of Egypt claimed independence and their leaders ruled as pharaohs. After the decline of the Old Kingdom, Egyptians no longer believed that only the pharaoh and his servants could gain immortality. Anyone who could afford a tomb and a funeral could expect the same life after death as the ruler.

One Egyptian of the period described what was happening:

❝ The robber is now the possessor of riches . . . the ways are not guarded roads. Men sit in the bushes until the benighted traveler comes, to take away his burden and steal what is upon him. . . . Noble ladies are now gleaners [people who pick up leftover grain after harvesting] and nobles are in the workhouse. **❞**

The changes caused chaos throughout Egypt. Even the pyramids were robbed.

The Middle Kingdom. Order was restored in 2080 B.C., with the beginning of the Middle Kingdom. Then a new pharaoh came to

Detailed drawings from a Theban tomb tell about life in ancient Egypt. The top bands show scenes of ruling families. Below are pictures of ordinary life.

power who united the land once again and established a ruling dynasty. Pharaohs of the Middle Kingdom moved the Egyptian capital to Thebes, but never regained the personal power of the earlier rulers. They had to share revenue and power with the priests and local government officials.

These Theban pharaohs led their armies south along the Nile and eastward into Asia. As a result of conquests, Egyptian trade expanded into Syria, Mesopotamia, and Nubia, a kingdom located on Egypt's southern boundary. Archaeologists have discovered Mesopotamian pottery in Egypt and Egyptian goods in Sumer.

The New Kingdom. The Middle Kingdom ended in disorder about 1780 B.C. Eventually, other strong pharaohs ruled Egypt. The period from about 1550 to 1085 B.C. is called the New Kingdom. During this period, Akhenaton (AH keh NAH tuhn), a pharaoh famous for bringing about important social and religious changes, ruled Egypt.

Akhenaton, Pharaoh of Egypt

FOCUS ON PEOPLE

Amenhotep IV (ah muhn HOH tehp) ruled Egypt from 1379 to 1362 B.C. He inherited the throne at a time when Egypt was the richest and most powerful kingdom in the ancient world. At that time Egypt dominated Palestine, Syria, and Nubia.

Amenhotep IV broke with Egyptian tradition by changing his name, moving the capital, and worshiping a new god.

For centuries before Amenhotep, Egyptians had practiced polytheism, worshiping many gods, whom they represented in human or animal forms. The two most important Egyptian gods were Amen, the king of the gods, and Re, the sun god. Amen protected the capital, Thebes. Re was the special god of the Egyptian city of Heliopolis.

Amenhotep began to worship only one god, a new form of sun god, Aton, who had no human or animal form. Aton was depicted as a disk representing the blessings and life-giving power of the sun. To establish this new god, Amenhotep tried to erase all traces of Amen by having the god's name removed from the temples.

In his religious zeal, Amenhotep, whose name meant "Amen is satisfied," changed his name to Akhenaton, "he who serves the Aton." To further emphasize his break with traditional ways, Akhenaton abandoned the old capital of Thebes. He built a new capital dedicated to Aton at Amarna.

Because of his preoccupation with religion, the pharaoh paid little attention to the army and even less attention to ruling the empire. Trade declined sharply, and local officials began to pocket taxes earmarked for the pharaoh. Conquered lands rebelled against Egyptian rule. Egyptian priests did not like Akhenaton's reforms because they left the priests with little power. Finally, the priests and the army rebelled against the new religion.

When Akhenaton died, about 1358 B.C., his very young son-in-law, Tutankhaton, succeeded him. The priests forced him to change his name to the now-famous name Tutankhamen (TOOT ahngk AH muhn), King Tut, to show his devotion to Amen. He also was forced to abandon the capital at Amarna. The priests, firmly in control once again, sought to erase all evidence of Aton's existence. The new god's name was removed from buildings and records.

Historians have learned a great deal about ancient Egyptians by studying their works. Much less is known about a third civilization that emerged around 2550 B.C. in the Indus River valley, present-day Pakistan. Evidence of the first Indus Valley civilization was discovered only in the early 1920s, when archaeologists uncovered the ancient valley cities of Harappa and Mohenjo-Daro (moh HEHN joh-DAH roh). ■

The Indus River Valley

Like the Tigris, Euphrates, and Nile rivers, the Indus River flows from well-watered high country, down through arid land and finally to the sea. See the map, Indus Valley Civilization, on page 41. The Indus Valley, although not so isolated as the Nile, is also

Akhenaton and Nefertiti are shown with their young daughters in this relief. Unlike earlier pharoahs, Akhenaton showed open affection for his family.

Indus Valley Civilization, 2300 B.C.

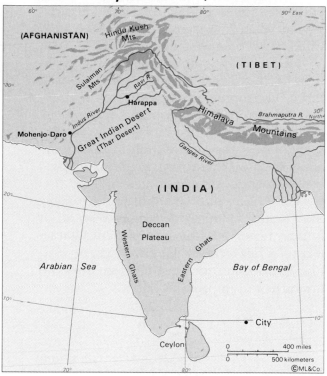

Map Skills **1.** Name three natural barriers that surround the Indus Valley. **2.** Are Harappa and Mohenjo-Daro located on a river? If so, what river?

protected by natural barriers. In the north, the towering Himalaya and Hindu Kush mountains separate India from the rest of Asia. The rugged Sulaiman Mountains form a barrier to the west, and the Great Indian Desert bars the east. These natural barriers, however, did not keep the Indus River valley civilization safe from invasions.

During the spring floods, the Indus River deposits a rich soil over a vast area. Inhabitants of the flood plain could plant their crops after the floods just as did the Egyptians. Unlike the Nile, the spring floods on the Indus are unpredictable.

The ancient Harappa civilization was centered about 200 miles from the Arabian Sea on the Ravi River, a tributary of the Indus. In addition to the cities of Harappa and Mohenjo-Daro, more than 70 other ancient towns and villages have been discovered in the area.

Harappan Civilization, 2500–1700 B.C.

Historians know far less about the Indus River valley civilization than about those of Egypt and Mesopotamia. To excavate more extensively, expensive engineering work would be needed to remove the ground water from the archaeological digs. In addition, scholars have been unable to decipher the ancient writing of the people who inhabited the cities.

Evidence indicates that both Harappa and Mohenjo-Daro were well-planned cities. They were laid out so that the streets met at right angles. Even the bricks were made in standardized sizes. Both cities included a walled central city where the rulers lived and where large granaries stored surplus crops and taxes. The inhabitants even used a standard system of weights.

Over the centuries, river floods have washed away much of Harappa. However, remains of Mohenjo-Daro show that the people there enjoyed indoor bathrooms, an extensive public drainage system, and a large ceremonial bathhouse. Ritual bathing, still an important part of the Indian religion, may have begun in Harappan times.

Like other early civilizations, the Harappan civilization was supported by agriculture. Harappans grew wheat and cotton and kept cattle, especially the water buffalo.

The Harappans traded with Mesopotamia. The route from Iran and Afghanistan to northwest India was a vital highway for the exchange of products and ideas between India and southwest Asia. Products from Harappan cities have been found in Sumer. Harappans used resources that came from as far away as southern India and Tibet.

About 1750 B.C., the Harappan cities underwent some kind of crisis. Streets were no longer laid out in careful patterns, and houses, pottery, and drainage deteriorated. Around 1700 B.C., Mohenjo-Daro seems to have been destroyed in a catastrophe. Excavators found homes abandoned, hoards of jewelry and tools, and skeletons of people caught in the debris. Nevertheless, enough of Harappan culture must have survived in the neighboring towns and villages to form the basis of later civilization.

The Huang He River Valley of China

About 1600 B.C., civilization began in the fourth great Eurasian river valley, the Huang He (Yellow River) in northern China. See the map, Early Chinese Civilization, on page 62. Chinese civilization began where the Huang He flows across a plain toward the East China Sea. Like the Indus River, the unpredictable spring floods of the Huang He caused considerable death and destruction, earning the river the name "China's Sorrow."

Despite difficulties, farmers in the Huang He Valley lived in villages and grew millet. Farmers here took advantage of the rich loess (lehs), soil blown in from central Asia. This soil, deposited during the Ice Age, was fertile, light, and easily worked with small hoes. Farm surpluses allowed the population in the region to increase. Because of this growth, the first cities developed about 1600 B.C. These cities became centers for trade with the pastoral people in the surrounding hills.

Life in Early China. The site of the earliest civilization in the Huang He Valley is Pan Po. For thousands of years, people in villages like Pan Po lived and died at the mercy of the Huang He.

Archaeologists have also found evidence of two villages near Pan Po. In excavating these villages, they discovered bronze ceremonial vessels, jewelry, and other articles. These articles found in graves are evidence of social classes, indicating that some inhabitants were rich and others poor.

In China, as in Mesopotamia, Egypt, and India, the development of civilization involved agriculture, specialization of labor, trade, and technological developments. By themselves, however, these changes do not explain why civilization occurred at these particular times and places. The most important factor was human ingenuity and willingness to experiment.

The river valleys presented great problems for the men and women who first lived there. The solutions they found to the problems of taming the rivers and making the valleys bloom were triumphs of the human spirit. The earliest cities built in the valleys were tributes to the intelligence, energy, and courage of many people.

The invention of civilization is probably the greatest change that occurred in all of human history. Its most important characteristic is not technology, buildings, or writing, but an attitude of mind that seeks to organize and improve society.

SECTION 3 *Study Skills*

Developing Vocabulary Explain the role of each of the following terms in Egyptian civilization: **1.** cataract. **2.** delta. **3.** pharaoh. **4.** hieroglyphics. **5.** bureaucracy.

Reviewing Main Ideas **1.** Why did the Egyptian people build pyramids? **2.** Describe three accomplishments of Harappan society. **3.** Explain how Akhenaton tried to change Egyptian society.

Understanding Geography **1.** How did the Nile River contribute to making the land of Egypt fertile? **2.** Compare the advantages and disadvantages of living in the Nile River valley and the Indus River valley. **3.** Where did Chinese civilization begin?

Understanding Chronology **1.** When were the ancient cities of Harappa and Mohenjo-Daro discovered? **2.** About when did the Chinese develop a civilization? **3.** Draw a time line showing about when each of the three river valley civilizations discussed in this section began.

Challenge Are civilizations today centered around water? Explain.

CHAPTER 2 *Summary & Review*

Summarizing Main Ideas

Culture refers to all the objects, ways of doing things, and ideas that members of a group have in common. A society is a group of people who share a common culture. Civilizations share a number of characteristics: an agricultural surplus, specialization of labor, social classes, government, cities, a written system of communication, and a common view of the world.

Not all societies develop civilizations. Agricultural and pastoral societies seldom develop all of the characteristics of a civilization.

The earliest civilizations grew up in four river valleys of Eurasia: the Tigris and Euphrates in Mesopotamia, the Nile in Egypt, the Indus in India, and the Huang He in China. These civilizations traded a variety of goods and ideas.

River Valley Civilizations

Sumer (Mesopotamia), 4000–1792 B.C.
1. Established first city-states
2. Developed cuneiform writing
3. Built ziggurats and irrigation canals
4. Developed bronze weapons and armor

Babylonia (Mesopotamia), 1792–1500 B.C.
1. Invaded Sumer
2. Conquered city-states of Mesopotamia
3. Developed a written code of laws

Egypt (Nile River valley), 3200–2200 B.C.
1. Developed hieroglyphic writing
2. Devised a solar calendar
3. Established a government bureaucracy

India (Indus River valley), 2500–1400 B.C.
1. Built well-planned cities
2. Used standardized weights and measures
3. Developed a written language

China (Huang He River valley), 2000–1100 B.C.
1. Lived in agricultural villages
2. Used bronze vessels
3. Developed numbers and other symbols
4. Grew millet and raised silkworms

Questions for Critical Thinking

COMPREHENSION Interpreting Events
1. How were the physical environments of the first river valley civilizations similar?
2. Explain why the growth of civilization made law codes necessary.

ANALYSIS Identifying Trends
1. Explain how environment affected cultural development in one of the four river valley civilizations of Eurasia.
2. Explain why some societies developed into civilizations but others did not.

APPLICATION Comparing Past to Present
1. How are American cities similar to cities of early civilizations?
2. Compare the role of government in ancient and modern societies.

SYNTHESIS Developing Research Skills
1. Look up the Code of Hammurabi. Describe five areas, other than those in the textbook, covered by the code.
2. Beginning in 1977, an exhibit of artifacts from the tomb of Tutakhamen was shown at several museums. Read newspaper and magazine accounts of the public reaction to the museum tour. Write a two-page report describing the reaction.

EVALUATION Weighing Consequences
1. Egypt was more isolated than other civilizations in southwest Asia. How did this affect its civilization?
2. Compare the effect of trade on ancient and modern cultures.

CHALLENGE
1. As civilizations developed, people increasingly depended on government to regulate society. Explain why this may have occurred.
2. For each civilization in the chart on this page, indicate which accomplishments were influenced by developments in other civilizations.

CHAPTER 3
Civilizations in the Age of the Chariot

GLOBAL TIME LINE

	1700 B.C.	1650 B.C.	1600 B.C.	1550 B.C.

TIME

2080–1550 B.C. Period of Egyptian Middle Kingdom

1700–1200 B.C. Bronze Age invaders raid river valley civilizations

1700 B.C. Two-wheeled chariots and bronze weapons are invented

PEOPLE

1700 B.C. Hittites move into Anatolia (Turkey)

1700 B.C. Kassites invade Babylon

1700 B.C. Aryans attack Harappans

1640–1570 B.C. Hyksos conquer and rule Lower Egypt

1600 B.C. Mycenaeans settle Balkan Peninsula

PLACE

1700 B.C. *Middle East;*[1] Babylon becomes capital of an empire

1600–1400 B.C. *Crete;*[2] Minoan civilization reaches height

Linking Past to Present

The Tuttle family of Dover, New Hampshire, has occupied the same farm since 1635. This achievement seems remarkable in the United States where families often leave their homes for employment in a new place.

The migration of people has occurred since human beginnings. The population of the United States includes migrants from around the world. In ancient times, groups of people migrated to engage in trade, to find more fertile land, or to conquer their neighbors.

In this chapter, you will learn about the adventures of the chariot-riding warriors as they crossed the grasslands of central Asia. You will also learn about the people of the Mediterranean region who sought new ports for trade and new lands to colonize.

Charioteer Tutankhamun defeats his Syrian enemies in this painting found in his tomb.

00 B.C.	1450 B.C.	1400 B.C.	1350 B.C.	1300 B.C.	1250 B.C.	1200 B.C.

1550–1085 B.C. Period of Egyptian New Kingdom

1500 B.C. Hittites plunder northern Mesopotamia

1500 B.C. Assyrians conquer Akkad

1300 B.C. Hittites invade northern Syria

1300 B.C. Zhou and Shang war in northern China

1500–1200 B.C. *Egypt;*[3] Egyptian culture flourishes

1500–1200 B.C. *Mediterranean;*[4] Phoenicia conducts trade in Mediterranean basin

1400 B.C. *India;*[5] Harappan civilization is destroyed

45

1 Invaders from the Eurasian Steppes

OBJECTIVE: *To understand that the early people of the steppes of Asia had a lasting impact on world history*

The Steppe Environment

The world's largest arid zone extends across northern Africa from the Atlantic Ocean, through Eurasia, to the Pacific Ocean. This vast arid zone includes many deserts, such as the Sahara in Africa, the Arabian in western Asia, and the Gobi in east central Asia.

The arid zone also includes steppes, or dry grasslands. In Eurasia, the steppes stretch from present-day Hungary through the southern Soviet Union, to the northern edge of China.

The Steppe People

The nomadic people who invaded and conquered the river valley civilizations be-

tween 1700 and 1200 B.C. spoke Indo-European languages. These Indo-European languages were the ancestors of many of the modern languages of Europe, the Middle East, and south Asia. English, Spanish, Persian, and Hindi are all languages of the Indo-European family.

Distribution of Languages. Languages are grouped into families. The languages in each family are related to one another. The Indo-European and Afro-Asiatic languages are major families. The Semitic languages of the Middle East, such as Arabic and Hebrew, belong to the Afro-Asiatic family. In the Bronze Age the Akkadians and the Babylonians spoke Afro-Asiatic languages.

The Indo-European peoples originated in the region north of the Black and Caspian seas. As their population expanded, they carried their languages in all directions. Slavic-speaking people migrated to the north and west. Germanic-, Celtic-, and Italic-speaking people traveled even further west. Greek- and Iranian-speaking people moved to the south. All these people spoke languages of the Indo-European family.

Another Indo-European group developed farther to the east when the Aryans invaded the Indus Valley. The language they spoke evolved into the Indic group of languages. Gradually, Aryan Sanskrit became the classical language of India.

Common root words show relationships among language families. For example, in

---

VOCABULARY DEVELOPMENT

steppes (stehps) *noun:* dry grasslands of central Eurasia; called prairie in North America and pampas in Argentina. From the Russian word, *step,* meaning lowland.

Indo-European peoples *noun:* people who once lived in the grasslands north of the Black and Caspian seas and migrated in successive waves into Europe, India, and southwest Asia.

tribe (tryb) *noun:* a group of people whose members believe they are descended from a common ancestor.

barbarian (bar BER e an) *noun:* one of a group of people whose culture is regarded as inferior or savage. From the Latin word, *barbaricus,* meaning foreign.

Migrations and Invasions, 1700–1200 B.C.

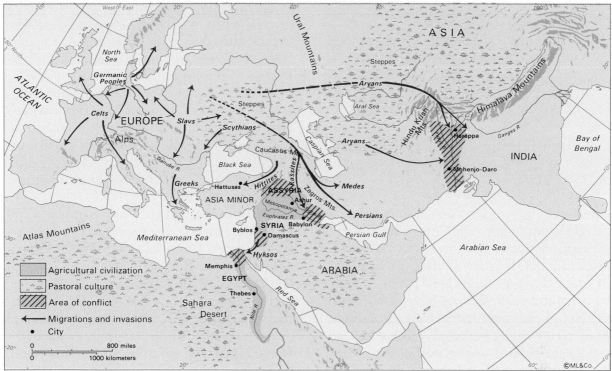

Map Skills **1.** In which direction did the Medes and Persians travel to reach the Arabian Sea? **2.** Name three seas located to the east of the Mediterranean Sea.

Sanskrit the word for father is *pitar;* in Latin the word for father is *pater.* The Slavic word for god, *bog,* is similar to the Old Indic word *bhagas* and the Old Persian word *baga.*

Even though the people of the steppes did not all speak the same language, they shared a common culture shaped by their environment. People responded to the arid grasslands of Eurasia and Africa by developing a food supply that could survive with little water. Most people in the steppes became herders and led their livestock across the plains in search of grass and water.

Life On the Steppes. Most of these nomads lived on the steppes of central Asia. Here, farming was risky because of the lack of water. Herding and hunting, though, provided a comfortable way of life.

The people who lived on the steppes counted their wealth in the form of animals. Their animals continually consumed their grazing lands so the herders needed to move on to other grasslands. They did not build permanent homes. The people of the steppes were often traders as well as herders because their travels led to contacts with many other people.

The nomads of the steppes lived in small, mobile groups, or tribes. Members of a tribe believed they were descended from the same ancestor and were, therefore, united by blood. Almost all pastoral peoples of Eurasia and Africa lived in tribes. Nomadic tribes were divided into smaller groups whose animals shared the same grazing lands. Settled people, living with the benefits and burdens of civilization, came to call these pastoral peoples barbarians. Barbarians were viewed as people who were foreigners outside the influence of civilization.

Nomads Encounter Civilization. During the past 4,000 years, pastoral groups have

A relief depicts Hittite charioteers, who learned the fine points of chariot management from their Mitannian neighbors.

repeatedly migrated from the grasslands into the river valleys. Their movements can be seen on the map, Migrations and Invasions, page 47. Historians offer two explanations for the migrations.

First, the nomads may have had several reasons to abandon the arid environment. They could have needed an increased food supply for their growing population. They could have needed more grazing land for their growing herds. All these factors could have pushed the people out of the steppes in search of greener pastures.

A second explanation suggests that the people of the steppes left their arid environments because of the lure of the wealth in the cities of Eurasian river valleys. For whatever reasons, groups of nomads left the steppes and attacked neighboring farms and towns. They plundered grain stores, made prisoners their slaves, and grazed their herds in farmers' fields and gardens.

War Chariots Invented

The nomads from the steppes invented a secret weapon to gain an advantage over their civilized neighbors. Sometime around 1700 B.C., the steppes people first combined the powers of horses and wheels and invented the chariot. The chariot changed warfare and stunned the foot soldiers protecting the river valley civilizations.

The war chariot was a two-wheeled vehicle drawn by as many as four horses. The chariot could turn sharply and move quickly across an open field. In warfare, the chariot carried both a driver who handled the horses and an archer or perhaps a spearman. Chariot warfare developed in the Bronze Age, after 1700 B.C.

Chariot warfare was effective but expensive. The costs of a fighting chariot involved horses, a driver, and a variety of craftspeople who could make wheels, axles, armor, and a great supply of arrows. Only wealthy chiefs, nobles, and kings could afford to be chariot warriors.

During the 500-year period from 1700 to 1200 B.C., wave after wave of nomad warriors invaded the river valley civilizations of Mesopotamia, Egypt, India, and northern China. With their horses and chariots, they arrived at the door of river valley civilizations in clouds of dust from the deserts and grasslands of Eurasia. At first, civilizations were taken by surprise and conquered. Gradually, the barbarian and civilized people borrowed ideas and skills from each other. New ways of living developed that spread beyond the Eurasian river valleys.

SECTION 1 *Study Skills*

Developing Vocabulary 1. List two other names for steppes. **2.** From what region did Indo-European people come? **3.** What is a tribe? **4.** What is the root word for barbarian?

Reviewing Main Ideas 1. Describe the lifestyle of the steppes people. **2.** From what parent language did the languages of the people of the steppes come? **3.** When was the war chariot developed?

Understanding Geography 1. On the map, locate the world's largest arid zone and describe its appearance. **2.** Why was the development of the war chariot a significant improvement in transportation?

Challenge List three advances in technology during your life that have changed the way you and your family live.

Locating Places on the Global Grid

Maps are among a geographer's most important tools. Geographers use maps to show where places and things are located on the earth. The people who make maps are called cartographers.

To make maps, cartographers use reference points, fixed points that are easy to recognize. The daily rotation of the earth provides cartographers with basic reference points. The earth rotates on an axis, an imaginary line through the center of the earth. The points at each end of the axis are the North Pole and the South Pole. The axis and the two poles are the three basic reference points upon which other reference points are based.

Imaginary lines drawn on the earth's surface connecting the two poles are called meridians, or lines of longitude. These lines extending north and south measure distances east or west. Imaginary lines extending east and west and measuring distances north and south are called parallels, or lines of latitude. The combination of meridians and parallels is called the geographic grid. The grid is useful for identifying locations of places on earth. See the map, Global Grid Line, on this page.

Latitude and Longitude

The parallel halfway between the North Pole and the South Pole is called the equator. The equator divides the earth into the Northern Hemisphere and the Southern Hemisphere. Each parallel, or line of latitude, is labeled according to how far north or south it is from the equator. The unit used to measure the distance from the equator is called a degree. A degree is a unit used to measure angles and curves. The symbol

for degree is °. A full circle is 360°. A half-circle is 180°. The earth is a sphere. Therefore, any line going completely around the earth is a 360° circle.

For more precise measurement, each degree can be divided into 60 equal parts called minutes. The symbol for a minute is '. Each minute can be divided into 60 seconds. The symbol for a second is ".

The equator is labeled zero degrees, or 0°. Moving away from the equator, parallels are labeled in increasing numerical order. The point farthest north on the earth, the North Pole, is one-quarter of the distance around the earth from the equator. The North Pole, then, is located at 90° north. The South Pole is 90° south.

The other part of the geographic grid system consists of meridians, or lines of lon-

Global Grid Line

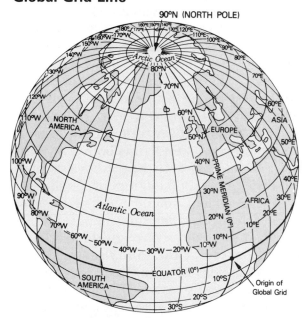

Map Skills **1.** What is the latitude of the equator?
2. What is the longitude of the prime meridian?
3. Near what continent do the equator and the prime meridian intersect?

Using a compass, a seventeenth-century navigator charts an ocean voyage.

gitude. One of the meridians, the prime meridian, is used, like the equator, as the reference point for labeling the lines of longitude. The prime meridian is 0°. The meridians in the half of the world east of the prime meridian are labeled between 0° and 180° east. The meridians in the half of the world west of the prime meridian are labeled between 0° and 180° west. Therefore, the meridian halfway around the world from the prime meridian is both 180° east and 180° west. Because the earth is a sphere, it is divided into 360 degrees of longitude.

By agreement among most of the nations of the world, the prime meridian is the meridian that passes through the old location of the Royal Observatory in Greenwich (GREHN ihj) near London, England.

Relationships in the Grid

The meridians and parallels in the geographic grid have certain characteristics. First, all meridians are equal in length. Each extends from one pole to the other, a distance of about 12,500 miles. Second, parallels vary in length. The longest parallel is the equator. The shortest parallels are nearest the poles. Third, all meridians meet at the poles. Fourth, parallels never intersect.

Fifth, the distance between any two meridians varies. They are farthest apart at the equator. The distance between two meridians narrows as they approach the poles. For example, the distance between 120° east and 121° degrees east is about 69 miles at the equator, 0°. The distance between meridians steadily decreases as they move north from the equator. At 90° north, the North Pole, the meridians intersect. Sixth, the distance between any two parallels is constant. One degree of latitude is always about 69 miles. Seventh, all intersections between meridians and parallels are right angles.

Only a globe can accurately show these relationships. The map on this page, Geographic Grid, indicates many of these traits accurately. This map does not, however, show the intersections of meridians and parallels as right angles.

The latitude and the longitude of a place indicate its location on the earth's surface. For example, the center of Chicago, Illinois is at 41°52′52″ north, 87°37′47″ west. The latitude and longitude of a place are its coordinates. Coordinates are useful for locating a place on a map or globe.

STUDY SKILLS Reading Maps

1. What is the name of the meridian at 0°?
2. What is the name of the parallel at 0°?
3. What body of water includes the point 43° north, 35° east?
4. Use the map on page 49 to estimate the coordinates of the Nile River delta.
5. Explain how meridians and parallels differ in length.
6. Estimate your community's coordinates.

2 Empires Expand the Influence of Civilization

OBJECTIVE: *To understand how civilization spread beyond the original river valley civilizations*

People of the Fertile Crescent

In the period from 1700 to 1200 B.C., the many city-states and kingdoms of the fertile crescent not only fought one another but also faced the invasions from the surrounding barbarians. After centuries of conflict, the strongest states survived; civilizations changed and spread throughout Eurasia.

The Hittites. The Indo-European people who invaded the plateau of Anatolia, present-day Turkey, were called Hittites. These barbarians from the northern steppes started several kingdoms in Anatolia and warred among themselves. In time, they came to use the skills and ideas of the fertile crescent civilizations and eventually built an empire that reached into Mesopotamia.

The Babylonians. In lower Mesopotamia, on the Euphrates River, lay the great city-state of Babylon. About 1700 B.C., Babylon was attacked by an Indo-European people called the Kassites, who invaded from the mountains to the east. Although the area continued to be called Babylon, Kassite kings ruled over it for 576 years.

The Assyrians. Farther north, on the Tigris River, lay another city, Ashur, the center of the kingdom of Assyria. The Assyrians conquered northern Mesopotamia. Like the original Babylonians, the Assyrians spoke a Semitic language related to Hebrew and Arabic. The Assyrian civilization was less advanced than that of the Babylonians, but Assyrian merchants lived and traded in all the surrounding countries.

The Hittite Empire

The Hittites migrated from the central Asian steppes and conquered the people of the eastern Anatolian plateau. The Romans later called the plateau of Anatolia, along with its coasts, Asia Minor. Today the name Asia Minor refers to the entire peninsula between the Mediterranean and Black seas.

When the Hittites migrated to Anatolia about 1800 B.C., they were barbarian nomads. In time, however, the Hittites borrowed from their civilized neighbors, learning to conduct business using the cuneiform tablets and the system of record

---

VOCABULARY DEVELOPMENT

Asia Minor *noun:* a peninsula of western Asia (Anatolia) between the Black Sea and the Mediterranean Sea; present-day Turkey.

infantry *noun:* soldiers who fight on foot.

economy *noun:* the structure of economic life, how the people of a country produce, distribute, and use goods and services.

standing army *noun:* a permanent army of paid soldiers.

vassal (VAS uhl) *noun:* **1.** A person who received land from an overlord in return for pledging loyalty, fighting for the lord, performing other duties; **2.** a subordinate, subject, servant, or slave. From the Latin word, *vassalus,* meaning manservant.

The Fertile Crescent, 1700–1200 B.C.

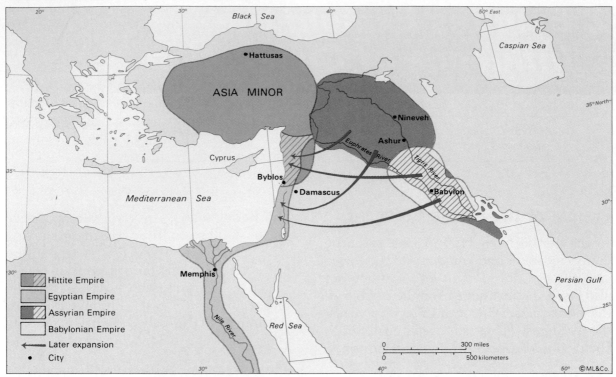

Map Skills **1.** What cities were located in the fertile crescent? **2.** What rivers flow through the lands of the fertile crescent?

keeping invented by the Sumerians. Hittite leadership was also influenced by Mesopotamian ideas and customs. At first, Hittite nobles elected their leader, or king. The king had an advisory council of noble warriors who were nearly his equals.

Over time, however, the Hittite king became more like the high priest in Mesopotamian civilization. The king assumed religious responsibilities and was protected by special bodyguards. The Hittite king remained a military leader, however, who led the army into battle.

Chariot Warfare. The military success of the Hittites rested on their war chariots which were much lighter and faster than the carts other people used. The Hittites fought only in summer months when the weather was good. Once they decided on war, they usually surprised or tricked the enemy to gain an advantage.

The king and his nobles rode to the attack armed with bows and arrows and wielding battleaxes and short, curved swords. Infantry, soldiers on foot, used swords and spears to guard the camp and supplies. The Hittites sacked conquered cities, taking everything of value, burning buildings, and making some conquered people slaves. Conquered nations had to supply soldiers, chariots, and weapons for the king's army.

Hittite Law Codes. The Hittite kings issued a new code of laws that was more humane than the codes of Hammurabi and Egypt. The new code of laws reduced the fine for stealing cattle from 30 to 15 head of cattle for each head stolen. For murder, the death penalty was not required. Instead, a person who committed murder was normally required to replace the dead victim with a slave or one of his own children. According to the code, the penalty for injury to a slave was only half as severe as for injury to a free person.

Hittite Religion. Like other early people, the Hittites believed in many gods and practiced polytheism. Their gods were immortal, human in form, and worshiped in temples of all sizes. In general, they had gods of the earth and gods of the sky. An important weather god, named Teshub, controlled clouds and storms. The Hittites also added myths and legends from Mesopotamian civilization to their own religion.

Treaties and Alliances. As a result of their conquests from 1400 to 1200 B.C., the Hittites ruled an empire that included most of Asia Minor. The Hittites often made treaties with the Egyptians and Mesopotamians against the powerful Assyrians. About 1250 B.C., the Egyptian queen begged the Hittite king to send one of his sons to take the place of her dead husband as king of Egypt. Such a proposal would have united, without war, the two most powerful empires. When the young Hittite prince arrived in Egypt, however, he was seized and killed. The two empires thus became bitter rivals.

The Hittite Empire ended in 1190 B.C. when the Phrygians (FRIHJ ee uhns), barbarians from the north, burned the capital. The Phrygians were part of the second great wave of barbarian invasions. The southern part of the Hittite Empire, however, survived in Syria for another 500 years.

Contributions to Civilization. The Hittites contributed to the spread of civilization throughout Asia Minor in two ways. First, they borrowed writing, business, religious, and government customs from Mesopotamia, adapted them, and brought this modified civilization to conquered people. Second, they introduced the use of iron throughout the interacting zone of communication. Hittite artisans worked with iron, a stronger metal than bronze, to craft weapons and tools.

The Assyrian Empire

Around 3000 B.C. a small group of people called Assyrians settled in northern Mesopotamia. They spoke a Semitic language, used cuneiform, and traded with the Sumerians. The Assyrians defended their frontiers, often unsuccessfully, against neighbors to both the north and south.

Assyrian Expansion. Between 2500 and 1600 B.C., the Assyrians built an army and expanded their land to the Mediterranean Sea. Expansion was important because the Assyrians needed metals from the west as well as a port on the Mediterranean Sea.

Assyrian Society. The Assyrian people dressed in tunics and wore sandals. The men had long hair and often grew beards. Many people were farmers who lived in small villages. Others were artisans who lived in the cities. They used slaves, most of whom were prisoners of war or debtors.

The Assyrians borrowed religious ceremonies and gods from both the Sumerians and Babylonians. The Assyrians' main god was Assur after whom they named both their country and chief city. The Assyrian king was ruler and chief priest of Assur.

Cuneiform symbols on the rim of this Hittite seal helped to decode the message inside which says: "Tarriktimme, king of the country of Erme."

The Babylonian Empire

During the Bronze Age, 3500 to 1000 B.C., the Babylonians, as well as the Assyrians, occupied Mesopotamia. The Babylonians, living in the south, had inherited ideas and practices from the centuries-old Sumerian civilization. Assyria, by contrast, had fewer cultural traditions. The Assyrians often borrowed Babylonian ideas and customs.

Between 1700 and 1200 B.C., Babylon and Assyria were alternately friends and enemies. At times, as during the reign of Hammurabi from 1792 to 1750 B.C., Babylon and Assyria were united under a single king and government.

Leadership of Babylon. From 1700 to 1200 B.C., Mesopotamian cities continued to develop. During that time, the cities of Babylon increased in size and influence. To protect themselves from the fury of invaders, Babylonians built massive walled cities with unbaked mud bricks. The walls, 20 to 30 feet high, were as much as 20 feet thick. Defenders of the cities could shoot arrows or drop boiling water on their enemies through openings in the towers.

Kings and the priests were important to the defense and economy of Babylonian cities. The king collected taxes, organized the army, and seized booty and prisoners of war. The priests owned lands and collected contributions used to build and repair the god's house, and conducted ceremonies for the success of armies and farmers.

Ways of Life. Except for the ruler and a few slaves, most people in Mesopotamia belonged to the same social class. Occupation accounted for the main difference in the way people lived.

Families were small, and the eldest son inherited the father's property. Daughters received dowries—money or property—to help them find husbands. To keep farmland from being divided, sons often lived with their parents. The identification of people by family names became common.

The Egyptian Empire

Although Egypt was isolated from neighboring people by natural barriers, contacts with barbarian foreigners increased at the end of the Middle Kingdom, 2080 to 1640 B.C. By 1700 B.C., Hittite pressure forced some people living in the mountains around the fertile crescent into Egypt. These displaced people, the Hyksos (HIHK sohs), thundered into Egypt on swift, horse-drawn chariots. Using their bronze weapons, the Hyksos defeated the delta Egyptians and by 1640 B.C. had established a kingdom there.

The Hyksos adopted many Egyptian customs. They also borrowed the Egyptian religion and government institutions. They did, however, bring their own changes to Egypt. The Hyksos continued to use bronze weapons and tools, drive light, spoke-wheeled war chariots, and weave their cloth on standing looms.

Egyptian Independence. The Egyptians, accustomed to being secure, resented the foreign rulers. The pharaoh determined to regain Egyptian independence. About 1570 B.C., the Egyptians rebelled and drove the Hyksos out of the delta.

To maintain their independence, the Egyptians made some changes. Instead of relying on farmers for military service, the pharaoh organized a professional standing army. His army included chariot units, archers, and infantry. Chariots, new bronze weapons, and the use of foreign soldiers made the Egyptians a powerful force. With this army, Egypt created an empire.

Egypt Founds an Empire. Egyptian armies turned south and conquered Nubia, in present-day Sudan. Then, they marched into the fertile crescent as far as the Euphrates River valley and conquered Palestine and Syria.

Egyptian soldiers were stationed in Palestine, Syria, and Nubia. Local kings who pledged loyalty to Egypt remained in power, but they became vassals of the pharaoh.

Their sons were sent to Egypt to be educated and were held as hostages to ensure their fathers' loyalty. Egyptian pharaohs also gave gifts to their vassals to help win their loyalty and support.

Rule of Ramses. In 1298 B.C., Ramses II (RAM sees), an army general, founded a new dynasty and ruled until 1225 B.C. For over 20 years, he led a fierce struggle against the Hittites for control of northern Syria. After reaching a stalemate about 1275 B.C., the two forces agreed to end their rivalry with the following peace treaty.

Two versions of the treaty exist. An Egyptian version was recorded in hieroglyphics on the walls of the pharaoh's temple in Thebes. A Hittite version was found in their capital inscribed on clay tablets.

Differences in the two versions show the political biases of each side. The Egyptian version always places the name of the pharaoh, Ramses II, before that of the Hittite king, Hattusilis. In the Hittite version, the order of names is reversed.

Early Peace Treaty

FOCUS ON SOURCES

The treaty, which was divided into several sections, brought a 70-year peace between the Egyptians and the Hittites. The following clauses of the treaty are taken from the Egyptian version.

❝ The treaty which the great prince of the Hittites, the mighty Hattusilis . . . has inscribed upon silver tablets for Ramses II, the great and mighty ruler of Egypt, . . .

Carved into a sandstone cliff, the Great Temple at Abu Simbel was built by Ramses II. Four seated statues of him, each 67 feet high, guard the entrance.

shall create peace and brotherhood between the two kings, their children, and their lands forever . . . and neither king will invade the territory of the other.

Defensive Alliance. . . . If some enemy, however, marches against the land Ramses II . . . has chosen to rule, and Ramses sends for help from the great prince of the Hittites, then the Hittite prince shall come to Ramses' aid and slay his enemy. [Ramses then made a similar pledge to Hattusilia.]

Written in Akkadian, the ancient language of Mesopotamia, this fragment is part of a peace treaty between Egypt and the Hittite Empire.

Return of Political Refugees. . . . If any important person or even ordinary person should flee from the land of Egypt and come to the great prince of the Hittites, let the great Hittite prince take him captive and have him sent back to Ramses II, the great lord of Egypt. Nevertheless, if any person is sent back to Ramses, the pharaoh shall allow no one to bring any criminal charges against him, shall protect his wives and children

from harm, and shall safeguard the person from injury and death. [A similar clause takes up Hittite refugees fleeing to Egypt.]

Conclusion. . . . As for these words that are written upon these silver tablets, whosoever does not obey them, may the thousand gods of the land of Egypt and the thousand gods of the land of the Hittites destroy his house, his land, and his servants. . . . But whosoever abides by these words, may he receive the blessing of the thousand gods of the land of Egypt and the thousand gods of the land of the Hittites. **"**

The treaty of peace with the Hittites, however, did not save Egypt from future enemies. A new wave of invaders fighting with iron weapons conquered parts of Egypt around 1200 B.C. Egypt lost all territory outside the Nile Valley. Upper and Lower Egypt were separated, and Egypt never again regained its former power. ■

SECTION 2 *Study Skills*

Developing Vocabulary Use each of the following in a sentence: **1.** Asia Minor. **2.** infantry. **3.** economy. **4.** standing army. **5.** vassal.

Reviewing Main Ideas **1.** How did the Hittites contribute to the spread of civilization? **2.** Why did the Egyptians rebel against the Hyksos? **3.** Why did the Egyptians and the Hittites agree to sign a peace treaty in 1275 B.C.?

Understanding Geography **1.** Where was the city-state of Babylonia located? **2.** Use the map on page 47 to trace and describe the travels of the Hyksos. Where did they set up their capital? **3.** Where was the center of the kingdom of Assyria?

Understanding Chronology **1.** About when did the Hittite Empire in Syria end? **2.** How long did Ramses II rule Egypt?

Challenge How does warfare today differ from that in the period between 1700 and 1200 B.C.?

3 Invaders of China, India, and the Mediterranean

OBJECTIVE: *To understand how Indo-European people influenced the river valley civilizations and helped spread civilization into new lands*

Phoenicians Spread Civilization

About the same period that barbarian nomads from the steppes were riding their chariots into the fertile crescent, great seafaring traders, the Phoenicians, were crisscrossing the Mediterranean Sea. They transmitted civilization and expanded the interacting zone through trade.

Trade Routes of the Mediterranean. The Phoenicians were one of the earliest people to build a network of trade routes and trading settlements that linked the people of the Mediterranean Basin. The Phoenicians settled on the east coast of the Mediterranean Sea near modern-day Lebanon about 3000 B.C. See the map, Aegean Civilizations, on page 58.

The Phoenicians were well-known traders whose most important cities were the ports of Tyre, Sidon, Byblos, and Berot (present-day Beirut). This eastern Mediterranean area of the ancient world was well suited for trade because the sea routes of the Mediterranean joined the land routes of the fertile crescent.

The Phoenicians were also famous sailors, brave and daring in exploring new sea routes. They skillfully powered their boats with square sails and oars. They used the pole star, Polaris, to navigate on the open sea. The seamen also kept detailed records of their journeys but refused to share those records with rivals.

Phoenician Alphabet. One of the most famous contributions of the Phoenicians was the written alphabet. Neither hieroglyphics nor cuneiform included a true alphabet of written letters that represented sounds. Egyptian hieroglyphics was a complicated system of writing that only a handful of professional writers, called scribes, could use. Hieroglyphics was based on pictures rather than sounds. Cuneiform contained the symbols for syllables only, not individual letters.

Phoenician traders simplified the symbols of Egyptian hieroglyphics into 21 signs, or letters, for single consonants. The inven-

---

VOCABULARY DEVELOPMENT

Peloponnesus (PEHL uh puh NEE suhs) *noun:* the southern tip of the Balkan Peninsula.

fortress cities *noun:* cities strengthened against attack by a fort or surrounding walls. From the Latin word, *fortis,* meaning strong.

siege (seej) *noun:* the surrounding of a fortified place, such as a city, by an opposing armed force, preventing people and supplies from entering or leaving. From the Latin word, *obsidere,* meaning to besiege

epic poem *noun:* a long narrative poem, in a dignified style, about the deeds of a legendary or historical hero.

Zhou (joh) *noun:* pastoralists of Asia who lived on the northwest border of Shang China, until recently translated in English as Chow.

military aristocracy *noun:* rule by a small group of individuals who control their own personal armies.

tion of the alphabet made it easier to read, write, and keep better records.

At first, the Greeks were suspicious of the paper with the small black markings that the Phoenician merchants used. In time, however, the Greeks came to use and perfect the alphabet, adding new signs for vowel sounds.

Phoenician Trade. The skilled Phoenician craftspeople sent metalwork, glass, embroidery, fine linen, and purple dye to people around the Mediterranean. Phoenicians also imported many materials, such as papyrus, ivory, and metals.

Phoenician Colonies. Phoenicians set up trading centers and colonies in places as far away as the island of Malta, Cadiz in Spain, and Carthage in Africa. Phoenicians also traded with the people living on the island

of Crete in the Aegean Sea. Here, between 1600 and 1400 B.C., the inhabitants created an advanced civilization called Minoan, after Minos, a legendary king of the island.

King Minos of Crete

FOCUS ON

PEOPLE

According to Greek legend, a powerful king named Minos once ruled Crete. The king was thought to be the son of Zeus, the supreme god of the Greeks, and Europa, the beautiful daughter of the king of Tyre, a Phoenician city. Minos supposedly married the daughter of the sun and had two daughters and two sons.

In return for help in obtaining the throne, King Minos promised to sacrifice a special bull to Poseidon, the god of the sea. Minos, however, prized the animal and decided to keep it. As a result, the angry Poseidon plagued Crete with a monster called the Minotaur, part man and part bull.

Minos entrusted one of his subjects, Daedalus, to make a prison for the Minotaur. The prison contained a complicated system of passages. Known as the labyrinth, this structure was a maze from which escape seemed impossible.

Shortly after the Minotaur was imprisoned in the labyrinth, a son of King Minos visited the king of Athens. While there, the Minoan prince was killed. Minos blamed the king of Athens for his son's death. He conquered Athens and imposed a terrible penalty. Each year Athenians were required to send seven maidens and seven youths to Crete to be sacrificed to the Minotaur.

Theseus, the son of the Athenian king, decided to end the terrible sacrifices or die in the attempt. He went to Crete in place of one of the doomed youths. When the daughter of King Minos, Ariadne, saw Theseus, she fell in love with him. Ariadne gave Theseus a ball of thread to unwind as he entered the labyrinth and a sword to kill the

Aegean Civilizations, 1600 B.C.

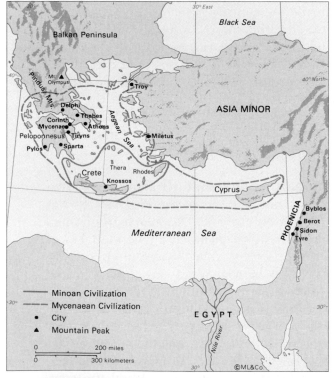

Map Skills **1.** What was the ancient name for the present-day city of Beirut? **2.** In which direction would an ancient Greek travel to reach Asia Minor?

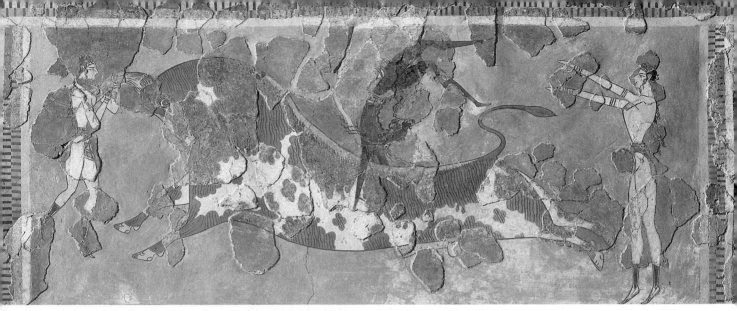

A powerful bull charges between human figures in this fresco from Knossos. The picture illustrates sacred rites that perhaps explain the story of Theseus.

Minotaur. After killing the monster, Theseus and the other intended victims used the thread to retrace the path that led out of the maze. Aided by Daedalus, Ariadne and Theseus eloped.

For helping Theseus escape, Minos imprisoned Daedalus and his son. They managed to escape and flee to Sicily, where they were granted protection. Minos died pursuing them.

The story of King Minos, with a cast of gods, humans, and monsters, contains many elements of legend. Few people believed the tale until Sir Arthur Evans, a British archaeologist, excavated Knossos in 1900. There he found evidence of a complex civilization. The floor plan of the palace was like the labyrinth of the Minoan legend. Evans honored King Minos by giving the name Minoan to the civilization on Crete. ▪

Minoan Civilization

The Mediterranean island of Crete is rocky and mountainous, a discouraging environment for farming. Still, the Minoans grew crops on small plains in the central and eastern parts of the island.

The Minoans also built several cities and towns on Crete and nearby islands. The most important city was Knossos (NAHS uhs),

the home of King Minos. At Knossos, archaeologists found a royal palace with spacious living rooms, vast storerooms, huge courtyards, and an athletic arena.

The Minoan Economy. Since their small island produced few crops, the Minoans turned to the sea for their livelihood. Minoan merchants traded with Egypt in the south and the islands of the Aegean Sea in the north. They established regional trading centers on various Aegean islands and at Miletus in Asia Minor.

Minoan Art and Architecture. The Minoan civilization set high standards in architecture and art. The architecture of the palace at Knossos rivaled structures anywhere in the ancient world. The building was surrounded by reception halls, living quarters, and storage rooms. Colorful paintings of men and women decorated the walls. In fact, women may have had a social status equal to that of men in Minoan civilization. They took part in sports events and other public activities.

The Minoans dominated the Aegean Sea until about 1400 B.C., spreading their influence through trade. Then Indo-European invaders conquered Crete and sacked Knossos, ending Minoan importance.

The Ancient Greek Civilization

Less than 100 miles north of the island of Crete lies the Balkan Peninsula, the homeland of the ancient Greeks. See the map, Aegean Civilizations, on page 58. The peninsula takes its name from the Balkan Mountains, which extend from the Black Sea to the Mediterranean.

Geography Influences History. Greece is divided into two geographic parts, the main peninsula and the Peloponnesus (PEHL uh puh NEE suhs). The Peloponnesus, almost an island by itself, is divided from the rest of Greece by the Gulf of Corinth. The Greek mainland and Peloponnesus form the southern region of the Balkan Peninsula.

Geography influenced the Greeks in several ways. First, the mountains of Greece provided a source of timber, which enabled them to build ships.

Second, the irregular coastline offers many good harbors. From earliest times, Greeks have been good sailors and fishermen. The many inhabited islands near Greece encouraged the growth of sea trade.

Third, whenever population grew beyond the numbers the mountainous land could support, Greeks left the mainland. They colonized the many islands and neighboring lands, such as Asia Minor, along the coasts of the Mediterranean Sea.

Early Mycenae, 1600–1200 B.C. About 1900 B.C., the Mycenaeans (MI suh NEE uhnz), Indo-European invaders, entered the eastern Mediterranean from the north. They spoke a language related to Greek. By 1600 B.C., these early Greeks were living throughout the entire Balkan Peninsula.

They built fortress cities at Pylos, Tiryns, and other sites. Mycenae (my SEE nee), their most important city, was located in the northeastern part of the Peloponnesus. This city gave the name Mycenaean to the culture of the entire region.

Being so close to Crete, Mycenae quickly assimilated the ideas and customs of the Crete civilization. For protection, the people of Mycenae built the king's fort on a high hill, overlooking the countryside. Guard towers protected the main roads.

Mycenaean society included several social classes. Kings lived in luxury in their palaces. They used beautiful vessels and ornaments of gold, silver, ivory, and bronze, many of which were decorated with precious stones. Warrior nobles lived on their own lands and were required to fight for the king. Artisans, farmers, and shepherds lived simple lives in much smaller houses. At the bottom of society were slaves, prisoners captured in battle.

The Story of Troy. From their settlements on the mainland, early Greek chieftains and their warriors advanced throughout the lands around the Aegean Sea. The most famous of these assaults was the siege of the city of Troy in Asia Minor, described in the *Iliad*. The *Iliad*, a Greek epic poem told by the poet Homer, relates the story of how King Agamemnon of Mycenae and his allies attacked Troy. The poem sings the praises of ancient Greek heros and gods. In the 1860s, Heinrich Schliemann, a devoted student of Homer, located the ancient city. He

A red-clay portrait of the Greek goddess Athena building the Trojan horse dates from 460 B.C.

found it buried under a 125-foot mound in present-day Turkey. He also unearthed the mighty fortress of Mycenae.

Expanding the Communicating Zone. The Greeks, rivals of the Phoenicians, traded throughout the Aegean and Mediterranean seas. Greek merchants traveled to Syria and Egypt. Greek settlers founded colonies on the north coast of Africa, in Sicily, and in Italy. In this way, the Greeks spread their culture and language to a wide area. The Greeks, as well as the Phoenicians, contributed to the growing economic interdependence and cultural interchange of the Mediterranean region.

The Aryan Invaders of India

As in the fertile crescent and the eastern Mediterranean, barbarian invaders attacked the early civilization in the Indus River valley during the Bronze Age and brought an abrupt end to the Harappan civilization.

As early as 2000 B.C., invaders from the steppes of central Asia attacked the cities of the Indus Valley. These invaders, like those who attacked the people around the Mediterranean, spoke an Indo-European language. They were called Aryans (AIR ee uhnz), a name related to Iran and to Eire, the old name for Ireland. The Aryan invasions reached their peak about 1500 B.C. However, centuries passed before the Harappan civilization completely collapsed.

Aryan Culture. The Aryans, nomadic herders who lived on the edges of civilization, raised cattle, sheep, goats, and horses. They used cows as a measure of wealth. According to Aryan law, the punishment for killing a man was the payment of 100 cows.

The nomadic Aryans did not build cities. Neither did they know how to read or write. Knowledge of the Aryan culture comes mostly from oral tradition. Like many pastoral people, they loved poetry and songs. To preserve stories about their adventures and

their gods, they made up long poems. Students spent months listening to, memorizing, and reciting verses.

The Aryans conquered the Harappans with bronze weapons and war chariots. The Harappans had few, if any, horses and did not use bronze weapons. Wars between the Aryans and Harappans lasted for centuries. The Harappans fortified their cities and resisted attacks. Finally, those cities were destroyed and abandoned.

A New Aryan Civilization. The Aryan invaders learned to farm from the Harappans and began to develop their own elements of civilization. The new civilization they built combined the Harappan culture with their own and shaped the future history of India.

The Shang Dynasty

Farther to the east, changes were also occurring in north China. The Shang civilization in east Asia began during the Bronze Age.

Shang Government. Archaeological evidence shows that strong continuity existed in north China from the Stone Age to the Bronze Age. Population expanded, and larger cities were built in the valley of the Huang He. About 1500 B.C., a dynasty called the Shang came to power and ruled until 1122 B.C., about 400 years. The Shang lands lay between the Yellow River and the uplands occupied by pastoralists called the Zhou. To protect themselves from raiding barbarians, the Shang established a military aristocracy. The kings were chosen from the heads of ruling warrior families.

Life in Shang China. Shang society was divided into rigid classes. At the top were the rulers, who used bronze implements and weapons. The upper class relied on warriors, artisans, and administrators. At the bottom of society were the peasants, who worked their fields and served as soldiers. Shang military campaigns required armies of as many as 10,000 people.

Early Chinese Civilization, 1600 B.C.

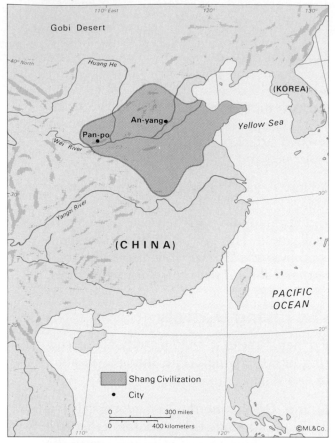

Gobi Desert

Huang He

An-yang

Pan-po

Wei River

Yangzi River

(KOREA)

Yellow Sea

(CHINA)

PACIFIC OCEAN

Shang Civilization
● City

0   300 miles
0   400 kilometers

©ML&Co.

Map Skills **1.** What rivers flowed through the Shang lands? **2.** What body of water is located to the east of the Shang lands? to the south?

Metalsmiths working with bronze reached a high level of sophistication. Bronze was used to make such weapons as arrowheads, swords, spear points, battle-axes, and armor. The most important use was in making ritual vessels, such as pots, wine jugs, and cups.

The Afterworld. The Shang view of the world was similar to the Egyptian view in that they believed in a close link between the worlds of the living and the dead. The ruler of the afterworld, the Lord on High, Shang Di, was served by the spirits of dead kings, queens, and nobles. The Shang ruler was the link between the world of the living and the afterworld.

The tombs of Shang kings were cross-shaped pits 40 feet deep. Accompanying the body of the dead king were valuable objects and sacrificed humans and animals. One royal tomb contained 440 bronze objects and 750 jade carvings. Another held the bodies of more than 160 humans along with 12 horses and 11 dogs in addition to the body of the king. All were killed to accompany the king in death.

The Spread of Civilization. From 1700 to 1200 B.C., civilization spread from the river valleys to the barbarian tribes of Indo-Europeans living on the fringes of civilization. These nomadic tribes migrated from their homeland in the central Asian steppes to Asia Minor, Mesopotamia, and Europe, as well as Iran and India. People, such as the Hyksos, Hittites, and Aryans, shared in the culture of more advanced people.

SECTION 3 *Study Skills*

Developing Vocabulary Define each of the following terms: **1.** Peloponnesus. **2.** fortress cities. **3.** siege. **4.** epic poem. **5.** Zhou. **6.** military aristocracy.

Reviewing Main Ideas **1.** What caused the Phoenicians to become great seafaring traders? **2.** How did Sir Arthur Evans cause people to reconsider their beliefs about the legend of King Minos?

Understanding Geography **1.** Where was the Minoan civilization located? **2.** Where is the Peloponnesus? **3.** Explain three ways geography influenced the ancient Greeks. **4.** On the map on page 47 trace the Aryan migrations. About how far did they migrate?

Understanding Chronology **1.** When did the Mycenaeans invade the Mediterranean area? **2.** When was Troy excavated? **3.** Why is 1122 B.C. significant in Chinese history?

Challenge How do new ideas spread among civilizations today?

CHAPTER 3 *Summary & Review*

Summarizing Main Ideas

Over a 4,000 year period, steppe nomads migrated to the river valleys of the south. Gradually the conquerors and conquered exchanged ideas, and new ways of living spread. The Hittites, Babylonians, and Assyrians at one time or another ruled over the various areas of several different river valleys.

One of the most important trading empires, Phoenicia, developed a written alphabet. The Phoenicians spread the use of language through the Mediterranean.

Great civilizations also developed in India and China. These civilizations had less contact with other peoples than did the Mediterranean civilizations. By 1200 B.C., though, a network of inter-communicating zones was established.

Migrations of People, 1700–1200 B.C.	
Invaders/Origins	**Lands Conquered**
Hittites–Steppes north of Black and Caspian seas	Eastern Asia Minor and northern Mesopotamia
Kassites–Zagros Mountains around present-day Iran	Babylonia
Hyksos–Palestine and Syria on west coast of Mediterranean	Lower Egypt
Celts–Steppes north of Black and Caspian seas	Moved through eastern Europe to France, Spain, and Britain
Phoenicians–Unknown	Settled throughout Mediterranean Basin
Mycenaeans–Steppes north of Black and Caspian seas	Settled over entire Balkan Peninsula
Aryans–Steppes of central Asia	Indus valley
Zhou–West Wei River valley	Shang China

Questions for Critical Thinking

COMPREHENSION Interpreting Events

1. Explain why the use of war chariots gave some people a military advantage over other groups of people.
2. Describe why the peoples of the steppes moved into the river valleys.
3. How did the Hittites treat the people in the areas they conquered?

ANALYSIS Identifying Trends

1. Discuss the impact of migrations on the development of each of the civilizations described in this chapter.
2. Identify the influence that the Minoans and the Mycenaeans had on the Greeks.

APPLICATION Comparing Past to Present

1. Compare the civilizations studied in Chapter 3 with those in Chapter 2. What advances allowed the later civilizations to trade more widely and to create empires?
2. Suggest three steps a civilization today can take to encourage its development. Use examples to indicate how successful each approach has been in the past.

SYNTHESIS Developing Map Skills

1. Describe the locations of the major civilizations discussed in this chapter.
2. What environmental factors did early civilization have in common?

EVALUATION Weighing Consequences

1. Summarize the role of writing in helping civilizations advance.
2. How were the views towards life and death of the Egyptians and the Shang similar?

CHALLENGE

1. Use examples to explain why civilizations with superior mobility often dominated neighboring civilizations.
2. Which groups listed in the chart on this page came from the steppes of Central Asia?

CHAPTER 4
Civilizations in the Iron Age

GLOBAL TIME LINE

	1200 B.C.	1150 B.C.	1100 B.C.	1050 B

TIME

1500–1000 B.C. *Rigveda* is composed in India

● **1200 B.C.** Iron Age reaches the fertile crescent

PEOPLE

● **1240 B.C.** Moses leads Hebrews out of Egypt

PLACE

1200–900 B.C. *Middle America;¹* San Lorenzo is most important Olmec site

Linking Past to Present

Can openers, pickaxes, motorcycles, and suspension bridges contain some iron or steel. Look around you and count the things made of these metals. Useful objects of iron or steel are so common in our everyday lives that we take them for granted. In 1700 B.C., however, people did not know how to make iron. When ancient Asians invented a way to melt and work iron around 1400 B.C., far-reaching changes occurred. Iron changed the way societies farmed, manufactured goods, traded, and fought.

In this chapter, you will learn about the Iron Age and its consequences. You will also learn how two world religions, Judaism and Hinduism, started. The third section introduces the first civilization in the Western Hemisphere, the Olmecs of Middle America.

Townspeople being led into captivity by the Assyrians during the seventh century B.C.

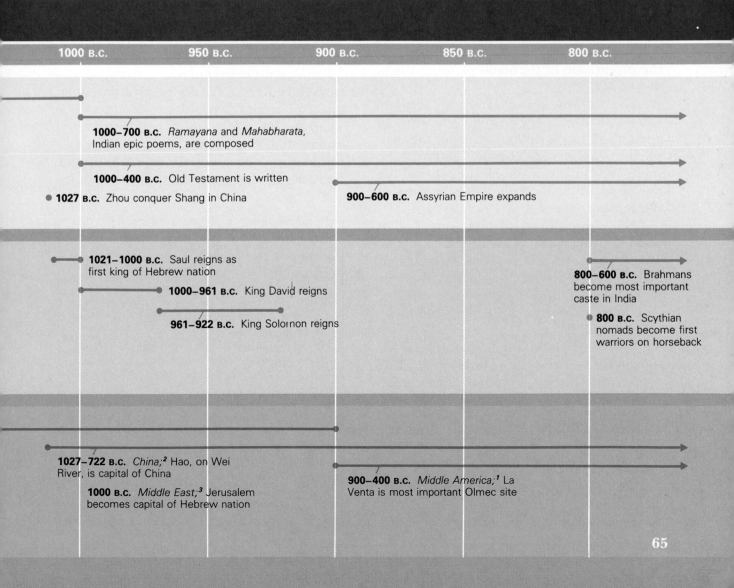

1000 B.C.	950 B.C.	900 B.C.	850 B.C.	800 B.C.

1000–700 B.C. *Ramayana* and *Mahabharata*, Indian epic poems, are composed

1000–400 B.C. Old Testament is written

1027 B.C. Zhou conquer Shang in China

900–600 B.C. Assyrian Empire expands

1021–1000 B.C. Saul reigns as first king of Hebrew nation

1000–961 B.C. King David reigns

961–922 B.C. King Solomon reigns

800–600 B.C. Brahmans become most important caste in India

800 B.C. Scythian nomads become first warriors on horseback

1027–722 B.C. *China;²* Hao, on Wei River, is capital of China

1000 B.C. *Middle East;³* Jerusalem becomes capital of Hebrew nation

900–400 B.C. *Middle America;¹* La Venta is most important Olmec site

65

1 *The Assyrian and Hebrew Nations*

OBJECTIVE: *To understand the development of the Assyrian Empire and the importance of the Hebrew nation*

Consequences of Iron Age

The period from 1200 to 800 B.C. produced far-reaching social and economic changes throughout the interacting zone. A single, but immensely important development in technology caused many of these changes: the production of tools and weapons made of iron.

The Hittites, nomads from the steppes, ruled Anatolia. They learned ironworking technology in the 1300s B.C. from the people they conquered. Around 1200 B.C., the trade and travels of the Hittites spread the new skills and tools throughout the lands of the fertile crescent.

The earliest iron objects were not as good as those made of bronze because artisans were just learning to work with the new metal. Later, however, as people became more skilled, iron implements became cheaper than bronze implements and much more plentiful.

Tools such as iron axes enabled people to cut timber and clear forests. Workers using iron chisels, saws, and knives could shape wood into furniture, build boats, and construct buildings.

Iron sickles and plows made plowing, planting, and reaping crops faster and easier. Because farmers could grow more food during the Iron Age, human populations increased in many parts of Eurasia and Africa. As the population grew, people started new towns and cities. They quickly realized the advantages of the strong, new iron tools and weapons. A brisk trade in iron products developed between towns.

Iron workers fashioned rims on chariot wheels, and made swords, lance points, and armor. The improved quality and increased quantities of the iron products changed cultures throughout the fertile crescent. Rulers, for instance, could provide stronger weapons for soldiers and build up larger armies than ever before. For the first time, ordinary people could afford weapons and become soldiers. As a result, wealthy nobles

---

VOCABULARY DEVELOPMENT

cavalry (KAV uhl ree) *noun:* combat troops mounted on horses.

vassal state *noun:* a state owing tribute to, and recognizing the authority of, another more powerful state. From the Latin word, *vassus*, meaning servant.

ethical monotheism (EHTH ih kuhl MAHN uh thee ihz uhm) *noun:* the belief in only one God, and in right conduct based on God-given laws.

prophets (PRAHF ihts) *noun:* religious leaders believed to speak for a god. From the Greek word, *prophetes*, meaning interpreter of a god's will.

Messiah (meh SY uh) *noun:* the expected king of the Hebrews, who would renew national strength and restore past glory. From the Hebrew word, *mashiah*, meaning anointed.

Assyrian kings thought hunting lions with a bow and arrow was the best training for the battlefield. King Kalakh, who lived in the ninth century B.C., is pictured here.

with chariots no longer had a monopoly on fighting. Instead rulers greatly increased the size of their armies.

Cavalry, Revolutionary Warfare

Around 800 B.C., another revolutionary development with far-reaching consequences occurred. Armies began to use cavalry, warriors on horseback. The cavalry had greater speed and mobility than soldiers in chariots. On horseback, they rode across the flat, grassy steppes that reached westward along the Black Sea from the Don River to the mouth of the Danube. This area is the present-day Ukraine.

The Assyrians of northern Mesopotamia were the first warriors to fight from horseback. They learned how to shoot arrows while controlling a galloping horse. In a chariot, one man controlled the horses while another used a bow and arrow. Ancient Assyrian carvings show early riders using the same technique. At first, two horsemen rode next to each other. One rider held the reins of both horses while the other shot arrows. Later, each rider learned to shoot while controlling the horse.

The Assyrian Empire

The chief activity of the Assyrians was war. Around 1300 B.C., the Assyrian king sent armies from northern Mesopotamia to conquer neighboring territory. They defeated the Babylonians in southern Mesopotamia, then moved west to the Mediterranean and took control of the coast of Syria. By 650 B.C., the Assyrians controlled the entire fertile crescent as well as northern Egypt. One Assyrian king called himself "King of Everything." See the map on page 69.

Assyrian Army. The huge Assyrian army included both cavalry and chariots. In addition, heavily armed infantry marched carrying shields, iron spears, and swords. Other troops included archers, famous for their accuracy, and soldiers who could hurl heavy stones with their slings. The army traveled with men trained to dig under the walls of an enemy's city, and large battering machines used to break down walls.

The cruelty of the Assyrians was legendary. They moved conquered populations from their homelands and made them slaves. Enemies captured in battle were savagely put to death. To put down a rebellion, the Assyrian king, Sennacherib (suh NAK uhr ihb), destroyed the city of Babylon. His boastful account has been translated:

" The city and its houses, foundations and walls, I destroyed, I burned with fire. The wall and the outerwall, temples and gods, temple-towers of bricks and earth, as many as there were, I razed [tore down] and dumped them into the Arahtu canal. Through the midst of that city I dug canals, I flooded its site with water, and the very foundations thereof I destroyed. I made its destruction more complete than by a flood. That in days to come, the site of that city, and its temples and gods, might not be remembered, I completely blotted it out with floods of water and made it like a meadow . . . . **"**

Later his sons killed the cruel Sennacherib. Then in 680 B.C., one of them ordered Babylon rebuilt.

Assyrian Government. The great power of the Assyrian Empire lay in its system of governing conquered peoples. Assyrian rulers did not rely on the loyalty of their vassal states, lands they had conquered. Rather, the king appointed a loyal governor to each Assyrian province. The governor's duty was to defend his province, collect taxes, and recruit soldiers for the Assyrian army. This system of delegating authority became the model for ruling later empires.

The Assyrian system brought increased trade and prosperity. They built a network of highways to move troops through the empire and to promote trade. Aramaic, the language of Syrian traders, was widely used throughout the interacting zone. As the Assyrian Empire spread and conquered people were forced from their homelands, an exchange of ideas took place among people of different cultures.

The Assyrians governed the largest empire the world had yet seen. One of the people they ruled were the Hebrews. The Hebrews did not develop or transmit iron

making techniques. Instead, they developed religious views that have continued to influence people throughout the world. They contributed to three great religious traditions: Judaism, Christianity, and Islam.

The Impact of Hebrew Beliefs

In the midst of widespread polytheism, the Hebrews held to a belief in only one God who demanded right conduct from his people. This belief in one god with moral standards is called ethical monotheism. The story of the Hebrews and their God is told in the Old Testament, a collection of books in the Bible. These books were written over a period of about 600 years, from 1000 to 400 B.C. The Old Testament is an important source for the study of ancient history.

Hebrew History. The Hebrews trace their origins to a nomadic herder named Abram from the Sumerian city of Ur. According to tradition, Abram left Sumer at the command of his God, who promised to make him the head of a great nation. Abram and his family eventually arrived in Canaan, the land between the Jordan River and the Mediterranean Sea. In that land, Abram changed his name to Abraham, meaning father of many. See the map, Travels of the Hebrews, on page 69.

One of Abraham's descendants, Jacob, had a large family that migrated to Egypt during a famine in Canaan. For hundreds of years, the Hebrews, the descendants of Abraham and Jacob, lived in Egypt. Eventually however, the pharoah enslaved the Hebrews. Moses led the Hebrews out of Egypt about 1240 B.C.

Moses took the people across the Red Sea into the desert. They traveled to Mount Sinai, where God appeared to Moses and made a covenant, or agreement, with the Hebrews. Under the covenant, God promised eternal love and protection to the Hebrews. In exchange, the Hebrews accepted God's rule and promised to obey God's laws.

Travels of the Hebrews, 1960–600 B.C.

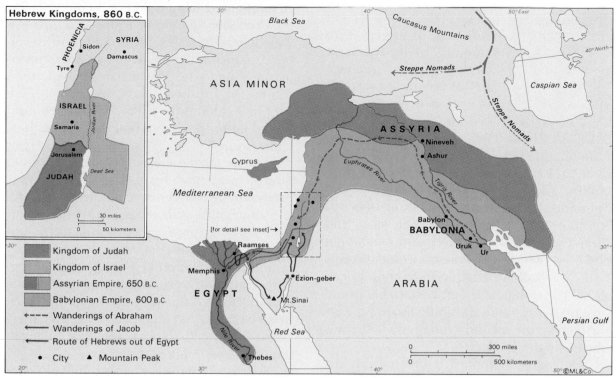

Map Skills **1.** Through which ancient cities did Abraham, and later Jacob, travel in their wanderings? **2.** To what land did the Hebrews go when they left Egypt?

The Ten Commandments, the rules for worship and moral conduct that God gave to Moses, express this covenant. Shortly after Moses' death, the Hebrews reached Canaan, the ancient homeland of Abraham, also known as Palestine.

The Hebrew Kingdom. The Hebrews were not a united people but lived in twelve tribes. Each tribe had its own ruler and military leaders. In 1021 B.C., a leader named Saul united the Hebrew tribes under a single government, Israel, and became their first king. Saul's successor, David, became the greatest of the Hebrew kings.

David began his career as an aide at Saul's court. He became a popular military hero and close friend of Saul's son, and he married Saul's daughter. King Saul became jealous of David's popularity and plotted to kill him. David, however, escaped to Judah, the desert frontier of his country, where he

organized other outlaws and refugees. Many who were in trouble, in debt, or discontented with the king joined him. David became a sort of Robin Hood. He and his followers protected the people from local bandits and helped the poor. David's popularity spread.

When Saul and his son were killed in battle, the people asked David to be their king. David ruled for almost 40 years, from 1000 to 961 B.C. He built his capital at Jerusalem. Leading the Hebrew armies against other nearby states, David expanded his kingdom to include lands east of the River Jordan, as well as part of Syria.

After David's death, his son, Solomon, ruled until 922 B.C. King Solomon equipped the Hebrew armies with chariots and built a huge palace and temple in Jerusalem. He also established trade networks, especially with the Phoenicians, the famed sailors and traders of the Mediterranean world.

Solomon: King of Israel

FOCUS ON PEOPLE

About 960 B.C., David chose his youngest son, Solomon, to be the next king of Israel. A legendary story of Solomon's wisdom involves two women who lived in the same house. Each gave birth to an infant on the same day. One of the babies died, and each woman swore the surviving child was hers. When they appeared before Solomon, he could not be certain who was the mother. He listened to their story and then ordered a soldier to cut the remaining child in two. Each woman would receive half. One woman accepted Solomon's decision. The other cried out that she would give up her claim to the child. Solomon gave the baby to the second woman, since she was obviously the mother.

The name Solomon is taken from the word *shalom*, meaning peace. King Solomon lived up to his name, teaching his people the value of law and order and trying to end war and discord. He divided his kingdom into 12 districts, deliberately crossing tribal boundaries. He hoped to reduce the separatism of the tribes and unite them into one people. He also formed alliances and economic ties with neighboring states. Marriages between leading Hebrews and neighboring allies strengthened King Solomon's rule.

Probably Solomon's closest alliance was with King Hiram of Tyre. Solomon developed a profitable exchange of food products to send to the Phoenician city of Tyre in return for finished goods. In return, Tyre supplied Solomon with the timber and skilled labor needed to build a fleet of merchant ships.

At the port of Ezion-Geber, Solomon built a huge blast furnace to smelt copper ore from the mines of the nearby Sinai. The constant winds of this region provided a natural bellows for a process similar to that used in 20th century smelting. The refinery established Solomon as a great copper king. The copper industry provided a valuable export that could be exchanged for such luxuries as ivory and peacocks. His merchant fleet, centered on the Red Sea, engaged in the copper trade.

Solomon used his wealth to beautify Jerusalem. Dominated by its great temple, Jerusalem became the spiritual and political center of Israel. The beauty of the temple, overlaid with gold and silver, added to the glory of Solomon's reign. Another great structure was the king's palace which required 13 years to build.

Israel prospered; towns grew in size and number. Because of the many building projects, however, taxes were high. Each of the 12 districts had to raise enough food to supply the palace in Jerusalem for one month each year. The list of daily requirements included 30 cors (over 6 U.S. bushels) of fine flour, 60 cors of meal, 10 fat oxen, 20 pasture-fed cattle, 100 sheep, gazelles, roebucks, and fatted birds. By present-day standards, that daily supply could provide a gourmet table for 5,000 to 6,000 people.

Solomon collected tolls from all caravans passing through Palestine, as well as taxes from his subjects. The state controlled trade in yarn, horses, and chariots. Despite Solomon's wealth, the costs of his building projects were higher than his income.

When King Solomon ordered cedar trees from Lebanon, they were sent from the Phoenician port of Tyre in ships like those shown here.

Portraits of King Solomon and the Queen of Sheba were woven into a Persian rug. Symbols of the tribes of Israel form the borders.

One of the most unpopular measures was the *corvée*, or forced labor. Solomon forced his subjects to work in Lebanon, cutting timber for his building projects. Forced labor and high taxes bred hostility toward the king, particularly among the lower classes. After Solomon died, his son, Rehoboam, could not hold the Hebrew Kingdom together. The 10 northern tribes revolted and became the kingdom of Israel. Its capital was Samaria. The two southern tribes kept their capital at Jerusalem and united as the kingdom of Judah. ■

Decline of the Hebrew Kingdom

By the 700s B.C., Assyria had conquered the 10 tribes of Israel and led almost 30,000 Israelites off to slavery in Assyria. Because Judah did not resist the Assyrians, it was spared and became a vassal state.

In 609 B.C., the Medes, the Persians, and other nations formed an alliance and defeated the Assyrian Empire. The new Babylonian Empire then emerged and conquered Judah. The Babylonians destroyed the temple in Jerusalem and led the people of Judah off to Babylon in captivity.

In Babylon, the Jewish prophets, religious leaders the Hebrews believed were inspired by God, reminded the captive people that a new king would come. The Hebrews believed this king would renew their strength and restore them to glory. The Hebrews called this savior they had long awaited, the Messiah.

From 1200 to 800 B.C., the Jews' belief in one God gave them courage and faith to survive as they gained and lost a kingdom. During this period, other important changes took place. The use of iron and the ability to ride horses revolutionized both the way work was done and the way wars were fought. The Assyrians used iron and mounted horsemen to extend their empire throughout neighboring lands.

SECTION 1 *Study Skills*

Developing Vocabulary 1. How do cavalry troops differ from other troops? **2.** What is the Latin root for the word vassal? **3.** What is ethical monotheism? **4.** What is the origin of the word prophets? **5.** What did the Hebrews expect the Messiah to do?

Reviewing Main Ideas 1. List two advantages of iron over bronze. **2.** List two advantages cavalry had over soldiers in chariots. **3.** What was the chief activity of the Assyrians? **4.** What did Moses accomplish as leader of the Hebrews?

Understanding Cause and Effect 1. How did the use of iron promote the growth of cities? **2.** How did the use of iron allow ordinary people to become soldiers? **3.** Why were taxes high under Solomon? **4.** How were the Jews able to survive as a people between 1200 and 800 B.C.?

Challenge Compare and contrast the activities of Solomon's government with those of the government of the United States today.

2 Changing Cultures of India and China

OBJECTIVE: *To understand the causes and consequences of the changing civilizations in India and China from 1200 to 600 B.C.*

India from Oral History

Sometime between 1200 and 800 B.C., techniques for smelting iron reached India. Invaders may have brought iron, or perhaps wandering nomads brought the process for smelting the new metal.

Because no written records exist, nothing is known about the life of ordinary Indians or how the use of iron may have affected their lives during the period from 1200 to 800 B.C. Presumably, the use of iron changed the lives of the Indian people just as it had changed the lives of people in other regions. In warfare, soldiers with iron weapons could defeat those using bronze weapons. Farmers using iron tools could clear and plant more land than those using stone implements.

Problems in Early Indian History. Historians face three major problems when studying the history of India during this period. First, since no written records existed, they must piece together information from poems and hymns that the Aryans composed after they invaded northern India. Second, these poems and hymns were composed by priests and holy men who left out everything that did not interest them. Third, Indian literature was oral, memorized and repeated, and changed from generation to generation. When such works were finally written down, there was no way of telling what parts were very old and what parts had been added later.

The oldest known accounts of the Aryans are religious poems called *Vedas*, after the Sanskrit word *veda*, meaning spiritual knowledge. The oldest of these *Vedas*, the *Rigveda*, was composed during the period from 1500 to 1000 B.C. It is made up of 1,028 hymns to various Aryan gods. From the river names used in the hymns, historians know that the Aryans were living in the Punjab, a region of grassy plains between valleys of the Indus and Ganges rivers.

Indian Epic Poems. The *Ramayana* and the *Mahabharata*, composed between 1000 and 700 B.C., indicate that the Aryans were mov-

VOCABULARY DEVELOPMENT

reincarnate (REE ihn KAHR nayt) *verb:* to be born again in a new earthly body.

karma (KAHR muh) *noun:* **1.** the belief that the combined effects of a person's actions transfer from one life to the next; **2.** fate or destiny

caste system (kast SIHS tehm) *noun:* **1.** the social system of India based on exclusive social classes; **2.** the system of hereditary Hindu social classes, each traditionally forbidden to socialize with the others. From the Latin word, *castus*, originally meaning separated.

fief (feef) *noun:* land granted by a lord to another noble in exchange for service.

primogeniture (PRY muh JEHN ih chuhr) *noun:* the right of the first child to inherit the family's property. From the Latin words *primus*, meaning first, and *geniture*, meaning born.

ing eastward across the Punjab into the Ganges Valley. The *Mahabharata*, with 90,000 stanzas, is one of the longest poems in the world. It tells the story of wars between kingdoms in the area around modern-day Delhi, in the north Indian plain. The power struggle ends in an 18–day battle that destroys most of the fighters. Only five brothers survived.

The *Ramayana* is set farther to the east. Clues in the poem indicate that the Aryans were beginning to push southward into the Indian peninsula. The *Ramayana* is an epic, a long poem about the legendary deeds of a hero. A masterpiece of world literature, it is still popular among audiences throughout India and southeast Asia. It tells of events in the life of King Rama, who probably lived between 1000 and 700 B.C. The poem took its present written form more than 1,000 years ago.

The *Ramayana*

FOCUS ON SOURCES In the epic, Rama wins the hand of the beautiful Sita in an archery contest. Despite his royal birth, Rama is forced by his stepmother to give up his claim to the throne in favor of his half-brother. Accompanied by Sita, Rama withdraws to a forest populated by holy men and demons. While Rama is away hunting, Ravana, the demon king of the island of Lanka, abducts Sita. (The ellipses, sets of dots, represent parts of the original poem which have been left out.)

❝ . . . Ravana came boldly across the clearing toward Rama's house covered with the disguise of an old holy man . . . . Sita saw him coming . . . .

Ravana . . . stood silently by Sita's house, as holy men do when begging their daily food. There was no sign of . . . Rama. All around them there was only the forest land of green and brown.

Sita . . . said, "Worshipful brahmana [holy man], be our guest. Sit, take some water, wash, and I will bring food. . . ."

"How do you come to live here alone, my girl, in [this] perilous . . . land?" He stood looking at her. "By the Book, fair are your jewels."

"I am Sita. These jewels were presents. Don't fear demons for my husband Rama will be back soon. . . ."

"Beautiful," said Ravana. "I am the Rakshasa King Ravana. I rule the universe. Come to me, Sita. I will take you to Lanka

This picture from the *Ramayana* shows Sita captured by the twenty arms of the evil Ravana.

. . . and I will put you over all my other queens."

Sita laughed . . . "Never." Sita looked again at the quiet forest and could see no one.

. . . Ravana clapped his hands and his disguise fell away. He was tall as a tree. He had ten dark faces and twenty dark arms, and twenty red eyes rimmed like fire. . . . He licked his lips with sharp tongues. He wore golden armor, long heavy gold earrings, . . . gold bracelets, gold armbands, ten golden crowns set with golden pearls, gold belt-chains crashing and gold rings all over his fingers. Fragrant white flower garlands went over his shoulders and around his ten necks . . . .

"I will have you!" said Ravana. "Princess Sita, you are half divine, why mingle more with men? Rule every world with me . . . . You will forget Rama with me!"

. . . Sita knelt . . . hiding her face, clinging to a tree . . . . Ravana reached for her . . . . He caught her . . . in two of his right arms and lifted her, and his demon chariot came to meet him through the air. . . .

. . . Sita cried, "Rama! Rama!" many times and struggled to get free, but it was useless. Ravana was on the chariot, holding Sita like a fireball in his bare arms, and the chariot began to move. . . .

. . . Sita saw a great huge vulture asleep high in a treetop and cried aloud to him, "Tell Rama!" **"**

The vulture was killed by Ravana, and could not help Sita. After more adventures, however, Rama and his brother arrive with an army of talking monkeys and bears. They rescue Sita after a fierce battle. Rama and Sita are reunited and return home where Rama is crowned king.

Both Rama, the central character in the *Ramayana* and Krishna, a central character in the *Mahabharata*, were really Indian gods in human form. Both poems were intended to point a moral or explain some local custom or religious practice. ■

A thirteenth-century B.C. sculpture illustrates how people of Indian upper castes draped a sacred thread to distinguish themselves from people of lower castes.

Hindu Religion Develops

The religion of India, Hinduism (HIHN du wihz uhm), developed over thousands of years. It combines beliefs of the conquering Aryans and the original inhabitants.

Believers of the Hindu religion held that people not only experienced life and death, but also were reincarnated, born again in a new earthly body. A related idea was that all the actions in a people's lives made up their karma and determined their fate in the next life. People acquired good karma by obeying caste rules.

Between the years 800 and 600 B.C., the Hindu priests of India, the Brahmans, became the most important caste. They devoted themselves to searching for religious truths in the Aryan Vedas. They wrote their opinions in Brahmanas (BRAH muhn uhs). According to the Brahmanas, the priests were necessary to carry out the rituals and maintain the favor of the gods. They also lived the best lives and acquired more good karma than others. When reincarnated, they continued their good lives.

Caste System Develops

The basic rules of Indian society also developed during this period from 1200 to 600 B.C. The Aryan conquerors were very conscious of skin color differences between themselves and the darker Harappans. Because of their strong sense of racial superiority, the Aryans tried to prevent any social contacts with their despised subjects. Therefore, a system of four hereditary castes evolved.

The Hindu religion affected every act of the Indian's life. The caste system assigned a social status to every occupation and task. The first three social groups, or castes, were only for the Aryans and included priests and religious scholars, noble warriors, and merchants and landowners. The lowest caste, farmers, included the original Indian inhabitants, the Harappans. The Aryans called them *shudras* or *dasas*, meaning slaves.

Below these four castes was another group of people, the pariahs. All other castes avoided them. Eventually, this lowest group became known as the untouchables. The untouchables were people working in trades or crafts regarded as unclean, such as hunting, gravedigging, and scavenging. People in the other castes were afraid they would be polluted by any contact with the untouchables. Therefore, until recently, this lowest group never went outside their houses without striking a pair of clappers to warn others of their approach.

Over time the Brahmans justified the caste system in religious terms. People in lower castes had acquired bad karma in a previous life and were therefore less good

than the Brahmans. The priests also believed that members of different castes should not associate with, eat with, or marry one another.

Historians do not know how much of the caste system developed between 1200 and 600 B.C. As far back as records exist, Indian society was organized into castes.

Zhou Dynasty in China

Like the Indians, the people of China were undergoing many changes. The Zhou finally conquered the Shang, with whom they had been fighting since 1300 B.C. This victory began a new dynasty in China in 1027 B.C. See the map, China under the Zhou, page 76.

Changes that took place in China during the centuries from 1200 to 800 B.C. did not bring China into the Iron Age. Instead, the Chinese continued to make bronze objects until 500 B.C. China's bronze technology, however, reached a high level in both quality and number of objects produced.

This detailed bronze tigress from 1200 B.C. shows the high degree of skill Shang artisans developed.

The Zhou Dynasty Begins. The Zhou, a pastoral people, lived on the western fringe of the Shang state. They traded with the tribal peoples of Tibet and Mongolia.

Around 1300 B.C., the Shang Dynasty attacked the Zhou and later defeated them. From the Shang, the Zhou learned the ways of civilization. Many Zhou abandoned their pastoral ways and settled in towns and cities. Zhou cities became centers for bronze casting. Some Zhou learned how to write using the Shang script.

While a vassal to the Shang, the Zhou's king, whose name was Wen, used war and diplomacy to increase his power. Gradually he united the Zhou and they became powerful enough to challenge the Shang. About 1100 B.C., while the Shang army was away fighting barbarians, the Zhou rebelled. Zhou timing, leadership, and strength enabled them to conquer the Shang.

China under the Zhou, 700 B.C.

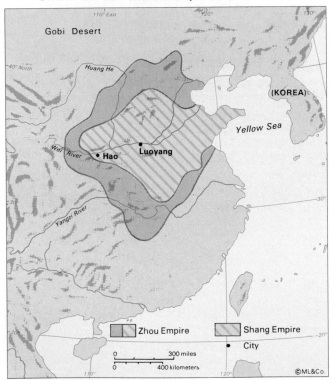

Map Skills 1. In which direction did the Zhou travel to move their capital to Luoyang? **2.** Was the Zhou empire larger or smaller than that of the Shang?

The Zhou capital was located at Hao on the Wei River close to the point where it flows into the Huang He. To control rebellious subjects to the east, the Zhou built another capital at Luoyang, on the Huang He. With these two capitals, the Zhou were able to control both their original territory and that of the former Shang Dynasty.

Zhou Government. The centuries from 1100 to 771 B.C. are called the Western Zhou Period because the Zhou ruler stayed in the western capital at Hao. Zhou kings built a strong central government. Assisting the king were two inspectors responsible for the two sides of the empire, east and west. Relatives and supporters of the Zhou ruler were given grants of land called fiefs in various parts of China.

Five ranks of nobility existed below the king. They were similar to the English duke, marquis, earl, viscount, and baron. In addition to a title and a grant of land, the Zhou ruler gave his nobles gifts of slaves, chariots, horses, and bronze vessels—symbols of the king's favor. Many of the best records of Zhou history are the long inscriptions on the bronze vessels the king gave as gifts to his loyal vassals.

Titles given to Zhou nobles were hereditary, meaning they could be passed from father to son. The Zhou began a new system in which the father's title went to the oldest son of the first wife. This system, called primogeniture, helped to prevent fights among relatives over who would inherit the father's title.

The king visited all the fiefs of his empire every year. Sometimes he held archery contests for his nobles in which he took part. The king also kept in touch with the common people through symbolic acts. For example, at the beginning of the planting season he went to the fields and plowed a strip of ground. For centuries after, Zhou Chinese emperors plowed the first furrow to show that they were concerned about the peasants and their farms.

A painting of King Wen, the Zhou ruler, listening to his wise man read an astrological chart.

Decline of the Zhou Kings. Early in the Zhou rule, the kings were powerful and controlled their lords. Later, kings became weaker and some nobles became stronger. Others made alliances with the barbarians and became independent of the Zhou king. As a result, China was divided into many small states.

In 771 B.C., barbarian raiders entered the Wei River Valley, attacked Hao, and murdered the Zhou ruler. The remaining Zhou members moved to the eastern capital at Luoyang.

Between 1200 and 600 B.C., the technology of ironworking contributed to the rise of new empires and the expansion of trade in the Mediterranean region, southwest Asia, and India. In China, many elements of that country's distinct civilization came into focus during this period. Also during this period, the first American civilization developed in complete isolation from the events occurring in Eurasia and Africa.

Religion under the Zhou. The Shang and the Zhou worshiped different gods. The Shang worshiped a god called the Lord on High; the Zhou worshiped a god they named T'ien (Tee EHN), meaning Heaven. The Zhou god was the sky but also the spirits of dead Zhou kings. Heaven rewarded or punished rulers according to their behavior.

The Zhou believed that T'ien favored their cause and ordered them to conquer the Shang. Heaven was unhappy with the Shang ruler because he did not look after his people. Thus, Heaven took away the Shang's mandate or command to rule and gave the Zhou the Mandate of Heaven. Ever since Zhou times, the Chinese believed that if a ruler was cruel, lazy, or did not care for his people, they should overthrow him. The people carried out God's punishment, the removal of the Mandate of Heaven.

SECTION 2 *Study Skills*

Developing Vocabulary Use each of the following in a sentence: **1.** caste system. **2.** reincarnate. **3.** karma. **4.** fief. **5.** primogeniture.

Reviewing Main Ideas **1.** What information does the *Ramayana* provide historians? **2.** Why did the Aryans develop a caste system in India? **3.** Why was primogeniture begun by the Zhou? **4.** According to the Zhou, under what conditions could people remove a ruler's Mandate of Heaven?

Understanding Chronology **1.** When was the *Rigveda* composed? **2.** When did the caste system develop in India? **3.** How long was the Western Zhou Period?

Challenge **1.** Do you agree with the Chinese attitude about the right of a people to overthrow their ruler? Explain. **2.** Does the United States have anything similar to a caste system today? Explain.

3 Life in the Americas, A Land Apart

OBJECTIVE: *To understand the causes of the agricultural way of life that developed in the Americas*

American Big Game Hunters

The people of the Western Hemisphere developed civilizations and learned to work with metals later than did people of the fertile crescent and the other river valleys. Americans did not invent bronze casting until about A.D. 1000. The American Indians did not learn to smelt iron until the Europeans arrived.

The first people who migrated to the Americas probably crossed the land bridge from Siberia to Alaska during the last Ice Age. The earliest remains of human beings, discovered in places as far apart as Peru and Canada, date back more than 20,000 years.

Early Americans, ancestors of American Indians, were hunters and gatherers. By 10,000 B.C., they were killing giant bison with horns 6 feet across, camels, moose, mastodons, and the elephant-like mammoths. They also hunted giant beavers and huge armadillos weighing about 300 pounds, and an American lion that looked much like the African lion of today.

American Agriculture Begins

Around 7000 B.C., the weather became warmer, and many of the big animals died out. Hunters adapted to the changing food supply by eating less meat and more plants. Seeds and fruits became more important, and people gradually learned to grow nourishing plants.

In the Western Hemisphere, the development of agriculture began around 5000 B.C. in Middle America. People in the highlands learned how to plant and harvest such crops as pumpkins, beans, and chili peppers. The first remains of domesticated maize, or Indian corn, date from around 2500 B.C.

Importance of Maize. Maize offered the early Americans many advantages. It was very nutritious and easy to raise, and could be stored. Kernels of corn could be ground into flour by rubbing a hand-held grinding stone over a base stone. The flour, mixed with a liquid, could be patted into a flat cake to be cooked. Tortillas, a thin corn pancake, are still prepared in this way.

Other important American foods were tomatoes, peppers, avocados, and pineapples. All of these crops were unknown in the Eastern Hemisphere. Crops familiar to Eurasians and Africans, such as wheat and rice, were unknown in the Americas. This

---

VOCABULARY DEVELOPMENT

mesa (MAY suh) *noun:* a high, flat hill rising above surrounding land. From the Latin word, *mensa*, meaning table.

terra cotta (TEHR uh KAHT uh) *noun:* a hard, brown-red, glazed or unglazed fired clay used in making statues, vases, and other objects of art. From the Italian word, *terra cotta*, meaning baked earth.

Middle America, 600 B.C.

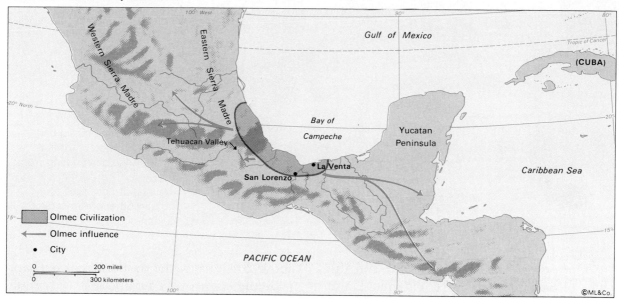

Map Skills **1.** In which direction would a resident of La Venta go to reach San Lorenzo?
2. Near what peninsula did the Olmecs live?

fact shows the independent way that agriculture developed in the isolated Western Hemisphere.

Unlike Eurasian farmers, American farmers did not invent plows. Neither did they have oxen or cattle to use as work animals. Americans developed cultures without the use of any wheeled vehicles. In constructing buildings, they did not use the arch and had no glass. They played drums and flutes but had no stringed musical instruments. All these facts illustrate that cultures in the Americas developed independently from those in the Eastern Hemisphere. Apparently, no communication with the Eurasian civilizations existed.

Olmec Civilization Begins

As in Eurasia, farmers in the Western Hemisphere lived in agricultural villages. Around 2500 B.C., village life developed in Middle America and in the Andes Mountain range of South America. The major areas of village life were the Tehuacán Valley of central Mexico and the coastal plain along the

Gulf of Mexico. See the map, Middle America, on this page. Maize agriculture formed the basis of this village life. Sometime after 1500 B.C., the American Indians of Middle America began to produce an agricultural surplus, the key to civilization.

The Olmecs of southern Mexico developed the first American civilization. They lived on the coastal plain along the Gulf of Mexico. Around 1250 B.C., the Olmecs established a city at a site called San Lorenzo. It was located on a high, flat hill rising above the surrounding land, called a mesa.

San Lorenzo was occupied from 1200 B.C. until 900 B.C., when it was abandoned. La Venta, about 50 miles northwest and closer to the Gulf, was the most important site from 900 B.C. to 400 B.C.

Olmec Society. The Olmecs were divided into two classes. The ordinary people were farmers who lived in villages of 10 or 12 families near San Lorenzo, along the river banks. These farmers produced a surplus of maize, the crop on which Olmec civilization depended.

The Olmec clay figurine at left is part jaguar and part human. In the center is a mother and child dating from 1000 B.C. The Olmec jade figurine at right was found among other ceremonial figurines.

The other class of Olmecs lived in the cities of San Lorenzo and La Venta. These city Olmecs included the religious and political leaders, or aristocracy, who dominated society. Olmec life on the mesa of San Lorenzo was vastly different from that in the agricultural villages.

The Olmec city boasted huge buildings suitable for Olmec leaders. These, and huge earthen pyramids topped with temples, crowned the mesa and dominated the area.

Olmec Culture.

The Olmecs did not have a fully developed writing system, but used some characters or symbols on carvings and works of art. Like the writing found in the ancient Indus Valley, that of Middle America has not yet been deciphered.

The Olmecs worshiped many gods, among them a jaguar rain god, a corn god, a fire god, and a feathered serpent. All are versions of gods worshiped by later peoples of Middle America. Olmec priests had great authority. They studied their calendar, which they believed could help them predict events. To keep the gods happy, the Olmecs offered human sacrifices.

Olmec Cities.

San Lorenzo contained a cluster of mounds and courtyards with small ponds for water storage. Workers brought stone to make drains for the plazas. Only about 200 houses, the residences of perhaps 1000 members of the aristocracy, were built on the mesa top.

The most spectacular sights on the mesas were huge stone heads with fierce faces in helmet-like headdresses. The stone for the sculptures had to be brought from more than 50 miles away. The biggest pieces weighed as much as 44 tons. To move such massive stones without the aid of wheels or machines of any kind was an outstanding feat and must have involved skillful organizing of great numbers of laborers.

Archaeologists have discovered many terra cotta, fired clay statues, representing people playing a kind of ball game, perhaps part of a religious ceremony. A solid rubber ball was used on a stone court. Stone walls enclosed the rectangular courts. The players wore heavy leather pads on their knees, elbows, and hips.

The second city, La Venta, was built on an island in a swamp. Laid out in a symmetrical pattern, the city included large pyramids. Platforms were built to hold houses, but no remains have survived. The people of La Venta created "pavements" of beautiful green stones laid out in delicate patterns. Mysteriously, the "pavement," when finished, was covered with dirt and a second layer of decorative stones laid down, then a third layer, and a fourth.

This Oaxcaca ballcourt, with its high walls and spectator seating, is similar to Olmec courts.

Olmec Trade. The Olmecs may have used their cities as centers of a trading network. Merchants may have left the cities of San Lorenzo and La Venta to trade among the peoples of Middle America. Items, such as obsidian, jade, cacao, and iron ore, were brought to the Olmec centers over long distances. Obsidian was used to make stone knives; jade was carved into sculptures. Cacao beans were the source of chocolate, and iron ores were ground into mirrors.

At the edges of the Olmec cultural areas were outposts or colonies. Some Olmec merchants traveled to distant places to secure the goods they needed. Olmec objects have been found throughout Middle America. Other Olmecs defended the frontiers against less civilized peoples.

Decline of Olmec Civilization. The ruins of the city of San Lorenzo show that the city

This carved stone head, which is 9 feet high and weighs 25.3 tons, is believed to be the portrait of an Olmec king.

Comparison of Olmec and Assyrian Cultures, 1250–400 B.C.

	Olmecs	Assyrians
Way of Life	Farmers and city-dwellers	Farmers, city dwellers, and fierce warriors
Language Writing	Undeciphered hieroglyphics written on clay tablets and monuments	Early Semitic language, cuneiform writing; later Aramaic language written with ink on parchment
Trade	Imported obsidian for knives, jade for sculptures, and iron for mirrors	Took tribute in animals, cedar, and metals. Built network of highways
Architecture	Large earthen pyramids and huge stone monuments	One-story, flat-roofed buildings as well as temples and palaces
Religion	Practiced human sacrifice to many gods	Food and precious objects offered to many gods
Technology	Worked in stone and clay	Worked iron into shields, spears, and swords
Importance	First advanced culture in the Western Hemisphere, influenced later American civilizations	Spread culture and language to neighboring people; developed a system of ruling conquered lands that became a model for later empires

was intentionally destroyed about 900 B.C. The great stone heads were toppled, defaced, and buried. The same thing seems to have happened to La Venta some years later. Jungles gradually covered the remains of Olmec civilization.

The Olmecs left a valuable legacy for later American people. Like the Olmecs, later inhabitants depended on maize, built cities and pyramids, and worshiped similar gods. They also renewed the trading network of the Olmecs.

Civilization in the Americas first developed in isolation from the Eastern Hemisphere. The Atlantic and Pacific oceans prevented the Americans from sharing in the interacting zone that linked one Afro-Eurasian civilization with another. For example, the technology for working metals, which gradually spread from the fertile crescent to the Indus Valley and later to China, did not reach the Americas. Therefore, the people of the Western Hemisphere developed their own independent solutions to the problems of taming their environment and developing their cultures.

SECTION 3 *Study Skills*

Developing Vocabulary 1. What is a mesa? **2.** What do the Italian words *terra cotta* mean?

Reviewing Main Ideas 1. What evidence suggests that civilization developed separately in the Americas and in Eurasia? **2.** Where did village life develop in the Americas around 2500 B.C.? **3.** How were the classes in Olmec society divided geographically?

Understanding Cause and Effect 1. What change in climate caused people in the Western Hemisphere to eat less meat and more plants? **2.** Why did the Olmecs offer human sacrifices? **3.** What evidence causes historians to believe that the Olmecs were able to organize great numbers of laborers?

Understanding Chronology 1. During what period did the first people migrate to the Americas? **2.** When did agriculture first develop in the Western Hemisphere? **3.** How long was La Venta's supremacy?

Challenge Give examples from art, food, and technology of the interaction among cultures of the world today.

Map Projections

A globe is the most accurate representation of the world. Like the earth, a globe is a sphere. Globes can show the shapes, areas, and locations of all parts of the earth. However, globes are awkward to carry, and landforms and other physical features often appear quite small on them. To show the east to west boundaries of Syria 9 inches apart on a globe, the globe would have to be 12 feet in diameter.

Flat maps are easy to carry and they can show enlarged portions of the world. Flat maps, however, always distort the world. Anyone who has tried to giftwrap a basketball knows the difficulty of fitting a sphere-shaped object to a flat sheet of paper. Cartographers face a similar challenge. A representation of the earth on a map is called a projection. Cartographers have created many different projections. No projection can show all characteristics of the earth accurately.

Mercator Projection

One of the best known map projections is the Mercator projection, created by Gerardus Mercator in 1569. Mercator, a sixteenth century Flemish cartographer, wanted a projection suitable for sailors. He kept all meridians and parallels meeting at right angles. He could not, however, also show the meridians intersecting at the poles.

The Mercator projection keeps shapes of landmasses reasonably accurate but it distorts their sizes and distances between them. The distortion gets worse nearer the poles. In the Mercator projection, Greenland appears to be larger than South America. In reality, Greenland is approximately one-

Mercator Projection

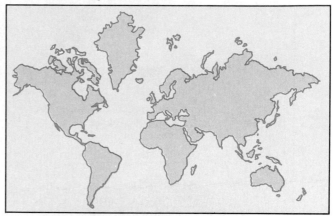

Peters Projection

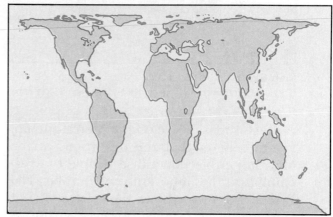

Map Skills 1. In the Mercator Projection, which is larger, Greenland or South America? 2. How do the shapes of Greenland and South America on the Peters Projection compare to those on the Mercator Projection?

eighth the size of South America. Europe, since much of it lies fairly far north, is also enlarged. Mercator's projection continues to be used by ship and aircraft pilots today.

Other Projections

Recently, Arno Peters, a West German historian, proposed a new projection to avoid

Alternative Projections

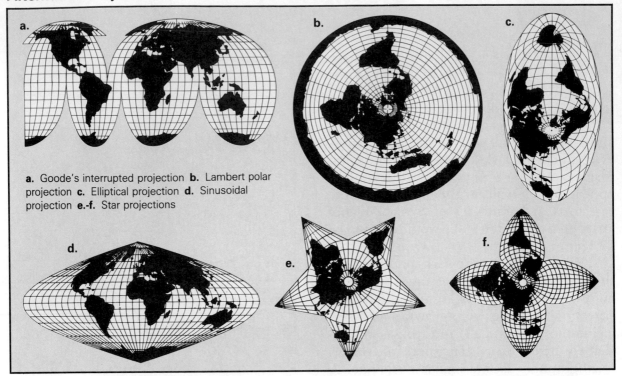

a. Goode's interrupted projection **b.** Lambert polar projection **c.** Elliptical projection **d.** Sinusoidal projection **e.-f.** Star projections

Map Skills **1.** Which map projections break the oceans into several areas? **2.** Which distort the shape of the land? **3.** Which show the correct size and shape for the land masses?

the distortions of size on the Mercator map. Peters believes that the distortions of the Mercator projection cause people to over-emphasize the importance of Europe. The Peters projection shows the relative size of land masses accurately, however, it distorts their shapes.

The Robinson projection is used for many of the world maps in this book. In the Robinson projection (see page 87 for an example) the meridians are curves rather than straight lines.

On an interrupted projection, such as the one on this page, the correct size of land and water areas are shown. However, the land shapes are somewhat distorted. Land distortions can be corrected by breaking the oceans into several areas.

Some projections center on a particular part of the earth. For example, the polar map centers on the North Pole. This projec-

tion can help navigators find the shortest and most direct routes between regions. An example of a polar projection is shown on this page.

Cartographers often choose a particular projection to highlight certain information. No map, however, can match the accuracy of a globe.

STUDY SKILLS Reading Maps

1. What advantages does a flat map have compared to a globe?
2. What is incorrect about the meridians on a Mercator projection?
3. According to Arno Peters, how does a Mercator projection influence how people think?
4. How is the Peters projection distorted?
5. Explain why the meridians on a Robinson projection are more realistic than the meridians on a Mercator or Peters projection.

CHAPTER 4 *Summary & Review*

Summarizing Main Ideas

Between 1200 and 800 B.C., the civilizations using iron caused great social and economic changes. For example, the Assyrians wielding iron weapons and charging on cavalry conquered other peoples. Iron tools made work easier on farms and in cities.

Historical knowledge of early India mostly comes from two epic poems, the *Ramayana* and the *Mahabharata*. India's caste system assigned a social status to every occupation. By 600 B.C., Hindu priests had become the most important caste in India.

In 1027 B.C., the Zhou became the rulers of China, and established a new dynasty that lasted until 771 B.C. Unlike other Eastern Hemisphere civilizations, China did not participate in the Iron Age until 500 B.C.

The Olmecs of southern Mexico developed the first American civilization. They did not use iron or the wheel.

Questions for Critical Thinking

COMPREHENSION Interpreting Events

1. How did Solomon try to encourage unity among the Hebrews?
2. Compare the Zhou culture to the culture of India at the same time.
3. According to the Zhou, when was revolution against a ruler justifiable?

ANALYSIS Identifying Trends

1. Explain how the introduction of iron weapons and cavalry changed warfare.
2. What causes a powerful culture to lose its influence over time? Use examples from this chapter to support your view.

APPLICATION Comparing Past to Present

1. Explain why monotheism is more common today than it was 3,000 years ago.

2. Compare India's Caste System with social classes in modern society.
3. Identify the factors that hindered trade in the ancient world. Which of these still hinder trade today?

SYNTHESIS Developing Research Skills

1. Write a two page report on one of the following: Assyrians, Hebrews, Zhou, Olmec. Analyze the civilization's accomplishments and identify its important leaders.
2. Check out the *Ramayana* or the *Mahabharata* from a library. Summarize one section.

EVALUATION Weighing Consequences

1. Summarize the problems associated with studying a culture that relies on oral history.
2. Why was a surplus of maize important to American civilizations?

CHALLENGE

1. Contrast the religion of the Hebrews and the Hindus. How might these differences have affected the development of their culture?
2. How does the cartoon on this page make a humorous point about the carved statues of early civilizations such as the Olmecs?

UNIT 1 *Review*

Critical Thinking for Today's World

ANALYSIS Understanding People

1. Give examples from this unit to show that, as humans learn to make more specialized tools, their level of production increases.
2. Compare and contrast the items people traded in ancient times with items traded among nations today.
3. Phoenicians helped spread writing to the common people in the Mediterranean Basin. Why is it an advantage for civilizations to have citizens who can read and write?
4. Since the time of the Neanderthals, human population has almost continually increased. Some historians believe that the number of confrontations between peoples has also increased. Explain why this may be so.
5. Describe the cultural differences between the Neanderthals and the Cro-Magnons.
6. Compare and contrast the influence on religion of Abraham and Amenhotep.
7. Why was the development of Hammurabi's Code an important advancement?

ANALYSIS Recognizing Change Over Time

1. Summarize the changes in culture caused by the knowledge of how to control fire.
2. The Agricultural Revolution was one of the most significant changes in history. Describe how changes in agriculture can still affect the modern world.
3. Explain why the most powerful modern civilizations are not as dependent on river valleys as were the early centers of civilization.
4. Make a timeline that includes the five most important events that happened between 12,000 and 500 B.C. Explain why you chose each of these events.

APPLICATION Solving Problems

1. Over the centuries civilizations have developed a variety of water sources. Describe how three of these methods have met people's need for water.
2. Ancient people learned to use metals to improve their way of life. Give three or more examples of improvements in technology during your lifetime that have enhanced the way people live.
3. Give examples of cases in which civilizations in Eurasia and Africa worked out different solutions to similar problems.
4. Throughout history, people have migrated when problems became too great. Choose one example of a migration described in this unit. Analyze how migration changed the culture.

SYNTHESIS Developing Global Citizenship

1. Today some feel that each individual is a citizen of Earth, rather than a citizen of a single civilization. Identify the reasons civilization developed. Then give evidence that global citizenship is or is not developing.
2. Explain why the number of individuals involved in governing society grew as civilization developed.
3. Conflicts between cultures are one barrier to global citizenship. Summarize the causes of conflicts between early civilizations.

EVALUATION Learning Lessons from the Past

1. As human technology in metal working improved, so did the number and quality of weapons. What relationship seems to exist between changes in technology and new forms of warfare? Use examples from both ancient and recent history.
2. Early civilizations often grew large through conquest. Later, the conquered people overthrew the conquerors. How may this recurring cycle of conquest have encouraged the development and spread of civilization?
3. India's caste system began as a way to regulate interactions among people. Evaluate the advantages and disadvantages of the system.

The Interacting Global Community to 800 B.C.

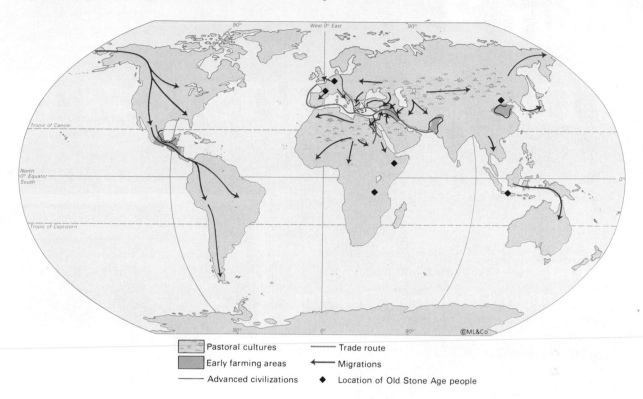

Pastoral cultures — Trade route
Early farming areas ← Migrations
Advanced civilizations ◆ Location of Old Stone Age people

A Global Perspective

From the time of the first humans to 800 B.C., people spread across the earth and established several strong civilizations. The green areas on the map above show where people developed early farming cultures. The tan areas containing grass indicate where people developed pastoral cultures based on herding domesticated animals.

The arrows on the map represent the movements of people. Note the several arrows moving away from the steppes in central Asia. Pastoralists from this region frequently attacked civilizations in China, India, and Mesopotamia.

The blue lines indicate the trade routes that existed by 800 B.C. Trade was an important means of spreading new ideas and technology.

COMPREHENSION Interpreting Maps

1. List four civilizations located in river valleys. What cities are located in these civilizations?
2. Which two continents have large regions where people were pastoralists?

3. Which two continents show the least trade or migration prior to 800 B.C.?
4. What body of water separates the continents of Africa and Europe?
5. Which two oceans included the most trade routes in 800 B.C.?
6. Identify the major centers of civilizations that existed prior to 800 B.C.?
7. Identify the areas where people were influenced by the centers of civilizations.
8. Compare the location of civilizations that developed before and after 2000 B.C.

ANALYSIS Recognizing Global Trends

1. The pastoralists from the steppes of central Asia moved east, south, and west. Explain why they probably chose not to move north.
2. Explain why the trade routes and migration routes seem to follow one another.
3. Explain why the civilizations in the Americas were less likely to learn from other peoples than were southwest Asian civilizations.

UNIT 2
The Expansion of

Civilizations 800 B.C.–A.D. 200

Consul of Rome watches a circus from his chariot in this inlaid-marble scene, from A.D. 360.

CHAPTER 5

Major World Cultures Develop

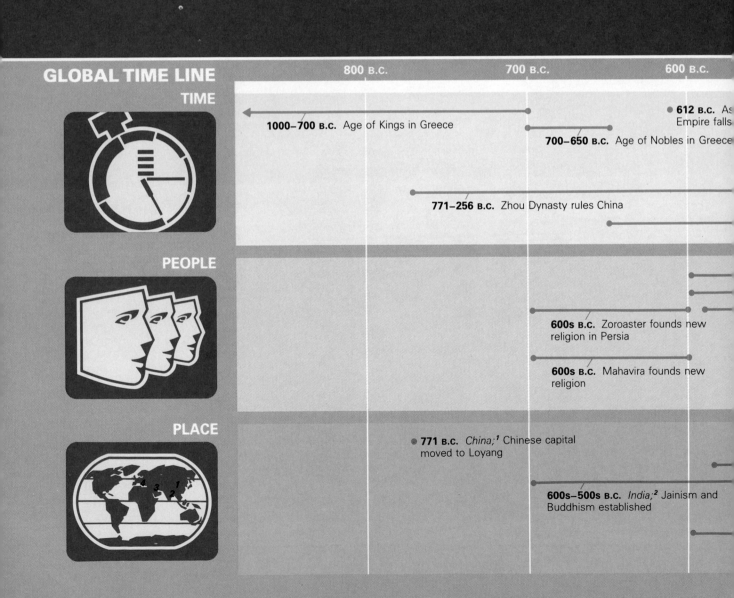

	800 B.C.	700 B.C.	600 B.C.
TIME			

1000–700 B.C. Age of Kings in Greece

700–650 B.C. Age of Nobles in Greece

612 B.C. As... Empire falls

771–256 B.C. Zhou Dynasty rules China

PEOPLE

600s B.C. Zoroaster founds new religion in Persia

600s B.C. Mahavira founds new religion

PLACE

771 B.C. *China;¹* Chinese capital moved to Loyang

600s–500s B.C. *India;²* Jainism and Buddhism established

Linking Past to Present

The Greeks, Persians, Indians, and Chinese who lived between 800 and 200 B.C. have greatly influenced today's world. The Greeks introduced democracy, and Greek philosophers laid the groundwork for modern scientific reasoning. The Persians built the largest empire the world had yet seen.

In India, the same centuries saw the beginnings of Hinduism and Buddhism, two major world religions still practiced by millions of people. Also, the moral teachings of Confucius were affecting the values, thoughts, and actions of the Chinese, Japanese, and Koreans.

The following chapter describes the causes and consequences of these developments in Greece, Persia, India, and China.

Greek merchants show their goods to the king, 600 B.C.

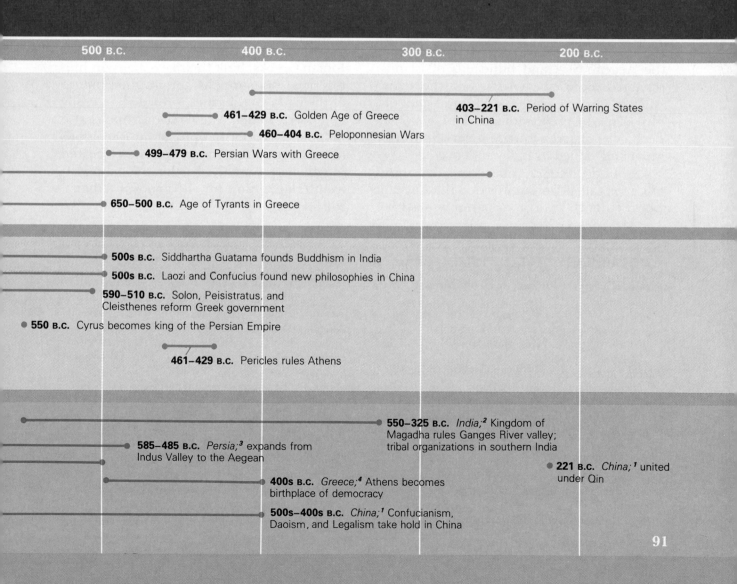

500 B.C.   **400 B.C.**   **300 B.C.**   **200 B.C.**

461–429 B.C. Golden Age of Greece

403–221 B.C. Period of Warring States in China

460–404 B.C. Peloponnesian Wars

499–479 B.C. Persian Wars with Greece

650–500 B.C. Age of Tyrants in Greece

500s B.C. Siddhartha Guatama founds Buddhism in India

500s B.C. Laozi and Confucius found new philosophies in China

590–510 B.C. Solon, Peisistratus. and Cleisthenes reform Greek government

550 B.C. Cyrus becomes king of the Persian Empire

461–429 B.C. Pericles rules Athens

550–325 B.C. *India;*[2] Kingdom of Magadha rules Ganges River valley; tribal organizations in southern India

585–485 B.C. *Persia;*[3] expands from Indus Valley to the Aegean

221 B.C. *China;*[1] united under Qin

400s B.C. *Greece;*[4] Athens becomes birthplace of democracy

500s–400s B.C. *China;*[1] Confucianism, Daoism, and Legalism take hold in China

91

1 *The Greek City-States*

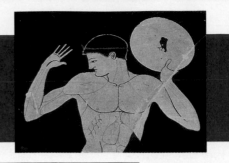

OBJECTIVE: *To understand the causes and consequences of the development of city-states in Greece*

The Greek City-States

The early Greeks developed independent city-states partly because water and mountain ranges separated each community. Greeks inhabited the Balkan Peninsula, the coasts of Asia Minor, the eastern shore of the Aegean Sea, and hundreds of islands scattered along the coasts. See the map, Ancient Greece, page 93. Physical geography shaped Greek traditions and customs. Each city created a unique form of government and valued its independence.

Around 1200 B.C., tribes speaking a form of Greek called Dorian invaded the Aegean world from the north, apparently destroying the splendid Mycenaean civilization. In its place, the Dorian Greeks established agricultural villages that, over several centuries, grew into small city-states. In time, these city-states influenced and controlled the surrounding territory.

Some of the Dorian Greeks, as well as Ionian Greeks, built their city-states on hilltop sites. An acropolis, the fortified hilltop of the early Greek cities, provided an easily defended citadel. The Greek acropolis also became a center for public and religious life. The most famous acropolis was located in Athens. There the Parthenon, a magnificent temple built for the goddess Athena, still stands.

VOCABULARY DEVELOPMENT

citadel *noun:* a fortress that commands a city, a stronghold.

oracle (AWR uh kuhl) *noun:* **1.** the place where gods were consulted; **2.** the response of a medium or priest. From the Latin word, *oraculum,* meaning to speak.

clan (klan) *noun:* **1.** a number of households that believe they are all descended from the same ancestor, have the same family name, and follow the same chieftain; **2.** a division within a tribe.

aristocracy (AR ihs TAHK ruh sih) *noun:* **1.** government by the best individuals or by a small privileged class; **2.** government by the upper class, usually a hereditary nobility. From the Greek words *aristos,* meaning best, and *kratia,* meaning rule.

tyrants (TY ruhnts) *noun:* **1.** absolute rulers without legal authority. From the Greek word, *tyros,* meaning master.

phalanx (FAY lanks) *noun:* an ancient military formation of infantry in close and deep ranks with shields joined and overlapping. From the Greek word *phalanx,* meaning line of battle.

archon (AHR kahn) *noun:* highest elected officials in ancient Greece; appointed officials and made laws. From the Greek word *archon,* meaning leader.

democracy (dih MAHK ruh see) *noun:* government in which the people hold power either directly or through elected representatives; rule by the people. From the Greek words *demos,* meaning people, and *kratia,* meaning rule.

Greek Religion

The Greeks worshiped many gods. Zeus, the god of the sky, was king of the gods. Hera, the sponsor of women and marriage, was his queen. The Greek people believed that each city had a special protector. The city of Sparta, for example, revered Ares, the god of war. Athenians believed that Athena, the goddess of wisdom, protected their city. The citizens of Corinth sought the favor of Apollo, the god of music and poetry.

The Greeks also believed that their gods had human characteristics and human failings. The Greeks sought advice from their gods through oracles, the places where gods were consulted through priests. The most famous oracle was at Delphi. People from all over Greece traveled to oracles to hear prophecies and advice.

Ancient Greece, 600 B.C.

Map Skills 1. How far is Athens from Sparta? 2. What is the name of the geographic region that includes Greece?

The Early Olympics

FOCUS ON SOCIETY

Periodically, athletes gathered from all over Greece to please the gods and honor dead heros by participating in athletic festivals, the Panhellenic Games. The most famous, the Olympic Games, were stopped in A.D. 394 but were revived in 1896. Dedicated to the god Zeus, the Olympics began in 776 B.C. They took place every four years. Some 40,000 Greeks crowded into their stadium built in Olympia. During the Olympic Games, wars between Greek city-states were suspended.

The earliest Olympics featured footraces. Later, athletes also competed in boxing, wrestling, and the pancratium, a combination of boxing and wrestling. Some athletes trained for the pentathlon. This event included running, jumping, wrestling, and discus and javelin throwing. Chariot races were added in 680 B.C.

In a special ceremony, the winner of each event received a wreath of olive branches as a prize. When the successful athletes returned home, enthusiastic crowds gave them lavish honors and gifts. Contestants who did not finish first received no recognition. The Greeks thought second place was no better than last.

Greek women were not allowed to compete in, or even watch, the Olympic Games. Some wealthy Greek women, however, owned teams of horses that competed in the chariot races.

After Rome conquered Greece in the second century B.C., the Olympic games lost their prestige and religious significance. The Roman Emperor Theodosius ended the Olympic Games in A.D. 394. ■

Evolution of Greek Government

As the Greek villages grew into city-states, power passed gradually from the hands of tribal chiefs, or kings, to the clan chiefs, or nobles. These nobles grew wealthy from their extensive land holdings. When crops failed, farmers fell into debt to large landowning nobles. When the farmers could not repay their debts, the nobles claimed their small farms.

Wealthy nobles maintained many horses and formed armies of cavalry. These nobles waged war and kept law and order in the city-states. Assemblies of nobles made governmental decisions and eventually replaced the kings. Rule by nobles, a wealthy, educated class, is called an aristocracy.

The nobles fought constantly among themselves for control of the city-states. At the same time, people became discontented as population increased and land grew scarce. Eventually, the common people became tired of warfare and chaos, and looked for new leaders.

In many Greek city-states, powerful individuals, called tyrants, gained control of the government by appealing to the poor and discontented for support. The term tyrant later came to mean a harsh or brutal ruler. In ancient Greece, however, tyrants were not always harsh. Many supported large public works projects because their position of power depended on pleasing the people.

The Phalanx Changes Society

Between 650 and 500 B.C., a change in military tactics brought a profound change in Greek society. The Greeks developed a new battle formation, the phalanx. A phalanx consisted of eight rows of foot soldiers, each carrying a spear in one hand and a shield in the other. The men stood so close together that their shields seemed to form a solid wall. Even cavalry could not stop the advance of this mass of men. Attack from the side or rear was the enemy's only chance to defeat the phalanx.

This military formation required the use of thousands of foot soldiers who had trained together for many months. For hours, male citizens practiced marching and running in step. In battle, each man's safety depended on the courage and discipline of his neighbor.

The larger the phalanx, the safer and stronger was the city-state. Safety, therefore, depended on the citizen farmer who lived modestly and could equip himself to fight with a spear, shield, and helmet. The system that had allowed wealthy landowners to take over the small farms of their poor neighbors gradually ended.

Sparta, a Military City-State

Sparta, a powerful city-state in a valley on the Peloponnesus, altered its way of life to accommodate the phalanx. Unlike many city-states, Sparta was not walled for defense. Spartans boasted that: "A wall of men is better than a wall of brick."

Social Classes in Sparta. The people of Sparta were divided into three groups, or classes: citizens, free subjects, and helots. Citizens were the descendants of the Dorian invaders who became the landowners and controlled the government.

Free subjects could never become citizens. Some free subjects grew wealthy as merchants and craftsworkers.

Helots, the lowest group, were slaves who farmed the land that Spartan citizens owned. Helots greatly outnumbered citizens and other subjects.

The Spartan Army. Near the end of the seventh century, the Spartans introduced the Lycurgan constitution. This document set up a system of lifelong military training for every citizen. The Spartan boy left home at the age of seven to become a soldier. Boys trained all day and lived in military barracks until they were 60 year old men.

The Government of Sparta. Two assemblies governed Sparta. The Assembly, composed of male citizens over 30 years of age, elected officials and voted on major issues. The Council of Elders proposed the laws on which the Assembly voted. Five elected officials called ephors carried out the laws the Council passed. These men controlled education, examined children at birth, and prosecuted court cases. They had unlimited power to act as guardians of Sparta.

Life in Sparta. The life of an average Spartan citizen was harsh and militaristic. Girls stayed at home and prepared themselves to be the wives and mothers of soldiers. Babies judged unfit to be future soldiers were abandoned on mountain tops. The role of women in Spartan society, as in all the Greek city-states, was restricted. Only Spartan men could speak at public gatherings, vote, and hold office.

Democracy in Athens

Life in Athens, influenced by reformers, was dramatically different from that in Sparta. When the need arose in Athens for

Democracy places a wreath on a citizen, reminding Athenians to value their freedom in this relief from ancient Athens.

a large supply of citizen soldiers for the phalanx, Athenians chose a reform-minded aristocrat, named Solon, to be archon, the highest official. His reforms helped the citizen farmer survive.

Reforms of Solon. Solon made three important changes. First, he ended the practice of enslaving people who could not pay their debts. Second, land was returned to people who had lost it because of indebtedness. Third, Solon rewrote the laws to make them humane.

Because of the importance of the citizen soldiers, Solon gave the Assembly of citizens the right to veto any laws of which it did not approve. He also allowed the Assembly to elect a Council of Four Hundred to enforce the laws.

About 560 B.C., a relative of Solon, Peisistratus (py SIS tra tuhs), plotted to seize control of Athens. To gain the sympathy of the people, he slashed himself and the mules of his chariot, and made a dramatic entrance into the marketplace. Peisistratus claimed that his enemies had wounded him. The people voted to provide him with a bodyguard of citizens armed with clubs. Peisistratus took over the acropolis and gained personal control of Athens.

Reforms of Peisistratus. In 560 B.C. the people of Athens gave power to the tyrant Peisistratus. He continued the reforms of Solon. Nobles who protested were exiled and their large estates divided among people who had no land. Public construction projects provided many jobs.

Peisistratus also advanced Athenian culture. He invited sculptors, painters, and poets to live and work at his court.

Reforms of Cleisthenes. The next reformer, Cleisthenes (KLYS thuh neez), belonged to a leading Athenian family. He became the most powerful statesman in Athens about 510 B.C. He went beyond Solon and Peisistratus to bring democracy, rule by the people, to Athens.

The Evolution of Democracy in Greece		
Approximate Time Period	**Form of Government**	**Cause of Downfall**
900–700 B.C.	**The Age of Kings:** rule by a king who gained power by inheriting the throne.	Landholding nobles grew more powerful than tribal kings.
700–650 B.C.	**The Rise of Nobles:** control by a few important nobles; a period of colonization and consolidation of power in the hands of a few people.	Hardship and discontent among the poor led them to support tyrants. Merchants and artisans also resented the powerful nobles.
650–500 B.C.	**The Age of Tyrants:** government control by a tyrant who gained support from the poor and the discontented.	Rulers began as popular reformers who later often limited the freedom of the people.
500 B.C.	**Democratic Government:** rule by citizens who proposed, passed, and enforced laws.	Geographic factors and strong independent spirit led to disunity.

Cleisthenes allowed all free Athenian males 18 years of age or older to register as citizens having the right to vote and hold office. He also created a Council of Five Hundred to advise the Assembly. All citizens participated in drawing lots to choose members of the council. The revolutionary result was a council made up of people in all social classes. More important, the Assembly was given the power to introduce and pass laws. The Assembly then became the real political power in Athens.

Athenian Democracy. Women, slaves, and non-Athenians had no political power. However, about 30,000 adult males of the total population of almost 350,000 participated in government decisions. These men were eligible to serve on the council and be present at any assembly meeting.

Athenian democracy worked for almost a century. It created a feeling of community and cooperation in Athens. Citizens participated directly in government. They debated and discussed the great issues of the day in the Assembly.

While Greek government was evolving, changes were taking place to the east, on the Iranian plateau. From there, a mighty and well-organized empire developed. Ruled by the Persians, this new empire expanded and threatened Athens, as well as its neighboring city-states.

SECTION 1 *Study Skills*

Developing Vocabulary 1. Explain the difference between the origins of the words aristocracy and democracy. **2.** How did an archon differ from the leader of a city-state in a tyranny? **3.** How are a citadel and a phalanx related? **4.** How do a clan and a tribe differ? **5.** Why did Greeks visit an oracle?

Reviewing Main Ideas 1. What characteristics did Greek gods exhibit? **2.** Describe the role of women in Greek life. **3.** List three reformers of Athenian government. **4.** Summarize the differences between Athens and Sparta.

Understanding Geography 1. Describe the physical geography of Greece. **2.** How did the geography of Greece affect the development of government in Greek cities? **3.** What was the purpose of the Olympics?

Challenge How did Athenian democracy differ from the present-day form of democracy in the United States?

2 Achievements of Persia

OBJECTIVE: *To become familiar with the rise of the Persian Empire, its accomplishments, and its beliefs*

The Iranian Plateau

The Iranian Plateau, homeland of the Persians, is more than 10 times larger than Greece. This plateau forms part of the great arid zone extending across Africa and Eurasia. It is bounded on the west by the Zagros Mountains. The northern boundary of the plateau stretches from the southern shore of the Caspian Sea to the mountains of the Hindu Kush. Today, the countries of Iran and Afghanistan occupy the Iranian Plateau.

The climate of this highland is hot and dry. Most of the region is made up of steppes that give way to deserts in some places and rugged mountains in others. The first inhabitants of the Iranian plateau were nomads who herded cattle, sheep, and horses across the grasslands. Later, after learning to irrigate, some of the nomads farmed and settled in permanent homes.

The Medes and Persians

The Medes and Persians were nomadic Indo-European tribes. They migrated to the Iranian plateau around 1500 B.C. from what is now part of the Soviet Union. The name Persia came from *Persis*, the Greek name for the region.

The Medes lived on the northwestern part of the plateau, and the Persians settled in the southwestern part. Both peoples lived in tribal groups and paid taxes to the mighty Assyrian Empire. In 612 B.C., however, the Medes and Persians formed an alliance with the once-powerful Babylonians. Together they defeated the Assyrians.

Cyrus the Great Creates an Empire. In 585 B.C., the Medes, looking for new lands, conquered their former ally, the Persians. The Persians proved loyal subjects, and the Mede ruler allowed his daughter to marry a Persian prince. A child of this marriage was Cyrus, later called Cyrus the Great.

A legend tells that Cyrus' grandfather tried unsuccessfully to have the infant killed. He believed that a child who combined the characteristics of both the Medes and the Persians would overthrow him. A shepherd protected Cyrus, who later formed an army of Persians and did overthrow his grandfather.

The warriors of Persia had great skills as horsemen and riders. Led by Cyrus, they extended the Persian Empire from the Indus River valley to the shores of the Aegean Sea. Later, in 525 B.C., Cambyses, the son of Cyrus, pushed the boundaries of the empire

---

VOCABULARY DEVELOPMENT

satrapy (SAY truh pee) *noun:* a province of ancient Persia.

satrap (SAY trap) *noun:* the governor of a satrapy.

universal (YOO nuh VUHR sil) *adj:* including all, or a major part, as all people. From the Latin word, *universus*, meaning all together.

The Persian Empire, 500 B.C.

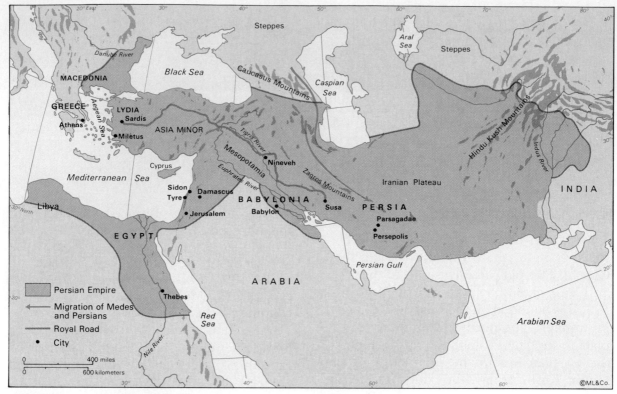

Map Skills **1.** Approximately how far apart are the Aegean Sea and the Indus River? **2.** How far is Thebes from the Black Sea? **3.** Name the cities located along the Royal Road.

into Africa by defeating Egypt and Libya. See the map, The Persian Empire, above.

Darius, Cambyses' successor, ruled the vast Persian empire at its height, from 521 to 485 B.C. His armies crossed into Europe, taking control of Thrace and Macedonia. As the Persian ruler, Darius governed an empire larger than any in world history up to that time. The Persian Empire included many of the centers of ancient civilization: Mesopotamia, the Indus Valley, Egypt, Syria, and Anatolia.

Persian Government. The Persians governed efficiently and with justice. They improved the earlier Assyrian practices of appointing a few governors to oversee provinces. The Persians divided their empire into 20 districts, or satrapies. Each satrapy had a governor, or satrap, appointed by the Persian king from among noble Persian

families. Then, inspectors called "the King's Eyes and Ears" checked district governors to be sure satraps used their power wisely.

Each satrap checked on local leaders and gathered taxes in the provinces. Military commanders kept order and recruited soldiers for the army. Persian kings sent their inspectors to ensure that taxes were fair.

Persian Architecture. The Persian kings celebrated their military and political successes by constructing splendid buildings in their cities. These magnificent structures displayed not only the Persians' wealth but also the cultural influences of different parts of the empire.

The palace that Darius built at Persepolis around 510 B.C. showed a blending of styles within the empire. The fluted columns found in the throne hall and audience chamber were fashioned in the Greek manner. Carved winged bulls were similar to Assyrian decorations. The reliefs on the walls resembled the work of Egyptian artists.

The Palace of Darius

FOCUS ON SOURCES

In his book, *Flames Over Persepolis*, Sir Mortimer Wheeler described the palace Darius built at Persepolis. Wheeler, a noted archaeologist, directed excavations in Great Britain, France, India, and Pakistan. He wrote the following description:

❝ At Persepolis, work was inaugurated by Darius in the years following 520 B.C. and was continued . . . until about 460 B.C. . . . Towards the north were two formal gateways, admitting to two richly columned halls; towards the south were residential buildings and a large treasury. The whole . . . was set within towered defenses of mud brick and approached by monumental staircases, richly pictured in relief.

The palace was on a scale worthy of a mighty empire at its prime, a work of high originality, designed and carved with assured mastery. The bare bones of the two feast halls today do little more than hint at former splendour. The western [hall], begun by Darius before 513 [B.C.], was two hundred feet square internally, and its thirty-six columns carried the timber roof at a height of some sixty feet above the floor.

Doors, and possibly other parts of the structure, were rivetted with ornamental bronze plates: rosettes and the representation of a griffen [a mythical animal having the head and wings of an eagle and the body, hindlegs, and tail of a lion] are mentioned, and gold-covered nails. . . . It has been calculated . . . that ten thousand people could be packed into the hall.

The main bulk of the palace buildings at Persepolis were of mud brick, which has long since dissolved. Occasional tile-

Guards in uniforms from Media and Persia stand watch on the stairway to Persepolis.

veneering has been mentioned. Major doorways and window frames were of limestone, the surface of which was often highly polished; a feature which we shall observe significantly . . . in India. ❞ ■

Zoroastrianism

The religion of the Medes and Persians had much in common with that of the Aryans who invaded India about 1500 B.C. Until about 600 B.C., the Persians worshiped many gods. The people sacrificed animals, and drank an intoxicating beverage that they believed brought them close to their gods. About 600 B.C., however, a religious reformer named Zoroaster was born. He became dissatisfied with the Persian religion of many gods and sacrifices.

A New God. At the age of 20, Zoroaster left his home and young wife to seek religious truth. After 10 years, he came to believe in only one god, Ahura Mazda (AH hoo ruh MAHZ duh), the source of light and truth. Zoroaster also believed that an evil spirit called Ahriman (AH rih muhn) lurked in the universe. A constant struggle took place between the forces of good and evil. According to Zoroaster, people must serve Ahura Mazda and live a good life in preparation for future salvation.

Over the years, Zoroaster taught others the truths that he believed Ahura Mazda had given him. Later, after Zoroaster's death, his followers developed sacred writings known as the *Avesta*. These writings contain Zoroaster's sayings called *Gathas*, as well as forms of religious ceremonies, laws, hymns, and prayers.

A Universal Religion. Zoroaster's religion never gained a large following. It did, however, influence the ideas of later religions such as Christianity and Islam. Both included the struggle on earth between good and evil and a final judgment. Zoroastrianism had a universal message, one for all people. To choose between good and evil, a person did not have to belong to a particular tribe or nation. This universalism was a feature of both Christianity and Islam, which emerged much later.

Islam later replaced Zoroastrianism as the majority faith in Persia, and the few people who still practice Zoroastrianism are a persecuted minority. The Parsis of India who came from Persia in the early 700s B.C. still practice the religion.

The Persian Interacting Zone

To move troops, supplies, and trade goods rapidly from one part of the empire to another, the Persians developed a remarkable and extensive interacting zone of communication. A Royal Road extended over 1,500 miles (2,400 kilometers) from Susa, the site of a Persian palace, to Sardis, capital of Lydia in Asia Minor. Along this road, the Persians built more than 100 supply stations and inns where travelers could stop for food and lodging.

As an official language, the Persians kept Aramaic, which the Assyrians had used. Scribes, therefore, had a common language that could be understood from one end of the empire to the other. In this way the Persians created a network of communication that blanketed southwest Asia, as well as Egypt and part of the Balkan Peninsula.

The creation of this interacting zone of communication provided a cultural diversity that enriched the Persian Empire. The Persians provided an environment in which people's talents could flourish. From the west came Greek architects, stone masons, and sculptors. At Pasagadae, Persepolis, and Susa, the three capitals of Persia, they built the palaces of the kings. From the Indus Valley on the eastern edge of the empire, rice was introduced for the first time into Mesopotamia. Merchants carried trade goods of all kinds across the empire under the protection of the Persian army.

An international army of thousands of bowmen and cavalry kept control within the Persian Empire and extended its borders through conquest. Persia even extended its power to Greece, threatening the independence of Greek city-states. Cyrus conquered the Greek city-states in Asia Minor in 550 B.C., and made them pay taxes to him. Then, in 490 B.C., the Persian ruler Darius invaded Greece. That move set the scene for a 20-year struggle between Greece and Persia.

SECTION 2 *Study Skills*

Developing Vocabulary Use each of the following in a sentence: **1.** satrapy. **2.** satrap. **3.** universal.

Understanding Cause and Effect 1. How did Cyrus contribute to the development of the Persian Empire? **2.** How did the Royal Road make the Persian government more efficient? **3.** List three ways in which Zoroastrianism influenced later Christianity.

Understanding Chronology 1. What is the significance of the year 585 B.C. in the history of the Medes and Persians? **2.** When was the Persian Empire at its height? **3.** What events were taking place in Greece during the period of Persian expansion?

Challenge How was the Persian culture similar to the culture of the United States?

3 Classical Culture of Greece

OBJECTIVE: *To recognize the cultural contributions of Greece and understand why Greek influence in the Mediterranean declined*

The Greek Wars with Persia, 499 to 449 B.C.

Unrest between Greece and Persia began around 550 B.C. when the Persian king Cyrus conquered Asia Minor and required Greek city-states to pay taxes to Persia. The city-state of Miletus resisted and led an unsuccessful revolt against Persia from 499 to 494 B.C. To help the rebels of Miletus, Athens sent a fleet across the Aegean to Anatolia. The Greeks burned the capital of the Persian province. See the map, The Greek Wars, on page 102.

In retaliation, the Persian ruler Darius launched an invasion of Greece in 490 B.C. Against great odds, a small Athenian force crushed the Persian army on a Greek plain called Marathon.

According to legend, Greece's swiftest runner, Pheidippides, carried the news of victory to Athens. Running into the city, he gasped, "Rejoice, we conquer," before falling dead. The marathon race of today is a course of 26 miles and 385 yards (42.2 kilometers), the same distance that Pheidippides ran in 490 B.C.

Eager to even the score, the Persians invaded Greece again in 480 B.C. This time, the huge Persian army faced a small group of Spartans at Thermopylae. A Greek warrior, seeing the great size of the Persian forces, exclaimed: "Excellent, if the Persians darken the sun with their arrows, we shall be able to fight in the shade." Nevertheless, this time the Persians defeated the heroic Spartans, killing them all. The conquerors then marched toward Athens.

The Greeks, however, planned a surprise for the Persians. The Athenians evacuated the city and let the army enter unopposed. The Persian army looted and burned the city. When the Persians were convinced of victory, the Greeks lured the Persian fleet into the Strait of Salamis.

In the narrow strait, the outnumbered Greek ships rammed the Persian ships, breaking off their oars. Greek warriors then boarded the Persian ships and fought a hand-to-hand battle. The Persian ruler Xerxes watched the battle from a great throne on cliffs overlooking the strait. After the Greeks inflicted a smashing defeat on the Persian navy, Xerxes fled back to Persia.

VOCABULARY DEVELOPMENT

marathon (MAR uh THAHN) *noun:* a footrace of 26 miles and 385 yards, run over an open course, especially as an event of the Olympic Games. After the legend of the Greek runner who ran from Marathon to Athens to tell of the Greek victory over the Persians (490 B.C.).

sophist (SAHF uhst) *noun:* in ancient Greece, any of a group of teachers. From the Greek word, *sophistes*, meaning wise person.

philosopher (fih LAHS uh fuhr) *noun:* a person who investigates the basic principles of being, knowledge, or human conduct. From the Greek words *philos*, meaning loving, and *sophos* meaning wise.

The Greek Wars, 500–400 B.C.

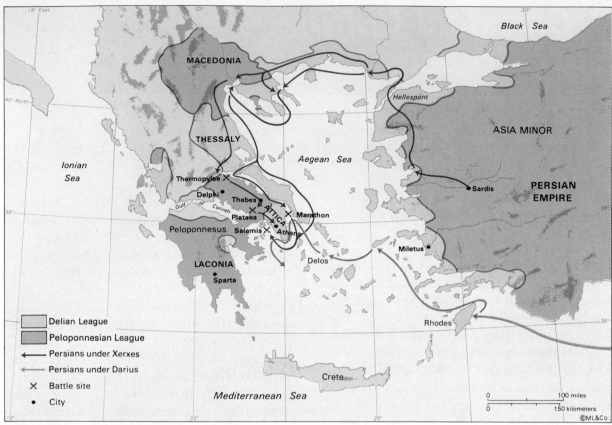

Map Skills   1. Which major cities and regions were in the Delian League? **2.** Which cities belonged to the Peloponnesian League? **3.** What sea separated Greece from Persia?

The next year, 479 B.C., Greek forces destroyed the myth of Persian invincibility. On the plain at Plataea, they again overwhelmed part of the Persian army that had been left behind. Regular naval campaigns against the Persians continued until 446 B.C. and the Greeks maintained their military strength and independence.

The Athenian Navy. The battles of Marathon, Thermopylae, Salamis, and Plataea became symbols of the successes of the small Greek city-states against the giant Persian Empire. After 479 B.C., however, the Athenian navy took the lead in the campaigns against Persia. Sparta, with the greatest army in the Greek world, refused to send its soldiers against Persia after the immediate threat of Persian invasion had faded.

Since Athenian military power relied on its navy, the rowers of the fleet became as politically important as the soldiers of the phalanx had been 100 years earlier. Rowers influenced decisions of the Assembly because, when home, they had time to attend Assembly meetings. They encouraged regular naval campaigns because their livelihood depended on their military wages and the booty collected after successful battles. Other citizens, who also enjoyed the new wealth that victory brought, supported the annual military engagements.

Athens Leads Greece

Cooperation among the independent Greek city-states was unusually strong during the wars with Persia. Even after the wars, many

Greeks continued to cooperate because they suspected that Persia was waiting for another opportunity to strike. In 479 B.C., Athens organized an alliance of city-states into an anti-Persian league.

The Delian League. The terms of the alliance, known as the Delian League, required that the Athenian navy continue the war against the Persians. Other cities that had no soldiers or ships promised to contribute money. Each city-state had one vote, and no city-state could leave the league without the consent of all members.

At first, membership in the Delian League was voluntary. Gradually, however, Athens used force to maintain and increase membership in the league. Many Greeks began to resent the league, which they believed was a tool Athens used to dominate Greece. Sparta organized a rival group of city-states into the Peloponnesian League.

After defeating the Persians, the Athenians prospered. They traded olives, pottery, and wine for wheat grown in other Mediterranean lands. The marketplace in Athens bustled with activity. To protect its trade, Athens assumed the role of police officer in the Aegean. It settled disputes between member cities of the Delian League and enforced the league's rules.

The Age of Pericles. The prosperity of Athens, together with the tradition of citizen participation in public life, encouraged artistic and intellectual creativity. In 461 B.C., Pericles, a popular Greek orator known for his honesty, became the principal leader of Athens.

Under Pericles, more citizens participated in government discussions and decisions. He believed all citizens should take an active part in the government. He claimed, "We . . . regard a man who takes no interest in public affairs not as a harmless but as a useless person."

Under Pericles, Athens also flourished as a center of cultural achievement. The Athenians rebuilt the acropolis, the hilltop center of their city. They also built the Parthenon, a great temple to Athena, and the Propylaea, the entrance gate to the acropolis. These structures became symbols of the glory of Greece.

Socrates: Seeker of Truth

FOCUS ON

PEOPLE

In the last half of the fifth century B.C., Greek teachers who were called sophists explored the questions of politics and philosophy. The sophists stressed public speaking and practical knowledge to train successful political leaders in Athens and other city-states. An Athenian philosopher, Socrates, opposed the sophists' emphasis on practical knowledge.

Socrates was born in Athens around 469 B.C. After his schooling, he worked as a stonecutter, following the Athenian custom of working at his father's occupation. While he never enjoyed the work, Socrates appreciated the opportunity to meet and talk with many people. In democratic Athens, people could speak publicly, discussing topics from sports and politics to war and religion.

Socratic Ideas. Socrates wanted individuals to understand how abstract ideas, such as justice, beauty, truth, and patriotism affected them. His motto was "know thyself."

To help individuals understand themselves and learn to think, Socrates developed a method of questioning that is called the Socratic method. First, he asked a question such as, "What is courage?" As the question was answered, he asked further questions, one leading to another. He might convince a person to agree, for example, that courage is noble. He would then point out that courage in the face of certain death, however, is foolish. Thus, courage is both foolish and noble. Socrates pointed out the contradictions that people commonly ac-

Italian painter Raphael, depicted Aristotle and Plato discussing philosophy.

cept. In this way, he forced people to examine their beliefs.

The Trial of Socrates. About 400 B.C., a group of men called The Thirty came to power in Athens. The Thirty resented people who criticized the government or suggested changes. Socrates continued his teaching, reminding the people of their mistakes and urging them to question their new leaders. Democracy was restored, but since some of the teachings of Socrates were considered dangerous, the 70-year-old philosopher was brought to trial in 399 B.C.

Athens charged Socrates with three crimes: denying the gods, corrupting youth, and attempting to overthrow the government. Athens promised that Socrates would receive only minor punishment if he confessed that his teachings were false. At his trial, Socrates boldly told the people to continue to search for the truth. The jury sentenced him to death.

Socrates was ordered to drink a poison known as hemlock. He thanked the jury for allowing him to find out what death was like, then he calmly drank the poison. ■

Greek Thinkers and Writers

Socrates never wrote down his ideas. His teachings are contained in the writings of Plato, his greatest student.

Plato formulated a theory of reality. Real things, Plato believed, were not the material objects of the world. Real things existed only as immaterial ideas.

Plato's primary concern was to define the ideal state, a state founded on truth and justice. In his most famous book, *The Republic*, he explained that people should be guided by eternal principles, such as love, justice, and honor. In the ideal state, people would perform those jobs for which they were best fitted. The wisest people would rule, skilled artisans would produce needed products, and warriors would fight.

The philosopher Aristotle, like Plato and Socrates before him, questioned the nature of the world and of human belief, thought, and knowledge. Aristotle was a professional thinker who came close to summarizing all the knowledge up to his time. He perfected a method for arguing according to rules of logic. Then, he applied his method to problems in the fields of science, physics, and biology. His work provides the basis of the scientific method used today.

Advances in Science and Math. Greek scientists and mathematicians also used reason to arrive at truth. Scientists questioned the composition of the universe. The Greek scientist, Democritus, first hypothesized that a substance, which he called an atom, was the basic building block of matter.

Most Greek scientists preferred to contemplate scientific questions and arrive at answers based on the results of their thinking. The physician, Hippocrates, however, carefully recorded his patients' symptoms and used the information to treat others with similar symptoms.

Hippocrates believed that diseases had natural causes and were not punishments inflicted by the gods. He is known as the Father of Medicine, and physicians still take the Hippocratic Oath based on his teachings about patient care.

Some Greeks believed that numbers offered the answers to the mysteries of the universe. Pythagoras (pih THAG oh rus), a philosopher and mathematician, emphasized knowledge and science as the paths to salvation. He discovered some of the principles of geometry. Students remember him today for the Pythagorean theorem.

Greek Literature. Drama was one of the most important forms of literature during the Age of Pericles. The most famous of the Athenian dramatists were Aeschylus (EHS kuh luhs), Sophocles (SAHF uh kleez), Euripides (yoo RIHP uh deez), and Aristophanes (air is TAHF uh neez). Aeschylus wrote about 90 plays. Among them is *Oresteia* (oh REHS tee uh), which takes place during the Trojan War.

Sophocles wrote more than 120 plays. The best known are *Antigone* (an TIHG uh nee) and *Electra*. The main characters of both plays are women, but men played the parts. Women were not permitted to perform on the Greek stage.

The plays of Euripides show people dealing with deep emotional problems that in some ways seem familiar in our time. His best known plays are *Alcestis* (al SEHS tihs) and *Medea* (meh DEE uh).

Aristophanes wrote comedies that poked fun at the Athenians and helped them to see their weaknesses. In *Lysistrata* (LIH sihs TRAH tuh), he begged the Greek leaders to end their constant warfare.

During the Age of Pericles, Herodotus and Thucydides (thoo SIHD uh DEEZ) pioneered the writing of history. Herodotus wrote about the Greek wars with Persia. Thucydides described the Peloponnesian Wars, the wars between Athens and the city-states on the Peloponnesus.

The Peloponnesian Wars, 460 to 404 B.C.
Some cities in the Delian League resented Athenian domination and tried to withdraw. Athens refused to consent. City-states, an-gered by the growing Athenian power, appealed to Sparta for aid. When Sparta joined other city-states with troops, war started. Between 460 and 404 B.C., Athens and Sparta fought each other at intervals for 35 years.

In the end, victory went to Sparta, but the wars were a disaster for both winners and losers. The earlier Persian Wars created a common cause and solidarity for Greek city-states. The Peloponnesian Wars destroyed the sense of community among Greek city-states.

The wars had two other important results. First, commercial life and international politics became more complex. Public servants needed more specialized knowledge than most ordinary citizens had. Second, as trade increased, wealthy citizens could afford more imported goods. Differences between rich and poor and slaves and citizens became more apparent.

As Greek civilization diversified, changes also occurred thousands of miles to the east. In India and China, new religions and philosophies were emerging in reaction to the political instability in these areas.

SECTION 3 *Study Skills*

Developing Vocabulary 1. Explain how the distance for the modern marathon was established. **2.** How are the origins of the sophist and philosopher similar?

Reviewing Main Ideas 1. Who was Pericles? **2.** Summarize the contributions of Socrates, Plato, and Aristotle. **3.** List four important Greek dramatists.

Understanding Cause and Effect 1. What happened as a result of the battle of Thermopylae? **2.** Why did the Greeks win the battle at Salamis? **3.** What caused the decline of the ideals of Greek life after the Peloponnesian Wars?

Challenge Choose one of the Greek writers, philosophers, or leaders and explain how his ideas are still applicable today.

4 *Foundations of Eastern Cultures*

OBJECTIVE: *To understand how new guidelines for living developed in India and China*

Government in India

Little is known about everyday life in India between 800 and 300 B.C. Information about Indian government and public practices during that time is more available. In the southern part of India, tribal cultures were common. In the north, small states ruled by kings of Aryan origin had been established by 550 B.C.

From 550 to 325 B.C., the largest Indian kingdom was that of Magadha located in the Ganges (GAN jeez) River valley. Magadha's location enabled it to control communication and trade on the Ganges River. The river also provided a link between Magadha and the busy ports in the Ganges Delta. Under powerful early kings, Magadha grew into an empire that included nearly all of northern India. Magadha exerted leadership throughout India until about 325 B.C.

The kings of Magadha controlled farming and trade and collected taxes. These revenues supported large armies and thousands of war elephants. The kings paid for vast irrigation systems and jungle clearing projects. Sea trade between western India and Mesopotamia flourished about 800 B.C.

South of the Ganges plain, tribal customs prevailed. The heads of clans joined together in tribal assemblies to make decisions. The leader of the assembly had the title raja, which originally meant a chief.

Darius Conquers the Indus River Valley.

About 510 B.C., Darius the Great of Persia led his armies into the Indus River valley. The Persian armies defeated the kingdom of Gandhara and incorporated that land into the Persian Empire.

Because of the difficulty of maintaining control of a region so far away, however, the Persian occupation of Gandhara lasted only a few years. Nevertheless, some remnants of Persian influence remained in the use of

---

VOCABULARY DEVELOPMENT

raja (RAH juh) *noun:* **1.** an Indian prince or chief; **2.** a title of nobility among the Hindus. Originally, chief of a tribal assembly in India; derived from the Indo-European word, *reg*, meaning to direct.

asceticism (uh SEHT uh siz uhm) *noun:* the practice of self-denial to develop personal and spiritual discipline. From the Greek word, *askein*, meaning to train the body.

nirvana (nihr VAH nuh) *noun:* in Buddhism, the state of freedom from all desire and individual consciousness and from the cycle of rebirth.

Qin (chin) *noun:* a Chinese dynasty that was founded in 221 B.C.; until recently, translated into English as Ch'in.

Laozi (low dzuh): founder of Chinese Daoist philosophy; until recently, translated as Lao Tzu.

Dao (dow) *noun:* Chinese philosophy that emphasizes conformity to nature; until recently, translated into English as Tao.

Kong Qiu (kung chyoo): Chinese philosopher also known as Confucius; until recently, translated into English as K'ung Ch'iu.

India, 500 B.C.

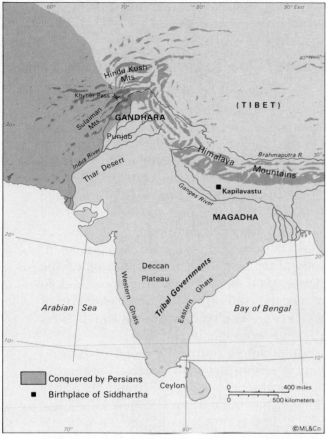

Map Skills 1. What are the two major rivers of India? **2.** Where does each river begin? Into what body of water does each flow?

coins and the development of a script based on Aramaic writing. Trade ties between Gandhara and Persia also continued.

Jainism Emerges in India

Before 700 B.C., Indians combined the religious ideas and rituals brought by the Aryans with the religious ideas and rituals of the people who had built the Indus civilization. From 700 to 300 B.C., this religion experienced many changes. During the 600s B.C., a religious teacher whose name was Mâhavira (man hah VEE rah) gained a large following.

Mâhavira grew up in northeastern India but left his home and family to search for religious truth. Twelve years later he claimed victory in his search. The Sanskrit word jaina (JY nuh) means victorious. The way of life Mâhavira founded is called Jainism (JY nihz uhm).

Jainism is based on the belief that every living thing consists of an eternal soul and a temporary physical body. The soul is imprisoned in the body as a result of involvement in worldly activities. To free their souls, individuals must take six vows: to injure no life, to be truthful, to not steal, to possess no property, to remain chaste, and to practice asceticism.

Buddhism Develops, 500s B.C.

While Jainism was attracting followers, an Indian prince named Siddhartha (sid DAHR tuh) Gautama (gwah TAH muh) started another religion called Buddhism. This new religion, like Jainism, was based on the religious experience of one man's search for truth.

Siddhartha was born into a wealthy family in the hill country near the Himalayas, present-day Nepal, about 563 B.C. His father tried to shield him from the world's problems. Siddhartha was in his late twenties before he first left his palace and saw the way most people lived.

The pain and injustice that Siddhartha saw beyond the palace gates so distressed him that he left his home permanently to search for religious truth. He followed the practice of extreme asceticism, self-denial. He dressed in clothes made of coarse cloth, sat on a couch of thorns, and let dirt accumulate on his body. Stories tell us that he lived on one grain of rice a day. Yet, Siddhartha's extraordinary self-discipline did not bring him an understanding of suffering and death.

Siddhartha's Enlightenment. At length, Siddhartha decided that asceticism was not the path to enlightenment. It did not reveal religious truth. He gave up self-denial and began to eat heartily. Then, one day as he sat at the foot of a fig tree, thinking about his experiences, his enlightenment came.

Siddhartha continued to accept some of the Indian ideas about reincarnation and karma. He believed that the goodness or wrongness of a person's behavior in each life determined the person's karma or fate in the following life. However, he rejected the traditional idea of castes, or social classes, based on karma. Siddhartha introduced the idea that the human soul could eventually earn nirvana, meaning freedom from the cycle of rebirth.

He preached a sermon at Sarnath that revealed his religious views. In this famous sermon, Siddhartha proclaimed the Four Noble Truths. First, the world is full of suffering. Second, suffering is caused by human desire. Third, ending human desire is the path to salvation. Fourth, salvation may be achieved through following the Eightfold Path of Right Views, Right Hopes, Right Speech, Right Conduct, Right Livelihood, Right Effort, Right Thinking, and Right Meditation.

Spread of Buddhism. Siddhartha attracted many followers who so admired his views that they called him the Buddha, meaning the Enlightened One. Buddhism was a personal religion that needed no priesthood or special place of worship.

China: The Later Zhou Period

Political turmoil often brings exciting developments in philosophy and culture. Such was the case in Greece following the Persian Wars. Political turmoil also led Chinese thinkers to search for guidelines for life.

In 771 B.C., barbarians had attacked the Zhou, forcing them to move their capital to Luoyang. (See Chapter 4, Section 2, page 77.) This action began the Later, or Eastern, Zhou Period. The period marked the beginning of the Zhou's decline. In setting up the new capital in the east, the king had to accept the land offered to him by the lord of the region. The land was much less than his previous holdings in the west.

In addition, one of the emperor's vassals kept a strong army to protect the empire against further invasions from the north. This vassal built a state called Qin (chin), which soon competed with the royal family for power. On the edges of the land the Zhou controlled, other states also fought for control in China. The period from 403 to

Prince Siddhartha rides away from his palace in the quiet of the night to seek enlightenment in this second-century B.C. stone relief.

Warring States of China, 403–221 B.C.

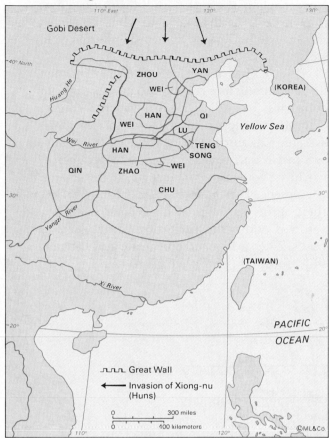

Map Skills **1.** Which three of the states border the Yellow Sea? **2.** Which of the states are divided into two parts?

221 B.C. is called the Period of the Warring States. See the map, The Warring States of China, above.

Changes in Chinese Life. Between 700 and 200 B.C., rice, rather than millet, became the main food of China. Large-scale irrigation projects, the use of animal-drawn plows, and the greater use of fertilizer increased the food supply. More food resulted in a larger population, as well as an increase in the wealth of states.

Cities in China grew in number and size. Prosperity made possible larger and better-equipped armies. The use of iron led to improved military weapons. One was a crossbow with a trigger to shoot iron-tipped arrows. In addition, the Chinese borrowed the practice of using a cavalry supported by infantry to strengthen their military power.

By the third century B.C., even with a more efficient army, the Zhou emperors lost effective control over the country. Individual states fought one another for land and control of China.

Chinese Civilization Spreads. During the Period of the Warring States, the influence of Chinese civilization spread to the coastal regions of north China and as far south as the Yangzi (yang see) Valley. Many Chinese, eager to escape the violence of the civil wars, migrated toward the frontiers of Chinese civilization. They carried Chinese culture with them to their new homes. In addition, local Chinese rulers, eager to make allies of surrounding barbarians, also spread Chinese culture by contacts.

Political Chaos Brings New Philosophies, 551 to 221 B.C.

During the violence of the Period of the Warring States, hundreds of thousands of Chinese died. The state of Qin eventually united China under a new dynasty.

Though the Period of the Warring States was politically chaotic, it was culturally creative. Three important philosophies, or ways of life, emerged in China: Daoism, Legalism, and Confucianism.

Daoism. The first Daoist, Laozi (low dzuh), lived sometime during the fifth century B.C. Laozi believed that people should deal with political chaos by withdrawing from public life and meditating on the Dao, the Way.

For Laozi, the Dao was the force of nature that brought things into being, sustained life, and directed the outcome of all events. Laozi thought that people could do little to influence this natural force. Instead, they should focus on the Dao and try to share in the natural force. Daoism offered communion with nature as an alternative to the political chaos.

Legalism. People pursued other alternatives to the political chaos by emphasizing a society that placed the welfare of the state above the welfare of individuals. This approach was called Legalism, and its founder was Shang Yang, a fourth century minister to the ruler of Qin. Shang Yang believed that people were better off when the state was powerful and prosperous.

According to Legalism, law forms the basis of society. The Legalists did not believe people would conduct themselves properly through a sense of duty. They needed strict laws to enforce the emperor's power.

Confucianism. A third school of philosophy was developed about 500 B.C. by Kong Qiu (kung chyoo), known as Confucius. He was born in 551 B.C. and lived until 479 B.C. Confucius was a teacher who had enormous influence on Chinese government and society.

Confucius was most concerned with moral behavior. He spoke very little about religion or the Chinese gods. His teachings concern how people should act and how government can encourage proper behavior among the people.

Confucius spoke of five relationships that required attention: the relationship between (1) ruler and subject, (2) parent and child, (3) elder brother and younger brother, (4) husband and wife, and (5) friend and friend. People in a superior position were to treat others humanely. Inferiors were to respond to their superiors with appropriate respect.

Everyone was responsible for contributing to the common good. Unlike Laozi, Confucius believed that people should not withdraw from the world but should actively serve their families and the state.

Cultural Foundations. Confucius's ideas, together with strong elements of Legalism, became the basic principles for government in China. Daoism and Legalism never achieved the importance of Confucianism. Nevertheless, these three philosophies gave the Chinese the threads with which to weave the most enduring cultural pattern the world has known.

Both China and India developed guidelines for living as a reaction to events in their countries. In India, Jainism and Buddhism offered people an alternative to the caste system. Legalism, Daoism, and Confucianism in China provided a sense of order in a world of constant warfare.

Greece, Persia, India, and China earned their status as major civilizations. Each developed enduring institutions and philosophies. They advanced culturally and formed solid foundations on which to build.

SECTION 4 *Study Skills*

Developing Vocabulary Use each of the following in a sentence: **1.** raja. **2.** Qin. **3.** asceticism. **4.** Dao. **5.** Laozi. **6.** Kong Qiu.

Reviewing Main Ideas **1.** Explain the ideas of Mâhavira. **2.** What are the Four Noble Truths? **3.** Compare the ideal of good government contained in the three Chinese philosophies.

Understanding Geography **1.** Where did Confucianism develop? **2.** Where did Buddhism and Jainism offer an alternative to the caste system? **3.** How did governments north of the Ganges River differ from those to the south?

Understanding Chronology **1.** When was the kingdom of Magadha an important empire? **2.** Describe the condition of China between 481 and 221 B.C. **3.** Make a time line showing when each of the following religions or philosophies first developed: Hinduism, Jainism, Buddhism, Daoism, Legalism, Confucianism.

Challenge Are the ideals of good government, contained in the philosophy of Kong Qiu, still useful today? Explain.

The Challenge of Climate

Throughout history, people have adapted their way of living to their climate. Climate is the normal weather pattern of a place. Two of the main elements of climate are temperature and precipitation. The combination of these two elements affects almost every aspect of an individual's life.

Temperature and Precipitation

The sun strongly influences the normal temperature pattern of a region. The axis on which the earth rotates is tilted slightly. Consequently, the sun's rays hit different parts of the earth at different angles. The areas around the equator receive rays most directly, so these are the warmest areas. The areas around the poles are never hit directly by the sun's rays, so these areas are the coolest. In between the equator and the poles are the temperate zones. The temperate zones have the greatest variation in temperature during a year.

The second element of climate is precipitation. Precipitation includes any moisture which falls to earth.

The sun plays an important role in causing precipitation. The heat of the sun causes water to evaporate into water vapor, microscopic droplets of water. Clouds are composed of water vapor. As air cools, it holds less moisture. When the water-filled air cools, some form of precipitation will fall. Wind often causes precipitation by blowing warm moist air and cool air together.

Koppen's Climate System

There are many different climates on the surface of the earth. In 1918, Dr. Wladimir Koppen of Austria developed a system to describe the earth's climates based on combinations of temperature and precipitation. Dr. Koppen identified five general climates in the world. These climates are shown on the map on the following page.

One is a tropical rainy climate such as that found in Mindanao in the Philippine Islands. This type of climate is warm and humid throughout the year and has heavy annual rainfall.

A second is a dry climate such as the Iranian Plateau. Regions with this type of climate are usually very warm and have very little rain.

A third climate region is one that is mild and humid. This climate has both warm and cold seasons and moderate to high rainfall. The Balkan Peninsula is an example of this type of climate.

A fourth is a snowy-forest climate that has a long cold season and a short warm season. Much of northern Europe has a snowy-forest climate.

The fifth climate region in Koppen's system is the polar climate, which is very cold throughout the year.

The five general climate regions are identified by a color key on the map on page 112. A sixth climate region, complex mountain areas, is also noted. This variation on the Koppen system shows areas where the climate changes radically as one travels from the base to the top of a mountain. All six regions contain several variations.

Climate and Civilization

Climate played an important role in the development of early civilizations. The three earliest civilizations, those in Mesopotamia, Egypt, and the Indus Valley, are about as near to the equator as present day Florida,

Climates of the World

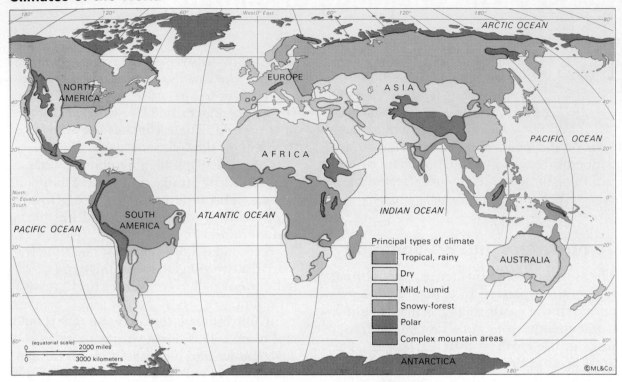

Principal types of climate
- Tropical, rainy
- Dry
- Mild, humid
- Snowy-forest
- Polar
- Complex mountain areas

©ML&Co.

Map Skills **1.** What part of the world has the highest temperatures? Why? **2.** What part of the world has the lowest temperatures? Why? **3.** Where are the moderate climate zones? Why?

and have warm climates. The warmth of the climate made growing crops easier.

The early civilizations used river water to grow crops. In Mesopotamia, for example, farmers watered their crops by digging irrigation ditches. In the Nile and Indus Valleys, yearly flood waters, along with irrigation, helped the crops to grow.

Efforts to meet challenges of climate affected people's relationships with each other. For example, one Mesopotamian farmer working alone would have found it difficult to dig the many ditches necessary to irrigate his crops. However, if that farmer and others cooperated, they could all benefit. Increasing cooperation was one of the reasons for the development of the great civilization of Mesopotamia.

Later civilizations, such as the Hittites and the Canaanites, developed in rain-watered areas. Eventually, civilizations developed in other areas as well. Today, people can adapt to any climate on earth.

STUDY SKILLS Reading Maps

1. What are the two basic elements of climate in the Koppen system?
2. What are the six general climates in the world?
3. Explain how the climate of Mesopotamia encouraged the development of a civilization.
4. Describe the climate of Greece as shown on the map on this page.
5. Identify the climate of the region in which you live.
6. Identify the challenges each type of climate presents to the people who live in it.
7. Explain why civilization first developed in areas that had to be irrigated.

CHAPTER 5 *Summary & Review*

Summarizing Main Ideas

Four major cultures developed in Eurasia between 800 and 200 B.C. In Greece, Persia, India, and China, people developed forms of government, religion, and philosophy that greatly influence cultures today.

In Greece, development of the phalanx as a military tactic promoted the growth of democracy. Athens became the center of intellectual development in the western world.

The Persian Empire included diverse and rich cultures. Through the Zoroastrian religion, the Persians influenced the Jewish and Christian religions. In the fifth century B.C. the Persians fought a series of battles with the Greeks, their rivals for trade. The Greeks finally won.

Farther east in Eurasia, states developed in India and China. In each region, philosophies developed. Buddhism and Confucianism still influence people.

Differences Between Athens and Sparta		
	Sparta	**Athens**
Social Groups	Citizen soldiers	Citizens
	Free subjects	Non-Athenians living in Athens
	Helot slaves	Slaves
Government	General Assembly of all citizens approved laws and elected officials	General Assembly of all citizens discussed matters of state, voted on laws, and elected officials
	Council of Elders proposed laws	Council of Five Hundred proposed laws and served as jurors
Economy	Farming by slaves provided for basic needs	Slave labor important in mining and farming

Questions for Critical Thinking

COMPREHENSION Interpreting Events

1. Why were the Olympic Games important?
2. How did Greek life change after the wars between Athens and Sparta?
3. What did the construction of the palace of Darius indicate about the Persian Empire?
4. What new ideas developed in China during the Period of the Warring States?

ANALYSIS Identifying Trends

1. What influence did Zoroastrianism have on later religions?
2. How did the gap between various groups in Athenian society change over time?
3. Compare and contrast the ideas of Socrates and Plato. How did Socrates influence Plato?

APPLICATION Comparing Past to Present

1. Is Athens or Sparta more like the United States today? Explain.
2. Explain how the role of transportation in uniting society has changed from ancient times to the present.

SYNTHESIS Developing Writing Skills

1. Write an outline of this chapter. Use section titles as the basic divisions.
2. Write a report comparing and contrasting the founders, development, and ideas of Buddhism and Confucianism.

EVALUATION Weighing Consequences

1. How did political disunity affect Greece, Persia, India, and China?
2. How are Jainism and Buddhism similar?
3. How are Legalism, Daoism, and Confucianism similar?

CHALLENGE

1. Explain how changes in military tactics affected politics in Athens.
2. Which ancient philosopher or religious leader discussed in this chapter expressed ideas that are closest to what most people believe today?

CHAPTER 6
The Spread of Civilization

GLOBAL TIME LINE

TIME

800 B.C.   **700 B.C.**   **600 B.C.**

800–300 B.C. The Mediterranean interacting community expands

800–300 B.C. Iron technology spreads to sub-Saharan Africa, Europe, India, and China

800–300 B.C. Mounted riders change life on the steppes

PEOPLE

800–500 B.C. Etruscans control the Italian Peninsula

800–300 B.C. Celts spread throughout Western Europe

800s B.C. Scythians become the first steppe nomads to ride horses

600s B.C. Assyrians and Babylonians conquer large empires and Greeks establish colonies throughout the Mediterranean Basin

PLACE

800–300 B.C. *Australia;*[5] Aborigines inhabit Australia

715 B.C. *Egypt;*[1] Kushites conquer Egypt

600s B.C. *Mesopotamia;*[2] Assyrians and Babylonians conquer large empires

Linking Past to Present

American culture has influenced peoples of other lands in countless ways. Americans have introduced other people to democratic ideas, computer electronics, blue jeans, and hamburgers. The movement of ideas, technology, or habits of living from one culture to another is an ancient theme in world history.

Earlier chapters showed how ancient civilizations developed. Chapter 6 focuses on the spread of ideas from centers of civilization to neighboring peoples. You will learn how merchants, colonists, and even conquering armies created cultural links between these older civilizations and distant peoples in central Asia, Europe, Africa, and Southeast Asia. You will also be introduced to developments in Australia, a continent isolated from others.

This clay funeral urn from fifth-century B.C. Rome shows a married couple.

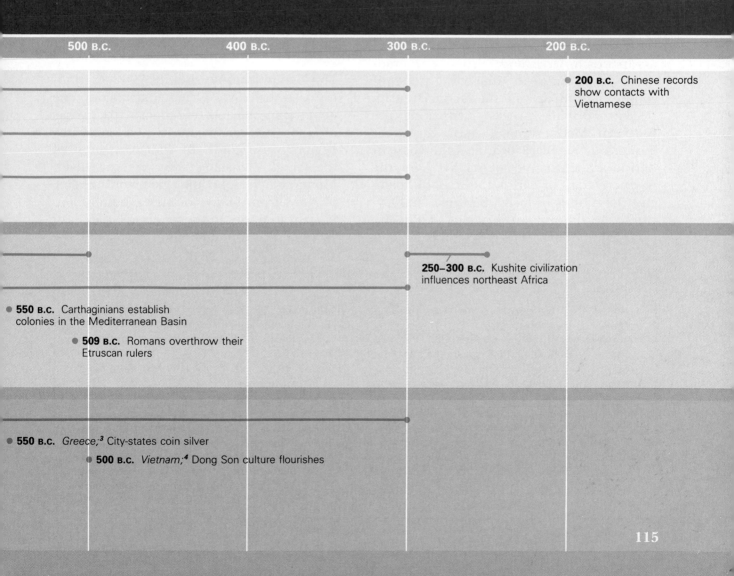

500 B.C.   400 B.C.   300 B.C.   200 B.C.

200 B.C. Chinese records show contacts with Vietnamese

250–300 B.C. Kushite civilization influences northeast Africa

550 B.C. Carthaginians establish colonies in the Mediterranean Basin

509 B.C. Romans overthrow their Etruscan rulers

550 B.C. *Greece;³* City-states coin silver

500 B.C. *Vietnam;⁴* Dong Son culture flourishes

115

1 Exchanges in the Mediterranean Basin

OBJECTIVE: *To understand the causes of the spread of civilization along the shores of the Mediterranean Sea*

Traders and Colonists

Early civilizations originated in Greece, Phoenicia, and Egypt, along the eastern rim of the Mediterranean Sea. Between 800 and 300 B.C., those civilizations exported their ideas, skills, and products to the lands washed by the Mediterranean. Peoples living in north Africa and Europe were gradually drawn into an interacting zone of communication around the Mediterranean.

By 550 B.C., Greeks lived along the northern Mediterranean coast, the areas bordering the Black Sea, and the coast of Africa. Phoenician colonists lived on the northern coast of Africa, the coast of Spain, and the islands of Sicily, Sardinia, and Cyprus. See the map, Migrations of Phoenicians and Greeks, 800–300 B.C., page 117.

Cultural Exchange. Colonization and trade led to the exchange of ideas throughout the Mediterranean interacting community. This exchange brought about improvements in technology and new dreams for the inhabitants. The Greeks learned more about navigation as they traded stories and ideas with Phoenician sailors.

The Use of Money. Before 700 B.C., traders used the barter system, exchanging one item for another. As trade increased, people of the Mediterranean region gradually began to use coins. By 550 B.C., most of the Greek city-states were coining silver. Moneychangers, people who knew the value of coins from many countries, became important to trade. In the bustling Greek port of Piraeus, moneychangers called out the

---

VOCABULARY DEVELOPMENT

barter *verb:* to trade by exchanging goods or services without using money.

commerce *noun:* the buying and selling of goods, especially on a large scale, between cities, states, or countries; trade. From the Latin prefix *com-*, meaning together, and word *merx*, meaning merchandise.

Gaul (gawl) *noun:* ancient region in western Europe, consisting of an area that now is mainly France and Belgium.

confederation (kuhn FEHD uh RAY shuhn) *noun:* a league or alliance of independent nations or states whose main purpose usually is limited to common defense or foreign relations.

fibula (FIHB yoo luh) *noun:* in ancient Greece or Rome, a buckle or clasp used to fasten flowing robes. From the Latin word, *figuere*, meaning to fasten or fix.

aqueduct (AK wuh DUHKT) *noun:* a bridgelike structure for transporting water from a distant source. From the Latin words *aqua*, meaning water, and *ductus*, meaning to lead.

republic (rih PUB lihk) *noun:* a state or nation in which political power comes from all the citizens entitled to vote; that power, or authority, is exercised by the representatives that citizens elect. From the Latin words *res*, meaning affair or interest, and *publica*, meaning public.

Migrations of Phoenicians and Greeks, 800–300 B.C.

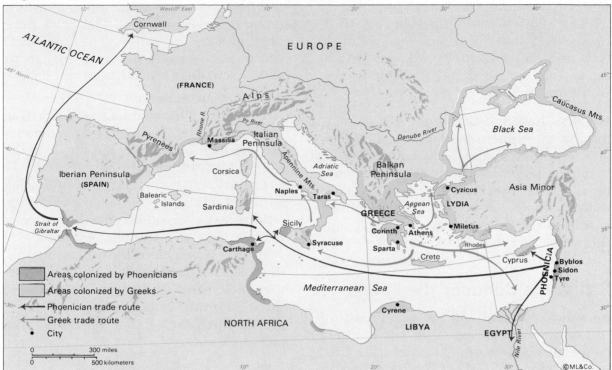

Map Skills **1.** In which direction did a Phoenician sailor travel to trade with the people of Athens? **2.** Name the three largest islands in the Mediterranean Sea.

latest exchange rates for the various currencies they traded.

At first, coins from many states were widely accepted. Later, however, three currencies were favored: the gold coins of Persia, the silver coins of Athens, and the silver coins of the Greek city-state of Cyzicus. The use of coins in trade led to other advances in commerce, that is the buying, selling, and transporting of large quantities of goods.

Civilization Spreads West. Gradually, between 800 and 600 B.C., the Greek and Phoenician colonies around the Mediterranean separated from their founding city-states. The colonies governed themselves and relied on their own armies for defense. They did, however, maintain their Greek or Phoenician cultural identity.

Carthage. One of the most important Phoenician colonies was Carthage, located on the northern coast of Africa near present-day Tunis. Originally a colony of the city-state of Tyre, Carthage was a seaport with two excellent harbors. Merchants, sailors, and craftsworkers were attracted to the port city, and Carthage grew rapidly.

The Carthaginians gradually extended their influence and power over other Phoenician settlements in the western Mediterranean. By 550 B.C., Carthage had established overseas settlements in northern Africa, southern Spain, and the islands of Sicily and Sardinia. By this time, Carthage had also become the leader of the western Phoenician world.

Economy of Carthage. As transmitters of the Phoenician seafaring tradition, the Carthaginians traveled far and wide, trading with countries throughout the Mediterranean interacting community. Carthaginian merchants grew wealthy. Carthage became the recognized leader of commerce in the western Mediterranean Basin.

The Phoenicians imported products from Spain and Africa, and sold them in Gaul and Italy. Much of Carthage's wealth came from the silver and lead mines they controlled in Spain and Sardinia.

Greeks Challenge Carthage. Greek colonists in the western Mediterranean region also were traders, and they challenged Carthaginian power in the Mediterranean. After 600 B.C., Greek colonies became trade centers. From these cities, Greek culture spread to the Celts of western Europe and the people of the Italian Peninsula.

Etruscans Conquer the Latins

Between 2000 and 1000 B.C., a group of Indo-Europeans moved south into the Italian peninsula. One group of tribes, the Latins, settled south of the Tiber River on the western coast. Their land, called Latium, included the small settlement of Rome.

The location of Rome had many natural advantages. The city was built on seven hills rising above the fertile plain that extended along Italy's west coast. The nearby Tiber River provided Romans with a link to the sea and was also a source of food. About 800 B.C., however, the Latins were conquered by the Etruscans (ih TRUHS kuhns), their neighbors to the north.

The Etruscans, who may have come originally from Asia Minor, moved into an area of northern Italy between the Arno and Tiber rivers. The region, known as Etruria (ih TROOR ee uh), was bounded on the east by the Apennine Mountains and on the west by the Mediterranean Sea. See the map, Italian Peninsula, 500 B.C., on this page.

The Etruscans built many fortified towns on hills. They already controlled most of Italy when the Greeks tried to colonize that area. It was because the Etruscans were strongest in northern Italy that the Greeks established their colonies in the south.

Etruscan Government. The Etruscans lived in city-states. A small group of aristocrats governed each city. The cities were joined in a confederation. The confederation, however, was not strong enough to prevent wars between Etruscan city-states.

The Etruscan Economy. Many Etruscans were wealthy. This wealth came partly from the sale of metal, but mainly from agriculture and their ability to control trade in the western Mediterranean.

Etruscan cities specialized in producing particular crafts or products. One city, Fafluna (FAF luh nuh), became the center of the iron industry. Another, Tarquinii (tahr KWIHN ee), was famous for bronze utensils. Metalworkers there made weapons, household implements, and sculptures that were the finest on the Italian Peninsula.

The fine jewelry and metalwork from lands around the Mediterranean stimulated

Italian Peninsula, 500 B.C.

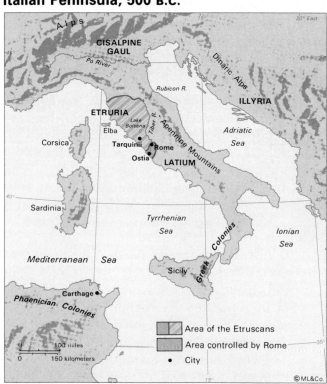

Map Skills   1. Which mountain range stretches through the Italian Peninsula? **2.** In which direction would you travel to reach Gaul from Rome?

the Etruscans to create superb new styles. They were particularly skilled in working with gold. Their version of the *fibula*, a kind of safety pin, was an intricate work of art.

Etruscan Engineers. The Etruscans also excelled in engineering. To avoid soil erosion and flooding, they channeled streams and rivers by digging a series of underground passages. These passages were a yard wide and tall enough for a person to stand in. Frequent shafts, opening from the underground passages to the surface, provided entrances for workers.

The Etruscans built bridges and a network of roads. They developed an arch, known as the Etruscan arch, that is one of the great architectural gifts they passed on to the Romans. Etruscan arches were used in the construction of aqueducts, raised brick channels for carrying water. Engineers also built bridges and large domed buildings utilizing the Etruscan arch.

Decline of the Etruscans. In 509 B.C., the Latin tribes successfully revolted against their Etruscan rulers. To govern themselves, the Latin tribes set up a new form of government, a republic, electing officials to pass and enforce laws. The new nation became known as the Roman Republic. With an attitude of conquer or be conquered, the Romans built a strong army that, by 270 B.C., had brought all of the Italian Peninsula under their control.

Etruscan Achievements. The importance of the Etruscans lies in the contributions they passed on to the newly formed Roman Republic. The Etruscans' legacy includes art, architecture, customs, dress, religion, and social and military organization.

Romans used the Etruscan alphabet, worshiped Etruscan gods along with their own, and adopted Etruscan building techniques. The Roman magistrate's chair, a folding chair with curved legs and no back, was an Etruscan design.

This fifth-century B.C. relief from a situla, or bronze bucket, shows women and men carrying goods.

From 800 to 300 B.C., the ideas of advanced cultures spread around the shores of the Mediterranean. The Phoenician colony of Carthage grew larger and more powerful. In the sixth century B.C., the Etruscans conquered and controlled much of the Italian Peninsula until, by 270 B.C., the Romans, their former subjects, defeated them.

SECTION 1 *Study Skills*

Developing Vocabulary 1. What is the relationship between barter and commerce? **2.** Where was Gaul? **3.** What is the difference between a confederation and a republic? **4.** Define *fibula*. **5.** What is the meaning of each root word of aqueduct?

Reviewing Main Ideas 1. What benefits did the Greeks receive from trade? **2.** What were the three most widely used currencies in the Mediterranean Basin? **3.** What type of government did the Latins establish after revolting?

Understanding Chronology 1. When was currency first used widely? **2.** When did the Phoenicians begin to establish overseas settlements? **3.** How long did the Etruscans live in Italy? **4.** What important development in the history of Rome occurred in 509 B.C.?

Challenge Identify the advantages and disadvantages of having a universal form of money used throughout a trading network.

Landforms

The earth's surface includes mountains, valleys, plains, and other landforms. Each has influenced how people in the past lived. This feature describes the forces of nature that cause landforms to develop and erode.

The earth's surface has developed very slowly over hundreds of millions of years. Geologists use terms of geologic time when they refer to the formation and erosion of the earth's landforms.

The geologic time frame is divided into four major eras. The oldest era is the Precambrian. The Precambrian Era began 4.6 billion years ago, when the earth was formed, and ended 570 million years ago. Scientists have found little evidence of life during the Precambrian Era. The time between 570 and 225 million years ago is called the Paleozoic Era. During this era, life became abundant on the earth.

The Mesozoic Era spans the period from 225 to 65 million years ago. The Mesozoic Era began when the first mammals and dinosaurs appeared. The extinction of dinosaurs 65 million years ago marked the end of the Mesozoic Era and the beginning of the Cenozoic Era. Nearly all of the landforms visible today were formed during the Cenozoic Era.

Landforms Develop

The landforms on the earth are the result of two forces, tectonic and volcanic, working from beneath the earth's surface. Tectonic activity involves the movement of large plates that compose the crust of the earth. The crust is the rocky outer portion. It is from 3 to 37 miles (5 to 60 kilometers) thick. Tectonic activity determines the location of the continents (see pages 10–11). This activity still occurs today as the earth's crust shifts in blocks.

The process of creating a landform by tectonic activity may begin with a break or a fault, a weak point, in the earth's crust. Faults may extend for many miles. Sudden shifts along the fault line can cause the crust to slip. This slippage creates a landform when the land on one side of the fault becomes lower than the land on the opposite side. The diagram of Faults on page 121 shows tectonic activity.

Mountains are created by a process called folding, or crustal compression. In this process, a piece of the crust is squeezed between two other pieces of the crust. The part of the crust being squeezed folds under the pressure. The diagram of Folds on the following page shows how this process occurs. The mountains of Greece and the Appalachian Mountains in the United States were largely the result of the compression of the earth's crust.

The other process shaping landforms is volcanic activity, the movement of molten rock. Volcanoes occur when molten rock, called lava, and heated gases from deep within the earth, escape to the earth's surface. This action is called an eruption.

Volcanoes erupt in one of two ways. Some eruptions are violent and devastating. Other eruptions are gradual.

Weathering of Landforms

Tectonic and volcanic activity create landforms. Weathering wears them down. Weathering refers to the action of weather and other forces on landforms. The four major causes of weathering are frost action, temperature changes, water erosion, and wind erosion.

Tectonic Activity

Folds

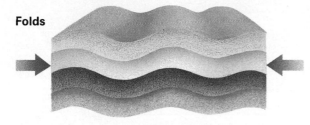

Faults

Folds cause the earth's crust to squeeze into a series of ridges, forming mountains. Faults cause the crust to slip, creating uneven landforms.

The Canadian Rockies in Alberta. Many peaks of the Rockies were formed millions of years ago by upheavals of the earth's crust.

In cold climates, frost action is a major force in weathering. Moisture works its way into the tiny cracks in rocks. When the moisture freezes, it expands. This expansion pushes against the rock, creating a great deal of pressure. Over time, the frost action breaks the rock apart.

In hot climates, the daily heating and cooling of rock can also have significant effects. Heating causes the rock to expand; cooling causes the rock to contract. Over a period of many years, the repeated expansion and contraction can cause the rock to crack or to break.

On any sloped surface, the action of water can change the landform. Rainwater flowing down a mountain or hill slowly wears away or erodes the rock in its path. Over many millions of years, great mountains can be worn down dramatically.

Wind is also an important element in the weathering process. In areas where the soil is loose, the wind can cause great damage as it carries away fertile soil. Plants and trees can help prevent erosion. Trees break the wind while the roots hold the soil down.

Landforms and People

Landforms are important to people for many reasons. For example, the flat plains region near Rome is well-suited for farming. Other landforms, such as mountains, act as natural barriers to human communities. The Alps formed a natural barrier that made contact between the ancient Romans and the people of northern Europe more difficult. Throughout history, the location of plains, mountains, and valleys has influenced people and has shaped the course of human events.

STUDY SKILLS Understanding Geography

1. What are the four eras in geologic time?
2. What are the two major natural forces that create landforms?
3. What is the tectonic process by which mountains are formed?
4. What are the four forces that wear down landforms?
5. Why do we speak of landform creation in a geologic time frame?

2 Peoples on the Fringes of Civilization

OBJECTIVE: *To understand the tension and interaction between the frontier peoples on the edges of civilization and the civilized peoples of Eurasia*

Horse Riders Cause Change

Peoples living near the edge of major civilizations interacted with their civilized neighbors in many ways. Sometimes, they traded peacefully; at other times, they waged war against each other. Whether trading or fighting, frontier people and civilized people enriched each other's cultures.

Among the peoples living on the fringes of civilizations were the Scythians, who inhabited the area known today as southern Russia. The Celts in western Europe, the Kushites in the upper Nile River valley, and peoples of Africa south of the Sahara also lived on the edges of the civilized world.

The Scythians were pastoralists whose original homeland was the Altai Mountain region of central Asia. See the map, Migrations of the Scythians and Celts, page 123. In the eighth century B.C., the Scythians migrated to the land around the Black Sea.

The Scythian nomads were the first people of the steppes to ride horses. Mounting horses changed life on the steppes in many ways. First, on horseback the pastoralists could travel greater distances in their search for good pasture. Second, horses provided people with the advantage of speed when hunting large, swift animals. Third, mounted riders could control larger herds of cattle and horses. Fourth, fighting from horseback changed warfare.

The Cavalry Revolution. By 700 B.C., steppe people were riding and fighting on horses. Tribes of nomad warriors had military striking power far superior to any infantry. This cavalry revolution changed life for the entire human community. In a time when most nations relied on foot soldiers and chariots, the Scythians galloped into history on horseback.

Scythian soldiers had bearded, weathered faces and long hair snarled by the wind. They rushed into battle with loud war whoops while shooting arrows. They collected the scalps of their enemies, and often attached enemy skulls to their belts and used them as cups. The Scythians wore suits of leather or scale armor for protection.

Steppe People Migrate West. As population in the steppes increased and herds grew larger, tribes were forced to move west in search of better pasture. Tribes formed alliances to defeat rivals for grassland.

Fighting was the nomads' way of life. They valued success in raiding and in war and used surprise and speed to their advan-

---

VOCABULARY DEVELOPMENT

scale armor *noun:* a thin layer of metal made of small scales or plates used to protect the body against arrows.

Druids (DROO ihds) *noun:* Celtic religious leaders. From the Indo-European word, *druwid*, meaning oak-wise.

Migrations of the Scythians and Celts

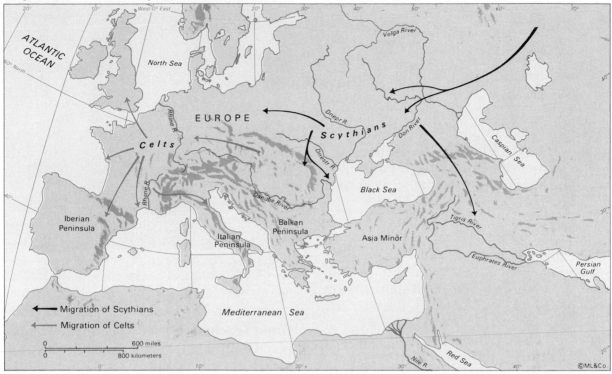

Map Skills   1. Describe the migration route of the Scythians. Use directions and list natural features such as seas and mountains along the route. **2.** Where did the Celts settle?

tage. Nomads soon learned that the quickest way to wealth was to raid someone else's herds. The migrating tribes threatened the security of farmers. Often living outside the protection of the distant urban centers, farmers learned to cooperate with their aggressive neighbors. An uneasy truce prevailed on the frontiers of civilization.

The Celts

As Indo-Europeans left the steppes, they pushed other Indo-Europeans from the outer fringes of civilized areas into cities. The Celts, thought to be originally from central Asia, migrated to the area around what is now southern Germany.

In the eighth century B.C., about the same time the Scythians occupied the north and west shores of the Black Sea, the Celts learned how to ride horses. Using their new mobility, the Celts spread across most of Europe from Hungary to the British Isles. The Celts brought into Europe the aggressive, warlike qualities that marked later European culture.

Celtic Culture. The Celts lived in more than 70 tribal societies. No king ruled all of the vast territory they inhabited. Leaders were chosen by the heads of major clans. The most influential Celts were the warrior aristocrats, members of the wealthiest and most powerful families in each tribe.

Most of the Celts became farmers and herders, though some were artisans and merchants. The Celts brought the use of iron and a new style of culture to western Europe.

A small group of Celtic religious leaders, called Druids, traveled among the Celtic tribes. They acted as judges and teachers, and performed religious rites.

The Druids

FOCUS ON PEOPLE

Druid tradition maintained that on the eve of November 1, Halloween, the spirits of the dead returned as ghosts and traveled through the world of the living. The night of October 31 marked the beginning of the Celtic festival, Samain. On this occasion, the Druid priests performed religious ceremonies to calm the vengeance of the roaming spirits.

The Druids carried Celtic customs of religion, science, and law to the people. Training for the Druid priesthood took up to 20 years. Student priests, drawn from Celtic nobility, were expected to memorize long passages of verse.

Druid Religious Leaders. The Druids, dressed in long, flowing white robes, protected the people from dangerous ghosts. The Druids also interceded with their hundreds of different gods, who were worshiped through animal and, sometimes, human sacrifice.

Druid Astronomers. The Druids also were astronomers who studied the relationship of the sun, moon, and stars. With their findings, they developed a way to record time and forecast future events. They created a lunar calendar in which time was calculated in nights rather than days. The calendar divided the year into the four seasons to schedule religious celebrations.

Druid Judges. Once each year Druids met at a place that may have been near present-day Chartres, in France. People who had legal or personal disputes gathered there to hear the judgments.

The Celts followed a well-defined code of conduct. The Druids dealt with tribal disputes, family problems, and property rights. They also resolved cases of murder and other crimes.

This three-headed deity on a second-century B.C. clay vase illustrates the Celtic belief in the threefold nature of divinity.

Druid Teachers. The Druids further dominated Celtic life through their role as teachers. The Celts accepted the Druids as the source of all knowledge. Druids educated the young nobility and were responsible for ceremonies and sacred rituals. As traveling educators, priests, and judges, the Druids preserved a common culture throughout Celtic society. ■

The Rise of Kush

The Scythians and the Celts lived along the northern fringes of the Mediterranean civilizations. To the south, in the upper Nile valley, the Kush civilization developed. See the map, The Kingdom of Kush, page 125.

For over 2,000 years, the Egyptians tried to extend their authority as far south as possible along the Nile River. Egyptian soldiers were stationed in fortresses between the first and third cataracts of the Nile in Nubia, the country now called Sudan. Control of Nubia provided Egypt with gold, ivory, and ebony, a hard, dark wood.

South of Nubia, between the third and sixth cataracts, was Kush, Africa's oldest and greatest inland empire. In the sixteenth and fifteenth centuries B.C., the Egyptians dominated Kush.

When the Egyptian Empire declined about 1000 B.C., the Kushites gained a new independence. In 751 B.C., the Kushites conquered Egypt and moved their capital north to Thebes, establishing the twenty-fifth dynasty of pharaohs.

The Assyrians Expand into Egypt. The kings of Kush wanted to become pharaohs and tried to restore Egypt to glory. Their triumph, however, was short-lived. In 671 B.C., fierce Assyrian armies marched through Israel to the Nile Delta, where they allied themselves with Egyptians. The Kushites, armed with bronze weapons, were no match for the Assyrians using iron weapons. The Kushites were pushed back up the Nile as the Assyrians occupied the valley.

The Kushites Move South. After losing Egypt to the Assyrians, the kings of Kush moved their capital farther south, to the lands beyond the fifth cataract. In a fertile plain along the Nile, the Kushites built a new capital at Meroe. The Kushites may have chosen the site of their new capital because rich iron ore deposits were nearby. Tall heaps of slag, the waste product of iron-working, can still be seen there.

During the third century B.C., the development of iron agricultural tools and weapons helped the Kush Empire to become a powerful economic and military force. The Kush civilization influenced northeast Africa until the fourth century A.D.

Culture of Kush. The Egyptians strongly influenced the government and religion of Kush. As in Egypt, the kings of Kush exercised the power of ruler and high priest. The Kush people worshiped many Egyptian gods, including Amen. After the Kush capital was moved south to Meroe, however, Kush culture developed with greater independence and creativity.

The people of Meroe developed an alphabetic writing. New gods and new forms of worship replaced Egyptian ones. A Kush lion god challenged the Egyptian gods. Kush artisans created original styles in architecture and pottery. The Kushites also domesticated the elephant, using the animal as a war tank and in royal ceremonies.

The Kushites were enterprising traders. They traded with Egypt to the north and engaged in profitable trade with east Africa, Arabia, and India from ports on the Red Sea. Their trade contacts may have extended as far east as China. Through trade, they helped to spread ironworking skills and tools to other parts of sub-Saharan Africa, Africa south of the Sahara.

The Spread of Iron to Sub-Saharan Africa. The techniques of iron smelting, first used in Asia Minor, spread rapidly southward after 1200 B.C. Ethiopians were the first African people to use iron. Iron objects dating

The Kingdom of Kush, 200 B.C.

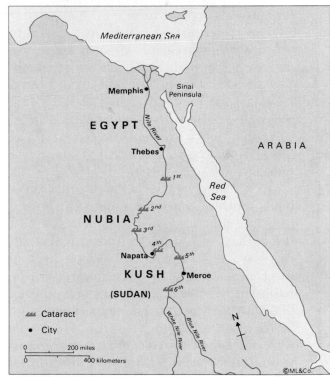

Map Skills **1.** In which direction did an Egyptian travel to reach Nubia? **2.** Into what body of water does the Nile River flow?

As his family watches, King Nastasen of Kush, on the left, presents his armor to a god. This engraving is from Ethiopia.

from 800 B.C. have been found in Ethiopia. Apparently, smelting techniques arrived there by way of Middle East trade on the Red Sea. The knowledge of iron spread down the east African coast and into the continent's interior. Soon after the Ethiopians learned about iron technology, the Kushites also began to smelt the metal.

How information about iron smelting reached other areas of Africa is unknown. Travelers from Kush may have carried stories, skills, and tools westward. Ironworking may also have spread with traders moving across the Sahara from Carthage. Most of sub-Saharan Africa went directly from the Stone Age to the Iron Age. Bronze was never widely used there.

Iron-using villages began in the grasslands south of the Sahara sometime during the thousand years before Christ. One of the earliest iron-using cultures of west Africa was the Nok. The Nok people lived in the central part of the area that is now the nation of Nigeria. The Nok thrived between 900 B.C. and A.D. 200. Historians know from archaeological diggings that the Nok people were farmers and iron users. Nok artisans produced beautiful ceramic sculptures of human and animal figures.

The Scythians, the Celts, the Kushites, and the people of sub-Saharan Africa were important societies. All lived on the fringes of the older and more advanced civilizations. All helped to spread new ideas to the lands of Europe and Africa far from the original river valley civilizations of the Nile, Tigris-Euphrates, Indus, and Huang He.

SECTION 2 *Study Skills*

Developing Vocabulary **1.** What is the advantage of scale armor? **2.** Explain the origin of the word Druid.

Reviewing Main Ideas **1.** Identify three cultures that lived on the edge of the Mediterranean civilizations. **2.** Describe the organization of Celtic society. **3.** Explain the importance of Druids in Celtic society. **4.** How did the cultures of Kush and Egypt differ?

Understanding Cause and Effect **1.** Why did the Scythians migrate? **2.** Explain how the use of horses altered the way people lived in the steppes.

Understanding Geography **1.** Describe the migration of the Celts. **2.** Where did the Scythians live originally?

Challenge Explain why English today contains the words of several languages.

3 Peoples of Southeast Asia and Australia

OBJECTIVE: *To understand the causes and consequences of early cultural developments in Southeast Asia and Australia*

Southeast Asia

Between 800 and 200 B.C., the established civilizations of the Mediterranean Basin, India, and China, were enlarging their influence throughout the interacting zone of Afro-Eurasia. On the southeastern fringe of that zone, complex cultures developed later and more slowly in the humid, tropical lands of Southeast Asia.

The Lands of Southeast Asia. Southeast Asia includes two distinct regions: a peninsula and off-shore islands. The largest region is the Indo-Chinese Peninsula, a subcontinent south of China and east of India. See the map, Southeast Asia and Australia, page 129. The peninsula juts south from Asia into the South China Sea. Today, the countries of Burma, Thailand, Laos, Vietnam, and Kampuchea, formerly Cambodia, occupy the Indo-Chinese Peninsula.

The other region of Southeast Asia includes the islands off the shores of the Indo-Chinese Peninsula. Among the present-day countries occupying these islands are Malaysia, Indonesia, Singapore, the Philippines, and Brunei.

The Southeast Asian peninsula is mountainous. Its principal rivers originate on the lofty plateau of Tibet. Like the Nile River, several of these rivers create fertile deltas. The largest deltas are at the mouths of the Irrawaddy River in Burma and the Mekong River in southern Vietnam.

Because Southeast Asia is close to the equator, the climate is hot and humid. Monsoon winds bring heavy rains twice each year. Southeast Asia receives an annual rainfall of 80 or more inches. The hot weather and abundant rainfall make the river valleys suitable environments for rice growing.

Early Southeast Asian Cultures

Since little archaeological work has been done in Southeast Asia, much of the region's early history remains a mystery. Historians know that sometime between 40,000 and 13,000 years ago people migrated to Southeast Asia. By 3000 B.C., the people in the area now known as Thailand were growing

---

VOCABULARY DEVELOPMENT

theory *noun:* an educated guess about how something might have been or might be done. From the Greek word, *theoria*, meaning to look at or contemplate.

marsupial (mahr SOO pee uhl) *noun:* an animal with a pouch for carrying its young—for example, a kangaroo. From the Greek word, *marsypos*, meaning a pouch or bag.

extinct *adj:* no longer in existence or use.

aborigines (AHB uh RIHJ uh NEES) *noun:* first inhabitants, usually applied to the original peoples of Australia. From the Latin prefix *ab-*, meaning from, and word *origine*, meaning the beginning.

kinship *noun:* being related to, sharing common ancestors.

---

rice. No evidence exists, however, to show that the cultivation of rice brought about any increase in population.

The Non Nok Tha Culture. By 2500 B.C., people of the Non Nok Tha culture in ancient Thailand were making bronze tools and other implements. The Bronze Age, therefore, began in Southeast Asia before it reached China.

The Dong Son Culture. Other people of Southeast Asia also participated in the Bronze Age. Bronze working in the area reached its height around 500 B.C., when the Dong Son culture flourished in northern Vietnam. The Dong Son people created huge bronze drums decorated with beautiful designs. Other bronze work included bracelets, belt hooks, buckles, and swords.

A Dong Son Vietnamese artisan created this bronze lamp-bearer between 500 and 300 B.C.

The Dong Son people lived in farming villages. Some cities may have developed about 1000 B.C. with the rise of the Thur Dynasty. This dynasty may have brought Chinese influence to Vietnam. Written references to Vietnam begin with Chinese records of Vietnamese contacts about 200 B.C.

Trade in Southeast Asia. For thousands of years, the people living along the coasts of Southeast Asia conducted a lively seagoing trade. Trade increased when they learned to build stronger boats with sails that caught the wind and propelled the boat. Using the monsoon winds, the people easily traveled the waters between the subcontinent and the nearby islands, as well as the distant islands of Indonesia.

The Australian Environment

Unlike the people of Southeast Asia, the inhabitants of Australia could not share in the exchange of ideas and technology characteristic of interacting civilizations. Instead, the island continent of Australia was isolated from the communicating zone that was spreading across Africa and Eurasia.

Australia is located in the Southern Hemisphere, far to the south of Asia and the islands in the South China Sea. The island's climate is primarily hot and dry. Deserts occupy the west central art of Australia. To the north and east are grasslands. Eucalyptus forests and swamplands cover the northern shore, whose climate is tropical like that of Indonesia. See the map, Southeast Asia and Australia, page 129.

A vast dry plain called the Nullarbor stretches almost 1,000 miles along the southern coast. Covering the plain are short grasses and some trees. Mountains span the eastern coast from present-day Melbourne in the south to the Cape York Peninsula in the north.

Early Inhabitants. Historians are not sure when people reached Australia. One theory,

Southeast Asia and Australia

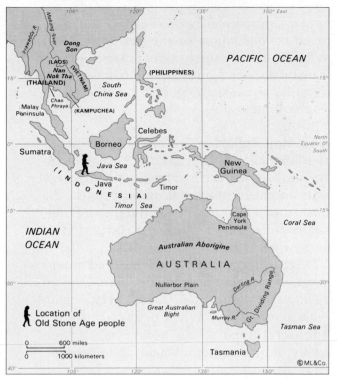

Map Skills **1.** In which modern countries are Sumatra, Borneo, and Java located? **2.** What rivers flow into the Indian Ocean?

or educated guess, suggests that the first inhabitants of Australia arrived about 30,000 years ago, during the Ice Age. Then, the islands of Sumatra, Java, and Borneo made up a single land mass connected to the Indo-Chinese Peninsula. New Guinea, Australia, and Tasmania formed another land mass. Seagoing people traveled around a chain of islands that lay between the two land masses and could have migrated from Southeast Asia to a new home in Australia.

When the first people arrived from Southeast Asia, they may have been startled by the unique kinds of animals they saw. Australia had been isolated from Eurasia for about 200 million years. Australian animals, therefore, did not develop in the same way as those on other continents. Giant kangaroos, huge lizards, and emus, large flightless birds, inhabited the island. Plant-eating marsupials, as large as the present-day rhi-

noceros and hippopotamus, roamed the land. Marsupials are animals that carry their young in pouches. Though such marsupials as the kangaroo still exist, the giant animals became extinct, died out, sometime around 15,000 B.C.

As the Ice Age ended, the waters of the world's oceans rose. Like the people who had migrated to the Americas, the aborigines, the first settlers of Australia, were isolated from other societies because of geographic changes.

Culture of the Aborigines. The first inhabitants of Australia developed a culture well suited to survival on the hot, dry continent. The people were hunters and gatherers. They also fished along the rivers and coasts. Their culture changed little over the centuries because they were cut off from the growing communicating zone of Eurasia. As a result, when the first Europeans arrived in the 1600s, they found the aborigines still using Stone Age tools.

Australia's aborigines divided into several hundred tribes of about 600 members each. The men did most of the hunting and fishing. Women provided the most dependable food supplies, gathering fruits, nuts, and vegetables.

The aborigines moved about constantly, each tribe searching for food within its territory. Tribal territories ranged from as many as 60,000 square miles in desert areas to as few as 300 square miles along the more fertile coasts.

To survive in the desert, the tribes had to know where the various animals lived, as well as the locations of edible plants and water supplies. Members of the desert Walbiri tribe could identify 103 different plant species and recognize 138 different types of animals. They classified plants and animals as food or medicine, or as having ceremonial or tool uses.

All of the tribes used similar tools: hammers, knives, scrapers, axeheads, spears, and digging sticks. Tool construction differed somewhat according to regions. Coastal people used bone tips on their weapons; desert tribes used stone-edged weapons. Some tribes had boomerangs, some had canoes, and some had woven bags. The aborigines did not develop metal-working technology.

Trade between Tribes. Aborigine tribes traded with their neighbors. Coastal tribes traded shell and marine products for stone tools made by inland peoples. Trade was not important to the aborigines, however, because, as wanderers, they did not accumulate many possessions.

Aborigine Customs. Tribes considered their territory sacred and did not try to take the lands of another tribe. Warfare between tribes, therefore, was limited. Even within a tribe, conflict was rare, perhaps because bonds of kinship were strong. A boy might call any woman in the tribe mother. A man might call any girl in the group daughter.

Occasional conflicts occurred over marriage arrangements or the performance of religious ceremonies. Generally, however, Australian aborigines seem to have been very good at keeping peace within their communities.

Common Beliefs. The aborigines believed that long ago, in "Dreamtime," great ancestors walked the earth. These ancestors were part human, part animal, and part bird. The ancestors' spirits lived in all things, and their life-creating force continued to be passed on to new generations.

According to the aborigines, all things originated from the same life force. Human beings, therefore, had a close relationship with all of nature. When people died, their spirits returned to the source of creation and entered an eternal state of dreaming.

Aborigines believed that sacred cave paintings like the one shown here were created by *Wandjinas*, spirits who emerged during monsoons and painted their images on cave walls before dying.

The Prosperous Hunters

Geoffrey Blainey, who is a present-day Australian historian, believes that the aborigines, also called aboriginals, had a relatively high standard of living. In his book, *Triumph of the Nomads: A History of Aboriginal Australia*, Blainey points out that the aborigines enjoyed a general abundance of food, a warm climate, and the use of tools. By the standards of the year 1800, when Great Britain organized colonies in Australia, the aborigines' material life could be compared favorably to life in many parts of Europe. The Europeans thought of the tribes as poor, however, because they were hunters.

" Aboriginals in most parts of Australia appear to have had an impressive standard of living at the time of the European invasion [in the late 1700s]. But the window through which we see them is so smoky or misted that only with difficulty can we recognize the kind of abundance in which they lived.

We often judge the material success of ancient empires by their surviving monuments and the remains of their temples and city walls, and by that test the aboriginals failed. But elegant, long-standing buildings were essentially a sign of a sedentary [settled] society, and often those buildings reflected the extreme contrast between the wealth of the rulers and the poverty of their subjects. Indeed, some stately palaces in ancient societies were built only by sacrificing the standard of living of ordinary subjects whose daily food, even in good years, was probably less in volume and variety than that of aboriginals. Similarly, the aboriginals were usually naked; and to Europeans, especially in the nineteenth century, nakedness was seen as evidence of material poverty.

This bias was understandable in cold lands, but clothing was an irrelevent criteria of well-being for people in a warm climate. It was also easy to overlook how often the aboriginals were extravagantly dressed. Their ceremonial dress, however, took the form of body paints, gaudy feathers from birds, and ornamental scars and coverings which provided decoration and not unwanted warmth. As the aboriginals were nomads, they had few possessions, and that also lowered them in the eyes of a civilization which believed that well-being and possessions were identical. . . .

The later Australians were unable to believe that the aboriginals usually found plenty of food. The disbelief was understandable. The vital role of aboriginal women as food-gatherers was not understood. Moreover aboriginals seemed to live from hand to mouth, and such a habit is associated more with the poor in a settled society. Likewise, many foods favoured by aboriginals seemed unappetizing to later Australians, and so the myth arose that aboriginals had to rely on the land's second-rate foods which Europeans ignored. Aboriginals, of course, relied on those foods because they preferred them to many other foods which they could have caught or picked.

The astonishing range of foods which grew in Australia before the coming of potatoes, cattle, and wheat has been forgotten. Almost everything eaten in Australia today belongs to species of flora and fauna introduced to the continent within the last 200 years. Accordingly the plentiful foods available to aboriginals slowly slipped from common knowledge. . . .

Conditions approaching famine were rarely observed by those Europeans who had the opportunity to see the aboriginals' tribal life before it disintegrated. Even when British explorers passed through countryside which was almost shaved bare by drought, they rarely noticed that aboriginals were on the brink of starvation. When they did report destitution, their report was sometimes nullified by their own ignorance

This aboriginal bark painting from Groote Eylandt, an island off Australia's north coast, shows a fishing scene. These islanders often painted scenes from everyday life.

of what aboriginals ate. . . . It was a popular mistake to imagine that they have small means of subsistence, or are at times greatly pressed for want of food. When food became scarce they simply moved camp more frequently. That was the very advantage of the nomadic life: the ease with which scarcity in one area could be circumvented by moving to a new area. **" ■**

Changes in History

History is the story of movement and change. Cultures and civilizations grow and change, and sometimes are conquered by new groups of people.

Between 800 B.C. and 200 B.C., ideas spread across a growing communicating zone. The people of the Mediterranean Basin traded and exchanged ideas with one another. Iron technology spread into sub-Saharan Africa. The peoples of Southeast Asia developed thriving cultures, and the aborigines of Australia had adapted to their environment and continued unchanged.

SECTION 3 *Study Skills*

Developing Vocabulary Write a sentence using each of the following: **1.** theory. **2.** marsupial. **3.** extinct. **4.** aborigines. **5.** kinship.

Reviewing Main Ideas 1. Explain why trade was a possible occupation for people living on the coasts of Southeast Asia. **2.** Describe why aborigine culture changed very little until the 1600s A.D. **3.** Approximately how many people live in a tribe of aborigines? **4.** Why was trade not important to aborigines?

Understanding Geography 1. Describe the two major regions of Southeast Asia. **2.** What are the major features of the geography of Australia? **3.** Identify three unique animals found in Australia today.

Understanding Chronology 1. When did the first people arrive in Southeast Asia? **2.** What development changed life for the Non Nok Tha by 2500 B.C.?

Challenge Explain why the culture of the Australian aborigines is likely to change dramatically in the future.

CHAPTER 6 *Summary & Review*

Summarizing Main Ideas

Civilizations in the Mediterranean Basin continued to develop between 600 and 200 B.C. By 550 B.C., traders were using currency rather than barter to carry on their exchanges in this region. The Greeks and Phoenicians established rival trading colonies throughout the Mediterranean. The Etruscans developed a strong civilization that lasted from 800 to 300 B.C.

People outside the Mediterranean Basin developed new skills and empires. Scythian nomads learned to ride horses. The Celts became adept at forging metal. The Africans of Kush built an iron-using civilization in the upper Nile Valley. In Southeast Asia, the Non Nok Tha and Dong Son cultures developed the use of bronze and built cities.

Settlers first reached Australia about 30,000 years ago. The aborigines remained outside the influence of other civilizations until recent times.

"So by a vote of 8 to 2 we have decided to skip the industrial revolution completely, and go right into the electronic age."

Questions for Critical Thinking

COMPREHENSION Interpreting Events

1. Explain why an economy based on the barter system does not expand as rapidly as one using currency.
2. Explain why the Greek and Etruscan civilizations were willing to trade with the Celts.

ANALYSIS Identifying Trends

1. Why did the early civilizations want to produce more and improved military technology? Provide examples to show whether or not nations still use resources for this priority.

APPLICATION Comparing Past to Present

1. Compare the impact of trade rivalry between Phoenicia and Greece with conflicts over trade between countries today.
2. Provide three examples of how the climate affects the peoples and cultures of the mainland and islands of Southeast Asia.

SYNTHESIS Making Decisions

1. How did the Kushites solve the problems created by declining Egyptian power?
2. How did Celts explain natural occurrences?

EVALUATION Weighing Consequences

1. Several ancient societies were confederations. Explain possible problems associated with a confederation.
2. Explain possible advantages and disadvantages to a country of having colonies.
3. What was the purpose of the regular ceremonies conducted by the Druids?
4. Explain why the Kushite civilization developed and lost influence so quickly.

CHALLENGE

1. What traits in aboriginal society might be useful to more technological civilizations? Explain your answer.
2. Today the world shares ideas across a global intercommunicating zone. What advantages and disadvantages does global exchange have for modern people?

CHAPTER 7
Hellenistic Culture Spreads

GLOBAL TIME LINE

350 B.C.　　　325 B.C.　　　300 B.C.

TIME

323–200 B.C. Hellenistic culture spreads throughout the interacting global community

303–232 B.C. Mauryan Dynasty rules India

PEOPLE

359 B.C. Philip becomes king of Macedonia

356 B.C. Alexander is born in Pella, Macedonia

336 B.C. Philip dies; Alexander becomes king of Macedonia

324 B.C. Alexander and 10,000 of his soldiers marry Persian brides

323 B.C. Alexander the Great dies of a fever in Babylon

PLACE

333 B.C. *Asia Minor;*[1] Alexander gains control of Asia Minor

332 B.C. *Eastern Mediterranean;*[2] Alexander gains control of Syria and Phoenicia

332 B.C. *Egypt;*[3] Egypt surrenders to Alexander

331 B.C. *Persia;*[4] Alexander defeats the Persian army

325 B.C. *India;*[5] Alexander conquers the Indus River Valley

Linking Past to Present

Such cities as New York, Paris, and London are cosmopolitan because people from around the world are able to work, live, or do business in them. In cosmopolitan cities, people are not limited to local or national attitudes. Instead, a worldwide perspective is encouraged.

Some individuals in earlier times had the vision and ability to introduce a cosmopolitan perspective to others. One such person was Alexander the Great, a Macedonian Greek. In the fourth century B.C., he created an empire that extended far beyond Greece. He united cities in Greece, Egypt, and the Middle East under one government. These cities became centers of trade and cultural exchange. As you read, think about what causes people to develop cosmopolitan attitudes.

Photo of modern-day Alexandria, Egypt.

---

250 B.C.   **225 B.C.**   **200 B.C.**

265 B.C. Rome gains control of the Italian Peninsula

221–207 B.C. Qin Dynasty rules China

250–170 B.C. Parni establish the Parthian Empire

200s B.C. Greek colonists settle throughout Syria and Asia Minor

269–232 B.C. Ashoka governs India

210 B.C. Death of Shi Huangdi, Emperor of China

213 B.C. *China;[7]* Emperor Shi Huangdi orders burning of books by Confucius

264–146 B.C. *Mediterranean Basin;[6]* Rome and Carthage fight the Punic Wars

1 The Empire of Alexander the Great

OBJECTIVE: *To understand how Alexander the Great introduced the Hellenistic culture throughout his empire*

Alexander Builds an Empire

Seldom does one person change history. Progress and major changes in human history generally result from trends involving large groups of people, such as the gradual development of ideas and technology. Real heroes—people of vision, insight, daring, and achievement—are rare. Alexander the Great was such a hero. His ambition, courage, and leadership changed the world.

In 334 B.C., at the age of 21, Alexander of Macedonia led an army into Asia. When he died 11 years later, he had conquered more of the world than anyone before him.

Constant Warfare. The end of the Peloponnesian Wars between Athens and Sparta, in 404 B.C., did not bring peace to

Greece. The Persians supported rival Greek city-states to promote disagreement, and the allegiances of city-states often shifted. Armies of Greek mercenaries, paid soldiers, fought for the side that paid the most. Often, Greek soldiers fought for the Persian king.

The Rise of Macedonia. Macedonia, a fertile and mountainous country north of Greece, was famous for its horses, cattle, and timber. The Macedonian people were Greeks and spoke their own Greek dialect. The inhabitants of the Greek city-states, however, thought that the Macedonians were barbarians because they had not developed an urban civilization.

Unlike the more democratic Greek city-states, the Macedonian warrior tribes were ruled by a king. His power was directly related to the strength of the Macedonian army he led.

Macedonia became a major power in the Greek-speaking world under the leadership of King Philip. As a young noble, Philip lived in the Greek city-state of Thebes. There, he watched the Theban army train and studied its battle plans. He saw the way the Thebans used the phalanx in battle.

Macedonian Conquests. When Philip returned to Macedonia and became king in 359 B.C., he reorganized the royal army after the Theban model. He created the strongest fighting force in the world. Ironi-

---

VOCABULARY DEVELOPMENT

mercenaries *noun:* professional soldiers hired to serve in a foreign army, sometimes called soldiers of fortune. From the Latin word, *merces*, meaning pay or wages.

regent (REE jehnt) *noun:* a person appointed to rule a country when the king is absent, too young, or otherwise unable to rule.

Hellenic culture *noun:* the achievements and way of life of the Greeks between 700 and 400 B.C. From the Greek word, *hellene*, meaning Greek.

Hellenistic culture *noun:* the blending of Hellenic culture with the cultures of Egypt and Asia.

---

cally, he used Greek techniques to conquer the Greek peninsula.

By 338 B.C., Philip had defeated the allied armies of Thebes and Athens, and successfully invaded Sparta. The Greek city-states, falling one by one before his victorious army, finally agreed to form a league with Philip as their leader.

Philip's ambitions, however, went beyond merely ruling Greece. He planned to invade the Persian Empire. Before he could carry out his plans, though, he was assassinated. The conquest of the Persian Empire was left to his 20-year-old son, Alexander.

Alexander the Great

FOCUS ON PEOPLE

Alexander's accomplishments were even greater than those of his father. Alexander was born in Pella, Macedonia, in 356 B.C. His father was the very powerful Macedonian king, Philip. His mother, Olympias, was an Illyrian princess.

Alexander was an excellent rider. As a young boy, he dared to ride a horse that no other person had been able to tame. Watching the horse's behavior while others tried to ride him, Alexander observed that the horse was afraid of his own shadow. When Alexander rode, he kept the horse's head facing into the sun. In this way he tamed Bucephalus, the horse whose spirit and courage matched those of Alexander.

Alexander grew up in a military environment, and he loved combat. As a boy, he learned to use weapons and endure hardship. Philip, however, rarely took Alexander on military campaigns. Once, after Philip returned from a successful campaign, Alexander complained, "Father is going to do everything; he won't leave any lands for me to conquer."

King Philip guided Alexander's education in the Greek tradition. By the age of

This Indian painting tells a legend about Alexander, who asked artisans to make him a glass barrel so he could observe life under water.

nine, he could sing, recite, and debate in Greek. After Alexander had tamed Bucephalus, Philip recognized his son's potential and hired Aristotle to teach Alexander. Legend says that Alexander acquired his love of reading from Aristotle.

As a youth of 16, Alexander governed Macedonia in his father's absence. At the age of 18, he proved his military leadership by helping Philip to defeat the Greeks at Chaeronea (KEHR uh NEE uh). This decisive victory in 338 B.C. gave Philip of Macedonia control of most of the Greek city-states.

Philip's next goal was to attack Persia. However, two years later, before the king could begin that military campaign, he was assassinated. Alexander became king of Macedonia and ruler of the Greek city-states at the age of 20.

Thebes, as well as several other Greek cities, tested the strength of the new ruler by revolting. Alexander swiftly put down the revolt, destroyed the city of Thebes, and enslaved its people. The other Greek cities quickly recognized his authority.

Alexander promptly pursued his father's dreams of conquest. Within two years after taking the throne, Alexander invaded Asia Minor with an army of almost 40,000 soldiers. On the way through Asia Minor, he and his army marched into the city of Gordium. The city was famous for a knot made with a leather thong. The knot was so complex that no one had been able to untie it. A legend foretold that whoever undid the knot was destined to rule the world. Alexander unsheathed his sword and cut the knot.

The legend was reinforced when Alexander conquered Egypt, Mesopotamia, Persia, central Asia, and the Indus Valley. As his successes multiplied, Alexander's subjects began to view him as a god-king. See the map, The Empire of Alexander the Great, on page 140.

The young ruler left a lasting impression on the world. His conquests linked the civilizations of the Mediterranean with southwest Asia and the Indus Valley, expanding the interacting global community. A new culture, combining Greek and non-Greek customs, spread throughout the lands of Alexander's vast empire. ■

Alexander's Style of Leadership

When Alexander defeated the Persian army, he freed the Greek cities from Persian rule. The Greek cities were allowed to govern themselves and were exempt from paying tribute to the Macedonians.

In 333 B.C., with Asia Minor under his control, Alexander pursued the Persian king, Darius III. The Macedonians met the Persians near the boundary between Asia Minor and Syria. Again Alexander triumphed, defeating a huge Persian army and capturing the royal treasury. He claimed the riches of Babylon and the royal palaces at Persepolis and Susa.

Further Conquests in Southwest Asia. During 332 B.C., Alexander's armies marched south through Syria, Phoenicia, and Egypt. The awed Egyptians surrendered without a fight and made Alexander their pharoah. Before leaving Egypt, Alexander planned Alexandria, a new city on the Mediterranean coast at the western edge of the Nile delta. Alexandria was one of the earliest of more than 25 cities the Macedonian king established throughout conquered territories.

In 330 B.C., Alexander moved north into Media. There he attacked Darius near the Caspian Sea. The Persian king, however, was murdered by one of his governors, who hoped by his deed to gain Alexander's favor.

Alexander Enters India. Even when his empire included most of the civilized world known to the Greeks, Alexander had not realized all of his ambitions. He wanted to include India in his new empire. Between 329 and 325 B.C., Alexander led his army over the towering Hindu Kush Mountains, to enter northern India through the Indus River valley.

Alexander wanted to continue farther east to conquer the Ganges Valley, which he thought was the end of Asia. His weary army, however, refused to go on. He, therefore, marched his forces south through the Indus Valley and along the coast of the Arabian Sea to return home.

On his return to Babylon, he fell ill with a fever. He died on a hot day in June, 323 B.C. A golden coffin was made for him. His body, over which hung a gold-embroidered purple cloth, was covered with precious spices. At his death, his Persian wife, Roxanne, was expecting their first child.

The Hellenistic Kingdoms

Alexander left no plans for the vast lands he had conquered. Some of his generals wanted to act as regents until Alexander's infant son was old enough to rule. These commanders hoped to keep the empire unified. Other generals, however, wanted to divide Alexander's empire among themselves. Within a few years of the conqueror's death, war broke out among the Macedonian generals.

When their struggles ended, Alexander's empire was divided into three great kingdoms. Antigonus I (an TIHG uh nus) and his descendants ruled Macedonia and part of Greece. Ptolemy (TAHL uh mee) and his descendants claimed Egypt. Seleucus (seh LOO kus) and his heirs, the Selucids (sih LOO sihds), ruled the largest territorial division. The lands of the Seleucids extended from the coast of Asia Minor east through Persia and central Asia. See the map, The Empire of Alexander the Great, page 140.

Hellenistic Culture. Alexander's ambitions were cultural as well as military and political. Most Greeks limited their political horizons to a particular city-state. Alexander, however, saw himself as the bearer of Greek culture to the world.

He started new cities as outposts of Greek culture. These cities, from Egyptian Alexandria in the west to the Asian Alexandrias in the east, followed the Greek patterns and customs. Each had open market squares, Greek style temples, assembly halls, and stadiums.

Alexander gave Macedonian and other Greek soldiers gifts of land in the new Asian cities so that they would introduce Greek culture to Asia. The soldiers married women in the conquered lands and became the governing class of the new cities. The Greek-speaking residents of all these cities formed a cosmopolitan society. These Hellenistic cities were linked by trade, as well as by shared Greek culture and the Greek language. This interacting zone extended from the Mediterranean Sea to the Indus River valley.

Greek and Persian cultures combined symbolically shortly before Alexander's death. In 324 B.C., Alexander chose a Per-

Alexander and Darius fight hand-to-hand in this Persian painting. The two rulers never battled this closely in real life.

sian bride and ordered 80 of his officers and about 10,000 soldiers to marry Persian women. He hoped that the soldiers would remain in Asia.

Just as Alexander brought the Hellenic or Greek culture to distant lands, he also adopted some regional customs. He wore the clothing of a Persian king to make himself acceptable to the people of the Persian Empire. He allowed himself to be worshiped in Egypt as the son of the Egyptian god, Amen. The Greeks of the new cities also were encouraged to worship the local gods

The Empire of Alexander the Great

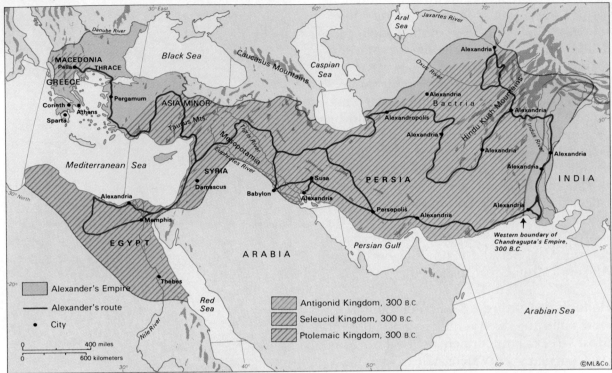

Map Skills 1. What major river lies to the east of Alexander's Empire? **2.** Through what lands did Alexander travel to reach the Indus Valley from his home in Macedonia? **3.** What great empire existed in India in 300 B.C.?

but to give them Greek names. The combination of Greek culture with other cultures came to be called Hellenistic culture.

Results of Alexander's Conquests.
In addition to spreading the Greek culture and language, Hellenistic culture had other lasting effects. The use of gold and silver coins and the development of a commercial economy spread throughout Alexander's empire. Most important, wherever he went, Alexander founded cities modeled after Greek cities. His successors continued to transform western Asia by starting other Hellenistic cities.

SECTION 1 *Study Skills*

Developing Vocabulary 1. What is the difference between Hellenic and Hellenistic cultures?
2. Who are mercenaries? **3.** Why would an area pay tribute to another area?

Reviewing Main Ideas 1. Why are great movements in history often more influenced by groups than individuals? **2.** Explain why the Greeks thought the Macedonians were barbarians. **3.** Describe how Alexander treated conquered lands. **4.** Explain how Alexander spread Greek culture.

Understanding Cause and Effect 1. Explain the influence of Alexander's education on his future. **2.** What happened to Alexander's empire after his death?

Understanding Geography 1. What areas did Alexander conquer? **2.** What geographical features limited the expansion of Alexander's empire to new lands?

Challenge Explain whether individuals or groups are more likely to make decisions in modern government.

2 The Hellenistic World of Southwest Asia

OBJECTIVE: *To understand the Hellenistic societies that prospered throughout Macedonia, Greece, Egypt, and Asia*

Alexander's Successors

Soon after Alexander the Great died, his enormous empire split into three kingdoms ruled by the Ptolemies, the Seleucids, and the Antigonids. The generals who began new dynasties in each of these lands encouraged local traditions while transplanting Greek culture.

Hellenistic Kings. Hellenistic rulers used such words as savior and benefactor in their titles to emphasize their power to help their subjects. The Ptolemies and the Seleucids thought of themselves as Greeks and successors to Alexander, but they lived and ruled in a style more like the Persians and Egyptians they had conquered.

Hellenistic rulers were trained as military leaders because war between Hellenistic kingdoms was almost constant. Kings spent much of their wealth and energy maintaining large and powerful mercenary armies. In addition, they tried to develop new strategies for siege warfare.

Before the end of the third century B.C., parts of the Hellenistic world had gained independence from the three great kingdoms. Even these independent areas, however, often had Greek rulers. They kept the Hellenistic traditions of monarchy and ruled with the help of a bureaucracy.

Hellenistic Achievements

Imitating the dreams of Alexander, his successors, the new kings, planned Hellenistic cities built on a grander scale than Greek cities. Hellenistic kings and wealthy citizens paid for enormous buildings, elaborate statues, and public monuments.

Hellenistic rulers tried to transplant elements of Greek culture to their new cities. Hellenistic cities enjoyed festivals and theater performances in the Greek tradition of Athens and Olympia.

International Language. In 500 B.C., the Assyrian and Persian empires used Aramaic as a common language throughout their lands. Hellenistic rulers of the third century B.C. promoted the use of Greek. The Greek language was used in schools, businesses, and government.

VOCABULARY DEVELOPMENT

koine (koy NAY) *noun:* the Greek language the common people spoke during the Hellenistic period. From the Greek word, *koinos*, meaning common.

rhetoric (REHT uhr ihk) *noun:* the skill of using words effectively in writing or public speaking. From the Greek word, *rhetor*, meaning orator.

deduction *noun:* a process of reasoning from a generalization to specific information.

dissection *noun:* to separate into pieces for scientific examination; analysis part by part.

The Greek language that developed during Hellenistic times, however, differed from the Greek of the classic Athenian writers and philosophers. The Greek spoken in the cities of the Hellenistic kingdoms became known as *koine* (koy NAY). *Koine* is the Greek word for common. *Koine* was the popular spoken language rather than the more formal language of classical literature.

Koine enabled educated people and merchants to communicate throughout the Hellenistic world. The 80 to 90 percent of the population that lived in rural areas beyond Hellenistic cities, however, continued to speak their own languages. They did not share in Hellenistic culture.

The Wealthy Gain Power. Alexander encouraged the cities that he founded to rule themselves. Hellenistic cities, however, departed from the Athenian legacy of democracy. The Hellenistic cities were not ruled by all the citizens. Instead, the wealthy citizens gained political influence and controlled city government.

In Hellenistic cities, ordinary citizens did not play much part in politics. Instead, the rich gained influence by donating money for public buildings and monuments. In addition, Hellenistic officials had to work with the king to whom they paid tribute and pledged loyalty.

Education Improves at the Gymnasiums. In ancient Greece, the gymnasium was a place for athletic training. In Hellenistic cities, sports and exercise for male citizens were also important. A Hellenistic gymnasium included a track, a court for wrestling, and rooms for various ball games.

The Hellenistic gymnasium became the center of intellectual, as well as athletic, life for the Greek ruling class. Private tutors and parents provided primary education. Gymnasiums offered more advanced training and often were supported by taxes or contributions from wealthy citizens. At gymnasiums, boys between 15 and 17 years old

This painting on marble shows girls in ancient Herculaneum playing a game called "knucklebones."

studied music, philosophy, and rhetoric, the art of using words skillfully. They heard lectures on such topics as philosophy, geometry, and astronomy. Through the gymnasium, Greek language and culture were passed on to the young.

Status of Women Improved. Hellenistic women shared public life and family responsibilities with men. Married women were not restricted to their homes as they had been in Athens. Marriage contracts regulated the behavior of husbands and wives, and women were permitted to own slaves and property. Probably the most important gain for upper class women was the opportunity to attend schools.

Women of the ruling classes occupied high social positions. Hellenistic princesses, for example, built temples, founded cities, paid mercenary soldiers, commanded armies, and acted as regents. Women of royal families ruled sometimes with their husbands or brothers.

As poets, scholars, and artists, women contributed to Hellenistic civilization. The opportunities available to women of the royal and wealthy classes were not available to commoners, though. Generally, men still dominated every part of society.

Slavery Extended. Much of the economic activity in Alexander's Empire relied on slavery. Many slaves lived and worked in Greece and the lands around the Mediterranean Sea. Prisoners of war were sold as slaves, and a growing number of pirates earned a living by selling captives in slave markets. Sometimes debtors sold their children into slavery to raise money.

Slaves did much of the work in the Hellenistic world. They provided heavy labor for construction, farming, and mining.

More fortunate slaves worked in the households of the wealthy.

A Hellenistic City. Alexandria, Egypt, became a city of more than a half million people. More Greeks and Macedonians lived there than in any other city. Teeming with both native Egyptians and people of many other countries, the city became the most cosmopolitan in the ancient world.

Alexandria, with its great harbor, was a wealthy trade center. Ships from ports throughout the Mediterranean Basin carried goods in and out of Alexandria. The city was famous for its world-class museum and library. The museum was dedicated to the Muses, goddesses of the Greek arts. The king paid scholars from the entire interacting Eurasian world to study Greek literature and philosophy at the museum.

The library in Alexandria was linked to the museum. Ptolemy I, its founder, sent

This first-century B.C. mosaic shows a temple on the Nile.

scholars throughout the Hellenistic world to find and copy works of Greek literature, science, and geography. The library may have contained 500,000 papyrus scrolls.

Non-Greeks in Hellenistic Cities. Alexander the Great's successors generally did not share his respect for non-Greek cultures. Most Hellenistic Greek settlers considered foreigners to be barbarians. The Greeks did not bother to learn the language of the peoples they conquered. Even when Greeks ruled other lands, they denied full citizenship to the original inhabitants. These people were called resident aliens. They were allowed to share in the economic and cultural life of the city but they could not vote or share in the government.

Generally, the wealthy and educated non-Greeks became "culture-Greeks." That is, they learned to speak *koine*, sent their sons to the gymnasium, and adopted Greek names. However, they still retained some of their original customs.

In Egypt, Syria, Asia Minor, and other places across the Hellenistic world, this new cosmopolitan class became a part of Greek commercial life. Gradually, they gained citizenship. Through these educated non-Greek merchants, Greeks interacted with the culture of countries they had conquered.

Life in Rural Areas. Many people in the Hellenistic world shared in the exchanges and benefits of the new cosmopolitan society. Local customs, especially those of the poor, changed little.

Different social, economic, and political interests divided the Greek-speaking people of the Hellenistic cities and the native-speaking people of the countryside. These differences created an imbalance in society that would contribute to further changes.

Scientific Achievements. Scientists made remarkable advances without the use of microscopes, telescopes, or other tools for measuring and observing. Aristarchus (AR is TAHR kus) of Samos wrote a book arguing that the earth revolved around the sun. He proposed this theory almost 2,000 years before the world generally accepted the idea.

Eratosthenes (ehr uh TAHS thuh neez) of Cyrene, the librarian at Alexandria about 200 B.C., calculated the circumference of the earth with an error of less than 1 percent. Hipparchus (hih PAHR khus) of Nicaea used trigonometry, and he accurately calcu-

A doctor treats a patient in this fourth-century B.C. relief. Hellenistic scholars made many advances in medicine.

lated the length of the lunar and solar years, and cataloged the stars.

The mathematician Euclid (YOO klihd) worked in Alexandria on problems of reasoning by deduction. He wrote a textbook, *The Elements*, that contained many elements of present-day geometry.

Using dissection of animals, doctors at Alexandria made important discoveries about digestion, the nervous system, and various organs of the body. These advances resulted from the Hellenistic interest in combining observation of the natural world with theory and systematic reasoning.

Hellenistic Philosophy. Like the Greeks, Hellenistic people believed that the universe followed rational principles and that philosophy offered the best way to understand these principles. The teachings of Plato and Aristotle continued to be very influential in Hellenistic philosophy.

In the third century B.C., however, philosophy added new ideas and principles to aid in understanding the workings of the universe. New schools of philosophy were concerned with how people should live their lives. People came to believe that fate and chance controlled public affairs. Two major philosophies developed during the Hellenistic period, Epicureanism and Stoicism (STOH ih sihz uhm). These philosophies showed people how to find permanent values in their lives even though fate or chance determined events.

A Cypriot named Zeno taught the most popular philosophy called Stoicism. Zeno and the Stoics believed that humanity was part of a universe governed by natural law. People should live a virtuous life in harmony with the natural law. Stoicism explained nature, provided an ethical approach to life, promoted social duty, and taught how to endure pain.

Epicurus (EHP uh KYUR uhs) developed a philosophical alternative to Stoicism. He taught that the universe was composed of atoms and ruled by gods who had no interest in humans. Epicurus believed that the only real objects were those that the five senses perceived.

The main goal of humans, he said, was to achieve harmony of body and mind. People could achieve the most pleasure in virtuous living and could learn to avoid pain by limiting their wants to the simplest needs.

Other philosophical doctrines, such as those of the Cynics and the Skeptics, were even more doubtful of human abilities to understand or change the universe. All of these schools focused on the individual. None of the newer Hellenistic philosophies taught that politics was an important part of the ideal life.

The Hellenistic kings who ruled in southwest Asia and Egypt brought Greek language and culture to their lands. Cities were modeled after the Greek cities of the fifth century, and boys were educated at gymnasiums similar to those of classical Greece. The Hellenistic culture did not reach the rural areas where between 80 and 90 percent of the people lived. The new culture, therefore, was a thin overlay on the societies of Egypt and Southwest Asia.

SECTION 2 *Study Skills*

Developing Vocabulary Use each of the following in a sentence: **1.** *koine*. **2.** rhetoric. **3.** deduction. **4.** dissection.

Reviewing Main Ideas 1. Explain how language helps unite an area. **2.** What was the importance of the Gymnasium? **3.** Describe the life of women in Hellenistic society. **4.** Identify some of the major scientific achievements during the Hellenistic period.

Understanding Cause and Effect 1. How does the existence of slavery influence people in a society? **2.** What effect did Hellenistic culture have on life in rural areas?

Challenge Are the ideas expressed by Zeno useful in the modern world? Explain.

GEOGRAPHY IN HISTORY

Water and Waterways

Humans, animals, and crops require water to survive. From the earliest settlements in Mesopotamia between the Tigris and Euphrates Rivers, civilizations have developed in areas with adequate supplies of water from either rivers or rain. This feature discusses waterways, how they developed, and how they have influenced history.

Oceans, Seas, and Lakes

Oceans cover about 70 percent of the earth's surface. In some places, the ocean is more than 19,680 feet (6000 meters) deep. The ocean along the coasts of continents is relatively shallow, though. These areas, less than 656 feet (200 meters) deep, are referred to as the continental shelf.

The ocean's floor is not a flat surface. Just as tectonic and volcanic activity on land produces irregular land forms, these forces also produce irregular landforms beneath the water. Tectonic and volcanic activity on the ocean's floor can create new islands. For example, volcanic activity underwater created Iceland and Hawaii.

A sea is a large body of water partially or completely enclosed by land. Seas were created by the same tectonic and volcanic activity which created oceans and continents. The Arabian, the Mediterranean, and the Caspian are examples of seas.

A lake is a large body of water located inland. Most lakes are smaller than seas and have different origins.

Sometimes a lake is formed in hollows carved out of the land. If the hollow has no outlet, it fills with rain or underground water and becomes a lake. Tectonic activity can create hollows. Shifts in the earth's crust can cause low spots. In some areas, ice age glaciers scooped out hollows just by the sheer weight of the slowly flowing ice.

Lakes may also be formed by two other methods. Rivers changing course may leave behind oxbow lakes. These are discussed later. People may build dams on streams or rivers, preventing a release of water and creating a lake.

Water slowly evaporates from all bodies of water. As water evaporates, it leaves behind salt and other minerals. In bodies of water with no outlet, the salt content is high. The oceans and most seas are salty. Bodies of water that are not salty are considered fresh. Most lakes are fresh water.

Streams and Rivers

A stream is a body of running water. A stream generally flows into a larger body of water, such as a lake or a river. A river is a large stream which empties into a larger body of water, usually an ocean or a very large lake. The streams flowing into a river are called its tributaries.

Development of a River. Streams and rivers have a characteristic pattern of development. River water comes from rain or melted snow. As the water flows downhill, it gradually creates a groove in the land. As this groove deepens, a river forms.

In the early stages of a river's life, water may accumulate in pools on flatter surfaces along the river's path. If the river flows over hills and sharp drops, waterfalls may develop. Over time, the river cuts a deep enough path to eliminate most pools and waterfalls. Flooding helps to smooth out the course of the river.

Some rivers flood every year. Others flood only when precipitation is unusually high. The land covered by the floodwaters

Life of a Stream

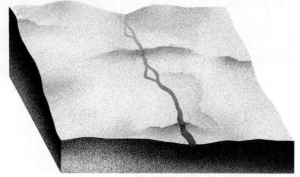

In Stage I, a stream is made of lakes, waterfalls, and rapids.

Falls and rapids persist in Stage II, as a river valley begins to develop.

By Stage III, a deep river valley has formed while rapids and falls have disappeared.

A stream reaches full maturity in Stage IV, marked by meanders, oxbow lakes, and a broad flood plain.

of a river is its flood plain. The flood plain of a very large and powerful river can stretch for miles on either side.

Under certain flood conditions, a river may change its course. Powerful flood waters may cause the river to overflow its banks and carve out a new course away from its previous course. Once the flood stage passes, the river then uses the new course.

When a river changes course, water may be trapped in the groove previously used. The water trapped in this way forms a type of lake with a unique "U" or oxbow shape. This type of lake is called an oxbow lake.

People and Water

Throughout history, people have found that living near water may have both great advantages and great disadvantages. The floods which improve the land's fertility also have the power to destroy everything in their paths. The value of water resources changes over time. At one time, the oceans seemed an unconquerable barrier to trade. As people developed their ability to sail, the ocean became a transportation route. Even today, in an age of highways and air travel, water transportation is a vital element of the world's economy.

STUDY SKILLS Understanding Geography

1. What two forces created the oceans?
2. How are seas and lakes different?
3. Explain how an oxbow lake is formed.
4. How did the development of sailing change the value of the ocean for people?

3 The Legacy of Alexander's Conquests

OBJECTIVE: *To understand the consequences of Hellenistic culture for people today*

The Impact of Hellenization

The Hellenistic world of cities, gymnasiums, and Greek learning was concentrated around the eastern Mediterranean. In the middle of the third century B.C., a Greek-speaking traveler would have seen similar sights in the cities along the coast of the Mediterranean Sea from Greece through Asia Minor, Syria, Phoenicia, and Egypt. Travelers also would have seen familiar sights in Seleucia, a great new city on the Tigris River in Mesopotamia. Farther to the east or west of the Mediterranean world, Greek culture influenced people less, and different cultures flourished.

The Seleucid Empire. Thousands of Greek colonists settled in the Seleucid lands of Asia Minor and Syria, changing them into a network of Greek-style cities. In some of those cities, the Greek conquerors included non-Greeks in their society and government. Often, the original inhabitants living in Hellenistic cities assimilated, or adapted, much of the Greek culture.

VOCABULARY DEVELOPMENT

assimilate *verb:* to take over and make part of an existing cultural tradition.
philhellene *noun:* an admirer of Greek culture. From the Greek words *phil*, meaning love of, and *Hellene*, meaning Greek.

Syria, particularly, was Hellenized. The Syrians adopted the Greek educational system and gave Greek names to their temples. In contrast, the Greeks who settled in Mesopotamia adopted the learning of the Mesopotamians with whom they lived.

In the new colonies and cities in Mesopotamia, especially Seleucia, a great trade center, Greek colonists encountered the traditions of the earliest river valley civilization. Hellenistic colonists learned Mesopotamian astronomy and mathematics and allowed old priesthoods to continue.

Persia and India. Persians and their immediate neighbors found Greek civilization more impressive than any they had known before. Bactria, a Greek kingdom, arose between India and central Asia. From Bactria, Greek influence spread into India.

In Persia, Greek and Persian cultures remained separate as long as the Seleucids ruled. Government officials were Greek, and Greeks were in the majority in Hellenistic cities. Persian nobles lived in the country removed from Hellenistic centers.

During the third century B.C., Persia and the Indus Valley broke away from the Seleucid empire. Nevertheless, some Greek influence remained, especially in their art and architecture.

The Mauryan Dynasty Begins in India. Alexander's lands in India were the first that his successors lost. According to Greek writers, in 303 B.C. Seleucus gave Indian territories to Chandragupta (CHUHN druh GUP tuh) Maurya (MAH ur yuh) in return for valuable new war weapons, 500 elephants.

Elephants became an important part of the Hellenistic armies. In A.D. 217, Indian elephants helped the Seleucids win a victory against Egyptian forces. The Egyptians had large African elephants. However, the Seleucids, on smaller Indian elephants, won the battle because their riders controlled their animals more skillfully.

Capturing Elephants for War

The Roman writer Arrian wrote a book about India called *Indike*. Arrian's account is valuable because he based his description on earlier works that now are lost. His account of hunting and taming elephants in India was based on the writings of Megasthenes (muh GAHS thuh neez), the Seleucid ambassador to India in 302 B.C.

❝ The hunters, having selected a level tract of arid ground, dig a trench all around it, enclosing as much space as would suffice to encamp a large army. The earth they throw up in the process of digging, they heap in mounds on both edges of the trench and use it as a wall. . . .

They next station some three or four of their best trained she-elephants within the trap. They leave only a single passage by means of a bridge thrown across the trench. The framework of the bridge they cover over with earth and a great quantity of straw, to conceal as much as possible. . . .

Now the wild elephants do not go near inhabited places in the daytime, but during the nighttime they wander about everywhere, and feed in herds . . . As soon, then, as they approach the enclosure, and hear the cry and catch scent of the females, they rush at full speed in the direction of the fenced ground. Being arrested by the trench, they move around its edge until they find the bridge, along which they force their way into the enclosure.

The hunters, meanwhile, seeing the wild elephants enter, hasten to take away the bridge. Others, running off to the nearest villages, announce that the elephants are within the trap. The villagers, on hearing the news, mount their most spirited and best-trained elephants, and as soon as mounted, ride off to the trap.

Though they ride up to it, they do not immediately engage in a conflict with the wild elephants, but wait til these are sorely pinched by hunger and tamed by thirst. When they think their strength has been enough weakened, they set up the bridge anew and ride into the enclosure. A fierce assault is then made by the tame elephants on those that have been entrapped. Then, as might be expected, the wild elephants, through loss of spirit and faintness from hunger, are overpowered.

Those elephants too young or too weak to be worth keeping, their captors allow to escape to their old haunts. Those which are retained they lead to the villages where, at

Alexander was attracted to the exotic world of India where he discovered a new military weapon, the Indian elephant shown here.

first, they give them green stalks of corn and grass to eat. The creatures, however, having lost all spirit, have no wish to eat. The Indians, standing round them in a circle, soothe and cheer them by chanting songs to the accompaniment of the music of drums and cymbals, for the elephant is of all brutes the most intelligent.

Some of them, for instance, have taken up their riders when slain in battle and carried them away for burial; others have covered them, when lying on the ground, with a shield; and others have borne the brunt of battle in their defense when fallen. There was one even that died of remorse and despair because it had killed its rider in a fit of rage. **"** ■

Chandragupta Creates an Indian Empire

The trade of elephants for land benefited both Chandragupta and Seleucus. Chandragupta established the first great Indian empire by extending his lands from the Ganges to the Indus valley. He ruled Magadha in northeast India and began the new Mauryan Dynasty of Indian rulers.

Government of Mauryan India. According to the report of a Greek ambassador at the Indian capital, Chandragupta used an enormous government bureaucracy to rule his subjects. Laws covered many details of society, even requiring washerwomen to beat the clothes on smooth stones.

The capital spread over 14 square miles of land. Surrounding it was a wooden wall with 570 watchtowers and 64 gates. Chandragupta and his successors built a network of roads to unify their kingdom.

The Rule of Ashoka. The Mauryan Empire reached its height during the reign of Chandragupta's grandson, Ashoka, who governed from 269 to 232 B.C. Ashoka, the greatest of the Mauryan rulers, began his reign by conquering the kingdom of Kalin-

These lions sit atop a Hellenistic column erected by Ashoka in 250 B.C. in the city of Sarnath. The sculptures on Ashokan columns are the best remaining examples of Mauryan imperial art.

ga, thus bringing almost all of the Indian peninsula under his control. See the map, Trade Routes 200 B.C., page 152.

Ashoka is best known for his wisdom and humanity. He converted to Buddhism but enforced tolerance for all religious beliefs. He appointed special officers to travel around his kingdom, spreading his ideas and working for the welfare of his subjects.

Cultural Assimilation in India. The links between Mauryan India and the Hellenistic kingdoms grew strong. Traders, soldiers, and missionaries exchanged ideas and customs. During the Mauryan Dynasty, 303 B.C. to 232 B.C., Greeks still lived in the cities of northwest India and often were employed in the government. Other Greeks came to India as ambassadors from the Seleucid kings. To improve communication with the west, Indian rulers made travel between India and Persia more pleasant by widening the roadways, planting shade trees, and building inns.

Ashoka sent missionaries as far west as Epirus (ih PY ruhs) in Greece to spread Buddha's teachings. The vast empire borrowed from Persian and Hellenistic models. Architecture best illustrates Persian influence. Chandragupta's palace appears to have resembled the Persian palace at Persepolis. Buildings and sculptures commissioned by Ashoka also reflected Persian styles.

Greek Influence in Parthia

Between 250 and 170 B.C., new invaders called the Parni moved from the central Asian steppes onto the Iranian plateau. They won control of Persia from the Seleucids. Their empire, Parthia, expanded to include the Seleucid lands in Persia and Mesopotamia. It became a major world power. See the map, Trade Routes 200 B.C., page 152.

The rulers of Parthia followed the Persian custom, allowing the conquered countries to rule themselves and keep their language and culture. However, Greek remained as the language of city government, and Greek officials stayed in office. Since the Parthians had no written language, they used Greek and Aramaic to communicate with their subjects.

This silver Persian dish shows a Parthian mounted archer taking aim at the enemy. Parthian archers were famous for their amazing riding and shooting skills.

Parthia Spreads Hellenistic Culture. During the middle of the second century B.C., Mithridates I, was the Parthian ruler. He conquered Mesopotamia and other eastern Seleucid provinces to give Parthia control of the communicating zone between Asia and the Mediterranean Basin. With the addition of Mesopotamia, where the Seleucids had developed great Hellenistic cities, Greek influence in Parthia increased. Mithridates I was called a philhellene because he supported Greek culture.

Hellenic Culture in the Western Mediterranean

In 300 B.C., the western Mediterranean was still on the fringes of the civilized world. The trading empire of Carthage and the Greek cities of southern Italy and Sicily dominated the region. However, Greek culture had already influenced part of the western Mediterranean Basin.

Carthage had close ties to the Hellenistic world. Carthaginians traded with Egypt and Greece, and many Greeks lived in Carthaginian lands. By the third century B.C., the government of Carthage, like that of Greece, had a constitution and a popular assembly. Although their Phoenician heritage remained strong, some of the citizens of the upper classes spoke Greek and wore Greek clothing and jewelry.

The Etruscans had spread their own cities throughout Italy. By 405 B.C., however, the Etruscans had lost control of the Italian Peninsula. Slowly the Latins, from the city of Rome, came to power.

Greek civilization influenced the Latins, or Romans, as they were called later. From the beginning of their history, Roman civilization translated much of the Greek culture and institutions into Latin.

By 200 B.C., the western Mediterranean was united under the Romans, who spread Hellenic culture throughout their lands. Long after the kingdoms of Alexander's suc-

Trade Routes, 200 B.C.

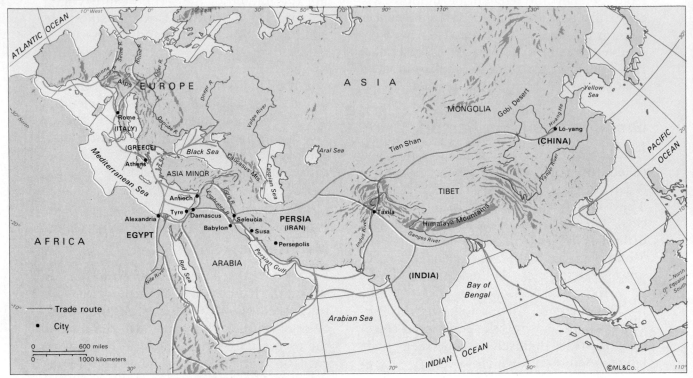

Map Skills 1. What bodies of water would a traveler cross to reach Antioch from Rome?
2. If merchants traveled southeast on the Red Sea, what body of water would they reach?

cessors disappeared, the people of the Roman Empire spread their version of Greek ideas to the people of the west.

The Legacy of Alexander the Great. Alexander's conquests linked the major centers of civilization from southeast Europe to India, expanding the interacting global community. These civilizations gained a common culture centered around cities, gymnasiums, and the Greek language. Expanding trade also tied them together.

The Greeks also learned from other cultures. Hellenistic discoveries in astronomy could not have happened without the Mesopotamian astronomical records made available after Alexander's conquests. By 200 B.C., much of the political domination of the Hellenistic rulers had ended, and Greek influence diminished.

SECTION 3 *Study Skills*

Developing Vocabulary 1. Give an example of assimilation. **2.** What are the meanings of the root words of *philhellene*?

Reviewing Main Ideas 1. Provide evidence of cultural exchanges between Mesopotamia and Greece. **2.** Why were the people who lived east of Alexander's empire less affected by Hellenistic culture? **3.** Explain how Chandragupta was successful in conquering India. **4.** What were the long-term results of the conquests of Alexander the Great?

Understanding Geography 1. Where was the Hellenistic world centered? **2.** What areas traded with Carthage?

Challenge Give examples of cultural achievements from the Hellenistic period that are still apparent today.

CHAPTER 7 *Summary & Review*

Summarizing Main Ideas

The Peloponnesian War ended in 404 B.C. Philip, King of Macedonia, expanded his army and soon defeated the Greeks. His son, Alexander the Great, conquered lands all the way to India by 323 B.C. When he died, Alexander's empire was divided among his generals.

The Hellenistic civilization was noted for its contributions to science, philosophy, and mathematics. Much of the work in the Hellenistic world was done by slaves.

On the edge of the Alexandrian Empire, the Persians, Mauryans, and Parthians were affected to a lesser degree by Greek ideas. Still Greek influence, from language to art, affected much of the known world as a direct result of Alexander the Great's conquests.

This silver dish from Alexandria, Egypt blends symbols of Greece and Egypt. The lion is Greek; the snake is Egyptian.

Questions for Critical Thinking

COMPREHENSION Interpreting Events

1. Explain the influence Alexander the Great had on the spread of Greek culture.
2. When Alexander the Great died, his empire was split among several generals. Analyze the results of this division on the development of Hellenistic civilization.
3. Why was the rule of Ashoka important to the history of India?

ANALYSIS Identifying Trends

1. Explain why scholarly activity usually increases when an empire is growing, and decreases when an empire is losing influence.
2. Why were Alexander's generals unable to maintain his empire?

APPLICATION Comparing Past to Present

1. Explain how Philip of Macedonia defeated the Greeks by using their own tactics.
2. Alexander the Great tried to give much of the known world a common culture. Give two modern examples that indicate people are developing a common culture today.

EVALUATION Weighing Consequences

1. After Alexander's death, the expanded interactive world did not revert to its previous limitations. Why not?
2. Explain how language unified the Mediterranean world.
3. How does the platter shown above reflect interaction between the Greek and the Egyptian cultures?

SYNTHESIS Developing Writing Skills

1. Write a two-page report on the accomplishments of Alexander the Great.
2. Compare and contrast the education of women in ancient society with the education of women today.

CHALLENGE

1. List two similarities and two differences between the empires of Alexander and Persia.
2. Compare the influence of Alexander's empire with that of the United States today.

CHAPTER 8

The Roman and Han Empires

GLOBAL TIME LINE

TIME

265–146 B.C. Rome and Carthage fight a series of wars

146 B.C. Romans defeat the Carthaginians

221 B.C. to 207 B.C. Qin Dynasty rules China

206 B.C. to A.D. 220 Han Dynasty rules China

PEOPLE

221 B.C. King Zheng (Shi Huangdi) conquers the warring states and founds the Qin dynasty of China

210 B.C. Shi Huangdi dies

206 B.C. Liu Bang overthrows the Qin dynasty

73 B.C. Spartacu leads a rebellion against Rome

100 B.C. Hippalus uses monsoons to sail directly from Africa to India

100 B.C. Parthians raise large, strong horses

PLACE

110 B.C. *Vietnam;*[1] Han gain control of northern Vietnam

108 B.C. *Korea;*[2] Han gain control of northern Korea

Linking Past to Present

Today an Italian businesswoman can board an airplane at the Rome international airport for China. Flying by way of Hong Kong, she lands in Beijing after a flight of twenty-one and a half hours.

In the second century A.D., Roman merchants took many months or even years to travel to China. They did, however, go. Travel from one end of Eurasia to the other became a reality in the early centuries A.D. The rise of the Roman Empire in the Mediterranean region and the Han Empire in China stimulated such communication.

This chapter will introduce these two empires, which unified huge territories and millions of people. You will also learn how adventurous caravan merchants and sea captains linked Rome and China.

Roman aquaduct in Segovia, Spain.

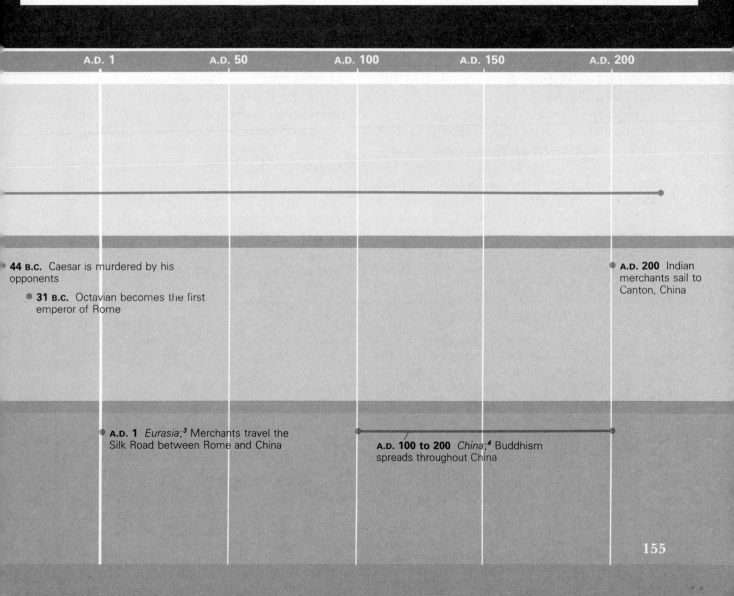

| A.D. 1 | A.D. 50 | A.D. 100 | A.D. 150 | A.D. 200 |

44 B.C. Caesar is murdered by his opponents

31 B.C. Octavian becomes the first emperor of Rome

A.D. 200 Indian merchants sail to Canton, China

A.D. 1 *Eurasia;[3]* Merchants travel the Silk Road between Rome and China

A.D. 100 to 200 *China;[4]* Buddhism spreads throughout China

1 *Rome Unifies the Mediterranean Basin*

OBJECTIVE: *To understand the events that led to the rise of Rome.*

Foundations of Rome

Rome began as a group of Latin villages along the banks of the Tiber River. About 700 B.C., Etruscans captured the villages and used them as their headquarters. Between 700 and 500 B.C., the villages merged to form Rome, a major city from which trade routes fanned out in all directions. The Etruscans ruled the Romans from 755 to 509 B.C. Then the Romans rebelled and overthrew the Etruscan king.

Before 100 B.C., Romans belonged to one of two social classes. Wealthy nobles made up the patrician class. Farmers, artisans, and common people composed the class called plebes or plebeians. Uniting both classes of Romans were shared customs and the fear of attack by neighboring barbarians. About 100 B.C., a third class, the equites, developed. The equites were wealthy businesspeople and merchants who were not members of the hereditary patrician class but formed a new middle class.

The Spread of Roman Control

To protect their borders, the Romans often battled neighboring tribes. By 265 B.C., Rome had conquered all of the people on the Italian Peninsula from the Appennine Mountains to the Mediterranean Sea.

While Rome was gaining control of the Italian Peninsula, Carthage, located on the northern coast of Africa, was building an empire. In the third century B.C., Rome and Carthage, the former Phoenician colony, became rivals. They fought a series of wars from 264 to 146 B.C. that were called the Punic Wars.

During these wars, Hannibal, a Carthaginian general, assembled a great army in the country now called Spain. With about

---

VOCABULARY DEVELOPMENT

ally (AL eye) *noun:* a nation associated with another by treaty or alliance. In ancient Rome, a conquered country with some self-government. From the Latin word, *aligare*, meaning to bind to.

century (SEHN chuhr ee) *noun:* usually means 100; in the army of ancient Rome, 100 men. From the Latin word, *centuria*, meaning one hundred.

decimation (DEHS uh MAY shuhn) *noun:* the practice of killing every 10th person as punishment; destroying a large part of the population. From the Latin word, *decimus*, meaning tenth.

veto *verb:* to forbid an action. From the Latin word, *veto*, meaning I forbid.

republic *noun:* a government in which power is held by a group of citizens who elect government officers to represent them. From the Latin words *res*, meaning thing or interest, and *publica*, meaning public.

paterfamilias (PAH tehr fah MIH lih ahs) *noun:* Latin word meaning father of the family.

latifundia (LAT uh FUHN dee uh) *noun:* in ancient Rome, a large farming estate worked by slaves and tenants. From the Latin words *latus*, meaning broad, and *fundus*, meaning estate.

publicani (PUHB lih kuhn ee) *noun:* in ancient Rome, collectors of public taxes.

60,000 soldiers and 40 war elephants, Hannibal marched through southern Gaul, now France, and across the Alps into Italy.

Hannibal defeated the Roman army in several major battles and remained in Italy for the next 15 years. The Romans refused to admit defeat, but they never again fought the skillful Carthaginian commander in Italy. Finally, in 204 B.C., the Roman general Scipio drove the Carthaginians from Spain and invaded their homeland in Africa. Hannibal returned home to defend Carthage and was defeated in 202 B.C. He later fought for other states against the Romans. In 183 B.C., unable to escape the Romans who demanded his surrender, Hannibal poisoned himself.

In 146 B.C., the Romans again defeated the Carthaginians. The Romans plowed and salted the fields of Carthage so that nothing would grow.

With Carthaginian power effectively destroyed, Rome took a major step toward controlling the lands around the Mediterranean Sea. Victory gave Rome the islands of Sicily, Sardinia, and Corsica, as well as most of the land that is present-day Spain, and the northern coast of Africa.

During the second century B.C., Roman armies also marched through Macedonia and Greece. By 133 B.C., Rome ruled most of Greece and Asia Minor. See the map, Roman Expansion, page 160.

Several factors accounted for Rome's success in gaining and holding such a large empire. Among these factors were: (1) fair treatment of conquered peoples; (2) military organization; (3) a government that could change in new situations; and (4) family values.

Allies. A people the Romans conquered became an ally. Rome's fair treatment of these people won their loyalty. Allies were allowed to keep their local government, but Rome controlled their relations with other countries. Allied peoples, however, were required to fight for Rome during wars.

Roman soldiers linked their shields above their heads to protect themselves during battle.

The Roman Army. Early Roman victories depended on the skill of citizen soldiers who owned their swords and shields and fought without pay. Each soldier belonged to an infantry unit of 100 men called a century. A captain, or centurion, led the unit. Between 40 and 60 centuries (4,000 to 6,000 soldiers) made up a Roman legion. The army also included special units of cavalry.

The army was well trained and discipline was strict. The centurion's badge of office was the vine-staff he used to beat men who broke the rules. Officers also enforced discipline through the practice of decimation. If an army unit showed cowardice in battle, every 10th man was executed.

The Roman army served as a training ground for Roman statesmen. No Roman citizen could be elected to a government office without first having served on 10 campaigns in the army.

Republican Government. The Romans, combining the practices of their old tribal culture and the newer city-state government, set up a republic. Citizens elected magistrates, or officials, to make and enforce laws. The complicated government had three assemblies, a senate, and many magistrates.

The Assembly of Tribes represented the 35 districts. Its members voted on laws.

Soldiers belonged to the Assembly of Centuries. They chose two consuls, the most important of all governing magistrates, and voted on laws. The amount and quality of his military equipment determined the number of votes each soldier could cast.

To counterbalance this advantage of the wealthy, the plebes created their assembly, the Council of Plebeians. They elected tribunes, who had the power to veto any action of the consuls. In Latin, veto means "I forbid." In 287 B.C., the Council of Plebeians also gained the power to pass laws.

The Roman Senate, made up of 300 patricians, was the most powerful governing body. Senators, appointed for life, were former magistrates. By 367 B.C., wealthy plebeians who had served the government were also admitted to the Senate.

The Senate proposed laws and sometimes acted as a court. Senators tried to settle problems among themselves before bringing any important questions before one or another of the assemblies.

Public decisions often led to lengthy debate. Yet, during wartime, emergencies demanded immediate action. Therefore, in time of crisis, the Senate appointed a dictator to serve a term of six months.

Roman Magistrates. Before 367 B.C., only patricians could hold elected office. The consuls, tribunes, and censors were members of the nobility.

Two consuls, elected for one-year terms, were the chiefs of the government and the commanders of the army in wartime. Each had to approve the acts of the other. If they did not agree, the act or policy was not approved.

Tribunes representing the plebeians could veto or overrule any government action. The decisions of praetors, or judges, formed a tradition of Roman law, the rights and responsibilities that applied to all. Censors kept records for taxation and enrollment in the Assembly of Centuries. After 318 B.C., censors chose senators.

Life in Rome. Roman children learned the responsibilities of citizenship from an early age. They were encouraged to work hard, to develop courage to fight for the republic, and to remain loyal to their city. Roman Citizens took pride in their civic duties.

The oldest man in a Roman family, the *paterfamilias*, was the head of the family. He had full control over the lives of his sons and daughters. A father usually arranged marriages for his daughters when they reached their early teens. Boys became citizens at the age of 14.

By the first century B.C., some Romans had begun to hire Greek tutors to educate their children. Other wealthy families sent their children to private schools. Upper-class girls sometimes were as well educated as the boys. Children of an artisan usually learned their father's trade.

The Romans worshiped many gods. In each household was a shrine where family members gathered to make offerings. As in Greece, public religious festivals and games in Rome were dedicated to individual gods and goddesses.

Women in Rome were freer than Greek women. Romans did not restrict women to a separate area of the house, as was the Greek custom. Roman women supervised the children and slaves, kept family accounts, appeared at public ceremonies, and often attended the theater. Women could make wills, own property, and also control their own money.

The Use of Money

FOCUS ON SOCIETY

The Roman government minted money for its citizens' use. The word *coin* is derived from the Latin word, *cuneus*, meaning wedge. From about the beginning of the third century B.C., the Romans minted bronze and silver coins. Before the use of coins, trade was limited by barter.

The use of coins by the Romans, Chinese, and Sumerians encouraged trade. The Roman coin at left, from 137 B.C., shows a citizen voting. The Chinese fish-shaped coin at right is from the late Chou period. The disk at bottom is a Sumerian writing tablet.

A farmer who wanted to trade some surplus wheat for a new plow faced a number of problems. The farmer needed to find someone who had an extra plow and wanted some wheat. A central marketplace where many people could gather eventually evolved. Transporting goods to the marketplace presented additional problems.

Determining a standard of value was yet another major problem. The worth, or the value, of goods could change from time to time and from person to person.

Development of Money. Using money solved many of the problems of the barter system. Any object can be used for money if everyone in a society agrees to accept it. The ancient Babylonians and Assyrians used metal cast into standard weights and sometimes stamped with signs to indicate weight and purity. In Hammurabi's time, silver shekels were the standard of value.

Lydia, a kingdom located in Asia Minor, created the first official government coinage in 640 B.C. Lydian coins were a mixture of gold and silver, and the metal content of the coins determined their value or worth. Coins, because they are portable, made trade easier and more efficient.

Marco Polo wrote about another form of currency, paper money, used in China by A.D. 1270. Paper money, unlike silver or gold coins, had no real value. The Chinese, like modern-day people, relied on the government to maintain the money's value.

The use of money solved problems involving trade and increased commerce within the lands Rome held. However, the republic faced many other problems. ■

Problems in the Republic

Between 509 and 133 B.C., the Roman Republic grew from a group of villages in central Italy to an empire of several million subjects. Such growth created problems in agriculture, in the social structure, and in governing provinces.

Changes in Farming. Conquered lands provided Rome with a vast source of land. By 133 B.C., senators and other wealthy citizens owned large estates called *latifundia* Slaves farmed these estates.

Owners of small farms in Italy could not compete with the latifundia in production. Many farmers left their fields to seek work in Rome.

The Rich and the Poor. Unemployed people flocked to Rome. The senate, however, occupied with problems of the empire, often ignored the city's needs.

Many people in business grew rich using slave labor. This practice reduced the number of jobs available, and the poor and unskilled grew poorer. The gap between rich and poor widened dramatically.

The growing number of slaves in Rome led to a revolt in 73 B.C. In southern Italy, Spartacus, a Greek slave, led a rebellion of about 70,000 runaway slaves. The Romans were unable to defeat the rebels and kill Spartacus until 71 B.C.

Governing the Provinces. Rome did not give citizenship to the conquered people of the provinces. The government considered the overseas provinces as sources of land and raw materials. Romans obtained grain

Roman Expansion to 133 B.C.

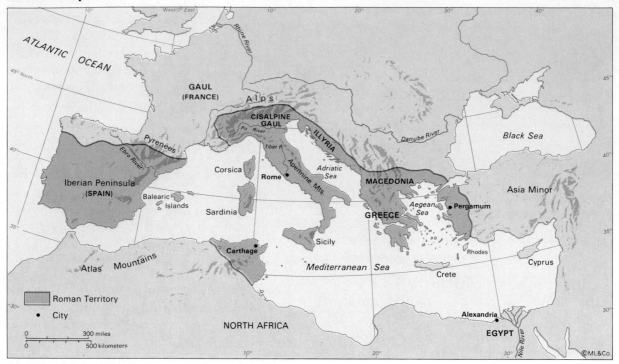

Map Skills 1. Where are the Alps, Pyrenees, and Atlas mountains located? **2.** How did mountains affect Roman expansion?

from Sicily. Metals, such as silver and copper, came from Spain and north Africa. Greece supplied marble, and Asia Minor provided carpets, medicines, and parchment. See the map, Trade in the Roman Empire, page 163.

The Senate appointed a governor for each province. The governor, who received no salary, had absolute power in the province for his one-year term. Many provincial governors grew rich using illegal or questionable methods to raise money, such as taking their subjects' land or imposing new taxes on them.

The provinces were also at the mercy of tax collectors, called *publicani*. The publicani paid a fixed sum to Rome as taxes for the province. Any amount they collected above the required sum, they kept.

Between 509 and 133 B.C., Rome's rapid growth brought many problems. Eventually, Rome tried to institute reforms.

SECTION 1 *Study Skills*

Developing Vocabulary Use each of the following terms in a sentence: **1.** ally **2.** century **3.** decimation **4.** veto **5.** republic **6.** *paterfamilias* **7.** *latifundia* **8.** *publicani*.

Reviewing Main Ideas 1. Why did the Romans often battle neighboring tribes prior to 265 B.C.? **2.** List four reasons why the Romans were able to build and control an empire. **3.** Explain why the Roman Senate appointed a dictator during wartime. **4.** How did the rights of Roman women differ from those of Greek women?

Understanding Chronology 1. About how many years did the Etruscans rule the Romans? **2.** Put these three events in chronological order: Romans make bronze and silver coins; Chinese print paper money; Lydians make gold and silver coins. **3.** When did a Roman Senate begin admitting wealthy plebeians?

Challenge Which problems that the Roman Republic faced also confront the United States?

2 Rome Dominates the Mediterranean World

OBJECTIVE: *To understand the Roman contributions to civilization*

End of the Roman Republic

In 133 B.C., some Roman leaders tried to introduce reforms to solve problems the republic faced. A tribune named Tiberius Gracchus wanted to break up the great estates and divide the land among the city poor. For his efforts, he was murdered in an election riot. Tiberius' brother became tribune 10 years later. He also failed in his attempt to weaken the great power of the Roman senators.

By 100 B.C., the Roman Empire required a professional army to defend its long frontiers from invaders. To give jobs to Rome's unemployed, as well as defend the borders, the army recruited volunteer soldiers from among the poor and landless.

Julius Caesar. By 60 B.C., generals were competing with one another for control of the Roman government. The two most successful generals were Pompey (PAHM pee)

and Julius Caesar (SEE zuhr). Pompey was popular because he cleared the Mediterranean Sea of pirates. He also added Syria, Phoenicia, and Palestine to the lands Rome ruled.

Caesar, also popular, gained military fame and a loyal army from an expedition that began in 58 B.C. He conquered the land that today constitutes France, Belgium, and Switzerland, and invaded England. Caesar proved his military genius by losing only two battles during his nine-year campaign. His description of the expedition, *The Gallic Wars*, is one of the best known works in Latin literature.

Caesar and Pompey made an alliance to control Rome. By 50 B.C., however, the alliance had collapsed and they were engaged in a civil war. In two years, Caesar defeated Pompey's armies in Greece, Asia, Spain, and Egypt. While in Egypt, Caesar met and fell in love with the legendary Cleopatra.

Caesar's victories marked the end of the Roman Republic. When he returned to Rome, the Senate appointed him dictator for life.

As dictator, Caesar began many reforms. To make the Senate more representative, he appointed 300 new senators. They included leading citizens of provincial cities as well as chieftains of tribes conquered in Gaul. He also granted citizenship to many people in the provinces.

Caesar's rivals, afraid of losing their influence, stabbed him to death in 44 B.C. Again, civil war broke out and spread over

---

VOCABULARY DEVELOPMENT

imperator (ihm puh RAYT uhr) *noun:* a Roman title of honor used by military and political leaders. From the Latin word, *imperativus*, meaning commanding.

procurator (PRAHK yuh RAYT uhr) *noun:* Roman official in charge of collecting revenue in a province.

aqueduct (AK wuh duhkt) *noun:* a structure used to transport water over a long distance. From the Latin words *aqua*, meaning water, and *ductus*, meaning to lead.

primary source *noun:* an eyewitness account.

the empire. Caesar's nephew, Octavian, finally ended the war in 31 B.C. by defeating his chief rival, Mark Antony.

Beginning of the Empire

Octavian became the ruler of Rome. He did not call himself king because he claimed that he was restoring the republic. He reinstated the election of magistrates and consulted the Senate on matters of importance. Nevertheless, this republic was a new Roman Empire, ruled not by elected representatives but by one man.

Octavian took the name Augustus, meaning great and revered. He also used his military title, imperator. The word emperor comes from this word.

Augustus and the emperors who followed him gradually developed a professional bureaucracy to govern the Roman Empire. The government hired administrators to carry out its policies efficiently. Thus, the government could continue to function even during periods of unrest.

Augustus was proud that he had virtually ended warfare in the Roman Empire. Peace prevailed from 27 B.C. to A.D. 180 with only two brief interruptions. This era is called the *Pax Romana*. In no other period of European history have so many people, about 60 million, enjoyed peace for so long a time. There were two major reasons for the two centuries of peace.

First, by about A.D. 200 the Roman Empire included all of the lands around the Mediterranean Sea and most of northwest Europe. See the extent of the Roman Empire on the map, page 163. Rome negotiated peace treaties with the Parthian Empire, the one organized state that touched Rome's borders. The Parthians controlled the trade routes to the east.

Second, life was comfortable for many Romans. Roman cities, like the cities of the Hellenistic world, had water and sewage systems, theaters, and public baths. The wealthy had comfortable villas with central heating systems. The Roman upper class probably lived more comfortably than at any earlier time.

Life in the Roman Empire

The Roman peace brought comfort and security for the wealthy landowning class, but not all shared the prosperity. The gap between rich and poor remained.

To occupy the people's work-free time, the emperors often staged public entertainment. Up to 260,000 people crowded into the Roman Circus Maximus to watch chariot races. The Colosseum, another great amphitheater seating 50,000 people, was the site of other popular events.

Governing the Provinces. Under the emperors, government of the provinces improved. Roman procurators, officials in charge of government revenue, were appointed to collect taxes. Provincial cities, though much smaller than the capital, patterned themselves after Rome, thus helping to spread Roman culture into the provinces.

Roman Law. Romans enforced a single system of law throughout the empire. Each citizen had the right to bring disputes before local judges and to appeal the decision to judges in Rome or to the emperor.

Roman law included all the main branches of public and private law that exist today. Skilled lawyers, called *juris prudentes*, meaning experts in law, interpreted the vast number of laws.

Engineering. The greatest accomplishment of Roman engineering was the improved system of roads. Roman roads, designed by surveyors, were straight highways paved with gravel or stone. Workers cut away hillsides, carved tunnels, and built raised surfaces over swampy ground. Many Roman roads are still used today.

Another major Roman engineering feat, gently sloping aqueducts, brought fresh water from the mountains over valleys and

Trade in the Roman Empire, A.D. 200

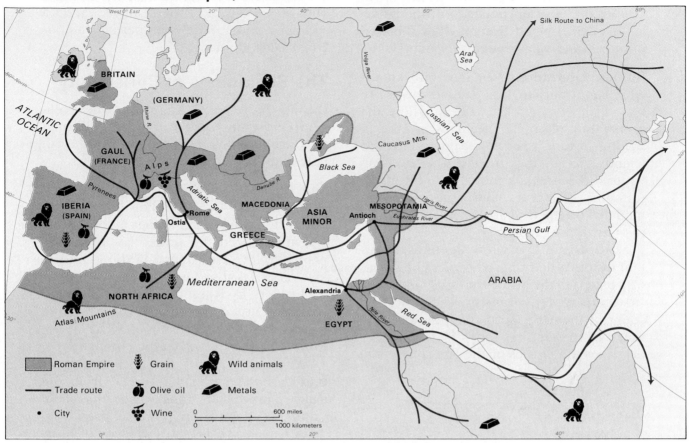

Map Skills **1.** Identify four major grain producing regions of the Roman Empire. **2.** What goods were traded between Rome and Alexandria?

plains to Roman cities. By A.D. 97, nine aqueducts were bringing about 85 million gallons of water a day from mountain springs to Roman cities.

Language. Latin, the language of the Romans, forms the basis of the Romance languages: French, Italian, Spanish, Portuguese, and Romanian. Latin was used in most European universities until the seventeenth century. It is the official language of the Roman Catholic Church.

Rome and Hellenistic Culture

The Greek colonies in the southern part of the Italian Peninsula influenced Roman ideas as early as 500 B.C. After the Romans conquered the Hellenistic world in the sec-

ond century B.C., Greek culture flooded into Rome. Wealthy Romans filled their homes with Greek statues and copies of Greek art.

In addition to art treasures, Romans brought slaves from Greece to teach their children. Romans also rebuilt their cities using Hellenistic plans and architecture.

Greek and Latin were official languages of the empire, and all laws and documents were written in both languages. The Roman alphabet of 23 letters was adopted from the Greek alphabet. The Roman alphabet is the basis for the alphabet used today in languages of the Western world.

Spread of Roman Culture. The Romans founded cities in northern Africa, Spain, and Europe north of the Alps. In this way, they extended the range of Hellenistic life to regions different in climate, soil, and population. Undefended Roman cities replaced hill forts, and villas dotted the countryside.

Roman Literature. Much of our knowledge about ancient Rome comes from primary sources, works written when the events took place. The Romans excelled in writing history, poetry, and long letters to friends. Virgil, the greatest Roman poet, wrote the *Aeneid*, a fictional account of the founding of Rome. This epic poem was modeled on the *Iliad* and *Odyssey*, written by the Greek poet Homer.

Tacitus and Livy wrote the most important historical accounts of Rome. The *Annals* of Tacitus tell the history of Rome under the first emperors. *Germania* gives the best account of the early Germanic peoples living north of the empire. Livy's *History of Rome* describes the virtues of the Roman Republic. Plutarch, a Greek who lived in the second century A.D., wrote *Parallel Lives*, a series of biographies comparing famous Greeks and Romans.

The Beginnings of Christianity

During the reign of Augustus, a new religion, Christianity, began in Judaea, a Roman province near Syria. There, Jesus, a Jewish holy man, began to preach to the Jews.

The Message of Jesus. Jesus described God as a loving father, and he urged people not to fight their enemies but to love them. He summarized the Jewish law by telling people to love God above all things and to love others as they loved themselves.

Leaders in Palestine objected to Jesus' ideas and urged the Romans to arrest him. Jesus was put to death by crucifixion, the Roman method of executing criminals.

After Jesus' crucifixion, his followers reported that Jesus had returned from the dead. This belief transformed the small group of followers into powerful preachers. They believed that the resurrection of Jesus proved that he was Christ, the Son of God, and the Messiah foretold by Jewish prophets.

The First Christians. By the middle of the first century A.D., the followers of Jesus had begun to be called Christians. Christian communities spread throughout the Roman Empire.

By the end of the third century A.D., Christians had a group of sacred books. The first four books, known as the Gospels, or Good News, were the works of some of Christ's early followers—Matthew, Mark, Luke, and John. Paul, a later convert, wrote a series of epistles, or letters, to inform others about Christianity.

The growth of Christianity presented a problem to the Roman political leaders. They did not know how to respond to the growth of a new religion. One of the leaders who had to deal with Christians was Pliny the Younger.

By worshiping in underground chapels, or catacombs, early Christians hoped to avoid persecution by the Romans.

Letters of Pliny the Younger

FOCUS ON SOURCES

Pliny the Younger, born in A.D. 62 in Como, Italy, was a well-educated politician and lawyer. In A.D. 100, the Emperor Trajan appointed him consul. He later became governor of the Roman province of Bithynia (bih THIHN ee uh) on the southern coast of the Black Sea. The 10 volumes of Pliny's letters describe the life and interests of a well-educated Roman.

Pliny Requests Advice. The following letter was written to the Emperor Trajan during the second century A.D.

❝ It is my invariable rule, Sir, to refer to you in all matters where I feel doubtful. Having never been present at any trials concerning those who profess Christianity, I am unacquainted with the nature of their crimes or the measures of their punishment.

The method I have observed towards those who have been brought before me as Christians is this: I asked them whether they were Christians; if they admitted it, I repeated the question twice, and threatened them with punishment. If they persisted, I ordered them to be at once punished.

An anonymous [unsigned] information was laid before me containing a charge against several persons, who upon examination denied they were Christians or had ever been so. They repeated after me an invocation to the gods and offered religious rites with wine and incense before your statue. . . . [They] even reviled the name of Christ: whereas there is no forcing, it is said, those who are really Christians into any of these compliances. I thought it proper, therefore, to discharge them. . . .

This contagious superstition is not confined to the cities only, but has spread its infection among the neighboring villages and country. Nevertheless, it still seems possible to restrain its progress. ❞

Trajan's Reply. The response Pliny received from the Emperor Trajan was based on Roman law rather than Trajan's personal desire to punish the Christians.

❝ You have adopted the right course in investigating the charges against the Christians who were brought before you. It is not possible to lay down any general rule for all such cases. Do not go out of your way to look for them. If indeed they should be brought before you, and the crime is proved, they must be punished. . . .

Anonymous information should not be used in any sort of prosecution. It is introducing a very dangerous precedent, and is quite foreign to the spirit of our age. ❞ ∎

The Reign of the Romans

The letters from Pliny and Trajan showed the efforts of Roman leaders to confront new developments in their empire. For 500 years, the Romans dominated Europe and the land around the Mediterranean.

SECTION 2 *Study Skills*

Developing Vocabulary 1. List two other words that come from the same root as imperator. **2.** What was the job of a procurator? **3.** List two words using the same root words as aqueduct. **4.** Give an example of a primary source.

Reviewing Main Ideas 1. Why was a bureaucracy beneficial to Rome? **2.** What did Augustus consider his major accomplishment? **3.** What role did Paul play in spreading Christianity?

Understanding Cause and Effect 1. Why did Caesar's rivals oppose his reforms? **2.** Explain two causes of the *Pax Romana*. **3.** Describe the ways that Rome's conquest of the Hellenistic world affected Roman culture.

Challenge Compare and contrast the role of entertainment in the Roman Empire and in the United States today.

3 The Qin and the Han Unite China

OBJECTIVE: *To understand the development and achievements of the Han Dynasty of China*

King Zheng Unifies China

From 200 B.C. to A.D. 200, the Romans dramatically influenced the development of civilization in western Eurasia. At the eastern end of Eurasia, 6,000 miles away, the Chinese developed another dominant civilization. Between 234 and 222 B.C., King Zheng (jehng) fought a series of battles that brought all of China's warring states under his rule.

King Zheng of the state of Qin (chin) conquered an area that included all of present-day China. He extended his control over lands from Manchuria to the northern edge of Vietnam and from the China Sea to the foothills of the Kunlun Mountains. See the map, Empires of China, page 167.

To impress his subjects, King Zheng changed his name to Shi Huangdi (shih hwahng dee), meaning First Emperor. Before this time the word *huangdi*, or emperor, had been used only for gods and mythical heroes.

To exert his control over the newly conquered states, the First Emperor needed to destroy the power of the former noble families. He moved more than 100,000 families to his capital city, Xianyang (shih ahn yang), destroyed their local fortresses, and melted down the weapons in their arsenals. He then centralized the administration of China by dividing the old warring states into 36 military districts. Civil and military governors ruled each district.

Like the Roman emperors, the First Emperor of China built a system of roads to move his army quickly from one place to another. The emperor also traveled the roads to inspect his district governments.

Impact of Shi Huangdi. Even though Shi Huangdi ruled for only 11 years, he made such radical changes that his dynasty marks a turning point in Chinese history. The emperor standardized weights, measures, and coinage for use in trade. He even set a standard axle width for wagons.

Most important, Shi Huangdi standardized the Chinese writing system. He wanted government officials and educated people

---

VOCABULARY DEVELOPMENT

Qin (chin) *noun:* one of the warring states of China, until recently, Ch'in in English.

arsenal *noun:* **1.** a building where weapons are manufactured or stored; **2.** a collection of weapons.

dialects *noun:* regional varieties of a language differing distinctively from the standard language. From the Greek word, *dialektas*, meaning conversation.

Beijing (bay jihng) *noun:* city in northeastern China; until recently, Peking in English.

Xiong-nu (shy uhng noo) *noun:* barbarian nomads living on the northern borders of China; until recently, *hsuing-nu*.

subsistence farm *noun:* a farm that provides a family with the minimum amount of food and shelter needed to survive.

seismograph (SYZ muh graf) *noun:* a device that detects the occurrence of earthquakes and measures their severity.

---

to be able to communicate with one another in a standard written language. In China, people spoke many different dialects, or regional varieties, of Chinese, making communication difficult.

Shi Huangdi, A Mighty Emperor

FOCUS ON PEOPLE

In 1974, a group of farmers made a startling discovery about 500 miles west of Beijing (bay jihng). While digging wells near the ancient capital of Xianyang, they unearthed an army of life-sized clay soldiers. Later, archaeologists excavating the site found over 6,000 clay figures of men and horses. Shi Huangdi, the First Emperor of China, had the clay army buried to protect his tomb when he died in 210 B.C.

Shi Huangdi fought for 12 years before he conquered all of the warring states. By 221 B.C., however, he had united China by defeating all his rivals "like a silkworm devouring a mulberry leaf."

Shi Huangdi completed the Great Wall of China. Earlier Chinese rulers had built portions of the wall to keep out the Xiongnu (shy uhng noo), aggressive nomads who lived along the northern borders of China. Shi Huangdi linked the various sections of the wall to form the 1,500 mile (2,400-kilometer) Great Wall.

When completed, the Great Wall was 15 to 30 feet (4.5 to 9.0 meters) wide at its base

Empires of China, 221 B.C.–A.D. 220

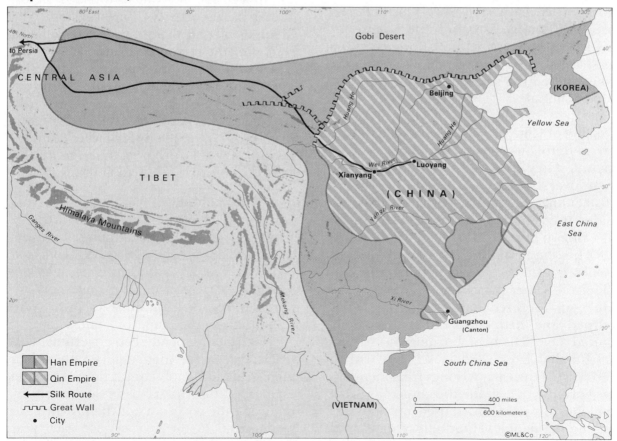

Map Skills **1.** Identify the three major rivers in China. **2.** Why did the Chinese build the Great Wall? **3.** What mountains form a border between China and Tibet?

and 40 to 50 feet (12 to 15 meters) high. As many as 25,000 watch towers may have been built, and up to 15,000 free-standing outposts stood just outside the wall. Each outpost was supplied with enough provisions to withstand a siege of four months.

By linking the various walls together, Shi Huangdi gave China long periods of peace from invading nomads. Nevertheless, Shi Huangdi worried about security almost from the moment he became emperor.

The emperor's concern about security extended to his preparations for the next life. He directed as many as 700,000 workers over 36 years to prepare a secure tomb. Artisans molded statues of soldiers and horses from clay to accompany him in death. The statues were fired at high temperatures and painted brilliant colors. The soldiers varied in height from 5 feet, 9 inches to 6 feet tall. They held actual weapons, and the clay horses were harnessed to real chariots. To protect the tomb from intruders, an automatic crossbow was set up before the grave was sealed. The bow would shoot anyone who entered the sealed tomb after the emperor's burial.

Decline of Qin. Shi Huangdi and his advisers were followers of the philosophy of Legalism. They stressed the authority of the state over the people through the use of clear, uniform, and detailed laws. The emperor used the laws to regulate all aspects of Chinese life.

The emperor tried to rid China of Confucianism because it supported the traditions of the prior Zhou Dynasty. Shi Huangdi ordered all Confucian books burned and had 460 Confucian scholars buried alive. His book burning was so successful that later Chinese scholars had to reconstruct the early writings from memory.

Forced labor on the the emperor's great building projects also caused unhappiness among the people. Hundreds of thousands of workers were needed to construct the Great Wall and imperial palaces.

According to Chinese tradition, a farmer, Zhe Sheng (che jheng), started a rebellion against Shi Huangdi's successor about 206 B.C. Floods had delayed him from reaching his work assignment on time. To avoid punishment, he started a rebellion that spread throughout the empire. The Qin Dynasty was overthrown in 206 B.C. However, the centralized bureaucracy of Shi Huangdi formed the basis for the rule of all later Chinese emperors. ■

The Han Dynasty

Eight years of civil war followed the overthrow of the Qin Dynasty. Finally, a commoner, Liu Bang (lyoo bahng), defeated his rivals to become the new emperor of China. He took the name Han after the Han River. His dynasty, which ruled China from 206 B.C. to A.D. 220, was one of the most significant dynasties in early Chinese history. The Chinese still call themselves the people of Han after the important Han Dynasty.

Han established new policies to end suffering and discontent. He set less severe penalties for breaking laws. He also reduced taxes for farmers to one-fifteenth of each year's crop. Although people were required to work on public projects, their service was limited to one month of each year.

Han Government. The Han emperors developed a professional administrative system for governing the empire. The governor in charge of the 108 districts collected taxes based on a yearly census taken by the head of every village. The governors reported to regional administrators who were responsible to the emperor's ministers.

Han rulers depended on government officials chosen for their ability rather than their wealth or family connections. The Han established the first civil service system by requiring the governors of the provinces to recommend to the civil service each year "worthy and morally correct men." The candidates then went to the capital to take a written examination that determined whether they were suitable for a government position.

Local officials also recommended boys for higher education based on their ability to read and write. The most able students attended the Grand College in the capital, one of the oldest schools of higher education in the world.

The system of selection for government service and higher education, though greatly improved, did not ensure unprejudiced selection. Local officials often recommended their friends and relatives. Also, women were ineligible for admission to the Grand College and for government employment. Nevertheless, the examination system provided China with skilled civil servants and led to the development of an effective government bureaucracy.

The Han under Wu Di. Literature and scholarship revived slowly after the First Emperor's suppression of learning. During the early Han Dynasty, scholars rewrote the Chinese classics from their own memories.

After 140 B.C., the Han emperor Wu Di (woo dee) made Confucianism the official state philosophy. Confucian scholars believed that rulers had duties to the people and could not do whatever they wanted. Education and scholarship, rather than force or rule by the upper class, formed the basis of government.

Wu Di promoted Confucianism and the civil service system, but he also protected his empire against invasion. The Chinese, like the Romans, saw themselves as a civilized world surrounded by barbarians. They used conquest and expansion to deal with the threat of barbarian invasion.

The greatest threat to the Han came from the Xiong-nu, who lived north of the empire and were skilled in fighting on horseback. From 121 to 119 B.C., Wu Di, whose name means "warrior emperor," pushed the Xiong-nu farther from the borders of China. By 110 B.C. he had extended

This portion of a twelfth-century silk handscroll shows the first Han emperor's army marching through the Yellow River region.

his rule into northern Vietnam. In 108 B.C., Han armies marched into northern Korea. These areas were absorbed into the economy and culture of China.

Life in China under the Han. Although some Chinese lived in large cities, the economy of Han China was based on agriculture. Most peasants lived on subsistence farms that provided them with the minimum food and shelter necessary to live.

Gradually, wealthy families gained control of more and more land. Their wealth allowed them to support private armies on their estates. By the first century A.D., some estates had grown to include many villages and thousands of peasants and soldiers. The glaring difference between the wealth of the great landowners and the poverty of most of the peasant farmers persisted into the twentieth century.

Han Achievements. Chinese historians regard the Han Dynasty as the greatest period in early Chinese history. Its importance is related largely to the development of technology in a number of areas.

Until the first century A.D., books were written on silk cloth or bamboo slats laced together. During the Han period, the Chinese learned to make paper from rags and bark. Paper became a Chinese export. Fine glazed pottery similar to porcelain also was produced and exported.

The Chinese under the Han improved farming methods. Chinese farmers developed shoulder collars for horses and oxen so that the animals could be used to pull wagons and plows. Rice farmers in the hilly lands of western China invented the water wheel to move water up the slopes from one level to another.

Han scientific achievements, in contrast to those of the Hellenistic world, involved practical solutions to problems. A Han scholar constructed the first seismograph to detect earthquakes and measure their inten-

This pictorial stone unearthed in Mizhi, Shaanxi shows a farmer using an ox-drawn plow and millet plants, which yielded an important grain.

sity. Another scholar wrote a medical text still used in traditional Chinese medicine.

The Chinese and the Romans. The empire that developed under the Qin and Han dynasties was in many ways similar to the Roman Empire in the West. Both developed centralized governments under an absolute ruler and his officials. Both also had a standard written language. If Roman travelers had journeyed to China in A.D. 100, they could have traveled between cities on an imperial road system similar to the system that linked the Roman Empire.

A Roman visitor, however, would have marveled at much in Han China. Imperial cities and palaces would have surpassed Roman buildings in size and splendor. The Great Wall that defended the empire against the northern barbarians had no equal in the Roman world. The Grand College and such technological inventions as paper and the water wheel would not be introduced in Europe for many centuries.

SECTION 3 *Study Skills*

Developing Vocabulary Define each of the following terms: **1.** Qin. **2.** arsenal. **3.** dialects. **4.** Beijing. **5.** Xiong-nu. **6.** subsistence farm. **7.** seismograph.

Reviewing Main Ideas Summarize the accomplishments of Shi Huangdi that changed China. **1.** Why did many laborers dislike Shi Huangdi? **2.** List five achievements of the Han. **3.** How had the distribution of wealth changed in China by A.D. 100? **4.** List three similarities between the Roman Empire and the Qin and Han dynasties in China.

Understanding Geography **1.** In relation to Beijing, where was the tomb of Shi Huangdi located? **2.** What part of the border of China did the Great Wall protect? **3.** List three regions that Wu Di's forces conquered.

Challenge Explain why a nation can be united more easily today than it could be during the time of the Qin and the Han.

4 *Links Across the Hemisphere*

OBJECTIVE: *To understand that by* A.D. *200 all of Eurasia was linked by trade*

Trade Routes between Rome and China

The Roman and Han empires were separated by a vast region of windswept steppes, high mountains, and desert. Yet, Alexander the Great had established a connection between southwest Asia and India before 320 B.C. His successors, the Seleucids, maintained diplomatic and trade relations with the Maurya Empire of India. By A.D. 100, the Roman and Han empires were linked by caravan routes across central Asia.

Before 100 B.C., however, China had almost no links to the lands of southwest Asia. In 102 B.C. the sixth Han emperor, Wu Di, sent an army west to central Asia. Some of his men returned with grapevines, alfalfa, and large-boned warhorses. Wu Di's expedition opened the way for the exchange of ideas and goods between China and central Asia. Later, these ties linked China with the Roman world.

The Silk Road. Within a century, silk brought from China became one of the most prized luxuries in the Roman world. Merchants with caravans of camels, horses, and mules traveled across Eurasia exchanging spices, cloth, and other products.

Romans called the route linking China with the Roman world the Silk Road. It started in the Wei Valley of China, crossed over the Pamir Mountains, and moved along a string of oases through central Asia into Mesopotamia. The route ended finally in Antioch, Syria. See the map, Trade Routes of Eurasia, on page 172. In Syria, the heavy cloth brought from China was unraveled and rewoven into a thin, almost transparent fabric.

Probably no single caravan ever crossed the entire route from the Wei Valley to Antioch. Rather, Chinese, Greek, Persian, and Roman traders each traveled part of the route. Products changed hands many times before reaching their destination. Because of the cost of financing a caravan and protecting it from robbers, only costly, nonbulky items as silk and spices could be profitably transported the entire distance.

Sea Routes to India. Before the first century A.D., Indian ships traveled from port to port along the coast of the Indian subcontinent. Sailors relied on the wind and stayed within sight of land. The time, direction, and distance they could sail was limited.

Travel by ship between Egypt and the east involved a slow and dangerous voyage through pirate-infested waters off the coasts of Arabia and western India. Alexandria,

---

VOCABULARY DEVELOPMENT

armor plate *noun:* a heavy metal protective covering.

bodhisattva (boh duh SAHT wuh) *noun:* in Buddhist belief, a soul who waits to enter nirvana in order to save others.

lacquerwork *noun:* wood covered with a clear or colored coating that dries to a glossy finish.

Trade Routes of Eurasia, A.D. 200

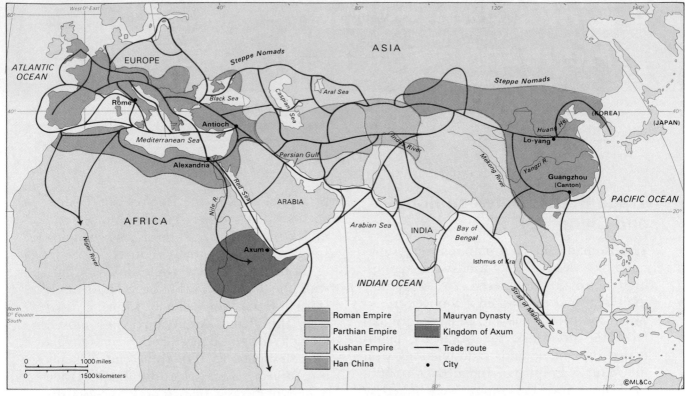

Map Skills 1. What empires did a traveler visit on a trip between Antioch and Luoyang?
2. What bodies of water would a sailor cross on the route between Axum and Canton?

Egypt, became the important link between traders in the Mediterranean Sea and those traveling to the East. Goods were brought through the Red Sea to Egypt from Arabia, Persia, India, Southeast Asia, and China. In Egypt, they were carried overland to Alexandria. See the map, Trade Routes of Eurasia, above.

A Direct Sea Route. About 100 B.C., mariners began to sail directly between the Red Sea and India across open water. By taking advantage of the monsoon winds, they were able to sail across the Arabian Sea. Seasonal temperature differences between the lands of Eurasia and the Indian Ocean caused the monsoons to blow from the southwest in the summer and from the northeast in the winter. Mariners, therefore, could sail across the Arabian Sea to India in late summer and return in winter.

By the second century A.D., over 100 Greek ships sailed between Egypt and India each year using the monsoon winds. Travel across the open sea was faster and safer than traveling along the coast. The regular monsoon winds enabled sailors to calculate the time needed to sail between ports.

A South Seas Trade Network. Merchants in India used the monsoon winds to sail east across the Bay of Bengal to Malaysia and Thailand. By A.D. 200, sailors were bringing goods from India around the straits of Malacca to Canton, China. The seas south of Eurasia formed a single trade network.

Other Indian merchants went overland to China. They traveled north from the Indus River to the land now known as Afghanistan. They then went eastward across the Asian steppe to northern China where they obtained silk.

Growth of Trade Centers

Trade between Rome and China affected people who lived along the trade routes. Trade centers grew into cities. Eventually, organized states developed whose economies depended on trade.

The Kingdom of Axum. Roman sea captains sailed south on the Red Sea to the northeast corner of Africa. There, they traded Roman goods such as glass and metals for ivory, tortoiseshell, and incense. The city of Axum became the center of a kingdom where power and wealth depended on trade. The African rulers of Axum eventually controlled several important ports on the Red Sea.

The people of Axum developed a system of writing and made coins. Greek inscriptions on coins and tablets show the Hellenistic influence on Axum.

The Parthian Empire. Parthia, Rome's rival on the eastern border of the Roman Empire, controlled part of the Silk Road. Trade between East and West was important to Parthian kings. They maintained roads and resting places, offered protection, and collected tolls for all caravans. Foreign traders were not allowed to enter Parthia.

Parthian horsemen in suits of armor were fearsome opponents for Roman footsoldiers. This mail-clad lancer is from about A.D. 200.

In addition to being a rival to Rome and an important link on the Silk Road, Parthia was well known for its horses. Sometime before 100 B.C., the Parthians began to raise alfalfa as food for their horses in winter rather than grass. They found that their horses grew larger and stronger than the ponies bred by the nomads on the steppes.

As the larger horses were able to carry heavier loads, the Parthian warriors were able to protect themselves and their horses with armor plate. With their armor and their large horses, the warriors could withstand attacks by the light cavalry of the steppe nomads. The armored horses and warriors of Parthia became the model for cavalry troops in both Asia and Europe in future centuries.

Impact of Trade throughout Eurasia

Other trade routes connected the people living along the Silk Road with barbarians living on the edges of civilization. An amber trade route developed between the Baltic and Black seas. Camel caravans also began to cross the Sahara linking west Africa with Roman north Africa.

Trade Spreads Disease. Trade along the growing network spread disease as well as ideas and products. Roman writers refer to severe epidemics that swept the Roman world after A.D. 100. Since few records were kept, however, present-day physicians do not know the nature of the diseases.

Missionaries Travel the Silk Road. According to tradition, the Kushan ruler, Kanishka, helped to spread new ideas along the trade routes. He encouraged missionaries to teach a new branch of Buddhism along the Silk Road.

Buddhism originally taught that the way to achieve nirvana was through meditating and recognizing the impermanence of the world. By the first century A.D., however,

This Chinese princess defied the law when she used her crown to smuggle precious silkworms out of China.

The Interacting Zone Expands

Although China and Rome were separated by over 4,000 miles, by A.D. 100, merchant caravans were regularly bringing Chinese goods, such as lacquerwork, to the Roman world in exchange for Western products. At about the same time, sea routes between the Arabian Peninsula and India, and across the Bay of Bengal to Southeast Asia also linked China, India, and the Roman world. No record exists that Chinese merchants or ambassadors met the Roman emperor. Still, Han writings record the arrival of Roman merchants in China in 166 A.D.

These new trade routes between empires expanded the communicating zone and brought much more than an exchange of valuable products. People living along the routes gained new importance. Merchants transported culture, ideas, and diseases, as well as products, along trade routes.

most people believed that the only way to achieve nirvana was to become a monk. The teaching that developed in Kanishka's time, Mahayana Buddhism, taught that ordinary people could be helped to achieve nirvana.

In Mahayana Buddhism, the souls of saintly people postponed their entry into nirvana to help others. These souls were called bodhisattvas (boh duh SAHT wuhz). Through their compassion and suffering, bodhisattvas helped people free their souls from the sorrows of this world.

Buddhism Spreads to China. Buddhist missionaries preached this message along the trade routes. Mahayana Buddhism had great appeal for the ordinary believer who wished to be saved but did not want to practice the self-discipline of a monk.

By the second century A.D., a Buddhist temple had been built in the Chinese capital, and Chinese scholars were traveling to India to study Buddhism. In later centuries, Mahayana Buddhism became popular in China and also spread to Korea and Japan.

SECTION 4 *Study Skills*

Developing Vocabulary 1. What is armor plate? **2.** How did bodhisattvas help others? **3.** Describe laquerwork.

Reviewing Main Ideas 1. When and how was China linked to southwest Asia? **2.** What important discovery did sailors make regarding the time to sail between ports? **3.** How did Mahayana Buddhism spread beyond India?

Understanding Cause and Effect 1. Why did the growth of trade increase the influence of people in Axum and Parthia? **2.** What caused Parthian horses to grow larger and stronger? **3.** How did trade help spread diseases?

Understanding Geography 1. Describe the route of the Silk Road. **2.** Where did the Kushans live? **3.** In what countries did Mahayana Buddhism become popular?

Challenge Are major cities today more or less likely than were cities in A.D. 200 to be located on trade routes? Explain.

Vegetation Around the World

By A.D. 100, some people had discovered that useful plants could be grown only in certain environments. Roman and African products were traded for exotic Chinese spices and silks, which were not available in the West. This feature describes where certain kinds of vegetation are located and some of the ways people have used vegetation.

Natural Vegetation

Natural vegetation includes the plants which grow in a region without the influence of people. Several factors that do influence the natural vegetation of a region include precipitation, temperature, soil type, and land features.

The amount of precipitation in an area affects what vegetation will grow there. Some plants, like rice, require a great deal of water to grow. Other plants, such as grasses, require much less water.

Temperature, particularly the length of the growing season, influences the success of different types of plants. The growing season is the warmer period during the year which is without frost. Frost is produced when the temperature drops below the freezing mark, 32 degrees Fahrenheit, or 0 degrees Celsius. Near the equator, the growing season can be year-round. Nearer to each of the poles, however, the growing season is much shorter.

Soil is also important because it provides an anchor for the plant's root system. The soil also stores nutrients which feed the plant throughout its lifetime.

Just as soil influences vegetation, vegetation influences soil. A plant helps to keep the soil in place by absorbing rainwater which would otherwise erode the soil. After a plant dies, it contributes nutrients to the soil. The decayed plant matter becomes part of the soil.

Land features play an important role in vegetation. The slope of the land affects the location and type of vegetation. A flat area helps to keep both moisture and nutrients at the plant's roots. A flat area may hold moisture too long, causing the plants to drown. On a steep slope, however, water flows down the slope before a plant can use it.

Biomes

Vegetation plays a major role in the types of animal life on earth. A system of plants and animals interacting together is called a *biome*. Each biome is named after a dominant type of vegetation found in it. Each biome is also characterized by a certain mixture of water in the soil and heat. There are five major types of biomes on earth: forest, savannah, grassland, desert, and tundra.

A forest has a relatively high amount of soil-water and heat. Savannahs are drier than forests. A savannah, however, is not as dry as a grassland. Grasslands have a moderate shortage of water. A desert has an extreme shortage of soil-water. Both grasslands and deserts have adequate heat for a wide variety of plants to grow. The tundra is too cold for most plants to grow. The map on the next page shows the location of biomes on the earth.

Vegetation and People

Vegetation has been important to people throughout history. About 4 million years ago, hominids learned to gather edible vegetation as food. Farming began around 13,000 B.C. as people discovered how to sow seeds and grow plants. As farming became

Natural Vegetation of the World

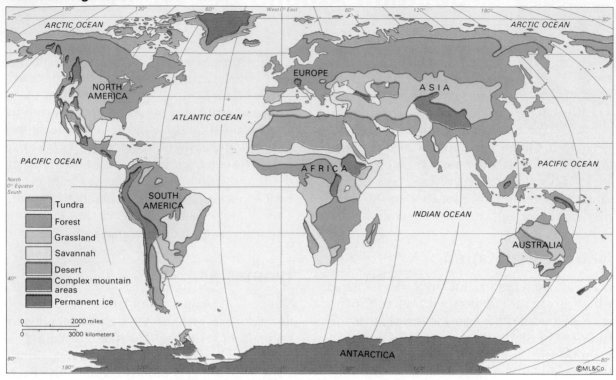

Map Skills **1.** Do the desert regions of the world lie directly along the equator? Explain your answer. **2.** Describe the vegetation environment of northern Asia and northern America.

more productive, surplus food made cities and civilization possible.

The reason that early peoples located in steppes and along river valleys is in part due to the fertile soils in these areas. The land of the steppes is fertile partly because it is dry. Without much rainfall, nutrients stay in the soil. The development of irrigation enabled people to use the natural fertility of the steppes and grow crops. A river valley is fertile because the flood waters deposit rich soil on the land as they subside.

In addition to supplying food for people and animals, vegetation has other important uses in trade. For instance, plant fibers, such as cotton and flax, have been woven into fabrics for thousands of years. The Carthaginians used another plant fiber, esparto grass, to make rope. The first fabric dyes were made from vegetable juices. Richly colored fabrics were a valuable trade item.

Just as vegetation affects people, people affect vegetation. The Kushites used the land on which they lived very intensively. They grazed and farmed the land so much that nutrients were lost and fertility declined. The land produced fewer crops. When Kush farmers harvested smaller surpluses, the Kush nation declined.

In recent years, human influence on vegetation has increased. The influence of vegetation on humans remains strong.

STUDY SKILLS Reading Maps
1. What four factors determine the vegetation of an area?
2. What is a biome?
3. What are the five major biomes?
4. List ten items you use regularly that come from plants.
5. Identify the biome of the region in which you and your family live.

CHAPTER 8 *Summary & Review*

Summarizing Main Ideas

The Roman and Han empires influenced much of Eurasia between 200 B.C. and A.D. 200. Each established an empire based on centralized administration, a good transportation system, and trade. Each empire expanded its borders by conquering neighboring peoples.

The Roman Republic was founded in 509 B.C. In 146 B.C., Rome defeated its long-time rival, Carthage. In A.D. 27, Augustus became the first emperor of Rome. The Roman Empire lasted for more than 400 years. The Greeks heavily influenced Roman culture. A new religion, Christianity, during the first century A.D., developed in the Roman Empire.

The Han overthrew the Qin Dynasty in 206 B.C. The Qin, under Emperor Shi Huangdi, had unified China and completed the Great Wall. The Han maintained the centralized government of China. Emperor Wu Di made Confucianism the official state philosophy.

By A.D. 100, the Roman and Han empires were trading with each other. The major trade routes were overland along the Silk Road and by sea across the Indian Ocean.

Questions for Critical Thinking

COMPREHENSION Interpreting Events

1. Why was Rome's defeat of Carthage an important event in the development of the Roman Empire?
2. Explain why Julius Caesar was a popular Roman general.
3. How was Rome able to maintain the Pax Romana for so many years?
4. Why did the Roman leaders view the spread of Christianity as a problem?
5. What was the purpose in building the Great Wall of China?

6. List three accomplishments of the Chinese emperor Wu Di.
7. How did the development of the shoulder collar and the water wheel change life for farmers under the Han?
8. How did monsoon winds promote trade between the Romans and Chinese?

ANALYSIS Identifying Trends

1. Explain what happened to the life of the poor in Rome between 200 B.C. and A.D. 200.
2. What important trend in Chinese history began under Shi Huangdi?

APPLICATION Comparing Past to Present

1. List five ways in which life in the United States today reflects developments that occurred in the Roman Empire.
2. What was the function of the civil service in China? Describe the same function in countries today. Explain.

SYNTHESIS Making Decisions

1. What enabled the Romans to make quick decisions during wartime?
2. How did the Han solve the problem of communication between Chinese who spoke different dialects?

EVALUATION Weighing Consequences

1. Summarize the efforts of Roman leaders to reform the government of Rome. Describe how successful they were.
2. How did the Romans and the Han each try to unify their empire?

CHALLENGE

1. List the costs involved in building the Great Wall of China.
2. Write a brief essay explaining the conditions in which a country benefits from centralizing its government.

UNIT 2 *Review*

Critical Thinking for Today's World

ANALYSIS Understanding People

1. Give examples of influential ideas developed by Socrates, Plato, and Aristotle.
2. How were the accomplishments of Alexander the Great and Shi Huangdi similar?
3. What are three personality traits of a successful leader? Use examples from this unit to support your view.

ANALYSIS Recognizing Change over Time

1. Reforms in Athens between 700 and 500 B.C. allowed more people to participate in government. Which large groups of people were still not able to participate in Athenian government in 500 B.C.?
2. Describe three main changes in Roman government between 509 and 133 B.C. that aided the growth of the state.
3. How did changes in philosophy from the time of Socrates to the time of Epicurus reflect the societies of their times?

APPLICATION Solving Problems

1. List and explain three ways the aborigines of Australia responded to the environment in which they lived.

2. Compare two different responses to the problem of invasion that people described in this unit developed.
3. Give examples of methods that three different cultures used to promote stable, popular government.

SYNTHESIS Developing Global Citizenship

1. Explain how the development of money eased interaction between different regions and cultures.
2. How did Alexander the Great unite people of different cultures?
3. Describe three ways that Ashoka strengthened Indian ties with cultures to the east and to the west.
4. Compare the religions, philosophies, and literatures of Greece, Persia, India, and China.

EVALUATION Learning Lessons from the Past

1. Use two examples from this unit to illustrate the political and social conditions which influence a culture to develop a new philosophy or new way of life.
2. List four methods the Romans or the Han used to strengthen their control over their empire. List and explain which of these methods nations still use in establishing a modern empire.

Eurasian Contributions to Culture, 800 B.C. to A.D. 200				
	Greece	**Persia**	**India**	**China**
Religion and Philosophy	Foundations of western thought	Zoroastrianism	Hinduism, Jainism, Buddhism	Daoism, Legalism, Confucianism
Technology and Communication	Advances in mathematics and science	Improved roads and irrigation techniques	Perfected the Sanskrit language	Used iron, silk porcelain, and paper
Architecture	The Parthenon, Propylea, and Erechtheum	Elaborate and monumental buildings	Buddhist stupas and inscription pillars	The Great Wall

The Interacting Global Community, 800 B.C.–A.D. 200

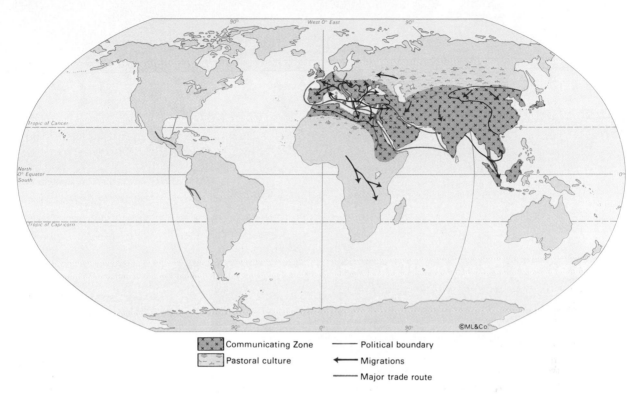

Communicating Zone — Political boundary
Pastoral culture ← Migrations
— Major trade route

©ML&Co

A Global Perspective

In A.D. 200, much of the Eastern Hemisphere, including parts of Europe, Asia, and Africa, was linked in an interacting zone. Within this zone, the influence of civilization radiated from Rome, Persia, India, and China.

In the Western Hemisphere, other centers of civilization drew people into another interacting zone. The Americas were isolated from the Eurasian interacting zone.

Two of the important forces linking civilizations in Eurasia were conquest and trade. Alexander the Great, for example, spread Hellenistic culture in southwest Asia and India. The silk trade helped to spread new ideas and ways of life.

COMPREHENSION Interpreting Maps

1. List the centers of civilization in A.D. 200.
2. Identify the physical features that helped and hindered trade among the early civilizations.

3. Which cultures were considered pastoral?
4. List one major city located in each of the following civilizations: Greece, Persia, Rome, India, and China.
5. How far is Rome from China? India? Greece? Carthage?
6. If traders wanted to go to Persia from Rome, in which direction would they travel?
7. Identify three cultures that the dominant civilizations influenced in A.D. 200.

ANALYSIS Recognizing Global Trends

1. Look at the communicating zone on the map. Identify geographical features that may have limited the size of the zone.
2. In what type of climate are most of the communicating zones located?
3. Compare the migration routes on this map with those shown on the map on page 87. Explain why the routes have changed.

UNIT 3
Links Throughout

180

ETVE LIS·VENTO·PLE NI
NIT·INTE RR A
VVIDONIS
COMITIS

A Bayeux Tapestry scene shows Harold crossing the sea in 1066. With special authorization of the City of Bayeux.

CHAPTER 9
Migrating Peoples Change Eurasia

GLOBAL TIME LINE

TIME

| A.D. 200 | A.D. 250 | A.D. 300 | A.D. 350 |

A.D. 200–600 Barbarian tribes invade western Europe

A.D. 224–65 Sassanid Dynasty rules Persia

A.D. 320–535 Gupta Dynasty rules India

PEOPLE

A.D. 224 Persian prince, Ardeshir, overthrows Parthian king

A.D. 285 Anthony of Alexandria founds the first Christian monastery

A.D. 283 Emperor Diocletian divides the Roman Empire

A.D. 330 Constantine mov the capital of the Roman Empire to Byzantium

PLACE

A.D. 313 *Roman Empire;*[1] Edict of Milan allows Christians freedom of worship

A.D. 301 *Armenia;*[2] Christian monks introduce Armenians to Christianity

Linking Past to Present

Americans seldom visit central Asia, a region far from North America. The vast region of central Asia is made up of mountains, deserts, and steppes. Populations are scattered and large cities few. Central Asia seldom appears in the news.

In earlier times, however, central Asia played an important role in world history. The pastoral people who inhabited the area were fierce nomads. Between A.D. 200 and 600, these nomads of central Asia attacked the Roman Empire, Persia, India, and China. In this chapter you will learn how the invasions of cavalry armies changed the course of history in these civilized regions. As you read, try to determine what recent events have altered history.

A Kazak mother and daughter travel by horseback in northwest China.

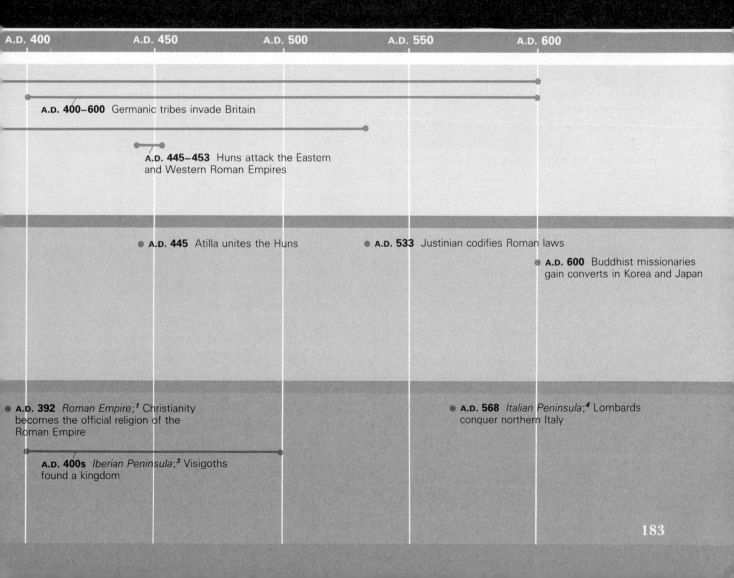

| A.D. 400 | A.D. 450 | A.D. 500 | A.D. 550 | A.D. 600 |

A.D. 400–600 Germanic tribes invade Britain

A.D. 445–453 Huns attack the Eastern and Western Roman Empires

A.D. 445 Atilla unites the Huns

A.D. 533 Justinian codifies Roman laws

A.D. 600 Buddhist missionaries gain converts in Korea and Japan

A.D. 392 *Roman Empire;*[1] Christianity becomes the official religion of the Roman Empire

A.D. 400s *Iberian Peninsula;*[3] Visigoths found a kingdom

A.D. 568 *Italian Peninsula;*[4] Lombards conquer northern Italy

1 New Invaders from Central Asia

OBJECTIVE: *To understand the effects of the barbarian invasions on the great civilizations*

The New Invaders

During the Bronze Age, between 1700 and 1200 B.C., the Kassites, Aryans, Hittites, and other nomadic peoples from central Asia overran the civilizations of Eurasia. These invaders charged into India, Mesopotamia, and Egypt, with their war chariots and superior weapons. From A.D. 200 to 600, new waves of invaders from the forests and steppes of Eurasia attacked the civilized centers of power.

In western Europe, Germanic people from beyond the Rhine and Danube rivers broke through the defenses of the Roman Empire. In central Asia, the Xiong-nu disrupted the civilizations of India and China.

VOCABULARY DEVELOPMENT

inure (ihn YOOR) *verb:* to accustom someone to something difficult or undesirable

prescience (PREE shee uhns) *noun:* knowledge of an event before it happens. From the Latin word, *praescire*, meaning to know beforehand.

infamy (IHN fuh mee) *noun:* great wickedness, disgrace. From the Latin word, *infamis*, meaning not famous or having a bad reputation.

odious (OH dee uhs) *adj.:* hateful, disgusting. From the Latin word, *odium*, meaning hateful, disgusting.

contiguous (kuhn TIHG yoo wuhs) *adj.:* touching along all or most of one side. From the Latin word, *contigere*, meaning to touch on.

horde *noun:* a wandering tribe or group.

The Germanic Tribes. About 1000 B.C., aggressive Indo-European tribes left the shores of the North and Baltic seas to enter the area that is now Germany. The Romans called all the invaders, Germani, even though that was the name of only one tribe. The tribes that migrated into western Europe included the Saxons, Franks, Vandals, Ostrogoths, and Visigoths. The Saxons continued their move west into England. County names in England, such as Wessex, Sussex, and Essex, originally referred to the West, South, and East Saxons.

By 200 B.C., some of the Germanic tribes had settled along the Rhine and Danube rivers, which formed the northern frontier of the Roman Empire. In northern Europe, the Franks crossed the Rhine River and settled in Gaul. In 50 B.C., Julius Caesar conquered all of Gaul which included present-day France and Belgium, as well as parts of what are now Holland, Germany, and Switzerland.

The Ostrogoths migrated from the area of Sweden to the lands north of the Black Sea. The Visigoths, who lived on the Hungarian Plains, raided villages throughout the Balkan Peninsula. The Vandals also moved south, eventually settling in north Africa. See the map on page 185.

The German Barbarians. The Romans considered the nomadic Germani to be barbarians because they were outsiders to civilization and could not read or write. Still,

Barbarian Invasions, A.D. 600

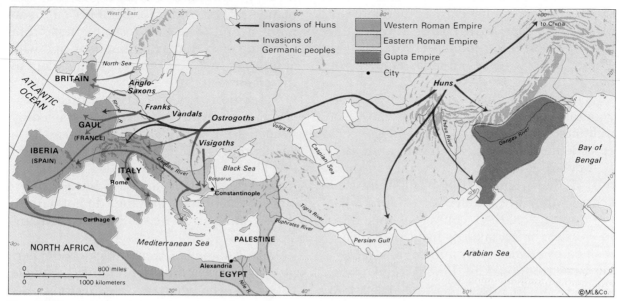

Map Legend:
- Invasions of Huns
- Invasions of Germanic peoples
- Western Roman Empire
- Eastern Roman Empire
- Gupta Empire
- City

Map Skills **1.** Which of the Germanic tribes traveled the farthest before settling in a new land? **2.** What lands were invaded by the Huns?

---

many Romans admired German warriors for their courage and German women for their fair-haired beauty. Fashionable Roman women with dark hair sometimes wore wigs made of hair imported from the Germans in the north.

Members of Germanic tribes sometimes united to plunder or fight a common enemy. German warriors rode into battle screaming loud war whoops. Their wild appearance and long hair, plastered in place with rancid butter, helped them frighten and repel their enemies.

The German Tribes

FOCUS ON SOCIETY

Much of the information about the early German people comes from Roman writers. One of Rome's greatest historians, Tacitus, wrote a description of Germany, *On the Origin, Geography, Institutions, and Tribes of the Germans*, usually shortened to *Germania*. Tacitus, writing in A.D. 98, relied on the works of earlier Roman writers, such as Julius Caesar, and reports of soldiers and merchants who returned from the Roman frontier. *Germania* provides insights into German society of the first century. Tacitus described how the Germans lived, governed themselves, and fought.

“ For my own part, I agree with those who think that the tribes of Germany are free from all taint of intermarriages with foreign nations, and that they appear as a distinct, unmixed race, like none but themselves. Hence, too, the same physical peculiarities throughout so vast a population. All have fierce blue eyes, red hair, huge frames, fit only for a sudden exertion. They are less able to bear laborious work. Heat and thirst they cannot in the least endure; to cold and hunger their climate and their soil inure [accustom] them.

. . . They carry a spear (*framea* is their name for it), with a narrow and short head, but so short and easy to wield that the same weapon serves, according to circumstances, for close or distant conflict. As for the horse-soldier, he is satisfied with a shield and spear; the foot-soldiers also scatter showers of missiles, each man having several and hurling them to an immense distance. . . . Their horses are remarkable neither for beauty nor for fleetness. . . .

They choose their kings by birth, their generals for merit. These kings have not unlimited or arbitrary power, and the generals do more by example than by authority. If they are energetic, if they are conspicuous, if they fight in the front, they lead because they are admired. . . . And what most stimulates their courage is that their squadrons or battalions, instead of being formed by chance or by a fortuitous gathering, are composed of families and clans. Close by them, too, are those dearest to them, so that they hear the shrieks of women, the cries of infants. They are to every man the most sacred witnesses of his

Dying Gaul, a third-century B.C. Roman copy of a Greek bronze original, commemorates the victories of Attalus I of Perganum over the Gauls.

bravery—they are his most generous applauders. The soldier brings his wounds to mother and wife, who shrink not from counting or even demanding them and who administer both food and encouragement to the combatants.

Tradition says that armies already wavering and giving way have been rallied by women who, with earnest entreaties, have vividly represented the horrors of captivity. . . . They even believe that the [female] sex has a certain sanctity and prescience [knowledge of the future], and they do not despise their counsels, or make light of their answers. . . .

About minor matters the chiefs deliberate, about the more important, the whole tribe. Yet even when the final decision rests with the people, the affair is always thoroughly discussed by the chiefs. They assemble, except in the case of a sudden emergency, on certain fixed days. . . .

In their councils, an accusation may be preferred or a capital crime prosecuted. Penalties are distinguished according to the offense. Traitors and deserters are hanged on trees. . . . Lighter offenses too, have penalties proportioned to them; he who is convicted, is fined in a certain number of horses or of cattle. Half of the fine is paid to the king or to the state, half to the person whose wrongs are avenged and to his relatives. . . .

When they go into battle, it is a disgrace for the chief to be surpassed in valour, a disgrace for his followers not to equal the valour of the chief. And it is an infamy [disgrace] and a reproach for life to have survived the chief, and returned from the field. To defend, to protect him, to ascribe one's own brave deeds to his renown, is the height of loyalty. The chief fights for victory; his vassals fight for their chief. If their native state sinks into the sloth of prolonged peace and repose, many of its noble youths voluntarily seek those tribes which are waging some war, both because inaction is odious [disgusting] to their race, and because they win renown more readily in the midst of peril, and cannot maintain a numerous following except by violence and war. . . .

It is well known that the nations of Germany have no cities, and that they do not even tolerate closely contiguous [touching] dwellings. They live scattered and apart, just as a spring, a meadow, or a wood has attracted them. . . . No use is made by them of stone or tile; they employ timber for all purposes. . . .

They all wrap themselves in a cloak which is fastened with a clasp, or, if this is not forthcoming, with a thorn, leaving the rest of their persons bare. They pass whole days on the hearth by the fire. The wealthiest are distinguished by a dress which is not flowing . . . but is tight, and exhibits each limb. They also wear the skins of wild beasts. . . . The women have the same dress as the men, except that they generally wrap themselves in linen garments, which they embroider with purple, and do not lengthen out the upper part of their clothing into sleeves. The upper and lower arm is thus bare. . . .

On lending money on interest and increasing it by compound interest they know nothing—a more effectual safeguard than if it were prohibited. . . .

Such on the whole is the account which I have received of the origin and manners of the entire German people. . . . **"** ■

The Huns

While the Germans were invading the Roman world from the north, another group of fierce nomads attacked from the east. Around 100 B.C., the Han empire of China defeated a group of the Xiong-nu whom the people of southwest Asia and Europe called the Huns. Blocked from advancing into China, these Huns began to move west. They left northern China and traveled through the Altai Mountains, across the lands now called the Soviet Union and Hungary, and through the northern Balkans.

The Huns, in contrast to the "huge-framed" Germans, were short and often

Barbarians surrender to Marcus Aurelius in this relief from a Roman arch.

bowlegged, because they spent long hours in the saddle. They traveled in a horde, or large group, carrying the food they needed, their few possessions, and extra horses.

These barbarians lived off the land, taking food and booty as they migrated. Fighting fiercely with bows and javelins, they destroyed anything and anyone in their path. A Roman writer described the Huns as "eaters of raw meat, drinkers of blood, ugly, and foul-smelling."

The Huns invaded the valley of the Volga River, between the Black and Caspian seas, around A.D. 320. From there, they moved farther west, pressuring the Ostrogoths and Visigoths. Those German tribes then moved west and south, to the borders of the Roman Empire, to escape the Huns.

The Parthians' Defenses

The Parthian Empire, Rome's neighbor to the east, also faced the threat of barbarian invaders. From 248 B.C. to A.D. 224, the Parthians ruled lands that included the Iranian plateau and Mesopotamia.

The Parthians were expert horsemen and archers. Their warriors wore heavy armor and rode a new breed of large, strong horses. The arrows of the Huns merely shattered or bounced off the armored Parthians. The Parthians, however, could not pursue the Huns across the steppes because their large horses required more grass than did the smaller ponies of the Huns.

Feeding warhorses, buying armor, and training warriors became very expensive for the Parthian kings. To reduce military costs, kings encouraged local self-defense. Parthian warriors lived in villages throughout the empire and collected rents from local peasants to pay their expenses.

The Parthian system of local self-defense had advantages and disadvantages. The king was spared large military expenses, and trained warriors protected Parthia from invaders. Nevertheless, the king had little control over these independent cavalrymen, who became powerful, landowning aristocrats. Despite drawbacks, the Parthians' system of local self-defense helped them to resist steppe invasions successfully and preserve the civilization transmitted to Parthia.

The Sassanid Dynasty of Parthia. In A.D. 224, Ardeshir, a Persian prince, overthrew the Parthian king. Ardeshir started the Sassanid Dynasty, which ruled the Persian Empire on the Iranian plateau and in Mesopotamia from A.D. 224 to 651.

Sassanid rulers, like the earlier Parthians, took advantage of trading opportunities. Since the Iranian plateau and Mesopotamia linked China, India, and the Mediterranean world, the Sassanids collected heavy tolls on goods passing along the caravan trade routes. See the map, The Byzantine and Sassanid Empires, A.D. 600 to 630, page 231. Taxing the silk trade between China and Rome was especially profitable for them.

The Sassanid Dynasty was one of the most powerful and fierce ever to rule the Iranian plateau. The Sassanid army relied on the use of both light and heavy cavalry. The heavy cavalry wore armor and fought with long lances. The more maneuverable light cavalry fought mainly with bows and arrows. The army also included infantry units. Between A.D. 450 and 600, the Huns repeatedly attacked the Persian Empire. The Sassanids successfully resisted, however, the effort drained their economic and military resources.

Although the center of the civilized world held off the barbarian invaders, the Roman Empire was less successful. In the years between A.D. 200 and 600, the Romans faced both the German invaders on the north and the Huns on the east. Like the Persians, the Romans changed their government and military to meet the challenge.

SECTION 1 *Study Skills*

Developing Vocabulary Use each of the following terms in a sentence: **1.** horde. **2.** inure. **3.** odious.

Reviewing Main Ideas **1.** Name the five main tribes of Germanic peoples that migrated into western Europe. **2.** Why did the Romans call the Germans barbarians? **3.** Describe how German warriors lived. **4.** Compare the physical appearance of the Germans and the Huns. **5.** Explain why the Parthians adopted a defensive response toward the nomads. **6.** What trading advantages did the Sassanids enjoy?

Understanding Geography **1.** From where did the Germanic peoples come? **2.** Where did the most important Germanic tribes settle? **3.** What people did they displace?

Challenge Discuss whether or not any area of the world today could still be considered barbarian.

2 The Roman Empire under Attack

OBJECTIVE: *To understand the causes and consequences of the collapse of the Roman Empire*

Problems of the Roman Empire

Between A.D. 200 and 400, the Roman Empire faced major problems. Causes of the problems included the threat from German tribes along the empire's north borders, a crisis in the Roman economy, the increased size of the army, and the complexities of ruling a vast empire.

German Tribes Threaten Rome. During the second and third centuries, the Roman government decided to let tribes of Germans settle on Roman lands. These tribes became allies of the Romans. As allies, the Germans swore loyalty to Rome and agreed to defend Roman borders. In return, they received land to farm inside the empire from the Roman government.

From the third century on, many Germans also enlisted in the Roman legions. Many held high positions in the army. Even so, the pressure of attacks by independent tribes showed no sign of decreasing.

Economic Crisis. Governing an immense empire also created serious economic difficulties. Rome relied on taxes to pay for government services. However, tax money did not expand with the growth of the empire. Many wealthy landowners refused to pay taxes and hired private armies. Poor landowners could not afford to pay. The rich and the poor made tax collection so difficult

that some citizens were forced to serve as government tax collectors.

Public expenses for the Roman Empire included both military expenses and the construction and maintenance of public buildings and roads. Sources of revenue were taxes and forced service.

Some emperors tried to create more money by reducing the amount of precious metals, such as gold and silver, in the coins they minted. The Emperor Severus (seh VEER uhs) reduced silver by 40 percent in coins minted during his reign. Although this practice increased the amount of money in circulation, the value, or buying power, of the money declined. Prices increased to make up for the declining content of precious metals in coins. Inflation, a general

---

VOCABULARY DEVELOPMENT

inflation (ihn FLAY shuhn) *noun:* a general rise in prices. From the Latin word, *inflare,* meaning to blow up.

Byzantium (buh ZAN she uhm) *noun:* a city, overlooking the straits between the Black and Mediterranean seas, founded by the Greeks in the 600s B.C. In 324 B.C., Byzantium was renamed Constantinople and became the capital of the Eastern Roman Empire, later called the Byzantine Empire. The Turks conquered Constantinople in 1453 and later renamed it Istanbul.

pyre (pyhur) *noun:* a woodpile for burning a dead body.

rise in prices, weakened the economy and further widened the gap between the rich and poor of Rome.

In addition to taxes and inflation, the use of slaves had contributed to the economic problems. The use of slaves discouraged new ideas in technology and made free people feel contempt for hard work. Thus, productivity declined.

The Increased Size of the Army.

Between A.D. 200 and 400, the vast borders of the Roman Empire were attacked repeatedly. The Germans in the north, African Berbers, Picts in northern Britain, nomads of Arabia, and powerful organized Persians in the east continually threatened the empire's frontiers. As frontier pressure intensified, the Roman army expanded to include more than 500,000 men. Eventually, the army's size and influence enabled powerful generals to choose the emperors and control the Roman government.

Complexities of Ruling a Large Empire.

Administrative problems developed because of the vast size of the Roman Empire. One leader could no longer govern such a large and diverse population. In addition, a single person could not control the soldiers neces-sary to defend more than 10,000 miles of border. To solve these problems, Emperor Diocletian (DY oh KLEE shuhn) divided the empire in two parts. One emperor ruled the Eastern Roman Empire while another governed the Western Roman Empire. See the map, Barbarian Invasions, page 185.

Both emperors held the title, "Augustus," revered one. Each had an assistant, called a caesar, who was a trained successor, or junior emperor. This system was intended to promote government stability and reduce the danger of civil wars over the emperor's successor.

The solution of dividing the empire created other problems, however. Sometimes the emperors and the caesars of the east and west plotted against each other. The loyalties of the separate armies were tested frequently. Meanwhile, Germans, Berbers, Picts, Arabs, and Persians waited impatiently to take advantage of any weakness within the empire.

When Diocletian divided the empire, he became emperor of the Western Empire. He chose Flavius Valerius Constantius as his caesar. Maximian became emperor of the Eastern Empire. Diocletian retired in A.D. 305, and Constantius became emperor of the Western Empire.

Found in Germany, this stone relief shows an active scene of Roman tax collections in the second century A.D.

Constantine the Great

Constantine was born at Naissus, a city in the area that is now Yugoslavia. Although his parents were not wealthy, his father, Flavius Constantius, rose through the ranks of the army to become emperor of the Western Empire. Constantine's mother, Helena, is thought to have been the daughter of an innkeeper.

A professional soldier, as was his father, Constantine probably had little formal education. He spent his youth at the court of Diocletian. There the emperor held him hostage to ensure his father's loyalty.

In A.D. 305, Constantine learned that his father was seriously ill and requested permission to go to him. Diocletian refused, but Constantine managed to escape and find Constantius. Soon after their reunion, Constantius died. Constantius' troops, impressed by the young son's daring, proclaimed Constantine successor to his father despite his age.

Constantine's desire to increase his control of the Western Empire led him to attack his major rival, Maxentius. On the eve of the important battle, Constantine had a vision or dream that changed both his life and the history of the world. According to tradition, just before the battle Constantine saw a cross and the Latin words, *In hoc signo vinces*—Latin for "In this sign you will conquer." He believed this vision was a sign from the Christian God that his victory over Maxentius was assured.

The next day, Constantine ordered his soldiers to march into battle with the symbol of Christ painted on their shields. Constantine's forces were victorious. Believing he owed his victory to the Christian God, Constantine accepted Christianity. Thus, he became the first Christian Roman emperor.

During his reign, Constantine tried to solve some of the empire's problems. To

This drawing tells a legend about Constantine, who used the Christian cross as his battle symbol after dreaming that it would bring him victory.

promote the economy, he established a stable money system based on gold. To make government more efficient, he separated the administration of civil and military functions and officials. To keep a strong tax base, he required people to stay in one occupation for life. For instance, a peasant could not move or give up farming, according to Constantine's law. To ensure stable transfer of power, Constantine started a system of hereditary succession of rulers. ■

The Divided Empire

Constantine became sole ruler of the Roman Empire in A.D. 324 by defeating Licinius, emperor in the east. To celebrate the victory, Constantine established a new capital at Byzantium (buh ZAN shee uhm). He then renamed his new capital city Constantinople, after himself.

The Greeks founded the city of Byzantium in the 600s B.C. It became part of the Roman Empire in the 100s B.C. The city was located in the eastern part of the Roman Empire, where people spoke Greek rather than Latin. See the map, Barbarian Invasions, page 185.

Overlooking the Bosporus (BAHS puh rehs), Constantinople was well situated to guard the strategic junction between the Black Sea and the Mediterranean Sea. The city became a military stronghold, guarding a major crossroads of world trade. Its location also was the key to the emperor's control of the valuable eastern provinces. Fortified with defensive walls, Constantinople became the center of a remarkable civilization called Byzantine, after the original city. It was a civilization that lasted a thousand years.

The Western Roman Empire. After Constantine died in A.D. 337, the empire was again divided into the Roman Empire in the west and the Byzantine Empire in the east. This time, the division of the empire became more permanent.

In the middle of the sixth century A.D., Justinian, then emperor of the Byzantine Empire, launched a campaign to reunite the empire. His forces advanced as far west as Spain. Justinian, however, was never able to subdue the Franks. After Justinian died, the lands he won in north Africa and Spain had to be given up when new invaders from the east attacked the frontiers of the Roman Empire.

Justinian is remembered for revising and reorganizing the great body of Roman law. His code of laws, issued in A.D. 533, made up of four volumes, is known as the *Corpus Juris Civilis* or *Body of Civil Law*. Justinian's Code became the foundation for many later European legal systems.

The Byzantine Empire, with more people, cities, and trade than the Western Empire, remained prosperous and strong. Constantinople became a thriving center of industry and culture. The economic decline and political troubles continued in the Western Empire. By A.D. 400, the government

The Germanic States, A.D. 526

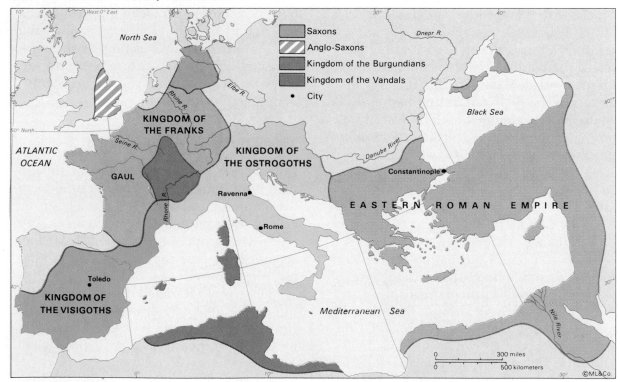

Map Skills **1.** List the Germanic tribes and the lands each settled. **2.** After A.D. 526, what lands remained part of the Roman Empire?

there was no longer able to keep tribes of German barbarians from flooding into the Roman Empire.

The Germans living on the border of the Western Empire assimilated many characteristics of the Romans. The Germans learned Roman ways through trade, religion, the army, government, and marriage. Roman merchants traded such products as jewelry, tools, utensils, and Roman coins to the Germans. The Germans had no money of their own. The increasing contacts between Romans and frontier barbarians resulted in a narrowing of the gap between the two cultures.

In return for the use of Roman land, German tribes gave the Romans their sworn loyalty, as well as slaves taken as prisoners of war. The Romans used these slaves as gladiators, servants, and field hands. Thousands of people called Slavs were among the prisoners from the conquered tribes in northeastern Europe. The name Slav meant glorious in the Slavic language. However, as thousands of Slavs were sold into slavery, the word slav came to mean slave.

German Invasions. In A.D. 378, the Visigoths defeated a Roman army and killed the emperor. The Visigoths and other Germanic tribes swarmed across the Roman borders. Scenes of violence and destruction became commonplace in Gaul. A Roman poet, Orientius (oh ree ENT ee uhs), wrote:

❝ In the villages and country houses, in the fields and in the countryside, on every road—death, sorrow, slaughter, fires, and lamentation. All Gaul smoked in one great funeral pyre. ❞

Between A.D. 406 and 572, German barbarians invaded the Western Empire, creating chaos and confusion among the people of the empire. Gradually, new societies emerged as the German invaders settled among the Roman populations.

In A.D. 568, a Germanic tribe called the Lombards turned against the empire and

This sixth-century mosaic from a church in San Vitale, Ravenna, Italy shows Justinian, local officials, and clergy attending a service.

took control of northern Italy. The Byzantine Empire managed to retain control of many locations in southern Italy and pockets of land around Rome and Ravenna. See the map, The Germanic States, page 192.

In Gaul, the Franks settled along the Rhine River frontier. Their leaders were related to the great chieftain, Merowech. This family of Frankish rulers was known as the Merovingian (MER oh VIN jih uhn) Dynasty.

In Spain, the Visigoths founded a kingdom. In England, very little of the Roman civilization survived after the Angles, Saxons, and Jutes invaded the island. Central leadership no longer existed in England. The Germanic invaders brought their language to England. Gradually, the Anglo-Saxon language developed as a mix of German tongues spoken on the European mainland, taking on unique English characteristics.

The Huns Invade the Byzantine Empire. In addition to the invading Germans, the Huns from Eurasia (see page 187) threatened the Roman Empire. Until the fifth century A.D., the Romans had fought only small groups of Huns. The Huns had not been united as a single group, following a single leader. Because the Huns lacked unity, Romans could bribe them or defeat

A fierce, stern portrait of Attila the Hun was carved into this medallion by an Italian sculptor centuries after the Hun's death.

Roman Empire in the west, destroying some Roman customs and assimilating others. The end of the Roman Empire ushered in a period that some call the Dark Ages. The term is inaccurate, however, since the period managed to preserve much of Roman civilization. At the same time, new trends and customs were taking root throughout western Europe.

Roman culture also survived for another thousand years in Constantinople and the Byzantine Empire. The Christian church preserved Roman customs and ideas. Roman civilization contained numerous elements of Greek culture. These elements were transmitted through the church, the Byzantine Empire, and the conquering barbarians, to later people of Eurasia.

them when they pressured the frontier. In A.D. 445, however, a powerful chief, Attila, united the Huns of Europe.

These Huns attacked the Byzantine Empire, defeated imperial troops, and advanced on Constantinople. They never seized the city, but the Byzantine Empire paid Attila a huge sum of gold as tribute.

The Huns Invade the Roman Empire. Attila then turned his army against the Roman Empire in the west. In A.D. 451, Attila led his hordes, or tribes, into Gaul. An army of Visigoths and other barbarian allies of Rome defeated him.

In A.D. 452, Attila led his army into Italy. Famine and disease, however, forced him to withdraw. He led his army back to the area now called Hungary. There, in A.D. 453, Attila died. After his death, the confederation of Huns broke apart. They ceased to be a major threat to the Roman Empire.

The Transmission of Roman Culture. Between A.D. 200 and 600, the divided Roman Empire developed as two separate civilizations. Eventually, barbarians invaded the

SECTION 2 *Study Skills*

Developing Vocabulary Explain the meaning of inflation.

Reviewing Main Ideas 1. Why did Diocletian divide the Roman Empire? **2.** What main advantage did the Germans gain from the Roman Empire? **3.** What main advantage did the Romans gain from the Germans? **4.** Explain the significance of some of the main achievements of Constantine.

Understanding Chronology 1. Explain two major problems the Roman Empire experienced between A.D. 200 and 400. **2.** How long was Constantine the Great, emperor? **3.** When did the Lombards take control of northern Italy? **4.** In what year was the Roman Empire divided into an Eastern and Western empire?

Understanding Cause and Effect 1. Explain the economic consequences of reducing the amount of precious metal in coins. **2.** What were two major effects of Diocletian's decision to divide the Roman Empire?

Challenge Compare the causes of the decline of the Roman Empire with problems the United States faces today.

3 The Influence of Christianity

OBJECTIVE: *To understand the causes and consequences of the spread of Christianity*

The Early Church

Between A.D. 180 and 300, barbarians repeatedly attacked Rome and civil wars disrupted the empire. Some Romans explained these disasters as the gods' punishment for the spread of a new religion, Christianity. Because of such a notion, some Christians were tortured and put to death.

The Roman government also persecuted Christians because they refused to worship the emperor and to make public sacrifices to the Roman gods. Christians sometimes refused to serve in the Roman army because the preachings of Jesus stressed peace. Despite Roman persecutions, Christianity continued to attract followers.

The Appeal of Christianity. Christianity spread throughout the Roman Empire for several reasons. First, Christians thought of their religion as catholic, or universal, and they accepted all people. Christians taught that Christ promised life after death for anyone who believed in his message. Ordinary people, therefore, could share in immortality. Hope was appealing to the underprivileged majority of the people in the empire who suffered poverty and oppression.

Second, people were attracted to the Christian faith because Christians followed a moral code that made them help one another, especially when they fell sick or suffered some disaster. Well-educated people, familiar with earlier Greek and Hellenistic philosophies, recognized that Christianity also provided a moral guideline for living.

Third, the unity of the Roman Empire enabled word of the new religion to reach

---

VOCABULARY DEVELOPMENT

vouchsafe (vowch SAYF) *verb:* to graciously grant or give.

beneficence (buh NEHF uh suhns) *noun:* kindness or generosity. From the Latin words *bene*, meaning well or good, and *facere*, meaning to do.

indulgence (ihn DUHL juhns) *noun:* a favor or privilege.

exchequer (ihks CHEHK uhr) *noun:* a treasury.

peremptorily (puh REHMP tuh ruh lee) *adj.:* in a final or decisive manner.

unambiguously (uhn am BIHG yoo wuhs lee) *adj.:* clearly; not having more than one meaning or interpretation. From the Latin word, *ambigere*, meaning to wander.

theologian (THEE uh LOH juhn) *noun:* a specialist in the study of religious faith and practice.

Nicaea (nih SEE uh): ancient city in Asia Minor.

ascetics (uh SEHT ihks) *adj.:* people who live lives of self-denial and contemplation for religious purposes. From the Greek word, *askein*, meaning to train the body.

monastery (MAHN uh STUR ee) *noun:* a place of residence for a group of people, especially monks, who have taken religious vows. From the Greek word, *monazein*, meaning to live alone.

monk (muhnk) *noun:* a man who joins a religious order, living away from the world and taking religious vows of obedience, chastity, and poverty.

Christian bishops at the Council of Nicea composed the first official definition of the relationship between God the Father and God the Son.

many people. Missionaries, new converts, and merchants used the well-traveled roads and the common language to take the ideas and writings of the Christians to people throughout the empire.

Fourth, the persecution of Christians united the faithful and strengthened their belief. Between A.D. 249 and 313, Christians were persecuted and many were executed.

Leadership of the Christians. By A.D. 200, Christianity had spread to Egypt, Spain, and England. The earliest Christian groups managed their affairs independently of other communities.

As members grew in various cities, the Christians chose a bishop, a leader from the clergy, to administer their own church affairs. The bishops appointed priests to serve smaller congregations, called parishes. The bishops in the larger cities of Rome,

Constantinople, Alexandria, Antioch, and Jerusalem were called patriarchs, meaning fathers of the church.

Authority of the Pope. On the split of the Roman Empire, the Patriarchs of Alexandria and Constantinople came to exercise independent religious leadership over Egypt and Byzantium.

The Patriarch, or Bishop, of Rome was called Pope, from a Greek word meaning father. The Pope was the supreme authority in the church in the West. In addition, the church in Rome held a special place in the minds of early Christians because Peter, the leader of the disciples of Jesus, established it. Many Christians believed the Bishop of Rome exercised leadership over all Christians in both the east and the west.

Doctrinal Disputes. As the number of Christians grew, disputes over church teachings occurred. New members, from widely different social and religious backgrounds, often disagreed about church teachings. Some ambitious priests took advantage of quarrels over church doctrine and rituals to advance among the church's leadership.

Religious thinkers disagreed about the nature of Christ. Some argued that Christ was God and, therefore, not human. Others maintained that Christ was human and, therefore, not God. Christians wondered, if Christ was both human and divine, how much of each quality was in his nature? Christians also disagreed about the nature of God and the relationship of the divine persons in the Trinity—the Father, Son, and Holy Spirit.

Constantine and Christianity. After Constantine united the empire, he officially ended persecution of Christians in the Roman Empire. Reversing earlier Roman policy, Constantine began to favor them. In A.D. 313, he issued the Edict of Milan, which provided for free exercise of all religions throughout the empire.

The Edict of Milan

FOCUS ON SOURCES

The reading excerpted below is taken from *Of the Manner in which the Persecutors Died*, the work of a Roman writer, Lactantius. The writer quoted from the Edict of Milan, which allowed Christians and all others to practice the religion "which to each of them appeared best."

" We judged it a salutary measure, and one highly consonant to right reason, that no man should be denied leave of attaching himself to the rites of the Christians, or to whatever other religion his mind directed him, that thus the supreme Divinity, to whose worship we freely devote ourselves, might continue to vouchsafe [grant] His favour and beneficence [charity] to us. And accordingly we give you to know that, without regard to any provisos in our former orders to you concerning the Christians, all who choose that religion are to be permitted, freely and absolutely, to remain in it, and not to be disturbed any way or molested.

And we thought fit to be thus special in the things committed to your charge, that you might understand that the indulgence [favor] which we have granted in matters of religion to the Christians is ample and unconditional; and perceive at the same time that the open and free exercise of their respective religions is granted to all others, as well as to the Christians. . . .

Moreover, with respect to the Christians, we formerly gave certain orders concerning the places appropriated for their religious assemblies; but now we will that all persons who have purchased such places, either from our exchequer [treasury] or from anyone else, do restore them to the Christians, without money demanded or price claimed, and that this be performed peremptorily [immediately] and unambiguously [clearly]; and we will also that they who have obtained any right to such places by form of gift do forthwith restore them to the Christians: reserving always to such persons, who have either purchased for a price, or gratuitously acquired them, to make application to the judge of the district, if they look on themselves as entitled to any equivalent from our beneficence.

. . . So shall that divine favour which, in affairs of the mightiest importance, we have already experienced, continue to give success to us, and in our successes make the commonweal [people] happy. And that the tenor of this our gracious ordinance may be made known unto all, we will that you cause it by your authority to be published everywhere. " ■

The Church after A.D. 313

When the Christians were no longer a persecuted minority in the Roman Empire, one of the bonds that had united them disappeared. Rival theologians attracted followers while they denounced one another as teachers of false and misleading doctrines.

The Nicene Creed. To settle theological disputes, Emperor Constantine held a meeting, or council, of all the Christian bishops at Nicaea in A.D. 325. The council members composed the Nicene Creed, the first official definition of the relationship between God the Father and God the Son.

Quarrels among Christians, however, did not end. Christians of Syria and Egypt refused to accept the Nicene Creed. They established the Syriac and Coptic, or Egyptian, Christian churches. Arius, a priest from Alexandria, maintained that Christ was created by God the Father and therefore was not equal to Him. Arius' teachings, called Arianism, attracted a wide audience.

Monasticism. Like the earlier Chinese and Greeks, the Romans looked for a way of life to help them cope with war and suffering. Christian ascetics and hermits sought to es-

St. Gallen Monastery in Switzerland. Religious members of monasteries lived a solitary life of labor, prayer, and contemplation.

Christianity beyond the Roman Empire. Early Christianity spread quickly throughout the lands Rome ruled. Its appeal, however, extended beyond the Roman Empire. The first barbarian ruler to become a Christian was an Armenian in Asia Minor. According to Armenian tradition, their king was converted to Christianity in A.D. 301. His people also became Christians.

Africans in Nubia and Ethiopia, both south of Egypt, also accepted the Christian religion. Like the Christians of Egypt, those of Nubia and Ethiopia remained independent of the authority of the patriarchs in both Constantinople and Rome.

In A.D. 432, Patrick, a British Christian, traveled to Ireland and converted many to Christianity. When the Germanic tribes invaded the British Isles, however, they stamped out Christianity.

SECTION 3 *Study Skills*

Developing Vocabulary 1. Define vouchsafe. **2.** What is the difference between beneficence and indulgence? **3.** What is an exchequer? **4.** Explain the meanings of the Latin roots for the word unambiguous. **5.** Give an example of an act done peremptorily. **6.** Describe the life of an ascetic. **7.** What is the relationship between a monastery and a monk?

Reviewing Main Ideas 1. List three reasons why Christianity appealed to many people. **2.** What is a bishop? **3.** Explain two early doctrinal disputes in Christianity.

Understanding Chronology 1. What happened to Christianity in the Roman Empire after A.D. 313? **2.** When were the first monasteries established?

Understanding Cause and Effect 1. Explain the relationship between Roman politics and the persecution of the Christians. **2.** What was the main impact of the Nicene Creed?

Challenge Why does Christianity continue to have more influence in the western world than in the east?

cape from the world and to devote themselves to a life of prayer and contemplation. The earliest Christian ascetics were hermits who went into the desert and lived alone.

One of the first Christians to practice asceticism was Anthony of Alexandria, who lived around A.D. 300. Anthony believed that a good Christian should give everything to the poor. About A.D. 285, Anthony founded the first monastery. The term monastery comes from the Greek word, *monazein*, meaning to live alone. The monks, as the religious members were called, gathered to eat but otherwise lived a solitary life of labor and prayer.

About A.D. 500, Benedict of Nursia, a young Roman noble disgusted with the corruption in Rome, left the city to become a hermit. In time, he attracted many followers and established a monastery on Monte Cassino, in Italy. Benedict wrote a set of rules for the monks who came to live there.

4 The Gupta Empire of India

OBJECTIVE: *To understand the causes and consequences of the rise and fall of the Gupta Empire in India*

India After the Mauryans

When the Roman Empire was just beginning to expand in the third century B.C., India was coming to the end of a period of unity under the Mauryan Dynasty. Soon after the great ruler, Ashoka, died in 232 B.C., India again became divided into small states. During the long period from 184 B.C. to A.D. 320, northern India was invaded several times. Just as the Aryans had done hundreds of years earlier, these invaders swept down through the mountain passes of the northeast, creating disorder.

A Period of Invasions. The first invaders after 184 B.C. were Greeks from the kingdom of Bactria, located in present-day Afghanistan. Following the Greek invaders, were Scythian nomads of the steppes, whom the Indians called Shakas. The Scythians invaded, conquered, and were barely established before they, too, were driven out by the Parthians, called Palavas in India.

VOCABULARY DEVELOPMENT

treatise (TREET ihs) *noun:* a formal book or article on a subject.

suttee (suh TEE) *noun:* an Indian practice requiring a widow to throw herself on her husband's funeral pyre.

ravage (RAV ihj) *verb:* to destroy violently, usually in a series of attacks over a period of time.

The Kushanas. Finally, the Kushanas, a central Asian people whom the Chinese forced west, pressured India. The Kushanas were a nomadic tribal people who grazed their herds near the Great Wall of China. Their peaceful way of life changed after the fierce Xiong-nu (see page 167) forced the Kushanas to move. The Kushanas invaded northern India and ruled there from about A.D. 78 to 227.

The Kushana rulers supported Buddhism, as had Ashoka. They also protected the trade routes along which products and Buddhism were brought into China and Southeast Asia. During this period, Buddhism almost replaced Hinduism as the major religion of India.

The Gupta Dynasty

An Indian king, Chandragupta, ruled the lands of Magadha in the lower Ganges River valley. In A.D. 320, he launched a series of invasions on neighboring lands in northern India. Within a century, the Gupta Empire had claimed all the lands from the Bay of Bengal to the Arabian Sea. See the map, The Gupta Empire, page 200.

As the Gupta emperors conquered new lands, they allowed the defeated rulers to remain in control. The Guptas appointed officials to the courts of the vassal Indian kings and received tribute from them.

During the reign of the Gupta Dynasty, India was free from the barbarian invasions

The Gupta Empire, A.D. 400

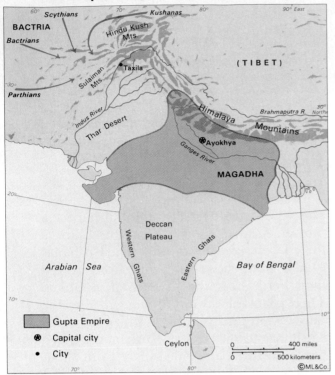

Map Skills **1.** What was the capital city of the Gupta Empire? **2.** In what direction would a resident of the capital travel to reach the Bay of Bengal?

that weakened both China and the Roman Empire. Consequently, about A.D. 350, Indian civilization entered a golden age that other Indian generations called classical.

Government under the Guptas. Despite the long years of Gupta rule, little information on its political, military, or geographic history is available. Most information on the Guptas is found in the written reports of Chinese, Ceylonese, and other Buddhist pilgrims, and in Indian literature.

The Gupta rulers held all government power. They followed the early Indian tradition of supporting Hinduism.

The highest Hindu caste, the Brahmans, held government positions. Although the Guptas tolerated Buddhism, the Brahmans worked to restore Hinduism to its former influence. By the end of the Gupta period, Buddhism had declined in India but had

gained strength in other parts of Asia. Hinduism became the dominant religion. Hindus and Buddhists, however, lived peacefully together, and Buddhist monasteries continued to exist.

Most northern Indians survived by farming. Only the people at the top of the caste system lived in luxury.

Women in India were less influential than men. The *Code of Manu*, a legal treatise, recommended that a wife worship her husband as a god. Some Indians practiced polygamy—marriage to more than one wife. During the Gupta dynasty, *suttee* also became common among the upper castes. The practice of *suttee* required a widow to commit suicide by throwing herself on her husband's flaming funeral pyre.

Literature in the Golden Age. Under the Gupta rulers, Indian literature was finally written, rather than preserved by the telling and retelling of stories. Indians wrote their stories and poems in Sanskrit, an Indo-European language very distantly related to Greek and Latin.

Kalidasa, a master of Sanskrit literature, is known for his plays and his epic and lyric poems. His most famous play, *Shakuntala*, tells the story of a king who marries the daughter of a wise man. The king is then called away and, because of a curse, loses his memory of the marriage. His wife gives birth to a son, and the lovers are reunited.

India's two great epics, the *Mahabharata* and the *Ramayana* were completed during the Gupta Dynasty. The *Mahabharata*, which the Indians regard as a book of religious instruction, is about three and a half times longer than the Bible. The *Mahabharata* and the *Ramayana* remain popular literature in India today.

Indian Achievements in Science and Mathematics. Indian science and mathematics also progressed under the Guptas. Indians invented the numeral system, now called Arabic. The important new concept of zero, allowing the position of a number to indicate its value, makes calculations easy and rapid. Without this concept, advanced mathematics based on the decimal system could not have developed. The Indian numeral system spread to Arabia in the tenth century but did not reach the Western world until the twelfth century.

Aryabhata, an Indian mathematician who lived in the fifth century, explained the daily rotation of the earth on its axis. Indian astronomers identified the seven planets that can be seen without a telescope. They knew that the planets and the moon shone because of light reflected from the sun. Indian astronomers also predicted eclipses, calculated the diameter of the earth, and developed a theory of gravity.

Indian Ideas Spread East. Buddhist missionaries spread Mahayana Buddhism along the trade routes to China and Southeast Asia. By A.D. 600, missionaries had traveled north to Korea and from there to Japan. They traveled by sea along the trade routes between India and China. See the map, The Expansion of Buddhism, page 202.

Indian traders used the monsoon winds to sail around the Malayan peninsula, where north-blowing monsoons carried them past the coast of Vietnam to China. Port cities and trade centers grew up along the mainland coasts of Southeast Asia and the major islands of Java and Sumatra. These communities became centers for the spread of Indian culture, languages, and religion.

Indian merchants often married local women and settled in new communities. Local princes adopted Buddhism and learned to write in Sanskrit. They rode elephants and sat under white umbrellas, symbols of royalty for Indian rulers.

About A.D. 400, the first great state in Southeast Asia, Funan, grew in what are today Vietnam and Cambodia. The culture of Funan was based on Indian ideas. Indian influence throughout Southeast Asia remained strong for centuries.

Wall frescoes from Ajanta caves near the city of Aurangabad, India.

The Decline of the Gupta Empire. Gupta rule ended in A.D. 535, when a group of Huns invaded northwest India. A league of Indian princes succeeded in keeping the Huns from advancing into south India. However, the invaders ravaged the north. In the seventh century, the Huns migrated to new pastureland. The rulers of many small kingdoms fought for control of India.

Links with East and West. During the entire period of the Gupta Dynasty, India was linked to other Eurasian civilizations through trade. Throughout India, archaeologists have found coins and finished goods from the Greek and Roman civilizations. Historians know that the Romans maintained trading stations on the west coast of India. Archaeologists also discovered a Roman trading station on the east coast. Pottery, beads, lamps, and glass are among the Roman objects found there.

Expansion of Buddhism to A.D. 600

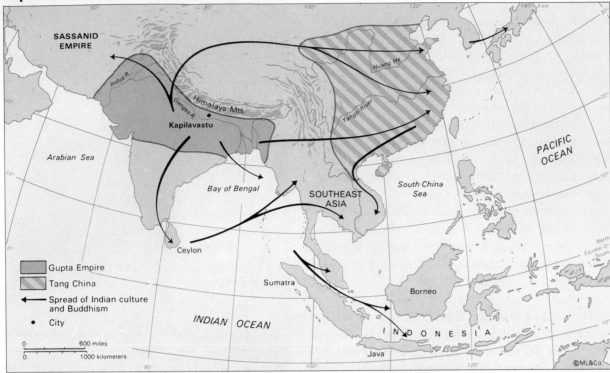

Map Skills 1. In what country did Buddhism originate? **2.** In what direction did Buddhism spread? **3.** What is the significance of Kapilavatsu?

Traders also traveled the Silk Road across Asia during the Indian Golden Age. A large amount of silk was carried from China to Taxila in the Indus Valley. From there the silk was shipped to ports on the Indian Ocean.

Chinese Buddhists traveled along the Silk Road from India, too, spreading Mahayana Buddhism. Buddhism moved east to Sri Lanka and southeast Asia where it gained many followers. See the map, The Expansion of Buddhism, above.

Missionaries from the West brought Christianity to India. The Christians living in Sassanid Persia sent preachers by ship through the Persian Gulf and the Indian Ocean. By this route they reached the region around Bombay, on the west coast of the subcontinent. The Christian church made little progress in Hindu India. India did, however, serve as a supply station for trips to the Pacific coast of China.

SECTION 4 *Study Skills*

Developing Vocabulary 1. What is a treatise? **2.** Explain the practice of *suttee*. **3.** Use the word ravage in a sentence.

Reviewing Main Ideas 1. List two of the peoples who invaded India between 184 B.C. and A.D. 320. **2.** Describe government under the Guptas. **3.** What was the main occupation in northern India? Why? **4.** Describe the main action in the play *Shakuntala*. **5.** Describe four Indian achievements in science and mathematics. **6.** Explain the main link between the Gupta Dynasty and other Eurasian civilizations. **7.** What significant factors contributed to the decline of the Gupta Empire?

Understanding Chronology Why was the period between 184 B.C. and A.D. 320 unstable for the people of India?

Challenge Describe similarities between government under the Guptas and under the Roman Empire.

Culture Realms

India is part of the great landmass called Eurasia, one of the seven continents. Other continental landmasses include Europe, Africa, North America, South America, Australia, and Antarctica. These seven landmasses and their nearby islands have 4.5 billion people living in some 200 different countries and territories. The term culture realm is more helpful to understand the history of these people than the term continent. A culture realm includes peoples who share a common history and culture. The Indian culture realm includes not only India but other countries of south Asia such as Pakistan and Bangladesh. The region has been isolated from the rest of the world by natural mountain barriers.

Worldwide, there are 11 culture realms. They are Latin America, Anglo-America, Europe, Australia, the Soviet Union, China, Japan, India, southeast Asia, sub-Saharan Africa, and the lands of north Africa and southwest Asia.

While each culture realm as a whole is unique, it may share some similarities with neighboring cultures. Mapmakers draw precise boundary lines between continents or countries, but culture realms tend to merge with one another.

North Africa, Southwest Asia

North Africa and southwest Asia form a culture realm that extends beyond the border between two continents. This area has a common environment, history, and culture. Egypt, on the African continent, and Syria, on the Asian continent, have more in common with each other than with countries in their own continent but in a different culture realm.

Many Different Names. Some people call this region or culture realm the Dry World. Much of the area, including the Sahara and Arabian deserts, receives little rainfall. However, along such major rivers as the Nile, in the mountainous regions, and along the Mediterranean coast water is more plentiful.

This region is called the Arab World, because most people speak Arabic or a related language, but other languages, such as Turkish and Persian, also are spoken.

Yet another name for this culture realm is the Islamic World. Islam is the dominant, though not the only, religion practiced in the region. Most Israelis practice Judaism, for example.

Americans and Europeans often refer to north Africa and southwest Asia as the Middle East. Middle East is a term referring to the region's relationship to Europe. From a European perspective, China and Japan are in the Far East.

Taken together, north Africa and southwest Asia make up the southern and eastern rim of the Mediterranean Sea. The most common land forms are hills, low plateaus, and mountains. Fertile plains are found along the Nile River, on the north African shore of the Mediterranean, and in the land between the Tigris and Euphrates rivers. An important feature in north Africa is the Sahara Desert.

A Common Culture. The culture realm of north Africa and southwest Asia share much history in common. Until this century, most people made their living in agriculture. Agriculture is still important. In moist regions, and where irrigation makes it possible, people continue to farm the land. In the arid and semiarid regions and in mountainous terrain, people often raise sheep, goats, and dromedaries.

Populations in North African and Southwest Asian Countries, 1985

	Egypt	Iran	Israel	Libya	Morocco	Saudi Arabia	Turkey
Area (in thousands of square miles)	387	636	8	679	172	830	301
Area (in thousands of square kilometers)	1,002	1,647	21	1,759	445	2,150	780
Population (in millions)	45	43	4	3	21	10	47
Annual birth rate (per 1,000 population)	37	43	24	46	44	44	34
Annual death rate (per 1,000 population)	10	11	7	11	12	13	9
Number of years to double population	28	26	41	17	24	17	29
Population projected by A.D. 2000 (in millions)	65	65	5	6	37	20	67
Annual death rate of infants under 1 year (per 1,000 births)	102	115	14	91	98	121	131
Life expectancy at birth	58	60	74	58	52	56	63
Percent of population urban	45	53	90	61	43	71	45
Per capita food supply (as percent of requirement)	128	119	119	152	110	129	122
Total GNP (in billions of U.S. dollars)	33	75	22	16	15	111	51
Per capita GNP (in U.S. dollars)	700	not available	5,370	8,480	760	12,230	1,240
Percent of adult population illiterate	56	58	8	48	72	75	40

Among the people who live by raising livestock, movement is a way of life. These people, called nomads, travel with their herds in search of water and grazing land. Nomads follow rather regular routes which are based on the availability of water and grazing land from season to season.

Nomads travel together in family groups. Within each group, some people make wood or metal objects or rugs from the wool of their animals.

During this century, life for many people in north Africa and southwest Asia has changed dramatically. Two of the statistics in the chart on this page measure the total value of the production in a year. The total value of goods produced is called the gross national product (GNP) of a country.

The chart shows figures for each country's total GNP and per capita GNP. Per capita means per person. Libya, Saudi Arabia, and other oil-producing countries have high per capita GNP figures, indicating that the country is wealthy. Their wealth increases their influence in world affairs.

STUDY SKILLS Understanding Geography

1. Name three major features of the landscape of the north African and southwest Asian culture realm.
2. Explain the reasons for three of the names given to the culture realm including north Africa and southwest Asia.
3. Explain the difference between a continent and a culture realm.
4. Explain the meaning of the phrase, the Middle East.
5. Describe the life of nomads.
6. According to the statistics in the chart, what will be the population of Israel by A.D. 2000?
7. Which country listed on the chart has the highest per capita GNP?

CHAPTER 9 *Summary & Review*

Summarizing Main Ideas

Between A.D. 200 and 600, Germanic tribes from the north and Huns from the east frequently attacked the Roman Empire. Rome's cost of protecting the frontiers was high.

The Parthians, unlike the Romans, could defend themselves without high costs. Their lands lay across main trading routes between Europe and China. The Parthians established an efficient system of local self-defense.

The unity of the Roman Empire favored the spread of Christianity within its borders. The religion continued to grow in the years after the empire collapsed.

During the same period, changes were occurring in India. In A.D. 320, Chandra Gupta began a dynasty that led to a Golden Age of Indian achievements in the fields of literature, science, and mathematics.

"I found the old format much more exciting."

Questions for Critical Thinking

COMPREHENSION Interpreting Events

1. In the cartoon, what is meant by "old format"?
2. Explain why the movement of Germanic tribes caused problems in the Roman Empire.
3. Discuss the relationship between the movement of the Germanic tribes and the movements of the Huns.
4. Explain how invasions of the Huns affected the peoples of Eurasia.

APPLICATION Comparing Past to Present

1. Rome faced severe economic problems because of the cost of protecting the empire. List two of these problems. Do modern countries face similar difficulties? Explain.
2. During the period A.D. 200–1000, the economy of northern India was mostly agricultural. Does such an economy seem likely today? Explain.

SYNTHESIS Developing Writing Skills

1. Research and summarize the main points of one of the following: Edict of Milan, Nicene Creed, the rules of Benedict of Nursia.
2. Read Edward Gibbons' description of the invasion of the Huns in *The Decline and Fall of the Roman Empire*. Write a paragraph summary of Gibbons' account.

EVALUATION Weighing Consequences

1. Explain the long-range effect of Diocletian's decision to split the Roman Empire.
2. What was the impact of directives such as the Nicene Creed and the Edict of Milan on the future of Christianity?
3. What effect did the doctrinal disputes have on the Christian Church during the third and fourth centuries A.D.?

CHALLENGE

1. Predict the impact on the culture and government of Rome, had the empire in the west survived another 1,000 years.
2. Why does inflation remain a problem today?

CHAPTER 10
China, Africa, and America Change

GLOBAL TIME LINE

TIME

| A.D. 200 | A.D. 250 | A.D. 300 | A.D. 350 |

300 B.C.–A.D. 300 Olmec ideas influence Middle America

A.D. 200–600 Mayan civilization dominates Middle America

A.D. 304–439 North China divid[ed] into sixteen kingdoms

PEOPLE

A.D. 200–600 Bantu-speaking people migrate into sub-Saharan Africa

A.D. 300–800 Indonesian people settle Madagascar and the eastern coast of Africa

PLACE

A.D. 200–600 *Sub-Saharan Africa;*[1] Bantu-speaking people migrate to sub-Saharan Africa

A.D. 220–586 *South China;*[2] South China ruled by six dynasties

A.D. 250–600 *Yucatan Peninsula;*[3] Mayan Empire centered in the Yucatan Peninsula

Linking Past to Present

In America today, only 2 percent of the people in the labor force make their living by farming. Nevertheless, civilization in this country was built on the labor of American farmers and ranchers who opened new land to settlement and fed the urban population.

Between A.D. 200 and 600, civilization expanded for the first time into south China. Peasants dug irrigation channels, greatly expanding the land available for growing crops. In Africa, too, pioneer farmers opened vast new areas to agriculture during this period. In Middle America, farmers who grew corn produced the surpluses that made Mayan civilization possible. In reading about these regions, keep in mind the important role that farmers have always played in building civilization.

Rice fields in the Guangdong Province.

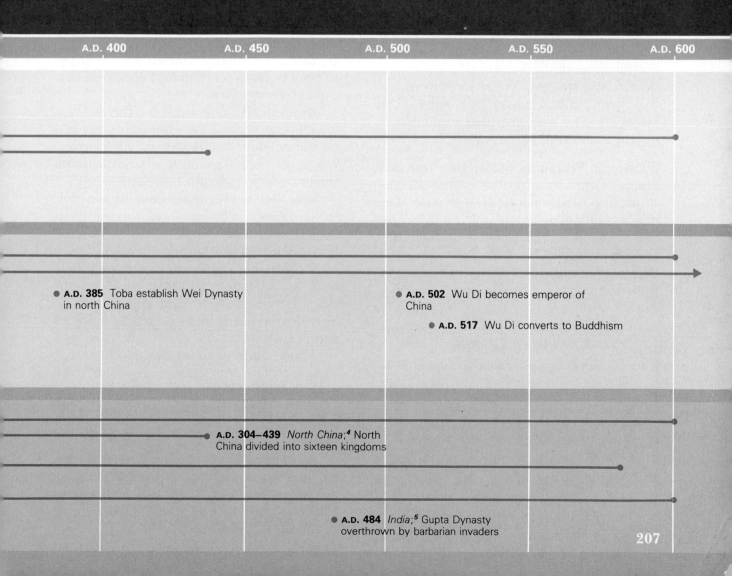

A.D. 400   A.D. 450   A.D. 500   A.D. 550   A.D. 600

● **A.D. 385** Toba establish Wei Dynasty in north China

● **A.D. 502** Wu Di becomes emperor of China

● **A.D. 517** Wu Di converts to Buddhism

● **A.D. 304–439** *North China;*[4] North China divided into sixteen kingdoms

● **A.D. 484** *India;*[5] Gupta Dynasty overthrown by barbarian invaders

207

1 New Ideas in a Divided China

OBJECTIVE: *To understand the causes and consequences of the fall of the Han Dynasty and the effects of Buddhism on Chinese civilization*

Northern China, A.D. 100

The pressure of invaders from the north contributed to the fall of both the Han Empire in China and the Roman Empire in the West. The Romans protected their northern borders along the Rhine and Danube rivers from the barbarians they called Germans. The Chinese built a series of walls to keep out the nomadic barbarians of the northern deserts and steppes. These sections of wall had been united under the ruler, Shi Huangdi. The wall provided some protection against invaders.

Economic Problems of the Han Dynasty.

Some of the same problems that affected Rome also weakened the Han Dynasty. One major problem was economic. The Han, like the Romans, found defense of their long northern frontier increasingly expensive. It became difficult to provide sufficient support to the army.

VOCABULARY DEVELOPMENT

tenant farmer: a person who farms land that someone else owns and pays rent in the form of cash or a share of the crops.

equal field system: the government grants to an individual land that reverts to the government at that person's death; the system prevents the formation of large estates.

collective responsibility system: each individual is held responsible for the conduct of everyone in the group.

By A.D. 100, powerful families who owned large estates controlled Chinese society. The rich landlords placed members of their families in official court posts. These government officials then removed their family names from the tax rolls. Tax evasion was widespread. Even though China's population increased, the government census of the late Han Empire showed fewer people on the tax registers than had appeared in a much earlier census.

Widespread tax evasion by the wealthy forced poor peasant farmers with no political connections to pay very high taxes. When they could no longer pay, peasants tried to escape taxation in several ways.

First, some sold their land to the rich estate owners, who then removed it from the tax registers. These peasants became tenant farmers, working for landlords.

Second, other peasants abandoned their land and became bandits. Some bandit chiefs became so powerful that rich landowners paid them to protect their families and possessions.

Third, some peasants fled south. In the Yangzi valley, they found much undeveloped land where they settled with little fear of government interference. By fleeing south, peasants also escaped the danger of barbarian invasions.

As tax revenue declined, Han rulers found it impossible to pay for the large army needed in the north. They, like the Romans, allowed some of the northern barbarians to settle along their frontier. The Han believed that the settled tribes would provide a screen to protect China from invasion. The plan worked for a while, but the new settlers could not protect China from its own internal civil wars.

Civil War in China. About A.D. 160, the Han emperor faced two crises. Powerful families at the Han court began to fight for power. At about the same time, Chinese peasants rebelled.

One group of peasants called their cause, The Way of the Great Peace. Inspired by Daoist religious ideas, they wore yellow sashes as a badge of unity and called for the end of the Han Dynasty. The name of another group of rebels reflects their membership fee, The Five Pecks of Rice Sect. They also called for an end to the Han Dynasty.

The emperor commanded Han armies to stop the rebellions. The soldiers, however, were more loyal to their generals than to the emperor. Before long, the generals were fighting one another for control of sections of the Han Empire.

The Three Kingdoms of China. By about A.D. 200, China was divided into three kingdoms. In the north was the state of Wei. In the west, a relative of the Han ruled a small kingdom that he called Han. In the Yangzi Valley, to the south, was the state of Wu.

Known as the Three Kingdoms, the states of Wei, Han, and Wu were constantly at war. The period is remembered for political intrigue, battlefield heroism, and treachery. For centuries afterward, Chinese looked back on the Three Kingdoms as one of the most colorful times in all of history. The folktales and legends of the turbulent period are contained in a famous Chinese epic, *Tales of the Three Kingdoms*.

Barbarian Conquests of North China. Without the forces of the Han Empire to hold them back, barbarian tribes invaded north China in great numbers about A.D.

The Kingdoms of China, A.D. 200–304

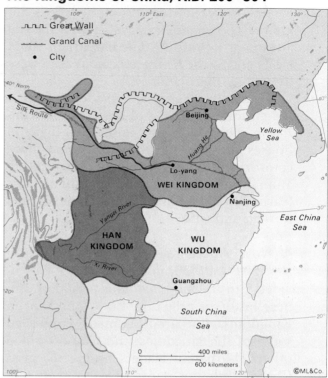

Map Skills **1.** Name the three kingdoms and the area of China which each dominated. **2.** In which kingdom was the Great Wall located?

These sixth-century painted clay figurines of horsemen, warriors, and Chinese civil officials were found in tombs in northern China.

304. The invaders were pastoral nomads who rode fast horses and tended flocks of animals. Their horses gave them a natural advantage in warfare. The barbarians could easily escape the Chinese farmers who were defending their land.

Gradually, barbarian invaders adopted the customs and ideas of the Chinese civilization. The conquerors found that living in houses and wearing silk clothing was more comfortable than living in tents and wearing animal skins. Many of the new inhabitants learned to speak Chinese, and some learned to read and write.

A New Aristocracy Develops. Between A.D. 304 and 439, northern China was divided into 16 kingdoms. This period of Chinese history is called the Era of the Sixteen Kingdoms. Barbarian nomads controlled some of the kingdoms; the Chinese ruled others. Barbarian leaders often employed Chinese administrators able to read and write, to keep records, draw up law codes, and collect taxes. In Chinese-ruled states, the northern newcomers served as generals and soldiers.

The Chinese and their new neighbors sometimes married one another. In this way, a new aristocracy developed that included both Chinese and non-Chinese characteristics. The ruling families, for example, were skilled at riding, archery, and hunting. This new elite formed the core of the ruling aristocracy that would dominate Chinese society between A.D. 600 and 900.

Buddhism Spreads to North China. During the Era of the Sixteen Kingdoms, the former north boundary of China was no longer defended. Nomads, armed bandits, and camel caravans entered and left China freely. Merchants carried Buddhism to communities from Afghanistan to northern China. Buddhist missionaries traveling the Silk Road brought the new religion to China. Buddhism spread throughout northern China for three major reasons.

From an eight-piece series, this silk painting shows the poet Bai Juyi visiting a Buddhist monk.

First, the north frontier of China was no longer defended. Buddhist merchants and missionaries freely traveled throughout northern China. During the political turmoil, the missionaries made many converts.

Second, the chaos that the barbarian invasions and civil wars caused, created a spiritual crisis. The traditional advice of Confucius, which recommended moderation, did not address the needs of the struggling Chinese people. One peasant folksong of the period laments:

❝ Long ago, when we started, the willows spread their shade. Now that we turn back, the snowflakes fly. The march before us is long, we are thirsty and hungry, our hearts are stricken with sorrow but no one listens to our plaint. ❞

Just as the Romans found that Christianity offered hope during a period of chaos and civil disorder, the Chinese discovered the strength of Buddhism. Buddhism taught the Chinese how to become detached from the troubles of the world. Buddhists believed that worldly troubles were only an

illusion. Mahayana Buddhists expected eternal peace through prayers to bodhisattvas [potential Buddhas] who would help them end the chain of reincarnation.

Third, Buddhism spread in northern China because the barbarian rulers welcomed foreign Buddhists at their courts. The Buddhist priests and monks could read and write. The new rulers, who never entirely trusted their Chinese officials, employed Buddhists to balance the influence of the Chinese. Over the next four centuries, Buddhism as it developed in China came to differ from Buddhism in India.

Chinese Travel to India

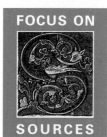

FOCUS ON SOURCES

Efforts of the Chinese to get correct knowledge and true images of Buddha led several Chinese pilgrims to travel to India. One such traveler, Fa Xian (FAH shuh EHN), left China in A.D. 399 and returned home 15 years later. In his "crabbed and difficult style," Fa Xian described some of the lands he passed through.

" In this desert [the Gobi Desert north of China], there are a great many evil spirits and hot winds. Those who encounter the latter perish to a man. There are neither birds above nor beasts below. Gazing on all sides, as far as the eye can reach, in order to mark the track, it would be impossible to succeed but for the rotting bones of dead men which point the way. . . .

This country [Sri Lanka, an island southeast of India] had originally no inhabitants; only devils and spirits and dragons lived in it, with whom the merchants of neighboring countries came to trade. When the exchange of commodities took place, the devils and spirits did not appear in person, but set out their valuables with the prices attached. Then the merchants, according to prices, bought the things and carried them off. But from the merchants going backwards and forwards and stopping on their way, the attractions of the place became known to the inhabitants of the neighboring countries, who also went there, and thus it became a great nation. The temperature is very agreeable in this country; there is no distinction of summer and winter. The trees and plants are always green, and cultivation of the soil is carried on as men please, without regard to seasons. " ∎

The Toba of Northern Wei

Some of the most important changes in northern China took place under a non-Chinese dynasty, the Toba. Between A.D. 385 and 534, the Toba, a tribe of northern barbarians, established a new state called Wei. In just over 50 years, the Toba conquered all of northern China and established the Northern Wei Dynasty. This dynasty illustrates the way Chinese and non-Chinese interacted in the north.

The culture of Wei combined elements of Chinese civilization and barbarian customs. The barbarians became soldiers, while educated Chinese became advisers at the

These drawings depict Chinese innovations: the chain pump used to irrigate rice paddies, the millstone used for grinding, and the silk weaving loom powered by a foot treadle.

court. Before long, the Toba found themselves defending northern China against other central Asian peoples. As part of that defense, they reconstructed part of the Great Wall, which had fallen into disrepair.

The Equal Field System.

In administering the new state, the Chinese made several important contributions. First, they established the equal field system. In this system, the government gave grants of land to families. Generally, a husband and wife would be given 140 units of land (almost 20 acres).

When the person to whom the land was granted died, the land went back to the government for reassignment. Thus, the land was publicly owned. In the equal field system, everyone worked, the government raised tax revenue, and land could not be combined into great estates.

The Collective Responsibility System.

The second major contribution of the Wei was the collective responsibility system. This system made people responsible for one another's behavior, kept order, and raised taxes.

Every five families were organized into a neighborhood. Five neighborhoods made up a village, and five villages made up an association. Every neighborhood had a chief, as did every village and association. Each of these three chiefs was responsible for collecting taxes and checking people's conduct. The whole group was responsible to the government. Thus, if one family did not pay its taxes, all five families were held responsible. The same was true if someone committed a crime.

In such a collective responsibility system, all the people watch their neighbors and put pressure on other members to behave properly. This system has been widely used in China, even in modern times.

As time went on, Chinese advisers increased their influence on Toba rulers. The Toba dressed in Chinese clothing, followed Chinese marriage customs, and even used Chinese names. When the Toba were ordered to give up their native language in favor of Chinese, though, they revolted and the Northern Wei state collapsed. Nevertheless, Toba rule was an outstanding example of the cultural combination of civilized people and barbarians in one state.

Southern China

Conditions in southern China were much more stable than those in the north. Between A.D. 220 and 589, six dynasties ruled the south portion of China. All of the dynasties were related to the Han, and all had their capitals at Nanjing.

About A.D. 200, when the north was invaded, more than half of the wealthy families fled to the south. As many as 2 million people made the trip south to the Yangzi valley. The northern refugees caused great changes in the south. They were better educated than the people already living there.

The wealthy refugees from the north bought land and carried on the way of life they had previously enjoyed. They preserved Chinese literature and learning. They also dominated the court at Nanjing. All their efforts to regain control of the north, however, failed.

Advantages of the Yangzi Valley. South China was a region of great potential. The Yangzi region was warmer than northern China and received more rainfall. The short growing season in north China favored crops such as wheat and millet. In the south, however, the land, climate, and water supply were favorable for growing rice.

In the longer growing season of the south, two or even three rice crops could be grown on the same land. Abundant rice production allowed the population of the south to grow rapidly. By A.D. 600, the south had grown wealthier and more densely populated than the north.

Between A.D. 200 and 600, China went from a civilization united under an emperor, to a group of rival states. In addition, assim-

ilation of some customs of the barbarian invaders changed the earlier Chinese culture. Many peasants left north China and migrated south. During the same period, another major migration of people was occurring in Africa south of the Sahara.

Early Chinese Dynasties	
Dynasty	**Dates**
Legendary Hsia	2000 B.C.–1500 B.C.
Shang	1500 B.C.–1000 B.C.
Chou	1000 B.C.– 221 B.C.
Qin	221 B.C.– 206 B.C.
Han	206 B.C.– 220 A.D.

SECTION 1 *Study Skills*

Developing Vocabulary Use each of the following terms in a sentence that describes the production of food: **1.** tenant farmer. **2.** equal field system. **3.** collective responsibility system.

Reviewing Main Ideas **1.** How were the problems of the Han Dynasty and those of Rome similar? **2.** List two ways in which Chinese peasants could escape taxation. **3.** Describe two ways that north China influenced invaders. **4.** List and explain three contributions of the Toba.

Understanding Geography **1.** Locate the area in China that faced the greatest risk of invasion. **2.** Identify the Three Kingdoms in China. Where were they located?

Understanding Chronology **1.** What date marks the fall of the Han Empire? **2.** When did the Toba start the Wei Dynasty?

Understanding Cause and Effect **1.** The Han emperor expected his armies to suppress rebellion. Why was he wrong? **2.** Explain the three reasons why Buddhism spread throughout northern China.

Challenge Give two examples of collective responsibility in the modern world.

2 People on the Move in Africa

OBJECTIVE: *To understand the causes and consequences of the spread of iron technology and agriculture throughout Africa between* A.D. *200 and 600*

Geography of Africa

Between A.D. 200 and 600, when Christianity and Buddhism were gaining new converts, African people were migrating over broad areas of their continent. As the last Ice Age ended, Africa's climate changed, forcing people to migrate in search of food. The diversity of Africa's topography, or landforms, and climate dramatically influenced this movement of people.

The Challenge of the Land. The enormous size of Africa, the world's second-largest continent in area, was a key factor in its history. The continent's 11.5 million square miles is more than triple the area of the entire United States including the states of Alaska and Hawaii.

Africa is divided into several zones of contrasting climate and vegetation. The map, Africa A.D. 600, page 215, shows the pattern of these zones. On both the south and north coasts of Africa, are strips of fertile land. Both rainfall and temperatures are moderate. These lands, however, quickly give way to vast deserts: the Kalahari (KAH lah HAH ree) and Namib in the south, and the even larger Sahara in the north. Bordering the deserts are narrow bands of open grassland or lightly wooded lands called savannas. At the equator, a large tropical rain forest sprawls across nearly 1 million square miles of Africa.

This pattern of zones is not perfectly regular. In some places, high plateaus or mountain ranges rise above the surrounding lands. Here the climate is cooler than at lower altitudes. The Ruwenzori mountain range, for example, soars over 16,500 feet and is always capped with snow and ice.

As African people migrated in search of food, they faced the challenge of adapting their way of life to the varying climate features. The natural environment greatly influenced when, where, and how migratory movements took place.

African Migrations

Between 16,000 B.C. and 8000 B.C., the climate of Africa was different. The Sahara and the savannas were lush and green. Later, the rivers slowly dried up and the vegetation died. As food became scarcer and

---

VOCABULARY DEVELOPMENT

topography (tuh PAHG ruh fee) *noun:* the surface features of a region, including rivers, lakes, and such manmade features as roads and bridges.

nutrient (NOO tree uhnt) *noun:* a nourishing substance that aids growth.

leach *verb:* to dissolve out, to remove nutrients.

tributary (TRIHB yoo TAIR ee) *noun:* a stream or river flowing into a larger one.

cocoyam (KOH koh yam) *noun:* a yam grown in cacao (cocoa) groves.

---

life more difficult, people left their home-lands in search of food and a more favorable environment. Some traveled north to the lands around the Mediterranean Sea. Others, who settled in the fertile land along the Nile, eventually developed Egyptian civilization and the kingdoms of Nubia and later Kush. Still others moved southward toward the savanna and the forest.

Africa South of the Sahara. Africa south of the Sahara (sub-Saharan Africa) is immense. The land below the Sahara measures 3,500 miles from north to south and, at its narrow southern end, 2,000 miles from east to west.

Sub-Saharan Africa contains wide grasslands. The soil of these lands, however, is not fertile. African farmers of the savannas and forests have always had to combat intense heat and heavy rains that strip nutrients from the soil.

The Sahara Desert.

Africa, A.D. 600

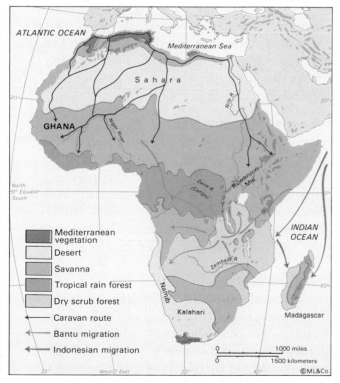

Mediterranean vegetation
Desert
Savanna
Tropical rain forest
Dry scrub forest
Caravan route
Bantu migration
Indonesian migration

Map Skills 1. Name the major rivers that flow through Sub-Saharan Africa. **2.** What direction is Indonesia from southeastern Africa?

A savanna in Kenya.

A rainforest in Ghana.

Most of the broad rivers of sub-Saharan Africa wander gently for hundreds of miles through the interior of the continent. These rivers are natural channels for trade and migration. However, swamps or waterfalls usually block entry to the rivers from the coasts and limit their use.

The People of Sub-Saharan Africa. Even though the earliest human societies almost certainly developed in Africa, the area south of the Sahara Desert was sparsely populated 2,000 years ago. Only a few areas supported farming peoples living in large villages. These areas were the Upper Nile Valley (the modern nation of Sudan), the Ethiopian Highlands along the coast of the Red Sea, and the savanna country of west and central Africa just south of the Sahara.

Everywhere else south of the Sahara, people lived in small communities scattered over huge areas. In the highlands of east Africa, small groups of people raised cattle and grew a few food crops. Bands of hunters and gatherers still lived in the tropical rain forests of west Africa and the Zaire (Congo) River basin. They used stone tools and probably did not grow crops. Other hunting, gathering, and cattle-keeping people lived from the southern savanna zone to the tip of the continent.

During the last thousand years B.C., farmers of the Upper Nile Valley, Ethiopia, and the west African savanna lands learned how to smelt iron. People using iron tools and weapons became more skilled farmers and hunters. In west Africa, where farmers grew millet, rice, and sorghum, crop production expanded, population increased, and villages grew larger.

The Development of Early Kingdoms. Social class differences began to distinguish privileged families of chiefs from the common people living in these villages. Historians believe that during the first 500 years A.D., the earliest kingdoms began to form in the savanna lands of west Africa.

Bushmen, living on the Kalahari, walk home from their waterhole. Their intimate understanding of nature helps these hunter-gatherers survive.

As in ancient Egypt and Mesopotamia, early west African states developed the belief that kings were sacred. The people's prosperity depended on a king who performed special religious rituals.

Africans Migrate South. As population increased, some people began to look for new lands to settle. Africans found difficult alternatives: to the north was the parched Sahara; to the south was a dense tropical rain forest. Migrating people chose to meet the challenge of the rain forest. There, however, the soil was poor. The high rainfall, more than 8 feet a year, leached the nutrients from the soil.

Bands of pioneers who pushed into the forest found that they could not grow their usual crops of millet and other savanna grains. Livestock, sickened by tropical diseases, could not thrive in the rain forests. To survive, early settlers burned clearings in the forest and planted tropical vegetables. They also fished along the numerous rivers.

Some people may have traveled quickly from the Sahara through the rain forests in canoes. The Zaire River and its tributaries provided natural routes for crossing the forest zone from north to south. Small groups of settlers probably reached the savanna country south of the rain forest sometime in the early centuries A.D. Here they could again grow familiar cereal grains.

Uncovering Early African History. The names and exact routes of these early migrants remain a mystery. The people of sub-Saharan Africa had no written languages and so left no written records. Historians are working to piece together information on the routes these pioneers used.

To reconstruct the history of early Africa, historians must rely mainly on two kinds of evidence. One is archaeological. Ancient village sites and cemeteries have been excavated in various regions of sub-Saharan Africa. Archaeologists have found stone and iron tools, copper ornaments, pieces of pottery, and beads. After dating, analyzing, and carefully comparing these artifacts, historians try to determine the way of life of the people who used them.

Language provides the other major clue to population movements in Africa. Historians study and compare the structure and vocabulary of languages spoken in Africa today. They use maps to plot the locations in Africa where basic words have the same or similar sounds. Examples of basic words are god, king, banana, canoe. Using these techniques, historians try to interpret when and by what route a language spread from one region to another.

Migrations of the Bantu. From the study of languages, historians discovered that the African peoples advancing into the southern half of the continent spoke languages of the Bantu family. The Bantu family of languages includes more than 400 languages.

Historians do not know whether the earliest farming people who moved from the savannas into the forests spoke Bantu. They do know, however, that Bantu-speaking groups of people gradually spread over central and southern Africa during the first thousand years A.D. They did not invade like the Huns who galloped across Eurasia. Rather, communities of farmers or cattle raisers drifted slowly southward, seeking new lands. This gradual movement is one of the major migrations in human history.

As the Bantu-speaking people advanced, they gradually replaced the original inhabitants. Today, the descendants of pre-Bantu inhabitants of central and southern Africa can be found only in remote areas. These descendants include the Pygmy communities living in the deep forests of Zaire and the Bushmen of the Kalahari Desert in south Africa and Namibia.

Bantu Peoples Develop Complex Societies. As Bantu-speaking societies grew, they became more complex. Archaeologists working in the southern part of Zaire, at a place called Sanga, uncovered a huge cemetery used between the seventh and ninth centuries A.D. Objects buried with the people show that the inhabitants of Sanga hunted, fished, and farmed. They produced both iron and copper implements, and built sturdy furniture. Many of the people wore beautiful copper jewelry. They also carried on trade with people along the coast of the Indian Ocean.

Historians have not been able to tell whether Sanga had a centralized government. An aristocracy of ruling families or wealthy traders may have existed. Historians do know, however, that within a few centuries, Bantu-speaking kingdoms began to appear in many parts of central and southern Africa.

Migrants from Across the Sea

Another migration, of an entirely different kind, also had an important impact on early African history. Between A.D. 300 and 800,

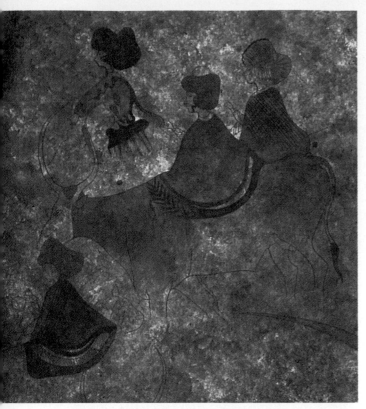

Saharan women ride horned oxen as they move their camp. This painting reflects the elegance and status that women held among the early Saharan cultures.

people from the islands of Indonesia, in Southeast Asia, sailed across the Indian Ocean toward Africa. A study of languages shows that communities of these explorers settled on the great island of Madagascar, off the coast of east Africa. Malagasy, the principal language of Madagascar, is related to the languages of Indonesia but not to Bantu or any other African language.

These newcomers brought food plants from the humid forests of Indonesia. They probably also brought iron tools and weapons. With these aids they built a flourishing farming society on Madagascar.

No evidence has been found to show that the Indonesian migrants also settled along the east coast of Africa. Nevertheless, the Indonesian food plants such as bananas, Asian yams, and cocoyams were somehow introduced to the mainland.

These new crops, which thrived in the tropical forests of west and central Africa, spread quickly among Bantu-speaking peoples. As a result, the tropical forestlands could now support a much larger population of farming people than before. The appearance of more complex societies, and eventually of large kingdoms, in the forest zone was related to the spread of the crops from Indonesia.

By A.D. 600, the African continent, from the tropical forest south, was more heavily populated than it had been at the time of Christ. The region was ready for important developments in trade, town-building, and the establishment of kingdoms.

African advancements occurred without the advantage of much contact with the civilizations of Eurasia. Across the Atlantic, in the Western Hemisphere, people had no contact with Eurasia or Africa. The people of Middle America, however, created a thriving civilization in the early centuries A.D.

SECTION 2 *Study Skills*

Developing Vocabulary Use each of the following terms in a sentence: **1.** topography. **2.** nutrient. **3.** leach. **4.** tributary. **5** cocoyam.

Reviewing Main Ideas **1.** What main advantage did the people of west Africa have over other areas in Africa? **2.** Describe two difficulties that faced Africans who migrated to the tropical rain forests. **3.** Describe the two ways in which historians reconstruct early African history. **4.** Identify the approximate number of Bantu languages. **5.** What is significant about the way in which the Bantu took over central and southern Africa? **6.** Why were the food plants brought to Africa by Indonesian immigrants so important?

Understanding Geography **1.** Describe the main climatic zones of Africa. **2.** Describe the topography of sub-Saharan Africa. **3.** What areas are best for farming in Africa? **4.** Where in Africa did the first large kingdoms develop?

Challenge Well over 100 major languages still exist in modern Africa. What problems might this diversity cause for countries in Africa?

The Changing Value of Oil

African farmers learned to make iron tools during the last thousand years B.C. The eventual economic consequence was increased farm production. This increase in food supported a larger population. That in turn encouraged the development of the first kingdoms. The development of the automobile, some 3000 years later, also had far reaching economic consequences.

North Africa and southwest Asia have two-thirds of the oil resources known to exist in the world. The wealth from oil production has reshaped many of the countries in the region.

Development of the Oil Industry

For most of human history, people did not consider oil an important natural resource. For thousands of years, the enormous oil resources of north Africa and southwest Asia had no trade value. Although oil could be burned, wood and coal were more popular for heating purposes. Wood was especially popular as a heating fuel because it was cheap and found nearly everywhere.

In the middle 1800s, people began to burn kerosene, a fuel made from oil, in lamps. Not until the development of the automobile, around 1900, did demand for oil increase sharply.

The rapid growth in demand for oil encouraged exploration for new reserves. The first large oil reserves in the Middle East were found in Iran in 1908.

Types of Resources. Oil is a nonrenewable resource. Nonrenewable resources are those that cannot be replaced quickly by nature. The oil people use today was formed during the age of the dinosaurs.

Wood is an example of a renewable resource. When one tree is cut down, another can take its place. People can learn to manage tree farms so that the supply of wood is constantly being renewed.

International Trade and OPEC

Although north Africa and southwest Asia hold most of the world's known oil, people in the region use relatively little oil. Car ownership is not common in this region. The average number of persons per car in the United States is 1.8, in the world generally 13, and in Iran 31. The number is calculated by dividing total population figures by total car figures.

Industrialized nations use the greatest quantities of oil. Together, the United States, Canada, Europe, and the Soviet Union use about 60 percent of the world's annual oil consumption. The countries of north Africa and southwest Asia trade their surplus oil to the more industrialized nations. This trade brings money to the oil-producing countries.

In 1961, 5 oil-producing nations joined together to create OPEC, the Organization

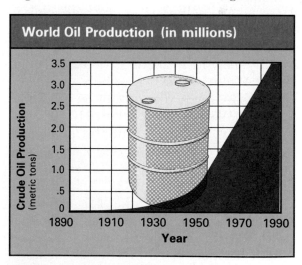

World Oil Production (in millions)

Crude Oil Production (metric tons)

3.5 / 3.0 / 2.5 / 2.0 / 1.5 / 1.0 / .5 / 0

1890 / 1910 / 1930 / 1950 / 1970 / 1990

Year

Members of OPEC

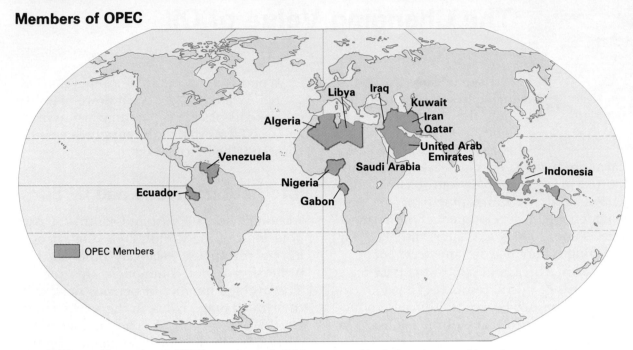

Map Skills **1.** Name the 13 OPEC members. **2.** Oil imports to North America are shipped over a vast distance. What is the most direct route between the Middle East and North America?

of Petroleum Exporting Countries. Today, OPEC has 13 members. In the Islamic region these are: Algeria, Iran, Iraq, Kuwait, Libya, Qatar, Saudi Arabia, and the United Arab Emirates. OPEC also includes two South American nations, Ecuador and Venezuela, and two African nations, Gabon and Nigeria. The 13th member of OPEC is the Asian nation of Indonesia. By withholding their oil from the world market, OPEC succeeded in raising the price of oil from $3.00 a barrel in 1973 to about $34.00 a barrel in 1982. When OPEC members compete, rather than agree, the price of oil can come down. In 1986 the price fell to $10.00.

OPEC is a cartel, a group of producers who joined together to control the price, production, and sale of oil. Cartels are illegal in many countries.

The revenue from the sale of oil increased the wealth of several nations in north Africa and southwest Asia. This wealth has been used in a variety of ways.

Saudi Arabia and Kuwait modernized their cities, created jobs, and raised the standard of living for most people. In some nations, however, poor management of the wealth has prevented significant improvements in the overall quality of life for their citizens.

Since the early 1980s, the price of oil has declined. Despite this decline, oil continues to be a major source of income for many nations in north Africa and southwest Asia.

STUDY SKILLS Understanding Geography

1. Explain the difference between renewable and nonrenewable resources.
2. Are there any similarities in climate and land forms of the OPEC countries?
3. Why was oil not considered to be a valuable natural resource for most of human history?
4. Suggest three different developments that could decrease the need for oil produced in north Africa and southwest Asia.
5. Which of the leading oil-producing countries are members of OPEC?

3 The Age of Mayan Civilization in America

OBJECTIVE: *To understand how the Mayans adapted elements of the Olmec culture and built an advanced civilization*

Origins of Mayan Civilization

From A.D. 200 to 600, while the Han Empire was falling and Bantu-speaking people were spreading throughout sub-Saharan Africa, a complex civilization flourished in the Western Hemisphere. Spanish explorers traveling through Middle America in the 1500s found evidence of the civilization. They discovered magnificent ruins in the jungles of the Yucatan (YOO Kah TAHN) Peninsula.

One Spaniard described them:

" . . . in all the discoveries in the Indies none so fine has been found. Buildings of big and well-carved stones—there is no record of who built them. **"**

The Spanish explorers believed the ancestors of the Indians living in the area had built them.

The Mayan civilization still fascinates archaeologists, travelers, and historians. Named after the Indians who now inhabit the area, the Mayan civilization flourished and then mysteriously disappeared. Archaeologists have uncovered much information about the Mayans, but much more remains to be discovered. The hieroglyphic symbols carved on Mayan buildings and stone slabs are not yet completely understood.

Olmec Influence. Geography isolated the peoples of Middle America from the interacting community of Eurasia and the Mediterranean Basin. Middle Americans shared, however, a common culture influenced by the earlier Olmecs. Between 300 B.C. and A.D. 300, Olmec ideas formed the basis of civilizations in Middle America.

The society of the Mayans, like that of the Olmecs, developed around ceremonial centers that became true cities. Mayans built temples, palaces, and official buildings as centers for religious ceremonies. Most of the people, however, lived in rural areas. Like the Olmecs, the Mayans played a ball game on stone courts.

Early Mayan History. By 300 B.C., the population of the Yucatan Peninsula had begun to expand rapidly. The people of the area built enormous pyramids. By about A.D. 250, the Mayans were using hieroglyphic symbols. This time marks the beginning of the great age of Mayan civilization.

VOCABULARY DEVELOPMENT

stelae (STEE lee) *noun:* upright slabs or stone pillars containing an inscription or carved design. From the Greek word, *stele*, meaning slab or pillar.

glyph (glihf) *noun:* a carved symbol; a hieroglyph. From the Greek word, *glyphein*, meaning to carve or cut out.

metate (may TAH tay) *noun:* a stone with a flat or concave surface used with a smaller stone called a *mano* to grind corn into flour.

sedan chair *noun:* a covered chair mounted on poles and carried by two people.

The Land of the Mayans. The Mayans lived around a number of ceremonial centers built in the jungle areas of the Yucatan Peninsula in the present countries of Mexico and Guatemala. The region the Mayans inhabited contained two kinds of land— highlands and lowlands. The highlands were made up of a series of steep ridges. The tops and sides of the ridges were the only lands suitable for farming. Those slopes were well drained so that water ran off during the rainy season.

The valleys between the ridges became swamps where water collected during the rainy weather. Temperatures ranged between 80 and 90 degrees Fahrenheit during the day and dropped into the 70s at night. Humidity was very high, especially during the rainy season. Clothes not aired in the sun were soon covered with green mold.

Mayan Agriculture. Rain forests covered much of Middle America. As in tropical Africa, the soil, stripped of nutrients by the rains, wore out quickly when the forest was cleared. Mayan farmers, like their modern descendants, used slash-and-burn agriculture. They cut down trees and burned all the natural vegetation from the land they intended to farm.

After two years of cultivation, fields had to be abandoned because the soil was already worn out. The land could not be farmed again for 7 to 10 years. Because of the poor quality of the soil, enormous amounts of land were required to support a large population.

Recently, archaeologists have discovered how the Mayans probably increased their food supply. They ate nuts from the breadfruit trees and many snails and mollusks from the swamps. However, these sources of food were still insufficient.

Airborne radar photography has identified another source of food production. Radar images show that the Mayans drained huge areas of low, swampy land to create raised fields that could be permanently cul-

The ancient ruins of Tikal have been restored to highlight the towering Temple of the Jaguar. This great plaza was once the center of a Mayan metropolis covering 50 square miles.

tivated. The lowlands were also unusually fertile because soil nutrients collected in the valleys. Raised fields may have been the crucial technique that allowed the Mayans to produce the agricultural surplus needed to support civilization.

Mayan Centers. Mayan society differed dramatically from the societies that existed at the same time in Eurasia. The Mayan city of Tikal (ti KAHL) had none of the bustling crowds that characterized, for example, Constantinople. Instead, most Mayans lived in small villages. Tikal, over 6 square miles in area, probably had a population of only 10,000 people.

The most impressive buildings in Tikal were the five temple pyramids built over the tombs of rulers. Pyramids were built by covering great earth mounds with stone blocks. At the tops of the pyramids were small, dark temples. Often, several pyramids faced one another around an open plaza. Stone slabs with carvings and hieroglyphic inscriptions stood in the plazas near the temples. A ball court, long buildings with many rooms, and a sweatbath were the other buildings.

The major groups of buildings were connected by wide, elevated roads with white plaster surfaces. Surrounding this impressive center were miles of smaller temples, palaces, and suburbs. Thousands of people filled the plazas on ceremonial days.

Mayan Religion. Historians do not yet fully understand the Mayan religion. They know that the Mayans worshiped a number of nature gods. One Mayan manuscript mentioned more than 160 gods. Many of the Mayan gods were similar to those worshiped by the Olmecs and other people of Middle and South America. The jaguar rain god appeared in many carvings.

Each day of the Mayan year had special religious importance, and religious festivals in honor of particular gods took place throughout the year. Priests played an important role in religious ceremonies and probably made up an aristocratic class. The priests performed the cycle of rituals and ceremonies required to please the gods.

The Mayans also observed special ceremonies when burying their dead. The corpses were painted red and wrapped in straw mats along with some of their personal belongings. They were buried under the floors of the houses in which they had lived. Mayan rulers and important persons were buried in their finest clothes within the pyramids. As in the Sumerian culture, servants were killed and buried with important people, along with jewelry and utensils.

Mayan Society. The Mayans were divided into several specialized classes. Nobles, who lived in the centers, wore elaborate clothes and jewelry. Their daily life was portrayed in murals.

Lower down the Mayan social scale were specialized groups, such as scribes, potters, and entertainers. Most of the people were at the lowest level of society, working as laborers or farmers. Each occupation appears to have been hereditary, and people could rarely move from their social class.

Mayan Hieroglyphics. To observe special occasions, Mayans erected large, carved slabs of stone called stelae (STEE lee). For centuries no one was able to read the hieroglyphic inscriptions on the stelae, temples, and few surviving manuscripts. Only since 1960 have historians begun to decipher the writing. The inscriptions have helped to better understand the Mayans.

Stelae were erected by the rulers of such centers as Tikal to commemorate important events of their reign. A king who passed his power on to his descendants ruled each of the great Mayan centers. Mayan kings, like those of ancient Sumer and Egypt, claimed to be associated with the gods. Rulers of the centers often were related to one another by marriage. Several of the stelae also show powerful women who may have been rulers of Mayan cities.

Cultural Centers of the Americas, A.D. 600

Map Skills **1.** Name the two bodies of water which border the Yucatan Peninsula. **2.** In which hemisphere is the Yucatan Peninsula located?

A New Mayan King

FOCUS ON

PEOPLE

Even though Mayan writing is not fully understood, enough can be deciphered to picture some events that occurred in Mayan cities. In their book, *The Mysterious Maya*, archaeologists George E. and Gene S. Stuart tried to recapture some of the events that occurred in the Mayan city of Tikal on May 8, A.D. 682, when a new king was installed. The names of the two rulers discussed, Stormy Sky and Double-Comb, have been derived from their name glyphs. A sky symbol, surmounted by a long-nosed god with arms extended and a curious smoking object in his forehead, was translated as Stormy Sky.

❝ The eastern horizon slowly reddens as Lord Sun prepares once again to emerge triumphant from his underworld passage. From the house compounds and the clusters of modest pole-and-thatch dwellings begin the sounds of dawn-barking dogs and the rhythmic click of *mano* stones against *metates* as women begin grinding breadnuts for the day's tortillas. The acrid smoke of wood cook fires hazes the clearing as men, shadowy forms in the half light, begin the long walk to their fields. . . .

Downtown, Lord Sun lifts majestically above the treetops and illuminates the sides of brightly painted temples in the North Acropolis. Nearby, just inside the doorway of a red stucco-covered building, an elderly priest sits on a wooden stool before a low cedar table. The coarse matting of the door-curtain has been tied to one side to let the morning light in. . . .

Today, the old man has already calculated, Lord Sun has completed 1,386,000 passages to reach the Long Count date of 9.12.10.0.0. . . .

Through auspicious fortune, Double-Comb [the new king] had been able to arrange the date of his accession to the rule of Tikal precisely 13 katuns—93,600 days—after the inauguration of the great Stormy Sky [the former king].

Maybe now, thought the old priest, the times of trouble would be over. Perhaps, he hoped, the sculptors could even begin carving stelae. None of those now living at Tikal ever had, for the last monument had been erected more than a century ago. . . .

Where the crowd has left an open lane at the west side of the plaza, an attendant raises his hand as he sights Double-Comb's procession. . . .

In the lead come four men with giant parasols made of basketry and bedecked with rare plumage. Others follow with tall banners of blue, red, and yellow cloth. Three subrulers, clad in the jaguar pelt of nobility, bear wooden carvings of the long-nosed god with the serpent foot—insignia of the Sky lineage. Behind them, carefully in step, come the litter bearers. They carry the heavy polished wooden sedan chair roofed with green plumage and holding the young ruler. . . . The head of the procession stops before the North Acropolis stairway, before the red temple that hides the tombs of Stormy Sky and his predecessor. The new ruler is assisted from his sedan chair by two courtiers. . . .

Smoke begins to creep from the dark doorway of the red temple memorializing Double-Comb's distinguished ancestors. Four days ago, as the accession ceremony approached its height, forty men had assembled for an important task. With ropes and log skids, they had hauled the great broken stela depicting Stormy Sky—the monument carved 236 years before—up the staircase and into the rear chamber of the red temple. Now, as the incense smoke pours into view, the crowd knows that the completion of the stela ceremony has confirmed Double-Comb's accession to power. **"** ■

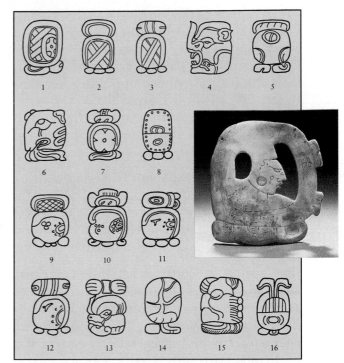

Hieroglyphic symbols represent the eighteenth month of this Mayan calendar. A Mayan shell pendant, inset, represents a day in their calendar.

Mayan Achievements

Historians and archaeologists have also translated enough of the Mayan hieroglyphics to appreciate their achievements in mathematics and astronomy. The Mayans developed a number system based on multiples of the number 20, in contrast to our system based on 10. Bars and dots depicted numbers. A shell-shaped symbol represented zero.

Like our modern number system, the position of the symbol determined its value. This system made addition and subtraction rather easy, and multiplication and division possible. Europeans, in contrast to the Mayans, still used Roman numerals and did not yet use zero.

The Mayan Calendar. The most important Mayan use of the numerical system was in calculating dates. The Mayan calendar was based on a solar year similar to modern calendars. Their calendar was based on 18 months of 20 days plus an unlucky 5-day period. Special omens were associated with each day.

The Mayans also calculated time from a single date, or zero date, in the past, in the way we use B.C. or A.D. These dates, which began in our equivalent of 3114 B.C., were known as the Long Count. The result of all these systems was a complex calendar requiring specialists to do calculations.

Civilizations of Mexico and Peru

In addition to the Mayan civilization, advanced societies also developed in the coastal valley and uplands of Peru and in central Mexico. Around A.D. 500, the Mexican city of Teotihuacán (TAY uh TEE wah KAHN) was an active metropolis and the center of a great empire. In Teotihuacán, the people built giant pyramid temples. Joining the pyramids of the Sun and the Moon was a wide street now called the Avenue of the Dead. Ball courts, a central marketplace, and magnificent palaces existed along with over 2,000 apartment compounds where between 20 and 100 people lived. Crowded slums also stood on the eastern edge of the city. As many as 200,000 people may have lived in Teotihuacán at its height.

Religion in Teotihuacán. Religion in Teotihuacán centered around the worship of a rain god and the feathered serpent, Quetzelcoatl (keht SAHL koh AHT uhl). However, pictures of jaguars were popular here, too.

Civilization in Peru. A separate center of civilization existed from early times in Peru. At the time of the Mayans, the Andean civilization was flourishing along the desert coast, in irrigated river valleys, and in the highlands around Lake Titicaca. The Moche, named for the river valley where they lived, left especially interesting remains.

They built great pyramids of adobe bricks and became accomplished metalworkers. Some of their finest achievements were represented in their pottery. They made pots decorated with modeled figures and paintings that show many of their everyday activities, from soldiers to women carrying their babies on their backs. Other Peruvian people of this time wove beautiful woolen textiles that have been found wrapped around the mummified bodies of their dead.

By about A.D. 600, new states had developed in the highlands of Peru. The ruins of Tiahuanaco (TEE uh wuh NAHK oh), over 10,000 feet high near the shores of Lake Titicaca, include giant sculptures of people and temple complexes. The Peruvian cultures did not use writing, and archaeologists have not studied them as intensively as the Mayans. Little is known about their history. The beauty of their pottery, goldwork, and textiles demonstrates the importance of these civilizations.

The people of the Americas lacked several elementary devices that were important to Eurasian civilizations. The civilizations of the Mayans, Peruvians, and Mexicans all lacked the wheel. The people knew nothing of iron smelting, and they had few domesticated animals. Dogs and the llama of the high Andes in Peru could not make up for the cattle, sheep, horses, camels, donkeys, goats, chickens, and pigs that expanded the resources of the Eurasian people.

In addition, the civilizations of the Western Hemisphere started late when compared with the civilizations of Eurasia and Egypt. They remained behind the older civilizations in skills and knowledge. Nevertheless, these early civilizations illustrate the ability of people to conquer their environment and accomplish great feats.

SECTION 3 *Study Skills*

Developing Vocabulary Describe the Mayan stelae.

Reviewing Main Ideas **1.** What Olmec influences were most important to the Mayans? **2.** Describe Mayan religion. **3.** Describe the three main social classes of the Maya. **4.** Why are stelae important to modern researchers? **5.** In what way were Mayan mathematics more efficient than contemporary European mathematics? **6.** Identify the Long Count. **7.** Discuss two major differences between Eurasian and American civilizations. How did these differences affect the peoples of each civilization?

Understanding Chronology During what years did the Mayan civilization flourish?

Understanding Geography **1.** Explain how the two main geographic features of Mayan lands influenced Mayan society. **2.** What did the Mayans do to get as large a food supply as possible?

Challenge What is the significance of the independent development of American civilizations for countries there today?

CHAPTER 10 *Summary & Review*

Summarizing Main Ideas

Like Rome and India, China underwent numerous changes after A.D. 200. About A.D. 160, the Han Dynasty began to lose control of China. Along with political changes came the growth of Buddhism and the acceptance of new ideas invaders from the North introduced.

Africa's geography has been a challenge to the African people. In the centuries after A.D. 200, African populations increased. Bantu-speaking peoples migrated to populate much of southern Africa. These peoples developed diverse societies. In the Western Hemisphere, the Mayans developed and ruled the Yucatan Peninsula. At the same time another civilization dominated Peru. In general, the civilizations in the Western Hemisphere developed more slowly than Eurasian civilizations. Nevertheless, American civilizations used their environments and resources to produce remarkable achievements.

Interaction of Cultural Influences	
Peoples	**Influence**
China	Indian Buddhism
India	Aryan, Persian, Greek art and ideas
Greece	Mycenean, Minoan, Persian art and ideas
Rome	Greek, Etruscan, Persian, Phoenician, Egyptian arts, skills, and ideas
Sub-Saharan Africa	Indonesian food
Mayan	Olmec architecture and religion
Arabs/Moslems	Bedouin, Judaic, Persian, Greek knowledge and philosophy

Questions for Critical Thinking

COMPREHENSION Interpreting Events

1. Compare and contrast Christianity and Buddhism in their responses to times of distress.
2. Mayan civilization was complex, yet never reached the power and influence of civilizations in Eurasia. What three factors may account for this difference?

APPLICATION Comparing Past to Present

1. Why do areas of early American civilization not exert much influence on world culture today?
2. Explain why civilizations interacting with other cultures seem to grow and become more powerful.

SYNTHESIS Developing Map Skills

1. Draw a map of Eurasia and label the intercommunicating zone. Identify the civilizations that ruled empires.
2. Refer to pages 775–784 and identify the topography and climate of the civilizations discussed in the chapter. What relationship between topography, climate, and civilization is apparent?

EVALUATION Weighing Consequences

1. If Mayan civilization could have been included within the Eurasian intercommunicating zone, what changes probably would have affected both areas?
2. Using the chart, analyze which peoples had a variety of outside influences on their culture and which had few.

CHALLENGE

1. Use three examples to compare and contrast the developments of the Eurasian civilizations with those in the Western Hemisphere.
2. Contrast the influence of religious ideals on the cultures of both India and China between 200 and 600 A.D.

CHAPTER 11
The Rise of Islam

GLOBAL TIME LINE

	A.D. 600	A.D. 625	A.D. 650

TIME

● **A.D. 613** Sassanid Persians invade Syria and Egypt

A.D. 644–656 Arabs conquer Egypt and much of the Middle East

PEOPLE

● **A.D. 570** Muhammad is born in Mecca

A.D. 623–628 Byzantine Emperor, Heraclius, successfully resists the Persians

● **A.D. 632** Muhammad dies; Abu Bakr chosen Caliph

PLACE

● **A.D. 628** *Persia;*[1] Persian capital of Ctesiphon temporarily occupied by the Byzantines

A.D. 634–644 *Mesopotamia;*[2] Arabs conquer Mesopotamia

Linking Past to Present

Islam is the youngest of the major world religions. Like Judaism and Christianity, Islam is a monotheistic religion; its followers profess the belief in one God.

Followers of the Islamic religion are called Muslims, or Moslems. Today, more than 800 million people, about one-fifth of the world's population, are Muslims. Between 2 and 3 million Muslims live in the United States.

During the seventh century A.D., the commitment of Arabs to spread the Islamic religion enabled them to create a large empire. The rise of Islam created a new civilization that dominated the history of much of Eurasia and Africa up to the sixteenth century. As you read the chapter, consider how the religion of Islam differs from Christianity and Judaism.

Pilgrims to Mecca walk around the Kaaba, honoring this symbol of the one God.

A.D. 675   A.D. 700   A.D. 725   A.D. 750

A.D. 661–750 Umayyad Dynasty rules the Islamic Empire

A.D. 716 Arab armies conquer Lisbon

A.D. 680 Islam splits between Sunni and Shi'ite Muslims

A.D. 661 Caliph Mu'auiyya establishes the Umayyad Dynasty

A.D. 693 Byzantine Emperor, Justinian II, defeated by Arabs

A.D. 732 Charles Martel defeats the Arabs and ends their westward advance

A.D. 712 Muhammad ibn Kasim establishes a Muslim state in India

A.D. 670 *North Africa;*[3] Muslims begin conquest of north Africa

A.D. 711 *Iberian Peninsula;*[4] Arabs conquer the Iberian Peninsula

A.D. 732 *Gaul;*[5] Franks defeat the Arabs and end Islamic expansion in western Europe

1 *The Beginnings of Islam*

OBJECTIVE: *To understand the causes and consequences of the development of the Islamic religion*

Islam's Foundations

During the seventh century A.D., Arabic-speaking people forged an empire that extended from Spain to the frontiers of China. Like the Germans and Huns, who attacked the Roman Empire in the fourth and fifth centuries, the Arabs invaded Persia and the Byzantine Empire. Unlike the Huns and Germans, however, the Arabs were unified by their new religion, Islam.

Before the Arab invasions, two large civilizations dominated the western third of the interacting zone. One was the Byzantine Empire. The other was the Persian Empire ruled by the Sassanid Dynasty.

VOCABULARY DEVELOPMENT

sect (sehkt) *noun:* a religious denomination, a faction.

Orthodox (AWR thuh dahks) **Christianity** *noun:* official religion of the Byzantine Empire. From the Greek words *orthos,* meaning correct and *doxa,* meaning opinion.

Monophysite (muh NAHF uh SYT) **Christian** *noun:* Christian who believes in the single divine nature of Christ, a view commonly held by members of the Coptic church. From the Greek words *monos,* meaning single, and *physis,* meaning nature.

dromedary (DRAHM uh dair ih) *noun:* a swift, one-humped camel of Arabia. From the Greek word, *dromos,* meaning running.

idol (EYE duhl) *noun:* an image, or other object, worshiped as a god. From the Greek word, *eidos,* meaning image.

The Byzantine Empire. In the sixth century, the Byzantine Emperor, Justinian, failed in his attempt to reunify the old Roman Empire. His successors, however, continued to rule the Byzantine Empire. It included Asia Minor, southeastern Europe, Syria, Egypt, and the coast of north Africa as far west as Morocco. The empire also controlled parts of Italy, as well as Sicily, Cyprus, and other major islands in the Mediterranean Sea. See the map, Byzantine and Sassanid Empires, page 231.

The prosperity of the Byzantine Empire depended on agriculture and trade. Constantinople, the capital, was one of the largest cities in the world. By contrast, the former Western Empire was divided into several Germanic kingdoms. Towns in the west declined and were often abandoned. Long distance trade hardly existed.

Problems of the Byzantine Empire. The Byzantines faced two serious problems in the early part of the seventh century. First, the Sassanid Empire of Persia threatened Byzantine lands. In A.D. 613, the Sassanids successfully invaded Syria and Egypt. The Persians even threatened Asia Minor, the heart of the Byzantine Empire. The Byzantine Emperor resisted the Persians. In A.D. 628, Byzantine armies temporarily seized the Persian capital of Ctesiphon. However, 15 years of war between the Byzantines and Persians had exhausted the military power and resources of both empires.

The second great problem the Byzantines faced was the conflict among different groups within the Christian religion. Severe disagreements over church doctrine divided the Christian church between hostile sects, or factions.

The official religion of the Byzantine Empire, called Orthodox Christianity, was dominant among the Greek-speaking people of the empire. The Christians of Syria and Egypt were Monophysites. They believed that the nature of Christ was only divine rather than both human and divine.

The people of Syria spoke mainly Aramaic; the Egyptians spoke Coptic, an Afro-Asian language derived from the ancient Egyptian languages. Neither the Syrians nor the Egyptians felt any loyalty to the Greek-speaking governors and tax collectors who ruled them. Many people throughout the Byzantine Empire resented its power after they were forced to pay more taxes and accept the Orthodox religion. As a result, deep social discontent undermined Byzantine rule in Syria and Egypt.

The Persian Empire. The Sassanid Dynasty ruled the people living on the mountains and plateaus of present-day Iran and Iraq. The dynasty preserved the great traditions of Persian civilization. The capital, Ctesiphon (TEHS ih fahn), was a magnificent city on the banks of the Tigris River. The Sassanids, however, had problems similar to those of their Byzantine enemies.

First, religious conflicts divided the Persians. The ruling class was comprised mostly of followers of Zoroaster. (See page 99.) However, a large Christian minority, especially in Iraq, wanted no part of Zoroastrianism. Second, the long war with the Byzantines financially weakened the Persian government. Third, economic problems caused social unrest. Most Persians were peasants and

Byzantine and Sassanid Empires, A.D. 600–633

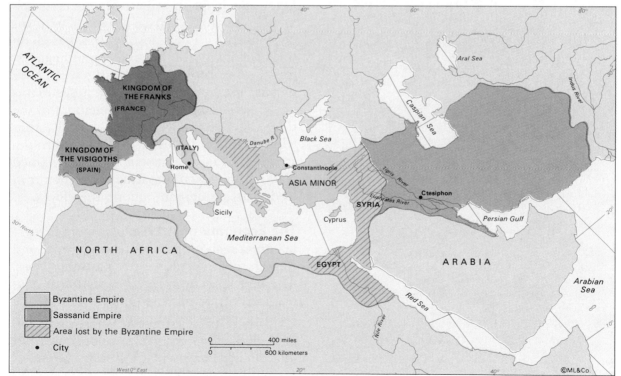

Map key:
- Byzantine Empire
- Sassanid Empire
- Area lost by the Byzantine Empire
- City

0 400 miles
0 600 kilometers

Map Skills **1.** Compare the size of the Byzantine and Sassanid Empires. **2.** In what direction did an Indian merchant travel to reach Egypt?

herders who were taxed heavily and, therefore, resented government oppression. These three problems weakened the Persian Empire and contributed to its decline.

Arabia in the Seventh Century

The Arabian Peninsula lies almost entirely in the arid zone of the Eastern Hemisphere. Arabs in the seventh century adapted to their challenging environment by living either as nomads or in settled communities.

The People of Arabia. The largest group of Arabs lived in the southwest portion of the Arabian Peninsula, a region known as the Yemen. See the map, Arabia, A.D. 600, below. Adequate rainfall and fertile soil in the Yemen enabled many farmers to grow crops. The Yemen was also a link in the trade route extending from the Indian

Arabia, A.D. 600

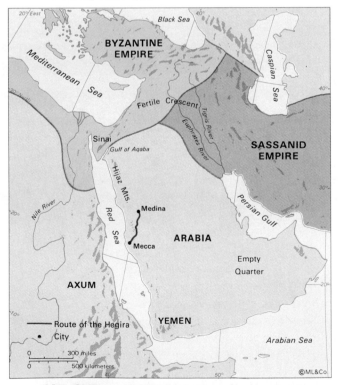

Map Skills 1. Name the bodies of water that border the Arabian Peninsula. 2. What countries now occupy the Arabian Peninsula?

Ocean through the Red Sea to Egypt or Syria. In A.D. 575, the Persians occupied the Yemen and controlled the trade routes. Sassanid power was not entirely secure, however, because of the Yemen's distance from the rulers of Persia.

Other Arabs lived in scattered communities outside the Yemen where water was available from springs and wells. Two important cities, Mecca and Medina, were located in the Hijaz (HEH jaz). The Hijaz is a hilly region extending along the western length of the peninsula parallel to the Red Sea coast.

The nomadic people of Arabia lived by herding dromedaries and trading. Nomads inhabited the central plateau of the peninsula where just enough rain fell to provide pastureland part of the year. They also traveled along the fringes of an area called the Empty Quarter, a vast sand desert that spread over southeastern Arabia.

Tribal Society. The people of the Arabian Peninsula lived in tribes. Members developed loyalty to their tribe instead of to towns or countries. Their loyalty was based on their belief that they shared common ancestors. For example, in Arabic the word *banu* means "the people of" or "the descendants of." If an Arab said he was a member of the tribe called Banu Nadir, he and all other tribe members believed that they were descended from an ancient ancestor named Nadir. Members of the tribe chose their own leaders by agreement among the elders.

The Economy of Arabia. Farmers in Arabia grew such crops as dates and grain, and traded their surplus with pastoral tribes. The best known products of southern Arabia were frankincense and myrrh. Made from plant juices, frankincense and myrrh were in great demand in the Middle East as incense, perfume, and medicine.

In the larger communities of the Yemen and the Hijaz, many people were merchants and traders. Arabian traders bought and sold luxury goods brought to the Yemen by ship from India and China. Some Arab traders led camel caravans from the Yemen north to the cities and towns of Egypt, Syria, and Mesopotamia. One center of trade along this route was the town of Mecca.

The Role of Mecca. Located in an extremely desolate and dry region, Mecca got most of its water from one well. Much of its food had to be imported. Despite its environment, Mecca thrived because it was an important religious center.

In the seventh century, most Arabians practiced polytheism, worshiping many gods of nature. Nomadic tribes usually possessed idols, which they placed in special tents for worship. A structure called the Kaaba dominated the center of Mecca. The Kaaba was the home of several important gods. Pilgrims came to Mecca from miles around to worship these idols. Wealthy merchants, who profited from the religious pilgrims, dominated the life of the town.

Muhammad, Messenger of God

FOCUS ON PEOPLE

About A.D. 570, Muhammad was born in Mecca. Both his father and mother died before Muhammad was six years old. He lived for a while with his grandfather and later with an uncle who was a merchant. According to tradition, Muhammad accompanied his uncle on caravan trips to Syria.

Muslims believe that on one of these journeys the caravan stopped at the retreat of a Christian monk. While talking to Muhammad, the monk noticed a mark on Muhammad's back. The monk declared this mark to be a sign from God that Muhammad would be a great prophet and that he should be looked after with care.

In A.D. 595, when Muhammad was 25 years old, he met a widow named Khadija. She owned her own trading business. Kha-

A sixteenth-century illumination from a Persian manuscript shows Muhammad ascending to Paradise.

dija's camel caravans traveled between the city of Mecca and Syria. On the recommendation of Muhammad's uncle, Khadija hired Muhammad to lead one of her caravans. She was pleased with Muhammad's work and, eventually, they decided to marry.

Khadija's father was dead. According to Arab tradition, she needed her uncle's permission to remarry. Khadija, however, planned the wedding without first receiving permission. When the wedding party assembled at her house, she encouraged her uncle to drink large amounts of wine. The wine made him sleepy. While he slept, Khadija and Muhammad were married. When her uncle awoke, Khadija told him that he had indeed consented and given her away.

Muhammad was in the habit of spending long hours meditating in a remote place outside Mecca. One day, when he was 40 years old, he thought he saw a vision of the angel Gabriel. The angel told him he was to be the Messenger of God and should proclaim to the world there was but one God.

Muhammad continued to receive revelations about God, creation, and the next life. Muhammad preached these revelations to the people of Mecca. His wife, Khadija, was his first convert. As Muhammad continued to preach, he became known as a prophet, and his new religion became known in Arabia as Islam. ∎

The Religion of Islam

In his early years as a prophet, Muhammad taught that God, called Allah in Arabic, was all-powerful, good, and always merciful to his people. However, he was also just and punished sin.

Muhammad also believed that people could work toward salvation by leading a life of morality and goodness and by consistently obeying God's will. In Arabic, the word Islam means surrender, or submission to the will of the one God.

Muhammad's emphasis on belief in one God was not much different from the monotheism of the Jews and Christians. Muhammad, however, believed that he was the final prophet of God. His mission was to complete the revelations God had given earlier to Adam, Abraham, Moses, Jesus, and others told of in the Bible.

Muhammad at Medina. Muhammad attracted a few followers in Mecca. Most of the population, however, opposed him. Muhammad wanted to destroy the idols in the Kaaba. This action would end pilgrimages to Mecca and be very bad for business. Merchants led the opposition to Muhammad, which became so strong that his life was threatened. In A.D. 622, he and a little band of converts left Mecca.

Muhammad and his band traveled to Medina, a farming and commercial town about 250 miles north of Mecca. Tribal feuds divided the people of Medina. Impressed by what they heard of Muhammad's preaching, the leaders of the tribes invited him to help them settle their differences.

Muhammad's journey from Mecca to Medina is called the *hegira*. This event marks the beginning of the Muslim calendar.

In Medina, Muhammad attracted many converts. He also became the new leader of the city. He ended tribal conflicts by forming a single united community.

Muhammad's leadership at Medina was so successful that many tribes from a wide surrounding area accepted his religion. When military forces from Mecca tried to stop him, Muhammad defeated them. In A.D. 630, Muhammad returned to Mecca, where the people accepted Islam.

In Mecca, Muhammad smashed the idols in the Kaaba. He then dedicated this structure to the one God, as the prophet Abraham had originally done centuries earlier. Muhammad also declared that the city would continue to be a religious center. Mecca remains special for Muslims.

SECTION 1 *Study Skills*

Developing Vocabulary Use each of the following terms in a sentence: **1.** sect. **2.** dromedary. **3.** idol.

Reviewing Main Ideas **1.** Identify the major difference between the Muslim invaders and invaders of the Roman Empire. **2.** Discuss three major problems the Byzantine Empire faced. **3.** Identify and describe the main problem of the Sassanid Empire. **4.** Describe four of Mohammad's beliefs. **5.** Explain the importance of Medina to the Muslim religion.

Understanding Geography **1.** What is the importance of the dominant physical feature of southeast Arabia? **2.** Why is Mecca important to people today?

Understanding Chronology **1.** For the Islamic people, what is the significance of A.D. 622? **2.** What happened in A.D. 630 that changed Arabian history?

Challenge Why was the Byzantine Empire the center of trade after the fall of Rome?

2 The Arabs Create an Empire

OBJECTIVE: *To understand the causes and consequences of Arab conquests*

Islam Unites the Arabs

After Muhammad and his followers gained control of Medina and Mecca, most of the tribes of Arabia submitted to his leadership. When Muhammad died in A.D. 632, he certainly could not foresee that the Arabs, united by Islam, would conquer a vast area of Eurasia and Africa.

Problem of Succession. Muhammad's sudden death, without a designated successor, created a problem for the new religion. Without a strong leader, the Muslim community faced the possibility of disintegration. In A.D. 632, influential Muslims gathered to choose a new leader. After discussion, they selected Abu Bakr (uh BOO BAHK ehr) to become the caliph, or successor, of the prophet. Abu Bakr was Muhammad's father-in-law by a later wife. He ruled

only two years before he died. Early in his reign, several tribes attempted to renounce Islam. Abu Bakr and his allies defeated them in battle, and they repledged their loyalty and submission to Allah.

Causes of Arab Invasions. Abu Bakr and the caliphs who succeeded him sent armies to conquer new territory. These Muslim invasions probably were the result of two major factors. First, Muslim leaders believed that they had a divine mission to expand the Islamic community. They felt compelled to introduce God's law as Muhammad had preached it. Second, Arab leaders wanted to keep the diverse Arabian tribes united under Islam. They may have believed that the best way to avoid tribal feuds was to attack a common enemy in the rich lands and cities to the north.

Reasons for Arab Successes. The sudden Arab conquest of Syria, Persia, and Egypt was one of the most remarkable military feats in history. The military skill and courage of the Arabs, along with the weakness of the Byzantine and Persian empires, help to explain the Arabs' success.

Two other factors also were important. First, the people of Syria, Iraq, and Egypt felt oppressed by their rulers, and did little to stop the Arabs. Second, the Muslim conquerors generally respected the religion and way of life of the Christians and Jews of the Middle East. The Arabs had no policy of converting people to Islam by force.

VOCABULARY DEVELOPMENT

caliph (KAYL ihf) *noun:* head of the Muslim religious community. From the Arabic word, *khalifa,* meaning successor.

mosque (mahsk) *noun:* a Muslim house of worship.

Dark Ages: the years between A.D. 500 and 1000, when trade, urban centers, and literacy declined in Europe as a result of Germanic invasions. These years also are called the Early Middle Ages.

Shi'ite (SHEE eyet) *noun:* an Islamic sect.

Sunni (SOON ee) *noun:* the major Islamic sect.

This miniature painting by an eleventh-century Persian historian shows Kenan Pasa riding through Macedonia to celebrate his victory for Islam.

Early Arab Conquests, A.D. **630–640.** Abu Bakr ordered Arab warriors to raid frontier settlements in Byzantine and Sassanid territory. The second caliph, Omar, who led the Muslims from A.D. 634 to 644, invaded Syria and Persia. The Arab attacks out of the desert surprised the already weakened Byzantine and Persian empires. In addition to surprise, the Arabs had a tactical advantage. They could quickly return to the desert where the heavily armored Persian and Byzantine warriors could not pursue them.

In August A.D. 636, Arab and Byzantine forces fought a decisive battle at the Yarmuk River, near the present-day border of Syria and Jordan. The Muslim warriors, outnumbered four to one, forced the Byzantine army to retreat.

The battle took place during a scorching summer dust storm. Many retreating Byzantine soldiers, blinded by the sand, fell into a ravine where they died. After this victory,

the Arabs rapidly drove the remaining Byzantine armies out of Syria. See the map, Spread of Islam A.D. 622–733, page 237.

Meanwhile, in the east, Muslim forces advanced to Mesopotamia, now Iraq, where they fought Persian forces. The Arabs won a major battle at Qadisiya (KAHD uh SEE yuh), in lower Mesopotamia. Within a year, they had seized the beautiful Persian capital of Ctesiphon (TEHS ih fahn) and controlled the rich agricultural lands of Mesopotamia. Over the next 10 years, the Arabs conquered the remainder of Persia. See the map, Byzantine and Sassanid Empires A.D. 600–633, page 231.

In A.D. 640, Arab forces crossed the Sinai Peninsula and invaded the Nile valley. The Byzantine emperor evacuated the great port city of Alexandria, refusing to fight at all.

After the Arab victories, thousands of Arabs moved permanently into the fertile lands of the Middle East. Some settled in towns while others continued their pastoral way of life.

Continued Arab Expansion. The third caliph, Uthman (UHTH muhn), who ruled from A.D. 644 to 656, sent Arab armies both east and west. Large raiding parties advanced far up the Nile Valley. Arab forces crossed the Libyan Desert to attack the Byzantine province of Ifriqiya (if ree KEY ah), today called Tunisia. Arab armies completed the conquest of most of Persia and advanced as far as the Amu Darya (Oxus) River, near the frontiers of Turkestan. Turkestan lies northeast of Iran and is currently part of the Soviet Union.

Uthman also ordered his generals to build a fleet of war ships. This Arab fleet conquered the large Greek-speaking islands of Cyprus and Rhodes.

Problems of the Arabian Empire. Rapid military expansion strained Arabian unity. Old feuds between Arabian tribes surfaced. Opposing political factions competed for the office of caliph. In A.D. 656, a band of

Muslim rebels assassinated Caliph Uthman. For five years, civil war raged among Muslim factions.

The Umayyad Caliphate, A.D. 661–750.
Through conquest, the Arabs gained the heavily populated farmlands extending from the Nile River to the Amu Darya River. Under Arab rule, Egypt and the Middle East were united for the first time since the days of the Roman Empire.

The Arabs needed a system to govern their newly acquired empire. Muhammad had laid the beginnings of a new kind of political organization based on common allegiance to God and his laws. Muhammad, however, had not worked out a plan for governing a huge empire with millions of people of different cultures.

To govern their lands, the Arabs set up a hereditary ruler. The main responsibility of the caliph, or ruler, was to defend the community of Islam and the laws of God. In reality, however, Mu'awiyya (mu AH wih ya), who successfully claimed the caliphate to end the civil wars, established the Umayyad (u MY yad) Dynasty. The office of caliph then passed from father to son, or to some other descendant, in a single family line.

The Umayyad caliphs adopted Byzantine and Sassanid customs. Mu'awiyya moved the capital from Medina to Damascus, the heart of the new Islamic empire. He and his successors also continued the government bureaucracy the empires had developed. The Umayyads even used Byzantine coins engraved with pictures of the Greek emperor.

In cities throughout the Umayyad lands, many people converted to Islam. As a result, the new rulers built mosques—Muslim houses of worship. Muslims believe that they must face Mecca when they pray. The most important element of a mosque was

Spread of Islam, A.D. 622–733

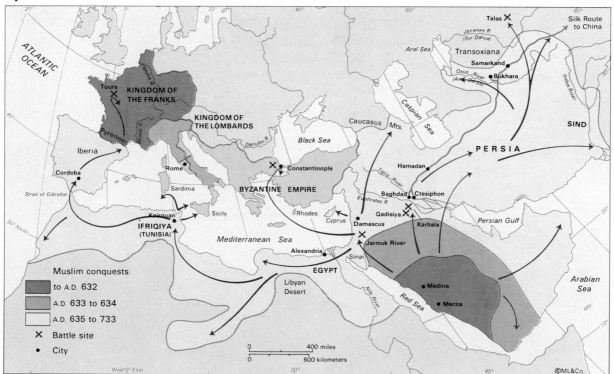

Map Skills **1.** Where did Islam originate? **2.** What is the most important city in the Islamic religion? **3.** Name five countries now occupying land conquered by the Muslims.

the *mihrab*, an alcove showing the direction of Mecca. Mosques usually were built so that the greatest number of worshipers could stand close to the *mihrab* and be closer to Mecca.

Later Arab Conquests, A.D. 650–750

To increase revenue, the Umayyad caliphs began a second series of conquests. They wanted to expand their territories and thus expand their tax base. They also wanted to keep independent Arabs from rebelling against the central government. The caliphs, therefore, sent their armies on new adventures of conquest for Islam.

Conquests to the West, A.D. 670. West of Egypt lies north Africa, currently occupied by the states of Tunisia, Algeria, and Morocco. The Arabs called this region the Maghreb, meaning land to the west. The Byzantine emperor still held coastal areas and the major port towns of north Africa.

The people living in north Africa, called Berbers, were divided into two groups. One group lived in the towns, and made their living as merchants, artisans, and workers. Many were Christians. The majority of Berbers inhabited the interior plains and mountains, and farmed or herded sheep or camels. Belonging to numerous tribes, the Berbers paid little attention to the Byzantine governors in the towns.

In A.D. 670, Muslim forces began their conquest of north Africa. The coastal cities the Byzantines held were strongly fortified, and the Berber tribes resisted the Arab invaders. Muslim armies fought in north Africa over several decades before finally gaining control of the land.

By the end of the seventh century, Muslims had added all of the Maghreb, except the interior mountain and desert regions, to the Arab empire. Christianity gradually lost influence, and Islam replaced it. Culturally, the Mediterranean Basin was split between Christians in the north and Muslims in the east and south. An important Christian minority remained in Egypt under the Coptic church. Jewish minority communities also continued to thrive and make important cultural and economic contributions.

Byzantine warriors used "Greek fire" as they battled Arab armies after A.D. 675. This "fire" was a highly flammable mix of oil, sulfur, and pitch.

The Umayyads intended to destroy the Byzantine Empire. To do so, however, they had to capture the great fortress capital of Constantinople. In the 670s, and again between A.D. 717 and 718, Arab army and navy units laid siege to the city. Christian forces beat them back both times.

The secret weapon of the Byzantines was "Greek fire." This highly flammable chemical mixture was shot from bronze tubes that could be mounted on ships or the walls of a city. The mixture began to burn when it hit the enemy, causing severe damage.

Conquests to the East. To the east, Muslim armies pushed through Persia to the lower valley of the Indus River. They found northern India divided into small Hindu states that were unable to resist their forces. The Muslim forces conquered the lower Indus Valley and introduced the Islamic religion to the region.

Arab Forces Defeat the Chinese. Farther to the east, the Arab armies reached the frontiers of the Chinese Empire. The Sui (swih) Dynasty had united the Chinese in A.D. 590 and ruled until A.D. 618. The next dynasty, the Tang (tahng), further strengthened Chinese unity. One of the great achievements of the Tang rulers was to advance Chinese military power westward to the grasslands of Turkestan. This expansion gave the Tang control of the rich trade in luxury goods along the Silk Road.

Early in the eighth century, Arab forces crossed the Syr Darya River into Turkestan, seizing the rich commercial cities of the Silk Road. See the map, Spread of Islam, page 237. In A.D. 751, the Arabs fought a great battle against the Chinese army. The Muslim victory forced the Tang to withdraw from the region.

Introduced into Turkestan, Islam gradually replaced Buddhism as the dominant faith. Even though the Tang army retreated eastward, trade between Islamic lands and China increased over the next 200 years.

The Arabs Invade Europe. During the lifetime of Muhammad, Europe west of the Byzantine Empire was still divided into a number of states ruled by Germanic tribes. The chieftains of these states were generally hostile toward the original inhabitants. The years between A.D. 500 and 1000 often are called the Dark Ages because the Germans cared little about trade, town life, or civilization. Learning and literacy thrived only in the Christian monasteries.

As the Arabs conquered north Africa, their forces moved west until they arrived at the Strait of Gibraltar. Less than 20 miles wide, the strait separates the Iberian Peninsula from Africa.

The countries of Spain and Portugal now occupy the Iberian Peninsula.

In A.D. 711, Muslim forces crossed the strait and entered Spain. The Muslims rapidly conquered most of Iberia, which became part of the Umayyad Caliphate.

North of Spain, the Kingdom of the Franks developed. When the Arabs crossed the Pyrennes mountains in A.D. 732, the Franks defeated them. The battle took place near Tours, in the central part of France.

The Battle of Tours did not destroy the Arab Empire. It did mark the end of Arab expansion into western Europe. The Muslims strengthened their hold on Iberia. This area became an important Islamic center and continued to be for many years.

The Fall of the Umayyad Empire

At its height, the Umayyad Empire extended across more than half of the Eastern Hemisphere. The empire, however, had numerous problems. The most serious difficulty was the dominance of a small group of Arab families. These influential families discriminated against poorer Arabs and non-Arab Muslims, as well as unbelievers.

Many converts to Islam wanted more control over the government. These discontented Muslims argued that Muhammad

This page from a Turkish history traces Muhammad's family tree back through Noah to Adam's son Seth. Below Muhammad are the first four caliphs.

had founded a social community in which all believers would live together as equals under God's law.

Islam Splits between Shi'ites and Sunnis. Many opponents of the Umayyad family were supporters of the Caliph, Ali, who had been assassinated in A.D. 661. They believed that the Umayyad family had stolen the office of caliph, which rightly belonged to descendants of Muhammad. Ali was Muhammad's cousin and the husband of Fatima, Muhammad's daughter. After Ali was killed, rebellious groups rallied around his son, Husayn (hu SA ihn). These opponents of the Umayyads were called Shi'a or Shi'ites.

In A.D. 680, an Umayyad army defeated Husayn and his followers. Husayn was killed and his head cut off. The murder of the prophet's grandson shocked many Muslims. Thereafter, Shi'ism developed into a sect within Islam, teaching that a descendant of Husayn would one day come to rule.

Religiously, Shi'ites stood in opposition to the majority of Muslims, called Sunnis. The Sunnis accepted the legitimacy of the Umayyad caliphs. Sunni Muslims historically believed that the rightful caliph was the leader the community of believers accepted. They rejected the idea that the office belonged to blood descendants of the prophet. In most other Muslim beliefs, differences between the Sunnis and Shi'ites were not great. Today, most of the citizens of Iran, formerly Persia, are Shi'ite Muslims. Large communities of Shi'ites also live in Lebanon, Iraq, and other countries.

Finally, in A.D. 747 a major revolt broke out under the leadership of Abu al-Abbas (uh BUL uh BUHS), a descendant of an uncle of Muhammad. The Umayyads were completely defeated and the Abbasids gained control of the caliphate. Despite the grave crisis and a change of power at the top, Islam continued to gain new converts.

SECTION 2 *Study Skills*

Developing Vocabulary Write a sentence using both caliph and mosque.

Reviewing Main Ideas 1. What impact did Muhammad's death have on Islam? 2. Discuss three main reasons for the Arab invasions and their success. 3. Explain the main reason why the Umayyad caliphs began a second series of conquests. 4. How did the Byzantine Empire defend itself against the Muslims? 5. Describe two problems the Umayyad Dynasty faced.

Understanding Geography 1. Name three continents involved in Muslim expansion. 2. What European area did Muslims conquer?

Understanding Chronology 1. What is important about A.D. 636 in the development of Islam? 2. When did the Islamic conquests of western Africa begin? 3. When did the Muslims conquer Spain?

Challenge Explain whether or not a new religion today could spread as rapidly as did Islam.

Major Cities Then and Now

Muhammad's flight to Medina changed the importance of that town forever. The role of other towns has also changed. Archaeologists often find old cities buried beneath newer cities. This feature analyzes the importance of cities.

The Development of Cities

Cities develop only where a food surplus exists. The earliest cities developed in areas where agriculture had progressed most, such as in Mesopotamia. Cities can support more specialized workers, such as artists and musicians. In modern times, cities usually are based on industry and manufacturing.

In ancient times, one benefit of living in the city was protection from invaders. Cities often were built on hills. The rugged landscape limited access to the city. City governments also built walls around their boundaries to stop attacks. The remains of ancient walls are one way in which archaeologists know the size of an ancient city.

Modern cities rarely rely on geographical features and walls for protection. Cities today depend on the military strength of their nation to defend against invasion.

Ancient cities also differed from modern cities in appearance. Early cities provided few services to their residents. Aqueducts for distributing water, sanitation systems for collecting sewage and garbage, and paved streets were not found in the first cities. The lack of these services affected the layout of the city. For example, people tried to live as closely as possible to the source of fresh water. The Romans were among the first people to build an extensive system of aqueducts within their cities. Aqueducts allowed people to spread out within cities.

Modern cities provide their citizens with a wide variety of services and systems. Some features of modern city life, such as water and sewage systems, are updated versions of services the Romans and earlier Harappan and Chinese cities provided. Some features, such as telephone and electrical lines, are more recent developments.

The Location of Cities

The location of a city influences many of its traits. Great cities developed in both Egypt and Mesopotamia. The cities were quite different, however. A desert surrounded Egypt. Consequently, most Egyptian cities were somewhat isolated.

Ancient Cities Today		
City	Earliest Known Settlement	Status Today
Baghdad	4000 B.C.	Population, 2.9 million; Village until A.D. 752; 1 million people in A.D. 800
Akkad	2300 B.C.	No longer exists
Tehran	1000 B.C.	Population, 4.5 million
Susa	2300 B.C.	Declined after the fourteenth century A.D.
Persepolis	500 B.C.	Declined after 330 B.C.
Medina	200 B.C.	Population, 198,000
Mecca	2000 B.C.	Population, 250,000
Ctesiphon	129 B.C.	Deserted after A.D. 763

This photograph of modern-day Istanbul, Turkey shows the beauty of the exotic city with its blend of Islamic and European architecture.

Foreigners heavily influenced cities in Mesopotamia. Mesopotamia was the crossroads of trade between east and west Eurasia. Mesopotamia had no mountains, deserts, or dense forests to protect it. Invaders who rode into the regions brought new ideas and forms of technology.

The location of certain cities made them important throughout history. Istanbul, formerly called Constantinople, in Turkey, is one such place. Istanbul is located at the eastern-most edge of Europe. The city is very hilly and overlooks the Bosporus Strait separating Europe from Asia. The Bosporus is the key transportation link between the Black and the Mediterranean seas. For over 1,500 years, Istanbul has been an important city because of its location on the Bosporus. The country controlling Istanbul has been able to prevent ships from passing through the Bosporus. Consequently, Istanbul has been and continues to be a vital trade and military center.

Today, Istanbul carries the marks of its long history of importance. Palaces and fortresses dating from the 300s stand next to modern office and apartment buildings. As long as water transportation is used, Istanbul will continue to be an important city.

STUDY SKILLS Understanding Geography

1. How did ancient Egyptian cities differ from cities of ancient Mesopotamia?
2. How did the widespread use of aqueducts change the way cities were organized?
3. Why has the location of Istanbul in Turkey helped it to remain an important city?
4. How many of the ancient cities listed in the chart still exist?

3 Islamic Civilization Develops

OBJECTIVE: *To understand the characteristics and achievements of Islamic civilization*

The Islamic Religion

By the end of the Umayyad Dynasty in A.D. 750, civilization, in the interacting zone from the western Mediterranean to northern India, was developing in new ways. The new ideas and customs of Islam combined with the traditional civilizations of Persia and the Hellenistic world to create the new Islamic civilization.

Within the first century of Islam's existence, the new religion grew to include people of many different languages and customs. Nevertheless, all Muslims have shared certain common beliefs and practices. Muslims must perform five duties, sometimes called the Five Pillars of Islam. As in other world religions, these basic duties symbolize a member's religious faith and commitment.

The Five Pillars of Islam. The first duty of a Muslim is to profess wholeheartedly that there is only one God and Muhammad is his prophet. A Muslim must state this belief openly and often.

The second duty is prayer. Muslims should pray at five set times each day.

VOCABULARY DEVELOPMENT

alms (ahmz) *noun:* money or gifts to the poor.

hajj (haj) *noun:* the pilgrimage to Mecca that every Muslim is expected to make at least once.

Prayers are recited at dawn, noon, midafternoon, sunset, and late evening. Each prayer involves certain ritual actions. The worshiper must face Mecca and recite words from the holy book of Islam, the Koran. This prayer is to be read at dawn:

❝ By the light of day, and by the fall of night, your Lord has not forsaken you, nor does He abhor you.

The life to come holds a richer prize for you than this present life. You shall be gratified with what your Lord will give you.

Did He not find you an orphan and give you shelter?

Did He not find you in error and guide you?

Did He not find you poor and enrich you?

Therefore, do not wrong the orphan, nor chide away the beggar. But proclaim the goodness of your Lord. ❞

The third pillar of Islamic faith is to voluntarily give alms, or offerings. The Muslim community uses these contributions to pay for many religious, charitable, and government expenses.

The fourth duty of a Muslim is to fast during daylight hours throughout the month of Ramadan, the ninth month of the Muslim year. During Ramadan, a Muslim must not eat, drink, or smoke between dawn and sunset. The purpose of this fast is to show a new commitment to God and to make amends for any sins.

Mecca is shown as the center of the world on the cover of this Arabic atlas from A.D. 958. The Islamic nations are named in the order of their distance from the Kaaba.

The final obligation is to make a pilgrimage, called the *hajj*, to the holy city of Mecca at least once in a lifetime. Three special days are set aside during the final month of the Muslim year for special prayers and ceremonies in Mecca and the neighboring area. Some of the activities take place before the Kaaba (KAHB uh), which stands in the courtyard of the central mosque in Mecca. Muslims make the journey to Mecca as an act of rededication to Allah.

Since the early days of Islam, Muslim pilgrims throughout the world have traveled to Mecca to perform the *hajj*. Pilgrimages to holy shrines form a part of most world religions, but Islamic pilgrimages are an unusually important unifying force. Today, between 1 and 2 million Muslims from around the world make the *hajj* every year.

Muhammad's Revelation. The Koran is the holy book of Islam. As the Jews refer to the Torah for the word of God, Muslims read the Koran. The Koran contains the revelations Muhammad received.

After moving to Medina, Muhammad shared many of his revelations with his followers, who began to memorize and write them down. Some time after his death, these writings were compiled and called the Koran, meaning recitation. Like the New Testament for Christians, the Koran is the basic statement of Islamic doctrine. Unlike the New Testament, however, the Koran contains specific rules for organizing Muslim society in accordance with God's will. The Koran deals with important Islamic religious subjects as well as rules for behavior among people. The Koran was used as the foundation for a system of laws to govern the entire Islamic civilization.

The Holy Book of Islam

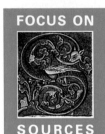

FOCUS ON SOURCES

The Koran has 114 chapters. Read in Arabic, the language of the Koran is powerful and poetic. Muslims believe that the Arabic language is sacred because Muhammad's revelations were written in Arabic. Below are excerpts from the Koran specifying required behavior, as well as the resulting rewards and punishments:

❝ In the month of Ramadan the Koran was revealed, a book of guidance with proofs of guidance distinguishing right from wrong. Therefore, whoever of you is present in that month let him fast. But he who is ill or on a journey shall fast a similar number of days later on.

Allah desires your well-being, not your discomfort. He desires you to fast the whole month so that you may magnify him and render thanks to Him for giving you his guidance. . . .

The first temple ever to be built for men was that at Beccah [Mecca], a blessed place, a beacon for the nations. In it there are veritable signs and the spot where Abraham stood. Whoever enters it [the first temple] is safe. Pilgrimage to the House is a duty to Allah for all who can make the journey. As for the unbelievers, Allah can surely do without them. . . .

Men have authority over women because Allah has made the one superior to the others, and because they spend their wealth to maintain them. Good women are obedient. . . .

Serve Allah and associate none [no other God] with him. Show kindness to your parents and your kindred, to the orphans and to the needy, to your near and distant neighbors, to your fellow travelers, to the wayfarers, and to the slaves whom you own. Allah does not love arrogant and boastful men, who are themselves niggardly [stingy] and enjoin others to be niggardly also; who conceal the riches which Allah of his bounty has bestowed upon them (We have prepared a shameful punishment for the unbelievers); and who spend their wealth for the sake of ostentation, believing neither in Allah nor in the Last Day. He that chooses Satan for his friend, an evil friend has he. **"** ∎

Islamic Sacred Law

The laws that govern Islamic society are based on the words and actions of Muhammad, as well as on the Koran. People who knew Muhammad tried to remember everything he said and did, as the best model for living their own lives and regulating conduct with others. These traditions were first passed along by word of mouth, as were the Gospels of the New Testament.

During the Umayyad period from A.D. 661 to 750, Muslim scholars began to write down the remembered words and actions of Muhammad. Islamic laws developed from several sources, but mainly from the Koran and the traditions of Muhammad.

Islamic laws made no distinction between religious and civil law. According to Muslim teaching, the sacred law, called the *Shari'a*, was the only correct guide to life because it contained God's revelation.

Islamic law did not specify only religious worship and personal conduct. It covered all aspects of life, including marriage, family life, inheritance, government, and business relations. For example, Islamic law contained simple rules for paying taxes. Muslims were required to pay a voluntary tax, *zakat*, to be used for religious purposes and charity. Non-Muslims in the Islamic Empire had to pay certain additional taxes. Unlike other empires, the holy law frowned on any government that constantly forced subjects to pay new kinds of taxes.

Islamic law also declared that Jews and Christians were to be regarded as People of the Book. That is, they shared in earlier prophetic revelations from God and, therefore, should not be forced to convert. Muslims, however, regarded these groups as their religious inferiors.

The law also protected non-Muslims and their property and permitted them to govern their own community affairs. Islam, like Judaism, emphasizes a person's actions as regulated by specific laws. The study and practice of law, therefore, has always been important in Islam just as it is in Judaism. While Christianity also stresses a person's conduct, the study of law is not emphasized.

Stress on Equality in Islam. Christian civilizations have stressed brotherly and sisterly love; Islam emphasizes social cooperation. Muhammad taught that all human beings are equal to one another in the sight of God. They should, therefore, cooperate with one another to carry out God's will. Islam does not exclude love but puts greater emphasis on people working together to build a society that obeys God's law.

Islam did not do away with the inequalities between rich and poor. No world religion or empire has yet eliminated poverty or inequality. Islam maintains that people should treat one another as equals, and governments should be fair and just. This ideal had great influence on the character of Islamic civilization.

For instance, the idea of equality meant that Islamic civilization did not include priests in its religious structure. The claim that certain individuals—priests—have special powers to communicate with God, goes back to the earliest civilizations. Early Christianity relied on priests to perform ceremonies and serve as intermediaries between God and people. Islam, however, did not include priests with special religious functions. Instead, the principal religious leaders of Islam were scholars called *ulama* (OO luh MAH) who mastered the Koran and other law books. Members of the *ulama* served as teachers, judges, and lawyers for the less-

Major Eurasian Religions and Philosophies, to A.D. 800

Religion	Founder	Scripture	Beliefs	Concentration of Believers
Hinduism	No single founder	*Vedas* Upanishads Mahabharata Ramayana	All souls are part of world soul Reincarnation One's actions will always have reactions Goal is Nirvana—release from rebirth	India
Buddhism	Siddhartha Gautama, sixth century B.C.	*Pali canon* plus a variety of scriptures by several subgroups	Four noble truths: (1) world is full of suffering, (2) caused by desire, (3) ending desire is path to salvation; (4) to be achieved through eight-fold path of right behavior	East and Southeast Asia
Daoism	Laozi, fifth century B.C.	Tao Te Ching	Withdraw from great activity Meditate on Dao to relate to force of Nature	China, Southeast Asia
Confucianism	Confucius (Kong Qiu) fifth century B.C.	*Analects*	Importance of moral behavior Humane relationships improve family and state	China, Southeast Asia
Judaism	no single founder	Torah	One God	Middle East, Europe
Zoroastrianism	Zoroaster, sixth century B.C.	*Avesta*	Dual forces of good and evil Final victory of good	Small groups in Persia and India
Christianity	Jesus, first century A.D.	Bible	One God; Jesus son of God Love of others Equality before God Monophysites believed Jesus was solely divine, not human.	Europe
Islam	Muhammad, seventh century A.D.	Koran	One God; Muhammad is his prophet Five Pillars of Faith Equality before God	Middle East, North Africa

educated majority. Most Muslims respected these leaders for their piety and learning, not for any special religious rank.

The Islamic acceptance of equality also meant that Muslims resisted class distinctions in their society. By contrast, the Hindu religion reinforced social inequality through the caste system. (See page 75.) In Hinduism, people belong to fixed social classes, and some classes have more privileges than others. In Islamic society, despite great differences in wealth and power, people could improve their social status. Further, Muslims of differing wealth, occupation, and race tended to mix more freely together than did people in other cultures. This spirit of equality and toleration gained new converts and helped the expansion of Islam.

The Position of Women in Islam. In Islamic civilization, women have occupied a subordinate position to men despite its stress on equality. According to Muslim law, women are inferior to men in several respects. Before Islam and the teachings of the Koran, however, the legal and social position of Arab women was worse. Then, women were treated almost as slaves, and a man could have as many wives as he wished and could support.

Muhammad limited the number of wives to four. He also commanded that a man should have only as many wives as he could treat with total equality. In addition, Islamic law gave women definite rights in such areas as marriage, inheritance, and the ownership of personal property.

In Islamic and other early civilizations, women generally filled the roles of wives and mothers and were excluded from public life. Exceptions must have existed, however, because Muhammad's first wife was a trader with independence and power. Khadija was not confined to the low status reserved for most Arab women before the time of Muhammad. Some Arab women influenced politics and society indirectly through their husbands and other male relatives.

The Spread of the Arabic Language. Arabic became the major language of Islamic civilization. Since it was the language of the Koran and therefore sacred, every Muslim, whether Berber, Persian, or Turk, was encouraged to learn Arabic and recite the Koran. Learning Arabic became a status symbol for converts to Islam. Arabic became the major language of Islamic scholars and Islamic literature.

Even before the time of Alexander the Great, Greek was the major language throughout the eastern Mediterranean. In the eighth century, Greek influence declined as Arabic gained importance throughout Islamic lands. Greek did, however, remain the language of the people of the Byzantine Empire and the Greek Orthodox religion.

A Persian painting of an old man of letters.

An Egyptian caravan, the traditional way of travelling through the desert. Inset, a thirteenth-century illustration of travellers from al-Harīrīs's *Maqāmāt*.

In Iraq, Syria, Egypt, and north Africa, Arabic gradually dominated the older Aramaic, Coptic, and Berber languages. Today, Arabic is the principal language of many countries in Africa and the Middle East.

The Spread of Islamic Civilization. By A.D. 750, Islam was the most dynamic civilization in the Eastern Hemisphere, bringing new political and religious energies. The Byzantine Empire was forced to give all the rich territories in Africa and Syria to its Arab conquerors. In Europe, the Muslims destroyed the Kingdom of the Visigoths and occupied the Iberian Peninsula. To the east, Muslims challenged Hindu society and Buddhism. The Arabs also forced the Chinese army to retreat from Turkestan. Following Arab conquests, Islamic culture spread throughout the conquered lands.

SECTION 3 *Study Skills*

Developing Vocabulary   Write a sentence using each of the following words: **1.** alms. **2.** *hajj*.

Reviewing Main Ideas   **1.** List the Five Pillars of Islam. **2.** What is the Koran? **3.** Under Islamic law, how are the People of the Book to be treated? **4.** What is the most important social value in Islam? **5.** What is the function of the ulama? **6.** How is Islam similar to Christianity and Hinduism? **7.** What is the status of women in Islamic law?

Understanding Cause and Effect   **1.** What are some results of Muslim pilgrimages to Mecca each year? **2.** How is it possible for a modern society to base its legal system on Islamic law?

Challenge   Compare women's role in Islamic societies with their earlier role.

CHAPTER 11 *Summary & Review*

Summarizing Main Ideas

In the seventh century, the Byzantine Empire dominated trade in the eastern Mediterranean lands. The empire's capital was Constantinople, and its major religion was Orthodox Christianity.

The Arab-speaking peoples were not united at the beginning of the seventh century. Islam began in A.D. 595, under the leadership of Muhammad. Muhammad quickly attracted converts throughout the Middle East.

Between A.D. 622 and 733, Islam spread over a huge area of the intercommunicating zone. The Umayyad caliphs created a strong central authority and held power until a series of revolts defeated the dynasty in A.D. 750.

The spread of Islam, combined with the traditions of Persia and the Hellenistic world, created a new civilization throughout the intercommunicating zone. By A.D. 750, Islam had replaced Byzantium as the dominant political and cultural force in the Mediterranean Basin and the western part of Asia.

Questions for Critical Thinking

COMPREHENSION Interpreting Events

1. How did Justinian's failure to reunite the Roman Empire affect the people of western Europe?
2. How did Islam affect the history of the Arab people?
3. The results of the Islamic conquests in Asia and Africa are important today. Identify three of these significant results.
4. Explain two relationships between Islamic law and the Muslim conquests.

APPLICATION Comparing Past and Present

1. Identify the areas of the world that are Islamic today, as a result of the conquests of the seventh century.
2. Identify four Islamic traditions that many people of the modern world seem to have adopted.

SYNTHESIS Developing Reading Skills

1. Read three sections of the Koran. Briefly summarize what was written.
2. Read one of the many biographies of Muhammad. Describe his life.

APPLICATION Weighing Consequences

1. If people of the Islamic faith had not conquered parts of Eurasia, how might those areas be different today?
2. Explain three of the cultural changes Islam caused in the Middle East.

CHALLENGE

1. Explain the rapid spread of Islam.
2. Which belief systems shown on the chart below have over 400 million followers?

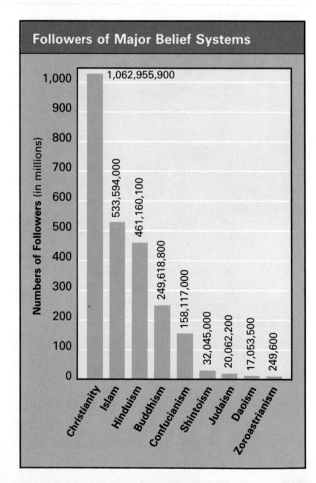

Followers of Major Belief Systems

Numbers of Followers (in millions)

- Christianity: 1,062,955,900
- Islam: 533,594,000
- Hinduism: 461,160,100
- Buddhism: 249,618,800
- Confucianism: 158,117,000
- Shintoism: 32,045,000
- Judaism: 20,062,200
- Daoism: 17,053,500
- Zoroastrianism: 249,600

CHAPTER 12
Asia and Europe Develop

GLOBAL TIME LINE

A.D. 750   A.D. 800   A.D. 850

TIME

A.D. 618–907 Tang Dynasty rules China

A.D. 800s Confucianism replaces Buddhism in China

A.D. 800s Magyars and Muslims invade Europe

PEOPLE

A.D. 800 Pope crowns Charlemagne, Emperor of the Holy Roman Empire

A.D. 813–833 al-Khwarizmi writes "al-jabr" extending the knowledge of algebra

A.D. 815 Caliph Ma'mun founds the "House of Wisdom" in Baghdad

PLACE

A.D. 750 *Baghdad;*[2] Baghdad made the capital of the Islamic Empire

A.D. 800s *Europe,*[4] Magyars and Muslims invade Europe; Vikings raid northern Europe

A.D. 843 *France;*[5] Treaty of Verdun divides Charlemagne's empire

A.D. 700s *China;*[1] The Tang capital becomes the largest city in the world

A.D. 794 *Japan;*[3] Kyoto becomes the capital of Japan

Linking Past to Present

In 1980, Tim Severin, an English explorer, followed the route of many Muslim sailors of the eighth and ninth centuries A.D. Muslim voyages that crossed two-thirds of the the Eastern Hemisphere were part of the growth of long-distance communication between A.D. 750 and 1000.

Tim Severin began his adventure from Oman, on the southeastern coast of the Arabian Peninsula. There, with the help of craftspeople from Oman and India, he built and launched a ship exactly like the ones that sailed the Indian Ocean 1200 years ago.

After a 6,000-mile voyage lasting seven and a half months, Severin and his crew arrived at the Chinese port of Canton. In the eighth and ninth century, journeys like Severin's stimulated communication and trade.

An ancient Arab ship passes a modern oil-rig off the coast of Singapore.

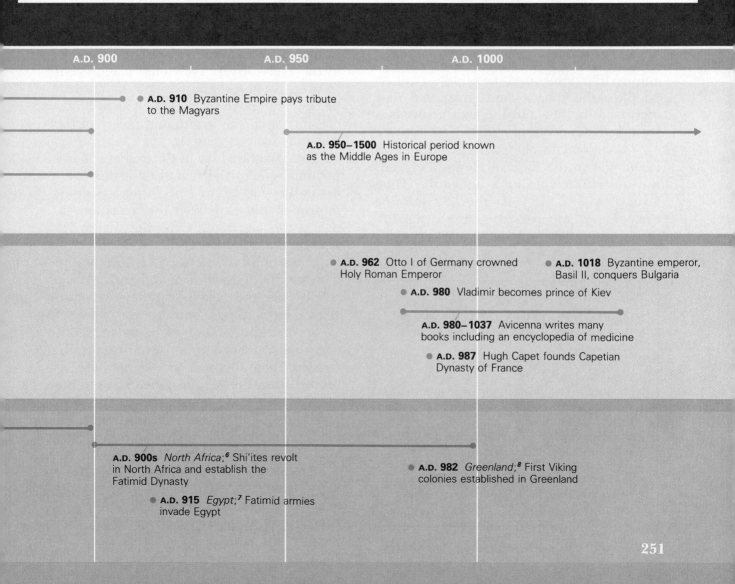

A.D. 900 A.D. 950 A.D. 1000

A.D. 910 Byzantine Empire pays tribute to the Magyars

A.D. 950–1500 Historical period known as the Middle Ages in Europe

A.D. 962 Otto I of Germany crowned Holy Roman Emperor

A.D. 1018 Byzantine emperor, Basil II, conquers Bulgaria

A.D. 980 Vladimir becomes prince of Kiev

A.D. 980–1037 Avicenna writes many books including an encyclopedia of medicine

A.D. 987 Hugh Capet founds Capetian Dynasty of France

A.D. 900s *North Africa;*[6] Shi'ites revolt in North Africa and establish the Fatimid Dynasty

A.D. 982 *Greenland;*[8] First Viking colonies established in Greenland

A.D. 915 *Egypt;*[7] Fatimid armies invade Egypt

251

1 The Abbasid Caliphate

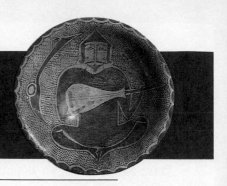

OBJECTIVE: *To understand the causes and consequences of the rise of the Abbasid Caliphate*

Changes for Islamic Civilization

Between A.D. 750 and 1000, trade and communication across the Eastern Hemisphere increased dramatically. Two important developments stimulated this growth.

First, the Abbasid Caliphate came to power in A.D. 750. The Abbasid rulers organized a powerful and wealthy Muslim empire that dominated the Middle East. As people of the Abbasid lands prospered, they increased the demand for luxury products from India and China.

The second development that stimulated exchanges in the Eastern Hemisphere was the unification of China under the Tang Dynasty in A.D. 618. Like the Abbasids, the early Tang emperors encouraged agriculture, communication, and overseas trade.

VOCABULARY DEVELOPMENT

Middle East: a large region that includes Egypt, the Arabian Peninsula, Syria, and the Iranian Plateau.

bazaar (buh ZAHR) *noun:* a marketplace selling many kinds of goods, a street of shops.

typhoon (ty FOON) *noun:* a violent, destructive storm originating in waters off the Asian coast.

syllogistic premise: a form of argument consisting of two statements assumed to be true and a conclusion drawn from them. For example: the two statements, teenagers go to school, and he is a teenager, lead to the conclusion, therefore, he goes to school.

The Rise of the Abbasid Caliphate.

In A.D. 750, the Umayyad Caliphate that ruled the Arab lands was overthrown in a civil war. A new dynasty, the Abbasids, replaced the Umayyads. Most of the Abbasid supporters lived in Mesopotamia and Persia. The new rulers,therefore, moved their capital from Damascus in Syria to Baghdad on the banks of the Tigris River. They built magnificent palaces, mosques, and bazaars, or marketplaces. The move from Damascus to Baghdad increased the wealth and power of the Abbasids for two reasons.

First, Baghdad lay in the heart of Mesopotamia, one of the richest agricultural areas in the world. The early Abbasid caliphs improved and expanded the irrigation canals of the Tigris and Euphrates Valley. As agricultural production increased, the Abbasids used their increased tax revenue to increase their government and army. As the caliphs became wealthier, they strengthened their empire's central government.

Second, the location of Baghdad, at the crossroads of two ancient trade routes, increased Abbasid power. One trade route extended from the Mediterranean Sea to the Persian Gulf and then by seaways to India and China. The second route crossed overland through the Middle East to central Asia and China.

Baghdad developed into a center of world trade. The merchants filled the markets of Baghdad with spices, textiles, perfumes, and other luxury goods from Asia.

Trade in Abbasid Lands, A.D. 750

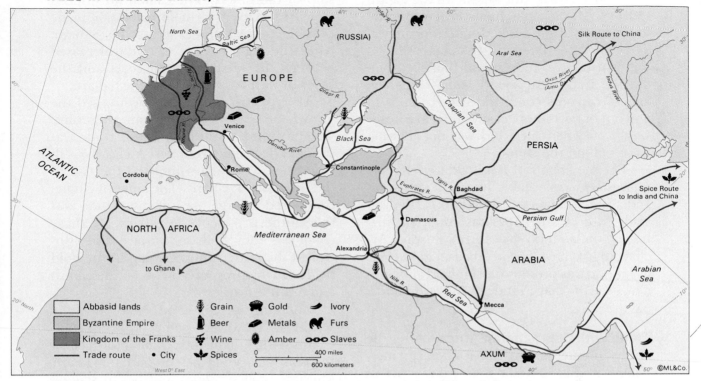

Map Skills **1.** Name the northernmost land to which trade extended. **2.** Where is Axum located? **3.** Which two major trade routes passed through Baghdad?

Government under the Abbasids.
The Abbasid caliphs adopted many aspects of Persian government. They did not live simple lives as had the prophet Muhammad and other early leaders of Islam. Instead, they lived in large palaces and kept themselves isolated from the common people. They imitated the Persian rulers by dressing in beautiful silk robes and tall cone-shaped hats. They became absolute rulers.

Devout Muslims, who believed in the equality of all people, resented the behavior and grand style of the caliphs. Still, most Muslims realized that the huge Islamic Empire could not be ruled by the simple governmental style of Muhammad's time.

Trade and Communication Increase.
During the eighth century, both the Chinese and Islamic empires encouraged trade. Long-distance caravan trade over the Silk Road flourished again for the first time since the A.D 200s. Changan, the capital of China under the Tang, attracted thousands of merchants from the Middle East and central Asia. Some were Christians and Jews. Many were Muslims from Persia and Syria.

At the same time, Arab and Persian sailors from the Middle East made regular ocean voyages to India, Southeast Asia, and China. Muslim sailors could travel from the Persian Gulf to China and return in about a year and a half. The long trip, however, was both dangerous and uncomfortable. Their ships did not have enclosed cabins, and crew members cooked and slept under the sun and stars. Along the way, typhoons threatened in the Indian Ocean.

Muslim merchants helped to spread the ideas and customs of Islamic civilization. Some settled down in port towns in India, Ceylon, and other places along the route. In this way, merchants introduced Islam to the Indian Ocean region.

Abbasid Trade in the West. In the eighth century, Muslim merchants began to trade in the lands around the Mediterranean Sea. They used the lateen, a triangular-shaped sail, which gave ships greater mobility than did the traditional square sails. Using the lateen, captains could move their ships in and out of ports more easily and make headway even when the wind was not blowing from behind the ship.

The merchants of Baghdad were largely interested in profitable luxury goods from India and China, but they also carried on trade with Europe. Muslims imported furs, honey, timber, and slaves from Europe. Archaeologists have found Abbasid gold coins as far north as present-day Finland and Sweden. (See the map, Trade in Abbasid Lands, page 253.)

Trade with Sub-Saharan Africa. After the Arabs conquered north Africa, Muslim merchants organized trading expeditions across the vast Sahara to the gold fields of west Africa. The dromedary camel became their

African slaves, shown at a slave-market in Yemen. This illustration from A.D. 1237 shows captives being sold into slavery in the Islamic world.

ship of the desert. The camel, introduced from Arabia to Africa in Roman times, made possible regular trade across the Sahara. After the eighth century, trade increased between the Mediterranean coast and the lands of west Africa south of the Sahara.

The African commerce encouraged the growth of several west African kingdoms. The most important item in this trade was the gold that came from west Africa. Wealth from the gold trade stimulated the rise of the Kingdom of Ghana. The kings of Ghana conquered a large area of grasslands and the southern part of the Sahara. By these conquests they built an empire and controlled the trade routes leading to the gold fields. Ghana prospered between the eighth and ninth centuries A.D.

The kings of Ghana probably were not Muslims. However, some Muslim merchants settled in the little trading towns near the southern edge of the Sahara. There, Muslims built mosques and began schools for their children.

Soon, some local African merchants converted to Islam, partly to improve their business connections with the Muslim traders. In this way, Islam gradually became an important religion in west Africa. By A.D. 1000, west Africa profited from its link to the interacting zone of Islamic trade.

Arab Scientific and Cultural Achievements. A united Middle East under Islam stimulated an exchange of ideas, as well as trade. Early Muslim scholars learned from the older Greek and Persian civilizations. New ideas about technology and science entered Baghdad, along with the silks and spices, because of the strong trade links to India and China.

Arab and Persian scientists stretched their understanding of mathematics, astronomy, natural science, medicine, chemistry, and geography during the Abbasid period. Ma'mun, who ruled from A.D. 813 to 833, was one of the greatest of the Abbasid caliphs. He founded a House of Wisdom in

Baghdad about A.D. 815. It included an enormous library and an astronomical observatory for studying the heavens.

Abbasid scholars adopted the Indian system of mathematics based on ten and the concept of zero. The most famous Abbasid mathematician, al-Khwarizmi, could be called the father of algebra. Al-jabr, one of al-Khwarizmi's ideas about mathematical integration, gives us the word algebra.

One of the giants of Abbasid science was the Persian scholar Ibn Sina, also called Avicenna (AV ih SEHN uh). In his lifetime, he wrote 99 books on astronomy, geometry, theology, philosophy, and art. He was best known for his work on medicine. He combined his own medical ideas with those of the Greeks and Persians. Centuries after his death, Avicenna's encyclopedia of medicine became the basis of medical practice throughout Europe.

Persian physician and wanderer, Avicenna, discussing medicine. Avicenna wrote the *Canon of Medicine*, used to teach doctors for more than 600 years.

Avicenna's Autobiography

FOCUS ON SOURCES

The Muslim world produced many scholars who explored many interests. The genius, Avicenna, was a physician, philosopher, mathematician, and theologian, as well as an astronomer. Avicenna's dedication to learning is evident in the following excerpt from his autobiography.

“ I now occupied myself with mastering the various texts and commentaries on natural science and metaphysics, until all the gates of knowledge were open to me. Next, I desired to study medicine, and proceeded to read all the books that have been written on this subject. Medicine is not a difficult science, and naturally I excelled in it, in a very short time, so that qualified physicians began to read medicine with me. I also undertook to treat the sick, and methods of treatment derived from practical experience revealed themselves to me such as baffle description. At the same time, I continued between whiles to study and dispute on law, being now 16 years of age.

The next 18 months I devoted entirely to reading; I studied Logic once again, and all the parts of philosophy. During all this time I did not sleep one night through, nor devoted my attention to any other matter by day. I prepared a set of files; with each proof I examined, I set down the syllogistic premises and put them in order in the files, then I examined what deductions might be drawn from them. I observed methodically the conditions of the premises, and proceeded until the truth of each particular problem was confirmed for me. Whenever I found myself perplexed by a problem, or could not find the middle term in any syllogism, I would repair to the mosque and pray, adoring the All-Creator, until my puzzle was resolved and my difficulty made easy. . . . ” ■

Industry and Technology

In addition to achievements in the sciences, Arabs also advanced in technology. Baghdad and other cities of the caliphate were busy centers of industry. Their workshops produced beautiful pottery, fabrics, rugs, metalwork, glass, and jewelry. Artisans used ideas and techniques from China and India to improve their products.

Arabs adapted the technology of papermaking. In A.D. 751, when the Arabs defeated a Tang army in central Asia, they captured some Chinese artisans skilled at making paper. These Chinese prisoners set up a paper mill in the Middle East.

Over time, the skills of papermaking spread from the Middle East to north Africa and Europe. Paper had several advantages over parchment, the traditional writing material. Paper was much cheaper and faster to make. Therefore, books became cheaper and easier to make. Since owning books became more common, knowledge spread throughout the Eastern Hemisphere faster and reached more people than ever before in history.

Philosophy. Between the eighth and tenth centuries, Muslim, Christian, and Jewish scholars translated most of the surviving books of ancient Greek philosophy into Arabic. The Shi'ite branch of Islam was especially interested in Greek philosophy.

A great debate arose about natural law. Some leaders disagreed with the Greek idea of a natural law that used definite rules of cause and effect to explain natural events. These laws explained the rotation of the planets and other natural events. Critics of the Greek idea of a natural law preferred to believe that God is directly responsible for every individual action and every event that occurs.

By the eleventh century, the Muslim opponents of Greek philosophy had gained influence. The majority of Muslim scholars decided that Greek ideas would not be taught in the schools of Islamic lands. Islamic civilization, therefore, did not adopt much of Greek tradition in philosophy, even though Islamic scholars had translated the Greek writings into Arabic.

The Breakup of the Abbasid Caliphate

Even during the long period when trade, industry, and learning flourished throughout Arab lands, serious political and religious problems existed. The Abbasids did not have the military power to control all of the conquered territories from Spain to India. Between the eighth and tenth centuries, many frontier regions of the original empire revolted against the caliph. In some places, local people, discontented under Baghdad's rule, organized revolts. In other places, the caliph's own governors or generals ignored his authority.

Music played an important role as Islamic armies celebrated victory. This fourteenth-century illustration from al-Jazart's *Automata* shows a military band on a mechanical water-clock.

The Umayyad Caliphate of Spain. The first major revolt took place in Iberia in A.D. 750, while the Abbasids were still trying to overthrow the Umayyad Dynasty. The leader of the rebellion, Abd al-Rahman (uhb DUL ra MAHN), was a young member of the Umayyad family who had escaped from the Abbasids during the civil war. He swam across the Euphrates River and wandered in disguise through Syria and north Africa, often pursued by Abbasid spies.

When he reached Spain, he found that the Arab military forces there did not support the government. They accepted him as their leader and helped him to overthrow the governor.

The southern part of Iberia, known as Andalusia (AN duh LOO zhuh), was fertile farmland. Muslims from north Africa migrated to Andalusia. They developed advanced techniques for irrigating the land and raising such crops as grain, olives, and grapes. They also introduced rice, oranges, sugarcane, cotton, apricots, and peaches to lands of Andalusia.

Farmers prospered, the population of Iberia increased, and cities grew. The capital that Abd al-Rahman built at Cordova soon rivaled Baghdad and Constantinople. Cordova had miles of paved streets lighted by streetlamps, as well as numerous mosques, public bathhouses, and palaces. The Grand Mosque, part of which still stands, was one of the most beautiful buildings in the Islamic world.

More Crises for the Abbasids. The revolt in Spain was only the first of several against the Abbasid Caliphate. Shi'ite groups opposed the authority of the caliph because he was not a descendant of Ali.

Even with these revolts, the Abbasids might have kept control of the heartland of the Middle East were it not for other problems. First, farm production declined in Mesopotamia because the irrigation system was not well maintained. Second, the caliphs of the later ninth and tenth centuries were weak rulers. They oppressed the peasants and spent extravagant sums of money building palaces and entertaining themselves.

A third problem developed when foreign mercenaries were used in the ninth century. Most of these soldiers were Turkish-speaking cavalry experts from central Asia. As the caliphs became weaker, these foreign soldiers gained more power in the government. In time, they controlled the caliph, but they had little interest in keeping the empire strong and prosperous.

Finally, in A.D. 945, a group of Persian warriors known as the Buyids took control of Baghdad. They ruled without consulting the caliph. By this time, the great Abbasid Empire was reduced to many separate Muslim kingdoms.

Islam, however did not decline along with the Abbasid Caliphate. The rebellions were against the rule of the extravagant caliphs, not against Islam itself. The religion continued to spread during the declining years of the Abbasid Caliphate.

SECTION 1 *Study Skills*

Developing Vocabulary 1. Give a modern example of a bazaar. **2.** Explain why the term Middle East is not exact. **3.** Give an example of a syllogistic premise. **4.** What is a typhoon?

Review Main Ideas 1. List five products Muslims traded with other cultures. **2.** Describe three Arab achievements in industry and technology. **3.** Why did the Shi'ite groups revolt?

Understanding Chronology 1. Explain two developments that expanded trade between A.D. 750 and 1000. **2.** What happened in A.D. 750 that changed Arabian history?

Understanding Cause and Effect Why did moving the capital from Damascus to Baghdad increase the wealth and power of the Abbasids?

Challenge What Arab influence can still be seen in the modern scientific community?

2 Tang Dynasty Expands China

OBJECTIVE: *To understand the causes and consequences of the expansion of the Chinese Empire*

The Reunification of China

Muslim merchants were drawn to China to trade because the Chinese people were again united and prosperous. In A.D. 589, rulers of the Sui (swih) Dynasty had set about uniting China.

China A.D. 600–900. Two major dynasties ruled China between the sixth and tenth centuries. The Sui Dynasty ruled from A.D. 589 to 618 and the Tang from A.D. 618 to 907. See the map, China A.D. 750–1000, page 260.

During the reign of these two dynasties, the population of China increased dramatically. Cities, trade, and transportation expanded. Religious changes also occurred, and Chinese ideas spread to the people of Korea, Vietnam, and Japan.

The Growth of Cities. On the decline of the Han Dynasty around A.D. 200, thousands of Chinese peasant farmers migrated from northern China to the warmer southern regions. Many settled in the Yangzi River valley. They drained the wet soil and built irrigation systems for rice farming. However, wealthy nobles owned most of the good land and employed the peasants as tenant farmers.

The high rice yields from new farmlands supported growing numbers of Chinese. Between A.D. 750 and 1250, the population of China probably doubled. Large cities grew where transportation was available along the coasts and in the major river valleys such as the Huang He and Yangzi.

Changan, the Tang capital in north central China, was the largest city in the world during the eighth and ninth centuries. Almost a million people lived within its great walls, and another million lived in the surrounding suburbs.

The streets of Changan were laid out at right angles. Wealthy families lived in two-story houses with enclosed gardens. Near the city, the emperor built a large public park and zoo. In the bustling marketplaces, visitors from Persia, Vietnam, Korea, and Japan mingled with the residents to watch acrobats, musicians, and jugglers.

Transportation and Trade. During the Tang era, China had the best transportation system in the world. Yang Chien, the first

VOCABULARY DEVELOPMENT

parasite (PAIR uh syt) *noun:* organism that lives on others without making any return. From the Greek prefix *para-*, meaning beside, and the Greek word *sitos*, meaning food.

civil service system: method for selecting government employees that emphasizes hiring qualified workers through testing.

Shinto (SHIHN toh) *noun:* religion of Japan whose followers worship many gods representing the forces of nature.

veneration (VEHN uhr AY shuhn) *noun:* reverence, deep respect. From the Latin word, *venus*, meaning love.

Kaifeng replaced Changan as China's capital by the twelfth century. This silk painting from the twelfth-century shows the sophisticated, prosperous city.

Sui ruler, employed thousands of peasants to build the Grand Canal linking the Huang He and Yangzi rivers. Alongside the Grand Canal, the government built tree-shaded roads and rest houses for weary travelers.

Even when the central government grew weak, the network of canals and roads helped to unify China economically and culturally. Boats carried goods from one part of the country to another over the growing canal system. Merchants shipped northern wheat to south China, and southern rice traveled north.

By A.D. 750, the extensive canal system was transporting goods quickly and efficiently throughout China. The Chinese court received, as tax payment, more grain than it could use. The court instructed local tax officials to sell part of the grain and buy fine porcelain, lacquer, and embroidered cloth for the emperor and his court.

Because China's wealthy landowners had much surplus grain to sell, they also could afford to buy luxury goods. Industries developed in the cities and towns to produce porcelain dishes, silk fabrics, and other luxury items. Many of these products were exported to India and the Middle East. A ninth-century Arab scholar noted with amazement:

❝ The Chinese have pottery of excellent quality of which they fashion bowls as thin as flasks of glass; one may see the glint of water through them, although they are made of clay. ❞

While the standard of living of China's peasants remained low, a prosperous middle class of merchants slowly developed. They were the leaders of economic change in China, but they never gained great power. The wealthy landowners, who viewed merchants as parasites because they did not create goods, remained the social and political leaders.

The increase in population, the growth of the transportation system, and the prosperous trade, linked northern and southern China more closely than ever before. Even when the power of the Tang government weakened, Chinese merchants continued to trade with India and the Middle East.

China, A.D. 750–1000

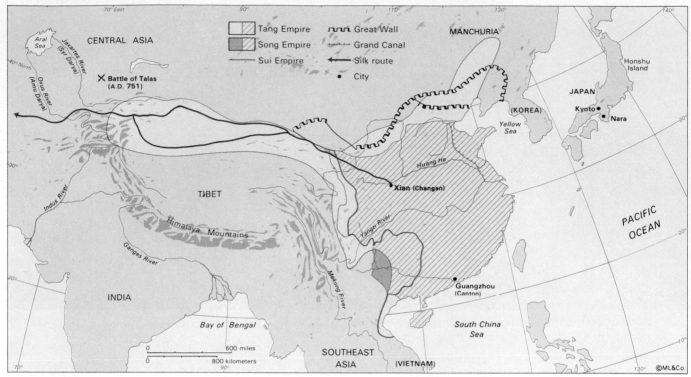

Map Skills **1.** Name the major cities of Tang China. **2.** What rivers are linked by the Grand Canal? **3.** What mountains did a Buddhist monk cross when traveling from India to China?

Religious Change under the Tang. When the Tang Dynasty came to power in A.D. 618, Confucianism, Buddhism, and Daoism were important religions in China. Buddhism had entered China from India (see page 176).

During the sixth and seventh centuries, Buddhism continued to gain new converts in China. In the ninth century, however, the number of followers of Buddhism declined. By then, Buddhist worship had become shallow and superstitious. Also, the powerful scholars of Confucianism viewed Buddhism as a foreign religion and resented it.

Throughout China, thousands of Buddhist monasteries had become wealthy landowners. The Tang government finally took over many of the monasteries and forced Buddhist monks and nuns to pay taxes. One Tang emperor destroyed 40,000 Buddhist shrines and over 4,000 monasteries. After the 800s, when these events occurred, Bud-

dhism was never again strong enough to challenge Confucianism.

The Chinese Civil Service System. Chinese scholars studied Confucianism with great care. One important Confucian idea was that talent and ability, not family connections, should enable individuals to qualify for government jobs. This idea opened government service to the educated. Government officials needed a strong education in Confucianism.

The Chinese civil service system for hiring government officers, accountants, and scribes developed during the Tang period. A young person who wanted a career in government was required to study many years to master the classical Confucian books. Then came a difficult written examination that 99 of 100 students failed.

The few applicants who passed the examination then underwent a grueling interview at the Department of Personnel. There, more examiners evaluated the candidate's writing ability, moral attitude, and personal appearance. Survivors of the testing process could rise eventually to a high office in the government.

Even though anyone could take the examinations, only the rich could afford to give their children the long, expensive education necessary. Therefore, despite the civil service system, most of China's officials came from wealthy families. Occasionally, a wealthy person might support a bright boy from a poor family by paying for his education and preparation for the exams.

The educational and civil service system performed a valuable function. Bright, dedicated people generally managed China's affairs. Even when dynasties fell or barbarians invaded China, the Confucian scholars kept government departments running. This government bureaucracy was an important element in the continuity of Chinese civilization during civil war.

China's Influence on Its Neighbors

The powerful Tang Empire and impressive Chinese culture influenced other east Asian peoples. China's neighbors in Korea, Vietnam, and Japan adopted some Chinese ideas and customs.

China Influences Korea and Vietnam. Chinese armies invaded Korea and Vietnam several times. Under the great Han Emperor, Wu Ti, China took control of Korea and Vietnam in the second century B.C. The Tang rulers invaded as well, but enjoyed only temporary success in Korea.

Both the languages and the cultural traditions of the Koreans and the Vietnamese set them apart from the Chinese. Still, the

As a result of Confucius's belief in a merit system scholars took difficult examinations to become Chinese government officials. Here they wait for their scores to be posted.

ideals of Chinese Confucianism attracted the educated people. Scholars learned to read and write the Chinese language and studied the Confucian classics. The rulers of Korea and Vietnam organized their governments following Chinese patterns.

Two factors continued to keep Korea and Vietnam separate from China. First, each maintained its own distinctive language. Second, Buddhism was the most important religious influence in both countries. Even after Buddhism declined in China, it remained strong throughout neighboring lands.

Early Japan. Like the Koreans and Vietnamese, the Japanese were influenced by Chinese ideas and customs. The Japanese lived on mountainous islands 100 miles from the east Asian mainland. Their language and basic culture also greatly differed from those of the Chinese. They practiced a religion called Shinto, which emphasized worship of spirits in nature and veneration of one's ancestors.

Like the Chinese, most Japanese were farmers, growing rice and other crops. Japan remained a rural country until the sixth century. By then, Chinese culture had begun to influence Japanese life, and cities started to develop.

Buddhism Arrives in Japan. Buddhist monks began to make the sea voyage from the mainland to Japan in about the sixth century. Some of these missionaries were Koreans; many were Chinese. Buddhism was more complex than Shintoism. Its teachings, as well as the beauty and mystery of its ceremonies and art, impressed many Japanese. Soon immigrant monks and Japanese converts began to build lovely Buddhist temples in the Chinese style.

Japanese Writing Develops. The Japanese language, like those of Korea and Vietnam, belongs to a family of languages completely different from Chinese. In the 500s, some educated Japanese learned to read and write Chinese. Scholars worked out methods of writing Japanese using the Chinese system of characters. Eventually, a Japanese script evolved. The Japanese writing, although different from Chinese, showed Chinese influences.

The New Japanese Government. Japan had no central government before the sixth century. The population was organized in large kinship groups, or clans. About A.D. 500, the Yamato was the most powerful clan. It controlled a rich agricultural region called the Osaka Plain, in the southern part of Honshu, Japan's largest island.

The Yamato leaders endorsed Confucian ideas of government. They imitated the Tang system of government. In the middle of the seventh century, the Yamato ruler declared that he was the emperor of all Japan. Even though he did not control the entire country, or even much of it, the Japanese people gradually accepted this Chinese idea of a single ruler.

In A.D. 710, the Yamato emperor began construction of a capital city, Nara. The new city was patterned after the Tang capital of Changan, though on a smaller scale. The Buddhist temples built at Nara are the oldest wooden buildings in the world that are still in existence.

The Japanese ruler built a second capital, also patterned after Changan, in A.D. 794. This second new city, Kyoto, remained the imperial capital of Japan for almost 1,100 years.

Japanese Ambassadors to China. During the eighth and ninth centuries, many exchanges between Japan and China took place. The Japanese government sent many large diplomatic missions to Changan to discuss politics and trade with the Tang. Japanese students, carefully chosen for their intelligence and talent, traveled to China to study Confucianism, Buddhism, art, music, and technology. When they returned to Ja-

A Japanese temple dedicated to the Buddha of healing was built in the Chinese style with a large central hall and two side pagodas. This is the Golden Hall of the Yakushiji at Nara.

pan, they introduced many Chinese ideas and customs.

By the late ninth century, Chinese influence on Japan began to decline for several reasons. Since the Tang Empire was losing influence, the Japanese were less impressed by their once-powerful neighbor. In A.D. 838, the last official Japanese mission went to China. After this visit, the Japanese decided that they had nothing further to learn from the Tang.

As contacts with China decreased, the Japanese returned to their cultural heritage. They could reject Chinese models more easily than could the Koreans or the Vietnamese because the East China Sea separates Japan from China.

Nevertheless, Buddhism, as well as many other ideas of Chinese origin, remained a permanent part of Japanese life. Even Buddhism, though, changed to accommodate more traditional Japanese beliefs.

SECTION 2 *Study Skills*

Developing Vocabulary Use each of the following terms in a sentence. **1.** parasite. **2.** veneration. **3.** civil service system.

Reviewing Main Ideas **1.** Describe Changan. **2.** Why did Buddhism decline in China? **3.** How did the Chinese civil service system influence the stability of the Chinese government? **4.** Give two reasons why Korea and Vietnam could maintain their separation from China.

Understanding Chronology **1.** What dynasties ruled China from A.D. 618 to 907? **2.** When did Japanese government develop?

Understanding Cause and Effect **1.** What lasting impact did the network of roads and canals have on China? **2.** What Chinese ideas influenced Japan?

Challenge What were the consequences of the ancient Chinese attitudes toward merchants and traders for China and other countries?

Birthplace of Three Modern Religions

Buddhism was born in India and was carried to China and Japan. Southwest Asia was the birthplace of three other religions: Judaism, Christianity, and Islam. These three religions have strongly influenced that region and the world.

Similarities and Differences

These religions have much in common. All three religions consider Adam to be the first human. Both Christians and Jews believe that God promised to send a messiah.

Jews and Muslims trace their heritage back to a descendant of Adam, called Abraham or Ibrahim. However, Jews and Muslims believe they descended from different children of Abraham. Abraham's wife, Sarah, bore him no children for many years. In order to assure himself offspring, Abraham married another woman, Hagar, who had a son whom they named Ishmael. Sarah had a son, Isaac, shortly thereafter, and asked Abraham to send Hagar and Ishmael away. Ishmael and Hagar finally made their way to Mecca, a city located in the area that is now Saudi Arabia. Muhammad, the founder of Islam, is considered to be a descendant of Ishmael. Jews believe they are descended from Isaac.

Each religion has its own holy book. The Jewish Torah, the Christian Bible, and the Islamic Koran are collections of sacred writings. Some of the writings are the same. For example, the Torah is also part of the Christian Bible.

The Spread of Religions

Religions can be classified as either universal or ethnic. A universal religion tries to appeal to all people and seeks to attract new followers. Both Christianity and Islam are universal religions. The crusades represent a period during which Christians and Muslims tried to bring new followers to their religions—by force, if necessary.

An ethnic religion is generally held by people who belong to one ethnic group or live in one location. Judaism is an ethnic religion because Jews around the world consider themselves part of one ethnic group. The area where Judaism began is called the Holy Land. This region, especially Jerusalem, is important to Jews.

A map of world religions shows that the two universal religions, Christianity and Islam, are more widespread than the ethnic religion, Judaism. This map shows that Judaism is dominant only in Israel. Christians are most numerous in Europe, Australia, and the Americas. Islam is the dominant religion in north Africa, southwest Asia, and parts of Indonesia.

The spread of ideas, including religion, is called diffusion. Judaism, Christianity, and Islam each have a unique pattern of diffusion over the earth's surface.

Christianity is the most widely diffused of all the world's religions. One billion people, roughly one-quarter of the world's population, are Christian. The timing and location of its origin helped to diffuse Christianity. Christianity originated in Palestine when that land was a province of the Roman Empire. Early followers of Jesus traveled throughout the Roman Empire over land and by sea, spreading the news of Jesus Christ. Merchants and soldiers were the first to hear the doctrines of Christianity because they lived and worked along the land and sea routes of the Roman Empire. Eventually, people throughout the Roman Empire accepted Christianity.

World Religions in the Twentieth Century

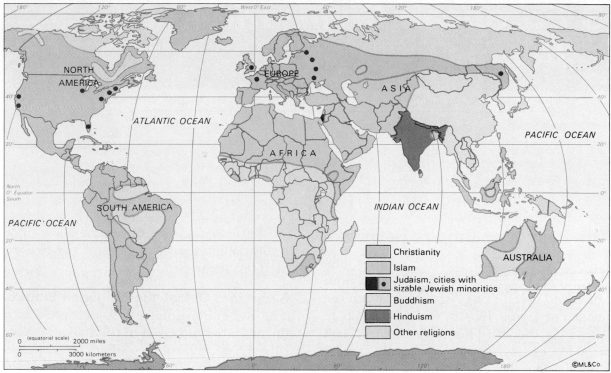

Map Skills **1.** Where are Christians most numerous? **2.** Where is Judaism dominant?
3. Where is Islam the major religion?

By 1500, Christianity was firmly in place in Europe. After 1500, Europeans introduced Christianity throughout the world.

The diffusion of Islam occurred rapidly following the death of Muhammad. Within a century, the Muslim troops and missionaries reached Palestine, India, north Africa, the Iberian Peninsula, and later Asia and Indonesia. Eventually, some blacks in America adopted Islam because of Islam's connection with their African heritage.

Jews have migrated, often to flee persecution. Since about A.D. 70, most Jews have lived outside of the Holy Land. However, they have not converted people in their new homelands as Christians and Muslims have done. Jews have emphasized preserving their faith in spite of religious persecution in their adoptive countries.

Many of the conflicts in southwest Asia today are, in part, religious conflicts. In Lebanon, Christian, Israeli, and Islamic conflicts have almost destroyed the capital city of Beirut. In Israel, Jews and Muslims have fought three wars in the past 40 years. The country of Israel was created in 1948 to provide a homeland for the Jews. The Jewish claim to this land is based on ancient Biblical ties to the area.

As the Jews moved in, many Arab Palestinians felt forced to move. Palestinians continue to claim the area that Israel now occupies in the Middle East.

STUDY SKILLS Understanding Geography

1. Name the Buddhist nation that is farthest east on the map.
2. Explain how Christianity was spread throughout the world.
3. What major areas of the world are influenced by religions not of Middle Eastern origin?

3 European Civilization Begins

OBJECTIVE: *To understand the causes and consequences of the rise of feudalism*

The Byzantine Empire Revives

In the seventh and eighth centuries, the Byzantine Empire lost all of its African lands and much of its Asian territory to the armies of Islam. In A.D. 674 and again in A.D. 717, the Muslims unsuccessfully laid siege to Constantinople, the great Byzantine capital. The Byzantine Empire survived, though greatly reduced in size.

In A.D. 867, an energetic new dynasty of emperors came to power in Constantinople. The first emperor, Basil I, was born in Macedonia, and the new dynasty was called the Macedonian Dynasty.

At the same time, the Abbasid Caliphate was weakening. Taking advantage of this weakness, Byzantine soldiers reconquered some of the territory previously lost to Islam. The Byzantine Empire recovered all of Asia Minor, Armenia, Crete, and much of northern Syria. The Byzantine navy once again dominated the waters of the eastern Mediterranean Sea.

Byzantines Defeat the Bulgarian Empire. The Byzantine Empire also expanded into the mountainous lands of the Balkan Peninsula. There, Byzantine soldiers faced a powerful rival, the Bulgarians. The Bulgarian people were descendants of Slavic invaders from the region that is now the Soviet Union. The Byzantine and Bulgarian empires fought each other for many years. About 1018, Basil II, the Byzantine emperor known as the Bulgar slayer, captured 14,000 Bulgarian prisoners. He blinded 99 out of every 100 men, leaving just a few of his victims with one good eye to lead the other men home. Shortly after Basil's capture and the torture of the Bulgarian prisoners, Bulgaria surrendered.

VOCABULARY DEVELOPMENT

count (kownt) *noun:* a member of the nobility in European countries.

missi dominici: Charlemagne's agents, or spies, messengers of the lord.

feudalism (FYOOD uhl ihz uhm) *noun:* an economic, political, and social system, in which vassals received the use of land in exchange for services to the overlord. Serfs farmed the land. The feudal system developed in Europe about A.D. 900. Similar feudal systems existed in China under the Zhou during the second and third centuries B.C., and in Japan between the ninth and nineteenth centuries A.D.

lord *noun:* the owner of a feudal estate.

homage (HAHM ihj) *noun:* a public vow of allegiance by a vassal to his lord.

serf *noun:* in feudal times, a person bound to the lord's land and transferred with the land to a new owner.

European Invasions, A.D. 800–1000

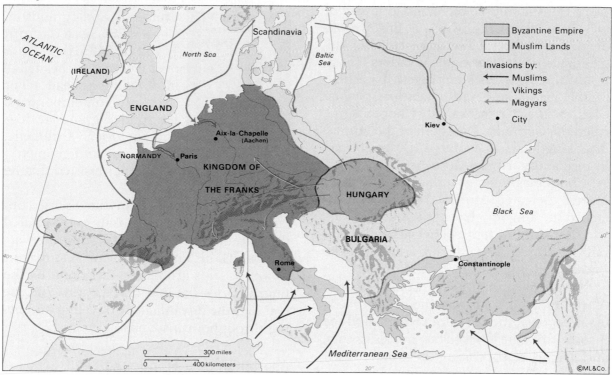

Map Skills **1.** In what lands did the Magyars settle? **2.** What lands were raided by the Vikings? **3.** Identify the people who invaded the Byzantine Empire.

The Greek Orthodox Religion. The revival of Byzantium also strengthened the Greek Orthodox church. The affairs of the government and the church were traditionally connected. The emperor, as head of the church as well as the state, ordered the church to introduce Christianity to neighboring people.

In the ninth century, the emperor sent Greek monks north to introduce Orthodox Christianity to the Slavic peoples. Like Buddhist missionaries in China, these Christians converted many people with their piety and learning. Cyril, a monk, invented an alphabet for writing the holy scriptures in Slavic languages. This alphabet, known as the Cyrillic alphabet, is still used in the Soviet Union today.

Bulgaria converted to Orthodox Christianity in A.D. 865. At about the same time, Byzantine missionaries founded an Orthodox church at the trading city of Kiev. See the map, European Invasions A.D. 800–1000, above. The Russian prince of Kiev was baptized in A.D. 988. This event opened the way for the Orthodox church to expand throughout the vast area of Russia.

Western Europe Develops Slowly

Despite a shared Christian heritage, western Europe, during the seventh and eighth centuries A.D., differed from Byzantium in many ways. The Byzantines had a strong central government, a standing army, public hospitals, trade networks, and an economy based on agriculture.

Western Europe, in contrast to its eastern cousin, was sparsely populated. Little trade occurred with Byzantium or the Islamic civilization. No European towns rivaled Constantinople or Baghdad in size or influence. Politically, western Europe was divided into several kingdoms ruled by descendants of the Germanic invaders.

Europe's fortunes improved for a time in the eighth and ninth centuries, when Charles the Great, called Charlemagne, ruled the Germanic Kingdom of the Franks. This kingdom was centered in present-day France and northern Germany.

Charlemagne's grandfather, Charles Martel, defeated Muslim raiders who attacked the kingdom from Spain in A.D. 732. Charles Martel's foot soldiers faced a new military force, the Muslim cavalry. The Franks had little cavalry of their own.

After defeating the Muslims, Charles Martel granted lands to some of his followers. In return, the new landowners used the income from the lands to buy horses, spears, and armor, thus creating an armored cavalry. These armored and mounted warriors were called knights. Later, Pepin, Charles Martel's son, used a cavalry of knights to help the pope of Rome.

The Papal States. In A.D. 754, the pope crowned Charles Martel's son, Pepin, King by the Grace of God. At the same time, he asked Pepin to help him defeat the Lombards, a Germanic tribe that had settled in northern Italy. The Lombards were raiding central Italy and threatening Rome. The king agreed to help the pope.

Pepin led his army, which now included a few knights to strengthen the infantry, on a victorious campaign into Italy. He then gave the land around Rome to the pope. This land became known as the Papal States and was ruled by the popes until 1870.

Pepin's son, Charlemagne, was even more successful than his father or grandfather. Charlemagne used the army created by his grandfather to help build an empire. In Latin, his name is Carolus Magnus. He gave his name to a dynasty of kings, the Carolingian Dynasty.

Charlemagne, King of the Franks

Charles Martel's grandson, Charles, was born on April 1, 742 or 743. He grew to over 6 feet, 3 inches tall—more than a head taller than his contemporaries. He studied grammar, logic, rhetoric, arithmetic, music, and some astronomy and geometry. His deeply religious mother insisted that he learn church doctrine.

Charles' father, Pepin the Short, conquered part of northern Italy and founded the Carolingian Dynasty. Charles often accompanied his father on military campaigns as well as trips around his kingdom. By the time Charles became king in A.D. 768, he had had the advantage of traveling and living throughout his lands.

Charlemagne's Empire, A.D. 843

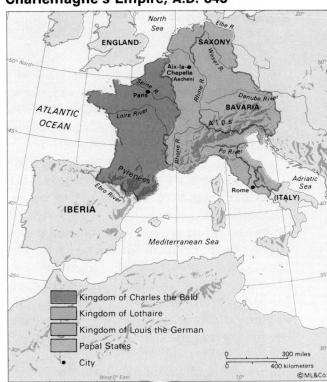

Map Skills 1. Which brother received the western part of the empire? 2. In whose lands was Paris located? 3. Whose lands included present-day Germany?

This illuminated manuscript shows Pope Leo III crowning Charlemagne in A.D. 800. Charlemagne became the Christian king of what was later called the Holy Roman Empire.

An energetic and courageous king, Charlemagne conquered the Lombards of Italy, as well as the kingdoms of Saxony, Bavaria, and Hungary. Charles appointed officials known as counts to administer his empire. To balance the power of the counts, Charles sent agents called *missi dominici*, or messengers of the lord, throughout his empire. This system of checks and balances enabled the king to rule effectively.

Charles built his capital at Aachen, also known as Aix-la-Chapelle, in what is now western Germany. See the map, The Division of Charlemagne's Empire, page 268. The city became famous for its palace, chapel, and school.

Charlemagne developed a close alliance with the pope in Rome, the leader of western Christianity. He supported the pope against the Lombards and the Byzantine emperor, both of whom held territory in southern Italy.

On Christmas Day, A.D. 800, Pope Leo III was present when Charlemagne was crowned Emperor of the Holy Roman Empire. This event suggested that the pope had political as well as religious authority over the Christian rulers of Europe.

Although Charlemagne regretted appearing to rule by the pope's authority, he tried to expand Christianity. When he conquered the people of Saxony, he forced them to become Christians.

Charlemagne invited Christian scholars from England, Ireland, and Italy to study at Aix-la-Chapelle. There they copied ancient Latin texts. ∎

New Invasions Trouble Western Europe

Charlemagne's empire began to crumble during the reign of his only son, Louis the Pious. When Louis died, the Holy Roman Empire was divided among Louis's three sons. After quarreling over the division, the brothers agreed, in A.D. 843, to a settlement called the Treaty of Verdun. The treaty divided Charlemagne's empire into three parts so that each brother would rule a separate kingdom. See the map, The Division of Charlemagne's Empire, page 268.

Later descendants of Charlemagne fought among themselves for control of the land. These feuds, as well as new waves of invaders in the ninth and tenth centuries, tore apart the empire. While the Byzantines enjoyed a period of growth and prosperity, western Europe was slipping back into disorder and stagnation.

Viking Invasions. Germanic warriors of Scandinavia, called Vikings or Norsemen, began to raid the coast of Europe as early as the ninth century A.D. The Vikings invaded

Viking raiders invaded and terrorized Charlemagne's empire. This twelfth-century drawing shows Danish Vikings arriving to attack England.

and conquered parts of northern Germany and France. In the 860s, a Frankish scholar wrote:

ᴸᴸ The number of ships increases, the endless flood of Vikings never ceases to grow bigger. Everywhere Christ's people are the victims of massacre, burning, and plunder. The Vikings overrun all that lies before them, and none can withstand them. **""**

In the British Isles the Vikings were called Danes. They invaded and destroyed many monasteries there.

The Magyars and Muslims Invade Europe. In the ninth century, Muslims and nomads from central Asia, called Magyars, also invaded western Europe. Migrating west in search of good pastures, the Magyars arrived on the grassy plains of Hungary in the late ninth century. From there they raided the crops and herds of farmers in Germany, France, and Italy, spreading terror and destruction throughout the area.

Muslim forces from north Africa also launched attacks against western Europe in the ninth century. They took the island of Sicily from the Byzantines, sent raiding parties far up the Rhone valley in France, and attacked Rome. The attacks of Vikings, Magyars, and Muslims produced instability, disorder, and suffering for the people of western Europe.

The Development of Feudalism

During the Viking, Magyar, and Muslim invasions of the ninth and tenth centuries, the rulers of Europe were too weak and poor to maintain large armies. To pay for military service, rulers used their most abundant resource, land. Rulers rewarded their best warriors with grants of land from their royal estates. These warriors became nobles who used the income from the land to arm knights and foot soldiers to form an army and fight for their ruler.

The grant of land was called a fief. The terms feudal and feudalism are derived from the Latin word for fief, *feudum*. When a person accepted a fief, he became a vassal of the lord or ruler who granted the land. In turn, vassals could grant smaller fiefs to sub-vassals. By accepting a fief, or large estate, and then granting part of it to another knight, a noble could at the same time be a lord to one and a vassal to another. A vassal might possess a number of fiefs granted by several different lords and therefore, owe them all service.

The feudal system set up social classes so that each person had a place. Vassals swore an oath of homage to their lord. At the bottom of the aristocracy was the single knight who was the lord of an estate. Below the knight were peasants who worked the land for the noble. Serfs, bound to the land, made up the lowest social class. Serfs could not leave their place of birth without breaking the law.

Feudal Responsibilities. The lord who granted the fief promised to protect his vassal and to resolve the vassal's grievances at his court. In turn, the vassal owed three major obligations to his lord.

First, the vassal promised to provide a certain number of knights and foot soldiers to fight for the lord. Second, he promised to contribute to the payment of ransom money should the lord be captured in war. Third, the vassal was expected to house and feed the lord and his nobles when they visited the vassal's fief.

A lord retained ownership or title to the fief, but a vassal had the right to pass the use of the land on to his eldest son. All lords and vassals were members of the noble, or aristocratic, class. The peasant populations farmed the great estates in return for military protection, but they had no role in the feudal relationships between noble lords and vassals.

The end of barbarian invasions did not bring peace to Europe. Europe's noble

A feudal knight swears an oath to his king in an illustration from a thirteenth-century bible. Rulers of Europe rewarded their best warriors with grants of land in exchange for military service.

knights constantly made war on one another, keeping Europe in a fragmented state for several centuries. By the eleventh century, lords and vassals had built great fortresses, called castles, throughout Europe to protect their fiefs. Then western Europe suffered from internal attacks instead of external invasions.

The feudal system developed in western Europe as a military and economic response to repeated invasions. It created a political and social system that provided local self-defense in the absence of a strong central ruler. It also contained internal forces for change that would transform western Europe. Feudalism would encourage the rise of powerful rulers who would create strong and enduring nations.

The Latin Christian Church Expands. Between A.D. 750 and 1000, two important developments occurred to strengthen the Latin Christian church. First, the Latin church, centered in Rome and using the

Holy Roman Emperor Otto III meets with clergy and dignitaries in this illumination from a late tenth century manuscript.

Latin language, drew apart from the Greek church of Constantinople.

The Byzantine emperor regarded himself as the leader of all Christians, including the pope of Rome. The Byzantines, however, could no longer control all of Italy. In addition, the pope commanded the support and protection of the kings and nobles of western Europe. The pope, therefore, ignored orders from Constantinople. In A. D. 1054 the pope became the head of the Latin Christian church completely separate from the authority of Constantinople.

The church headed by the pope became known as the Roman Catholic church. The church headed by the Patriarch of Constantinople became the Eastern or Greek Orthodox church.

A second development also strengthened the Roman Catholic church. The church continued to expand in western Europe, even during the most troubled periods. Monks preached their faith to the peoples of central and eastern Europe. In

those regions they sometimes competed successfully against Greek missionaries from Constantinople. The Vikings and Magyars eventually converted to the Roman church.

By the year A.D. 1000, the Greek Christian church was largely centered in eastern Europe. The Latin church, adding many believers throughout western Europe, began to influence the ideas and customs of western European civilization.

The people of western Europe experienced invasions and civil wars between A.D. 750 and 1000. The chaos resulted in feudalism, developed to help people cope with the unstable conditions. The Greek-speaking Byzantine Empire remained an important center of civilization. The Latin church, however, gained many converts and rivaled the Greek Orthodox church as leader of the Christian population.

SECTION 3 *Study Skills*

Developing Vocabulary 1. Who were the *missi dominici*? **2.** Explain the connections between these terms: vassal, lord, serf, feudalism. **3.** What is a fief?

Reviewing Main Ideas 1. Who was the founder of the Cyrillic alphabet? **2.** Identify three ways in which feudal Europe differed from Byzantium.

Understanding Geography 1. Where was Charlemagne's capital? **2.** Where was the Vikings' homeland?

Understanding Chronology 1. When did the Macedonian Dynasty take power? **2.** When did Charlemagne become king?

Understanding Cause and Effect 1. Explain the significance of Charlemagne's association with the pope. **2.** What was the main impact of the invasion of Europe between A.D. 750 and 1000?

Challenge What impact did Charlemagne have on modern Europe?

CHAPTER 12 *Summary & Review*

Summarizing Main Ideas

Between A.D. 700 and 1000, traders spread Islamic culture into sub-Saharan Africa and southern Spain. Arab traders also began regular ocean journeys to eastern Asia after A.D. 750.

In China, the Sui and Tang dynasties enforced unity between A.D. 589 and A.D. 907. During this period, Chinese population, cities, trade, and transportation grew. The development of a civil service provided a continuity to Chinese government that was lacking in many of the other civilizations.

Europe struggled against invaders from A.D. 750 to 1000. For a brief time, western Europe was united under the Carolingian Dynasty. After Charlemagne died in A.D. 814, new waves of invaders swept through Europe.

Viking, Magyar, and Muslim invasions promoted the growth of feudalism. The Christian church based in Rome became the most important religion and institution in western Europe.

"There they go again, searching new horizons, challenging the unknown. Why do they do it? What drives them on?"

Questions for Critical Thinking

COMPREHENSION Interpreting Events

1. Why are the people in the cartoon venturing into the unknown?
2. Explain the long-range effects of the Sui and Tang dynasties.

ANALYSIS Identifying Trends

1. Explain the effect on China of the change from Buddhism to Confucianism during the ninth century.
2. Why did the advent of feudalism mark the beginning of the return of safety and prosperity to western Europe?

APPLICATION Comparing Past to Present

1. Today, western Europe is divided into relatively small nations. How did European feudalism encourage this division?
2. What two achievements of China, during the period A.D. 750–1279, are still evident today?

SYNTHESIS Developing Graphic Skills

1. How is the cartoonist raising questions about the accuracy of the historical record?
2. How might the questions the cartoon raises influence the interpretations of history?

EVALUATION Weighing Consequences

1. Describe the long range results of the development of feudalism.
2. How did the period of barbarian invasions in western Europe affect Christianity?

CHALLENGE

1. Identify and explain the aspects of modern society that are direct results of the growth of Islam and Christianity between A.D. 750 and 1000.
2. Explain the lasting impact of Chinese culture on the other civilizations of Asia.

UNIT 3 *Review*

Critical Thinking for Today's World

ANALYSIS Understanding People

1. Explain why the people of China found Confucianism more appealing than other belief systems such as Buddhism.
2. Compare and contrast the expansions of Christianity and Islam by A.D. 1000.
3. Explain the advantages and disadvantages of feudalism to the European peasants.
4. Throughout history, scholars have influenced society and government. Describe the role that scholars have had in the development of Islamic civilization.

ANALYSIS Recognizing Change Over Time

1. Explain why Christianity and Islam are more widespread than Judaism is today.
2. Dynasties rose and fell in the civilizations discussed in the unit. Explain why this cycle occurred in several geographic regions.
3. Explain why the Byzantine Empire was able to survive until past A.D. 1000.
4. Explain how the way of life of Germanic tribes changed as they migrated into the Roman Empire.
5. How did the changes in climate affect the Germanic people?

APPLICATION Solving Problems

1. Religions and philosophies offer rules for individuals and social behavior. Explain why such rules were necessary in early civilizations. Analyze the role of those rules in civilization today.
2. How did Muslims respond to the problems created by the death of Muhammad?
3. How are the problems faced by people today similar to the problems faced by people in feudal times? Compare and contrast how people then and now have responded to these varying problems.

4. Consider the sources of information historians have for sub-Saharan Africa, Mayan civilization, the Gupta Dynasty, and the Arab expansion. What kinds of problems must historians solve to understand a civilization?
5. What geographical factors may explain why European countries were smaller than the Muslim Empire?

SYNTHESIS Developing Global Citizenship

1. Trade routes multiplied across Eurasia and Africa between A.D. 200 and 1200. Analyze five exchanges that occurred throughout the interacting zone because of trade.
2. Give examples to show how Islamic culture combined with Mediterranean cultures to create a new way of life.
3. Explain why neither the Chinese civilization nor the Islamic civilizations included all of the continent of Asia.
4. How did geography exclude sub-Saharan Africa, Mayan, and Peruvian people from the interacting zone?
5. Compare the achievements of the Gupta Dynasty with the Umayyad Caliphate.

EVALUATION Learning Lessons From the Past

1. Discuss how continued invasions both benefited and harmed the people of the Mediterranean interacting zone.
2. Both Islamic and Byzantine scholars preserved works from the Romans and Greeks. Explain the impact such knowledge has had on modern times.
3. Explain how the Chinese civilization of A.D. 1000 developed from the base of an older Chinese civilization.
4. Explain why the following cities were important in A.D. 1000: Baghdad, Mecca, Rome, and Kyoto. Do major cities today have similar reasons for their importance?
5. Analyze why cities such as Constantinople have remained important throughout much of history.

The Interacting Global Community to A.D. 1000

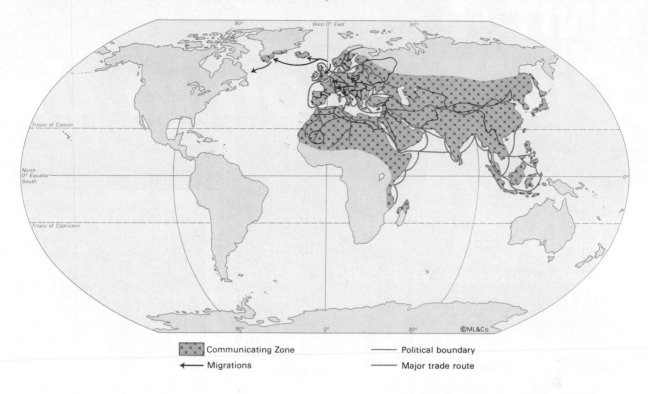

Communicating Zone   **Political boundary**
Migrations   **Major trade route**

A Global Perspective

By A.D. 1000, the Mediterranean interacting zone was enlarged by the spread of Islam and contacts with east Asia. Increased trade helped cities such as Venice, Alexandria, and Baghdad to grow. The map shows both trade in the Eastern Hemisphere and migrations of peoples to the Western Hemisphere.

Islamic civilization continued to expand its influence. Constantinople and Baghdad were located at the crossroads of east-west trade. Muslim trade also expanded into India and along the African coast.

European states became more unified. In northern Europe, Viking explorers ventured westward to Iceland and Greenland. In Africa, Bantu-speaking people migrated south. They developed complex societies ruled by a single individual.

Though Eurasian trade routes did not stretch to the Americas, peoples of the Americas nevertheless interacted among themselves through the exchange of goods.

COMPREHENSION Interpreting Maps

1. Name the three seas shown on the map above that had the most active trade routes. Refer to the map on page 777 for proper names.
2. Name the trade route that crossed Asia from Baghdad to Beijing.
3. How did trade change the communicating zone in Africa between A.D. 200 and 1000? Refer to the map on page 179.
4. Describe and explain the relationship between the sea trade routes and the coastlines.
5. What people migrated the farthest?

ANALYSIS Recognizing Global Trends

1. Explain how Muslim traders helped spread Islamic religion and culture.
2. Islam influenced which European areas? See page 237.
3. What improvements in sailing techniques helped bring about dramatic changes in the world between A.D. 200 and 1000? See page 179.
4. What role did the Arabs play between China and Europe?

UNIT 4
Civilization in the

Middle Ages
1000–1450

Benozzo Gozzoli's fifteenth-century painting *Journey of the Magi* was actually a portrait of the Medici family.

CHAPTER 13

Power Centers in Asia and Europe

GLOBAL TIME LINE

TIME

1000   1050

960–1279 Song Dynasty rules China

900s Venice, Genoa, and Paris become important cities

1000s Domesday Book records landholdings in England

PEOPLE

900s Mahdi establishes the Fatimid Dynasty in North Africa

● **960** Tai Tsu founds the Song Dynasty in China

1000s Chinese invent the printing press, gunpowder, and establish iron industries

PLACE

900s *Egypt;*[1] Mahdi builds Al-Qahira (Cairo) in Egypt as his capital

1000s *China;*[2] Chinese develop the world's first large scale commercial economy

1000s *Europe;*[3] Advances in farming contribute to an increased food supply

Linking Past to Present

An army of Turkish invaders bringing a new style of government to the Middle East, Chinese engineers building a steel suspension bridge, French farmers opening new land with heavy iron plows—these people were agents of change. They represent important developments taking place in world history between 1000 and 1200.

Those agents of change have their counterparts today. New ideas and inventions spread quickly around the world. Superpowers today compete for influence. Modern engineers continue to improve the techniques of building bridges. Underdeveloped countries with large populations seek ways to cultivate more land.

As you read this chapter, think about how new political ideas or technologies changed society.

Chupu bamboo suspension bridge in Sichuan Province.

1100	1150	1200

1066 European astronomers record seeing Halley's comet for the first time

1164 Ayyubid Dynasty unites Syria, Palestine, and Egypt

1096–1291 Christian crusaders battle the Turks

1200s Engagement rings come into fashion in Europe

1092 Seljuk Empire splits into several small kingdoms

1066 William the Conqueror defeats King Harold of England at the Battle of Hastings

1170 Saladin overthrows the Fatimid Dynasty of Egypt and founds the Ayyubid Dynasty

1071 Turks defeat the Byzantine army at the Battle of Manzikert and gain control of most of Asia Minor

1096 Pope Urban II organizes the First Crusade

1100s *Eastern Europe;*[4] German monks convert the people of Hungary to Christianity

1206 *India;*[5] Delhi becomes the new Turkish capital

279

1 The Rise of the Turks

OBJECTIVE: *To understand the causes and consequences of the rise of the Turkish people*

Origin of the Turks

In the eleventh century, a group of nomads called Turks migrated from central Asia to India and the Middle East. Sometime before the fourth century A.D., these people had moved to the grasslands that stretched from the Altai Mountains to the Caspian Sea. This region became Turkestan. See the map, The Spread of Islam, page 237.

Little is known about the Turks before the fourth century A.D. The Chinese, however, recorded a legend about the origin of the Turks. Many centuries ago, a central Asian tribe was defeated in battle. The last survivor was a 10-year-old boy. The victors did not kill him but cut off his feet and left him in a swamp. When he grew up, he had 10 sons by a female wolf. One of these children founded the first Turkish tribe.

Muslims Influence the Turks. Between the fourth and the eleventh centuries, several Turkish groups founded kingdoms in Turkestan. Buddhist missionaries spread their religion among the Turks. In the eighth century, however, Arab Muslims invaded and conquered part of Turkestan. The influence of Muslim merchants and scholars gradually converted the Turks from Buddhism to Islam.

Turkish Society. Some of the Turkish people herded sheep and horses, and lived as pastoral nomads. Others were merchants and artisans who lived in towns. Tribes of nomadic Turks traveled over the steppes in large wagons pulled by oxen or camels.

Turkish women enjoyed greater social equality with men than other Muslim women. A Turkish woman could buy, sell, and manage property. The wife of a Turkish chief was not kept out of view in a harem Instead, she could appear in public.

The Turks Expand Their Territory. During the eleventh century, the lands of India and southwestern Asia were divided into several Muslim or Hindu kingdoms. The rulers could not effectively defend their lands against invaders. As a result, warriors from Turkestan poured into both India and the Middle East.

Throughout history, central Asian nomads often crossed the high passes of the Hindu Kush Mountains to invade Afghanistan and northern India. Near the end of the tenth century, Turkish warriors also invaded and conquered these lands. The first

---

VOCABULARY DEVELOPMENT

harem *noun:* a secluded part of a house where the women of a Muslim household live. From the Arab word *harim*, meaning sanctuary.

sultan *noun:* a Muslim ruler; king.

madrasas (muh DRAH suhs) *noun:* Muslim colleges.

sans (sanz) *prep.:* without. Adapted into English directly from the French.

Turkish dynasty, the Ghaznavids (GUHZ nuh vihdz), built the capital city of Ghazna in what is now Afghanistan.

From 998 to 1038, the greatest Ghaznavid ruler, Mahmud the Conqueror, expanded his kingdom to include northeastern Persia. He also sent armies through the Khyber Pass to invade the small Hindu kingdoms of the northern Indus River valley. Mahmud's soldiers destroyed wealthy Hindu temples and carried back gold and Indian slaves. With this wealth, Mahmud built Ghazna into an important center of Islamic learning and architecture.

Turkish Influence in India. After Mahmud died, the Ghaznavid Empire shrank in size. Turkish armies, however, continued to raid India. In 1206, a Turkish general took the title of sultan and founded a new kingdom, placing its capital at Delhi. This city was in the fertile plains of north India, between the Indus and Ganges river valleys. See the map, Seljuk and Delhi Sultanates, page 282.

A privileged and powerful social class of Turkish and Afghan warriors governed the Delhi Sultanate. They collected taxes from thousands of Hindu peasant villages. Most Indians never accepted the Islamic religion. Hinduism remained an important part of Indian life. However, Muslims continued to rule much of India for more than 500 years.

Turkish Power in the Middle East and Africa

Early in the eleventh century, a powerful confederation of Turks migrated to the arid lands north of Persia. Called the Seljuk (sehl JOOK) Turks after their first leader, they had been converted to Islam a century or so earlier. In part, Islam unified the Seljuk and Ghaznavid Turks. The Seljuk Turks, however, turned on the Ghaznavids in northern Persia and conquered them.

Several small states occupied the Middle East at that time. Therefore, the Seljuks had little trouble conquering the region. In 1055, they entered Baghdad, the seat of the Abbasid caliph. The Seljuk leader did not depose the caliph, who was the supreme spiritual leader of all Muslims. Instead, he declared that, as sultan, he would rule in the caliph's name. The caliph was too weak to disagree. Like the pope who had acknowledged Charlemagne's right to rule (page 268), the caliph's approval gave the Seljuks authority in the eyes of Muslims.

In the second half of the eleventh century, the Seljuk Turks expanded their empire from eastern Persia to the Mediterranean Sea. Turkish forces advanced west into Asia Minor, territory of the Byzantine Empire. In 1071, the Seljuks defeated a large Byzantine army at Manzikert (MAN zuh

A fourteenth-century Turkish manuscript shows Mahmūd of Ghazna using a catapult to attack rebels in their mud-brick fortress. Islamic armies used siege tactics to gain control of cities.

KUHRT), in eastern Asia Minor. The Turks even captured the Byzantine emperor and held him until a ransom was paid.

The Battle of Manzikert in 1071 enabled the Seljuks to win control of most of Asia Minor. During the next three centuries, thousands of Turks migrated from northern Persia to Asia Minor. The Greek Christian population gradually declined, and Asia Minor became the Muslim and Turkish-speaking region that is now called Turkey.

In 1092, members of the ruling family quarreled and split the Seljuk Empire into several small kingdoms.

The Order of Assassins. An organization of Muslim revolutionaries and terrorists, the Assassins, was founded in the eleventh century by Shi'ite Muslims. They rejected the caliph in Baghdad.

The Turks were Sunni Muslims. They believed, along with the majority of Muslims, that religious leadership belonged to the caliph. Shi'ite groups, therefore, resented and opposed the Turks because the Turks accepted the caliph.

The Assassins, also called Ismaili Shi'ites, were headquartered in a huge fortress in the mountains of northern Persia. From there, they sent terrorist bands to start revolts against the Turks and murder political leaders. For 200 years, the Order of Assassins caused disruption in the Middle East. By the thirteenth century, however, their membership and influence had declined.

The Fatimid Dynasty of North Africa. In the early tenth century, a Shi'ite Muslim called the Mahdi, or Savior, gained the support of many Berbers in north Africa. He established the Fatimid Dynasty in the area that is now Tunisia.

In 969, a successor of the Mahdi led an army of Berber warriors across Libya and

Seljuk and Delhi Sultanates

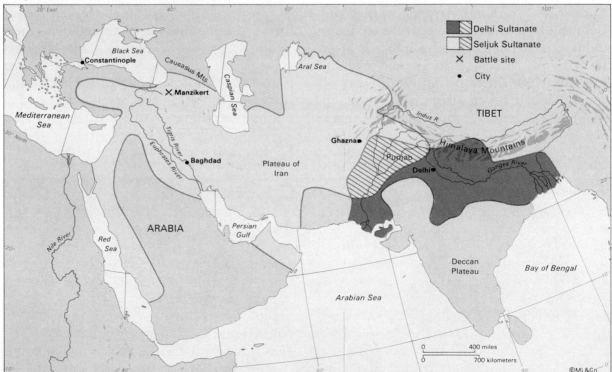

Map Skills 1. How many kilometers apart are the cities of Ghazna and Delhi? **2.** In what direction would an invader travel to reach the Deccan Plateau from the Himalaya Mountains?

The English King Richard I is shown unhorsing the Arab King Saladin during the Third Crusade.

invaded the Nile Valley. He built a new walled city in Egypt to serve as the capital. He called it Al-Qahira (al-KAH hee RAW), or Cairo, meaning The Victorious. Cairo became an important city of the Muslim world in the eleventh and twelfth centuries. Its mosques, palaces, and public bath houses were famous for their beauty. A traveler from Persia wrote that the city had 20,000 stores and shops, that 52,000 camels carried water from the Nile to it every day, and that every night 1,000 soldiers guarded the Fatimid ruler's palace.

By the late tenth century, the Fatimid rulers of Egypt, like the Abbasid caliphs of Baghdad two centuries earlier, had settled into a life of luxury and pleasure. They lost their zeal for Shi'ite revolution and in 1170 were overthrown.

The Rise of Saladin. The Middle East remained divided into a checkerboard of states throughout the twelfth century. For a short time, however, Egypt, Syria, and Palestine were united under a ruler known in Europe as Saladin.

Saladin, the son of a military officer, was an expert archer and swordsman. He became an officer under a Turkish prince of Iraq. In 1164, Saladin commanded troops in the successful invasion of Fatimid Egypt. When only 30 years old, he took control of

Egypt and founded a new dynasty called the Ayyubid. He united Syria and Palestine with Egypt. After Saladin died in 1193, his empire was again divided into rival states.

Islamic Learning and Culture

Even though the Islamic world suffered repeated invasions and political upheavals in the eleventh and twelfth centuries, scientific research and learning continued. The Turkish military rulers supported writers, philosophers, and other teachers. The Seljuk sultans gave money to build Muslim colleges, called *madrasas* (muh DRAS uhs).

These colleges were built in the Middle East and north Africa at about the same time Oxford and Cambridge colleges were founded in England. Some of the most important were located in Baghdad, Damascus, and Cairo. Young Muslims came from throughout Islamic lands to study religion, law, grammar, and other subjects. They lived in dormitories, did homework by candlelight, and earned diplomas after seven or more years of study.

In Ghazna in the early eleventh century, the Persian poet Firdawsi wrote the famous *Shah-nama* (SHAH NAH muh). This book, an epic poem of about 60,000 verses, tells of the great deeds of the warrior-kings of Persia before Islamic times.

An important Muslim philosopher of the twelfth century was ibn Rushd, known in Europe as Avérroës (uh VEHR oh eez). He wrote books on the teachings of Aristotle and Plato, and also developed his own philosophy. His writings, translated from Arabic into Latin, influenced Christian Europe after the fourteenth century.

The *Rubáiyát* of Omar Khayyám

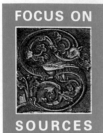

FOCUS ON SOURCES

Omar Khayyám (OH mahr ky YAHM), a poet, astronomer, and mathematician, lived in Baghdad under the Seljuks. He is known for his long poem, the *Rubáiyát* (ROO bih yaht), meaning a collection of four-line verses. Some of the lines are longer than the columns of this book, however, making the stanza appear longer than four lines. In the *Rubáiyát*, Omar Khayyám wrote about nature, the shortness of life, and the pleasure of love.

" Here with a Loaf of Bread beneath the Bough,
A Flask of Wine, a Book of Verse—and Thou
Beside me singing in the Wilderness—
And Wilderness is Paradise enough.

"How sweet is mortal sovereignty!"— think some:
Others—"How blest the Paradise to come!"
Ah, take the Cash in hand and waive the Rest;
Oh, the brave Music of a distant Drum!

• • •

Lo! some we loved, the loveliest and best
That Time and Fate of all their Vintage prest,
Have drunk their Cup a Round or two before,
And one by one crept silently to Rest.

• • •

Ah, make the most of what we yet may spend,
Before we too into the Dust descend;
Dust into Dust, and under Dust, to lie,
Sans Wine, sans Song, sans Singer, and—sans End!"

• • •

There was a Door to which I found no Key:
There was a Veil past which I could not see:
Some little Talk awhile of Me and Thee
There seemed, and then no more of Thee and Me. " ■

Between 1000 and 1200, Muslim scholars and writers contributed to the knowledge and literature of the interacting lands of Eurasia and north Africa. Partly because of the Turkish invasions and two centuries of warfare, the people of the Middle East did not make significant advances in agriculture and industry. The Chinese, however, made astonishing strides.

SECTION 1 *Study Skills*

Developing Vocabulary Use each of the following terms in a sentence: **1.** harem. **2.** sultan. **3.** sans. **4.** madrasas.

Reviewing Main Ideas **1.** Why did the Turks change their religion? **2.** Explain the importance of the Battle of Manzikert. **3.** How did the Order of Assassins disrupt the Middle East?

Understanding Chronology **1.** About how long did the Turks live in Turkestan? **2.** What areas were conquered in the eleventh century?

Understanding Cause and Effect Explain two factors that helped the Turks' conquests.

Understanding Geography **1.** What was the capital of the Turkish Ghaznavid Dynasty in Afghanistan? **2.** Describe the location of Delhi.

Challenge Compare the status of women in eleventh century Turkish society with their status in modern Turkey.

2 Advances During the Song Dynasty

OBJECTIVE: *To understand the economic, scientific, and technological advances that occurred in China during the Song Dynasty*

The Rise of the Song Dynasty

After the fall of the Tang Empire in 907, China remained divided for several decades. In 960, a general, given the title Taizu (ty dzoo), founded the Song Dynasty.

Taizu's most important task was to reunite the country and stop the constant wars that weakened China. He gradually replaced regional warlords with officials from his civil service. He also created a professional army, which was controlled by the central government.

Taizu favored his second son, who had advised him to lead a revolution and claim the Chinese throne. His jealous brothers tried to poison the favorite. When this attempt failed, they set an ambush for him outside the palace gates. The favorite, later called Taizong, heard about the ambush and was prepared. In the fight that ensued, both his older and younger brothers were killed. His grief-stricken father abdicated, and Taizong became the Song emperor.

A Government of Scholars. Taizu and his successors created a civilian government that contrasted with the Turkish military governments in the Middle East. After 1065, Song emperors scheduled civil service examinations every three years in each district of the empire. Those who passed the local tests (fewer than 10 percent) took further examinations. Examiners followed elaborate procedures to mark papers fairly. A government scribe copied each test so that no one could recognize the original handwriting. Names of candidates were removed from their papers, and three people read every exam.

VOCABULARY DEVELOPMENT

warlord *noun:* a military commander using force to govern a limited area.

commercial economy: a system of producing, distributing, and consuming goods on a large scale.

gluten (GLOOT uhn) *noun:* a gray, sticky protein substance found in grains, that gives dough its tough, elastic property. From the Latin word, *gluten*, meaning glue.

canal locks: enclosed parts of artificial waterways equipped with gates so that water levels can be changed to move boats from one level to another.

alchemist (AL kuh mihst) *noun:* a person in the Middle Ages who tried to combine magic and chemistry. Many alchemists tried to turn a base metal, such as iron, into gold.

abacus (AB uh kus) *noun:* a frame holding beads that slide back and forth; used to solve arithmetic problems. From the Greek word, *abax*, meaning counting board.

acupuncture *noun:* a Chinese practice of puncturing the body with needles at specific locations to relieve pain and cure disease.

anatomical (AN uh TAHM ih kuhl) *adj.:* having to do with the structure of the body.

pig iron *noun:* crude iron as it comes from the blast furnace; so called because of its shape and size.

The Song Dynasty thus developed a remarkable government of scholars. English-speaking people have called these high government officials mandarins, after the Portuguese word, *mandarin*, meaning to command. Mandarins showed their rank by the color of the buttons on their caps. Governors and generals wore red coral buttons, lieutenant governors and judges blue, and lower officials other colors.

Each mandarin had an official robe. The military robe was embroidered with beasts, the civil robe with decorative birds. Judges wore plainer robes.

To ensure their honesty, government officials were never assigned to the province from which they came. They could neither marry nor acquire property in the province to which they were sent, and could not serve over three years in one province.

Most of the great poets and philosophers of the age were government officials. Both their scholarly writings and their practical policies were based on Confucianism.

Eleventh century Confucian scholars proposed reforms in landholding, education, and government.

Military Crises. Government officials and scholars became the most highly respected members of Song society. Since soldiers were no longer so highly respected, recruiting became difficult. A popular saying was: "The best iron is not to be used for nails, and the best men are not to be used for soldiers." This attitude differed greatly from that in both Japan and Europe, where society prized military skills.

Song rulers were always fearful that powerful generals would become warlords. They limited the size and strength of the army until it could no longer defend the northern borders against barbarian tribes. Song rulers, therefore, gave the barbarians tribute to keep them from invading China.

Steppe invaders, however, learned to use new Chinese military inventions, such as the crossbow, steel armor, and gunpowder. In

Song and Jin China, 1000–1200

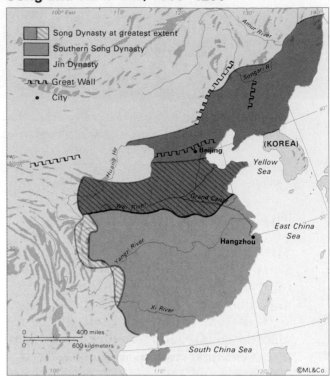

Map Skills 1. What Chinese rivers are linked by the Grand Canal? **2.** What region of China does the Great Wall protect?

1126 and 1127, a steppe people, the Jurchen (JUR chen), overran northern China.

The Song emperor was forced to flee to southern China, giving up the north to the Jurchen. In the south, the emperor established a new capital at Hangzhou, south of the Yangzi River. For this reason, the Song Dynasty from 1127 to 1279 is called the Southern Song.

Cities and Commerce Grow

China was the most populous and advanced country in the world during the eleventh and twelfth centuries. Almost 100 million people lived in China, and at least 10 cities housed more than 1 million people. Chinese cities had theaters, parks, and restaurants. The increase in population and the growth of cities resulted from expanded farming, industry, and transportation.

Advances in Farming. By the twelfth century, Chinese farmers were producing enough rice and wheat to feed the people living in the large cities. They also raised silkworms to make the luxurious cloth sold both in China and abroad. Farmers were part of a market network that stretched in many areas from rural peasants, to large-city dwellers, and finally to overseas traders.

The people of China could buy and sell products to fill their basic needs. No longer did each family have to supply all of its necessities. The Chinese developed the world's first large-scale commercial economy.

Government policy was one of the most important reasons for change. Government officials were sent from region to region with instruction manuals and pictures to encourage farmers to work harder and adopt new farming techniques.

New varieties of rice ripened so fast that two crops could be grown each year. Chinese farmers used manure as fertilizer, and workers built dikes to increase the available farmland. A thirteenth century official described a province of hard-working farmers as follows:

❝ The soil is rich in Wu, and can give two harvests in one year. Silkworms can be brought to maturity eight times in one year. . . . In Wu, the people open up the wastelands and swampy depressions for the cultivation of rice of moderate gluten content, and they also plant vegetables, wheat, hemp, and beans. ❞

Advances in Transportation. Transporting crops from farmlands to cities was as important as growing more food. In the eleventh and twelfth centuries, the Chinese improved transportation. Water transportation was the most efficient way to move large loads. Major Chinese cities were located on rivers linked together by canals.

In the 1200s, the Chinese invented canal locks. The locks enabled boats to go up and down rivers with rapids. By the thirteenth century, Chinese rivers and canals were filled with barges carrying supplies all over

A scroll by Chang Tse-tuan shows the crowded streets and open-air market of Kaifeng, the twelfth-century capital of northern Song China.

the country. Several hundred tons of rice were unloaded at the capital city of Hangzhou every day to feed the people.

Advances in Commerce. Commerce depends on the exchange of merchandise in convenient markets using an accepted system of money. The Chinese had strings of copper for money. As trade expanded, however, the supply of copper could not match the demand. In the tenth century, the government began to issue paper money as a copper substitute. The Chinese were the first people in the world to accept paper money widely. To further expand the money system, merchants began to allow their customers to purchase items on credit.

Chinese Society. The advances in farming, transportation, and commerce led to much more complex specialization in occupations. The growing cities needed more government officials, workers, managers, and merchants. City people also needed more doctors, teachers, and pharmacists. Chinese cities even had employment agencies for cooks, gardeners, chair porters, singers, and other specialized workers.

For upper class women, however, life became more restricted during the Song period. One practice that restricted women was the demand of fathers and husbands that women have small feet. About the tenth century, tiny feet became the standard of beauty for Chinese women. The feet of young, upper class girls were tightly bound. Eventually, the arches of their feet broke, and their toes curled under. They hobbled around, and servants waited on them. This custom persisted until the twentieth century. These upper class Chinese women grew up with "lily-feet," a symbol of wealth.

Science and Industry Advance

Eleventh century Chinese made important discoveries in science and technology. Chinese inventors developed the printing press and gunpowder. In the eleventh century, Chinese artisans were learning to make energy-powered spinning machines.

Chinese Printing. As early as the seventh century, the Chinese printed pictures and books. Workers carved pictures and whole sections of text on wood blocks. The blocks then were inked and used to print books. Using this method, the government printed and distributed educational manuals. By the tenth century, all of the Confucian and Buddhist texts were in print.

In the eleventh century, a printer, Bi Sheng, invented movable type made of baked clay. He made separate pieces for each Chinese character and put them in iron frames for printing. Movable type never became very important in China, however, because 4 to 5 thousand characters were needed for a book.

The Invention of Gunpowder. A Chinese alchemist who made a mistake invented gunpowder. According to the story in a Chinese textbook:

" There was a case in which sulphur and realgar [a mineral consisting of arsenic sulfide] were mixed with saltpeter and honey, and burnt. Flames leapt up, burning the alchemist's hands and face and incinerating the building. **"**

From this mistake, scientists went on to develop a "fire-drug" that was used for bombs, grenades, and rockets. Someone thought of filling bamboo tubes with gunpowder and attaching them to arrows or lances. These devices may have been the ancestors of the cannon. The Chinese used explosives in their wars from the eleventh century on. Within the next 300 years, the technology of making gunpowder weapons spread westward from China to India, the Middle East, and Europe.

Mathematics and Medicine in China. Important advances also occurred in mathematics. Arithmetic books in the eleventh

This scene from a twelfth-century silk scroll shows a doctor using moxibustion, the burning of a soft material on the skin, to treat a disease or disorder.

century showed the use of algebra and trigonometry to survey land, calculate exchange rates and business costs, and measure objects. By the end of the Song period, Chinese merchants and accountants were using the abacus, a device for doing complex arithmetic. Merchants used the abacus for the same purpose that the calculator is used in the present day.

During the Song Dynasty, Chinese medicine provided the best treatment available in the world. Physicians carefully observed the symptoms of diseases and wrote accurate descriptions. Books contained information about thousands of plants used as medicines. An official government drugs office tested and approved new remedies.

Chinese doctors used acupuncture, puncturing patients with needles to relieve pain and cure diseases. The Chinese dissected human bodies to develop better anatomical charts and models. Using these charts, they improved acupuncture.

The Chinese Technological Revolution.
Artisans searching for solutions to their problems made important technological advances. When timber became scarce in

northern China, for example, manufacturers learned how to use coal and turn it into coke. In the eleventh century, they began to use coke in blast furnaces to make iron and steel. By the middle of the eleventh century, up to 125,000 tons of iron were produced each year.

The Chinese used iron and steel for nails, hoes, statues, coins, and even suspension bridges and armored war wagons. Factories employing many workers produced these iron and steel items. One iron manufacturer employed 700 coal miners, 1,000 iron ore miners, and 1,000 blast furnace workers. He produced 14,000 tons of pig iron a year.

By the thirteenth century, the Chinese had made great advances in science and technology and in industrial production. Many historians believe that the Chinese were beginning an industrial revolution in Song times. China at this time was more productive than any other region.

SECTION 2 *Study Skills*

Developing Vocabulary 1. Describe a commercial economy. **2.** What is an abacus? **3.** What English word shares its Latin root with *gluten*? **4.** How are alchemists and chemists different? **5.** What is acupuncture?

Reviewing Main Ideas 1. Describe three precautions taken to insure fairness in Chinese civil service exams. Why were such steps necessary? **2.** Identify specific achievements by the Chinese in each of four different areas of knowledge.

Understanding Chronology 1. When did the Song Dynasty begin regularly scheduled civil service exams? **2.** When did the Chinese begin using explosives in warfare?

Understanding Cause and Effect Why was it possible for such a large part of the Chinese population to live in cities?

Challenge Compare the methods of twelfth century Chinese farmers with the farming methods used in China today.

Asia, Land of Diversity

Asia, the largest continent, has great variety in geography, culture, and religion. Asia includes the culture realms of India, China, Japan, and part of the Soviet Union. At times Asia was isolated from the rest of the world. At other times, Asia was a highway for far-reaching exchange.

Physical Environment

Asian climate ranges from very cold northern areas, to hot, tropical regions in the south. Most of northern Asia is part of the Soviet Union. This region is a vast plain with a harsh climate. No month is completely free of frost in parts of northern Asia. The cold climate makes agriculture almost impossible. Some people are nomads who make a living herding or hunting. Most of the remainder of the Soviet Union is subarctic with long cold winters and short cool summers in normal years.

Much of central Asia is dry and at a high altitude. Central Asia includes parts of Mongolia, China, and Tibet. The Gobi Desert lies in southern Mongolia.

Southern Asia is much warmer than the Northern part of the continent. In general, Southeast Asia receives much more rain than southwest Asia.

Mountain ranges help define the borders of nations. The Hindu Kush divides Pakistan from Afghanistan. The Tien Shan forms a northwestern boundary for China. The towering Himalayan Mountains separate China from India. Mount Everest, the world's tallest peak, is part of the Himalayan chain. Two nations, Nepal and Bhutan, nestle entirely within the Himalayas.

The variations in climate within Asia affect how people live. For example, northern China has a cold, dry climate. The people in this region grow wheat and millet. In southern China, wet winds from the east bring large amounts of rain. This rain, combined with the warmer temperature, allows people to grow rice. As a result of these differences in climate, people eat different kinds of food. Northern Chinese cooking features wheat noodles. Southern Chinese cooking emphasizes rice.

Cultural Diversity

Although Asian countries share the same continent, they do not share the same culture. For example, the majority of people in China are Han Chinese. However, a census of China also includes other groups of people such as Mongols, Turks, Koreans, Manchus, and Tibetans. The Chinese culture has been the dominant one for most of recorded history.

Some countries have not had one dominant culture. Consequently, these countries, such as Indonesia, are even more diverse than China. For example, entertainment in Indonesia might feature instruments from the Middle East and music influenced by the traditional Chinese Court. There a puppet theater, the wayang, might feature puppets acting tales from a Hindu epic that is called the *Ramayana*.

Religious Diversity. For the past one thousand years the major religions in Asia have been Hinduism, Buddhism, and Islam. Confucian and Daoist ways of thinking (see page 109) have influenced east and southeast Asia. Shinto developed as a local religion in Japan. Hinduism developed, and largely remained, in India, although it has influenced much of Southeast Asia. Buddhism developed in northern India and

Data on Countries in Asia

	Bangladesh	China	India	Indonesia	Japan	Philippines	Vietnam
Area (in thousands of square miles)	56	3,696	1,269	741	145	115	128
Area (in thousands of square kilometers)	144	9,572	3,287	1,919	377	300	331
Population (in millions)	87	1 004	685	147	119	53	52
Annual birth rate (per 1,000 population)	45	19	33	30	13	32	32
Annual death rate (per 1,000 population)	17	7	13	13	6	7	11
Number of years to double population (projected)	30	60	33	40	not available	28	29
Population projected by A.D. 2000 (in millions)	127	1 257	961	198	128	75	79
Annual death rate of infants under 1 year (per 1,000 births)	133	56	117	106	6	50	35
Percent of population under 15 years	47	34	40	40	22	41	42
Percent of population over 64 years	5	7	5	5	12	4	not available
Life expectancy at birth	47	70	53	52	77	65	57
Percent of population urban	15	28	24	22	76	36	19
Per capita food supply (as percent of requirement)	85	105	90	106	123	102	94
Total GNP (in billions of U.S. dollars)	12	313	173	199	1,215	30	9
Per capita GNP (in U.S. dollars)	140	308	249	570	10,120	598	160
Percent of adult population illiterate	71	32	64	28	0	11	6

spread south and east. Islam was carried to Asia through trade links and military action. Several of the Soviet Union's republics are now largely Muslim. Malaysia, Pakistan, and Bangladesh are Muslim nations. Sections of western China and much of Indonesia are also Muslim. (See page 246.)

Isolation and Influence. Asian nations such as China and Japan have, at times, sought to reduce their contacts with outsiders. Other nations lay in the path of the changing currents of trade and conquest. The Great Wall of China was built to keep out foreign invaders. The 1,500 mile long wall is a symbol of China's efforts to be culturally pure. However, Chinese culture has influenced neighbors such as Japan, Korea, and Vietnam.

In some instances, contact with other cultures has not been by choice. For instance, northern India was influenced by a succession of invaders including the Aryans, Greeks, and Muslims. In modern times, India was a colony, an overseas possession, of Britain until the 1940s. The Philippines were dominated first by Spain and then by the United States. As a result of the influence of the United States, the English language is commonly used today in business in the Philippines.

STUDY SKILLS Understanding Geography

1. Identify the location of two major mountain ranges in China.
2. What three religions are dominant in Asia?
3. Explain how the variations in China's climate affect the type of food people eat.
4. Cite three examples of the diversity found in the culture of Indonesia.

3 European Civilization Comes of Age

OBJECTIVE: *To understand the causes and consequences of the development of European civilization during the Middle Ages*

Europe during the Middle Ages

Europe was a rustic land of forests and fields in the tenth century. No large cities interrupted rural life; stone buildings were rare. Even kings and knights wore homespun clothes and did not know how to read or write. In contrast to the civilization of Song China, Europe was a barbarian land on the outskirts of the interacting world.

Nobles Control the Countryside. At the beginning of the eleventh century, feudal knights dominated most of Europe. Knights controlled the countryside from the castles they held as fiefs from their feudal lords. Each lord governed his own territory, operated his own court and collected rent and taxes from peasants. Kings had little power.

In the late tenth century, however, some great nobles began to win firmer control over lesser nobles. These great nobles built their own castles to control the countryside.

Divine Right Kings. As had Charlemagne, other European kings claimed that their rule came from God's authority. To reinforce the notion that God gave them the authority to rule, these divine right kings developed elaborate rituals of coronation. Despite their claims, European rulers did not exercise as much power as the mighty emperors of the Byzantine Empire and

---

VOCABULARY DEVELOPMENT

homespun *noun:* cloth made of yarn spun at home.

divine right kings: kings who believed their right to rule came directly from God.

chivalry *noun:* a code of behavior knights were supposed to follow. From the French word, *cheval*, meaning horse.

joust *noun:* a competition in which two knights on horseback galloped at each other with lances lowered, each seeking to unseat the other. From the Latin word, *juxtare*, meaning to approach.

moldboard *noun:* a piece of wood or iron attached to the side of a plow so as to turn the soil over. Moldboard plows opened more land to farming.

fallow (FAL oh) *noun:* land left uncultivated, or not seeded, for one or more growing season, to allow farmers to plow under the weeds and increase subsequent productivity.

manor: the agricultural estate over which a feudal lord held authority.

commune (KAHM yoon) *noun:* a local body created for self-government in towns during the Middle Ages. From the Latin word, *communis*, meaning common.

charter *noun:* a written grant of specified rights from a ruler, government, or business to a group of people.

literacy (LIHT uhr uh see) *noun:* the ability to read and write. From the Latin word, *littera*, meaning letter.

lay investiture: the authority of a lay person, such as a king, to grant religious offices to clergy.

laity *noun:* the people who practice a religious faith, as distinct from those who are members of the clergy.

China. In fact, the kings of Europe shared power with their feudal vassals. The strongest vassals often had more real power than the kings they served.

The feudal king of France actually controlled little more than the city of Paris in the eleventh century. Gradually, other energetic French kings increased the area they controlled. For instance, when vassals died without heirs, the French king claimed their fiefs as his own. The king punished rebellious knights and took away their fiefs. The French king required vassals to come to the French court to learn about royal policies. In 1066, a French lord from Normandy invaded England, and introduced feudalism to the British Isles.

Feudalism Arrives in England. At the beginning of the tenth century, a group of Vikings conquered northwest France. They became known as Normans, from the word Norsemen.

The Normans were adventurous warriors who expanded their lands by conquest. In 1066, William, the Duke of Normandy, led an army across the English Channel to England. His forces and those of the English king, Harold, fought a decisive battle near the village of Hastings. William's knights defeated the English armies, and William won the title William the Conqueror.

William the Conqueror

FOCUS ON PEOPLE

William was born in Normandy about 1027. His ancestors were Norsemen who had settled in northern France about a century before his birth. He was the illegitimate son of the Duke of Normandy and a peasant girl. For this reason, his enemies always called him William the Bastard.

In 1066, the king of England, a cousin of William's father, died without an heir. William claimed the English throne. Two other

This scene from the Bayeux Tapestry shows a messenger bringing news of Harold to William in 1066. With special authorization of the city of Bayeux.

men, the king of Norway and an Anglo-Saxon noble, Harold Godwinson, opposed William's right to rule England.

When the Anglo-Saxon, Harold, was crowned king, William decided to invade England. He recruited knights and archers and built a fleet of ships. Meanwhile, the king of Norway, Harold's former ally, invaded England from the north. Harold defeated the Norwegians, then raced south to Hastings to confront the new threat to his throne. In October 1066, William's army met Harold's soldiers and defeated them at the famous Battle of Hastings. Harold died after a Norman arrow struck him in the eye.

As ruler of England, William made great changes in government and society. He introduced feudalism and the French language to England. William divided England into fiefs, granting them to a number of his followers. He built stone castles along the borders to protect his lands. For the next 200 years, Norman kings ruled both England and much of France.

William also ordered an official survey of his newly acquired lands and people. He had the results compiled in the Domesday Book. Many of these records still survive.

William remained a warrior, and spent much of his time fighting rebellious nobles. He died in 1087, during a battle in France. His contemporaries often described William as brutal, but they recognized that he brought security and order to England and Normandy. One English chronicler described William at his death:

" This King William was a man of great wisdom and power and surpassed all his predecessors in honor and strength. Although severe beyond all measure to those who opposed him, he was gentle to good men who loved God. . . . Amongst other things, the good security he made in this country is not to be forgotten—so that any honest man could travel over his kingdom without injury with his pockets full of gold; and no one dared strike another, however much wrong he had done him. " ∎

The Age of Chivalry

A code of conduct called chivalry developed in the 1100s. The word chivalry comes from the French word, *cheval*, meaning horse. Chivalrous conduct was expected of knights, whose status symbol was the horse. Chivalry emphasized the virtues of Christian piety and public service rather than violence. Chivalrous knights idealized upper class women and promised to protect them.

Sons of nobles began early to train for knighthood and learn the code of chivalry. At about the age of seven, a boy went to a lord's castle to serve as a page. In that position, he learned knightly manners, horsemanship, and military skills.

Around the age of 14, the page became a squire and served an individual knight. His new duties included caring for the knight's horse and weapons. When he was judged competent, he accompanied the knight in battle to prove his abilities. At about the age of 21, the squire was dubbed a knight.

During the twelfth century, fighting between knights declined. Instead, tournaments where knights could practice their military skills became common. Gradually, orderly government replaced fighting as knights administered their estates, presided over local law courts, advised the king, and jousted in tournaments. Political life in Europe became more stable and orderly.

Advances in Farming. After 1000, the landowners and peasants of Europe developed improved methods of farming. Two factors contributed to these advances. First, population growth required more crops and created pressure to clear new land for farming. Second, advances in technology increased farm productivity.

The most important development was the introduction of the heavy moldboard plow. The soil of northern Europe was rich, but also wet and heavy. A heavy-wheeled plow, equipped with an iron cutting edge and a curved moldboard to turn the soil had come into wide use by the end of the twelfth century. Teams of oxen, and later horses, pulled these moldboard plows. Farmers also began to use bigger iron tools, such as scythes, to harvest their crops faster.

Another important development was crop rotation. Farmland had to be regularly left fallow, without crops, to allow farmers to plow under the weeds. In the early Middle Ages, peasants usually farmed only half of their land. In the eleventh century, however, some began to grow crops on two-thirds of their fields each year. Farmers also learned to plant crops that left natural fertilizers in the soil.

The Manor System. Most European peasants lived in villages on land owned by a lord. Peasant families farmed land for the lord, or owner, as well as a small strip of their own land. Estates containing the lord's house, farmland, and villages were called manors. Each manor tried to be self-sufficient.

Some peasants living on the manor were freemen who rented their land from the lord of the manor. Others were serfs who

This page from the Luttrell Psalter from 1390 shows farmers using the German plough. The plough, pulled by a team of community-owned oxen, drained the ground and dug long furrows.

were bound to the land. In late Roman times, peasants were fixed to the land, or enserfed. A legal code that Emperor Theodosius established in A.D. 395, demanded labor services to a lord and forbade peasants to leave the land. If serfs left the land where they were born, they broke the law and could be severely punished. Serfs provided a work force to ensure that the land of the estate would be farmed.

The Growth of Towns. As European farmers became more productive, towns and trade began to grow. In the year 1000, European towns were small and enclosed within walls for protection against barbarian invaders. Often these towns were built inside the ruins of old Roman towns. Farmers brought their surpluses and merchants brought their goods to towns. A few grew into cities of from 5,000 to 10,000 people.

As sea trade increased on the Mediterranean, such ports as Venice and Genoa grew into cities. Capitals such as Paris and London became important as more people came to the king's court on business.

Towns prospered by producing and selling tools, cloth, and luxury goods. The young cities and towns welcomed newcomers. If a serf ran away to a town and lived there unclaimed for a year and a day, he could stay as a free man.

The increased agricultural and commercial activity in the twelfth century created new expectations. Old customs did not cover new situations. City people demanded, and

eventually gained, the right to govern their own affairs. They organized communes, associations of citizens, to govern themselves. Townspeople often rebelled against the lord who owned the land. When they rebelled successfully, they protected their independence with a charter from the king or local noble. The charter guaranteed their right to govern themselves and to hold their own law courts. Rulers often were willing to grant charters because prosperous towns provided tax money. In addition, prosperous merchants could lend large sums of money to rulers, who were often short of funds.

Self-government made European cities of the twelfth century very different from those in other parts of Eurasia. Leaders of Islamic cities had no legal rights to control their own affairs. They were at the mercy of Turkish or other military rulers who taxed the cities heavily and seized surplus wealth. By contrast, European townspeople felt more secure about investing money in business enterprises. Such investment stimulated growth.

The Spread of Knowledge. As European cities became more prosperous, the demand for learning grew. In Europe, bishops developed schools to train priests. Some universities evolved from these schools.

By the end of the twelfth century, education was spreading in western Europe. Governments, the Latin church, and merchants needed people who could read, write, and keep accurate accounts. Increasingly, trained lawyers settled disputes. The first European university was founded at Bologna in Italy in the eleventh century, to train people in law.

The universities of southern Europe formed around schools of law or, sometimes, medicine. The University of Paris, which became the model for universities of northern Europe, formed around schools of theology.

Changes in education led to the growth of literacy in Europe. At that time, formal education was always in Latin and emphasized philosophy and logic. Practical subjects, such as engineering, were not taught in schools.

The Christian Church in the Middle Ages

The Latin Christian church touched the lives of most European people in the eleventh to thirteenth centuries. Parish priests with little education prayed over and guided these people. Bishops managed religious districts called dioceses. They appointed priests and managed church property. Generally, the kings or nobles chose the bishops, who often were sons of feudal lords.

The Growth of Papal Power. In all parts of Europe, the Latin church controlled vast amounts of land. Kings and nobles appointed bishops and abbots to manage lands under their rule. Frequently, relatives or loyal followers were appointed to important church positions. Often a king even chose the pope, the head of the church, who held the office of bishop of Rome.

Many church leaders, however, believed that the church should be independent of political rulers. The churchmen thought that the people and the clergy of a diocese should choose their bishop. Monks should elect their abbot.

In the tenth century, the church and European rulers disagreed on the issue of lay investiture. The church opposed the practice of allowing rulers, who were laity and not religious leaders, to grant positions to the clergy. This problem was solved in different ways in the various lands of western Europe.

In the agreement, or Concordat, of Worms (vorms), reached at the city of Worms, Germany, church leaders and nobles agreed that church officials should elect bishops and grant them spiritual powers. The German emperor promised not to influence those elections. Rulers, however, were allowed to grant lands and secular, or political, powers to the elected church officials in a separate ceremony.

The Church Expands to Germany and Spain. In Germany, ambitious knights moved eastward to conquer new territory. German monks and peasants followed them across the Elbe River, spreading Christianity and opening lands to farming. Independent Christian kingdoms developed in Poland and Hungary before the twelfth century. Then, restless German warriors turned northeastward to conquer and convert Baltic peoples.

Another target for Christian expansion was the Iberian Peninsula. In the eleventh century, Muslims ruled most of this area. Church leaders urged Christian knights to invade Islamic Spain as a religious crusade. The small Christian kingdoms of Leon, Castile, and Navarre led this effort. The military campaigns, which the Spanish called the *reconquista*, or reconquest, lasted throughout the Middle Ages. Eventually, Seville, Cordova, and most of the other great Muslim cities fell to the Christians. In the mountainous country of far southern Spain, however, the little Muslim kingdom of Granada survived until 1492.

The Pope Appeals for a Crusade. The Seljuk Turks conquered central Asia Minor in the last half of the eleventh century. This Turkish threat persuaded the Byzantine emperor to appeal to the pope in Rome for help. He asked for mercenary soldiers to drive the Turks from Byzantine lands.

In 1096, Pope Urban II proclaimed a crusade against the Turks. The word crusade comes from the Latin word, *cruciata*, meaning marked with a cross. His appeal brought an overwhelming response. Several thousand knights set out for Palestine in 1096 carrying banners marked with the cross of Christianity. These crusaders went to help the armies of the Byzantine Empire regain territories lost to the Turks. From the beginning, however, crusaders and the Greek Orthodox peoples of Byzantium distrusted each other.

Armies from France, Germany, and Italy traveled through the Balkans to Constantinople to free Jerusalem and the Holy Land from Muslim control. The crusaders captured the city of Antioch and, in 1099, took Jerusalem. They set up four small states along the eastern coast of the Mediterranean. They chose kings for these states and divided the land into fiefs. See the map, The Crusades, page 298.

In 1147, the Second Crusade was organized. The crusaders were defeated in Asia Minor and never reached the Holy Land.

The rise of the Muslim ruler, Saladin, brought unity to the Muslims. After his conquest of Egypt, Saladin attacked the European crusaders' lands in Palestine. Saladin defeated the crusader knights at the Battle of Hattin, in 1187, and recaptured Jerusalem. One of Saladin's men described their strategy against heavily armored European knights:

❝ Clothed from head to foot with a coat of mail that makes him resemble a block of iron, [the knight] is not affected by repeated blows, but as soon as his horse is killed the knight is thrown over and captured. **❞**

After this battle, Saladin's army easily recaptured Jerusalem, which the Europeans had held for 88 years. The crusaders contin-

Townspeople bartered and bought what they needed in local markets and at annual fairs. St. Denis is shown blessing a fair and preaching to the people.

ued to hold on to some coastal cities for about another century.

The pope called for the Third Crusade in 1189. Saladin and the Muslims, however, defeated the combined forces of the kings of England, France, and Germany. By the thirteenth century, nearly all of Asia Minor was under Turkish control. About 300,000 Christians and Muslims lost their lives in the Third Crusade.

Crusades were attempted even after 1291, when the Muslims recaptured the city of Acre. However, the crusaders never again regained the Holy Land, which remained firmly in Muslim hands.

Although the crusades did not keep the Holy Land permanently under Christian rule, they did strengthen Europe's economy. The knights and merchants who went to Palestine acquired a taste for many of the products of the Middle East, India, and

The Crusades, 1096–1291

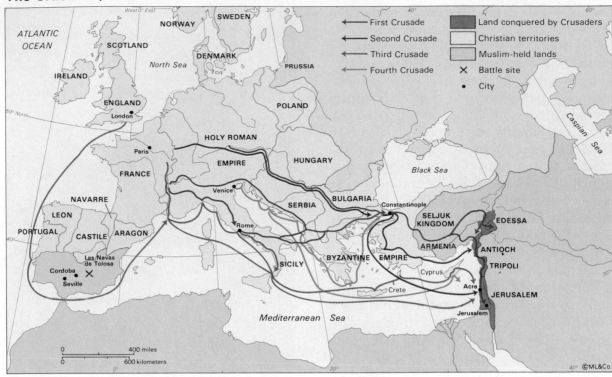

Map Skills **1.** Did the majority of Christian lands lie north or south of the Mediterranean Sea? **2.** What empires did the Crusaders travel through to reach Jerusalem?

China that were available in Palestine. The crusades stimulated trade that contributed to the commercial expansion of Europe.

Between the eleventh and thirteenth centuries, Europe was transformed from a rustic, barbaric land into an energetic partnership of town and country; of church and state. The European population increased rapidly. The people cleared forests and drained the marshes of Holland. They built and defended great stone castles and churches. Some moved to towns that grew into cities.

SECTION 3 *Study Skills*

Developing Vocabulary **1.** Describe chivalry. **2.** What is the connection between the moldboard plow and fallow land? **3.** Explain the relationship between communes and a charter.

Reviewing Main Ideas **1.** How did the relationship between kings and nobles begin to change in the eleventh century? **2.** How did the new plow introduced in Europe during the Middle Ages aid farmers? **3.** What change in education occurred between the eleventh and the thirteenth centuries? **4.** In what ways did the crusades accomplish something different from what they set out to do?

Understanding Chronology **1.** In what year did William, Duke of Normandy, win the Battle of Hastings? **2.** Pope Urban II urged a crusade against the Turks at the end of which century? **3.** When did the Muslims recapture Acre?

Understanding Cause and Effect **1.** Why might a lord willingly grant a charter? **2.** Explain the importance of Aristotle to education in the eleventh and twelfth centuries.

Challenge Compare European towns of the year 1000 with European towns of today.

CHAPTER 13 *Summary & Review*

Summarizing Main Ideas

Muslim Turks established their power and religion over much of western Asia in the eleventh century. Turks formed the Ghaznavid Dynasty and the Delhi Sultanate. Seljuk Turks pushed into Asia Minor and the Fatimid Dynasty controlled north Africa. Saladin briefly united Egypt, Syria, and Palestine.

Song China in the twelfth and thirteenth centuries was governed by a scholar bureaucracy. The Chinese made advances in water transportation, canal building, mathematics, and medicine. They developed the printing press and gunpowder.

In Europe, nobles and kings gained tighter control of society. Improved plows and crop rotation enabled feudal manors to produce more food. A larger food supply made possible larger town populations. Pope Urban II inspired many Europeans to go off to fight in the Middle East during the crusades.

"It doesn't matter if the salesman convinced you—you just don't put aluminum siding on a castle, and that's that."

Questions for Critical Thinking

COMPREHENSION Interpreting Events

1. Why did Chinese commerce, technology, and industry grow so rapidly after 960?
2. Why was it significant that China developed a professional civil service?
3. How did the use of money allow the Chinese to expand their economy and trade?
4. Explain how improvements in farming influenced the development of civilization in European countries.

APPLICATION Comparing Past to Present

1. Compare the role of towns in trade in 1200 with their role today.
2. List similarities and differences in the way the government chose civil servants in eleventh century China with how civil servants are chosen in the United States today.
3. In the cartoon, why is the mention of aluminum siding humorous?

SYNTHESIS Developing Research Skills

1. Write a report on one of the major crusades. Describe the crusade's immediate and long range effects.
2. Write a one page report on one of the following leaders: Pope Urban II, Richard the Lionhearted, Saladin.

EVALUATION Weighing Consequences

1. Describe the impact on the people of southwest Asia of the eleventh century Turkish conquests.
2. What was the result of feudal lords winning control over knights?
3. How might the climate of the Holy Land have contributed to the failure of the crusades?

CHALLENGE

Compare the reasons for participating in a crusade against Muslim Turks in the 1100s with the reasons people today may crusade for a clean environment or world peace.

CHAPTER 14

Eurasian Sea Trade Exchanges

GLOBAL TIME LINE

TIME

794–1185 Heian period of refinement and culture in Japan

858–1160 Fujiwara family dominates Japanese government

1000s Khmer people build temple of Angkor Wat in Kampuche

PEOPLE

900s Lady Murasaki Shikibu writes the first novel

1020 Yaroslav the Wise codifies Russian law

900s King Vladimir of Kiev converts to Orthodox Christianity

PLACE

1000–1100 *Byzantine Empire;*[2] Byzantium becomes a cultural center for the Christian world

1000–1200 *East Africa;*[1] People of east Africa import silks, glassware, and porcelain from China

1000   1100

Linking Past to Present

Consider the variety of foods from around the world available in modern supermarkets. People today often think of worldwide trade as a modern development. In reality, trade between widely separated parts of the world has been going on for 2,000 years or more.

Between 1000 and 1200, people in Eurasia and Africa increased the amount of goods they exchanged. Germans spiced their meat with pepper from India. People of India played chess with pieces made from ivory collected in east Africa. East African families ate from porcelain dishes made in China. All of this trade indicates that the peoples of Eurasia and Africa were influencing one another's ways of life. As you read this chapter, analyze the ways trade influences people's lives.

A Chinese "junk" sails past Hong Kong.

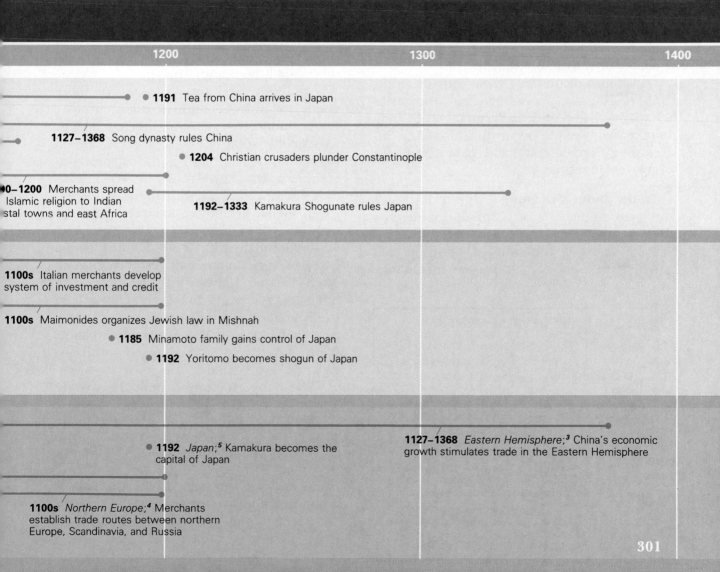

	1200		1300		1400

1191 Tea from China arrives in Japan

1127–1368 Song dynasty rules China

1204 Christian crusaders plunder Constantinople

…0–1200 Merchants spread Islamic religion to Indian …stal towns and east Africa

1192–1333 Kamakura Shogunate rules Japan

1100s Italian merchants develop system of investment and credit

1100s Maimonides organizes Jewish law in Mishnah

1185 Minamoto family gains control of Japan

1192 Yoritomo becomes shogun of Japan

1192 *Japan;*[5] Kamakura becomes the capital of Japan

1127–1368 *Eastern Hemisphere;*[3] China's economic growth stimulates trade in the Eastern Hemisphere

1100s *Northern Europe;*[4] Merchants establish trade routes between northern Europe, Scandinavia, and Russia

1 Growth of Trade in East Asia

OBJECTIVE: *To understand the developments in trade and culture in east Asia between 1000 and 1400*

Chinese Trade

Trade grew rapidly along the major sea routes of eastern and southern Eurasia between 1000 and 1200. In this period, an individual trader did not carry goods all the way across Eurasia. Instead, groups of merchants relayed their wares from one trade center or port to another.

China's economy grew rapidly after about 700 (see pages 258–259). Industries expanded, and trade between parts of China increased. People began to use money, including copper coins and paper notes, in greater quantities.

Trade under the Song. One of the most important aspects of China's commercial economy was the expansion of foreign trade. During the Song Dynasty, which lasted from 960–1279, Chinese merchants, shipbuilders, and sailors built thriving port cities along China's southern and eastern coasts. Chinese ships sailed to Korea, Japan, Southeast Asia, India, and Ceylon. Occasionally, they ventured as far as the Persian Gulf and the coast of east Africa. These ships were filled with rice, sugar, iron and copperware, silk fabrics, porcelain dishes, silver, gold, books, and paper.

Chinese merchants exchanged these goods for spices, cotton textiles, incense, ivory, rhinoceros horns, and tortoise shells. Eventually, some Chinese traders settled permanently in foreign ports, especially in Southeast Asia. These traders, carrying Chinese ideas and skills with them, extended the influence of Chinese civilization. See the map, page 303.

Traditionally, the emperors of China had looked down on wealthy merchants and often treated them with suspicion. The Song government, however, encouraged trade. It allowed foreign traders to do business in Chinese ports. Foreign merchants from as far away as India and southwest Asia came to China.

The Song rulers also built the world's largest navy. By the thirteenth century, 52,000 sailors were serving in the Chinese navy. The navy's main mission was to patrol and protect China's seacoasts and rivers.

Ships and Technology. Chinese scientists, engineers, and seamen made important advances in shipbuilding and navigation dur-

---

VOCABULARY DEVELOPMENT

etiquette (EHT ih kuht) *noun:* behavior established by custom as acceptable in social relations. From the French word, *etiquette*, literally, ticket.

phonetic (fuh NEHT ihk) **alphabet**: having a separate symbol for every speech sound.

contemplative (KΛHN tuhm PLAYT ihv) *adj.:* thoughtful, meditative. From the Latin word, *contemplatus*, meaning to gaze attentively, to observe.

samurai (SAM uh RY) *noun:* a member of the aristocratic military class in feudal Japan.

Chinese Overseas Trade, 1000

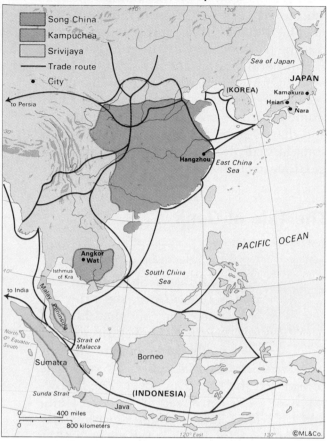

Map Skills **1.** In A.D. 1000, what empire controlled the Strait of Malacca and the Sunda Strait? **2.** On what peninsula was Angkor Wat built?

ing the Song period. For example, the Chinese used iron nails to increase the strength of their ships. Chinese ships, called junks, were the world's largest at that time. The Chinese sometimes referred to them as whales. The biggest junks had five huge sails and several levels of decks.

On the ships were comfortable cabins for merchants and other passengers. Some of these cabins even had private bathrooms. Crew members sometimes took their families along on voyages. On long trips, sailors grew vegetables and spices on shipboard in large wooden tubs.

Junks also were equipped with firefighting equipment, lifeboats, and special equipment for taking samples of sea life from the ocean floor. Naval ships carried weapons such as catapults for hurling firebombs, and bamboo tubes for firing small rockets with gunpowder. A Chinese writer described the great junks this way:

❝ The ships . . . are like houses. When their sails are spread they are like great clouds in the sky. Their rudders are several tens of feet long. A single ship carries several hundred men. It has stored on board a year's supply of grain. ❞

Chinese sea captains were experts at navigating the China Sea and the Indian Ocean. Like Arab and Indian sailors, they used the monsoon winds to aid their travel. By the early twelfth century, Chinese captains were using compasses to help them navigate. It was not until 200 years later that European sailors began to use compasses.

China's Importance. China, the most powerful and populous country in Eurasia, was exporting and importing more goods than ever before by 1200. This economic growth stimulated trade all across the Eastern Hemisphere. Ships from many different countries carried larger quantities and more varieties of goods from port to port. A single web of trade connected China to the Mediterranean. The growth of China's commercial economy was probably the factor most responsible for the increase in trade across much of Eurasia.

Japan Comes of Age

One of China's important trading partners was Japan. The Sea of Japan separates this country of mountainous islands from China and Korea. Chinese junks sailed to Japanese ports carrying silk, sandalwood, porcelains, books, copper money, and other products. For them, the Japanese traded gold, silver, mercury, lumber, steel swords, and beautiful furniture.

The contacts between China and Japan involved much more than trade goods. Between the sixth and ninth centuries, the Japanese aristocracy adopted many aspects of Chinese life. Japanese nobles borrowed China's language and system of government. Buddhism also was imported to Japan and gained some acceptance. Still, Chinese culture never greatly influenced Japanese farmers and workers.

The center of society in Japan was the capital where the emperor lived. In the eighth century, the emperor and his court moved from Nara to Heian (HAY ahn), a city later called Kyoto (kee OHT oh).

During the Heian period in Japanese history, 794–1185, the noble families of Japan gathered at the royal capital. Gentlemen and ladies of the court valued politeness, personal appearance, and romantic love. They appreciated the arts of writing poetry and judging the beauty of flowers or shells. Etiquette was extremely important. Loud laughter or mismatched clothing, for instance, was embarrassing. Japanese aris-

tocrats looked down on the common people who could not share in court refinement.

The Japanese fascination with Chinese culture had declined by the middle of the Heian period. After about A.D. 1000, Japanese literature, painting, and architecture became more distinctly Japanese. Educated women of the palace began to write poetry and diaries in a Japanese script based on a complicated phonetic alphabet, rather than in Chinese characters.

The Tale of Genji

FOCUS ON SOURCES

The best of the Japanese court writers was Lady Murasaki Shikibu. In *The Tale of Genji*, she wrote an account of the life of Prince Genji (JEHN jee) and other members of the imperial court. This book is considered the first true novel. The following excerpt, a conversation between Genji and his friend Tō no Chūjō, illustrates the romantic quality of life at the court.

" It had been raining all day. There were fewer courtiers than usual in the royal presence. Back in his own palace quarters, also unusually quiet, Genji pulled a lamp near and sought to while away the time with his books. He had Tō no Chūjō with him. Numerous pieces of colored paper, obviously letters, lay on a shelf. Tō no Chūjō made no attempt to hide his curiosity.

"Well," said Genji, "there are some I might let you see. But there are some I think it better not to."

"You miss the point. The ones I want to see are precisely the ones you want to hide. The ordinary ones—I'm not much of a hand at the game, you know, but even I am up to the ordinary give and take. But the ones from ladies who think you are not doing right by them, who sit alone through an evening and wait for you to come—those are the ones I want to see."

Emperor Go-Toba spent years making swords after his abdication and exile in 1221. He hoped to forge the perfect blade to kill the man who deposed him.

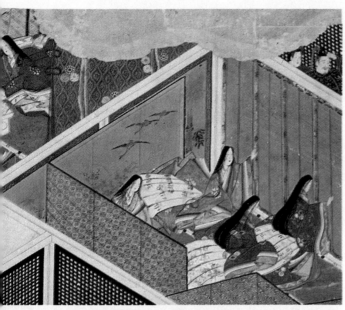

An illustration from the first novel ever written, *The Tale of Genji*. The book was a romantic character study written in Japanese by Lady Murasaki Shikibu around 1000.

It was not likely that really delicate letters would be left scattered on a shelf, and it may be assumed that the papers treated so carelessly were the less important ones.

"You do a have a variety of them," said Tō nō Chūjō, reading the correspondence through piece by piece. This will be from her, and this will be from *her*, he would say. Sometimes he guessed correctly and sometimes he was far afield, to Genji's great amusement. Genji was brief with his replies and left out no secrets.

"It is I who should be asking to see *your* collection. No doubt it is huge. When I have seen it I shall be happy to throw my files open to you."

"I fear there is nothing that would interest you." Tō nō Chūjō was in a contemplative mood. "It is with women as it is with everything else: the flawless ones are very few indeed. This is a sad fact which I have learned over the years. All manner of women seem presentable enough at first. Little notes, replies to this and that, they all suggest sensibility and cultivation. But when you begin sorting out the really superior

ones you will find that there are not many who have to be on your list. Each has her little tricks and she makes the most of them, getting in her slights at rivals, so broad sometimes that you almost have to blush. Hidden away by loving parents who build brilliant futures for them, they let word get out of this little talent and that little accomplishment and you are all in a stir. They are young and pretty and amiable and carefree, and in their boredom they begin to pick up a little from their elders, and in the natural course of things they begin to concentrate on one particular hobby and make something of it. A woman tells you all about it and hides the weak points and brings out the strong ones as if they were everything, and you can't very well call her a liar. So you begin keeping company, and it is always the same. The fact is not up to the advance notices. " ■

Japanese Politics and Society

During most of the Heian period, the nobles usually practiced Japanese Buddhism. To be a good Buddhist, a person was expected to read holy scriptures, practice complicated rituals, and recite prayers over and over again. Buddhist monastaries were centers of political and economic power. Some of them had private armies of monks.

Buddhism began to spread among the common people beginning around the year 1000. Buddhism became a more distinctly Japanese faith by absorbing aspects of Shinto, the ancient native religion of Japan. Buddhist temples and statues of gods and goddesses became less Chinese and more Japanese in appearance. Buddhism gradually became the major religion of Japan despite its decline in China.

Japanese Feudalism. Important political changes also occurred during the Heian period. The emperor's government rapidly declined in power. Instead of managing the empire, the emperor and his officials pursued court ceremonies and luxury. From 858 to 1160, the Fujiwara (foo jeh wah rah) family dominated the administration of the Japanese government. Other families rivaled them in remote areas of the country.

A decentralized feudal system developed in Japan in the tenth and eleventh centuries. As in Europe, feudal lords provided law and order and controlled local regions. Japanese lords ruled with the help of professional warriors called samurai. Like the knights of Europe, the samurai were nobles holding special ranks and privileges that commoners did not share. Sometimes, the samurai fought on horseback like European knights. They wore armor made of strips of gleaming steel tied together with thongs. While the knights of Europe were using lances in battle, the samurai fought with razor-sharp steel swords and with bows that shot arrows 4 feet long.

Samurai lived by a strict code of honor later known as *bushido*. According to this code, warriors were expected to fight with reckless courage. If a samurai warrior was defeated in battle or dishonored in some way, he was obligated to commit suicide in a ceremony called *seppuku*.

Japanese feudalism differed from European feudalism in important ways, however. The samurai usually were not rewarded with land, as were the knights of Europe. Instead, Japanese warriors received a fixed quantity of the rice paid to their lord by peasants of the region he controlled. Japanese warriors, unlike European knights, did not regard women as weak creatures to be idealized and defended. Rather, Japanese noble women lived by the same rules of honor and courage. Japanese women also could own and inherit land and titles, in contrast to European women of the time.

Japan's Economy. Japan's commercial economy grew during the Heian period. Peasants increased food production and opened new lands to agriculture. People improved roads and bridges, and trade be-

Japan's mighty feudal warriors, the samurai, defend Japan from Mongol invaders in this detail from a thirteenth-century scroll.

tween parts of Japan increased. By the end of the twelfth century, towns were beginning to develop as centers of commerce.

Rise of the Shogun. Another important political change occurred in Japan near the end of the twelfth century. By 1185, the Minamoto family had won control of all Japan. Seven years later, the family's leader, Yoritomo, took the title of shogun, or supreme commander. In theory, he served the emperor. In fact, he became a military dictator. He built a new capital city of his own at Kamakura. His government, the Kamakura Shogunate, lasted until 1333. The Japanese feudal system continued during this important period.

By the end of the Kamakura Shogunate, China's influence on Japan's government and culture had declined. In the established Japanese pattern of government, the emperor reigned officially, but the shogun actually ruled. This type of government lasted until the middle of the nineteenth century.

Empires in Southeast Asia

Sea trade from Japan or China to the Middle East or Europe passed through one of two straits in Southeast Asia. The Strait of Malacca separates the Malayan Peninsula from the island of Sumatra. The Sunda Strait divides Sumatra from the island of Java. See the map, Chinese Overseas Trade, page 303. Any kingdom that controlled these straits could prosper by encouraging and taxing the trade passing through them.

Such a kingdom, Srivijaya (SREE wih JAW yuh), arose near the end of the seventh century. Most of the Srivijayans were rice farmers, sailors, or merchants. They spoke the Malay language. Many of the people of Srivijaya held beliefs and practiced rituals that combined Buddhism and Hinduism.

The kings of Srivijaya were called maharajas, a term borrowed from India. Their capital stood on the island of Sumatra. These rulers concentrated on collecting taxes on trade. An old legend says that the maharaja of Srivijaya was always trying to make the spirits of the ocean happy. Every day he would throw a gold brick into the sea. As he did so, he would say, "Look, there lies my treasury!"

Srivijaya was at the height of its power about A.D. 1000. Trade through the straits grew more important than ever after 1000, but parts of the empire broke away from the central government's control. Even so, Srivijaya lasted until the fourteenth century.

As Srivijaya slowly declined after 1000, another kingdom of Southeast Asia increased its power. This kingdom was the land of the Khmer (KH mehr) people of Kampuchea (KHAM poo CHEE uh). Whereas Srivijaya was a sea-oriented empire, the Khmer state controlled a large area of rice-growing land in Indochina.

The Khmer did not keep written records until the 600s, so little is known of Kampuchea's origin. The people were mostly Buddhists, though influenced by Hinduism. The great Hindu-Buddhist temples built in the eleventh and twelfth centuries show that Kampuchea was prosperous and powerful.

The most famous temple was Angkor Wat. Its nine huge towers, at one time, were plated with gold. Beneath the central tower stood a gold statue of the Hindu god, Vishnu. A moat measuring almost 2 miles long surrounded the temple complex. Angkor Wat has fallen into ruin today, but it remains one of the largest religious buildings in the world.

The Khmers formed an unusual empire for the period from 1000 to 1200. They did not depend on trade. Other leading empires in Asia, however, did prosper by taxing trade. Empires in China, Japan, and Srivijaya were becoming linked more closely with western Eurasia via the Indian Ocean.

SECTION 1 *Study Skills*

Developing Vocabulary Use each of the following terms in a sentence: **1.** etiquette. **2.** samurai. **3.** phonetic alphabet.

Reviewing Main Ideas **1.** How did the Song Dynasty encourage the growth of trade? **2.** What arrangements would merchants make to move trade goods from one end of Eurasia to the other? **3.** How was feudalism in Japan different from feudalism in Europe? **4.** What does the story of Genji reveal about court life in Japan? **5.** What was the role of the shogun?

Understanding Chronology **1.** How much earlier did Chinese sailors use the compass than the Europeans? **2.** Explain the name of the period in Japanese history from 794 to 1185.

Understanding Cause and Effect **1.** Describe the impact on the Japanese government of the way of life led by the Japanese upper class. **2.** Why did the Srivijaya Empire prosper? **3.** Trace the influence of Indian culture on the Srivijaya and Khmer empires.

Challenge Explain how the trade and cultural exchanges between China and Japan in the thirteenth century influenced each culture.

2 The Indian Ocean Region

OBJECTIVE: *To understand the impact of Muslim traders on India and east Africa*

Traders in the Arabian Sea

Between the years 1000 and 1200, more and more ships sailed the busy seaways of the Indian Ocean. Muslim merchants carried the goods of China and Southeast Asia across the Arabian Sea to the west. Hindu, Buddhist, and Muslim merchants carried products of the Middle East, Africa, and Europe across the Bay of Bengal to the east. The wares of almost all nations of Eurasia and east Africa traveled the Indian Ocean.

In the Arabian Sea, merchants sailed in ships called *dhows* (douz). These vessels had two or three masts and triangular-shaped sails. Most dhows were built in India of teakwood from India's tropical forests. Indian shipbuilders used no nails in constructing these ships. They drilled holes in the planks and stitched the boards together side to side with rope made of coconut fiber. They sealed the cracks between the boards with pitch. Indian dhows were less sturdy than Chinese junks, but they were strong enough to sail in the Indian Ocean where the monsoon winds were usually steady.

The Horse Trade. Horses were an important item of trade in India. Rulers of Indian kingdoms needed horses for their armies. Because these animals did not breed well in India, they usually were imported. Muslims in Arabia and Persia raised excellent cavalry horses. Merchants then herded their horses onto large dhows and transported them to the ports of India. Travelers who sailed on boats carrying large shipments of horses often found the trip unpleasant.

Islamic Influence in India. Muslim merchants helped to spread Islam in India. The number of Muslims grew in the eleventh and twelfth centuries, particularly along the west coast of India. Muslims intermarried with local people who were Hindus or Buddhists. The new settlers built mosques and opened schools for their children. Gradually, Islam became the dominant way of life in many coastal towns.

The spread of Islam in India led to many conflicts between Muslims and Hindus. Muslims considered the beliefs of Hindus offensive to God. Muslims worshiped one God, Allah; Hindus honored several. Mus-

---

VOCABULARY DEVELOPMENT

monsoon (mahn SOON) *noun:* a seasonal wind over the Indian Ocean and south Asia. It blows from the southwest from April to October, and from the northeast the rest of the year.

frankincense (FRANG kuhn SEHNS) *noun:* a gum resin from various Arabian and northeast African trees. It is often burned as incense.

myrrh (mur) *noun:* a sweet-smelling but bitter-tasting gum resin from certain plants of Arabia and east Africa, used in making perfume and as incense.

sheik (sheek) *noun:* the chief of an Arab tribe, family, or village. From the Arabian word, *shakha*, meaning to grow old.

---

lims believed all people to be equal in the sight of Allah; Hindus followed a caste system. Muslims rejected the use of statues; Hindus created beautiful statues of the gods they worshiped. Yet, Hindus and Muslims lived together in the same communities.

The Chola Kingdom

The leaders in trade in the southern part of India were Hindu merchants. They specialized in carrying goods between India and the Far East. See the map, Indian Ocean Region, page 310.

The Chola (CHOH luh) Kingdom, one of several Hindu states of India in the eleventh and twelfth centuries, supported these merchants. The people of the kingdom spoke Tamil. Tamil is still the main language of southern India and part of Ceylon, now called Sri Lanka.

The Chola kings ruled from cities dominated by huge Hindu temples. Chola craftworkers created beautiful sculptures of Hindu gods and goddesses. These works of art are among the finest ever made in India.

In the thirteenth century, the Chola Kingdom fought several long wars with neighboring states. The kingdom declined as a result of these wars. As the kingdom declined, Muslim merchants gradually took control of trade in the Bay of Bengal. This takeover represented one more step in the expansion of Islamic influence.

Muslim Influence in East Africa

At the same time that Muslim influence was growing in India, Arab and Persian traders were sailing down the east coast of Africa. They traveled south with the winter monsoon wind and returned north in April or May with the early summer monsoon. They called east Africa the Land of Zanj.

People speaking Bantu languages lived in villages and little towns along the coast in the period from 1000 to 1200. They raised rice, coconuts, and bananas. In addition, they fished in the coastal waters. When Muslim merchants began to arrive, trade became increasingly important in the life of the Bantu.

An important east African trade good was ivory. Deep in the interior of the continent, hunters killed elephants and removed

Muslims have used Arab dhows like the one at left for centuries to conduct trade between the east African coast and far Asia. Above, a twelfth-century Arab ship sails the Persian Gulf.

their ivory tusks. Then traders carried these tusks along overland routes to the coast. There, Muslim sea merchants bought the prized ivory and shipped it to the Middle East, India, and China. Though elephants also lived in India, ivory from African elephants was harder and easier to carve. Carvers made jewelry, dagger handles, and other goods from ivory.

Other products that were exported from east Africa included slaves, incense, and lumber. Incense is an oil or a resin from trees that gives off a pleasant smell when it is burned. Frankincense and myrrh are two common types of incense.

The east African coastal towns imported goods from as far away as China. Among the products were cotton and silk textiles, beads, glassware, and Chinese porcelain. The coastal people used most of these goods; however, merchants carried some of the wares to the interior.

Mixing of Cultures. As trade expanded, the population of the coastal towns grew. Most of the townspeople were Bantu-speaking Africans. In the eleventh and twelfth centuries, though, Muslim immigrants from south Arabia and the Persian Gulf region also settled in those coastal towns. Many of these people were merchants. Others, however, were scholars, lawyers, and artisans. These Muslims introduced the Islamic system of law, Arabic language and literature, and Middle Eastern art and architecture into east Africa. They married local Africans and raised their children as Muslims. East African towns gradually became part of the Islamic world that was located around or near the Indian Ocean.

The Muslim culture of the Indian Ocean combined elements of African and Middle Eastern culture. For example, by the fourteenth century, Swahili was the principal language of the coast. Swahili is basically a

Indian Ocean Region, 1000

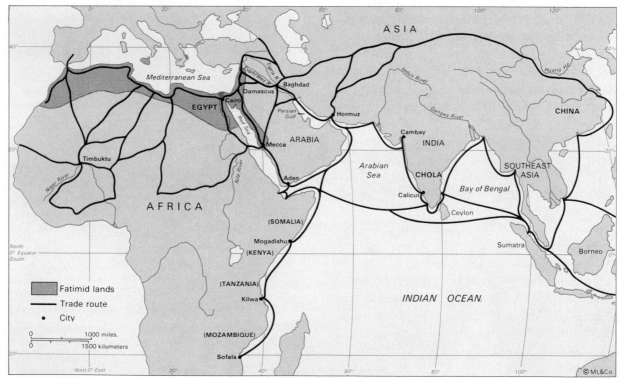

Map Skills **1.** How many miles would a merchant travel to reach Baghdad from Cairo.
2. In what direction would a traveler sail to reach Mogadishu from Calicut?

This illustration from al-Harīrī's *Maqāmāt* shows musicians before a parade for the Great Festival, a celebration during the annual pilgrimage to Mecca.

Bantu language, but includes many Arabian words. Today, it is spoken throughout Kenya, Tanzania, Uganda, and in parts of other African countries.

City Life. One of the most important towns along the coast was Mogadishu (MAHG uh DIHSH oo), now the capital of Somalia. The life of Mogadishu and other towns centered on the port area, where big oceangoing dhows unloaded their cargos. The buildings of each town were set very close together, and the streets were narrow and winding. The most important building in a community was its stone or wooden mosque. Muslims attended services at the mosque each Friday, the Islamic holy day.

Most east Africans were farmers, fishers, sailors, or artisans. They lived in small houses made of wood and mud plaster. Successful merchant families, however, lived in stone houses sometimes three stories high. Many houses had sunken courtyards. The members of wealthy families wore imported silk and cotton clothing and used Chinese porcelain. A Muslim traveler of the fourteenth century who visited Mogadishu tells of his experience at mealtime:

❝ The food of these people is rice cooked with butter, served on a large wooden dish. With it they serve side dishes, stews of chicken, meat, fish, and vegetables. They cook unripe bananas in fresh milk, and serve them as a sauce. . . . One of them eats as much as several of us: they are very fat and corpulent [overweight]. **❞**

Each of the important towns along the coast had its own government. The rulers were called *shayk*, or sheik. These leaders were often wealthy.

The African people of the coast relied on the sea for their livelihood. They did not have much direct contact with the Bantu-speaking societies and kingdoms of the continent's interior. Therefore, Islam remained mostly unknown in the interior of east Africa until the nineteenth century.

The Muslim civilization of east Africa continued to flourish between 1200 and 1500. The growth of trade across Eurasia and Africa contributed to its prosperity.

SECTION 2 *Study Skills*

Developing Vocabulary Explain the importance of monsoons, frankincense, and myrrh in promoting trade.

Reviewing Main Ideas 1. Why did travel in the Indian Ocean increase rapidly between the years 1000 and 1200? **2.** Why did conflict develop between Muslims and Hindus in India? **3.** What was the role of the Hindu merchants of the Chola Kingdom? **4.** Explain why Swahili developed into an important language.

Understanding Geography 1. Describe the trade routes used by the Chinese, the Muslims, and the Cholas. See maps on pages 303 and 310. **2.** Name two important trading cities in Africa, Italy, India, and east Asia.

Challenge Compare the Muslim role in Indian Ocean trade in the twelfth century, with Muslim trade in the Indian Ocean today.

Monsoons and Their Impact

Sea trade between Africa and Asia depended on the monsoons. The monsoon cycle also affected lifestyle and culture. Monsoons are seasonal winds of south and southeast Asia that bring wet weather in summer and dry weather in winter. The timing of these rains determines the growing season.

The Cause of Monsoons

The vast size of Asia is one of the major reasons why monsoons occur there. Water and land warm up at different rates and hold heat for different lengths of time. Water heats up more slowly than land. Water also keeps heat longer than does land.

The heating and cooling of land and water have an important effect on the local barometric pressure, the pressure of the air on the surface of the earth. During winter, large land masses lose heat more rapidly than does the nearby ocean. The difference in rates of cooling causes a difference in the barometric pressure over the two regions. The sharp cooling of the land creates a higher pressure over the land than it creates over the ocean.

The combination of barometric pressure that is high over the land, and low over the ocean, creates a wind. Wind always moves from a high pressure area to a low pressure area. In winter, therefore, wind blows from the land towards the ocean.

During summer, the situation is reversed. The land heats up quickly, while the ocean warms slowly. This change causes the barometric pressure over the ocean to be higher than the pressure over land. Again, the difference in pressure creates wind. In summer, the wind blows off the ocean toward the interior of the land mass.

The shifting winds, which result from the seasonal heating and cooling of the land, cause monsoons over south and southeast Asia. In the winter, the winds are dry, since they come off the land. In the summer, however, the winds come off the ocean carrying much moisture.

The Influence of Monsoons

Regions with monsoon climates generally have a high annual rainfall. That rainfall, however, comes almost entirely during the summer months. To understand the seasonal rains, see the graph, Rainfall in Cochin, India, page 313. The graph shows that Cochin usually receives 28 inches (70 centimeters) in June and about 25 inches (62.5 centimeters) of rain every July. The winter months, in contrast, are very dry.

Asian mountain ranges, such as the Himalayas, keep the monsoon rains from coming very far into the interior. The mountains break up the rain pattern. As the moisture-laden air comes from the ocean, it is pushed up the mountainsides, cools, and falls as rain. Monsoon rains are, therefore, concentrated in the coastal regions and on the island nations of Southeast Asia.

The Dangers of Monsoons. Monsoons are both welcomed and feared. Monsoon rains in India vary from year to year. In a year when the rains do not come, crops fail. The people face great hardships. In some cases, the monsoon rains are exceedingly strong, and the wind that brings them is powerful. Unusually heavy monsoons can cause severe flooding. At the end of the 1970 monsoon season, a violent storm struck Bangladesh. Over 200,000 people died from the flooding and destruction that resulted from the violent storm.

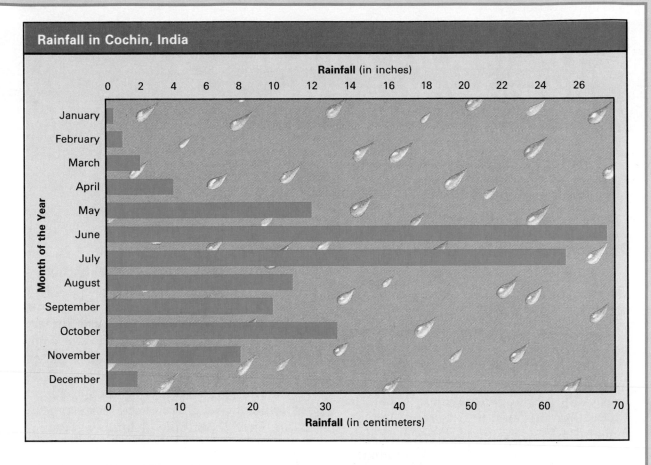

Rainfall in Cochin, India

Rainfall (in inches)

0 2 4 6 8 10 12 14 16 18 20 22 24 26

Month of the Year

January
February
March
April
May
June
July
August
September
October
November
December

0 10 20 30 40 50 60 70

Rainfall (in centimeters)

Monsoon Area Crops. Many types of trees and plants can grow in a monsoon climate. Two of the most important are the teakwood tree and the rubber tree. Teakwood is used to make fine furniture. Rubber trees are native to South America. European explorers brought rubber trees from America to Southeast Asia.

The unique monsoon climate has a major influence on the diets of people living in Southeast Asia. The climate is perfectly suited to growing rice. Early residents developed an agricultural system based on rice. Eaten with some of the many locally available vegetables, rice makes a meal which is nutritious, filling, and tasty. Rice is the mainstay of the diet of one-quarter of the world's population.

The monsoon climate has just the right characteristics for rice production. Rice growing requires plentiful water. After the rice has matured, however, there is need for a dry harvest season. During the warm, wet summers, the rice has time to mature. When weather becomes dry, harvest occurs.

The monsoons sometimes bring with them great destruction. They also bring with them the means for feeding one of the world's largest populations.

STUDY SKILLS Understanding Geography

1. Why does wind direction affect rainfall in Southeast Asia?
2. What effect do mountains have on the location of monsoon rains?
3. Explain why a diet based on rice is popular in many countries.
4. What two valuable trees are found in Asia's monsoon forests?
5. Why is a monsoon climate so well-suited for growing rice?

3 The Mediterranean World and Russia

OBJECTIVE: *To understand the shift from Muslim to Italian dominance in Mediterranean trade*

Italian Merchants

Muslims were the leading traders in the Mediterranean Basin in the year 1000. Hundreds of ships sailed back and forth each year from such seaport cities as Beirut and Alexandria. These ships went to Morocco, Tunisia, Spain, and Sicily in the west and to India in the east. Trade was heaviest in the southern Mediterranean. In 1200, 200 years later, traffic in the Mediterranean Basin was entirely different. Italian and other European ships outnumbered Muslim vessels. Islamic merchants came to rely on Italian customers. Changes in European society had transformed the Mediterranean world in 200 years.

Venice and such other Italian port cities as Genoa, Pisa, and Amalfi became the leading trading centers in the Mediterranean Basin. See the map, The Mediterranean World A.D. 1000, page 317. Italian nobles built mansions in the city and invested in trade. By the twelfth century, merchants were cooperating with nobles to set up city governments called communes. The communes' policies protected and encouraged trade in the Mediterranean.

Several advantages reduced competition for Italian merchants in the Mediterranean Basin. First, the supply of lumber for shipbuilding was plentiful. Second, Italian shipbuilders outstripped their competition by using a new, cheap form of ship construction. Third, an abundant supply of labor provided the Italian city-states with a military advantage. Sailors were trained for hand-to-hand combat. They served when necessary to protect Italian shipping.

Of the three, the military advantage in ship-to-ship combat probably was the most important. Italian sailors and merchants valued fighting more highly than did Muslim merchants. Thus, Muslim shipping was gradually pushed out of long-distance Mediterranean trade.

Trade Risks Cause Changes. Sea trade offered tremendous profits but involved very high risk. Ships were expensive to build. Storms and pirates could destroy them. Even after a safe and successful voyage, profits were uncertain. Traders had no guarantee that they would receive high prices for their goods. To lessen the risk to

---

VOCABULARY DEVELOPMENT

invest (ihn VEHST) *verb:* to put money into something for the purpose of obtaining income or profit.

confiscate (KAHN fuh SKAYT) *verb:* to seize private property, appropriate. From the Latin word, *confiscare*, meaning to lay up in a chest.

tapestry (TAP ihs tree) *noun:* a heavy cloth with decorative designs and pictures, and used as a wall hanging. From the Greek word, *tapētos*, meaning carpet.

envoy (EHN voy) *noun:* an agent sent by a ruler or a government on a diplomatic mission, a messenger.

---

one person, Italian sea traders borrowed a system of investment from the Arabs and Chinese. Individuals could buy a share in a ship and its cargo. Investors included relatives, friends, and merchants. Even religious convents invested in the trading ventures.

Another way to reduce the risk was through the use of credit. Italian merchants learned about credit from Islamic and Byzantine merchants. In the twelfth century, Italian merchants began to deposit their money with a banker. They conducted business with credit based on their bank deposits instead of money. This practice was the beginning of a European banking system.

The career of Romano Mairano, a Venetian merchant, is an example of the risks and rewards of trade. In 1155, Romano borrowed money to buy a ship. He persuaded some investors to pay the cost of a voyage to Constantinople with a cargo of lumber. On this single voyage, he made enough profit to pay back most of his loans. He was soon hired for other trips. He owned and sold part of the cargo that was carried on the ships on which he sailed. After a few years, he owned his own ship.

In 1171, however, Romano's ship was in the harbor of Constantinople when the Byzantine emperor seized all cargo belonging to Venetians. The emperor's confiscation of the goods was part of an on-going trade battle. The Byzantine merchants resented losing their business to merchants from Italy. Romano spent the next 12 years paying off his losses. He built and sailed ships on voyages to Syria, Palestine, and Egypt until he was almost 70.

Trade with Northern Europe. Trade between northern and southern Europe increased greatly after the crusades. Italian merchants prospered by shipping silk, spices, citrus fruit, wine, salt, and tapestries to northern Europeans in exchange for wool, cloth, furs, honey, iron, and timber.

North-south trade was not at first concentrated in special ports or cities. Instead, merchants traveled overland to attend regularly scheduled fairs in the French province of Champagne. Italian merchants loaded their pack animals with goods from the Mediterranean Basin and Asia. The merchants then crossed the snow-covered Alps to France. Here they met merchants from Flanders, England, Germany, and France who had brought northern goods to sell.

Northern European merchants, in turn, developed trade routes north to Scandinavia and east toward Russia. During the eleventh and twelfth centuries, merchants moved into the Scandinavian countries of Denmark, Norway, and Sweden. Traders also pushed farther east into Prussia and Russia. A German priest who visited the Prussians in the twelfth century described them:

❝ Although the Prussians do not yet know the light of the [Christian] faith, [they are] men endowed with many natural gifts. . . .

A manuscript drawing from 1338 captures the bustling commercial spirit of Venice. Prosperous merchants lived in palaces along the Grand Canal.

They have an abundance of strange furs . . . [which] they offer for the woolen garments called *faldones*. "

Byzantine Civilization

As an energetic young civilization was developing in western Europe between 1000 and 1200, the civilization of the Byzantine Greeks was being attacked. Normans from Italy, Seljuk Turks from Asia Minor, and crusaders from Europe all invaded. The crusaders did the most severe damage.

In 1204, the Fourth Crusade set out for Palestine. On their way, the crusaders stopped to help a Byzantine prince try to take control of the imperial throne. Western knights besieged Constantinople for weeks. Finally, they captured and looted the city.

A Latin knight, Count Baldwin, took the title Byzantine Emperor. The crusaders divided Byzantine territories among themselves and ruled them as feudal fiefs for about 50 years. The crusaders' attacks eventually caused the downfall of the Byzantine Empire.

Byzantine Influences on Russia. Despite the Byzantine Empire's political fall, it remained a strong cultural force. People in the Byzantine Empire believed that their society transmitted learning of the ancient Greeks and Romans. Byzantine influence was strongest in Russia, Serbia, and Bulgaria.

Byzantine missionaries first went to Russia in the ninth century. At the end of the tenth century, King Vladimir of Kiev made Orthodox Christianity the religion of his country.

According to a Russian legend, Vladimir interviewed missionaries from many countries. He turned down Islamic envoys when he discovered that their religion did not allow drinking. Vladimir reasoned that "Drinking is the joy of the Russians; we cannot exist without it." Jews also were rejected when Vladimir found that they did not have their own country. After he sent advisers to visit Bulgaria, Germany, and Byzantium, he decided on Orthodoxy because of the beauty of its churches and services. In addition, he made a political alliance with the empire by marrying a Byzantine princess.

The decision of the state of Kiev to accept Orthodox Christianity had long-lasting consequences. One result was that Russia would have closer relations with Orthodox than Latin Christian countries.

Yaroslav the Wise

FOCUS ON PEOPLE

When Vladimir the Great died, his sons fought to succeed him. Vladimir had married several times, so many of his sons had different mothers. This difference increased the competition among them. After 21 years of fighting, at least four of Vladimir's sons had died. A fifth, Yaroslav the Wise, gained control of Kievian Russia.

After defeating his brothers, Yaroslav turned on the states surrounding Russia. He attacked the Poles, the Turks, and the Byzantines. He expanded Russia's territory.

Yaroslav was one of the first Russian rulers to strengthen links between Russia and western Europe. Yaroslov's daughters married kings of Norway, Hungary, and France. Three of his sons married German princesses, and another son married a Byzantine princess. Yaroslav himself married the daughter of a Swedish princess.

Europeans considered Kiev under Yaroslav a strong and progressive kingdom. For example, Yaroslav's daughter, Anna, learned how to write. When she married Henry I, king of France, she was able to sign the marriage certificate. Henry, though a king, could not even write his name. He signed the marriage certificate with an X.

Under Yaroslav, the laws of Kiev were written in an orderly manner for the first time. Yaroslav based the Russian law code

The Mediterranean World, 1000

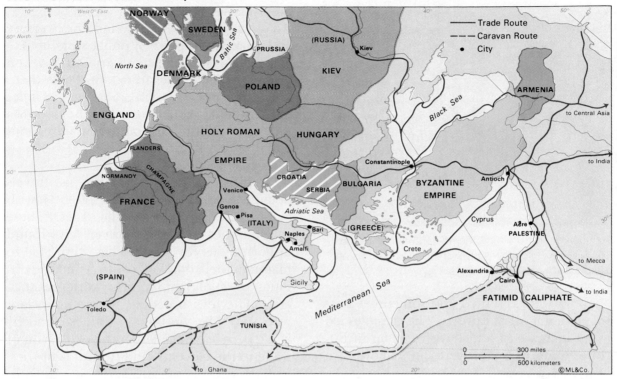

Map Skills **1.** What cities are linked to Venice by trade routes? **2.** List two geographical features that contributed to the growth of Venice as a center of trade.

on Byzantine models. The law code of Kiev was very mild. Physical punishments, including executions, were rarely used.

In addition to establishing a law code, Yaroslav greatly influenced Russian culture. To promote the spread of Christianity in Russia, he hired writers to translate Greek religious literature into Russian. He helped to build several great cathedrals and monasteries. The most famous cathedral is St. Sophia's, in Kiev. Yaroslav hired artists to beautify Kiev and other Russian cities.

Yaroslav hoped to prevent battles over who would succeed him. He established guidelines to determine which of his sons should govern each part of his kingdom. Soon after Yaroslav's death in 1054, however, his descendants went to war with one another over control. Yaroslav's wisdom could not prevent the fighting that went on after his death. ■

Jewish Culture and Trade

As Yaroslav was developing a Russian state, another culture was developing without a state. Jews were scattered throughout the cities of Europe, northern Africa, and western Asia.

Persecution of Jews was rare in the Islamic world. Jews participated freely in trade and intellectual pursuits. They often served as advisers to caliphs.

Moses ben Maimon, or Maimonides (my MOHN ih deez), was one of the greatest Jewish thinkers of the twelfth century. He was the physician to a high official in Saladin's court. Maimonides is remembered, though, because he systematized all of Jewish law into an organized code called the *Mishnah Torah*. He also wrote a work that analyzed the relationship between faith and reason by examining Aristotle and the Bible.

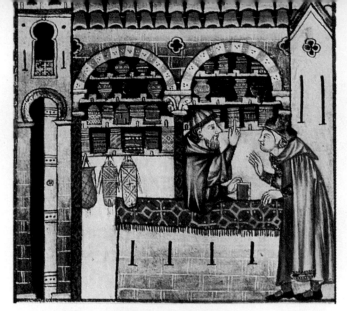

An illustration from a thirteenth-century manuscript shows a Spanish-Jewish merchant selling herbs and spices from the Orient.

Jews were resented and sometimes persecuted in most of Europe. The crusades led to an increase of anti-Jewish feeling in Europe. Only in Spain were Jews allowed to live freely.

In the eleventh century, Christians gradually forced European Jews out of trade. By the end of the twelfth century, the main line of business Jews were allowed to follow in much of Europe was money-lending. Church leaders prohibited Christians from charging interest on loans.

In Asia and Africa, Jews were among the most active traders. Their caravans traveled from southern Arabia all the way across the Silk Road to China (see page 287). Wherever Jews traveled or settled, they maintained their religion and culture. In the twelfth century, a rabbi from Spain, Benjamin of Tudela, took a 10-year trip around the Mediterranean world. He wrote an account of his travels, describing the cities he saw and the people he met. Here is his description of his visit to Egypt:

❝ The pyramids, which are seen here, are constructed by magic; and in no other country or other place is anything equal to them. They are composed of stones and cement, and are very substantial. In the outskirts of the city is the very ancient synagogue of our great master Moses, upon whom be peace. An old and very learned man is the overseer and clerk of this place of public worship. He is called Al-Sheikh Abunasar. Old Mizraim [Memphis] is 3 miles in extent. From there to the land of Goshen, 8 parasangs [28 miles or 45 kilometers]. It is called Belbeis (bihl BAYS), is a large city, and contains about 3,000 Jewish inhabitants. ❞

Benjamin's description of his travels demonstrates the important role of Jewish communities in the Middle Ages. These communities existed wherever Jews found opportunities for trade. They were able to maintain their religion, culture, and the tradition of scholarship in many different societies. The Jewish people, in one important way, were like the Italian, Chinese, and Islamic peoples. Each led in the expansion of trade in the eleventh and twelfth centuries.

SECTION 3 *Study Skills*

Developing Vocabulary Write one paragraph using all of the following words: **1.** confiscate. **2.** invest. **3.** envoy.

Reviewing Main Ideas **1.** What were the most important exports from Europe carried by the Venetian traders? **2.** Identify the advantages Italians had in gaining control of the Mediterranean trade. **3.** Describe the Mediterranean trade area in the 1200s. **4.** How did the crusades influence the Byzantine Empire? **5.** Give evidence that indicates that the Byzantine Empire was the cultural center of the Christian world. **6.** How did the crusades stimulate trade in northern Europe? **7.** Summarize the influence of Yaroslav the Wise on Russia.

Understanding Chronology **1.** What crusade disrupted the Byzantine Empire in 1204? **2.** When did King Vladimir decide to convert Russia to Christianity?

Challenge Is a single world religion possible? Explain your answer.

CHAPTER 14 *Summary & Review*

Summarizing Main Ideas

During the Song Dynasty, Chinese merchants traded in Japan, Southeast Asia, India, and east Africa. South Indian merchants carried goods into eastern Asia. The Khmer and Srivijaya empires in Southeast Asia learned of Indian culture through such trade.

Muslim traders introduced their religion and culture into India and east Africa. In India, many conflicts between Hindus and Muslims occurred. Trading cities, combining Muslim and African culture, grew on the east African coast.

Italian merchants led expanded trade in the Mediterranean region by 1200. Returning crusaders increased European demand for silks and spices. In northern Europe, merchants conducted trade at scheduled trade fairs.

Orthodox Christianity spread even though the Byzantine Empire crumbled. Russia linked itself with eastern Europe by accepting Orthodox Christianity. Although a scattered people, the Jews developed their own culture, and were important in trade.

Logs to be shipped from Abidjan, a port on the Ivory Coast.

Questions for Critical Thinking

COMPREHENSION Interpreting Events

1. Explain how improved ship building techniques helped Chinese merchants lead Asian trade.
2. Explain two reasons why Italians became involved in Mediterranean trade.

ANALYSIS Identifying Trends

1. What impact did the collapse of the Byzantine Empire have on the expansion of trade between Europe and Asia?
2. Discuss the long range results of Russian conversion to Orthodox Christianity.
3. Identify several ways that China influenced Japanese society.

APPLICATION Comparing Past to Present

1. How do the trade patterns of the eleventh to thirteenth centuries help explain the fact that modern African cities are usually located on coasts?
2. Discuss the importance of credit to twelfth century trade and to trade today.

SYNTHESIS Developing Map Skills

1. Which cities were important stops on the Mediterranean trade routes of the Italians?
2. See the map, Chinese Overseas Trade, on page 303, and describe the geographical features that trade routes and trading cities have in common.

EVALUATION Weighing Consequences

1. What influence did Chinese visitors have on Japanese religion?
2. How did Muslim trade in the Indian Ocean influence the Hindus?
3. Why did trade increase when Mediterranean products began to reach northern Europe?

CHALLENGE

Compare the trade and interdependence of peoples in the thirteenth century with that of nations today.

CHAPTER 15

The Mongol Conquerors

GLOBAL TIME LINE

| | 1200 | 1225 | 1250 |

TIME

1100s Court jesters entertain in Europe

1100–1300 Italian cities dominate trade and banking, and Belgian cities dominate the woolen cloth industry

1211–1227 Mongol Empire expands under Genghis Khan

1215 Magna Carta guarantees rights of English citizens

1236–1241 Mongols terrorize Russia, Poland, and Hungary

PEOPLE

1206 Temujin proclaimed the Great Khan by tribal leaders

1211 Genghis Khan invades China

1215 King John of England signs the Magna Carta

1240 Batu founds Khanate of the Golden Horde

PLACE

1240–1480 *Russia;*[1] Golden Horde rules Russia

Linking Past to Present

A new migration of nomads from the Asian steppes occurred in the thirteenth century. The Mongols under Genghis Khan created the largest empire the world has ever known. At its height, this empire stretched from eastern Europe to the Korean Peninsula.

The Mongol conquests were extremely violent and destructive. In the Middle East the Mongols killed hundreds of thousands of people and destroyed cities and irrigation works. Western Europe, by contrast, escaped a Mongol assault. This may help explain why, in modern times, the Middle East remained a less developed part of the world than western Europe. As you read the chapter, analyze the ways migrating peoples alter the cultures of lands they invade.

Nomadic Mongol women were skillful riders.

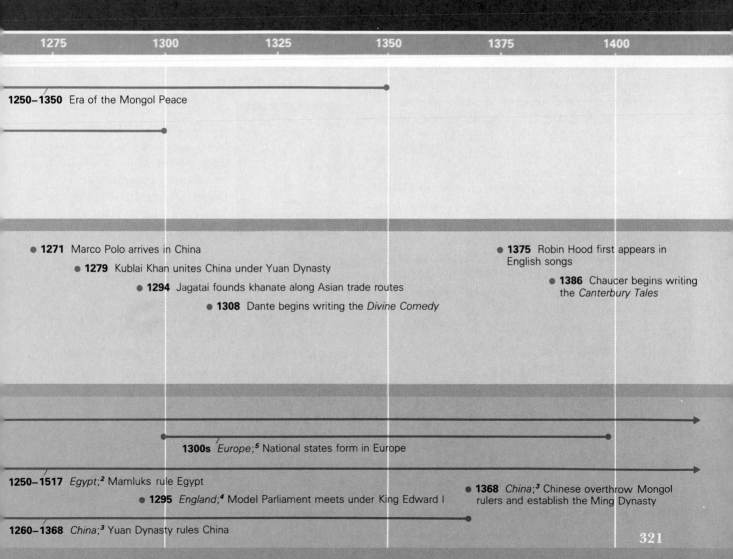

1275   1300   1325   1350   1375   1400

1250–1350 Era of the Mongol Peace

- **1271** Marco Polo arrives in China
- **1279** Kublai Khan unites China under Yuan Dynasty
- **1294** Jagatai founds khanate along Asian trade routes
- **1308** Dante begins writing the *Divine Comedy*
- **1375** Robin Hood first appears in English songs
- **1386** Chaucer begins writing the *Canterbury Tales*

1300s *Europe;*[5] National states form in Europe

1250–1517 *Egypt;*[2] Mamluks rule Egypt

- **1295** *England;*[4] Model Parliament meets under King Edward I
- **1368** *China;*[3] Chinese overthrow Mongol rulers and establish the Ming Dynasty

1260–1368 *China;*[3] Yuan Dynasty rules China

321

1 Genghis Khan and the Mongols

OBJECTIVE: *To understand the development of the Mongol Empire based in central Asia*

The Rise of the Mongols

The Mongols had little influence on world history before the thirteenth century. Then, the dynamic Genghis Khan (JEHNG gihs KAHN) and his cavalry charged across the steppes and changed the course of Eurasian history for all time.

Early Mongol culture was similar to that of other nomadic peoples of central Asia. Mongols herded horses and sheep, moving throughout the year in search of grazing land. They lived in *yurts*, or wood frame tents covered with felt. When a Mongol family traveled, its *yurt* and other belongings were loaded on a large wagon.

Mongol boys learned to ride horses when they were three years old. Women took charge of household duties and child raising. Mongol women also rode expertly.

Most of the Mongols believed in a god they associated with the sky and the night heavens. They also honored priests called shamans, who interpreted the will of god, predicted the future, and protected people from harm with the help of various rituals.

VOCABULARY DEVELOPMENT

confines (KAHN fynz) *noun:* boundary, border. From the Latin prefix *com-*, meaning with, and word *finis*, meaning end, limit.

lamented (luh MEHN tihd) *adj.* expressed sorrow for, regretted. From the Latin word, *lamentum*, meaning a mourning.

Like other tribes of the Asian steppes, the Mongols formed into clans. The members of each clan claimed to be descended from a common ancestor. Frequently, these clans fought among themselves for the best grazing land. At times, an unusually forceful leader, or khan, managed to unite all the clans for war with a common enemy.

Genghis Khan

FOCUS ON PEOPLE

One such forceful leader was Genghis Khan. He was born about 1167, the son of a minor clan chieftain. His original name was Temujin. When he was about 12 years old, a rival chief poisoned his father. Temujin was too young then for clan leadership, and the clan deserted him. Temujin, his mother, and his four brothers survived by hunting and fishing.

Temujin was a ruthless and strong-willed boy. When his half-brother stole some wild game from him, Temujin shot and killed him with an arrow. When he was a teenager, the leaders of a rival clan captured him. Temujin was held prisoner with a wooden yoke around his neck. He escaped, however, by floating down a river.

As a young man, Temujin attracted attention because he was a warrior of unusual strength and intelligence. When a tribe kidnapped his new wife, he organized a small force of cavalry to rescue her. Temujin and his soldiers caught up with his enemies, defeated them in battle, and rescued his wife. After this episode, more Mongol warriors accepted Temujin as their military leader.

In 1206, the tribal leaders met in a great assembly and proclaimed Temujin the great khan of "all who dwell in tents of felt." They gave him the honorary title, Genghis Khan. In the Mongol language, this term meant "lord of the world." The Mongol tribes were thus united in a great confederation. Over the next 21 years, they would conquer much of Eurasia. ■

The Mongols Conquer China

When Genghis came to power in the early thirteenth century, China was split between the Southern Song Empire and the Jin State. See the map, Song and Jin China 1000–1200, page 286. The Mongols invaded China in 1211. Four years later, Genghis attacked the Jin capital of Beijing and massacred many of its inhabitants. By the end of the thirteenth century, the Mongols had conquered China.

Mongol Tactics. Genghis Khan was one of the greatest military strategists in history. He used various tricks to confuse his enemies. Sometimes, a small Mongol cavalry unit would attack, then pretend to gallop away in flight. The enemy usually gave chase. Then, the rest of the Mongol army would appear suddenly and slaughter the exhausted enemy forces.

Another strategy was to make the enemy believe the Mongol calvary was larger than it actually was. Sometimes, prisoners of war were forced to put on Mongol clothing. These prisoners then were driven ahead of the main army to take the first shock of enemy arrows. Mongols sometimes put life-like dummies on horses to look like warriors. Spies were sent regularly into enemy territory to spread rumors that the approaching Mongol forces were enormous.

This illumination from a Persian manuscript shows the nomadic Genghis Khan holding court in his palace, a tent.

Genghis and his generals kept all Mongol units in communication with one another. Sometimes they used a system of flags and fires to send signals. A Mongol messenger might spend many hours in the saddle without stopping to cook food or sleep. One way that messengers refreshed themselves was by sucking warm blood from a small gash in their horse's neck.

The Mongol Army. The Mongol army was made up of cavalry units. Each warrior carried two bows and two or three quivers of arrows, as well as a shield of thick leather and a sword or lance. The Mongol bow was so strong that it could shoot an arrow 350 yards. Skilled archers could hit a target while riding at full gallop.

Every member of the Mongol cavalry wore underwear of raw silk. Often the silk would not break when an arrow struck it. Rather, the silk would be drawn into the wound. The arrow then could be pulled out with less damage to the flesh.

Learning from the Chinese. Genghis Khan despised what he considered the soft ways of civilization. Still, he adopted useful ideas from peoples he conquered. For instance, he employed Chinese engineers to build catapults to hurl stones at city walls and gates. The Mongols also learned from the Chinese how to make bombs.

The Mongols Sweep Westward

Long before completing the conquest of China, Genghis turned his attention to the Islamic region west of Mongolia. In 1218, a Mongol army conquered most of the steppe region north and west of the Tian Shan Mountains. Many of the herding tribes in that region were Turkish Muslims. Thousands of Turkish cavalry troops were recruited into the Mongol army.

Mongols and their Turkish allies destroyed numerous Islamic cities over the next four years. In Nishapur in northern Iran, for example, the Mongols massacred almost the entire population. Then, they hunted down the dogs and cats and killed them. Nishapur fell into ruin, never to recover. The Mongols herded the population of Merv, another Iranian city, onto a nearby plain. Each warrior was assigned a certain number of people, including women and children, to kill with his sword.

Genghis returned to Mongolia in 1222. There he built his capital at Karakorum. He resumed his drive to conquer China but died in 1227, while fighting. His armies probably had killed more people than any previous conqueror in history. Genghis organized his empire so well, however, that it continued to expand for another half century after his death.

Mongol Expansion into Europe. In accord with Mongol custom, the empire of Genghis Khan was divided among his four sons after he died. The Mongol leaders elected the third son, Ogadai (AHG uh TY), to be the emperor, or great khan. In 1236,

Ogadai ordered his cavalry into Russia and eastern Europe. The Christian princes of Russia were politically divided and failed to cooperate in resisting the Mongols. City after city fell to the fierce invaders.

From Russia, the Mongols moved into eastern Europe. In winter of the year 1241, they galloped into Poland, crossing rivers on the ice. Another force advanced to the southwest, terrorizing Hungary. One raiding party came within 60 miles of Venice.

Now the pope and the kings of western Europe feared that Mongols would attack Germany and Italy. These invaders from the steppes seemed to strike Europe like lightning. Terrified Europeans thought the Mongols were allies of the devil. An English scholar of the time wrote:

❝ Swarming like locusts over the face of the earth, they have brought terrible devastation to the eastern parts of Europe, laying them waste with fire and carnage [death].... They come with the swiftness of lightning to the confines of Christendom, ravaging and slaughtering, striking everyone with terror and incomparable horror. ❞

Suddenly, in the spring of 1242, word reached the Mongol generals in Europe that the Great Khan, Ogadai, had died the prior

Northmen, called the Rus, settled in Novgorod. They were spared an attack by the Mongols when a spring thaw turned their steppelands to mud in 1240.

December. The officers had to return to Karakorum to help choose a new leader. In this way, western Europe was saved from devastation. The Mongols established a government over Russia, but they never resumed attacks on Poland and Hungary.

The Kingdom of the Il-Khans. Hulagu (hoo LAH goo), a grandson of Genghis Khan, founded the Kingdom of the Il-Khans in southwest Asia in 1260. This kingdom included Iran, Iraq, and parts of Syria and Asia Minor.

As rulers of the Middle East, the Il-Khans slowly abandoned the nomadic culture of the steppes. By the end of the thirteenth century, they had converted to Islam. Like other Mongols, the Il-Khan leaders encouraged trade. They allowed merchants from all lands to use routes that passed through their khanate.

The Il-Khan conquest of the Middle East was more destructive than the Mongol conquest of China. In 1258, Hulagu broke through the gates of Baghdad, the capital of the Abbasid Empire. His warriors burned part of the city and massacred thousands of inhabitants. Many of the city's libraries and works of art were destroyed. According to some accounts, Hulagu executed the last caliph by having him rolled up in a carpet and trampled to death by horses.

The most damaging attacks were on the irrigation works of the Tigris and Euphrates valleys. By destroying canals, the Mongols ruined much of the agricultural land on which Mesopotamian civilization had relied for 4,000 years.

One Iranian historian lamented:

❝ There can be no doubt that even if for a thousand years to come no evil befalls the country, yet will it not be possible completely to repair the damage, and bring back the land to the state in which it was formerly. ❞

Mongol destruction and a climate change help to explain the relative lack of economic growth in the Middle East after 1258. However, caravan traffic in the Middle East soon revived and the cities of the region continued to serve as important centers of trade.

The Il-Khans became involved in long, costly wars with neighboring Mongol kingdoms. These wars emptied the treasury of the Il-Khans and depleted their resources. Consequently, the government fell apart rather suddenly in 1335.

India and Egypt Escape. Like western Europe, India and northern Africa were spared Mongol domination. The Mongols raided but never conquered India. In Syria, the Mongols confronted a powerful military force, the Mamluks, based in Egypt. In 1260, the Mamluks defeated the Mongols.

Though the Mamluks defeated the Mongols, the legacy of Genghis Khan's empire continued. For a century, the Mongols controlled most of Asia.

SECTION 1 *Study Skills*

Developing Vocabulary Use each of the following words in a sentence: **1.** confines. **2.** lamented.

Reviewing Main Ideas 1. Describe the lifestyle of the Mongols. **2.** How was Temujin able to become the "lord of the world?" **3.** What strategies did the Mongols use to confuse their enemies? **4.** Describe Genghis Kahn's cavalry. **5.** What did the Mongols do to strike terror among those they wished to conquer?

Understanding Chronology 1. How long did the Mongols dominate Eurasia? **2.** Who served as Khan longer, Temujin or Ogadai? **3.** What happened in 1242 that may have saved Europe from Mongol control?

Challenge Mongol warriors struck terror in settlements throughout Asia. Today, bands of terrorists can create fear throughout the world. Have the purposes and methods of terrorists changed through the years? Explain.

2 The Era of the Mongol Peace

OBJECTIVE: *To understand the consequences of the interactions of people within the Mongol Empire*

The Mongol Kingdoms

The period from the middle of the thirteenth century to the middle of the fourteenth century is sometimes called the Mongol Peace. This term refers to the period of stability and law and order that characterized much of Eurasia under Mongol rule. During this time, land and sea traders traveling across the Eastern Hemisphere were more active than ever before.

In theory, one descendant of Genghis Khan was designated the great khan, to rule the entire empire. In practice, quarrels and civil wars among the descendants often divided the empire. By 1260, the Mongol lands were split into four khanates. A descendant of Genghis ruled each. See the map, Khanates of the Mongol Empire, 1294, page 328. The Il-Khans ruled in the Middle East. The other three Mongol khanates were in China, central Asia, and Russia.

VOCABULARY DEVELOPMENT

ritual (RIHCH oo wuhl) *adj.:* the observance of set forms or rites, as in public worship.

famine (FAM uhn) *noun:* a serious general shortage of food. From the Latin word, *fames*, meaning hunger.

alienate (AYL yuhn AYT) *verb:* to change from a friendly to an unfriendly relationship.

refine (rih FYN) *verb:* to free from impurities. From the French word, *raffiner*, meaning to purify.

Mongol Rule in China. Kublai Khan (KYOO bly KAHN), Genghis Khan's grandson, conquered and united China, ending the Southern Song Dynasty in 1279. Kublai founded a new dynasty called the Yuan (yoo AHN). The Yuan lasted from 1260 to 1368. Kublai united all of China, Korea, and parts of Indochina under his rule. The Mongol calvary was almost unstoppable. Mongol naval attacks, though, were less successful.

Kublai tried to invade Java and Japan by sea but failed. He first attempted to invade Japan in 1274 with a force of 25,000 men. Soon after the first troops landed, a typhoon suddenly hit Japan and destroyed more than 200 of the Mongol ships. Seven years later, Kublai tried again to invade Japan. This time he sent 140,000 troops. Again a typhoon destroyed his navy. Fewer than 30,000 of his troops managed to return to China. The Japanese called the saving typhoons Kamikazi (KAH mih KAH zee), or divine wind.

The Mongol conquerors of east Asia were less cruel than their comrades in the Middle East. The Mongols apparently did not slaughter masses of people in China as they had in central and southwestern Asia. When the conquest was complete, Kublai quickly restored public order and peace. He moved his capital from Karakorum to Beijing. Moving the capital was a sign that he intended to become emperor of China. In memory of his steppe heritage, however, he planted a stretch of prairie grass on the grounds of his summer palace near Beijing.

Kublai ruled China intelligently. To increase his acceptance by the Chinese people, he performed the Confucian public rituals, as had previous Chinese emperors.

Under his leadership, China soon recovered much of its former economic prosperity. He improved the country's roads, canal network, postal system, and navy. He also started a system for storing surplus grain to guard against famine. According to a European visitor, Marco Polo, Kublai provided food for 30,000 poor people every day.

Kublai also encouraged trade. The Yangzi River valley remained the main commercial highway of the empire. Marco Polo, the merchant, visited the Yangzi River valley and wrote the following:

❝ More vessels and more rich merchandise pass up and down this river [the Yangzi] than upon all the rivers and all the seas of Christendom. **❞**

Kublai invited foreign merchants to visit China. Most of them were Muslims from India, central Asia, and Iran.

After Kublai Khan died in 1294, Mongol rulers had increasing difficulties in governing China. Economic problems developed, and conflicts with native Chinese weakened Mongol control. A Chinese rebel seized Beijing in 1368 and proclaimed a new dynasty, the Ming. The Ming Dynasty ended Mongol rule in China.

The Jagatai Khanate. The Jagatai Khanate (JAHG uh TY KAHN ayt), the second great Mongol kingdom, was named for Jagatai, one of Genghis Khan's sons. The Jagatai kingdom in central Asia straddled the main trade routes connecting China and western Eurasia. The khans of Jagatai encouraged merchants of all countries to pass through their realm. This open trade policy made possible increase of trade across Eurasia that was a feature of the Era of Mongol Peace. The Jagatai khans ruled until the 1370s.

Kublai Khan, grandson of Genghis Khan, leads his Mongol riders across a desert.

The Khanate of the Golden Horde. In Russia, a grandson of Genghis Khan founded the fourth of the great Mongol kingdoms. This grandson, Batu, led the Khanate of the Golden Horde. Historians are uncertain why the empire was considered golden. However, horde comes from the Turkish word, *ordu*, meaning the camp or headquarters of the ruler. The capital was Saray, a city on the Volga River.

Like other Mongol rulers, those of the Golden Horde had a wide outlook. They maintained passage roads for merchants traveling overland from the Black Sea toward China. They also permitted Buddhist, Christian, and Muslim missionaries to preach freely in the kingdom.

Early in the fourteenth century, however, the khans made Islam their official religion. Islam soon spread rapidly in the region north of the Black and Caspian seas. Today, Islam is still a major religion in parts of the Soviet Union.

The Mongols did not interfere with the practice of Orthodox Christianity in Russia. When the khans accepted Islam, however, they alienated many Russian Christians. Mongol rule also isolated the Russians from other Christians for the next 250 years. The Russian Orthodox church became increasingly independent of the Greek Orthodox church. Russia fell behind western Europe in technology and scientific advancement during the long rule of the Mongols.

The Golden Horde ruled over several small Russian princes. In the late fourteenth century, the Russian rulers of Muscovy increased their power. Under the prince of Moscow, Ivan III, Russia achieved complete independence from the Mongols in 1480. Muscovy, with its capital city of Moscow, was the core of a new Russian state that would grow steadily in the following centuries.

The Khanate of the Golden Horde shrank in size as the Russian state grew. It was not until the middle of the sixteenth century, however, that the last of the four Mongol khanates had finally collapsed.

The Spread of Turkish Influence. Turkish influence had begun to spread through India and the Middle East in the eleventh and twelfth centuries. This expansion continued in the thirteenth and fourteenth centuries. The Mongol Empire spread in part because

Khanates of the Mongol Empire, 1294

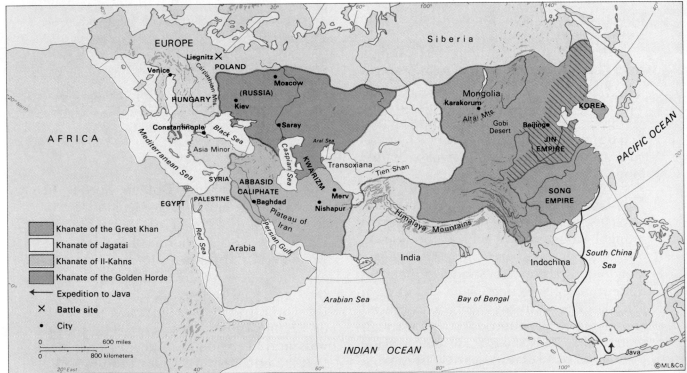

Map Skills **1.** Name the mountain ranges that lie between Beijing and Baghdad. **2.** Which Mongol Khanate was farthest north? **3.** Which bordered on the Pacific Ocean?

many Turkish horsemen joined the Mongol cavalry. Consequently, as the Mongol Empire grew, Turkish culture also spread.

In India, the Delhi Sultanate (see page 281) remained strong throughout the thirteenth century. After the middle of the fourteenth century, however, ineffective government and rebellions weakened the kingdom. It soon lost much of its territory.

Turks continued to take land from the Byzantine Empire in Asia Minor. This process had begun at the Battle of Manzikert in 1071 (see page 281). By the end of the fourteenth century, advancing Turks controlled all of Asia that had once belonged to the Byzantine Empire.

The Mamluk Kingdom

In the middle of the thirteenth century, an Islamic government ruled Egypt. Islamic rulers commonly employed slaves as soldiers. One Arabic word for slave is *mamluk*. Many mamluks were Turks from central Asia. In 1250, a group of these slave-soldiers overthrew the government of Egypt. They established the Mamluk Kingdom.

Cairo was the capital of the Mamluk sultans. Under their rule, it became a center for trade and for Islamic learning. Cairo was the largest city in the world outside of China. Its population may have exceeded 500,000 in the fourteenth century. In 1481, a traveler from Europe found Cairo awesome:

❝ If I were to write and describe the glory and wealth of the city and the men therein, this book would not suffice [be enough]. . . . I swear that if it were possible to place all the cities of Rome, Milan, Padua, and Florence together with four other cities, they would not, the whole lot of them, contain the wealth and population of the half of Cairo, and this is true. ❞

The Mamluks ruled Egypt for 267 years. Theirs was one of the longest lasting dynasties in Islamic history.

The Spread of Knowledge

During the Mongol Peace, people traveled more freely across Asia than they had ever done before. The exchange of ideas and skills that resulted often had an important effect on the culture into which they were introduced.

China's Exchanges. From China, people in western Eurasia learned about gunpowder, printing, and the compass. Each caused dramatic changes in western Eurasia. The use of gunpowder led to new weapons. Printing revolutionized the spread of knowledge in Europe. The compass encouraged exploration in the search for trade because sailors could navigate even when they could not see the sun or stars.

China also benefited from exchanges with other people. From Egyptians, the Chinese learned how to refine sugar. Carrots, pistachio nuts, grape wine, and a grain called sorghum were introduced to China from western lands.

The Spread of Islam. Religions, particularly Islam, spread rapidly during the thirteenth and fourteenth centuries. Turkish conquerors, Muslim merchants, and traveling scholars spread the Islamic religion. Hundreds of thousands of people in central Asia, India, Southeast Asia, and west Africa chose Islam in this period. See the map, Spread of Islam, page 330.

The Traveler, Ibn Battuta. Muslims of the Mongol Age often traveled thousands of miles for business or study. One unusually ambitious traveler was Abu Abdallah ibn Battuta. He was born in Tangier, Morocco, in 1304. As a boy, he learned Islamic religion and law. In 1325, he left home to make the holy pilgrimage to Mecca. Then he spent the next 29 years of his life traveling as far as India and China.

He made the holy pilgrimage several more times. In addition, he went to study with great scholars in different cities and to

Spread of Islam, 1300 – 1500

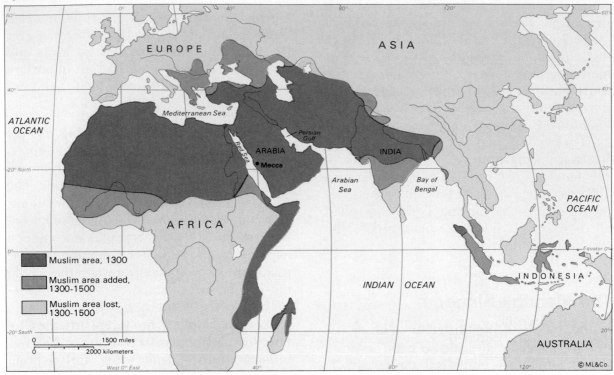

Map Skills **1.** What lands did the Muslims conquer between 1300 and 1500? **2.** What body of water lies between Africa and India? **3.** What bodies of water border the Arabian Peninsula?

work as a judge. He married several times during this period and fathered several children. Whenever he took to the road, though, he divorced his wife and left his children behind with her.

Over the years, Ibn Battuta had many adventures that nearly cost him his life. The guide he hired while traveling in south Arabia tried to rob and murder him. In Asia Minor, he became lost in a snowstorm. In northern India, he fought with bandits and was wounded. As he was sailing along the coast of India on a merchant ship, pirates attacked him. They robbed him of all his possessions and marooned him on a beach.

When Ibn Battuta finally returned home in 1354, the sultan of Morocco ordered him, with the help of another scholar, to write a book about his travels and the things he had seen. Today, historians use Ibn Battuta's book for information on fourteenth-century society and culture.

SECTION 2 *Study Skills*

Developing Vocabulary Write a paragraph in which you use three of the following terms: ritual, famine, alienate, refine.

Reviewing Main Ideas **1.** Explain what the Mongol Peace had in common with the Pax Romana. **2.** How did Kublai Khan use Chinese customs to help rule China? **3.** What were two traits of Mongol rulers?

Understanding Chronology **1.** How long did Mongols rule Russia? **2.** How long did the Mamluks rule Egypt? **3.** When did Ibn Battuta write about his amazing travels?

Understanding Cause and Effect **1.** Describe several problems that led to the downfall of the Mongol rule in China. **2.** How did Mongol rule affect Russia's relationship with Europe?

Challenge Contrast the missionary efforts of the Mongols and the Turks.

Environment and Warfare

Throughout history, people have fought wars to control important areas. Often the geography of a region has helped determine the outcome of a battle. An area's climate has also influenced history.

Geography Influences Warfare

The causes of war are complex. Countries commonly fight to expand their land or control strategic areas.

Motives for War. Gaining access to seaports has often been a motive for war. Russia, whose major ports are in the north and thus subject to winter freezing, has fought numerous battles in its push to gain warm water ports such as those on the Black Sea. Peter the Great (1689–1725) and his successors wanted to make Russia a great naval power for both military and trade reasons.

Some wars occurred because leaders wanted to increase the size of their empires. Genghis Khan, whose name means "Lord of the World," led his Mongol warriors in the thirteenth century to conquer lands throughout central Asia.

The outcome of battles has often been influenced by control of key geographical features, such as straits or mountain passes. In 1071, at the Battle of Manzikert, the Seljuk army trapped the Byzantine army in a valley. Unable to fight their way out, the Byzantine force surrendered. The Seljuk victory at Manzikert led to the Turkish conquest of most of Asia Minor.

Barriers to Warfare. Major landforms such as deserts, mountains, and oceans can limit or complicate warfare. Such barriers often serve as boundaries between countries. Island nations such as Japan, Indonesia, and the Philippines are separated from other nations by oceans. The ocean has helped protect these countries from past invasions.

In some countries, there are no such barriers to warfare. In these places, wars have been relatively common through the ages. Korea is just such a nation. The hills of Korea do not deter invaders. For much of its history, Korea has been under the domination of either China or Japan.

Climate Affects Warfare

Fighting a war on foreign soil can be difficult. Problems created by weather conditions can make fighting nearly impossible. Such features often aid people defending against invasion.

Modern warfare is complicated. Huge numbers of people are involved. By the end of World War II, the United States army alone had 8,266,373 soldiers. Soldiers must be fed, clothed, sheltered, and given medical care. Soldiers need guns, ammunition, and a variety of vehicles. All the vehicles need fuel.

Countries fighting on foreign soil must transport all the supplies they need. An army defending its homeland, therefore, has an advantage and can damage its enemy severely by cutting off its supplies.

Winter Invasions. The Soviet Union has successfully cut off invaders' supply lines. In 1812, a French army under Napoleon invaded Russia. His soldiers did not have the clothing and equipment to withstand a Russian winter. Suffering from the cold, they retreated.

During World War II, German troops had a similar experience. They had planned to conquer the Soviets before the coming of

This 1530 battle scene is from the *Baber Nama,* or history of Baber's reign. Baber was the founder and first emperor of the Moghul Dynasty in India.

Soviet troops invaded Afghanistan in 1979. This photo of a downed Soviet helicopter shows the mountainous terrain that hindered Soviet efforts.

winter. Therefore, they also were not well supplied when winter came on. The German army caused great destruction but was unable to conquer the Soviet Union. Like the French over a century earlier, the Germans failed to understand the influence of geography and climate on warfare.

Summer Invasions. Climate also played a role in the D-Day invasion of World War II. Ocean currents and prevailing winds cause frequent storms and rough seas in the English Channel.

In June, 1944, United States and British forces gathered in England across the channel from Normandy, France. Over 156,000 troops in 9,000 seacraft and 11,000 aircraft waited for clear weather. As in the amphibious invasion by the Spanish Armada in 1588, few things went right. Crashing waves

kept frogmen from blowing up the underwater fortifications along the beaches of Normandy. The rough seas sank 27 of 32 amphibious tanks. While wading to shore, many soldiers lost their footing in the rough sea and drowned.

The Allies landed troops on three main beaches. The most bloody was Omaha Beach where 9,836 American soldiers died.

STUDY SKILLS Understanding Geography

1. Why did Genghis Khan want to conquer lands throughout Asia?
2. What is the military importance of mountains, deserts, and oceans?
3. What problems are related to fighting on foreign soil?
4. What feature of the Soviet Union has enabled it to emerge victorious in past wars?

3 Europe in the Mongol Age

OBJECTIVE: *To understand the growing importance of trade, cities, and nationalism in Europe*

Expansion of European Trade

The Mongols retreated from Poland and Hungary in 1242. They never again threatened western or central Europe. Consequently, European civilization continued to develop without interruption during the thirteenth century. Cities continued to grow as centers of trade, industry, and learning.

European merchants had been expanding their trade throughout the Mediterranean Basin since the eleventh century. Most of them were citizens of Venice, Genoa, Pisa, and other city-states of Italy. See the map, Trade Routes 1350, page 334. The merchants profited immensely by transporting crusaders to Palestine to fight against the Muslims. At the same time, the Venetians traded peacefully with Muslims in Alexandria, Cairo, and other cities.

The open trade policies of the Mongol Empire created new commercial opportunities. The Mongols welcomed merchants of all nations and religions.

Marco Polo Describes Asia

FOCUS ON SOURCES

Among the Italian merchants who visited China were two Venetian brothers, Niccolo and Maffeo Polo. They took along Niccolo's 17-year-old son, Marco, on their second trip to east Asia. The Polo family remained in China for seventeen years. Marco worked for Kublai Khan in a job that required him to travel extensively.

A few years after Marco returned to Venice, he wrote a book called *Description of the World*. Many people refused at first to believe the things he said about China. The wealth and customs he described, though,

---

VOCABULARY DEVELOPMENT

guild (gihld) *noun:* a union of men in the same craft or trade formed to uphold standards and protect the members. From the Old English word, *gyld*, meaning association (of paying members).

flying buttress (BUHT rihs) *noun:* a projecting structure, usually of stone or brick, built against a wall to support or reinforce it.

heresy (HAIR uh see) *noun:* a religious belief that differs from the orthodox doctrines supported by church leaders.

friar (FRY uhr) *noun:* a member of a religious order in which no one held any personal or community property but lived mostly by begging for charitable contributions.

common law: the law of a country or state based on custom, usage, and the opinions and decisions of a law court.

Parliament *noun:* a lawmaking body; the national legislative body of Great Britain. From the French word, *parler*, meaning to speak.

---

made people more curious about the lands of Asia. The following excerpt from Marco Polo's book describes the palace of Kublai:

❝In the middle of [the city] rises the Great Khan's palace, which is built as I shall tell you. It is the largest that was ever seen.... On each side of the palace is a great marble staircase, which leads from the ground to the top of the marble wall, and by which one reaches the palace. The inside walls of the halls and rooms are all covered with gold and silver, and on them are painted beautiful pictures of ladies and knights and dragons and beasts and birds and divers [various] other things. The ceiling is also made in such a way that one sees nothing else on it but pictures and gold. The great hall is so vast and large that quite 6,000 men could banquet there. There are so many rooms as to surpass all belief. The beauty and size of this palace are so great that no one on earth, who had the necessary skill, could have planned or built it better. The roof is varnished in vermillion [red], green, blue, yellow, and all other colors; and so well and cunningly is this done, that it glitters like crystal, and can be seen shining from a great way off all round. And you must know that the roof is so strongly and firmly built that it lasts for years without number. ❞

In the middle of the fourteenth century, the Mongol khanates declined in power. Without the order and protection of the Mongols, overland trade once again became more dangerous. For about 150 years after Polo, few Europeans visited China. ∎

European Cities

Cities grew rapidly in Europe in the twelfth and thirteenth centuries. Cities in northern Italy, such as Genoa and Venice, thrived.

Trade Routes, 1350

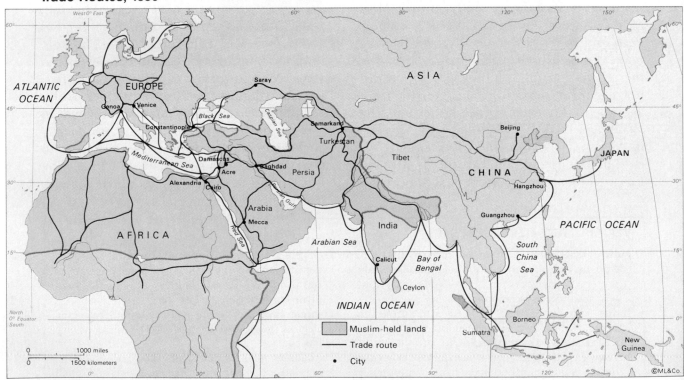

Map Skills **1.** On what continent is the city of Cairo located? **2.** Name two Italian cities that became important trading centers. **3.** What is the name of the island just south of India?

Several cities developed in Flanders, a region that today is part of Belgium. The cities of Bruges, Ghent, and Ypres were the leading centers of Europe's expanding woolen cloth industry.

Many former serfs flocked to the towns to look for jobs and opportunities. As a result, towns grew into cities. Until the nineteenth century, though, most Europeans were still farmers.

Growth of Guilds. As towns grew, new problems and special interests emerged. Skilled workers and craftspeople, for instance, had specialized concerns. Some artisans and merchants started guilds. These associations set standards and protected the special skills and interests of their members. For example, the woodworkers of a town formed one guild, the bakers another.

Gothic Churches. Soaring churches were built in many European cities in the late twelfth and thirteenth centuries. The biggest were cathedrals, the headquarters of a bishop. The massive churches demonstrated new engineering and artistic skills in Europe. Earlier churches had required thick walls to hold up their heavy roofs. Consequently, they had small windows. This style of architecture is called Romanesque. During the twelfth century, architects learned to support roofs by using exterior supports called flying buttresses. The walls then had less weight to support. Churches thus could be taller and have thinner walls and more windows. Today, this style of architecture is called Gothic.

New Religious Orders. Many Christians believed the church was too concerned with its own wealth and power. Heresies (HAIR uh seez), religious opinions not officially approved by the church, multiplied.

Christians tried to reform the church by starting new religious orders. The members of these orders were called friars. For example, St. Francis of Assisi founded the Franciscan order in 1209. The Franciscans served the poor and needy in the towns of Italy and northwestern Europe. St. Dominic started the Dominican order in 1216 to preach against heresy and to educate students.

The Universities. Several new universities opened during the thirteenth century.

A student usually entered a university at age 14. Every student was a male. He rented a room in the town and lived on his own. Students attended classes in their professors' homes or in rented rooms. Shopkeepers often charged students high prices for food and lodging. Sometimes, students protested these prices by rioting in the streets. Students frequently had money problems, as this letter from a young man to his parents shows:

❝ This is to inform you that I am studying at Oxford with the greatest diligence [careful, steady effort], but the matter of money stands in the way of my promotion, as it is now two months since I spent the last of what you sent me. The city is expensive and makes many demands; I have to rent lodgings, buy necessities, and provide for many other things which I cannot now specify. Wherefore I respectfully beg your paternity [fatherhood] that by the promptings of divine pity you may assist me, . . . ❞

A fourteenth-century illustration shows a professor and his students at the University of Paris.

The Rise of National Monarchies

Powerful monarchies began to develop in Europe during the twelfth and thirteenth centuries. The rise of new kingdoms was closely related to Europe's economic growth. Kings taxed expanding agriculture and trade to help build up their armies and governments. Also, they borrowed money.

Monarchy in France. In the eleventh century, the kings of France governed less territory than some of their own vassals. However, two thirteenth-century kings, Philip Augustus and Louis IX, expanded their lands and made France into the largest and richest kingdom in Europe.

Monarchy in England. King Henry II ruled England from 1154 to 1189. His reforms of the legal system strengthened the English monarchy. He appointed royal judges to travel through the country, holding court. Soon, more cases were tried in the king's courts than were tried in the courts of feudal lords.

Henry and his successors tried to make laws uniform throughout England. Each year, the most important court decisions were collected and written. These written decisions then became the basis for future court decisions. This type of law, based on judges' decisions rather than on a code of laws, is called common law. The laws were common to all of England.

Limits on the Monarch. Kings of England often needed more money to run their kingdom. In 1215, the nobles forced the unpopular King John to sign the Magna Carta, a document that guaranteed specific rights to the king's subjects. According to the Magna Carta, the king could not collect any new taxes without the consent of the Great Council, a body of important nobles and church leaders who advised the king. Nobles engaged in a dispute or accused of a crime were to be tried by members of their own social class. The king also agreed not to take property without paying for it. The Magna Carta established the idea that the king, as well as his subjects, must abide by the laws of the land.

Parliament (PAHR luh muhnt), England's lawmaking body, also originated in the thirteenth century. In most of the kingdoms of Europe, rulers occasionally called together councils of the leading nobles and bishops to explain royal policy or ask for advice. Some of the councils also acted as courts of law. Their meetings were called *parlements* in France and parliaments in England. The word is derived from the French word, *parler*, meaning to talk.

In 1295, King Edward I called an assembly that included great barons, church leaders, lesser nobility, lower clergy, and delegates from the towns. This assembly, called the Model Parliament, became the ancestor of Britain's Parliament of today.

Nations Develop in Europe. As strong monarchies developed in England and elsewhere in Europe, so did the idea of a nation. A nation is a group of people who share a common language, history, culture, and region. Many groups were beginning to think of themselves as distinctive nations.

SECTION 3 *Study Skills*

Developing Vocabulary Use each of the following terms in a sentence: **1.** guilds. **2.** flying buttresses. **3.** heresy. **4.** common law.

Reviewing Main Ideas **1.** What impact did the Mongol Peace have on Europeans? **2.** Explain the purpose of guilds. **3.** Why were the Franciscan and Dominican religious orders started? **4.** List four characteristics commonly shared by the people of a nation.

Understanding Cause and Effect **1.** What influence did St. Francis of Assisi have on the Christian Church? **2.** What influence did the Magna Carta have on the development of English government?

CHAPTER 15 *Summary & Review*

Summarizing Main Ideas

In the thirteenth century, Mongols, under the leadership of Genghis Khan, made conquests in China, Iran, and Russia. Only the death of the khan halted their westward march before reaching Germany.

For about one hundred years the Mongols maintained an uneasy peace in central Eurasia. The Mongols divided the land into four khanates: the Yuan in China, the Jagatai in central Asia, the Il-Khans in southwest Asia, and the Golden Horde in Russia.

European merchants continued to expand their trade in the thirteenth century. Marco Polo traveled, lived, and wrote about China. Such information informed western Europeans and encouraged trade. Guilds gained importance in European cities and the people of the towns took greater part in ruling their lives. Europeans built great cathedrals and established universities.

Questions for Critical Thinking

COMPREHENSION Interpreting Events

1. How did Chinese life change following the invasions by the Mongols?
2. Compare how Kublai Khan and Alexander the Great treated people they defeated.
3. Describe the effect Mongol rule had on Russia.
4. Explain how educated Muslims helped spread Islam.

ANALYSIS Identifying Trends

1. What impact did the Mongol invasions have on the development of the Middle East?
2. Explain the connection between economic changes in Europe and the growth of nations.

APPLICATION Comparing Past to Present

1. Give three examples of ideas exchanged during the Mongol Age that are still important in the interactive zone today.

2. Do organizations similar to guilds exist today? Give examples and compare their purposes.

SYNTHESIS Developing Reading Skills

1. Read Marco Polo's *Description of the World* and write a book report.
2. In the cartoon, what problem do the king and his advisers have?

EVALUATION Weighing Consequences

1. Discuss the immediate and longterm effects of the Mongol conquests.
2. Why are Ibn Battuta's writings important to modern historians?

CHALLENGE

The leaders of a thirteenth-century khan's army kept in constant communication with each other during the many battles that they fought. Compare the importance of military communications in the thirteenth century with the importance of military intelligence as it is used in warfare today.

"Perhaps we've cut the royal budget too much."

CHAPTER 16
National States and Empires

TIME	1300	1325	1350

1000–1400s Anasazi Indians develop pueblo-building societies in the southwestern area of North America

1330–1350 Plague spreads from central Asia to China, Europe, and Africa

1200s–1500s Mound builders settle in the Mississippi River valley of North America

1337–1453 England and France fight the Hundred Years War

PEOPLE

1312–1337 Mansa Musa rules the Mali Empire

1360s Petrarch, an Italian scholar, develops the ideal of humanism

PLACE

1300–1450 *Africa;*[1] Kingdoms of Mali and Songhai expand as a result of trade, sub-Saharan Africa trades with Muslim merchants across the Indian Ocean

1352 *Africa;*[1] A geographer, Ibn Battuta explores Sahara Desert

Linking Past to Present

One day in 1347, a merchant ship sailed into the harbor of Alexandria, Egypt. When the ship docked, the port officials found a terrible sight. Of the 332 people on board, 287 were dead. The remaining 45 sailors and merchants died in port shortly thereafter.

The people on the ship died of plague, called the Black Death, a disease that spread across the Eastern Hemisphere. People still contract plague. Posters in the mountain parks of California warn tourists that squirrels carry plague. Deaths from plague in Vietnam increased from 15 cases per year in 1960 to over 4,000 per year in 1970. As you read the chapter, consider whether the consequences of a modern epidemic would be similar to the effects of plague on fourteenth-century societies.

A fifteenth-century view of London Tower.

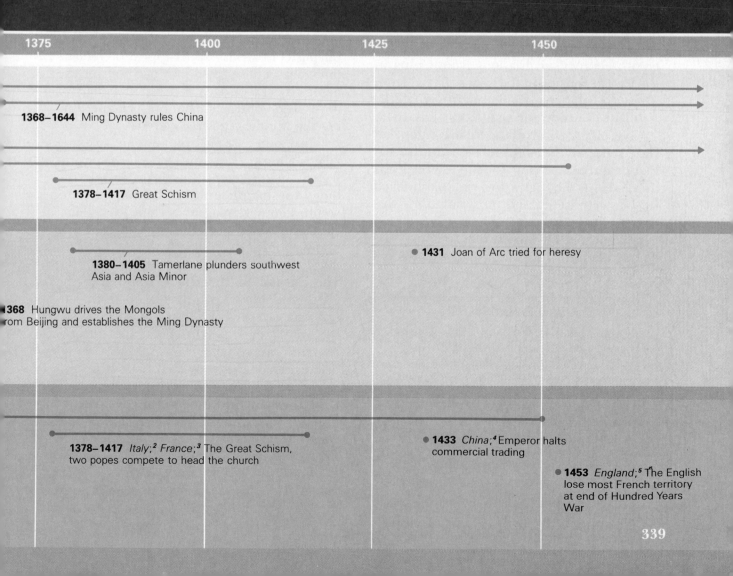

| 1375 | 1400 | 1425 | 1450 |

1368–1644 Ming Dynasty rules China

1378–1417 Great Schism

1380–1405 Tamerlane plunders southwest Asia and Asia Minor

1431 Joan of Arc tried for heresy

1368 Hungwu drives the Mongols from Beijing and establishes the Ming Dynasty

1378–1417 *Italy;*[2] *France;*[3] The Great Schism, two popes compete to head the church

1433 *China;*[4] Emperor halts commercial trading

1453 *England;*[5] The English lose most French territory at end of Hundred Years War

1 The Black Death in Eurasia

OBJECTIVE: *To understand the causes and consequences of the Black Death in Asia*

Origins and Effects of Plague

The peoples of the Eastern Hemisphere during the thirteenth and fourteenth centuries were coming into closer contact with one another through trade and the exchange of ideas and inventions. Epidemic diseases, as well as trade goods, could also spread along the trade routes. In the fourteenth century, civilizations from China in the east to Europe in the west suffered from a deadly plague. About one-third of the people of Europe and the Middle East died.

The Black Death of the Middle Ages first flared up in the steppes of central Asia. Plague spread among rodents there. Fleas that lived in the fur of these animals picked up plague bacteria and transmitted the diseases to humans.

Plague occurs in two main forms. The characteristics of one, called bubonic plague, are extremely high fever, chills, delerium, and in most cases, death. The germs causing bubonic plague collect in the lymph nodes, particularly those in the armpits and groin. The nodes become enlarged and extremely painful. The swellings are called buboes (BYOO bohz), from which the name bubonic plague is derived. In some cases, purplish or blackish spots appear on the victim's skin. These spots may account for the name, the Black Death. Less than half of those who contracted bubonic plague during the Middle Ages recovered.

The other type, pneumonic plague, killed almost everyone who became infected. In this type, the germs invade the lungs, causing pneumonia. During the fourteenth century, plague became pandemic, spreading over a wide area and affecting many people.

The Spread of the Black Death. In the 1330s and 1340s, plague spread from central Asia eastward to China and westward to the Middle East, north Africa, and Europe. Experts stress the hemisphere's long-distance trade routes as the key to the extensive spread of the disease. Infected rats and fleas traveled the trade routes in loads of grain or furs, moving both overland and on ships. Travelers carried plague-infected fleas from town to town.

The map, Black Death Attacks Eurasia and Africa, page 341, shows the timing and directions of the spread of plague. Caravans

---

VOCABULARY DEVELOPMENT

pandemic (pan DEHM ihk) *adj.:* occurring over a wide geographic area and affecting an exceptionally large proportion of the population, as a pandemic outbreak of a disease. From the Greek word, *pandemos*, meaning of all the people.

obliterate (uh BLIHT uh rayt) *verb:* wipe out, remove all traces of. From the Latin words, *ob litteras scribere*, meaning to erase.

genealogy (JEE nee AHL uh jee) *noun:* an account of the descent of a person, family, or group from an ancestor.

Black Death Attacks Eurasia and Africa

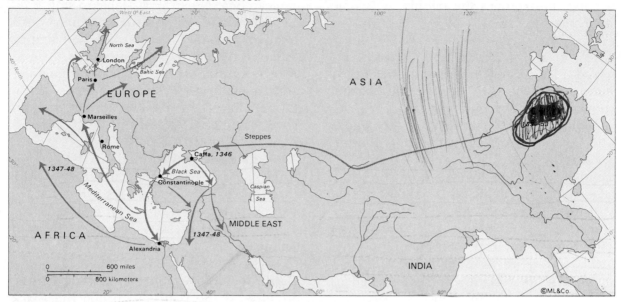

Map Skills **1.** In what year did the Black Death reach the furthest west in Africa? **2.** In what general direction did the Black Death spread? **3.** What is the distance in miles between Paris and London?

from central Asia probably introduced it to China. Between 1331 and 1353, plague killed millions of Chinese.

Plague reached southern Russia before it reached Europe. In 1337, a Mongol army laid siege to the trading port of Caffa on the Black Sea. The merchants of Genoa controlled Caffa and many Italians lived there.

When plague broke out among the Mongol army during the siege, the leader knew he would have to abandon it. According to legend, before retreating, he used his catapults to hurl plague-infested bodies over the walls of Caffa.

Soon the people of Caffa contracted plague. Some of the Genoese survivors sailed to Constantinople and Italy, where they spread plague. From there, merchant ships carried the disease to ports all around the Mediterranean Basin.

Effects of Plague in Islamic Lands. The Black Death struck the Islamic countries in the Middle East and north Africa in 1347 and 1348. A Muslim writer who lost both his parents to plague described its terrible effects this way:

❝ Civilization, both in the East and the West, was visited by a destructive plague which devastated nations and caused populations to vanish. It swallowed up many of the good things of civilization and wiped them out. . . . Cities and buildings were laid waste, roads and way signs were obliterated, settlements and houses became empty, dynasties and tribes grew weak. The entire inhabited world changed. ❞

Trouble in Islamic Lands

A century of economic decline and political troubles followed the Black Death in Islamic southwest Asia and north Africa. Plague killed huge numbers of people, including farmers, skilled artisans, and scholars. Agriculture, craft industries, and learning all suffered. The great craft industries of Cairo and Damascus declined. Trade on the Red Sea route also decreased.

For a century or more after 1350, very few large, stable kingdoms existed in the Islamic region. Numerous small states competed for territory and power.

The Conquests of Tamerlane 1380–1405.
Among the troubles the people in Islamic lands faced was the rise of Timur, a Muslim Turk. Timur began his career as a military officer of a Mongol kingdom. After he received a leg wound in battle, he was called Timur the Lame. In Europe, he became known simply as Tamerlane.

Tamerlane saw himself as the leader who would revive the great Mongol Empire of Genghis Khan. Probably, he was not descended from Genghis Khan, but he had a fake genealogy made up to show that he was. In 1380, he led a great horde of steppe nomads in an invasion of southwest Asia and India. They captured and plundered such great cities as Baghdad, Delhi, and Damascus. Tamerlane's forces reached as far as Moscow and across Asia Minor to the Aegean Sea. No army was able to stop him.

Tamerlane was a cruel conqueror. In many of the cities he captured, he killed or enslaved the entire population. He inspired fear by cutting off the heads of his enemies and stacking them into pyramids. Even though he was a Muslim, he killed thousands of fellow Muslims, as well as Christians, Jews, and Hindus.

Tamerlane's invasions damaged agricultural productivity and upset city life throughout Islamic lands just when the region was trying to recover from plague. When he died in 1405, his huge kingdom fell apart.

Cultural Achievements in Islamic Lands.
In spite of the political turmoil the Black Death caused, Muslim peoples continued to make contributions to art and scholarship. They excelled especially in architecture. Tamerlane founded a magnificent capital at Samarqand (SAM uhr KAND), a city in central Asia that now is part of the Soviet Union. His tomb, topped by a great blue dome, is one of the most beautiful Islamic buildings.

At the other edge of the Muslim world was Granada, a small Muslim kingdom in the mountains of southern Spain. In the fourteenth century, the rulers of Granada constructed the stunning palace known as the Alhambra.

In scholarship, Ibn Khaldun (IHB uhn kal DOON), who lived from 1332 to 1406, towers above other Muslim thinkers of the period. Born in Tunis, he traveled and studied in several countries, including Morocco, Granada, and Egypt. He wrote a number of books on religion, philosophy, and history. Ibn Khaldun is best known for developing a theory to explain how and why societies change. He showed that climate, geography, and many other factors influence history. He looked for patterns in history, something no earlier writer had done in a systematic way. Ibn Khaldun has been called the father of modern social science.

This miniature shows Tamerlane's armies using sheer numbers to overwhelm an Islamic fort.

Ming China

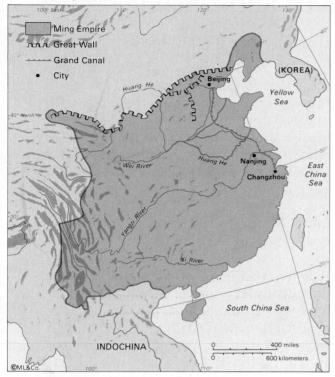

Map Skills 1. Name the two longest rivers in China. **2.** What two bodies of water touch China's coasts?

Rise of the Ming Dynasty

Outbreaks of plague caused huge losses of life in China during the fourteenth century. The Chinese also suffered from severe floods and droughts. These disturbances weakened the Mongols' rule. The Chinese, who regarded Mongols as uncivilized foreigners, rebelled against them in 1350.

One of the rebel leaders was a Buddhist monk who took the title Hongwu (hung woo) meaning "vast military power." He and his followers drove the Mongols from their capital at Beijing in 1368. Within a few years, Hongwu controlled all of China and was proclaimed emperor. He established a new Chinese dynasty known as the Ming, or "Brilliant," Dynasty. The Ming Dynasty ruled China until 1644.

The Ming rulers founded their first capital at Nanjing but later moved it to Beijing.

Ming emperors built 14 miles of walls around Beijing. The center of government was a cluster of magnificent palaces, temples, and gates. It was known as the Forbidden City because only the emperor's household could enter. A moat surrounded the Forbidden City.

Hongwu ruled until 1398, and his successor, Yongle, ruled until 1424. They restored order and prosperity to China, encouraging the expansion of agriculture, trade, and industry. Between 1405 and 1433, Ming naval and merchant fleets visited many ports of Southeast Asia and the Indian Ocean, including the coast of east Africa. China exported large quantities of beautiful porcelain, or chinaware, as far as Africa and Europe.

Plague had a lasting effect on societies across Eurasia. Islamic countries fell to Tamerlane. Mongol rulers of China were overthrown. In Europe, plague also brought social, economic, and political changes.

SECTION 1 *Study Skills*

Developing Vocabulary Use each of the following words in a sentence: **1.** pandemic. **2.** obliterate. **3.** genealogy.

Reviewing Main Ideas 1. Explain where and why death rates from plague were the greatest. **2.** Summarize the influence of Tamerlane on history. **3.** Why was Ibn Khaldun called the father of modern social science?

Understanding Geography 1. Where did the Black Death spread? **2.** Locate and describe the Forbidden City.

Understanding Chronology 1. During what years did plague devastate the population of Eurasia and Africa? **2.** How did plague benefit Tamerlane? **3.** How many years did the Ming Dynasty rule China?

Challenge What can people today do to prevent or end a global epidemic, such as influenza?

Population Growth and Decline

In Ming China the plague greatly reduced population. Today huge population increases in some parts of Asia are of great concern. Other parts, such as the northeastern part of the Soviet Union, have a very sparse population. The study of population is called demography. Demographers study why population grows or declines and the factors influencing population density.

Elements of Population

For most of human history, the world's population has increased sporadically. In recent years, the rate of growth has been even faster. World population doubled between A.D. 1 and 1500. Population doubled again by 1825 and again by 1925. Between 1925 and 1976 the number of people on planet Earth doubled again.

Population constantly changes, as people are born, move, live, and die. Population may increase in two ways: through birth and through migration. Migration into an area is called immigration. People can leave an area in two ways: by death and by migration. Migration out of an area is called emigration.

Thus, there are four elements of population: births, deaths, immigration, and emigration. The balance among these four elements determines the population or population change in an area.

The combination of birth and death rate is important. For most of human history, the birth rate, the number of children being born, was very high. In addition, the death rate was high. While many babies were being born, many other people were dying. This situation kept the population from increasing greatly. A slowing of the death rate, then, would bring an increase in population.

In the 1600s, the worldwide birth rate was about 35 per 1,000 people. The death rate was about the same. By 1939, the birth rate had risen very slightly. However, the death rate had dropped to 26 per 1,000. Since the death rate was far below the birth rate, the world's population was growing quite rapidly.

Infant Mortality. An important part of the death rate is infant mortality. Infant mortality refers to the death of children younger than one year of age. A high infant mortality rate usually indicates that the overall level of health in an area is poor.

Infant mortality is also significant because children are an important resource. In many parts of Asia, children must help their parents by working in the fields with them. In poor societies where people consume most of what they produce, people have little chance to save for their retirement. Parents rely on their children to care for them when they are elderly. When infant mortality is high, parents must accept the harsh fact that not all of their children will live to become adults. Thus, they may have seven or eight children, hoping that three or four of them will survive infancy and reach adulthood.

Improved Health Care. Important improvements in health care have made longer life possible. In the past century, societies have developed better ways to provide people with clean water and sanitary living conditions. Better medical treatment has also helped to extend people's lives. For example, the number of deaths from diseases such as tuberculosis and small pox are a small fraction of what they were in 1900.

Improvements in health and a decline in infant mortality have led to a decline in the

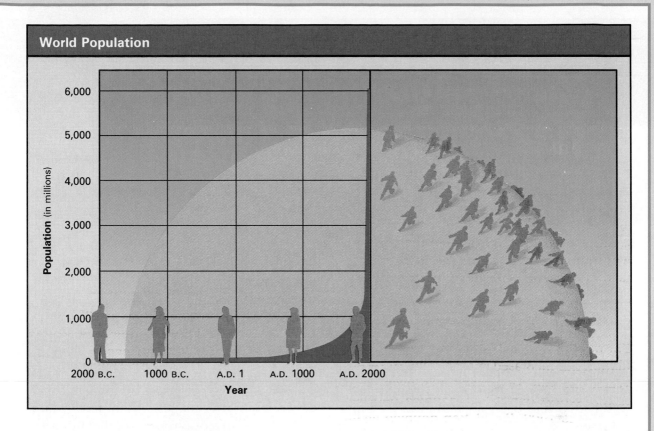

World Population

Population (in millions) — 6,000, 5,000, 4,000, 3,000, 2,000, 1,000, 0

Year — 2000 B.C., 1000 B.C., A.D. 1, A.D. 1000, A.D. 2000

birth rate. Parents realize that they do not need to have so many children just to insure that some will reach maturity.

The Demographic Transition

Demographers call the shift from high to low birth rates and death rates the demographic transition. Making the demographic transition is a major challenge for a country. Lowering the death rate has become relatively easy.

The difficult part of the demographic transition is lowering the birth rate. There are several reasons. First, people respond slowly to a lower death rate. They do not decide immediately to have smaller families, so the birth rate does not drop when the death rate declines. Second, tradition or religion may encourage people to have large families. Third, having children may be considered a sign of prosperity. Fourth, means for limiting births may not be available.

Countries with a low death rate and a high birth rate face rapid population growth. In the Philippines, for example, the birth rate is 44 per 1,000 people. The death rate is 11 per 1,000 people. Some countries in Asia have begun campaigns to limit family size. In China, couples are encouraged to have only one child. The government will not assist the parents with the needs of any but the first child. China has a birth rate of 27 per thousand and a death rate of 14. The challenge of meeting the needs of a rapidly growing population requires special efforts by these heavily populated countries.

STUDY SKILLS Understanding Geography

1. What is demography?
2. What are the four elements of population?
3. What is the demographic transition?
4. What are three reasons why decreasing the birth rate is difficult?
5. Using the chart, determine when population levels began to rise dramatically.

2 Europe in the Middle Ages

OBJECTIVE: *To understand how people in fourteenth century Europe lived*

Europe's Climate Changes

Plague attacked western Europe at a time when the population had already been weakened by repeated famines. In part, changes in Europe's climate had caused many of the food shortages that resulted in famines. From about 1300 to 1850, the earth's climate was considerably colder and wetter than had been normal in preceding centuries.

Unpredictable weather conditions included cold, wet growing seasons when the crops did not ripen. Famines occurred every 10 years or so during the late Middle Ages. When the Black Death struck in the middle of the fourteenth century, people were suffering from periodic food shortages.

VOCABULARY DEVELOPMENT

trencher *noun:* a platter on which to serve food.

schism (SIHZ uhm) *noun:* a split in an organized group, especially a church, as a result of a difference of opinion. From the Greek word, *schizein*, meaning to cut.

humanism *noun:* the secular, cultural, and intellectual movement started by the study of Greek and Roman literature.

potential (puh TEHN shul) *noun:* all that a person is capable of being or becoming.

Renaissance (REHN uh SAHNS) *noun:* the great European revival of interest in literature, art, and learning, stimulated by humanism during the fourteenth through sixteenth centuries.

Life in the Middle Ages

FOCUS ON SOCIETY

Unsanitary living conditions during the Middle Ages contributed to the rapid and devastating spread of plague. Most people were poor peasants or serfs who lived in small villages. Often, six or more people lived in a one-room wooden hut with their small animals.

They slept on bags filled with straw, which attracted fleas, lice, and other insects. They ate black bread, eggs, poultry, and some vegetables but could seldom afford meat. Peasants could not hunt or fish because animals on the manor belonged to the lord. Europeans knew little about sanitation. People dumped their wastes into rivers from which they also drank.

Life in the Castles. Even in great castles, servants and visitors slept in the great hall with only screens for privacy. Poultry, dogs, and other animals roamed everywhere. The floors were covered with straw containing insects and garbage.

Although nobles could afford meat, it was seldom fresh. People used sauces to disguise the rotten taste. Spices for the sauces were very expensive. At dinner, each place in the great hall was set with a thick slab of day-old bread called a trencher, which served as a plate. The upper crust was eaten by the nobles. After dinner, the gravy-soaked lower crusts were thrown to the dogs in the hall or sent to the poor.

Life in the Cities. As more people moved to the cities in the fourteenth century, wooden houses were crowded along narrow streets only 6 to 10 feet wide.

When people needed more room in their houses, they added upper stories. Each story jutted out over the street a little farther than the one below. People on the streets dodged garbage thrown from windows, as well as pigs and chickens in the streets.

Many Europeans believed that baths were dangerous. People rarely washed themselves or their clothes. Rats were so common that they were not noticed unless their numbers increased enough to threaten the food supply. Epidemics were frequent.

This fifteenth-century scene shows peasants along the left bank of the Seine River, planting and tilling their fields.

Disease and early death were expected. Medical theories were often wrong and treatment useless or dangerous. Among the cures suggested for plague were eating poultry, not sleeping past dawn, and smoking a pipe. Many children died before reaching the age of six. Mothers often died in childbirth. The average life expectancy of those who survived childhood was 35. ■

The Black Death Spreads through Europe

The Black Death spread from ports around the Mediterranean to France, Germany, and England. By the time the Black Death came to an end in 1351, about one-third of the people of Europe had died.

Plague struck people in both the countryside and the cities. The death rate, however, was usually highest in cities, where large numbers of people and large numbers of rats were crowded together. For example, almost a third of the population of Paris died. In Scandinavia and eastern Europe, some communities disappeared completely as plague swept through.

Neither Muslims nor Christians had any understanding of the cause of plague. Most Christians believed that God had brought plague to punish people for their sins. In several parts of Europe, frightened Christians thought Jews caused plague. They said Jews were poisoning the water supply.

Even though the pope and other leaders condemned this ridiculous idea, some Jewish communities were cruelly persecuted. The entire Jewish population of one Swiss city was burned to death. Many Jews fled from western Europe to Poland and Russia, where their descendants remained for the next 600 years.

Long-Term Effects of the Black Death. Plague devastated Europe. Documents in England show the extent of plague. In August 1349, the mill on the manor of Sladen was abandoned because the miller had died and no tenants were left to bring corn to be ground. The land lay untilled and useless. In Bedfordshire, a mill was declared of no value because the mill and land were deserted, and no buyers could be found.

Owners of large estates lost many of their tenants and serfs to the epidemic. The owners were forced to rent out their estates or turn them into sheep or cattle farms. Serfdom almost disappeared.

Plagues and famine returned every few years to kill more people. The resulting population decline had drastic effects. Much of the abandoned land remained empty. The decline in population, however, brought higher wages for the common people as employers competed for workers.

Cities became more important. People who survived the famines and plague had more money to spend. This income stimulated the growth of new industries in the cities to satisfy the demand for goods. Cities became central to economic life.

The shortage of workers in Europe also stimulated the invention of labor-saving devices. A shortage of mine workers in Europe, for example, led to the invention of more efficient water pumps for mining.

The Hundred Years War 1337–1453. In some parts of Europe, war caused as much suffering and misery as plague and famine. Wars during the early Middle Ages often involved only small armies of mounted knights. However, in the fourteenth and fifteenth centuries, wars were more frequent and far more destructive.

The kings of France and England fought each other periodically from 1337 to 1453 in The Hundred Years War. They battled over control of the English-owned lands in northern France. At first, the English won most of the battles. Later, in the early 1400s, a peasant girl, Joan of Arc, rallied the French.

Joan believed that she had received visions from God directing her to lead the French army. Dressed in men's clothing, she helped the French to lift an important siege on the city of Orleans. The English captured her in 1431, tried her for heresy, and burned her to death. Joan of Arc became a symbol of patriotism and unity for the French. In 1453, when the war finally ended, the English lost almost all of their territory in France.

Changes in Warfare. Important changes in the way wars were waged compounded the misery of life in the late Middle Ages. The most remarkable development was the use of gunpowder, which spread from China to Europe in the fourteenth century. European bronze workers made cannons with the techniques previously used for casting church bells. In the middle of the fifteenth century, the French used giant cannons to destroy English castles and win the final battles of the Hundred Years War. The firearms of that period were huge, clumsy, and inaccurate. Cannons, however, ended for a time the effectiveness of stone castles and made long sieges unnecessary.

Another change in warfare was the involvement of common people. The kings and nobles who began the Hundred Years War regarded it as a contest of chivalry and honor. By the end of the war, however, ordinary peasants and townspeople also were fighting. Later wars involved whole countries rather than just trained knights and noblemen.

Crises in the Latin Church

At the beginning of the thirteenth century, most Europeans believed that they were part of a single Christian society headed by the pope. Popes were powerful leaders in political affairs. They ruled their own territory in Italy, and headed a large bureaucracy of officials and lawyers.

By the fourteenth century, however, popular respect for the papacy was declining. In the late 1200s, popes and kings argued more over political power than over religious issues. Rulers began to oppose the right of the pope to control church affairs in their kingdoms, and the pope began to challenge the authority of the kings.

Boniface VIII, pope from 1294 to 1303, refused to allow priests to pay taxes to King Philip IV of France. The king, therefore, sent soldiers to kidnap Boniface. Although he was released quickly, Boniface died soon afterward.

Philip called together representatives of the clergy, nobility, and townspeople to explain the quarrel and seek their support. This meeting was the first such assembly in France. The assembly came to be called the Estates-General. Later, French kings summoned the Estates-General when they wanted special taxes or when they sought the support of the people.

The Babylonian Captivity. Shortly after Boniface's death, Philip IV had one of his French counselors elected pope. The new pope moved the seat of the papacy from Rome to Avignon (ah vee NYON), a city in southern France. From 1303 to 1378, the French controlled the popes who continued to live in Avignon. This period in church history of French control is called The Babylonian Captivity.

The Great Schism. In the last decades of the fourteenth century, rival popes lived in Avignon and Rome. Each claimed to be the true leader of the church and attracted supporters. This Great Schism lasted from 1378 to 1417 when a church council deposed both the French and the Italian popes and agreed that a new pope should be chosen in a new election.

All the problems of the church bewildered and angered most Christians. The church lost much of its prestige and moral influence in Europe for more than a century following the Great Schism.

Nation-States of Europe, 1470

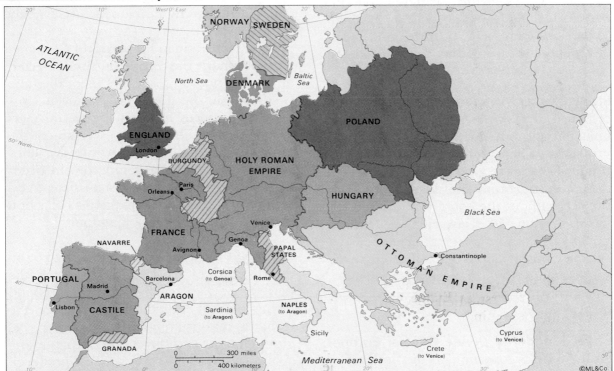

Map Skills **1.** Which nation-states border the Mediterranean Sea? **2.** Which western European nation is the largest? **3.** Which nation-states border France?

Centralized Power

The fourteenth and fifteenth centuries were times of crises for European rulers. Kings struggled with their nobles for control of the government. Rulers were in constant need of money to pay for wars. In some parts of Europe, people rebelled against heavier taxes. The results of these struggles in England, France, Germany, and Spain were very different. In every case, however, the struggles laid the foundations for modern European states. See the map, Nation-States of Europe, 1470, on page 349.

The Growth of Parliament in England.
English kings focused their energies on governing England after the end of the Hundred Years War. By the beginning of the fourteenth century, all of England, including the mountainous region of Wales, was united under a strong British monarchy.

After the signing of the Magna Carta, English kings turned more and more to Parliament when they needed money. In time, Parliament took an increasingly important part in making laws and acting as a high court. Representatives of towns and counties eventually formed their own group, the House of Commons, in Parliament.

French Kings Increase Power.
The kings of France developed a strong monarchy and built an able bureaucracy to govern their provinces. They did not have to call the Estates-General to raise money. Rather, in the fifteenth century, they began to tax their subjects without the consent of a representative assembly. They also employed professional advisers to manage their money.

The English kings gained strength by cooperating with a representative assembly. In contrast, the French kings gained power by avoiding it.

Small Kingdoms Divide Central Europe.
Strong central governments did not exist in most other parts of Europe. Italy and Germany remained divided into numerous

The Renaissance ideal of benevolent despotism is shown in this fresco, *The Effects of Good Government*. The figure of Security is offering protection to the citizens of Siena.

city-states or small feudal states. German princes ruled their own small states, but no national monarchy developed in Germany for centuries.

The Holy Roman Emperors of Germany did not inherit the throne but were elected by leading nobles. A law of 1356, called the Golden Bull, specified that the seven most powerful princes in Germany would elect the emperor. These princes retained the power to govern their own territories. They therefore elected weak emperors in order to retain as many rights as possible. As a result, central Europe remained a collection of small states and weak kingdoms.

European Cultural Vitality.
In spite of all the disasters of the late Middle Ages, the period saw great creativity in the arts and technology. In addition to gunpowder, the compass, and printing, Europeans were beginning to use such inventions as paper, the spinning wheel, and eyeglasses. The development of national languages continued in the fourteenth and fifteenth centuries.

Birth of Humanism. In Florence at the end of the fourteenth century, a group of scholars began to study the works of ancient Greek and Roman writers. These works so inspired them that they wanted to use the writers' ideas as models for their own lives. Such studies led Petrarch (PEE trahrk), an Italian scholar, as well as Boccaccio and other writers and thinkers of the time, to develop the idea of humanism.

Humanists believed that they were reviving the glory of ancient literature and thought. They saw their age as a kind of rebirth, or renaissance, of classical literature. They invented the term Middle Ages to separate their society from the societies of earlier centuries.

Humanism for these scholars meant an emphasis on Greek and Roman learning, a lifestyle based on the moral teachings of ancient civilization, and an appreciation of the natural world around them. They believed that an education that emphasized the subjects of grammar, rhetoric, history, and poetry, and that used classical texts for the teaching of those subjects, would lead people to realize their natural potential. These subjects came to be called the humanities.

Humanists admired the dignity, intelligence, and achievements of humans. Such ideas were very different from the teachings of the church in the Middle Ages that stressed human sinfulness and that life on earth was a preparation for life after death.

At the same time, statues that had survived from ancient Greece and Rome were inspiring Italian artists. They began painting in a more natural style, showing a better understanding of human anatomy. These developments marked the beginning of a cultural rebirth known as the Renaissance.

Monarchs were increasing their power during the fourteenth and fifteenth centuries. At the same time, national cultures and languages were emerging in Europe. The English, French, Spanish, Portuguese, and other peoples continued to think of themselves as nations—that is, as communities of people sharing a common culture, language, history, and political destiny.

SECTION 2 *Study Skills*

Developing Vocabulary Describe the relationship between humanism and the Renaissance.

Reviewing Main Ideas 1. Describe the impact of the depleted population of Europe on the feudal economy. **2.** After the plague, how did the importance of cities change? **3.** What advances in technology were made between 1350 and 1500? **4.** What two changes in warfare occurred during the Hundred Years War? **5.** Explain the Great Schism. **6.** Give an example of the pope's loss of influence during the fourteenth and fifteenth centuries. **7.** What change in language occurred in the late Middle Ages?

Understanding Chronology 1. Europe's climate changed to wet and cold during what centuries? **2.** When was the Hundred Years War? How long did it actually last?

Challenge The change in climate had a dramatic effect on Europe. What impact would such a change have today?

3 Kings and Empires in Sub-Saharan Africa

OBJECTIVE: *To understand the causes and consequences of the rise of empires in sub-Saharan Africa*

Sub-Saharan Civilization

The Black Death did not reach African peoples living south of the Sahara Desert. The vast Sahara, with its sparse population, acted as a barrier against the plague.

Even though the Black Death did not cross the Sahara, communication between one side of the desert and the other developed steadily in the fourteenth century. Muslim merchants transported goods southward across the desert in large camel trains. These caravans carried textiles, copper and silver, books, spices, horses, and other goods from commercial towns of north Africa to the people of west Africa. They also carried great slabs of salt taken from mines deep in the Sahara. When the caravans returned from west Africa, they carried gold, ivory, ostrich feathers, kola nuts, hides, and slaves.

Gold collected from the riverbeds of west Africa was the most important item in this trade. Gold was in great demand in both Muslim countries and Europe. In the thirteenth century, the expanding European economies required gold for currency. About two-thirds of the gold in use in Eu-

rope in the fourteenth century probably came from west Africa.

Empires of the Sudan. Just south of the Sahara lies a wide belt of open and wooded grassland called savanna. This belt of savanna, the Sudan, stretches from the Atlantic Ocean to the mountains of Ethiopia. In Arabic, the Sudan indicates the "land of the black people." South of the African Sudan lies a vast band of tropical rain forest. See the map, Africa, 1000–1500, page 354.

Trans-Saharan caravan trade stimulated the rise of major kingdoms in the Sudan. Some of their wealth came from agriculture and herding. The rest resulted from control of the caravan trade routes that passed between the tropical rain forest to the south and the Sahara to the north.

The Mali Empire. A west African people, the Malinke (MAH ling KAY), founded the Mali Empire in the thirteenth century. This kingdom was not the first large one to arise in the savanna region (see page 254). More is known about Mali, however, because Muslim geographers and north African travelers wrote books about west Africa.

Mali began as a small state in the savanna not far from the main gold mining areas. Early kings, called mansas, conquered lands to the east and west, and gained control of the important north-south trade routes. Mansas of Mali used the wealth derived from taxes on trade and agriculture to build an army of bowmen and armored cavalry.

VOCABULARY DEVELOPMENT

savanna *noun:* grasslands holding scattered trees.

mansas *noun:* early kings of west Africa.

By the early fourteenth century, the well-governed Mali empire extended from the forest in the south to the edge of the Sahara in the north. The Niger River ran through the heart of the empire. Great canoes sailed up and down the river carrying trade goods and soldiers.

Caravans from north Africa brought Muslim merchants and scholars to west Africa. Many settled in the trading towns of the Sudan and spread the religion of Islam. The kings of Mali, their officials, and most of the merchants of the Sudan became Muslims. Most of the peasants, however, did not convert to Islam until several centuries later.

Mansa Musa of Mali

FOCUS ON PEOPLE

The most famous ruler of Mali was Mansa Musa, who reigned from 1312 to 1337. His empire stretched from the Atlantic Ocean on the west to the borders of present-day Nigeria. Today's countries of Mali, Senegal, and Gambia were part of Mali. Mansa Musa ruled Mali during a golden age of peace and prosperity.

Mansa Musa kept order in his kingdom with an army of slave soldiers and cavalry. During Mansa Musa's reign, a merchant could travel from one end of Mali to the other without fear of bandits. When the king appeared in public, his subjects fell to the ground before him and threw dust over their heads to show submission. No one was allowed to wear sandals or to sneeze in the king's presence.

In 1324, Mansa Musa made a pilgrimage to Mecca. The journey across the Sahara Desert to Egypt took over a year. To prepare for the trip, the king assembled over 60,000 people to guard and serve the mansa and his household. Each of the 500 slaves carried a bar of gold weighing about 4 pounds, as well as provisions for the trip.

Mansa Musa and his vast caravan passed through Cairo on their way to Mecca. They spent so much gold there that its value in Egypt declined by about 25 percent. The king's wealth attracted so much attention in Egypt that trade increased between Egypt and Mali.

Musa's fame spread to northern Africa and Europe. He and other kings of Mali exchanged diplomatic envoys with the rulers of Morocco and Tunisia.

A Catalan map from 1375 shows Mansa Musa of Mali holding a gold nugget as he barters with a trader.

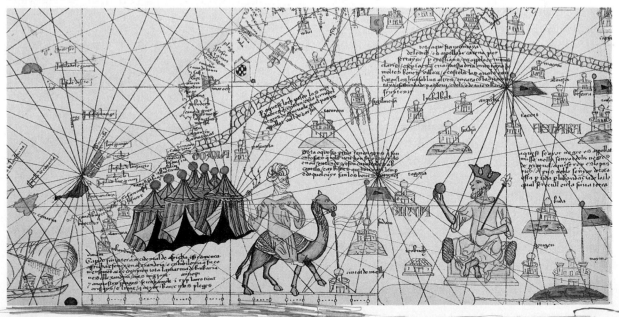

Africa, 1000–1500

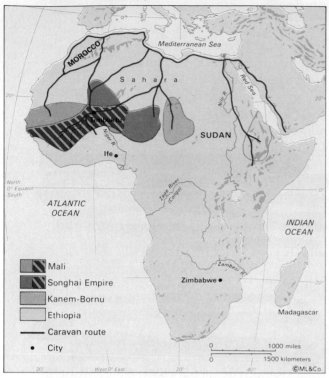

Map Skills 1. Which African empire extended the farthest east? 2. In what area of Africa is the city of Timbuktu?

When he returned to his kingdom, Mansa Musa brought a Muslim architect to design new buildings. This artisan introduced a new technique for making bricks. Mosques and palaces in Mali towns were constructed using these new bricks.

The Moroccan traveler, Ibn Battuta, visited Mali in the 1350s. He described the king's audience:

❝ The sultan sits on certain days in the palace yard to give audience. There is a platform under a tree with three steps. . . . It is covered with silk and has pillows placed on it. . . . The sultan comes out from a gate in the corner of the palace, bow in hand, his quiver between his shoulders, and on his head a cap of gold tied with a golden band. . . . The singers go out before him carrying gold and silver [musical instruments] and behind him come 300 armed slaves. ❞

Later in that century, Mali faced many problems. Members of the royal family fought one another for the right to be mansa. The lands of the empire were too large to be governed effectively over a long time. Weak leaders were unable to stop rebellions. Nomads from the Sahara raided the farmlands. After 1350, Mali declined. ∎

The Songhai Empire

As Mali declined, a people known as the Songhai (SAWNG hy) built a larger empire in the Sudan. The Songhai, who lived along the banks of the Niger River, had successfully revolted against Mali. Two forceful kings, Sunni Ali and Askia Muhammad, ruled between 1464 and 1528. Their conquests expanded the Songhai Empire past the boundaries of Mali. Like Mali, Songhai was a Muslim kingdom that grew wealthy by controlling trade across the Sudan.

During the fifteenth century, the city of Timbuktu grew into an important center of trade and Islamic learning. Located on the southern fringe of the Sahara, Timbuktu attracted great caravans from both north and south. At several colleges founded in the city, Islamic scholars taught theology, law, and other subjects.

Leo Africanus, a visitor, described Timbuktu in the sixteenth century:

❝ Here are many shops of artificers [skilled artisans] and merchants, and especially of such as weave linen and cotton cloth. And hitherto the [north African] merchants bring cloth of Europe. . . . Here are a great store of doctors, judges, priests, and other learned men, that are bountifully maintained at the king's cost and charges, and hither are brought diverse [varied] manuscripts . . . which are sold for more money than any other merchandise. ❞

Songhai declined in the late sixteenth century. In 1591, soldiers from Morocco invaded Songhai and overthrew the ruler.

The Sultan of Morocco wanted to control the southern end of the trans-Saharan caravan trade. Morocco was never able to rule the Sudan effectively, though, because it was so far away. Songhai, however, never again became a powerful empire.

Ethiopia, Outpost of Christianity. Islam was the only major religion to expand significantly in Africa between the eighth and sixteenth centuries. The kingdom of Ethiopia in northeastern Africa was the only Christian nation. In the fourth and fifth centuries, monks brought Christianity to Ethiopia. They converted the king, who claimed to be descended from King Solomon of the Old Testament.

Between the fifth and fifteenth centuries, Ethiopia was isolated from other Christian lands for two reasons. First, the jagged mountains and deep valleys of Ethiopia made communication difficult. Second, Islamic states to the east and north blocked Ethiopia's contact with the Mediterranean region. The Ethiopian church developed doctrines and rituals that differed from those of other Christian churches. For example, Ethiopian Christians, like Muslims and Jews, do not eat pork.

The mountainous terrain made Ethiopia a difficult country to unify. From the twelfth to the sixteenth centuries, however, the region experienced a long period of unity, military expansion, and cultural achievement. King Lalibela (lah LEE buh lah), who ruled in the early 1200s, conquered large territories. He also ordered his craftsmen to build a number of churches. These buildings, carved out of solid rock, are marvels of engineering. Artists decorated the interior walls with paintings of Christ and the Apostles and used geometric designs that showed Islamic and African influences.

The kingdom of Ethiopia was one of the longest lasting monarchies in world history. Haile Selassie (HY lee suh LAS ee), the last emperor who traced his descent from Solomon, was overthrown in 1974.

Other African Kingdoms

In the lower half of Africa, from the tropical rain forest south, population was sparse until about the year 1000. However, in the following centuries, farming peoples using iron tools steadily pushed into the southern forests and grasslands (see page 216). Population grew and communities became larger.

The Artisans of Ife. One of the earliest towns in the west African forest region was Ife (EE fay), located west of the Niger River in an area that today is the Republic of Nigeria. The people who inhabited Ife left no written records. They did produce beautiful terra cotta and bronze sculpture, though. Statues have been found of the heads or entire bodies of kings and queens who lived as early as the eleventh century.

These statues required highly skilled artisans. To support these artists, Ife must have been a prosperous society organized on a large scale. It may have been a center of trade linking peoples of the forest with those of the savanna to the north. By the fourteenth century, more states had appeared in the west African forest.

An Ethiopian king is crowned in front of the Axum Cathedral of St. Mary of Zion.

Ruins from the ancient African city of Zimbabwe indicate that its first inhabitants lived during the Iron Age. The walls shown here were 32 feet high.

The Karanga of Zimbabwe. The vegetation and climate south of Africa's tropical forests are similar to those of the west African savanna. By the twelfth century, most of the savanna region was inhabited by people who spoke Bantu languages and used iron implements. These migrants from the north founded Zimbabwe (zim BAH bweh). See the map, Africa, 1000–1500, page 354.

The inhabitants of Zimbabwe were a people known as the Karanga. They established a political and religious center at Great Zimbabwe. There, in the eleventh century, the Karanga began to construct temples, walls, and other structures of cut stone ingeniously fitted together. This construction method, which also was used in other parts of southern Africa, continued on and off for almost 400 years.

The people of Zimbabwe left no written records. Their society must have been complex and wealthy, however, because they left evidence of engineering skill and artistry.

Like the kingdoms of west Africa, Zimbabwe gained much of its wealth by control-ling trade in gold. From southern Africa, gold was carried eastward to the Indian Ocean. From there, Muslim merchants shipped it to India, China, and the Mediterranean region.

In return for the gold, African traders brought textiles and other manufactured goods from the coast to Zimbabwe. The king and the ruling class wore gowns of imported silk or cotton, and they dined on imported Chinese and Persian dishes.

The Sahara partially isolated the peoples of tropical Africa from the civilizations of north Africa and Eurasia. The presence of imported goods and the expansion of Islam, however, shows that the peoples of sub-Sahara Africa were linked to the commercial world of the Mediterranean Sea and Indian Ocean. In contrast, the people of the Americas continued to develop independently of the Eastern Hemisphere.

SECTION 3 *Study Skills*

Developing Vocabulary 1. Describe the African savanna. 2. Who were the mansas?

Reviewing Main Ideas 1. Why did gold become the most important African trade item during the fourteenth century? 2. What source of information do historians have about the Mali Empire? 3. What problems did the Mali Empire have in common with other empires throughout history? 4. What evidence suggests that Zimbabwe had trade links with Asia?

Understanding Geography 1. Describe the location of the Sudan. 2. Explain why Christianity was stronger than Islam in certain parts of Africa. 3. What area does the climate and vegetation of Zimbabwe resemble?

Understanding Chronology 1. When did the Songhai Empire fall? 2. When was the last Ethiopian emperor overthrown?

Challenge Compare the strengths of Christianity and Islam in Africa today.

4 Empire Building in the Americas

OBJECTIVE: *To understand the causes and consequences of the development and decline of early American empires*

Warrior Empires of Mexico

The Black Death did not reach the peoples of the Americas because they were isolated from the Eastern Hemisphere. Amerindians did not share in the ideas and technologies that spread along the trade routes of Eurasia and Africa. They did not know how to work iron or use the wheel. They did not use oxen, horses, or camels to carry heavy loads because these animals were unknown in the Western Hemisphere.

Nevertheless, important cultural developments occurred in the Americas in the centuries after A.D. 1000. Mexico as an urban civilization had a long history. Between the fourth and ninth centuries, dozens of Mayan city-states thrived in southern Mexico and Guatemala. The Mexican city of Teotihuacán was a center of imperial power and artistic brilliance (see page 225).

By around 800, however, Teotihuacán was in ruins. The city probably declined gradually, but invading tribes from the arid lands to the north finally destroyed it. They surged into the fertile highlands of central Mexico much as German tribes flocked into the Roman Empire or Turkish nomads invaded the Middle East.

The Toltecs. Between the eighth and tenth centuries, Mexico suffered numerous wars between cities and migratory peoples. Then, shortly before 1000, a new empire grew on the central plateau of Mexico. The founders, a people called the Toltecs, invaded from the north. After conquering central Mexico, they expanded southward into territories that had once belonged to the Mayans.

The Toltecs, like the Mayans, were great builders and artisans. Tula, their thriving capital, was built not far from modern Mexico City. Toltecs built temples and plazas, as well as large stone courts for playing ceremonial ball games. Their artisans fashioned beautiful pottery and stoneware. They were also among the first people of Mexico to make decorative jewelry and useful objects out of gold and copper.

The Toltec Empire declined in the twelfth century. A long period of drought and famine occurred, and a new wave of invaders swept down from the arid north. The invaders, who came in several groups, were known as the Chichimecs (CHEE chuh MEHKS), or "dog people." These barbarians seized Tula about 1223.

VOCABULARY DEVELOPMENT

Amerindian *noun:* an American Indian.
chinampas (chuh NAM puhz) *noun:* man-made farmland created in shallow lakes.
causeway *noun:* a raised road or highway.
khipus noun: colored pieces of string whose colors and patterns of knots recorded statistics and past events.
pueblos (PWEHB lohz) *noun:* communal dwellings with flat roofs, resembling apartment houses, and made of stone or adobe.

The Aztecs. One of the Chichimec groups, the Mexica, or Aztecs, arrived in the highland basin known as the Valley of Mexico in the twelfth century. They were a small tribe and probably paid tribute to powerful city-states in the region.

The Aztecs first built small settlements in marshland at the edge of Lake Texcoco, one of several shallow lakes in the valley. They learned from neighboring peoples how to create large areas of fertile farmland called chinampas (chuh NAM puhz).

To construct a chinampa, workers staked down huge mats of vegetation on the lake. They piled numerous layers of plants on top of these mats, then added layers of fertile mud dredged from the bottom of the lake. These chinampas, used for agricultural purposes, were laid out in grid patterns, separated from one another by canals. People moved by boat from one chinampa to another. Chinampa land produced bountiful harvests of maize, beans, squash, tomatoes, avocados, and other crops.

By the fourteenth century, the Aztecs had built a capital called Tenochtitlán (tay NAWCH tee TLAHN). The city extended across several small islands and chinampas near the edge of Lake Texcoco. Gradually, other Aztec towns arose in the lakes region. The valley formed a natural route across central Mexico. By the end of the fifteenth century, the Aztecs dominated all of central Mexico from the Caribbean Sea on the east to the Pacific Ocean on the west.

Mexican emperors usually permitted defeated people to govern themselves. However, they insisted on receiving huge amounts of tribute in the form of food, cloth, and slaves. Any group that failed to pay the large tribute was severely punished.

Because of the tribute pouring into Tenochtitlán, the city resembled Rome. The population increased to between 122,000 and 200,000. In the city were soaring temples, lush greenery, and flowing water.

Canals, clogged with the boats of merchants and farmers, crisscrossed the city. Four huge causeways, raised roads, connected the city to the mainland. Tenochtitlán, like the Mayan and Toltec cities, was built without the aid of the wheel, iron tools, or strong beasts of burden.

The City of Tenochtitlán

FOCUS ON SOURCES

In 1520, the Spanish explorer, Hernán Cortés, wrote with wonder and awe about the Aztec capital in a letter to his emperor, Charles V. In the following excerpt from one of his letters, Cortés describes the brimming markets, magnificent temples, and luxurious palaces of Tenochtitlán:

❝ Most powerful Lord, an account to Your Royal Excellency of the magnificence, the strange and marvelous things of this great city . . . will, I well know, be so remarkable as not to be believed, . . .

This great city . . . is built on the salt lake, . . . There are four artificial causeways leading to it, and each is as wide as two cavalry lances. The city itself is as big as Seville or Córdoba. The main streets are very wide and very straight; some of these are on the land, but the rest and all the smaller ones are half on land, half canals where they paddle their canoes. . . .

This city has many squares where trading is done and markets are held continuously. There is also one square . . . where more than 60,000 people come each day to buy and sell, and where every kind of merchandise produced in these lands is found; provisions as well as ornaments of gold and silver, lead, brass, copper, tin, stones, shells, bones, and feathers.

There are streets of herbalists where all the medicinal herbs and roots found in the land are sold. There are shops like apothecaries, where they sell readymade medicines as well as liquid ointments and plasters. There are shops like barbers where they have their hair washed and shaved, and shops where they sell food and drink.

. . . There are many sorts of spun cotton, in hanks [coils] of every color, and it seems like the silk market at Granada, except here there is a much greater quantity. They sell as many colors for painters as may be found in Spain and all of excellent hues. . . .

There are, in all districts of this great city, many temples or houses for their idols. . . . Amongst these temples there is one, the principal one, whose great size and magnificence no human tongue could describe, for it is so large that within the precincts, which are surrounded by a very high wall, a town of some 500 inhabitants could easily be built. All round inside this wall there are very elegant quarters with very large rooms and corridors where their priests live. There are as many as 40 towers, . . . and the most important of these towers is higher than that of the cathedral of Seville. . . .

There are in the city many large and beautiful houses, and the reason for this is that all the chiefs of the land, who are Mutezuma's [Montezuma's] vassals, have houses in the city and live there for part of the year; and in addition there are many rich citizens who likewise have very good houses. All these houses have very large and very good rooms and also very pleasant gardens of various sorts of flowers both on the upper and lower floors. . . . " ■

A Diego Rivera mural of the founding of Tenochtitlán suggests the prosperity and trade that impressed early Spanish explorers.

Life in Tenochtitlán

Aztec society was divided into social classes. At the top were the ruler, his relatives, the warrior-noble families, and the priests. Aztec priests directed religious worship, education, and record keeping. They alone had knowledge of the complex Aztec writing system. Free farmers and artisans made up the second class. The lowest classes were serfs and slaves.

The aristocratic families controlled all political power and enjoyed a much higher standard of living than the common people.

Priests taught religion, astronomy, the calendar system, history, and proper manners to the sons of nobles. Aristocratic girls attended separate schools to learn temple rituals and domestic duties. Few common people received formal education.

The Aztecs worshiped several vengeful, unpredictable gods. Their religion taught that at an unknown time in the future the sun and the earth would come to an end. Until then, the sun had to be "nourished" by human hearts.

When the Aztecs went to war they tried to capture their enemies rather than kill them. These prisoners were brought to the temples of Tenochtitlán to be sacrificed to

Civilizations in the Americas

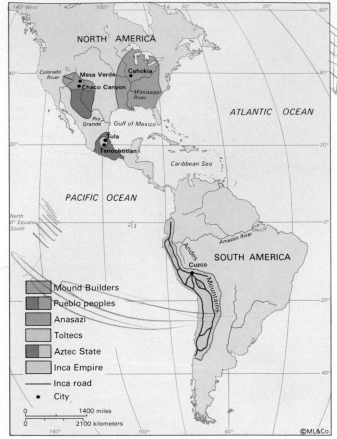

Mound Builders
Pueblo peoples
Anasazi
Toltecs
Aztec State
Inca Empire
Inca road
● City

0   1400 miles
0   2100 kilometers

©ML&Co.

Map Skills **1.** Along what river did the mound builders live? **2.** Which of the Amerindian civilizations developed in South America?

their gods. At one temple ceremony in 1487, 80,000 victims were killed.

During the reign of Montezuma II, between 1503 and 1519, the king and the aristocratic families isolated themselves from the common people. They demanded more tribute and more victims for sacrifice. The empire may have been in decline in 1519, when European invaders discovered and destroyed it.

The Empire of the Incas. A number of small kingdoms existed in the valleys of the high Andes Mountains in South America between the eleventh and fifteenth centuries. The center of one of the kingdoms was the town of Cuzco, more than 10,000 feet

above sea level. The people of Cuzco became known as the Incas.

From 1435 until nearly the end of the century, the Incas attacked neighboring states. At the same time, they became highly skilled at diplomatic negotiations and political organization. By 1500, they were ruling millions of people. Their empire extended about 3,000 miles along the Andes Mountains. The Inca Empire included the area of modern Peru, Bolivia, Ecuador, and parts of Chile and Argentina.

Unlike the Aztecs, the Incas created a highly integrated society. They developed a complex bureaucracy that reached into the most remote Andean villages. The army constantly moved about the empire to keep order and peace.

The central government did not tolerate opposition, but it did try to create a united people. The government developed a network of communications that even the ancient Persians or Romans would have admired. To link the distant parts of the empire, the Incas built about 14,000 miles of roads. Rope suspension bridges were built across deep gorges. Soldiers, government couriers, merchants, farmers, and the emperor traveled along these narrow mountain highways.

Another policy designed to integrate the people of the empire was especially innovative. After the Incas conquered distant lands, loyal subjects were sent to form colonies there. Conquered people who resisted Inca authority were resettled in the center of the empire. These population exchanges increased the ruler's control and brought a cultural richness to the Inca Empire.

Only government officials, army units, and people working for the state lived in Cuzco and other Inca cities. Most of the population lived in rural hamlets, raising maize and other crops on steep mountain hillsides. The terracing and irrigation methods of Andean farmers were so ingenious and effective that agricultural scientists still study them.

The ruins of Machu Picchu, an ancient Incan city, stand on a mountain about 8,000 feet high. Inset, a ceremonial gold and turquoise knife made in Peru between 1300 and 1500.

Unlike the Aztecs, the Incas had no system of writing to keep government records and send messages. They did, however, use *khipus*, knotted pieces of string. The knots, tied in different colors and styles, recorded government statistics and the empire's history. Only highly trained specialists could read a *khipus*.

The Inca Empire was one of the best organized states in world history, but it did not last long. In 1525, a civil war broke out over control of the throne. At the same time, a band of Spanish warriors took advantage of the political turmoil to seize the empire.

Smaller Indian Societies

A great variety of Indian societies and cultures existed outside the great centers of civilization in Middle America and Peru. Some of these Indian farming communities created complex cultures after the year 1000.

Pueblo Builders. Between the eleventh and thirteenth centuries, the Anasazi Indians lived in the region that is now the southwestern United States. They built settlements of pueblos, flat-roofed apartment houses. Chaco Canyon in northwestern New Mexico was a center of impressive pueblo building. One apartment house was four stories high and had more than 800 plastered rooms. An ingenious irrigation system brought water to their fields.

Drought or the possibility of invasion may have caused the Anasazi to abandon their pueblos by the end of the thirteenth century. Nevertheless, pueblo-building societies continued to thrive in central and southern New Mexico and Arizona in the fourteenth and fifteenth centuries.

Mound Builders. Indian societies grew steadily after the eighth century in a wide area of North America centering on the

Above, an Indian mound in Ohio in the shape of a serpent. At right, pueblos built by Anasazi cliff dwellers in Mesa Verde, Colorado.

Mississippi River and its tributaries. New, productive strains of corn enabled the population to increase. Some Indians built towns clustered around flat-topped mounds of earth. On some of these mounds, the local ruler built his residence. On others, the people took part in religious rituals.

The shape and uses of these mounds are remarkably similar to those of Middle America. In fact, historians believe that the civilizations of Mexico influenced the Mississippi people.

Mound-building societies became more complex about the thirteenth century, and towns grew larger. Craft specialists produced beautiful pottery, furniture, and sculpture. The Indians of the Mississippi region were on the verge of creating a new civilization in this rich agricultural land. This process was interrupted when European conquerors and settlers began to arrive in the seventeenth century.

Between 1300 and 1500, Amerindians built complex civilizations in the highlands of South America. Indians in North Amer-ica also developed rich cultures. Surprisingly, these achievements occurred in total isolation from the civilizations of the Eastern Hemisphere.

SECTION 4 *Study Skills*

Developing Vocabulary   Use the following in a sentence: **1.** chinampas. **2.** khipus. **3.** Amerindian. **4.** pueblos. **5.** causeway.

Reviewing Main Ideas   **1.** Why did diseases such as the Black Death and inventions such as the wheel not reach the Americas? **2.** Describe the basic traits of Aztec society. **3.** How did the Incas carry on communications in their empire? **4.** Describe the buildings made by the pueblo building Indians.

Understanding Chronology   **1.** When was the reign of the last Aztec ruler? **2.** When were the Incas at the height of their power?

Challenge   What is the legacy of Inca or Aztec society in modern Latin American societies?

CHAPTER 16 *Summary & Review*

Summarizing Main Ideas

Disease and invasions disrupted many civilizations in the fourteenth and fifteenth centuries. Plague spread throughout Eurasia and Africa. The high death rate led to a commercial and agricultural decline. Tamerlane and his followers also disrupted culture across central Asia. In China, Hongwu drove out the Mongols and established the Ming Dynasty. Ming rulers at first promoted trade, but later they encouraged isolation.

A climate change, war, plague, and unsanitary conditions combined to drastically reduce Europe's population. The survivors, however, lived in a world of growing cities, stronger kings, and developing national literature.

Trans-Saharan caravan trade stimulated the rise of Muslim-ruled kingdoms in west Africa. Farther south, cultures developed in Ife and Zimbabwe. Gold was often a key to trade.

In the Americas, the Toltec Indians, and then the Aztecs, developed civilizations on the plateau of Mexico. In the Andes Mountains, the Inca Empire grew. Smaller Indian societies developed in North America.

A physician treats a patient and a woman visits the apothecary in this French illumination.

Questions for Critical Thinking

COMPREHENSION Interpreting Events

1. Compare the conquests and rule of Tamerlane to those of Genghis Khan.
2. Describe the results of plague in China.
3. Identify the results of the development of France and England as nations.
4. List those characteristics in both Aztec and Inca civilizations that led them to dominate Central and South America.

ANALYSIS Identifying Trends

1. Describe the long range results of the Black Death on European society.
2. What were the consequences of moving the pope's headquarters to Avignon?

APPLICATION Comparing Past to Present

1. List the basic ideas of humanism and indicate which are widely accepted today.
2. Gold mined in Africa was important to thirteenth century Europe. Is African gold still important today? Explain.

SYNTHESIS Developing Writing Skills

1. Write a report describing the trade and cultural accomplishments of both the Aztec or Inca societies.
2. Research and write a description of life in Europe during plague years.

EVALUATION Weighing Consequences

1. Discuss the impact of the plague on the Jews of Europe.
2. Explain how life in Europe was changed by the climate change of the fourteenth century.

CHALLENGE

1. Discuss the possible direction European society may have taken if the Black Death had not occurred.
2. What was the result of the isolated development of the Amerindians before 1519?

UNIT 4 *Review*

Critical Thinking for Today's World

ANALYSIS Understanding People

1. Explain why upper classes, such as the knights in Europe and the samurai in Japan, became more interested in the arts as their classes became more established.
2. What heritage did the monasteries preserve?
3. After the year 1000, empires rose in west Africa and the Americas. Explain the similarities and differences between these empires.

ANALYSIS Recognizing Change Over Time

1. Throughout Europe, education became more and more important as cities and trade grew. What relationship might exist between cities and education?
2. Concern with salvation began to decrease as humanism grew in popular thinking. Explain why this occurred.
3. Chinese, Indian, and Muslim traders influenced the people with whom they traded. Give three examples of that influence.

APPLICATION Solving Problems

1. As Chinese cities grew, so did their need to provide food for the population. The same is true in the modern world. Identify and explain the problems of and solutions for supplying food to cities then and now.
2. The reduction in population brought about by plague had complex results in European society, economics, religion, and politics. What were the results?

SYNTHESIS Developing Global Citizenship

1. How did trade lead to a growing awareness of other cultures? Is this still the case? Give some examples.
2. Marco Polo gave Europe its first widely read description of China. Give some examples of written accounts that have influenced exploration and immigration during other times in history and explain.

EVALUATION Learning from the Past

1. The Mongols were extremely harsh rulers. Their empire lasted only a short while. What conclusions can be drawn from these statements? Give reasons for the conclusions.
2. Europeans who went on the crusades had many reasons for going. List four of the reasons. How might these reasons still be utilized in modern society to convince citizens to support governmental policies?
3. When the crusaders returned, they brought with them goods unknown to Europe. Within a brief time, such things as silk and spices were considered necessities of life. Identify four items that are necessities today that were new only a few years ago. How has international trade had an effect on these items?
4. Using Russia as an example, explain how religion can benefit and yet isolate an area.
5. Would a reader need knowledge of history to understand the cartoon? Explain why or why not.

"I skimped a little on the foundation, but no one will ever know it."

The Interacting Global Community, 1000–1450

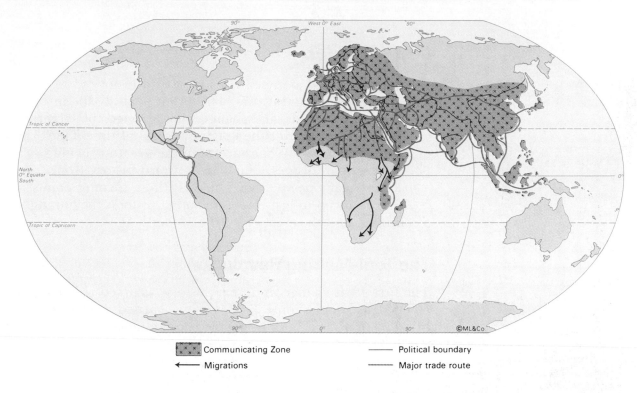

Communicating Zone   Political boundary

⟵ Migrations   Major trade route

A Global Perspective

From about 1000 to 1450, the zone of trade controlled by the Muslims grew. As trade routes were established to the east, Muslim and Chinese goods were available throughout the zone.

Trade regions near the Mediterranean expanded both north and south. Sub-Saharan traders moved goods inland in Africa. These traders also provided products, primarily gold, for the Middle East and southern Europe. Traders of Europe sailed throughout the Mediterranean basin and north to Scandinavia. Crusaders returned to Europe with a desire for luxuries they had seen in Palestine. Mongol rulers in central Asia encouraged trade across their lands to increase prosperity.

In the Western Hemisphere, America built empires and conducted trade. Emperors, khans, and kings all found economic and social advantages in encouraging trade. National states developed as kings became more powerful. Towns grew along trade routes.

COMPREHENSION Interpreting Maps

1. List the African locations where people were carrying on trade with the Muslims in 1450.
2. In what areas might rivalry have existed between Muslim and Chinese traders?
3. Which ocean or sea seems to have the most trade routes? Why are there so many in that general location?
4. What groups of people lived outside the communicating zone in 1450?
5. What trade connections existed at that time in the Americas?

ANALYSIS Recognizing Global Trends

1. Using the maps on pages 334, 349, 354, and 360, list the major centers of civilization in the global community.
2. What areas are influenced by these civilized centers?
3. Compare the map on this page with the map on page 179. In what directions has the global community expanded?

Dear Reader,

Sometimes I imagine myself teaching world history to a classroom of space travelers. They want to study the important events, trends, and changes that affected the largest number of humans over the longest periods of time. One of these aliens asks: "What have been the greatest turning points in human history?" Looking at world history from a space traveler's perspective, I suggest those turning points could be reduced to just three: inventing of tools, beginning of farming, and the creation of the Modern Age.

The Tool-Making Revolution

The first great change in human history occurred about 500,000 years ago. Some early humans learned to make and use stone tools. With tools, people became more efficient

Since the invention of tools about 500,000 years ago, humans have used increasingly complex tools to change and control their environment.

workers. They cut, dug, pounded, and shaped. They built shelters, hunted animals for food and clothing, and made baskets and bowls to store roots and berries. Tools made life more secure and comfortable. Tools also encouraged human cooperation in hunting and gathering which involved the forming of simple social groups. The earliest societies were made up of small bands of people who used tools to hunt, gather, and store food.

The tool-making revolution allowed humans to change and control their natural environment. The rate of change was extremely slow, however. For half a million years, the number of tool-making societies remained very small. Gradually, stone-tool-makers fashioned stronger and more complex tools. Tools were invented for a variety of purposes including farming, traveling, making war, and making goods. Tools of bronze, iron, steel, and plastic are all consequences of that first stone-tool-maker's skill. The tool-making revolution affected people everywhere, in all ages, over half a million years to the present time.

The Farming Revolution

The second great turning point in human history was the invention of farming. About 10,000 years ago, in the hill country of southwest Asia, people first learned to grow grain for food instead of relying on hunting and gathering. Within the next few thousand years, farmers planted crops in the fertile river valleys in southwest Asia, India, China, and the Americas.

Farming made civilization possible. Societies that eventually raised crops and animals produced surplus food regularly. That surplus allowed some people time to develop new skills as priests, merchants, artisans, or soldiers. By 3500 B.C., the first cities thrived in the Tigris-Euphrates Valley. There, temples, public buildings, and market places served neighboring farm villages as well. Early civilization developed in those and similar cities in other river valleys. Early civilization depended on farmers' surpluses and taxes. Civilization with its cities, specialists, government, and writing was a significant consequence of the revolution of farming.

The patterns of civilization spread from the early river valleys to rain-watered areas across Eurasia and northern Africa. The spread of civilization caused important changes in the organization of human society. Larger numbers of people depended on one another. Laws, moral teachings, and systems of records were needed to regulate people's behavior and relationships. Religion, government, and economic activity became more organized and complex.

Civilizations were built with farmers' plows.

The invention of farming enabled cities and civilizations to develop and continues to make urban life possible.

As civilizations became more complex, the rate of change quickened. More and more people had time to plan, invent, teach, and experiment. After the invention of writing, people could use the knowledge gathered by previous generations.

In addition, the civilizations in Eurasia and Africa had more frequent contacts with one another. Trade, migrations, and conquests created an ever-expanding zone of interaction and links among peoples. New ideas, inventions, products, and skills spread from one civilization to another. Sometimes new ideas and inventions were rejected. Sometimes a new idea was accepted and produced an unexpected chain reaction. For example, Buddhist monks in India probably invented the concept of zero about the fourth century A.D. In the next several centuries that idea spread across the Eastern Hemisphere and revolutionized mathematics, accounting, engineering, and science. This and countless other changes are the result of farmers producing surpluses that allowed for the creation of civilizations.

Creation of the Modern Age

A short time after A.D. 1500, the third great turning point in history occurred. That time marks the beginning of the Modern Age. This revolution that began 500 years ago is characterized by (1) continuous global exchanges of ideas, products, and information; (2) an emphasis on reason, science, and technology; (3) the pursuit of human rights, values, and meaning; (4) accelerated change.

Truly great exchanges began in 1492. The exchange of plants, animals, products, peoples, and ideas that resulted from the linking of Europe and the Western Hemisphere affected human life in countless ways. Now every part of the world is linked by land, sea, or air.

A reliance on reason, science, and technology also characterize the Modern Age. The discovery and application of the laws of physics, chemistry, and biology, expressed in mathematical equations, has occurred mostly in the past few hundred years. Understanding and applying science in everyday life have resulted in more changes in the natural environment than people living before 1500 could have imagined.

The ideas that ordinary people should have authority over their own government and that individuals have natural rights developed only in the past 300 years. These powerful ideas have released great energies in the modern world.

Finally, an obvious characteristic of the Modern Age is the ever increasing rate of change itself. You expect your life to be different from that of your parents. Two thousand years ago, however, most children expected to live a life very similar to their parents. Compared to the lives of the hunters of 20,000 B.C. or the farmers of 10,000 B.C. the world is changing at a dizzying speed. In the past, governments and religions generally wanted to prevent change and preserve traditions. In the Modern Age, by contrast, we expect change and plan for improvements.

It is hard to get a perspective on this third revolution because it is still taking place. We are living within the Modern Age. Ancient farmers planting the first grains had no idea that they were building civilization. Likewise, we have no clear idea of the consequences of the Modern Age. The story of the Modern Age continues.

Best wishes,

Ross E. Dunn

Scientific theories and inventions since Newton's time continue to change the ways people think and live.

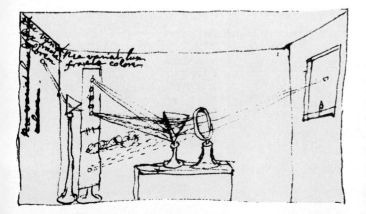

UNIT 5
The Age of Global

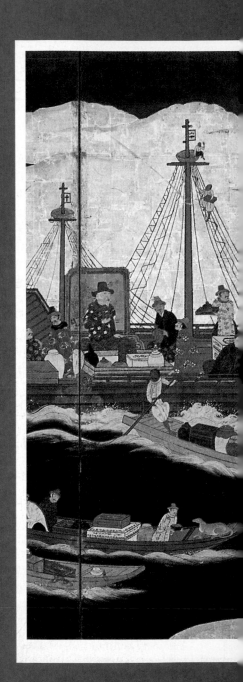

Communication

1450 - 1650

A Portuguese ship arrives in Japan, from a seventeenth-century Japanese screen.

CHAPTER 17
Exploration Links the Hemispheres

GLOBAL TIME LINE

1450   **1475**   **1500**

TIME

1368–1644 Ming Dynasty rules China

1400s Muslim and Italian merchants monopolize trade between Europe and Asia

1400s Europeans improve ship-building technology, navigation instruments, and naval weapons

1453 Ottoman Turks capture Constantinople

PEOPLE

1487 Bartholomeu Dias rounds the tip of Africa the Cape of Good Hope

1492 Columbus reach the West Indies

PLACE

1368–1644 *China;[1]* Chinese emperors isolate their country from the western world

1500–1650 *South America;[3]* Dise and slavery reduce the Indian population by up to 90 percent

1500s *Spain;[2]* Spanish king become the wealthiest rule in Europe

Linking Past to Present

Before the fifteenth century, peoples of the Eastern and Western hemispheres were separate, moving only within their own interacting zones. Then in 1492, an Italian sponsored by Spain, Christopher Columbus, sailed westward, hoping to reach Asia. Instead, he found his path blocked by America. His accidental discovery established a link between the two hemispheres.

The linking of peoples in the two hemispheres shaped the world of today. Exchanges of ideas, plants, diseases, and peoples reshaped cultures in each hemisphere. Most people in the Americas today have ancestors who crossed the Atlantic or Pacific Ocean after 1492. The global system that links the world today developed from that 1492 voyage.

An immigrant family on Ellis Island gazes at the Statue of Liberty.

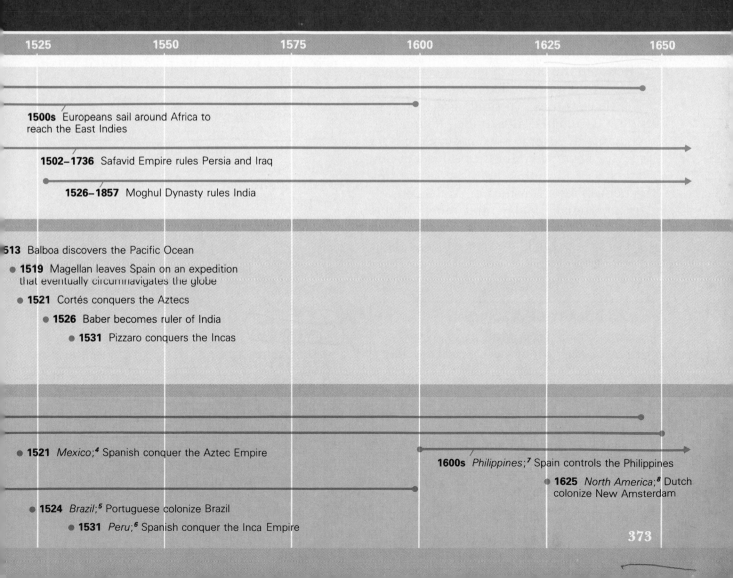

| 1525 | 1550 | 1575 | 1600 | 1625 | 1650 |

1500s Europeans sail around Africa to reach the East Indies

1502–1736 Safavid Empire rules Persia and Iraq

1526–1857 Moghul Dynasty rules India

1513 Balboa discovers the Pacific Ocean

1519 Magellan leaves Spain on an expedition that eventually circumnavigates the globe

1521 Cortés conquers the Aztecs

1526 Baber becomes ruler of India

1531 Pizzaro conquers the Incas

1521 *Mexico;*[4] Spanish conquer the Aztec Empire

1600s *Philippines;*[7] Spain controls the Philippines

1625 *North America;*[8] Dutch colonize New Amsterdam

1524 *Brazil;*[5] Portuguese colonize Brazil

1531 *Peru;*[6] Spanish conquer the Inca Empire

373

1 *Trade in the Eastern Hemisphere, 1400s*

OBJECTIVE: *To understand the Chinese and European challenges to Muslim trade dominance*

Muslim Control of Trade

During the fourteenth and fifteenth centuries, a giant commercial zone linked most of Eurasia and Africa. Merchants traded goods across Eurasia along two major sets of routes. First were the overland trails across central Asia. Second were the routes of the southern seas.

Between the eleventh and fifteenth centuries, Muslims controlled most of the trade along these routes. No single great Muslim empire dominated this trade. Rather the merchants of several Muslim states in Asia and Africa competed for the business of carrying spices and other luxury goods across the hemisphere. Muslims of Arab, Persian, African, Indian, Malay, and other origins worked together in highly organized commercial networks. Their religion gave them a basis of cooperation and trust.

China exported a greater number and variety of products than any other single country. Early in the fifteenth century, the Chinese began sending fleets of ships west.

Under the Ming Dynasty, which reigned from 1368 to 1644, the Chinese revived the tribute system. China sent officials to neighboring countries to collect gifts for the Chinese court. Even distant rulers offered gifts in recognition of China's power.

After 1398, Chinese leaders had an additional reason to send out naval expeditions. The first Ming emperor, Hongwu, died in 1398. His son, Yunglo, and nephew, Chien Wen, battled for control of the empire. It was thought that Chien Wen died in the struggle, but his body was never found. According to one rumor, Chien Wen had escaped. He was rumored to be in Southeast Asia, preparing to invade China and overthrow his cousin. The expeditions Yunglo sent out watched for signs of Chien Wen.

Cheng Ho

FOCUS ON PEOPLE

The leader of several naval expeditions Yunglo sent out was Cheng Ho, a court official. Cheng Ho was born in 1371 to a Muslim family in Yunnan Province. Yunnan (yoo NAHN), a landlocked area in southern China, was the last Chinese province the Mongols controlled. When Cheng Ho was

---

VOCABULARY DEVELOPMENT

tribute system: a system whereby one ruler or state regularly pays money or goods to another stronger ruler or state. From the Latin word, *tribuere*, meaning to pay.

exotic (ihg ZAHT ihk) *adj:* foreign and unfamiliar rather than native. From the Greek word, *exotikos*, meaning outside.

monopoly (muh NAHP uh lee) *noun:* the exclusive control of a given market that virtually eliminates free competition. From the Greek words *monos*, meaning single, and *polein*, meaning to sell.

10, the Chinese conquered Yunnan. They took Cheng Ho prisoner and sent him to be a servant in the army. At age 10, he seemed an unlikely choice to become a great Chinese admiral.

The Chinese gave Cheng Ho greater responsibilities as he grew older. He learned more about war and diplomacy, and became a respected court official. Yunglo appointed him to oversee some expeditions west.

Preparations for the first expedition were enormous. The fleet included 62 ships carrying 27,870 sailors. The largest ship measured 444 feet or 135 meters, by 180 feet or 55 meters. This ship weighed over 1,500 tons. In 1405, the expedition left China for a two-year voyage. The fleet traveled to Malaya, Ceylon, and southwest India before returning to China. On later voyages, Cheng Ho sailed to Burma, India, the Philippines, the Persian Gulf, the southern coast of Arabia, and the Red Sea.

The expeditions of Cheng Ho were generally peaceful. Cheng Ho did not seek personal fortune. Instead, he brought Chinese silk and porcelain to leaders of distant lands in exchange for the formal recognition of the superiority of the Ming emperor. Later, Chinese merchants and immigrants settled in parts of Southeast Asia and Indonesia explored by Cheng Ho.

Only on a few occasions did Cheng Ho need to use force. On the third voyage of his fleet, the ruling family in Ceylon demanded huge payments of Chinese silk and gold in exchange for protecting Cheng Ho's expeditionary force. Cheng Ho marched on the capital and took the royal family captive. He then set sail for China. When the prisoners agreed to acknowledge the Chinese emperor, they were allowed to return home.

China's Trade and Power Expand. Although Chien Wen was never found, trade between China and neighboring countries increased as a result of Cheng Ho's expeditions. Cheng Ho brought luxury items, agricultural products, gems, metal, medicine,

A Ming Dynasty artist depicted the arrival of the first in China in 1414. The giraffe was a gift from African ruler.

cloth, and exotic animals to China. Among the animals that dazzled the Chinese court were ostriches and giraffes. Some Chinese believed that the giraffe was the mythological unicorn. Lions, tigers, and zebras were other animals brought to Yunglo from Africa. These animals eventually became part of the zoo that is in Beijing today.

Cheng Ho established contact with over 50 countries as far west as the African coast. Colonies were also formed in Java, Sumatra, and the Philippines. See the map, Chinese Trade and Exploration, page 376. Foreign lands paid tribute in exchange for peaceful relations with the Ming Dynasty. Ambassadors from over 16 countries attended the imperial court. Vast lands were opened to the influences of Chinese civilization.

Just before Cheng Ho left on his seventh and last expedition, he carved the following boastful inscription into stone:

❝ The Imperial Ming Dynasty, in unifying seas and continents, . . . even goes beyond the Han and Tang dynasties. The countries beyond the horizon and at the ends of the earth have all become subjects, and to the most western of the western or

Chinese Trade and Exploration, 1500

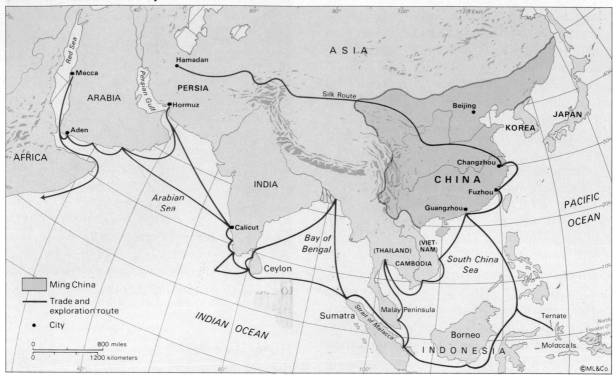

Map Skills **1.** Name the farthest continent reached by Ming admirals. **2.** Through what bodies of water did ships of the Ming Empire pass? **3.** Which city is farthest north, Fuzhou or Changzhou?

the most northern of the northern countries, however far they may be, the distances and the routes may be calculated. Thus the barbarians from beyond the seas, though their countries are truly distant, have come ... bearing precious objects and presents. **"**

Cheng Ho's Legacy. When Cheng Ho completed his final voyage, China was capable of making direct contact with Europe. China had challenged the Muslim control of trade in the Indian Ocean. The government of China, though, stopped sponsoring great expeditions. People soon forgot the achievements of Cheng Ho. Jealous members of the Ming government even destroyed the journals and narratives of his voyages. However, Cheng Ho's fame has survived in legend in many lands he visited. For centuries, people in a temple in Thailand have made sacrifices in his name. The Chinese consider him founder of their early colonies. ■

China's Trade Declines

Several factors caused the decline of Chinese seagoing expeditions and trade. Yunglo died in 1424. His successors were less interested in expanding China's influence. Many Chinese criticized the policy of sending costly expeditions overseas. Additionally, critics argued that since Chinese culture was far superior to all others, such contacts were useless. They claimed that China could only be corrupted by contact with foreigners and foreign cultures.

The expensive expeditions became a large tax burden on China. The Chinese had to bolster their defenses in the north in order to ward off Mongol attacks. The higher defense costs meant that Chinese spending on sea expeditions had to be limited.

After the voyages ended, China became more isolated from the Indian Ocean region and western Eurasia. Chinese withdrawal enabled Muslim merchants to regain dominance over trade in the Indian Ocean. The next challenge to Muslim trade networks came, not from powerful China, but unexpectedly from upstart Europeans.

Europe Challenges the Muslims

For many centuries Muslim merchants sold spices from the Indian Ocean coastlands to Italians. The Italians then traded the spices to other Europeans. As Europe recovered from the Black Death, European merchants considered ways to gain direct access to those goods.

The Importance of Spices. The supply of spices came from several small islands now part of Indonesia. For example, the tiny island of Ternate (tuhr NAHT ee) was one of the few places where a particular type of evergreen tree grew. The dried flower buds of this tree are the spice called cloves. Other islands nearby supplied nutmeg, mace, cinnamon, and ginger, as well as other spices.

Spices were needed for making medicines, dyes, incense, and perfumes. They were also used in preparing and preserving food. The diet of most Europeans had little variety. It was made up mainly of bread, beans, cabbage, and cheese. Beer was the common beverage. Fresh meat in Europe usually was scarce, and without refrigeration, soon spoiled. Spices could conceal the taste of partly spoiled meat and improve the flavor of vegetables.

Europeans, however, found that spices were extremely expensive. Therefore, they used them mainly on special occasions, such as weddings and at the end of Lent. The high cost was due to the fact that most Europeans had no direct access to these spices.

Europeans Desire Direct Trade. As Italians and Muslims grew wealthy from the spice trade, powerful nations were developing along the Atlantic coast. In the later fifteenth century, monarchs of such nation-states as England, France, Portugal, and Spain assumed leadership in Europe.

These monarchs envied the merchants who were making high profits in the spice trade. Each monarch wanted to break the Italian and Muslim trade monopoly. The vast wealth of the spice trade could greatly strengthen a monarch. In addition, as Christians, the monarchs resented the Muslims' power. The desire to take the Holy Land from the Muslims had never died.

Religious zeal was combined with a desire for profit and national pride. Together, these three forces motivated Europeans to seek an all-water route around the Muslim lands. In the process, the Europeans helped to establish the first global interacting zone.

SECTION 1 *Study Skills*

Developing Vocabulary 1. How did the tribute system demonstrate the relationship between two countries or empires? **2.** What is a monopoly? **3.** Why did the Chinese consider giraffes exotic in the fifteenth century?

Reviewing Main Ideas 1. What was the main purpose of Cheng Ho's voyages? **2.** Describe three factors that led to the decline of Chinese sea-going expeditions. **3.** Why was the cost of spices so high throughout Europe? **4.** Explain three reasons Europeans sought an all-water route around Muslim lands.

Understanding Geography 1. Across what bodies of water did the African animals given to Yunglo travel? **2.** Use the map, Chinese Trade and Exploration, page 376, to measure the distance between the east coast of China and the farthest point reached by Cheng Ho. **3.** Why did some of the islands of Indonesia become particularly desirable to Europeans?

Challenge Give examples that indicate that the factors that contributed to European exploration in the fifteenth century also caused exploration at other times.

2 European Age of Exploration

OBJECTIVE: *To understand the causes of the European Age of Exploration*

European Developments Promote Exploration

Several trends in the fifteenth century combined to make European exploration possible. Among them were: the desire to expand trade, strong national rulers with money to unify their countries, new sailing inventions and sturdier ships for ocean travel, a growing sense of curiosity, and the transmission of skills from the Chinese and Muslims.

Desire for Trade. Europeans wanted spices, silk, and other items from Asia. Merchants who traded in these goods often became rich. Expanding trade meant expanding wealth. In addition, finding a new trade route linking Europe to eastern Asia would allow Europeans to make greater profits on trade. Europeans usually purchased Asian goods through Muslim merchants. A direct trade route would allow Europeans to deal directly with the people of China and southeastern Asia.

Rise of Nations. The new development of strong nations in western Europe promoted European exploration. As nations developed, their monarchs controlled greater wealth than had earlier rulers. Consequently, these monarchs could more easily afford to fund risky ventures. The leaders in exploration in the fifteenth and sixteenth centuries were Spain, Portugal, England, and France. They also were among the first nations to develop in Europe.

Improvements in Technology. Before the year 1000, Europeans used ships that had single, square-rigged sails. Such ships could not use headwinds but relied on tailwinds and sometimes oarsmen, for propulsion. Muslims had developed a better type of sail that could use both tailwinds and headwinds—the lateen sail. Lateen sails were triangular. With these sails, ships could travel against the wind by tacking. To tack means to zigzag across the wind. As a result boats with lateen sails could travel upwind. Once ships could tack, they could go anywhere without waiting for a tail wind.

VOCABULARY DEVELOPMENT

astrolabe (AS truh LAYB) *noun:* an instrument used to find the altitude of a star; the sextant replaced it. From the Greek words *astron*, meaning a star, and *lambanein*, to take.

innovation (IN uh VAY shuhn) *noun:* something new, a change in the way of doing things

diverse (dy VUHRS) *adj.:* different, varied. From the Latin word, *divertere*, meaning to turn aside.

mutiny (MYOOT uhn ee) *noun:* revolt; forcible resistance to authority, especially among soldiers or sailors. From the Latin word, *movere*, to move.

amnesty (AM nihs tee) *noun:* a general pardon for past offenses against a government. From the Greek prefix *a-*, meaning not, and word *mnasthai*, meaning remember.

depict (dih PIHKT) *verb:* picture, show, represent in a drawing. From the Latin word, *depingere*, meaning to paint.

European Age of Exploration

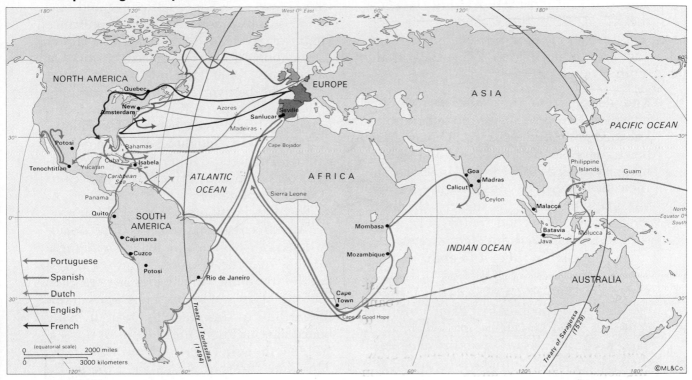

Map Skills **1.** How many miles did Columbus travel from Portugal to reach the West Indies?
2. Which of the explorers whose routes are shown on this map traveled the farthest in their explorations?

A second development in ship technology was an improvement in steering. Traditionally, Egyptian, Roman, and Viking captains steered their ships using oars fixed on either side of the boat. The Chinese, in the first century A.D., developed a method of using a single rudder attached at the rear of the ship. The Chinese system made steering more dependable and permitted greater power than had the steering oar. Muslims borrowed the idea from the Chinese and passed it on to Europeans in the late thirteenth century.

A third development that aided European navigation was the use of several masts. Again, this was a Chinese innovation that spread to Europe. By the end of the fifteenth century, three-masted ships were common in European waters. The Portuguese developed a sturdy three-masted ship called the caravel.

Europeans also learned about better navigation skills and instruments from Muslim and Chinese traders. Chinese sailors had used magnetic compasses since the twelfth century. The pointer of the first compass was a metal spoon balanced on water in a bowl. Such spoons were replaced with metal needles in the ninth century.

Another version of the Chinese compass consisted of a disk of lodestone, an iron ore with magnetic properties. This disk was engraved with the directional points and mounted on a block of wood that was floated in a bowl of water. Gradually, Muslims learned to use the compass, and by the thirteenth century Europeans were using it.

Another important navigational instrument was the astrolabe. An astrolabe helped the navigator determine location by measuring the altitude and position of stars. With it, a navigator could plot latitude on a map. The Greek scientist, Hipparchus, invented the astrolabe in the second century B.C. Arab astronomers improved the astrolabe and reintroduced it to Europeans in the tenth century A.D.

Knowledge from the Muslims.

Muslims provided Europeans with the geographical knowledge to produce accurate maps. Muslim traders pictured the lands and seas on maps showing a round world. In addition to their own maps, the Muslims gave Europeans maps made by the ancient Greeks as long ago as the second century A.D., when the Greeks explored the Mediterranean.

Europeans of the fifteenth century would have been ill equipped to explore without the knowledge of seafaring technology that many peoples had gained over the centuries. The knowledge passed on from earlier centuries, as well as improvements of their own, helped Europeans to change the world forever.

The Portuguese Sail Eastward

The Portuguese were among the first to use the knowledge and experience of Muslim and Chinese sailors. They also used innovations developed by the Venetians to construct stronger hulls. About 1500, the Portuguese mounted heavy cannons on their sturdy ships. Such cannons gave the Portuguese a tremendous military advantage on the seas. Traditionally, ships fought by ramming, boarding, or setting on fire the enemy ships. Now they could destroy enemy ships from a distance.

Even with these innovations, there were obstacles to exploring any great extent of ocean. Ignorance and fear of the unknown had to be conquered. Some sailors feared that beyond the sight of land they would find boiling waters, terrible sea beasts, and the edge of the world. At that edge, they were sure the sea would drop like a waterfall into space.

Prince Henry the Navigator.

One person who helped to conquer ignorance and fear of the seas through education was Prince Henry of Portugal. In 1415, Prince Henry used national funds to establish a school at Sagres (SAH greesh) Point in Portugal. At that school, the best mathematicians, mapmakers, astronomers, sea pilots, sailors, and writers gathered to exchange information.

Prince Henry sought advice from diverse experts. Portuguese ships then followed Africa's coast to pursue Prince Henry's dreams of ocean exploration.

By 1432, Portuguese crews had followed the African coast as far south as Cape Bojador (BAHJ uh DAW uhr). Still, many Portuguese thought that the horrors of the sea began beyond this point. Gil Eanes (zhihl YAH nehsh) was one of several sea captains whose crew forced him to turn back for fear of being boiled alive or lost to the demons of the sea. In 1434, though, Eanes led a second voyage. This time the ship passed the cape and a psychological barrier was broken.

When Prince Henry died in 1460, Portuguese caravels had sailed a third of the way to Africa's southern tip. By 1484, Diogo Cão (koun) had sailed nearly 6,000 miles south of Portugal, erecting stone pillars to mark important points along the way.

Dias Reaches India.

In 1487, Bartholomeu Dias (DEE uhsh) followed Cão's route. After he passed Cão's last pillar, he continued, despite strong winds that pushed him farther from the coast. After the winds died down, Dias tried to find the African coast. He then realized that the direction of the coastline was generally northeastward, meaning that his ship had rounded the southern tip of Africa. His tired and homesick crew mutinied and forced Dias to turn back. In Portugal, they named the southern tip of Africa, Cape of Good Hope, since Portugal hoped to be the first European country to establish a water route to India.

Dias advised the Portuguese fleet that finally traveled all the way to India. Vasco da Gama (GAH muh) was the fleet's commander. After rounding the Cape of Good Hope, da Gama and his crew arrived at the port of Mozambique. Their eyes grew wide at the sight of Muslim dhows loaded with cloves, pepper, coconuts, gold, silver, pearls, and precious stones. From Mozambique, da Gama and his crew sailed to the nearby island of Mombasa.

Mombasa's king provided da Gama with an experienced Muslim pilot for the trip across the Indian Ocean. On May 20, 1498, da Gama and the crew reached Calicut, on the western coast of India. Declaring that he had come "seeking Christians and spices," da Gama found many more spices than Christians. Da Gama returned to Portugal in 1499 with a cargo of pepper and cinnamon worth 60 times the cost of the voyage.

By 1510, Portuguese ships were rounding Africa regularly. They soon controlled most European trade with Asia. The dreams of Prince Henry the Navigator were fulfilled.

At the top, a portrait of Prince Henry. At the center, Domenico Ghirlandajo's portrait of Christopher Columbus. At the bottom, a drawing of Ferdinand and Isabella.

The Spanish Sail Westward

Many of the sailors and merchants who sailed for the Portuguese were Italian by birth. The most famous of all the Italian born sailors of this time was Christovao Colom of Genoa, Italy.

Better known as Christopher Columbus, this experienced sailor was convinced, through a miscalculation of the earth's geography, that the shortest route to Asia involved sailing west. He sought funding from King John II of Portugal, but a panel of experts counseled the king to reject Columbus.

A stubborn dreamer, Columbus went to Spain. For six years he pleaded his case before the Spanish court. Again, experts counseled rejection of Columbus's request. Isabella of Castile and her husband, Ferdinand of Aragon, considered the possible gains for Spain. At last, Isabella approved a voyage westward to reach Asia.

Columbus was happy for the chance to sail west. He was not so happy, though, with his flagship, the *Santa Maria*, a clumsy little vessel. Columbus called it "a dull sailor and unfit for discovery." With Columbus and the *Santa Maria* were the *Nina* and *Pinta*.

Columbus's crew was not the best. Some of its members were experienced sailors; others were unemployed men, desperate to improve their lot in life. Some were ex-convicts to whom Isabella and Ferdinand only recently had granted amnesty.

Columbus had carefully studied the maps of the ancient Greek scientist Ptolemy. These maps depicted the earth as smaller than its actual size. Consequently, Columbus expected to reach the Indies, the name for all the vast Asian lands from India and the southeast Asian Spice Islands to China, in one or two months.

On August 3, 1492, Columbus and his crew set out. As the trip stretched on for al-

Eastern Hemisphere Trade, 1500

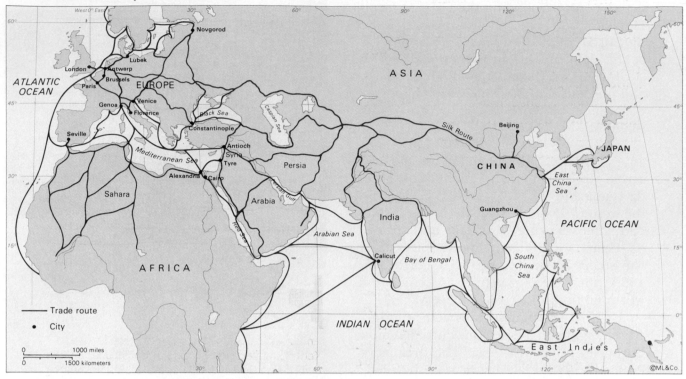

Map Skills **1.** Through which countries would a caravan travel to reach Constantinople from China? **2.** Which bodies of water would a ship sail through to get to Alexandria from Beijing?

most 40 days with no sign of land, the crew grew restless. Columbus tried to calm their fears by understating the distance traveled each day, so that the crew would not feel so far from home. Nevertheless, by October 10 the crew was ready to mutiny. Two tense days went by. Then at 2 A.M. on October 12, a sailor named Rodrigo de Triana called out. He had spotted land! Columbus and his crew were both relieved and excited. They believed they had found the Indies.

What they found was probably Watlings Island in the Bahamas. Columbus thought it was a remote island of the Indies. They sailed on, first to Cuba and then to Hispaniola. They found some unfamiliar plants and fruits. They even found a bit of gold. Still, they saw no sign of the great cities of Asia, no grand civilization, no Great Khan. They found no spices or silks or pearls. Yet they had proved that land could be reached by sailing west.

An accident off the coast of Hispaniola ruined the *Santa Maria*. Columbus left the ship's crew on Hispaniola and boarded his favorite of the three ships, the *Nina*. Accompanied by the *Pinta*, that ship brought Columbus and the crew back to Spain in January 1493.

A Letter from Columbus

FOCUS ON SOURCES

Columbus described the lands and people that he had seen on his first voyage in a letter to Gabriel Sanchez. Sanchez was the treasurer for King Ferdinand. Here is an excerpt from that letter:

❝ All these people lack, as I said above, every kind of iron; they are also without weapons, which indeed are unknown; nor are they competent to use them, not on account of deformity of body, for they are well formed, but because they are timid and full of fear. They carry for weapons, however, reeds baked in the sun, on the lower ends of which they fasten some shafts of dried wood rubbed down to a point; and indeed they do not venture to use these always; for it frequently happened when I sent two or three of my men to some of the villages, that they might speak with the natives, a compact troop of the Indians would march out, and as soon as they saw our men approaching, they would quickly take flight, children being pushed aside by their fathers, and fathers by their children. And this was not because any hurt or injury had been inflicted on any one of them, for to every one whom I visited and with whom I was able to converse, I distributed whatever I had, cloth and many other things, no return being made to me; but they are by nature fearful and timid.

Yet when they perceive that they are safe, putting aside all fear, they are of simple manners and trustworthy, and very liberal [generous] with everything they have, refusing no one who asks for anything they may possess, and even themselves inviting us to ask for things. They show greater love for all others than for themselves; they give valuable things for trifles, being satisfied even with a very small return, or with nothing; however, I forbade that things so small and of no value should be given to them, such as pieces of plate, dishes and glass, likewise keys and shoestraps; although if they were able to obtain these, it seemed to them like getting the most beautiful jewels in the world. . . .

In all these islands there is no difference in the appearance of the people, nor in the manners and language, but all understand each other mutually; a fact that is very important for the end which I suppose to be earnestly desired by our most illustrious king, that is, their conversion to the holy religion of Christ, to which in truth, as far as

An early nineteenth-century painting by Frederick Kemmelmeyer, *First Landing of Christopher Columbus*, illustrates the theme of the Old World meeting the New World.

I can perceive, they are very ready and favorably inclined. . . .

In all these islands, as I have understood, each man is content with only one wife, except the princes or kings, who are permitted to have twenty. . . . "

Columbus believed he had reached the fringes of Asia. He convinced Isabella and Ferdinand that he had. Spain gave Columbus a hero's welcome. Those who had laughed at him now apologetically sought his favor. ■

Magellan Follows Columbus

Between 1493 and 1502, Columbus made three more voyages to the west. Each time, he returned without evidence that he had reached Asia. After Columbus's fourth and final voyage, the goodwill of the Spanish court had been exhausted. Columbus died in 1506, after an extended illness and the embarrassment of being stripped of his titles and honors.

Another person who believed a westward route to Asia was possible was Ferdinand Magellan, a Portuguese sailor. He appealed to his country's monarchs to support an expedition to the west. Portugal was satisfied, though, with its profits in the Indian Ocean trade. The Spanish court, however, decided to gamble again on the westward route.

Magellan Sets Sail. On September 20, 1519, Magellan commanded a fleet of five ships sailing westward out of Sanlucar, Spain. Magellan and his crew reached South America and followed the coast southward. They huddled in the relative safety of a bay to wait out the cold season. Sailors mutinied. Magellan executed three mutineers and left two stranded on land. As the weather warmed, Magellan and his crew continued their journey southward to the tip of South America. After a terrifying stormy journey around the continent, the fleet headed for the Spice Islands.

During the long voyage across the Pacific Ocean, the crew's supplies deteriorated. Worms filled the flour they used for biscuits. The smoked penguins they carried with them began to spoil. The drinking water turned yellow. Sailors had to hold their noses to make drinking it bearable. The lack of fruits and vegetables caused sailors to contract scurvy, a disease marked by body sores, swollen gums, and loose teeth.

Magellan pulverized maggots, wormlike insect larva, as a potential protein source to add to the catch of fish and seabirds. Enterprising sailors trapped rats and sold them to one another for food. Some sailors boiled leather into broth to fill their stomachs.

Finally, in March 1521, Magellan and his crew landed at Guam in the Mariana Islands chain. Here they traded and dined with friendly inhabitants. On Mactan Island in the Philippines, though, Magellan died of a spear wound.

One Ship Returns. Juan Sebastian del Cano (dehl KAH noh), a leader of the mutiny along the South American coast, took command. He led the expedition across the Indian Ocean and around Africa. At last, one of the five ships sailed into Seville, Spain on September 8, 1522. Of the original 275 crew members, only 18 returned. Yet they were not empty-handed. Magellan's crew had eventually found the Moluccas.

The Magellan voyage demonstrated the true size of the earth. Magellan's crew sailed around the world and proved that a westward route to Asia was possible, if not practical. The voyages of Columbus and Magellan linked the hemispheres for the first time.

SECTION 2 *Study Skills*

Developing Vocabulary   **1.** Explain how astrolabes and compasses aided sailors. **2.** How is a mutiny different from other types of rebellions? **3.** Name a recent innovation in auto design.

Reviewing Main Ideas   **1.** Describe five trends that helped make European exploration possible. **2.** Identify the countries or groups of people from whom the Europeans learned new sailing technology. **3.** What was the contribution of Prince Henry the Navigator to exploration? **4.** Explain why Columbus misinterpreted the results of his voyage. **5.** Which belief of Columbus did Magellan's voyage prove correct?

Understanding Geography   **1.** Why did the Spanish begin sailing westward to reach Asia? **2.** Explain the name, Cape of Good Hope.

Understanding Chronology   **1.** How long after the opening of Prince Henry's school did the Portuguese reach India? **2.** Approximately how many days did Columbus travel on his first voyage before reaching Watlings Island?

Challenge   Explain whether explorations in space have changed civilizations today as much as the explorations in the fifteenth and sixteenth centuries changed Europe.

3 The First Global Empires

OBJECTIVE: *To understand how European empires in the Americas linked the Eastern and Western hemispheres*

Conquest in Mexico

The Spanish eventually realized that Columbus had not reached Asia. They then set about searching for wealth in the land he did reach. In this process, the Spanish confronted and conquered two great Indian empires, the Aztec and the Inca. Other Europeans soon followed the Spanish into the Americas. See the map, European Age of Exploration, page 379.

The Spanish established their base for exploration on the island of Cuba. In the spring of 1519, Hernan Cortés, a Spanish noble, led an expedition from Cuba to explore the mainland. Cortés soon encountered the great and fierce Aztec civilization. Aztecs relayed reports of the strange, light-skinned creatures to their ruler, Montezuma. Montezuma and others wondered whether the leader could be Quetzalcoatl, the god of Aztec legend who was someday to return to Mexico. The Aztec ruler sent his representatives to investigate.

Cortés awed the Aztecs with his horses and weapons. The Aztecs, in turn, awed the Spaniards with their gold and silver jewelry, decorated cotton cloth, and feathered ornaments. Cortés's ambition grew as he viewed the dazzling wealth of the Aztecs. He sent a ship loaded with Montezuma's gifts to the Spanish king, Charles V. Cortés included a letter explaining what he had done with the rest of his ships:

❝ Believing, therefore, that if the ships remained there would be a rebellion . . . whereby all that in the name of God and Your Highness has been accomplished in the land [Mexico] would be prevented, I devised a plan, according to which I declared the ships unfit to sail and ran them aground. ❞

Some of the soldiers under Cortés were ready to return to Spain, so he destroyed the remainder of his fleet. Then his men had no choice but to battle for survival in this strange land. Cortés now headed to Tenochtitlán to meet Montezuma.

On the way, Cortés made allies of the Totonac and Tlaxcalan Indians. These Indians disliked the Aztecs and wanted to help overthrow them. Cortés communicated with his Indian allies through two interpreters. One was a Spaniard, Geronimo de Aguilar

---

VOCABULARY DEVELOPMENT

negotiate (nih GOH shee AYT) *verb:* to confer, discuss, or bargain with a view to reaching an agreement. From the Latin word, *negotiari*, meaning to carry on business.

terrain (tuh RAYN) *noun:* ground or earth with its topographical features. From the Latin word, *terra*, meaning earth.

mercantilism (MUR kuhn tihl ihzm) *noun:* the doctrine that the economic interests of a nation can be strengthened by tariffs, increased foreign trade, monopolies, and a surplus of exports over imports. From the Latin word, *mercari*, meaning to trade or buy.

Hernan Cortés is given a necklace by the Aztecs. Cortés later conquered the Aztec Empire, renamed it New Spain, and rebuilt the city of Tenochtitlán.

(ah gwee LAHR), who spoke Mayan. He had been shipwrecked and had lived for eight years as a slave of the Maya in the Yucatan. The other interpreter was a young Indian woman, Malintzin, who spoke both Mayan and Aztec. Cortés spoke Spanish to Aguilar, Aguilar spoke Mayan to Malintzin, and Malintzin spoke Aztec to the Indians Cortés encountered. Eventually, Malintzin learned Spanish, was baptized, and bore Cortés a son. The Spaniards called her Doña Marina. In Mexico she is known as Malinche.

Cortés Meets Montezuma. Cortés rode into Tenochtitlán on November 8, 1519. Cortés wished the emperor good health. Montezuma and Cortés exchanged gifts of necklaces. Then the Aztec ruler led Cortés to a residence reserved for gods that had been prepared for his visit.

Cortés tried to convert Montezuma to Christianity. When this failed, Cortés resorted to force and imprisoned Montezuma. When the Aztec ruler died in captivity, war broke out. In less than two years, the Spanish conquered the Aztec Empire. Cortés captured Tenochtitlán and destroyed the temples. He then rebuilt the city as the capital of Spain's empire in Middle America, called New Spain.

Disease and Spanish Success. Three factors contributed to the Spanish conquest of the Aztecs. First, iron weapons, horses, and gunpowder gave the Spanish a tremendous military advantage. Second, the Aztecs were such oppressive rulers that many Indians joined the Spanish forces.

The third factor cannot be underestimated. Diseases the Spanish brought caused the Indian population to decrease dramatically. One writer reported that Indians "died in heaps . . . like bedbugs." Entire villages and cities were destroyed by chicken pox, smallpox, whooping cough, malaria, and yellow fever. Indians had never been exposed to these diseases. Consequently, they had no resistance to them. In the early 1500s, the population of Mexico may have been 25 million. By the middle of the 1600s, it was probably under 1.5 million. In North and South America, the Indian population declined by as much as 90 percent.

The ravages of disease destroyed the ability of the Aztecs and other Indians to resist Spanish conquest. Without soldiers to fight, or leaders to negotiate, or people to carry on the traditional way of life, Aztec culture was virtually destroyed. Elements of the once-flourishing civilization that survived, blended with Spanish culture to form the basis of modern Mexican society.

Conquest in Peru

In Peru, another Spaniard conquered another Indian empire. Francisco Pizarro (pih ZAHR oh), a crude, ambitious man, heard rumors of the wealth of the Incas. In 1531, Pizarro and his forces landed in northern Peru. He headed for Cajamarca (KAH huh MAHR kuh), home of the leader of the Incas, Atahualpa (AHT uh WAHL puh). Atahualpa had recently defeated his brother in a battle for control of the Inca Empire.

Once in Cajamarca, Pizarro slaughtered most of Atahualpa's attendants and confined the leader to a cell. Desperate, Atahualpa offered to fill a room just like his 17 by 12 foot cell to a height of 7 feet with plates and vessels of gold. In addition, he would fill it twice over with silver. All this

Peruvian children re-create a court scene leading to the execution of the last Inca king. Lizards and toads make up the audience.

would be Pizarro's, Atahualpa promised, if Pizarro would free him. Pizarro accepted the ransom, but instead of releasing Atahualpa as promised he had him strangled.

As in Mexico, disease greatly aided Spanish conquest in Peru. Like the Aztecs, the Incas were nearly destroyed by European diseases. However, Spanish conquest in South America was slowed down by pockets of Indian resistance and the unfamiliar terrain. The Spaniards finally were able to control Peru completely, by the end of the sixteenth century. By the next century, Spain controlled most of South America.

Spain's Rivals Seek Empires

Spain's empire in the Americas made its government the wealthiest in sixteenth-century Europe. Much of this wealth came from silver mines in Mexico and Peru. Other European rulers wanted to establish American empires that would enrich them as well. England, France, Portugal, and the Dutch Republic were eager for overseas trade and territory. All five of these countries were guided by the economic theory of mercantilism

According to the theory of mercantilism, a country's supply of gold and silver determines the country's power. To increase its wealth, a country should export more than it imports. Thus, more gold and silver would flow into the country than flowed out. Colonies could provide raw materials to a country. These raw materials would be used to produce finished products for sale on the international market. Eventually, colonies themselves could buy finished goods made in the home country.

Spain took an early lead in the race for colonies in America. Spaniards continued to explore the Caribbean, South America, and North America going as far as the area that is now California and Kansas. Some of these explorers hoped to find the legendary fountain of youth. Others searched for the mythical Seven Golden Cities of Cibola, a group of cities of unmatched splendor. Explorers representing England and France searched for the Northwest Passage, a supposed all-water route to Asia around the northern part of America. Though they failed to find the route, each explorer established his country's claims.

Another country exploring and claiming land in the Americas was the Dutch Republic. Now called the Netherlands, it won its independence from Spain in 1648. The Dutch established trading colonies in the Caribbean and in North America. Their colony on that continent was called New Amsterdam, which later became New York.

Portugal Claims Brazil. Portugal seemed likely to be Spain's chief rival in the Americas. Under Prince Henry the Navigator, Portugal developed into a major seapower

Theodor de Bry's engraving from 1592 shows flying fish landing aboard a Portuguese ship in West Indian waters.

(see pages 380–381). The year after Columbus returned from his first voyage, Spain and Portugal attempted to divide between them the newly discovered lands. In the Treaty of Tordesillas (TORD ih SEE yuhs), negotiated in 1494, the two countries established a line of demarcation, or dividing line, in the Western Hemisphere. Land to the east of the line belonged to Portugal. Land to the west belonged to Spain. On the basis of this treaty, Portugal claimed Brazil. Spain eventually claimed the rest of the South American continent.

Competition in the East Indies. The Portuguese controlled trade between Europe and Asia through much of the sixteenth century. Portuguese colonies included Malacca and Macao. The Dutch challenged the Portuguese with the formation of the Dutch East India Company in 1602. By 1658, the Dutch had taken control of much of the spice trade. By then, the Dutch had established a colony at Capetown, on Africa's southern tip. This colony was a supply station for ships traveling from Europe to Southeast Asia.

The First Global Interacting Zone

The efforts of Spain and its rivals created one interacting global community. By the end of the sixteenth century, the coasts of Eurasia, Africa, and the Americas were linked together for the first time. Europeans used knowledge gained from the Muslims and the Chinese to make the links. When Columbus set sail in 1492, the people of the Eastern and Western hemispheres did not know of each other's existence. After contact was made, the lives of people everywhere changed. In the years following 1492 exchanges between the hemisphere grew, establishing the first interacting zone between hemispheres.

SECTION 3 *Study Skills*

Developing Vocabulary Use each of the following terms in a sentence: **1.** negotiate. **2.** terrain. **3.** mercantilism.

Reviewing Main Ideas 1. List three factors that helped the Spanish conquer the Aztecs. **2.** Explain why European diseases affected Indians so seriously. **3.** How were the Spanish able to conquer Peru? **4.** Why were the Americas important to Spain?

Understanding Geography 1. Why did Brazil become a Portuguese colony rather than a Spanish colony? **2.** Explain why Capetown was an important colony to the Dutch. **3.** Explain the provisions of the Treaty of Tordesillas. How did the treaty affect Spain and Portugal?

Understanding Cause and Effect 1. The Spanish allied themselves with various Indian tribes to oppose the Aztecs. Explain the importance of these allies to the success of the Spanish conquest of the Aztecs. **2.** Why did mercantilism lead to exploration and colonization?

Challenge European settlement in the Americas significantly changed cultures on each continent. Discuss two areas where new settlers are changing the culture today.

Latin America

Latin America is the part of the Western Hemisphere that includes Mexico, the Caribbean Islands, and Central and South America. The major languages of the area, Spanish and Portuguese, developed from Latin. Despite similarities in language, the region's ethnic diversity reflects the influence of its varied history and geography.

The Land and Climate

The southern portion of Latin America is the continent of South America. South America includes two major land forms, the Andes Mountain Range and the Amazon River Basin. See the map, South America, page 783. The Andes Mountains stretch the entire length of South America along the western coast, a distance of 4,500 miles, or 7,240 kilometers. The Amazon River Basin is a densely forested lowland area in the northern part of Brazil. The river itself is 4,000 miles or 6,437 kilometers long. Only the Nile River is longer. The Basin covers an area of 2,722,000 square miles or 7,050,000 square kilometers. The Amazon Basin is one of the few areas where trees which contain latex grow. Latex is used to make rubber.

Mexico and Central America are crisscrossed with mountains and high plateaus. Central America is a narrow strip of land connecting South and North America. At the narrowest point, in Panama, only 40 miles of land separate the Pacific Ocean and the Caribbean Sea. The Panama Canal was built in the early twentieth century to provide a passage for ships traveling between the Atlantic and the Pacific oceans.

The Climate. Most of Latin America lies between 30 degrees north and 30 degrees south of the equator. Consequently, most of the area has a warm climate. The southern part of Latin America, however, extends to 50 degrees south latitude and has cold, harsh winters.

Rainfall is heaviest in Central America and the Amazon Basin, where it can amount to as much as 120 inches or 3000 millimeters a year. Northern Mexico and the southern tip of South America are drier, with rainfall of less than 10 inches, or 250 millimeters, every year.

Natural Resources and the Economy. Much of the land of Latin America is not highly productive. Therefore, many people live at subsistence level, raising only enough food to feed themselves. In eastern Mexico, parts of Central America, and in the northern and eastern lands of South America, people live by raising livestock and farming. The large plains of Brazil and Argentina, called pampas (PAM puhs) provide excellent grassland for cattle grazing. Leather from cattle has contributed to a booming shoe industry in Brazil.

Latin America contains many minerals. Chile and Peru, for example, have more than 20 percent of the known copper reserves in the world. Bolivia and Brazil produce more than 15 percent of the world's tin supply. Venezuela and Mexico export large quantities of oil.

The People

As a result of its history, Latin America has a diverse population. The various groups of people who have come to Latin America have settled, or been forced to settle, in different regions. As many as 5 million Africans were brought to the islands as slaves. Black slaves were brought to work on cof-

Data on Countries in Latin America

	Argentina	Brazil	Chile	Cuba	Mexico	Nicaragua	Venezuela
Area (in thousands of square miles)	1073	3,286	285	43	756	49	352
Area (in thousands of square kilometers)	2780	8,512	737	114	1,958	127	912
Population (in millions)	30	135	10	10	76	3	15
Annual birth rate (per 1,000 population)	25	23	23	16	34	44	32
Annual death rate (per 1,000 population)	9	6	6	6	5	11	6
Number of years to double population	47	19	41	67	28	20	23
Population projected by A.D. **2000** (in millions)	37	187	16	not available	115	5	25
Annual death rate of infants under 1 year (per 1,000 births)	44	75	24	17	39	102	32
Percent of population under 15 years	30	46	32	not available	40	48	30
Percent of population over 64 years	12	4	1.9	9	6	1.1	5
Life expectancy	70	63	67	73	66	57	67
Percent of urban population	83	68	81	70	66	55	86
Per capita food supply (as percent of requirement)	128	105	112	117	120	102	107
Total GNP (in billions of U.S. dollars)	72	191	22	15	157	3	64
Per capita GNP (in U.S. dollars)	2,560	1,505	1,920	1,592	2,165	1,140	3,880
Percent of adult population illiterate	5	25	4	9	17	90	15

fee plantations in Brazil and sugar plantations on the Caribbean Islands. Today, these countries have a high percentage of blacks and people of mixed races.

Indians continued to live in areas European colonists could not reach easily. Today, the Indian population of Latin America is concentrated in the mountains of Ecuador, Peru, Guatemala, Bolivia, and Paraguay. Over 90 percent of Guatemalans have Indian ancestors.

Europeans preferred to settle in the moderate climates. Consequently, less than 5 percent of the population of the Central American country of Belize is of European descent. In Argentina, over 98 percent of the people have some European ancestry.

The various ethnic groups within Latin American countries, at times, disagree over the use of land, minerals, and other natural resources. The variety of ethnic groups in Latin American countries have created a dynamic culture. The people of these countries need to work together to develop their economic resources.

STUDY SKILLS Understanding Geography

1. What land areas make up Latin America? What parts of the Western Hemisphere are included in Latin America?
2. What are the two major land forms in South America?
3. List three valuable mineral resources found in Latin America.
4. Identify the causes and consequences of ethnic diversity in Latin America.
5. During the 1600s, buccaneers lived on the islands in the Caribbean. Research the origin of the term buccaneer and the way of life of these Caribbean pirates.

CHAPTER 17 *Summary & Review*

Summarizing Main Ideas

During the fourteenth and fifteenth centuries, Muslims controlled major trade routes linking Eurasia and Africa. During the late fourteenth century, Chinese traders challenged the Muslim monopoly. In the following century, European merchants also began to challenge Muslim control of trade.

Several trends, including stronger national rulers, new sailing inventions, a sense of curiosity, and desire to expand trade combined to stimulate European exploration. Christopher Columbus, searching for a westward sea route from Europe to Asia, landed in the Americas in the year 1492.

After Columbus, contacts between the hemispheres increased. New diseases destroyed much of Indian culture. Europeans established empires in the Americas.

Questions for Critical Thinking

COMPREHENSION Interpreting Events

1. Describe the impact Europe's awareness of the Americas had on trade and colonization.
2. What problems faced other countries that wanted to colonize the Americas after Spain, Portugal, France, and England had made their claims?

ANALYSIS Identifying Trends

1. How did European ideas about exploration change as colonization proceeded?
2. What trend declined in China following the death of Yunglo in 1424?

APPLICATION Comparing Past and Present

1. Public opinion influenced fifteenth century exploration. Describe how public opinion influences exploration today.
2. Compare the methods by which the Europeans learned of Muslim and Chinese sailing techniques with the methods used to transmit knowledge today.

SYNTHESIS Developing Writing Skills

1. Write a report on one explorer.

2. Compare and contrast the responses of the Incas and Aztecs to the Spanish.

EVALUATION Weighing Consequences

1. Since Columbus did not reach Asia, why did his voyages cause a sensation in Europe?
2. If Europeans had not developed mercantilism, would exploration and settlement have developed in the same way? Why?

CHALLENGE

What can nations learn from Portugal's success as a leader of exploration?

European Explorers, 1487–1682		
Explorer	Dates of Exploration	Achievement
Bartholomeu Dias (Portugal)	1487–1488	Rounded the Cape of Good Hope
Christopher Columbus (Spain)	1492–1504	Reached the Western Hemisphere
Vasco da Gama (Portugal)	1497–1498	Sailed to India
Juan Ponce de León (Spain)	1513	Explored Florida
Ferdinand Magellan (Portugal)	1519–1521	Led first voyage around the world
Hernán Cortés (Spain)	1519–1521	Conquered Mexico
Francisco Pizarro (Spain)	1531–1535	Conquered Peru
Jacques Cartier (France)	1535	Explored the St. Lawrence River
Sir Francis Drake (England)	1577–1580	Sailed around the world

CHAPTER 18
The Renaissance and Reformation

GLOBAL TIME LINE

	1450	1475	1500	1525

TIME

1300–1600 Artists strive for realism and accuracy of detail

1455–1485 War of the Roses is fought by the York and Lancaster families for England's crown

1489 Plus (+) and minus (-) symbols come into use

1500s Use of large firearms ends the military advantage of fuedal castles and knights

PEOPLE

1400s Leonardo da Vinci tries to show movement in his art

1440s–1458 Johann Gutenberg constructs a printing press with moveable type

1469 King Ferdinand of Aragon's marriage to Queen Isabella of Castile unites Spain

1508 Michelangelo begins painting the ceiling of the Sistine chapel

1508 Raphael begins decorating the popes quarters with frescoes

1512 Machiavelli begins writing his political essay, *The Prince*

1516 Charles Hapsburg becomes Charles I

PLACE

1450s *Italy;*[1] Florence becomes the center of the Renaissance movement

1500s *Switzerland;*[2] Zwingli and Calvin establish Protestantism in Switzerland

1517 *Germany;*[3] Martin Luther posts his 95 Theses the church door in Wittenb

Linking Past to Present

The citizens of each of the nations in the western world share a common culture and history that differ from those of other countries. All of the countries of the western world, however, share similar artistic and religious heritages and beliefs.

During the fifteenth century, religious reformers in Europe criticized the Roman Catholic church and founded new Christian denominations. Artists, scholars, and writers began to concentrate on the present as well as on the next life. There was a vigorous rebirth of creativity. This rebirth began in Italy and quickly spread throughout Europe. As you read the chapter, think about how the individualism expressed during the Reformation and Renaissance affects your ideas and beliefs.

A printing office about 1500.

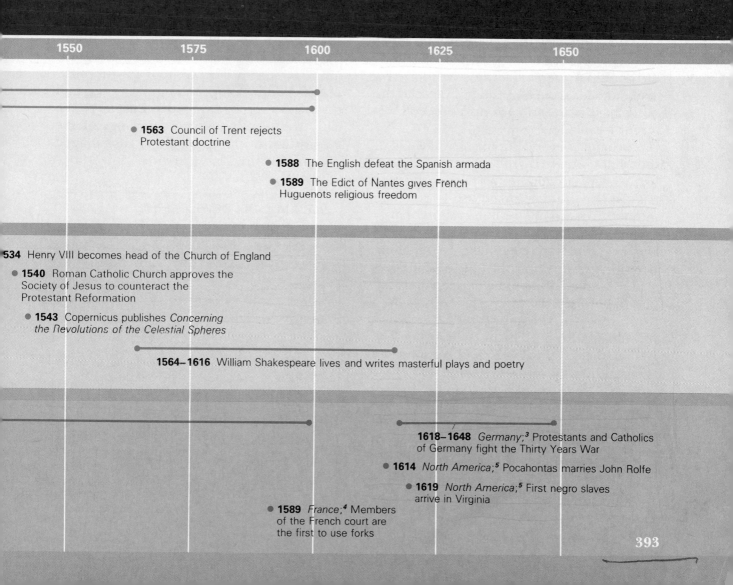

| 1550 | 1575 | 1600 | 1625 | 1650 |

1563 Council of Trent rejects Protestant doctrine

1588 The English defeat the Spanish armada

1589 The Edict of Nantes gives French Huguenots religious freedom

1534 Henry VIII becomes head of the Church of England

1540 Roman Catholic Church approves the Society of Jesus to counteract the Protestant Reformation

1543 Copernicus publishes *Concerning the Revolutions of the Celestial Spheres*

1564–1616 William Shakespeare lives and writes masterful plays and poetry

1618–1648 *Germany;[3]* Protestants and Catholics of Germany fight the Thirty Years War

1614 *North America;[5]* Pocahontas marries John Rolfe

1619 *North America;[5]* First negro slaves arrive in Virginia

1589 *France;[4]* Members of the French court are the first to use forks

393

1 The Growth of European National States

OBJECTIVE: *To understand the causes and consequences of the growth of national states in Europe*

European Nations Grow

During the Middle Ages, people of Europe identified with their local village or town. The local lord, not some remote king or emperor, affected their daily lives.

Thousands of dukes, barons, and other feudal nobles jealously guarded their own territories. A merchant who transported a load of goods from one end of France to the other paid tolls and customs to several different local rulers.

A change began to occur near the end of the Middle Ages. By the sixteenth century, many people in developing European countries were becoming linked to a larger community or nation. The link resulted partly from the Hundred Years War, which united warring allies and enemies. In addition, people in various European countries shared a common language, religion, ruler, and literature.

In the early fifteenth century, the kings of England, France, Spain, and Portugal, as well as the Russian tsars, had consolidated their authority over large territories. These rulers created strong national states. In contrast, Holland and Sweden emerged somewhat later as important national states. Germany and Italy, in contrast, remained divided into numerous city-states and principalities until the 1860s. The invention of gunpowder facilitated the formation of national states in western Europe.

Guns and National States

FOCUS ON SOCIETY

The use of gunpowder and firearms in Europe was closely related to the rise of strong national states. The Chinese may have invented the earliest guns. The technology for making both gunpowder and guns, however, had spread to Europe by the early fourteenth century. Drawings of the earliest European guns show vase-shaped objects that fired large arrows.

VOCABULARY DEVELOPMENT

national state: in the 1500s, large territories that a ruler had consolidated under one government. People in these lands generally shared a common cultural heritage.

facilitate (fuh SIHL uh TAYT) *verb:* to make easy or easier.

artillery (ahr TIHL uhr ee) *noun:* large guns, such as cannons. From the Latin word, *ars*, meaning skill, art.

limited monarchy: a government, ruled by one person, in which power is limited. In England, Parliament limited the monarchy.

Court of the Star Chamber: a special court appointed by King Henry VII in order to seize the estates and fortunes of rebellious or disloyal nobles. Trials were held in secret and without juries.

absolute monarch: person whose power to govern is not limited by laws.

By the fourteenth century, European metal workers were building huge bronze tubes that fired heavy stones. These large guns, called bombards, were used as siege weapons to destroy the walls of castles or towns. They were so heavy and awkward, though, that they were difficult to move.

Defense Against Bombards. As bombards became common, Italian military experts found ways to defend towns or forts against the new artillery. These experts told kings to surround their strongholds with a barrier of loosely packed earth and a wide ditch. Such a ditch made direct approach to castle walls difficult for the enemy. When the bombards were fired, the heavy stones would thud harmlessly into the earthworks around the walls.

Cannons Become Portable. By 1470 the French were using smaller mobile siege guns called cannons. Armies learned to attach cannons to gun carriages pulled by big horses. Cannon warfare spread rapidly across Europe. Later in the next century, cheaper iron artillery replaced bronze cannons. Hand guns called arquebuses (AHR kwuh buhs uhz), or muskets, were invented at the end of the fifteenth century.

Cannons, muskets, and earthwork fortifications were extremely expensive. Metal had to be mined, hundreds of artisans employed, and thousands of laborers put to work. Lords controlling relatively small territories could not afford to equip their armies with firearms.

Effect of Firearms. The kings of Europe, however, could afford firearms by imposing taxes and borrowing funds from the towns. The age of the feudal knight safe in his castle was over. Nevertheless, no European king was wealthy or powerful enough to dominate all of Europe with cannons and muskets. Instead, national monarchies, rather than a single giant empire, shaped the future of Europe.

A painting of the Battle of Rosebecque during the Hundred Years War.

Firearms also made conflicts among European states more destructive. By the fifteenth century, rival states were competing in furious arms races to produce the deadliest guns. Greater numbers of soldiers died or were mutilated in wars, often struck down by bullets they could not even see. "Would to God that these wretched instruments had never been invented," wrote one sixteenth-century European. ■

Royal Power in Europe

England was the first of the strong national monarchies to develop in Europe. The English kings of the late Middle Ages slowly strengthened their power at the expense of the great nobles. They balanced the power of the nobility by encouraging the influence of the middle class. English monarchs allowed middle class town leaders and lower ranking nobles to meet in Parliament, giving them a voice in the government. For this reason the English monarchy was a limited monarchy.

English kings gradually accepted Parliament's right to levy new taxes. Only Parliament could grant funds for war and royal administration. In return, Parliament helped to unite England under royal authority.

The monarchs of England struggled throughout most of the fifteenth century to keep the great barons from regaining their power. In 1455, a bloody civil war broke out between two branches of the royal line, the Lancaster and York families. Each family claimed the crown. English barons supported one or the other of the families.

This struggle was called The War of the Roses, because a white rose was the symbol of the York family and a red rose indicated a Lancaster. The war threatened to destroy England's strong monarchy. In 1485, however, Henry Tudor, of the Lancaster family, defeated the Yorkists and won the throne.

The Reign of Henry VII. Henry, the new Tudor king, promoted peace by marrying a princess of the York family. Many nobles who had resisted royal authority had died in the war and thus were no longer a threat.

As Columbus and others sailed the seas in search of a new route to the east, Henry and his successors continued to increase their power at home. Henry VII worked to restore and expand royal authority. A cold and shrewd man, he packed Parliament with friends and supporters from the lower nobility and the wealthy urban middle class. These groups became loyal supporters of the king because they profited from the peace and commercial prosperity that a strong central government provided.

Henry chose his key advisers and local officials from among the large landowners who were not nobles. He personally appointed local officials called justices of the peace. He also outlawed private armies.

Finally, Henry dealt ruthlessly with the great barons. He created a special court called the Court of the Star Chamber. To this court he appointed judges who interpreted English law to favor the crown. Then he proceded to seize the estates and fortunes of the great nobles. The Star Chamber Court held trials in secret and without juries. In modern times, any government court that is rigged against the defendant is called a star chamber court.

Henry was so successful at seizing the barons' wealth that his government almost became financially independent of Parliament. The English people, tired of war and disorder, accepted the strong government of Henry VII.

The French Monarchy. In the Middle Ages, feudalism was more firmly established in France than anywhere else in Europe. Great nobles were always ready to defend their privileges from the king's interference. Gradually, however, prosperous leaders of the towns supported the French kings' efforts to strengthen their bureaucracy and army. A strong monarchy meant protection on roads and waterways.

Louis XI Increases French Lands. King Henry VII had a counterpart in France, King Louis XI, who ruled France between 1461 and 1483. Louis XI was small and lame. He surrounded himself with people of low birth; one of his royal advisers had even been his barber. Louis usually wore old, threadbare clothes and an ancient hat covered with religious medals. He also was cruel. It was said that he enjoyed visiting prisons to be sure that prisoners were safely locked up and badly treated.

Louis's opponents called him the Spider King because he used any method to trap his enemies and expand his territories. Louis's greatest foe was Charles of Burgundy, who ruled most of eastern France.

In 1477, Charles attacked the Swiss, hoping to rule them. However, Swiss footsoldiers using long spears, called pikes, killed Charles at the battle of Nancy. King Louis then added part of Burgundy to the realm of the French monarchy.

Louis took additional land when, in 1480, the Duke of Anjou died without an heir. At the deaths of the counts of Maine and Provence, Louis regained those provinces for the crown. The only great province Louis did not control was Brittany, in northwestern France.

When Louis died, France was emerging as a powerful national state. The country had a standing professional army of about 25,000 troops. Louis' successor, Charles VIII, married the heiress to Brittany, consolidating all of the French provinces.

By 1500, French and English kings, often aided by the middle class, were building strong national states. Centralized government bureaucracies and royal courts helped to increase the power of the monarchies. Between 1450 and 1600, the monarchs of Spain also consolidated their power.

A Spanish Nation. The nation of Spain developed after 1469, when King Ferdinand of Aragon married Queen Isabella of Castile. Ferdinand and Isabella ruled jointly in both kingdoms. They began to strengthen their rule in each of the kingdoms by decreasing the power of the noble families. They also gained control over all appointments to important church positions. They worked toward becoming absolute monarchs, with complete authority over the governments of Aragon and Castile.

By persecuting non-Christians, the Spanish monarchs also used the Roman Catholic church to unify the nation culturally. For centuries, Christians, Jews, and Muslims had lived in Spain in relative harmony. Then, in 1479, Ferdinand and Isabella created the Inquisition. This court, made up of clergy, was formed to suppress heresy—beliefs unacceptable to the church. The Inquisition persecuted, and sometimes tortured, Jews, Muslims, and others in the

In this baptism scene from the Granada Cathedral, Muslim women still wear their veils as they choose Christianity over persecution by Spanish Christians.

kingdom whose beliefs differed from church doctrine.

In 1492, the monarchs expelled more than 150,000 Jews who refused to convert to Christianity. This policy cost Spain the loyalty and skills of many productive and educated citizens.

Ferdinand and Isabella had Muslims persecuted and expelled as well. Also in 1492, Spain's army invaded and conquered Granada, the small Muslim kingdom in the mountains of southern Spain. According to legend, the last sultan of Granada shed tears as he left his magnificent palace, called the Alhambra.

The conquest of Granada was a triumph for Spain. As a result, Ferdinand and Isabella ruled all of Iberia except Portugal, which remained an independent and rival national state.

In 1493, Ferdinand and Isabella's daughter, Joanna, married Philip Hapsburg of Austria. Their oldest son, Charles, would one day rule all of Spain.

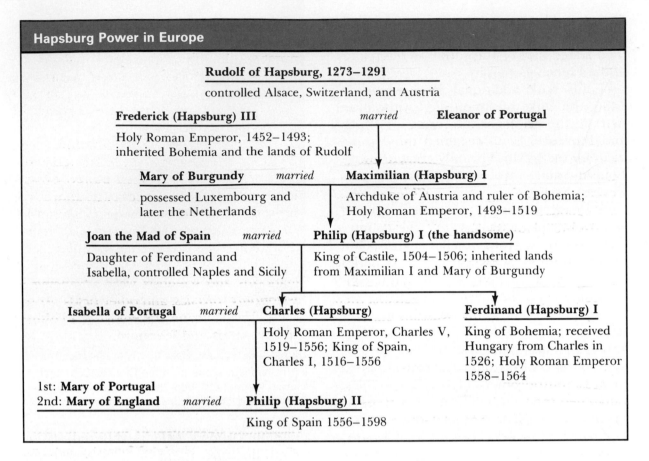

Hapsburg Power in Europe

Rudolf of Hapsburg, 1273–1291

controlled Alsace, Switzerland, and Austria

Frederick (Hapsburg) III   *married*   **Eleanor of Portugal**

Holy Roman Emperor, 1452–1493;
inherited Bohemia and the lands of Rudolf

Mary of Burgundy   *married*   **Maximilian (Hapsburg) I**

possessed Luxembourg and
later the Netherlands

Archduke of Austria and ruler of Bohemia;
Holy Roman Emperor, 1493–1519

Joan the Mad of Spain   *married*   **Philip (Hapsburg) I (the handsome)**

Daughter of Ferdinand and
Isabella, controlled Naples and Sicily

King of Castile, 1504–1506; inherited lands
from Maximilian I and Mary of Burgundy

Isabella of Portugal   *married*   **Charles (Hapsburg)**   **Ferdinand (Hapsburg) I**

Holy Roman Emperor, Charles V,
1519–1556; King of Spain,
Charles I, 1516–1556

King of Bohemia; received
Hungary from Charles in
1526; Holy Roman Emperor
1558–1564

1st: **Mary of Portugal**
2nd: **Mary of England**   *married*   **Philip (Hapsburg) II**

King of Spain 1556–1598

The Holy Roman Empire. The trend toward strong national states did not reach Germany. Around 1500, that land was divided into about 300 separate political states. The princes of the more important German states elected a ruler called the Holy Roman Emperor.

In theory, the emperor actually was the lord of the German states. In reality, the German princes usually went their own way. The emperor ruled only the provinces he inherited. In 1273, the electors chose a noble of the Hapsburg family. For the next 300 years, most of the Holy Roman Emperors were from the Hapsburg family.

Although the emperor gave Germany the appearance of unity, he had few powers. He could not force subjects of other German provinces to obey him, pay taxes, or cooperate in common policies.

One of the emperor's rights, however, was to reassign any fiefs that became vacant from lack of heirs. Takeovers of these fiefs, as well as fortunate marriages, increased the Hapsburg family's lands. One German, referring to the way the Hapsburgs went about obtaining land, said, "Let others wage war; you, happy Austria, marry."

Charles was the oldest son of Philip Hapsburg of Austria and Joanna of Spain. In 1516, he became the king of Spain and all its possessions. In 1519, when he was only 19, the German princes elected him Holy Roman Emperor. His territory included not only Austria, Bohemia, and Spain but also the Netherlands, Milan, Sicily, and southern Italy, as well as the Spanish empire in the New World.

Charles wanted to defeat France and unite much of western Europe. He spent a great deal of time and resources in long, exhausting, unsuccessful wars with France. In his own empire, he was never able to control all of the German princes.

The Russian Nation. In eastern Europe, the Russian kingdom of Moscovy emerged as a powerful state in the sixteenth century. Three centuries earlier, the Mongols, sweeping westward across Asia, had conquered Moscovy (see page 324). For about 250 years, the Mongols demanded regular tribute from the Grand Prince of Moscow. Under Mongol influence the Russians remained cut off from western Europe. Russians did, however, travel the long route to China to bring back goods and ideas.

In 1480, Ivan the Great, Grand Prince of Moscow, refused to continue paying tribute to the Mongols, who were no longer strong enough to enforce their demands. Ivan's forces, using artillery and musketeers, then conquered neighboring Russian states to create a vast new empire.

Under Ivan the Terrible (Ivan IV), who ruled from 1533 to 1584, Russia became the largest European state. Ivan's musketeers marched the length of the Volga River valley to the Caspian Sea, defeating Mongol cavalry as they went. These victories added vast new territories to the Russian state.

Ivan centralized Russian government. He earned the title, Terrible, by murdering large numbers of Russian nobles who opposed him. In a blind rage, he also murdered his son. He ruthlessly collected taxes from the peasants. Despite his cruelty, Ivan transformed Russia into a powerful state.

National States in the Sixteenth Century

Between 1450 and 1600, the monarchs of England, France, and Spain increased their lands and power at the expense of the nobility and, sometimes, one another. They continually engaged in wars for power.

All of the new nations had the ability to expand their territories. They were under pressure to build powerful armies and navies, and create efficient governments. By 1618 the Hapsburgs controlled extensive lands and threatened other European nations. The destiny of Europe was not yet clear. Instead of remaining divided into a number of nations, Europe could still be consolidated into a single, large empire by a strong monarch. Events between 1600 and 1640 proved important to the fortunes of the people of Europe.

The fifteenth and sixteenth centuries in Europe brought revolutionary changes. While kings increased their power, explorers searched for new trade routes and, in the process, stumbled on new markets and resources. During the same period, writers and religious leaders tried to reform the Roman Catholic church. Meanwhile, mathematicians and scientists were advancing in astronomy, physics, and other fields. At the same time, Europe was enjoying a cultural rebirth in art and literature.

SECTION 1 *Study Skills*

Developing Vocabulary 1. What is the difference between an absolute monarchy and a limited monarchy? **2.** What was the Court of the Star Chamber? **3.** How is a national state different from an empire?

Reviewing Main Ideas 1. Explain how the growth of nationalism changed how people viewed their community. **2.** List the characteristics of national states. **3.** Explain two advantages of a strong central government. **4.** Describe two ways Louis XI increased the power of the French monarchy. **5.** Describe the methods used by the Hapsburgs to gain power in the Holy Roman Empire.

Understanding Cause and Effect 1. Describe the impact of portable cannons on European warfare. **2.** Explain how the development of firearms aided the development of national states. **3.** What was the result of the War of the Roses?

Challenge How was the pressure on sixteenth-century national states to have large armies similar to the pressure on modern governments to have large military forces?

2 The Renaissance in Europe

OBJECTIVE: *To understand the causes and consequences of the intellectual and artistic Renaissance in Europe*

The Renaissance Begins in Italy

The Renaissance was a period of great artistic creativity that began in Italy and spread throughout Europe. As early as the 1300s, some scholars began to study the works of classical Greek and Roman artists and thinkers. These scholars, who came to be called humanists, laid the foundations for the Renaissance, as they turned to ancient Greek and Roman architecture, art, and writing for inspiration.

By the fifteenth and sixteenth centuries, a mature civilization was evolving in Europe. Population, trade, and industry expanded. In fifteenth century Italy, cities approached the size of the larger cities of the Middle East.

Italian cities grew wealthy from trade between Asia and Europe. City rulers, rich merchants, and church officials spent large sums of money to build and beautify churches and public buildings. They also supported artists and writers. The cities of Italy, therefore, became cultural centers.

Rather than emphasizing religious ideas, humanist writers and artists expressed more concern for human, rather than spiritual, matters. Although religion continued to be important, Renaissance thinkers concentrated on the problems and experiences of the present life rather than the next one. Painters realistically portrayed nature and the human body. Writers told stories of everyday life.

The Realism of Giotto. Giotto (JAHT toh) di Bondone was an important painter of the 1300s. The son of a poor shepherd, he began as a young boy by sketching on a rock with a sharp stone. Like other contemporary artists, he was employed to decorate the walls of churches and other religious buildings. He painted only sacred scenes. In contrast with earlier painting, however, Giotto's people looked solid and real.

VOCABULARY DEVELOPMENT

Renaissance (REHN uh SAHNS) *noun:* a movement or period of vigorous artistic and intellectual activity; a rebirth or revival. The Renaissance in Europe spanned the years 1350 to 1600.

perspective *noun:* the technique of making scenes, painted on a flat surface, appear to be three dimensional.

fresco (FREHS koh) *noun:* the art or technique of painting with watercolors on wet plaster. From the Old High German word, *frisc,* meaning fresh.

Utopia (yoo TOH pee uh) *noun:* an imaginary island with a perfect social and political system, described in a book by Thomas More. Today the word has come to mean any perfect place or situation. From the Greek word, *topos,* meaning place and *ou,* meaning not.

essay (EHS ay) *noun:* a short, analytical literary composition written from a personal point of view. From the French word, *essai,* meaning an effort or attempt.

Giotto tried to make his paintings appear three dimensional rather than flat. He drew objects in the foreground larger than those in the background. Later, other artists discovered this technique called perspective.

The Italian Renaissance reached its peak during the late fifteenth and early sixteenth centuries. Three major artists dominated this period: Leonardo da Vinci, Raphael, and Michelangelo.

The Genius of Leonardo da Vinci. Leonardo da Vinci, an architect, musician, botanist, anatomist, and engineer, was born near Florence, Italy, in 1452. In the late 1460s, he was apprenticed to Andrea del Verrocchio, a famous painter and sculptor.

Later, Leonardo assisted Verrocchio on the painting, *The Baptism of Christ*. This painting illustrates the change in artistic styles during the Renaissance. The parts Leonardo painted are softly shaded and shadows conceal the edges. The people are shown in the act of moving. Verrocchio's figures, in contrast, are sharply defined, representing the stiffer style used during the early Renaissance.

During his lifetime, Leonardo recorded his observations and ideas in notebooks. The notebooks contain plans for a flying machine, a parachute, and a tank, as well as drawings of the human body showing how bones, tendons, and muscles work.

Leonardo studied anatomy by dissecting human corpses and the bodies of animals. Dissection was not only against the law but also prohibited by the church. Leonardo, however, believed that an understanding of how the body worked was essential to an artist. His drawings are the first accurate pictures of human anatomy.

One of Leonardo's most famous paintings is the *Mona Lisa*. It is a portrait of Lisa del Giocondo, the young wife of an Italian merchant. The *Mona Lisa* is famous for her mysterious smile. Actually, Leonardo showed the woman's face moving either into, or out of, a smile.

A charcoal drawing of Leonardo da Vinci, believed to be a self-portrait sketched by the artist at age sixty.

In 1517, the king of France invited Leonardo to live in the city of Tours. Leonardo died there in 1519.

The Frescoes of Raphael. The artist, Raphael (RAY fih uhl) Santi, lived and worked in Italy during the Renaissance. Famous for his madonnas—pictures of Mary, the mother of Jesus—he was a master of design.

Among Raphael's most famous works are frescoes he painted to decorate the pope's quarters in the Vatican. Each wall in the room has an arch to support the curved ceiling. Raphael brilliantly incorporated the arches into the paintings. The best known of these paintings is the *School of Athens*.

The Art of Michelangelo. The third famous artist of the late Renaissance, Michelangelo, was an architect, sculptor, and painter. His scenes on the ceiling of the Sistine chapel still impress visitors to Rome.

Michelangelo Buonarroti was born in a village near Florence, where his father was a government official. Michelangelo attended school until the age of 12, when he was apprenticed to the most popular painter in Florence. Before his apprenticeship was finished, however, Michelangelo decided that he wanted to become a sculptor.

In 1494, Michelangelo moved to Rome. While there, at the age of 23, he carved one of his most famous statues, *The Pieta*. This magnificent work, carved in marble, shows the dead Christ lying across the knees of his mother. The statue is currently in St. Peter's Church in Rome.

In 1508, Michelangelo began his most famous work. The pope asked him to paint the ceiling of the Sistine chapel. The curved ceiling, covering an area of more than 5,000 square feet, is larger than a basketball court. The frescoes had to be painted quickly before the plaster dried.

Michelangelo worked on a wooden platform, 65 feet above the floor of the Vatican's Sistine Chapel. For four years he painted, bent over backward or lying on his back, with paint dripping onto his face.

Michelangelo lived for his art. He was never satisfied with his own work and could not tolerate anything that was not perfect. He harshly judged the work of other artists, one of whom broke his nose in a fight. In his later years, Michelangelo devoted himself to architecture and poetry.

Northern Renaissance Artists

The ideas of the Renaissance traveled northward across the Alps in the fifteenth century. Merchants, bankers, diplomats, and scholars introduced the new styles in art to such countries as France, Germany, England, and Spain.

The earliest Renaissance paintings outside Italy were done in Flanders, now a part of Belgium and Holland. There the painter, Jan Van Eyck (van EYEK), used his observation of detail to paint realistic pictures. He emphasized lighting and used vivid colors to make his paintings come alive.

In Germany, the painter, Albrecht Dürer, was the first major artist to paint realistic nature pictures. He was also a master portrait painter. He is best remembered, however, for engravings in copper showing people going about their everyday affairs.

Dürer also wrote books on geometry and artistic theory. He was the first writer to publish scientific literature in German.

Writers and artists throughout western Europe shared in the ideas of the humanists. The introduction of printing in the late 1400s was responsible for the rapid spread of new ideas.

The Printing Press and Renaissance Writers

The knowledge of printing traveled slowly across the communicating zone, probably from China to Europe. In the 1440s, Johann Gutenberg of Mainz, Germany, constructed a printing press with movable type. The oldest complete surviving book printed by Gutenberg is the *Constance Missal*. A book of Masses for the German diocese of Constance, it was printed in 1450.

The effect of the printing press in Europe was revolutionary. Previously, copyists had labored a whole year to copy two books. The Renaissance printer could produce hundreds, and later thousands, of books in the same time.

Printing helped to spread humanist ideas quickly throughout Europe. The printing press reduced the price of books since so many copies could be produced in a relatively short time. More people could now afford to own books. As both the reading audience and interests grew, the variety of books written and published also grew.

The Reform Spirit. Among the most famous writers of the Renaissance were Erasmus and Sir Thomas More. Erasmus was a Dutch priest and scholar. In his best-known book, *In Praise of Folly*, Erasmus ridiculed lawyers and professors, and especially church officials. Erasmus, though a Christian, thought the clergy were greedy, ignorant, corrupt, and superstitious. He believed that the church needed to be reformed, and that reform could begin within the church itself.

Sir Thomas More, another great Renaissance scholar, was born in England in 1477. For the title of his book, More coined a new word, *Utopia*. Utopia has come to mean an ideal society.

Like Erasmus, Sir Thomas More demonstrated the spirit of reform in his writings. In *Utopia*, More criticized his society by describing an ideal world. His Utopia emphasized religious toleration, communal rather than private property, a simple way of life, and social equality.

The French Renaissance writer, Michel de Montaigne (mahn TAYN), pioneered a new literary style, the essay. True to the humanist emphasis on the individual, Montaigne's essays offered his personal views. Montaigne believed that people were rational and could decide how to live their own lives. The church and clergy were not the only sources of wisdom.

The Writings of Shakespeare. William Shakespeare, born in England in 1564, wrote plays and poems that many consider to be among the best in the English language. Shakespeare's characters illustrate universal human qualities. His plays, therefore, have meaning beyond the time during which Shakespeare lived.

Many lines from his plays and poems have become part of our everyday speech. He created such familiar phrases as "fair play," "catch cold," "foregone conclusion" and "all's well that ends well."

Niccolo Machiavelli (MAH kyah VEHL lee) also was an influential writer during the Renaissance. Like Thomas More and other humanists, Machiavelli's writings concentrated on politics.

Above, the only oil portrait of Shakespeare believed to be authentic, from about 1610. At left, John Gilbert's painting celebrates scenes from Shakespearean plays.

403

Machiavelli's Practical Politics

FOCUS ON SOURCES

Machiavelli was born in Florence, Italy, in 1469, the son of a lawyer. He obtained a clerical job in the Florentine government in 1498 and later became a diplomat. He traveled to every important Italian city-state. In his political essay, *The Prince*, Machiavelli used his observations to set down rules for a prince or leader of a state. The following is taken from the essay.

" I say that every prince ought to desire the reputation of being merciful, and not cruel; at the same time, he should be careful not to misuse that mercy. . . . A prince, therefore, should not mind the ill repute of cruelty, when he can thereby keep his subjects united and loyal; for a few displays of severity will really be more merciful than to allow, by an excess of clemency, disorders to occur. . . .

It will naturally be answered that it would be desirable to be both feared and loved; but as it is difficult to be both at the same time, it is much more safe to be feared than to be loved, when you have to choose between the two. For it may be said of men in general that they are ungrateful and fickle, dissemblers [liars], avoiders of danger, and greedy of gain. . . . And the prince who relies upon their words, without having otherwise provided for his security, is ruined; for friendships that are won by rewards, and not by greatness and nobility of soul . . . cannot be depended upon in time of adversity.

Besides, men have less hesitation in offending one who makes himself beloved than one who makes himself feared. . . . A prince, however, should make himself feared in such a manner that, if he has not won the affections of his people, he shall at least not incur their hatred; for being feared, and not hated, can go very well together. **"** ■

Renaissance Europe

During the Renaissance, the people of Europe rediscovered their ancient heritage. The Greek and Roman emphasis on the worth and creative potential of human beings profoundly affected people.

Renaissance thinkers also emphasized accuracy in translating ancient works. They wanted to understand the original meanings in Greek and Roman writings. This scholarly emphasis on unbiased truth is a major aspect of modern academic research.

Europeans also explored both hemispheres during the Renaissance. The Renaissance writers criticized the Roman Catholic church, and later reformers attacked the church for being corrupt. Early in the sixteenth century these criticisms turned to widespread revolt.

SECTION 2 *Study Skills*

Developing Vocabulary   Use each of the following terms in a sentence: **1.** Renaissance. **2.** perspective. **3.** frescoe. **4.** Utopia. **5.** essay.

Reviewing Main Ideas   1. Explain how Giotto's art differed from earlier European art. **2.** List three major artists of the Italian Renaissance and give one example of the work of each. **3.** Compare and contrast the ideas of Erasmus and Sir Thomas More. **4.** Explain why Shakespeare's plays and poems are still meaningful today. **5.** Explain the importance of the Greek and Roman writers to Renaissance thinkers. **6.** According to Machiavelli, why should a leader aim to be more feared than loved?

Understanding Geography   1. In which country did the Renaissance begin? **2.** List four countries where the northern Renaissance was influential.

Challenge   Compare the influence of the printing press in fifteenth-century Europe with the influence of the computer in the twentieth-century world.

3 The Religious Reformation

OBJECTIVE: *To understand the causes and consequences of the Protestant Reformation*

The Troubled Church of 1500

Such reformers as Erasmus and Sir Thomas More criticized the Roman Catholic church during the sixteenth century. Earlier reformers also had spoken out against many church practices.

The Teachings of John Wycliffe.
During the fourteenth and fifteenth centuries, heretics preached doctrines unacceptable to the leaders of the church. In England, John Wycliffe, a professor at Oxford in 1356, was among the most influential of the heretics. Wycliffe believed that the church too often interfered in the political affairs of countries. He also attacked the wealth and immorality of the clergy. His ideas influenced reformers of the 1400s.

Political Power of Popes.
Renaissance popes were administrators, diplomats, and patrons of the arts. They built churches and palaces, but often ignored the spiritual life of Christians.

For example, Julius II, pope from 1503 to 1513, schemed in Italian politics and fought in battles against local city-states. He also began construction of St. Peter's Church in Rome. He employed Leonardo da Vinci, Raphael, and Michelangelo to work on the church and decorate his lavish private quarters.

One of the ways that popes raised funds for their building projects was by selling indulgences. Church leaders built cathedrals and universities with some of the money people paid to buy indulgences. An

---

VOCABULARY DEVELOPMENT

heretic (HAIR uh tihk) *noun:* a church member who holds beliefs opposed to church dogma. From the Greek word, *hairetikos*, meaning able to choose.

indulgence (ihn DUHL juhns) *noun:* a means the Roman Catholic church developed to pardon sinners from part of the penalty for their sins. For example, a person could contribute money to a specific cause rather than go on a pilgrimage. The practice was sometimes abused as a means of raising money.

Protestant (PRAHT ihs tuhnt) *adj:* a member of any of the Christian churches that resulted from the Reformation; one who protests, or testifies for, the truth as he or she sees it. From the Latin

prefix *pro*, meaning for, and word *testari*, meaning to testify or affirm.

Reformation *noun:* the sixteenth-century religious movement that aimed at reforming the Christian church.

deliberative body *noun:* a group which thinks about and discusses issues and reaches decisions carefully.

predestination (pree DEHS tuh NAY shuhn) *noun:* in theology, the doctrine that one's fate or destiny in life has been preordained by God. From the Latin prefix *prae*, meaning before, and *destinare*, meaning to fasten down, to secure.

armada (ahr MAH duh) *noun:* a fleet of warships, such as those Spain sent against England in 1588.

indulgence was believed to cancel some of the punishment necessary to atone for sins. The purchaser could use the indulgence personally or for the soul of anyone who had died. Some Catholics, such as Martin Luther, believed that the church was wrong to sell indulgences to the people.

Martin Luther

FOCUS ON PEOPLE

Martin Luther was born in Germany in 1483. Even as a young man, Luther was intensely religious. He began to study law but gave up his studies to become a monk. The story of Luther's decision to become a monk begins in 1505.

Luther was traveling to Erfurt, Germany, when a storm approached and the sky grew dark. A lightning bolt struck Luther and knocked him to the ground. He was sure that God was punishing him for some dreadful sin. He thought he would meet fewer temptations in life as a monk than as a layman. Shortly thereafter, Luther joined a group of Augustine monks.

Luther later became a priest and then a professor at the University of Wittenberg in Saxony. Luther did daily good deeds and continually worked hard to save his soul. He worried that God was displeased with him and with his actions.

Fear of eternal damnation left Luther one day when he read St. Paul's letter to the Romans: "He, who through faith is righteous, shall live." Luther interpreted the passage to mean that faith alone, not good deeds, could bring salvation. People could not wipe out the punishment for sin by praying and performing good works. Instead, salvation was God's gift to those who had unquestioning faith.

Luther Objects to the Sale of Indulgences. As a result of his belief in salvation, or justification, by faith alone, Luther opposed the sale of indulgences. In 1517, when Pope Leo X's representative arrived in Saxony to raise money, Luther publicly challenged the sale of indulgences.

As was the custom in a public disagreement, Luther posted 95 theses, or statements, on the church door in Wittenberg. These statements identifed the points Luther was prepared to defend in public debate against anyone who cared to argue. Luther hoped that his statements would lead the church toward reform. Instead, his actions began the Protestant Reformation

Luther Breaks with the Church. Defenders of the papacy soon labeled Luther's views as heresy. In 1520, Luther published three pamphlets defending himself. His arguments attracted many followers in Germany. Most Christians, including the clergy, admitted that the church needed reform. Besides, the people, and the rulers of the German states, did not like to see German money going to support the church in faraway Rome.

In June 1520, Pope Leo X warned Luther to take back his statements. Luther burned the letter. In January 1521, the pope excommunicated, or expelled, Luther from the church. Charles V called Luther before the Diet of Worms, the supreme deliberative body of the Holy Roman Emperor, to discuss Luther's case.

As the defender of the pope and the Christian church, the emperor demanded that Luther take back his views. Luther refused, saying:

❝ I cannot revoke anything—since to go against one's conscience is neither safe nor right. Here I stand; I cannot do otherwise. God help me. Amen. **❞**

Luther continued to write pamphlets, usually in German so that more people could read them. In addition, he translated the New Testament into German. The popularity of his Bible helped to create a national German language. ∎

Reformation leaders gather around their protector, John Frederick the Magnanimous. John Frederick's family offered Luther shelter when he refused to give up his heretical ideas.

Lutheranism Spreads

Luther and his followers did not believe that the church should own property. They also thought that rulers should appoint clergy as they did officials for other public offices. Many German rulers sincerely agreed. Others agreed because they had much to gain. They confiscated church lands, closed monasteries, and appointed church officials.

When Luther died in 1546, most of northern Germany and Scandinavia had followed his reforms. Parts of southern Germany remained Roman Catholic. See the map, Protestant and Catholic Europe, page 408. The Holy Roman Emperor, Charles V, failed to force them to restore the Roman Catholic church.

In 1555, a compromise was reached at Augsburg. Called the Peace of Augsburg, it allowed every German ruler to choose Lutheranism or Roman Catholicism for his subjects. Most rulers of northern Germany chose Lutheranism; most in southern Germany remained Roman Catholic.

The Protestant Reformation Spreads. Two religious thinkers in Switzerland, Huldreich Zwingli and John Calvin, helped to spread the Protestant Reformation.

Zwingli, a Roman Catholic priest, studied the humanist writers and believed that the church needed reform. He agreed with Luther on most points.

Zwingli's ideas spread and, in 1523, the Zurich magistrates called a public meeting to decide between Catholicism and Zwingli's Protestantism. Zwingli's side won. The people of Zurich adopted Protestantism, closed monasteries, and abolished religious statues and pictures. By 1528, the major Swiss cities had become Protestant. In more conservative rural areas, however, the people remained Roman Catholic.

Civil war broke out between Protestants and Catholics. Zwingli was killed in battle. After the war each district of Switzerland chose its own form of religion.

John Calvin Spreads New Ideas. John Calvin, a French lawyer, settled in Switzerland in 1536. Calvin agreed with many of Luther's ideas but emphasized predestination. He also simplified religious rituals and abandoned statues and organ music. Calvin, like Luther, believed that God grants salvation to the faithful alone. Since God knows everything, he knows who will be faithful and be saved. God makes the choice, not each individual.

Calvinists were never absolutely sure they had been chosen for salvation. They believed that upright moral conduct was a sign of God's favor. Fighting, swearing, laughing in church, playing cards, dancing, and theatergoing were all prohibited. Like other Protestants, they believed they could find religious truth in the Bible.

Most importantly, Calvin developed a pattern of church government that separated church officials from civil control. Calvinists in Geneva were one of the first Protestant churches in Europe to gain independence from civil government. Calvin's reforms spread throughout Europe. John Knox brought Calvinist ideas to Scotland and founded Presbyterianism. French Calvinists, called Huguenots (HYOO guh NAHTS), became a minority in France. English Protestants, influenced by Calvin, were called Puritans. In Dutch provinces, Calvinists formed the Dutch Reformed Church. Peo-ple in Poland and Hungary also became Calvinists but later were reconverted to Roman Catholicism. See the map, Protestant and Catholic Europe, 1600, below.

The Reformation in England

Protestantism spread to England for political rather than religious reasons. Henry VIII, who ruled from 1509 to 1547, wanted a son to continue the Tudor line. However, his wife, Catherine of Aragon, bore only a daughter, Mary.

The Act of Supremacy. Henry appealed to Pope Clement VII in 1527 to annul his marriage. Henry hoped to marry Anne Boleyn, a pretty young lady at court. The pope might have granted Henry's request; however, Catherine was the aunt of the Holy Roman Emperor, Charles V. Rather than offend Charles, the pope refused.

Protestant and Catholic Europe, 1600

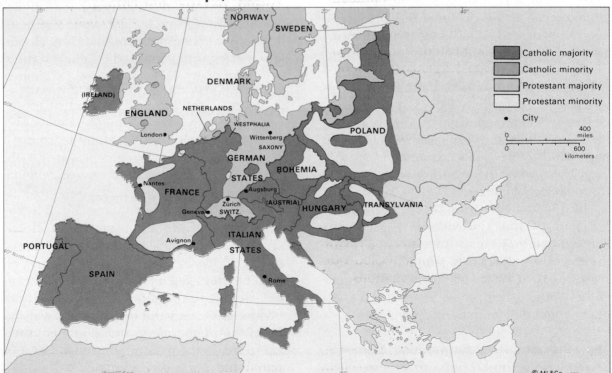

Map Skills   1. In what country is the city of Geneva? **2.** Were the German states primarily Catholic or Protestant? **3.** Were more western Europeans, Protestant or Catholic?

Finally, in 1534, Henry asked Parliament to declare him the head of the Church of England. Parliament passed the Act of Supremacy, making the ruler of England the supreme head of the Church of England.

Henry's marriage to Anne Boleyn did not last long. She bore a daughter, Elizabeth. When Anne resisted divorce, Henry had her beheaded. He married four more times. Only his third wife bore him a son.

Henry VIII's Successors. When Henry died in 1547, his 10—year-old son became King Edward VI. Edward's advisers, influenced by Lutheran and Calvinist ideas, changed many Catholic rituals and made the Church of England more Protestant.

Edward died in 1553, and his half-sister, Mary, succeeded him. Queen Mary, daughter of Catherine of Aragon and wife of Philip II of Spain, tried unsuccessfully to restore Roman Catholicism to England. Mary died, however, without an heir.

Mary's successor and half-sister, Elizabeth, ruled for 45 years. Queen Elizabeth I insisted on a strong national church and returned England to Protestantism. In 1563, Parliament approved the Thirty-nine Articles, the official religious statement of the Church of England.

Under the Thirty-nine Articles, the Church of England, or Anglican church, kept ceremonies and the organization of the Catholic church. Church services, however, were in English rather than Latin, and priests were allowed to marry.

Some people in England thought that the Thirty-nine Articles did not go far enough and that the church needed further reform. Many of these people, called Puritans, formed their own congregations.

Catholic Counter Reformation

Luther and Calvin did not intend to set up separate churches. Like most religious leaders of the time, they believed that all Christians should belong to one true church.

For 20 years, the popes failed to take effective action either for or against the reformers. However, the Protestant arguments, and the conversion of much of Europe to new Christian denominations, demanded attention. Pope Paul III finally made the first major reforms in the 1540s.

The Society of Jesus. In 1540, Pope Paul III approved the request of Ignatius of Loyola to establish a new religious order called the Society of Jesus. Ignatius, a Spanish noble and soldier, spent much of his time reading and thinking about the lives of Christ and the saints.

Ignatius left the army and attended the University of Paris. There, he and a small group of friends organized themselves into a religious order.

Members of the Society of Jesus, known as Jesuits, thought of themselves as soldiers of Christ. Their goal was to end the spread of Protestantism and reconvert people who had left the Roman church. Jesuits brought Poland, Bavaria, and Hungary back to Roman Catholicism. They also helped stop the spread of Calvinism in France.

The Council of Trent. In 1545, Pope Paul III called a council of church leaders to meet in Trent, Italy. This council was to make needed reforms in the Roman church. The council rejected Protestant teachings.

The Council of Trent declared that the Bible was not the only source of religious truth. Church traditions also contained religious truths. Council members refused to accept any of the Protestant reforms and reaffirmed the pope as the head of the Roman Catholic church.

The council did ban the sale of indulgences and the buying or selling of church offices. Bishops were instructed to see that members of the clergy were well-educated and lived moral lives. The council also prepared the *Index of Prohibited Books*, listing books the church considered immoral or dangerous to the faith.

Effects of Religious Upheaval. The Protestant Reformation and the Catholic Counter Reformation affected Europe in a number of ways. First, Europeans became more informed about Christian doctrine. Several interpretations and forms of worship were now available, which encouraged people to think for themselves.

Second, since reading and understanding the Bible were necessary for salvation, Protestants stressed education. Many schools were set up to teach people to read. Catholics built universities to educate priests.

Third, kings and national governments used religious controversy to increase their power. Monarchs generally exercised both religious and civil authority.

Finally, wars often had religious, as well as political, causes. Catholic and Protestant rulers fought to gain religious converts as well as to increase their power.

Catholic France. The last member of the royal house of Valois, which had ruled France since 1328, died in 1589. Two families then fought for the French throne. Henry of Navarre, a Huguenot member of the Bourbon family, claimed the throne, as did the Catholic Guise family. In 1594, Henry gave up his Protestantism and accepted the faith of the majority of his subjects and became King Henry IV.

To bring peace to France, Henry issued the Edict of Nantes. This edict granted the Huguenots religious freedom. Huguenot leaders were allowed to fortify and govern about 100 French towns.

The Hapsburg Empire. The Holy Roman Emperor, Charles V, inherited Bohemia, Austria, most of Italy, Spain, and the Netherlands in the early 1500s. Along with his titles, Charles inherited many responsibilities. In Spain, he was responsible for maintaining the large overseas empire and defending Spain against its rivals, France and England. As Holy Roman Emperor, he was responsible for defending Europe

In France, the religious conflict erupted in the St. Bartholomew's Day Massacre in 1572, when the French queen ordered the slaughter of Huguenots.

against the Turks. In Germany, he was responsible for upholding the Roman Catholic cause against the Protestant princes.

In 1556, after 40 years of ruling Spain and almost as long as Holy Roman Emperor, Charles abdicated the throne and retired to a monastery. His brother, Ferdinand, inherited Bohemia, Austria, and the title, Holy Roman Emperor. Charles's son, Philip II, received the Spanish possessions.

Philip thought of Spain as the defender of the Roman Catholic church. He decided to invade England. In addition to returning England to the Roman Catholic church, he hoped to stop English attacks on Spanish shipping. Philip had to conquer England or give up control of the sea. In 1588, Philip sent the Spanish Armada, a great fleet, to pick up Spanish troops from the southern Netherlands and then attack England.

The Spanish armada was made up of 130 ships carrying about 8,000 sailors and 19,000 Spanish soldiers. Philip planned to attack England by land and sea.

The armada was so large that it could not be assembled in one port. The English discovered the Spanish plans, and the English adventurer, Sir Francis Drake, destroyed 37 ships at Cadiz before the armada set sail for England.

The large ships of the Spanish armada were better suited for the calm waters of the Mediterranean Sea than for the unpredictable English Channel. The English ships in the makeshift collection that met the armada were small and maneuverable. The English guns fired faster and had a longer range than those of the Spanish. The English damaged many of the Spanish galleons and sunk a few as they tried to sail the Channel on their way to the Netherlands.

The remaining Spanish ships were severely damaged, and the commander decided to return to Spain. Rather than move through the English Channel again, he sailed north around Scotland and Ireland. Off the Irish coast, the ships were caught in a violent storm. Less than half of the once proud Spanish force returned to Spain.

The Thirty Years War. Between 1618 and 1635, Ferdinand II of Austria, a grandnephew of Philip, and the Austrian Hapsburg, tried to reunite the divided German territories. The Thirty Years War began when the Protestant nobles of Bohemia revolted against Hapsburg control. Ferdinand defeated the Bohemians.

The war brought Protestant Denmark and Sweden and even Catholic France into the conflict against the Hapsburgs of Germany and Spain. The fighting left Germany devastated. The war was ended with the Treaty of Westphalia in 1648. The treaty greatly reduced the size and authority of the Holy Roman Empire.

First, the Treaty of Westphalia made German rulers almost independent of the Holy Roman Emperor. They could make war or peace without the emperor's interference. Second, rulers agreed to recognize the Dutch Netherlands and Switzerland as independent nations. Third, the French received Alsace, an important area along the Rhine River. Sweden received control of German lands along the Baltic coast.

The devastation of Germany eliminated the Hapsburg threat to other nations. In contrast, the gains of France and Sweden made them powerful. France became the dominant power in European politics.

The New Europe. For centuries, most western Europeans had supported the Roman Catholic church. Beginning in the fifteenth century, people began to call for church reform. The people of Europe experienced a religious upheaval. By the middle of the 1600s, they could choose from a number of Christian denominations. Religious wars changed the map of western Europe.

SECTION 3 *Study Skills*

Developing Vocabulary 1. Who is a heretic? 2. What is an indulgence? 3. Define armada. 4. Explain the doctrine of predestination.

Reviewing Main Ideas 1. Explain the importance of John Wycliffe's beliefs. 2. Explain two Lutheran ideas that appealed to German nobles. 3. What were the results of the Peace of Augsburg? 4. Compare the actions and influence of Luther, Zwingli, and Calvin. 5. What was the main goal of the Jesuits?

Understanding Cause and Effect 1. Explain why the sale of indulgences caused unrest among Catholics. 2. Explain three reforms brought about by the Council of Trent. 3. How were the causes of the Reformation in England different from the causes of Luther's break with Catholicism? 4. What were the effects of the Thirty Years War?

Understanding Chronology 1. How long after Luther posted the 95 theses was he excommunicated? 2. In what year did Spain send out an armada to fight England?

Challenge What are the advantages and disadvantages of having a ruler, such as Henry VIII, make both religious and political decisions?

4 Europe and Modern Science

OBJECTIVE: *To understand the causes and consequences of the advances in science during the Renaissance*

The Search for Truth

One of the most important consequences of the Protestant Reformation was to end the Catholic church's control of people's beliefs about God, nature, and the universe. The Protestant religions encouraged individuals to go directly to the Bible and find the truth. The search for knowledge was no longer controlled by a single authority.

In contrast, leaders of the Islamic world and China generally remained in agreement about the truths that guided creation, nature, and the universe. Chinese and Muslims made advances in science during the fifteenth and sixteenth centuries. However, religious and cultural leaders put narrow limits on free inquiry. In Europe, inquiry about the universe was opening up.

European scientists of the sixteenth century inherited a great storehouse of scientific knowledge from the ancient Chinese, Greeks, Romans, Arabs, Indians, and other peoples. They were aware of the scientific advances made in the Middle Ages.

Scientists of the Renaissance were able to use several important new inventions that allowed them to see and measure more accurately. Among the new tools invented about 1600 were the microscope, the thermometer, the telescope, and the barometer. Using these instruments, Renaissance scientists conducted experiments with light, air, water, and magnetism. New discoveries went far beyond the scientific knowledge of the past.

The Inventions of Leonardo da Vinci. The brilliant and curious mind of the artist, Leonardo da Vinci, led him to investigate many areas. He was fascinated by water and designed pumps, canals, and studied the causes of waves. He also wrote a treatise on geometry.

In his notebook, Leonardo da Vinci drew designs for a helicopter, a giant crossbow, a rapid-fire crossbow, a finned missile, a mortar with shrapnel, a drilling machine, a diving suit, and floats for walking on water. If his designs for new machines had been pub-

---

VOCABULARY DEVELOPMENT

heliocentric (HEE lee oh SEHN trihk) *adj.:* the theory that the sun is the center of the universe. From the Greek words *helios*, meaning sun, and *kentron*, meaning center.

geocentric (JEE oh SEHN trihk) *adj.:* the theory that the earth is the center of the universe. From the Greek words *ge*, meaning earth, and *kentron*, meaning center.

quadrant (KWAHD ruhnt) *noun:* an instrument for measuring altitude in navigation and astronomy.

elliptical (ih LIHP tih kuhl) *adj:* a less than perfect circle. From the Greek word, *elleipein*, meaning to fall short.

deductive reasoning: reasoning from a general principle to a specific conclusion.

inductive reasoning: reasoning from particular facts to a general conclusion.

---

lished, technology might have advanced rapidly. Leonardo da Vinci believed in experimentation. He wrote in his notebook:

❝ Those sciences are vain and full of errors which are not born of experiment, the mother of all certainty. ❞

The Universe of Copernicus. After the death of the Polish astronomer Nicolaus Copernicus in 1543 his book *Concerning the Revolutions of the Celestial Spheres* was published. The book changed the way educated people thought about the universe.

For over 30 years, Copernicus studied books that had been written about astronomy. In his reading, he discovered the writings of Aristarchus of Samos, who lived in the 200s B.C. Aristarchus believed that the universe was heliocentric, meaning that the sun was at the center of the universe. Planets revolved around the sun, rather than it around them.

In his book, Copernicus brilliantly defended the heliocentric view of Aristarchus. He disagreed with the traditional view of the universe that dated from the Greek scientist, Ptolemy, in the second century A.D. (see pages 139 and 143–144). Ptolemy, and most later scholars, believed in the geocentric theory. This theory maintained that the earth was the center of the universe. The sun and planets revolved around it.

Few people paid any attention to Copernicus. People could see and feel that the earth was not moving. Therefore, the planets and sun must move. In addition, many people rejected the new idea because it contradicted the views of the Catholic church.

Copernicus did not test or prove his new theories. However, a Danish scientist, Tycho (TEE koh) Brahe (BRAH huh), who lived from 1546 to 1601, supplied supportive evidence.

Over the course of 21 years, Brahe accurately recorded the travel of the planets through their orbits. Brahe used astrolabes, quadrants, and other instruments to track the planets. The telescope had not yet been

Polish astronomer Nicolaus Copernicus observes the skies. Copernicus believed the sun, rather than the earth, was at the center of the universe.

invented. Brahe's records showed that the planets did not travel in perfect circles.

Elliptical Orbits. The German scientist and mathematician, Johannes Kepler, a former assistant of Brahe, continued the work of Copernicus and Brahe. Kepler noticed that Brahe's data indicated irregularities in the movement of Mars.

Kepler could not find a circular path that agreed with Brahe's observations. He searched for an explanation using mathematical calculations. Eventually, he reached an exciting conclusion. People had long believed that the planets move in circular orbits. Kepler realized that Mars, and all the planets, move in elliptical orbits. However, only mathematicians could understand Kepler's proof.

The Ideas of Francis Bacon. The ideas of Francis Bacon, who lived from 1561 to 1626, marked the beginning of a new era in

European science. Bacon, an English philosopher and statesman, was an influential supporter of the use of scientific methods to solve problems. He planned to write a six-volume work surveying the methods, theories, and achievements of experimental science. Only the first two volumes were completed before his death.

Bacon believed that if people eliminated four prejudices, they could discover the truth. The first prejudice is the tendency to generalize or form general rules from only a few specific examples. For instance, people suppose a greater order and regularity in nature than actually exits.

Second, people make judgments and decisions based on their state of mind, social background, and previous experience. People of different backgrounds judge matters in different ways. Bacon urged people to judge information objectively.

Third, words are not precise. Since people communicate with words, confusion arises in determining exact meaning.

Fourth, previous learning and philosophies influence people. Earlier knowledge is not always correct.

Bacon said that people should not rely on deductive reasoning based on biased observation and previous knowledge. Instead, they should use an inductive, or experimental, method to solve problems. Using inductive reasoning, a person examines particular cases or instances of a phenomenon and applies the facts to form a general rule.

Descartes and Analytic Geometry.

René Descartes (day KAHRT) was born in France in 1596. He was able to pursue a life of study when an inheritance freed him from the need to earn a living. Trained by Jesuits and gifted in mathematics, he combined the ideas and techniques of algebra and geometry to develop analytic geometry.

Descartes believed that questions of philosophy and theology could be answered by using techniques of mathematical reasoning. Each step in the solution would follow logically and naturally from the prior step. Descartes believed that he logically proved his own existence with the statement, "I think, therefore I am."

The Work of Galileo.

An Italian astronomer and physicist, Galileo (GAL uh LEE oh), has been called the founder of modern experimental science. Using a primitive telescope, Galileo was the first person to see the mountains on the moon, rings around Saturn, the satellites of Jupiter, and sunspots. He realized that the heliocentric theory of Copernicus was true.

Galileo was born in Pisa, Italy, in 1564. He made his first important scientific discovery at the age of 20 when he discovered the principle of the pendulum. According to a story, Galileo watched the swinging of a chandelier in the cathedral of Pisa. He timed the swings of the lamp with his pulse beat and found that each swing, even as it slowed and moved a shorter distance, took the same amount of time. This observation was later applied in making the pendulum clock and accurately measuring time.

Galileo emphasized testing theories by observation and experimentation. At the age of 25, he discovered the law of falling bodies. This law was counter to Aristotle's belief that the heavier the object, the faster it falls. According to legend, Galileo dropped two unequal weights from the top of the Leaning Tower of Pisa. A crowd of people saw both objects strike the ground at about the same time. This fact laid the foundation for the study of matter in motion, or mechanics.

In 1609, Galileo made his first telescope. A telescope magnifies objects seen from far away, such as the planets. Most historians think that a Dutch optician made the first telescope. Galileo, hearing about the invention, also built one.

Galileo's telescope magnified objects only 33 times. It could be focused on only a small area, about one-fourth the size of the moon. Nevertheless, using his telescope,

Galileo, at center, explains the law of falling bodies in this fresco. Giovanni de Medici watches glumly on the side.

Galileo was the first person to see that the moon did not shine by its own light. Galileo also studied the Milky Way. He observed that the Milky Way contained stars "so numerous as to be almost beyond belief."

In 1632, Galileo published his findings in *Dialogue on the Two Great Systems of the World*. Galileo's observations supported the Copernican theory of the universe. Some scholars supported Galileo; others scoffed at his work.

The Catholic church disapproved of Galileo's work, but he continued to support the heliocentric theory. Church officials placed the works of Copernicus on the *Index of Forbidden Books*. The church summoned Galileo before a court. After a long trial, Galileo was forced to say publicly that he would give up his belief in the theory. Privately, however, he did not change his views.

The court sentenced Galileo to an indefinite prison term. Instead of being put in prison, he was confined to his house in Florence, Italy. He died there in 1642.

Progress in Biology. Andreas Vesalius (vih SAY lee uhs), a Belgian scientist, pioneered the study of anatomy. Vesalius wanted to know what made the human body work. For example, how did his body make his arm move when he lifted his hand and how did he move his legs to walk?

He dissected human bodies to find the answers to his questions. In 1543, he published the results of his studies in *On the Fabric of the Human Body*. The book explained everything Vesalius had discovered about the parts of the body, the veins, the muscles, and even the brain.

Vesalius made many mistakes. He did not know that the heart pumps blood through the body. He did, however, discover where the veins are and how the heart is made. His book, with nearly 300 illustrations, was beautiful, and the printing was clear and easy to read.

An English physician, William Harvey, was the first person to understand and describe how the blood circulates through the body. He also understood the function of blood vessels. He published *An Anatomical Treatise on the Motion of the Heart and Blood in Animals*, in 1628.

Galileo, Brahe, Kepler, Harvey, and others scientists of the seventeenth century dramatically altered people's perception of the earth in relation to the universe. They tested their theories by careful, scientific experiments. When evidence from experiments contradicted the Bible, or the church's interpretation of the Bible, scientists searched for explanations. When scientific evidence contradicted earlier theories, scientists gave up previous ideas.

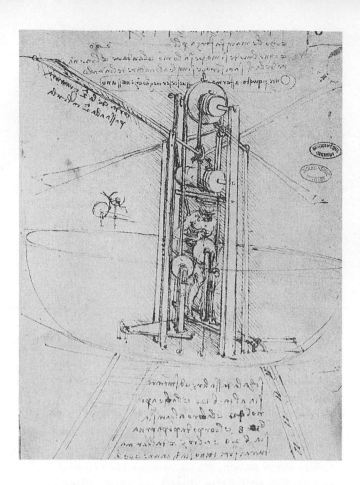

At left, Leonardo da Vinci's drawing of manned flight in a "standing ornithopter," from 1490, anticipates the invention of the modern-day helicopter at right.

A new scientific reasoning replaced the Renaissance tendency to build on Greek and Roman ideas. Scientists, explorers, and religious leaders tested traditional views, and the ideas of the Greeks and Romans, against new evidence. Using a rational approach and a sense of adventure, the pioneers of the sixteenth and early seventeenth centuries laid the foundations for a new view of nature and the universe. Scientists of the sixteenth and seventeenth centuries, however, continued to hold firm religious beliefs. Religious ideas played a major role in shaping European civilization.

SECTION 4 *Study Skills*

Developing Vocabulary 1. What is the difference between heliocentric and geocentric views of the universe? 2. Explain the difference between deductive and inductive reasoning.

3. What is the meaning of the Greek origin of the word elliptical?

Reviewing Main Ideas 1. Why do Francis Bacon's ideas represent the beginning of a new era of science? 2. List and explain the four prejudices that Bacon felt kept people from learning the truth? 3. Which philosopher is associated with mathematical logic? Why? 4. Describe Kepler's and Galileo's contributions to the study of astronomy.

Understanding Cause and Effect 1. Describe the effect on Renaissance science of improved tools for seeing and measuring accurately. 2. Explain why the ideas of Copernicus were not immediately accepted.

Understanding Chronology 1. How old were the ideas about the universe that Copernicus challenged? 2. What was the significance of the book Galileo published in 1632?

Challenge Describe the Renaissance attitude that encouraged scientific exploration. Does that attitude still exist?

The Geography of Capital Cities

A national capital is both the showplace and nerve center of a nation. The location of the capital can be a statement of a nation's past as well as its present priorities and interests. Examples from Latin America demonstrate how geography as well as a country's heritage can influence the location of a nation's capital.

Locating the Capital

The capitals of many countries are located near the geographic center of the country. One advantage of a centrally located capital is that the government is as close as possible to all parts of the state. Panama, Colombia, and Chile are some of the Latin American countries with centrally located capitals.

Coastal Capitals. Some capital cities are at an edge of the country's territory. In cases such as Buenos Aires, capital of Argentina, topography makes the location desirable. Located where the La Plata river reaches the ocean, the capital is the center of shipping and communication. Across the La Plata river is Montevideo, the capital of Uruguay. At the northern edge of South America lies Caracas, the capital of Venezuela. Caracas relies on two coastal cities for importing and exporting goods.

Historic Site. Governments sometimes locate capitals in places that have political or historical meaning. A nation which has fought to win land from another nation may locate its capital within the newly won territory. This is a sign that the nation means to stay on the new land. For example, after the Spanish conquered the Aztecs, they built Mexico City on the site of Tenochtitlán.

Bolivia's Divided Capital. Bolivia is one of the few countries in the world with a divided capital. The official capital is Sucre. Since 1898, however, most government offices have been in La Paz. The government moved to La Paz because it has better transportation to the rest of the country.

The Case of Brasília

Most nations have their capitals in major cities. Occasionally, however, nations intentionally build their capital far from any population center. In April 1960, Brazil dedicated a partially finished capital city set in the country's interior.

The creation of a new capital for Brazil was a very important decision. Prior to 1960, Brazil's capital city was Rio de Janeiro. Rio is a large city on the Atlantic coast. This location reflected the nation's colonization by the Portuguese. In the 1950s, the government of Brazil decided to reduce its emphasis on past European connections. Brazil wanted to focus on its future. That future lay in the resources of its largely undeveloped interior, including the savannah area chosen for the new city.

Attracting New Settlers. The Brazilian government wanted to attract settlers to the Amazon region. One way to do this was to move Brazil's capital to a location about 400 miles inland from the Atlantic Ocean. This new city required planning. The plan had to include streets, government buildings, housing, and shops. Workers built railroads to transport goods into the city from the coast. In order to attract people to the new location, the national government provided economic incentives. People who worked in the new national capital were paid high sal-

At left, a paper mill in Brazil. Above, a panoramic view of Brasília, the capital of Brazil. Both show how people change the environment.

aries and wages. Even with economic incentives, attracting people to Brasília was not easy. Professional people were needed in the new capital, but many people were firmly tied to the old capital. They had family and friends there. They enjoyed its warm, luxurious beaches. Rio had a wide variety of cultural attractions.

Growth and Problems. Initially, the growth of Brasília was slow. A presidential palace, a chapel, a cathedral, the congress building, and a hotel were among the first buildings. Later, private investors came to the city and played a role in its continuing development.

By the mid-1980s, Brasília had grown to become a metropolitan center with a population of some 2.5 million people. Residents from rural areas moved to the city, drawn by the possibility of finding jobs in the capital.

Though the government paid many of its workers well, other jobs in Brasília were low-paying. Brasília needed janitors, porters, and maids. Still, for many poor Brazilians today, these jobs represent a beginning.

Many of these people from the rural areas live in shacks which they have built from whatever materials they were able to find. Bits of wood, metal, or cardboard are shaped into shelters on the edge of the city. Through hard work, they may be able to move to more permanent housing. The new city is part of a bold attempt to tap the resources of the Brazilian interior.

STUDY SKILLS Understanding Geography
1. What is a capital city?
2. What is the benefit of a centrally-located capital city?
3. Give three reasons why a nation's capital might not be centrally located.
4. Why did the Brazilians develop Brasília in the interior of their nation?
5. What is unusual about Bolivia's capital?

CHAPTER 18 *Summary & Review*

Summarizing Main Ideas

Between 1450 and 1650, national states led by strong monarchs developed in England, France, Spain, and Portugal. Military strength, linked to the development of firearms, promoted the development of these nations.

The Renaissance, a new pursuit of learning and an interest in ancient culture, began in Italy in the 1300s. Renaissance ideas spread to northern Europe.

In religion, leaders such as Martin Luther and John Calvin challenged the teachings of the Roman Catholic church. Efforts to reform the Catholic church led to the formation of several new groups of Christians.

New attitudes toward observation and experimentation encouraged scientific development. Scholars studied physics and examined the human body.

Questions for Critical Thinking

COMPREHENSION Interpreting Events

1. Explain the significance of a national ruler breaking with the established church.
2. Compare and contrast the ideas expressed in Luther's 95 Theses and Parliament's Thirty-Nine Articles.

ANALYSIS Identifying Trends

1. Analyze the impact of the Reformation on the power of the Catholic church.
2. Examine the importance of the War of the Roses and the Thirty Years War for the growth of national states.

APPLICATION Comparing Past and Present

1. People in the new national states developed strong patriotism, which led to rivalry among nations. List three recent examples where this pattern has reoccurred.
2. Compare the distribution of Catholics and Protestants on the map titled Protestant and Catholic Europe, 1600, on page 408. Does either religion have a majority?

SYNTHESIS Developing Research Skills

1. Compare and contrast the doctrines of Martin Luther and John Calvin.
2. Write a report on one of the following Renaissance scientists: Kepler, Copernicus, Galileo, Brahe, or da Vinci.
3. Compare and contrast the styles of the artists: Giotto, Michelangelo, and da Vinci.

EVALUATION Weighing Consequences

How did the use of the printing press make possible the rapid spread of the Protestant Reformation?

CHALLENGE

Discuss the long term effect of Renaissance scientists on scientific thought.

Renaissance and Reformation Writers	
Author	**Title**
Erasmus	*In Praise of Folly* (1511)
Sir Thomas More	*Utopia* (1516)
William Shake-speare	*Romeo and Juliet* (1595), *Hamlet* (1601)
Niccolo Machiavelli	*The Prince* (1513)
Martin Luther	*Ninety-Five Theses* (1517)
John Calvin	*Institutes of the Christian Religion* (1536)
Nicolaus Copernicus	*Concerning the Revolutions of the Celestial Spheres* (1543)
William Harvey	*An Anatomical Treatise on the Motion of the Heart and Blood in Animals* (1628)
René Descartes	*Discourse on Method* (1637)
Galileo	*Dialogue on the Two Great Systems of the World* (1632)
Andreas Vesalius	*On the Fabric of the Human Body* (1543)

CHAPTER 19

Three Muslim Empires

GLOBAL TIME LINE

TIME

1502–1736 Turkish warriors rule the Safavid Empire of Shi'ite Muslims in Iran

PEOPLE

1453 Sultan Mehmed II conquers Constantinople, changes the name to Istanbul, and makes the city his capital

1467–1520 Selim I expands the Ottoman Empire into Syria and Egypt

1500–1524 Shah Isma'il conquers Persia and Iraq and forcibly converts people to Shi'ism

PLACE

1400s *Soviet Union;*[1] Azerbaijan becomes the homeland of the Safavid Turks

1453 *Turkey;*[2] Constantinople falls to the Ottoman Turks

1500s *England;*[3] Black lead pencils first used for writing

1450   1475   1500

Linking Past to Present

January 20, 1981, was a dramatic day in American history. In Washington, D.C., a new president was being inaugurated. Simultaneously, 52 Americans who had been held hostage in Iran for more than a year were being released. At that time, Iran was undergoing a revolution. Its leaders were Muslims of the Shi'ite sect.

Shi'ism was the dominant Muslim sect in Iran in the sixteenth century under the Safavid rule. Two other powerful Muslim states developed at about the same time—the Ottoman Empire in Asia Minor and the Moghul Empire in India. These states ruled a vast area in Eurasia and northern Africa. This chapter describes the important effect that these three Muslim empires had on the course of world history.

A sixth-century Christian cathedral in Istanbul used as a mosque after 1453.

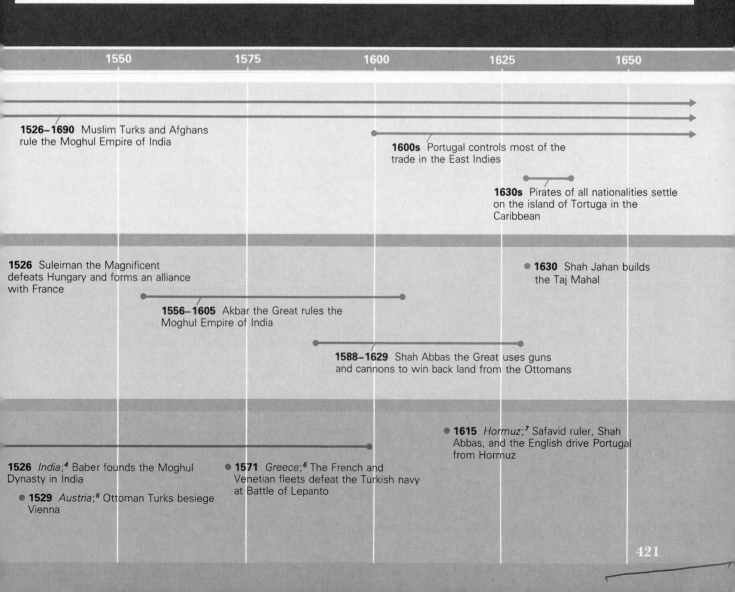

1550   1575   1600   1625   1650

1526–1690 Muslim Turks and Afghans rule the Moghul Empire of India

1600s Portugal controls most of the trade in the East Indies

1630s Pirates of all nationalities settle on the island of Tortuga in the Caribbean

1526 Suleiman the Magnificent defeats Hungary and forms an alliance with France

1630 Shah Jahan builds the Taj Mahal

1556–1605 Akbar the Great rules the Moghul Empire of India

1588–1629 Shah Abbas the Great uses guns and cannons to win back land from the Ottomans

1615 *Hormuz;*[7] Safavid ruler, Shah Abbas, and the English drive Portugal from Hormuz

1526 *India;*[4] Baber founds the Moghul Dynasty in India

1571 *Greece;*[6] The French and Venetian fleets defeat the Turkish navy at Battle of Lepanto

1529 *Austria;*[5] Ottoman Turks besiege Vienna

1 The Ottoman Empire

OBJECTIVE: *To understand the expansion of the Ottoman Empire in the fifteenth and sixteenth centuries*

Rise of the Ottomans

Most of Asia Minor in the fourteenth century was divided into several small states ruled by Turkish princes. Osman, a warrior who lived from 1258 to 1324, founded one of these states, in northwestern Asia Minor. He led his mounted warriors on raids against both the Byzantine cities and the neighboring Muslim states.

Osman was the first of a line of 10 sultans who conquered territory throughout the Middle East and southeastern Europe. The empire they developed was known by a form of Osman's name, Ottoman. See the map, Ottoman Empire, page 424. The Ottoman Empire existed until 1922. Few other empires in history have endured as long as the Ottoman Empire.

VOCABULARY DEVELOPMENT

elite (ih LEET) *noun:* the group regarded as the best, most distinguished, or most powerful. From the French word, *eslire*, meaning to choose.

Flemish (FLEHM ihsh) *adj.:* of the people of Flanders. In the Middle Ages, Flanders was a country on the North Sea. Today the area along the coast of the North Sea is a part of France and Belgium.

deficit (DEHF uh siht) *noun:* an excess of losses over profits or expenditures over income. From the Latin word, *deficere*, meaning to lack or to fail.

The Conquest of Constantinople. By the beginning of the fifteenth century, the Ottoman Empire had conquered most of Asia Minor and part of the Balkans. The empire had conquered the land on all sides of the great fortress city of Constantinople. In 1453, the Ottoman sultan, Mehmed II (meh MEHT), concentrated his army and navy around Constantinople. The city that had once ruled the powerful Byzantine Empire was prepared to make a strong stand against the new challenger. A Turkish writer, Ashikpashazade, recorded the following:

❝ For fifty days the battle went on by day and night. On the fifty-first day, the Sultan ordered free plunder. They attacked. On the fifty-first day, a Tuesday, the fortress was captured. There was good booty and plunder. Gold and silver and jewels and fine stuffs were brought and stacked in the camp market. They [the soldiers] began to sell them [the goods]. They made the people of the city slaves and killed their emperor, and the ghazis (GAH zeez) [soldiers] embraced their pretty girls. . . . On the first Friday after the conquest they recited the communal prayer in Aya Sofya [Hagia Sophia, the largest Christian church in Constantinople], and the Islamic invocation was read in the name of [the] Sultan . . . ❞

The conversion of Hagia Sophia into a Muslim mosque symbolized the success of the Muslims over the Byzantine Empire.

The Ottoman Government. Mehmed did not destroy Constantinople. Instead, it became the capital of the Ottoman Empire, and the center of imperial government.

The Ottoman government was made up of four major branches. The first was the palace of the sultan. Members of the palace helped the sultan to conduct his personal business. This group included the sultan's advisers, servants, bodyguards, wives, and female slaves. The wives and female slaves inhabited the part of the palace known as the harem. These women always stayed within the palace walls. Sometimes they had great influence on the sultan's policies.

The second branch of government was the bureaucracy that administered the empire. Directing the bureaucracy was the grand vizier (vih ZIHR), the most powerful person in the empire under the sultan. The bureaucracy was responsible for running the imperial treasury and collecting taxes. Jews and Christians had to pay special taxes, but they could govern their own affairs.

The government's third branch supervised education and religious affairs. Muslim scholars and other officials also operated the Islamic law courts.

The Ottoman Army. The army was the fourth department of the government. In the early days of the Ottoman Empire, the army relied on Turkish cavalry. Gradually, the sultans formed an army of infantry soldiers who were their personal slaves. Since these slaves had no property or family ties, they were totally loyal to the sultan.

Most slave soldiers came from the Christian population of the empire. This system of recruitment was called *devshirme*, (dehv SHUHR may) or boy levy. About every fourth year, government officials would visit a village. The officials would obtain from the village priest a list of boys between 12 and 20 years old. Then the officials would order all of the boys to attend a meeting where each would be evaluated. The boys evaluated as the best potential soldiers, or the most in-

A sixteenth-century Turkish miniature depicts a battle between the Ottoman sultan, Bayezid II, and the Byzantines.

Ottoman Empire, 1650

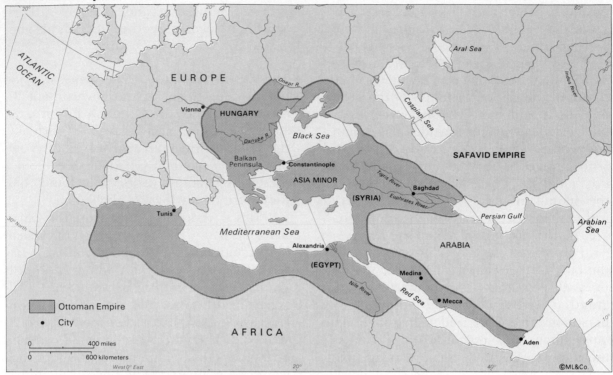

Map Skills **1.** What bodies of water border the Ottoman Empire? **2.** What major rivers flow through the Ottoman Empire?

telligent, would be drafted into service. Orphans, only sons, and married youths usually were exempted.

Some of the Christian boys taken by the slave recruiters were trained to serve as government officials. In these jobs, intelligent and ambitious boys could become powerful and wealthy administrators. To do so, they had to convert to Islam, vow to serve the sultan loyally, and learn the special customs and etiquette of the government leaders. Christian families who wanted their sons to become powerful sometimes brought them voluntarily to the slave recruiters.

The army provided excellent military training. Soldiers learned to use handguns and cannons with skill. The best soldiers were placed in an elite fighting force called the Janissary (JAN uh SER ee) Corps. Janissaries were not permitted to marry or own land, and they had to live in special barracks.

They fought in all of the great Ottoman military victories in the fifteenth and sixteenth centuries.

The Ottoman Strength

FOCUS ON SOURCES

The power of the Ottoman Empire frightened European Christians. Few people in Europe had actually traveled to the Middle East, but many heard of the Turks' conquests. In 1589, a Flemish man, Augier Ghislain de Busbecq (BOOZ BEHK), published a book describing the life of the Ottomans. The book was based on four letters de Busbecq wrote while serving as Hapsburg ambassador in Constantinople. In this excerpt, de Busbecq describes two reasons for the strength of the Ottoman

Empire—their system of promoting individuals and the Janissaries. He then contrasts Muslim and Christian soldiers:

Promoting Individuals. " In making his appointments the Sultan pays no regard to any pretensions [claims] on the score [basis] of wealth or rank, nor does he take into consideration recommendations or popularity; he considers each case on its own merits, and examines carefully into the character, ability, and disposition of the man whose promotion is in question. It is by merit that men rise in the service, a system which ensures that posts should be assigned only to the competent. . . . Those who receive the highest offices from the Sultan are for the most part the sons of shepherds or herdsmen, and so far from being ashamed of their parentage, they actually glory in it, and consider it a matter of boasting that they owe nothing to the accident of birth; for they do not believe that high qualities are either natural or hereditary, nor do they think that they can be handed down from father to son, but that they are partly the gift of God, and partly the result of good training, industry, and unwearied zeal . . .

This is the reason that they are successful in their undertakings, that they lord it over others, and are daily extending the bounds of their empire. These are not our ideas, with us there is no opening left for merit; birth is the standard for everything; the prestige of birth is the sole key to advancement in the public service. . . .

The Janissaries. At Buda I made my first acquaintance with the Janissaries; this is the name by which the Turks call the infantry of the royal guard. . . . They are scattered through every part of the empire, either to garrison the forts against the enemy, or to protect the Christians and Jews from the violence of the mob. There is no district with any considerable amount of population, no borough or city, which has not a detachment of Janissaries to protect Christians, Jews and

An Ottoman commander and the Janissary Corps enter the capital of Persian Georgia in this sixteenth-century Turkish miniature.

other helpless people from outrage, violence, and wrong.

A garrison [force] of Janissaries is always stationed in the citadel of Buda. The dress of the men consists of a robe reaching down to the ankles, while to cover their heads, they employ a cowl [hood], part of which contains the head, while the remainder hangs down and flaps against the neck. On their forehead is placed a silver-gilt cone of considerable height, studded with stones of great value.

The Turkish monarch going to war takes with him over 20,000 camels and nearly as many baggage mules, of which a great part are loaded with rice and other kinds of grain. . . . The invading army carefully [avoids eating this food] at the outset; as they are well aware that when the season for campaigning draws to a close, they will have to retreat over districts wasted by the enemy, or scraped bare by countless hordes of men and droves of hungry animals, as if they had been devastated by locusts; accordingly they reserve their stores [food] as much as possible for this emergency. Then the Sultan's magazines are opened, and a ration just sufficient to sustain life is daily weighed out to the Janissaries and other troops of the royal household. The rest of the army is badly off, unless they have provided some supplies at their own expense. . . . On such occasions they take out a few spoonfuls of flour and put them into water, adding some butter, and seasoning the mess with salt and spices; these ingredients are boiled, and a large bowl of gruel is thus obtained. Of this they eat once or twice a day, according to the quantity they have, without any bread, unless they have brought some biscuit with them. . . . Sometimes they have recourse to horseflesh; dead horses are of course plentiful . . . and such beasts as are in good condition when they die furnish a meal not to be despised by famished soldiers.

The Turks and Europe. From this you will see that it is the patience, self-denial and thrift of the Turkish soldier that enable him to face the most trying circumstances and come safely out of the dangers that surround him. What a contrast to our men! Christian soldiers on a campaign refuse to put up with their ordinary food, and call for dainty dishes! . . . It makes me shudder to think of what the result of a struggle between such different systems must be; one of us must prevail and the other be destroyed, at any rate we cannot both exist in safety. On their side is the vast wealth of their empire, unimpaired resources, experience and practice in arms, a veteran soldiery, an uninterrupted series of victories, readiness to endure hardships, union, order, discipline, thrift and watchfulness. On ours are found an empty exchequer, luxurious habits, exhausted resources, broken spirits, a raw and insubordinate soldiery, and greedy quarrels; there is no regard for discipline, license [abuses of liberty] runs

riot, the men indulge in drunkenness and debauchery [immorality], and worst of all, the enemy are accustomed to victory, we to defeat. Can we doubt what the result must be? The only obstacle is Persia, whose position on [the Ottomans'] rear forces the invader to take precautions. The fear of Persia gives us a respite, but it is only for a time. " ■

Ottoman Influence Spreads

The administrative and military strength of the Ottoman Empire led to continued expansion. Under the leadership of Selim I (seh LEEM) and Suleiman (soo lay MAHN) the Magnificent, in the early 1500s, the empire expanded east, west, and south. Each spring the massive army left Istanbul, formerly Constantinople, to campaign with its cannons, musketeers, and cavalry.

The Ottomans attacked other Muslim states to expand their control of the populous lands of the Middle East. To the east, the Ottomans fought a long series of wars with the Safavid Empire of Iran. Ottoman victories gave them brief control of the rich valley of the Tigris and Euphrates rivers. To the south, an Ottoman army attacked the Mamluks in Egypt. The Mamluk cavalry kept to the tradition of fighting only with bows, swords, and lances. These weapons were no match for the Ottoman artillery that in short order mowed down the Mamluk horsemen. The Ottomans conquered the Mamluks and added the Nile valley to their empire in 1517.

Northward, the forces of Suleiman the Magnificent fought brilliant campaigns against the Christian states of Europe led by the Hapsburgs. At the Battle of Mohács in 1526, the Turks defeated the Christian army and then swarmed over the rolling plains of Hungary. At the same time, Suleiman made an alliance with France against the Hapsburgs. In this way, the Ottoman Empire came to play an important part in European politics.

The Seige of Vienna. In the summer of 1529, the Turks attacked Vienna, the capital of Austria. All Europe feared that if the Ottomans took the city, the German states might fall next.

The Turks laid mines under the walls of Vienna and battered the walls with their cannons. The infantry almost succeeded in breaking through. The Janissaries, though, feared the end of summer. They knew that the autumn rains would make the long march back to Istanbul slow and difficult. Consequently, they convinced Suleiman to withdraw. The Ottoman advance into Europe halted.

Ottoman Naval Power. In addition to their land forces, the Ottomans built a powerful navy. In the sixteenth century, this fleet dominated the eastern Mediterranean and the Black Sea. Two Turkish sea warriors, known as the Barbarossa brothers, conquered the coastlines of northern Africa. In 1571, the Ottoman navy lost more than 200 ships in a battle against the fleets of Spain and Venice. This contest, known as the Battle of Lepanto, was a temporary setback for the Ottoman Empire. The Turkish navy continued to control the eastern Mediterranean well into the seventeenth century.

The Ottomans carried naval warfare into the Indian Ocean in the 1500s. Turkish ships attacked the Portuguese, who were newcomers to trade there. These attacks did not expel the Portuguese from the Indian Ocean, however.

Ottoman Culture. The stability and wealth of the Ottoman Empire encouraged Islamic art and learning to flourish. In major cities, skilled workers made beautiful textiles, carpets, ceramics, and illustrated books. The sultan and his officials were highly educated. They encouraged the work of scholars, poets, and painters. In Ottoman universities, scholars produced important works in mathematics, medicine, astronomy, geography, and history. One seventeenth-century scholar traveled around the empire and Europe for 40 years. He then wrote a 10—volume history of his journeys.

The wealth of the empire was expressed in magnificent mosques, palaces, and various public buildings in Istanbul and other cities. The most ingenious Ottoman architect was Sinan (sih NAHN), a Christian of Greek origin, who later converted to Islam. He later became the sultan's royal architect. Sinan designed more than 300 buildings. In Edirne (ay DIHR nuh), a city about 120 miles, or 200 kilometers, west of Istanbul, he built a mosque that fulfilled a special dream:

" Christians say that they have defeated the Muslims because no dome has been built in the Islamic world which can rival the dome of St. Sophia [a church in Istanbul]. It greatly grieved my heart that they should

Brightly colored Turkish galleys tow foreign ships back to port in a 1622 miniature celebrating the victory of Admiral Ali Pash.

say that to build so large a dome was so difficult a task. I determined to erect such a mosque, and with the help of God . . . I made the dome of this mosque six cubits [1 cubit is about 20 inches, or 51 centimeters] wider and 4 cubits deeper than the dome of St. Sophia. "

Signs of Trouble in the Empire. By the beginning of the seventeenth century, the Ottoman Empire was one of the largest and most powerful states in the world. Yet it was no longer expanding, and political and economic problems were becoming worse.

A major problem was bad leadership. After 1574, a series of weak rulers governed for about a century. Some of them were only children when they came to power. Others cared nothing about the affairs of state and devoted themselves entirely to amusement. One sultan was even insane.

These weak rulers could not control their own officials and soldiers. Therefore, factions within the government and army fought one another for control of the powerful offices. The Janissaries threatened to rebel if they were not paid more money. Bribery and corruption in government became widespread. The administration of the empire became less efficient and less fair to the common people.

Many government officials were honest and dedicated, but the empire was running short of money. The government depended on new conquests for its prosperity. However, the huge army had gone as far as its supply lines could reach during its summer campaigns. When the empire reached the limits of territorial expansion, revenue from war and taxes declined. Therefore, the treasury began to build up a big deficit. Underlying these economic problems were two important factors.

First, the population of the empire doubled in the sixteenth century and continued to grow. Yet the lands and city workshops were not producing enough food and goods to keep up with the population increase.

Thus the standard of living declined for many people, while officials made money.

The second factor was inflation. Prices increased throughout Europe in the sixteenth century because of the increased supply of gold and silver from Latin American mines. In the Ottoman Empire, prices rose so high that the government could not pay its expenses. Ordinary people could barely afford to buy bread in times of shortage.

Despite these troubles, the state remained a powerful force in world affairs in the seventeenth century. The empire remained intact, influencing the politics of Europe and the Middle East. Istanbul remained one of the greatest cities of Eurasia. The empire that Osman founded would outlast other Muslim empires of the era.

SECTION 1 *Study Skills*

Developing Vocabulary 1. Name a group that could be considered elite in modern society. 2. What would happen to a business that consistently runs a deficit?

Reviewing Main Ideas 1. What was symbolic about the conversion of Hagia Sophia in 1453? 2. What were the four departments of the Ottoman government? 3. According to de Busbecq, why was the Ottoman army so successful? 4. What stopped the Ottoman advance at Vienna? 5. Describe cultural accomplishments of the Ottoman reign.

Understanding Cause and Effect 1. What two problems faced the Ottoman Empire when it could no longer expand? 2. Explain two economic factors that caused the decline of the Ottoman Empire.

Understanding Chronology 1. Explain why the year 1574 may be considered a turning point in the history of the Ottoman Empire. 2. How long did the Ottoman Empire last?

Challenge Provide five examples of empires that have gained and lost power. What generalization applies to all your examples?

2 The Safavid Empire

OBJECTIVE: *To understand the important role of the Safavid Empire in the Muslim world*

Iran's Shi'ite Empire

The second great Islamic empire of the sixteenth and seventeenth centuries, the Safavid, was centered in Iran. Like the Ottoman Empire, this empire's founders were nomadic Turkish warriors. Their homeland was the mountainous region west of the Caspian Sea known as Azerbaijan (AZ uhr by JAHN). See the map, Safavid Empire of Persia, page 430.

In the century before the rise of the Safavid Empire, Iran was divided among a number of small states or tribal groups. In Azerbaijan, several Turkish tribes joined together in a religious organization. They became known as Safavids because the name of the organization's founder was Safi al-Din. People nicknamed the members of the organization Redheads because they wore cone-shaped red hats.

The Safavids were Shi'ite Muslims. Throughout the fifteenth century, they made vigorous, sometimes violent, efforts to convert people to their beliefs. One of their beliefs was that someday a descendant of Muhammed's grandson, Husayn, would emerge to rule as a savior (see page 240). In 1501, a Safavid leader arose who many Shi'ites believed was the savior. This leader's name was Isma'il (ihs MAH EEL).

Shah Isma'il. When Isma'il was three, his father died in a battle against Sunni Muslims. Loyal family servants protected the young boy and his brother from death at the hands of Sunni soldiers.

At age 14, Isma'il set out to conquer a kingdom. He had seven supporters. Within a year, though, he commanded over 7,000 soldiers. He captured Tabriz (tuh BREEZ), the major city of Azerbaijan, and proclaimed himself shah, or king. Within 10 years, he and his army controlled most of Iran and the valleys of the Tigris and Euphrates.

Before Isma'il's reign, most Iranians were Sunni Muslims. Isma'il, however, tried to force everyone to convert to Shi'ism. His supporters warned him that the majority of Muslims might object. He replied:

> " God and the Immaculate Imams [a group of Islamic leaders] are with me and I fear no one. By God's help, if the people utter one word of protest, I will draw the sword and leave not one of them alive. "

Isma'il carried out his threat. He executed or exiled many Sunni religious leaders because they disagreed with him.

VOCABULARY DEVELOPMENT

caravansary (KAIR uh VAN suh ree) *noun:* a kind of inn where caravans stop for the night. From the Persian words *karwan*, meaning caravan, and *sarai*, meaning inn.

calligraphy (kuh LIHG ruh fee) *noun:* handwriting, especially as an art. From the Greek words *kallos*, meaning beauty, and *graphein*, meaning to write.

Safavid Empire of Persia, 1650

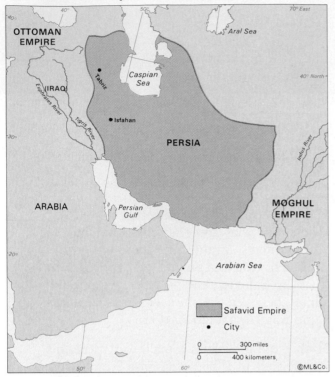

Map Skills   1. Was the Safavid Empire larger or smaller than the Ottoman Empire? **2.** Which bodies of water washed its coasts?

Conflict with the Ottomans.   The Safavids stirred up rebellion in Asia Minor, but the Ottoman Empire controlled the region. Much of the conflict was over religious issues. The Safavid and Ottoman rebels were Shi'ites. Most Muslims in the Ottoman Empire were Sunnis. In 1514, Ottoman leader, Sultan Selim, sent a letter to Isma'il attacking the Safavid leader's religious beliefs:

❝ . . . Only by practicing the true religion [will man] prosper in this world and merit eternal life in the other. As to you, Amir [ruler] Isma'il, such a recompense [reward] will not be your lot [fate], because you have denied the sanctity of the divine laws; because you have deserted the path of salvation and the sacred commandments; because you have impaired the purity of the dogmas [beliefs] of Islam; because you have dishonored, soiled, and destroyed the altars of the Lord, . . . because you have raised the standard of irreligion and heresy; because yielding to the impulse of your evil passions, and giving yourself up without rein to the most infamous disorders, you have dared to throw off the control of Muslim laws and to permit lust and rape, the massacre of the most virtuous and respectable men, [and] the destruction of pulpits and temples . . . [therefore] our doctors have pronounced sentence of death against you, perjurer [one who lies under oath] and blasphemer [one who is irreverent to God], and have imposed on every Muslim the sacred obligation to arm in defense of religion and destroy heresy and impiety in your person and that of all your partisans. **❞**

Isma'il responded to the letter by claiming that he did not want war with the Ottomans. He suggested that when Sultan Selim wrote the letter he was under the influence of the drug opium. Isma'il even sent a box of opium to the sultan.

Throughout 1514, the Ottomans attacked the Safavids. Isma'il's warriors fought on horseback with bows, spears, and swords. Like the Mamluks in Egypt, they thought that fighting with gunpowder was cowardly. The Ottomans crushed the Safavid forces with their artillery.

This defeat so depressed Shah Isma'il that he gave up hope of conquering the Islamic world for Shi'ism. When he died in 1524, his kingdom faced both internal rebellions and new Ottoman invasions.

Reign of Shah Abbas the Great

The Ottomans were unable to completely conquer the Safavids. Isma'il's successors held the state together during the next several decades. They resisted Ottoman attacks, put down tribal revolts, and gradually rebuilt their authority throughout Iran.

The Safavid state reached the peak of its power and wealth under Shah Abbas I, who ruled from 1588 to 1629. Like Suleiman the

Shah Abbas I guided the Safavids to the height of power. He greets a Turkish ambassador in this scene from a lacquer document box made in 1609.

Magnificent of the Ottomans, Shah Abbas was a brilliant military leader. One reason for his success was that he convinced his soldiers to trade their bows and spears for muskets and cannons. He also created a large standing army that was ready to fight at a moment's notice.

At the heart of Shah Abbas's army were regiments of elite troops that came from Armenia and the Caucasus Mountains. Like the Janissaries in the Ottoman Empire, these soldiers were the personal military slaves of the ruler. Shah Abbas gave them special training in the use of firearms. He expected these soldiers to be completely devoted to him. Shah Abbas and his personal army regained much territory in the west that had been lost to the Ottomans.

Shah Abbas ruled his kingdom with a firm hand. He punished any official who was cowardly or incompetent. Despite his strong rule, his subjects loved Shah Abbas. He wore simple clothes, and he often visited cafes to converse with his people. Sometimes he walked around bazaars, Muslim marketplaces, in disguise, to see that merchants were selling goods at fair prices.

Trade Expansion under Shah Abbas. Iran remained an agricultural empire under the Safavids. Shah Abbas did much, though, to encourage manufacturing and trade. Iran's workshops produced beautiful textiles, carpets, and ceramics. Their silk was in great demand in many lands. Caravans carried goods along the roads that crisscrossed the empire. The shah built numerous caravansaries, or rest stations, along these roads. At a caravansary, merchants and travelers could find protection and free lodging.

The Armenians Trade. Armenian merchants conducted much of the long-distance trade of Safavid Iran. Armenia is a region located in eastern Turkey and the Soviet Union. Armenians shared a common language and the Christian faith. A large community of Armenians occupied a suburb of Isfahan (IHS fuh HAHN), the capital of Iran. From there, they organized caravans to many lands. Groups of Armenian merchants lived along the trade routes to India, Russia, the Mediterranean, and Europe.

Conflicts with Portugal. Shah Abbas generally encouraged trade with Europe. However, he opposed Portuguese control of the key port of Hormuz. By dominating this town, located at the mouth of the Persian Gulf, the Portuguese could control trade from the Indian Ocean to Iran. In 1615, Shah Abbas joined with the English to attack Hormuz and expel the Portuguese. After 1615, more English and Dutch merchants entered Iran. They brought pepper and other spices from east Asia in return for silk. Iran became involved in world trade.

Safavid Culture

Islamic art and literature, as well as medicine, mathematics, and astronomy, flourished in Safavid Iran. Persian artists were famous for their textile and carpet designs, manuscript illustrations, and calligraphy.

Persian Literature. One of the greatest artistic works of the period is an illustrated manuscript of the *Shahnama,* or *Book of Kings.* This epic is written in beautiful calligraphy. More than 250 delicate paintings depict Persian life. Shah Abbas, a lover of fine handwriting, at times held a candle to light the page for his calligrapher.

Persian was used as the language of scholarship, poetry, and diplomatic documents throughout much of the Islamic world. For example, most Muslim scholars and government officials in both the Ottoman Empire and India could read, write, and speak Persian.

The Glory of Isfahan. The single greatest cultural achievement of Shah Abbas was the construction of Isfahan, his capital. The city lay in the midst of a lush oasis surrounded by dry steppes and distant mountains. The population of Isfahan was about 1 million, making it one of the largest cities in the world in the early seventeenth century.

The center of Isfahan was a great public square called the Maydan. Domed mosques surrounded the 20-acre square. Soldiers paraded, jugglers performed, and Shah Abbas played polo in the vast square.

Near the Maydan was a bazaar covering over 11 acres. This bazaar included shopping arcades, warehouses, fire stations, mosques, and theological colleges. Musicians played in a gallery over the main gate of the bazaar at sunrise and sunset each day that the Shah was in residence.

The End of Safavid Iran

A European traveler said about Shah Abbas, "When this great prince ceased to live, Persia [Iran] ceased to prosper." After Shah Abbas, poor leadership weakened Iran as it did the Ottoman Empire. Each of the four rulers who followed Shah Abbas was addicted to alcohol. The Shi'ite religious leaders lost their respect for the shah and took more power into their own hands. The common people suffered as taxes became more oppressive to support government spending. The army became corrupt. The Ottomans retook the western part of the empire.

In 1722, a horde of 20,000 Afghans took advantage of the Safavids' weakness to invade the country. The Afghans captured Isfahan and brought the Safavid Empire to an end. Iran would remain politically weak and divided until the twentieth century.

SECTION 2 *Study Skills*

Developing Vocabulary 1. Who would have used a caravansary? **2.** What is the difference between calligraphy and ordinary handwriting?

Reviewing Main Ideas 1. Describe the difference between the religious beliefs of Safavids and Ottomans. **2.** Discuss four qualities that made Shah Abbas an effective ruler. **3.** What was the effect on Iran of the cooperation between Shah Abbas and English and Dutch merchants and traders?

Understanding Geography 1. What empires were on the borders of Safavid Iran? **2.** Where is Armenia? **3.** Why is the port of Hormuz important? **4.** Describe the city of Isfahan. **5.** In what areas was the Persian language important for communication?

Understanding Cause and Effect 1. Explain four reasons why the Safavids lost control of Iran. **2.** How did religious differences lead to conflict among Muslims?

Challenge Compare and contrast reasons that Hormuz and Istanbul were important cities.

Amazon Rain Forest

The Amazon Basin and the Andes Mountains are the two dominant land forms in South America. The basin is the land drained by the tributaries that flow into the Amazon River, the second longest river in the world. The river flows through the northern part of South America, mostly in Brazil, and empties into the Atlantic Ocean. The Amazon Basin includes one of the largest rain forests in the world.

Rain Forest Characteristics

The Amazon Rain Forest is the product of several interacting factors. First, the land is largely flat. Most of the region is composed of plains and plateaus. This flatness tends to hold moisture from the rain, rather than allowing the land to dry completely.

Second, the climate of the Amazon Basin is hot and humid. The average rainfall in the basin is 40 to 80 inches, or 101 to 203 centimeters. Some basin areas are washed with 80 to 200 inches, or 203 to 508 centimeters a year.

A third important factor is the soil. Most of the Amazon Basin has a reddish type of soil called oxisol. The color of the oxisol is the result of great amounts of rain. As the water flows through the soil, most of the nutrients are carried away. Two minerals, the oxides of iron and aluminum are not carried away. They remain in the soil and give it its characteristic red color.

The Amazon Basin supports lush vegetation in spite of the soil's infertility. Trees are the dominant type of vegetation. The trees are so close together that they provide dense shade for the ground beneath them. Small plants and bushes cannot grow in this dense shade. Consequently, the floor of the rain forest is generally open with little plant life. The rain forest does not have the dense undergrowth so often depicted in movies.

Workers construct the Amazon Highway between Brasília and Belem.

Other types of plants in the typical rain forest are epiphytes, plants which cling to other plants for physical support and nutrition. Epiphytes include ferns, orchids, mosses, and vines.

Despite poor soil, the Amazon Rain Forest supports 3000 varieties of trees. Trees of the same species are often widely dispersed. Lumber companies find it uneconomical to cut trees of only one species. Therefore, total lumbering is common. This practice threatens the ecology of the rain forest.

The trees and other plant life in the Amazon Rain Forest thrive on the nutrients which come from the decaying plant matter, including fallen branches, leaves, and dead trees. The hot climate and the heavy rainfall enable bacteria and fungi to destroy the fallen plant material rapidly. The decayed vegetation is quickly used for nourishment by the living plants. Without this decayed vegetation, very little formation of valuable humus, the dark-colored, highly fertile layer of soil, can occur.

Value of the Rain Forest

The Amazon Basin is largely uninhabited. Efforts to use the resources of the Amazon Rain Forest have so far been a failure. Farmers have tried to cultivate the land by cutting trees and planting crops. At first the soil produced good yields. Unfortunately, the crops quickly used up the natural fertility of the soil and cultivation has been diminished. To turn the rain forest into farm land would require the addition of great amounts of expensive fertilizer.

Oil and Gas. Along the western edge of the Amazon Basin, in Peru, people have discovered oil. This region became Peru's most important source of both oil and natural gas in the 1970s. A 525 mile, or 840 kilometer, pipeline to the coastal city of Bayovar carries the oil and gas. The pipeline, built with the economic help of Japan, runs through part of the rain forest, and across the Andes Mountains. The crude oil is refined in Bayovar, and used within Peru or sold to Japan or Brazil.

Current projects that utilize the resources in the rain forest include cattle ranching, forestry, and iron mining. With each project, scientists gain new understanding of the unique qualities of the Amazon Rain Forest.

Global Importance. The most important use of the rain forest is actually threatened by efforts to develop it commercially.

The rain forest is important as a source of oxygen. People and animals use oxygen as they breathe, and return carbon dioxide to the air. Plants use carbon dioxide and return oxygen to the air. Thus there is a balance of carbon dioxide and oxygen for both plant and animal life.

The Amazon Rain Forest is important in this process because of the great number of plants which grow there. They release enormous amounts of oxygen into the air. Oxygen from the region is circulated by global air currents to Iran as well as other parts of the world.

The Amazon Rain Forest continues to produce a steady release of oxygen. However, destruction of the rain forest may cause problems. The current balanced system of oxygen-carbon dioxide transfer could become imbalanced. The long-term effects of such an imbalance are uncertain.

STUDY SKILLS Understanding Geography

1. Where is the Amazon Rain Forest located?
2. What factors interact to produce the Amazon Rain Forest?
3. What is oxisol?
4. Name three projects that have been developed to use the natural resources of the Amazon Basin.
5. What is the global significance of the Amazon Rain Forest?

3 The Moghul Empire

OBJECTIVE: *To understand the contributions to history of the Moghul Empire of India*

Foundations of the Empire

The most populous Muslim empire in the sixteenth century was the Moghul Empire of India. See the map, Moghul Empire of India, page 436. Prior to the 1400s, India was divided among several kingdoms. Some rulers were Hindus, as was the great majority of India's population. Muslim monarchs governed other states, especially in northern and central India. The ancestors of these monarchs had invaded India from central Asia centuries earlier.

Baber the Tiger.   To the northwest of India lay the rugged land of Afghanistan. There, a brilliant war captain, Baber (BAH buhr), came to power shortly after 1500. His ancestors included the great central Asian conquerors Genghis Khan and Tamerlane. Attracted by the riches of the Indus and Ganges valleys, Baber led his army on raids into these areas.

VOCABULARY DEVELOPMENT

decree (dih KREE) *noun:* an official order of a government, church, or court. From the Latin prefix *de-*, meaning from, and word *cernere*, meaning to judge.

legacy (LEHG uh see) *noun:* anything handed down from, as from an ancestor. From the Latin word, *lex*, meaning law.

faction *noun:* a group of people in an organization working against other groups or the main body.

In 1526, Baber launched a large-scale assault on the Delhi Sultanate, a weak Muslim dynasty (see pages 281–282). When the sultan of Delhi counterattacked with a wall of nearly a thousand war elephants, Baber's artillery destroyed them. After ending the Delhi Dynasty, Baber then defeated an alliance of Hindu princes that tried to oppose him. Soon, he was master of northern India. He and his warriors became known as Moghuls (MOO guhlz), the Persian word for Mongols. In fact, these conquerors were mostly Turks and Afghans, not Mongols.

Baber's followers called him "the Tiger" because he was a brave and ruthless conqueror who gave no mercy to his enemies. He was also a gifted leader much beloved by his soldiers. In his autobiography, *Memoirs of Baber*, he tells of being caught in a winter blizzard with his army at the top of a mountain pass:

❝ We reached a small cave; I took a hoe and dug in the snow breast-deep. In this hole I sat. They begged me to go inside, but I would not. I felt that for me to be in shelter and comfort while my men were in the snow was not to do my duty by them. In the morning I found four inches of snow on my head. ❞

In another part of his autobiography, Baber describes the land and people of Hindustan, a region in northern India. As a Muslim military leader, Baber was unimpressed with the Hindus.

The Moghul Empire, 1650

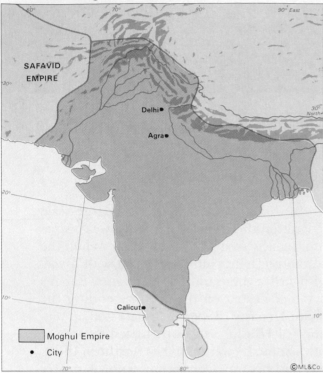

Map Skills **1.** In what direction would a merchant from Delhi travel to reach Calicut? **2.** The Moghul Empire bordered what other empire?

❝[Hindustan] is a wonderful country. Compared with our countries, it is a different world; its mountains rivers, jungles and deserts, its towns, its cultivated lands, its animals and plants, its people and their tongues, its rains and its winds, are all different . . . Most of the inhabitants of Hindustan are pagans. [The] people have no good looks; of social [customs] paying and receiving visits, there is none; of genius and capacity none; of manners none; in handicraft and work there is no form or symmetry, method or quality; there are no good horses, dogs, grapes, muskmelons or first-rate fruits, no ice or cold water, no good bread or cooked food in the bazaars, no hot baths, no colleges . . . ❞

Baber was successful as both a military leader and a writer. In addition, he composed poetry, and studied botany.

Humayun Almost Loses the Empire. Baber died in 1530, after ruling his Indian empire for only four years. His son, and successor, Humayun (hoo MAH yoon), was a much less talented leader. He nearly lost the empire altogether when rebel forces chased him out of India in 1540. He sought refuge with the Safavids in Iran. However, 15 years later he returned at the head of a new army and reconquered the lost territories. Humayun was more a man of learning and culture than a warrior. He did, however save the Moghul Empire from extinction. He died after only six months back in power, the result of a fall down the steps of his library.

Akbar the Great

FOCUS ON PEOPLE

Moghul leaders kept news of the death of Humayun secret for two weeks. They wanted Humayun's 13–year-old son, Akbar, to take the throne without opposition. As soon as the new ruler was firmly in control, he acted quickly against one of the strongest opponents of the Moghuls, an army led by Hemu, a rebellious Hindu.

The forces of Akbar and Hemu met at Panipat, a city 50 miles, or 80 kilometers, north of Delhi. At first, Hemu's forces seemed stronger than those of Akbar. As Hemu was preparing a final assault on the Moghul army, he was hit in the eye with an arrow and lost consciousness. Without his leadership, Hemu's army panicked and fled. Akbar and the Moghuls won the battle. The Moghuls, under Akbar's leadership, expanded their control over northern India. During his reign, Akbar extended his empire to include over 100 million subjects.

Ruling an Empire. Akbar was an extraordinary man. Although he could barely read or write, he had a great love of learning. To increase his knowledge, he brought scholars to his court, including architects, poets, philosophers, priests, and artists from many countries. Like Ashoka, who had ruled so many years before him (see page 150), he cared for the interests of all of his subjects, Hindu and Muslim alike.

In 1562, Akbar married the daughter of a Hindu prince. The emperor decreed that his wife's relatives, even though they were Hindus, should be regarded as members of the royal family.

Akbar's government took steps to show respect for the rights of Hindus. Akbar abolished the special tax on Hindus that Muslim rulers had imposed in the past. His government paid for building both Muslim mosques and Hindu temples. He forbade Muslims from killing and eating cows, which Hindus considered sacred. Akbar believed that "Miracles occur in the temple of every creed . . . each person according to his condition gives the Supreme Being a name."

Akbar loved children. He once said, "children are the young saplings in the garden of life; to love them is to turn our minds to the Bountiful Creator." For several years he was concerned about his failure to produce an heir. Finally, he visited a Muslim mystic who prophesized that he would father three sons. Akbar's Hindu wife soon gave birth to the first of their three sons.

In his delight, Akbar built a huge mosque in Fatehpur Sikri (FAHT uh pur SEE kree), the mystic's village. He soon transferred his court to the village, making it the new capital of India. Unfortunately, Fatehpur Sikri did not have a sufficient water supply to support a large city. Akbar had to abandon his capital after only 14 years. To this day, Fatehpur Sikri remains an enormous and well-preserved ghost town.

During his 49-year reign, Akbar introduced a series of administrative reforms. These changes made the government more efficient and just. During his reign, Akbar made the Moghul Empire a well-governed land. The administrative system that he devised survived for centuries after him.

Mogul Emperor Akbar, seated, receives his son Jahangir and grandson Khurram in this opaque water-colored miniature from the seventeenth century.

Continuing Debates over Religion. Akbar called together Muslim, Hindu, Zoroastrian, Jewish, Jain, and Christian scholars to debate religious and philosophical issues in 1572. Some Muslims, including Akbar's half-brother, believed that these debates threatened Islamic influence in the empire. The rebellion they started became the most serious crisis of Akbar's reign. By 1581, the open rebellion had been put down.

Akbar created his own religious brotherhood known as Divine Faith. It included ideas from several religions but never gained popularity outside the royal court. It died out after Akbar's death in 1605.

Akbar left a glorious legacy to the Moghul rulers who followed him. Under his capable leadership, art, architecture, and literature flourished. Northern India became an orderly, unified state that was well-administered. ■

Prosperity and Decline

Akbar's kingdom benefited from developments in other cultures, particularly the Persian culture of Iran. Persian was the language of diplomacy, administration, and learning in the Moghul Empire. Persian poets, artists, and architects worked at Akbar's royal court. More than 100 painters served the emperor, producing marvelous book illustrations, portraits, and pictures of birds and animals. Both Persian and Hindu traditions influenced these artists.

India's Long-Distance Trade. Taxes on agriculture paid for most of the luxury of Akbar's royal court and the expenses of his government. Under Akbar, India became increasingly involved in trade. The country's most valuable export was cotton cloth, produced by thousands of Indian spinners and weavers. These cotton goods were exported to Asia, east Africa, and Europe. India also exported pepper, indigo, carpets, and other products.

Foreign lands did not produce many items that Indians wanted. Therefore, most of India's exports were sold for silver or gold. These metals poured into the country.

Unlike the Ottomans, the Moghuls did not build a navy to protect their sea merchants. Europeans slowly increased their share of India's export trade. In the sixteenth century, Portuguese traders became dominant. In the seventeenth century, the Dutch and English displaced the Portuguese traders.

Jahangir and Shah Jahan. After Akbar died, his son, Jahangir (jah HAHN geer), and grandson, Shah Jahan, ruled. During their reigns, 1605–1657, the Moghul Empire was one of the greatest states.

Neither Jahangir nor Shah Jahan was so gifted or open-minded as Akbar. However, they inherited a well-organized empire and kept it stable and productive under their rule. They also conquered more territories in central and southern India. While Jahan-

Jahangir steps across the globe to embrace Shah Abbas of Persia and pushes him into the Mediterranean in this seventeenth-century painting.

gir ruled, his Persian wife, Nur Jahan, wielded great power.

The Taj Mahal. Both Jahangir and Shah Jahan spent vast amounts of tax money to build new fortresses, palaces, and mosques to glorify their reigns. Shah Jahan ordered his architects to build an entirely new city.

Shah Jahan's wife, Mumtaz, died at the age of 39 while giving birth to her fifteenth child. In her memory, Shah Jahan ordered a beautiful tomb to be built for her in the city of Agra. It required 20,000 workers and 20 years to build the wondrous white marble tomb in the midst of a Persian-style garden of trees, flowers, and reflecting water. Called the Taj Mahal, people still regard this tomb as one of the most beautiful buildings in the world. When Shah Jahan died in

1658, his remains were put to rest beside the casket of Mumtaz Mahal.

The Last Great Emperor. The last of the great Moghul emperors was Aurangzeb (AW ruhng zehb). He inherited an empire that was facing serious problems in the mid-1600s. Government toleration of non-Muslims was declining. Taxes on peasants had risen to pay for administration, conquests, and the expenses of the royal court.

Like Akbar, Aurangzeb was a man of great energy. Unlike Akbar, though, he discriminated against his non-Muslim subjects. He forbade the building of Hindu temples, and reintroduced the special tax on non-Muslims. He ended the partnership between Hindus and Muslims that Akbar had nurtured, and, as a result, alienated the Hindu population.

Aurangzeb's style of living was simple, the opposite of his three predecessors. He stopped the building of grand palaces, and he forbade music, dancing, and showy clothing in the royal palace.

Conquests and Revolts. Aurangzeb spent huge sums on military campaigns. He was determined to conquer southern India. He campaigned with 50,000 camels, 30,000 elephants, and thousands of soldiers and camp followers.

Providing supplies to this huge army was a challenge. The soldiers and animals stripped the countryside bare of food wherever they marched. Transporting food, weapons, and other supplies became an increasing problem as the supply line lengthened. Aurangzeb did conquer southern territories, but he could not hold them. Communications were too poor to allow control of areas so far from Delhi.

As Aurangzeb's demands for taxes increased, more and more peasants faced economic ruin or starvation. An anonymous critic wrote to the emperor:

" Your subjects are trampled underfoot; every province of your empire is impoverished; depopulation spreads and difficulties accumulate. . . . **"**

The Taj Mahal, built by Shah Jahan in the seventeenth century as a tomb for his wife, Mumtaz.

Eventually, Indian peasants revolted. The largest rebellion was among the Marathas (muh RAHD uhz). They were a Hindu people who lived in the hills and arid highlands of west central India. The Marathas defied Aurangzeb's campaigns to crush them. In 1705, two years before he died at the age of 88, Aurangzeb gave up his efforts to defeat the Maratha rebels. He returned to the north, a broken man.

Decline of the Moghuls. Aurangzeb died leaving India in turmoil, revolt, and economic hardship. Rival political factions competed for control of government. The Marathas established their own independent kingdom. Other territories successfully revolted as well. In 1739, an army from Iran invaded India and sacked Delhi. The invaders even stole the emperor's jeweled throne.

By the mid-eighteenth century, India was again divided into several kingdoms and minor states. Along the coasts, British merchants were slowly building up their political power. In the nineteenth century, Britain would conquer and reunite India.

The Islamic Empires in Decline

The Moghul Empire, like the Safavid and Ottoman empires, never regained the power it had in the sixteenth and seventeenth centuries. None of these empires had used its wealth to develop sustained growth. One historian labeled the governments of the three empires "revenue pumps." They pumped out the wealth of their empires without doing anything to restore it.

The three Islamic empires shared other traits in common. All were governed by military leaders of Turkish origin who ruled through a powerful central government. All three had strong militaries that used cannons and firearms. All three empires included peoples of different languages, cultures, and religions.

Despite the decline of the three great Islamic empires, Islam continued to expand.

One important area of growth was Africa south of the Sahara. In both eastern and western Africa, Muslim merchants and religious preachers continued to convert large numbers of people to Islam. Muslim traders and holy men were active in Southeast Asia during the sixteenth and seventeenth centuries. They transformed much of Indonesia from a Hindu and Buddhist country to an Islamic country. Today, Indonesia is one of the largest Muslim nations in the world. While Islam was expanding, Europeans increasingly were assuming political and economic power in the world.

SECTION 3 *Study Skills*

Developing Vocabulary Use each of the following terms in a sentence: **1.** decree. **2.** legacy. **3.** faction.

Reviewing Main Ideas **1.** Summarize Baber's accomplishments as a leader. **2.** Describe four reforms introduced by Akbar. **3.** What does the Divine Faith brotherhood indicate about Akbar's attitude toward religion? **4.** What was India's most valuable export during Akbar's reign? **5.** Why was the Taj Mahal built? **6.** By the mid-eighteenth century, how was control of India changing? **7.** Explain four common traits of the Islamic empires of the seventeenth century.

Understanding Geography **1.** What were the areas that were included in the Moghul Empire? **2.** List the areas which received Indian exports. **3.** Why was conquest of southern India so difficult for Aurangzeb? **4.** Why was Fatehpur Sikri a failure as a capital?

Understanding Cause and Effect **1.** What characteristics of Akbar made him an effective ruler? **2.** How did Aurangzeb's rule make the problems of the Moghul Empire worse? **3.** Explain how the decline in the Moghul, Safavid, and Ottoman Empires was in part caused by how they used their wealth.

Challenge Based on the history of the Moghul Empire, suggest three ways a country can promote prosperity.

CHAPTER 19 *Summary & Review*

Summarizing Main Ideas

By the fifteenth century, the Ottoman Empire had conquered most of Asia Minor and the Balkans. The Ottomans fought surrounding Muslims as well as European Christians. In 1529, the Turks' movement into Europe was stopped at Vienna. Despite difficulties, the Ottoman state remained powerful in the seventeenth century.

In Iran, the Safavid Empire consolidated power during the sixteenth and seventeenth centuries. The Shi'ite Safavids fought a series of battles with the Sunni Ottomans. As trade increased, so did contacts with Europe.

Baber, the Tiger, organized the Empire of India. His successors expanded control throughout much of India, and sponsored trade with Asia, Africa, and Europe. In the 1700s the Moghuls, like the Safavid and Ottomans, became weak. By the mid-eighteenth century the Muslim empires were coming under the increasing influence of European nations.

Questions for Critical Thinking

COMPREHENSION Interpreting Events

1. Discuss the significance of the conversion of Hagia Sophia to a mosque.
2. What were the long range effects of the Turkish failure to conquer Vienna?
3. Explain the impact of Isma'il's rule on the spread of Muslim influence.
4. Discuss the impact of inflation on the Ottoman government's ability to maintain and expand its empire.
5. Why did the Moghul Empire begin a rapid decline when Aurangzeb died?

APPLICATION Comparing Past and Present

1. Identify a bureaucracy today and compare it with the Ottoman bureaucracy.
2. Iran remains the center of Shi'ite Islam. Find out how this affects Iran's relationships with other Islamic countries today.

SYNTHESIS Developing Graphic Skills

1. Create a time line comparing the developments in the Islamic kingdoms with those in Europe during the sixteenth century.
2. Develop a chart listing the three Muslim empires, and the important leaders in each.

CHALLENGE

1. Compare how the Ottoman, Safavid, and Moghul Empires treated people within their empire who had religious beliefs different from the leaders.
2. Akbar was an effective administrator. Discuss the importance of effective administration in maintaining an empire.

"You mean no one remembered to bring a rock?"

CHAPTER 20
The Effects of Global Exchanges

TIME	1450	1475	1500	1525	15

1492–1650 Active exchange of plants and animals between the Old and New Worlds

1500–1700 Population of America decreases due to Columbian Exchange

PEOPLE

● **1440** King Ewuare rules the Benin Empire in Africa

● **1497** Cabot explores the North Atlantic coast for England

1535–1542 Coronado explores North America and reaches California

1539–1541 De Soto explores Florida and discovers the Mississippi River

PLACE

1500s–1600s *Central and South America;[1]* Spanish colonize the New World

● **1510** *India;[2]* Portuguese use Goa as base for their spice trade

● **1513** *China;[3]* Portuguese reach Canton

Linking Past to Present

Between 1450 and 1650, the European discovery of the Americas resulted in a chain of events. First, the lure of a New World brought many European colonists. Next, the colonists tried to duplicate the Old World in the New World, by bringing European plants and animals to the new land. Later, explorers brought New World plants back to their homelands.

As you read the chapter, think about many of the things you eat every day—bread, beef, pork, lettuce, citrus fruits. European explorers and settlers brought these products along with them on their voyages. Many of these plants and animals prospered in the New World. The original inhabitants saw pigs, chickens, and sheep for the first time.

Pieter Brueghel's painting of ocean terrors, 1566–69.

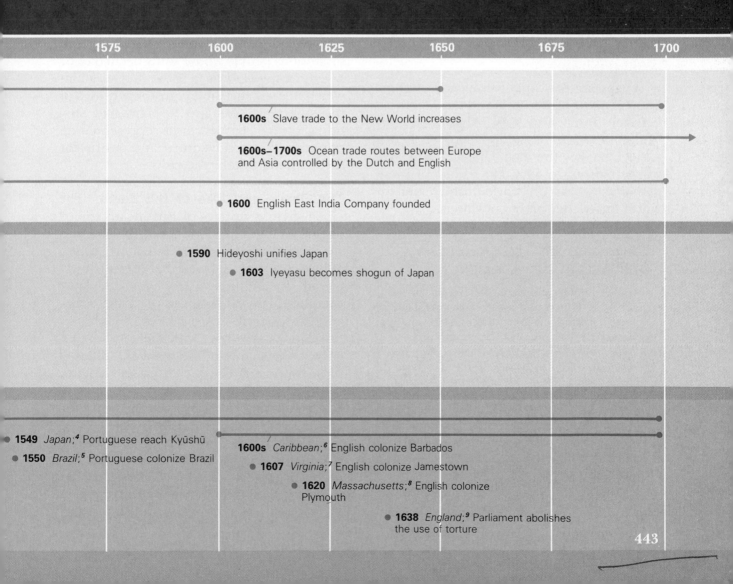

1575	1600	1625	1650	1675	1700

1600s Slave trade to the New World increases

1600s–1700s Ocean trade routes between Europe and Asia controlled by the Dutch and English

1600 English East India Company founded

1590 Hideyoshi unifies Japan

1603 Iyeyasu becomes shogun of Japan

1549 *Japan;*[4] Portuguese reach Kyūshū

1550 *Brazil;*[5] Portuguese colonize Brazil

1600s *Caribbean;*[6] English colonize Barbados

1607 *Virginia;*[7] English colonize Jamestown

1620 *Massachusetts;*[8] English colonize Plymouth

1638 *England;*[9] Parliament abolishes the use of torture

443

1 The New World Meets the Old World

OBJECTIVE: *To understand the consequences of global exchanges between Eurasia and the Americas*

World Knowledge Expands

In the sixteenth century, numerous ships sailed out of European ports to visit Africa, Asia, and the Americas. For the first time in history, people in the Eastern and Western hemispheres heard stories about each other. When Europeans intruded into America, the interacting global community almost doubled in area.

European sea captains sailed their ships between their home ports and the Americas, between India and west Africa, between Mexico and east Asia, and between Persia and China. See the map, Global Trade Network 1650, page 445. The effects of these global networks on world history and on world knowledge were enormous.

VOCABULARY DEVELOPMENT

intrude (ihn TROOD) *verb:* to force oneself on others without being asked. From the Latin word, *intrudere*, meaning to thrust or push.

mammal (MAM uhl) *noun:* an animal that is a warm-blooded vertebrate, usually hairy, and feeds its young with milk secreted by mammary glands. From the Latin word, *mamma*, meaning breast.

predator (PREHD uh tuhr) *noun:* an animal that lives by capturing and feeding on other animals. From the Latin word, *praeda*, meaning prey.

Columbian Exchange: the exchange of plants and animals between the Old World and New World following Columbus's trips.

New Global Horizons. The age of overseas exploration expanded the horizons of Europeans. Stories, rumors, and artifacts of the people and lands of India, Africa, and Asia circulated in Europe.

European sailors told tales of strange crops, unbelievable wealth in gold and silver, conquests of magnificent cities, and mysterious people whose souls needed to be saved. America was a new world about which neither the Bible, nor the writings of the ancient Greeks and Romans had anything to say. The new land represented an opportunity for adventure and profit for those willing to take the risks.

The Shape and Size of the Earth. The globe-circling voyages of Europeans forced drastic changes in ideas about the size and shape of the world. Maps and charts drawn after the voyages showed that the earth was round. In addition, Europeans calculated that the earth was larger than earlier scholars had thought.

Mapmakers drew, with more or less accuracy, the shapes of the main coastlines of most continents. They charted the Atlantic coasts of the Americas, the Pacific coast of South America, the whole outline of Africa, and the coasts and islands of Asia.

Partial information about interiors of continents also was available. Explorers had mapped some inland areas. De Soto, for instance, explored the part of North America between Florida and the Mississippi.

Global Trade Networks, 1650

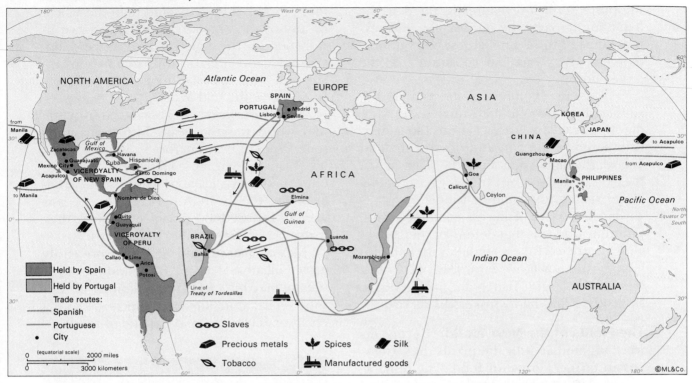

Map Skills **1.** In what country is the city of Seville? **2.** In what direction would a Spanish merchant travel to reach the New World? **3.** On what bodies of water would the merchant travel?

Coronado led a group into North America. Cartier (KAHR TYAY) sailed up the St. Lawrence River into present-day Canada.

After Vasco da Gama rounded the Cape of Good Hope, European sailors learned the global wind system. At about 20 degrees latitude north of the equator, winds in the Atlantic and Pacific Oceans blow northeast. At 20 degrees latitude south, they blow southeast. At about 50 degrees latitude, both north and south of the equator, winds blow mostly from the west. In the Indian Ocean, monsoons vary with the seasons. This knowledge helped Europeans estimate the best routes for their voyages.

The Migration of Plants and Animals

On October 12, 1492, Christopher Columbus and a group of his sailors landed in the Bahama Islands. From that day to the present, the people of the Eastern and Western hemispheres have been bound together. The two worlds, which in 1492 were very different, began exchanges that created common interests and characteristics.

The Animals of the New World. Until Columbus sailed to America in 1492, the Eastern Hemisphere and the Americas were completely isolated from each other. Consequently, many plants and animals thriving in the Americas were unknown to Eurasians and Africans.

In America, Columbus and his crew were surprised by the unfamiliar animals. Columbus was also puzzled that he did not find the animals that Europeans used for food. He remarked:

❝ I saw neither sheep nor goats nor any other beast, but I have been here but a short time, half a day; yet if there were any I couldn't have failed to see them. . . . **❞**

The Indians of the New World had domesticated only a few animals: the dog, the llama and alpaca, the guinea pig, and several kinds of fowl. The largest beast of burden was the llama, no substitute for the larger horse or ox.

European explorers wondered at the small size of the mammals they saw in Middle America. The largest cat was the jaguar. Compared to the lion and tiger of the Old World, the jaguar was a middle-sized cat. In the West Indies no four-legged animal larger than a fox could be found.

The rivers of America contained rays, piranhas, and eels that defended themselves with electricity. Rivers teemed with fish previously unknown to European explorers. One of the largest fish swam in the Mississippi River and had whiskers like a cat.

The Plants of the New World. Europeans were unfamiliar with the plants that Amerindian farmers grew for food. The remarkable variety of Indian food plants included corn and potatoes, cassava, tomatoes, avocados, sweet potatoes, peanuts, beans, pumpkins, and squash.

When brought to Europe, these plants increased food supplies and contributed to rapid population growth. Corn, maize, was the most important because it grew in a wide variety of climates. Corn needed only a short growing season, and contained large amounts of carbohydrates, sugars, and fats. This plant was an ideal supplement to the food supplies of the Old World.

In cool, moist soils, the potato yielded more food per acre of land than did wheat or any of the grains traditionally grown in Europe. As the amount of farmland decreased, and towns and population increased, the potato became a valuable resource to the Old World.

The most varied crop borrowed from the new world was the bean. Europeans grew some types of beans before Columbus made his historic voyage. However, the soy, butter, kidney, French, navy, and string bean grew only in America. When beans were introduced to Eurasia and Africa, they thrived in a wide variety of climates.

Maize, cassava, and peanuts were easily grown in sub-Saharan Africa, and the sweet potato in China. The populations of Europe, Asia, and all Africa increased as a result of improved and expanded foods.

World Population (in millions)				
	1650	**1750**	**1800**	**1850**
Africa	100	95	90	95
Asia (excluding Russia)	327	475	597	741
South America	12	11	19	33
North America	1	1	6	26
Europe and Russia	103	144	192	274
Australia	2	2	2	2
Total	545	728	906	1,171

English artist John White sketched the wildlife of the Americas during the sixteenth century. The "allagato" is probably the man-eating reptile that Columbus reported sighting in Panama 100 years earlier.

A llagatto: This being but one moneth old was 3. foote 4. ynches in length. and lyue in water.

446

As Europe's population increased in the seventeenth century, many people sought relief and opportunity by moving to the Americas. Within a century, because of the European settlers' arrival, more than 85 percent of the Amerindian population was wiped out by disease and warfare.

Colonists Bring New Plants to America. The explorers and settlers who arrived in the Americas felt strange in their new environment. They were unfamiliar with both the plants and the animals, and found survival difficult. Their solution was to ship plants and animals from their homelands to the New World.

When Columbus sailed to America the second time, he brought many Old World seeds and plant cuttings. He introduced wheat, chickpeas, melons, onions, radishes, salad greens, grapevines, sugarcane, and many fruits. A few years later, European colonists brought horses, pigs, cattle, chickens, sheep, and goats. The new plants and animals prospered, causing a biological revolution in the Americas.

Wheat and the other European grains failed to grow in the West Indies, as did grapevines and olive trees. Spanish colonists, therefore, had to live without three traditional staples: bread, wine, and oil. Many crops did prosper, however, among them cauliflowers, cabbages, radishes, lettuce, and European melons.

The Spanish also planted sugarcane wherever the climate was favorable. Charles V sent experienced sugarcane farmers and mill technicians to the West Indies. He lent settlers enough money to build sugar mills in Hispaniola, now called Santo Domingo.

Later, Spanish settlers discovered that wheat would grow in the highlands of Mexico. The government controlled the planting of wheat to assure that enough was raised to feed the local Spanish population.

By 1551, the new settlers were successfully growing grapes in Peru and Chile. They produced enough wine from the grapes to export. Olive trees also grew in Peru and Chile. Eventually, an olive oil industry developed.

Augmenting the fruits and vegetables that settlers and explorers brought to feed themselves were many others that arrived accidentally. Seeds crossed the ocean in folds of cloth, and clods of mud, and in many other ways. Kentucky bluegrass, daisies, and dandelions did not grow in the New World until Europeans arrived.

Old World Animals Prosper in America. An astronaut observing the ships arriving in the Americas might have guessed that the settlers' goal was to replace people with pigs, dogs, and cattle. The Indian population rapidly declined while the supply of domesticated animals rose. Few American predators or diseases existed to deplete the growing population of new animal arrivals.

These new competitors for available land and water increased rapidly. In April 1514, a Spanish settler who had brought pigs to Cuba wrote to the king that his herd had increased to 30,000. Another Spaniard reported that great numbers of cattle inhabited Hispaniola.

Although horses were slower to adapt, their numbers also increased. Like the pigs and cattle, horses were running wild in Hispaniola by the middle of the 1500s. In Mexico by 1550, horses were available for little more than the effort to catch them.

As Europeans moved north, to a climate more suitable for horses, the number of horses increased even faster. The horse enabled the Indians of North America to develop a new way of life. Before the horse arrived, only a few Indians could live on the great plains of the Midwest. They could not farm because the sod was so thick. Hunting was difficult because Indians on foot could not kill enough animals to provide a dependable supply of food.

When Indians learned to ride horses, they also discovered a new way to hunt buffalo. Most Indians of the Great Plains be-

Mounted conquistadors' great mobility and speed terrified Inca troops. A scene from Compañon's history shows Spaniards rounding up their mounts.

came mounted nomads. An Indian on horseback was different from one without a horse. George Catlin, a nineteenth-century American artist known for his paintings of American Indians, described the change:

" A Comanche on his feet is out of his element, and comparatively almost as awkward as a monkey on the ground, without a limb or a branch to cling to; but the moment he lays his hand upon his horse, his face even becomes handsome, and he gracefully flies away like a different being. **"**

The Columbian Exchange. The exchange of plants and animals between the Old and New Worlds, called the Columbian Exchange, affected the Old and New Worlds differently. In Eurasia and Africa during the 17th and 18th centuries, it contributed to an increase in population. New crops, such as potatoes in Europe, corn in Africa, and sweet potatoes in China, brought a more varied and healthier diet. Therefore, people lived longer.

In the New World, by contrast, the Indian populations declined drastically. In the sixteenth century Indians died from epidemics of Old World diseases. Europeans took advantage of this situation to conquer and occupy large areas in the Americas.

SECTION 1 *Study Skills*

Developing Vocabulary Define each of the following terms: **1.** intrude. **2.** mammal. **3.** predator. **4.** Columbian Exchange.

Reviewing Main Ideas **1.** How did the age of exploration change European perceptions of the world? **2.** List five plants from the New World that grew well in Asia and Africa. **3.** List ten plants and animals introduced into the New World by Europeans. **4.** Why were some of the plants and animals introduced to the New World more successful than others? **5.** Explain why the movement of plants and animals between the New and Old World is called the Columbian Exchange.

Understanding Cause and Effect **1.** Explain how the wind patterns influenced travel across the Atlantic Ocean. **2.** How did the introduction of the horse change the way of life of some American Indians? **3.** Compare the effects of the Columbian Exchange on the populations of the New World and the Old World.

Challenge Give three specific examples of new products in the past twenty years that have changed how people live. Have these been as influential as the horse and sugar plantations were in the Americas?

The Earliest Hemispheric Links

After Christopher Columbus reached the Americas from Spain, the Eastern and Western hemispheres were linked in regular global interaction. Columbus may not have been the first person to link the two hemispheres. Historians have found evidence suggesting that Phoenicians from North Africa and Vikings from Scandinavia may have reached America long before Christopher Columbus did.

Convincing evidence of previous contacts is scarce. If earlier travelers arrived in the Americas, they left few indications of their visits. The Columbus expeditions resulted in the first permanent settlements in the Americas by Europeans. Evidence of earlier visits in Central or South America may have been destroyed by the hot, humid climate of the region.

The Vikings

The Vikings were well-known as traders and pirates who used their navigational skills well. Between the years 700 and 1100, the Vikings were involved in large-scale exploration and resettlement. They established colonies in Kiev, Normandy, England, Scotland, and Ireland. The Vikings sought new lands for growing crops and new waters for harvesting fish.

Most of what has been learned about the voyages of the Vikings comes from written records of their explorations. According to adventure stories called sagas, Vikings colonized Iceland in 860, and Greenland in 986. Archaeological research has shown that the Vikings built thick-walled homes of stone and earth in these colonies.

The first Viking to see America was probably Bjarni Herjulfson. He arrived in Iceland in 986 with a cargo from Norway. He planned to spend the winter with his father. He discovered that his father had just moved to Greenland. Bjarne set sail for the new settlement. After losing his way in a fog, he found instead a flat, wooded land. Knowing that this land could not be icy Greenland, Herjulfson turned the ship around and made his way to Greenland where he finally found his father. The exact location of the wooded land Herjulfson saw is uncertain. Many scholars think the land was North America.

Sixteen years later, Leif Ericson, a Viking living in Greenland, bought Herjulfson's ship. He sailed west and also found land. Noticing the abundant wild grapes which grew there, Ericson called the land Vinland, meaning the land of vines.

Other Vikings followed Ericson, and even attempted to settle in Vinland. However, conflicts with people already living there, fights among themselves, and death from plague ended the settlement.

Forged Evidence. Viking records have been uncertain and further confusion resulted from faked records. In 1898, a flat stone with a carved inscription in Scandinavian letters was uncovered on a farm in Kensington, Minnesota. After considerable debate, the general conclusion was that the stone was a forgery.

In 1965, the discovery of a map raised the issue of Viking contact with North America. The map, which appeared to have been drawn somewhere around 1440, showed an island labeled "Island of Vinland, discovered by Leif and Bjarni in company." In 1974, a test of the map's ink indicated that the map, too, was a forgery. However, in 1961, archaeologists discovered evidence of a settlement at L'anse Aux Meadows,

Newfoundland. Radiocarbon tests date the site at the time of Viking exploration.

Phoenician Exploration

Some people claim the Phoenicians of northern Africa explored the Americas even earlier. There is little physical evidence of this. However, the Phoenicians were excellent navigators who built sturdy ships, and prevailing ocean currents could have carried a ship from Africa to the Americas.

In the interior of Africa, boat-travel and navigation were common. Throughout history, the rivers of Africa have been navigated by local peoples in sturdy boats made of reeds. Africans developed ships with both sails and oars.

Modern Evidence. A Norwegian named Thor Heyerdahl tried to show that Africans could have reached America. In the late 1960s, he built a boat of papyrus reeds and

The *Ra* II, shown here, successfully sailed across the Atlantic from Africa, providing evidence that ancient Egyptians could have traveled to the New World.

called it Ra (rah). The word *Ra* meant sun in ancient Egypt, as well as in parts of America. The similar meaning of the word Ra in both places is one reason to suspect some early contact between Egypt and America.

On May 25, 1969, Heyerdahl set out from Safi, a city on the Atlantic coast of North Africa. The boat was within a few days of America when a serious problem developed because Heyerdahl had misinterpreted the paintings from which he modeled his vessel. Unfortunately, the trip could not be completed.

Later, a smaller boat, Ra II, was designed using the information Heyerdahl had gained from his attempt. A native American group, the Aymara, built the boat and sailed it successfully across the Atlantic from Africa. In this way, Heyerdahl and his followers provided evidence that early discovery of the Americas by Africans, such as the Phoenicians, was possible.

In addition to the Vikings and Phoenicians, other people, such as the Irish and Chinese, may have reached the Americas before Columbus. Throughout history, people have overcome geographical barriers. Perhaps future historians will discover other evidence that Columbus was not the first sailor to conquer the ocean barriers surrounding the Americas. Nevertheless, his voyages resulted in permanent settlements and a linking of the hemispheres through trade. For this achievement, Columbus deserves to be honored.

STUDY SKILLS Understanding Geography

1. Why has it been difficult to prove that people came to the Americas from other lands before Columbus did?
2. Why did the Vikings leave Scandinavia?
3. Where did the Vikings establish colonies?
4. On what basis did people make claims for early contact with the Americas by Phoenicians from North Africa?
5. What did Thor Heyerdahl accomplish?

2 European Overseas Empires

OBJECTIVE: *To understand the causes and consequences of the development of European Empires*

The Portuguese Empire

The Portuguese were the first Europeans to build an overseas empire. When Prince Henry died in 1460, Portuguese ships had sailed a third of the way to Africa's southern tip. In 1487, Bartholomeu Dias rounded the the Cape of Good Hope and in 1498 Vasco da Gama entered Calicut harbor, on the southwestern coast of India (see page 381). Muslim merchants held a trade monopoly in the Indian Ocean. They gathered spices and shipped them from southern India up the Red Sea to Egypt. From Egypt, merchants forwarded them to Venice and other Italian cities for sale in western Europe.

Da Gama and his men found that the people of India had little interest in the goods they brought to trade. Eventually, though, they were able to trade the goods for a cargo of pepper and cinnamon. When they returned home, they sold the spices for 60 times the cost of the expedition.

Da Gama was the first European to carry the spices in a single voyage to Lisbon, Portugal. This route made Lisbon, not Venice, the main port receiving spices for Europe.

Controlling the Trade Route. Muslim states around the Indian Ocean did not maintain large navies. Muslim merchants were unable to stop the Portuguese from taking over their trade. Portuguese ships were outfitted with heavy cannons that could fire as far as 200 yards. Such cannons made obsolete the old tactics of ramming, or using grappling hooks and boarding an enemy ship. Portuguese used their cannons to attack and sink Muslim vessels.

In order to control trade along their new route, the Portuguese often resorted to terrorism. For example, on a later voyage, da Gama captured several unarmed vessels returning from Mecca. He took the cargo from the ships and then set fire to them, burning the Muslim crew and the pilgrims on board.

The Portuguese quickly seized control of much of the trade across the Indian Ocean. They also captured Socotra (suh KOH truh) and Hormuz, strategic islands that guarded entry to the Red Sea and the Persian Gulf. In India, they seized Goa, a port city on the western coast, and set up their naval headquarters there.

VOCABULARY DEVELOPMENT

obsolete (AHB suh LEET) *adj.*: no longer usable, out-of-date. From the Latin word, *obsolescere*, meaning to go out of use.

grappling hook: an iron bar with claws at one end for grasping and holding.

sacrament (SAK ruh muhnt) *noun:* in Christianity, certain rites regarded as a means to make humans pure and morally strong. Protestants generally recognize baptism and Holy Communion. Roman Catholics and Eastern Orthodox churches recognize seven. From the Latin word, *sacrare*, meaning to consecrate, to set apart as holy.

Portuguese Trade in Asia. Using the naval base of Goa as headquarters, the Portuguese set up forts and naval stations around the Indian Ocean. In 1511, they captured Malacca at the tip of Malaya. This gave them control of the strategic straits leading to China. Two years later, the first Portuguese ship reached the Chinese port of Canton. The Chinese gave the Portuguese the right to establish a warehouse and settlement at Macao, near Canton.

Portuguese traders reached Japan in 1549, landing on a small island off the southern tip of Kyūshū (kee YOO SHYOO). Portuguese ships returned to Japan, where their merchants got along well with the Japanese. The Portuguese brought Chinese goods to Japan and traded the goods for silver from the Japanese.

Portuguese Colonies in America. Besides Asian and African trading colonies, the Portuguese colonized the area of South America now called Brazil. In 1530, the king of Portugal offered large land grants to nobles who would set up colonies there. By about 1550, the Portuguese controlled 15 towns along the coast.

Christian Missionaries in the Colonies. Christian missionaries followed Portuguese explorers, often with little success. In India and China, the people thought of Christianity as the religion of a small group of foreigners. In Muslim countries, extremely few people accepted Christianity.

In Japan, however, Christian missionaries gained some converts. St. Francis Xavier (ZAY vee uhr) and a group of other Europeans reached Japan in 1549. Some Japanese adopted European clothing and converted.

Portuguese missionaries also converted many Indians in Brazil. They were unable, however, to protect the Indians' rights or improve their living conditions.

The Spanish Empire in America

By 1550, Spain had gained control of a vast empire consisting of the West Indies, Central America, southern North America, and a large part of South America. The Spanish king set up a centralized government in Madrid to govern the American holdings with a firm hand. He gradually replaced the Spanish soldiers with government administrators and officials.

Governing the Americas. The Spanish king created the Council of the Indies, located in Spain, to govern the new American colonies. The council appointed and supervised colonial officials. Spain continually sent new officials to America and recalled others back to court.

Europeans in the Americas

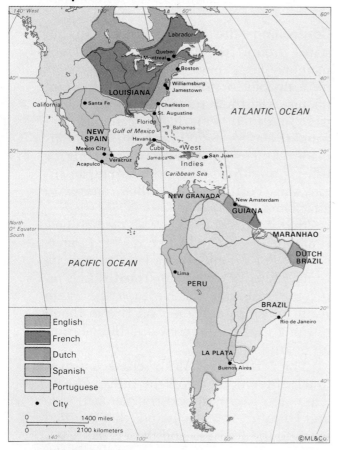

Map legend:
- English
- French
- Dutch
- Spanish
- Portuguese
- City

1400 miles
2100 kilometers

©ML&Co.

Map Skills **1.** List the European countries that had colonies in the New World. **2.** After each country, list the names of its colonies.

A Peruvian mountain of silver, discovered in 1545, was Spain's greatest asset. A 1584 drawing shows llamas carrying ore to the mine's refinery.

Colonial leaders had to be *peninsulares*, persons born in Spain. *Creoles* (KREE ohlz), people of pure Spanish blood born in America, had no political power. Creoles, however, prospered as landowners and businesspeople. *Mestizos* (mehs TEE zohs), people of both Spanish and Indian ancestry, along with the Indians, became the laborers in the mines and on the plantations.

Organizing Mining. The government controlled mining to add to royal and public revenues. Administrators and tax collectors supervised the mines. Government officials also worked in the ports of the Americas and Spain to discourage smuggling.

The mines of the New World produced more silver than Europeans had ever seen before. Between 1503 and 1660, Spain received 18,600 tons of silver and 200 tons of gold through government ports. In addition, to avoid taxes, many Spaniards smuggled the precious metals into Spain.

Silver mines in Peru and Mexico made Spain's rulers the wealthiest in sixteenth-century Europe. Colonists, however, did not benefit directly from the wealth in silver. Most colonists worked in agriculture or professions and trades.

Spanish Treatment of the Indians. The Spanish king granted land to the explorers and other nobles. These landowners also received villages of Indians to provide labor. Colonists used the Indians to farm, work the mines, and do household work. The landowners were supposed to protect the Indians and convert them to Christianity. In reality, they treated Indians like slaves.

The Spanish Mission System. In 1493, the pope granted the Spanish government the right to appoint bishops and other church officials in the New World. The Spanish sent missionaries to all their colonies to work among the Indians who were persuaded to become Christians.

Some missionaries, interested in the Indians' religious welfare, also became defenders of Indian rights. Bartolomé de las Casas (lahs KAH sahs) was a strong champion of Indian rights.

Las Casas Defends the Indians

FOCUS ON PEOPLE

Bartolomé de las Casas was born in Seville, Spain, in 1474. He was 19 years old when Columbus returned from his first trip to the New World. Las Casas watched as Amerindians and colorful parrots were paraded through the streets of Spain. Las Casas's father accompanied Columbus on his second voyage to the Americas. When he returned, he gave Bartolomé an Indian slave that he brought back with him.

In 1502, Bartolomé traveled to the New World where the king granted him a large estate. He used Indians to farm his lands and work in the mines. In 1511, while attending Mass, Bartolomé heard a sermon in which the priest condemned the treatment of Indians. The priest refused to give las Casas the sacraments because Bartolomé treated his Indians as slaves.

Las Casas thought about his relationship to God and his treatment of the Indians. In 1512, at the age of 38, he became a priest. He probably was the first Spanish American to become a priest. Las Casas believed that the Indians were mistreated and he should work to improve their lives.

In 1514, he publicly returned his Indians to the Spanish governor. Las Casas then went to Spain to try to obtain legal rights for the Indians. He urged the government not to use Indians as laborers but to use African slaves instead. Later, when the importation of black slaves increased, he regretted this suggestion.

Las Casas persuaded King Charles V to sign laws to improve the condition of the Indians. One law freed the children of Indians who were slaves. Las Casas was given the title, Protector of the Indians.

Later, he returned to the Americas, this time as a bishop. He tried to establish model settlements where free Indians could work together with Spanish farmers. The settle-ments were not popular, and las Casas was forced to abandon the idea. He entered a Dominican monastery and began to write the history of the Spanish in the Indies. In his book, he described the treatment of the Indians:

❝ The Christians, with their horses and swords and lances, began to slaughter and practice strange cruelty among them [the Indians]. They penetrated [forced their way] into the country and spared neither children nor the aged, nor . . . women, . . . all of whom they ran through the body and lacerated [tore jaggedly], as though they were assaulting so many lambs herded in their sheepfold.

They made a gallows just high enough for the feet to nearly touch the ground, . . . they put wood underneath and, with fire, they burned the Indians. . . .

They generally killed the [Indian] lords and nobles in the following way: they made wooden gridirons [framework of bars used for broiling food] of stakes, bound them upon them, and made a slow fire beneath; thus the victims gave up the spirit by degrees, emitting cries of despair in their torture. . . . ❞ ■

An illustrated eyewitness account by las Casas shows Spanish conquerers burning chieftain Hatuey at the stake.

Decline of the Spanish Empire

The Spanish Empire declined for several reasons. First, Charles V and Philip II used the huge treasure from America in their religious wars against Turks and Protestants, including the outfitting of the Spanish armada. Charles V paid an army to fight the Turks on the eastern border of his lands.

Second, the Spanish nobility looked down on work and lived off the rents from their lands. Nobles made up only 2 percent of the population of Spain but owned almost all the land. Since these aristocrats looked down on careers in commerce and industry, so did the rest of the population. When merchants became successful, they bought estates and titles and gave up their businesses. In addition, Spain had expelled the Jews and Muslims, whose commercial enterprises and taxes had helped to support the government.

Finally, the new wealth, in the form of gold and silver, caused severe inflation in Spain. Prices in Spain rose more than 400 percent in a century. More important, prices in other European countries rose only half as much. Spanish wages were, therefore, much higher than those in other countries. Any young industry in Spain was at a disadvantage. The wages paid to workers made Spanish products much more expensive than those manufactured in countries where wages were lower.

The English and Dutch began to challenge the Spanish trade monopoly, just as the Spanish and Portuguese had tried to break the Muslim monopoly. By the end of the sixteenth century, the French, Dutch, and English were gaining colonies in the Americas and reducing Spanish influence in the New World.

Settlement of North America

Although England had developed overseas trade by the 1500s, the English kings recognized the power of the Spanish and Portuguese. Instead of competing with the Spanish in the Caribbean, the English concentrated on the North Atlantic. Henry VII sent John Cabot on a voyage of exploration to North America. In 1497, he explored the coasts of Newfoundland, Nova Scotia, and New England. His explorations gave the English a claim to the New World.

Exploration in North America did not end English interest in obtaining spices from the east. They began to search for a northwest passage around North America to Asia. Their attempts proved unsuccessful, but one English explorer tried going eastward and landed in Russia. After spending time at the court of Tsar (tsahr) Ivan IV, he and his fleet returned to England. Eventually, the English set up the profitable Muscovy Company for direct trade between England and Russia.

English interest in North America stimulated colonization. During the 1600s, the English founded several colonies along the east coast of North America. The first permanent settlement, Jamestown, was established in 1607 in the area that is now Virginia. The second settlement, Plymouth, was founded in 1620, in the present-day state of Massachusetts.

Settlements were established in the Caribbean with the hope that they would make a profit. Settlers were to raise products such as sugar that England normally had to import.

The Dutch and English in Asia

Both the English and the Dutch used their geography to develop trading empires. The Dutch Netherlands bordered on the North Sea. Dutch merchant ships carried goods to and from Asian lands. They then distributed the goods to other countries of Europe in fluyts, or flyboats. These were slow, ugly ships able to carry large cargos. The Dutch did not try to establish large colonial territories. Rather, they became wealthy by transporting the goods of other nations.

An eighteenth-century painting shows merchants selling their wares while groups of Indians watch the procession of the viceroy.

The English in India. In 1600, to encourage trade with India, Queen Elizabeth granted a charter to some private businesspeople to start the English East India Company. Trading posts were set up in the Indian cities of Madras, Bombay, and Calcutta. The English worked with local rulers, and gradually the East India Company became wealthy and powerful.

The Dutch Trading Empire. At the end of the sixteenth century, the Dutch challenged Portugal's empire in the east. A Dutch fleet sailed around the tip of Africa to the East Indies. The voyage took two and a half years, and only 89 of the 289 crew members returned. Nevertheless, investors, those who put money into a business, made a substantial profit. A second expedition was even more fortunate, making a 400 percent profit. In 1598, 5 fleets of ships sailed to the east. The Dutch soon surpassed the Portuguese. The Dutch were better sailors and could transport a cargo more cheaply.

In 1602, Dutch investors formed the Dutch East India Company. By 1629, they had driven most of the Portuguese from the East Indies. Later, the Dutch also occupied Malacca and Ceylon. They established a base on Formosa, and controlled the trade to China and Japan as well as the Indies.

Relationships with Japan

While strong monarchs were developing trading networks in the East Indies, powerful warlords were consolidating their power in Japan. In 1192, the Minamoto family leader took the title shogun and became a military dictator (see page 306). The family was not strong enough, however, to control local warrior lords. Between 1300 and 1500, the Japanese suffered through a long series of civil wars.

The Tokugawa Shogunate. In 1590, a powerful general, Hideyoshi (hih deh yuh shih), defeated his opponents and unified Japan. His successor was Tokugawa Ieyasu (ih yeh yah soo), a powerful *daimyo* or local lord from Edo, now Tokyo. In 1603, Ieyasu, like the leader of the earlier Minamoto family, took the title of shogun. His dynasty, the Tokugawa Shogunate, lasted until 1868.

An Isolated Land. The emperor, under the Tokugawa, continued to live in a palace in Kyoto. However, he was only a figurehead who had no power. The Tokugawa shogun ruled over all the daimyos.

To consolidate his control of Japan, the shogun forced all the daimyos to swear loyalty to him. To ensure their loyalty, he forced members of the daimyos' families to remain in Edo as hostages. Every other year the daimyos had to travel to Edo and live in houses around the shogun's castle.

Fearing that new wars would break out and destroy his power, the shogun tried to prevent change. The Japanese were not allowed to travel to other countries. European merchants were banned from Japan.

Portuguese monk, St. Francis Xavier, gained some Christian converts after arriving in Japan in 1549. Here monks and Japanese merchants meet.

The Japanese in the southern island of Kyūshū who had become Catholics were forced to give up their faith. Some missionaries and Japanese converts were crucified. Others were made to trample on the crucifix.

Changes Occur in Japanese Society. Japanese isolation was not complete, however. One Dutch ship a year was allowed to come to Nagasaki. The ships could dock only at an island in the middle of the harbor.

The Japanese were very curious about the western world. A few scholars went to the tiny island to study Dutch merchants. These Japanese began to question the authority of the respected Chinese.

Japanese scholars noticed, for example, that descriptions of internal organs of the body in Dutch medical textbooks differed from those of the Chinese. They wondered whether the Chinese and Europeans had different organs. When the Japanese dissected a human body, they found that the organs corresponded to those in the Dutch book. They concluded that the Dutch knew more than the Chinese.

During the Tokugawa Shogunate, towns and cities grew around the castles of the daimyos. The daimyos' need to travel between the city of Edo and their castles led to the development of a national road system.

The artisans and merchants who lived in the cities became richer and more powerful. Under the influence of Confucian ideas, the Japanese previously had looked down on merchants. Gradually, however, commerce became more important. The daimyos, like the European kings, often were forced to borrow money from wealthy merchants.

The European overseas empires grew out of a search for sea routes to Asia. Between 1500 and 1600, the Spanish and Portuguese dominated trade. From 1600 to 1700, the Dutch and English established colonies and controlled trade. Spain, Portugal, England, and the Netherlands all transported, sold, or used slaves. In the 1700s, slave trade grew in importance.

SECTION 2 *Study Skills*

Developing Vocabulary Use each of the following terms in a sentence: **1.** grappling hook. **2.** obsolete. **3.** sacrament.

Reviewing Main Ideas 1. What military advantage did Portuguese ships have over Muslim ships? **2.** Describe the system used by Spain to rule its New World empire. **3.** Why was las Casas given the title, Protector of the Indians? **4.** What was the goal of English explorations in the Americas?

Understanding Cause and Effect 1. Give three reasons why the Spanish Empire began to decline. **2.** What impact did St. Francis Xavier have on Japan?

Challenge Identify the top five nations in international trade today. Explain what these nations have in common with those who dominated trade in the sixteenth century.

3 The Atlantic Slave Trade

OBJECTIVE: *To understand the causes and consequences of the slave trade that developed between Africa and the Americas*

Peoples and Kingdoms of Africa

The European voyages of discovery in the fifteenth and sixteenth centuries opened sea routes that linked Europe and the Americas with Africa. For the first time in history, west African peoples who lived south of the Sahara Desert established contact by sea with other parts of the globe. After 1492, west Africa became increasingly involved in an interacting Atlantic world of trade and migration. For 300 years, Africa's role in the Atlantic trade world was to supply slaves to American plantations.

Many of the African slaves originally lived along the coasts of west and central Africa. When Portuguese sailors visited this region in the fifteenth and sixteenth centuries, they found villages and small towns of people who farmed and used iron tools. Some of these peoples engaged in long-distance trade. West African forest people, for example, traded gold, ivory, and kola nuts, as well as slaves, to merchants who transported the goods north. The Portuguese also traded with these people.

The Kingdom of Benin. One of these west African states was Benin, in the southern part of the region that now is Nigeria. The history of this forest kingdom may have begun as far back as the tenth century. The king, called the *oba*, ruled with the help of a staff of officials and an army. Beginning about 1440, King Ewuare, known in African tradition as a great warrior, according to legend conquered 201 towns. His conquests transformed Benin into an empire.

In Benin City, the capital, merchants bought and sold the products of the forest, blacksmiths fashioned iron tools, and artists created beautiful bronze sculptures. A Dutch visitor described seventeenth-century Benin City:

❝ The King's palace . . . is a collection of buildings which occupy as much space as the town of Harlem [in Holland], and which is enclosed with walls. There are numerous apartments for the Prince's ministers and fine galleries, most of which are as big as those on the Exchange at Amsterdam. . . . The town is composed of 30 main streets, very straight and 120 feet wide, apart from an infinity of small intersecting streets. The houses are close to one another, arranged in

---

VOCABULARY DEVELOPMENT

indentured (ihn DEHN chuhrd) **servant:** one who is bound by contract to work for another for a given length of time.

chattel (CHAT uhl) *noun:* a piece of personal property, such as furniture, a car, livestock, or [archaic] a slave. From the Old French word, *chatel*, meaning cattle.

stereotype (STAIR ee uh TYP) *noun:* a fixed idea about a person or group, held by a number of people, without allowing for critical judgment.

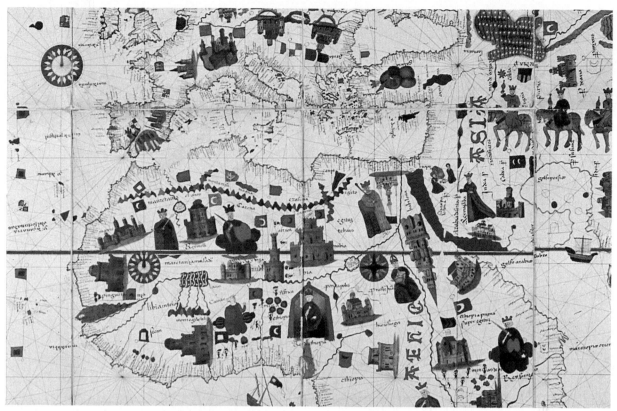

A 1493 Portuguese map of Africa shows the legendary Christian kingdom of Prester John along the Nile River. Portuguese explorers first reached the African coast in 1444.

good order. . . . These people are in no way inferior to the Dutch as regards cleanliness; they wash and scrub their houses so well that they are polished and shining like a looking-glass. . . . **"**

Slavery in Africa. Slaves were used in Islamic, European, and most other civilizations until quite recent times. Slaves served in African societies as farm laborers, domestic workers, soldiers, and servants of rulers. The treatment of slaves varied with different masters.

In most African societies, slaves had some legal rights and often were integrated into the families of their masters. Slaves in Africa were permitted to marry nonslaves, and the children of slaves often were freed. In contrast to North America, the practice of herding big gangs of slaves to work on plantations and isolating them from the free population was unusual.

The Origins of the Slave Trade

When Europeans first sailed to Africa to trade, they returned home with gold, ivory, and small numbers of slaves. By the end of the sixteenth century, however, the slave trade was beginning to dominate relations between Europe and west Africa.

Europeans demanded increasing numbers of slaves to satisfy the economic needs of their colonies in the Western Hemisphere. In Brazil, the West Indies, and other tropical areas of America, Europeans created huge plantations to grow such products as sugar, tobacco, and coffee. These plantations required large labor forces. Workers also were needed to mine gold and silver.

Indian and European Laborers in America. At first, Spanish and Portuguese plantation and mine owners used Indian laborers, often enslaving them. However, new diseases from the Old World, together with warfare and mistreatment, drastically reduced the Amerindian population. For example, 40,000 Indians were enslaved in Bahia, Brazil, in 1563; 20 years later only 3,000 were still alive. Indian labor could not meet the demands of the plantations.

Plantation owners tried to get Europeans to come to America and work in their fields. Between the sixteenth and eighteenth centuries, thousands arrived in America as indentured servants. These individuals agreed to work without wages for a certain number of years. In return, the holders of their contracts of indenture paid the fares to America. Indentured servants often were worked very hard, treated badly, and severely punished if they tried to run away.

Indentured servitude, however, did not entirely satisfy the demand for labor in the Americas. Indentured servants seldom stayed as plantation workers after their contracts ended. Instead, they moved to towns or farmed their own land. Tropical diseases also depleted the supply of European workers. Europeans who worked in tropical areas often died within a year of their arrival. In the seventeenth century, many Europeans thought of America as a dangerous and unhealthy place. According to one English story, a convicted criminal told the judge he would rather be hanged than sent to a Caribbean island as an indentured servant.

Slave Labor from Africa. Even before the discovery of America, Europeans were growing sugar on Madeira and the Canary Islands, just southwest of Europe. Planters there preferred to use small numbers of African slaves rather than enslave fellow Christian Europeans.

When settlers opened sugar plantations in Brazil and the Caribbean, they also employed African slaves. Trading ships sailed down the west coast of Africa, picked up a cargo of slaves, then sailed west across the Atlantic Ocean to the Caribbean islands or the coast of South America.

The use of African slaves offered planters several advantages. First, as slaves, the Africans did not require wages and could be controlled for life. Thus, plantation owners could grow sugar and other crops more cheaply with the help of slaves than with laborers who worked for wages. Second, slaves could be easily isolated from the free population. Africans differed in appearance from Europeans and Indians and could be found easily if they ran away. Third, African slaves tended to live a little longer in the plantation environment than did either Indians or Europeans. Africans came from homelands with tropical climates. Therefore, their resistance to the tropical diseases in America was better.

Even though Africans resisted tropical diseases, the death rate of newly arrived slaves was still very high. Many died, not only from diseases but also from the change in climate, overwork, beatings, and suicide. The plantation societies of America regarded slaves as chattel, the property of the master and nothing more. Slaves had no legal rights. Those on West Indies plantations could not expect to survive more than an average of eight years.

The Slave Trade to America. The cultivation of sugar and other crops on large plantations was a profitable business in the Americas. During the seventeenth and eighteenth centuries, European planters demanded more and more African slaves to meet their needs. European governments granted special licenses to merchants or trading companies to buy slaves along the African coast. The Spanish and Portuguese dominated the slave trade until the seventeenth century, when the Dutch, English, and French began to take a larger role.

African Kingdoms and the Slave Trade. The slave trade in Africa was highly organized. Long-distance trade routes, market centers, and professional merchant firms made the slave trade possible. Some African

A colored engraving from 1872 depicts the slave market in Zanzibar.

"We entered Commassie [Kumasi] at two o'clock. . . . Upwards of five thousand people, the greater part warriors, met us with awful bursts of martial music. . . . The dress of the captains was a war cap, with gilded rams horns projecting in front, the sides extended beyond all proportions by immense plumes of eagles' feathers and fastened under the chin with bands of cowries. . . . The king, his tributaries, and captains, were resplendent in the distance, surrounded by attendants of every description. . . . At least a hundred large umbrellas, or canopies, which could shelter thirty persons, were sprung up and down by the bearers with brilliant effect, being made of scarlet, yellow and the most brightly colored cloth and silks. "

rulers refused to take part in the slave trade. Others, however, used the slave trade to increase their wealth and territory.

One of the kingdoms that profited from slave trading was Ashanti, located in the region of west Africa that today is the Republic of Ghana. Ashanti was founded in the late seventeenth century. Its first great military and political leader was Osei Tutu. According to legend, he became king when a powerful Ashanti priest caused a golden stool to fall from the sky onto Osei Tutu's lap. From then on, the golden stool was the symbol of royal authority in the nation.

Osei Tutu and his successors built a powerful army using guns purchased from Europeans. With these weapons, they conquered weaker neighbors. Some of the prisoners taken in these wars were sold to European slave traders in return for more guns and other goods. This trade enriched Ashanti's royal family, officials, and leading merchants. An English traveler who visited Kumasi (kyoo MAH see) in 1817 described the Ashanti capital:

Slave Factories. European trading companies and governments founded settlements, called factories, along the west African coast. Slaves were collected and sold at these settlements. Europeans did not need to conquer a large African territory or raid for slaves in the interior. In fact, Europeans rarely traveled into the forest interior. African kingdoms and merchant groups controlled the overland slave trade to the coast and used military power if necessary to prevent Europeans from interfering in their slave trading business.

Slave Trade. Slaving ships sailed out of such European ports as Nantes in France and Liverpool in England. Their holds were loaded with textiles, beads, iron bars, alcohol, firearms, and other goods. When they reached the African coast, they sold or bartered these goods to African merchants or rulers. In return, they filled their ships with slaves, gold, timber, and palm oil. The ship then set sail for America.

The majority of slaves were transported to Brazil or the West Indies to work on sugar or coffee plantations. The first slaves arrived in North America when 20 Africans landed at Jamestown, Virginia, in 1619.

The Journey to America.

Most of the Africans sent to America were first enslaved as prisoners of war. Just as the Christian nations of Europe frequently warred with one another in the seventeenth and eighteenth centuries, so strong African states fought over territory and attacked their weak neighbors. Prisoners taken in combat had no rights. Their captors enslaved them, killed them, or sold them to slave merchants. Africans also were sold into slavery if they were rebels, enemies of the king, criminals, or refugees from famine or war.

The Middle Passage.

The voyage of slave ships from Africa to America was called the Middle Passage. The trip took an average of 2 months and was a horrifying experience. Slaves were crammed below deck into stifling spaces only 4 or 5 feet high. The male captives usually were chained together in pairs with leg irons. The slaves were given a meager diet and little water. Sometimes, if food ran short or disease broke out, slaves were thrown overboard.

The ship's captain and crew feared slave uprisings. A slave who refused to eat or cooperate was severely beaten. Many slaves died during the Middle Passage from disease, bad food, overcrowding, or despair. On the Dutch ships that crossed the Atlantic between 1596 and 1650, for example, 17 percent of the slaves died.

The Experience of a Slave

FOCUS ON SOURCES

Olaudah Equiano was kidnapped as a young boy from his home in the area that now is Nigeria. He was sold to British slave traders in 1756 and sent to the Caribbean island of Barbados. In 1766, he managed to buy his freedom with money he earned in trade. He then traveled to England, where he worked as a barber and servant. He became involved in the antislavery move-

Olaudah Equiano's autobiography detailed his experiences as a slave in the Caribbean. This portrait is from the title page of the first edition.

ment, and in 1789 published a book telling of his experiences. The following excerpt tells of his passage to the West Indies:

❝ The first object which saluted my eyes when I arrived on the coast was the sea, and a slaveship, which was then riding at anchor, and waiting for its cargo. These filled me with astonishment, which was soon converted into terror, which I am yet at a loss to describe, nor the then feelings of my mind. When I was carried on board I was immediately handled, and tossed up, to see if I were sound, by some of the crew; and I was now persuaded that I had got into a world of bad spirits, and that they were going to kill me. Their complexions differing so much from ours, their long hair, and the language they spoke, which was very different from any I had ever heard, united to confirm me in this belief. . . .

When I looked round the ship and saw . . . a multitude of black people of every description chained together, every one of their countenances expressing dejection and sorrow, I no longer doubted of my fate; and, quite overpowered with horror and anguish, I fell motionless on the deck and fainted. When I recovered a little, I found some black people about me, who I believed were some of those who brought me on board, and had been receiving their pay; they talked to me in order to cheer me, but all in vain. I asked them if we were not to be eaten by those white men with horrible looks, red faces, and long hair. They told me I was not . . .

I was soon put down under the decks, and there I received such a salutation in my nostrils as I had never experienced in my life; so that, with the loathsomeness of the stench, and crying together, I became so sick and low that I was not able to eat, nor had I the least desire to taste any thing. I now wished for the last friend, death, to relieve me; but soon, to my grief, two of the white men offered me eatables; and, on my refusing to eat, one of them held me fast by the hands, and laid me across, I think, the windlass, and tied my feet while the other flogged me severely. . . .

In a little time after, amongst the poor chained men, I found some of my own nation, which in a small degree gave ease to my mind. . . . but still I feared I should be put to death, the white people looked and acted, as I thought, in so savage a manner; for I had never seen among any people such instances of brutal cruelty; and this not only shown towards us blacks, but also to some of the whites themselves. One white man in particular I saw, when we were permitted to be on deck, flogged so unmercifully with a large rope near the foremast, that he died in consequence of it; and they tossed him over the side as they would have done a brute. . . .

The stench of the hold while we were on the coast was so intolerably loathsome, that it was dangerous to remain there for any time, and some of us had been permitted to stay on the deck for the fresh air; but now that the whole ship's cargo were confined together, it became absolutely pestilential. The closeness of the place, and the heat of

A British sailor's picture of the lower deck of a slave ship in 1846 depicts the crowded conditions during the voyage.

the climate, added to the number in the ship, which was so crowded that each had scarcely room to turn himself, almost suffocated us. This produced copious [many] perspirations, so that the air soon became unfit for respiration, from a variety of loathsome smells, and brought on a sickness amongst the slaves, of which many died, thus falling victims to the improvident avarice [stupid greed], as I may call it, of their purchasers. This wretched situation was again aggravated by the galling of the chains, now become insupportable; and the filth of the necessary tubs, into which the children often fell, and were almost suffocated. The shrieks of the women, and the groans of the dying, rendered the whole a scene of horror almost inconceivable. Happily perhaps for myself I was soon reduced so low here that it was thought necessary to keep me almost always on deck; and from my extreme youth I was not put in fetters. " ∎

The Effects of the Slave Trade

Some African rulers and merchants profited handsomely from the slave trade, as did European planters, merchants, traders, and shippers. Many smaller, weaker African societies, which had no guns to defend themselves, suffered disastrously from warfare and slave raiding.

Population Decline. The population of west and central Africa may have declined as a result of the slave trade. During this same period, however, new American crops, such as maize, peanuts, and cassava, were introduced to Africa. These new foods provided a better and more varied diet. Population growth from improved diet may have offset the loss from the slave trade.

African Relations with Europe. The slave trade had a negative effect on the cultural and economic relations between Africa and Europe. Europeans developed stereotypes of Africans to justify their enslavement. The slave trade took from Africa its most productive resource, its people. More than three centuries of slave trade held back Africa's economic development.

Africans in America. Historians have estimated that between 9 and 10 million Africans were taken from their homelands to America. Between 1701 and 1810, more than 5.5 million Africans crossed the Atlantic. Slave trade did not end until about 1870. The movement of Africans to America was one of the major migrations in world history. Until the nineteenth century, more Africans than Europeans crossed the Atlantic to live in North or South America.

Even though Africans went to the New World by force, they contributed to building a new civilization. Slaves preserved many aspects of their original cultures. Art forms, musical instruments and styles, forms of speech, cooking, religious beliefs, and folktales all survived. African slaves contributed skills, as well as backbreaking labor, to America's economic development. In South Carolina, for example, slaves from west Africa taught European settlers the best way to plant and grow rice.

Communication and trade across the Atlantic Ocean after 1492 linked Europe, Africa, and America. For more than 300 years, Africa played a part in this Atlantic world. People of African descent became major contributors to economic growth and cultural development in the Americas.

SECTION 3 *Study Skills*

Developing Vocabulary Explain how each of the following terms is related to the development of the African slave trade: **1.** indentured servant. **2.** chattel. **3.** stereotype.

Reviewing Main Ideas 1. List three differences between slavery in Africa and slavery in the Americas. **2.** Describe three reasons planters preferred Africans as slaves. **3.** Why did some African tribes participate in the slave trade? **4.** Cite three passages from the excerpt by Equiano describing the treatment of slaves.

Understanding Geography 1. Why did most American slaves originally come from west and central Africa? **2.** To what areas were most African slaves taken? **3.** Where was the kingdom of Benin located?

Understanding Chronology 1. How did the composition of the population of the Americas change between 1500 and 1650? **2.** What significant development in North American population began in 1619? **3.** How long did the slave trade continue?

Challenge Consider how the development of the Americas might have been different if there had been no slave trading.

CHAPTER 20 *Summary & Review*

Summarizing Main Ideas

Between 1450 and 1650, Europeans explored and settled the New World. Plants and animals were introduced to both Europe and the Americas. Europeans migrated to the Americas and began to control much of the land. Many of the American Indians died of the newly introduced and deadly diseases.

Europeans established trade empires and colonies throughout the New World and southern Asia. The Spanish set up an empire in the Americas based on close control by Spanish administrators. Some countries, such as Japan, tried to prevent widespread contact with Europeans.

The need for labor on New World plantations prompted the growth of the African slave trade. African tribes often aided European slave traders. Blacks became an important part of the newly developing societies of the Americas. By the end of the eighteenth century, the Atlantic intercommunicating zone was well established.

"Look! Look, gentlemen! . . . Purple mountains! Spacious skies! Fruited plains! . . . Is someone writing this down?"

Questions for Critical Thinking

COMPREHENSION Interpreting Events

1. What influence did Christian missionaries from Europe have on the people of Africa and Asia?
2. Why did slavery make the plantation system of farming practical?

ANALYSIS Identifying Trends

1. How did population movements during the Columbian Exchange influence the peoples of the Americas?
2. How did the Columbian Exchange affect life in Europe?
3. How did changes in Japanese society affect the way that the Japanese and Europeans interacted with each other?

APPLICATION Comparing Past and Present

1. Give three examples of the legacy of European control still evident in former colonies.

2. Use the example of Tokugawa, Japan, to demonstrate the difficulties a nation today would have in keeping out foreign influences.

SYNTHESIS Developing Map Skills

1. On a map, draw the major Spanish and English trade routes across the Atlantic.
2. Draw a map showing the sources of African slaves and the routes used to bring them to the New World.

EVALUATION Weighing Consequences

1. Use the chart on page 446. What was the consequence of the slave trade on the African population?
2. What influence did the precious metals that were brought to Spain from the New World have on the European economies?

CHALLENGE

Compare the situation shown in the cartoon on this page with Columbus's actual discovery of the New World.

UNIT 5 *Review*

Critical Thinking for Today's World

ANALYSIS Understanding People

1. Explain why Latin American Indians accepted Europeans at first. What might have happened if the Indians had fought the Europeans immediately?
2. Europeans decided to conquer and exploit, rather than cooperate with, the Indians. Suggest reasons based on European history that might explain this policy.
3. What advantages did Europeans expect to find in the unknown lands?
4. The Chinese traded throughout Southeast Asia in the fourteenth century. Why did they not continue to expand their trade beyond the Indian Ocean?
5. How did religious conflicts influence the development of the Safavid Empire?
6. What method did kings such as Henry VII in England and Louis XI in France use to strengthen their power?
7. How did the art of Leonardo da Vinci represent the spirit of the Renaissance?
8. What literary changes occurred during the Renaissance?

ANALYSIS Recognizing Change Over Time

1. Between 1450 and 1650, technology in Europe changed rapidly. Give three examples of such change. Explain how each change made the life of the common people different.
2. How were the Ottoman, Safavid, and Moghul empires alike?
3. What were three traits common to nations in western Europe in the sixteenth century?
4. How did gunpowder contribute to the development of strong national states?
5. How did the development of Russia as a national state differ from the development of western European nations such as France?
6. Explain how the development of the printing press stimulated and influenced the spread of humanist ideas.

7. Religious leaders of the sixteenth century objected to abuses of power in the Catholic church. How did these objections lead to major religious and political changes?

APPLICATION Solving Problems

1. As demand for foreign products grew, so did the pressure to increase trade and find alternate routes. How did Europeans deal with this challenge?
2. How did European colonists attempt to solve the problem of unfamiliar surroundings in the Americas?
3. Machiavelli sought to solve the political confusion in Italy by advising rulers. How would his advice help a ruler stay in power?

SYNTHESIS Developing Global Citizenship

1. When settlers moved to the New World they faced a problem of loyalty. Discuss the factors that might influence whether colonists were more loyal to a European monarch or to a local authority.
2. Explain why sailors might be considered global citizens.
3. Europeans in the sixteenth century began challenging existing ideas. How did these challenges influence lands beyond Europe?

EVALUATION Learning Lessons from the Past

1. What problems faced plantation owners who decided to use slaves to work their land? Which of these problems are still faced by people who hire workers today?
2. In their race to claim land and settle colonies, Europeans did not understand the environment of the new areas they were changing. How might nations avoid such mistakes as they explore the undersea and outer space worlds today?
3. Renaissance scientists challenged traditional ideas and were, therefore, often unpopular. Give examples of how people today react to those who challenge accepted beliefs.

The Interacting Global Community, 1450–1650

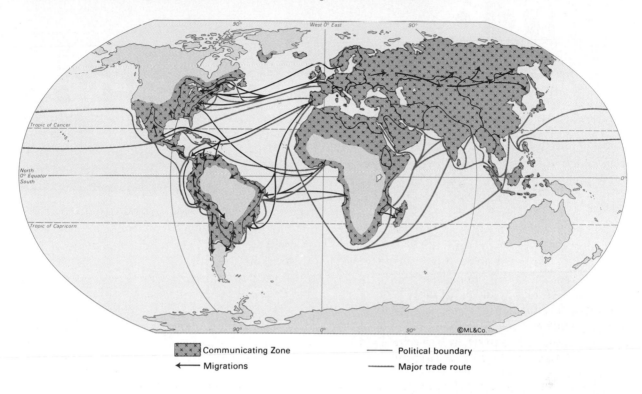

✕✕✕ Communicating Zone	—— Political boundary
⟵ Migrations	═══ Major trade route

A Global Perspective

Between 1450 and 1650, a world intercommunicating zone became reality when trade opened between the Eastern and Western hemispheres. Trade and settlement linked the coastal areas of all inhabited continents.

European demand for Asian goods prompted Portugal, Spain, England, France, and other nations to search for new routes to Asia. After reaching the Americas, Europeans were attracted by the gold, silver, land, and natural resources found there.

By 1650, New World settlements, such as New Amsterdam and Mexico City were prosperous centers of European-style civilization. European trade with China, India, and Japan helped complete the worldwide communicating zone.

COMPREHENSION Interpreting Maps

1. Using the map on page 445, calculate the trade route distances from Seville to Mexico City; from Lisbon to Goa; and from Calicut to Macao.

2. Using the map, describe the advantages of reaching east Asia by an all water route. What are the disadvantages?
3. List the areas of Asia, Africa, and the Americas that were claimed before 1650 by the following European nations: England, France, Portugal, Spain, and the Netherlands.
4. Using the map on page 452, list the European colonies of 1650 located between the southern tip of South America and Hudson Bay.

ANALYSIS Recognizing Global Trends

1. Describe the areas on this map not included in the communicating zone.
2. Why are some areas not included in the communicating zone?
3. How does the communicating zone on the above map differ from the communicating zone shown on the map, The Interacting Global Community, 1000–1500 on page 365?
4. Using the map on page 452, determine which two countries seem the most powerful based on the amount of land they claim. Does land alone make a nation powerful?

UNIT 6
Revolutions and

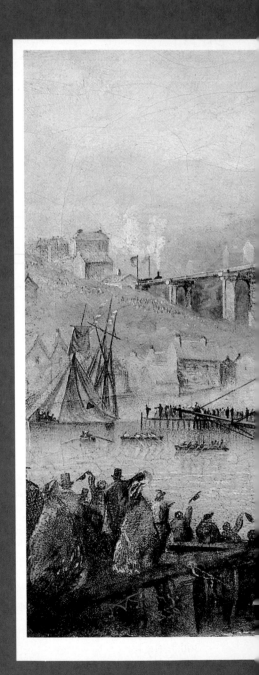

468

Enlightenment

1650–1850

British engineer I. K. Brunel's Saltash Bridge over the Tamar River in England was built during the 1800s.

CHAPTER 21
European Power Expands

GLOBAL TIME LINE

	1650	1670

TIME

1600–1700 Absolute monarchs rule much of Europe

PEOPLE

1643–1715 Louis XIV rules France as an absolute monarch

1689–1702 William and Mary share the English throne

PLACE

1643–1715 *France;¹* Louis XIV makes France the cultural center of Europe and builds Versailles

1650 *Europe;²* Population of Europe increases

1660 *England;³* Constitutional monarchy returns

1663 *England;³* English introduce toll charges for use of roads

Linking Past To Present

An American tourist traveling in tropical Africa pays for a meal with a plastic credit card. Eventually, the cost of the dinner will be deducted from his checking account in a bank in the United States and deposited in the restaurant's African bank. The use of credit cards is one aspect of the worldwide system of capitalism.

The capitalist world economy of today began to develop at a fast pace only 300 to 400 years ago as population increased and transportation improved. This chapter will show how technological advancements stimulated the rise of capitalism in Europe in the seventeenth and eighteenth centuries. As you read the chapter, try to determine whether recent technological advances have contributed to the world's prosperity.

Technological banking: a cash machine.

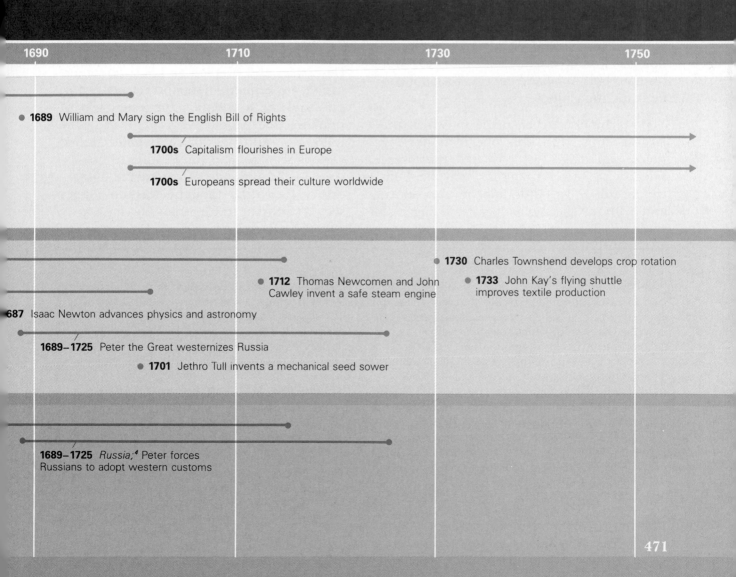

| 1690 | 1710 | 1730 | 1750 |

1689 William and Mary sign the English Bill of Rights

1700s Capitalism flourishes in Europe

1700s Europeans spread their culture worldwide

1730 Charles Townshend develops crop rotation

1712 Thomas Newcomen and John Cawley invent a safe steam engine

1733 John Kay's flying shuttle improves textile production

1687 Isaac Newton advances physics and astronomy

1689–1725 Peter the Great westernizes Russia

1701 Jethro Tull invents a mechanical seed sower

1689–1725 *Russia;* [4] Peter forces Russians to adopt western customs

1 *A Technological Revolution Begins*

OBJECTIVE: *To understand the causes and consequences of the European technological revolution*

The Birth of Modern Technical Society

The thirteenth-century philosopher and scientist, Roger Bacon, described a world where science and technology worked together. He believed that science and technology would create machines to save humans both time and energy. Bacon imagined such machines:

" Machines may be made by which the largest ships, with only one man steering them, will move faster than if they were filled with rowers; wagons may be built which will move with unbelievable speed and without the aid of beasts; flying machines can be constructed in which a man may beat the air with mechanical wings like a bird. . . . **"**

The technology for these machines was related to the scientific revolution developing in the 1600s. Such scientists as Galileo, Descartes, and Kepler emphasized observation, experimentation, and reason. Thus, they laid the foundation for a new way of thinking (see pages 413–415). During the following centuries, more people studied various sciences and found ways to use science in the pursuits of commerce and industry. Scientific thought was no longer seen as a threat to Christian ideas.

VOCABULARY DEVELOPMENT

technology *noun:* the body of knowledge available to a civilization that is of use in making tools, and extracting or collecting needed materials. From the Greek word, *tekhne*, meaning skill or art.

specimen (SPEHS uh muhn) *noun:* one individual of a class or group used as a sample or example. From the Latin word, *specere*, meaning to see.

stagnant (STAG nuhnt) *adj.:* not moving or flowing; inactive, such as stagnant water. From the Latin word, *stagnum*, meaning standing water, pond, or swamp.

microorganism (MY kroh AWR guh nihz uhm) *noun:* any animal or plant that cannot be seen without magnification.

microbiology (MY kroh by AHL uh jee) *noun:* the branch of biology that deals with microorganisms.

capillary (KAP uh LEHR ee) *noun:* a small blood vessel that connects arteries and veins. From the Latin word, *capillus*, meaning hair.

corpuscle (KAWR puhs uhl) *noun:* a cell that is capable of free movement in a fluid such as blood or lymph. From the Latin word, *corpus*, meaning body.

trajectory (truh JEHK tuh ree) *noun:* the path of a moving particle or body curved by gravitational force. From the Latin word, *trajectus*, meaning to throw across.

intervene (IHN tuhr VEEN) *verb:* to come between so as to change or modify. From the Latin prefix *inter-*, meaning between, and word *venire*, meaning to come.

European society in the seventeenth century was unique because people were combining the results of scientific inquiry with technology in a systematic way. Scientists provided an understanding of nature and its laws. A number of factors came together in Europe between 1650 and 1750 to create a modern society. These factors enabled people to use scientific principles to solve practical problems.

European Reliance on Technology. For centuries Europeans had been trying new technology. New sources of energy replaced beasts of burden and expanded the power people used to reduce their workloads. Early sources of energy included water and wind. Later, people used steam and electricity. Gradually, reliance on technology resulting from scientific experiments became a characteristic of European life.

Humanistic Attitudes. The development of humanistic attitudes during the Renaissance paved the way for technical progress in Europe. Humanism, the emphasis on life in this world rather than the next, encouraged scientific study. In the Middle Ages, Europeans had translated some ancient Greek books from Arabic into Latin. Knowing that this learning existed, Italian humanists aimed to rediscover many more classical Greek and Roman texts. They searched in libraries and monasteries. The revival and translation of these texts contributed greatly to European knowledge in the early modern age.

Population Growth. The last serious plagues to affect Europe ended in the 1700s. After 1730, the European population increased an average of about 1 percent a year. Increased population created new demands for food, shelter, and clothing. These demands in turn stimulated economic activity and technological advances. At the same time, the increasing population provided a larger labor force that raised economic productivity.

Interest in science led to the founding of scientific societies that sponsored research and education. Here, a tutor instructs students in astronomy.

Scientific Societies. After 1650, the scientific revolution was advanced by scientists meeting for the first time specifically to discuss experiments. They organized groups such as the Royal Society of London and France's Academy of Science.

The societies published records of their meetings, as well as scientific papers. Members also wrote to one another. A European communications network developed among scientists. For example, Benjamin Franklin and his experiments were well known to most European scientists. This network of communication stimulated further interest in new fields.

Scientific societies also supported research. Some established museums; some created botanic gardens containing specimens for study. Patrons began to support scientific work as earlier counterparts had supported the arts during the Renaissance.

Europe's Scientific and Technical Advances

Europeans advanced in chemistry, biology, physics, and mathematics between 1650 and 1750. Among the scientific pioneers was Robert Boyle of England, who developed the science of chemistry. By carefully studying a wide variety of liquids and gases, Boyle came to believe that certain elements formed the basis for all things in the universe. His pioneering work in the study of chemical mixtures and compounds helped to establish chemistry as a science.

During the late 1600s, men expanded knowledge in the fields of biology, natural science, and medicine. Anton van Leeuwenhoek (LAY vehn hook), a Dutch cloth merchant, used principles of optics to construct a microscope. He wanted a better way to examine the quality of cloth.

Using his microscope, Leeuwenhoek also studied such things as stagnant water, teeth scrapings, and blood cells. He discovered previously unknown bacteria and other microorganisms. Called the father of microbiology, Leeuwenhoek recorded his findings systematically.

An Italian physician, Marcello Malpighi (mahl PEE geh), used Leeuwenhoek's invention to examine a dissected frog. He discovered capillaries, the small blood vessels that connect arteries and veins. He also was the first person to describe in detail the red blood corpuscles and the structure of the lungs, spleen, and kidneys. His studies provided a better understanding of living organisms and stimulated further advances.

Another scientist, Isaac Newton, contributed to advances in physics, mathematics, and astronomy during the middle of the 1600s. Before the seventeenth century, Europeans accepted the theories of Greek scientists such as Aristotle to explain the workings of the universe. However, by 1650, evidence was growing that the ancient theories might be wrong. Isaac Newton's findings contributed to this evidence.

Sir Isaac Newton

FOCUS ON PEOPLE

Newton is considered to be one of the greatest scientists in history. He explained the law of gravity, developed calculus, and proposed the theory of color, all within 18 months from 1665 to 1667.

Newton was born in 1642, the year Galileo died. As a young boy, Newton was considered a poor student. He was more interested in making mechanical devices than in studying. While in his teens, he invented a small windmill that could grind wheat. He also invented a water clock and a sundial.

At the age of 23, following Galileo's exacting methods of observation and experimentation, Newton formulated the law of gravity. According to legend, Newton's interest in gravity was awakened when an apple fell from a tree and hit his head.

In stating the single law of gravity, Newton combined the ideas of Kepler and Galileo to explain how gravity governs the orbiting of planets around the sun and the falling of objects to the earth. Newton also used mathematics to show how the gravitational pull of the sun and moon causes tides in the oceans.

At the time he made his discoveries, however, Newton did not complete his investigations or publish his findings. In 1684, three scientists—Edmond Halley, Robert Hooke, and Christopher Wren—were trying to determine what law produced the motion of the planets around the sun.

Halley met Newton in Cambridge and discovered that Newton had worked out a complete proof of the law of gravity. Halley persuaded Newton to publish his findings. Besides paying all of Newton's expenses, Halley postponed his own work to correct the proofs. In 1687, Newton's *Principia Mathematica* was published. The book, a scientific account of gravitation, explained the movements of every planet, as well as those of the moon, comets, and stars.

To work out the law of gravity, Newton developed a new mathematical method called calculus. Newton's calculus formulas could be used to calculate the orbit of a comet or the path of an iron ball shot from a cannon. The trajectories of missiles and the orbits for spacecraft and satellites are based on Newton's formulas.

Newton also conducted a variety of experiments with sunlight. He discovered that sunlight is a mixture of light of all colors. He split sunlight into the colors of the rainbow using a prism. The study of light led Newton to consider constructing a new type of telescope using a reflecting mirror. He invented a reflecting telescope that was only 6 inches long. The telescope used a mirror, instead of a lens, to magnify an image up to 150 times.

Newton became active in public life after the publication of *Principia*. He was the president of the Royal Society of London, a member of Parliament, and an author.

Newton's book, *Opticks*, published in 1704, contained detailed accounts of white light, the color spectrum, and the construction of the reflecting telescope. When Newton died in 1727, he was buried in Westminster Abby, an honor usually reserved for kings and national leaders. ∎

At right, an eighteenth-century anonymous portrait of Isaac Newton. Below, Newton's sketch of light passing through a lens and a prism, causing a spectrum of colors.

European Advances in Agriculture

The introduction of new crops from the Americas accounted in part for Europe's steady population growth after 1730. The practical application of science and technology to agriculture also contributed to population growth by increasing Europe's supply of food.

New World Foods Increase the Food Supply.

The introduction of maize and potatoes increased the supply of food in Europe. Maize was grown in southeastern Europe. Potatoes grew well in the cool climate of northern and western Europe. There, farmers had previously been limited to growing oats and rye. On favorable soil, potatoes produced nearly 4 times as many calories per acre as oats and rye.

Crop Rotation Raises Food Production.

In addition to growing new crops, European farmers learned to farm more efficiently. Charles Townshend, a wealthy farmer, experimented with rotating crops rather than leaving the land fallow. He discovered that certain crops, such as clover and alfalfa, add nutrients to the soil and that turnips make a fine feed crop for animals.

At first, Townshend was nicknamed "Turnip Townshend" and ridiculed. Eventually, however, other farmers adopted his system of rotating crops, and in some parts of Europe food production increased up to 33 percent.

Before crop rotation, farmers did not have enough feed for livestock through the winter months. Most animals were slaughtered in the fall, and meat was preserved with salt. Clover, alfalfa, and turnips, however, could be used to feed livestock through the winter. Fresh meat became readily available year-round.

Cultivation Increases Crop Yields.

Another farmer, Jethro Tull, discovered that frequent cultivation of the soil by hoeing increased crop yields. Hoeing was difficult, however, because crops were not planted in rows. Farmers used the broadcast method of sowing seed. They took handfuls of seed and scattered them across their fields. Tull invented a mechanical seed drill to sow seeds in rows. He also invented a horse-drawn hoe.

Breeding Techniques Increase Animal Size.

During the late 1700s, Robert Bakewell and others developed new breeding techniques that increased the size of animals. He was determined to breed animals that matured faster.

Sheep traditionally had been bred for wool. They fattened too slowly to be raised for meat. Bakewell developed a Leicestershire (LEHS tuhr shuhr) breed of sheep that fattened quickly. This meat became known as mutton. It grew in popularity among the English. The chart shows how farmers increased the size of animals by improved breeding techniques. This increased the amount of food available.

Importance of Advances in Farming.

Improvements in farming increased crop yields and profits. Some English landowners, therefore, began to plant crops on all of their land. They no longer left fields fallow for peasants to graze their animals. The peasants were often forced to become farm laborers or move to cities in search of jobs. The revolution in agriculture contributed to the decline of rural peasant society in parts of England.

Average Market Weight of Livestock (in pounds)		
	1710	**1795**
Oxen	370	800
Calves	50	150
Sheep	38	80

Thomas Newcomen's steam engine aided the mining industry. The engine pumped water from the mines, and, as shown in the painting, raised heavy loads of coal safely to the surface.

The Spread of Advances in Farming. Some European farmers began to experiment systematically in the seventeenth century. As they tried new techniques, they kept accurate records of the seed, labor, and yield involved per acre. They also communicated their results to other interested landowners through agricultural journals and newsletters.

Advances in Manufacturing

Many forests of western Europe disappeared during the 1600s and 1700s. Farmers cleared forests to provide additional farmland. They also cut down trees for fuel. The supply of available lumber greatly decreased. Eventually shipbuilders had to import timber from Sweden, Russia, and North America.

The Development of Coke to Produce Iron. Ironmakers, like shipbuilders, needed large amounts of wood. Iron manufacturers used charcoal to heat their furnaces.

Charcoal is wood that has been partly burned. Coal could not be used although it was abundant, because chemical impurities in coal made the iron too brittle.

In 1709, an English ironmaster, Abraham Darby, discovered that he could burn off the impurities in coal. The resulting coke then could be used to produce iron. Coke was cheaper than charcoal. As the production of iron increased, prices fell. Builders began to use iron instead of wood in the construction of such things as machines, bridges, and farm tools.

A Safe Steam Engine. Another artisan, Thomas Newcomen, designed a steam engine to pump water from mine shafts. Newcomen, a blacksmith and hardware dealer, teamed with John Cawley, a plumber. In 1712, they invented a safe steam engine that performed heavy work without danger of a possible explosion.

The Flying Shuttle. John Kay increased textile production in 1733 with the invention of the flying shuttle. Kay's invention

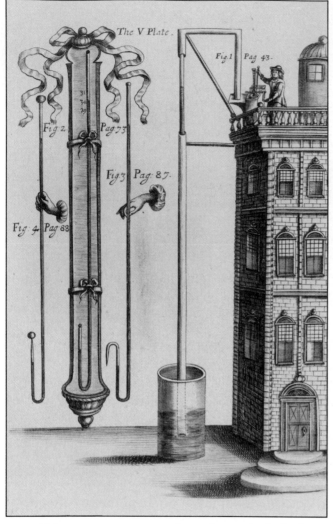

Using a vacuum pump, a long pipe, and a tank of water, Robert Boyle proved that air pressure prevents water from being forced up higher than thirty feet.

physical matter in the heavens and on earth. Individuals began to search for natural laws that regulated other aspects of human affairs, such as government and economics.

In religion, a new view of God emerged. Many people began to regard the universe as a giant machine, started by God and left to run according to well-defined laws. Some people began to question whether God actively intervened in the world.

Scientific discoveries, as well as trial and error, led to advances in practical technology. For example, the invention of an improved water pump for use in the mines increased coal production. This advance stimulated improvements in the iron industry where coal was used. European society of the seventeenth and eighteenth centuries was the first in the world where continuous technical change became commonplace.

SECTION 1 *Study Skills*

Developing Vocabulary **1.** What is the difference between science and technology? **2.** Compare the meaning of corpuscle with the meaning of *corpus*. **3.** How is microbiology related to microorganisms?

Reviewing Main Ideas **1.** Why were scientific societies important to the development of European technology? **2.** List three scientific inventions that advanced European technology. **3.** Describe two of Sir Isaac Newton's scientific contributions.

Understanding Cause and Effect **1.** In what way was the development of humanistic attitudes an aid to European technical progress? **2.** Describe two inventions that increased food production in Europe. **3.** How did improved farming techniques contribute to the end of peasant society? **4.** Name two factors that led to the decrease in European forest lands in the 1600s and 1700s.

Challenge During the Scientific Revolution one new invention often led to several others. Is that process still true? Explain.

doubled the amount of cloth that weavers could produce. The flying shuttle also produced a wider bolt of cloth. This labor-saving device was the first in a series of inventions and improvements that increased textile production.

Effects of the Scientific Revolution. The scientific discoveries and technical advances of the seventeenth and eighteenth centuries affected the way people viewed their world. Newton brought order to the universe with a set of laws that explained the motions of

2 Europe's Political Systems before 1750

OBJECTIVE: *To understand the European systems of government before 1750 and the causes and consequences of their development*

European Political Systems

A few European states grew in power during the 1600s and 1700s. Central governments under absolute rulers aided such growth. The practice of absolute rule varied from country to country. Nevertheless, certain general characteristics developed.

First, an absolute monarch legally had unlimited power. The monarch was above the law, responsible only to God for all policies and decisions. Second, the ruler personally controlled the military. Third, the absolute monarch controlled a bureaucracy of officials who enforced royal policies. Rulers worked to develop a prosperous economy able to support a large standing army.

Absolute Monarchy in France. Louis (LOO ih) XIV, the third king of the Bourbon (BOOR buhn) Dynasty, inherited the throne of France in 1643, when he was only five years old. He reigned 72 years, longer than any other monarch in modern European history. Louis, who chose the sun as his royal emblem, is often called The Sun King.

As an absolute monarch, Louis tried to remove any challenges to his authority. He took personal responsibility for all aspects of French government. Louis made all the decisions affecting the affairs of the state, the church, and even the royal household.

The Economy under Louis XIV. Louis and his finance minister, Jean Baptiste Colbert (kohl BAIR), encouraged new industries and improved roads. They adjusted taxes to make them more uniform and easier to collect. They standardized currency and encouraged trade.

Religion in France. Louis extended the concept of political absolutism to religion. He controlled the Catholic church in France. He directed church policy in all matters except doctrine. The French clergy generally supported Louis's policies.

In 1685, Louis revoked the Edict of Nantes, which had given French Protestants the right to practice their religion openly in France. Huguenots faced torture, persecu-

---

VOCABULARY DEVELOPMENT

pension (PEHN shuhn) *noun:* a regular payment, not a fee, that a sponsoring person or government gives to someone, such as an architect or artist.

diplomacy (dih PLOH muh see) *noun:* the conduct of business between nations, such as making treaties.

treason (TREE zuhn) *noun:* betrayal of one's country, as in aiding the enemy. From the Latin prefix *trans-*, meaning over, and word *dare*, meaning to give.

commissioning (kuh MIHSH uhn ing) *verb:* giving permission to, authorizing. From the Latin word, *commissio*, meaning delegating business.

balance of power: a fairly even distribution of military and economic power among nations so that no nation will become too strong or too dangerous.

tion, and the destruction of their churches. Thousands were imprisoned or sent to the Mediterranean to row galleys in the French navy. Many left France, escaping to England, Holland, Prussia, or the American colonies. France lost many skilled craftsmen, professionals, and business leaders to these other countries.

French Culture under Louis XIV. Louis made France the cultural capital of Europe. He assembled and encouraged the finest artists, writers, and musicians. He granted talented individuals a government pension so that they could devote their time to art.

To demonstrate the greatness of France, Louis built the palace of Versailles (vuhr SY) a few miles outside Paris. The palace, which took 40 years to build, is more than 1/4 mile long and has about 1,300 rooms. Two smaller palaces also are located on the 250 acres of Versailles.

The French court under Louis became the model for the courts of Europe. Versailles became the ideal palace, and many other rulers built similar residences. French clothing, manners, and cooking also were imitated. The French language was used in diplomacy throughout Europe.

French Military Power. Louis established the strongest standing army in Europe. He put almost 250,000 French soldiers in uniform under his command. French soldiers were well-trained and equipped. Louis also increased the size and strength of the navy.

Louis's Military Ambitions. Louis fought four major wars to expand French territory. However, the alliances of other countries always checked his ambitions. In 1700, Louis fought his last war in an effort to put his grandson on the Spanish throne.

The Spanish Hapsburg king had died without an heir. In his will, he left his throne to Louis's grandson, Philip of Anjou. Philip, a member of the Bourbon family, was distantly related to the Spanish Haps-burgs. Many European nations were afraid that one day the Bourbons would unite the kingdoms of Spain and France.

England, Holland, Austria, and other states allied to stop the French. The War of the Spanish Succession engaged much of Europe, as well as the American colonies, from 1701 to 1713. The war ended in a compromise reached in the Treaty of Utrecht.

The treaty contained three main provisions. First, the treaty recognized Louis's grandson as the king of Spain. However, it stated that the French and Spanish crowns were never to be united. Second, Spanish possessions in Italy and the Netherlands were transferred to Austria. Third, England received Gibraltar from Spain and Nova Scotia and Newfoundland from France.

The War of Spanish Succession proved that the Austrian Hapsburgs and the British were the military equals of France. Years of war and the lavish life at court had drained France's treasury. Perhaps, realizing the economic drain, Louis advised his heir not to "imitate me in my fondness for buildings nor in my fondness for war."

Disadvantages of Absolutism in France. Louis's desire to control and regulate all areas of French life brought about restrictions on personal freedoms. Louis used spies, secret police, and other agents to catch and punish opponents of his policies. Many were imprisoned without being charged or tried publicly.

Louis's practice of absolutism served as a model for other nations. In eastern Europe, the rise of absolutism in the 1600s brought major changes in life and government to the people.

Central and Eastern Europe

In the seventeenth century, three strong states—Austria, Prussia, and Russia—were developing in central and eastern Europe. The rulers of these states copied the absolutist practices of France.

The Austrian Empire. Austria, ruled by the Hapsburg family, occupied the geographic crossroads of central Europe. From the hereditary lands of Austria and Bohemia, the Hapsburgs expanded eastward and southward, driving back the Ottoman Turks. By 1700, Hapsburg rulers had pushed the Ottomans out of Hungary and become its hereditary kings.

The Austrian Empire grew in size between 1650 and 1750. Hapsburg rulers, however, never centralized the administration of the empire. Each principality or kingdom kept its own form of government and administration.

Maria Theresa Rules Austria. In 1740, at the death of her father, Maria Theresa inherited the throne of Austria. Though only 23 years old, she was the monarch of an empire that consisted of a patchwork of people. Among those living within the empire were Germans, Hungarians, Italians, Belgians, Romanians, and Poles. Also included were several Slavic peoples, such as Bohemians, Serbs, Croatians, and Slovenians. See the map on this page.

Maria Theresa and her successors tried to govern the lives of their people from the Austrian capital at Vienna. The variety of languages, religions, and cultures within the empire challenged the Hapsburg ability to rule successfully. In addition, surrounding Austria were rivals who at times formed alliances against the Hapsburgs. Prussia was a major rival of Austria.

The Growth of Prussia. The Hohenzollern (HOH uhn TSAHL urn) family ruled the German state of Prussia. Under the absolute rule of Frederick William from 1640 to 1688, Prussia became a centralized and carefully administered state. He created a strong, efficient army because Prussia lacked natural geographic defenses.

Force and favors persuaded the Prussian nobility, called Junkers, to support Frederick William's plans. In return for military

Peoples of Eastern Europe

Map Skills **1.** Name four ethnic groups that lived on the Balkan Peninsula. **2.** Name three ethnic groups ruled by Maria Theresa of Austria. **3.** What people were neighbors of the Lithuanians?

service and loyalty, Frederick William exempted the Junker class from taxes. They also were given legal authority over their peasants. The Junkers became the military officers and loyal bureaucrats needed to build a strong, efficient state. Discipline and obedience became Prussian values.

The Growth of Russia. On the eastern frontier of Europe, absolute monarchs ruled Russia. For years, Russian tsars executed or exiled those who opposed them.

In 1650, Russia was an agricultural country with a very small middle class and only limited commercial contact with western Europe. Nobles controlled estates farmed by serfs.

Peter the Great traveled throughout Europe in 1697. This nineteenth-century painting by Daniel Maclise shows Peter at Deptford dockyard, England.

The lack of a seaport for overseas trade was a major problem for Russia. The country had no access to the Atlantic Ocean or the Mediterranean Sea. Sweden blocked access to the Atlantic Ocean through the Baltic Sea. Even if Russian ports could have been established on the Baltic, the water froze for months in the winter. To the south, the Ottoman Empire controlled the straits, the Dardanelles (DAHR duh NEHLZ), that led from the Black Sea to the Mediterranean Sea). (see pages 503–504).

Peter the Great Westernizes Russia. Russia gained seaports and joined the modern world under Peter the Great. Peter, who was almost seven feet tall, ruled from 1689 to 1725. He traveled to western Europe in 1697. Peter visited England, the Dutch Netherlands, Prussia, and Austria. In the Netherlands, he worked as a carpenter in a shipyard to learn how ships were made. He visited schools, factories, and hospitals. The scientists and artisans Peter met impressed him. He persuaded some to go to Russia with him.

With missionary zeal throughout the remainder of his reign, Peter worked to westernize Russia. He wished to follow the model of western European countries in political, economic, and cultural development. He forced the nobles of his court to cut off their traditional long beards and to wear western clothes. Peter even executed his son, Alexis, for opposing his reforms.

Peter chose people of ability for high military and administrative offices, rather than relying on hereditary privileges. He compelled Russian nobles to serve the state in some capacity. He sent the sons of nobles abroad to study. Peter created a nobility that had little in common with the rest of Russian society and depended on the tsar.

Peter adopted many ideas from Germany, Sweden, and France. He reorganized his army along western lines and adopted the best European weapons. After seeing western monarchs controlling the churches in their countries, Peter took control of the Russian Orthodox church. He deposed the patriarch of Moscow and appointed state officials to administer the church's property.

Under Peter, Russia became strong enough to engage Sweden in a long war for power in the Baltic region. In 1721, after a 20-year struggle, Peter forced Sweden to give up important territories along the Baltic Sea. The area included part of Finland and the ports of Riga, Reval, and Viborg.

Peter built a new capital near the Baltic Sea and named it St. Petersburg, after himself. He called the new capital his "window to the west." Soon French governesses and German tutors, as well as other Europeans, arrived in Russia.

Russia under Catherine. Catherine the Great ruled Russia from 1762 to 1796. She was a German princess who had come to Russia at the age of 16 to marry the heir to the throne. The marriage was a complete failure. In 1762, she and a group of nobles deposed her weak and neurotic husband and later had him murdered.

Catherine promoted western European culture, especially French, and continued the policies of Peter the Great. She also fought a successful war against the Turks. Her prizes were the Sea of Azov and most of the northern shore of the Black Sea. Russia also gained the right to send ships from the Black Sea through the Bosporus and the Dardanelles to the Mediterranean Sea.

Catherine, at about the same time, sought to expand westward into Poland. The Polish king did not have the political, military, or economic resources to develop a strong, centralized government. The king of Poland, like the Holy Roman Emperor, was elected. Independent Polish nobles tended to choose a weak monarch whom they could control. Prussia, Austria, France, and Russia each plotted to put its favorite candidate on the Polish throne.

In 1772, Russia, Prussia, and Austria each took a piece of Polish territory in what is called the First Partition of Poland. In 1793, Russia and Prussia partitioned Poland a second time. Finally, in 1795, Russia, Prussia, and Austria agreed to a Third Partition, dividing the remainder of Poland among themselves. Thus, Poland disappeared from the map as an independent nation. See the map on this page.

England Develops a Constitutional Monarchy

Absolute monarchies promoted order and stability in most European states. England, however, developed into a strong nation without absolute monarchs. The effective voices of both lords and commoners in the English Parliament limited the power of English monarchs.

Between 1600 and 1750, some English kings accepted the increasing power of Parliament, though kings tried to limit the assembly's power. Kings who resisted argued that Parliament overstepped its authority in limiting the monarch's power to tax, form religious policies, and carry out justice.

English Kings Oppose Parliament. Two early seventeenth-century English monarchs, James I and Charles I, resisted Parliament's efforts to limit royal power. Their efforts led to civil war as supporters of Parliament fought supporters of the king. The war ended in 1649. Charles was convicted of treason and other crimes in a special session of Parliament. He was then publicly beheaded.

The issue of the rights of the king and Parliament was not the only one in bringing England to civil war. Religious issues also divided England. Many people believed that the Church of England was still too much like the Catholic church. They said it needed to be purified of Roman doctrines and elaborate ceremonies. Called Puritans by their critics, these people gained control of Parliament and the army. Their leader was Oliver Cromwell.

Partition of Poland, 1772–1795

Map Skills **1.** What three nations annexed Polish land? **2.** How many miles would a traveler cover on a trip from Russia to Lithuania?

After the civil war, the army gave Cromwell the title Lord Protector of England. Cromwell and the army ruled England in a military dictatorship from 1649 to 1658.

Under the Puritans, life in England was strictly regulated. Such entertainments as dancing, card playing, and theatergoing were banned. In 1660, two years after Cromwell's death, Parliament restored a monarch to the throne. Charles II was the son of Charles I. His brother, James II, succeeded Charles in 1685.

The Glorious Revolution. Influenced by his exile in Europe, James II was determined to rule as an absolute monarch. People resisted, and James fled to France.

Parliament then invited William of Orange, ruler of the Dutch Netherlands, and his wife, Mary, to rule England. Mary was the daughter of James II. Parliament's action of putting William and Mary on the throne of England is known as the Glorious Revolution. In 1689, William and Mary were recognized as rulers of England.

A Constitutional Monarchy. As a condition of receiving the English throne, William and Mary agreed to accept the English Bill of Rights. This document outlined basic rights and powers.

The English Bill of Rights

FOCUS ON SOURCES

Parliament passed the Bill of Rights, and William and Mary signed it in December 1689. Like the Magna Carta, the Bill of Rights is considered a major step in the development of constitutional government. By choosing new monarchs and passing the Bill of Rights, Parliament brought stability to England. Here are some of the rights and powers guaranteed in The Bill of Rights:

Parliament exemplified English democracy. Karl Anton Hickel's 1793 painting shows a lively debate in the House of Commons. The House's two opposing political parties face each other.

"1. That the pretended [claimed] power of suspending laws, or the execution of laws, by regal authority without consent of Parliament, is illegal.

2. That the pretended power of dispensing [doing away] with laws, or the execution [carrying out] of laws, by regal authority as it hath been assumed and exercised of late, is illegal. . . .

3. That the King is prohibited from commissioning special courts to avoid going through the normal channels. . . .

4. That levying money [collecting a tax] for or to the use of the Crown . . . without grant of Parliament . . . is illegal.

• • •

6. That raising or keeping a standing army within the kingdom in time of peace, unless it be with consent of Parliament, is against the law.

• • •

9. That the freedom of speech and debates or proceedings in Parliament ought not to be impeached [challenged]. . . [except by] Parliament.

10. That excessive bail nor excessive fines [be] imposed, nor cruel and unusual punishments inflicted.

• • •

13. And that for redress of all grievances [setting right all wrongs], and for the amending, strengthening, and preserving of the laws, Parliament ought to be held frequently. **"**

Under this Bill of Rights, absolutism died in England. The agreement between Parliament and William and Mary also ended the threat that James II would regain his English throne. James also claimed the throne of Scotland, England's northern neighbor. From Scotland, he or his heirs could attack England. To avoid that, England and Scotland united under one government in 1707. The united countries were named Great Britain. The people were called British. ■

The European Balance of Power

Between 1650 and 1750, competition between the strong states of England, France, Prussia, Russia, and Austria often led to war. Large standing armies and better organized economies encouraged aggressive monarchs to try to expand their lands.

War was considered a legitimate and effective way to settle political disputes. Success in war brought glory, new markets, and more territory and power. To increase their ability to wage war or defend themselves, rulers sought allies.

In the 1600s, governments often cooperated to help maintain peace. They hoped to avoid war by maintaining the balance of power. Since war was costly, rulers tried to settle disputes with diplomacy.

The struggle to balance political, economic, and military power went beyond the European continent. Colonies became important factors in European power politics. Ambitious rulers divided, traded, or sacrificed territories from Asia to the Americas.

SECTION 2 *Study Skills*

Developing Vocabulary   1. How did Louis XIV use pensions? **2.** What is treason? **3.** Is a balance of power among nations beneficial to all those involved? Explain.

Reviewing Main Ideas   1. Identify three characteristics of an absolute monarch. **2.** List three reforms of Peter the Great. How did they change Russia?

Understanding Chronology   1. What was the importance of the war fought from 1701 to 1713? **2.** List the results of Russia's victory over Sweden in 1721.

Understanding Cause and Effect   1. Explain the causes of the Glorious Revolution. **2.** How did the partitions of Poland change Europe?

Challenge   Find five similarities between the English and the American Bill of Rights.

3 Capitalism and Global Trade

OBJECTIVE: *To understand the causes and consequences of the growth of mercantilism and capitalism as economic systems*

European Economies

By the 1700s, France, Holland, Sweden, England, Portugal, and Spain controlled colonies throughout much of the world. European trade expanded. See the map, Europe and Global Trade, 1763, page 487. This overseas trade and expansion stimulated a commercial revolution that dramatically changed European economic life.

Mercantilism. Colonies were an important part of an economic system called mercantilism. Many European monarchs were mercantilists. The supporters of mercantilism believed that the nation with the most gold and silver was the wealthiest and, therefore, the most powerful. European rulers recognized that their political power was based on wealth. They obtained their wealth from land ownership and trade. In the mercantilist system, the government regulated the country's economy.

Monarchs could help to increase their country's supply of gold by maintaining a favorable balance of trade. To achieve this advantage, a country must sell, or export, more goods to other countries than it buys.

Payment for foreign trade goods at that time was paid in gold and silver. Therefore, the difference between exports and imports resulted in a net increase or decrease in the country's supply of gold and silver.

Spain, for example, did not maintain a favorable balance of trade. Spanish kings used their vast wealth from the New World to pay military expenses and buy the supplies they needed. As a result, Spain imported more than it exported. Thus, its gold

---

VOCABULARY DEVELOPMENT

tariff (TAIR ihf) *noun:* a tax that a government places on goods imported into the country. From the Arabian word, *arafa*, meaning to inform.

raw material: material still in its original state before processing or manufacturing.

laissez faire (LEHS ay FAIR): the practice of letting owners of industry and business set working conditions without government control or regulation. French words meaning let people do as they please.

capitalism (KAP uh tuhl ihz uhm) *noun:* an economic system in which individuals or companies own and operate businesses for profit.

entrepreneur (AHN truh pruh NYOOR) *noun:* a business manager or organizer who assumes the risk of forming a business for the sake of profit. From the French word, *entreprendre*, meaning to undertake.

consumer goods: goods that satisfy people's needs.

redeem (rih DEEM) *verb:* to buy back. From the Latin prefix *re-*, meaning back, and word *emere*, meaning to buy.

domestic (duh MEHS tihk) *adj.:* made or produced in the home country, native. From the Latin word, *domus*, meaning home.

Europe and Global Trade, 1763

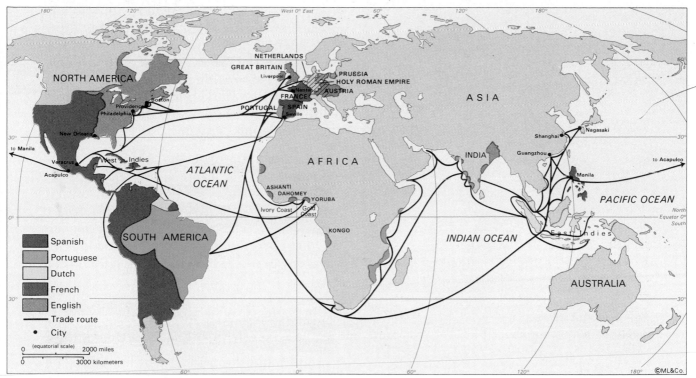

Map Skills   1. In what directions would a merchant travel to take his goods from Boston to Veracruz? **2.** What European countries held colonies in Africa?

and silver quickly disappeared into the treasuries of other nations.

Nations could take several steps to establish a favorable balance of trade. First, the government could impose tariffs, taxes on imports, to limit goods coming into the country. Tariffs raised the price of foreign goods so that people were discouraged from buying them.

Second, countries could increase the value of their exports. Manufactured goods were the most valuable exports. Their sale brought a higher price than did raw materials. Mercantilist countries, therefore, encouraged manufacturing.

Third, to maintain their gold supply, countries could aim to become self-sufficient and thus reduce imports. In this way, nations also could decrease their need to rely on other countries. Self-sufficiency was particularly important to countries often at war with one another.

Fourth, colonies could help a country to gain a favorable balance of trade. Mercantilist countries wanted colonies to supply raw materials to the manufacturing industries of the home country. Colonies also became buyers, or markets, for products manufactured in the home country.

During the 1800s, the mercantilist systems of some European countries gradually gave way to another economic policy called *laissez faire* (LEHS ay FAIR). Merchants and businesspeople came to believe that government restrictions upset the natural laws regulating the economy. The French words *laissez faire* mean let people do as they wish.

The Capitalist System

The desire for fewer government restrictions grew out of the desire of business leaders to make a profit. This profit motive is a driving force behind capitalism, an econom-

Commerce and piety are shown together in Quentin Metsys's 1514 painting. A banker weighs his earthly goods while his wife looks through a religious book.

ic system in which individuals and private companies, rather than the government, own and operate businesses.

The Development of Capitalism.
Capitalism developed in Europe over a long period of time. The growth of towns and trade gradually created a new economic system. Between 1650 and 1750, capitalist economies based on the profit motive became more active. Capitalism expanded as individuals and nations recognized the economic benefits of the new system.

The Workings of Capitalism.
Individuals invest capital, or money, in a business in order to manufacture and sell goods. Capitalists invest in order to make a profit. Much of the profit is reinvested to produce more goods, capital, and profits.

The capitalist system that evolved in Europe had five major characteristics. First, individuals owned the means of production—factories, farms, mines. Second, individuals invested their capital, or money, hoping to make a profit. Third, money, credit, and

banking, rather than barter, were used. Fourth, producers competed with one another for better products and prices. Fifth, the labor of people was no longer regarded as an aspect of family, village, or feudal duties, but as something to be bought or sold freely in the marketplace. These features distinguished commercial capitalism from other economic systems.

Individuals Control the Means of Production.
In the capitalist system, individuals, rather than the government, owned the factories, farms, mines, and other means of production. Generally, in the late 1700s, governments reduced restrictions on the way in which individuals used their capital assets or ran their businesses.

The Profit Motive.
Individuals also invest their capital to make a profit. A profit is the difference between the cost of making a product and the price at which it sells. The profit motive helps to determine what is produced, how it is produced, and how much is produced. The profit motive is the driving force behind the capitalist economy.

Individuals known as entrepreneurs (AHN truh pruh NYOORZ) accepted business risks, hoping to make a profit. They tried to produce or supply products to meet the demands of the growing population. Europe's increased demand for sugar, coffee, cotton, tobacco, and rice led entrepreneurs to establish plantations in European colonies around the world. Eventually, the plantations produced such large quantities of these items that they were no longer luxury goods. The entrepreneurs' profits soared.

Use of Money and Credit.
Another characteristic of commercial capitalism was the extensive use of money and credit. Money was necessary to finance new businesses, voyages of exploration, and armies to conquer new lands. Investment capital had to be easily used and exchanged. Capitalism grew with new money management methods used to finance business expansion.

Competition. Commercial capitalism encourages competition. Entrepreneurs compete with one another for profits. In theory, this competition results in the best product at the lowest possible price. Competition also encourages entrepreneurs to produce and distribute goods efficiently in order to increase their profits.

In practice, however, competition and the profit motive did not always result in the best product or the lowest price. Businesses sometimes cooperated to keep prices high. Without government regulation, greed and the profit motive often led to low wages, poor working conditions, and poor quality products and goods.

During the early years of capitalism, the middle class in Europe was growing. Two distinct groups existed: the middle class, who owned and controlled the capital; and the workers, who were employed to produce and distribute the products.

Workers exchanged their labor for wages. Although workers produced the goods and services, they did not share in the profits. Workers received only a small share of the wealth they created.

Reasons for the Growth of Capitalism

Capitalism developed in Europe during the 1700s for a number of reasons. Among them were: the search for trade routes, leading to the discovery of new lands; the increase in population; and changing attitudes toward making a profit. All stimulated the development of the capitalist system.

Discovery of New Lands. Probably the greatest single reason for the growth of commercial capitalism was the connection between the Eastern and Western hemispheres during the Age of Exploration.

When Europeans colonized the Americas, the center of economic activity shifted first to Spain and Portugal, and later to northern Europe. Spain and Portugal used their new wealth to purchase goods from the northern European states. Merchants in France, Holland, and England welcomed the opportunities for investment and profit. Gold and silver flowed from the treasuries of the Iberian states and stimulated the economies of other nations. The merchants of northern Europe reinvested their profits in a variety of commercial activities. These countries developed prosperous capitalist economic systems.

Growth in Population. The European increase in population after 1730 created a demand for manufactured products. Manufacturers and merchants concentrated on producing popular consumer goods rather than in providing luxury items. New businesses began, and old industries expanded to meet the new demand.

Changing Attitudes. Changing attitudes about the value of business activity and profits stimulated capitalism. Before 1650, the Roman Catholic church discouraged trade. St. Thomas Aquinas summarized the traditional attitude of the Catholic church toward commerce when he wrote:

" . . . trading, considered in itself, has a certain debasement attaching thereto, [and], by its very nature, it does not imply a virtuous or necessary end . . . trading engages the mind too much in worldly cares and withdraws it from spiritual cares . . . "

Early Protestant leaders also criticized economic activity, especially the lending of money for interest. As commercial exchanges multiplied, the church began to accept the value of trade and reasonable interest rates on loans. Profits were justifiable because merchants risked the loss of some or all of their investments.

By 1650, Calvinists, influential Protestants, were supporting capitalist practices. About the same time, the Catholic church also accepted the practice of charging interest on money lent for business purposes.

Commercial Capitalism Changes Life in Europe

The rise of commercial capitalism brought important changes to European life. Each change supported and depended on other economic developments also occurring in Europe. Taken together, these changes produced economic growth and altered European economic life.

The Development of Banks. Entrepreneurs needed large sums of capital, or money, to begin or expand a business. Banks developed as a few European families, who had gained wealth through trade, began to lend money to entrepreneurs, governments, and the church. The wealthy Medici family of Florence, Italy, made loans to entrepreneurs and rulers in the 1300s. A German merchant, Johann Fugger (FOO guhr), founded a banking firm in Germany in the late 1300s. By the 1500s, the Fugger family was one of the richest in Europe. Annual profits often ran as high as 50 percent.

Until about 1700, any money European monarchs borrowed to run the government was considered their personal debt. A new monarch often felt no obligation to repay his predecessor's loans. The Fugger bank was ruined because of the Spanish crown's inability to repay its loans.

To protect their investments against nonpayment of government debts, bankers usually charged high interest rates to all borrowers. This practice limited people's ability to borrow and, therefore, a country's economic development.

Development of National Banks. Banking changed when banks began to distinguish between a king's personal debts and the public debt. Some banking families were replaced when national banks assumed responsibility for managing the national debt. The first national bank was established in Sweden. In 1694, the Bank of England was established. Other national banks were set up soon afterward.

Government revenues from taxes and tariffs, as well as the funds of individuals and other countries, were deposited in national banks. Investors believed that their money was safe and that interest payments would be made on schedule.

Investments in national banks were so great that banks usually could guarantee the payment of government debts. The capital, built up from deposits and loan payments, was used to finance unusually large public expenses, such as waging a war.

The Use of Bank Notes. Business benefited from techniques for handling large amounts of money. Shipping gold, silver, or other currency between places was neither safe nor practical. Yet, merchants from one area often had to purchase goods and raw materials from distant sources.

Banks solved the problem of payment by issuing bills of exchange. An English merchant, for example, could deposit funds in an English bank. The bank then issued a bill of exchange for the deposited amount. The merchant could use the bill of exchange to pay for goods in other countries.

The English merchant could, say, buy goods in Amsterdam using a bill of exchange. The Amsterdam merchant then would redeem the bill of exchange for money at the Bank of Amsterdam. The two banks would settle their accounts later.

The use of checks soon followed. Eventually, national banks began to issue bank notes. This paper currency was a substitute for gold and silver. On demand, the bank would redeem the bank note for precious metal. Business flourished because the banks were fairly secure and payments prompt.

Joint Stock Companies. As trade expanded, enterprising capitalists looked for new ways to finance businesses. One method was to form a joint stock company. Business investors pooled their money and started a company. Other individuals could buy shares of stock in the company.

If the company succeeded, all the investors shared in the profits according to the percentage of their investment. If the company lost money, all shared in the losses. The joint stock company became popular because profits were often high and the risks were shared by many stockholders.

European monarchs sometimes granted charters to joint stock companies. A charter gave the company the exclusive right to trade in a particular area. Charters reduced competition among merchants.

As part of their responsibilities, chartered companies sometimes governed the areas they controlled. Many had the power to negotiate treaties and maintain armies. Each company also was expected to establish markets for goods manufactured in the home country and to acquire precious metals. The Dutch East India Company had exclusive trading rights in the East Indies. The British East India Company, chartered by Parliament, eventually ruled much of India. The London Company controlled all of colonial Virginia.

The Domestic System. To meet the demands of Europe's expanding population, manufacturers needed new production methods. Guild regulation of membership and production limited the amount of goods available. Thus, manufacturers started the domestic system.

In this system, manufacturers provided raw materials to farm families. The families earned money by doing such jobs as spin-

An engraving of Brunswick Dock on the Thames River in Blackwall, England. The dock was built in 1789–1790 to accommodate and protect British East India Company ships.

In the domestic system, farm families spun wool and weaved cloth in their homes. This painting depicts a weaver's home in 1650.

ning wool or weaving cloth in their homes. This system is also called cottage industry. The merchant, or entrepreneur, directed the entire process. Entrepreneurs brought raw materials, rented equipment, contracted workers for each task, and arranged for the sale of the finished product.

Both the entrepreneur and the peasant gained something from the domestic system. Workers received wages. However, competition among workers was great. Therefore, entrepreneurs could keep wages and prices low.

The domestic system eventually weakened the guild system. However, cottage industries also created a gap between workers and employers that did not exist in the guilds. In the domestic system, the worker did not participate in all the steps needed to complete a product. Instead, the worker became a link in the chain of production. Gradually, some entrepreneurs brought workers together in large shops to carry out work previously done in the home. The factory system developed from this practice.

As the domestic system became more widespread, capitalists accumulated more money. They reinvested these funds in in-dustries that required a large amount of money to set up. For example, such businesses as shipbuilding, printing, mining, and ironmaking required a large capital investment to purchase expensive machinery. European business activity thrived.

Expanding Economies. European monarchs saw the advantages of increased trade and production. Kings could tax the wealth flowing into their countries and receive new revenues. This money could be used to purchase expensive military hardware, maintain large standing armies, or pay debts.

Europe's prosperous economies provided a strong foundation for political, military, and commercial domination of the world. Merchants spread European customs and culture to many parts of the globe. European conquests also influenced the way Europeans viewed the world. Conquests filled them with the belief that their way of life was superior to that of most other peoples. Europeans came to believe they had a natural right to expand their civilization.

SECTION 3 *Study Skills*

Developing Vocabulary **1.** Why do countries impose tariffs? **2.** What is an entrepreneur? **3.** How do individuals profit from capitalism?

Reviewing Main Ideas **1.** Explain the steps a nation could use to maintain a favorable balance of trade. **2.** List four characteristics of European capitalism. **3.** What factors influenced the growth of capitalism in Europe? **4.** What were the advantages and disadvantages of the domestic system of production?

Understanding Cause and Effect **1.** How did bills of exchange and checks change trade? **2.** What advantages did joint stock companies have over privately owned businesses? **3.** Explain the development of banks from the late 1300s to 1700.

Challenge How do *laissez faire* and mercantilism affect trade in the modern world?

Europe's Land, Climate, and People

The European culture realm contains many common historical and natural elements. Europe is located in the Northern Hemisphere. The land varies from warm sea-level beaches to ice-capped mountains with glaciers. The climate ranges from very warm along the southern Mediterranean, with water temperatures above freezing, to the cold temperatures of the Arctic Circle. The skin of Europeans, on the whole, is lighter than the skin of other peoples. For centuries Europeans have influenced world affairs. An awareness of the diversity in the land, climate, and people will aid in understanding cultural differences.

Land

The land of Europe extends from the Arctic Ocean in the north to the Mediterranean Sea in the south. The western boundary of Europe is the Atlantic Ocean. The eastern boundary extends into western Russia and connects with western Asia. Since no body of water separates Europe and Asia, some geographers classify them as a single continent called Eurasia.

Mountains. Some of the world's most famous mountains are in Europe. The Alps cover the larger part of Switzerland and Austria between Germany and Italy. Mount Blanc, the highest peak of the entire chain, continues to be a great challenge for skiers and mountain climbers.

There are other mountain chains as well. The Apennines run north and south in Italy. The Pyrenees separate Spain from France. The Kjølen mountains separate the northern half of Norway and Sweden. Northern Great Britain and central Spain have rough, hilly terrain. Mountains have influenced the lives of many Europeans.

Peninsulas. Peninsulas are important landforms of Europe. At the western edge of Europe, the Iberian Peninsula separates the Atlantic Ocean and the Mediterranean Sea. The countries of Spain and Portugal make up the Iberian Peninsula. Italy extends southward, in the shape of a boot, from the European continent. East of Italy lies the Balkan Peninsula, which includes the nations of Yugoslavia, Romania, Bulgaria, Albania, and Greece along with a small part of Turkey. A large part of Scandinavia is located in the Scandinavian Peninsula.

Islands. Several major islands are part of Europe. To the north, Iceland, Ireland, and Great Britain, which includes England, Scotland, and Wales, are islands in the Atlantic Ocean and the North Sea. To the east of Spain are the Balearic Islands. To the west of Italy are the islands of Corsica, Sardinia, and Sicily. Greece, in addition to its mainland area, has four hundred islands.

Climate

The temperatures of Europe vary widely, from the arctic winters of the north to the mild winters of the south. The differences in temperature from north to south make possible a variety of farm produce. Wheat, barley, and other grains grow in the north. The southern Mediterranean region is warm enough to support a citrus crop.

Europe has a milder climate than parts of North America at the same latitude. This is the result of the Gulf Stream, a powerful ocean current that warms the winds that flow across the Atlantic Ocean. Since much of Europe lies within 300 miles of the At-

Data on Countries in Europe

	Bulgaria	France	West Germany	Greece	Poland	Spain	Sweden
Area (in thousands of square miles)	43	210	96	51	121	194	158
Area (in thousands of square kilometers)	111	544	249	132	313	504	411
Population (in millions)	9	54	61	9	37	36	8
Annual Birth Rate (per 1,000 population)	14	14	10	13	19	13	11
Annual Death Rate (per 1,000 population)	11	10	12	9	9	7	11
Number of years (projected) **to double population**	population decreasing	NA	population decreasing	66	78	82	population decreasing
Population projected by A.D. 2000 (in millions)	10	58	59	12	41	43	8
Annual death rate of infants under 1 year (per 1,000 births)	18	9	10	14	25	7	11
Percent of population under 15 years	22	21	16	22	25	9	19
Percent of population over 60 years	16	18	20	17	25	11	26
Life expectancy at birth	72	74	74	74	71	74	76
Percent of population urban	64	73	85	58	60	74	87
Per capita food supply (a percent of requirement)	141	135	132	145	135	136	117
Total GNP (in billions of U.S. dollars)	26	531	625	34	134	156	88
Per capita GNP (in U.S. dollars)	2,920	9,770	10,171	2,500	3,710	4,105	10,650
Percent of adult population illiterate	5	1	0	7	1	7	0

lantic Ocean, the people benefit from these warm winds. Europeans living along the coast of the Mediterranean Sea also enjoy a mild climate.

People

There are an estimated 696,433,000 people in Europe. Within each of the 34 European countries, there is a unique and important cultural heritage. Europeans speak many languages and have traditions and customs that are hundreds of years old. Many Americans trace their roots to Europe, the birthplace of western civilization. The chart on this page compares data in various European countries. Some countries show no projected growth in population, while others show an increase.

STUDY SKILLS Understanding Geography

1. Describe the diversity of Europe's landforms.
2. Name three European crops.
3. Describe the climate of Europe.
4. Discuss three reasons for the cultural divisions among European people.
5. Which country on the chart has the greatest projected increase in population by the year 2000?

CHAPTER 21 *Summary & Review*

Summarizing Main Ideas

After 1650, European reliance on technology increased. Craft workers, artisans, and scientists gained respect. Fewer farmers produced large crop yields. Rural unemployment forced many into the new industrial cities.

Absolute monarchs rose to power as nation-states developed in the 1500s. The French monarch, Louis XIV, represented absolutism at its height. In 1649, Charles I was beheaded, marking an end to absolutism in England.

Economics dominated political thought in the late 1600s. Capitalism fulfilled the desires of a profit-minded middle class. Joint stock companies developed to expand trade. As European merchants spread customs and cultures, European civilization gained power throughout the global community.

Questions for Critical Thinking

COMPREHENSION Interpreting Events

1. Explain how Leeuwenhoek's inventions had wide applications.
2. As global trade expanded, so did the power of the nations most involved in it. Why?

ANALYSIS Identifying Trends

1. How can machines destroy pride in a job?
2. How did the conditions in Europe between 1600 and 1750 encourage a Technological Revolution?

APPLICATION Comparing Past and Present

1. Explain why steam engines are not as common today as in the 1700s.
2. Compare and contrast an absolute monarchy and a constitutional monarchy. Which is most likely to work in the modern world?
3. Explain why similarities exist between the English Bill of Rights and the first 10 amendments of the U.S. Constitution.

SYNTHESIS Developing Research Skills

1. Report on one of the inventors from this chapter. Explain the invention and its immediate and long-range importance.
2. Research and report on conditions in France during the rule of Louis XIV.

EVALUATION Weighing Consequences

1. Describe the problems caused by the movement of people from the country to the city during the Technological Revolution.
2. Could the Technological Revolution have occurred without the development of capitalism? Explain.

CHALLENGE

1. Discuss: Absolutism was doomed after the Technological Revolution began.
2. What does the cartoon on this page suggest about scientific discoveries?

"Nothing yet . . . How about you, Newton?"

CHAPTER 22
Trade in the Atlantic World

TIME

1650	1675	1700	1725

1650s Slavery becomes part of the Atlantic economic system

1700s Philosophes spread new ideas

1650–1815 Europe emerges as the strongest power in global affairs

● **1680** Dodo bird becomes extinct

PEOPLE

● **1690** John Locke publishes his *Second Treatise on Civil Government*

PLACE

● **1652** *South Africa;*[1] The Dutch establish Cape Town

1689–1725 *Russia;*[2] Peter the Great westernizes Russia

Linking Past to Present

In early 1986, the people of the Philippines rejected Ferdinand Marcos, the man who had ruled them for two decades. The belief that people have a right to rebel against an unjust government developed from the ideas of French and English philosophers in the seventeenth and eighteenth centuries.

This revolutionary doctrine was put into practice when American colonists rebelled against the government of Great Britain in 1776. Since that time, the idea that governments should be accountable to the will of the people and not the ruler has been a powerful force in world history. This concept remains powerful even today. It has been the rallying cry in numerous rebellions, both large and small, throughout the world.

A mural painted by Diego Rivera commemorates the Mexican Revolution of 1910.

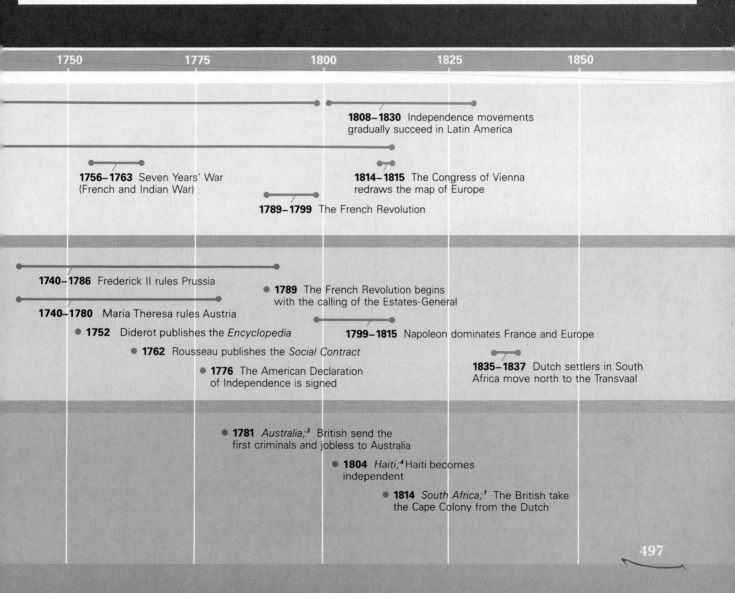

| 1750 | 1775 | 1800 | 1825 | 1850 |

1808–1830 Independence movements gradually succeed in Latin America

1756–1763 Seven Years' War (French and Indian War)

1814–1815 The Congress of Vienna redraws the map of Europe

1789–1799 The French Revolution

1740–1786 Frederick II rules Prussia

1789 The French Revolution begins with the calling of the Estates-General

1740–1780 Maria Theresa rules Austria

1752 Diderot publishes the *Encyclopedia*

1799–1815 Napoleon dominates France and Europe

1762 Rousseau publishes the *Social Contract*

1776 The American Declaration of Independence is signed

1835–1837 Dutch settlers in South Africa move north to the Transvaal

1781 *Australia;*[3] British send the first criminals and jobless to Australia

1804 *Haiti;*[4] Haiti becomes independent

1814 *South Africa;*[1] The British take the Cape Colony from the Dutch

1 European Settlement and Trade

OBJECTIVE: *To understand the expansion of European influence around the world through trade and settlement*

The Atlantic Economic System

In the 1600s, the Europeans developed extensive trade across the Atlantic Ocean. The northwestern European countries of England, France, and the Netherlands grew prosperous by controlling this trade.

England and France followed mercantilist policies more successfully than did other countries. The money that flowed into their treasuries provided funds for purchasing goods from home industries. In addition, England and France built powerful armies and navies. The wealth from trade also financed new jobs in the government.

In part because of their loyal bureaucracies, France and England effectively exercised their new found global power.

European leaders believed that acquiring colonies was important. Colonies provided raw materials that would otherwise be bought from other nations. Colonies also served as markets for finished products made in domestic industries. Further, nations wanted ports around the world to secure supplies. Atlantic Ocean trade, based on the development of colonies, is known as the Atlantic economic system.

Colonizing America. The desire for colonies caused several European nations to conquer parts of the Americas. In the Americas, Europeans could grow crops formerly bought from Asia, such as sugar, cotton, and rice. Growing and harvesting these crops required the hard labor of large numbers of unskilled workers. The need for a plentiful, cheap labor supply led to the growth of slavery.

Slavery and Triangular Trade. After 1650, slavery became an essential part of the Atlantic economic system. European merchants established a profitable trade that included markets in Europe, Africa, and America. Since this trade involved three major trade routes, it became known as triangular trade. See the map, Europe and Global Trade, 1763, page 487. At ports on the west coast of Africa, Europeans traded

---

VOCABULARY DEVELOPMENT

exploit (ihk SPLOYT) *verb:* to use productively; to take advantage of or use unjustly. From the Latin word, *explicare*, meaning to unfold.

Caribbean (KAIR uh BEE uhn) **Sea** *noun:* part of the Atlantic Ocean, bounded by the West Indies, Central America, and the north coast of South America. From the Carib Indians, who once lived there.

Boer (bawr) *noun:* a South African whose ancestors were Dutch colonists. From the Dutch word, *boer*, meaning farmer.

Cossack (KAHS ahk) *noun:* a member of a people of southern Russia, famous for fighting on horseback. From the Turkish word, *qazaq*, meaning adventurer.

incentive (ihn SEHN tihv) *noun:* something that encourages one to take action. From the Latin prefix *in-*, meaning on, and word *canere*, meaning to set the tune.

---

their manufactured goods for slaves. Merchants then took the slaves to the Americas and traded them for raw materials, such as sugar and lumber. From the Americas, traders took these raw materials back to Europe.

The increase in imports and exports promoted economic growth in Europe. To a lesser extent, the growth of trade also influenced people in Africa and the Americas. Europe supplied the manufactured goods that African slave traders and African rulers needed. Europe received a steady flow of raw materials from the Americas.

The states of western Europe created the system of trade across the Atlantic for their own benefit. The European states became wealthy using the labor of Africans and American Indians, as well as Europeans. Colonies provided the materials and markets. Africans supplied much of the labor. Europe supplied the capital and the organization. As trade increased, merchants gained more money to invest.

British Expansion

In the seventeenth and eighteenth centuries, England and France were rivals for colonies around the world. Neither country discovered in North America the gold or silver they hoped to find. Each did, however, exploit other sources of wealth: fertile land, fish, timber, and furs.

France called its territory in America, New France. See the map, Europeans in the Americas, page 452. The French king carefully regulated his colonists, discouraging self-government and independent economic activity. Also, predominantly Catholic France prohibited French Protestants from settling in New France.

The British Colonial System. British colonies in North America attracted far more settlers than did French colonies. Many colonists came to the British possessions to escape religious persecution. Others came for economic reasons. In Britain, large land-

The booming colonial trade is portrayed in this scene at the Customs House on the Thames River. The harbor is full of ships, the dock loaded with goods.

owners were forcing farmers off the land. These farmers could obtain land in the North American colonies, and achieve economic success through hard work and initiative. Such factors led to the growth of Britain's North American colonies.

Indian people resisted European settlement but failed to defend their lands successfully. Old world diseases had drastically reduced the North American Indian population by the sixteenth and seventeenth centuries. By 1776, the growing population in the British colonies led to widespread calls for self-government.

Britain Defeats France. Around the world, Britain and France competed both economically and politically. This competition resulted in a series of wars between 1689 and 1763. These wars were fought on both land and sea in Europe, Asia, and North America.

The decisive conflict occurred between 1756 and 1763. This war was called the Seven Years' War in Europe and the French and Indian War in North America. Britain won the war, in part because the large population in its colonies gave Parliament greater resources to draw on in the war.

The treaty ending the French and Indian War gave Canada, and the disputed land between the Appalachian Mountains and the Mississippi River, to Great Britain. The treaty allowed France to keep its possessions in the Caribbean Sea.

Expansion into India. France and Great Britain held little territory in India, but conducted an increasing amount of trade. Each nation built trading posts and fortifications to protect the investments of the joint stock

Baron Clive, an English soldier and founder of British India, and an Indian general, Mir Jaffier, meet after a 1757 battle to allow the British to fortify Calcutta.

companies that controlled trade. After 1763, French influence in India was severely restricted. Britain's role, though, would grow tremendously. Britain used India as a base for establishing its dominance in Southeast Asia.

Conflict in South Africa. Europeans also had expanded into southern Africa and Australia. In 1652, the Dutch established the trading colony of Cape Town on the southern coast of Africa. Dutch farmers, called Boers, as well as French Protestants seeking religious freedom, came to the region to farm. The Cape Town colony prospered agriculturally. As time passed, the settlers migrated north into the interior where they established huge farms and ranches. African peoples known as Khoisan (KOY san) resisted the European intrusion. Many of them died of smallpox and other diseases. Some intermarried with Europeans, some retreated into the interior, and many were enslaved.

In 1814, the British took over the Cape Town colony. The British governors tried to control the settlement of the Boers and regulate the way they treated the African population. Consequently, the Boers migrated northward, an event called the Great Trek. The Great Trek led to the establishment of the independent states of Transvaal and the Orange Free State in the South African interior. Tension between the Boers, native Africans, and British continued to dominate South African affairs.

British Settle in Australia. Europeans expanded into the Pacific very slowly prior to 1750. For centuries, Australia, the largest landmass in the southern Pacific, remained isolated from the ocean trade routes. In 1787, Britain sent the first of several groups of criminals and jobless people to Australia. The native people were not prepared for the newcomers. As in the Americas, disease and slaughter significantly reduced the population. Survivors retreated into the desert areas of the north. By 1793, a new wave of free settlers had established colonies along Australia's eastern coast.

Russian Expansion

The development of the Atlantic trading system expanded Europe's influence to the west and south. To the east of Europe lay the Siberian plain. This region, over 4,000 miles across, had an excellent river network. Russian explorers, trappers, and traders moved rapidly across the Siberian plain in the seventeenth century. See the map, Growth of Russia, page 502. At the same time, British and French pioneers were penetrating the interior of North America.

The native people of Siberia did not possess the military strength or organization to stop the Russian expansion. The Russian explorers, called Cossacks (KAHS ahks), established forts as they advanced. From these outposts, Cossack trappers and merchants engaged in a profitable fur trade with the native peoples. Russians exchanged the furs from Siberia, as well as iron and timber from Russia, for manufactured goods from western Europe. The Chinese halted the Russian advance along the Amur (ah MOO uhr) River, north of Manchuria. The Russians and the Chinese signed a treaty that set the border of Russia north of the Amur Valley. Like other European nations, Russia could not yet challenge Chinese power.

The Russians' drive eastward eventually reached into North America. In 1728, Captain Vitus Bering (BAY rehng) sailed into the waters that today take his name. His explorations of Alaska and the Aleutians opened the way for Russian settlement.

Fur traders quickly established a line of trading posts along the North American coast. To supply these posts with needed provisions, the Russians founded several settlements. Some of these settlements were as far south as California. Russia maintained its claims to territory in North America until 1867.

Russia's conquest of Siberia complemented its expansion into the Ukraine and the Baltic (see pages 481–482). By 1796, Russia was a powerful country in the global interacting zone.

Reasons for European Power

Between 1650 and 1815, Europe was emerging as the dominant power in global affairs. Europeans directly controlled many parts of the world. Much of the rest of the world was under the influence of a global trading system run to benefit European merchants. Four reasons help to explain Europe's success in expanding its power.

The first reason was Europe's superiority in science and technology. Much of its technical superiority was based on knowledge transmitted from the Muslims and Chinese. In particular, effective use of gunpowder to make weapons gave the Europeans a military advantage over peoples in Australia and the Americas.

A second advantage for Europeans was their aggressiveness. Europeans actively sought to expand their frontiers. Territorial expansion increased Europe's commercial and political power. Expansion heightened national glory and pride. It also provided new markets and the opportunity to establish naval ports. From these ports, trade and territory could be better protected.

A third reason for Europe's success was a genuine belief that expansion was moral. Devout Christians saw European expansion as a way to spread Christianity. The Spanish conqueror, Francisco Pizzaro, clearly expressed this attitude. In 1532, on defeating the Inca army and taking its leader, Atahualpa, prisoner, Pizzaro stated:

❝It was the will of heaven because you insulted the Holy Book. Take courage and trust me. We Spaniards are a magnanimous people. We have come to this land to spread the religion of Jesus Christ. No wonder we are victorious. ❞

Growth of Russia, 1533 – 1865

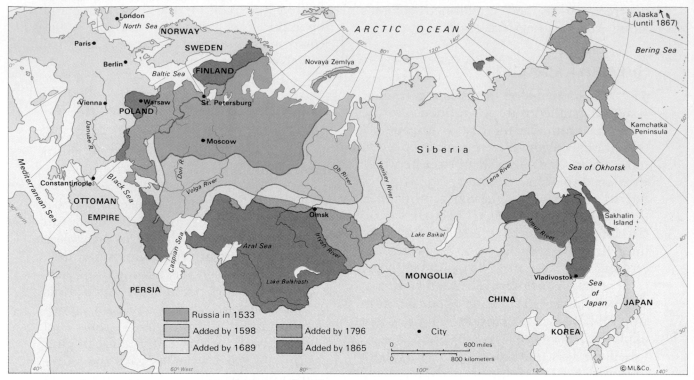

Map Skills **1.** What seas did Russia border in 1865? **2.** Where is Lake Baikal? **3.** How many miles separate Moscow from Sakhalin Island?

Peter the Great of Russia expressed similar feelings 150 years later. He sought to introduce European science and technology into Russia, "so that, having mastered them thoroughly, we can . . . be victors over the enemies of Jesus Christ."

Finally, Europe succeeded at expansion because national treasuries could afford expensive public policies. Conquest brought financial rewards from both wealth taken and the trade that resulted. This new wealth paid for continued expansion. In addition, wealth served as an incentive. Kings, investors, and members of the middle class all wanted a share of the wealth that could be gained through expansion. They actively sought wealth around the globe. This search led to the creation of an ever closer global communication system. European expansion increased contacts among people throughout the world.

SECTION 1 *Study Skills*

Developing Vocabulary **1.** Why are people or nations exploited? **2.** What incentive motivated governments to seek global expansion?

Reviewing Main Ideas **1.** Name three ways nations spent the money they obtained from trade. **2.** Diagram triangular trade. **3.** Explain four reasons for Europe's success in expanding its power. **4.** Construct a chart showing the many areas that were colonized by the French, British, Dutch, and Russians.

Understanding Cause and Effect **1.** Why did Russian expansion stop at the Amur River? **2.** Why did British colonies in North America attract more settlers than the French colonies? **3.** What were the results of the French and Indian War?

Challenge How do nations continue to influence their former colonies?

The Importance of Straits

A strait is a narrow waterway that connects two larger bodies of water. Straits are important for two reasons. First, they serve as passageways for ships. Second, their strategic location gives power to the countries that control them.

Europe has four important straits. The Strait of Gibraltar connects the Atlantic Ocean and the Mediterranean Sea. It separates Spain from Morocco, Africa. The English Channel is a passageway between the Atlantic Ocean and the North Sea. England is on one side, France on the other. The Dardanelles links Europe and Asia in Turkey. Together with the Bosporus to the east, these straits connect the Black Sea with the Mediterranean. Each of the four straits has been important to the countries through which it flows.

Strait of Gibraltar

The Strait of Gibraltar is a narrow body of water that connects the Mediterranean Sea and the Atlantic Ocean. The strait is about 32 miles long and varies from 8 to 23 miles wide. At the surface level, the water flows from the Atlantic Ocean into the Mediterranean Sea. Below the surface, the current is reversed. This movement helps to keep the Mediterranean Sea relatively clean.

On either side of the strait is a large rocky hill. On the Spanish side, a small peninsula, Gibraltar, extends like a finger into the Mediterranean Sea. The rocky hill on the peninsula is 1,396 feet high and is called the Rock of Gibraltar. On the other side of the strait is Mount Acho in Morocco, Africa.

Throughout history, the Strait of Gibraltar has been important as a trade route. The water is deep enough, 1,200 feet, to accommodate large ships. The location, where the Mediterranean joins the Atlantic, makes it a strategic military spot. Whoever controls the Gibraltar peninsula possesses influence in the Mediterranean Sea. Today, Gibraltar is a British dependency served by planes, ships, and a ferry service.

The English Channel

A channel, like a strait, connects two larger bodies of water, but a channel is wider. The English Channel is about 350 miles long and ranges from 21 to 100 miles wide. The narrowest part, between Dover, England, and Calais, France, is the Strait of Dover.

Ships in the English Channel must often fight rough weather. Currents from the Atlantic Ocean and the North Sea meet in the channel. The currents and strong winds cause roughness and often, dense fog.

Difficulty in crossing the English Channel has often protected England from invasion. The Spanish Armada in the 1500s, Napoleon's fleet in the 1800s, and Hitler's warships in the 1940s all failed to cross the channel. The fleet of William the Conqueror did succeed in 1066, and the Anglo-Saxons fell to the Normans.

Today the English Channel is a busy sea passage. About 600 ships daily sail through or across the Strait of Dover. Ferryboats and Hovercraft, ships that travel over land and water above a cushion of air, carry vehicles and people between France and England.

The Dardanelles

The Dardanelles is by far the narrowest of the straits, varying from 1 to 4 miles wide. The Dardanelles, along with the Bosporus to the east, connects Asia with Europe. The

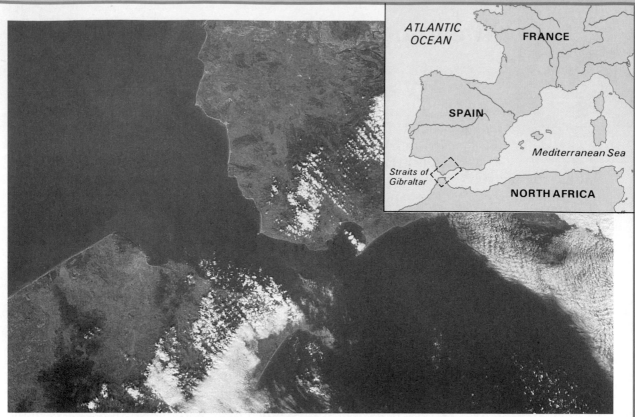

The Strait of Gibraltar, shown in a satellite photo, is the gateway to the Mediterranean. The nation controlling the strait also controls naval traffic in and out of the Mediterranean.

straits are part of a waterway that leads from the landlocked Black Sea through Turkey to the Mediterranean.

The Dardanelles has a strong surface current that flows toward the Aegean Sea. A powerful undercurrent flows east and brings salt water into the Black Sea.

Throughout history the Dardanelles has been the scene of power struggles. In 480 B.C., Xerxes I of Persia built a boat bridge and led an army to invade Europe. In 384 B.C., Alexander the Great led his army into Asia over a similar bridge. Many years later, the Byzantine Empire used the strait as a defense. Later, the Ottoman Turks ruled the Dardanelles. In 1841, European powers affirmed Turkey's control of the passage of ships. Although possession of the Dardanelles has been threatened, Turkey still remains in control.

Throughout the years, many wars were fought and treaties negotiated for the control and use of Europe's important straits. They are geographical features that have influenced history.

STUDY SKILLS Understanding Geography

1. Explain the difference between a strait, a channel, and a peninsula.
2. What effect does the current have on each of the European straits?
3. Describe a voyage from the Black Sea to the Mediterranean Sea. (See the map on page 511.)
4. Why have straits been strategic military spots?
5. Why do English Channel swimmers cross the channel at the Strait of Dover?
6. Write a description for a tourist's guide on one of the European straits.

2 Enlightenment and Revolution

OBJECTIVE: *To understand the power of ideas in shaping political revolutions*

The Enlightenment in Europe

During the seventeenth and eighteenth centuries, European nation-states expanded their power using distant colonies. At the same time, European intellectual leaders emphasized the power of reason. Seventeenth- and eighteenth-century European scientists and political thinkers explained the reliable laws of nature in a world that had seemed mysterious and unpredictable. They viewed reason as a light that would help people to see the world more clearly. As a result, the eighteenth century in Europe is called the Age of Enlightenment.

Isaac Newton, offering his brilliant explanations of planetary motion and light, did more to alter European opinion than any other scientist. Following Newton's ex-ample, other scientists explained the natural world using the scientific method of observation and experimentation.

One of the early thinkers whose ideas affected others was John Locke. Locke criticized the belief in absolute monarchy in his *Second Treatise on Civil Government*, published in 1690. Locke stated that people are born with equal rights to life, liberty, and property. Governments must protect these rights. Locke and other thinkers developed the idea of government as a social contract between the ruler and the citizens of a country. If a ruler tried to govern without the consent of the people, or did not obey the laws, subjects could justifiably revolt. They could defend their rights because their ruler had broken the social contract. Subjects could then try to form a better government.

The Philosophes

The ideas of the Enlightenment were spread through the writings of a group of people called the philosophes (fee law ZAWFS). The center of the movement was in France. Like Locke, many philosophes criticized the absolute power of government.

Attitudes Toward Government. One leading philosophe was a French thinker, the Baron de Montesquieu (MAWN TEHS KYOO). Montesquieu argued that government power should be divided among executive, legislative, and judicial branches. Each

---

VOCABULARY DEVELOPMENT

philosophe (fee law ZAWF) *noun:* the French word for philosopher. From the Greek words *philos,* meaning loving, and *sophos,* meaning wise.

deist (DEE ihst) *noun:* one who believes in the existence of a God but not in divine incarnation. From the Latin word, *deus,* meaning God.

intuition (IHN too WIHSH uhn) *noun:* the ability to perceive or know things without conscious reasoning. From the Latin prefix *in-,* meaning in, and word *tueri,* meaning to look at.

boycott *verb:* to refuse to buy, sell, or use something, to ban. From Captain C. C. Boycott, a land agent in Ireland in the 1880s.

Top right, Montesquieu. Left, Voltaire. Bottom, Diderot.

but they thought that religious differences were unimportant. Deists maintained that God created the universe to operate by natural laws and did not interfere with its daily workings. Miracles, superstition, prejudice, and ignorance had no place in such a world.

Hope for Education. Despite the obstacles and intolerance of rulers and citizens, the philosophes were optimists. The Marquis de Condorcet (KAWN DAWR SEH) expressed this optimism even while fleeing government persecution. He wrote:

❝ The time will come when the sun will shine only on free men who know no other master but their reason; . . . when we shall . . . learn how to recognize and so to destroy, by force of reason, the first seeds of tyranny and superstition. . . . **❞**

For Condorcet, war and prejudice would disappear in the face of reason. The philosophes believed that education would help people to learn to use their power to reason more effectively. Many philosophes worked hard to spread knowledge.

Perhaps the greatest effort to organize Enlightenment thought was the *Encyclopedia*. Under editor Denis Diderot, contributors to the *Encyclopedia* wrote articles to explain the natural world and human society. The articles in the work challenged traditional beliefs and institutions.

branch would check and balance the power of the other two. By separating the power, Montesquieu argued, no individual or group could gain absolute power.

In *The Spirit of Laws*, the Baron de Montesquieu stated:

❝ . . . experience shows us that every man invested with power is apt to abuse it . . . to prevent this abuse, it is necessary . . . that power should be a check to power. **❞**

Religion and Tolerance. Another theme of the philosophes was tolerance. Critics of the intolerant government or church were imprisoned, tortured, or killed. Francois Marie Arouet (AY EHR WEE), writing under the name Voltaire (vohl TAIR), was a strong critic of religious and political persecution and censorship.

❝ By what right could a being, created free, force another to think like himself? . . . tolerance has never brought civil war; intolerance has covered the earth with carnage . . . **❞**

Like many Enlightenment thinkers, Voltaire was a deist. The deists believed in God,

The Social Contract

FOCUS ON SOURCES

One French writer who did not share all the ideas of the philosophes was Jean Jacques Rousseau (ROO SOH). Rousseau was born in Geneva, Switzerland, in 1712. His mother died while giving birth to him. When he was 10, his father abandoned him. Six years later, Rousseau moved to France, where he spent much of his life.

Rousseau did not agree with the philosophes that reason would improve all aspects of society. He felt that intuition, rather than reason, was the best guide to proper behavior. On other issues, though, Rousseau agreed with the philosophes. In the following passage from *The Social Contract*, Rousseau argues that people originally lived without government:

"I assume, for the sake of argument, that mankind at some time reached a point when the disadvantages of remaining in a state of nature outweighed the advantages. Under these conditions, the original state of nature could no longer endure. The human race would have perished if it had not changed its ways.

Men, being human, cannot develop new powers. But they can unite and control the powers they already have. Men in the state of nature could get together, pooling their strength in a way that would permit them to meet any challenge. They had to learn to work together under central direction. . . .

Some form of association must be found which can rally the whole community for the protection of the person and property of each of its citizens in such a way that each man, because he is a voluntary member of the association, . . . remains as free as he was before. That is the basic problem solved by the social contract. . . .

The heart of the idea of the social contract may be stated simply: Each of us places his person and authority under the supreme direction of the general will [of society] and the group receives each individual as an indivisible part of the whole. . . .

In order that the social contract may not be a mere empty formula, everyone must understand that any individual who refuses to obey the general will must be forced by his fellows to do so. This is a way of saying that it may be necessary to force a man to be free; freedom in this case being obedience to the will of all." ■

Above, the title page of *The Social Contract*, printed in 1762. Inset, a portrait of Rousseau.

The American Revolution

The ideas of the Enlightenment, particularly those of Locke and Rousseau, had tremendous influence across the Atlantic Ocean in the colonies of Great Britain. The American settlers helped and benefited from Britain's rise to power. The American colonies numbered over one-third of Britain's total colonies. They generated a considerable share of Britain's trade. In accord with mercantilist theory, British power depended partially on the resources and revenues it received from America.

After 1751, Britain tried to tighten its control over colonial commerce and government. In that year, Britain issued the first in a series of Navigation Acts designed to regulate colonial trade. Most colonists believed the regulations allowed both Britain and the colonies to prosper. Opponents could avoid the laws by smuggling.

Changes After 1763. British policy changed in 1763, after the end of the Seven Years' War (see page 500). Victory over France and Spain gave Britain control of most of North America east of the Mississippi River. Governing and defending this empire and repaying the war debts were costly. Britain needed to raise money and, to do so, tried to enforce old laws more strictly.

Two other results of the war made the colonies less willing to support British taxes and regulations. After Britain's victory, American colonists no longer feared French and Spanish attacks. In addition, the colonists gained a sense of pride from fighting beside the respected British army.

Britain felt that the colonists had benefited from Parliament's expenditures in the war. Consequently, the British believed that the colonists should help pay the debt. In 1764, Parliament passed the Sugar Act. This act was one of a series of measures de-signed to raise revenue. Though the act reduced the tax on molasses by 50 percent, it added new taxes on the sale of coffee, wine, cloth, indigo, and sugar.

Americans generally argued against the Sugar Tax and other taxes for two reasons. First, the colonists claimed that their interests were not being represented in the British Parliament. Colonists resented being taxed without having the right of representation. Second, colonists argued that Parliament could regulate their trade, but that colonial legislatures should levy all taxes.

The British rejected the colonial arguments. Leaders in Parliament said that the colonies had become unprofitable, and stricter control was necessary. Furthermore, the American colonists were being treated in the same manner as other British subjects. In fact, many inhabitants of Britain had no say in choosing representatives in Parliament. In theory, Parliament consid-

Feelings against the British Crown ran high, as shown in this painting. A crowd of New Yorkers is toppling a statue of King George III from its pedestal.

ered the interests of all members of the British Empire, whether they were directly represented or not.

Massachusetts soon became the center of anti-British activities. Britain tried to discourage colonial protests by punishing Massachusetts. The British closed Boston's port, established military rule in Massachusetts, and prohibited political meetings. The practice of housing British troops in the homes of colonists also was revived. The colonists named these measures the Intolerable Acts.

Power of the Boycott. In 1774, colonial leaders met in Philadelphia to organize a response to the Intolerable Acts. Restrictive British policies and the influence of Enlightenment ideas about the right to rebel led increasing numbers of colonists to consider breaking away from Britain. Most leaders at the Philadelphia meeting, called the First Continental Congress, were not yet convinced that independence was necessary. Instead, these leaders called for a ban on the purchase of British goods. Previous bans, today called boycotts, had pressured Britain to change some of their policies.

Before adjourning, the First Continental Congress agreed to meet again in 1775. By the time the Second Continental Congress met, colonists and British soldiers had clashed in battles at Lexington and Concord, Massachusetts.

A New Nation. In 1776, the Second Continental Congress began work on declaring American independence from Britain. The major responsibility for writing the Declaration of Independence went to Thomas Jefferson. In the Declaration of Independence, Jefferson clearly expressed the ideals of the Enlightenment:

❝ We hold these truths to be self-evident, that all men are created equal; that they are endowed by the Creator with certain unalienable [not transferrable] rights: that among these are life, liberty, and the pursuit of happiness. That, to secure these rights, governments are instituted among men, deriving their just powers from the consent of the governed . . . ❞

The American colonies had made their decision to break with Britain. The Declaration established a new order for and by the people. By 1783, colonial America had fought for and won its independence. By 1787, the Americans reaffirmed their beliefs in beginning their Constitution with the words:

❝ We the people of the United States, in order to form a more perfect Union, . . . ❞

The Constitution of the United States influenced later constitutions written for other countries. The founding of the United States became a model and an inspiration for others suffering under oppression. Soon, the people of France and Latin America would also rebel.

SECTION 2 *Study Skills*

Developing Vocabulary 1. How does intuition differ from reason? **2.** Could the American Revolutionists have been philosophes? Explain. **3.** How would a ban, or boycott, affect a business? **4.** Define deist.

Reviewing Main Ideas 1. Explain Montesquieu's idea about division of power in government. **2.** How did Rousseau's philosophy differ from other philosophes' ideas? **3.** Why were the American colonies considered a vital asset to the British Empire? **4.** Why were American colonists less willing to go along with British policies after 1763?

Understanding Chronology 1. How did Locke's writings of 1690 influence the Age of Enlightenment? **2.** What laws did the British pass between 1751 and 1774 to tighten their control over the American colonies?

Challenge Is the Declaration of Independence important today? Explain.

3 Revolutions in France and Latin America

OBJECTIVE: *To understand the causes and consequences of the revolutions for greater political freedom in France and Latin America*

The French Revolution Begins

The revolutionary ideas that persuaded American colonists to rebel against Britain also influenced the French and Latin Americans. French thinkers, such as Rousseau and Montesquieu, questioned the right of monarchs to rule with absolute power.

In 1789, France was one of Europe's richest countries, but its government was bankrupt. The costs of past wars, the luxurious lifestyle of King Louis XVI's court, the burden of maintaining a large army, and large expenditures to help the Americans had emptied France's treasury.

Problems of the Third Estate. French society was divided into three groups, or estates. The First Estate, the clergy, and the Second Estate, the nobility, owned much of the land in France. These two groups paid virtually no direct taxes. The Third Estate represented all other groups in French society, about 97 percent of the people. This group paid almost all the money to support the French government. The First and Second Estates were powerful enough to reject efforts of the king to tax them.

Nobles also held most of the high military, church, and government positions. The children of nobles were encouraged to marry only other nobles, as well. Thus, even wealthy members of the Third Estate had less power than they felt they deserved.

Peasant members of the Third Estate faced their own problems. After 1750, the peasant population of France increased significantly. Since purchasing land was difficult, many peasants could barely support their growing families.

In 1787 and 1788, bad weather made the poor families' problems even worse. The poor harvests caused food prices to increase. Rising prices hurt the cities and brought hunger to many. Despite these problems, the crown continued to demand full payment of taxes.

The Estates-General Meets. Louis XVI had good intentions, but he was a weak and indecisive king. He did not have the skills needed to deal effectively with the problems he inherited on taking power in 1774. Some of the nobles encouraged him to call a meeting of the Estates-General, France's legislative assembly, to confront the government's financial problems.

VOCABULARY DEVELOPMENT

ratify (RAT uh FY) *verb:* to give official approval to; to confirm.

consul *noun:* one of the three highest officials of the French republic from 1799 to 1804. From the Latin officials of the same title.

arbitrary (AHR buh TRER ee) *adj.:* not fixed by rules, based on one's preference.

censor (SEHN suhr) *verb:* remove information that might be useful to an enemy. From the Latin word, *censere*, meaning to judge.

Napoleon's Empire, 1812

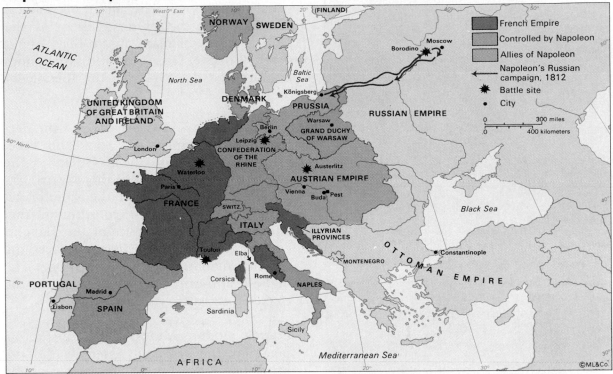

Map Skills 1. About how many miles did Napoleon's army march from Königsberg to Moscow? **2.** In what body of water is the island of Elba located? **3.** How far is Waterloo from Paris?

The Estates-General had not met for 175 years. The nobles hoped to control the assembly and to increase their power.

The Third Estate saw this first meeting of the Estates-General as its opportunity to change France. Inspired by the success of the English and American revolutions, members of the middle class also wanted to increase their power in French society. Third Estate representative Emmanuel Siéyès (SYAY YAYS), a member of the clergy, summarized their feelings saying:

❝ What is the Third Estate? Everything. What has it been thus far? Nothing. What does it demand? To become something. **❞**

In the past, the Third Estate had little influence in the Estates-General because each estate had one vote. The First and Second Estates outvoted the Third Estate, two to one. Members of the Third Estate echoed the American cry, "No taxation without representation!" They refused to meet until the voting system was changed.

The Third Estate pressured Louis into changing the Estates-General into the National Assembly. This change gave each individual representative a single vote. Leaders of the Third Estate believed that they could draw support for other reforms from the First and Second Estates.

The National Assembly. As the National Assembly was meeting in the summer of 1789, Louis made two decisions that changed the course of French history. On July 11, he dismissed his finance minister, Jacques Necker. The Third Estate viewed Necker as a supporter of reform. At the same time, Louis stationed troops around Paris and Versailles. Rumors spread that he would dissolve the National Assembly, ending the people's hope for change.

This scene shows members of France's Third Estate swearing an oath of unity in 1789. Locked out of their meeting rooms, they met in a tennis court.

"Men are born and remain free and equal in rights. . . . The aim of all political association is the preservation . . . of the natural rights of man. . . . No body or individual may exercise authority which does not proceed directly from the [people of the] nation."

King Louis XVI did not accept the declaration's principles. He could do little, however, to oppose them. He faced the growing political power of the citizens.

In the summer of 1791, the National Assembly ratified a new constitution that adopted several principles of the Enlightenment. The new government replaced the absolute monarchy with a limited one. The highest authority in France became the elected Legislative Assembly.

France under Attack. The constitution made by the National Assembly did not bring peace to France. The king resented the limitations on his power. He secretly tried to get support from the Austrian and Prussian monarchs. In April 1792, however, those two states went to war against France's revolutionary government.

The new government also faced opposition from people who wanted more reforms. In 1792, under the leadership of Georges Jacques Danton, the people of Paris forced the Legislative Assembly to set new elections. The elected representatives would meet to revise the infant constitution.

This new constitutional group was called the National Convention. The group's first act was to abolish the monarchy and declare France a republic. The convention put King Louis XVI on trial for his dealings with Austria and Prussia. The king was found guilty of treason and beheaded in 1793.

The Jacobins. Within the National Convention, a group known as the Jacobins gained control. They mobilized the nation and successfully met the challenge of Austria and Prussia.

Across France these two events triggered a series of reactions. On July 14, 1789, a group of Paris citizens stormed the Bastille (bas TEEL), a prison and symbol of absolutism and royal oppression. The crowd seized the Bastille in the name of the people.

The Upheaval Continues. The National Assembly tried to bring order and reform to a nation that seemed ready for revolution. Acting quickly, the Assembly abolished some of the taxes peasants were required to pay. It also ended the exemption granted to the clergy and the nobles. Church lands and the court system were reorganized. The National Assembly formulated the Declaration of the Rights of Man and Citizen. This document stated Enlightenment beliefs:

The execution of Louis XVI, though, was just the beginning of a bloody period in the French Revolution called the Reign of Terror. Under the leadership of Maximilien Robespierre (ROHBZ peer), the Committee of Public Safety executed individuals suspected of not supporting the revolution. In 1793 and 1794, between 20,000 and 40,000 people were put to death. As the turmoil continued, Robespierre was killed.

The Directory. The National Convention submitted its new constitution for France in 1795. A group of five leaders called the Directors headed the new government. The Directory, though, did not last long. In 1799, a young, popular general, Napoleon Bonaparte (BOH nuh pahrt), took over the government as First Consul.

Napoleon

FOCUS ON PEOPLE

Napoleon was born on August 15, 1769, on the Mediterranean island of Corsica where his father practiced law. Napoleon was educated at a military school in France. As a young man, he read up to 15 hours a day. He was strong-willed and displayed a fighting spirit. He said:

❝ Nothing [scared] me; I feared no one. I struck one, I scratched another. I was a terror to everyone. ❞

Napoleon's Rise to Power. During the years of the French Revolution, Napoleon proved himself to be a good soldier. By the time he was 25, he had become a general. His first real chance to display his talents came in 1793, when he helped to drive the British troops from the French seaport of Toulon (too LAHN). However, not until he won a series of impressive victories against Austrian forces in Italy, in 1796 and 1797, did he become a national hero. French

shopkeepers began to display his picture in their store windows. He was compared to Julius Caesar and Alexander the Great.

By 1799, the people were displeased with the Directory. They were tired of 10 years of war and revolution. They wanted a return to an orderly government and the ideals of the French Revolution. Napoleon took advantage of the situation. He returned to France from Egypt and quickly overthrew the government. He wrote a new constitution concentrating power in himself as First Consul for the next 5 years.

From Consul to Emperor. Napoleon wanted to rule for the rest of his life, then pass on his power to his descendants. The people of France voted to make Napoleon emperor for life and his authority hereditary. On December 2, 1804, in a magnificent ceremony at Notre Dame Cathedral, Napoleon crowned himself emperor.

As ruler of France, Napoleon wanted to dominate Europe. He said, "I love . . . power. I love it as a musician loves his violin." By 1812, he had reached the height of his power; he had conquered virtually all of continental Europe west of Russia. See the map, Napoleon's Empire, page 511.

The Rule of Napoleon. Besides his military accomplishments, Napoleon achieved many domestic reforms. One of his most important achievements was the establishment of a single code of laws for all of France, known as the Code of Napoleon. These laws abolished serfdom and feudalism. They guaranteed equality before the law, religious toleration, and trial by jury. The Code of Napoleon is still the basis of law in France, western Europe, and parts of Asia and Latin America. In the United States it influenced Louisiana law.

Napoleon also reformed the educational system. He created a government agency to supervise all levels of education in France, from primary grades through college. Finally, Napoleon put France back on a sound financial basis. He established the Bank of France to maintain a sound currency and promote economic prosperity in France.

To maintain absolute power, Napoleon used his secret police to spy on people and to make arbitrary arrests and imprison people. He censored speech and the press.

Downfall and Defeat. Napoleon's empire was too large for one man to control. France did not have the resources to continue his military campaigns. He tried to defeat France's rival, Britain, by preventing other countries from trading with that nation. This policy failed and created resentment throughout Europe.

In 1812, Napoleon suffered his first major military setback when he tried to invade Russia. Russia's large size, harsh climate, and determined people were formidable obstacles. Napoleon believed that a large-scale invasion would force a Russian surrender.

Napoleon at Mount St. Bernard Pass. Napoleon crowned himself emperor of France in 1804. He was exiled after a military defeat at Waterloo in 1815.

In the spring of 1812, he set off for Moscow with 600,000 soldiers. On September 14, Napoleon and his army entered the city. The Russians, however, had deserted Moscow. Later that night, fires raged throughout Moscow, probably set by the Russians.

Napoleon then made a costly decision. Instead of retreating immediately, he waited. As winter approached, Napoleon still had not conquered the Russians. He waited so long that his troops had to retreat through Russia in the dead of winter. Food, supplies, and clothing became so scarce that his soldiers fought one another for them. Many soldiers froze to death as the temperature fell to 30 degrees Fahrenheit, or 34 degrees Celsius, below zero. Fewer than 100,000 of his troops survived the march back to Paris.

Encouraged by Napoleon's failure to conquer Russia, several nations declared war on France. Prussian and Austrian armies both attacked the weakened French forces. Napoleon was defeated and sent into exile on the island of Elba off the coast of Italy. He escaped and returned to France.

The French welcomed Napoleon back to power, and for 100 days he ruled France. Finally, on June 18, 1815, a combination of British and Prussian troops defeated him at Waterloo, Belgium. This time, Napoleon was sent to the south Atlantic island of St. Helena, where he died on May 5, 1821. ■

Europe after Napoleon

After the first defeat of Napoleon in 1814, European leaders met to bring peace to Europe. This meeting, called the Congress of Vienna, completed its work in 1815, just before the final defeat of Napoleon at Waterloo. See the map on page 521.

The brother of Louis XVI, known as Louis XVIII, became king of France. Historians do not know what happened to Louis XVI's son. Austria and Prussia claimed control over more land in central

Europe. Together with Russia, these two countries became defenders of the old system of monarchy against rising nationalism and democracy.

The French Revolution and the Napoleonic Wars had a lasting impact throughout Europe. The revolutionary ideas of the Enlightenment and a new spirit of nationalism were even more popular than before 1789. Many people were horrified by the Reign of Terror and the wars of the period. Nevertheless, they had become believers in the right of people to freedom and equality and the need for popular government. The next stage for the expression of these ideas would be Latin America.

Revolutions in Latin America

In the early 1800s, tremendous changes occurred in Latin America. People were dissatisfied with high taxes, economic regulations limiting free trade, foreign control over political affairs, and a rigid colonial class system. Enlightenment ideas and the success of revolutionary events in the American colonies and France encouraged the Latin colonials.

Independence for Haiti. The first Latin American country to achieve its independence was the French colony of St. Domingue (SAN duh MAHNG). The leader of the revolt was Francois Domingue Toussaint (TOO SAHN), later known as Toussaint L'Ouverture (loo vehr TYOOR).

Toussaint had been born a slave in 1743. When he grew up, he became an overseer of slaves. Toussaint received his freedom at the age of 34. He dedicated the rest of his life to establishing peaceful race relations, eliminating slavery, and freeing the French colony.

A slave revolt broke out in St. Domingue in 1791. After ensuring his former master's safety, Toussaint joined the rebels. Dissatisfied with the rebel leaders, he formed his own army. In 1793, he joined Spain and

New Nations of Latin America, 1825

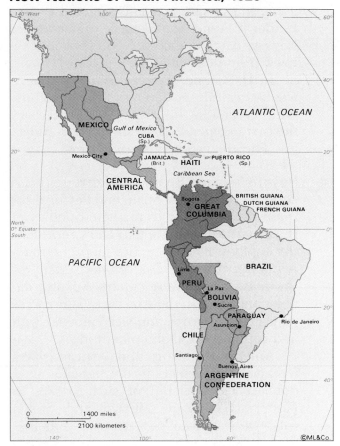

Map Skills 1. Which South American nation has the largest land area? **2.** What Caribbean island had gained its independence by 1825?

Britain in their war against France. On the battlefield, Toussaint was able to find a hole in his opponent's defenses. This skill won him the title L'Ouverture, a French word meaning the opening.

In 1793, the French government outlawed slavery. Impressed, Toussaint joined the French cause.

For eight years, Toussaint used his skills to gain control of the island of Hispaniola. He improved the economy and concluded trade agreements.

In 1802, peace in Europe gave Napoleon the opportunity to regain the former colony. He sent 30,000 troops to the island. For five months, Toussaint's army fought the French again. Heavy casualties forced Toussaint to seek peace. He agreed to surrender if France would agree to not restore slavery. After France agreed, Toussaint retired from political life.

In 1803, a new revolt for independence was successful. On January 1, 1804, Toussaint's followers in Hispaniola established the first independent nation in Latin America. They named it Haiti (HAYT ee).

Revolts against Spain and Portugal. Napoleon's conquest of Spain and Portugal cut these countries off from their colonies in the Americas. Beginning in 1808, rebellions throughout Latin America brought independence to numerous colonies. Many of the rebel leaders were creoles, Spanish descendants born in the Americas. Many were educated in Europe and were familiar with and supported Enlightenment ideas.

American Indians and African slaves were willing partners in the fight for freedom. The leadership of such creoles as Father Hidalgo in Mexico and Simón (seh MOHN) Bolívar (buh LEE vahr) and José de San Martín in South America was effec-

Father Hidalgo led Mexico to freedom from Spain. In this symbolic painting, he is shown crowning Mexico being freed from colonial chains.

tive. By 1830, they had driven the Spanish and the Portuguese from Latin America.

Problems of Independence. The independent Latin American countries faced several problems. Few of the new leaders or citizens had experience in self-government. Leaders disagreed sharply about how to set up their new governments. Individual leaders often did not want to share their political power. Geographic barriers divided people and hindered communication. Bolívar and San Martín had dreamed of a united, independent Latin America. In fact, Latin America divided into 20 independent countries. See the map on page 515.

The governments in most of the new Latin American nations showed the influence of Enlightenment political ideas. They had constitutions, political parties, division of authority among various branches of government, and election of leaders. In most new Latin American nations, however, strong leaders called *caudillos* (kaw DEE yohz) rose to power with the army's support. These *caudillos* were little more than military dictators.

SECTION 3 *Study Skills*

Developing Vocabulary 1. Define ratify. **2.** Why would articles or books be censored? **3.** What was a consul?

Reviewing Main Ideas 1. What was the major accomplishment of the Jacobins? **2.** List three of Napoleon's achievements. **3.** What was the purpose of the Congress of Vienna? **4.** Why was the French government bankrupt by 1789?

Understanding Chronology 1. Describe the difficulties facing the Third Estate before 1789. **2.** List and identify the significant dates in French history between 1789 and 1815.

Challenge What problems do the newly independent African countries share with Latin American countries?

CHAPTER 22 *Summary & Review*

Summarizing Main Ideas

With the development of trade routes in the 1500s, England, France, and to a lesser extent the Netherlands became the dominant world powers. As these countries conquered and colonized new lands, mercantilism became their most important foreign policy.

During the seventeenth and eighteenth centuries, new ideas like those of the Enlightenment emerged. Enlightenment thinkers popularized a belief in the right of people to choose their rulers and to revolt against injustice.

The Enlightenment beliefs in liberty, equality, and brotherhood led to the American Revolution, the French Revolution, and other revolutions throughout the world.

Questions for Critical Thinking

COMPREHENSION Interpreting Events

1. How was the Third Estates' dissatisfaction with the Estates-General a major cause of the French Revolution?
2. Why did the Directory fail to satisfy the French people?
3. Explain the positive and negative aspects of Napoleon's reign.

ANALYSIS Identifying Trends

1. Describe the advantages and disadvantages of mercantilism.
2. What influence did the philosophes have on the outbreak of revolutions in the late eighteenth and early nineteenth centuries?
3. Explain the common traits of the American Revolution and later European revolts.
4. Compare France's and Haiti's revolutions.

SYNTHESIS Developing Writing Skills

1. Write a report describing the Seven Year's War. Include the treaty and provisions which ended the conflict.
2. Make a detailed list of the causes of the French Revolution.
3. Write a biography of a philosophe.

Philosophers of the Enlightenment	
Name	**Ideas**
John Locke, English *Second Treatise on Civil Government*, 1690	• People's rights to life, liberty and prosperity • Social contract between ruler and citizen • Citizen's right to revolt to form better government
Voltaire, French *Candide*, 1759	• Rights to freedom of thought and speech • Abolishment of religious and political persecution
Jean Jacques Rousseau, French *The Social Contract*, 1762	• Intuition as guide to proper behavior • Man's ability to unite and control already possessed powers • Social contract for all to abide by

APPLICATION Comparing Past to Present

1. The American colonies used the boycott very effectively. Would a boycott be equally effective today? Explain.
2. Is it likely a figure such as Napoleon could dominate a modern nation? Explain.

EVALUATION Weighing Consequences

1. Discuss the long-range results of Napoleon's invasion of Russia.
2. What influence did the explorations of Captain Bering have on Russian expansion? Why?
3. What happened when Britain tightened its control of its North American colonies?

CHALLENGE

1. How have the ideas of the American and French Revolutions influenced modern governments in these two countries?
2. Study the chart on this page and decide which writers might have had the greatest impact on America's Founding Fathers. Explain.

CHAPTER 23
Industrialization Transforms Europe

GLOBAL TIME LINE

1750   1770   1790

TIME

1750–1850 Age of Canal building in Europe and North America

PEOPLE

1764 James Hargreaves invents the spinning jenny

1769 Richard Arkwright invents the water frame

1769 James Watt develops a steam engine that will run other machinery

1776 Adam Smith publishes *The Wealth of Nations*

PLACE

Linking Past to Present

Nationalist revolutions occurred in many countries between 1750 and 1850. Even now, in the twentieth century, many people around the world continue to rebel against governments for many reasons.

In the two decades after World War II, many Asian and African nations overthrew their colonial rulers. However, many other people still feel oppressed. Irish Catholics continue to demonstrate against British rule in northern Ireland. During the last 10 years, the black population of South Africa has rebelled seeking self-government and an end to segregation. As you read and hear news accounts of wars and demonstrations, consider the progress in self-government that people have made since 1750.

An English lithograph from 1897 depicts the triumph of steam and electricity.

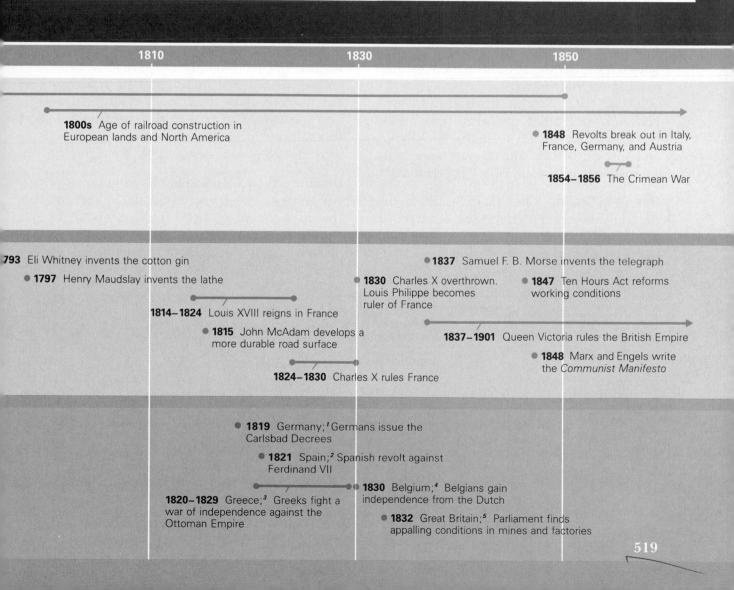

1810   **1830**   **1850**

1800s Age of railroad construction in European lands and North America

1848 Revolts break out in Italy, France, Germany, and Austria

1854–1856 The Crimean War

1793 Eli Whitney invents the cotton gin

1797 Henry Maudslay invents the lathe

1814–1824 Louis XVIII reigns in France

1815 John McAdam develops a more durable road surface

1824–1830 Charles X rules France

1830 Charles X overthrown. Louis Philippe becomes ruler of France

1837 Samuel F. B. Morse invents the telegraph

1847 Ten Hours Act reforms working conditions

1837–1901 Queen Victoria rules the British Empire

1848 Marx and Engels write the *Communist Manifesto*

1819 Germany;[1] Germans issue the Carlsbad Decrees

1821 Spain;[2] Spanish revolt against Ferdinand VII

1820–1829 Greece;[3] Greeks fight a war of independence against the Ottoman Empire

1830 Belgium;[4] Belgians gain independence from the Dutch

1832 Great Britain;[5] Parliament finds appalling conditions in mines and factories

519

1 Political Revolutions Continue

OBJECTIVE: *To understand the causes and consequences of the European revolutions that occurred in the nineteenth century*

Nationalist and Democratic Revolutions

Between 1750 and 1850, the ideas of the Enlightenment led to revolutions on both sides of the Atlantic Ocean. Even after the Congress of Vienna returned monarchs to European thrones and redrew political boundaries, democracy and nationalism remained popular ideas.

After 1815, Austria, Prussia, and Russia generally defended the ideas and agreements reached at the Congress of Vienna. In contrast, Britain and France were more sympathetic to revolutionary movements.

Revolt in Spain. The first indication of underlying discontent after 1815 occurred in Spain. King Ferdinand VII, who had seen his father hand the Spanish crown to Na-poleon, was restored to the throne after Napoleon's exile. In 1814, he suspended the liberal constitution implemented in 1812. He also decided to reestablish control over his restless colonies in the New World.

Ferdinand tried to send a large army to Central America. However, the army rebelled and demanded that he restore the former liberal constitution. Great Britain refused to aid Ferdinand, and he was unable to reconquer the former colonies. He also was forced to restore the constitution. Liberal revolutionaries in other countries were not all so successful as the Spanish.

Discontent in Germany. German university students staged demonstrations against the government in 1817. They demanded democratic reforms and the unification of all Germans under one government.

VOCABULARY DEVELOPMENT

implement *verb:* put into effect. From the Latin word, *implere*, meaning to fill up.

barricade (BAIR uh KAYD) *noun:* a barrier or obstruction. From the Italian word, *barricare*, meaning to fortify.

abdicate (AB duh KAYT) *verb:* renounce, give up, such as a throne or authority. From the Latin word, *abdicare*, meaning to deny.

plebiscite (PLEHB uh SYT) *noun:* a direct ballot on a political issue to determine the actual will of the voting people. From the Latin words *plebis*, meaning common people and *sciscere*, meaning to vote for.

jurisdiction (JUR ihs DIHK shuhn) *noun:* authority, legal power. From the Latin words *juris*, meaning law, and *dicere*, meaning to say or speak.

Crimea (kry MEE uh): a peninsula in southwest Russia extending into the Black Sea.

exile (EHG zyl) *noun:* a person who is forced to live away from his or her country, one who is banished. From the Latin word, *exilium*, meaning banished, or sent out to wander aimlessly.

seclusion *noun:* being apart from others, isolation, privacy. From the Latin prefix *se-*, meaning apart; word *claudere*, meaning to close; and suffix *-io*, meaning condition of being.

Europe in 1815

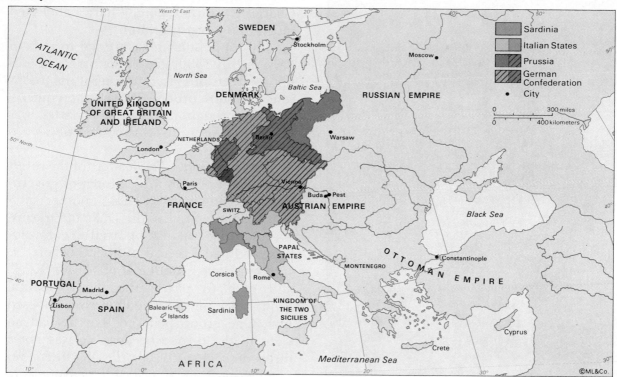

Map Skills   1. Compare this map with the map on page 511. List the changes to nations' borders made by the Congress of Vienna. **2.** Name three nations that border Switzerland.

The Austrian minister, Metternich, called the leaders of the German Confederation to a meeting at Carlsbad in Bohemia. There, he persuaded them to censor newspapers and disband nationalist student groups. Known as the Carlsbad Decrees, these measures were enforced with uneven severity in the German states.

Failed Revolutions.   Similar revolts in other countries during the 1820s also failed. Austrian and Russian troops crushed a Polish nationalist rebellion and executed many of the leaders. A revolution in Italy failed when the king of Naples invited the Austrian army into his kingdom to restore order. A revolution in Portugal also failed.

Greek Independence.   The movement for freedom did succeed in Greece, however. The Greeks managed to overthrow the rule of the Ottoman Turks that had lasted more

than 300 years. Many individual sympathizers from all over Europe fought with them.

During the 1800s, other peoples who had long been ruled by the Ottoman Empire also revolted in an effort to gain independence or autonomy. Egypt was granted independence in 1809, and Serbia and Romania later became autonomous.

Later Revolutions

Repression of the revolutions that took place in Europe during the early years of the 1800s did not discourage reformers. The ideas of both the Enlightenment and the French Revolution continued to inspire people's efforts.

Belgian Independence.   The European leaders who met at the Congress of Vienna united the Dutch and Austrian Netherlands under a Dutch king. The Belgians in the

The Duke of Orleans rides to the Hôtel de Ville during the Paris riots of 1830. Leaders of the revolution later chose the duke to be the next king of France.

south of the new country, however, did not speak Dutch and were mostly Protestants. Most Belgians were Roman Catholics.

In August 1830, the people of Brussels, Belgium, fought against Dutch rule. With British and French support, the Belgians won their independence.

The French Revolution of 1830. A Bourbon king again became the ruler of France in 1814. Louis XVIII was forced to accept a constitution that limited his power.

When Louis died in 1824, his brother, Charles X, became king. Charles abolished much of the constitution.

This unpopular measure led to riots in Paris in July 1830. People set up barricades in the streets of Paris and fought the troops sent to restore order. The rebellion quickly spread throughout France. Charles was forced to give up his throne and flee.

The Citizen King. The leaders of the revolt could not agree on a new form of government. Eventually, they chose another king, Louis Philippe. Louis, the Duke of Orleans, was Bourbon, had supported the revolution, and had a record of liberal beliefs.

Louis called himself the "Citizen King" and tried to please the many political groups of France. Some, however, opposed him. One group believed that he had no right to the throne because he was not a direct descendant of Charles X. Others, remembering French glory under Napoleon, wanted to restore the empire. Many French workers wanted to end the monarchy and set up a new republic.

Finally, in February 1848, Louis's critics organized a series of meetings to speak out against his policies. Louis issued a decree forbidding the final meeting. The people of Paris protested. When the National Guard joined the rioters, Louis abdicated.

The Second French Republic. The people of Paris established a republic in 1848. They elected representatives to a National Assembly that wrote a new constitution.

The constitution set up a republican government. A president and a representative legislature were to be elected by all adult males. The president was limited to a single four-year term. The citizens overwhelmingly chose Louis Napoleon, nephew of Napoleon Bonaparte, as president.

The Second French Empire. During his first years as president of the French republic, Louis Napoleon remained popular. He promised jobs to workers, encouraged trade, and defended property rights.

Under Louis, France enjoyed two decades of prosperity and stability. He became so popular that in 1851 he held a plebiscite asking for power to write a new constitution for the republic. The people approved his plan by a vote of almost 12 to 1.

The new constitution extended Louis's term as president to 10 years. It also established the Council of State to make laws. Members were appointed by the president rather than elected by the people.

Louis believed that only an emperor could bring France both liberty and glory. In 1852, he held another plebiscite. The people approved Louis's request to take the title Emperor Napoleon III. While France was returning to monarchy and empire, though, other nations of Europe were responding to the ideas of the Enlightenment in different ways.

Revolts in the Austrian Empire. The news of the overthrow of Louis Philippe in March 1848 inspired some Austrians to take similar action. Students, workers, and liberals demanded a constitution and the resignation of Metternich.

The revolt spread from Vienna to ethnic groups within the Austrian Empire. In Hungary, Louis Kossuth (kah SOOTH), a nationalist, persuaded the Magyars to demand a constitution and separate Hungarian government. The Czechs in Bohemia and nationalists in northern Italy revolted against Austria.

After several months, Austria regained control over Bohemia and Hungary. The Russian tsar, Nicholas I, helped the Austrians defeat the Magyars. Austrian soldiers also crushed the revolution in Vienna.

Foreign Policy of Napoleon III

Napoleon III, like his namesake, tried to win glory abroad. In the 1850s, both Russia and France claimed jurisdiction over Chris-

tian holy places in Palestine. These were under the authority of the Ottoman Empire. Both Great Britain and France feared Russia's growing stronger by gaining warm-water ports at Turkey's expense.

The Crimean War. The Ottoman Empire, backed by France and Great Britain, resisted Russian claims in Palestine. In 1854, the three allies went to war against Russia.

Early in the war, newspaper stories describing the suffering of soldiers in the Crimea (kry MEE uh) strongly affected British officials. They sent Florence Nightingale and 38 other nurses to help in Turkey.

After two years of fighting and losses on both sides, the allies defeated the Russian forces. The English and French forced Russia to give up any claim of protecting Christians in the Ottoman Empire. The allies also would not allow a Russian navy in the Black Sea.

The war led to better medical facilities for both the military and civilian population. After the war, Florence Nightingale continued to work for adequate hospital care. Her work inspired modern ideas about hospital administration and nursing.

The war inspired English poet, Alfred Tennyson, to write "The Charge of the Light Brigade," praising an English cavalry troop in the war. A British commander ordered the cavalry brigade to attack a part of the Russian army. His troops misunderstood the order and charged through a valley that was one and a half miles, or half a league, long. They were attacked from all sides. Only 247 of 673 soldiers survived. Here is an excerpt from the poem:

" Half a league, half a league,
  Half a league onward,
  All in the valley of Death
    Rode the six hundred.
  "Forward, the Light Brigade!
  Charge for the guns!" he said:
  Into the valley of Death
    Rode the six hundred.

• • •

Cannon to right of them,
Cannon to left of them,
Cannon behind them
　Volleyed and thundered:
Stormed at with shot and shell,
While horse and hero fell,
They that had fought so well
Came back through the jaws of Death
Back from the mouth of Hell,
All that was left of them—
　Left of six hundred. **"**

Napoleon Intervenes in Mexico. After the Crimean War, Napoleon III turned his attention to expanding the French colonial empire. He sent troops to strengthen French rule over Algeria in North Africa. He also chartered French engineers to begin work on the Suez Canal in 1859. The canal would connect the Mediterranean Sea and the Red Sea, cutting thousands of miles off the trip from Europe to Asia. Finally, Napoleon established a French colony in the country of Cambodia.

One of Napoleon's least successful colonial efforts was in the Americas. In 1863, French forces overthrew the Mexican government. The United States was involved in the Civil War and could not intervene.

Napoleon III asked the Archduke Maximilian, brother of the emperor of Austria, to rule Mexico. He and his wife, Carlota, had lost their positions as regents of Lombardy when Austria lost its control of northern Italy.

Maximilian agreed to accept only if the people of Mexico wanted him as their emperor. Napoleon and Mexican exiles in France furnished false proof to persuade Maximilian. He and his wife arrived in Mexico in 1864.

The Mexicans hated Maximilian, whom French troops kept in power. In 1865, the United States sent an army to the Mexican border and asked Napoleon to withdraw.

The Mexican army, with this support from the United States, defeated the French. When Napoleon withdrew his troops, Carlota went to Europe to beg the European kings to help her husband. She traveled to Paris, Vienna, and, finally, Rome. When she failed to receive any promises of assistance, Carlota suffered an emotional breakdown. The Mexicans executed her husband the following year, and she spent the rest of her life in seclusion.

Effects of the Revolutions. Europeans achieved some liberal reforms by rebelling against their kings. Greece and Belgium won their independence. All adult males won the right to vote in France and Prussia.

Most of the political revolutions, however, failed. Social class divisions remained strong. Reforms that middle class liberals demanded were too few for the more radical working class. In addition, many Europeans were afraid that any change would bring more upheaval. The countries where liberal reforms succeeded were those with a growing middle class, such as England.

SECTION 1 *Study Skills*

Developing Vocabulary 1. Why would a political leader call for a plebiscite? **2.** Define abdicate. **3.** Who is an exile?

Reviewing Main Ideas 1. Why was Ferdinand VII unsuccessful in regaining control of Spanish colonies? **2.** List the reasons for the success of the Greek Revolution. **3.** Compare the causes of revolts in France, Germany, and Austria.

Understanding Chronology 1. Describe the important events in Mexico from 1863 to 1865. **2.** What developments resulted from the Crimean War of 1854 to 1856?

Understanding Cause and Effect 1. What was the cause for the Carlsbad Decrees? Explain how they worked. **2.** What factors led to the abdication of Louis Philippe?

Challenge Liberal reforms generally occur in countries with a large middle class. What outcomes might we expect from revolts in third world countries today? Explain.

Housing and the Environment

While the revolutions of Europe and the Americas may have emphasized the differences in social classes, all people share some basic needs such as food and shelter. Social class determined how much could be spent on satisfying these needs. The type of shelter, peasant's hut or king's castle, depended on class. Shelter, however, is also influenced by climate and the available resources for building.

Early European Homes

Winters are cold in northern Europe, and forests are plentiful. Since earliest times, people who settled in what is now Scandinavia, Germany, Austria, Russia, Great Britain, and France used wood and grasses in building houses. Logs supplied the frames. Roofs were often made of straw called thatch. Floors were covered with rushes, grass-like plants that were changed when dirty. Windows were avoided for the sake of warmth. Roofs were steeply slanted so that the snow could slide off easily. Heavy snow could cause a flat roof to collapse.

In southern Europe, the climate is generally mild. Early houses were often built of clay-like mud plastered over sticks for support. Along the southern Mediterranean, in countries such as Spain, Portugal, Italy, and Greece, houses were low. Often they were constructed around gardens. These homes had only slightly slanted roofs and many windows to let in the breeze. White and pastel exteriors helped the buildings reflect heat and remain cool.

The ancient Romans learned to make buildings of cement. Their cement was so durable that many buildings, roads, and bridges still exist. To make cement the Romans mixed lime, water, and volcanic ash. Volcanic ash was readily available. The only active volcano on the mainland of Europe is Mt. Vesuvius, in Italy. After the fall of the Roman Empire in the 400s, the art of cement-making was lost. It was not rediscovered until 1756.

Castles of the Middle Ages

In feudal times, Europe was in an almost constant state of warfare. Homes were needed that could provide protection from enemies. People gathered together to build castles using stone as well as wood.

The location of the castle was important. Sometimes castles were built on flat land, but in places where northern Europe is hilly

A present day view of Santorini, Greece showing the variety in houses.

In feudal times, castles were built to provide protection from enemies. Shown here, Neuschwanstein Castle in Bavaria, Germany, a modern imitation.

year round. With only firelight and candlelight, the living quarters were dark and gloomy. The keep was the safest place to be, however. Because of the sturdy construction, the keep could be more easily defended than the rest of the castle.

Post-Middle Ages Homes in Europe

Houses made of bricks became popular in London after the Great London Fire of 1666. Bricks, of clay, shale, water, and other materials, were either dried in the sun or fired in a kiln to make them fire- and weather-resistant.

Brick is actually the oldest manufactured building material. Sun-dried bricks were made in the Middle East by 6000 B.C. Fired bricks were produced by 3500 B.C. The Romans learned the technique and used it wherever they went in Europe until the A.D. 400s. Other Europeans rarely used bricks until after the Middle Ages.

Europeans still use stone for foundations, walls, and steps. Popular stones include granite, limestone, sandstone, marble, and slate. Roofing and flooring is often made of slate because it splits into thin slabs.

Today, when building a home, modern Europeans can choose from a wide variety of building materials. It is still necessary, however, to consider climate and location when making that choice.

and mountainous, castles were built on the top of hills. Heavy walls built around the castle defended against invasion.

The strongest part of the castle was the keep. The keep was a high tower-like structure with thick walls. The feudal lord and lady lived on the upper floor. Servants and soldiers occupied the first floor. A cellar contained wells for water and storage space for food. In the cellar, cold air helped preserve food throughout the winter. Even in warm weather, food supplies were well-stocked to feed people for months at a time in the event of a siege. The cellars tended to remain cool. Drying and salting also aided food preservation.

Keeps had few windows so that invasion would be more difficult. Glass was unknown. The few openings were usually covered with wooden shutters. The stone walls kept dampness in, so fireplaces were lit all

STUDY SKILLS Understanding Geography

1. What should people consider when building a house?
2. Compare and contrast houses in warm climates with houses in cold climates.
3. How does climate influence the style of European housing?
4. Name five materials used to build houses.
5. Why are brick, cement, and stone preferable to wood and thatch as building materials?

2 The Industrial Revolution

OBJECTIVE: *To understand the causes and consequences of the Industrial Revolution*

The Origins of the Factory System

Manufacturing was a slow and expensive process in 1750. Production, especially in the textile industry, was by means of the domestic system (see page 491). Europeans paid high prices for clothing. As populations increased in the 1700s and 1800s, the demand for cloth became greater.

New Inventions Aid Manufacturing. The textile industry in England was mechanized during the 1700s. John Kay's flying shuttle, invented in 1733, enabled weavers to weave cloth twice as fast as previously. However, spinners, who made the thread from cotton and wool, could not keep pace with weavers who used the flying shuttle. Demand for cloth continued to outstrip supply. British textile merchants offered a prize for better spinning techniques.

In 1764, James Hargreaves (HAHR greevz), an English worker, won the prize. He invented a machine called the spinning jenny. It could produce eight times as much thread as a single spinning wheel.

The output of both Kay's and Hargreaves' machines was limited because both were hand operated. As weavers and spinners tired, they became less efficient and worked more slowly.

In 1769, Richard Arkwright invented a water-powered spinning machine called the water frame. Since Arkwright's machine was large and expensive, spinning could no longer be done in workers' cottages. Arkwright opened a spinning mill, which soon employed several hundred workers.

The Steam Engine and Mass Production. Each new invention inspired yet another invention or improvement. In 1769, James Watt, a Scottish engineer, produced a steam

---

VOCABULARY DEVELOPMENT

mechanize (MEK uh NYZ) *verb:* to do or operate by machine instead of by hand. From the Greek word, *mechane*, meaning machine.

lathe (layth) *noun:* a machine, still in use today, that shapes a piece of metal or wood by holding and turning it rapidly against the edge of a cutting tool. From the Middle English word, *lath*, meaning supporting stand.

factors of production *noun:* in economics, land, labor, and capital; the resources needed to produce goods and services.

enclosure *noun:* something that shuts in all around. From the Latin prefix *en-*, meaning in, and word *claudere*, meaning to close.

impulse *noun:* a momentary surge of electric current in one direction. From the Latin prefix *in-*, meaning in, and word *pellere*, meaning to drive.

patent *verb:* to obtain from the government the exclusive right to produce, use, and sell a product or invention.

breech-loading *adj.:* loading at the breech, or back part, of a gun instead of at the muzzle, or front.

The Industrial Revolution began with the mechanization of the textile industry. Here, factory workers use Samuel Crompton's spinning mule to make thread.

engine that could be adapted to run machinery. With steam engines to power machines, factories no longer needed to be near natural waterfalls or places where dams could be built. Instead, manufacturers could build factories near coal fields.

One more problem remained to be solved before machines could be made efficiently. Each of the first steam engines was unique. No standard parts could be used for repairs. An owner needed the services of a full-time engineer to repair any breakdown. In 1797, Henry Maudslay invented a lathe that could cut metal accurately to within a thousandth of an inch. This machine tool allowed people to make identical, interchangeable parts for other machines. In the United States, Eli Whitney experimented with interchangeable parts for making guns.

Further Advances in the Textile Industry.
In 1779, Samuel Crompton combined the best features of the spinning jenny and the water frame. His machine was able to spin cotton and wool fibers together into a fine, strong thread. Called the spinning mule, Crompton's device worked so well that soon weavers could not keep up with spinners.

In 1785, Edmund Cartwright restored the balance of productivity between spin-

ners and weavers. His invention, a power loom, increased the output of weavers so that they kept pace with spinners.

This series of improvements increased the supply of cotton cloth, thus lowering the price. As the price fell, demand increased still more. Soon a lack of cotton limited the production process again. Consequently, the demand for cotton increased. Cotton growing was not profitable, however, because removing seeds was too time-consuming and expensive.

In 1793, an American, Eli Whitney, invented the cotton gin. This new machine could remove cotton seeds quickly and cheaply. Cotton farming grew as did the demand for slaves to work the American cotton plantations.

The Factors of Production. The mechanization of the English textile industry began the Industrial Revolution. It eventually exported technology, products, and expectations throughout the world. Great Britain was in a position to take advantage of the new inventions. The country possessed an abundant supply of what economists call the factors of production. These are the resources needed to produce goods and services. The three basic factors of production are land, labor, and capital.

Land includes all the natural resources, such as fuel, water for power and transportation, and minerals. England had a supply of coal and iron ore, excellent harbors, and navigable rivers.

England also had an abundant labor force. Workers were available because changes in agriculture had forced many farmers from the land.

During the 1700s, England's small farmers suffered as a result of a movement called enclosure. The policy of enclosure required that the common land English villagers owned be divided among the village landowners. Landowners received portions of the common land based on the amount of land they already owned. The more land a person owned, the larger the share of common land received. Property boundaries also were redrawn so that each person's land was in one piece rather than scattered around the village. Landowners were required to fence in their property.

As a result of enclosure, farmers could no longer use the former common land. Many farmers did not have enough animals to farm their land or could not afford to build a fence. Farmers who owned small plots sold them to large landowners and became tenant farmers. Many moved to the cities to look for work. These families provided labor for the growing factory system.

Capital, the money needed for business investment, also was readily available. Wealthy English nobles and merchants were looking for investments.

Another factor besides those of production—land, labor, and capital—strengthened the Industrial Revolution in England. Its stable government encouraged business.

Industrialization Spreads. From England, the Industrial Revolution gradually spread throughout Europe. However, a lack of coal hampered some European countries. Coalfields extend in a belt across Belgium, the Ruhr region of Germany, and into the Ukraine and central Asia. Overland transport of the coal, though, was quite expensive. Most countries, therefore, could not take advantage of the early steam engines that were extremely wasteful of coal.

Not until the second half of the 1800s did other nations challenge British leadership in industrialization. Belgium, with large deposits of coal and iron and a willing labor force, closely followed the British lead. The United States, aided by European investment, surpassed Britain to become the leading industrial nation by the end of the 1800s.

A lack of unity hindered Germany in the 1850s and 1860s. Few of the many German states had all the factors necessary for industrialization. The nations of southern and eastern Europe remained largely agricultural throughout the 1800s. Governments in Spain, Italy, Austria, and Russia did little to encourage industrial growth.

The Transportation Revolution

The business changes the Industrial Revolution caused made better transportation necessary. Large quantities of raw materials required transport to factories. Finished products had to be transported to markets.

Road Construction. During the 1700s, roads often were nothing more than deeply rutted dirt trails. Wagons got stuck in the mud when it rained, and their drivers and passengers choked on dust during dry weather. In 1815, John McAdam, a Scottish engineer, brought road construction into the industrial age.

McAdam proposed putting layers of small stones directly on a hard, leveled bed of earth. This surface was called a macadam road after John McAdam. Traffic over the road compacted the stones and created a fairly smooth surface. Roads were constructed rapidly, and by 1825 England had nearly 4,000 miles of them newly prepared.

Canals Connect Waterways. Even over better roads, raw materials and finished products moved slowly and in limited amounts. Great Britain, however, had an extensive network of navigable rivers. On river highways, goods could be transported in large quantities, quickly and cheaply. To expand navigable waterways, the British began to deepen and widen rivers and streams by dredging.

Then, in 1759, the Duke of Bridgewater improved the transportation of his coal. He had a canal dug from his coal mine to the factory city of Manchester, 7 miles away. Using the canal, he could deliver more coal faster than before. Then he could reduce the price of his coal by 50 percent and still make a profit.

Global Transportation, 1850

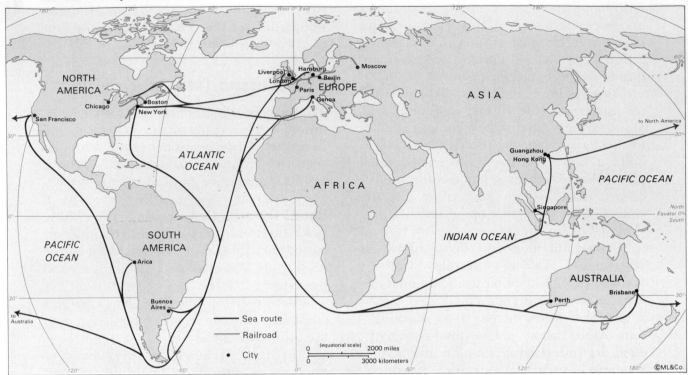

Map Skills **1.** Through which ocean did most trade routes cross? **2.** During the 1800s, what forms of transportation would take a traveler from New York to San Francisco?

Although the Chinese opened the Grand Canal in 605, canals did not become common in England until the 1800s. Canal building caught on, and by 1830 Great Britain had nearly 3,200 miles of canals. France, other western European countries, and the United States also expanded their water networks.

The Steam Engine Improves Transportation. Although canals made transportation within a country cheaper, they did nothing to improve trade over the expanding global community. Sailing ships still dominated trade routes. Steam-powered ships soon improved trans-Atlantic trade.

An American, Robert Fulton, adapted Watt's steam engine to power ships. In 1807, his steamboat, the *Clermont*, began regular trips on the Hudson River between New York City and Albany. In 1838, a British sidewheeler, *Sirius*, became the first ship to cross the Atlantic using only steam power. In 1840, Samuel Cunard and two partners established steamship mail service between Britain and the United States.

Steam power successfully applied to shipping was next applied to land transportation. A British engineer, George Stephenson, was one inventor of a locomotive a steam engine that ran on tracks. In 1830, an engine, the *Rocket*, pulled a string of rail cars from Liverpool to Manchester. At 29 miles per hour, it won a prize for speed.

By the middle of the 1800s, every country in Europe was building railways. See the map, Global Transportation, 1850, on this page. Over 20,000 miles of track crisscrossed the continent in 1850. Railroad construction stimulated economic growth. Railroads provided fast, cheap transportation for both passengers and large quantities of goods. As the boom in railroad building spread, so did the demand for iron and laborers.

A Ride on an Early Railway

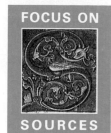

FOCUS ON SOURCES

By 1800, James Watt's steam engines were in use throughout Great Britain. In 1825, one of Watt's steam engines powered the first railway train between Stockton and Darlington, England. Five years later, the second railroad, between Liverpool and Manchester, opened. The following is Frances Kemble's description of a ride on the Liverpool-Manchester railway during its first year of operation:

❝You can't imagine how strange it seemed to be journeying on thus, without any visible cause of progress other than the magical machine. . . . We were to go only fifteen miles, that distance being sufficient to show the speed of the engine. . . . After proceeding through this rocky defile [a narrow gorge], we presently found ourselves raised upon embankments ten or twelve feet high; we then came to a moss, or swamp, of considerable extent, on which no human foot could tread without sinking, and yet it bore the road. . . .

We had now come fifteen miles, and stopped where the road traversed a wide and deep valley. Stephenson made me alight and led me down to the bottom of this ravine, over which, in order to keep his road level, he had thrown a magnificent viaduct [bridge] of nine arches, the middle one of which is seventy feet high, through which we saw the whole of this beautiful little valley. . . . We then rejoined the rest of the party, and the engine having received its supply of water, the carriage was placed behind it, for it cannot turn, and was set off at its utmost speed, 35 miles an hour, swifter than a bird flies (for they tried the experiment with a snipe [a slender-billed bird]). You cannot conceive what that sensation of cutting the air was; the motion is as smooth as possible, too.❞ ■

The Communication Revolution

Improvements in communication during the 1800s were as revolutionary as those in manufacturing and transportation. The Industrial Revolution increased the need for people to communicate over long distances. Factory managers needed to know when raw materials would be available. Merchants needed to communicate with factory owners about shipments and orders of goods to sell.

The Telegraph and Telephone Improve Communication. Samuel F. B. Morse invented the telegraph in 1837. He discov-

A French lithograph depicts Liverpool and Manchester Railway passenger trains in 1831. First-class riders traveled in closed cars while second-class passengers rode in open, dusty cars.

ered a way to send electrical impulses over a wire. The impulses created clicks at the other end. Morse worked out a code made up of dots and dashes to translate the clicks into letters of the alphabet.

In the 1850s, a telegraph cable was stretched from Dover in England to Calais in France. Other cables soon linked major cities in Europe. In 1866, waterproof cables were laid across the oceans. These cables linked the hemispheres.

By the 1870s, inventors were trying to send the human voice across wires. Alexander Graham Bell, one of these inventors, finally succeeded. His invention, the telephone, was patented in 1876.

Other Inventions Change People's Lives. An important invention of the early 1800s was the breech-loading handgun. The new gun had a hinge near the trigger and opened for reloading. Previously, people could only load muskets while standing. The ball and powder had to be rammed down the long barrel of the gun.

The breech-loading gun altered warfare. In 1866, Prussian soldiers were able to lie down on the ground while shooting at Austrian soldiers. The Austrians, without the new guns, became easy targets when they had to stand to reload their muskets. Officers had to devise new military strategies for both offense and defense to accommodate the breech-loading gun.

Many other inventions changed the way people lived. Among the new inventions of the 1800s were the camera, bicycle, and sewing machine. The reaper, first successfully built by Cyrus McCormick in 1831, enabled farmers to harvest grain more quickly and with less spoilage.

New Creative Movements in the Arts. The advances in transportation and communication were accompanied by a succession of new creative movements in the arts. Romanticism, a turning away from classical art to a focus on the personal expression of emo-tion, developed in the late 1700s. Romantic writers, painters, and composers looked back at the adventure and romance of the past and focused on their feelings, experiences, and love of nature.

Romanticism, which reached its peak between 1790 and 1840, broke from tradition and forged a path into the Modern Age. By 1830 a new movement, realism, began to dominate the arts. Writers, especially in fiction, depicted the world as they saw it.

By the late 1800s, painting also became more realistic, and other trends emerged. Painters, experimenting with color and light, developed a technique called impressionism to capture their impression of a scene. While the impressionist movement ended with the 1800s, the emphasis on creating art for its own sake and on personal expression continued.

SECTION 2 *Study Skills*

Developing Vocabulary **1.** How did enclosure affect farmers in England? **2.** Name the factors of production. **3.** Why would an inventor apply for a patent?

Reviewing Main Ideas **1.** What three resources aided the Industrial Revolution in England? **2.** How did steam engines improve manufacturing and transportation? **3.** What natural resources did factories use before and after the invention of steam engines?

Understanding Chronology **1.** Construct a time line showing inventions in manufacturing in the 1700s. **2.** Trace the communication improvements that occurred in the 1800s.

Understanding Cause and Effect **1.** What was the impact of Maudslay's invention? **2.** How did the McAdam process improve transportation?

Challenge Inventions changed people's way of living during the Industrial Revolution. Give five examples of inventions of the past 30 years that have changed our way of living.

3 New Patterns of Life Develop

OBJECTIVE: *To understand the causes and consequences of the changes that affected society in the 1800s*

Effects of the Industrial Revolution

For centuries, many people in Europe were self-employed. For them, working was deeply bound up with family, village life, and religious rituals. The Industrial Revolution dramatically changed people's lives. Workers in factories could not set their work hours. They had to be ready to work when the steam power was turned on. Families looking for jobs often had to leave the village to be near factories.

Mushrooming Cities. Industrial towns across Europe grew rapidly during the nineteenth century. In Britain, for example, Manchester and Leeds became centers of textile manufacturing, and Birmingham and Sheffield, centers of iron smelting. The population of these towns increased 10-fold between 1750 and 1850. During the same period, London's population rose from 900,000 to nearly 2.5 million. The growing cities filled the needs of the factory owner.

Living Conditions in the Growing Cities. Sanitary conditions in most cities did not keep up with the growth in population. City services such as water supply, garbage removal, and public schools, did not exist.

Families were often crowded into tenements. A tenement is an apartment building with minimal sanitation and comfort. Often, 12 or more people crowded into a single room. The testimony of a doctor before a parliamentary committee in 1819 described life in London:

VOCABULARY DEVELOPMENT

tenement *noun:* an apartment that is run-down and overcrowded. From the Latin word, *tenere*, meaning to hold.

compensation (KAHM puhn SAY shuhn) *noun:* payment to make amends for a loss, such as from injury, damage, or unemployment. From the Latin word, *compensatus*, meaning to weigh one thing against another.

socialism *noun:* an economic system in which all members of a community, often through its government, own the means of production; everyone shares the work and the products.

proletariat (PROH luh TAIR ee uht) *noun:* the class of people whose status is the lowest in a society.

From the Latin word, *proletarius*, meaning citizen of the lowest class, the working class, especially the industrial working class.

bourgeoisie (BOOR ZHWAH ZEE) *noun:* the social class between the aristocracy, or very wealthy, and the working class; middle class, usually with private property interests. From the Latin word, *burgus*, meaning castle.

communism *noun:* an economic system based on community or government ownership of all property; characterized by a classless society and equal distribution of goods, envisioned by Marx as being achieved through revolution rather than by gradual means.

"From three to eight people of different ages often sleep in the same bed. In general, there is only one room and one bed for each family.

Persons of the lowest class do not put clean sheets on their beds three times a year. Even when no sheets are used, they never wash or clean their blankets nor replace them until they are no longer usable. . . ."

In addition to poor living conditions, factory workers faced the threat of unemployment. The new machines produced great quantities of goods. If sales decreased, employers cut wages or laid off workers.

For example, between 1790 and 1815 the countries of Europe were engaged, off and on, in the Napoleonic Wars. The government required guns, ships, uniforms, and all the equipment necessary to wage war. When a military campaign ended, demand decreased. The boom conditions of wartime gave way to periods of high unemployment in peacetime.

Working Conditions. For the first time in history, many women and children were employed outside the home and fields. Women and children were hired for lower wages. Women also had previously been involved in the textile industry in their homes.

Working conditions were poor during the first century of the Industrial Revolution. Wages usually were low, barely enough to buy food and obtain shelter. The working day was often 14 to 16 hours long. Most factories were extremely noisy, dirty, and cramped.

Early machines had no safety devices. A worker who got sick or was injured had no source of income. Governments did not interfere with employment practices of factory owners or promote worker safety. No insurance for workers or compensation for injuries existed.

Many children worked in factories and mines from the age of five on. In coal mines, women and children pulled heavy coal carts through the tunnels on their hands and knees. Workers in coal mines seldom saw the sun, and black coal dust filled their lungs.

In some extreme cases, factory owners and supervisors fined workers for a variety of frivolous reasons. A worker could be fined for opening the window, having dirty hands, leaving an oil can out of place, or whistling. A sick worker might pay a high fine as well as the cost of the day's steam.

Child Laborers

FOCUS ON PEOPLE

The majority of textile factory workers in the 1700s and 1800s were women and children. In 1832, Parliament investigated working conditions, especially the treatment of children. Following are two excerpts from testimony about labor conditions. The first one is about conditions in the textile industry while the second is about the mines.

Testimony of William Cooper. This excerpt contains the testimony of William Cooper, a witness before the Sadler Commission in 1832. The **Q** indicates the question asked of Mr. Cooper. The **A** is his answer.

"**Q:** When did you first begin to work in mills or factories?

A: When I was about 10 years of age.

Q: What were your usual hours of working?

A: We began at five o'clock in the morning and got out at nine at night.

Q: What intermissions did you have for meals?

A: When we began at five, we went on until noon, and then we had forty minutes for dinner.

Q: Had you no time for breakfast?

Children carry clay in a nineteenth-century British brickyard. An 1833 Act of Parliament, the first in a series of reforms, shortened children's working hours.

A: No, we got it best as we could while we were working.

Q: Had you any time for an afternoon refreshment?

A: No, when we began at noon, we went on till night; there was only the one forty-minute break.

Q: Did you ever work even later than the time you have mentioned?

A: I cannot say that I worked later there. I had a sister who worked upstairs, and she worked till eleven at night.

Q: At what time in the morning did she begin to work?

A: At the same time as I did.

Q: To keep you at your work for such a length of time, what means were taken to keep you awake and attentive?

A: They whipped us at times. **"**

Testimony of Patience Kershaw. This second excerpt is the statement of Patience Kershaw. It was delivered before the Ashley Mines Investigation Commission of 1842 and illustrates the life of many children.

"I am Patience Kershaw, I am 17 years old. My father has been dead about a year. My mother is living and has ten children, five lads and five lassies. All my sisters have been coal carriers but three went to the mill. Alice went because her legs swelled from carrying coal in the cold water of the mine. I never went to school. I go to Sunday-school, but cannot read or write. I go to the [coal] pit at five o'clock in the morning and come out at five in the evening. I get my breakfast of porridge and milk first. I take my dinner with me, a loaf, and eat it as I go. I do not stop or rest any time for that purpose. I get nothing else until I get home, and then have potatoes and meat, not meat every day, though.

The bald place upon my head is made by pushing the coal cart. I push the cart a mile and more underground and back; they weigh over 300 pounds; I push 11 a day. I wear a belt and chain to pull the cart out. I am the only girl in the pit. There are about 20 boys and 15 men. **"**

Employers and government officials often used new economic theories to justify working conditions. They believed that natural laws governed economic life as well as nature. The deplorable living and working conditions of laborers, they believed, resulted from these economic laws. ■

New Economic Theories

The new economic conditions of the Industrial Revolution required new explanations for economic activity. Economists believed that natural laws governed economic life much as laws of nature governed the planets and life on earth. Interference with natural laws might result in disaster.

The Invisible Hand of Adam Smith.

One of the most famous of these economists was Adam Smith. His book, *The Wealth of Nations*, was published in 1776. In the book, Smith argued that progress results when individuals follow their own self-interests. Businesses follow their self-interest when they compete with one another for the buyers' money. Each producer tries to provide goods and services that are better and less expensive than those of competitors. Buyers compete with one another to purchase the best goods at the lowest prices.

The result of this competition—Smith called it an "invisible hand"—guides the market economy to produce the best product at the lowest price. Each individual who "intends only his own gain" is nevertheless "led by an invisible hand" to promote the good of society. Smith claimed that government need not interfere in the economy. Economists Thomas Malthus and David Ricardo supported Smith's ideas.

Malthus and Overpopulation.

Thomas Malthus, one of the Anglican clergy, became a professor of history and political economics. He is best known for his 1798 *Essay on the Principle of Population*.

Malthus believed that population tended to increase more rapidly than the food supply. Without wars and epidemics to kill off the extra population, most people were destined to be poor and miserable. The predictions of Malthus seemed to be coming true in the 1840s. Later, however, improved transportation and better methods of agriculture provided enough food for most people in Europe.

Ricardo's Iron Law of Wages.

David Ricardo was a leading British economist of the 1800s. He published his book, *Principles of Political Economy and Taxation*, in 1817.

Like Malthus, Ricardo believed that a permanent underclass would always be poor. In a market system, labor and other resources are cheap when plentiful and expensive when scarce. Ricardo believed that wages would be forced down as population increased. If a decrease in population brought higher wages, workers would have more children. Wages would again fall, and the cycle would repeat itself. This idea became known as the iron law of wages.

Reforms and Reformers

As more people crowded into the cities and began to work in factories, reformers began to demand changes. They supported legislation to protect workers from long hours and dangerous working conditions.

Factory Laws in Great Britain.

The first laws to protect British workers were passed in 1833. The Factory Act of 1833 forbade employers from using children under nine years of age in textile factories. The act also limited children between the ages of 9 and 13 to 9 hours of work a day, 48 hours a week. Children 13 to 18 could work only 12 hours a day and 69 hours a week.

In 1842, The Mines Act forbade mine owners from using women and girls in the mines. Boys could not work underground until they were 10 years old.

The Ten Hours Act in 1847 limited textile factory employment of women and children under 18 to 10 hours a day. Since factories were not profitable without the cheap services of women and children, the 10-hour day even applied to men.

The Union Movement.

The early factory laws were not very effective because they were not strictly enforced. In addition, the laws did not regulate wages. To obtain higher wages and improve their conditions, some workers tried to form unions.

Labor unions were illegal in Great Britain. An act of 1800 stated that persons who combined with others to demand higher wages, shorter hours, or better working conditions were liable to imprisonment.

Eventually, workers gained the right to protest. In 1825, Parliament passed an act that permitted workers to meet in order to agree on wages and hours. The National Association for the Protection of Labor, formed in 1845, helped persuade Parliament to allow peaceful picketing. Laws passed in the 1870s allowed workers to strike. In other countries, workers also forced changes in laws. Gradually, unions began to represent workers.

Utopian Socialist Ideas. The harsh living and working conditions in the early years of the Industrial Revolution stimulated ideas for reform. Among the reformers were Utopian Socialists, who blamed society's ills on private ownership of the factors of production. Laborers were at the mercy of employers thinking only of profit.

To improve conditions, socialists of the 1800s favored collective or common ownership of property. These reformers first

used the word socialism in the 1800s. Under socialism the factors of production would be owned by the public and operated for the welfare of all.

Utopian socialists tried to set up ideal communities where people could live better lives. Robert Owen was one of the most influential. He began to work at the age of 10 as a shopkeeper's apprentice. By the age of 28, he was managing one of the largest cotton mills in England. Owen created a model industrial community at his New Lanark, Scotland, textile mill. Unlike many factory managers, he treated his workers fairly.

Owen set up "villages of cooperation" in both Great Britain and the United States. Everyone in the villages worked, and everyone shared in what was produced. Each vil-

Below, an engraving of Robert Owen's communal society in New Harmony, Indiana. At right, a journal features a design for a utopian community.

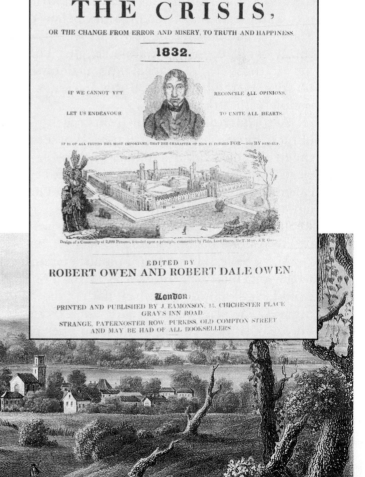

lage was supposed to be self-sufficient. His best known settlement was New Harmony, Indiana. These communities did not prosper and were disbanded after a few years.

Charles Fourier (FOO RYAY) and the Comte de Saint-Simon (KAWNT deh SAHN SEE MAWN) were French socialists. Saint-Simon wanted to bring about a new society where all people would have to work and would receive rewards equally for their labor. No one would be able to inherit wealth; therefore, all people would begin life on an equal economic basis.

Charles Fourier also thought that society would improve if private property were eliminated. However, he lacked the money to establish any cooperative villages.

Marx and the Communist Manifesto. Karl Marx, the most influential socialist of the 1800s, transformed his ideas for reform into a new economic system. Marx believed that all great movements in history were the result of an economic class struggle. The haves, those with political and economic power, took advantage of the have-nots, people with little power.

According to Marx, the Industrial Revolution intensified class struggle. Workers, called the proletariat (PROH luh TAIR ee uht), were exploited by employers, whom Marx called the bourgeoisie (BOOR ZHWAH ZEE). The labor of workers created the profits, or wealth, for employers. Workers, however, received none of these profits.

Marx believed that the capitalist system, which produced the Industrial Revolution, would eventually destroy itself in the following way. Factories would drive small artisans out of business, leaving a small number of great manufacturers to control all the wealth. The large proletariat would revolt, seize the means of production from the capitalists, and produce what society needed. Workers, sharing in the profits, would bring about economic equality for all people.

The workers also would control the government in a "dictatorship of the proletar-iat." After a period of cooperative living and education, the state would "wither away as a classless society developed." Marx called this final phase pure communism. Marxian socialism is also called scientific socialism. In 1848, Marx and a friend, Friedrich Engels, published their ideas in a pamphlet, the *Communist Manifesto*.

Between 1750 and 1850, revolutions in production, agriculture, transportation, and communication changed the lives of the people in western Europe and the United States. Many people in Europe opposed the new technology and mass production techniques. They especially disliked changes in traditional ways of living. Yet industrialization gave Europe tremendous economic power. The economies of Asia and Africa were still based on agriculture and small workshops. Much of Europe was gaining the capability to produce many goods faster and more cheaply. This production made non-Western countries increasingly dependent on Europe for many goods.

SECTION 3 *Study Skills*

Developing Vocabulary **1.** Explain the differences between the proletariat and the bourgeoisie. **2.** Describe living conditions in a tenement. **3.** How does socialism benefit members of a society?

Reviewing Main Ideas **1.** Why was unemployment common among factory workers, yet uncommon among farm workers? **2.** Describe conditions in factories during the Industrial Revolution. **3.** Define "invisible hand."

Understanding Cause and Effect **1.** According to Marx, what would cause the end of the Industrial Revolution? **2.** List important factory laws passed in Great Britain and explain their effects on factory workers.

Challenge Explain the quote, "Factory workers become slaves to the machine."

CHAPTER 23 *Summary & Review*

Summarizing Main Ideas

The ideas of both democracy and nationalism inspired revolutions on both sides of the Atlantic between 1750 and 1850. Countries such as Austria, Prussia, and Russia resisted change. The middle classes of Great Britain and France were more sympathetic to the reform movement.

Breakthroughs in manufacturing, transportation, communications, and farming altered traditional occupations and values. Beginning in the late 1700s, laborers, no longer needed on the farms poured into the cities seeking jobs.

Living and working conditions grew worse as industrialization continued. Worker welfare was of little concern to most factory owners. By the 1840s, unions had formed to protect factory workers from poor conditions and wages.

European life changed greatly by 1850. With increased production, trade became more global. Countries sought a balance of power in international affairs.

Questions for Critical Thinking

COMPREHENSION Interpreting Events

1. Discuss the issues of the Crimean War that reflect the growing concern over the balance of power in Europe.
2. What influences led to the passage of factory laws in Great Britain?

ANALYSIS Identifying Trends

1. What was the effect of the enclosure movement on English society?
2. Explain how improvements in industry led to improvements in communication. Give at least two examples.

APPLICATION Comparing Past and Present

1. Why are laws designed to protect employees still necessary?
2. How important is good transportation to modern industry? Explain and give several specific examples.

Inventions and Industrial Growth

Date	Name	Invention
1764	James Hargreaves	Spinning jenny
1769	Richard Arkwright	Water frame
1769	James Watt	Steam engine to run machinery
1779	Samuel Crompton	Spinning mule
1785	Edmund Cartwright	Power loom
1793	Eli Whitney	Cotton gin
1797	Henry Maudslay	Accurate lathe for cutting metal
1798	Eli Whitney	Interchangeable, replaceable parts for muskets
1807	Robert Fulton	Steamboat
1815	John McAdam	Macadamized roads
1837	Samuel Morse	Telegraph

SYNTHESIS Making Decisions

1. Why did the French people vote in 1852 to make Louis Napoleon emperor of France?
2. How did the decision to unionize benefit factory workers?

EVALUATION Weighing Consequences

1. Explain the long-range importance of the union movement.
2. Find out how the ideas of Karl Marx influenced social reformers of his time.

CHALLENGE

1. Why might emerging Third World nations adopt the ideas of Karl Marx?
2. Choose 4 inventions from the chart on this page and explain their effects at the time and their effects on modern life.

CHAPTER 24
Responses to European Power

TIME

● **1773** Waltz becomes popular dance in Austria

● **1779** Qajar Dynasty begins rule in Iran

PEOPLE

1701–1792 Ibn Abd-ul Wahhab begins the Wahhabi movement

1772–1883 Ram Mohan Roy reforms Hinduism

1757–1774 Sultan Mustafa III attempts reform in the Ottoman Empire

● **1762** Mozart, at age 6, tours Europe as musical prodigy

PLACE

● **1750** *China;*[1] Tea and opium become main products traded

● **1779** *Iran;*[2] Qajar rulers initiate European ideas and technology

Linking Past to Present

English and French are widely spoken throughout the world. In fact, today English alone is the language of about 350 million people. Additionally, at least 400 million more speak it as a second language. This is in part because Great Britain, the United States, and France dominated the world in the nineteenth century. The growing trade and military power of Europe and the United States forced the people of other countries to respond.

The power of the western industrialized countries threatened the economies and political independence of Asian and African societies. The challenge of the West stimulated movements for military, economic, and moral reform in several countries.

A British resident in India entertains at home around 1800.

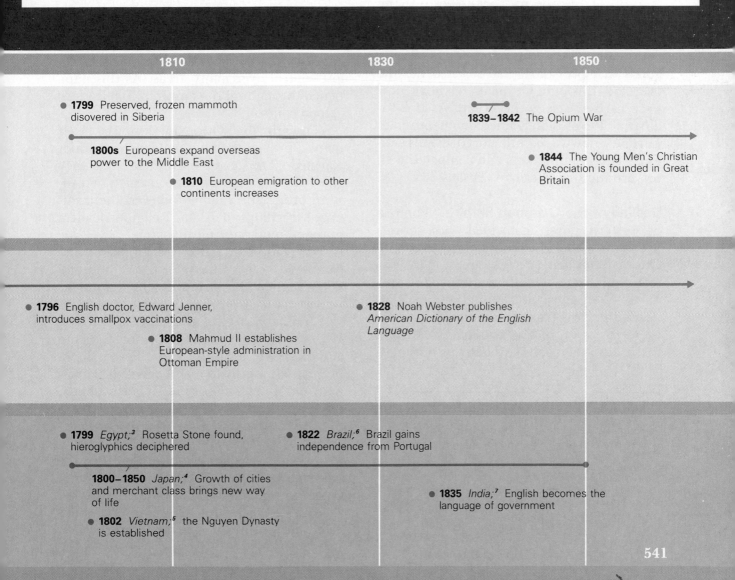

1810   **1830**   **1850**

1799 Preserved, frozen mammoth disovered in Siberia

1839–1842 The Opium War

1800s Europeans expand overseas power to the Middle East

1844 The Young Men's Christian Association is founded in Great Britain

1810 European emigration to other continents increases

1796 English doctor, Edward Jenner, introduces smallpox vaccinations

1828 Noah Webster publishes *American Dictionary of the English Language*

1808 Mahmud II establishes European-style administration in Ottoman Empire

1799 *Egypt;*[3] Rosetta Stone found, hieroglyphics deciphered

1822 *Brazil;*[6] Brazil gains independence from Portugal

1800–1850 *Japan;*[4] Growth of cities and merchant class brings new way of life

1835 *India;*[7] English becomes the language of government

1802 *Vietnam;*[5] the Nguyen Dynasty is established

541

1 *The Decline of Muslim Power*

OBJECTIVE: *To understand how Russia and Great Britain gained power at the expense of Muslim empires*

European Power Affects the Ottomans

By 1600, the commercial and industrial expansion of Europe had begun to hurt the Ottoman Empire. The Dutch and British developed trade routes by sea to India, Southeast Asia, China, and Japan. Trade goods that previously had reached Europe overland through Ottoman territory now were carried across the ocean. As the Industrial Revolution gained momentum in Europe, newly manufactured goods entered Ottoman markets and competed with the products of Ottoman artisans.

Decline of the Ottoman Empire. The rise of western power coincided with serious problems within the Ottoman Empire. The Ottoman population grew rapidly in the sixteenth and seventeenth centuries. Yet productivity in agriculture did not grow at nearly the same pace. Since individual farmers were not producing as much as they had in the past, their standard of living declined.

They could not pay as much in taxes, even though the government tried to collect higher taxes.

Farmers suffered from high taxes. Peasants left the land in large numbers to seek opportunity in the cities. Since jobs were few, many desperate peasants joined rebel bands as outlaws. The Ottoman government lost control over many areas. As this happened throughout the empire, local leaders gained control.

Though the Ottoman Empire faced many problems, the rulers were not alarmed. The leaders assumed that they ruled the greatest empire on earth. To restore order, the sultans followed the traditional teachings of Islam. Religious leaders opposed much technical change.

The Ottoman Empire was built on the combined power of armed forces and taxation of peasant farmers. The Ottomans valued three professions: government service, military service, and religious service. War and religion were important. Banking and finance were considered inferior. Banking was left mostly to members of the Christian and Jewish minorities. Consequently, the Ottoman rulers were slow to respond to the commercial and industrial revolutions.

European Influence Expands. In the eighteenth century, the Ottoman sultans began to understand the seriousness of the European challenge. They became interested in European knowledge, especially

VOCABULARY DEVELOPMENT

embassy (EHM buh see) *noun:* the official residence and office of an ambassador to a foreign country. From the Prussian word, *ambaissa*, meaning mission, task.

sepoy (SEE poy) *noun:* a native of India serving in the British army. From the Hindu and Persian word, *sipah*, meaning army.

military knowledge. The sultans wanted to use the knowledge to strengthen and increase their power.

Military technology, mapmaking, and shipbuilding were among the western accomplishments Turks prized.

As early as 1720, the sultan sent people to France to learn about technical matters. Some Ottoman leaders wanted to train an engineering corps for their army. Others wanted to organize a fire brigade for Istanbul. The first books printed in the Turkish language were published in the 1700s.

Europeans living in Turkey introduced much of the new technology to the Ottomans. For example, a Hungarian who had converted to Islam set up the first printing press. The first artillery school for military officers was established with help from a French nobleman, Count de Bonneval. De Bonneval came to Turkey in 1729, to escape legal troubles in France.

The Tulip Age.
After 1700, people at the sultan's court began to dress in the French style and to imitate European manners. With the French court at Versailles in mind, the sultan built huge summer palaces.

The years from 1717 to 1730 are known as the Tulip Age in the Ottoman Empire. Tulip-growing represented stylish copying of European fashions. Upper class people copied French manners, decorations, furniture, and portrait painting. The Tulip Age ended suddenly in 1730 when the Safavids from Iran defeated the Ottomans forcing the sultan to abdicate.

Opposition to Reform.
The influence of European technology did not dramatically change Turkish life for two reasons. First, the borrowing was limited largely to military technology. Second, various groups in Turkey, who had something to lose by change, opposed European technology. Printing, for example, was a threat to the scribes who made their living by hand-copying documents. Some feared that change in political or religious ideas would threaten traditional leadership. To the Ottomans, the radical ideas of the French Revolution held a great danger. One Turkish author described the revolution as a:

" . . . conflagration [a great fire] of sedition [rebellion] and wickedness that broke

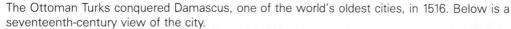

The Ottoman Turks conquered Damascus, one of the world's oldest cities, in 1516. Below is a seventeenth-century view of the city.

out a few years ago in France, scattering sparks and shooting flames of mischief and tumult in all directions. **"**

One of the Ottoman leaders who saw the need for reform was Sultan Mustafa (moos tah FAH) III. During his rule from 1757 to 1774, he realized that he would not be able to overcome opposition to reform. He hoped that his son, who became Sultan Selim III, would be more successful and would be able to put reforms into practice.

Selim III

FOCUS ON PEOPLE

Selim III was born in 1761. His father provided the best education for him and instilled in him the desire to reform the empire. Selim became an excellent poet and composer of Ottoman music. His efforts to reform the empire, though, turned out to be less successful.

When Selim III began to rule the Ottoman Empire in 1789, he faced a period of decline. The sultan's authority was defied in the frontier provinces of the empire. People in Syria, Palestine, and Greece rebelled. Greece was able to gain independence in the nineteenth century. Outdated weapons and methods of warfare along with a rebellious army prevented the Sultan from exerting effective control.

Military Reforms. Selim attempted to save the crumbling Ottoman Empire. He tried to reform the military and the economy but prevent other changes in society. Selim was convinced that reforming the armed services would result in the development of an effective military force. With this force, he could defeat the enemies of the empire.

Officers and technicians recruited from Europe trained the new military force. Appointments to military positions began to result from ability rather than influence or bribery. The navy was expanded and new ships were constructed.

Sultan Selim III attempted to reform the Ottoman Empire during his reign from 1789 to 1808. He is shown here, with Vizier Koca Yusuf Pasha.

The technical assistance Europeans provided led to diplomatic ties between various European countries and the Ottoman Empire. The Turks established embassies in London, Paris, Vienna, and Berlin. Foreign diplomats, merchants, and soldiers began living in the Ottoman Empire.

Economic Reforms. Selim also attempted to improve the economy of the empire during his reign. To help finance his government, he instituted taxes on tobacco, coffee, and other commodities. To reduce inflation, he had gold coins melted down, thereby removing them from circulation. These economic measures were, on the whole, unsuccessful.

City populations grew faster than the supplies of housing. Consequently, many people were homeless. The government tried to force some people to return to agricultural areas. Selim believed that defining the rank and social position of the people in the empire would help to preserve order. As a result, the government issued clothing regulations. For instance, only members of the ruling class were allowed to wear clothes made of silks and satins. Such government measures, however, were unsuccessful.

Continuing Problems. Selim's problems were compounded in 1798 when Napoleon Bonaparte invaded Egypt. The French captured Cairo and Alexandria without effective resistance. Selim, eager to halt Napoleon's advances, entered an alliance with Britain and Russia. This alliance drove the French from Egypt. The ensuing peace freed the Ottoman Empire from European domination for a while. However, Napoleon's invasion shocked the Muslim world by exposing its military weakness.

The peace with France did not end the turmoil within the empire. One of the leaders of the opposition to reform was Selim's cousin, Mustafa. He was extremely ambitious. In 1807, he led an attack on Selim and other reformers. On July 29, 1808, on the orders of Mustafa's henchmen, Selim was strangled to death. ■

Further Attempts at Reform

Selim's death did not end efforts for reform. His supporters continued to carry on his efforts. Within months of Selim's murder, another reform-minded sultan, Mahmud (mah MOOD) II, came to power.

After reforming the army, Mahmud tackled the civil government. He reduced the power of leaders in the Islamic community. He established European-style administration, built roads, and started a postal service. As a symbol of the reforms he sought, Mahmud replaced the traditional turban with the fez, a rimless felt hat with a tassel at the top. Individuals who wore fezes demonstrated their support for Mahmud's efforts.

Tanzimat Reforms. Mahmud's sons continued his reforms. Collectively, these reforms were called *Tanzimat*, the Turkish word for reform or reorganization. The Ottoman reformers created a national school system and a ministry of education. By 1869, primary school was supposed to be free and compulsory. In addition, French, British, and American missionaries started hundreds of Christian schools. Robert College, founded by Americans in 1863, still exists in Istanbul.

Despite internal reforms, the Ottoman Empire continued to lose territory during the nineteenth century. The Ottomans lost control of much of eastern Europe and the empire's northern frontiers.

In addition to the loss of territory, a decline in revenues further weakened the empire. At the end of the Crimean War, the Ottoman government was heavily in debt to the European powers. To ensure payment, the Europeans controlled revenue collection through an organization known as the Ottoman Public Debt Administration. This authority was a humiliating loss of power for this most powerful Islamic state.

Turkish Nationalism. Rapid changes and losses in wars left many Turks frustrated. In 1865, several individuals joined to form a nationalist organization called the Young Ottomans. The Young Ottomans were dissatisfied with the loss of imperial power. They also resented efforts to replace Islamic law with reform law based on the Code of Napoleon. Some of the Young Ottomans were ardent Muslims, but others were not at all religious. They believed the Turks needed a modern constitution. In 1876, a constitution was written, and in 1877, a parliament convened.

Most Turks opposed the reforms, however, and they quickly failed. Nevertheless, such efforts did set the pattern for the twentieth century. In 1908, another group, the Young Turks, emerged to lead a revolution. The efforts to combine reform and Islamic traditions led to strong Turkish nationalism in the twentieth century.

Decline of Muslim Empires

The Safavid Empire in Iran and the Moghul Empire in India were similar to the Ottoman Empire. All three empires were led by rulers who were both Muslim and Turkish. Most people in each empire were peasant farmers. None of the three was prepared to confront European power.

Decline of the Safavids. The Safavids ruled Iran from 1501 to 1722 (see pages 429–432). Iran, located between the Ottomans and the Moghuls in India, had more contact with these empires than with Europe. The Safavids made little effort to understand the rise of European industrial and military power.

Rise of the Qajars. In 1779, another dynasty, the Qajars (kuh JAHRZ), took power in Iran. They remained in power until 1925.

The Qajar rulers claimed religious authority, but they never had strong religious support. The ulama, experts in Muslim law, who did not always support the Qajar rulers, retained religious authority.

During the Qajar period, Iran became involved in the struggle between Russia and Great Britain. The Russians wanted to extend their influence southward to the Persian Gulf. The British wanted a buffer between Russia and their empire in India.

To resist, the Qajars tried to strengthen their defenses. In the nineteenth century, they initiated military reforms similar to those of the Ottomans. European advisers helped the Qajars to set up military schools and reorganize the government.

While the Qajars were making these changes, Europeans exploited Iran's economy. By the 1890s, the British had a monopoly over the Iranian tobacco crop. The British also were operating the Imperial Bank of Persia. The Customs Service was reorganized under the Belgians. The Qajars were losing control over their country.

Merchants and religious leaders were the first to oppose the loss of Qajar control in Iran. They attacked both the corruption of the government and foreign influence.

The conflict in Iran reflected a general conflict over European influence. Rulers tried to reform their societies using European technology and ideas. As Europeans gained more influence, however, opposition to them increased. Thus, the rulers of Iran were caught between lure of the benefits of western civilization and their own subjects. In Iran, the conflict between admirers of western civilization and opponents of foreign influence has continued.

Changes in India. Muslims from central Asia founded the Moghul Empire in India in 1526. Around 1600, agents of the British East India Company began trading along the Indian coast. Eventually, the company gained control of the coastal regions. From there they expanded inland.

A late eighteenth-century painting by an unknown Indian artist depicts a British officer riding in procession in India.

By 1850, the British ruled half of India directly and controlled the other half through agreements with local rulers. The surviving Moghul emperor at Delhi had little power and relied on a British pension to pay his expenses.

The East India Company administered India until 1858. However, governor generals of India answered to Parliament.

As conquerors and rulers of India, the British faced the same problems as the earlier Moghuls. India was a huge and diverse land of many languages and religions. The British debated how best to govern India. Some wanted to revive traditional Indian culture. Missionaries wanted to convert the Indians to Christianity. Reformers in Britain wanted to introduce science and technology and to reform the government.

At first, the British encouraged traditional learning in Arabic, Persian, and Sanskrit, the Hindu language. After 1835, however, English replaced Persian as the language of government. The British established schools that taught the English language and culture, both necessary to obtain government jobs. The rise in British influence caused a crisis for Indian culture. That crisis had many causes and responses for the British and the Indian people.

In 1857, a group of Indian soldiers, sepoys (SEE poyz), rebelled against the British. The British suppressed the Sepoy Mutiny with savage force.

Throughout the 1800s, Europeans expanded their overseas power to the Middle East. The Ottoman, Safavid, and Moghul empires reacted to the European challenge in different ways. The Ottoman rulers attempted to reform their government. The Safavids resisted outside influence. The Moghul Empire was divided into many states, none strong enough to resist.

SECTION 1 *Study Skills*

Developing Vocabulary 1. What is the purpose of an embassy? **2.** Use sepoy in a sentence that shows its meaning.

Reviewing Main Ideas 1. Give examples of European technology introduced to the Ottomans. **2.** What factors limited European influence in the Ottoman Empire?

Understanding Cause and Effect 1. What factors caused the decline of the Ottoman Empire? **2.** What common traits led to the decline of the Safavid, Moghul, and Ottoman empires? **3.** Why did groups such as the Young Ottomans and Young Turks develop? How successful were they? **4.** How did the Tulip Age affect the Ottoman Empire?

Challenge Explain how traditional Turkish cultures and religions were threatened by European influence.

2 Asian Responses to European Power

OBJECTIVE: *To understand how China, Japan, and Southeast Asia reacted to the growth of European power*

The Manchu Qing Dynasty

The Manchus replaced the Ming Dynasty in China in 1644. The Manchus came from Manchuria, the region northeast of the Great Wall. The government they established in Beijing, called the Qing (chihng) Dynasty, lasted until 1911.

Qing is the Chinese word for pure. The Manchus used the name to suggest that they would not be weak and corrupt like the Ming rulers they replaced.

Opposition to the Manchus. In 1644, fewer than 2 million Manchus ruled over more than 150 million Chinese. Consequently, the Manchus had to win the support of many Chinese. They did so by governing China efficiently. The Manchus maintained the law code and system of government the Ming Dynasty had used.

VOCABULARY DEVELOPMENT

queue (kyoo) *noun:* a braid of hair hanging from the back of the head, a pigtail. From the Latin word, *cauda*, meaning tail.

kowtow (KOU TOU) *verb:* to kneel and touch the ground with the forehead to show respect and submission. In Chinese, *kowtow* means a knock on the head.

petition (puh TIHSH uhn) *noun:* a written request to someone in authority, often signed by a number of people. From the Latin word, *petere*, meaning to ask.

The Manchus also required the Chinese to wear their hair in the Manchu style. The front of the head was shaved and the rest of the hair hung down the back in a braid called a queue (kyoo). The queue was a sign of Manchu conquest. Chinese who resisted the Manchu conquest were suppressed.

The Tributary System. The Chinese considered themselves to be superior to other peoples. The emperors of China insisted that all other rulers pay them respect by sending tribute in the form of gifts.

Foreign rulers or ambassadors had to kowtow before the emperor. Kowtow comes from the Chinese words for knock on the head. The person paying respect to the emperor had to kneel on the ground three times and tap his head on the ground nine times. The Chinese ruler then responded by giving valuable gifts to the official and holding a grand banquet.

After 1500, European merchants traveled to China to buy valuable goods, especially silk, tea, and high-quality dishes called porcelain. However, Europeans had little that the Chinese wanted. Consequently, Europeans had to pay with silver.

For 300 years, China accumulated silver from all over the world. Some of it came from Japan, but most came from America. The Spanish sent silver mined in Mexico to the Philippine Islands, their colony in the Pacific Ocean. From there, the Spanish traded the silver to Chinese merchants for Chinese goods. The goods were shipped back to Mexico and Spain.

Trade in Canton. After 1700, the British became the most important European traders in China. The British East India Company controlled all British trade with China. Every year the East India Company sent ships to China from India. The Chinese required that all foreign ships go only to the southern port of Canton. Europeans trading in China were not allowed to travel or even to talk with ordinary Chinese.

As the value of the trade grew, the British wanted to trade in different parts of China. They decided to send a representative to tell the Chinese emperor that the trade rules were too strict and the taxes too high. The representative was James Flint, probably the first British citizen to speak Chinese. Flint traveled north from Canton in 1757 with a petition to the emperor asking to expand trade.

The results of the Flint mission shocked the British. Chinese law strictly forbade anyone to travel to northern China except to pay tribute. Flint was arrested, sent back to the south, and imprisoned for several years. Then he was banished from China for life. The Chinese individual who had written the petition for him was executed. The emperor ordered trade in Canton restricted even more tightly. In his order, the Qing emperor gave his opinion of foreign trade:

" The products of China are abundant. What need have we for the small and insignificant goods of distant barbarians? **"**

After Flint's failure, the British tried to send ambassadors to China through the official system of tribute. Unwilling to recognize the superiority of the Chinese emperor, the British failed.

Tea and Opium. The volume of British trade in China grew rapidly after 1750. Tea was the main product traded. The British

government got about 10 percent of its revenue from taxes on the sale of tea. Though the tea trade was profitable, the British did not like to pay in silver. They continued to search for a product the Chinese needed.

In the late eighteenth century, the British discovered they did have a product the Chinese wanted—opium. Opium, extracted from the seed pods of poppy flowers, was long used as a medicine to stop diarrhea. In the eighteenth century, people began to mix it with tobacco and smoke it as a drug.

Opium also was taken from the poppy pods in the form of a white gum. The gum was heated over a flame and the opium addict would then inhale the fumes. Today, opium often is refined into other drugs, such as morphine and heroin.

By 1800, thousands of Chinese were addicted to smoking opium. Since opium smoking was illegal in China, the drug had to be smuggled in from abroad. India and Turkey were the main centers of production. In India, the British East India Com-

A watercolor scene shows a western merchant purchasing tea in the late 1700s.

pany controlled the production. The company sold opium to traders, who smuggled it into China.

A lively drug traffic developed all along the south China coast. In out-of-the-way coves and inlets smuggling ships would meet longboats with rowers. Called fast crabs and scrambling dragons because of their speed and splashing oars, these longboats could outrun the Chinese coastal patrols. The drug dealers also bribed Chinese officials. By 1838, the British were sending 40,000 chests of opium to China each year. Each chest weighed 133 pounds and could be worth 1,000 Mexican silver dollars.

Chinese officials complained to the emperor about opium smuggling. They worried about the number of people becoming drug addicts, the officials taking bribes, and the silver being spent. China was losing more on the drug than it was earning by selling tea. The emperor decided to stop the opium trade.

A Letter to the Queen

FOCUS ON SOURCES

The emperor appointed an official, Lin Zexu, to solve the opium problem. In 1839, Lin sent a letter to Queen Victoria of Great Britain concerning the opium trade. He believed that only with British support could the opium trade be stopped. However, his appeal to the moral conscience of the queen failed. Here is an excerpt from Lin's letter:

❝ But after a long period of commercial intercourse, there appear among the crowd of barbarians [Europeans] both good persons and bad, unevenly. Consequently, there are those who smuggle opium to seduce the Chinese people and so cause the spread of the poison to all provinces. Such persons who only care to profit themselves, and disregard their harm to others, are not

tolerated by the laws of heaven and are unanimously hated by human beings. His Majesty the Emperor, upon hearing of this, is in a towering rage. . . . **❞**

Appeals to Morality. **❝**We find that your country is [far] from China. Yet there are barbarian ships that strive to come here for trade for the purpose of making a great profit. The wealth of China is used to profit the barbarians. That is to say, the great profit made by barbarians is all taken from the rightful share of China. By what right do they then in return use the poisonous drug to injure the Chinese people? Even though the barbarians may not necessarily intend to do us harm, yet in coveting [desiring] profit to an extreme, they have no regard for injuring others. Let us ask, where is your conscience? I have heard that the smoking of opium is very strictly forbidden by your country; that is because the harm caused by opium is clearly understood. Since it is not permitted to do harm to your own country, then even less should you let it be passed on to the harm of other countries—how much less to China! Of all that China exports to foreign countries, there is not a single thing which is not beneficial to people: . . . when eaten, . . . used, or . . . resold: all are beneficial. Is there a single article from China which has done any harm to foreign countries? . . . **❞**

Penalties for Smugglers. **❝**Now we have set up regulations governing the Chinese people. He who sells opium shall receive the death penalty and he who smokes it also the death penalty. Now consider this: if the barbarians do not bring opium, then how can the Chinese people resell it, and how can they smoke it? The fact is that the wicked barbarians beguile [lure] the Chinese people into a deathtrap. How then can we grant life only to these barbarians? He who takes the life of even one person still has to atone [pay] for it with his own life; yet is the harm done by opium limited to the taking of one

The British East India Company's steamer *Nemesis* destroys Chinese war junks during the Opium War. The Chinese boats were no match for British guns and iron-covered steamships.

life only? Therefore in the new regulations, in regard to those barbarians who bring opium to China, the penalty is fixed at decapitation [beheading] or strangulation. This is what is called getting rid of a harmful thing on behalf of mankind. " ∎

The Opium War

Lin Zexu went to Canton to confront the opium dealers. He seized 30,000 chests of opium from the merchants at Canton and had the drug destroyed. The British, however, had first turned the opium over to a representative of the British government. Legally, the opium Lin destroyed was the property of Great Britain.

This incident created conflict between Britain and China. The conflict increased over an issue of legal authority and justice. British sailors in Canton became involved in

a fight that resulted in the death of a Chinese citizen. The Chinese demanded that the British sailor be brought to justice. The British agreed, but could not identify which sailor had caused the death. The Chinese, believing that the government was responsible for its people, demanded any sailor be turned over to them. The British rejected this demand and went to war.

The Opium War lasted from 1839 to 1842. British forces attacked throughout southern China. The Qing Dynasty's forces were poorly trained and badly organized. They were equipped with swords, spears, bows and arrows, and old-fashioned cannons. The Chinese were no match for the British equipped with guns and iron-covered steamships. Lin had effectively challenged the drug dealers, but he could not challenge the British military. He was sent in disgrace to northwest China.

Conditions of the Treaty. The British government forced the Qing ruler to sign a treaty ending the war. Simply signing the treaty was an insult to China because that act indicated an agreement between equals. The conditions of the treaty were even more insulting. The treaty gave Hong Kong to Great Britain as a colony. China also had to pay 21 million Mexican dollars to Great Britain for the cost of the war. The opium trade continued as before.

The most significant clause of the treaty required that China open five ports for British trade: Canton, Xiamen, Fuzhou, Ningbo, and Shanghai. These treaty ports marked the beginning of a new era in Chinese history. China lost the power to keep foreigners out. France and the United States quickly made treaties that gave them the same privileges as the British.

New Influences Change Japan

Like China, Japan strictly limited foreign influences. Within Japan, though, merchants were gaining respect. By 1800, merchants were lending money to the daimyo and samurai (see pages 305–306), many of whom were living in poverty.

Merchant Life. The rise of the merchants brought a new lifestyle to Japanese cities. Many small schools opened, and many city men learned to read. By 1850, about one-third of the population was literate. One-fourth of these people were women.

Printing grew rapidly. Publishers sold stories of city life with woodblock illustrations. One popular series of stories made fun of the samurai. These stories showed how city values were becoming more important to the people.

Artists also captured the colorful life in the city in woodblock prints. These prints demonstrated the new popular culture developing in Japan.

The changes in Japan during the time it was closed off from the rest of the world were similar to the changes occurring in Europe. The growth of cities and the merchant class helped to prepare Japan for contact with Europe and the United States.

The Opening of Japan. After 1800, more and more foreign ships made contact with Japan. Sometimes, sailors were shipwrecked in Japan. The United States wanted Japan to allow its ships to stop there on their way across the Pacific. The Japanese worried as

Travelers leaving a ship in the bustling harbor of Yokohama, Japan in the late 1800s.

they learned about the expansion of the Russian Empire and the Opium War.

In 1853, the United States caused a crisis in Japan that forced the shogun to decide how to confront the industrial world. The United States sent a fleet of 8 ships into Edo Bay. Commodore Matthew C. Perry left a letter for the Japanese emperor. He told the Japanese that he would return the next year to discuss trade relations.

After Perry's visit, the shogun asked his daimyo to consider Japan's response. The ships from the United States were better armed than any Japanese vessels. Perry returned as promised in 1854. The Japanese agreed to sign a treaty opening two minor ports to ships from the United States.

Perry's trip began the opening of Japan. Soon afterwards, Japan signed treaties with the British, the Russians, and the Dutch. These treaties gave foreigners the right to live and trade in more ports.

Korea and Vietnam Resist Europe. Korea and Vietnam were smaller countries than Japan, and more closely tied to Chinese culture. Korea followed the Chinese example. All outsiders were banned with such vigor that some people referred to it as the Hermit Kingdom. Vietnam, because it was closer to southeast Asia, had extensive contact with European traders.

The earliest Vietnamese state was formed in the tenth century in the Red River valley just south of China. That region, around the modern city of Hanoi, was a rich rice-growing area. Chinese influence was very strong there for many centuries. However, French missionaries had been in northern Vietnam since the early 1700s.

Over the centuries, the Vietnamese had gradually pushed southward to control the area on the coast near the city of Hue. By 1750, the Vietnamese had expanded into the delta of the Mekong River. The main city there was Saigon, now called Ho Chi Minh City. The south was less developed and less populous than the north.

Vietnam was torn by rebellions and civil war from 1771 until 1802. Then, in 1802, a new ruling family, the Nguyens (ehng GWY ahnz), took control of the country. They were aided by about 400 French citizens. The Nguyen Dynasty established its capital at Hue.

The first ruler of the Nguyen Dynasty was tolerant of Buddhism, Confucianism, and Christianity. Later emperors, however, were hostile to Christianity. In the 1850s, two French priests and a Spanish bishop were executed.

Following these executions, the French began to demand rights in Vietnam similar to those the British enjoyed in China. The French wanted to travel through Vietnam to reach southwest China. The French military occupation of Saigon in 1859 marked the beginning of the French conquest of Vietnam and Indochina. Vietnam, like much of Asia, was unable to resist the growth of European and American power.

SECTION 2 *Study Skills*

Developing Vocabulary 1. Explain the term kowtow. 2. What is the purpose of a petition?

Reviewing Main Ideas 1. How did the British East India Company affect Chinese trade? 2. List the provisions of the treaty ending the Opium War. 3. Compare the reactions of the Chinese, Japanese, Koreans, and Vietnamese to European trade from 1700 to 1860.

Understanding Cause and Effect 1. Why were the Manchus able to control China? 2. What were the effects of British opium smuggling on China? 3. What was the result of the 1854 treaty between Japan and the United States?

Challenge Since 1700, Europeans have tried to control Southeast Asia politically and economically. How might this explain the French and American involvements in Vietnam during the 1950s and 1960s?

3 Influence of Several World Religions

OBJECTIVE: *To understand how religions reacted to the growing power of western civilizations*

Muslims Respond to Western Civilization

Reform movements developed throughout the Islamic world in the nineteenth century. Muslims in the Ottoman Empire (see pages 422–427) and elsewhere believed that rising European power threatened the independence of Muslim countries and the traditional values of Islam.

Islam had been an expanding, conquering civilization for centuries. Suddenly, Islam seemed to be retreating before Western power. Muslim leaders searched for a solution to the crisis.

VOCABULARY DEVELOPMENT

vocation (voh KAY shuhn) *noun:* the career toward which one feels called. From the Latin word, *vocare*, meaning to call.

evolution (EHV uh LOO shuhn) *noun:* the theory that all species of plants and animals developed from earlier forms. From the Latin prefix *e-*, meaning out or forth, and word *volvere*, meaning to roll.

philanthropy (fih LAN thruh pee) *noun:* a desire to help humanity through charitable gifts. From the Greek words *philein*, meaning to love, and *anthropos*, meaning man.

cultural imperialism: the policy and practice of seeking to dominate the affairs and customs of a given people at a given time, especially those people in underdeveloped areas or weaker countries.

Some Muslims reacted by rejecting change. They wanted to return to an earlier, simpler time. Other Muslims wanted to adapt Islam to the industrial age by building modern armies, reforming governments, and constructing railways.

The Wahhabi Movement. One of the most influential Islamic reform movements took its name from Muhammad ibn Abd ul-Wahhab (IHB uhn uhb DUHL wuh HAHB), who lived in Arabia from 1703 to 1792. Ibn Abd ul-Wahhab wanted Muslims to return to a simpler, purer form of Islam. He believed that Muslims had betrayed God by failing to live according to the sacred Islamic law. The Wahhabis believed that divine law should govern all aspects of life. They did not recognize the claim of the Ottoman sultan to be the universal leader of Islam.

In Arabia, a local leader, Ibn Saud (IHB uhn suh OOD), converted to Wahhabi beliefs. He led a rebellion against the Ottoman Turks and established a state devoted to Wahhabi principles. In the early 1800s, the Saudi state took control of Mecca and Medina, the most important cities for Islamic pilgrims. Pilgrims visiting Mecca carried Wahhabi ideas to other Islamic lands.

The royal family of Saudi Arabia today are descendents of the Wahhabi reformers. They have continued the Wahhabi tradition of a conservative and fundamentalist approach to Islam.

Hindu pilgrims bathe in the sacred Ganges River in Benares, India. The Ganges is the holy river of more than 350 million Hindus.

In India, Muslims returning from Mecca preached Wahhabi ideas in the nineteenth century. Muslim rulers had governed most of India for hundreds of years but were rapidly losing power to the British. Wahhabi leaders declared that Islam could only become dominant again through sincere religious revival. The movement had no political success, but Wahhabi fundamentalism has remained an important religious force in the Islamic countries of Asia.

Hinduism in India

British rule in India also stimulated Hindu Indians to search for a new sense of identity. Hindus, who were by far the largest religious group in India, began to take their own religious heritage more seriously. In Bengal, in eastern India, leaders tried to eliminate Persian words that had entered the Bengali language during the period of Muslim rule (see pages 435–440). They re-placed all of these words with words of Sanskrit origin.

Reformers in northern India also tried to develop Hindi as a common language for Hindus. By developing a common language, reformers hoped to unify the Hindus. As in Bengali, words of Sanskrit origin replaced those of Persian origin. Hindus began to write their language with a Sanskrit alphabet. These changes in language and writing helped to emphasize the common heritage of Hindus in India.

The most famous Hindu reformer of the nineteenth century was Ram Mohan Roy who lived from 1772 to 1833. He came from an upper class Brahmin family of Bengal, but he decided early in life to study European religion and culture. He learned English and took a job in the British colonial government. He also took up a study of Christianity and eventually wrote a book called *The Precepts of Jesus*. Roy did not want to convert to Christianity. He wanted to find a common ground that would enable Hindus, Muslims, and Christians to understand each other.

He also worked to reform Hinduism by making its teachings more rational and more understandable to the West. He worked energetically for social and political reforms under British rule. He led a successful campaign to get the British to abolish suttee, the Hindu practice which forced a woman to burn herself on her husband's funeral pyre. Unlike Muslim Wahhabis, Ram Mohan Roy believed that Indians must adapt to Western culture and power. He was a founder of the modern nationalist movement in India.

As the numbers of educated Hindus like Roy increased, so did their demand for change. Hindu intellectuals developed political goals. In 1885, Indians formed the Indian National Congress. This group supported reforms to improve conditions in India. One reform in 1900 was to make Hindi the official language of the courts in some provinces of northern India. This decision alarmed the Muslims. In response, the Muslims formed their own organization, the Muslim League, in 1906. These two groups became rivals for power in India during the twentieth century. The Muslims felt persecuted by the Hindus.

The Revival of Buddhism

Throughout the nineteenth century, Buddhism continued to be the dominant religion in much of Southeast and East Asia. The faithful Buddhists prayed in their local temples, made offerings, and observed Buddhist festivals.

In Southeast Asia, men often spent months or years in monasteries, pursuing quiet reflection. By contrast, East Asian Buddhist monasteries and nunneries sheltered persons who had chosen a religious vocation for life. Monks went into the local community to perform rituals on holy days or at funerals.

By the middle of the nineteenth century, several Buddhist revival movements had developed in China. A leader of one movement was Yang Wenhui. Yang was born in 1837 into an educated Chinese family. When he was three years old, his family engaged him to a girl of nine. Childhood engagements were common in China at that time. Six years later, however, the girl caught smallpox. The disease badly scarred her face. Both families considered breaking the engagement. Yang, however, refused. He reasoned that if he did not marry the girl, no one would.

After Yang was married and had a son, he became interested in Buddhism. Yang searched bookstores for Buddhist texts, visited temples, and talked with monks. Since he had family responsibilities, Yang did not become a monk himself. Instead, he used his time and energy to collect and reprint Buddhist books. He founded three printing firms, which published more than a million volumes of Buddhist scripture.

Yang favored sending Chinese students to Europe for their education. He thought that modern science could be combined with Buddhism. He even started a small school to train Chinese Buddhists to be missionaries abroad. In 1909, Yang founded the Association for Research on the Buddhist Religion.

Yang Wenhui was not alone in trying to revive Chinese Buddhism. Many Buddhists carried on similar activities in the early twentieth century.

Expansion of Christianity on a Global Scale

Like Islam, Hinduism, and Buddhism, Christianity was energetic in the nineteenth century. Protestants from Europe and the United States led a great wave of missionary activity. Many Christians believed they had a duty to preach Christ's gospel to non-Christians around the world.

Challenges in Europe. Christian missionaries who went to Asia or Africa expected to see their new teachings opposed. Even in Europe, nineteenth century scholars challenged many beliefs of Christianity.

Some philosophers wanted to replace traditional church teachings about morality with reliance on reason. Others, such as revolutionary socialist Karl Marx, viewed religion as a dangerous delusion. Some Bible scholars argued that historical research indicated that Jesus was not divine. In their view, Jesus was a great teacher, but not God.

The most controversial challenges to traditional Christian teachings came from the sciences. In 1859, Charles Darwin published *On the Origin of the Species*, a book describing his ideas on evolution. To many, evolution appeared to contradict the biblical account of creation. In addition, the work of such geologists as Charles Lyell suggested that the earth was much older than some thought the Bible taught.

These challenges caused the Christian churches to lose numerous followers in the nineteenth century. Despite this, Christian churches made gains in other areas. In Britain, for example, the Young Men's Christian Association, YMCA, was founded in 1844. The YMCA tried to reach young people in the middle and lower classes. The Salvation Army was formed in 1878. Its members tried to bring the gospel to the poor and homeless.

Christianity on the Frontiers. The fastest growing areas of the Christian community were the frontiers of western civilization. In Australia, New Zealand, South Africa, and North America, European settlers brought the Christian faith with them.

The Christian church in North America grew rapidly as the United States expanded its territory across the continent. In the eighteenth century, few Christians were affiliated with churches. In 1800, only 7 percent of the people in the United States were members of Christian churches. By 1850,

A missionary preaches the gospel to the "heathens" in this title page from *The Origin and History of Missions*, published in Boston in 1832.

the number had doubled. By 1900, church membership in the United States had risen to 36 percent.

Changes in Christian Practices. Toward the end of the nineteenth century, many Christians began to emphasize efforts to improve life for people on earth. Wealthy individuals turned to philanthropy, a belief that they should help others. Two of the most famous philanthropists were Andrew Carnegie and John D. Rockefeller. Carnegie, a leader in the steel industry, and Rockefeller, whose money came from oil, donated millions of dollars to help others in the early twentieth century.

Christian denominations and congregations built hospitals, schools, and colleges to assist the poor. Christian effort to apply the teachings of Jesus in helping the poor is called the social gospel movement.

Missionaries in Africa and Asia.
As the Christian church grew on the frontiers of western civilization, Christianity also influenced non-Europeans around the world. The French were the most active European missionaries. The Society of Missionaries of Our Lady of Africa, also known as the White Fathers, preached Christianity in northern Africa.

Both Catholic and Protestant missionaries usually spread their beliefs through their country's colonial empires. The number of missionaries was never very high. In the early twentieth century, about 30,000 Christian missionaries were working among the peoples of Africa, Asia, the Pacific Islands, and South America.

The Impact of Christian Missionaries.
Despite the efforts of the missionaries, the percentage of Christians in Asian and African countries was low. Christian communities in Islamic, Hindu, and Buddhist countries were small and isolated. These communities depended on leadership and financial support from Europe and the United States.

Still, the significance of the missionary effort went beyond the individuals who were converted. The effort reflected the beliefs of the countries that sent out the missionaries. For church communities in Europe and North America, the effort to spread Christianity was an expression of faith. Church members made contributions or encouraged their sons and daughters to serve in foreign lands.

Churches often sponsored projects to provide relief for victims of famine and disease. Missionaries often started the first schools and hospitals in an area. In China, for example, Christians established a network of schools, colleges, and hospitals. Missionaries also promoted the study of the Chinese language and culture, the education of women, and education outside one's own country. The missionary effort focused on cultural change. Western influence, otherwise, was primarily military, political, and economic.

Some results of the missions' work were unpopular. Chinese scholars and officials saw the missionaries as a threat to their position in society.

Many people of Asia and Africa regarded Christianity as part of the Western effort to dominate the globe. Even when the missionaries were privately supported, non-Westerners viewed them as agents of cultural imperialism. The conflicts between cultures grew rapidly as the power of Europe and the United States increased.

SECTION 3 *Study Skills*

Developing Vocabulary 1. What is cultural imperialism? 2. Define evolution. 3. How could a philanthropist help an evangelist? 4. Explain the relationship between the word vocation and its Latin root.

Reviewing Main Ideas 1. How did the rise of nationalism create problems for Islamic states? 2. How did the Wahhabi movement affect the political and religious reforms in Arabia? 3. List positive and negative contributions of nineteenth century Christian missionaries in Africa and Asia.

Understanding Chronology 1. List in order the events of Asian religious reform. 2. Construct a time line of the growth of Christianity in the United States from 1800 to 1900.

Understanding Cause and Effect 1. What influence did scholars like Yang Wenhui have on China? 2. Why were organizations such as the YMCA and the Salvation Army founded?

Challenge Discuss whether or not missionary work of today is as successful as it was in the nineteenth century.

The Global Migration of Europeans

Some Europeans left for foreign lands as Christian missionaries. However, there were many additional reasons for migration. During the late 1800s and early 1900s, the greatest emigration of Europeans to other continents took place.

Population Growth

Between 1800 and 1914, the world's population grew from 900 million to 1.6 billion. The population of Europe grew even more rapidly—from 190 million to 423 million. A rising standard of living along with major improvements in health care significantly lowered the death rate.

As Europeans moved to other continents, they brought their language and culture with them. In 1810, only 5.6 million Europeans lived outside of Europe. By 1910, 200 million Europeans had left the continent. The heaviest migration was across the Atlantic to the Americas. From 1880 to 1910, about 15 million Europeans moved to South America. In the same period, about 17 million moved to the United States. The high point came between 1900 and 1914 when almost 1 million emigrants left Europe every year.

Today we are used to the fact that Europeans live all over the world. Russian-speaking peoples live in Siberia. Spanish- and Portuguese-speaking peoples occupy Central and South America. German-speaking peoples live in the United States. English- and French-speaking peoples are found in North America as well as in Australia, New Zealand, India, Pakistan, Southeast Asia, and many parts of Africa. Most of this movement of Europeans has taken place since 1800.

Reasons for Leaving Europe

Europeans left their homelands in the nineteenth century for many reasons. The main ones were political, religious, and economic.

Political Reasons. Political reasons, such as revolutions before the 1840s, forced millions of Europeans to emigrate. Additionally, Great Britain and Russia sent both political and other criminals to distant lands. In the 1800s, the Russian tsars sent thousands of people to Siberia as punishment. The cold climate made supplying basic needs a real challenge.

By 1867, Britain had sent 150,000 convicts, many of them debtors, to Australia. There they had to adjust to a land with a different climate as well as different plants and animals. Poisonous snakes, for example, were a real problem.

Many British went to India to govern that colony. The British government also sent people to govern their African colonies as well as almost 50 other colonies around the world.

Religious Reasons. The opportunity to worship freely without fear of criticism appealed to many Europeans. For example, between 1900 and 1914, Jewish persecution in Russia forced 1.5 million Jews to emigrate to the United States.

Economic Reasons. Some emigrants left their homes as a result of natural disasters. In 1845, the potato crop failed in Ireland and the lower Rhine valley of Germany. Food shortages led millions of Irish, Scots, and Germans to come to the Americas. Between 1845 and 1911, the population of Ireland fell from 8.1 million to 4.3 million. Many of these people sailed for Canada to begin a new life in a similar climate zone.

Migrations, 1880–1914

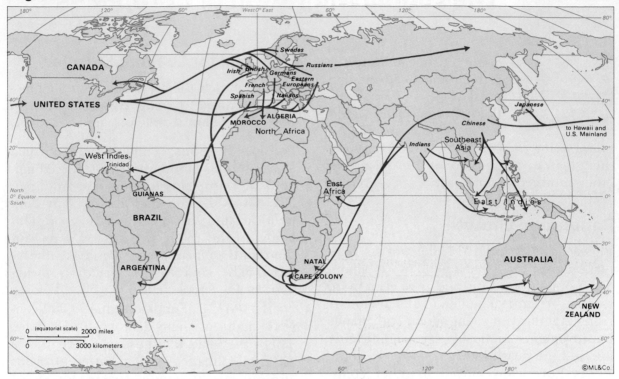

Map Skills **1.** Was the pattern of migration to the north or to the south? **2.** From what hemisphere did most of the migration come? **3.** Was the pattern of migration towards the Western Hemisphere or the Eastern Hemisphere?

How Mass Emigration Occurred

In the days of the *Mayflower*, tens of millions of people could not have crossed the seas. Advances in shipping and transportation permitted the mass migration of Europeans. By 1914, there were 30,000 steamships on ocean trade routes. Railways crossed the continents. In 1869, the first transcontinental railway in the United States was completed. In 1885, the first trans-Canada railway was finished. By 1905, there was even a Trans-Siberian Railway.

The movement of people to a new land often created a chain reaction. At first a few individuals would go. Perhaps young men and women would leave to seek their fortunes in a new land. If they were successful, they would send for their families. As whole families settled in a new homeland, word of their success spread. Letters and visits back

home encouraged more Europeans to move. Never before had one continent of the globe so completely dominated the others. European religion, culture, politics, and languages spread to all parts of the earth. The influence, in many locations, has lasted until the present day.

STUDY SKILLS Understanding Geography

1. Using examples, give three reasons why a nineteenth century global migration of Europeans occurred.
2. Explain why the mass migration was from Europe rather than some other continent.
3. What elements of geography affected the lives of the migrants?
4. What were the results of the mass emigration of Europeans?
5. In which direction did most of the emigrants go? Why?

CHAPTER 24 *Summary & Review*

Summarizing Main Ideas

By 1600, European expansion and internal problems began weakening the Ottoman Empire. European influence in military affairs, map making, and shipbuilding quickly replaced Turkish ways. New technologies and customs soon spread. Despite reform attempts, the Ottoman Empire continued to lose territory and influence during the nineteenth century.

In China, the Manchu replaced the Ming in 1644. When Europeans attempted to expand into the Chinese trade market, China resisted. European influence was slight until 1842 when the British were victorious in the Opium War. In 1854, the United States opened trade with Japan and the East became an integral part of the global trade network.

Religions were affected by the expansion of industrial Europe and the opening of new trade routes. Muslims came into greater contact with Jews and Christians. In India, followers of Hinduism revived and modernized their faith. By the end of the nineteenth century, Christian missionaries had spread religious beliefs and European culture throughout Africa and Asia.

Questions for Critical Thinking

COMPREHENSION Interpreting Events

1. Why did reforms fail in the Ottoman Empire?
2. How did Britain gain control of India?

ANALYSIS Identifying Trends

1. Why did political revolutions occur throughout much of the civilized world between 1650 and 1800?
2. Explain how the Europeans established a pattern of dominance over the countries with which they traded.

APPLICATION Comparing Past and Present

1. Explain the changes that occurred in Japanese trade policies after 1854.

Western Influences on Eastern Empires		
Eastern Empire	Dominant Western Power	Areas of Influence
Ottoman Empire	France	Trade, culture, military technology, mapmaking, shipbuilding, printing, religion
India	Great Britain	Trade, language, science, education, religion
China	Great Britain	Trade
Japan	United States	Trade

2. Explain why conflicts over foreign influence are still occurring in Iran today.

SYNTHESIS Developing Writing Skills

1. Write a summary of Hindu beliefs.
2. Write a report on the Sepoy Rebellion.
3. Write a defense of China's conduct in the Opium War.

EVALUATION Weighing Consequences

1. What were the long-range results of the Ottomans' resistance to reform?
2. How did China's defeat by the British in the Opium War benefit China?

CHALLENGE

1. Industrialization necessitated increased trade, which caused Europeans to try to control their foreign trade markets. Give examples of the long-range results.
2. Note the Western influences on Eastern empires shown on the chart. Why was outside influence minimal in China and Japan and more extensive in Turkey and India? What were the areas of influence?

UNIT 6 *Review*

Critical Thinking for Today's World

ANALYSIS Understanding People

1. Describe the conditions in seventeenth and eighteenth century Europe that allowed the common people to readily accept the ideas of the philosophes.
2. Give examples to show how changes in production methods alter people's attitudes toward manual labor.
3. Describe ways in which absolute monarchs served some useful purposes. Why would people follow such a ruler?
4. Draw a diagram to explain Triangular Trade. List the various types of people involved on each side.
5. How did Adam Smith's ideas affect the average citizen?

ANALYSIS Recognizing Change Over Time

1. In what ways did the reliance on machinery and scientific methods change people's ability to produce food?
2. When the steam engine was applied to transportation, travel and trade increased. What other improvements have added to this transportation revolution?
3. In what ways was Russia different after the rule of Peter the Great? How did these changes affect the common peasant?
4. Why was the Glorious Revolution the real beginning of British constitutional monarchy?
5. To the philosophes, free, universal education was one of the answers to many of the world's evils. How close is the United States to achieving the goals of the philosophes?

APPLICATION Solving Problems

1. As new machinery required different materials and sources of power, new inventions were developed. Give examples of such developments in modern life.
2. When natural waterways were not available to use for shipping, canals were built. List

ways in which modern man modifies or changes his natural environment to benefit commerce.
3. European states of the eighteenth and nineteenth centuries tried to achieve a balance of power. Give specific examples of which countries were involved, how they tried to balance power, and what resulted from their efforts.
4. The rise of industry in the nineteenth century created problems for cities. Choose two problems and explain how people attempted to solve them. Discuss whether or not they have been successful.

SYNTHESIS Developing Global Citizenship

1. With the spread of Christianity, European culture also spread. List some of the advantages and disadvantages that this spread brought to the native peoples.
2. Explain how the Eastern and Western nations prospered by the trade agreement of 1854 between Japan and the United States.

EVALUATION Learning Lessons from the Past

1. When colonial powers tried to dictate to their possessions, revolutions often resulted. How would this influence modern governments in their dealings with newly independent Third World nations?
2. How did the quality of life change following the Industrial Revolution?
3. Explain whether the French Revolution made the life of the Third Estate better or worse. Use specific examples.
4. What lesson should modern day conquerors, intent on controlling several different nations, learn from the experiences and defeats of Napoleon?
5. Give examples to show how a nation that wants to industrialize could obtain the factors of production.
6. Compare and contrast modern governments' efforts to achieve a balance of power to the efforts made in the seventeenth and eighteenth centuries.

The Interacting Global Community, 1650–1850

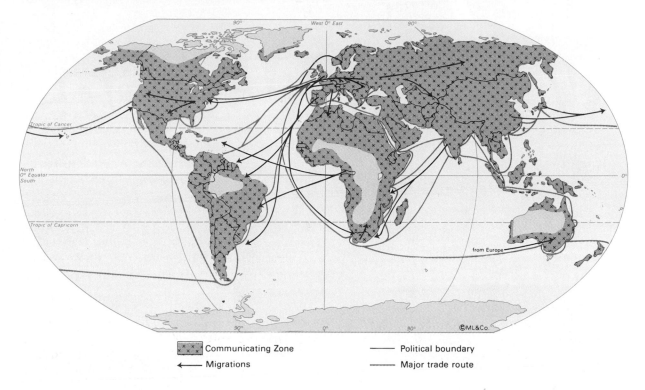

Communicating Zone   Political boundary
← Migrations   Major trade route

A Global Perspective

With the spread of trade, more areas came under the influence of Europe. European countries fought to control colonies. By the 1800s, England and France controlled the greatest number of colonies.

Colonial settlement tended to be restricted to coastal areas. Trade with the interior, especially in North America, was channeled through the river systems, to settlements at natural harbors like New York.

Trade routes to the East and North America became well established. Traditional routes, especially through the Middle East, began to lose traffic to newer routes. With the expansion of trade came a greater interchange of ideas. The revolutionary spirit of the late eighteenth century spread beyond Europe.

COMPREHENSION Interpreting Maps

1. How do the zones of communication differ between this map and the map on page 467?
2. How have the areas touched by European trade changed as a result?

3. Describe the routes most Europeans used to trade with the New World and the countries of Asia.
4. Explain any changes in the number, size, or location of nations since 1650.
5. List three geographical reasons for English, French, and Dutch dominance of world trade.

ANALYSIS Recognizing Global Trends

1. How did trade routes shift between the years 1650 and 1850? See page 467.
2. Explain the changes that occurred in the migration patterns of Europeans between the year of 1650 and 1850. See page 467.
3. If Europeans wanted to expand trade to areas not already involved, what areas might they consider?
4. In which direction does most trade flow between 1650 and 1850? How do these trade routes compare to earlier trade routes? See the map, Global Trade Networks, 1650, on page 445.

UNIT 7
Western Nations

Lead the World

1850–1945

The United Nations building in New York City. The UN was established in 1945 to promote international peace.

CHAPTER 25
Western Power Grows

	1850	1860	1870

TIME

● **1860** Garibaldi and his Red Shirts drive the Bourbons from Sicily

● **1866** Prussia and Austria fight the Seven Weeks War

● **1867** The Austrians and Hungarians create the Dual Monarchy

● **1870** France and Prussia fight the Franco Prussian W

PEOPLE

● **1848** Franz Josef becomes Emperor of Austria

● **1860** Victor Emmanuel II becomes king of a united Italy

● **1861** Alexander II institutes liberal reforms in Russia

● **1871** Wilhelm I, King of Prussia becomes the first German emperor

● **1871** Otto von Bismarck becomes Germany's chancellor

PLACE

● **1861** *Russia;*[1] Emancipation Proclamation frees the serfs

● **1867** *Japan;*[2] Japanese overthrow the shogun and install the Meiji Emperor

Linking Past to Present

St. Pierre and Miquelon, two small islands, lie just off the coast of Newfoundland, in Canada. These islands are not part of Canada. They are provinces of France. Like Hong Kong and Gibraltar, St. Pierre and Miquelon are tiny remains of a European empire.

Less than a century ago, western nations ruled almost the entire globe. The final surge of western imperialism overseas took place in the late 1800s. At the same time, however, ethnic groups in the Austrian Empire were demonstrating for self-government. The Ottoman Empire was losing territory, as new national states appeared in Europe. This chapter discusses both the rise of new nations on the European continent and the development of their power abroad.

Victoria, Hong Kong.

1880	1890	1900	1910

● **1882** Italy, Germany, and Austria form the Triple Alliance

● **1901** Europeans end the Boxer Rebellion in China

1904–1905 Russia and Japan fight the Russo-Japanese War

● **1907** Britain, France, and Russia form the Triple Entente

● **1896** First modern Olympic Games are held in Athens

● **1914** Europeans control most of Africa

● **1882** King Leopold II of Belgium claims the African Congo

● **1890** Wilhelm II forces Bismarck to resign

● **1900** Arthur Evans discovers the Minoan culture while excavating on Crete

● **1903** Emmeline Pankhurst and her daughters found the Women's Social and Political Union

● **1910** Sun Yat-sen founds the Nationalist Peoples Party in China

● **1877** *United States;*[4] First public telephones installed

● **1881** *Africa;*[5] French occupy Tunisia

● **1882** *Egypt;*[3] Egypt becomes a British protectorate

● **1885** *Great Britain;*[6] All adult males allowed to vote

● **1895** *Korea;*[7] Japanese defeat the Chinese and win control of Korea

● **1898** *Hawaii;*[8] United States annexes the Hawaiian Islands

● **1914** *Panama;*[9] Panama Canal Opens

1 Unification of Italy and Germany

OBJECTIVE: *To understand the causes and consequences of the unification of Italy and Germany*

Nationalism Leads to a United Italy

Between 1850 and 1914, two trends, liberalism and nationalism, dominated political feelings in Europe. Liberalism is a political philosophy based on establishing and protecting individual political and civil liberties. In Europe during the 1800s, liberals worked to obtain civil rights and equality before the law for all individuals. They carried on the ideas of Locke, Rousseau, and other writers of the Enlightenment.

Nationalism prompted people who shared a common history, culture, and language to unite under a single government. Many people in Europe, such as the Italians, Germans, Poles, and Serbs, thought of themselves as national groups. Each of these groups wanted to be united in an independent nation.

Nationalists Work to Unite Italy. After the Congress of Vienna in 1815, the Italian people remained divided among a number of states and provinces, as they had been for centuries. In northern Italy, Austrians ruled Venetia, Lombardy, Parma, Lucca, Modena, and Tuscany. See the map, Unification of Italy, 1858–1870, page 569.

Kings of the Bourbon family ruled the Kingdom of the Two Sicilies. This kingdom included the island of Sicily and the southern half of the Italian Peninsula. The pope governed the territory around Rome, called the Papal States. Victor Emmanuel II, an Italian king, ruled the island of Sardinia and the mainland regions of Savoy, Piedmont, and Nice.

After the unsuccessful revolutions of 1848 (see page 522), Sardinia became the leader of the struggle for Italian unification. Victor Emmanuel's kingdom included the

---

VOCABULARY DEVELOPMENT

liberalism *noun:* a political philosophy based on the establishment and protection of individual political and civil liberties.

prime minister: the head of a government.

mobilize (MOH buh LYZ) *verb:* to bring into readiness for active participation. From the Latin word, *mobilis*, meaning movable.

annex (AN ehks) *verb:* to add or incorporate within a political area. From the Latin prefix *ad-*, meaning to, and word *nectere*, meaning to bind.

realpolitik (ray AHL POH lih TEEK) *noun:* a German word meaning politics based on practical self-interest rather than on ideals.

indemnity (ihn DEHM nuht ee) *noun:* compensation for some loss or damage, repayment. From the Latin prefix *in-*, meaning not, and word *damnum*, meaning damage.

Reich (ryk) *noun:* Germany as an empire; the German government.

federation *noun:* a union of states or organizations.

---

only territory in northern Italy not dominated by Austria. Victor Emmanuel supported Italian nationalism and hoped to unite Italy under his leadership.

Another Italian nationalist was Count Camillo Cavour. He edited an Italian newspaper, *Il Risorgimento*. The name is an Italian term meaning resurgence or revival. Gradually, the entire Italian nationalist movement came to be called *Risorgimento*, and Cavour was its leader.

Cavour Becomes Prime Minister of Sardinia. In 1852, Victor Emmanuel appointed Count Cavour the prime minister of his government. Sardinia had a constitution and a parliament of elected representatives. Cavour wanted Sardinia to be a model for a united Italy.

He hoped to use the rivalries among more powerful European nations to drive the Austrians out of Italian lands. As a first step, he convinced Emperor Napoleon III of France to support Sardinia's nationalist aims. Napoleon was facing growing opposition in France. He needed to gain prestige for France and win back the people's support. Therefore, in 1858 Napoleon agreed to a secret alliance with Sardinia against the Austrians.

War with Austria. Cavour and Napoleon planned to trick Austria into declaring war on Sardinia. The French would then send troops to help the Sardinians defeat Austria. In return, France would gain the territories of Savoy and Nice just to the west of Piedmont. Napoleon secretly hoped that after the war France could dominate a weak confederation of Italian states.

To carry out this plan, Cavour encouraged Italian nationalists to revolt against the Austrians in Lombardy and Venetia. To aid the rebels, Sardinia mobilized; that is, it began to prepare for war. Austria demanded that Sardinia demobilize. When Cavour refused, Austria declared war and sent troops to the rebelling provinces.

Unification of Italy, 1858–1870

Map Skills 1. Which island is closest to the Italian mainland? 2. Are there more small states to the north or south of Rome?

France entered the war on Sardinia's side, and together the two states drove Austria from Lombardy. Enthusiastic nationalists overthrew their rulers in other Italian areas. They then petitioned to be annexed to Sardinia.

Sardinia's ally, Napoleon III, fearing that Prussia would join Austria, negotiated a separate peace. According to the treaty that ended the war, Sardinia received Lombardy. Austria retained control of Venetia and the other states of northern Italy.

King Victor Emmanuel agreed to the terms of the treaty. The people of Parma, Modena, and Tuscany again revolted against their rulers. The papal province of Romagna rebelled again as well. The people of these provinces set up popular governments. The new governments held plebiscites in which the people voted overwhelmingly to become part of Sardinia.

To avoid war with France, Cavour agreed in 1860 to let France keep Nice and Savoy. Napoleon III agreed not to stop Sardinia from annexing Parma, Modena, Tuscany, and Romagna.

Garibaldi Leads the Red Shirts. Nationalists now joined forces to expel the Bourbons in southern Italy and Sicily. Giuseppe Garibaldi, a popular Italian military leader, had fought the Austrians in 1859. He re-

turned to Italy and formed a volunteer army called the Red Shirts after the color of their uniforms. The Red Shirts attacked the Bourbon king's forces and drove them from Sicily in 1860.

Garibaldi and his victorious forces then crossed to the mainland. They soon drove the Bourbon king, Francis II, and his army north to the border of the Papal States. Cavour, though, was afraid that France or Austria might aid Francis. Cavour sent an army to stop Garibaldi. He persuaded Garibaldi to let King Victor Emmanuel annex Sicily and the Papal States. The pope, helped by Napoleon III's forces, retained control of Rome.

Italy Is United under Victor Emmanuel. In 1860, elections were held everywhere in Italy except Venetia and Rome. The Italian people voted to join Sardinia under King Victor Emmanuel. A parliament of elected representatives met in Turin in March 1861. They proclaimed Victor Emmanuel II king of Italy "by the grace of God and the will of the nation."

At left, a portrait of Giuseppe Garibaldi. Below, a painting by M. Bisi of King Victor Emmanuel's entrance into Milan.

The Unification of Germany

The German people, like the Italians, were divided into many states. The Congress of Vienna in 1815 loosely united these states into what became known as the German Confederation. See the map on page 521.

German nationalists wanted a single German nation. However, Austria, a leading member of the German Confederation, feared a strong, unified Germany. Moreover, the rulers of small states did not want to lose their power by being absorbed into a large German nation.

Prussian Leadership. Prussia was the most powerful state in the German Confederation. The Ruhr Valley in western Prussia contained the largest coal deposits in Europe. Prussia used this coal to build an industrial economy and fuel a large iron and steel industry.

Wilhelm I, like earlier Prussian kings, was an authoritarian ruler. He maintained the Prussian military traditions of discipline and obedience (see page 481).

The Junkers, the land-owning class of Prussia, were influential in the country's parliament. The chancellor of Prussia in the 1860s was Otto von Bismarck, a conservative Junker. Bismarck, a shrewd diplomat, shared Wilhelm's goal of a united Germany under Prussian leadership.

Otto von Bismarck

FOCUS ON PEOPLE

Bismarck was born in Schönhausen, Prussia on April 1, 1815. The son of a Junker, Bismarck studied law and politics. The young Bismarck was more interested in drinking beer and fighting duels than in studying. He did, however, manage to receive a law degree.

Shortly after finishing his education, Bismarck entered government service. He became a judicial administrator in Aachen. While there, he fell in love with an English woman. In 1839, he left his post for several months, without permission, to follow her across Germany. As a result, he was forced to resign his position.

In 1847, Bismarck successfully campaigned for a seat in the United Prussian Diet. As a representative, he opposed any attempt by liberals to transfer power from the king to the legislature. Bismarck's views led the king to appoint him ambassador to Russia in 1859 and, two years later, ambassador to France.

In 1862, Wilhelm I planned to increase the size of the army and unite Germany under Prussia's leadership. To help him, Wilhelm appointed Bismarck his prime minister. In this powerful position, Bismarck hoped to unite Germany "not with speeches . . . but with blood and iron." By this statement, Bismarck meant that he would resort to war and military might when diplomacy and speeches failed.

Bismarck also followed a policy of *realpolitik*, a German term meaning realism or practical politics. He believed that any actions were justified if they helped to attain a nation's goals. The legislature refused Bismarck's request for money to increase the army. Bismarck collected the necessary taxes and reorganized the army without the legislature's consent. ■

War with Denmark

Bismarck formed a military alliance with the Austrians. The purpose of the alliance was to annex the small states of Schleswig and Holstein. The people of Holstein were German; the population of Schleswig was a mixture of Germans and Danes.

King Christian IX of Denmark ruled both states. Under the Danish constitution, however, Schleswig and Holstein were independent of Denmark. In 1863, King Christian proclaimed a new constitution annexing Schleswig.

Unification of Germany, 1865–1871

Map Skills 1. What waterway is closest to the city of Berlin? **2.** To go from the Baltic Sea to France, what main rivers would you cross?

When Austria and Prussia protested, the king refused to back down. Then, Austria and Prussia defeated the Danish army and occupied Schleswig and Holstein. According to the peace treaty, Austria would govern Holstein and Prussia would govern Schleswig. Bismarck, though, wanted both of the northern German states and prepared to fight Austria.

War with Austria. Before going to war, Bismarck wanted to be certain that no other nations would aid Austria. By making vague territorial promises, he persuaded Napoleon III to remain neutral if war developed. Bismarck then asked France to put its territorial demands in writing.

Bismarck formed an alliance with Italy. He promised to give Venetia to the new nation if Prussia defeated Austria. The Russians promised to remain neutral.

In 1866, Bismarck provoked Austria into war using a dispute over Holstein. The Prussian army was well organized and trained. In seven weeks, the Prussian troops defeated Austria and its allies, the southern German states.

The Treaty of Prague ended the Seven Weeks War. Bismarck did not want Austria as a permanent enemy and stopped the war before Austria's defeat was total. The peace treaty gave Venetia to Italy, and Schleswig and Holstein to Prussia. See the map, Unification of Germany, 1865–1871, on this page. The treaty also forced Austria to approve the dissolution of the confederation of German states.

In 1867, the northern German states joined Prussia in the North German Confederation. Each state governed itself, but the king of Prussia was the hereditary president of the confederation. Prussia, the largest and most powerful state, also dominated the legislature of the confederation.

The Ems Telegram. Bismarck's handling of the Ems telegram is an example of his use of *realpolitik*. After the Seven Weeks War, only the states of southern Germany remained outside the new German confederation. Although the southern German states did not want to be dominated by Prussia, they also feared France. Bismarck wanted them to form a military alliance with Prussia against the French.

In 1870, a revolution in Spain helped Bismarck to unify Germany. The revolt forced Queen Isabella II to flee. The Spanish offered the crown to the German prince, Leopold, who was a cousin of the king of Prussia. If Leopold accepted, a member of the Hohenzollern family would rule both Spain and Prussia.

Napoleon III sent a note to Leopold, asking him to turn down the offer. He also sent a note to the Spanish, telling them to cancel the offer. Leopold remained in Germany. Napoleon then sent an ambassador to visit King Wilhelm I at his vacation resort

A. A. Von Werner's painting shows delegates from the allied German states at the Palace of Versailles in 1871, proclaiming a new German empire, the Second *Reich*.

in Ems, Germany. The French ambassador asked the king to guarantee publicly that no member of the Hohenzollern family would ever sit on the throne of Spain. Wilhelm refused to make such a promise and then sent a telegram to Bismarck, describing the recent meeting.

Bismarck edited the king's telegram to make it appear that the French ambassador and the king had insulted each other. He released the edited message to the press. The people of both France and Prussia demanded war. On July 15, 1870, France declared war on Prussia.

The Franco-Prussian War. The next step of Bismarck's plan for German unification was to win over the southern German states. He showed them the written demands regarding their territory that Napoleon III had made before the Seven Weeks War. These demands so angered the southern

states that they became allies of Prussia against France.

Within six months, Prussia had crushed France. German troops occupied Paris and captured Napoleon III. The French legislature proclaimed the end of the Second French Empire and established the Third French Republic.

The French resented the peace terms Bismarck imposed on them. Germany took the province of Alsace and part of Lorraine. France also had to pay 5 billion francs, about $1 billion, to Germany over three years. German troops were to occupy northern France until the indemnity was paid. The French were bitter over their defeat and the loss of land.

The German Empire. On January 18, 1871, delegates from all the allied German states met at the Palace of Versailles. They wrote a constitution for a new German empire made up of all the German states except Austria. Berlin, the capital of Prussia, became the capital of Germany. The representatives appointed Wilhelm I emperor. Bismarck became the chancellor of the new German empire.

The Germans called their new empire the Second *Reich*. *Reich* is a German word meaning empire. To German nationalists, the First *Reich* was the Holy Roman Empire. The new constitution united the German states in a federation. Each state had its own ruler and administered its internal affairs. The central government of the empire was responsible for common problems, such as national defense, foreign affairs, and tariffs.

A New Balance of Power. The loser in the wars with both Italy and Germany was Austria. Bismarck, however, had much in common with the Austrian emperor, Franz Josef I. Both Bismarck and Franz Josef I supported strong, authoritarian governments. In addition, Austria needed allies. Rival nationalities quarreled often in Austria, an empire composed of peoples of many different cultures. In 1879, therefore, Franz Josef I signed an alliance with the German emperor.

Bismarck persuaded Italy to join the German-Austrian alliance in 1882, making it the Triple Alliance. Bismarck also signed a secret treaty with Russia. Bismarck's purpose was to keep France from gaining allies and seeking revenge.

A New German Emperor. In 1888, the 29-year-old grandson of Wilhelm I inherited the throne. The new emperor, Wilhelm II, believed in a strong Prussian state. He increased the size of the army and set about building a navy to rival that of Great Britain. He resented Bismarck's power, however, and wanted to set policy for himself. In 1890, he forced Bismarck to resign.

To win popular support, Wilhelm introduced some liberal policies. He increased the social insurance programs passed under his grandfather. He also supported public schools, making Germany's schools among the best in the world. Wilhelm encouraged industry, and by 1900 Germany was the leading industrial nation in Europe. Wilhelm's policies contributed to nationalism in Germany, the people's strong sense of pride in their nation.

The building of national states was complete throughout western and central Europe by 1871. The people of eastern Europe and the Balkan Peninsula, however, were still part of the Austrian, Russian, or Ottoman empire. These empires ruled peoples of many different languages and traditions. As in Germany and Italy, nationalism and liberalism were growing among these people.

SECTION 1 *Study Skills*

Developing Vocabulary 1. Why would a country mobilize its army? **2.** What is an indemnity? **3.** Define *realpolitik*.

Reviewing Main Ideas 1. Describe Camillo Cavour's influence on the Italian nationalist movement. **2.** Why was Prussia the most powerful state in the German confederation? **3.** What was the outcome of the Franco-Prussian War?

Understanding Geography 1. Construct a chart showing the Italian provinces and who ruled them in 1815. **2.** What countries were involved in the Triple Alliance?

Understanding Chronology 1. What happened in 1860 that aided Italian unification? **2.** When was the Seven Weeks War fought? **3.** Construct a time line showing Bismarck's accomplishments between 1860 and 1890.

Challenge When Bismarck allied with Austria and Italy, the European balance of power changed. As alliances change today, the same thing happens. What problems can this cause?

2 Nationalism, Imperialism, and Democracy

OBJECTIVE: *To understand the causes and consequences of nationalism, imperialism, and democracy between 1850 and 1914*

Nationalism in Eastern Europe

During the early years of the 1800s, the Austrian, Ottoman, or Russian empire ruled the peoples of eastern Europe. In each empire were people of many different ethnic and religious backgrounds. Like the Germans and Italians, these ethnic groups developed pride in their national heritage and a desire for independence.

The Hungarians Revolt Again. Among the people of the Austrian Empire were Germans, Magyars, Poles, Czechs, Croatians, Slovaks, and Romanians. Between 1848 and 1914, many of these ethnic groups fought unsuccessfully to gain their independence.

Franz Josef became the emperor of Austria in 1848 at the age of 18. He inherited the task of holding the empire together. Yet during his reign of almost 70 years, nationalist movements almost tore Austria apart. Austria first lost its possessions in northern Italy. Between 1858 and 1860, Italy and France gained control of all the northern Italian states.

The Magyars of Hungary, after an unsuccessful revolt in 1849, continued to oppose Austrian rule. They demanded greater autonomy within the empire. Finally, in 1867, Franz Josef agreed to create a dual monarchy, the Austrian Empire and the Kingdom of Hungary.

Franz Josef became both the emperor of Austria and the king of Hungary. The two nations also shared ministers of war, finance, and foreign affairs. Each nation, however, had its own constitution and parliament. The Hungarian Parliament met in Budapest; members of the Austrian Parliament met in Vienna. Although the Dual Monarchy allowed the Hungarians limited self-government, other minorities still had no political power.

Revolts in the Ottoman Empire. The rulers of the Ottoman Empire also faced a growing nationalist movement among mi-

---

VOCABULARY DEVELOPMENT

autonomy (aw TAHN uh mee) *noun:* the right or power of self-government. From the Greek words *autos*, meaning self, and *nomos*, meaning law.

nullify (NUHL uh FY) *verb:* to cancel. From the Latin words *nullus*, meaning none, and *facere*, meaning to make.

Slavophile (SLAH vuh FYL) *noun:* a person who admires the Slavs and their culture. A Slavic term meaning friend of the Slavs.

pogrom (poh GRAHM) *noun:* an organized massacre of helpless people. From the Russian words *po*, meaning of, and *grom*, meaning thunder.

emigrate (EHM uh GRAYT) *verb:* to leave one's homeland and settle in another country. From the Latin prefix *ex-*, meaning out, and word *migrare*, meaning to move.

suffrage (SUHF rihj) *noun:* voting rights. From the Latin word, *suffragium*, meaning vote of approval.

nority groups. During the 1800s, ethnic groups within the Ottoman Empire revolted and gained some degree of self-government (see page 521). In 1830, Greece won independence. By 1850, Egypt and Arabia had won autonomy within the empire. On the Balkan Peninsula, Romania, Serbia, and Montenegro gained autonomy.

In 1875, Slavic peoples in the Balkan Peninsula again revolted against the Turks. This time, when the sultan sent troops to put down these nationalist movements, Russia aided the rebels. The Russians defeated the Ottoman Empire in 1877 and forced the sultan to sign the Treaty of San Stefano. The treaty set up the large new state of Bulgaria.

Delegates at the Congress of Berlin, shown in a painting by A. A. Von Werner, hoped to end international tensions in the Balkan Peninsula.

The Congress of Berlin, 1878. In the 1800s, Russia had the largest territory and population in Europe. Germany, located between France and Russia, feared both its enemy to the west and the giant to the east. Great Britain, Germany, and France shared concern that strong Russian influence in the Balkan Peninsula would cause more unrest. They, therefore, called an international conference at Berlin in 1878 and pressured the Russians to attend.

The representatives at the congress nullified the Treaty of San Stefano and reduced the size of Bulgaria. They also converted Bulgaria into an autonomous state within the Ottoman Empire. This ended Russia's access to the Aegean Sea.

The conference gave Serbia, Montenegro, and Romania complete independence from the Ottoman Empire. Great Britain received the island of Cyprus from the Ottomans. Austria-Hungary became administrator of the Serbian-speaking provinces of Bosnia and Herzegovinia. According to the agreement, the Austrians could not annex the provinces. In 1908, however, Austria ignored the Congress of Berlin settlement and annexed Bosnia and Herzegovinia.

The Russians left the congress feeling that they had been cheated. Many of the people in the Balkan Peninsula also were unhappy. The newly created states did not satisfy all ethnic groups. For example, many Serbs still lived in Hungary rather than the new state of Serbia. The conference members had hoped to settle nationalist unrest and international tensions in the Balkans. Instead, the area remained a powder keg.

Imperialism in Russia

Many different ethnic groups made up the Russian Empire in the 1800s. Ukrainians, some of whom hated their Russian rulers, lived in the south. Estonians, Lithuanians, Poles, Finns, and Moslem peoples, who resented their Russian conquerors, were also governed by the Russian tsar. In the Caucasus Mountains, a great variety of people lived together. All of them were restless under Russian rule.

Alexander II Institutes Reforms. The nationalist revolutions and liberal movements of the 1800s at first had little impact on Russia. The empire continued to be authoritarian. Millions of peasants were serfs, bound to the land.

By the middle of the 1800s, the liberal ideas of the times were influencing the educated aristocracy of Russia. In addition, factory owners who wanted industrial growth needed more laborers. These groups worked to free the serfs.

When Russia was defeated in the Crimean War, in 1856, both reformers and conservatives argued over the best way to strengthen their country. Reformers urged that Russia imitate the governments of western Europe. They claimed that the power of England and France resulted from their constitutional governments and from the people's liberties.

Conservative Slavophiles opposed these reformers. The conservatives wanted to preserve everything that was distinctively Russian and imitate no other countries.

Alexander II became tsar when his father died during the Crimean War. Alexander, like previous tsars, believed in autocracy. However, he thought that reforms were needed to strengthen Russia.

In 1861 Alexander II issued the Emancipation Edict, freeing all the serfs. The liberals hoped that Russia would follow the agricultural example of western Europe. They hoped that freed serfs would become independent farmers, working hard on land they owned. Therefore, productivity would increase, and rural unrest would disappear.

The tsar, however, did not give the peasants direct ownership of the land. Instead, the government assigned ownership to local communities. Community ownership of farmland by free peasants was customary in most of central Russia. Slavophiles hoped that this act would increase the strength of traditional Russian communities.

In addition to freeing the serfs, Alexander carried out other reforms. He gave Russian provinces some self-government. He also abolished most secret trials and established trial by juries.

The Return of Repressive Measures. Despite his reforms, Alexander did not win popular support. Fierce debate continued over whether Russia should imitate western nations. Reactionaries, those who resist change, opposed the reforms because they did too much.

Liberals opposed Alexander's reforms because they did too little. Groups of students began to meet secretly to discuss more radical changes for Russia.

Alexander was willing to consider further reforms. In 1881, however, he died at the hands of a Russian terrorist. The tsar was riding home in his coach. A bomb suddenly exploded near him, killing two people and wounding a Cossack officer. The tsar, unhurt, went to aid the victims. Then a second bomb went off, fatally wounding him. A young relative of the tsar described the scene later at the palace:

" The Emperor lay on the couch near the desk. He was unconscious. Three doctors were fussing around but science was helpless. . . . He presented a terrible sight, his right leg torn off, his left leg shattered, innumerable wounds all over his head and face. "

Frightened by this assassination and by another revolt in Poland, the new tsar, Alexander III, halted all reforms in Russia. Both he and his successor, Nicholas II, repressed liberal movements. Between 1881 and 1894, the government increased censorship and used spies and informers to locate and punish opponents.

Encouraged by the Slavophiles, Alexander and then Nicholas returned to a program of Russification. Under this program, all people within the empire had to use Russian when dealing with the government. Public education was only in the Russian language. Jews were unpopular and were persecuted throughout Russia.

Laws Governing Jews in Nineteenth-Century Russia

The Russian government strictly regulated the lives of Jews during the 1800s. Russian Jews were allowed to live only in certain areas, called the Jewish Pale of Settlement. The Committee of Ministers also established quotas restricting the number of Jewish students in secondary schools and universities. Even within the Jewish Pale of Settlement, Jews could make up only 15 percent of the student body.

On May 3, 1882, the Committee of Ministers, with Alexander III's approval, issued additional regulations to govern the Jews. Below are three measures contained in the May Laws:

" 1. As a temporary measure and until a general reexamination is made, in due form, of legislation concerning the Jews, they are forbidden henceforth to settle anew outside of cities and towns, an exception being made only in the case of existing Jewish agricultural colonies.

2. Until further notice, the registration of deeds of sale and mortgages in the names of Jews is forbidden, as well as the attestation [certifying as genuine], in the name of Jews, of leases on real estate situated outside of cities and towns, or of letters of attorney for the administration or management of such property.

3. Jews are forbidden to carry on trade on Sundays and on the twelve principal holy days. **"**

LIVE AND LET LIVE IN RUSSIA
"Your money, Jew, or your life!"—The cry for ages.

Jews living in the countryside received little or no protection. Soldiers on leave sometimes took part in pogroms (poh GRUHMZ) in which Jewish people were terrorized and sometimes murdered. Many Jews who could afford to emigrate fled to the democratic nations of Great Britain and the United States. Others fled to Palestine where Jews hoped to eventually establish an independent Jewish state. ■

Growth of Democratic Nations

While reformers in Russia struggled for change, western nations strengthened their democracies. The British claimed a heritage of unique political freedoms. In the second half of the 1800s, Parliament expanded these freedoms.

Great Britain Extends Democracy. By 1688, Parliament was exercising more power than the British monarch. The British government was not a true democracy, however, because only male property owners and a few other men were allowed to vote. In addition, they voted openly by voice rather than by secret ballot. Nobles and wealthy landowners often influenced voters or bought their votes.

Only males who owned property could be elected to the House of Commons. Members of Parliament received no salary. Representatives needed a private income.

During the 1800s, Parliament passed a number of laws that extended suffrage, the right to vote. The Reform Bill of 1832 gave representation to the new industrial cities and lowered property qualifications for voting. Britain adopted the secret ballot in 1872, and in 1885 gave the vote to all adult males. During the same year, the Redistribution Bill organized electoral districts that were about equal in population. Later laws took away the House of Lords' power to veto tax and budget bills. In 1910, Parliament voted to pay a salary to its members.

Women Struggle for the Right to Vote.

During the 1800s, women in both the United States and Great Britain worked to gain the right to vote. They gained that right gradually. In the United States, Wyoming allowed women to vote in 1869. Woman suffrage was granted in New Zealand in 1893, and in Australia and several Scandinavian countries in the early 1900s.

Emmeline Pankhurst and others worked for woman suffrage in Great Britain at the turn of the century. She and her daughters, Christabel and Sylvia, founded the Women's Social and Political Union, WSPU, in 1903. They organized marches, distributed pamphlets, and demonstrated to gain supporters. Finally, in 1918, Parliament passed a bill allowing women over the age of 30 to vote.

A police officer arrests a British suffragist about 1912. British women over the age of 30 finally gained the right to vote in 1918.

A photograph by Lewis Hine shows an Italian family after arriving at Ellis Island. European immigrants poured into the United States in the early 1900s.

The United States Becomes a World Power. The United States, a representative democracy like Great Britain, also grew and changed in the last half of the nineteenth century. In 1865, after the Civil War ended, the United States underwent dramatic economic and political growth.

The purchase of Alaska from Russia in 1867 added territory to the United States that was more than twice the size of Texas. American cities grew to rival, in size and industrial might, those of Europe. By 1900, 76 cities in the United States had populations over 50,000.

European immigrants poured into the United States. Between 1905 and 1907, more than 10,000 immigrants entered the country every day. Immigrants to the United States could expect to acquire citizenship after seven years of residence. With citizenship came the right to vote, and the opportunity to own property. Americans new and old felt pride in their country equal to that of European nationalists. Its prosperous economy, large population, and modern transportation made the United States a world power.

In the second half of the 1800s, the leading national states of the West were rich and powerful. These nations, particularly Great Britain, France, Germany, and the United States, could produce goods and mobilize citizens better than any other countries.

Between 1880 and 1914, these nations, together with Belgium and Portugal, began new imperialist adventures overseas. By the start of World War I, western nations ruled or economically dominated most of the inhabited globe.

SECTION 2 *Study Skills*

Developing Vocabulary 1. Explain the difference between immigration and emigration. **2.** What is a pogrom? **3.** Define autonomy.

Reviewing Main Ideas 1. Explain the importance of the Treaty of San Stefano. **2.** How did the nationalist movement affect Austria between 1848 and 1914? **3.** Give examples of ways in which Jewish life was regulated by the Russian government.

Understanding Cause and Effect 1. Why did Franz Josef create the dual monarchies of Austria and Hungary? **2.** Explain the Slavophile's impact on Russian reforms in the 1800s. **3.** List the factors that helped the United States become a world power.

Understanding Chronology. 1. Chart the revolts of various ethnic groups within the Ottoman Empire during the 1800s. **2.** Construct a chart showing England's suffrage laws from 1832 to 1918.

Challenge What problems does a nation with many ethnic groups encounter?

3 Imperialism Transforms the Globe

OBJECTIVE: *To understand the causes and consequences of the western world's domination of the globe*

Imperialism in Africa

During the last half of the nineteenth century, the armies and navies of the western national states conquered almost all of the African continent. They also occupied large areas of Southeast Asia and parts of the western Pacific.

The seven European nations of Great Britain, France, Germany, Portugal, Italy, Belgium, and Spain divided almost the entire African continent among themselves between 1880 and 1914. By the year 1914, only Liberia and Ethiopia had managed to maintain their independence from European colonial powers.

The Scramble to Partition Africa

During the 1850s, Europeans began to travel into the interior of Africa. Most western explorers searched for opportunities to develop trade or introduce Christianity. European governments wanted to trade with Africa. They regarded conquest as too expensive.

European Attitudes Change. In the 1870s, Europeans changed their attitudes about controlling Africa. European countries, for the first time, had become capable of conquering the continent through scientific and technological advancements.

VOCABULARY DEVELOPMENT

colony *noun:* an area where a foreign power gains political control over a region and its inhabitants.

protectorate (pruh TEHK tuhr iht) *noun:* a country that retains its own government but whose policies are guided by an imperial power.

imperialism (ihm PIHR ee uhl ihz uhm) *noun:* the policy of attempting to dominate the political, economic, or cultural life of another country or region. From the Latin word, *imperare,* meaning to command.

guerrilla (guh RIHL uh) *noun:* a member of a force of fighters, usually volunteers, who operate in small groups and usually make hit-and-run attacks against the enemy. From the Spanish word, *guerilla,* meaning little war.

intimidate (ihn TIHM uh dayt) *verb:* to influence or force by fear; to frighten. From the Latin pre-

fix *-in,* meaning in, and word *timidus,* meaning fearful.

cabinet *noun:* a group of official advisers to a nation's ruler. Members head the major branches of government.

sphere of influence: a region where an imperial power claims economic and political rights that are recognized by other nations.

archipelago (AHR kuh PEHL uh goh) *noun:* a group of many islands. From the Greek words *archi,* meaning chief, and *pelagos,* meaning sea (originally the Aegean Sea).

isthmus (IHS muhs) *noun:* a narrow strip of land having water at each side and connecting two larger sections of land. From the Greek word, *isthmos,* meaning narrow passage.

Above, Ethiopian Emperor Menelik II. At left, an Ethiopian painting depicts Menelik's victory over the Italians at Adowa in 1896.

First, scientists invented drugs that protected Europeans from tropical diseases. Then soldiers could march into the interior of Africa without many becoming extremely sick and dying.

Second, Europeans developed superior weapons. A revolution in weaponry made muzzle-loading muskets obsolete. The repeating rifle, developed in the 1870s, enabled soldiers to fire shots quickly, one after the other. By the 1880s, soldiers using the deadly machine gun could quickly kill large numbers of people.

Africans who resisted European conquest did not have the most modern guns. At a battle in the Upper Nile Valley in 1898, a British army used artillery and machine guns against a poorly armed African force. The British won the battle and suffered only a few casualties. After the battle, however, 11,000 Africans lay dead.

The French Expand Their Lands in Africa. New drugs and new weapons made the European invasions of Africa possible. The principal motive for the conquest was European political affairs.

France lost the eastern provinces of Alsace and Lorraine to Germany in the Franco-Prussian War. Bismarck, the chancellor of Germany, wanted to avoid another war with France over these territories. He therefore encouraged France to seek colonies overseas.

France controlled a small coastal colony in the Senegal River region of western Africa. In the 1870s, the French sent their forces up the Senegal River. They conquered African states as they moved east.

In 1881, the French also occupied Tunisia, in northern Africa. A small Turkish-speaking minority governed this largely Arab country. The Turkish ruler of Tunisia owed large debts to European banks. France, using the debts as an excuse, invaded the country from its neighboring colony of Algeria.

All European leaders feared that a rival country would gain an advantage by colonizing Africa. This advantage could upset the delicate balance of power. Therefore, when France took aggressive military action in western Africa, other countries began to compete for colonies. The conquest of Africa was an extension of balance-of-power politics in Europe.

The British Take Control of Egypt. After European engineers built the Suez Canal in 1869, Egypt became strategically important. The Suez Canal linked the Mediterranean and Red seas. European ships no longer had to sail around Africa to reach Asia.

Like the ruler of Tunisia, the Turkish ruler of Egypt also borrowed heavily from European banks. In 1876, when he could no longer pay the interest on his debts, France and Britain took control of Egypt's finances. Six years later, the British, angered by France's occupation of Tunisia, sent troops into Egypt. Meeting little resistance from the Egyptians, the British established a protectorate in Egypt.

Belgium Claims the Congo. Leopold II, king of Belgium, also wanted to carve out an African empire. To develop trade in the Congo River basin of central Africa, now Zaire, Leopold formed the International Association of the Congo in 1882. France, alarmed by Leopold's action, also claimed territory in the Congo region.

The Berlin Conference of 1884. Germany was left out of the accelerating race for colonies. In 1884, therefore, Bismarck called a conference of the European powers. The goal of the conference, which met in Berlin, was to ensure free trade on the Congo River for all nations. In fact, the delegates divided large areas of Africa among themselves. Af-

ricans were not invited to the conference and had nothing to say about the decision to encourage imperialism on the continent.

The Final Division of Africa. In the years between the Berlin conference and the start of World War I, seven European countries competed to establish colonial empires in Africa. France took control of a vast area stretching from the Mediterranean Sea southward across the Sahara to the Atlantic coast. See the map, Colonial Empires, 1914, page 584.

The British carved out widely separated colonies in all regions of the continent. Some areas, such as Egypt, Nigeria, and Kenya, were large and populous.

The Germans took territories in western, eastern, and southern Africa. King Leopold's soldiers and traders created a huge empire in the Congo basin. The Portuguese enlarged their existing colonies of Angola and Mozambique. They had held these lands since the days of the slave trade. The Italians began the conquest of Libya in 1911. Spain held minor territories, including the northern area of Morocco.

As in British India and Spanish America, small numbers of European officials, soldiers, merchants, and missionaries occupied and developed these new African empires. Few of the tropical colonies attracted European settlers and their families.

African Resistance Movements. The European occupation of Africa took many years to complete. African resistance often slowed European conquest. In some areas, standing armies of African states fought to preserve their freedom. In other areas, Africans organized guerrilla warfare in forests, deserts, or mountains.

Resistance movements in some parts of Africa lasted for many years. Even though the French gained control of Morocco in 1912, Berber warriors were still fighting the French as late as 1934. In general, however, most African resistance movements were

Colonial Empires, 1914

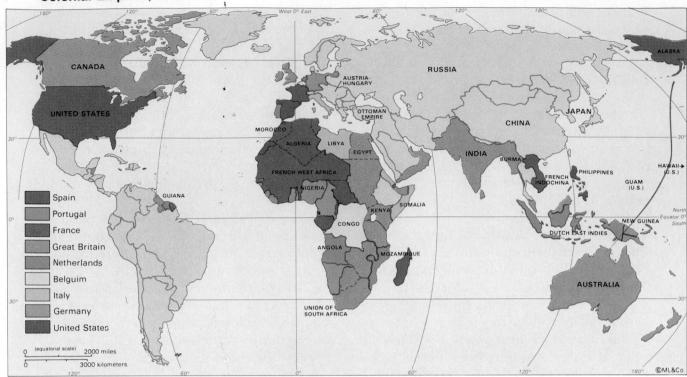

Map Skills **1.** In 1914, which continent was almost totally composed of colonies? **2.** Which colonial power controlled the largest section of Africa? **3.** What areas were held by the U.S.?

doomed to failure. Europeans possessed superior weapons and communication. By 1914, Europeans were firmly in control of most of Africa.

The Japanese Resist European Domination

Of all the people of Asia and Africa, the Japanese were the only ones who not only rejected European domination but also developed a powerful industrial nation. The Japanese opened their ports to foreign nations in 1854. This change eventually brought a new government to Japan.

The New Japanese Constitution. In 1867, a group of Japanese warriors overthrew the shogun and transferred authority to a new emperor who had just succeeded to the throne. He took the title Meiji (MAY jee) for his reign. The new ruler's goal was

to make Japan so strong that it would never again be intimidated by foreigners.

To strengthen Japan, the Japanese daimyo persuaded the emperor to industrialize and westernize the country. The emperor sent Japanese scholars abroad to study American and European government systems, military organizations, and schools.

In 1889, the Japanese adopted a constitution patterned after that of the Germans. Under the constitution, Japan retained a divine and supreme emperor. The emperor appointed a cabinet of ministers who were his advisers. The legislature could consider only bills the cabinet submitted. The emperor could veto any bill, summon or dissolve the legislature, make treaties, and declare war.

During the Meiji period, the Japanese copied the most modern machines and industrial techniques. They mechanized their textile industry, developed a steel industry, and expanded shipbuilding. They improved transportation and communication by building railroads and installing telephones and telegraph lines.

The Russo-Japanese War. The Japanese were so successful that in 1904 they were able to challenge Russia. During the year before, the Russians had moved more than 100,000 troops into Manchuria. China was not strong enough to stop this Russian aggression. The Japanese, however, regarded Manchuria as a future Japanese sphere of influence.

Before declaring war on Russia, Japan signed a treaty of alliance with Great Britain. Japan and Great Britain agreed that each had the right to defend its own special interests in China, Manchuria, and Korea. They also agreed to remain neutral if either nation became involved in a war.

The Japanese then demanded that Russia withdraw its troops from Manchuria. When the Russians were slow to negotiate, Japan attacked without first declaring war. The Japanese destroyed an entire Russian fleet of 32 ships; then, they defeated the Russian soldiers in Manchuria.

The Russians surrendered in 1905. The Treaty of Portsmouth ended the Russo-Japanese War. Russia withdrew its troops from Manchuria and returned it to China. Russia was forced to recognize Japanese interests and rights in Korea. In 1910, Japan annexed Korea, renaming it Chosen.

Japan's brilliant victory in the Russo-Japanese War showed the western world that this island nation had become a world power. Japan entered the twentieth century, not as a colonial possession, but as an important imperialist power.

European Imperialism in Asia

Across the Indian Ocean from Africa, Southeast Asia also fell under European control in the late nineteenth century. From their base in India, the British won new ter-

During the Meiji period, the Japanese adopted Western textile processing methods. An early silk-reeling factory is shown here.

ritory in Burma and Malaya in the 1880s and 1890s. The French extended their control over Indochina.

European Control of Southeast Asia. Between 1850 and 1890, the French gradually gained control of the three major regions of Indochina: Vietnam, Cambodia, and Laos. The Dutch had ruled coastal areas in the vast archipelago of Indonesia since the 1600s. In the 1800s, they extended their control to more islands and the interior.

In Southeast Asia, only Thailand escaped European colonial control. Thailand owed its independence to King Rama V, who ruled from 1868 to 1910. His life was depicted in the musical, "The King and I."

Rama V devoted himself to reforming and modernizing his country. He ended feudalism, abolished slavery, updated his bureaucracy and army, and opened a railway and telegraph line. He also negotiated with Great Britain and France to prevent either nation from attacking his country.

United States Expands in the Pacific. The United States, like European nations, took control of overseas lands. By the mid-1800s, United States citizens had developed sugar and pineapple plantations on the Hawaiian islands. In 1898, to protect American interests, the United States annexed the Hawaiian islands.

War with Spain. In the same year, the United States declared war on Spain. Earlier, the American press had played up incidents of Spanish abuse of the inhabitants of Cuba. On February 15, 1898, the United States battleship *Maine* mysteriously exploded in Havana harbor. The cause was never determined. The people of the United States demanded war.

The United States defeated Spain in the war and proceeded to occupy the Philippines, Cuba, and Puerto Rico. The Treaty of 1898 ended the short war. By the terms of the treaty, the United States received Puerto Rico, Guam, and the Philippine Islands. Thus, it became an important colonial power in east Asia.

The United States Builds the Panama Canal. To defend lands in the Pacific Ocean, such as Hawaii and the Philippines, the United States needed a navy based on the west coast. For many years, engineers had talked about a canal through the Isthmus of Panama. In 1903, the United States tried to negotiate a treaty with Colombia for permission to build a canal through Panama, then part of Colombia.

The people of Panama were eager to have the revenue and jobs provided by the construction of a canal. American agents encouraged a movement for independence. When Panamanians rebelled, the United States sent warships to prevent Colombian troops from putting down the revolution. The United States immediately recognized the independence of Panama.

Work began and the Panama Canal opened in 1914. The opening of the canal greatly improved American military and commercial access to the Pacific Ocean.

European Pressures on China. No European nation conquered China. The European states, however, along with the United States and Japan, increasingly dominated China's economy. They also interfered in its government in the late 1800s.

The Taiping Rebellion. Japan resisted European control by building an industrialized economy. Chinese leaders could not agree on how to resist western domination.

Many Chinese scholars, educated in Confucian classics, believed that Chinese government and culture were superior to those of the West. When the Europeans forced their policies on the Chinese emperor of the Manchu Dynasty, these Chinese turned against him.

Shortly after the Opium War ended in 1842 (see page 551), the people of southern China rebelled against Manchu rule. A young man, Hong, led the rebellion. Influenced by Christian missionary pamphlets, he dreamed that he was the son of God and brother of Jesus Christ. Believing in his mission to save China, he began a religious movement that turned into the largest rebellion in Chinese history.

The rebellion, or civil war, lasted from 1851 to 1864. Thousands of rebels captured 600 walled cities before being defeated. They seized control of southern China to the Yangtze River.

The rebellion pointed out the danger of replacing traditional Chinese cultural values: Many Chinese blamed Christian missionaries for the rebellion. The Taiping Rebellion weakened Chinese society as well as the Manchu Dynasty.

Chinese Efforts to Resist the West. After the unsuccessful Taiping Rebellion, many Chinese officials saw the need to change.

Supporters of the Manchu Dynasty used siege tactics to overcome the Taiping rebels. Thousands of rebels, led by Hong, captured 600 walled cities before being defeated.

They began a program they called self-strengthening. The goal was to learn enough from the West to keep China strong and independent. A strong China could resist more western influence. The self-strengthening program emphasized two strategies: better education and improved military technology.

In the 1870s, the government put Yung Wing, a Yale-educated administrator, in charge of an educational mission. Yung took 120 boys to Connecticut, where they lived with American families and attended American schools.

Officials of the Chinese court visited the students. They were horrified to find the young men hiding their queues under caps and playing baseball. The government quickly canceled the educational mission, fearing that young Chinese were being converted to western cultural values.

Like Rama V and other Asian rulers, the Chinese tried to strengthen their country by building a modern army and navy. They paid western engineers to show them how to construct steamships and naval guns. More than a dozen vessels were built, and naval cadets were trained in modern tactics.

In 1894 and 1895, China fought a war with Japan over control of Korea. The Chinese had great hope for their new fleet. The Japanese, however, destroyed it. In their defeat, the Chinese were humiliated and recognized the failure of their self-strengthening movement.

Chinese Dislike of Foreigners Grows.
Antiforeign sentiment became more violent during the last half of the 1800s. Educated Chinese, especially Confucian scholars, resented missionary activities. After the Taiping Rebellion, angry crowds occasionally attacked missionaries.

A serious outbreak of antiforeign sentiment took place in the 1890s. A religious movement called the Righteous and Har-

MAINTAINING HIS EQUILIBRIUM.

CHINESE EMPEROR: "Oh, do let me go! You're pulling me to pieces between you."
THE POWERS: "Don't be afraid. We're only maintaining your equilibrium."

From the *Westminster Budget* (London).

The English lion, the United States eagle, and the Russian bear each try to get a piece of China. They protest that they are helping China stand alone.

monious Fists spread in northern China. The British called the group the Boxers. The Boxers believed that their magic arts and rituals gave them special powers.

The Boxers attacked missionaries and Chinese Christians. They killed about 250 foreigners and many Chinese. The Manchus supported the Boxers and declared war on the foreign powers. In 1900, British and French along with Americans and Japanese sent an army of 20,000 into China to put down the Boxers. In the peace settlement, the defeated Chinese were forced to pay a huge indemnity. The uprising failed to end European domination of China.

The Open Door Policy. Europeans extended their influence farther into China during the 1890s. Various European nations divided China into spheres of influence, areas where each nation claimed special trading rights.

United States merchants did not want to be excluded from trade with China. In 1899, the United States government asked the European powers to recognize an Open Door Policy. That is, the United States wanted Chinese trade to be open to all nations. Not wanting to be the first country to refuse, all nations agreed.

The Chinese Nationalist People's Party. Some of China's intellectual leaders were educated in Europe, the United States, and Japan. They were critical of the Confucian scholars. Instead of maintaining traditional values, these western-educated Chinese wanted to build an industrialized economy. They also wanted a constitution and a democratic government.

One of the intellectuals, Sun Yat-sen, was among the young Chinese leaders who favored a democracy. He had lived in the United States, attended school in Hawaii, and studied medicine in Hong Kong. In the early 1900s, Sun Yat-sen founded the Guomindang (gwoh mihn dahng), the Nationalist People's Party. In 1911, a new wave of rebellion struck China. Nationalists forced the Manchus to abdicate and proclaimed the Chinese Republic.

SECTION 3 *Study Skills*

Developing Vocabulary Use each of the following terms in a sentence: **1.** colony. **2.** protectorate. **3.** imperialism. **4.** archipelago. **5.** isthmus.

Reviewing Main Ideas 1. What two factors led to the success of the Europeans in Africa? **2.** How was Japan westernized during the Meiji period? **3.** How successful was China's self-strengthening movement?

Understanding Geography 1. Chart the African possessions of France, Italy, England, Belgium, and Germany. **2.** List the Southeast Asian countries controlled by Great Britain and France in 1890. **3.** What islands did the United States gain from Spain in 1898?

Understanding Cause and Effect 1. Why was Ethiopia able to remain an independent country? **2.** Why did the United States declare war on Spain in 1898? **3.** List the causes of the Taiping Rebellion.

Challenge Is the Panama Canal as vital to the United States today as it was in 1914? Explain.

A View of Sub-Saharan Africa

Anthropological finds indicate that humans may have roamed Africa south of the Sahara Desert for over a million years. The culture that developed there first used stone tools and later iron technology.

By 1914, European colonies were established in much of Africa. Colonists south of the Sahara, in the sub-Saharan culture realm, found the area particularly rich in minerals and oil. Colonial powers used these to enhance their industrial growth. Today, the recently independent nations of sub-Saharan Africa must find a way to combine the best of many cultures in order to compete in a technological world.

Sub-Saharan Culture

Culturally, the area south of the Sahara is quite diverse. Nearly 6,000 different ethnic groups live in this region. A few of the more important languages of Africa are Hausa, Yoruba, Fulani, Swahili, and Zulu. The last two are members of the Bantu language group.

People in the area bordering the Sahara Desert, in the northern and coastal areas of eastern Africa, are strongly influenced by Islam. Many peoples of sub-Saharan Africa are Christians, especially in West, Central, and Southern Africa.

Climate and Geography

Africa south of the Sahara is generally warm except for areas in the highlands and the far south. The area just south of the Sahara Desert supports a grassland. In the middle of the continent, bordering the equator, is a tropical rain forest. South of the rain forest is another semi-dry grassland area.

Regions of Sub-Saharan Africa

The sub-Saharan realm of Africa is so large that it has four separate regions: West, East, Central, and Southern Africa. Each region has its own characteristics.

West Africa. West Africa lies to the south of the Sahara and borders the Atlantic. This section is Africa's most populous region. A few groups, such as the Yoruba of Nigeria, have lived in cities for hundreds of years. However, most African cities have grown up since European colonial days.

East Africa. Facing the Indian Ocean is a grassland and forest region known as East Africa. East Africa is centered on Lake Victoria and includes the countries of Uganda, Kenya, and Tanzania. Here, rainfall fills several large lakes and creates beautiful waterfalls. These lakes feed the waters of the Nile, the world's longest river. Here, herding and agriculture are the primary means of livelihood.

Central Africa. In the center of the continent, and bordering the equator, lies a tropical region. This area extends from the Central African Republic in the north to Zaire in the south, and the Cameroons to the west. Here the powerful Zaire River has its source and then flows westward. Central Africa is a region of jungle rain forest. The economy depends on agriculture and export of raw materials.

South Africa. To the south of Central Africa lies another savannah region known as South Africa. Southern Africa, which includes Zimbabwe, has some of the greatest concentrations of natural resources on the continent. There are deposits of gold, copper, diamonds, platinum, and iron ore.

Data on Countries in Sub-Saharan Africa

	Chad	Kenya	Nigeria	Tanzania	Uganda	Zaire	Zimbabwe
Area (in thousands of square miles)	495	224	356	365	93	905	150
Area (in thousands of square kilometers)	1,284	582	923	945	241	2,344	390
Population (in millions)	4	19	91	17	12	30	8
Annual birth rate (per 1,000 population)	43	54	50	35	45	46	54
Annual death rate (per 1,000 population)	22	13	16	10	13	19	13
Number of years (projected) **to double population**	33	17	27	23	22	23	25
Population projected by A.D. 2000 (in millions)	7	37	150	31	25	52	11
Annual death rate of infants under 1 year (per 1,000 births)	146	85	124	98	100	117	72
Percent of population under 15 years	42	48	47	46	45	46	51
Percent of population over 60 years	6	5	2	5	5	4	3
Life expectancy at birth	42	56	50	53	55	47	55
Percent of urban population	17	13	20	13	12	34	23
Per capita food supply (as percent of requirement)	76	89	99	87	80	96	80
Total GNP (in billions of U.S. dollars)	.5	6	68	4	3	5	4
Per capita GNP (in U.S. dollars)	125	355	775	260	220	171	590
Percent of adult population illiterate	82	53	66	26	52	42	39

Population and Economics

The diverse people of sub-Saharan Africa are primarily dependent upon agriculture and herding for their livelihood. About 80 percent of the inhabitants live in rural areas along the coast or near rivers; 75 percent of these people are involved in farming for their own families. Unfortunately, making a living through agriculture is difficult because of poor soils, frequent droughts, and the lack of modern fertilizers. Many Africans raise crops to be sold abroad, but crop prices on the world market are often low.

Challenge for the Future

Sub-Saharan Africa holds enormous natural resources. Besides the hardwood, ores, and minerals, Africa's rivers have the potential of providing hydroelectric power. Before Africa's productive potential can be reached, however, the continent must produce more food for its own people. Agricultural production of basic foods will go up only when more assistance and support is given to Africa's farmers.

STUDY SKILLS Understanding Geography

1. Why were the ores and minerals of Africa more important to European colonists than to the natives?
2. What effect has climate and geography had on the cultural development of the people in sub-Saharan Africa?
3. Describe the present and the potential use of Africa's rivers.
4. Suggest why Western Africa is the most populous area on the continent.

CHAPTER 25 *Summary & Review*

Summarizing Main Ideas

By the mid-nineteenth century, nationalism had become a strong force throughout Europe. Spurred on by victory over Austria, the states and provinces of Italy united in 1861. Germany joined Prussia to form the North German Confederation in 1867. The same year, the Austrian Empire gave equal status to Hungary.

By the middle 1800s, liberal ideas had reached Russia. Alexander II, though remaining authoritarian, abolished serfdom in 1861, and initiated other reforms. When Alexander was assassinated in 1881, reform stopped.

Following the Civil War, the United States grew dramatically. In foreign affairs, the United States acquired the beginning of a world empire with victory over the Spanish in 1898. As a world leader, the nation called for an Open Door in China and built the Panama Canal.

Questions for Critical Thinking

COMPREHENSION Interpreting Events

1. How did the Triple Alliance affect the balance of power in Europe?
2. What were the results of the opening of the Panama Canal?
3. Explain how the Japanese dealt with Westernization.

APPLICATION Comparing Past and Present

1. Bismarck manipulated the Ems Telegram for his own purpose. Could such a thing happen today? Explain.
2. Is it important today for a nation to have autonomy? Why?

ANALYSIS Identifying Trends

1. Why did the Europeans want to colonize Africa and Asia?
2. How did Sun Yat-sen influence the Chinese government?

Imperialistic Wars, 1870 to 1905		
Conflict	Countries Involved	Victorious Country
Franco-Prussian War 1870	France, Prussia	Prussia
Sino-Japanese War 1894–1895	China, Japan	Japan
Fashoda Affair 1898	France, Great Britain	Compromise reached
Spanish-American War 1898	Spain, United States	United States
United States vs. Philippine Republic 1899–1911	United States, Philippines	United States
Boer War 1899–1902	Great Britain, Boers in South Africa	Great Britain
Boxer Rebellion 1900	Chinese Boxers, International force from Europe and the United States	Major Powers
Russo-Japanese War 1904–1905	Russia, Japan	Japan

EVALUATION Weighing Consequences

1. What were the causes and effects of the Russo-Japanese War?
2. What problems did the unification of Germany and Italy cause the rest of Europe?

CHALLENGE

What were the long-term effects of the nineteenth-century policies of Europe?

CHAPTER 26

War on a Global Scale

TIME

1914	1915

1914–1916 A stalemate develops on the western front

1915 Germans sink the Lusitania

PEOPLE

1914 Archduke Franz Ferdinand assassinated by a Serbian terrorist

1915 Einstein develops a general theory of relativity

PLACE

1914 *Belgium;¹* Germans march through neutral Belgium

1915 *France;²* Poison gas used on the western front

Linking Past to Present

Preventing war is a concern for everyone today. Nuclear weapons threaten to make another war the last one ever. Understanding why past wars started may help to make war less likely in the future. In 1914, war broke out in Europe. Each of the combatants had its reasons for fighting. Few, however, predicted that millions of soldiers and civilians would be wounded or slaughtered. Likewise, no one could have foreseen that many cities and millions of acres of land would be destroyed.

The military and economic situations that existed in 1914 will never again be duplicated. Still, studying the causes, upheavals, and tremendous costs of World War I can and should encourage all people today to try harder to prevent wars in the future.

Colin Gill's *Evening after a Push*.

1916	1917	1918

1916 British introduce the tank at the Battle of the Somme

1917 German telegram to Mexico angers the United States

1917 The Russians revolt against the tsar

1918 The Ottoman Empire surrenders

1918 An armistice ends World War I

1916 Prince Faisal leads an Arab revolt against the Turks

1916 Lloyd George becomes British prime minister

1917 Nicholas II abdicates

1917 Kerensky forms a provisional Russian government

1918 Lenin signs the Treaty of Brest-Litovsk

1918 Kaiser Wilhelm II abdicates

1918 Nicholas II and his family murdered by revolutionaries

1916 *Italy;[3]* Italy declares war on Germany

1917–1920 *Russia;[4]* The Russians fight a civil war

1917 *Russia;[4]* Army units mutiny in St. Petersburg

1917 *Russia;[4]* Trans-Siberian Railroad completed

1918 *Great Britain;[5]* Women over 30 are allowed to vote

593

1 *Breakdown of the European State System*

OBJECTIVE: *To understand the causes of World War I*

The Causes of World War I

The Western world achieved military and economic dominance over the globe by the early 1900s. When the twentieth century dawned, European soldiers and officials ruled India, Southeast Asia, and most of Africa. Western diplomats and businesspeople manipulated the economic and political affairs of China, Persia, and the Ottoman Empire. In the Western Hemisphere, the United States, a latecomer to the company of Western powers, was becoming a major influence throughout the world.

Each nation in Europe pursued policies around the world designed to increase its power and influence. Often, they conflicted with the interests of other nations.

Conditions were developing that made likely the outbreak of a general war. These conditions eventually led to World War I: first, economic competition for markets; second, Europe's alliance system aligned nations against one another; third, all ethnic groups had strong nationalist feelings.

Economic Competition and the Arms Race. The industrial nations of Europe competed with one another for influence and trade. Britain was the leading industrial country in the world until 1870. Then, the newly united Germany rapidly industrialized, and built modern transportation and communication networks. German businesspeople began to compete successfully with British merchants in east Asia, the Middle East, and Latin America.

Weapons were an important product of European industries. European and American merchants competed to gain new markets for their weapons. In Europe, the major powers were stockpiling military hardware. Each nation wanted to keep its armed forces stronger than those of any potential enemy.

Competition for international trade also led to a naval arms race. The major European countries, as well as the United States and Japan, strengthened their navies to protect their shipping routes. Britain started a massive buildup of ships and naval guns in 1884. Germany, England's chief economic rival, soon followed.

In 1906, the British launched the super-battleship HMS *Dreadnaught*. This mighty

---

VOCABULARY DEVELOPMENT

kaiser (KY zuhr) *noun:* title the rulers of Germany used between 1871 and 1918. The German form of the Latin word, *caesar*.

autocratic (AW tuh KRAT ihk) *adj.:* having absolute power. From the Greek words *autos*, meaning self, and *kratos*, meaning power.

entente (ahn TAHNT) *noun:* a French word meaning an understanding or agreement between two or more governments.

ultimatum (UHL tuh MAYT uhm) *noun:* a final offer or demand of one of the parties engaged in a conflict. From the Latin word, *ultimare*, meaning to come to an end.

Britain controlled the seas with the world's largest navy prior to World War I. Shown here, from left to right, two cruisers, a torpedo catcher, a torpedo boat, and a battleship.

warship had 24 rapid-firing cannons and 10 guns with 12-inch-wide barrels. Five torpedo tubes increased its destructive power.

The *Dreadnaught* intimidated the other major powers, who began building their own giant battleships. Soon Germany, the United States, Austria-Hungary, Italy, and Japan had new battleships to add to their war fleets.

Europe's Two Alliance Systems. The states of Europe had engaged in balance-of-power politics since the sixteenth century. Whenever one country gained too much influence in European affairs, other countries formed alliances against it. Through war and diplomacy, Europeans preserved a balance of power. This system worked because alliances were flexible. Countries formed new alliances to meet changing economic and political circumstances.

Near the end of the 1800s, however, European alliances developed into two rigidly opposed blocks. In 1871, Germany defeated France in the Franco-Prussian War. Then the provinces of Alsace and Lorraine were occupied. To keep France isolated, Bismarck, still the German chancellor, formed an alliance with Austria-Hungary. In 1882, Italy, angry because France had seized Tunisia, joined the pact to form the Triple Alliance.

Germany lay between France on the west and Russia on the east. Bismarck thus feared that the two countries might ally with one another and attack Germany on two fronts. To prevent such attack, he remained friendly with Russia. However, in 1890, Kaiser Wilhelm II forced Bismarck out of office. Wilhelm, who had none of Bismarck's diplomatic skills, believed that the contrast between autocratic Russia and republican France would prevent an alliance.

Wilhelm was wrong. In 1894, France, searching for allies, joined with Russia to counter the threat of the Triple Alliance. Bismarck's fear of fighting a war on two fronts came one step closer to reality.

In the early 1900s, Germany's rapidly growing navy threatened Britain's naval supremacy. Britain tried to reach an agreement with Germany to end the naval arms race. When this effort failed, Great Britain also looked for allies.

In 1902, the British king, Edward VII, made an official visit to Paris. The French people received him with great enthusiasm. France and Great Britain signed the Franco-British Entente in 1904. In 1907, Britain also allied with Russia, enlarging the alliance into the Triple Entente. See the map on this page.

The major powers of Europe were now set against one another in two alliance systems, both bristling with armaments. The threat of a general war became greater. Suspicion and distrust made peaceful diplomacy increasingly difficult.

Alliances' Strengths and Weaknesses.

The nations of the Triple Alliance—Germany, Austria-Hungary, and Italy—bordered one another, enabling them to coordinate military operations when necessary. Since they also occupied a central position on the continent, however, they faced enemies to both the east and the west. In addition, Italy was a weak link in the alliance. Italy could not be depended on to support Austria, since both wanted provinces around the Adriatic Sea.

The nations of the Triple Entente controlled the seas and could surround the nations of the Triple Alliance. The Triple Entente countries, however, were less formally bound to one another than were those of the Triple Alliance. In addition, Britain and Russia disagreed over who should control the strategic Bosporus and Dardanelles. These two countries quarreled over territory in Asia, as well.

Nationalist Feelings Increase.

Nationalism involves a desire to build the power and prestige of one's own nation. This feeling was a powerful force throughout Europe in the late 1800s. Nationalist feeling was especially intense in the Balkan Peninsula, where many ethnic groups did not have political freedom. The Austro-Hungarian Em-

European Alliance Systems, 1914

Map Skills **1.** Which countries were part of the Triple Alliance? **2.** Which countries were part of the Triple Entente? **3.** What geographic advantage did each have?

pire ruled several Balkan peoples. Russia and the Ottoman Empire also wanted to preserve their interests in the Balkans. Several of the Balkan people spoke Slavic languages. The Russians, also Slavs, declared themselves protectors of oppressed Slavic groups under Ottoman rule.

Serbs, Czechs, Romanians, and other Balkan groups grew more discontented during the nineteenth century. The most obvious reason for their unrest was the oppressive rule of Austria and the Ottomans. A second reason was the rapid population growth in the rural communities of the Balkan Peninsula.

Countries on the Balkan Peninsula were not industrialized. Land for farming did not increase as population increased. Thousands of jobless people migrated from the Balkans to western Europe or America during the late nineteenth century. Still, the population problem remained. This situation angered and frustrated landless and unemployed young people.

The Austrian Empire ruled a huge population of Slavs. Nationalists in the small Slavic kingdom of Serbia stirred up anti-Austrian feeling among all the Slavs.

In 1908, Austria annexed Bosnia, a Slavic-speaking region. This action made the Serbs furious. Political instability increased in 1912 and 1913, when two short but violent wars broke out in the Balkans. The fighting involved Bulgaria, Greece, Romania, Serbia, and the Ottoman Empire.

Elsewhere, relations between France and Germany became more hostile. The French were still angry over their loss of Alsace-Lorraine. Germany also resisted French claims to have a sphere of influence in Morocco, Africa.

Act of Terrorism Leads to War

On Sunday, June 28, 1914, the Archduke Franz Ferdinand, heir to the throne of Austria, and his wife, the Duchess Sophia, were on a state visit to Sarajevo, the capital of Bosnia. As they drove through the city in an open car, a man named Gavrilo Princip ran forward and shot and killed them both. Princip was a member of the Black Hand, a Serbian nationalist organization.

The Austrians blamed the government of independent Serbia for the assassination, even though it was not directly responsible. Austria sent an ultimatum to Serbia. An ultimatum is a demand whose rejection ends negotiations and causes the use of force or other direct action. Austria demanded that Serbia allow Austrian officials to suppress anti-Austrian societies and publications in Serbia. Serbia was also to allow Austrian judges to try the assassin.

Serbia accepted most of the demands, but Austria was really looking for an excuse to attack its tiny neighbor. On July 28, 1914, Austria declared war.

Germany was determined to support Austria, its only major ally other than Italy. Russia was equally determined to help Serbia, its Slavic friend. The Russian army was the first to mobilize for war. The German government demanded that the Russians demobilize, fearing that Germany might have to fight both Russia and France at the same time. Russia refused, and on August 1, 1914, Germany declared war on Russia. Later, Germany declared war on France.

The Schlieffen Plan. In 1904, a decade before the war started, the German general staff had worked out a plan to fight a two-front war. The plan was named after General Alfred von Schlieffen, head of the general staff. He believed that at the start of a war, France, on the west, would be a more dangerous opponent than Russia, the giant to the east. Russia would take longer to mobilize its troops and prepare for war.

If war broke out, the Germans would send only a relatively small army to the east to face the Russians. The main German forces would quickly defeat France. With France out of the war, the Germans could then send all their forces to fight Russia.

The New York Times.

"All the News That's Fit to Print."

NEW YORK, MONDAY, JUNE 29, 1914.—EIGHTEEN PAGES.

ONE CENT In Greater New York, Jersey City and Newark. | Elsewhere TWO CENTS

VOL. LXIII...NO. 20,610.

CALIFORNIA GOES ON ROCKS IN FOG

Tory Island, Off Northwest Irish Coast, Scene of Mishap to Anchor Liner.

IN NO IMMEDIATE DANGER

STAYS IN AIR 21 HOURS.

Berlin Aviator's Feat Held to be a World's Record.

BERLIN, June 28.—Herr Landmann, an aviator, today concluded a non-stop flight of 21 hours and 48 minutes.

It is asserted that this flight constitutes a world record.

Twenty-one hours would be almost enough to carry the seaplane America either to the coast of Ireland, or to the Azores. Plans for the forthcoming trans-Atlantic flight are based on the America's reaching the Azores in twenty hours.

FEDERALS DESERT AGUASCALIENTES

Town South of Zacatecas Evacuated by Huerta's Forces, but Villa Turns Back.

IS CAMPAIGN ABANDONED?

Border Hears His Ammunition

DEWEY IN CANAL PARADE.

Propose Pan-American Memorial to Columbus

A splendid tomb topped by a great light is proposed to be erected in Santo Domingo, in the Caribbean Sea, by subscriptions from peoples of all lands. See NEXT SUNDAY'S TIMES.

OUR GUNS FIRE ON SANTO DOMINGO

HEIR TO AUSTRIA'S THRONE IS SLAIN WITH HIS WIFE BY A BOSNIAN YOUTH TO AVENGE SEIZURE OF HIS COUNTRY

Francis Ferdinand Shot During State Visit to Sarajevo.

TWO ATTACKS IN A DAY

Archduke Saves His Life First Time by Knocking Aside a Bomb Hurled at Auto.

SLAIN IN SECOND ATTEMPT

Lad Dashes at Car as the Royal Couple Return from Town Hall and Kills Both of Them.

LAID TO A SERVIAN PLOT

Heir Warned Not to Go to Bosnia, Where Populace Met Him with Servian Flags.

AGED EMPEROR IS STRICKEN

Shock of Tragedy Prostrates Francis Joseph—Young Assassin Proud of His Crime.

Archduke Francis Ferdinand and his Consort the Duchess of Hohenberg.

Slain by Assassin's Bullets.

Archduke Ferdinand and his wife, inset, moments before they were shot and killed in Sarajevo. The next day's *New York Times* reported the assassination of the couple.

Britain Enters the War.

Along part of the border between Germany and France are the thick Ardennes Forest and the Vosge Mountains. Schlieffen, therefore, planned to attack France by a northern route across the open plains of Belgium. The small country of Belgium was not part of any alliance system. Major powers, including Germany and Great Britain, had guaranteed Belgium neutrality in 1839 because of the country's size and strategic location.

On August 3, 1914, the Germans violated Belgian neutrality and attacked. The next day, Great Britain declared war on both Germany and Austria. Within a week of Austria's decision to attack Serbia, nations of the two great alliance systems were at war. German leaders promised their troops that they would be home from the war before the leaves turned colors and fell from the trees.

SECTION 1 *Study Skills*

Developing Vocabulary 1. Explain the relationship between kaiser and autocratic. 2. How could an ultimatum be used to intimidate? 3. Explain entente.

Reviewing Main Ideas 1. What conditions led to World War I? 2. Name the countries in the Triple Alliance and Triple Entente. List their strengths and weaknesses. 3. Explain the Schlieffen Plan.

Understanding Chronology 1. When was the first superbattleship built by the British? 2. When did Germany march into Belgium?

Understanding Cause and Effect 1. What was the effect of the assassination of Archduke Franz Ferdinand? 2. What event caused England to declare war on Germany and Austria?

Challenge Could a local conflict become a world war today? Justify your answer.

The Challenge of Disease

Imagine the death and destruction resulting from global war. It is often difficult to think of any positive accomplishments of those times. Yet the conquering of certain diseases was a positive result of the close global interaction of human beings.

Many diseases are related to climate and are found only in particular regions of the world. In earlier times, the study of such diseases was largely ignored by the people outside those regions. Around the time of World War I, faraway regions became accessible as well as politically and economically interesting to larger nations. The world became aware of many unusual diseases. Scientists began research to find the causes and the cures.

Illnesses in Tropic Regions

One example of global cooperation in the fight against disease is the story of Walter Reed. Prior to World War I, Reed, a United States Army doctor, was assigned to treat tropical diseases in Cuba. Dr. Reed discovered outbreaks of yellow fever among the people and troops both in Cuba and in Central America. Reed proved that this often fatal disease was carried by a particular type of mosquito. Using Reed's information, Army engineers began a war against these insects. Mosquito control measures, serums, and a vaccine developed by a South African doctor, have now eliminated yellow fever.

In tropical sections of Africa, other diseases threaten health. Malaria, a disease in existence since at least 500 B.C., as well as sleeping sickness, drew world attention through the suffering of European colonists. Both of these diseases require a vector to enter the human population. A vector is a carrier of the disease. In 1898 three Italian investigators discovered that certain mosquitoes are the vectors of malaria. The tsetse fly is the vector for sleeping sickness.

After the 1925 London Conference on sleeping sickness, a drug derived from arsenic was given to every infected person in the Cameroons. This action is credited with saving entire tribes from extinction. However, a cure for one mysterious African variety of sleeping sickness remains to be found. The disease drains its victims of energy and usually kills animals. In some areas, the disease is so severe that cows and horses cannot be raised there.

Conquering Smallpox

The story of smallpox is much more encouraging. Smallpox differs from malaria and sleeping sickness in several ways. First, the virus is not vector-transmitted. Instead, it is transmitted directly from one person to another like a cold. Second, the disease affects people worldwide, rather than just those in a particular region. Happily, smallpox is no longer a problem. It has been eliminated from the world.

The vaccine against smallpox was developed by an English surgeon, Edward Jenner, in 1796. He noticed that dairymaids who contracted a relatively harmless disease called cowpox never contracted smallpox. In May 1796, Jenner removed fresh cowpox lesions from a dairymaid's finger. Using the matter from her finger, he inoculated an eight-year old boy, using a new technique. The boy soon developed a slight fever and a low-grade lesion. Later, when he was inoculated with live smallpox, he did not contract the disease. Jenner had found a simple way to prevent this disfiguring and often fatal illness.

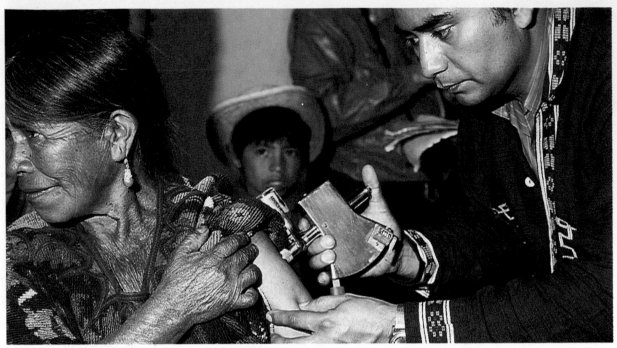

Vaccines and insect control measures have reduced deaths from such diseases as yellow fever and smallpox. Here, a Guatemalan doctor inoculates an Indian woman.

In spite of the existence of Jenner's vaccine, smallpox persisted almost everywhere until the 1940s, when, through vaccination, it was eliminated from North America and Europe. Developing regions, especially in Africa and Asia, were not able to wipe out the disease until two organizations, the World Health Organization and the United Nation's Children's Fund, took the lead in providing vaccinations against smallpox in 1966. These organizations were positive outgrowths of World War II. In Ethiopia in 1976, the world's last cases of smallpox were recorded by UN doctors.

The Challenge of the Future

Developing nations, with their low per capita income and sparse industry, find it difficult to protect the health of their populations. Disease continues to thrive in poor living conditions. Vector-carried diseases like malaria are especially difficult to eliminate in areas as vast as Africa. Insect-killing chemical sprays or drugs are not always safe, available, or affordable.

In the global fight against disease, much depends on the cooperation of such groups as scientists, educators, doctors, patients, travelers, and funding organizations throughout the world. Such cooperation is necessary to protect people as technological inventions increase the mobility of the interacting global community.

STUDY SKILLS Understanding Geography

1. How could a world war stimulate interest in the study of diseases?
2. Explain the difference between the way in which yellow fever and smallpox are transmitted to humans.
3. What method is used to prevent smallpox?
4. Why would it be hard to eliminate a vector-carried disease in Africa?
5. Describe how the elimination of the diseases yellow fever and smallpox was the result of cooperation around the world.

2 The Worldwide Battlefield

Come On!
buy more
LIBERTY BONDS

OBJECTIVE: *To understand how World War I became a war of stalemate*

The War of Stalemate

When World War I broke out in August 1914, the nations of both alliances expected to win quick victories. Everyone, however, miscalculated. The Russians mobilized rapidly. The French failed to anticipate the German attack through Belgium. The Italians refused to come into the war on the side of their German and Austrian allies. Austria, much to its embarrassment, failed to conquer even little Serbia.

The Germans Fail to Defeat France. Germany's Schlieffen plan worked well at first. The German forces drove through Belgium and onto the flat plains of northeastern France. Then, as soldiers and horses became exhausted, the German advance slowed down.

In September 1914, French forces stopped the German advance at the Marne River, just 37 miles from Paris. Called the Miracle of the Marne, this battle forced the German army to fall back. German forces formed a battleline that stretched from the coast of Belgium southward to the mountains of Switzerland.

The French and German armies dug in for the winter. By the spring of 1915, a double line of trenches and barbed wire ran across northern and eastern France. The war on the western front became stalemated, or deadlocked.

The Eastern Front. Meanwhile, the Germans were forced to divert some of their forces to the eastern front. There, they achieved two victories over the Russians. However, the Germans could not defeat and occupy Russia. A different kind of stalemate developed on the eastern front. The battleline moved back and forth over long distances, but neither side could win a complete victory.

VOCABULARY DEVELOPMENT

stalemate (STAYL MAYT) *verb:* to bring to a standstill or deadlock.

Allies: in World War I, the nations that fought against the Central Powers, especially Great Britain, France, Russia, and the United States.

Central Powers: in World War I, the nations that opposed the Allies: Germany, Austria-Hungary, and later Bulgaria and Turkey.

attrition (uh TRIHSH uhn) *noun:* a gradual weakening or wearing to the point of exhaustion. From the Latin word, *atterere,* meaning to wear or to rub away.

reconnaissance (rih KAHN un suhns) *noun:* observation and examination in order to learn something, especially for military purposes. From the Latin word, *recognoscere,* meaning to learn again.

dirigible (DIHR uh juh buhl) *noun:* a balloonlike airship filled with a gas that is lighter than air. From the Latin word *dirigere,* meaning to direct, and the English suffix *-ible,* meaning able.

"Oh, What a Lovely War." In Great Britain, many young men volunteered for military service. Government propaganda in Britain created popular support. The British public looked forward to a "lovely war" that would bring victory over the Germans.

A Call for Soldiers

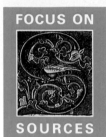

FOCUS ON SOURCES

In September 1914, David Lloyd George, chancellor of the exchequer, gave a speech in London. He called on the people of Great Britain to support the war effort. In the following excerpt, Lloyd George appealed to Britain's sense of honor. He also appealed to the sense of adventure and idealism:

❝ I am fully alive to the fact that every nation that has ever engaged in war has always invoked the sacred name of honor. Many a crime has been committed in its name; there are some being committed now. All the same, national honor is a reality, and any nation that disregards it is doomed. Why is our honor as a country involved in this war? Because, in the first instance, we are bound by honorable obligations to defend the independence, the liberty, the integrity, of a small neighbor that has always lived peaceably. . . . We entered into a treaty—a solemn treaty—two treaties—to defend Belgium and her integrity. Our signatures are attached to the documents. . . .

I envy you young people your opportunity. . . . It is a great opportunity that only comes once in many centuries to the children of men. For most generations sacrifice comes in drab and weariness of spirit. It comes to you today, and it comes today to us all, in the form of the glow and thrill of a great movement for liberty that impels [moves] millions through Europe to the same noble end. It is a great war for the emancipation [freedom] of Europe from the thralldom [slavery] of a military caste which has thrown its shadows upon two generations of men, and is now plunging the world into a welter [disordered state] of bloodshed and death. ❞ ■

Global Dimensions of the War

In the first months of the war, the two alliance systems expanded. Japan, as well as the little Balkan country of Montenegro, joined Britain, France, and Russia. All these nations were called the Allies. France and Britain also called up forces from their huge overseas dominions and colonial empires. By 1917 Greece, Portugal, Romania, and even Italy had joined the Allies.

Opposed to the Allies were the Central Powers: Germany, Austria-Hungary, and the Ottoman Empire. The Turks had formed a secret alliance with Germany just before the invasion of Belgium. Bulgaria also joined the Central Powers.

The United States kept to its tradition of isolation from European affairs and declared its neutrality. An American diplomat wrote to President Woodrow Wilson from London, "I thank heaven for many things— first the Atlantic Ocean."

The Major Fronts. The two main battlegrounds of the war were the eastern and western fronts. The western front stretched from the Swiss border through France to the North Sea. The eastern front extended through Poland and Russia. A third front opened in the Balkans in 1916.

The Allies attempted to establish a foothold on the Dardanelles in 1915 to defeat the Ottoman Empire. Thousands of Allied troops, many of them young Australians, died trying to fight their way up steep cliffs defended by Turkish artillery and machine guns. See the map on page 603.

After the Schlieffen Plan failed, the opposing sides dug networks of trenches. The trenches were about 6 feet deep and wide

World War I in Europe, 1914–1918

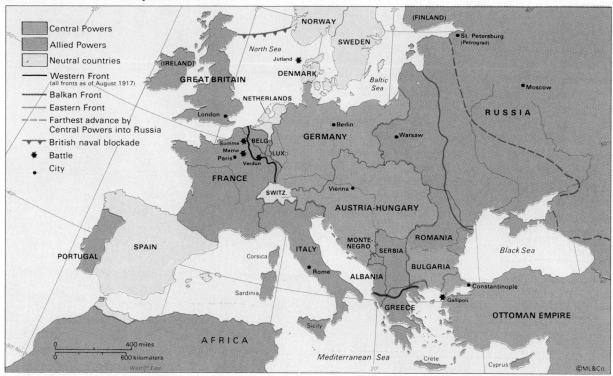

Map Skills **1.** Which countries formed the Central Powers? **2.** Which countries formed the Allied Powers? **3.** How close did the Central Powers advance to Paris during the war?

enough for two men to walk side by side. The opponents, facing each other across no-man's-land, realized they faced a long, bloody war on the western front.

War in the Middle East. In 1916, Arab subjects of the Ottoman Empire revolted against their Turkish masters. Led by Prince Faisal, an Arab of the noble Hashimite family, the rebellion spread from Arabia to Palestine and Syria. Both the British and the French supplied war materials and advisers to the Arab rebels. As the war progressed, the Ottoman Empire crumbled.

War in the Colonies. Early in the war, British, French, and Japanese forces attacked the German overseas empire. In Africa, Germany quickly lost all its colonies except German East Africa, later called Tanganyika. There, the Germans withstood the British, Portuguese, and Belgians.

Germany also held colonies in east Asia and the Pacific basin. Armed units from Australia, New Zealand, and Japan seized German Pacific island possessions. British and Japanese troops quickly drove the Germans from the Shantung Peninsula in China. As the German colonies fell, Japan emerged unchallenged as the most powerful imperial nation in Asia and the Pacific.

The New Weapons of Warfare. The defensive weapons on the western front were the technical products of industrialized countries. Weapons included high-powered rifles, air-cooled machine guns, and long-range cannons. These cannons, called howitzers, were designed to deliver deadly concentrated fire. A single shell could kill large numbers of people.

In 1915, the chemical industries of the opposing powers added poison gas to the horrors of war. Chlorine, and later mustard

Soldiers on the western front advance from their trenches in John Nash's *Over the Top.*

gasses, were blown into the wind to blind or kill thousands of soldiers.

War of Attrition. The fighting on the western front became a war of attrition. In a war of attrition, each side tries to outlast the other while inflicting heavier losses than are being suffered. Month after month, the armies killed each other's soldiers in a cycle of attack and counterattack.

Generals on both sides insisted that mass frontal attacks against the enemy were the only way to gain ground. Under cover of artillery fire, soldiers swarmed out of their trenches, clawing through the mud and barbed wire. They advanced only yards before the enemy's artillery and machine gun fire cut them down.

The Germans were in serious economic trouble by February 1916. To break the deadlock, the German general staff decided to attack the city of Verdun, France. They did not expect to win a major breakthrough of the Allied line. Instead, the Germans hoped to slowly destroy the French forces as the French fought to defend the city.

To take the pressure off the defenders of Verdun, a combined British and French force began a massive assault along the Somme River. On the first day of the Battle of the Somme, the British lost almost 60,000 men. Each minute during the first 24 hours, 15 British soldiers were killed and another 30 wounded.

During the Battle of the Somme, the British introduced another new weapon, the tank. A motorized armored tractor equipped with cannons and machine guns, the tank quickly became an important destructive weapon.

The battle at Verdun continued until December. There at Verdun, the Germans lost 330,000 soldiers and the French lost 350,000. Losses on the Italian front totaled about 300,000 troops. On the eastern front, perhaps as many as 2.1 million fell in battle. The Battle of the Somme claimed 1 million more casualties.

War under the Sea. The new German U-boats, submarines in English, were untested weapons of naval warfare. In 1915, the Germans began to use the undersea boats to blockade the British ports.

This submarine activity threatened the trading rights of neutral nations, such as the United States, who were supplying goods to the warring nations. Most of the United States trade was with Britain and France.

In naval warfare, combatants were required to tow nonmilitary ships to shore and release passengers and crews before seizing the ships. Submarines could not tow a vessel. When German U-boats began to sink ships bound for Allied ports, American lives were lost.

On May 7, 1915, a German submarine attacked and sank the British ocean liner, *Lusitania,* as it steamed through the Irish Sea. The ship sank quickly, taking 1,200 lives. Over 100 of those drowned were citizens of the United States. The *Lusitania* was secretly carrying arms and ammunition to Great Britain.

The sinking of the *Lusitania* brought the United States and Germany to the brink of war. Tensions increased during the next 10 months. On March 24, 1916, the Germans sank the French ship, *Sussex,* in the English Channel. Again, citizens of the United States were killed.

After the *Sussex* sank, Germans decided that their policy of unlimited submarine warfare would bring the United States into the war. To avoid this event, Germany stopped U-boat attacks on neutral ships. Attacks were limited to ships of nations at war with Germany. By 1916, however, the submarine was one of the most destructive weapons of war.

Fighting in the Air. World War I was the first air war in history. During the early stages of the war, countries used airplanes mostly for reconnaissance, scouting the positions of enemy troops. In 1915, the Germans began to use Fokker airplanes equipped with machine guns that could be fired through the whirling propeller. The Fokker became a powerful weapon.

The Germans also began to use large, heavier-than-air dirigibles, the Zeppelins. In January 1915, the Germans sent the first Zeppelins to bomb England. They launched 19 airship raids on the British Isles in 1915 and 41 in 1916.

The terrible bloodshed of the war caused the president of the United States, Woodrow Wilson, to try to negotiate an end to the fighting. He called for the nations to settle for "peace without victory." Wilson's appeal got nowhere. The combatants in Europe were not ready for peace. As the winter of 1916 approached, the armies stayed in their trenches.

SECTION 2 *Study Skills*

Developing Vocabulary Write a sentence using each of the following terms: **1.** stalemate. **2.** reconnaissance. **3.** dirigible. **4.** Explain what is meant by a war of attrition.

Reviewing Main Ideas 1. Why did World War I last longer than expected? **2.** Explain the result of the Battle of Verdun. **3.** How were airplanes and dirigibles used?

Understanding Cause and Effect 1. List new weapons developed for World War I. **2.** How did the Germans use submarines?

Understanding Geography 1. List the countries that fought for the Allies and for the Central Powers. **2.** Construct a map showing the major fronts of World War I.

Challenge Give examples of advances in technology during a war that benefit society after the war.

3 The Mexican and Russian Revolutions

OBJECTIVE: *To understand the causes and consequences of the Mexican and Russian Revolutions*

Twentieth Century Revolutions

World War I occurred during a time of widespread revolutions. In the early 1900s, revolutions in Persia, the Ottoman Empire, Mexico, and Russia reshaped the world.

The Mexican Revolution. In the early 1900s, aristocratic families and political strongmen dominated most Latin American countries. The working class and peasants lived in poverty and had no political power. Mexico was under the rule of a strongman named Porfirio Diaz who had the support of the land-owning families, foreign corporations, and the church. Mexico's peasants, who were mostly of Indian descent, were losing more and more of their land to great landlords. Diaz's rural police terror-ized them into submission. The country's growing middle class also felt deprived of power and urged liberal reforms.

Then in 1910, Francisco Madero, a middle class liberal, led a revolt against Diaz. The poor farmers inspired by Pancho Villa in the north and Emiliano Zapata in the south, joined the revolutionaries. Diaz fled the country, but fighting among revolutionary groups continued for ten years. The middle class wanted moderate reforms, but the oppressed peasants and urban workers wanted radical changes.

In 1917, the more radical groups wrote a new constitution for Mexico that created a democratic government with a strong presidency. The constitution limited the power of the church and gave the govern-

---

VOCABULARY DEVELOPMENT

hemophilia (HEE muh FIHL ee uh) *noun:* a hereditary condition in which blood does not clot. It occurs only in males but is transmitted by females.

hypnotize (HIHP nuh TYZ) *verb:* put someone into a state of altered consciousness. In this state the subconscious mind can respond to suggestions. From the Greek word, *hypnos,* meaning sleep.

conspirator (kuhn SPIHR uh tuhr) *noun:* a person who takes part in a conspiracy, a secret planning. From the Latin prefix *com-,* meaning together, and word *spirare,* meaning to breathe.

reactionary (ree AK shuh NER ee) *noun:* a person who resists change and prefers to return to a previous political or social system; an ultraconserva-tive. From the Latin prefix *re-,* meaning back; word *actus,* meaning moving; and suffix *-ary,* meaning relating to.

soviet (SOH vee iht) *noun:* any of the various governing councils in the Russian socialist system.

provisional (pruh VIHZH uhn uhl) *adj.:* temporary; for the time being. From the Latin prefix *pro-,* meaning before, and word *videre,* meaning to see.

military draft: the choosing of individuals for required service in a country's armed forces.

collective farm: a large farm formed by consolidating many small farms into a single, government-supervised unit.

ment the right to redistribute land to the peasants. It also controlled the activities of foreign companies, and set forth ambitious goals for labor reform and social welfare.

During the 1920s and 1930s, the government gradually carried out many reforms that benefited ordinary citizens.

The Russian Revolution

During World War I, a revolution in Russia affected the outcome of the war and much of later history.

Nicholas II Establishes a Duma. As in Mexico, the Russian people had suffered under autocratic rule for centuries. They won some self-government under Tsar Alexander II in 1881 (see page 577). His successors, Alexander III and Nicholas II, however, returned to a policy of oppression.

Then, in 1905, the Japanese defeated the Russians in a short war (see page 585). This embarrassing defeat revealed inefficiency in the Russian government. The loss also sparked a revolution. To weaken the revolutionaries, Nicholas II issued a decree called the October Manifesto. This document provided for the election of a parliament called the *Duma*. All new laws had to pass the Duma.

Causes of the Russian Revolution. The end of the Russo-Japanese War and the establishment of the Duma quieted reformers for a while. Then Nicholas again instituted autocratic policies. He dismissed two sessions of the Duma and changed the qualifications for voting to include only large and wealthy landowners.

During World War I, Nicholas II faced many of the same conditions that had led to the Revolution of 1905. In 1917, however, these conditions led to the Russian Revolution and a new government.

First, the Russian government was inefficient. This fact became apparent when the war effort was mismanaged. Food and

A Bolshevik poster from the Russian Revolution advocates a global revolution. The Bolsheviks proclaimed a soviet constitution for Russia in 1918.

fuel shortages led factory workers in St. Petersburg to organize a series of strikes.

Second, Russian losses on the battlefield shocked the people. Over 1.5 million Russians already had died, and another 5 million were wounded. About 2 million had been taken prisoner.

Third, members of the Duma criticized government management of the war and demanded reforms. Nicholas dissolved the Duma, but it continued to meet.

Fourth, when Nicholas called the army to put down an uprising by the factory workers, the soldiers joined the rioters. The revolt then spread to the countryside. Rebellious peasants wanted to own the land.

Despite the uprisings, however, many Russians continued to respect the tsar. They believed that he had been misled by his advisers or was unaware of the people's sacrifices and suffering.

Nicholas II was the last tsar of Russia. He is shown here with his wife, Alexandra, and their children shortly before the family was assassinated in 1918.

Nicholas II, Tsar of Russia

FOCUS ON PEOPLE

Nicholas II was born in St. Petersburg on May 18, 1868, the eldest son of Alexander III. Nicholas was brought up to believe in traditional, absolute rule even though some of the Russian people were ready for a change from the autocratic policies of the tsars. Nicholas married Princess Alexandra, whom he called Alix, of Hesse, Germany, on November 26, 1894, shortly after becoming tsar.

Alix was one of the numerous grandchildren of Britain's Queen Victoria. The first four children of Nicholas and Alix were girls. Disappointed at not having a male heir, the tsar sought help from fortune tellers, mystics, and any who offered hope.

The tsar and tsarina were, therefore, thrilled by the birth of their son, Alexis, on August 12, 1904. Their happiness changed to dismay. Doctors diagnosed the boy as having hemophilia, a disease causing uncontrollable bleeding.

Several advisers influenced Nicholas and Alix. Most unusual of the tsar's advisers was Rasputin (rahs POO tihn). A mysterious, brooding monk, Rasputin became the most powerful man in Russia. He seemed to hypnotize the young Alexis, at times stopping the dangerous flow of blood. This ability gave Rasputin control over the royal couple.

On Rasputin's advice, Nicholas dismissed the head of the army and directed the war effort himself. The cabinet was infuriated, and even the tsar's mother protested. Nicholas, however, went to the front. Soon after, the military situation worsened.

Meanwhile, the tsarina ruled Russia following Rasputin's advice. Russian leaders blamed Rasputin for the protests of Russian workers and soldiers. Finally, three members of the aristocracy set out to dispose of Rasputin. They first poisoned his food. The monk continued to eat and drink merrily. Then they shot him, but he roared and grabbed at his attackers. When Rasputin finally collapsed, they threw the supposedly dead body into the Neva River. A later autopsy showed that Rasputin had actually died by drowning.

The conspirators' murder of Rasputin solved no problems. The tsarina continued to listen to reactionary advisers and people lost faith in the tsar.

In March 1917, army units stationed in St. Petersburg mutinied. On March 12, opponents of the the tsar established a provisional government. Three days later, Nicholas II abdicated.

Nicholas II was the last tsar of Russia. In 1918, revolutionaries murdered him, his wife, and his children. ■

The Bolshevik Revolution

The Germans' inability to win on either the western or the eastern fronts led them to help a group of exiled Russian socialist revolutionaries, called Bolsheviks. The leader of the group was Vladimir Ulyanov, known in history as Lenin.

The Germans hoped that the Bolsheviks would stir unrest in Russia and hurt the Russian war effort. In April 1917, therefore, the German high command arranged to transport the group through Switzerland and Sweden back to Russia.

The Bolshevik Program. Lenin was a follower of Karl Marx. However, he modified the ideas of Marx to fit Russian conditions. Lenin advocated the formation of a disciplined party of revolutionaries. They were to organize the overthrow of the tsar's government. After the revolution, the party under Lenin would take over the factors of production. Lenin's adaptation of Marxism formed the basis for present-day Russian communism.

To gain the support of the Russian peasants, Lenin announced that the Bolsheviks would give them land. Lenin also promised to seize the factories and banks from their capitalist owners. Then he would improve working conditions. The Bolshevik slogan—Peace, Land, Bread—appealed to most Russian people. The party quickly became a major force in Russian politics.

The Petrograd Soviet adopted Lenin's ideas. The Petrograd Soviet was a council of workers from the major factories of Petrograd—the former name of Leningrad—that met to plan strikes. In 1917, most Soviet members became Bolsheviks.

The Provisional Government under Kerensky. In July 1917, four months after Nicholas abdicated, Alexander Kerensky became premier of Russia. Kerensky was a moderate socialist who had been a government minister under the tsar. Under Kerensky, the Russians launched an offensive on the east. Austria and Germany easily stopped them.

Lenin Overthrows the Provisional Government. Kerensky struggled on as head of the provisional government until autumn. However, the government had little power. Soldiers, deserting by the thousands, were returning home to claim their share of the land. Workers continued to strike.

Lenin organized a group called the Red Guards, after the popular color of European revolutionary socialists. The Red Guards were recruited from among the factory workers of Petrograd and Moscow. On November 6, 1917, they stormed the Winter Palace in Petrograd and overthrew the provisional government. This rising became known as the October Revolution.

Russia Leaves the War. Lenin viewed World War I as an international effort to benefit capitalism and promote imperialism. In order to achieve his objectives, Lenin needed to withdraw Russian forces and establish peace. In March 1918, he negotiated the Treaty of Brest-Litovsk with the Central Powers. Russia gave up Poland, Estonia, Latvia, Lithuania, Finland, and the Ukraine. They ceded land to the Turks and agreed to pay huge war reparations.

The price of peace was the loss of 34 percent of Russia's population and 32 percent of its best farming land. Lenin submitted to this humiliation because he believed

Soldiers hail the overthrow of the Tsar during a 1917 May Day parade through Palace Square in Petrograd. The banner reads, "Down with the old!"

that history was on his side. He felt that the revolution would eventually sweep out of Russia and overwhelm the world.

Communism in the Soviet Union

The Bolsheviks faced opposition in Russia. Supporters of the tsar, republicans, moderate socialists, and foreign military forces all opposed the Bolshevik revolutionaries.

In July 1918, Lenin proclaimed a soviet constitution for Russia. He changed the party's name to the Communist party. He also outlawed all rival parties and moved the government back to Moscow.

The Central Committee of the Communist party and its Politburo, or executive committee, held power in soviet Russia. Lenin and his assistants, Leon Trotsky and Josef Stalin, controlled the Politburo.

In 1918, an attempt on Lenin's life gave him the excuse to attack his enemies. He had many of his opponents killed, including intellectuals and professionals. Many people fled from Russia.

The Russian Civil War. Between 1917 and 1920, Russians fought each other in a civil war. Trotsky led the government army, called the Red Army. They eventually destroyed the disunited opposition, called the White Army. A military draft and strict discipline made the Red Army powerful.

The French and British intervened against the Bolsheviks in the Ukraine in 1919. They prolonged the civil war, but their support of the White Army was too little to bring victory. By the spring of 1920, the Bolsheviks controlled nearly the whole Ukraine. By the end of 1920, the Soviets had reestablished the old Russian frontiers in the Caucasus and central Asia.

The New Economic Policy. Most of the Allied occupation forces had withdrawn from Russia by 1920. Russian communism survived but at a terrible price. In the fighting and the famine that followed, 13 million people died. The Russian economy collapsed. Industrial production was about 15 percent of the 1913 level.

In 1921, Lenin introduced his New Economic Policy, NEP. The reforms under the NEP allowed peasants to sell farm products on the free market. Businesses had more freedom to operate. The NEP helped to restore some prosperity to the Soviet Union.

In 1922, Lenin reorganized the country into a vast federal republic. Each region became a republic controlled from Moscow. Together, these republics formed the Union of Soviet Socialist Republics, or USSR. Not until 1928, however, did the country recover to a point somewhat near its prewar level of economic production.

A Communist Government. Lenin died in January 1924, after a brief illness. Trotsky and Stalin immediately battled for control of the government.

Trotsky and his followers advocated an immediate international Communist revolution. Stalin and his supporters followed their motto—Today Russia, Tomorrow the World! Stalin believed that the Communist revolution had to be completed in Russia before it could be exported.

In 1926, Stalin won the struggle and expelled Trotsky and his supporters from the Politburo. Trotsky was forced into exile in 1929 and later assassinated.

Stalin's Five-Year Plans. Stalin began the first Five-Year Plan to promote rapid industrial growth. To strengthen the national defense, the government encouraged the development of heavy industry. At the same time, collective farms replaced the agricul-

tural system of the country. No individual farmers on collective farms own land.

Many peasants resisted Stalin's collectivization. Stalin suppressed opposition by having millions of rural people killed, sent to labor camps, or forced onto collective farms. Soviets suffered from a famine in 1932 and 1933 while farms were being turned into collectives.

In 1933, Stalin began his second Five-Year Plan. When the old Bolsheviks complained that Stalin was betraying the revolution, he reacted brutally. He executed many of his opponents in the Communist party and became the absolute dictator of the Soviet Union.

The Soviet Union changed during the 1920s, to a communistic society. Under the Five-Year Plans, the communist leaders encouraged industrialization. They began to build a new economic system but at a staggering cost to the Soviet people.

SECTION 3 *Study Skills*

Developing Vocabulary Write a sentence using each of the following terms: **1.** conspirator. **2.** reactionary. **3.** soviet. **4.** provisional.

Reviewing Main Ideas **1.** How did Lenin gain the support of the Russian people? **2.** What was the purpose of the NEP? **3.** What was the purpose of the Five-Year Plans? **4.** How did the Mexican Constitution of 1917 attempt to reform Mexico?

Understanding Cause and Effect **1.** List the causes of the Russian Revolution. **2.** Why did the Germans help Lenin and the Bolsheviks? **3.** Explain the causes and results of the Mexican Revolution.

Understanding Chronology **1.** Explain Lenin's actions of July 1918. **2.** List significant events in Russian history from 1905 to 1933.

Challenge What problems might the Five-Year Plans present in Russia today?

4 *The Cost of the Great War*

OBJECTIVE: *To understand the consequences of World War I*

The Last Years of the War

In January 1917, a German foreign minister, Alfred Zimmermann, sent a secret telegram to the German ambassador in Mexico. Zimmermann instructed his messenger to promise Mexico parts of the southwestern United States if it would attack its northern neighbor. The British intercepted the telegram, decoded it, and sent it to Washington. American newspapers published the message, and the people of the United States demanded war.

The United States Enters the War. In addition to the Zimmermann telegram, Germany's resumption of unlimited submarine warfare angered the United States. In February 1917, German U-boats sank 540,000

tons of merchant shipping. The United States Congress declared war on Germany on April 6, 1917.

The United States and its allies responded to the German attacks with the convoy system. Convoys were groups of ships that sailed together for protection. Huge merchant fleets began to move soldiers and supplies across the Atlantic. Guarded by American destroyers and subchasers, these convoys poured reinforcements into France.

German Advances. In March 1918, just 18 days after the signing of the Treaty of Brest-Litovsk, German troops could be transferred from the Russian front to the West. The Germans began a furious assault on the western front. They attacked with a heavy bombardment of artillery fire and gas bombs. They began to drive the British, French, and Belgian troops toward the sea.

The German army pushed forward, and by July had reached the Marne River. Four years earlier, at the beginning of the war, the French had stopped the German advance at this river. Here again, the Allies stopped the Germans at the Second Battle of the Marne. In September, the Allies began a counteroffensive.

Allied Counterattack. Bolstered by fresh troops from the United States, the Allied forces began to drive the exhausted Germans back toward the east.

VOCABULARY DEVELOPMENT

armistice (AHR muh stihs) *noun:* an agreement to temporarily stop fighting before signing a peace treaty. From the Latin words *arma,* meaning arms, and *stitium,* meaning stand still.

displaced person: someone forced to leave home and country, usually because of war.

epidemic (EHP uh DEHM ihk) *adj.:* spreading rapidly among the people; widespread. From the Greek prefix *epi-,* meaning among, and word *demos,* meaning people.

malnutrition (MAL noo TRIHSH uhn) *noun:* poor health resulting from a lack of proper food. From the Latin words *malus,* meaning bad, and *nutrire,* meaning to nourish.

The Armistice. In September, Bulgaria asked for an armistice. By the end of October, the Ottoman Empire had surrendered. On November 3, 1918, Austria-Hungary signed an armistice, or cease-fire ending its involvement in the war.

On November 7, 1918, the people of Bavaria, in southern Germany, rebelled against the German government. Within 48 hours, Kaiser Wilhelm II abdicated. The Prussian House of Hohenzolern had joined the Russian Romanovs and the Austrian Hapsburgs in exile. Revolutionaries marched in the streets of Berlin. On November 9, 1918, the Social Democrats proclaimed a German Republic.

Two days later, at 11:00 A.M. on November 11, 1918, a general armistice went into effect. The guns fell silent on the western front. At the eleventh hour of the eleventh day of the eleventh month, after more than four years of fighting, World War I finally came to an end.

Death and Destruction

In European history, few events equal World War I in destructiveness. Only the Black Death of the fourteenth century and the Thirty Years War of the seventeenth century were comparable. The tremendous destruction of the war resulted in physical, psychological, and economic hardship, as well as political change.

The Human Costs. The official statistics for World War I indicate that 9.1 million soldiers and sailors were killed in action, or died of wounds or disease. More than 21 million military personnel were wounded. Another 7.4 million were taken prisoner or were listed as missing in action. These figures do not include civilian casualties.

In addition, hundreds of thousands of innocent civilians were driven from their homes during or immediately after the war. Many of these people, called displaced persons, never returned to their native lands.

The Influenza Epidemic. Medical advances limited the outbreaks of typhoid and dysentery that usually accompanied war. Nevertheless, the health costs of the war were terrible. The hardships of war prepared the way for the great influenza epidemic of 1918–1919.

Dangerous shortages of food and fuel set the stage for an epidemic. Weakened and disheartened, many people were suffering from malnutrition. After four years of war, weakened people were nearly defenseless against a rapidly spreading epidemic of respiratory flu.

The flu reached its most critical stage at the end of the war and had disappeared by the spring of 1919. The epidemic left between 21 and 27 million people dead. About 45 percent of those who died were between 15 and 35 years old.

World War I caused tremendous physical and psychological destruction as suggested here in Kaethe Kollwitz's 1923 charcoal drawing, *The Survivors.*

More than 21 million military personnel were wounded and nearly 8 million taken prisoner during the war. This 1918 painting by Harvey Dunn is called *Prisoners and Wounded*.

The Psychological Costs. Between 1914 and 1919, as many as 42 million people lost their lives from war wounds, as well as war-related famine and diseases. Many of these victims were the young people who would have become the political, social, and economic leaders in their countries.

The war affected philosophers and artists deeply. Since the beginning of the Enlightenment, technological progress and political justice seemed to be bringing positive change. To technologically oriented people, the culture of Europe and the United States seemed superior to others. Yet, people of these cultures had fought the most brutal, deadly war in history. Technological power had made killing more efficient. The destructive power of the airplanes, tanks, and submarines developed and used in the war made some people question the value of the world's technological progress.

Further, the war shook many peoples' faith in European political systems. The leaders could not prevent a war that no one really wanted.

Literature and the War

FOCUS ON SOCIETY

Nine years after the end of the war, German author Erich Maria Remarque published a novel describing trench warfare. The book, *All Quiet on the Western Front*, described the suffering and senseless slaughter of the war. In this excerpt, Remarque describes being shelled:

❝ We come to the communication-trench and then to the open fields. The little wood reappears; we know every foot of ground here. There's the cemetery with the mounds and the black crosses.

That moment it breaks out behind us, swells, roars and thunders. We duck down—a cloud of flame shoots up a hundred yards ahead of us.

The next minute under a second explosion part of the wood rises slowly in the air, three or four trees sail up and then crash to pieces. The shells begin to hiss like safety-valves—heavy fire—

"Take cover!" yells somebody—"Cover!"

The fields are flat, the wood is too distant and dangerous—the only cover is the graveyard and the mounds. We stumble across in the dark and as though spirited away every man lies glued behind a mound.

Not a moment too soon. The dark goes mad. It heaves and raves. Darknesses blacker than the night rush on us with giant strides, over us and away. The flames of the explosions light up the graveyard.

There is no escape anywhere . . .

The dull thud of the gas-shells mingles with the crashes of the high explosives. A bell sounds between the explosions, gongs, and metal clappers warning everyone—Gas—Gas—Gaas.

. . . I wipe the goggles of my mask clear of the moist breath. . . .

These first minutes with the mask decide between life and death: is it tightly woven? I remember the awful sights in the hospital: the gas patients who in day-long suffocation cough their burnt lungs up in clots.

Cautiously, the mouth applied to the valve, I breathe. The gas still creeps over the ground and sinks into all hollows.

. . . Someone lies in front of us. We stop. . .

The man on the ground is a recruit [new member]. His hip is covered with blood. . . .

We cut off his trousers carefully. He groans. "Gently, gently, it is much better—"

If he has been hit in the stomach he oughtn't to drink anything. There's no vomiting, that's a good sign. We lay the hip bare. It is one mass of mincemeat and bone splinters. The joint has been hit. This lad won't walk any more. . .

. . . I say to the youngster who looks at us fixedly: "We're going for a stretcher now—"

Then he opens his mouth and whispers: "Stay here—"

"We'll be back again soon," says Kat. "We are only going to get a stretcher for you."

Kat looks around and whispers: "Shouldn't we just take a revolver and put an end to it?"

The youngster will hardly survive the carrying, and at the most he will only last a few days. What he has gone through so far is nothing to what he's in for till he dies. Now he is numb and feels nothing. In an hour he will become one screaming bundle of intolerable pain. Every day that he can live will be a howling torture. And to whom does it matter whether he has them [the days] or not— " ■

Economic Consequences of the War

The economy of combatant countries suffered from the enormous loss of land, property, and shipping.

Much of northeastern France, Poland, Serbia, and northeastern Italy was turned into wasteland. In France alone, nearly 3,000 square miles of forest lands had been burned and 8,000 square miles of farmlands destroyed. Around Verdun, for a generation after the war, mechanized farming was impossible because of the metal fragments that filled the soil.

Property damage presented economic hardship to the people of both rural and urban areas. Farmers lost over 1 million head of livestock. In the cities, over 600,000 buildings were destroyed or damaged. Bridges, highways, tunnels, canals, railroads, and telegraph and telephone lines had been torn apart or blown up.

The Price of the War. The monetary cost of war is difficult to measure. Human life cannot be assigned a monetary value. Destruction of property can be estimated only roughly. When all factors are considered, the approximate cost of World War I was between $330 and $375 billion.

The Legacy of the Great War. World War I was the most expensive and destructive

Combatant countries suffered enormous losses of land and property. Sir George Clausen's 1919 painting *Returning to the Reconquered Land* illustrates the losses.

conflict in history before 1914. The war broke the Russian, German, Austro-Hungarian, and Ottoman empires. The Romanov, Hohenzollern, and Hapsburg dynasties fell from power. Most of the map of Europe and southwest Asia was redrawn. The German overseas empire was divided among the winners.

The war devastated France and Russia. Italy, Germany, Austria, Belgium, and Great Britain were exhausted. The United States tried to retreat into isolationism. Famine, disease, and warfare had torn apart the old European national states and empires. Peace did come after four long years of slaughter. The Germans were not yet ready to accept their defeat. The next 20 years served as a prelude to an even greater and more terrible global conflict.

SECTION 4 *Study Skills*

Developing Vocabulary Define the following terms: **1.** displaced person. **2.** epidemic. **3.** malnutrition. **4.** Explain the difference between an armistice and a treaty.

Reviewing Main Ideas 1. How successful were convoys in protecting shipping? **2.** What was the dollar cost of World War I?

Understanding Cause and Effect 1. Why was the flu epidemic so destructive? **2.** How did the war affect people's faith in governments?

Understanding Chronology 1. When did the United States enter World War I? **2.** List the major events of October 1918.

Challenge Besides the loss of life, what other problems are associated with war?

CHAPTER 26 *Summary & Review*

Summarizing Main Ideas

In the century prior to 1914, each European nation pursued policies to increase its power. Alliances became necessary as countries looked for assistance to protect their interests. Europe was divided into opposing camps. Germany, Italy, and Austria-Hungary made up the Triple Alliance, while France, Great Britain, and Russia formed the Triple Entente. From August 1914 to the winter of 1918, World War I raged in Europe. Even with the introduction of new weapons, neither side was able to achieve a clear-cut victory.

In 1910, the peasants and middle-class liberals of Mexico began a ten-year struggle for changes. Pancho Villa and Emiliano Zapata led the revolutionaries, and a new constitution was written in 1917.

In 1917, a revolution in Russia established a new government. In 1918, Lenin outlawed all but the Communist party. Russia withdrew from World War I. In 1922, Lenin organized the Soviet Union.

Losses of World War I (in millions)			
Losses	Allied Powers	Central Powers	Total
Human Losses			
number of dead	5.2	3.9	9.1
number wounded	12.2	9.6	21.7
number missing	4.2	3.2	7.4
Monetary Losses			
war expenditure	$145.	$63.0	$208.0
property loss on land	*	*	$30,000.0
ship and cargo	*	*	$ 7.0
loss of production	*	*	$ 45.0
loss to neutrals	*	*	$ 2.7
war relief	*	*	$ 1,000.0
*no individual information available			

Questions for Critical Thinking

COMPREHENSION   Interpreting Events

1. How did Austria make war unavoidable?
2. How successful were the NEP and the Five-Year Plans?
3. Compare the motivations of the peasants and middle-class in the Mexican Revolution.

ANALYSIS   Identifying Trends

1. Explain how growing trade competition led to war.
2. How can nationalism be both a positive and a negative influence?

APPLICATION   Comparing Past and Present

1. How does trade competition cause tensions today?
2. Could discontent over war lead to the overthrow of a modern government, as it did in Russia in 1917? Explain.
3. Explain how attitudes toward war have changed since 1914.

SYNTHESIS   Developing Writing Skills

1. Write a book report on *All Quiet on the Western Front* or *Johnny Get Your Gun*. Discuss the author's views of war.
2. Compare and contrast the weapons introduced during World War I with those used during the American Revolution.

EVALUATION   Weighing Consequences

1. Explain how a world war resulted from the alliance system.
2. Can there be a winner in a war of attrition? Explain.

CHALLENGE

1. Do wars generally settle the basic problems that cause them? Give examples from World War I to explain your answer.
2. Use the chart to summarize the human and monetary losses that resulted from World War I.

CHAPTER 27
The Troubled Peace

1918   1920   1922   1924   1926

TIME

● **1918** Paris Peace Conference convenes

● **1919** Treaty of Versailles brings peace

● **1919** Allies establish the League of Nations

● **1921** United States passes restrictive immigration laws

PEOPLE

● **1918** President Wilson presents his peace plan, the Fourteen Points

● **1919** Mohandas Gandhi becomes the leader of India's Congress party

1920s Ibn Saud conquers much of Arabia

● **1921** Lenin introduces the New Economic Policy in Russia

● **1922** Mustapha Kemal becomes the military dictator of Turkey

PLACE

● **1919** *France;[1]* Delegates to the Peace Conference meet at Versailles

● **1920** *Arabia;[2]* Ibn Saud founds Saudi Arabia

● **1922** *Turkey;[3]* Turks defeat Greek invaders and reconquer much of Armenia

● **1922** *Iraq;[4]* Iraq becomes an independent state

● **1922** *Russia;[5]* Russia becomes the Union of Soviet Socialist Republics

● **1923** *Germany;[6]* Germans suffer from high inflation

Linking Past to Present

One of the forces for peace on the globe today is the United Nations. This organization, headquartered in New York City, provides an international forum for discussing solutions to worldwide problems. Through discussion, nations hope to avoid armed conflicts in the future.

The idea for an international organization like the United Nations was first acted on over 70 years ago. In 1918, many people believed they had fought World War I to make the world safe for democracy. In order to preserve the peace and foster democractic principles, the postwar leaders established the League of Nations. As you read the chapter, try to determine whether leaders of the powerful nations of the world in the 1920s could have strengthened the League of Nations.

A detail from Childe Hassam's *Allies Day, May 1917.*

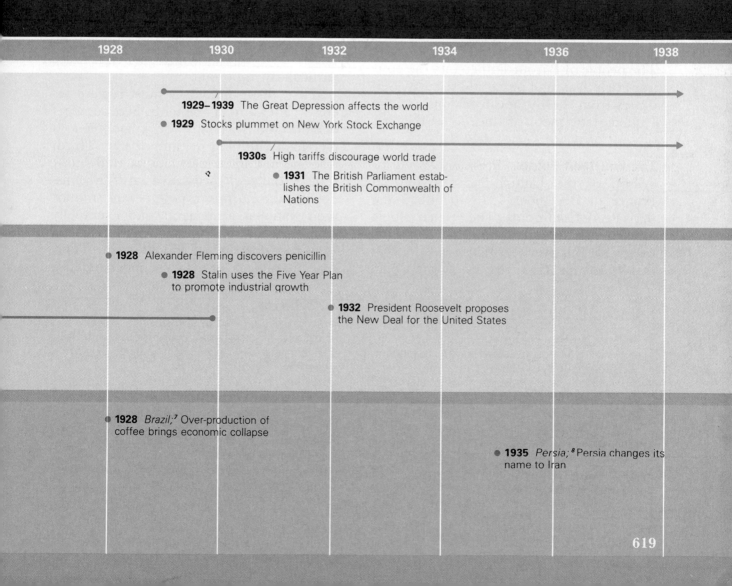

| 1928 | 1930 | 1932 | 1934 | 1936 | 1938 |

1929–1939 The Great Depression affects the world

1929 Stocks plummet on New York Stock Exchange

1930s High tariffs discourage world trade

1931 The British Parliament establishes the British Commonwealth of Nations

1928 Alexander Fleming discovers penicillin

1928 Stalin uses the Five Year Plan to promote industrial growth

1932 President Roosevelt proposes the New Deal for the United States

1928 *Brazil;*[7] Over-production of coffee brings economic collapse

1935 *Persia;*[8] Persia changes its name to Iran

619

1 *The Search for a Lasting Peace*

OBJECTIVE: *To understand the causes and consequences of the treaty signed at Versailles in 1919*

The Paris Peace Conference

World War I exhausted the resources of the great nations of Europe. For half a century, these nations had nearly dominated the world. The Great War, however, reduced populations and natural resources. The losses shattered confidence in the future. The people of Europe limped into the postwar era in search of peace and security. Delegates from the European nations and the United States met in France to set the conditions for peace.

The Fourteen Points. President Woodrow Wilson of the United States arrived in France in December 1918 to attend the Paris Peace Conference. The French people welcomed him with wild enthusiasm. One reason for this overwhelming reception was that Wilson had come to Europe with a plan that many believed would ensure a lasting world peace.

Wilson's plan, the Fourteen Points, sought to prevent future wars by dealing with the problems that caused the Great War. Wilson encouraged the adoption of certain international principles to reduce rivalries. Five of the Fourteen Points were particularly important.

First, open diplomacy must replace secret treaties and agreements. Second, freedom of the seas must be guaranteed to merchant shipping in time of war. Third, free and unlimited international trade must replace the high protective tariff systems. Fourth, the European powers must reduce their national armaments and eventually demilitarize. Fifth, nations must create a "general association of nations" to give "mutual guarantees of political independence

---

VOCABULARY DEVELOPMENT

delegate (DEHL uh giht) *noun:* a person chosen to speak for others at a meeting or convention; a representative. From the Latin word, *delegare,* meaning to send from one place to another, appoint, or assign.

professional diplomat: a person whose career involves the conduct of relations between nations.

premier (PREE mee uhr) *noun:* the prime minister of any of certain countries. From the Latin word, *primus,* meaning first.

compromise (KAHM pruh MYZ) *noun:* a settlement in which both sides make concessions, yield some

demands, or modify some possessions. From the Latin prefix *com-,* meaning together, and word *promittere,* meaning promise.

reparation (REHP uh RAY shuhn) *noun:* a making of amends by paying debts, such as by a nation defeated in war. From the Latin word, *reparare,* meaning to repair.

mandate *noun:* a command or formal order; a commission from the League of Nations to a country to administer a certain region; an authoritative order. From the Latin word, *mandatum,* meaning to entrust.

---

and territorial integrity to great and small states alike."

Wilson felt the fifth point was the most important. The association, called the League of Nations, was the first serious attempt to establish a form of global government.

The Armistice. The German leaders signed an armistice on November 11, 1918. The cease-fire required the Germans to withdraw from all occupied territory. They also had to surrender their heavy artillery, submarines, and most of the navy. The Allies sent an army to occupy Germany.

The Allies hoped to make it impossible for the Germans to fight another war. In order to tighten their control of Germany, the Allies maintained a naval blockade on all German ports. This action restricted shipments of vital food and medical supplies to the disabled German people. The Germans would not forget such treatment.

Delegates to the Peace Conference. In January 1919, delegates from 27 countries met at the Palace of Versailles, near Paris. Professional diplomats did most of the work at the conference. The major decisions, though, were reserved for the Big Four. These men were the leaders of the four most powerful nations. Woodrow Wilson represented the United States; Georges Clemenceau (KLAY MAHN SOH), France; David Lloyd George, Great Britain; and Vittorio Orlando, Italy. The Big Four determined the final terms of the Treaty of Versailles.

Orlando, representing Italy, was the least influential of the four leaders. Woodrow Wilson attempted to dominate the proceedings. He was convinced that he knew the best way to end war. Wilson believed that creating a League of Nations would lead to lasting peace.

Georges Clemenceau was known as the Tiger of France. The 78-year-old French

Europe after the Treaty of Versailles, 1923

Map Skills **1.** Which territories were lost by the Soviet Union? Which were gained? **2.** Identify the area between France and Germany that both countries wished to control.

premier hoped for security from the Germans. Clemenceau disagreed with President Wilson and referred to him as "another Savior come upon earth to reform men." Lloyd George of Great Britain tried to work out compromises between Wilson's idealism and Clemenceau's demands.

One of the sharpest disagreements between Clemenceau and Wilson was over treatment of the defeated countries. Wilson disliked the idea of punishing the Central Powers. However, to win support for his dream, the League of Nations, he agreed. He did, however, block some of the harshest demands of the French and Italian delegates. The Treaty of Versailles represented compromises among the Big Four.

The Treaty of Versailles

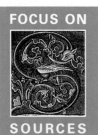

FOCUS ON SOURCES

The Treaty of Versailles formally ended war between the Allied Powers and Germany. The treaty was signed in the Hall of Mirrors in the Palace of Versailles on June 28, 1919. The Allies chose both the time and the place to humiliate Germany. The date was the fifth anniversary of the assassination of the Grand Duke, Franz Ferdinand, at Sarajevo. That event was the spark that began World War I. The place was the same hall where, in 1871, the German delegates had proclaimed the German Empire (see page 573). Following are several articles from the treaty:

" Article 42. Germany is forbidden to maintain or construct any fortifications either on the left bank of the Rhine or on the right bank. . . of the Rhine.

Article 43. In the area defined above the maintenance and the assembly of armed forces, either permanently or temporarily, and military maneuvers of any kind, as well as the upkeep of all permanent works for mobilization are in the same way forbidden.

Article 45. As compensation for the destruction of the coal-mines in the north of France and as part payment towards the total reparation due from Germany for the damage resulting from the war, Germany cedes to France in full and absolute possession, with exclusive rights of exploitation [using productivity], unencumbered and free from all debts and charges of any kind, the coal-mines situated in the Saar Basin as defined in Article 48.

Article 119. Germany renounces in favour of the Principal Allied and Associated [nations that supported the Allies] Powers all her rights and titles over her overseas possessions.

Article 231. The Allied and Associated Governments affirm, and Germany accepts, the responsibility of Germany and her allies for causing all the loss and damage to which the Allied and Associated Governments and their nationals have been subjected as a consequence of the war imposed upon them by the aggression of Germany and her allies.

Article 232. The Allied and Associated Governments recognize that the resources of Germany are not adequate, after taking into account permanent diminutions [decreases] of such resources which will result from other provisions of the present Treaty, to make complete reparation for all such loss and damage.

The Allied and Associated Governments, however, require, and Germany undertakes, that she will make compensation for all damage done to the civilian population of the Allied and Associated Powers and to their property during the [war]. . . . **"**

In addition to punishing Germany, the delegates to the treaty conference redrew the map of Europe. They attempted to redraw national boundaries. The delegates wanted to arrange the map to include similar ethnic groups within the same nation. See the map, Europe after the Treaty of Versailles, 1923, page 621.

A painting by James Guthrie depicts the Allied leaders of World War I. Winston Churchill is full-face at center. David Lloyd George from Great Britain sits third from the left.

Territorial Settlements

The Treaty of Versailles created several new nations which received their land from portions of Germany, Austria-Hungary, and the Soviet Union. The Soviet Union, though among the Allied Powers when the war began, lost the most territory.

The New Map of Europe. In eastern Europe, the Treaty of Versailles established Finland, Estonia, Latvia, Lithuania, Poland, and Yugoslavia as independent countries. In central Europe, Czechoslovakia became independent. The Austro-Hungarian Empire was dismantled, and Austria and Hungary became separate nations. Italy, Greece,

Romania, Belgium, and Denmark gained land at the expense of the former countries that were the Central Powers.

The creation of nine new countries complicated European politics. The new governments were inexperienced and unstable. Czechoslovakia and Yugoslavia had such diverse populations that neither had a strong sense of national unity. Not one of the nine new countries could defend itself if threatened. Thus, military alliances began to form shortly after the treaties were ratified.

The New Map of the Middle East. Boundaries and governments also changed in southwest Asia—the Middle East. The

Ottoman Empire, which had lasted nearly 600 years, finally came to an end. The Turks lost much of the territory they had once ruled. By 1922, however, the Republic of Turkey had emerged as a unified and generally stronger country. Mustafa Kemal (keh MAHL) Atatürk, a military strongman, was responsible for saving Turkey from being dismembered by the Allies. He crushed a Greek invasion of his country in 1922. He also undertook a radical program to modernize Turkey. The Turkish people regard Mustafa Kemal Atatürk as the father of their modern nation.

Lands formerly part of the Ottoman Empire were divided under the authority of the League of Nations. France was given a mandate over Syria and Lebanon. A mandate required the administering power to treat the territory as a temporary trust and prepare the people for self-government.

Great Britain gained a mandate over Trans-Jordan and Palestine. The British also took possession of most of Mesopotamia. In 1922, though, the independent state of Iraq was created, and Britain formed an alliance with the Iraqi government.

In Arabia, the Hijaz was recognized as an independent kingdom. During the 1920s, Ibn Saud conquered most of Arabia and proclaimed himself king. Saud was a strict Muslim of the Wahhabis sect (see page 554). In 1932, he renamed this kingdom Saudi Arabia.

The New Map of Africa and the Pacific. The peace treaty also changed the map of Africa. The victors were to supervise former German colonies for the League of Nations. The British took over the German colonies of Southwest Africa and East Africa, later called Tanganyika. South Africa was given control of South West Africa, now called Namibia, which it still holds today.

France received part of Togo and part of the Cameroons. In the Pacific, Australia, New Zealand, and Japan received mandates over former German colonies. The Japanese incorporated the Mariana, Marshall, and Caroline island systems into their empire. This move strengthened the Japanese position in the central Pacific. Japan's stronger position, though, increased the possibility of conflict between Japan and the other Pacific Ocean powers, especially the United States.

The Bitter Aftermath

The Treaty of Versailles was signed on June 28, 1919. That same day, Wilson entered into a military defense pact with Great Britain and France. This defense pact illustrated the uncertainty of the postwar era. Nearly everyone expected trouble in the aftermath of the Peace Conference.

Continuing Conflicts. President Wilson dreamed of eternal peace, but the Versailles settlement brought no real peace. Several countries continued to disagree over boundaries. Land conflicts pitted Poland against Germany, Czechoslovakia, Lithuania, and Russia. Austria and Hungary, Greece and Turkey, Italy and Yugoslavia, and Russia and Finland were all locked in similar boundary disputes. Ireland, Mexico, China, and Russia were fighting civil wars. War continued in Arabia. The British were fighting in Afghanistan, and violence was increasing in India. In conjunction with the Russian Revolution, communist uprisings occurred in several scattered spots throughout the world.

The Allies ended their blockade of Germany in July 1919. By then, many Germans were desperately hungry. Germany was in disorder. The new republican government had crushed several uprisings, but unrest and demonstrations continued.

Germans Object to the Treaty. The treaty made the Germans angry and resentful. The victorious countries stripped away large amounts of German territory. They abolished the German air force and dramatically reduced the size of the army and navy. One of the terms of the treaty was that Germany had to ship its valuable coal to France and Belgium for the next 10 years.

Germany was also expected to pay war reparations amounting to $5 billion within 2 years and an additional $33 billion over the next 30 years. The treaty severely handicapped the German economy.

The final blow to German pride was Article 231 of the Treaty of Versailles (see page 622). Called the War Guilt Clause, the article stated that Germany was fully responsible for starting the war. The Germans, however, were angered because they believed that the war started as a conflict between Austria-Hungary and Serbia.

Other Nations Object to the Treaty. Like Germany, other countries objected to the Treaty of Versailles. Italy felt cheated by the agreements. Italy had made secret treaties with the Allies in 1915. In return, Italy was to receive the Tyrol and Trieste, lands on Italy's northern border. Lloyd George, Wilson, and Clemenceau were willing to give Italy only the Tyrol. An embittered Orlando walked out of the conference.

The United States, despite Wilson's support, rejected the Treaty of Versailles. Since the treaty provided for a defensive alliance with Great Britain and France, the United States Senate was apprehensive. Senators also feared that the League of Nations might again embroil them in European affairs. The people of the United States did not want to be involved in Europe, and the Senate refused to ratify the treaty.

The French were also unhappy because they thought that the agreement did not sufficiently punish the Germans. Only some of the British seemed satisfied with the peace treaty.

The Treaty of Versailles left a legacy of bitterness. The peacemakers failed to solve the problems facing the postwar world. These problems dominated global relations for the next 20 years.

OVERWEIGHTED

President Wilson: *Here's your olive branch. Now get busy.*

Dove of Peace: *Of course I want to please everybody; but isn't this a bit thick?*

SECTION 1 *Study Skills*

Developing Vocabulary **1.** What are the differences and similarities between the roles of a premier and a prime minister? **2.** What compromises did delegates make during negotiations over the Treaty of Versailles? **3.** Why was Germany required to pay reparations after the war?

Reviewing Main Ideas **1.** Summarize the major parts of Wilson's Fourteen Points. **2.** What was the purpose of the Treaty of Versailles? **3.** As a result of the treaty, what happened to many countries' boundaries and territories?

Understanding Geography **1.** List the nine new European countries created by the Treaty of Versailles. **2.** Explain the European involvement in the Middle East.

Challenge Why is compromise so difficult among nations?

2 Postwar Shifts in Power

OBJECTIVE: *To understand the causes and consequences of the colonial independence movements and the shift in world power away from Europe*

Colonial Independence Movements

World War I exhausted the great nations of Europe. The centers of world power shifted to such rising nations as the United States and Japan. The war also reshaped the attitudes of many of the colonial peoples around the world. Colonies began to demand their independence.

The British Commonwealth. The far-reaching overseas dominions of the British Empire helped the Allies to win the war.

VOCABULARY DEVELOPMENT

commonwealth *noun:* an association of self-governing states that hold a common allegiance, as to the British crown; a nation, state, or other political unit.

corporation (KAWR puh RAY shuhn) *noun:* an association of employers and employees. From the Latin word, *corporare*, meaning to make into a body.

civil disobedience: nonviolent protest of a government policy or law by refusing to comply with it.

superficial (SOO puhr FIHSH uhl) *adj.:* apparent; seeming on the surface. From the Latin prefix *super-*, meaning above, and word *facies*, meaning face.

depression (dih PREHSH uhn) *noun:* a period of declining business activity, high unemployment, and falling prices and wages. From the Latin word, *depressus*, meaning to press down, to sink.

Dominions are self-governing nations that recognize the British monarch as their chief of state. The dominions of Canada, Australia, New Zealand, and the Union of South Africa all contributed money and soldiers to help Great Britain.

After the war, Canadians, Australians, and New Zealanders wanted complete self-government within the British Empire. Great Britain faced pressures for equality and freedom throughout its empire.

In late 1926, the British held an Imperial Conference in London. At this conference, delegates from British possessions determined the basic structure of a new imperial organization. In 1931, the British Parliament officially established the British Commonwealth of Nations.

Commonwealth members were independent states within the British Empire. Each member was equal in status but united by a common allegiance to the crown.

Some Commonwealth members enjoyed more self-government than others. Canada, Australia, New Zealand, and the Union of South Africa were in effect independent nations. Inhabitants of European ancestry dominated these countries. Other areas, such as Nigeria and Kenya, were British colonies having little self-government.

The French Empire. Like the British, the French called on their colonies for support during World War I. The French, however, differed from the British in rejecting the idea of a union of separate and equal countries. Rather, the Asian and African subjects of France were included in Greater France, a group of all French-speaking colonials. Other areas, though, were not treated as equals or prepared for self-government.

African and Asian colonies had given much to the Allied war effort. India had contributed 800,000 troops to the British cause. These colonial peoples, therefore, resented the fact that the Versailles conference ignored their hopes for greater self-government. The growing force of nationalism in Asia and Africa soon challenged Western imperialism.

Africa between the Wars. The African empires of Britain, France, and Belgium became even larger after World War I because these countries took over German colonies.

The colonial powers spent little money on education, agriculture development, or industry in Africa during the 1920s and 1930s. In 1939, for example, the British colony of Nigeria had only a dozen high schools serving a population of 50 million people. The Belgians spent more in the Congo but only on the primary grades.

The colonial governments concentrated instead on exploiting the agricultural and mineral resources of their colonies.

During the 1920s and 1930s, newly constructed railroads, bridges, and roads opened the interior of Africa to exploitation. Trucks carried farm goods over newly built roads. The first trans-Africa airplane flights started in the early 1920s. Between 1921 and 1932, the Belgians completed the first trans-Africa railway.

Colonial Economies. In the 1920s and 1930s, Europeans thought of Africa as having two types of economic zones. The area called the export zone had mineral resources and cash crops suitable for export. Included in the export zone were the min-

The Cape to Cairo Railway's first engine reached Salisbury, Rhodesia (now Zimbabwe) on September 2, 1899. The first trans-African railway was completed in 1932.

ing districts of the Transvaal in South Africa, the palm plantations of West Africa, and the vineyards of Algeria.

The other zone may be called the labor zone. Regions in this zone provided cheap labor. The use of cheap labor made the export zone a success. Without a cheap work force, the mining and export farming businesses could not prosper.

The Need for African Labor. Most of the peoples of Africa chose to live as independent subsistence farmers. The colonial administrations, therefore, came up with ways to move more Africans into the labor force in mines and on plantations. One way was to impose money taxes on Africans. To get the cash to pay their taxes and thus avoid fines or prison, men and women were forced to take wage-paying jobs. Another method was forced labor. Even though the colonial powers worked to end slavery throughout Africa, large gangs of Africans were often put to work on public projects against their will.

The work Africans did was often dangerous. Gangs of laborers recruited from the villages of the Belgian Congo constructed the Congo-Ocean Railroad. During an 11-year period, over 125,000 men worked at constructing the line. As many as 15,000 of these workers died on the job.

The Union of South Africa consumed workers at a furious pace. In the 1920s, over 325,000 men were employed in the Transvaal to mine gold, diamonds, and coal. Of that number, 90 percent of the miners were contract laborers drawn from all over the Union and neighboring colonies. The need for laborers in South Africa was so great that workers were recruited from India and China. The standard of living of these laborers, however, remained low, while the opportunities and quality of life of the white settlers steadily improved.

Europeans benefited from African labor. The increase in mineral production brought prosperity to such corporations as the French West African Company and the

Commercial Society of West Africa. The Lever Brothers Company, for example, manufactured soap from West African palm oil. These corporations exerted great political influence on the colonial governments. They did little, however, to develop African economies. Rather, the profits they made were sent back to Europe to pay dividends to shareholders.

Early African Nationalism. During the 1920s and 1930s, African peoples became increasingly discontented with European economic and social policies. Protest movements and even rebellions broke out. In northern Morocco, for example, Abd al-Krim, a Berber military leader, led his people in revolt against the Spanish. Only with French help did the Spanish crush the rebellion in 1926. In both British and French West Africa, Western-educated African lawyers, journalists, and teachers organized associations to promote colonial reforms. These organizations would grow into mass nationalist movements after World War II.

Indian Nationalism Grows. The British Empire included the modern countries of India, Pakistan, Bangladesh, Burma, and Malaya. These lands produced wheat, rice, fruits, vegetables, spices, sugar, palm oil, tea, and coffee. Raw cotton, cotton goods, and cotton yarn had long been major Indian exports. Jute, animal hides, silk, indigo, and opium were also exported.

From such great ports as Calcutta, Bombay, and Madras, the British exported Indian goods to the world. Few Indians, however, benefited from this trade and the resulting economic growth.

Nationalism in India had been growing since the mid-nineteenth century. The Congress party of India led the movement for Indian independence. This party represented all the people of the subcontinent—Hindu, Muslim, Sikh, and Christian.

The Muslims also supported another organization, the All-India Muslim League.

Mohammed Ali Jinnah, a tall, thin lawyer, became the leader of the Muslim League. At first a champion of Hindu-Muslim unity, Jinnah gradually came to believe that the majority of Hindus would never share power with the Muslims.

After 1919, the leader of the Congress party was Mohandas Gandhi, who came to be called *Mahatma* or Great Soul. He was trained in London as a lawyer and practiced law for a time in South Africa. After he returned to India in 1915, he rejected Western ways and took up the nationalist cause. He dressed in a simple *dhoti*, or loincloth, made of rough cotton cloth that he had spun and woven himself. He wore simple leather sandals. In this plain dress, the Mahatma traveled about India preaching the doctrine of home rule for India.

The Noncooperation Movement. Gandhi urged the boycott of all foreign goods, British schools, imperial law courts, and other British institutions. He encouraged all Indians to use peaceful means to resist British rule. Jinnah and the All-India Muslim League joined in the demand for home rule.

In addition to the noncooperation movement, the Mahatma launched a campaign of civil disobedience against the British government. Civil disobedience is the deliberate and public refusal to obey what is considered an unjust law. This policy is a form of personal and public protest to attract attention to and correct unjust policies. In India, nonviolent civil disobedience was known as *Satyagraha,* or truth-force.

Despite Gandhi's pleas for nonviolence, armed conflict played a major role in the independence movement. In 1922, rioters attacked a police station in Chauri Chaura. They burned 22 officers to death. Gandhi was arrested and sent to jail but was released two years later.

Gandhi and other leaders of colonial peoples spent many years of their lives in jail or exile. Their efforts, however, were gradually rewarded. In 1935, the British Parliament passed the Government of India Act, which provided local self-government and limited democratic elections. With this act, India was moving toward its independence from Great Britain, which would come in 1947.

A civil disobedience riot in India. Mahatma Gandhi launched civil disobedience protests to attract attention to and correct unjust British policies.

As Britain and France struggled after the war to contain the rising tide of colonial nationalism, the centers of world power shifted from war-torn Europe to the United States and Japan.

United States Economic Power

The United States was the leading supplier of weapons and other goods to Europe during and after World War I. Wealthy and influential corporations ruled global financial empires based in the United States. Among them were the United Fruit Company, International Telephone and Telegraph, U.S. Steel, and Standard Oil. After World War I, the United States was the world's leading producer of iron, steel, coal, petroleum, meat, grain, textiles, lumber, and electric power.

The United States automobile industry demonstrated the country's leadership in the world economy. In 1927, for example, 4,890,000 cars were produced worldwide. Of that number, more than 4,265,000 were manufactured in the United States.

Immigration Laws and High Tariffs. The United States dominated all international trade in the 1920s. By the middle of that decade, its merchant fleets transported goods worth $9 billion a year. Exports exceeded imports by up to $600 million a year. The United States had become a world power. Power, however, creates responsibilities and problems.

In 1921 and 1924, the United States Congress passed restrictive immigration laws. These measures were designed to protect the jobs of United States citizens. The laws severely limited the movement of people into the United States, especially from Asia. The limit on immigration offended the Japanese. When the law went into effect in 1927, relations between the two countries began to decline.

The Congress also passed higher tariffs to limit foreign imports and therefore protect United States industries. These tariffs, combined with isolationism, limited United States political and cultural dealings with the rest of the world.

Overproduction. United States economic prosperity became a serious problem in the 1920s. Agricultural and industrial production soared, but the demand for food and manufactured goods did not keep up. As European countries recovered from the war, they no longer imported large quantities of goods.

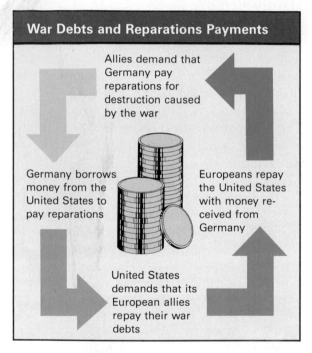

War Debts and Reparations Payments

Allies demand that Germany pay reparations for destruction caused by the war

Germany borrows money from the United States to pay reparations

Europeans repay the United States with money received from Germany

United States demands that its European allies repay their war debts

Debts and the Banking System. The world banking system, as well as that of the United States, faced problems in the 1920s. Banking and exports were linked. The United States accepted only American dollars when selling goods abroad. European countries, however, could not sell their goods in the United States because of high tariffs on imports.

To obtain American dollars, countries borrowed from United States banks. Since the Allied countries had already borrowed billions of dollars during the war, additional borrowing increased their debts.

The world banking system also was linked to war debts and German reparations. A circular system of money and credit developed. First, United States banks loaned money to Germany. Next, the Germans used these funds to pay reparations to European countries. Finally, the Europeans used the German payments to repay American bankers. This fragile system would collapse if any crisis disturbed one of the three links.

Despite these difficulties, the United States remained the richest and most powerful nation on the globe. The superficial economic prosperity caused many people to ignore serious postwar problems.

Japanese Industrial Power

Like the United States, Japan emerged from World War I as a strong nation. Compared to England or France, Japan suffered few losses and experienced little economic strain during the war. In fact, Japan gained former German colonies and became the most important economic force in east Asia. After the war, American and European nations recognized Japan as one of the five great powers.

The Japanese Economy. Japan's economy depended heavily on imported raw materials. Using these materials, Japan rapidly industrialized. The government and the industries of Japan worked closely together to promote economic growth. This alliance between the sword, or the government, and the yen, or big business, became the backbone of a strong Japan. By the 1920s, four large companies, or *zaibatsu*, dominated the Japanese economy. They were Mitsui, Mitsubishi, Sumitomo, and Nissan. The power of the *zaibatsu* rivaled that of the great international corporations that had prospered in the United States.

The growth of Japanese industry was closely linked to the military's need for weapons. At left, the first Japanese army formed by Saigo. At right, contemporary Japanese industry.

The growth of Japanese industry was closely linked to the army and navy. The military services were technically under the command of the emperor. In practice, they were free from civilian control. The military barely tolerated the elected constitutional government. Military leaders in Japan often abused their power. The emperor had little control over these officers.

The Japanese army and navy supported the development of heavy industries to produce weapons for their use. This need further strengthened the ties among the emperor, the *zaibatsu,* and the military.

Japan's Predicament. The rapidly growing Japanese population demanded economic expansion. In 1920, 56 million people lived in Japan. By 1940, the population had grown to over 73 million. Overseas colonies added another 25 million to the empire's population. Yet Japan lacked many important natural resources such as iron ore and coal. The country's industrial growth depended heavily on raw materials imported from other lands.

A second source of unrest was Japan's reliance on trade with the United States. Japan received more than 25 percent of its imports from the United States. Nearly 20 percent of Japan's exports went to the United States. This economic reliance on the United States worried many Japanese leaders. They feared that dependence on one country hampered Japan's ability to act independently.

The tariff policy of the United States in the 1920s threatened to destroy Japanese trade. Conflicts over immigration further complicated relations between the two countries. The Japanese resented United States immigration restrictions. The restrictions indicated that many people in the United States considered the Japanese inferior. In addition, the Japanese faced internal problems caused by their lack of raw materials and other resources and the rapidly growing population.

Japan's military leaders, the Imperial High Command, had a solution for these problems—expansion. Japan would secure greater resources and living space by seizing territory from such neighboring states as Manchuria and China. Although expansion might lead to conflict, the military believed that the benefits would be worth the risks. As the decade progressed, militarism was on the rise in Japan. Liberal democracy was fading away.

As the 1920s ended, world leaders faced serious problems including overproduction in the United States, the circular system of money and credit, and high tariffs. These problems led to a global depression in the following decade.

SECTION 2 *Study Skills*

Developing Vocabulary 1. Give an example of civil disobedience. **2.** List the three criteria for a depression. **3.** What is the major difference between a commonwealth and a corporation? **4.** Why was the economic prosperity of the United States called superficial?

Reviewing Main Ideas 1. How did colonial peoples' attitudes change after World War I? **2.** What benefit did European countries derive from their colonies? How was this accomplished? **3.** What factors led to the United States becoming a world power? **4.** What three groups joined forces to make a strong Japan?

Understanding Chronology List the following events in chronological order. Include the date of each event. **1.** Moroccans unsuccessfully revolt against Spain. **2.** Gandhi is elected leader of the Congress party. **3.** *Zaibatsu* dominate Japanese economy. **4.** United States restrictive immigration laws go into effect. **5.** The Imperial Conference begins. **6.** Parliament establishes British Commonwealth of Nations.

Challenge List reasons for and against restrictive immigration.

The Formation of Deserts

The mood in the decade after World War I was one of celebration. The war to end all wars was over, the Treaty of Versailles was complete, the League of Nations was expected to settle all future grievances, and the economy was booming. Few worried about the future. However, just as the activities of human beings can change the world, so can the forces of nature. Green fields can become a desert.

The Dust Bowl

Many people flocked to the Great Plains in the southwestern United States during and after World War I. An increased demand for grain encouraged them to try farming. Although improved tractors and other farm machinery made sowing and reaping easier, the new farmers did not become successful. They faced a difficult climate and had little knowledge of good farming practices.

Wind, rain, and severe dust storms eroded the land and blew away the topsoil. Poor farming practices and the grazing of too many animals had destroyed the protective covering of vegetation. Wheat, as it was grown during World War I, did not protect the ground from wind damage. By the 1930s, the lack of soil protection and a drought ruined the farms.

Thousands of hungry and homeless farm families were forced to flee to California and other places. Prairie grasses soon were replaced by desert vegetation.

Causes of a Desert

The Dust Bowl might have been avoided if people had understood the processes involved in the making of a desert.

Logging, if done indiscriminately, can destroy whole forested areas. A carelessly tossed match can do the same. Farming strips the land of its natural ground cover. Although new plants are grown, harvesting leaves the land unprotected.

Animals can damage the land in two ways. First, they eat the grass. Sometimes this leaves it too short to provide adequate protection of the soil from the elements. Second, their sharp hooves can damage the roots of plants. This kills the plants and again exposes the soil to the elements.

Stages in Desert Formation

There are four stages in the development of a desert. First, the natural vegetation is cleared. Second, the soil is dried out by the sun. Third, the wind sweeps away the topsoil. Fourth, the rain washes away the nutrients. The infertile soil that remains is a desert. However, planning can interrupt and reverse this process at any stage.

Deserts occur when the land is stripped of vegetation and left unprotected. During a period of drought, every effort should be made to leave plants in the soil. The roots help to hold the nutrients while the leaves protect the soil from the direct buffeting of wind and rain. Plants also slow down the evaporation of valuable ground water that collects during periods of wet weather.

Reclaiming Desert Land

Reclaiming large areas of land such as the Sahara, Arabian, or Kalahari deserts is difficult. Such a task is extremely expensive because there is no local source of non-salt water. Any fresh-water resource would have to be shipped in huge quantities. Some people have even suggested towing an iceberg

Nouakchott, the capital of the west African country of Mauretania, is located in the desert and surrounded by sand dunes.

to these areas. Others feel this could affect world climate adversely.

Israel is a good example of a country which has succeeded in reclaiming some of its desert land. Crop land in Israel has tripled since 1948. Swamps have been drained, irrigation expanded, and soil erosion ended. The Negev Desert, on Israel's southeastern side, has been made to bloom. Water from the Sea of Galilee is pumped southward through the National Water Carrier, a system of canals, pipelines, and tunnels 88 1/2 miles long. A network of regional systems connects with the carrier and extends to the southern Negev where the land is irrigated.

The Israelis have become experts at reclaiming land. Other nations that would like to reclaim desert land often study their effective techniques.

Challenge for the Future

Some scientists suggest that certain plants can actually promote rainfall. Research seems to indicate that pollen from grain crops provides a better-than-average surface for moisture condensation. Greater moisture condensation means more rainfall. Therefore, planting grain might feed starving people and, if properly cultivated, halt the formation of a desert.

In the 1930s, the farmers of the Dust Bowl region did not know how to prevent deserts. Today, people have knowledge of the way in which deserts are formed. This knowledge can be used to halt the desertification process and protect the land.

STUDY SKILLS Understanding Geography

1. Explain how vegetation helps to prevent the formation of deserts.
2. List three land uses that lead to the formation of a desert.
3. Where and why did the Dust Bowl occur?
4. Propose an original method which could be used to reclaim a desert.
5. How has Israel reclaimed desert land?
6. What effect might the elimination of all deserts have on the earth?

3 The Great Depression

OBJECTIVE: *To understand the causes and consequences of the global depression of the 1930s*

World Economic Problems of the 1920s

Despite signs of prosperity, the world economy of the 1920s suffered from serious flaws. The world went through a serious economic depression in the 1930s. The depression resulted from numerous factors, many the legacy of World War I.

War Debts and Reparations. One of the unresolved economic issues from the war was the debts the European countries owed the United States. Bankers and the United States government had loaned more than $10 billion to various governments to fight the war or rebuild their economies after the peace. To handle repayment of these loans, the United States set up the Foreign Debt Commission. Debtor nations were supposed to repay their loans over a 62-year period.

The principal debtor nations depended on reparations from Germany to repay these debts. Austria, Hungary, Bulgaria, and Germany had to pay reparations for the damages caused by the war. Germany, the most powerful of the losers, was assessed 132 billion gold marks, about $33 billion. This debt grew to 480 billion marks, or $120 billion, when paid with interest over a long period of time.

The Treaty of Versailles left the German nation bankrupt. By 1921, Germany was in default. It was unwilling and unable to pay its debts. To avoid an international crisis, the European powers forced the Germans to accept a new payment schedule. London banks loaned Germany 1 billion marks to help it pay reparations.

This borrowed money enabled the Germans to make their first payments. Within a year, though, they were in default again. In early 1923, the German government stopped the coal deliveries to Belgium and France as required in the terms of the Treaty of Versailles.

The French and Belgian armies invaded the Ruhr district of Germany and seized the coal mines. When German workers refused to cooperate, however, the armies withdrew from the area.

The German Inflation Crisis of 1923. Germany's economic problems led to rapid inflation. Faced with rising debts, governments issued more money to pay their bills. Following this practice, Germany printed more money, increasing the number of marks in circulation. This caused severe inflation.

VOCABULARY DEVELOPMENT

bankrupt (BANGK ruhpt) *noun:* legally declared unable to pay debts.

default (dih FAWLT) *noun:* a circumstance in which an individual or country fails to pay money due. From the Latin prefix *de-*, meaning away, and word *fallere*, meaning to fall.

During 1923, the value of the German mark dropped so low that the money was used as fuel for heat, as wallpaper, and as mattress stuffing.

At the beginning of 1923, the exchange rate for the German mark was 4 to the dollar. By August, the exchange rate had reached 1 million marks to the dollar. In December 1923, the exchange rate was 4.2 trillion marks to the dollar.

The German government was printing 46 billion new paper marks each day. This money dropped so much in value that people used it for wallpaper and mattress stuffing, or burned it for heat. Moreover, the German government's actions threatened the money systems of other nations.

A series of international agreements tried to restore order to the German economy. The German mark was revalued at 4.2 marks to the dollar. The United States government agreed to set up a commission to settle the reparations question. These agreements ended the inflation crisis.

The Dawes Plan and the Young Plan.

The head of the Reparations Commission of 1924 was Charles Dawes, a tough-talking, no-nonsense United States business leader. By the terms of the Dawes Plan, Germany agreed to pay 1 billion marks in 1924 and an increasing amount each year until 1929. In 1929, the nations of Europe would negotiate a final agreement. To allow Germany to make its first payment, the United States and other Allied nations loaned the Germans 800 million marks.

In 1929, Owen Young, another American business leader, worked out the details of the final reparations payment plan. Germany was to pay about 1.7 billion marks in 1929 and an increasing amount each of the next 36 years. After 1965, the payments would be fixed until they were completed in 1988. Within six months, though, the world economy collapsed. Then the entire reparations system broke down with it.

The Crisis of 1926–1928.

Collecting reparations and repaying debts were not the only economic problems facing Europe. In 1925, Great Britain tried to prevent inflation by establishing a gold standard. Under the gold standard, British currency could be exchanged for a fixed amount of gold.

Other European currencies began to fluctuate wildly in value. The French franc, for example, dropped from a rate of 5 to the dollar to 50 to the dollar. The economic crisis toppled the French government. In Belgium, the economic crisis was so severe that the Belgians granted the king dictatorial powers to deal with the problems.

By 1927, world economy was in danger of complete collapse. Representatives from Germany, Britain, and France met in the United States with members of the Federal Reserve. The Federal Reserve banking system controlled the amount of money in circulation and the credit available in the United States.

With support of the foreign representatives, the Federal Reserve tried to increase the number of dollars in circulation. This increased supply of money could be used to pay debts and stimulate consumer spending. In practice, the increased money only caused inflation, and global economic problems worsened.

One key indicator of American confidence in the economy of the United States is the price of stocks. When investors are optimistic about the economy, they buy stocks, expecting their value to increase. Despite the economic problems in the 1920s, many people expected stock prices to rise. As the number of investors grew, their purchases drove the value of stocks higher.

Between 1927 and 1928, many stocks had doubled or even tripled in value. For example, stock in Radio Corporation of America, RCA, rose from $90 per share to $382. Some people borrowed money to buy stocks. As long as prices increased, the buyer could always sell the stock at a profit and repay the loan.

In the summer of 1929, some investors worried that stock prices might fall. To avoid expected losses, these investors sold their stock. By fall, other investors were realizing that the slowing demand for stocks would bring down prices. Soon, people were selling stock as quickly as possible.

In the last week of October, stock prices plummeted. Investors lost millions of dollars. Many were unable to repay the loans they had used to buy stock. Closely following the Great Crash of the New York Stock Exchange in 1929 was a worldwide depression. Businesses were forced to close, and many people lost their jobs.

The Depression Spreads. By the end of 1930, the world was suffering from what became known as the Great Depression. Unemployment grew, businesses went bankrupt, and banks failed. Without jobs, workers had no money to spend. Without customers, businesses did not need workers.

Depositors gathered outside the Union Bank of New York City after the state ordered its doors closed on August 5, 1931. By 1932, more than 1,500 United States banks had closed.

By 1930, global trade was declining. The United States tried to protect its businesses by raising tariffs on imported goods 50 to 100 percent over what they had been in 1922. Economists all over the world tried to convince United States President Herbert Hoover not to sign the tariff bill. They knew that other countries would raise their import taxes on American goods.

Soon, 25 countries raised their tariffs, which discouraged trade even more. Between 1929 and 1934, world trade dropped from $69 billion to $23 billion. Even trade in goods not covered by these high tariffs declined dramatically.

The troubled economic system also led to the collapse of United States banks and the international banking systems. By 1932, more than 1,500 banks had gone out of business in the United States alone. Depositors who had money in these banks lost more than $172 million.

A similar collapse occurred in central Europe. In 1931, Credit-Anstalt, a huge Austrian bank, went bankrupt. The Bank of England tried unsuccessfully to save the Austrian bank by lending it 150 million Austrian shillings. Banks, corporations, and governments around the world lost their deposits. As a result, each was threatened with bankruptcy.

War Debt Payments End. The collapse of the American stock market and international banks, as well as declining trade, made further war debt and reparation payments impossible. In 1932, Germany stopped paying reparations.

The entire war payments system was in ruins. Only Finland continued to pay its World War I debts. In fact, Finland remains the only country in the world that repaid its war loans in full.

Global Economic Chaos. Almost no society in the world completely escaped the economic disaster. Not all countries suffered equally, though. The Soviet Union, for example, enjoyed increased trade during the hard times of the 1930s.

For most people, the 1930s were bitter times. For example, Japan's most important export was silk. However, very few customers could now afford luxurious textiles. Australia also depended heavily on a textile export, wool. When the price of wool dropped suddenly in 1929, the Australian economy collapsed. By 1932, the standard of living in Australia had dropped by more than 30 percent.

The depression also devastated the countries of Africa and South America. Between 1929 and 1932, Latin American exports dropped by 60 percent, and imports fell by 75 percent. Foreign investments disappeared, and banks and businesses failed. Military takeovers drove many governments from power.

In Europe, too, the increasing financial disaster caused several changes in government. Small nations, such as Belgium and the Netherlands, and such large states as France and Great Britain, granted emergency powers to their leaders to take the necessary steps to improve conditions.

The Depression in the United States. The once-strong United States economy also suffered disastrously. In 1933, the total economic production of the nation was about half of the 1929 level. Up to 25 percent of the working population was out of work and looking for employment.

In the 1932 presidential election, Franklin Roosevelt promised to give the people of the United States a New Deal. Roosevelt and the Democratic party won an overwhelming victory. They began emergency economic programs to promote relief, recovery, and reform. At his first inauguration, the new president told the people, "the only thing we have to fear is fear itself." This phrase became the United States' battle cry against the depression. It encouraged people to try harder and not to give up hope for a better future.

Franklin Delano Roosevelt

Franklin Delano Roosevelt was born in Hyde Park, New York, in 1882. An only child in a wealthy family, he was tutored at home until the age of 14. In 1900, Roosevelt entered Harvard where he was a reporter for the school newspaper, the *Crimson*. He was elected editor of the *Crimson* in 1903. In the same year, he became engaged to Eleanor Roosevelt, a distant cousin. Franklin and Eleanor were married in 1905.

In 1907, Roosevelt was admitted to the New York bar to practice law. He ran for his first political office, a seat in the New York Senate, in 1910. During his successful campaign, he toured the district, asking voters to "call me Franklin." Roosevelt thrived on politics and made it his career.

In 1921, Franklin went boating near his summer home in Campobello, New Brunswick, Canada. He helped put out a small forest fire on an island nearby. Then, he went swimming in the Bay of Fundy. The next day he suffered from severe pain in his back and legs. By the following day, he could not move his legs. His doctor diagnosed his condition as polio. For the rest of his life, Roosevelt wore 10-pound braces on his legs.

Not until 1928 did he again run for a political office. In that year, he began the first of his two terms as the Democratic governor of the state of New York.

In 1932, Roosevelt was elected to the presidency of the United States. As chief executive, he radiated confidence in himself, the New Deal, and the country. With his little dog, Fala, and his jaunty smile, Franklin Roosevelt was a symbol of hope and optimism. When he took office, he called a special session of Congress and made 15

Franklin Delano Roosevelt greets workers and their families while campaigning in Elm Grove, West Virginia in 1932.

proposals. Congress passed all 15 measures during the first 100 days of his presidency.

One morning, Roosevelt submitted a major banking bill to Congress. By afternoon, the bill had passed both houses and been signed into law. The American people felt that something new and bold was being done to solve their problems.

Roosevelt was the only United States president to serve more than two terms. He was president from 1933 until his death in 1945. While he was president, his wife helped him by observing and listening to the public as she traveled across the country. Roosevelt instructed Eleanor, "Watch the people's faces. Look at the condition of their clothes on the wash line. You can tell a lot from that."

In the 1930s, Roosevelt became a world leader. The people of the United States still preferred to remain isolated from Europe's problems. Roosevelt, however, led the nation away from isolationism. Eventually, he led the nation into an alliance to once again save the world for democracy.

Franklin Roosevelt's administration made the United States government responsible for the security of peoples throughout the world. On the day before his death, he worked on the draft of a speech. The speech ended with these two sentences which show his optimism:

" The only limit to our realization of tomorrow will be our doubts of today. Let us move forward with strong and active faith. **"** ■

The global depression had stunned the world. Franklin Roosevelt, Neville Chamberlain, and other world leaders tried to cope with the depression through economic reforms and social welfare programs. Yet the severity of the crisis led not only to poverty but to great frustration and bitterness, especially in Europe. In Germany and Italy, these feelings played into the hands of dictators who rose to power because they promised the people they would restore prosperity.

SECTION 3 *Study Skills*

Developing Vocabulary **1.** What would cause a country to default on a loan? **2.** Explain how Germany went bankrupt.

Reviewing Main Ideas **1.** What action by the German government caused their inflation crisis? How was it solved? **2.** Describe conditions of business and banking during the Great Depression. **3.** Give three examples of how Franklin D. Roosevelt tried to improve the United States' morale during the depression.

Understanding Cause and Effect **1.** Explain what Great Britain did to try to stabilize its currency. What effect did this have on other countries' currency? **2.** Explain the causes of the Great Stock Market Crash of 1929. **3.** Explain the effects of tariffs on importers and exporters.

Challenge Which government discussed in this chapter provided the best solution to global depression? Support your answer with facts.

Unemployment, 1928–1938

CHAPTER 27 *Summary & Review*

Summarizing Main Ideas

The Big Four—the United States, Great Britain, France, and Italy—met at the Paris Peace Conference in 1919 to write the Treaty of Versailles. They hoped that, by acting on Woodrow Wilson's Fourteen Points, they could establish lasting world peace. Despite these good intentions, many countries objected to the treaty's terms. The treaty reshaped the world's economy and established new boundaries.

The 1920s were a period of rapid economic growth and exploitation in many colonial nations. Countries controlling colonial territories were challenged by independence movements.

The United States and Japan emerged as world powers. However, by the end of the 1920s their economies, dependent on world trade, began to show signs of weakness.

Global economic collapse occurred in 1929. Unstable world currencies and banking practices were major causes of the depression. World leaders sought solutions to the crisis, but it continued through most of the 1930s.

Questions for Critical Thinking

COMPREHENSION Interpreting Events

1. Explain how Woodrow Wilson's hopes were crushed during and after Versailles.
2. Why did Germany have so much difficulty paying its debts?
3. What advantage did countries have in owning colonial territory? Use specific examples.

ANALYSIS Identifying Trends

1. How did the redistribution of world territories contribute to the global depression?
2. Explain how Japan's economic growth contributed to world power struggles.

APPLICATION Comparing Past to Present

1. Compare the rapid economic growth of the 1920s to a person today who suddenly wins the lottery. What lessons can be learned?

RESCUE MOTHER AND GIRL.

Danbury Police Find White Plains Pair Starving in Woods.

Special to THE NEW YORK TIMES.

DANBURY, Conn., Sept. 6.—Found starving under a rude canvas shelter in a patch of woods on Flatboard Ridge, where they had lived for five days on wild berries and apples, a woman and her 16-year-old daughter were fed and clothed today by the police and placed in the city almshouse.

The woman is Mrs. John Moll, 33, and her daughter Helen, of White Plains, N. Y., who have been going from city to city looking for work since July, 1931, when Mrs. Moll's husband left her.

When the police found them they were huddled beneath a strip of canvas stretched from a boulder to the ground. Rain was dripping from the improvised shelter, which had no sides.

A 1932 *New York Times* article features the rescue of a mother and daughter found starving and homeless after unsuccessfully seeking work.

2. Summarize depression conditions as described in the newspaper clipping above.

SYNTHESIS Developing Writing Skills

1. Assume the role of the girl in the newspaper clipping and write several diary entries.
2. Write a speech you would deliver if you were seeking independence in one of the colonies described in this chapter.

EVALUATION Weighing Consequences

1. How did the Treaty of Versailles lead to Germany's economic collapse?
2. How and why did Germany's economic collapse lead to economic disaster in other countries of the world?

CHALLENGE

1. Show with past and present examples how the economic conditions of one country are affected by conditions in another country.
2. Compare the negotiations and outcome of the Treaty of Versailles with a recent example of diplomatic negotiations.

CHAPTER 28
The Second World War, 1939–1945

GLOBAL TIME LINE

TIME

1939	1940	1941

1936–1939 Spanish fight a civil war

1939 Britain and France begin to rearm

1940 Germany invades Norway and Denmark

1941 United States declares war on Germany and Italy

PEOPLE

1939 Franco becomes dictator of Spain

1940 Churchill becomes prime minister of Great Britain

1941 Field Marshall Rommel of Germany leads Afrika Korps

PLACE

1939 *Albania;*[1] Italy invades Albania

1939 *Poland;*[2] Germany invades Poland

1939 *France;*[3] Germany attacks France

1941 *Hawaii;*[4] Japanese bomb Pearl Harbor

1941 *Russia;*[5] Germany invades Russia

Linking Past to Present

American Nazi party members often run as candidates for political offices in the United States. The members of the American Nazi party borrowed their uniform, philosophy, and goals from the National Socialist German Workers' party. The name of this German political party was shortened to Nazi. The first Nazi party gained support in Germany during the 1920s. Their leader was Adolph Hitler.

The popularity of the Nazi party in Germany led Hitler to believe that he could make Germany powerful enough to dominate Europe and the world. As you read this chapter, evaluate the philosophy and goals of the Nazi party both in Germany in the 1920s and 1930s and in the United States today.

From Picasso's 1937 mural, *Guernica*

1942   **1943**   **1944**   **1945**

- **1942** Battles of Midway and Coral Sea turn the tide of war in the Pacific
- **1942** Magnetic recording tape invented
- **1943** World's first nuclear reactor built in United States
- **1944** German V-2 rockets launched against British
- **1945** Germany surrenders
- **1945** Allies found the United Nations
- **1945** Big Three meet at Potsdam
- **1945** Japan surrenders

- **1942** Enrico Fermi splits the atom in the United States
- **1942** Selman Waksman discovers streptomycin as tuberculosis cure and coins word "antibiotic"
- **1945** President Franklin D. Roosevelt dies

- **1942** *India;⁶* Gandhi demands independence and is arrested.
- **1943** *Italy;⁷* Allies invade Italy, Mussolini resigns
- **1944** *France;³* Allies invade France
- **1945** *Japan;⁸* United States drops atomic bombs on Hiroshima and Nagasaki

Buy More
LIBERTY BONDS

MUST
CHILDREN DIE
AND MOTHERS
PLEAD IN VAIN
?

1 *The Peace That Failed*

OBJECTIVE: *To understand the causes and consequences of international hostility in the 1930s*

Efforts to Maintain Peace

In January 1920, delegates to the League of Nations met in Geneva, Switzerland. The covenant, or charter, of the League established a permanent secretariat headed by a secretary-general. The secretariat was responsible for the day-to-day administration of the new world organization. A council, or upper house, was made up of delegates from nine member nations. Legislative authority was granted to a general assembly.

The Weakness of the League of Nations.

The League of Nations was founded to help countries discuss and settle their disputes peacefully. However, the United States, the leading economic power in the world, refused to join. This greatly weakened it from the start. The Soviet Union and the defeated Central Powers were excluded from membership. The absence of these countries made peaceful settlement of world disputes difficult. Eventually, the nations first excluded from the League were given membership, but the United States never joined.

The main weakness of the first global organization was the absence of any real power. In disputes between nations, the League was limited to debate and suggestions for sanctions against aggressors.

The Washington Naval Conference. In
November 1921, President Warren Harding invited nine nations with interests in the Pacific to attend a naval armaments conference in Washington, D.C.

Representatives agreed to a series of treaties. The most important one was the Five Power Naval Armaments Treaty. This agreement proclaimed a 10-year naval hol-

---

VOCABULARY DEVELOPMENT

sanction (SANGK shuhn) *noun:* a penalty for breaking a law. From the Latin word, *sanctus,* meaning holy.

fascism (FASH ihz uhm) *noun:* a system of government characterized by one-party dictatorship, extreme nationalism, militarism and racism, and the suppression of opposition. From the Latin word, *fasces,* meaning a bundle of rods tied around an ax, used by Roman magistrates as a symbol of authority.

totalitarian (toh TAL uh TAIR ee uhn) *adj.:* a government controlled by one political party.

Orient (AWR ee uhnt) *noun:* Asia, especially the Far East, including China, Japan, and Korea. Sometimes, the term Orient also includes the countries of Southeast Asia as well as the Malay Archipelago.

Axis: the countries united against the Allies in World War II, originally Germany and Italy, later also Japan.

appease (uh PEEZ) *verb:* to quiet by giving in to the demands of, usually by the sacrifice of principles. From the Latin prefix *a-,* meaning to, and word *pax,* meaning peace.

During the worldwide depression in the 1930s, the Nazi party attracted support in Germany. People responded to Hitler's promises. In 1933, President Paul von Hindenburg appointed Hitler chancellor. Two years later, the Nazi party became the largest party in the German parliament.

Hitler Violates the Treaty of Versailles. Once in power, Hitler disbanded opposition parties and labor unions, controlled schools, and imprisoned his enemies. He encouraged his private army, the storm troopers, to attack Jews and communists. The Gestapo, a secret police force, gained power. Hitler took the title of leader, *der Führer* (duhr FYOOR uhr), in German.

Hitler reduced German unemployment. He started public works as well as a secret rearmament program. As unemployment declined, Hitler's support increased. He called his regime the Third Reich, and promised it would last 1,000 years.

Hitler believed that Germans were members of a superior race. He deprived people of their civil rights if he thought they were inferior to Germans. In 1936, Hitler marched his new German army into the Rhineland, the demilitarized area between Germany and France. The French government appealed to Great Britain for support. The British refused. Hitler then fortified the Rhineland, the frontier between the two countries. Most Germans applauded his defiance of the Versailles settlement.

The Birth of the Spanish Republic. Spain, which had remained neutral during World War I, lagged behind the rest of western Europe. Spain's economy was agricultural, and aristocrats owned much of the land. The powerful Roman Catholic church controlled Spain's educational system.

During the early 1900s, strikes, military plots, and political assassinations troubled Spain. Socialists, communists, and anarchists competed for control. Many people opposed the power of the church.

In 1930, revolutionaries overthrew the king and established a republic. Liberal representatives wrote a democratic constitution which provided for a one-house parliament and separation of the church and the state.

The new government instituted reforms. It took land from the church and nobles and gave it to the landless peasants. New laws gave workers shorter hours, higher wages, and a voice in management.

The Spanish Civil War. These reforms angered the aristocracy, the church, and other conservative elements. Army officers wanted to return to a monarchy. The conservatives organized a fascist party that they called the Falange (FAY lanj).

In 1936 the fascists led an army uprising that brought a bitter and bloody civil war. The Falangists, led by General Francisco Franco, called themselves Nationalists. Most of the army officers and troops joined the nationalist movement. The opposition were known as Republicans or Loyalists. Many Spanish workers and peasants joined the Republicans opposing the Nationalists.

The Spanish Civil War, waged between 1936 and 1939, soon involved much of Europe. Germany and Italy supported the fascist Falange with weapons and money. The Soviet Union supported the Republicans. Stalin sent planes, technicians, and military advisors from the Soviet Union. The Spanish Civil War became a testing ground for new weapons and military tactics used later in World War II.

The Nationalists won the war in March 1939. Franco set up a fascist dictatorship modeled after Mussolini's. He, too, assumed the title of leader, *el Caudillo* in Spanish.

The Threat to World Peace. The totalitarian rulers of Europe threatened peace. In the Soviet Union, Stalin wanted to extend his power. Mussolini dreamed of reestablishing the ancient Roman Empire. *Il Duce* hoped to dominate the Mediterranean and expand the Italian Empire in Africa.

A 1932 photograph of the Japanese invasion of China. When the League of Nations condemned the attack, Japan resigned from the organization.

One of the Nazi slogans was, Today Germany, Tomorrow the World! Adolf Hitler believed that whoever controlled central Europe could dominate the European continent and eventually control the world.

Japanese Aggression. The Japanese in the Orient also dreamed of conquest. In 1936, Emperor Hirohito (HIR oh HEE toh) appointed Koki Hirota prime minister. The new leader of the government was also leader of the militaristic Black Dragon Society. The appointment of Hirota signaled the victory of militarism and imperialism.

The Road to War

The Japanese army stormed into Manchuria in late 1931. In early 1932, the League of Nations officially condemned the attack. Japan answered by simply resigning from the world organization. In 1934, Hitler took Germany out of the League.

The League Fails to Maintain Peace. In 1934, Japan rejected the naval armaments agreements and began to expand the Imperial Navy. In 1935, Hitler condemned the Treaty of Versailles and worked to rearm Germany. The Italian army invaded Ethiopia in eastern Africa. Haile Salassie (HY le suh LAS ee), emperor of Ethiopia, appealed to the League for help. He received nothing but a few ineffective sanctions against Italy.

The League of Nations was totally discredited by 1936. In October of that year, Hitler and Mussolini formed the Rome-Berlin Axis, which they called the Pact of Steel. Soon after, Japan, Germany, and Italy signed the Anti-Comintern Pact, a treaty aimed at preventing the spread of international communism.

In the summer of 1937, the Japanese Imperial Army invaded northern China. The League had failed once again to maintain peace.

Hitler's Aggression. Hitler annexed Austria in 1938. Der Führer then demanded annexation of the Sudeten (soo DAYT uhn), German regions made part of Czechoslovakia in the Treaty of Versailles. In September, Hitler and Mussolini met with the prime ministers of Britain and France in Munich, Germany.

Neville Chamberlain, prime minister of Great Britain, tried to maintain the peace. He believed that Hitler would end German expansion if all Germans were brought together in a single nation. In addition, neither Britain nor France wanted nor was prepared for another war.

Chamberlain therefore agreed to a policy of conciliation and appeasement. The four chiefs of government agreed to transfer the Sudeten territories to Germany. In return, Hitler promised that he would make no more territorial demands.

On his return home, Chamberlain assured his people that he had achieved "peace in our time." In March 1939, however, Hitler seized the rest of Czechoslovakia. In April, Mussolini sent his army across the Adriatic Sea to invade Albania. As a result of this aggression, Chamberlain decided to resist any further German de-

Aggression in Europe and Asia, 1930–1940

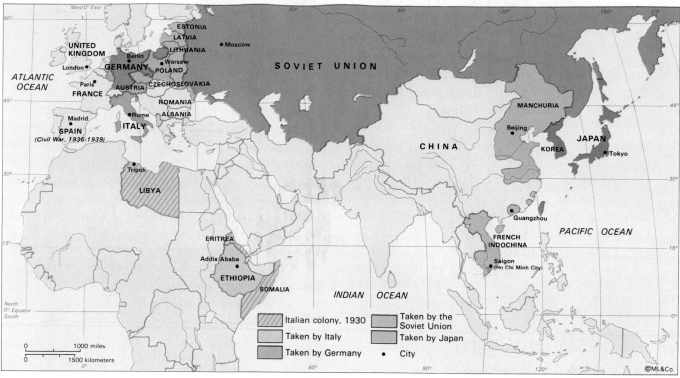

Map Skills **1.** What countries were aggressors in this period? **2.** Which areas did Italy control in Africa? **3.** By 1940, which European countries were under German control?

mands. Britain signed treaties guaranteeing the boundaries of Poland and Romania. Britain and France hurried to rearm.

In August 1939, Nazi Germany signed a non-aggression pact with communist Russia. Hitler wanted to remain friendly with Stalin so that he could avoid a two-front war. Stalin and Hitler pledged to avoid war with each other. Also, in a secret agreement, they planned to divide Poland.

On September 1, 1939, the German army smashed into Poland. They used a new military tactic called *blitzkrieg*, meaning lightning war. Tanks and armored trucks divided the enemy forces on the ground, encircled them, and forced their surrender. Dive bombers and fighter planes supported the ground forces. Polish army resistance quickly collapsed.

Within 48 hours, Great Britain and France declared war on Germany. The second global war had begun.

SECTION 1 *Study Skills*

Developing Vocabulary **1.** Define facism. **2.** Identify three nations that were called the Axis powers. **3.** Tell what the Orient includes. **4.** What are sanctions?

Reviewing Main Ideas **1.** Explain why the efforts to maintain peace after World War I failed. **2.** Name four dictators that came to power following World War I. **3.** Explain why Hitler was able to attract the support of the German people. **4.** How did Hirota's appointment affect Japan?

Understanding Geography **1.** Why did Mussolini want to conquer the Balkans and expand into Africa? **2.** Identify the first three countries Hitler's forces conquered in 1938 and 1939. **3.** Why did Hitler want to control central Europe?

Challenge What lesson can be learned from Chamberlain's policy of appeasement?

Africa in World War II

In Africa, World War II was fought mainly in the north. Before the war in Europe began, Benito Mussolini, the dictator of Italy, conquered Ethiopia. Later, in 1941, over 325,000 soldiers from South Africa joined the British to free Ethiopia. Some of these South African troops then joined forces with Britain's General Montgomery, Monty, in fighting the Germans.

Field Marshal Rommel led the German *Afrika Korps*. This brilliant tank commander was nicknamed the Desert Fox, because of his effective desert fighting tactics.

Allied Military Goals

The war in north Africa was fought for control of Egypt and the Suez Canal. The winning side would control the canal and thus be able to send its battleships and aircraft carriers directly to the Asian front. Ships from the losing side would have to go around Africa to reach the battle areas in Asia. This would be more costly.

The country that won control of north Africa would also have direct access to the oil-rich Middle East. This oil could be refined into gasoline for tanks and planes.

Montgomery developed his British and Commonwealth forces into a smooth-working, hard-hitting combination of air, infantry, and armored fighters. The Allies, blocked the Nazi advance at El Alamein, Egypt and launched a counterattack in 1942. They drove Rommel out of Egypt and captured 9,000 German soldiers.

When the Axis forces in north Africa surrendered, Churchill called the battle of El Alamein a turning point in British fortunes. "Up to Alamein we survived. After Alamein we conquered."

Non-Military Involvement

While the battles in Africa occurred in the north, the societies of sub-Saharan Africa also played a role in World War II. This role was strongly influenced by their position as colonies of European nations.

African societies could not establish their own policies toward other nations. As colonies, they followed the policies of their colonial masters. The chief way sub-Saharan Africa aided the war effort was by providing mineral resources for the Allies.

Mineral Resources. In the late 1800s, European settlers discovered diamonds in southern Africa. Diamonds were important to the war effort. Industrial diamonds are used to cut and drill through hard metal. Diamonds are used in such work because of their extreme hardness.

The chrome, platinum, and gold of South Africa was also important to the Allied war effort. South Africa is the world's major supplier of chrome, a metal used to produce a variety of steels. Steel was used to build tanks, ships, and planes.

Platinum is used in refining gasoline. The gold of South Africa did not have a direct function in the war. However, the possession of gold made a country rich and enabled it to purchase the supplies necessary for winning battles.

The mineral resources of the African colonies helped contribute to the Allies' victory in World War II. The mining of these resources and their industrial use had long-lasting consequences for the people of South Africa.

Apartheid's Beginnings. With the war, the population of South Africa shifted to urban areas, where factories needed workers for wartime production. South Africa

African mineral resources contributed to the Allied victory in World War II. Above, copper mines in Zaire. Inset, German Field Marshal Erwin Rommel in Africa in 1942.

has 48 percent of its population living in urban areas.

As more black people came to the cities to work, the white government reacted with a system of race separation. This system, called apartheid, is still in effect today.

Black miners are forced to live in enclosed dormitory buildings near the mines. If they work in city factories, they are made to live in township ghetto areas outside of the city. Once a year, the male workers are allowed to visit their wives and children, who must live in distant homeland areas.

It was not only in the urban areas that the races were treated differently. When the 325,000 South African soldiers went to help free Ethiopia, distinctions were also made. The 125,000 black soldiers from South Africa were not allowed to bear arms. They were distributed among the combat units as stretcher-bearers and physical laborers.

Sub-Saharan Africa was involved in World War II and affected by it. African soldiers and Africa's natural resources contributed to the success of the Allies. However, as colonies of Europe, sub-Saharan Africa did not have control over its level of participation in the war.

STUDY SKILLS Understanding Geography

1. In what region of Africa did World War II battles occur?
2. What factor determined Africa's involvement in World War II?
3. How did Africa help with the fighting of World War II?
4. What supplies did Africa provide for World War II?
5. What effect did World War II have on South Africa?

2 The War Spreads Around the World

OBJECTIVE: *To understand the causes and consequences of World War II*

The New War

When World War II began in Europe, the Germans were well prepared. Their weapons were new, and German army units were well trained. In September 1939, 53 German divisions drove into western Poland and crushed the badly outnumbered Polish army in four weeks. The Germans gave the world a clear demonstration of the new concept of lightning warfare. Meanwhile, the Soviets, according to a secret agreement with Germany, overran eastern Poland.

The Maginot Line. After World War I, France fortified its border with Germany. To prevent another invasion from the east, France built a series of steel and concrete bunkers nearly 200 miles long. These fortifications were called the Maginot line after the statesman who planned them. Most of the fortifications were underground.

Despite the lightning German attack on Poland, France felt secure behind the Maginot line. Unfortunately for the French, World War II proved to be a war of movement, fought in the air, on the ground, on the sea, and under the sea.

The Phony War. While Germany attacked Poland, French forces moved up to the Maginot line. British forces crossed the English Channel into northern France. The British navy blockaded Germany's ports.

The Germans massed their troops behind the fortifications Hitler had built in the Rhineland. These fortifications, called the Siegfried line, were a combination of tank traps, bunkers, machine-gun nests, and cement and steel barriers. For a time in early 1940, the world watched this silent confrontation and waited. The newspapers and radio broadcasters called this the *sitzkrieg*, the sitting war, or Phony War.

While this stalemate continued in the west, the Soviets in the east forced the Baltic states of Latvia, Estonia, and Lithuania into an alliance. Soviet troops also defeated the outnumbered Finnish army, restoring the old Russian borders.

The Phony War Ends. The quiet on the western front was broken suddenly in the spring of 1940. On April 9, German land, sea, and air forces attacked Denmark and

---

VOCABULARY DEVELOPMENT

bunker *noun:* an underground steel or concrete fortification containing weapons.

fifth column: any group of people who give aid to the enemy from within their own country. The term was coined in 1936 during the Spanish Civil War. General Mola, who was attacking Madrid, Spain, had four columns of troops marching toward the city and boasted of a fifth column within.

evacuate (ih VAK yoo WAYT) *verb:* to remove people from a place for their protection; to withdraw. From the Latin prefix *e-*, meaning out, and word *vacuare*, meaning to empty.

Norway. The Danes had no army and surrendered immediately. The Norwegians tried to fight but were defeated in only three weeks.

The conquest of the two Scandinavian countries was accomplished with the aid of local pro-Nazis called the fifth column. The term fifth column, coined during the Spanish Civil War, describes traitors within a country who aid the enemy.

One month after these conquests the full power of the *blitzkrieg* was turned against western Europe. On May 10, 1940, the Nazis attacked Belgium and the Netherlands. Employing naval forces, infantry, tanks, dive bombers, and paratroopers, the Germans overran the Low Countries and blasted around the Maginot line.

Germany Invades France. Hitler's alliance with Russia freed the German generals to concentrate their forces in the west during June 1940. The Germans attacked across France's northern plains, bypassing the Maginot line and reaching Paris in less than six weeks. On June 10, the Italians invaded southern France.

Dunkirk. As the Germans pushed their way to Paris, the French, Belgian, and British troops retreated. At the end of May, about 350,000 of these Allied troops reached Dunkirk, a seaport in northern France. Cut off from the major French forces in the south, they seemed trapped.

The British government decided to evacuate the troops across the channel. British civilians in fishing boats and yachts sailed alongside warships to bring the troops home. The British lost nearly a third of their craft but saved more than 338,000 men. All heavy equipment, however, was left behind.

France Falls, 1940. France surrendered to Germany on June 22, 1940. Marshal Henri Petain, an aged World War I hero, formed a new government and signed an armistice with Germany. To humiliate the French, Hitler held the armistice ceremony in the same railroad car in which the Germans had signed the armistice of 1918.

By the terms of the surrender, the French army was demobilized. The Germans occupied northern France, including Paris. Petain's government moved to Vichy to administer unoccupied southern France. In England, the British, led by a new prime minister, Winston Churchill, were determined to continue fighting.

Winston Churchill

FOCUS ON PEOPLE

When Norway fell to the Germans, Neville Chamberlain resigned as prime minister of Great Britain. Winston Churchill, who had warned the British about Hitler for years, succeeded Chamberlain.

Winston's father was Lord Randolph Churchill, a famous member of Parliament and a direct descendant of the Duke of Marlborough. His mother, Jennie Jerome, was an American, famous for her beauty.

Winston Churchill, who had warned the British about Hitler for years, succeeded Neville Chamberlain as prime minister of Great Britain in 1940.

Winston grew up in Blenheim Palace, one of England's famous stately homes.

Since Winston was the family's second son, he would not inherit its lands or title. Therefore, he chose to pursue a military career. After graduating from Sandhurst, the royal military college, Churchill served as a young officer in India and Africa. He resigned from the army in 1899. Then he became a newspaper correspondent and politician. His articles and books recounting his adventures in India, along the Nile, and in South Africa made him famous.

In 1901, Churchill won a seat in Parliament. Between 1901 and 1914, he held a number of high positions in the British government. When World War I broke out, he served as first lord of the admiralty in charge of naval affairs. A political disagreement forced him to resign in 1915.

Churchill's wit was often sharp and biting. A woman at a dinner party declared that she liked neither Churchill's politics nor his moustache. He replied, "Madame, you are as unlikely to come into contact with the one as with the other."

On another occasion, playwright George Bernard Shaw sent Churchill a pair of tickets to his new play. The accompanying note said, "Come to my play and bring a friend, if you have a friend." Churchill replied, "I'm busy for the opening, but I'll come to the second night, if there is a second night."

Churchill returned to politics in 1924 but from 1929 to 1939, he was never offered a cabinet post. His career seemed at a dead end. Then, in 1939, the British faced the threat of a powerful and aggressive Germany. Churchill, with experience as head of the British navy in World War I, was again appointed first lord of the admiralty. The next year, when Neville Chamberlain resigned, Churchill became prime minister of Great Britain.

Churchill is best remembered for his gift of oratory. During the battle for France, he delivered the following famous address to the House of Commons:

" We shall not flag or fail. We shall go on to the end, we shall fight in France, we shall fight on the seas and oceans, we shall fight with growing confidence, and growing strength in the air, we shall defend our island, whatever the cost may be, we shall fight on the beaches, we shall fight on the landing grounds, we shall fight in the fields and in the streets, we shall fight in the hills; we shall never surrender, . . . "

As he finished, he covered the microphone and muttered, "And we will hit them over the head with beer bottles, which is about all we have got to work with."

After the dramatic rescue at Dunkirk, only the British opposed Germany. Hitler made a public speech inviting the British to surrender. In a well-known speech answering Hitler, Churchill said:

" What General Weygand called the Battle of France is over. I expect that the Battle of Britain is about to begin. . . . Let us therefore brace ourselves to our duties, and so bear ourselves that, if the British Empire and its Commonwealth last for a thousand years, men will still say, "This was their finest hour." " ■

The Battle of Britain

In August 1940, a great air battle began in the skies over Great Britain. The German air force, the *Luftwaffe,* sent bombers in repeated waves across the English Channel and the North Sea. The British defended their island home with fierce determination.

The British Use Radar. While the *Luftwaffe* was raining death and destruction on the British, the German air force was also taking a terrible beating. The British claimed that in September 1940, during a single 24-hour period, 185 German planes were destroyed. In tribute to the brave British pilots, Churchill said, "Never in the field of human conflict was so much owed by so many to so few."

The RAF's superiority over the *Luftwaffe* was based in part on Britain's use of radar. In 1940, during the height of the Battle of Britain, radar gave the British a tremendous advantage. The RAF knew when and where the Germans were going to attack.

A great naval battle was waged in the Atlantic. German submarine wolf packs disrupted the supply lines to the British Isles. In the air, on the sea, and under the sea, the mighty battle raged.

The War Spreads

The war also expanded into the Balkans. Mussolini launched an attack on Greece in the fall of 1940. Hungary and Romania joined the Axis at the end of 1940. In early 1941, Bulgaria joined the fascist alliance.

In the spring of 1941, the Nazis invaded Yugoslavia and completed the conquest of Greece. In Africa, the Italian army battled the British in Somaliland and Egypt. By the spring of 1941, the fighting raged across the coast of north Africa. German Field Marshal Erwin Rommel, the Desert Fox, led the *Afrika Korps.*

Operation Barbarossa. Hitler lost patience with the western front as the Battle of Britain dragged on. *Der Führer* turned his attention to the east.

According to Hitler, fascism's true enemy was not weak-willed Western democracy but Marxist-Leninist communism. In addition, he believed that the conquest of the Soviet Union would be another step toward his world domination. On June 22, 1941, the Germans began Operation Barbarossa. German troops invaded the Soviet Union on a 2,000-mile front from the Baltic to the Black Sea.

The German air force began a great air battle over Great Britain in August 1940. A photograph from 1941 shows the damage caused by a raid on London.

World War II in Europe and North Africa, 1941–1945

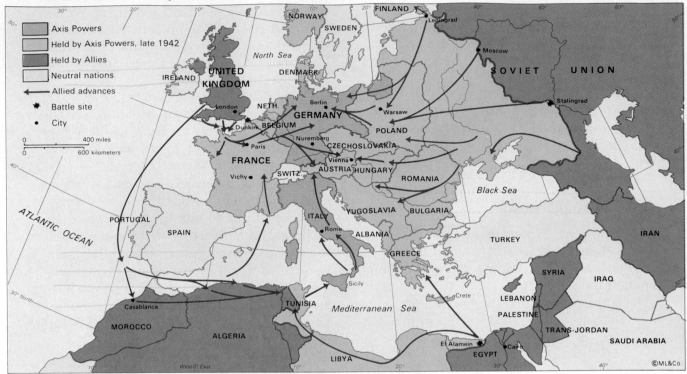

Map Skills **1.** From 1940 to 1942, which countries were added to the Axis Powers? Refer to previous map on page 649. **2.** Which countries maintained neutrality during World War II?

The Germans overran eastern Poland and the Baltic lands. The Nazis then pushed into central Russia and the Ukraine. In September 1941, they began a siege of Leningrad, which lasted 1,000 days. In October, the Nazis swept across the Ukraine and into the Crimea.

By November 1941, German troops and supplies were severely overextended. The great Nazi war machine began to show signs of strain. Equipment and ammunition were running short. Gasoline was in great demand, and supplies were growing scarce.

The Japanese Attack French Indochina.
While Hitler's armies were spreading across Europe, the Japanese continued their conquests in the East. Japan had a plan to dominate the East. The Japanese wanted to control a large area and use its land and natural resources.

Japan gained control of Manchuria in 1932. In 1937, Japanese and Chinese troops clashed near Beijing. The Japanese army took the city, then moved south. By 1939, the Japanese occupied about one-fourth of China. The Chinese, however, refused to surrender. They moved their capital up the Yangzi River and fought a guerrilla war.

In 1939, Japan took the island of Hainan and some small islands off the coast of French Indochina. This conquest endangered the British supply route from Hong Kong to Singapore.

In late 1940, Japanese forces expanded the war into Southeast Asia. They pressured the Vichy government of unoccupied France to place French Indochina under Japanese protection. Disturbed by these aggressions, the United States cut off all trade with Japan early in 1941 and seized Japanese financial assets in America.

The Japanese Attack Pearl Harbor. In October 1941, General Hideki Tojo became prime minister of Japan. Tojo, long an opponent of the United States, strongly supported the Axis alliance. He immediately ordered the Japanese Imperial Navy and Air Force to activate secret plans for a general attack on key British and American bases in the Pacific Ocean and on the coast of Asia.

On Sunday, December 7, 1941, the Japanese attacked American bases in the Hawaiian Islands and the Philippines, as well as British bases in Hong Kong and Malaya. The Japanese launched bomber squadrons from the decks of aircraft carriers. The planes attacked the United States Pacific Fleet resting at anchor in Pearl Harbor, a large base west of Honolulu. Japanese pilots destroyed or damaged 18 American warships, blew up over 180 airplanes, and killed over 3,500 men. The Japanese lost 30 planes and about 50 men.

The Japanese gained a tremendous advantage in the December 1941 attacks in the Pacific. By early 1942, they were advancing toward their goal of controlling most of East Asia. The Imperial Army drove into the jungles of Burma. Guam, Wake Island, and the Philippines were conquered. Hong Kong, Singapore, and the Dutch East Indies also fell. Japanese forces readied an attack on the British colony of India. They also advanced on Australia, New Zealand, the Aleutians, Midway, and the Hawaiian Islands. See the map, World War II in the Pacific, 1941–1945, on page 659.

By mid-1942, the enemies of fascism were in retreat on every front. Hitler, Mussolini, and Tojo seemed to have victory within their grasp. The Axis leaders underestimated the determination of their opponents, however. Winston Churchill, prime minister of Great Britain, Joseph Stalin, premier of the Soviet Union, and Franklin D. Roosevelt, president of the United States, joined forces to oppose the aggression of the Axis powers.

On Sunday, December 7, 1941, the Japanese attacked American bases in Pearl Harbor, destroying over 180 American airplanes and killing over 3,500 people.

SECTION 2 *Study Skills*

Developing Vocabulary 1. What is the connection between bunkers and the Maginot line? **2.** How did the term fifth column originate? **3.** Use the word evacuate in a sentence that shows its meaning.

Reviewing Main Ideas 1. Name five countries the Germans conquered during April, May, and June of 1940. **2.** How did Churchill's gift of oratory help him lead the British? **3.** Why was the British Royal Air Force so successful at fighting the *Luftwaffe*?

Understanding Chronology 1. Create a time line showing when Germany attacked Britain, Yugoslavia, Greece, and the Soviet Union. **2.** When did the United States become directly involved in World War II?

Challenge Discuss why the United States waited so long to enter World War II.

3 The Allies Defeat the Axis Powers

OBJECTIVE: *To understand the events and consequences of World War II*

Turning the Tide

After the fall of France, President Roosevelt of the United States did everything to aid Great Britain short of declaring open war. Though officially neutral, the United States sent Britain weapons left from World War I. All through 1940 and 1941, the United States navy aided the British fleet.

The Atlantic Charter. Four months before the Japanese attacked Pearl Harbor, Winston Churchill met with President Roosevelt. The secret meeting took place on board a battleship cruising off Newfoundland. There, the two leaders drew up a statement called the Atlantic Charter.

By the terms of this agreement, Great Britain and the United States pledged to defend freedom of speech, freedom of religion, freedom from fear, and freedom from want. The Atlantic Charter also committed both nations to end territorial expansion and guarantee the right of self-government to all nations. Finally, both pledged to preserve freedom of the seas and work for general disarmament after the war.

On January 1, 1942, 26 nations signed the United Nations Declaration pledging support for an alliance against the Axis. By the end of the war, 46 nations had signed the United Nations Declaration. The Allies pledged to fight until each of the Axis powers had been defeated.

The War in the Pacific. After the attack on Pearl Harbor, United States isolationism ended. "Remember Pearl Harbor!" became the country's battle cry. The United States geared its economy and industry for wartime production.

Admiral Yamamoto, who planned the attack on Pearl Harbor, warned his government that the Americans would fight back with great fury. American and Australian air and naval forces halted Japanese expansion in the Pacific in May 1942. The Japanese fleet, advancing toward New Guinea, was defeated in the Coral Sea after a five-day battle.

A month later, the United States fleet intercepted a larger Japanese fleet, moving east to attack Midway Island. For three days, Japan and the United States fought an air and sea battle north of Midway Island. The United States finally won.

VOCABULARY DEVELOPMENT

Allies: in World War II, the nations that fought against the Axis, especially Great Britain, the Soviet Union, and the United States.

amphibious (am FIHB ee uhs) *adj.:* a military operation in which troops are moved from ships to shore.

concession (kuhn SEHSH uhn) *noun:* something granted, as a right or privilege. From the Latin prefix *com-*, meaning with, and word *cedere*, meaning to grant.

nuclear (NOO klee uhr) *adj.:* operated by the use of atomic energy.

The battles of the Coral Sea and Midway turned the tide of war in the Pacific. United States victories opened the supply lanes to the southwest Pacific and to Guadalcanal.

On land, Japanese expansion ground to a halt in the jungles of New Guinea and Guadalcanal. On these islands, American and some Australian soldiers fought the long, difficult battle to drive out the entrenched Japanese forces.

German Retreat in Africa. Within a few weeks of the Battle of Midway, the British Eighth Army stopped Rommel's *Afrika Korps* at El Alamein in western Egypt. In mid-November, the *Afrika Korps* retreated into Libya while the British advanced.

Fighting in Eastern Europe. During the summer of 1942, a new German offensive pushed Soviet troops back to Stalingrad. There, the Soviets waged a bitter and bloody battle in defense of the city.

In November, the tide of battle turned. A Soviet counterattack pushed the Germans from the ruined city and encircled them. Hitler ordered his troops to continue fighting. However, on January 31, 1943, the German troops surrendered.

Allied Victories. Throughout the year United Nations forces won victory after victory. On the eastern front the Soviets drove the Germans from their land. In north Africa, the Allies routed the *Afrika Korps* and drove it across Libya into Tunisia.

During the summer of 1943, an Anglo-American force conquered Sicily. In September, the Allies invaded southern Italy. Mussolini resigned and was arrested. A newly formed Italian government tried to join the Allies. Instead, the Germans rushed their forces to Italy and took control. They freed Mussolini and set up a new government in northern Italy. During the last

World War II in the Pacific, 1941–1945

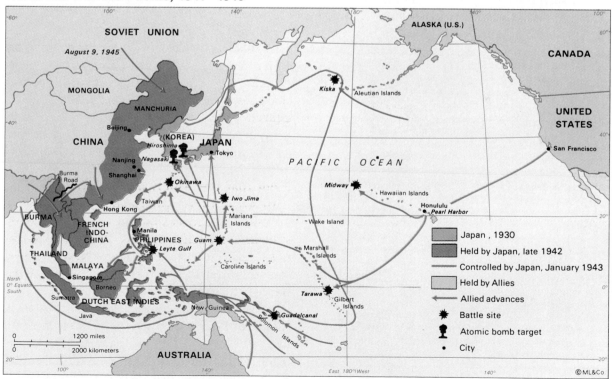

Map Skills **1.** Did Japan control more water or land areas in the Pacific arena? **2.** The Allied forces won strategic island victories. Where was the first victory in the Pacific?

months of 1943, the Allies fought bitter battles as they slowly pushed north. In the Pacific, the Allies were driving the Japanese from island to island.

The bloody, unrelenting struggle continued with growing fury into 1944. The Allied forces advanced slowly up the Italian Peninsula. With resources limited, Germany's armies in Italy and along the eastern front began to collapse. On June 4, 1944, the Allied forces entered Rome.

The Second Front

For months, Stalin had demanded that the Allies open a second front in Europe by invading France. Roosevelt, Churchill, and Stalin met at Teheran, Iran, in November 1943. They discussed a plan called Operation Overlord, an Allied invasion of France. Allied troops would cross the English Channel and land on beaches in Normandy.

D-Day. The Allies launched the greatest airborne and amphibious invasion in history on June 6, 1944.

More than 175,000 troops and tons of equipment were involved in the invasion. During the first 100 days after the D-Day landings in Normandy, more than 2 million Allied troops entered France.

After heavy fighting on the beaches, the Allies pushed into northern France. Shortly after, other Allied forces landed on the Mediterranean coast of France and fought their way north. On August 25, 1944, Allied troops freed Paris. In September, they faced the strongly fortified Siegfried line along Germany's western frontier.

In June 1944, the Soviet army drove the Germans west. By the end of 1944, the Red Army had taken Estonia, Lithuania, Latvia, Romania, and Bulgaria. Meanwhile, the British were driving the German troops from Greece.

D-Day Invasion and the Battle of the Bulge, 1944

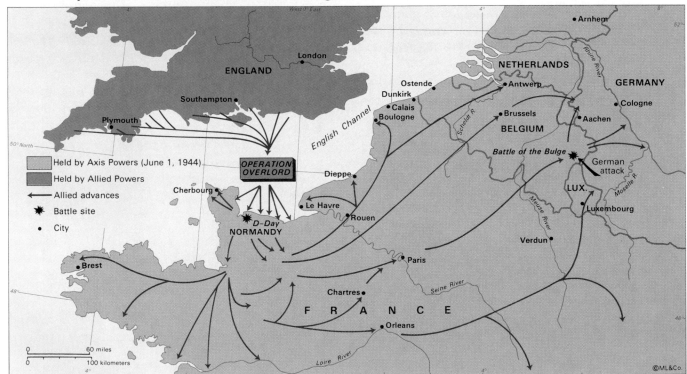

Map Skills **1.** From which country did the Allies launch the D-Day invasion? **2.** The D-Day invasion took place in what section of France? **3.** Where did the Battle of the Bulge occur?

German Rockets. German scientists, led by Werner von Braun, constructed an arsenal of rockets. The V-1 rocket, or buzz bomb, was in full production by the spring of 1944. The V-1s and later V-2s terrorized people and caused destruction in such cities as London and Antwerp.

These rockets could not save the Nazis. However, the V-2 series set the stage for later work on Intercontinental Ballistic Missiles, or ICBMs. The rockets that carried the first cosmonauts and astronauts into space in the early 1960s were the legacy of World War II science and technology.

In December 1944, the Nazis launched a counterattack against Allied forces in Belgium. Called the Battle of the Bulge, it was the last great effort of the dying German war machine. The Allies rallied and drove the Nazis into Germany.

The Big Three Meet at Yalta. In February 1945, Roosevelt, Churchill, and Stalin met at Yalta, a resort on the Black Sea. The Big Three, as they were called, expected a German surrender soon. The war against Japan, however, was still to be won. At Yalta, a tired Roosevelt secured Stalin's promise to join the war against the Japanese within three months after the war in Europe ended. In return, Stalin was promised territory in the Far East.

The leaders also tried to agree on how to settle affairs in Europe after the war. They planned to divide Germany into zones of occupation, one for each of the three major Allies plus France. The European countries, freed from Nazi control, were to elect their own governments. Roosevelt agreed to give the Soviets concessions in eastern Europe if the Soviets joined the UN.

The Allies Defeat Germany. On the eastern front, the Soviet army pushed through Poland. In the spring of 1945, angry Italians captured and shot Mussolini.

Berlin fell to the Russians in early May, after a bloody battle through the city's streets. Hitler committed suicide in his underground bunker. On May 8, 1945, Germany surrendered and the war in Europe ended. The Allies celebrated Victory in Europe Day, also called V-E Day.

The Pacific War Theater. The war against Japan still raged. The Allies drove the Japanese from the Marshall, Admiralty, Mariana, and Caroline islands. During 1944, led by General Douglas MacArthur, Allied forces landed in the Philippines after a fierce naval battle in Leyte Gulf.

The Japanese Surrender

Franklin Roosevelt died suddenly in April 1945. When Harry S. Truman became the new president, he was informed of the top secret Manhattan Project. Under this code name, a group of scientists and engineers was building the first atomic weapon.

Truman made the decision to test this weapon. On July 16, 1945, an atomic bomb was exploded in the desert near Alamagordo, New Mexico. One of the scientists present said, "I am sure that at the end of the world. . . the last man will see something very similar to what we have seen."

In the summer of 1945, Japanese forces were in full retreat on every front. A bloody battle on the island of Iwo Jima brought the Allies' forces to within 750 miles of Japan. In April, Americans landed in Okinawa.

In early August 1945, the war in the Pacific suddenly came to an end when the United States used nuclear weapons against Japan. President Truman had the responsibility of deciding whether or not to drop the atomic bomb. On July 26, the Allies issued an ultimatum to the Japanese government, demanding surrender. The government refused.

On August 6, 1945, the United States long-range bomber *Enola Gay* dropped an atomic bomb on Hiroshima (HIHR uh SHEE muh), a city in Japan. The bomb destroyed more than 60 percent of the city and killed more than 150,000 people.

Still, the Japanese would not surrender. On August 9, 1945, another B-29 dropped an atomic bomb on Nagasaki (NAH guh SAH kee), Japan, killing nearly 40,000 people. As many as 70,000 badly burned survivors remained as horrible evidence of the effects of a nuclear explosion. Radiation poisoning soon demonstrated the long-term destructiveness of nuclear warfare.

Announcing Japan's Surrender

FOCUS ON SOURCES

The atomic bomb dropped on Hiroshima exploded with a force never before felt. When an even more powerful bomb was dropped on the city of Nagasaki, Japan surrendered. On August 15, 1945, the *Nippon Times*, Japan's largest newspaper, printed the following letter from the emperor to the people of Japan:

" After pondering deeply the general trends of the world and the actual conditions obtaining in Our Empire today, We have decided to effect a settlement of the present situation by resorting to an extraordinary measure.

To strive for the common prosperity and happiness of all nations as well as the security and well-being of Our Subjects is the solemn obligation which has been handed down by Our Imperial Ancestors, which We lay close to heart. Indeed, We declared war on America and Britain out of Our sincere desire to ensure Japan's self-preservation and the stabilization of East Asia, it being far from Our thought either to infringe upon the sovereignty of other nations or to embark upon territorial aggrandizement [expansion]. But now the war has lasted for nearly four years. Despite the best that has been done by everyone . . . the war situation has developed not necessarily to Japan's advantage, while the general trends of the world have all turned against

her interest. Moreover, the enemy has begun to employ a new and most cruel bomb, the power of which to do damage is indeed incalculable, taking the toll of many innocent lives. Should We continue to fight, it would result not only in the ultimate collapse and obliteration [destruction] of the Japanese nation but also in the total extinction of human civilization. Such being the case, how are We to save the millions of Our subjects or to atone Ourselves before the hallowed spirits of Our Imperial Ancestors? This is the reason We have ordered the acceptance of the provisions of the Joint Declaration of the Powers. " ■

The Japanese surrendered on September 2, 1945. When the news of the surrender was broadcast around the world, huge crowds celebrated in every major Allied city. In the following weeks, the Russians occupied Manchuria. Japanese forces in Indonesia and Malaya surrendered to the British. United States forces occupied Japan and liberated China. The most destructive war in history was finally over.

SECTION 3 *Study Skills*

Developing Vocabulary 1. What is an amphibious invasion? 2. Contrast the members of the Allies in World Wars I and II. 3. Suggest a concession Roosevelt could have given to Stalin.

Reviewing Main Ideas 1. Why did Japan attack Pearl Harbor? 2. Explain why the Soviet Union wanted the Allies to invade France. 3. Why did Truman use atomic weapons? 4. How did the Japanese justify their eventual surrender?

Understanding Cause and Effect Did the Japanese bombing of Pearl Harbor justify the United States bombing of Hiroshima and Nagasaki? Explain.

Challenge List the major steps the Allies took to defeat the Axis.

4 *The Postwar World*

OBJECTIVE: *To understand the costs of World War II*

Postwar Agreements

During 1945, delegates from the Allied nations met to determine the status of the postwar world. They agreed to establish a world organization dedicated to peace and cooperation among nations. The Allies also settled the destiny of people in what had been Axis countries.

The Allies Establish the United Nations. Delegates from 50 Allied nations met in San Francisco from April to June 1945. They agreed to a charter for a world organization. All 50 nations joined the United Nations. Member nations agreed to maintain the peace, and promote equal rights and self-determination among peoples. They also pledged international cooperation.

VOCABULARY DEVELOPMENT

satellite nation: a nation that depends on a larger, more powerful state.

buffer zone: a neutral zone separating two potentially rival countries.

genocide (JEHN uh SYD) *noun:* the systematic killing of a whole ethnic group. From the Greek word, *genos*, meaning race of people.

holocaust: the systematic destruction of Jews by the Nazis before and during World War II.

atrocity *noun:* extreme cruelty or brutality.

penicillin (PEHN uh SIHL ihn) *noun:* any of a group of bacteria-destroying compounds obtained from certain molds.

synthetic fibers: threads produced chemically rather than from materials found in nature.

As did the League of Nations, the United Nations has a large assembly. The General Assembly is composed of delegates from all member nations. Real power, however, rests in the Security Council. The United States, Great Britain, France, the Soviet Union, and China hold permanent seats on this council. Six other nations are elected on a rotating basis.

Voting in the Security Council is by majority. Nevertheless, to pass a resolution the majority must include all five permanent members. In this way, each of the Big Five nations holds veto power over any council action. The Economic and Social Council, Trusteeship Council for former colonies, International Court of Justice, and the Secretariat for Administration complete the UN's main structure.

In addition to the United Nations, the Allies set up international agencies to administer emergency postwar relief. They also established an international bank to aid the nations bankrupted by the war.

Meeting at Potsdam. As nations voted on joining the new world organization, the Big Three met for the last time at Potsdam, a suburb of Berlin, in July 1945. President Harry Truman represented the United States in place of Roosevelt. Part way through the meetings, Churchill was voted out of office. The new prime minister of Great Britain, Clement Attlee, replaced Churchill. Joseph Stalin represented the Soviet Union.

The Big Three—Winston Churchill, Harry Truman, and Joseph Stalin—met for the last time at Potsdam, a suburb of Berlin, in July 1945.

At Potsdam, the Allies disagreed on numerous points. Great Britain and the United States were suspicious of Soviet policy in Poland. The Soviet Union seemed intent on making Poland into a satellite nation. Stalin also made it clear that he had no intention of allowing free elections in eastern Europe. Instead, he intended to set up a buffer zone of east European satellite countries between the Soviet Union and Germany.

The Big Three did agree to divide Germany into four zones. The United States, Britain, France, and the Soviet Union were to occupy and administer separate zones. Germany's capital of Berlin and Austria's capital of Vienna also were divided into four separately administered sectors.

The Nazi War Crimes. During the weeks after Germany surrendered, the world learned the extent of Nazi crimes against humanity. When Allied troops occupied Germany, they discovered the full extent of the horrors of Nazi crimes. After their victory in Poland, the Nazis shipped hundreds of thousands of Polish soldiers and civilians to Germany as slave labor for factories and farms. They emptied whole towns and refilled them with German settlers. They murdered or imprisoned 250,000 clergy, intellectuals, and other leaders.

Another horrifying practice was genocide, the deliberate and systematic killing of a group of people. The Nazi propaganda machine preached that Jews were inferior beings responsible for Germany's prewar problems. In 1939, the Nazis pursued a final solution of what they called the Jewish question. The plan was to exterminate all the Jews in Europe. This systematic murder of the Jews is known as the holocaust

The Germans set up a network of concentration camps in Europe, including six death camps in Poland: Auschwitz, Belsen, Chelmno, Majdanek, Sobibor, and Treblinka. Each camp contained huge gas chambers in which as many as 6,000 persons could be suffocated by cyanide gas each day. Their bodies were burned in special ovens. By the end of the war, the holocaust had consumed about 6 million Jews. Nearly as many non-Jews, including resistance fighters, also were murdered.

The War Crimes Trials. During 1945 and 1946, a special international court met at Nuremberg, Germany, to bring major Nazi leaders to trial. Judges representing 23 nations took part. United States Supreme Court Justice Robert H. Jackson was a chief counsel for the prosecution.

The German officials were accused of, first, waging aggressive war. Second, they were accused of violating generally accepted rules on the treatment of prisoners of war and civilians in occupied territory. Of the 22 defendants, 12 received death sentences, 7 received prison terms, and 3 were acquitted. Later, trials of lesser leaders were held. In all, about 500,000 Nazis were found guilty of war crimes.

Similar trials were held in Tokyo. Top officials were charged with war crimes and atrocities. Former premier Hideki Tojo and six other Japanese leaders were executed.

Terezin

FOCUS ON SOCIETY

In Czechoslovakia, the Nazis took over a walled town, Terezin, about 37 miles, or 60 kilometers, from Prague. By July 1942, they had evacuated the non-Jewish population. They used Terezin, also called Theresienstadt, as a camp for Jews. Terezin was meant to be a model camp. Representatives from humanitarian organizations could be shown the town.

About 15,000 Jewish children under the age of 15 passed through Terezin on their way to other camps. Of these children, only about 100 survived. Like children everywhere, they wrote stories and poems and drew pictures. Children interned there wrote the following poems. They are from the book, *I Never Saw Another Butterfly:*

"At Terezin". The following poem, "At Terezin," was written in 1943 in pencil on a piece of drawing paper. The author, a boy, Teddy, probably lived in children's home L 410.

❝When a new child comes
Everything seems strange to him.
What, on the ground I have to lie?
Eat black potatoes? No! Not I!
I've got to stay? It's dirty here!
The floor—why, look, it's dirt, I fear!
And I'm supposed to sleep on it? I'll get
    all dirty!

Here the sound of shouting, cries,
And oh, so many flies.
Everyone knows flies carry disease.
Oooh, something bit me! Wasn't that a
    bedbug?
Here in Terezin, life is hell
And when I'll go home again, I can't yet
    tell. ❞

Deported Jews arrive at the Auschwitz concentration camp in Poland. By the end of the war, about 6 million Jews, and nearly as many non-Jews, had been killed in the death camps.

"The Butterfly." This poem, "The Butterfly," written in 1942, is preserved as a typewritten copy in the collection of poetry by Pavel Friedmann. Pavel was born in 1921 in Prague. He was deported to Terezin in 1942. He died in Oswiecim, another Nazi concentration camp, in 1944.

" The last, the very last,
So richly, brightly, dazzlingly yellow.
  Perhaps if the sun's tears would sing
  against a white stone. . .

Such, such a yellow
Is carried lightly 'way up high.
It went away I'm sure because it
  wished to
  kiss the world goodbye.

For seven weeks I've lived in here,
Penned up inside this ghetto
But I have found my people here.
The dandelions call to me
And the white chestnut candles in the
  court.
Only I never saw another butterfly.

That butterfly was the last one.
Butterflies don't live in here,
  In the ghetto. "

Of the 141,000 inmates at Terezin from 1941 to 1945, over 33,500 died as a result of the dense crowding of the ghetto. The Nazis shipped another 88,000 on to extermination camps. Few of these people lived to see the end of the war. ■

The Costs of the War

The total cost of World War II cannot be measured. However, accurate estimates in a number of categories exist.

The Cost in Lives. The cost in lives was enormous. Between 40 and 50 million people were killed in World War II. About a quarter of these deaths occurred in the war in Asia. The United States lost about 300,000 members of its armed forces.

The main battlefield, though, was Europe, especially eastern Europe. The chart on page 670 shows the estimates of European war dead, both military and civilian.

These figures do not measure all the costs in terms of hardships to people. Many more people died after May 7, 1945. Asians and Europeans died of starvation and diseases in the aftermath of the war's destruction. The numbers include only the dead, not the people wounded and maimed.

The War's Cost in Money. The best estimates suggest that the money expenditures for the war totaled just over $1 trillion. The Allies spent about $230 billion more than the Axis powers. Much of this money came from the United States.

As the fighting ravaged the Allied countries of Europe, the United States increased production to supply war material. Early in the war, President Roosevelt challenged the United States to become the "Great Arsenal of Democracy."

The United States spent between $317 billion and $341 billion. Over $48 billion went to lend-lease aid for other members of the alliance. By 1944, the United States was spending over $90 billion annually on the war effort.

The Destruction of Property. Great cities, such as Warsaw, London, and Berlin, were heavily damaged. Dresden, Hiroshima, and Nagasaki almost disappeared. Previously populated areas of the world lay in ruins.

People throughout Europe and Asia lost their houses and farms, as well as their jobs. Cathedrals that had stood for centuries were reduced to rubble. Bombs and artillery shells demolished factories, roads, railways, and harbor installations.

Postwar Technology

During the war, governments mobilized the economies of their nations. They used the mass production techniques of the indus-

Europe after World War II, 1945–1948

Map Skills **1.** Which nations occupy West Germany? **2.** Which nation occupies East Germany? **3.** Which nation occupies land both east and west of Poland?

trial age to create the weapons of modern war. Factories produced record-breaking numbers of planes, tanks, artillery, machine guns, and ammunition.

Peacetime Uses of Technology. In addition to weapons, war research brought peacetime benefits. Penicillin, discovered in 1928, was first produced on a large scale during the war. Penicillin saved thousands of soldiers' lives. Since then, it has saved the lives of hundreds of thousands of civilians throughout the world.

Battle casualties stimulated research to improve techniques for storing blood and plasma. New techniques in plastic surgery were developed to reconstruct badly disfigured soldiers, sailors, and airmen. Now these techniques are used to aid victims of peacetime accidents and fires.

Radar also has peaceful uses. Air and sea navigation and traffic control now rely on radar. Synthetic fibers, such as the nylon used for parachutes, were developed during the war. Today, they have many uses in such articles as fishing nets, surgical thread, clothes, rugs, and upholstery fabrics.

German research for the V2 rockets led to the development of rockets for space exploration. The jet engine, developed during the war, revolutionized air travel.

The Atomic Age. The atomic bombs dropped on Hiroshima and Nagasaki were the result of years of scientific research begun in the early 1900s. In 1939, President Roosevelt appointed a secret special commission to determine whether an atomic bomb could be developed. When the commission agreed that it could, Roosevelt established the Manhattan Project eventually headquartered at Los Alamos, New Mexico. The goal of the program was to produce an atomic bomb as fast as possible.

Ben Shahn's 1945 painting *Liberation* was inspired by the sight of children swinging joyfully around a pole after learning that France was finally free of German occupation forces.

Scientists worked for three years to build the first atomic bomb. On July 16, 1945, a bomb was tested successfully in the Alamogordo desert. The world entered the Atomic, or Nuclear, Age.

Nuclear Power. After the war, research on nuclear weapons continued. Scientists, however, also developed nuclear energy to generate electrical power. In 1954, the United States Navy launched the first nuclear-powered vessel, the submarine *Nautilus*.

The first nuclear power plant began operation in 1956 in England. The United States opened its first nuclear power plant in 1957. Other industrialized countries also began to build nuclear plants to generate their electricity.

Although nuclear power had peaceful uses, countries continued to build and stockpile nuclear weapons. During the decades following the war, the nations of the world tried to control the spread of these weapons. The possibility existed that the people of the earth could be destroyed in a nuclear war.

SECTION 4 *Study Skills*

Developing Vocabulary. 1. Explain genocide and holocaust in the context of World War II. **2.** How did penicillin and synthetic fibers help the soldiers in World War II?

Reviewing Main Ideas. 1. Summarize the main points of the agreements the Allies made after the war. **2.** Compare the poems "At Terezin" and "The Butterfly." **3.** What was the cost of World War II in both lives and money? **4.** Name five technological benefits of the war.

Understanding Geography Explain why Germany was divided after the war, but not Japan.

Challenge Evaluate the positive and negative outcomes of World War II.

CHAPTER 28 *Summary & Review*

Summarizing Main Ideas

The League of Nations was formed in 1920 to promote world peace and cooperation. It was not effective and dictators, such as Hitler in Germany and Mussolini in Italy, rose to power. Postwar problems increased international hostilities.

From 1939 to 1940, Germany conquered eastern Europe. Churchill was elected prime minister of Great Britain in 1940 and mobilized the British people. The war spread to the Middle East, Africa, and Russia, as Hitler was joined by Mussolini. Japan's attack on the American base at Pearl Harbor in December 1941 brought the United States into World War II.

United States war material poured into the Allied nations to turn the tide of the war. Germany surrendered in May 1945. The Japanese surrendered in August after President Truman ordered atomic bombs dropped on Hiroshima and Nagasaki.

Following the war, the Allies divided Germany and formed the United Nations. World War II was more costly than any previous war in history.

"Fresh, spirited American troops, flushed with victory, are bringing in thousands of hungry, ragged, battle-weary prisoners . . ."   (News item)

Questions for Critical Thinking

COMPREHENSION Interpreting Events

1. Why did the peace treaty of World War I fail?
2. How did the war spread around the world?
3. What enabled the Allies to defeat the Axis powers?
4. Did the Allies or Axis powers pay a heavier cost for the war? Explain.

ANALYSIS Identifying Trends

1. Why was World War II more costly than World War I?
2. Discuss why there has not been another world war since 1945.

APPLICATION Comparing Past to Present

1. Compare the Allies' treatment of Germany following the two world wars.

2. How is the United Nations different from the League of Nations? How have these differences affected relations among the nations of the world?

SYNTHESIS Developing Writing Skills

1. Write a paragraph explaining the message of the cartoon on this page.
2. Write a poem about the costs of war.

EVALUATION Weighing Consequences

1. List the major changes that resulted from World War II.
2. Rank the outcomes of World War II from best to worst.

CHALLENGE

1. When can war be justified?
2. How can war be prevented?

UNIT 7 *Review*

Critical Thinking for Today's World

ANALYSIS Understanding People

1. Choose two important people who lived between 1850 and 1945. Explain their contributions to the history of the world.
2. The United States maintained its neutrality in World War I until 1917. What events triggered its declaration of war on Germany?
3. Explain how various Russian groups reacted to Stalin's five-year plans.
4. Give three examples from the 1920s and 1930s when world leaders' solutions to a problem actually made matters worse.
5. What were Hitler's reasons for sending an army into other countries?
6. Why did Truman use the atomic bomb?

ANALYSIS Recognizing Change Over Time

1. Describe two ways liberalism under Alexander II changed Russia.
2. Explain the changes in the Mexican government from 1910 to 1940.
3. Describe how World War I changed the political boundaries of Europe.
4. Show Japan's growth from an isolated island to a world power by using a chart with these headings: Date, Event, Result of Event.
5. Contrast the Allied treatment of Germany after World War I and after World War II.

APPLICATION Solving Problems

1. Explain how the Congress of Berlin created problems as well as solved them.
2. What steps did European countries take to protect their shipping routes and overseas markets?
3. List the major provisions of the Treaty of Versailles. Which problem of postwar Europe was each meant to solve?
4. How did President Roosevelt try to solve the social, political, and economic problems of the Great Depression in the United States?

SYNTHESIS Developing Global Citizenship

1. Give two examples of the way nationalism shaped world history.
2. What common bonds united countries before World War I?
3. What events led the Russian people to revolt?
4. What events caused a European conflict to become a global war?
5. What has the world done to prevent another world war?

EVALUATION Learning Lessons from the Past

1. Evaluate the advantages and disadvantages of new weapons using examples from this unit.
2. Give two specific examples of colonial exploitation. How did people react?
3. What lesson did the world learn about the policy of appeasement after World War II?
4. Both the Allies and the Axis used bombs in World War II. Give reasons why the dropping of two atomic bombs were events that led to almost immediate surrender.
5. Construct a chart listing the problems that led to World War II and how each was resolved.
6. Explain why advances in science and technology are more rapid during wartime. List three wartime advances that were valuable after the war.

Estimates of European War Dead, World War II	
USSR	20,000,000
Germany and Austria	6,500,000
Poland	6,000,000
Yugoslavia	1,600,000
France	600,000
Hungary	600,000
Romania	600,000
Italy	400,000
Britain	390,000
Czechoslovakia	270,000
Other countries	463,000

The Interacting Global Community, 1850–1945

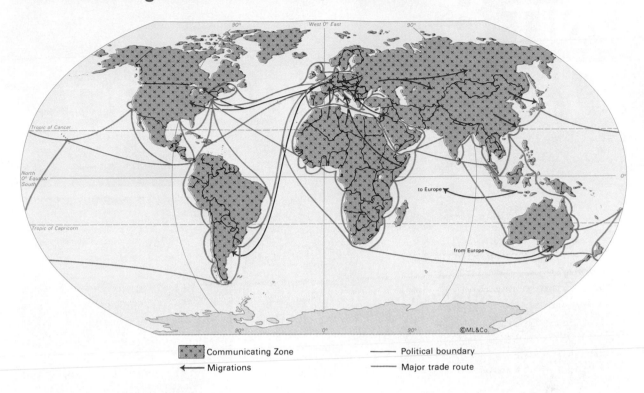

Communicating Zone   Political boundary

Migrations   Major trade route

A Global Perspective

During the period from 1850 to 1945, the global community experienced major changes. In less than a century, existing empires were challenged, independent nations emerged, and alliances changed.

In the first half of the 1900s, two world wars were fought. Between the wars, a Great Depression engulfed much of the world. Technological advances increased global communication. The U.N. was formed to promote world peace and international cooperation.

COMPREHENSION Interpreting Maps

1. What geographic feature gave people in the United States a feeling of safety during the two world wars?
2. Which parts of the American continent were in the greatest danger from submarine attacks and air raids?
3. How does Russia's location explain its need for a larger army and air force than a navy?
4. Using the map above, name the continents from which people migrated and the bodies of water they crossed to settle in Australia.
5. Using the map above, name the four continents to which Europeans migrated. For the proper names of the continents, see the geography feature on pages 10–11.
6. Name two large land areas that were not affected by migrations after 1850 because of their geographical features.
7. Using the map above, name the continent to which Africans migrated.

ANALYSIS Recognizing Global Trends

1. Compare the migration patterns of the 1600s with the 1800s. See the map on page 560.
2. What bodies of water are connected by the Panama Canal; the Suez Canal? In what ways have these canals simplified trade?
3. Compare the communicating zone of 1850–1945 to that of A.D. 1000 on page 275. How are they different? List five developments that changed the communicating zone.

UNIT 8
The Interacting

Courtesy of The Peace Museum/The Ribbon Project.

Modern World

Since 1945

A panel from the handcrafted ribbon of peace that was tied around the Pentagon on August 4, 1985.

CHAPTER 29

The World after World War II

GLOBAL TIME LINE

1945   1950   1955

TIME

- **1945** New French constitution establishes the Fourth French Republic
- **1950** North Korean troops invade South Korea
- **1947–1955** United States economy prospers
- **1948** Soviets take over Czechoslovakia
- **1949** Western nations form the North Atlantic Treaty Organization, NATO

PEOPLE

- **1929–1953** Joseph Stalin leads the Soviet Union
- **1944–1946** Charles de Gaulle heads the provisional French government
- **1949–1963** Konrad Adenauer brings stability to West Germany
- **1947** President Truman proclaims the Truman Doctrine to contain communism
- **1947** George C. Marshall proposes a European recovery plan

PLACE

- **1945** *Great Britain;*[1] Labor party nationalizes major industries
- **1947** *Italy;*[2] Italians adopt a new constitution establishing a republic
- **1948** *Korea;*[3] Korea is divided into the Republic of Korea in the south and the Democratic Peoples' Republic of Korea in the north
- **1948–1949** *Berlin;*[4] United States and Great Britain airlift supplies to West Berlin

Linking Past to Present

After World War II, the Allied countries continued to manage their peacetime economies as they had their wartime economies. Countries of western Europe followed the industrial example of the United States. They developed mass production, inexpensive goods, and mass markets. Trade barriers between nations were lowered. As a result, the economic recovery after World War II was much more rapid than the recovery after 1918.

The post World War II world was sharply divided between communist and non-communist countries. Both the United States and the Soviet Union worked to gain allies in the new countries in Africa and Asia. As you read the chapter, determine what conditions contributed to the division between the former allies.

An American plane airlifts supplies to Berlin during the Russian blockade in 1948.

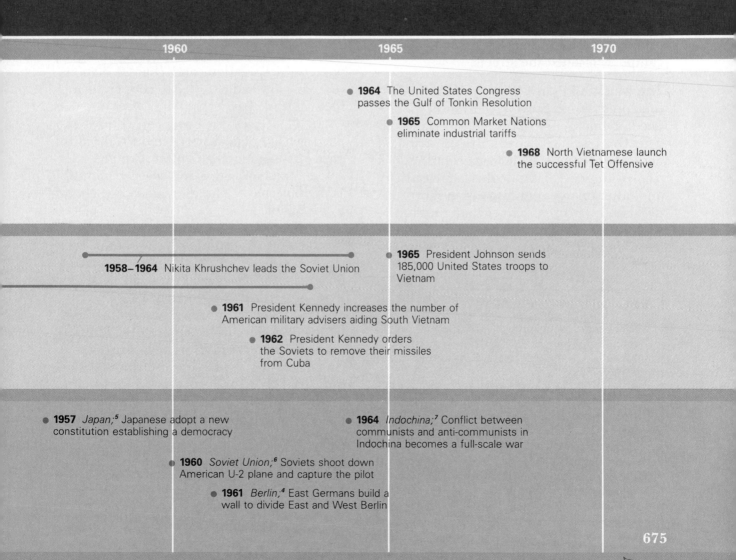

1960   **1965**   **1970**

1964 The United States Congress passes the Gulf of Tonkin Resolution

1965 Common Market Nations eliminate industrial tariffs

1968 North Vietnamese launch the successful Tet Offensive

1958–1964 Nikita Khrushchev leads the Soviet Union

1965 President Johnson sends 185,000 United States troops to Vietnam

1961 President Kennedy increases the number of American military advisers aiding South Vietnam

1962 President Kennedy orders the Soviets to remove their missiles from Cuba

1957 *Japan;[5]* Japanese adopt a new constitution establishing a democracy

1964 *Indochina;[7]* Conflict between communists and anti-communists in Indochina becomes a full-scale war

1960 *Soviet Union;[6]* Soviets shoot down American U-2 plane and capture the pilot

1961 *Berlin;[4]* East Germans build a wall to divide East and West Berlin

675

1 Rebuilding the World after World War II

OBJECTIVE: *To understand the causes and consequences of postwar aid to Europe and Asia*

Western Europe Rebuilds

When World War II ended, many of the cities, towns, and farming communities of Europe were in ruins. Transportation and communication systems, factories, and homes were destroyed. Millions of refugees, called displaced persons, filled special camps or roamed the streets.

The Marshall Plan. When the war ended, the countries of Europe were in desperate need of emergency relief and economic aid. The United States, Great Britain, Canada, and other nations made large contributions to provide relief. Despite this aid, electricity and other energy sources were in short supply. Food was even scarcer than during the war. President Truman sent former President Herbert Hoover to 22 countries to re-port on conditions. Hoover found many people near starvation.

In 1947, Secretary of State George C. Marshall addressed the Harvard College graduating class. He suggested the United States should aid all European nations in need. His offer was directed "not against any country or doctrine but against hunger, poverty, desperation, and chaos." Nations receiving aid had to agree to cooperate and remove trade barriers.

In all, 16 western European nations applied for aid. The Soviet Union refused to participate in Marshall's offer. Congress debated Marshall's idea for several months. Many objected to the estimated cost, about $12.5 billion.

In February 1948, however, Soviet tanks rumbled into Czechoslovakia and took over that country. An alarmed Congress promptly approved the European Recovery Plan, also called the Marshall Plan.

The Marshall Plan was a great success, both politically and economically. The appeal of communism in western Europe declined, along with malnutrition. The industrial life of Germany rapidly improved. By 1951, the production of goods in western Europe surpassed prewar levels.

Managing Nations' Economies. After World War II, governments in many democratic nations took a more active role in managing their economies. Some nations had started to direct their economies in the

---

VOCABULARY DEVELOPMENT

welfare state: a state in which the citizens' welfare—employment, medical care, retirement funds—is considered to be the government's responsibility.

chancellor (CHAN suh luhr) *noun:* the prime minister in some countries. From the Latin word, *cancellarius,* meaning secretary.

Jiang Jieshi (JYANG KY SHEHK): Pinyin spelling, formerly Chiang Kai-shek.

military dictatorship: a state in which the armed forces choose the leader of the country.

Mao Zedong (mou zuh DONG): Pinyin spelling, formerly Mao Tse-tung.

1930s to combat the Great Depression. The influential British economist John Maynard Keynes (kaynz) argued that during times of depression, governments should spend money on public projects to increase economic activity. By adjusting expenditures, governments could increase production, employment, and consumption. After the war, many governments managed their national economies and worked toward lowering trade barriers more or less as Keynes had suggested.

The Labor Party Governs Britain. The Labor and Conservative parties dominated British politics both before and after the war. The Labor party supported programs to help the working class. The Conservative party supported individual freedom and distrusted government controls.

In 1945, Winston Churchill and his Conservative party were defeated at the polls. The people, weary of war and sacrifice, elected a majority of Labor party candidates. The Labor government nationalized, or took over, such major industries as coal, steel, iron, transportation, communications, and banking. The goal of the Labor party was to protect consumers and workers, and to better manage the economy to achieve prosperity.

The Labor government passed new welfare measures. Education was free until students reached the age of 16. All people received free dental and medical care. Great Britain became a welfare state, a nation whose government assumed responsibility for the welfare of its people.

The war ended the British Empire. Great Britain lost some of its valuable overseas colonies and possessions during the war. The British later gave independence to India and most of the remaining colonies. Great Britain also lost its place as the leading industrial country of western Europe.

The Fifth French Republic. The Third French Republic ended when France fell to the Germans in 1940. During the Nazi oc-

The French used cranes at Le Havre, France, to unload the first shipment of American-made tractors sent under the Marshall Plan.

cupation, Charles de Gaulle (duh GAWL), a French general, formed a Free French government in exile, headquartered in London. His frequent radio broadcasts to France stirred patriotism and encouraged the French resistance movement. After the Allies liberated France in 1944, de Gaulle headed the provisional government that governed the country until 1946.

Charles de Gaulle was an imposing figure at 6 feet 4 inches, or 193 centimeters. Often stubborn and aloof, he loved France and was a fierce patriot. De Gaulle firmly believed he was the only person who could again make France a world power.

After the war, de Gaulle wanted a new French constitution that would give the president more power. Without it, the same politicians who, he believed, had mismanaged the country before the war would again govern France. Not trusting the assembly to write the constitution, he resigned.

This 1961 photo was taken during the Algerian Revolution against French rule. More than 250,000 French and Algerians died before Algeria gained independence in 1962.

In 1958, a rebellion against French rule in Algeria created a crisis. To prevent a civil war, the government again called on de Gaulle to lead the country. The general agreed, on the condition that political leaders support a new constitution giving greater power to the president. The constitution establishing the Fifth French Republic was approved in September 1958. For the next ten years, while President de Gaulle governed, France prospered.

West German Prosperity. By the end of World War II, the German economy was in ruins. In the United States zone of military occupation, 90 percent of German industry was totally destroyed. More than 2,000 bridges were demolished.

The zones of Germany occupied by the Western powers began rebuilding with hard work, intelligent planning, and aid from the Allied countries. In 1949, West Germany drafted a new democratic constitution. The two leading political parties under this new system were the Christian Democrats and the Social Democrats. The Christian Democrats, who held the majority of seats in the legislature, encouraged private enterprise. The Social Democrats were socialists who favored government control of the factors of production.

Konrad Adenauer (AD uhn ow ehr), leader of the Christian Democrats, became chancellor, or prime minister, of Germany in 1949. He was 73 years old. Under Adenauer's 14 years of firm leadership, West Germany became a major industrial and military power. Adenauer acknowledged Germany's responsibility for the war crimes committed against the Jews, and the government paid war reparations to Israel. He also allied Germany to a new era of peace with the Western nations.

Italy Lacks a Stable Government. After the war, the Italians also wrote a new constitution, which changed their nation from a monarchy to a republic. Italy, like West

Germany, chose an effective, experienced post-war leader. Alcide de Gasperi (al CHEE day duh GAS puhr ee), a member of the Italian resistance movement during the war, became prime minister of Italy in 1945.

Italy had a number of competing political parties after the war. The most popular parties were the Christian Democrat, the Socialist, and the Communist. Italy was the only western European country where the communists formed a major party.

De Gasperi, leader of the Christian Democrats, began a long-term land reform program to increase land ownership in southern and central Italy. He encouraged industry, constructed new power plants, and established close ties with the West. These measures helped prevent the Communists from gaining control of the government in Italy.

In 1953, the Christian Democrats lost control of the Italian legislature. Succeeding prime ministers seldom remained in office more than a year or two. No single party could win enough votes to control the legislature and form a stable government.

The Soviet Union Controls Eastern Europe

At the end of the war, Europe was divided between the free nations of the West and the Soviet-controlled nations of the East. Russia had often been invaded from western Europe. The Poles invaded in the seventeenth century and Napoleon in 1812. The Germans invaded in 1914 and in 1941. Each time, the Soviets suffered huge losses in life and property. Soviet leaders wanted a buffer zone under their control to prevent any west European country from attacking the Soviet Union again.

By refusing to withdraw Soviet military forces from Eastern Europe, Stalin, the Soviet dictator, created this buffer zone. It included the states of Poland, East Germany, Czechoslovakia, Hungary, Romania,

Bulgaria, and Albania. The states often were referred to as satellite countries of the Soviet Union. See the map, Europe after World War II, page 667.

The Satellite Nations of Eastern Europe.
Soviet Union control over its satellites was economic as well as military. The products of the satellites had to be sold at low prices in the Soviet Union. In turn, the satellites had to buy Russian goods at high prices. The satellites provided badly needed goods and services for the recovering economy of the Soviet Union.

In Poland, Hungary, Romania, East Germany, Czechoslovakia, and Bulgaria, the Soviets installed local communists to head the governments. In Albania and Yugoslavia, national leaders had already set up communist states. See the map, Europe after World War II, page 667.

Communism in Yugoslavia.
Marshal Tito (TEE toh) headed the Communist party of Yugoslavia. Tito and his resistance fighters had helped the Soviets to liberate Yugoslavia from the Germans in 1944. The popular Tito then became the dictator of Yugoslavia. Tito believed in communism, but he objected to Soviet control. In 1948, he announced that Yugoslavia would follow an independent course. Yugoslavia was the only eastern European country to successfully challenge Soviet control.

Asia after World War II

Much of World War II was fought in Asia. The Japanese conquered Southeast Asia, Manchuria, and parts of China during the war. Bombs destroyed transportation systems and disrupted the economies of Asian countries.

United States Occupation of Japan.
Before World War II, Japan was the most industrialized nation in Asia. When the war ended, most Japanese cities and factories

When Japan surrendered, United States troops occupied the Japanese home islands. Here, a United States flag waves atop a hangar at Japan's Atsugi Airport in 1945.

were in ruins. Only about 20 percent of Japanese industries escaped bombing.

When Japan surrendered, United States troops, headed by General Douglas MacArthur, occupied the island nation. Emperor Hirohito was allowed to remain on the throne. The emperor appointed ministers who carried out MacArthur's orders.

MacArthur and his advisers drafted a new constitution that went into effect in 1947. This constitution established a democracy, removing political power from the emperor. The Allies also abolished the Japanese army and navy.

By the time the United States occupation forces withdrew in 1952, Japan's industrial production equaled that of 1941. Japan's postwar economic growth, like West Germany's, astonished the world.

The Chinese Civil War. In China, the years after World War II witnessed the triumph of the Communist party. From 1912, when

the Chinese Empire came to an end, until the Communist victory in 1949, China experienced almost continuous upheaval. Sun Yat-sen, leader of the Nationalist People's Party, or Guomindang, tried to modernize China along Western lines. He never succeeded, however, in uniting the country (see page 588).

When Sun Yat-sen died in 1925, Jiang Jieshi (JYANG ky SHEHK), formerly spelled Chiang Kai-shek, a young general, became the new leader of the Guomindang. In 1927, Jiang and his nationalist army succeeded in uniting China. He set up his nationalist government in Nanjing and ruled China for the next ten years. This government was a one-party military dictatorship.

The Long March. During the 1920s, the communists set up the Chinese Soviet Republic in south central China. The nationalists attacked repeatedly, however, and forced the communists to retreat. Facing total defeat, Mao Zedong (mou zuh DONG), leader of the communists, made a desperate gamble. He led 100,000 communists on a 6,000 mile trek north and west to escape the Nationalist army. This Long March across swamps, mountains, and deserts ended in October 1935. About 3,000 of the travelers reached their goal.

These survivors reestablished the Chinese Soviet Republic in the north.

In 1937 Japan invaded China, forcing the nationalist government to abandon the eastern cities and retreat into the interior of southern China. Jiang Jieshi was not strong enough to defend China. The Chinese communists, however, organized guerrilla forces among the peasants. These forces grew into a popular, patriotic movement. Many peasants deserted the nationalist cause. By the end of World War II, the communists were well organized and strong.

Communist Victory. After the Japanese surrendered in 1945, civil war broke out in China. The nationalist government tried to

Communist soldiers, shown here, captured Nanjing in 1949. Jiang Jieshi retreated to Taiwan. Mao Zedong and the communists subsequently won control of mainland China.

regain control of the territory the Japanese had occupied. The United States backed the nationalists who controlled the cities in eastern and southern China. The communists, however, received aid from the Soviet Union and by 1946 went on the offensive.

When Mao's forces captured the nationalist capital at Nanjing in 1949, Jiang Jieshi and his supporters retreated to the island of Taiwan, also called Formosa, off the southern coast of China.

All of mainland China fell to the communists, who organized the People's Republic of China, placing its capital at Beijing. Under Mao Zedong, China was turned into a socialist state similar to that of the Soviet Union.

By 1950, Japan and the countries of western Europe had recovered from World War II. All had new constitutions and democratic governments. Communist dictators ruled the countries of eastern Europe, which had become satellites of the Soviet Union. The Soviet Union also influenced the communist government established in China. Increasingly, two superpowers came to dominate the world—the United States and the Soviet Union.

SECTION 1 *Study Skills*

Developing Vocabulary Write a sentence using the following words: **1.** welfare state. **2.** chancellor. **3.** Jiang Jieshi. **4.** military dictatorship. **5.** Mao Zedong.

Reviewing Main Ideas 1. What were the effects of the Marshall Plan on western Europe? **2.** How does a socialist government control the economy? **3.** What were the goals of the United States occupation of Japan? **4.** How did the government of Czechoslovakia differ from that of Yugoslavia?

Understanding Cause and Effect 1. How did the 1945 election of a Labor government affect the lives of the British? **2.** What impact did de Gaulle have on France from 1944 to 1968? **3.** How did de Gasperi influence Italy's growth after World War II? **4.** What events enabled the communists to develop a strong hold on China?

Understanding Geography 1. Construct a map showing the countries that made up the Russian buffer zone. **2.** How was the country of Germany divided after World War II?

Challenge Is foreign aid as important today as it was after World War II? Explain.

North American Geography

During World War II, citizens of the United States were grateful that their country was separated from Europe and Asia by wide oceans. Inhabitants of the American culture realm felt that the Atlantic and Pacific oceans protected them from invasion.

The North American continent includes Canada, the United States, Mexico, and Central America. The oceans have always challenged seafarers. The continents, too, have geographical features that offer challenges and affect the climate.

Landforms

Early explorers who traveled inland from the east coast of North America had to cross the Appalachian Mountains. This mountain chain sweeps southward from Quebec, Canada to Alabama in the United States. For more than 1,200 miles, or 1,900 kilometers, this broad system forms the rocky backbone of eastern North America. These rolling hills were once much higher. Since their birth some 280 million years ago, wind, rain, snow, and even glaciers have eroded them. The highest peaks now range between 6,000 and 7,000 feet.

Early travelers who ventured inland from the west coast came upon a much higher mountain chain. The Rocky Mountains extend all the way from Alaska to New Mexico. They are a part of the great mountain system that continues down the western part of South America to the southern tip of Chili. In North America the Rockies stretch about 3,100 miles, or 5,000 kilometers. The highest peaks are in Colorado and rise over 14,000 feet. This rugged mountain spine forms North America's Continental Divide. Waters on the western side flow into the Pacific Ocean while those on the eastern side flow to the Atlantic and Arctic oceans. The younger Rocky Mountains were born when a series of upheavals thrust them up above a shallow sea.

Between the Appalachian and Rocky Mountain chains is the mighty Missouri-Mississippi river system. From a source high in the Rocky Mountains, these rivers and their tributaries flow to the gulf of Mexico. This river system is the third largest in the world. The Mississippi alone is 2,348 miles, or 3,779 kilometers, long. Before joining it, the Missouri flows a greater distance— 2,466 miles, or 3,969 kilometers. The rivers drain lands from the Appalachian Mountains in the east to the Rocky Mountains in the west. This area includes all or part of 31 states and 2 Canadian provinces. Although periodic flooding is a challenge, this river system is responsible for the growth of many major cities. The Missouri-Mississippi river system continues to be an important shipping lane for products in the United States and part of Canada.

The United States and Canada share the largest group of fresh-water lakes in the world. The Great Lakes make up the most important inland waterway in North America. Both countries share four of the lakes: Superior, Huron, Erie, and Ontario. Lake Michigan lies entirely within the United States. The lakes were gouged out about 250,000 years ago. At that time, glaciers dug deep depressions in the earth. As the glaciers retreated about 10,000 years ago, melting ice filled the depressions and formed the lakes. Together, the Great Lakes have an area of 94,510 square miles, or 244, 780 kilometers. Lake Superior is the largest. These lakes are connected to the Atlantic Ocean by the St. Lawrence River. Lake levels are of different heights. How-

Data on Countries in North America		
	Canada	United States
Area (in thousands of square miles)	3,845	3,619
Population (in millions)	25	236
Annual birth rate (per 1,000 population)	15	16
Annual death rate (per 1,000 population)	7	9
Number of years to double population (projected)	58	78
Population projected by the year 2000 (in millions)	29	268
Annual death rate of infants under 1 year (per 1,000 population)	7	11
Percent of population under 15 years	23	22
Percent of population over 60 years	13	16
Life expectancy at birth	76	74
Percent of population urban	76	74
Per capita food supply (as percent of requirement)	126	138
Total GNP (in billions of U.S. dollars)	317	3,701
Per capita GNP (in U.S. dollars)	12,650	15,670
Percent of adult population illiterate	4	4

ever, a series of canals and locks solved this challenge. They permit large ocean vessels to reach inland ports.

Climate

The climate of North America ranges from arctic in northern Canada to humid, equatorial in southern Florida, Mexico, and Central America. The greater part of the continent has a temperate climate with warm summers and cold winters. Bodies of water and large landforms play an important role in the weather.

Oceans and large lakes absorb more heat from the sun than does the land. They also hold the heat longer. However, during the day, coastal lands warm faster than the seas. When wind blows across the water onto the land, the warm air above the land rises. Cooler sea breezes then replace the heat.

When an ocean wind blows against a mountain, the air is lifted and cooled. The water vapor forms clouds, and rain or snow falls. As air flows down the other side of the mountain, it becomes warmer and the clouds evaporate. Land on the far side may have dry or desert-like conditions as in the southwestern United States.

The Great Lakes and the Gulf of Mexico influence the weather in the eastern half of North America. Winds blowing across these bodies of water pick up moisture and usually bring rain. A northeast wind across Lake Michigan will eventually bring cool, wet weather to Illinois. A southwest wind from the Gulf will bring Illinoisans warm, wet weather. Generally, the Great Lakes have the greater influence in the winter; the Gulf of Mexico in the summer.

American Neighbors

Relations between the United States and its neighbors, Mexico and Canada, are generally good. Citizens can travel freely across the borders. No passport is needed at the border checks. However, certain rules apply to products that may be transported. Shared resources make it important to maintain friendly relations among the nations of the North American continent.

STUDY SKILLS Understanding Geography

1. Contrast the Appalachian and Rocky Mountains as to location, age, length, and height.
2. What is the Continental Divide?
3. Why is the land temperature often cooler near an ocean or large lake than it is inland?
4. Explain why large waterways are important to maintaining a nation's growth.
5. Use the information on the chart to compare and contrast Canada with the United States.

2 A World of Superpowers

OBJECTIVE: *To understand the causes and consequences of the rise of two superpowers*

Two Giants Vie for Influence

The alliance of Great Britain, the United States, and the Soviet Union began to crumble during World War II. As fascism and Nazism were defeated in Europe, little remained to hold the Western democracies and the Soviet Union together. The war had helped to create two military-industrial giants—the Soviet Union and the United States. Both competed for world influence after the war.

American Influence Increases. Weakened by two world wars, western Europe never regained its former influence throughout the world. After the war, the United States and the Soviet Union replaced the countries of western Europe as the world's strongest economic and military powers.

The Strong United States Economy. After the war ended, many economists in the United States expected a postwar depression. They thought that as war industries closed down, factories and workers

would become idle. Instead, Americans went on a shopping spree for houses, appliances, and cars.

Farmers also gained from America's wartime prosperity. Many Europeans who were fighting the war were unable to farm. The United States became the breadbasket of the world as great amounts of farm products were exported. Farm production grew more than 400 percent. After the war, farm products were used to feed the people of countries devastated by the fighting. With large overseas markets and high prices for their crops, American farmers prospered. Farm income was higher than ever before in United States history.

During the decade after 1945, United States influence spread throughout the world. The United States was the leading exporter of goods during and after World War II. American industry provided the goods that war-weary European and Asian countries could not produce.

The Soviet Union Rebuilds. The Soviet Union suffered terrible losses during the war, heavier than those of any of the Allies. German occupation of the industrialized western part of the Soviet Union destroyed factories, as well as communication and transportation systems.

When the United States offered Marshall Plan aid, Stalin refused. He feared that accepting capitalist assistance would weaken the appeal of communism. Instead, Stalin

---

VOCABULARY DEVELOPMENT

economist (ih KAHN uh mihst) *noun:* a specialist in economics, the science that deals with wealth and the related problems of labor. From the Greek word, *oikonomia,* meaning management of a household.

breadbasket: a region that supplies much grain.

---

introduced a new set of five-year plans designed to repair war damage. The new plans emphasized heavy industry rather than consumer products.

The goal of the five-year plans was to catch up with American industry. By 1956, Soviet factories produced three times as much as before the war. While output was less than the United States, it did equal or exceed that of most other nations.

Soviet Agriculture. An industrial economy cannot develop unless food is available to feed the growing number of factory workers. If farmers cannot increase their productivity, the government must buy food from other nations. The cost of importing food decreases the money that can be used to build and expand industry.

Increasing farm production, however, was a difficult problem for the Soviet Union. Harsh weather and poor yields made government efforts unsuccessful.

The cold war became a hot war when Soviet tanks invaded Prague, Czechoslovakia, in 1968. Here, a freedom fighter encourages his friends.

The Causes of the Cold War

FOCUS ON SOURCES

Most people of the world hoped that the victory over the Nazis and fascists, along with the founding of the United Nations, would lead to lasting peace. Deep distrust, however, developed between the Western world led by the United States and the communist countries led by the Soviet Union. This distrust and its consequences came to be called the Cold War.

The following excerpt from *Beyond the Cold War* examines the causes of the Cold War between the two superpowers. The author of the book, Professor Frederick L. Schuman, is an expert in the field of Soviet affairs and international relations:

❝At all events, what we have long been calling the Cold War did not begin in 1945, in the aftermath of World War II and of the Yalta and Potsdam conferences. In a broader sense it began with the second Russian Revolution of 1917. The communists were then convinced that the Russian Revolution would inevitably be followed by worldwide revolution and that it was their mission and duty to assist the inevitable to come to pass. . . .

Within ten months after Russia's October Revolution, Soviet Russia and the West were at war. And the war was not a cold war but a hot war, marked by many casualties and vast destruction. Be it remembered . . . that this was not begun by communists sending armies against the West but by the West sending armies against Soviet Russia. . . . The legacy of mutual fear and suspicion and hatred which nourished the Cold War of the 1940s and 1950s originated in the hot war between East and West in 1918–1921. . . .

The Cold War in the narrower sense began in the late summer and fall of 1945, immediately after the surrender of Japan, with early, repeated, and emphatic American and British protests against the imposition of Soviet hegemony [leadership] and communist power on Eastern Europe.... This vast and alarming extension of Russian power into central Europe and the Balkans was alleged [believed] in London and Washington to constitute a Russian violation of the Yalta and Potsdam agreements....

In international politics, as in our personal affairs, decisions have consequences. These consequences are often irrevocable .... They are with us today. They will be with us for a long time to come. **"**

The Cold War between the Soviet Union and the West was fought mostly with words. The result was growing hostility and mistrust among nations and an inability to solve world difficulties through the United Nations. The opposing sides competed in building up armaments and attracting the support of the nonaligned countries. This freeze continued in varying degrees until the mid-1980s when Mikhail Gorbachev became the Soviet leader. He proposed a restructuring, or *perestroika*, of the Soviet government and economy. The meltdown of the Cold War continued as it became more clear to the Soviets that a centrally controlled economy would not work.

Distrust between the Superpowers

As early as 1945, a major difference divided the United States and the Soviet Union. The United States followed the western European tradition of representative democracy and a free market economy. In the United States, private individuals and corporations owned the factors of production.

The Soviet Union kept its long tradition of a highly centralized and authoritarian government. The communists dictated political policy and also controlled the economy of the Soviet Union.

As the Soviet Union expanded into eastern Europe, the Western world became increasingly concerned. Winston Churchill, speaking in Fulton, Missouri, in 1946, said:

" From Stettin... to Trieste in the Adriatic, an iron curtain has descended across the continent. Behind that line lie all the capitals of the ancient states of central and eastern Europe. Warsaw, Berlin, Prague, Vienna, Budapest, Belgrade, Bucharest, and Sofia, all these famous cities and the populations around them lie in what I must call the Soviet sphere, ... **"**

The Truman Doctrine. On February 4, 1947, Great Britain told the United States that it could no longer afford to give economic help to Turkey. It also could no longer help the Greek monarchy, which was trying to put down a revolt by communist-led guerrillas. The guerrillas were receiving aid from Greece's communist neighbors, Yugoslavia, Bulgaria, and Albania.

President Truman faced a dangerous choice. If he did nothing, Greece might become another Soviet satellite. If he aided the anticommunists, another war might break out. Truman decided to act. He asked Congress for $400 million in economic and military aid for Turkey and Greece. Truman told Congress, "I believe it must be the policy of the United States to support free peoples who are resisting attempted subjugation [conquest] by armed minorities or by outside pressures."

This statement defined the Truman Doctrine, a policy to contain communism within the Soviet Union and the satellite countries it controlled.

The Berlin Airlift. In the summer of 1948, the United States and the Soviet Union confronted each other over the future of Germany. The division of Germany was a disturbing problem. The situation in Berlin was especially difficult. Located deep within Soviet-controlled East Germany, West Berlin depended on Western Europe.

With American postwar aid, West Berlin made an astonishing economic recovery in

Alliances, 1980s

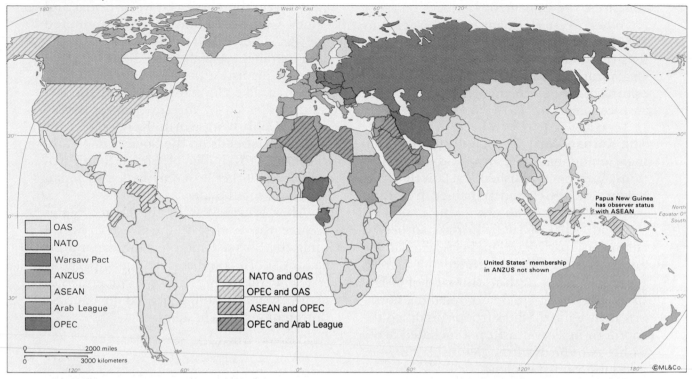

Map Skills   **1.** To what alliances does the United States belong? **2.** To what alliance does the United Kingdom belong? **3.** Name the nations that are allied in the Warsaw Pact.

contrast to East Berlin, where growth was slow. In July 1948, the Soviets, angered by a currency dispute in Berlin, blockaded the western sectors of the city. They refused to allow the Allies to use highways or trains to bring supplies to West Berlin.

The United States viewed the action as a direct threat to the postwar freedom of western Europe and the agreements made after the war. Acting on the Truman Doctrine, the United States and Great Britain began an airlift to relieve the city of West Berlin. They used every transport and cargo plane they could make available.

For 327 days, planes took off and landed every few minutes around the clock. In 277,000 flights, the airlift brought 2.5 million tons of supplies into West Berlin. Finally, in May 1949, the Soviets removed the blockade and allowed traffic from West Germany to cross through East Germany to reach West Berlin.

That same month, voters in the three western zones of Germany approved a constitution. The Western powers turned over government of their zones to the Federal Republic of Germany.

Cold War Alliances. After the Soviet advance into eastern Europe, many people feared further Soviet expansion. Increasingly, the Western nations saw the need for an alliance against the Soviet Union.

In April 1949, 12 nations signed a mutual defense pact. They formed the North Atlantic Treaty Organization, or NATO. The 12 nations were the United States, Great Britain, France, Italy, Portugal, Norway, Denmark, Iceland, Canada, and the Benelux countries of Belgium, the Netherlands, and Luxembourg. Joining them later were Greece, Turkey, and West Germany. All agreed that an attack on one would be considered an attack on all. They also agreed to resist an attack. See the map, Alliances, 1980s, page 687.

When West Germany joined NATO in 1955, the Soviet Union formed its own defensive union. Called the Warsaw Treaty Organization, it included Bulgaria, Czechoslovakia, East Germany, Hungary, Poland, and Romania.

The Korean War. Despite the intense feelings, emotional speeches, and confrontations, Europe established a relatively stable balance of power and remained free from warfare. Asia was the new battleground.

From 1910 to 1945, Korea had been a colony of Japan. Agreements reached at the end of World War II divided the Korean peninsula at the 38th north parallel of latitude. The Soviet Union occupied the northern half. United States troops occupied the southern half. South Korea included Seoul (sohl), two-thirds of the peninsula's people, and most of its farmland.

In 1948, a United Nations commission went to Korea to supervise elections for a government to rule the entire peninsula. The Soviets would not allow the commission into their zone. Therefore, elections were held only in the south.

The elections established the Republic of Korea. Syngman Rhee, an anticommunist educated in the United States, became president. The communists set up the Democratic People's Republic of Korea in the north. Led by Moscow-trained Kim Il Sung, it was a dictatorship.

In 1948, both sides withdrew their troops. The Soviets, however, had heavily armed the North Koreans. In June 1950, North Korean troops invaded the south. The United Nations, with support of the United States, sent troops to South Korea.

At first, North Korean forces pushed far south to the tip of the peninsula. Then, under General Douglas MacArthur's leadership, the United Nations forces boldly counterattacked. They drove the North Koreans back almost to the border of China.

As the United Nations forces neared the Yalu River, the border between Korea and China, Chinese communist troops entered the war. They drove the U.N. forces to the 38th parallel. A stalemate developed. Finally, an armistice was signed in 1953.

Korea, like Germany and Vietnam, is a country divided by the superpower rivalry of the Cold War. North Korea's socialist economy depends on the Soviet Union and the People's Republic of China. South Korea's free market economy is tied to Japan and the United States.

After World War II, the United States became the leader of the Western world while the Soviet Union led the communist nations. Both countries became superpowers. The differences in government, economic systems, and goals led to distrust. Both nations sought allies.

SECTION 2 *Study Skills*

Developing Vocabulary **1.** What is the job of an economist? **2.** What does the term breadbasket mean?

Reviewing Main Ideas **1.** Make a chart showing the geographic, industrial, and political similarities and differences between the United States and the Soviet Union. **2.** What were the goals of the Soviet five-year plans? **3.** Explain the Cold War.

Understanding Cause and Effect **1.** Explain why American farmers became more productive after World War II while the Soviet farmers did not. **2.** What was the iron curtain? **3.** How did the Truman Doctrine change United States foreign policy? **4.** What were the causes of the Korean War?

Understanding Geography **1.** Name the 12 countries that were original members of NATO. **2.** What countries were members of the Warsaw Pact?

Challenge What basic principles of the Cold War does the Korean conflict reflect?

3 The Cold War in the 1950s and 1960s

OBJECTIVE: *To understand the causes and consequences of the Cold War in the 1950s and 1960s*

European Cooperation

By the spring of 1950, the Marshall Plan had shown impressive results. In France and Italy, production levels were well above those of 1938. German industry had begun its extraordinary expansion. Also under the Marshall Plan, tariff barriers were being lowered. A new age of European economic cooperation was beginning.

The European Coal and Steel Community. National loyalties remained strong throughout Europe in the 1950s. Several leaders, however, agreed that Europe's future depended on economic cooperation among nations. Germany's prime minister, Konrad Adenauer, declared, "We will have to shake off this idea [of national loyalties] if Europe is to develop as. . . it deserves."

The new European spirit of cooperation showed practical results in 1950. The French foreign minister, Robert Schuman, proposed a plan to produce coal and steel without restrictions among western European nations. The resources of northwestern Europe included large deposits of coal and iron ore. National boundaries, however, divided the great supply of iron and coal resources among France, West Germany, Belgium, and Luxembourg.

In 1952, ministers from the four countries, plus the Netherlands and Italy, signed a treaty establishing the European Coal and Steel Community, ECSC. Member nations set up an international central authority to regulate production and prices.

The European Economic Community. The new European leaders pursued dreams beyond nationalism and cooperated with one another to bring prosperity. In the 1950s, the West Germans signed a treaty of friendship with their longtime enemy, France. In 1956, the six ECSC countries pooled their nuclear resources to form Euraton, the Atomic Energy Commission. The members agreed to share information on the peaceful uses of atomic energy.

The most important step toward European cooperation, however, came in 1957.

VOCABULARY DEVELOPMENT

comrade (KAHM rad) *noun:* used as a form of address in the Communist party; a friend.

peaceful coexistence: living together without conflict despite differences, as in political systems or among nations.

espionage (EHS pee uh NAHZH) *noun:* the act of spying; a government's use of spies to learn another country's military secrets.

refugee (REHF yoo JEE) *noun:* a person who flees his home to seek refuge elsewhere, as in time of war, natural disaster, or persecution. From the Latin word, *refugere,* meaning to retreat.

purge *verb:* to purify; to rid of individuals thought to be disloyal or undesirable. From the Latin word, *purgare,* meaning to cleanse.

bloc *noun:* a group of nations acting together in support of one another.

Then, the six countries of the ECSC founded the European Economic Community, also called the EEC or Common Market. The nations agreed to gradually abolish tariffs and import quotas among themselves. Between 1958 and 1966, industrial production within the EEC increased by almost 38 percent.

The Common Market was so successful that Greece, Turkey, and many newly independent nations of Africa asked to become associate members. They received tariff benefits and the right to eventually join as full members.

In 1965, the member nations approved a plan to eliminate all industrial tariffs. In 1967, a single European headquarters of the EEC was set up in Belgium.

The Outer Seven The success of the Common Market inspired cooperation among other European nations outside the Common Market. In November 1959, Great Britain, Switzerland, Austria, Portugal, Sweden, Denmark, and Norway signed an agreement establishing the European Free

Trade Association, EFTA. The purpose of that treaty was to reduce trade barriers among member nations. However, the economies of these seven countries did not share common resources, as did the Common Market nations. Great Britain's trade exceeded all the others combined. These factors limited the success of the EFTA.

While the European nations were drawing closer together, the Soviet Union strictly controlled its eastern European satellite nations. Joseph Stalin, dictator of the Soviet Union since 1929, cast a dark shadow over the Russian and Eastern European peoples.

Joseph Stalin, Man of Steel

FOCUS ON PEOPLE

Joseph Stalin was the undisputed ruler of the Soviet Union from 1929 to 1953. Stalin extended the Soviet Union's control over one-fourth of the globe. For Soviet citizens who refused to cooperate, he set up a network of concentration camps in Soviet Siberia.

Joseph was born on December 21, 1879, in a peasant's small cottage in the present-day Soviet Republic of Georgia, a mountainous region of the Caucasus. His parents named him Joseph Vissarionovich Djugashvili. He alone of his parents' four children survived infancy.

The boy's father was a shoemaker and an alcoholic. He beat Joseph brutally and eventually deserted his family. Joseph's mother then worked as a laundress to support her son. She earned enough money to send him to a parish school and later to an Orthodox Theological Seminary. Her ambition was to see her son become a priest.

While in the seminary, Joseph joined a secret socialist organization. He was caught reading the organization's radical literature and expelled from the seminary. Joseph then began to organize railroad workers and encourage strikes. The tsar's police

Stalin ruled the Soviet Union from 1929 to 1953. Although he created the myth that he was the country's savior, he killed many Russians in purges.

soon arrested him, however, and sent him to Siberia.

During the Russian revolution of 1905, Joseph escaped and returned to Georgia. At the time, Lenin was in Geneva, Switzerland, planning the Russian Revolution. Trotsky was forming the first Workers' Soviet in St. Petersburg. In Georgia, Joseph wrote fiery pamphlets. In one he said:

❝ Russia is like a loaded gun, at full cock, ready to go off at the slightest concussion. . . . Our committees ought at once to set out to arm the people . . . to set up regional centers for the collection of arms, to organize workshops, for the preparation of . . . explosives. **❞**

Joseph's pamphlets caught the eye of Lenin, who met the young radical at a party conference in Finland. Joseph began organizing oil workers and took the name Stalin, meaning Man of Steel. Early in 1922, Lenin created the post of general secretary of the Central Committee for Joseph Stalin.

Later that year, Lenin became ill. He dictated a testament reviewing possible successors. About Stalin, he wrote:

❝ Stalin. . . becomes unbearable in the office of general secretary . . . I propose to the comrades to find a way to remove Stalin. . . and appoint another man. . . more patient, more loyal, more polite and more attentive to comrades, less capricious etc. **❞**

In 1924 Lenin died. Immediately, Stalin and Leon Trotsky struggled for leadership of the Communist party. Stalin won and became the absolute dictator of Russia.

While having millions of fellow Russians killed, Stalin tried to create a myth that he was the country's father and savior. Every Soviet writer, musician, and painter was expected to devote artistic energies to supporting this policy. Many towns, factories, and streets in Russia were named for Stalin. Millions of copies of his collected works were printed. A new metal was called Stal-inite, an orchid was named Stalinchid. Children standing before their desks every morning said: "Thank Comrade Stalin for this happy life."

When Stalin died on March 5, 1953, the government announced:

❝ The heart of the comrade and inspired continuer of Lenin's will, the wise leader and teacher of the Communist party and the Soviet people—Joseph Vissarionovich Stalin—has stopped beating. **❞**

After Stalin died, several Soviet leaders struggled for control of the country. The party announced that a new collective leadership would govern. Nevertheless, by 1956 Nikita Khrushchev (KROOS chehv), the son of a coal miner, became the dominant figure of the party and the government. ■

Soviet Problems in the 1950s

Khrushchev differed from Stalin in both personality and attitude. He never attended school as a boy and probably did not learn to read until he was an adult. He fought with the Red Army during the Russian Revolution. He later worked as a laborer during the day and went to school at night. He was self-confident, outspoken, and proud of his self-education.

In 1956, Khrushchev addressed the Twentieth Congress of the Communist party of the Soviet Union. A stunned audience listened as he detailed the crimes of the Stalin era and denounced the dead dictator for his brutality and abuse of power. Khrushchev also declared that peaceful coexistence with the capitalist nations of the West was possible.

The suggestion of peaceful coexistence created shock waves throughout the communist world. Mao Zedong accused Moscow of abandoning Marxist-Leninist doctrines. Relations between the two communist giants, the Soviet Union and the People's Republic of China, became strained. Even more serious was the independent thought that communists in Poland and Hungary exerted. These countries were the most industrialized and Western-oriented.

A Revolt in Hungary. Imre Nagy, a liberal communist in Hungary, became a symbol of the people's desire for a freer life. The old Stalinist leaders refused to step down.

Khrushchev's speech to the Party Congress brought hope for liberal changes to Hungary. In October 1956, when no reforms occurred, a large crowd of protesters called for the resignation of the government. The secret police opened fire, and revolution suddenly swept the country.

Imre Nagy was elected premier. He soon pledged free elections and the withdrawal of Hungary from the Warsaw Pact. The Soviets responded by sending troops into Budapest, the Hungarian capital. On November 4, 1956, tanks fired on demonstrators. Hungarians fought back with Molotov cocktails, bottles filled with gasoline with rags for wicks. Liberals broadcast pleas for help. No country came to their aid.

The Soviet army put down the Hungarian revolt and returned loyal party members to power. About 250,000 Hungarians fled across the border to Austria. About 25,000 died. The Soviets executed Nagy.

The Cold War, 1955–1960

The events of 1956 marked a new era in the relationship between the superpowers. The failure of the United States to aid Hungary seemed to point to a retreat from the Truman Doctrine. However, the Soviets continued talk of peaceful coexistence seemed to indicate a backing away from world communist revolution. In 1958, the two coun-

Shopkeepers and customers watch members of the Hungarian revolutionary forces take aim against the secret police in Budapest on October 31, 1956. The Soviet army put down the revolt.

tries began negotiating limitations on the testing of nuclear weapons. Nevertheless, confrontations between the Soviets and the West continued to occur.

The U-2 Crisis. In 1955, the United States Central Intelligence Agency authorized secret high-altitude flights over Soviet territory. The plane used for these missions, the U-2, was designed to fly higher than Russian fighter planes and beyond the reach of antiaircraft fire. As a U-2 passed over the Soviet Union, its infrared cameras took detailed photographs of everything below.

On May 1, 1960, the Soviet Union announced that it had shot down a U-2 inside its borders. Khrushchev then personally announced that the pilot, Francis Gary Powers, had been captured.

President Eisenhower suspended further U-2 flights over Soviet territory. Powers was tried for espionage and sentenced to 10 years in a Soviet jail. After 17 months, however, he was exchanged for a Soviet spy convicted in the United States.

The Berlin Crisis. John Kennedy was elected president of the United States in 1960. In the summer of 1961, he and Khrushchev met to discuss the status of Berlin. For 15 years, the Soviets had protested the presence of Allied troops in the city. Khrushchev repeated an earlier demand that Berlin become a demilitarized free city. It would not be part of either West Germany or East Germany. Kennedy refused the Soviet proposal. Instead, he asked Congress to expand the armed forces.

Alarmed by the dispute, thousands of East Germans moved into West Berlin. In August, more than 4,000 refugees a day were crossing the border. Many of them were professional and skilled workers.

Shortly after midnight on August 13, Soviet tanks and East German police took up positions along the 25-mile border separating the two parts of the city. Under the protection of these guns, workers built a

An East German patrols the border at the Berlin Wall. The concrete and barbed wire wall was built in 1961 to prevent East Germans from escaping to the West.

stone and concrete wall topped by barbed wire to stop the stream of refugees.

By fall, it was clear to Khrushchev that the United States would not agree to demilitarize Berlin. Khrushchev extended indefinitely the deadline for withdrawal of troops. The crisis faded; the wall remained.

The Cuban Missile Crisis. One year later, an even more serious crisis developed in the Western Hemisphere. Fidel Castro, a lawyer turned guerrilla fighter, overthrew the military dictator of Cuba. Cuba is an island located about 90 miles off the coast of Florida. Within two years, Castro had purged the moderate members of his rebel movement, censored the press, and placed most of the land on the island under government control. Castro then announced that he was joining the communist bloc of nations.

In 1962, Kennedy learned that the Soviet Union was building missile bases in Cuba. From these bases, nuclear missiles could easily reach the United States. Kennedy ordered the navy to stop any Soviet ships from landing in Cuba. He also told

Delegates at the United Nations Security Council emergency session examine aerial photographs of missile launching sites in Cuba on October 25, 1962.

the Soviets to dismantle the missile bases, or United States planes would bomb them.

A dozen Soviet ships carrying weapons steamed steadily toward Cuba while the world held its breath. For almost a week nuclear war loomed. Then, as the Soviet ships approached Cuba, they turned back. Finally, in an exchange of letters with Kennedy, the Soviet premier agreed to dismantle the missiles under United Nations supervision in exchange for a United States promise not to invade Cuba.

Cuba remained a member of the communist bloc. The Soviets continued to buy most of Cuba's sugar and give billions of dollars in economic aid. They also supplied Cuba with Soviet weapons and manufactured goods. In return, Cuba still serves as a base for communist guerrilla movements in Central and South America. Cubans have also been sent to Africa to help Marxists.

The Cuban Missile Crisis marked the end of the first stages of the Cold War. The relative simplicity of the two alliances that had dominated world politics for 15 years was rapidly changing. An additional factor made world politics more complex. The newly emerging nations of Africa and Asia were demanding attention.

SECTION 3 *Study Skills*

Developing Vocabulary Define: **1.** comrade. **2.** peaceful coexistence. **3.** espionage. **4.** refugee. **5.** bloc. **6.** purge.

Reviewing Main Ideas 1. How did the personalities and attitudes of Stalin and Khrushchev differ? **2.** How did the Soviet Union react to the problems that occurred in Hungary? **3.** Explain the U-2 crisis.

Understanding Cause and Effect 1. What was the purpose of the Common Market? **2.** Why did the Soviets build the Berlin Wall? **3.** Explain the causes and results of the Cuban Missile Crisis.

Understanding Geography 1. Which countries formed the Common Market in 1957? **2.** Name the nations that formed the EFTA.

Challenge Explain the relationship between the United States and the Soviet Union today.

CHAPTER 29 *Summary & Review*

Summarizing Main Ideas

Various relief programs followed World War II. The most significant was The Marshall Plan, which was responsible for rebuilding much of western Europe. In 1957, the Common Market was formed to further the economic growth of western Europe. By 1965, the Common Market had eliminated tariffs on all industrial goods sold to member nations.

The end of the war also saw a breakdown in cooperation between East and West. Two new superpowers, the United States and the Soviet Union, emerged as the leading countries in a struggle between communism and democracy.

The Cold War between the superpowers took on new dimensions by the mid-1960s. The countries in Africa and Asia began demanding attention during the 1960s.

'Is Big Insult, Asking Me To Free MY Colonies!'

Questions for Critical Thinking

COMPREHENSION Interpreting Events

1. Why did large numbers of citizens support socialist governments after the war?
2. Why was Marshal Tito allowed to maintain some freedom from Russian control?
3. How successful were Soviet five-year plans?

ANALYSIS Identifying Trends

1. List several postwar relief programs and tell how effective they were.
2. What did the Berlin Airlift and Greek Crisis have in common?
3. Explain the statement, "The Cuban Missile Crisis was just another incident of confrontation politics."

APPLICATION Comparing Past and Present

1. Explain why the industrial countries were able to rebuild.
2. Is a buffer zone as important to the Soviet Union now as it was in 1945? Explain.
3. Why is the Common Market so important to European economic development?

SYNTHESIS Developing Writing Skills

1. Write a report on one of the following individuals, emphasizing his role in the postwar period. Mao Zedong, Douglas MacArthur, Marshal Tito, Konrad Adenauer, Charles de Gaulle, George C. Marshall, Harry Truman.
2. Write an essay on the causes or consequences of the Korean War.
3. Describe Joseph Stalin's importance to Russian history.

EVALUATION Weighing Consequences

1. What was the result of the nationalists' desire to rid China of communism?
2. What was the later impact of money saved by Americans during the war?

CHALLENGE

1. What does this cartoon tell about American views of Khrushchev?
2. Why did Americans build bomb shelters and hold disaster drills in the 1960s? Are they necessary today? Explain.

CHAPTER 30
The End of Colonial Empires

GLOBAL TIME LINE

TIME

PEOPLE

PLACE

1945

1950

1946–1954 French fight the North Vietnamese for control of Vietnam

1948 United Nations recommends the partitioning of Palestine into Arab and Jewish states

1949 Arabs and Jews sign an armistice

1940s Kwame Nkrumah works to liberate the Gold Coast from colonial rule

1946–1963 Jomo Kenyatta leads Kenya to independence

1949 Sukarno becomes Indonesia's first president

1947 *India;¹* Indians gain independence from Great Britain

1947 *India;¹* India is partitioned to form the Muslim state of Pakistan

1952–1961 *Africa;²* Mau Mau terrorize Europeans in Kenya

Linking Past to Present

Drought, famine, and political unrest have dominated news on Africa in the 1980s. In Cameroon, a tropical west African nation, the story was more hopeful. The economy leaped ahead, the standard of living rose, and democratic institutions flourished. Cameroon has rich oil resources, and leaders have managed them wisely.

Cameroon's success story, however, is an exception in Africa. The leaders of most African nations still struggle with social problems. Most nations on the African continent continue to experience severe economic troubles. Lack of rain has brought about a famine, increasing the suffering of the people. As you read the chapter, consider the great political and economic challenges these new nations faced in the past 30 years and continue to face.

A view of downtown Bombay, India.

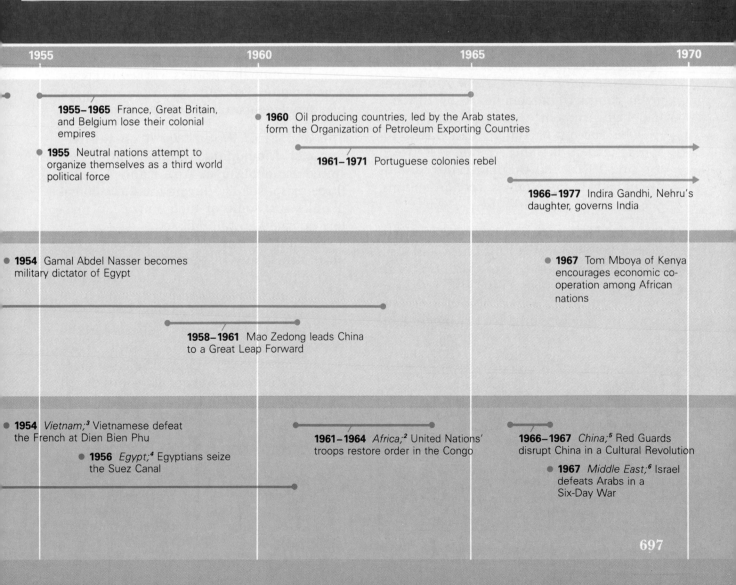

1955   1960   1965   1970

1955–1965 France, Great Britain, and Belgium lose their colonial empires

1955 Neutral nations attempt to organize themselves as a third world political force

1960 Oil producing countries, led by the Arab states, form the Organization of Petroleum Exporting Countries

1961–1971 Portuguese colonies rebel

1966–1977 Indira Gandhi, Nehru's daughter, governs India

1954 Gamal Abdel Nasser becomes military dictator of Egypt

1958–1961 Mao Zedong leads China to a Great Leap Forward

1967 Tom Mboya of Kenya encourages economic cooperation among African nations

1954 *Vietnam;*[3] Vietnamese defeat the French at Dien Bien Phu

1956 *Egypt;*[4] Egyptians seize the Suez Canal

1961–1964 *Africa;*[2] United Nations' troops restore order in the Congo

1966–1967 *China;*[5] Red Guards disrupt China in a Cultural Revolution

1967 *Middle East;*[6] Israel defeats Arabs in a Six-Day War

697

1 Nationalism in Africa and Asia

TO KEEP NIGERIA ONE IS A TASK THAT MUST BE DONE

OBJECTIVE: *To understand the causes and consequences of growing nationalism in Africa and Asia*

Nationalist Movements Grow

Between World War I and World War II, nationalists in the European colonies of Africa and Asia protested against social, political, and economic conditions. After the war, protests turned to demands for political independence. Nationalists won their first great victory in 1947, when India was given complete independence by Britain's Labor government.

The success of Indian nationalists inspired leaders in other colonies. Between the mid-1950s and the mid-1960s, dozens of colonies become new sovereign nations. See the map, page 701.

Colonial Nationalism. Many Western-educated colonial leaders in Africa and Asia adopted nationalism. However, twentieth century colonial nationalism differed from the European nationalism of the 1800s. Early nationalism in Europe centered on the desire of national groups, such as the Italians and Germans, to form a single government. In Africa and Asia most colonies were not made up of a single national or ethnic group. By 1945, few African or Asian colonies had grown into nations whose people shared the same culture. After World War II, nationalist leaders worked to create a new national identity by organizing popular movements to win independence.

The Impact of World War II on the Nationalist Movement. World War II inspired nationalism in Africa and Asia for three reasons. First, during the war colonial peoples saw some of their European masters defeated and humiliated.

Second, most colonial peoples supported the cause of their European rulers during the war. As a result, colonial peoples felt that they had earned respect and equal treatment after the war ended.

Third, colonial leaders, educated in the West, learned Western liberal ideas. They became more and more disturbed that these ideals of freedom and equality contradicted European colonial domination.

The End of the British Empire

As late as World War II, most British believed that one day in the distant future their colonies would be ready to govern themselves. Their timetable for indepen-

---

VOCABULARY DEVELOPMENT

ethnic (ETH nihk) *adj.:* designating the basic divisions of people as distinguished by such things as customs, characteristics, language, and common history. From the Greek word, *ethnos,* meaning people or nations.

martial law: temporary rule of military authorities over the civilian population, as in time of war or civil disturbances.

---

dence was speeded up repeatedly as nationalist movements became more powerful.

Indians Demand Independence. India was better prepared for independence than any other major colony. For over 50 years, the British had trained Indians for government posts. When the war ended, the Congress party (see page 629) led by Gandhi demanded complete independence. The Labor government of Great Britain agreed. A major complication, however, was the division between Muslims and Hindus in India. The Muslims wanted a separate state they called Pakistan.

The Muslims Win a State. After World War II, serious rioting broke out between Hindus and Muslims. The British were convinced that civil war would rip apart India if Hindus and Muslims shared the same nation. In 1947, the parties involved in the dispute agreed to divide India. Pakistan, the new Muslim state, was to occupy two separate areas. One state was located in northeast India and the other one was located in northwest India.

Widespread rioting and confusion broke out along the borders between India and Pakistan. More than 17 million Indians became refugees, and over 1 million Indians were killed. Gandhi personally went to Delhi to plead for fair treatment of Muslim refugees. While he was there, a Hindu fanatic shot and killed him.

The religious violence and Gandhi's death made the first years of independence difficult for India. Nevertheless, Indian leaders set about organizing stable governments. In 1950, the Indian nation adopted a constitution that set up a democratic system of government.

British Interest in Egypt. Egyptians disliked their monarch's extravagance, government corruption, and delays in promised reforms. In 1952, young army officers forced the king to abdicate. A year later, Egyptian leaders declared Egypt a republic.

Mahatma Gandhi walks with his grandchildren in 1944. After World War II, the Congress Party led by Gandhi demanded complete independence from Great Britain.

In 1956, the Egyptians elected a military officer, Colonel Gamal Abdel Nasser, to the presidency. He soon became the military dictator of Egypt.

The Suez Crisis. In 1955, Nasser asked the United States for aid to construct a dam on the Nile River at Aswan. He wanted the Aswan High Dam for generating electrical power and for controlling flooding on the land around the Nile.

At first, President Eisenhower refused. Nasser then persuaded the Soviets to build the dam for him. Angered, both the United States and Great Britain temporarily withdrew aid. In retaliation, Nasser seized the Suez Canal from the British in July 1956.

The British and French sent troops to the canal. Citizens of these countries held the majority of stock in the Suez Company. Aided by Israel, the British and French forces occupied the canal. The United Nations intervened, ended the fighting, and demanded troop withdrawal. Egypt retained control of the canal but paid dividends to the stockholders.

The British Withdraw from Africa. After the war, the British Labor government prepared its African colonies for independence. It turned over authority to nationalist leaders. Nationalists in the West African Gold Coast, an area that had few European settlers, worked to prepare their nations for independence.

Ghana Gains Independence. In the 1940s, Kwame Nkrumah (KWAH mee en KROO muh) worked to liberate the Gold Coast from the British. He organized strikes and boycotts and was often imprisoned. Finally, in 1957, the Gold Coast gained full independence. The former colony took the name Ghana. It became the first nation governed by black Africans to join the British Commonwealth. During the celebrations, Nkrumah told the crowds:

❝ There is a new African in the world, and that new African is ready to fight his own battle. . . .It is the only way in which we can show the world we are masters of our own destiny. ❞

Nigeria Becomes Independent. In the west coast colony of Nigeria, nationalists also organized a mass movement for independence. Three years after granting independence to Ghana, the British granted the Nigerians self-government. Britain's other west African territories, though smaller and poorer, soon became independent states governed by their own leaders.

Civil War in Kenya. British East Africa, unlike the west African colonies, included influential minorities of European settlers. The Europeans feared rule by an African government and insisted on retaining control over the colony.

Leaders of the nationalist movement in Kenya were members of the Kikuyu people. After World War I, the Kikuyu Association pressed for African rights. The association wanted land and political representation. Also, the Africans wanted to end the system of identity passes that Africans were required to carry. Jomo Kenyatta (kehn YAHT uh), a black nationalist, led the movement for self-government in Kenya.

The Africans in Kenya refused to accept white rule. They also protested white ownership of the best farmland. The Kikuyu formed a secret movement called the Mau Mau. The Mau Mau used terrorism to drive the whites from Kenya.

Between 1952 and 1961, the Mau Mau guerrillas killed 75 white settlers. In turn, the British army and police killed more than 13,000 Kenyans. Finally, in 1963, against the wishes of the settlers, Kenya won independence. Kenyatta became the leader of an independent Kenya.

Kenyan black nationalist Jomo Kenyatta was jailed in 1952 for his Mau Mau activities. He is pictured here immediately after his release from prison in 1961.

Newly Independent Countries, 1945 – Present

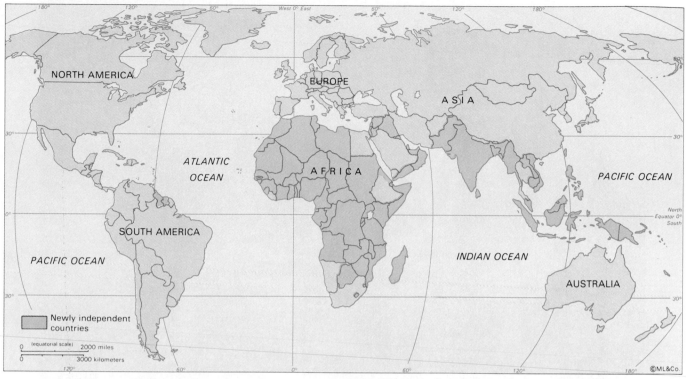

Map Skills **1.** Which was the first country to become independent after 1945? **2.** In which continent have the most nations become independent since 1945?

Nationalism in French Colonies

The French were much slower than the British to accept the idea of national independence for their colonies. After World War II, however, the tide of nationalism forced France to give up its colonies.

The Nationalist Movement in Vietnam.

Nationalists in Southeast Asia gained independence from France after World War II. Opposition to French rule there, however, began before the war. The French crushed a Vietnamese Nationalist party in 1930.

In the same year, a Vietnamese nationalist, Ho Chi Minh (hoh chee MIHN), formed the Indochina Communist party, or Viet Minh. Ho grew up in the French colony of Indochina. While working in France during World War I, he studied Marxism. Disappointed when the Versailles peace conference ignored the petitions of Indochinese

nationalists, Ho turned to Marxism to fight imperialism. The communists came to dominate the Vietnam nationalist movement.

A Divided Vietnam.

The Japanese expelled the French from Southeast Asia during World War II. When the war ended in 1945, the Japanese in northern Vietnam surrendered to the nationalist Chinese, who opposed European colonialism. The Chinese allowed the Viet Minh to declare the independent Democratic Republic of Vietnam. The French returned to south Vietnam, however, and made plans to reoccupy the entire country.

From 1946 to 1954, the French fought a long and bitter war with the North Vietnamese. The United States supplied no troops but paid as much as 80 percent of French costs in the fighting.

A general named Vo Nguyen Giap (woh nyehn GYEHP) led the Vietnamese commu-

In 1954, the French lost a long, bitter war to communist forces in North Vietnam. French General Cogny is shown here at Vietnamese army batallion headquarters in Indochina in 1954.

nist forces. In 1954, Giap attacked the French who were defending an isolated jungle outpost at Dien Bien Phu. In a bloody battle, Giap's forces defeated them.

Following the French defeat, a council of foreign ministers met at Geneva, Switzerland. The ministers agreed to divide Vietnam at the 17th degree of north latitude. Communist-ruled North Vietnam became the Democratic Republic of Vietnam. The anticommunist south became the Republic of Vietnam.

The Algerian Revolution. After the war in Indochina ended, France faced rising nationalism in its African colonies. Nationalists in the French north African colonies of Morocco, Tunisia, and Algeria demanded independence. Through negotiations and with little violence, France withdrew from Tunisia and Morocco in 1956.

France, though, strongly opposed Algerian independence. Algeria was the home of a million Europeans, about 15 percent of the population. Many families had lived in Algeria for three or four generations, and considered Algeria, rather than France, their home. They dominated Algeria's society and government.

Algerian Independence. Algerian nationalists revolted against the French in 1954, less than four months after the end of the Indochina war. By 1956, the French had sent more than 400,000 troops to Algeria. Forces on both sides used physical torture and cruelly treated their enemies. The war caused deep divisions in France and an appeal for De Gaulle to again lead the country. In 1962, France granted the nationalists' demands. Algeria became an independent Muslim nation.

Other New Nations

Great Britain and France ruled the largest colonial empires, but other countries also had overseas territories. Among them were Holland, Belgium, and the United States. Between 1945 and 1960, these nations gave up their Asian and African possessions.

Dutch East Indies Become Indonesia. When Japanese forces invaded Southeast Asia in 1942, they took control of the Dutch colonies in the East Indies. After the war ended, the Dutch tried to reestablish their control. Nationalists, led by Sukarno (soo KAHR noh), resisted. The Dutch were unable to defeat Sukarno, and in 1949 the Dutch East Indies became the independent republic of Indonesia.

The Philippines. The United States had controlled the Philippine Islands since 1898. Following the attack on Pearl Harbor, however, the Japanese took over the islands. A Filipino nationalist group, the People's Anti-Japanese Army, also called the Huk movement, fought the Japanese.

After the war, the United States granted the Philippines their long-promised independence. A constitution set up a democratic government. Because of a great gap between rich landlords and poor farmers, however, the Philippines did not achieve social stability. Communist-led Huks continued to wage guerrilla warfare in rural areas.

In 1972, the Philippines president, Ferdinand Marcos, declared martial law, temporary military rule ending the country's experiment with democracy. Marcos issued a new constitution that greatly increased the power of the president. The Marcos family became extremely wealthy while the condition of the peasants grew worse.

The End of the Belgian Empire. During the 1940s and early 1950s, the Belgian Congo was profitable. The standard of living was somewhat higher than in other parts of the continent.

The Belgians, however, did nothing to prepare the people of the Congo for self-government. The Congolese received only an elementary school education. No African Congolese were educated well enough to hold high government posts.

In 1957, the growing nationalist movement swept the Congo. The Belgians were taken by surprise and decided to abandon their huge colony. In 1959, Belgium announced that the Congo would be granted independence in 1960.

By 1965, the great empires had been dismantled. Only Portugal retained large colonies in Africa. New states at first rejoiced in their independence. Soon, however, they came to realize that independence did not solve any economic or social problems.

SECTION 1 *Study Skills*

Developing Vocabulary **1.** Explain the meaning of the term ethnic. **2.** When might martial law be declared?

Reviewing Main Ideas **1.** What is the difference between European nationalism and colonial nationalism? **2.** Explain the cause of the major problem India faced following independence. **3.** How did the Mau Mau work to achieve independence for Kenya? **4.** Why was Algeria important to France?

Understanding Chronology **1.** Construct a time line showing the year each of the following countries gained independence: India, Egypt, Ghana, Kenya, and Algeria. **2.** List the important events in Vietnam from 1930 to 1956.

Understanding Cause and Effect **1.** How did World War II inspire nationalism? **2.** Explain the cause and outcome of the Suez crisis of 1956.

Challenge List three advantages and three disadvantages former colonies experienced as a result of their break with the Western powers.

Place Names Tell a Story

Names of places tell a great deal about their history or environment. For instance, after the Belgian Congo achieved independence it changed its name to Zaire. This name is a form of the word river in many African dialects.

Throughout the United States and Canada, places have a wide variety of names. A number of interesting stories about why and how the names of places were chosen can be told.

Places and Names

Of the original 13 colonies, 7 were named in recognition of European royalty. Georgia, Virginia, Delaware, Maryland, New York, and North and South Carolina all were named in honor of royalty who supported the colonization of America. After the American Revolution this custom continued as many places were named in honor of those responsible for events in America's history. Washington, Lincoln, and Columbus are among the most common American place names.

Another custom was to name one place in memory of another place across the ocean. Oldenburg in Germany supplied the name of Oldenburg, Indiana, because the place reminded the immigrants of their hometown. Many towns were given biblical names in honor of places found in the Bible, thereby showing the religious feelings of the townspeople. Bethlehem, Nazareth, Emmaus, Zionsville, and Egypt are all town names found in the southeast corner of Pennsylvania. Naming a new town is an opportunity to make a statement about what the people value, whether it is a royal patron, a hometown, or a religion.

Heroic Names

Sometimes, heroic events are commemorated in place names. In 1824, two members of a Michigan surveying party led by John Mullet fought with two Indians near a stream. When it came time to name the land they surveyed for a city, they named it for the battle at the creek: Battle Creek.

Sometimes the events which are commemorated do not have heroic endings. A stream in southern Indiana, for example, is called Jack's Defeat Creek in reference to the fate of a local resident, whose horse became stuck in the muddy creek.

Some of the events commemorated in place names are sheer legend. For example, Phoenix, Arizona is named for the bird that in Greek legend, was destroyed but rose from its own ashes. The founders of Phoenix responded to the difficulties of building a city in a near-desert by recalling the rise of the Phoenix. They hoped that their new city would likewise rise up.

Topographical Names

Occasionally, places are named for local landforms or topography that is unique. In northwest Utah an enormous lake is fed by freshwater streams, yet it is much saltier than the oceans. The waters do not drain away but evaporate leaving salt behind. What better name could there be for this major landform than the Great Salt Lake? In turn, it has given its name to a nearby settlement, Salt Lake City.

Accidental Names

Sometimes, places acquire their names by accident. Gnome, Alaska, is an example. The surveyor who was sent to map the land that became Gnome prepared his map as usual. He drew the map, and labeled the important land features and settlements with the names by which they were known locally. He could not find out what one part of the land, a cape, was called.

When he filed his map with the government so that it could be offficially recorded, the surveyor wanted to make it clear that he did not know the cape's name. To do so, he wrote a question mark along with the word name. The government official who recorded the information apparently misread the writing. In his book of place names, he wrote Gnome. The name stuck.

Names Reflect Diversity

A look at a map of North America will show the range of people who have come to settle this continent. In the southwest, there are many Spanish names. Los Angeles and San Francisco are two examples from California. In Texas, San Antonio and Laredo are examples. In other regions, the French influence is dominant. Quebec, in Montreal, Canada, reflects the French influence. New Orleans is named for the city of Orleans in France. Many other nationalities are reflected in other place names.

The Cajun Region

The Cajun region of Louisiana is of special interest in connection with place names. The name Cajun reflects a migration pattern as well as the way local language and dialects alter names.

The easternmost part of Canada was settled by French people. Some of these settlers of Nova Scotia were so impressed by the beauty of the wooded land that they named the place Acadia. Acadia is a legendary place of great natural beauty.

In 1755, the British forcibly transported about 4,000 Acadians to Louisiana. They

French-Canadian migrants to Louisiana, formerly called Acadians, are known as Cajuns today. Shown here, a view of the French Quarter in New Orleans.

settled near Bayou Teche. Gradually, their French culture began to meld with the local culture. The name Acadians changed with local usage. The *a* sound disappeared entirely. The *di* was replaced by a *j* sound. Today, the descendants of the Acadian migrants are known as Cajuns.

Places may be named to honor heroes or heroic events. They may be named after a city in the old country or after landforms. They may even be named by accident. A look at a map will give us a hint of the fascinating variety of North American place names. These place names can tell interesting stories.

STUDY SKILLS Understanding Geography

1. Tell five ways places are named.
2. Explain how the names of American places show the diversity of the American people.
3. What is the origin of the name Cajun?
4. Explain the name of your town and suggest two new names for it.
5. Infer why the seven states named for European royalty did not change their names after the American Revolution.

2 New Nations Search for Stability

OBJECTIVE: *To understand the problems faced by newly independent nations in Africa and Asia*

A New Africa Faces the World

More than 30 nations in Africa won their independence between 1945 and 1965. Leaders of these nations worked to establish stable governments and prosperous economies. As the new nations proudly joined the United Nations, however, leaders faced overwhelming problems.

Problems of New Nations. Four major problems challenged leaders of newly independent countries. First, the percentage of literate, educated people in the new nations was very small. Few colonial powers prepared the people to govern.

Second, the new nations often included ethnic groups that did not share a common language and culture. These groups competed for land and political power.

Third, most Africans and Asians had no previous experience in self-government. Europeans had developed democracy over hundreds of years. The colonial powers tried to impose democratic governments on new nations. The social conditions in these nations, however, were very different from those in Europe. As a result, governments developed differently.

Fourth, most of the new nations suffered economic problems. Often, they lacked natural resources or the skills and technology to take advantage of existing resources. Most of the people were desperately poor. Leaders could not establish stable, democratic governments as long as poverty caused social unrest.

Crisis in the Congo. When the Congo gained independence from Belgium in 1960, most of the people were loyal to their region or group. They lacked a strong national identity. The first prime minister, Patrice Lamumba, had only regional support.

One of Lamumba's political rivals, Moise Tshombe (MOY shee shahm BAY), became prime minister of the Congo's wealthy province of Katanga. This area contained most of the Congo's mineral resources. Under Tshombe, Katanga seceded from the Congo and declared itself independent.

By the end of 1960, the Congo had broken into four separate regions that had no effective central government. The enemies of Patrice Lamumba assassinated him in February 1961.

The United Nations Restores Order. The United Nations sent a peacekeeping force to the Congo to restore order. UN troops,

---

VOCABULARY DEVELOPMENT

secede (sih SEED) *verb:* to withdraw formally from membership in a group or organization. From the Latin word, *secedere,* meaning to be apart.

kibbutz (kih BOOTS) *noun:* an Israeli collective farm.

separatist: a person or group that withdraws from a larger group.

A rebel officer, Gaston Soumialot, reviews his troops. They supported Patrice Lamumba in the Congo's civil war.

aided by Belgians, forced Moise Tshombe out of Katanga and reunified the country. United Nations forces withdrew in 1964. By 1971, black African government officials had replaced the Belgians and renamed the nation Zaire.

The Nigerian Civil War. The new country of Nigeria also lacked unity. People in more than 250 ethnic groups live there. In addition, Nigeria's natural resources, especially oil, are located in the southeast.

In the middle of the 1960s, rioters in the north killed hundreds of Ibo who had moved there. To escape persecution and protect their oil wealth, the Ibo seceded from Nigeria and proclaimed the Republic of Biafra in southeastern Nigeria.

Between 1967 and 1970, the Nigerian government fought a savage war against the Biafrans. They surrounded Biafra and stopped all trade. Almost a million people, many of them civilians, died of famine and disease as well as in the fighting between the two countries.

After Biafra was defeated, the central government, under military leader Lieutenant Colonel Gowan, worked to rebuild national unity. By 1971, Nigeria's economy was again prosperous. The nation became a leader in African affairs because of its size, wealth, and newly stable government.

Portugal Drags Its Feet. Portugal was the first European country to establish African colonies and the last to grant them independence. In 1951, Portugal declared that its two huge colonies, Angola and Mozambique, were overseas provinces of Portugal and could never be released.

In 1961, rebellion broke out in the Portuguese colonies. The ten-year war that followed threatened the stability of all southern Africa. The rebels received aid from both the Soviet Union and sympathetic African nations.

In 1974, the military leaders in Portugal publicly admitted that they could not defeat the African guerrillas. The army overthrew Portugal's dictator and established a military dictatorship. The new government quickly reached an agreement with the rebels. Mozambique declared its independence in June 1975. Angola became free in 1976.

Military Rule in Africa. A pattern of military rule developed in the new nations of Africa. Military leaders often seized control. Using the army to enforce their orders, they could govern the former colonies.

Nationalism in the Middle East

The Middle East, like Africa, is a diverse area. Inhabitants speak different languages and practice different religions.

The Founding of Israel. The Jewish national movement is one of the most unusual in modern times. In ancient times, the Jews were united as a nation. After the destruction of Jerusalem in 586 B.C., however, Jews migrated throughout Africa, Asia, and Europe. They were always a minority and often harshly treated.

In the 1800s, some Jews supported a nationalist movement called Zionism. The goal of Zionists was to create a Jewish homeland in Ottoman-controlled Palestine. As early as 1882, small groups of Jewish immigrants from Europe founded colonies in Palestine, then under Ottoman Turkish rule.

Jewish interest in Palestine grew during World War I as the Allies supported self-determination for ethnic groups. In 1917, the British issued the Balfour Declaration, saying they would "view with favor" the creation of a Jewish homeland in Palestine. However, to gain Arab support the British also led the Arabs to believe that they would govern themselves in the same area.

After World War I, Britain received Palestine and Trans-Jordan, later called Jordan, as League of Nations mandates (see page 624). The British faced a difficult problem. They had promised the Jews a homeland in an area populated by Arabs.

The problem grew worse in the 1930s. The rise of Hitler caused large numbers of European Jews to flee to Palestine. In 1935, 62,000 Jewish immigrants arrived. European Jews began to dominate the Palestinian economy. They also purchased large areas of land. This prosperity caused envy and discontent among the Arabs.

Both before and after World War II, Great Britain attempted to limit Jewish immigration into Palestine. In retaliation, Jewish nationalists blew up British-built railways, bridges, and government offices.

Finally, in 1947, the frustrated British announced that they would withdraw their forces from Palestine in 1948. They submitted the entire dispute to the United Nations. Jews seized part of Palestine. The United Nations recommended that Palestine be partitioned into an Arab state and a Jewish state ratifying the existing boundaries. The Jews controlled western Palestine, where, in 1948, they founded the Republic of Israel.

Nationalists Clash in Palestine. The creation of Israel angered many Arabs and stimulated Arab nationalism. The armies of Syria, Lebanon, Iraq, Trans-Jordan, and Egypt attacked. A surprised world watched as Israel held off the Arab forces. In 1949, the United Nations persuaded the Arabs and Jews to sign an armistice.

About 750,000 Arab refugees fled Israel during the Arab-Israeli War. The United Nations set up refugee camps in neighboring Arab lands to house these people. Few found jobs. Most hoped that someday they could return to their villages.

The Six-Day War. During the next ten years, tension increased as the Arab nations and Israel spent huge amounts to build up their armed forces. Israel feared that the Arabs were again preparing to attack. In 1967, to gain an advantage, Israel surprised the world by striking first. Israeli forces attacked airfields in Egypt, Jordan, and Syria.

The Arabs were defeated in six days. The Israelis then controlled Arab territory more than three times the area of Israel. Jordan's half of Jerusalem became a part of Israel in June 1967.

The Palestine Liberation Organization. The Six-Day War increased the refugee problem. During the war, another 200,000 Arabs fled to Jordan. After the war, several Palestinian Arab groups formed the Palestine Liberation Organization, PLO.

From refugee camps in Jordan and Lebanon, the PLO launched guerrilla attacks against Israel. Later, they expanded their terrorist strikes to include all powers or individuals that supported Israel. Israel retaliated with raids and attacks into surrounding Arab nations that supported the Palestinians and their cause.

The 1973 War. In October 1973, the Egyptians launched a successful attack against Israel. For several weeks, tanks and jet fighters battled. Israel then pushed the Egyptians back across the canal and Israeli forces entered Egypt.

Before the Israelis could inflict heavy damage, the major world powers, led by the United States, negotiated a cease-fire. Neither side, however, was prepared to sign a formal peace treaty.

During the 1973 War, Golda Meir (MEH ih uhr) was the prime minister of Israel. Meir, born in Russia, grew up in the United States. Her dedication to developing a homeland for Jews inspired her move to British-governed Palestine.

Golda Meir Decides How to Live

Waving knives, swinging clubs, and screaming at the "Christ killers," thugs terrorized Jewish communities in early twentieth-century Russia. When they swept through one city, two terrified little girls stood on a stairway holding hands. Their fathers tried to barricade the entrance to the apartment building.

Both families survived the pogrom. One of the little girls, Golda Mabovitch, was especially angry at the idea of an attack on her family just because they were Jewish.

Golda's father, a carpenter, left Russia in 1903. He hoped to make enough money in the United States to send for his family later. During her father's absence, Golda looked up to her older sister, Sheyna. She belonged to a group dedicated to socialism

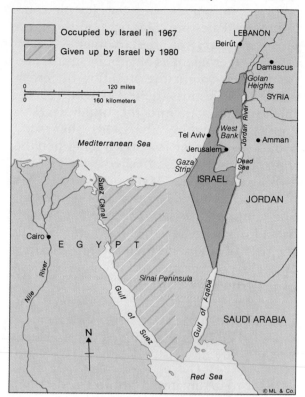

Israel and the Middle East, 1967-1980

Occupied by Israel in 1967

Given up by Israel by 1980

0 120 miles
0 160 kilometers

LEBANON
Beirút
Damascus
Golan Heights
SYRIA
Mediterranean Sea
Tel Aviv
West Bank
Jerusalem
Amman
Gaza Strip
Dead Sea
ISRAEL
JORDAN
Cairo
E G Y P T
Nile River
Suez Canal
Sinai Peninsula
Gulf of Suez
Gulf of Aqaba
SAUDI ARABIA
N
Red Sea
© ML & Co.

Map Skills   1. What part of Egypt did Israel occupy in 1967? **2.** On what river is the West Bank?

and Zionism. They wanted to remake Russia into a society that recognized human equality. They also were dedicated to the establishment of a Jewish state in Palestine. Such ideals were extremely dangerous. The girls' mother breathed a sigh of relief when, in 1906, Mr. Mabovitch sent for them.

The Mabovitch family settled in Milwaukee, Wisconsin. Their home was a gathering place for discussions among Zionists. Golda listened excitedly to the talk about Jews already in Palestine, working for a Jewish state. In 1921, after becoming a teacher, Golda left the United States to fulfill a dream. She and her husband of four years, Morris Myerson, moved to Palestine.

In Palestine, Golda and Morris first lived in a kibbutz, a Jewish communal settlement. In 1924, Golda, Morris, and their son moved to Tel Aviv and later to Jerusalem.

By 1928, Meir wanted to become more involved in establishing the Jewish community in Palestine. She became the executive secretary of the Women's Labor Council. Her talent as an administrator and fund raiser caught the attention of Jewish leaders in Palestine. In the 1930s and 1940s, she was accepted into the upper level of Zionist leadership. In 1948, she stood proudly with other Jewish leaders when the state of Israel was established.

In 1956, Golda Myerson changed her name to the more Hebrew-sounding Meir. She continued to serve Israel, first as ambassador to the Soviet Union, and later as minister of labor and then foreign minister. In 1969, she became prime minister, head of the Israeli government.

In 1971, Meir visited Milwaukee and talked to the students in her old elementary school. The spirit that guided her is evident in her address:

" It isn't really important to decide when you are very young just exactly what you want to become when you grow up. It is much more important to decide how you want to live. If you are going to be honest with your friends, if you are going to get involved with causes that are good for others, not only for yourselves, then it seems to me that that is sufficient, and maybe what you will be is only a matter of chance. **"**

When Golda Meir died of cancer in 1978, friends and enemies alike realized that they were witnessing the passing of a remarkable woman who had decided how to live in accordance with her own beliefs and ideals. ■

Crises in Asia

While the new state of Israel was fighting for its existence, newly independent India established a democratic nation. Independence for India, however, did not end the problems of that populous nation.

Nehru Governs India. Indians elected Jawaharlal Nehru (Juh WAH har lahl NAY roo) their first prime minister in 1953. Nehru, along with Gandhi, had led the Congress party and the nonviolence movement against the British. For the new prime minister, the greatest task was to hold the new nation together.

Nehru firmly supported democracy and worked hard to meet India's economic and social needs. His two major goals for India were to industrialize the country and to modernize its agriculture.

In order to advance industrial development, Nehru organized a mixed economy with both socialist and capitalist elements. The government controlled the basic industries but encouraged foreign investment and private enterprise.

India under Indira Gandhi. The political stability India enjoyed under Nehru ended with his death in 1964. In 1966, his daughter, Indira Gandhi (IHN dih ruh GAHN dee), became prime minister. She had been the constant companion of her father and shared his goals for India. However, she faced growing economic problems and student demonstrations.

In 1975, Indira Gandhi proclaimed a state of emergency. She arrested thousands of political opponents, banned several political groups, censored the press, and postponed elections. Gandhi's critics feared her dictatorial power and disliked the influence of her son, Sanjay. He was also a member of parliament and had become an influential adviser to his mother.

When elections were held in 1977, Gandhi was defeated. Her successors, though, were unable to solve India's problems. In 1980, in a dramatic turnaround, Indira and Sanjay Ghandi were again elected in a Congress party landslide. Sanjay, however, died in a plane crash in 1981. His younger brother, Rajiv, was elected to take his place in parliament. Rajiv developed a reputation as a reformer.

Since achieving independence, India has had to contain several separatist movements. Sikh religious extremists make up one group. They demanded an independent Sikh homeland in northwestern India. They stored ammunition and sheltered fugitives in their religion's shrine, the Golden Temple. In June 1985, Indira Gandhi sent Indian troops to storm the temple. Five months later, two trusted Sikh bodyguards assassinated her.

Gandhi's son, Rajiv Gandhi, succeeded his mother as the new Congress party leader. In 1985, Rajiv Gandhi became India's seventh prime minister.

The Formation of Bangladesh. The new nation of Pakistan faced problems more severe than those of India. Between the two areas making up Pakistan were 1,000 miles of hostile Indian territory. West Pakistan controlled the government. The people of East Pakistan felt that they had little control over government policies. In addition, the people of each area spoke different languages and had different customs. They shared only the Islamic religion.

As resentment grew in East Pakistan, nationalists formed an independence movement called the Awami League. In March 1971, East Pakistan declared its independence from West Pakistan. Hundreds of thousands of people were killed in a civil war. More than 10 million refugees fled to West Bengal, in India.

In December 1971, the West Pakistani army gave up the struggle. East Pakistan became the independent Muslim country of Bangladesh (BAHNG gluh DEHSH), meaning Bengal Nation.

China's Great Leap Forward. While India struggled successfully to preserve democracy, China became a communist dictatorship. In 1949, Mao Zedong forced the Chinese nationalists from China and became the communist dictator. He modeled the Chinese economy and government after those of the Soviet Union. Mao proclaimed a Great Leap Forward and emphasized heavy industry and agricultural production. He ended all private ownership of farmland. Under the close supervision and central planning of the government, farms were collectivized and new industries built.

The Cultural Revolution. By 1966, Mao was afraid that the people were beginning to lose their revolutionary spirit. He urged the people to make their own revolution. He campaigned against what he called the Four Olds: Old Thoughts, Old Culture, Old Customs, and Old Habits.

Indians in Bangladesh celebrate their independence from West Pakistan in 1971.

Red Guards rename the street in front of the Soviet Embassy "Anti-Revisionism Road" during a demonstration in Beijing on August 29, 1966.

To begin the war against the Four Olds, Mao closed all schools in China except primary schools. Youths were formed into units called Red Guards. Groups of Red Guards traveled across China to spread Mao's thoughts and attack the old ways of thinking and acting.

Red Guards attacked teachers and forced them to confess that they had been teaching wrong thoughts and ideas. Red Guards charged into factories and harassed workers. In the countryside, they interrupted farmwork, ate food supplies, and often terrorized peasants. Many people were killed.

In December 1966, Mao ordered the Red Guards to return home. They, however, refused, and the turmoil and disorder in China continued.

While the Red Guards roamed the countryside, Mao moved to eliminate his oppo-nents. He replaced many high officials, reorganized the party, and fired hundreds of officials.

After 1972, China slowly returned to normal. The Cultural Revolution slowed China's economic development and inspired a strong popular reaction against the Red Guard radicalism. When Mao died in 1976, China's leaders adopted more moderate policies.

During the first two decades of independence, the nations of Africa, the Middle East, and Asia continued to search for political stability and economic prosperity. The gap between the rich, developed nations and the nonindustrialized countries, however, continued to widen.

SECTION 2 *Study Skills*

Developing Vocabulary 1. Explain the relationship between secede and separatist. **2.** Where would a *kibbutz* be located?

Reviewing Main Ideas 1. List several problems faced by new African nations. **2.** Describe the common pattern of development that occurred when African nations became independent. **3.** What was the goal of Zionism? **4.** How did the United Nations resolve the Palestinian problem in 1948? **5.** What were Nehru's goals for India?

Understanding Chronology 1. List and explain important dates in the Congo's history from 1960 to 1971. **2.** Explain the significance of the Israeli action of 1967. **3.** What conditions led to the Great Leap Forward movement in China in 1958? How long did the movement last?

Understanding Cause and Effect 1. Why was disunity a problem in Nigeria? **2.** Why was the PLO formed? **3.** Why was the country of Bangladesh founded?

Challenge What common problems do developing nations have? Propose a possible solution for one of these problems.

3 Development in the Third World

OBJECTIVE: *To understand the causes and consequences of the differences in development among the countries of the third world*

Nations of the Third World

During the Cold War of the 1950s, several of the world's nations were not committed to supporting either the United States or the Soviet Union. Among them were India, Yugoslavia, Indonesia, and Egypt. These nations, as well as other newly independent countries, met in 1955 to form a union of nonaligned, or neutral, nations. They would remain free from the economic or political influence of the superpowers.

The nations became a third political force, or third world. The first and second worlds are those nations that the United States and the Soviet Union dominate. A third world nation is a state that remains uncommitted to either superpower.

The Less Developed Countries. Half of the almost 5 billion people in the world seldom have enough to eat, fewer than 1,500 calories per day. Most of these hungry people live in what the United Nations terms less developed countries, LDCs. LDCs have four general characteristics: their people have low incomes, their economies are based on subsistence farming, their technology is limited, and their populations are rapidly growing.

To develop economically, nations must produce a surplus, an amount left over after the needs of the people have been met. For example, if a farm family can produce a small surplus, it can trade its extra food for fertilizer, a hoe, or an ox, which will help to increase its production. As the family in-

---

VOCABULARY DEVELOPMENT

nonaligned: not cooperating closely, as in nations.

third world: the underdeveloped countries of the world, especially those in Africa and Asia.

calorie (KAL uh ree) *noun:* the amount of heat needed to raise the temperature of 1 gram of water 1 degree centigrade, a unit used for measuring the energy produced by food. From the Latin word, *calor,* meaning heat.

capital goods: items that are used to produce other goods, such as tools, fertilizers, farm animals, and machinery.

neocolonialism: economic domination of an independent country by a foreign power.

commodity (kuh MAHD uh tee) *noun:* an article such as food, clothing or metal that is bought and sold. From the Latin word, *commodus,* meaning suitable.

cartel (kahr TEHL) *noun:* an association of businesses established to control a commodity's price, production, and sale. The most famous recent cartel is OPEC. From the Latin word, *carta,* meaning a card, a paper.

embargo (ihm BAHR goh) *noun:* a prohibition of trade in a particular commodity. From the Latin prefix *in-,* meaning on and the word *barra,* meaning bar.

---

creases production, it eventually raises its standard of living.

In the same way, a nation must produce and invest a surplus to grow economically. The nation trades or invests the surplus to purchase capital goods, such as machinery or fertilizer. Using these goods, the nation increases production, thus increasing its surplus. Increased production creates jobs and improves the people's way of life. Investment is the key to economic growth.

When a country's population increases more rapidly than production, however, the country cannot invest the surplus in capital goods. Instead it must use the surplus to obtain food to feed the growing population. Many developing nations are trapped in a cycle of poverty.

Neocolonialism. Another factor that hinders economic growth in developing nations is neocolonialism, a term coined by the African leader Kwame Nkrumah (KWAH mee ehn KROO muh). This term describes the economic system in which the most developed countries in the Northern Hemisphere dominate the economies of the less developed countries in the South.

Large corporations sometimes invest in less developed countries to get raw materials and cheap labor. Governments in the North that want political and military power also influence trade. Nations of the North want allies and bases in the South. In return, they give economic aid and arms to less developed states.

Economic Growth in LDCs

Each nation must write its own plan for economic growth. Natural resources, educational level, and goals differ among all nations. However, an overriding problem all developing nations face is the need for capital (see page 488). Nations cannot achieve industrial development without capital to invest.

Since India became independent, the country has worked to industrialize. The Inde Ahmedabad power station generates electricity for Indian homes and businesses.

Aid to Developing Countries. For this reason, LDCs look for outside aid. Governments of industrialized nations offer grants or foreign aid to developing countries. Grants and foreign aid are gifts that require no repayment. Corporations invest in developing countries when they build plants or businesses that employ people or exploit a natural resource.

The World Bank, a United Nations organization, loans money to developing countries at low interest rates. Private banks also offer loans. Since this money must be repaid, it creates an even greater problem for the developing nation. The country may need to spend any surplus wealth to make interest payments on loans.

Trade in Developing Countries. Trade also offers LDCs a means to develop economically. Often, an LDC can obtain capital by selling its raw materials on the international market.

Exporting raw materials, however, presents two main problems. First, raw materials sometimes bring low prices. Yet, the developing country must pay for manufactured goods from the industrialized nations. Second, developing countries often become dependent on exports of a single commodity. When the price of that commodity falls, the developing country's economy may collapse. To control prices, LDCs have tried to organize cartels.

Importance of the Oil-Producing States. The Middle East contains the world's largest oil reserves. Since 1945, oil has been the chief item of trade for this region. In 1960, oil-producing countries of the Middle East formed a cartel called the Organization of Petroleum Exporting Countries, or OPEC. After the 1973 Arab-Israeli war, OPEC imposed an embargo restricting oil sales to many of the countries that supported Israel. Later they substantially raised the price.

As a result, oil-producing nations increased their earnings from $40 million in 1973 to $120 million in 1974. Money from the industrialized world poured into the less developed Arab nations.

The World Debt Problem. The high price of oil disrupted the entire world economy. It also began a chain reaction. First, individuals, businesses, and governments initiated measures to conserve fuel. Second, the search for alternative sources of energy spread and intensified.

Third, world trade decreased because rising oil prices forced up the prices of many other goods. Individuals and nations bought fewer of the more expensive products. Demand, therefore, decreased.

Fourth, conservation methods were successful. An oil surplus finally developed, causing prices to fall. Countries such as Mexico that had borrowed large amounts based on their revenues from higher oil prices could not repay their loans. The world banking system was seriously threatened. Banks instituted emergency measures. They rescheduled the payment plans of countries that could not meet their loan payments. Many of these countries are still unable to pay their debts.

Developing nations face many problems on the road to prosperity. Few have the ability to feed their populations well without aid. Many suffer from political instability.

The Challenge of Development

FOCUS ON SOURCES

In June 1967, African leaders met in Nairobi, Kenya, to discuss the problems of developing nations. Topics ranged from economic planning to social and cultural movements. Tom Mboya (ehm BOY yah), a young, dynamic Kenyan leader, was the most likely candidate to succeed Jomo Kenyatta. However, Mboya was assassinated in 1968. The following excerpt is from a paper Tom Mboya prepared:

The natural gas refinery in Hassi-R'Mel, Algeria, is evidence of Algeria's efforts to become economically self-sufficient.

"The achievement of rapid economic and social development of the developing countries will depend on these countries' own efforts. The major burden in this task is, and should be, on their shoulders. . . . Moreover, they cannot expect foreigners to do this work. If this happens, not only will the developing countries be disappointed in most cases, but the foreigners will try to get the maximum they can through the young nations' natural resources. In short, resources of these countries will be developed for the benefit of the foreigners, . . . neocolonialism will be the order of the day.

There are several things which the developing nations must do. First, they must avoid being involved in the power struggle and ideological [different ways of thinking] warfare which is raging on an ever-increasing scale. . . .

Second, the developing countries must be committed to, and believe in, rapid development. Such commitment is a precondition for sustained and maximum effort and sacrifice. To assume a fatalistic attitude [accepting every eventuality as a certainty] will be disastrous. It will be like an army going to war already convinced that it will be defeated. . . .

I now come to a most important action which developing countries can take, . . . to establish the necessary conditions for development to take place. This point must be grasped, for it means the matter is that much more urgent.

Economic cooperation among developing countries must include effective measures to increase trade among themselves. When one examines trade statistics of developing countries, one notices their trade is mainly with the industrial nations. . . .

What is perhaps not fully realized is that economic cooperation does not only mean tariff preferences. . . . To be effective, tariff preferences must be accompanied by cooperation in other sectors, for example in coordinated industrial programs. It must be accompanied by measures to improve transportation and means of communications among these countries. "

Tom Mboya's plans for LDCs to help themselves and one another have not yet brought prosperity. LDCs continue to face challenging problems. ■

SECTION 3 *Study Skills*

Developing Vocabulary Use each of the following words in a sentence: **1.** nonaligned. **2.** third world. **3.** calorie. **4.** capital goods. **5.** neocolonialism. **6.** commodity. **7.** cartel. **8.** embargo.

Reviewing Main Ideas 1. Explain the term third world. **2.** What are four characteristics of LDCs? **3.** Explain neocolonialism.

Understanding Cause and Effect 1. Explain two problems that result from exporting raw materials. **2.** What problems were created and solved by the development of OPEC? **3.** What were four reactions to the high price of oil? **4.** What did Tom Mboya state that developing nations must do to prosper?

Challenge Assume the role of a leader in an LDC. Explain how you would put Tom Mboya's advice into action.

CHAPTER 30 *Summary & Review*

Summarizing Main Ideas

Following World War II, nationalist movements became active throughout the world. With few exceptions, independence movements in the British Empire were peaceful. France fought long and expensive wars with its colonies. The Dutch, Belgians, and Americans granted their colonies independence between 1945 and 1960. By 1965, the great empires were dismantled.

Newly independent countries faced several problems which slowed their advancement. New nations often allowed powerful military leaders to take control.

In the Middle East, the desire for a Jewish state caused numerous problems. In 1948, the United Nations recognized the state of Israel.

Half of the world's population lives in LDCs, less developed countries. These nations find themselves in a cycle of poverty. LDCs often want foreign aid. To prosper they must cooperate with one another and help themselves.

Questions for Critical Thinking

COMPREHENSION Interpreting Events

1. How did the Indian government handle its problems with the Hindus in 1947? Explain your answer.
2. What did the Suez Crisis show about Europeans' ability to cooperate with one another?
3. Explain the Jewish and Palestinian claims to independent states in the Middle East.

ANALYSIS Identifying Trends

1. Why did many newly independent nations accept leadership by military dictators?
2. Are most of the former colonies subject to neocolonialism? Why?

APPLICATION Comparing Past and Present

1. Explain and give examples of how colonial powers still influence their former colonies.
2. How do nonaligned nations exert influence on world affairs?

Colonial Independence in Asia and Africa		
Country	**Year**	**From**
Asia		
Philippines	1946	United States
India	1947	Great Britain
Pakistan	1947	Great Britain
Burma	1948	Great Britain
Ceylon (Sri Lanka)	1948	Great Britain
North Korea	1945	Japan
South Korea	1945	Japan
Indonesia	1949	Holland
Cambodia	1954	France
Laos	1954	France
Vietnam	1954	France
Malayan Federation (Malaysia)	1957	Great Britain
Africa		
Tunisia	1954	France
Morocco	1956	France
Ghana	1957	Great Britain
Nigeria	1960	Great Britain
Algeria	1962	France
Kenya	1963	Great Britain
Zaire	1960	Belgium
Mozambique	1975	Portugal
Angola	1976	Portugal

SYNTHESIS Developing Writing Skills

Report on Indira Gandhi, Ho Chi Minh, Jomo Kenyatta, Gamal Abdel Nasser, or Mao Zedong.

EVALUATION Weighing Consequences

1. What impact does military control of new governments have on citizens?
2. What has been the outcome of the various Israeli-Arab conflicts since 1948?

CHALLENGE

Construct a map showing the colonial possessions on this chart.

CHAPTER 31

Currents of Change 1960—Present

GLOBAL TIME LINE

TIME

1973–1974 OPEC oil embargo causes worldwide inflation

1973–1978 Golda Meir governs Israel as prime minister

1973 The United States and North Vietnam sign a cease-fire agreement

1975 South Vietnam falls to the communists

PEOPLE

1971 President Nixon withdraws most United States troops from Vietnam

1972 President Nixon establishes friendly relations with the People's Republic of China

1972 President Nixon and Soviet Premier Leonid Brezhnev meet for the first time

1974 President Nixon resigns in the wake of the Watergate scandal

PLACE

1975 *Indochina;[1]* Civil war between communists and anti-communists begins in Cambodia

1976 *Indochina;[1]* Vietnam united to form the Socialist Republic of Vietnam

1976 *Middle East;[2]* Israeli troops occupy southern Lebanon

1970   1975

Linking Past to Present

A shopper, standing in the crowded aisle of a supermarket, stared at the rows of cereal. All around, other shoppers were speaking different languages. To the left, two women were speaking Spanish. To the right, a young couple was speaking Vietnamese. Others were talking in Arabic. Most of the shoppers were wearing jeans. Three wore headphones attached to radios.

This common occurrence illustrates two facts of our modern world. First, the technology and material products of the West have become the basis of a global culture. Second, interaction among people of differing cultures has become more intense than ever before. As you read the chapter, take notice of the evidence of a shared world culture.

A market in Saudi Arabia.

1980	1985	Present

1979–1981 Iranians hold 59 Americans hostage

1979 The United States and the People's Republic of China establish formal diplomatic relations

1980–1985 Indira Gandhi, Nehru's daughter, governs India as prime minister

1980 War begins between Iran and Iraq

1979 The Ayatollah Ruhollah Khomeini becomes the leader of Iran

1985 Rajiv Gandhi becomes prime minister of India

1979 Margaret Thatcher becomes prime minister of Great Britain

1986 Corazon Aquino becomes president of the Philippines

1979 Egypt and Israel sign a peace treaty

1980s Bishop Desmond Tutu pleads for nonviolent protests by blacks in South Africa

1979 *Afghanistan;*[3] Soviet troops invade Afghanistan

1982 *Middle East;*[2] An international peacekeeping force tries to restore order in Lebanon

1979 *Central America;*[4] Sandinistas overthrow Somoza and set up a socialist government

1985 *Poland;*[5] Communists crush opposition in Poland

1980 *Poland;*[5] Workers' strikes spread throughout Poland

1985 *Switzerland;*[6] President Reagan and Soviet Premier Gorbachev meet to discuss disarmament

1981 *Middle East;*[2] Israelis destroy Iraqi nuclear reactor

719

1 *The Superpowers Compete for Influence*

OBJECTIVE: *To understand the causes and consequences of the Atomic Age*

Relaxing Tensions Between the Superpowers

The Cuban missile crisis of 1962 was a turning point in recent world history. After that crisis, the United States and the Soviet Union pulled back from the brink of war. The two countries moved gradually toward reducing tensions.

From the 1960s to the present time, the United States and the Soviet Union have remained the greatest military powers on earth. These two superpowers still compete in a race to build the most weapons, both conventional and nuclear. They also compete for allies among third world countries. At times, however, the countries have taken steps to reduce hostility and tensions.

Superpowers Move toward Detente. Despite the Berlin airlift and the Cuban missile crisis, relations between the United States and the Soviet Union improved in the 1960s. After the Cuban missile crisis, leaders of both countries worked toward detente. Detente is a French word that means relaxation or easing of tension. In the 1960s, the term came to mean an easing of tensions between the Soviet Union and the United States.

In April 1963, the Soviets accepted a United States proposal for a special telephone, called the hot line, to link the White House and the Kremlin. This enabled leaders of the two nations to communicate quickly during a crisis. The line went into operation at the end of August 1963.

To further relieve tensions and reduce the arms race, President Kennedy of the United States announced, in June 1963, that he was suspending nuclear tests in the atmosphere. The next month, representatives of Great Britain, the United States, and the Soviet Union agreed to end all testing of nuclear weapons in the atmosphere, outer space, and underwater.

United States Detente with China. After establishing the People's Republic of China (see page 681), Mao Zedong set up a government and economic system modeled on that of the Soviet Union. The two countries signed a treaty of alliance against Japan in February 1950. The Soviet Union provided

---

VOCABULARY DEVELOPMENT

detente (day TAHNT) *noun:* a lessening of tension between nations, as through a treaty or trade agreement. A French word meaning to relax. From the Latin prefix *de-*, meaning from, and word *tendere*, meaning to stretch out.

domino theory: the theory that a certain result follows a certain cause the way a row of upright dominoes falls if the first one is pushed.

coup (koo) *noun:* a sudden, forcible overthrow of a government. A French word meaning a sudden blow or stroke.

draftee *noun:* a person chosen for required service in the armed forces.

---

technical assistance and loans for China's economic development. Thousands of Chinese went to the Soviet Union to study.

In the late 1950s, the two giants quarreled over the correct path to communism. They also disagreed over the border between China and the Soviet Union. In 1960, the Soviets withdrew all their technicians from China, and border skirmishes between their soldiers flared up.

After the communist takeover of mainland China, the United States and Communist China had no diplomatic, economic, or cultural relations. In February 1972, President Nixon took a giant step toward establishing friendly relations with the People's Republic of China. He met for eight days with Chairman Mao Zedong and Premier Zhou Enlai (JOH EHN LY). As a result, the two nations announced that both would cooperate in peacefully settling disputes. They also agreed to open trade and cultural relations. The United States recognized that Taiwan (see page 681) was part of China and promised to eventually withdraw American forces from the island.

One obstacle to diplomatic relations remained. China insisted that the United States withdraw its recognition of, and end its mutual defense pact with, Taiwan. In 1978, President Carter received assurances that the People's Republic of China would not attack Taiwan. He agreed to the conditions, and the two nations opened their embassies in Beijing and Washington.

After the deaths of Zhou Enlai and Mao Zedong in 1976, moderates led by Deng Xiaoping (dung sheeaw-ping) stressed modernization. By the mid-1980s, the nation had shifted toward a market-oriented socialism. China established commercial ties with the industrialized world, expanded relations with the United States, and tried to improve ties with the Soviet Union.

In 1989, China's economic reforms prompted students to demand equally significant political reforms. After more than seven weeks of peaceful demonstrations in Beijing's Tiananmen Square, army troops moved in with tanks, rifles, and bayonets. The man in the photo pleaded for an end to the killing but was pulled away. The bloodshed, seen live on worldwide television, shocked the West, especially when the Chinese government later claimed that the massacre had never happened. Many of China's trade partners reevaluated their foreign policies in light of these events.

The Communist Nations of Eastern Europe. The split between the Chinese and Soviets in the 1960s led the satellite countries of eastern Europe to work for more independence. Albania sided with the Chinese and left the Soviet bloc. The Romanians insisted on pursuing independent economic and foreign policies. By the mid-1960s, Romania had friendlier relations with China and Israel than with the Soviet Union.

In Hungary, the communist leader, Janos Kadar (YAH nohs KAHD ahr), decentralized economic planning and allowed some private enterprise. Economic conditions improved, and he granted the people more freedom. In 1964, more than 100,000 Hungarians were allowed to visit friends and relatives in Western countries.

The people of Poland also enjoyed more freedom than citizens of the Soviet Union. Like Romania and Hungary, Poland allowed more religious freedom. Farms in Poland were not collectivized. Most farms remained in the hands of individuals.

The Prague Spring. In Czechoslovakia, however, the Soviets refused to allow more autonomy. In 1968, the new first secretary of the Czechoslovak Communist party, Alexander Dubcek (DOOB chehk), along with other party leaders, instituted liberal reforms. They reduced censorship and granted the people more civil liberties. Political prisoners were released, and new political parties gradually formed.

The alarmed Soviets pressured the Czechoslovaks to cancel the reforms. When they refused, Soviet, East German, Polish, and Hungarian troops invaded Czechoslovakia on August 21, 1968. Dubcek was forced out of office. The new government brought back earlier authoritarian policies.

Despite the Soviet crackdown in Eastern Europe, detente continued. The United States accepted Eastern Europe as a Soviet sphere of influence and continued policies to relax tensions with the Soviets.

The War in Indochina

When the Vietnamese defeated the French in Indochina in 1954, President Eisenhower advanced the domino theory. According to this theory, all the nations of Southeast Asia would fall to communism like a domino chain reaction if Vietnam fell. Eisenhower, therefore, supported direct economic and military aid to South Vietnam, where communists sought to overthrow the government (see page 701).

Vietnam's Unstable Government. In the 1960s, war broke out between communist and anticommunist forces in Cambodia, Laos, and South Vietnam, the three nations that had been French Indochina. Communists wanted to set up communist dictatorships. The United States opposed communist governments.

In South Vietnam, the government of Ngo Dinh Diem (NYOH DIHN DIHM) was unpopular because it represented a Roman Catholic minority. Most Vietnamese were Buddhists. In addition, Diem rigged elections, imprisoned his opponents, and suspended promised land reforms. As opposition increased, Diem arrested Buddhist monks and destroyed temples.

A growing opposition fought a guerrilla war against Diem. Called the Viet Cong, meaning Vietnamese Communists, the guerrillas controlled the countryside. In cities, too, more and more people turned against the repressive policies and corruption of Diem's government.

The United States Increases Aid. In 1961, President Kennedy increased the number of American military advisers aiding South Vietnam. He also supplied Diem's troops with helicopters. By the fall of 1963, about 17,000 American advisers were working with the Vietnam army.

On November 1, a military *coup* (koo) occurred. The Diem regime was overthrown and Diem killed. Soon after, Kennedy agreed to send helicopters, reconnaisance

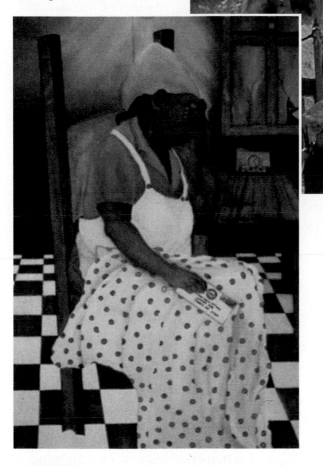

At right, American officers carry a wounded Vietnamese soldier. Below, Vietnam veteran Cleveland R. Wright's *We Regret to Inform You.*

planes, and American Green Berets trained in anti-guerrilla warfare to aid the new South Vietnamese government.

The new government, under a series of generals, proved even more unstable and ineffective than the Diem government. Land reform still lagged, corruption went on, and Viet Cong influence grew steadily. The Viet Cong controlled almost 80 percent of the countryside. Ho Chi Minh sent over 30,000 North Vietnamese to provide military assistance to the estimated 150,000 Viet Cong guerrillas.

When Lyndon Johnson became president in 1963, he and his advisers believed that only a small investment of American troops and money could defeat the Viet Cong. In August 1964, however, the conflict in Indochina grew into a full-scale war.

The Gulf of Tonkin Resolution. American naval vessels, supporting South Vietnamese raids on the coast of North Vietnam, were attacked in 1964. As a result, the American Congress adopted the Gulf of Tonkin Resolution. This allowed the president to "take all necessary measures to repel any armed attack against armed forces of the United States and to prevent further aggression." In 1965, President Johnson sent 185,000 United States troops to Vietnam. The United States also launched regular bombing raids on the North.

Opposition to the war grew in the United States. Pictures of dead and wounded American soldiers flashed on American television screens nightly. Americans took part in peace marches and sit-ins to oppose the war. Students marched in the streets chanting, "Hey, Hey, LBJ, how many kids have you killed today?" As the war dragged on, some Americans no longer believed the president's claims that victory was just around the corner.

A New Government for South Vietnam.

In 1967, the South Vietnamese government held elections. President Thieu (tyoo) and Vice-President Ky (kee) were elected. Widespread reports of election fraud raised questions in the United States. Thieu and Ky, however, brought greater political stability to the country.

The North Vienamese fought a war of attrition. They believed they could outlast the Americans just as they had the French. North Vietnam sent troops and supplies southward through a network of roads, paths, and tunnels that Americans termed the Ho Chi Minh Trail. Using the supplies and tunnels, they waged a guerrilla war.

Vietnam veteran Kenneth Willhite's 1981 painting reflects the theme that people can forget war as easily as they can rip down a poster and repaint a wall.

American troops faced many problems. They had difficulty dealing with both the geography and cultural differences. They seldom saw the enemy, who attacked and then slipped back into rice paddies or jungle tunnels. The army of South Vietnam, in contrast to the North's, was made up of draftees who often lacked motivation to fight during the early years of the war.

The Tet Offensive.

In January 1968, the North Vietnamese and Viet Cong successfully launched a heavy assault on towns throughout South Vietnam. South Vietnamese and United States troops struggled for weeks to drive the Viet Cong from the towns. "It became necessary to destroy the town to save it," one officer said, looking over the remains of the city of Ben Tre and the bodies of thousands of civilians. Finally, in 1968, delegates from both sides met in Paris to discuss peace. The meetings soon became deadlocked, however.

During the same year, opposition to the war increased in the United States. President Johnson announced a limited halt to the bombing of North Vietnam. He also stated that he would not be a candidate for reelection to the presidency.

Richard Nixon became the next president of the United States. He pledged to end the war "with honor." In June 1969, Nixon announced a plan to withdraw American ground troops gradually and let the South Vietnamese do their own fighting.

The United States and North Vietnam signed a cease-fire agreement on January 27, 1973. The United States withdrew its troops but continued to send economic and military aid to the South. North Vietnam released American prisoners of war.

War Continues in Southeast Asia.

The cease-fire did not end the war. North and South Vietnamese forces continued fighting. In the spring of 1975, North Vietnam launched a major attack. Its forces quickly fought their way south. On April 19, 1975,

South Vietnam fell when the communists captured Saigon, the capital. In 1976, North and South Vietnam were united to create the Socialist Republic of Vietnam. Saigon was renamed Ho Chi Minh City in honor of the communist leader who had died in 1969.

Civil War in Cambodia. In 1975, a civil war broke out in Cambodia. The United States aided the noncommunists in their fight against the Cambodian communists, the Khmer Rouge. In April 1975, however, the communists took over Cambodia, as well as neighboring Laos. They changed the name of Cambodia to Kampuchea (KAHM poo CHEE uh).

The communist Khmer Rouge under Pol Pot imposed a reign of terror on the people of Kampuchea. They tried to set up an agrarian society without a trace of foreign influence or modernization. They forced everyone to move to the countryside. Roads were clogged with refugees. Hundreds of thousands died from mass executions, starvation, and disease.

In 1977, however, a new civil war broke out in Kampuchea between communist groups. Vietnam intervened, drove out the Cambodian communist leader, Pol Pot, and established a puppet government. Pol Pot's forces, Khmer Rouge guerrillas, continued to fight the new government in remote areas of the country.

The Boat People

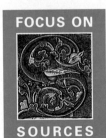
FOCUS ON SOURCES

During the 1970s, more than 1.5 million refugees fled Indochina. They preferred the uncertainty of life as refugees to life under the communists. The flight of these people, along with the upheaval in India, Pakistan, and Bangladesh in the 1940s, represents one of the great population shifts in recent history.

Many refugees were denied entrance to countries when they tried to land their crafts. This 1979 photograph shows the plight of Cambodian boat people.

The refugees were often called boat people because most left Indochina by boat. They bought their way out of Vietnam, Laos, and Kampuchea on illegally operated and unseaworthy freighters or any other boats they could find. The following excerpt is from the book, *The Refused: The Agony of the Indochina Refugees* by Barry Wain. The author is a diplomatic correspondent for *The Asian Wall Street Journal:*

❝ For a start, the boat people headed for southern Thailand, the nearest landfall. But the pattern changed when Thai pirates regularly began to attack and rob refugee boats, sometimes raping and killing the occupants. . . .

The gamble of the voyage was captured in verse by one anonymous refugee:

... we are the foam
floating on the vast ocean
we are the dust
wandering in endless space
our cries are lost
in the howling wind...

A sense of desperation propelled the boat people. Nguyen Van Phong (en GY yehn van FONG), ... took three months to assemble a drum raft with the help of his three sons....

Some voyages were nothing short of miraculous. A United States congressional subcommittee was told of 25 Vietnamese men, women, and children who made a 1,000 mile trip to southern Malaysia in a 30-foot boat.... Their sole navigational aids were an old rusty United States Army-issue pocket compass 2 inches in diameter and a [4 inch] fragment of a map of the world torn from a geography textbook. **"**

Many of the boat people were refused entrance when they tried to land their frail craft. Eventually, Western countries and China welcomed the largest number. The United States accepted about 500,000. ■

Detente under Nixon

Despite their disagreements in Vietnam and elsewhere, the United States and the Soviet Union continued to work toward detente. The nuclear arms race was a major source of tension. By the 1960s, both nations were spending enormous amounts on military hardware and new weapons systems.

Disarmament Treaties Lessen Tensions.
When Richard Nixon became president of the United States in 1969, he adopted a flexible approach to the Soviet Union and encouraged detente. In 1969, the two leaders, President Nixon and Premier Leonid Brezhnev (brezh NYOF), agreed to arms lim-

itation talks. Representatives from both countries met to work out an agreement.

In 1971, the United States and the Soviet Union finally signed a formal agreement on the status of Berlin. The Soviets promised to guarantee the Western powers access to West Berlin and to respect the city's independence. In return, the West agreed to recognize East Germany. This agreement removed what Khrushchev had called a "bone in the throat" of the Soviets.

In May 1972, President Nixon traveled to Moscow for a summit meeting with the Soviet premier, Leonid Brezhnev. Nixon was the first American president to visit the Soviet Union since World War II.

At the summit meeting, the two countries agreed to increase trade and to cooperate on space exploration. They also signed an agreement on arms control. The agreement, called the Strategic Arms Limitation Treaty, SALT, limited the number of offensive missiles and defensive missile sites that each nation could build.

In June 1974, Nixon and Brezhnev held another summit meeting in Moscow. Again, agreements were reached between the two countries to improve trade relations and increase cooperation in scientific matters. The United States and the Soviet Union also agreed not to test nuclear weapons underground. They were unable, however, to agree on a reduction of offensive missiles.

In 1974, President Ford signed a preliminary agreement with Premier Brezhnev to extend strategic arms limitations into the 1980s. In the same year, the two nations also agreed not to conduct underground nuclear tests of more than 150 kilotons.

The Helsinki Accords. Hopes for a more peaceful world rose in July 1975. President Ford joined leaders of 34 other nations in Helsinki, Finland, to sign several agreements. One set of agreements established borders for Poland and other East European countries. In return, the Soviets guaranteed more liberal exchanges of people

Polish Solidarity leader Lech Walesa appears before the U.S. Congress in November 1989 to request aid for Poland. He said, "The world is awaiting your signal. It is watching you. Do not let the world wait any longer."

and information between the East and West. They also agreed to recognize certain basic human rights.

The Soviets Invade Afghanistan. President Carter tried to maintain the spirit of detente, but Soviet actions made this difficult. In 1979, Soviet troops invaded Afghanistan, an area of interest to both the superpowers. Since World War II, Afghanistan has remained one of the poorest and least developed nations in Asia. As a result, no government has been able to retain power in Afghanistan for long.

In 1979, Babrak Karmal (bah BRAHK kahr MAHL), backed by the Soviet Union, became the leader of Afghanistan. To protect this puppet ruler, the Soviets sent over 80,000 troops to Afghanistan. Opposition to Karmal and resentment of foreign troops grew. Rebels began armed resistance. Fighting increased, and over a million refugees fled into Pakistan, which already had a severe population problem.

The Soviets Fight a Guerrilla War. The geography of Afghanistan, made up of mountainous lands, was ideal for guerrilla warfare. Soviet forces found it impossible to defeat the rebels.

Unrest in Poland. During the 1970s, the communist government of Poland continued to allow its citizens more civil rights. The country, however, suffered from economic problems. In July 1980, worker strikes to protest food shortages and high meat prices spread through the cities.

In mid-August, 16,000 workers struck in Gdansk (guh DAHNSK), a major seaport in Poland. They demanded the right to form labor unions independent of Communist party control. After long negotiations, the government recognized an independent trade union called Solidarity. The government also agreed to salary increases.

Lech Walesa (wah LEHN sah) led the new union. In March 1981, he led a nationwide protest against police brutality. Millions of Poles backed a referendum questioning whether the Communist party should continue to govern Poland.

The communist government, angered by the demands, declared martial law, suspended union activities, and arrested thousands of Solidarity leaders and members.

Tanks appeared on the streets of Warsaw and other Polish cities, crushing opposition and enforcing authoritarian rule.

Changes in the Soviet Union

The death of Soviet leader Leonid Brezhnev in 1982 brought two elderly Soviet leaders to power. Both died in office. In 1985 Mikhail Gorbachev became chairman of the Communist party. Gorbachev represented a younger generation concerned about economic growth.

Gorbachev backed a new program based on *glasnost,* or openness, and *perestroika,* or restructuring. His goal was to improve life for Soviet citizens. He cut back on military involvement and spending abroad and opened new paths to economic exchange.

Soviet Actions Reduce World Tension. Soviet aid to Vietnam helped finance that nation's occupation of Kampuchea. This drain on Soviet resources, as well as world condemnation of the occupation, led Gorbachev to encourage the Vietnamese to leave Kampuchea. Vietnam agreed to withdraw its troops by 1990.

Under Gorbachev the Soviet Union improved relations with China. The two countries signed a broad trade agreement in 1985 and later made progress toward resolving their border disputes. In Afghanistan the cost of war in money and Soviet lives led to Gorbachev's agreement to slowly withdraw Soviet troops.

Talks between President Reagan and Chairman Gorbachev led to a reduction in the number of intermediate ballistic missiles each side had positioned in Europe. Later, Gorbachev announced additional plans to reduce Soviet troops and conventional weapons in Europe.

Gorbachev Represents Change. Ethnic groups in the Soviet republics and the people of the satellite nations of Eastern Europe tested the limits of *glasnost* beginning in the late 1980s. For example, the people of Latvia, Estonia, and Lithuania demanded and received greater autonomy. Cries for change echoed throughout Poland, Hungary, and Czechoslovakia.

Gorbachev viewed his policies and the developments he was allowing in these communist strongholds as a revolution. The wall that had divided Berlin and had been a constant reminder of seemingly unbreachable differences between East and West crumbled in November 1989.

Changes in Soviet policy created social unrest and political division at home. However, events stimulated by Gorbachev's leadership made possible for the first time a peaceful end to the cold war.

SECTION 1 *Study Skills*

Developing Vocabulary 1. Explain detente. 2. Why might a country experience a *coup*? 3. Why would a country need draftees?

Reviewing Main Ideas 1. What actions were taken following the Cuban missile crisis to ease tensions between the United States and Soviets? 2. How did Janos Kadar change the government of Hungary? 3. Explain President Eisenhower's domino theory. 4. What is the purpose of SALT?

Understanding Chronology 1. List the five most important dates in the history of Soviet-American detente. 2. Construct a time line showing United States involvement in Vietnam. 3. How did American involvement in Vietnam change after January 27, 1973? 4. List events in Poland in 1980 and 1981 that triggered the declaration of martial law. 5. When and why did the Soviets invade Afghanistan?

Understanding Cause and Effect 1. Why was Taiwan a problem in American relations with Communist China? 2. Why did many South Vietnamese oppose Ngo Dinh Diem? 3. Explain the problems faced by American troops fighting in Vietnam.

Challenge Reread the Gulf of Tonkin Resolution. What impact could such a resolution have on United States policy today?

2 The Middle East, Danger Zone of World Affairs

OBJECTIVE: *To understand the causes and consequences of the unrest in the Middle East*

Problems in the Middle East

Today more than 160 nations coexist on the globe, more than twice as many as before World War II. Each nation pursues its own economic and political interests, often at the expense of its neighbors. At the same time, other groups of people still struggle for independence. The most dangerous clashes between national interests in the postwar period occurred in the Middle East. See the map on page 709.

The Arab-Israeli Agreement. Following the 1973 War between Israel and Egypt (see page 709), Anwar Sadat (suh DAHT), Egypt's president, received international attention. His early successes in the conflict showed that Egypt could successfully fight a military operation. After his limited victory, Sadat opened negotiations with the Israeli leaders.

To hasten an agreement, the United States mediated among Syria, Egypt, and Israel. Negotiations were carried on through shuttle diplomacy. United States Secretary of State Henry Kissinger shuttled between Damascus, Tel Aviv, and Cairo, the capitals of Syria, Israel, and Egypt.

To promote peace, Egyptian President Sadat took an unprecedented step. He traveled to Israel to visit the prime minister, Menachem Begin (muh NAHKH uhm BAY gihn), in November 1977. No major Arab leader had entered Israel, a country whose existence Arabs did not recognize. Sadat addressed the Knesset (KNEHS eht), Israel's parliament, and urged a direct peace settlement between Eygpt and Israel.

VOCABULARY DEVELOPMENT

mediate (MEE dee AYT) *verb:* to provide friendly or diplomatic intervention, usually by invitation, for settling differences between persons or nations. From the Latin word, *medius,* meaning middle.

nuclear reactor: a device for starting and maintaining a controlled nuclear chain reaction to produce energy.

escalate (EHS kuh LAYT) *verb:* to increase in amount, intensity, or scope; to expand from a local conflict to a general, especially nuclear, war. From the Latin word, *scalare,* meaning to climb.

leftist *noun:* a person who politically favors socialism or revolution to improve or reform the life of the people.

rightist *noun:* a person who politically favors the established order, traditional attitudes, national interests, and the security of private wealth and prosperity.

summit *noun:* a conference of the heads of governments. From the Latin word, *summus,* meaning highest.

martyrdom (MAHR tuhr duhm) *noun:* the assuming of an attitude of self-sacrifice or suffering for one's beliefs. From the Greek word, *martyr,* meaning a witness.

unilateral (YOO nuh LAT uhr uhl) *adj.:* of or affecting one side only. From the Latin words *unus,* meaning one, and *lateralis,* meaning side.

In the fall of 1978, President Carter offered personally to help the two leaders work out their differences. He invited them to the presidential retreat, Camp David, Maryland. While there, Anwar Sadat and Menachem Begin agreed to the terms of a peace treaty. Signed in the spring of 1979, the treaty returned the Sinai Peninsula to Egypt but did nothing to promote a Palestinian state. The rest of the Arab world, particularly the Palestinians, angrily criticized the treaty.

The Arab-Israeli Conflict Continues. During the late 1970s and the 1980s, relations between the Arabs and Israelis seemed trapped in a cycle of violence. The Arabs would strike at Israel, and the Israelis would retaliate. Then the Arabs would strike again. PLO artillery and commandos also continued to attack Israel from camps in Syria and Lebanon.

Israel Attacks Iraq. Another Arab nation, Iraq, also opposed Israel. Iraq, which includes the ancient land of Mesopotamia, became independent in 1933. In 1981, the Iraqis were completing a $260 million nuclear reactor. Nuclear reactors make plutonium, a needed component to manufacture atomic weapons.

The Israeli defense minister predicted that with the nuclear reactor the Iraqis would be capable of producing atomic bombs within four to six years. A member of Iraq's ruling Revolutionary Command Council had stated earlier, "The Arabs must get a bomb."

To stop the spread of nuclear weapons to the Arabs, the Israelis destroyed the reactor in June 1981 in a surprise air attack. After the attack, Iraq promised to make "bigger and better nuclear reactors." Israel retorted that it was ready to repeat its attack at any time.

International Conflicts in the 1980s

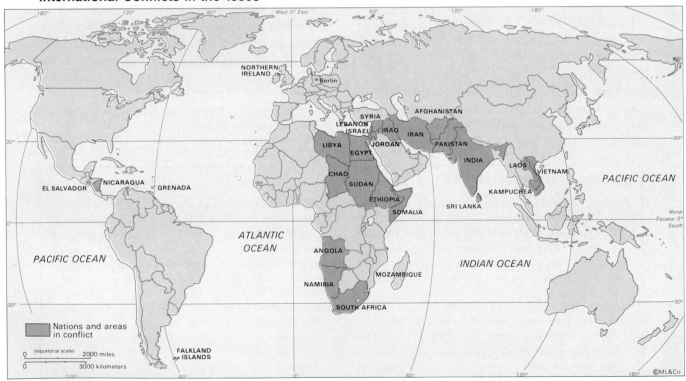

Map Skills **1.** Identify nations in Central America that have been tension areas during the 1980s. **2.** Which continents have been relatively free of tensions during the 1980s?

The Civil War in Lebanon, 1975-1976.

During the 1970s, border raids from Lebanon into Israel and Israeli retaliation escalated. The continued tensions and fighting spilled over to Lebanon, resulting in a bloody civil war.

Loyalties of the people of Lebanon are split among political, religious, and ethnic causes. Lebanon's population is about half Christian and half Muslim. Both the Muslims and the Christians are divided further. The leftists support reform and liberal policies. The rightists back a return to fundamentalist religious beliefs.

The main cause of the civil war, which began in 1975, was the political differences between Muslims and Christians. Other factors, however, also contributed to the war. Among them were interference of Israel and Syria in Lebanese affairs and the presence in Lebanon of Palestinian groups.

In 1982, Israeli planes and artillery bombarded Lebanese cities to destroy PLO bases, weapons, and supplies. This photo of Beirut was taken in May 1982.

Foreign Nations Prolong the Civil War.

During the 1960s and 1970s, many Palestinian refugees moved to Lebanon. The PLO set up a base there. Lebanese Christians and Muslims split over support of the PLO. Many Muslims supported the PLO.

When the civil war broke out between the Muslims and Christians in 1975, Syria invaded and occupied parts of Lebanon in an effort to keep order along its border. Syrians also wanted to protect the Damascus-to-Beirut highway, their main supply route from and to the Mediterranean. Palestinians launched attacks on Israel. The Israelis responded by attacking southern Lebanon. The United Nations stationed troops along the border between Lebanon and Israel. The bloodshed, however, continued as hundreds of Lebanese and Palestinians were killed.

During the first year of the civil war, a tangle of political alliances developed. Israel backed the Christians. President Assad (ah SAHD) of Syria supported the Muslims and Palestinians. By 1976, the Palestinians seemed to be taking control of Lebanon. Either the Christians would be defeated or Lebanon would be partitioned.

The Syrians were afraid Israel would intervene to defeat the PLO. To prevent Israeli intervention, Syria eventually moved toward support of the Christians. Syria supplied arms to the Christians and prevented the Palestinians from taking militarily strategic points.

During the summer of 1976, the Israeli army occupied sizable parts of southern Lebanon. In early June, Syrian military units entered the country with about 450 tanks and 20,000 soldiers.

Repeated attempts were made to bring the fighting to an end. Finally, a formal summit meeting late in October 1976 established an Arab League peacekeeping force of 30,000 troops, mostly Syrian. The forces were under the overall command of Lebanon. The civil war continued to drag on.

Israel Occupies Lebanon.

The Lebanese government lost popular support as fighting continued among political groups. Only the Phalangist party, which successfully led the Christians, remained politically strong. The Phalangist militia was the most powerful Lebanese military force.

To destroy Palestinian military bases and force Lebanon to curb PLO raids, Israel invaded Lebanon with 20,000 troops in March 1978. The next year, a small contingent of United Nations forces replaced the Israelis. Israel, however, continued to supply arms, money, and advisers to the Phalangist forces in the south. Israel's aim was to counteract PLO power by backing the Christian militia.

Syrians, Lebanese Christians, Lebanese Muslims, and the PLO continued to struggle over Lebanon in the early 1980s. Palestinians continued to raid Israel from bases in Lebanon. In 1982, over 60,000 Israeli troops and 500 tanks, along with jeeps, personnel carriers, and artillery, entered Lebanon. The Israeli vehicles were decked in red bunting so that Israeli pilots could easily identify them.

Passing United Nations peacekeeping forces on their way, the Israelis swept across the 63-mile long Lebanese border to destroy PLO bases, weapons, and supplies. Israeli planes and artillery bombarded Lebanese cities. Within 48 hours, the Israelis had destroyed many of the PLO's positions.

Israeli Prime Minister Menachem Begin spoke to the Knesset after the attack. He promised to end the fighting when Israel had secured a 25-mile buffer zone in southern Lebanon. After a week of fighting, Israel and the PLO agreed to a cease-fire. However, Israeli troops remained, as did the 15,000 to 20,000 PLO guerrillas. Syria doubled its forces in Lebanon.

International Peacekeeping Forces.
United States leaders called for a withdrawal of all foreign troops from Beirut. They also organized an international force to restore order. Troops from the United States, France, and Italy remained in Lebanon for 19 months.

During the occupation, United States Special Envoy Philip Habib worked to negotiate an agreement among Lebanon, Syria, Israel, and the PLO. An agreement reached in late August 1982 resulted in the evacuation of all PLO guerrillas. They were transferred to other Arab countries where they formed new camps.

The Bloodshed Continues.
Terrorism continued in Lebanon during the occupation. Christian Phalangists entered two Palestinian refugee camps in West Beirut and murdered 700 to 800 Palestinians, mostly women and children. Muslims, who felt that the international forces supported the Christians, bombed French and American troops. In 1984 the international forces left Lebanon, and in 1985 the Israelis withdrew their troops. Lebanon remained divided, and the violent civil war continued.

Israel and the PLO.
More than 20 years after the 1967 war, Israel still occupied the West Bank of the Jordan River and the Gaza Strip. Almost 2 million Palestinians live in these lands. In 1988 Palestinians there rioted to focus attention on their plight. The Israelis harshly repressed the *intifadeh,* or uprising, provoking worldwide criticism.

In 1988 Yasir Arafat, speaking for the PLO, recognized Israel's right to exist in peace and security. He also renounced terrorism in all its forms. These concessions opened the way for negotiations between the United States and the PLO over the Palestinian question. Israel, however, rejected all contact with the PLO.

Revolution in Iran

While Lebanon was being torn apart by civil war, Iran became engulfed in revolution. Iran is one of the largest Muslim countries in the Middle East. The people of Iran, however, are mainly Persian, not Arab. Since the sixteenth century, most of the population has been Shi'ite Muslim.

Iran Modernizes. During World War II, Britain occupied the southern part of Iran and the Soviet Union occupied the north. Both powers wanted to control Iranian oil production. At a conference in Teheran in 1943, the Big Three agreed that Iran should be independent after the war.

In 1945, the ruler, Shah Muhammad Reza Pahlavi (rih ZAH PAHL uh vee), was forced to flee when revolutionaries took over the country. A succession of governments, backed by the Soviets or the British, ruled the country. In 1953, with the support of the United States, the shah returned to the throne. He again set up an autocratic government. Savak, the security police, who gained a reputation for using torture, enforced the shah's policies.

The shah was determined that Iran would be strong enough to resist another foreign power occupation. With United States aid, he strengthened Iran's military forces. The United States bought large amounts of Iranian oil, and the shah bought American weapons on a massive scale. By 1965, Iran was the most powerful country in the Middle East.

When oil revenue increased sharply in the early 1970s, the shah used the money to modernize Iran and encourage westernization. He divided large estates among landless peasants, and built schools, highways, and industries. The shah also introduced social reforms, including the right of women to vote. Newly educated citizens and business leaders became increasingly influential in Iran.

Rapid economic development, however, brought growing inflation, corruption in government, and brutal repression of opposition. As a result, conservative Muslims opposed the shah. In the late 1970s, students joined with Muslim clergy to organize strikes and protest rallies.

Iran Becomes an Islamic Republic. Opponents of the shah supported an exile, the Ayatollah Ruhollah Khomeini (roo HOH luh

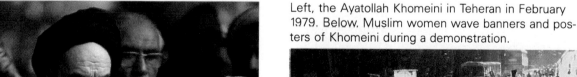

Left, the Ayatollah Khomeini in Teheran in February 1979. Below, Muslim women wave banners and posters of Khomeini during a demonstration.

koh MAY nee). This Muslim leader was living in France. In January 1979, when the shah was unable to maintain order, he, too, went into exile. The next month, Khomeini, a Shi'ite Muslim, returned to Iran and established an Islamic republic. Iran's population is 92 percent Shi'ite Muslim.

The Ayatollah and his supporters established a conservative Muslim government. Their aim was to restore Islamic law and traditional Islamic values. Shi'ites place great value in martyrdom. They see Christianity and westernization as cultural threats to their traditional ways of life.

The Hostage Problem. The Iranians blamed the United States for the shah's excesses. In 1979 Iranian militants occupied the United States embassy and took the 59-member staff hostage. For over a year, both sides negotiated, threatened, and denounced each other. The United States froze Iranian financial assets in American banks and attempted a rescue mission. Finally, in January 1981, an agreement was reached, which freed the hostages.

The taking of hostages in the Middle East remained a problem. Muslim extremists, thought in the West to be backed by Iran, took hostages throughout the 1980s, hoping they could trade them for jailed terrorists or obtain other concessions. The majority of these hostages continued to be Americans.

War between Iran and Iraq. The Iraqis, attempting to end the revolutionary government in Iran and settle old grievances, attacked Iran in September 1980. Both nations claim the Shatt al-Arab (SHAHT AHL AHR ubh), an important waterway at the mouths of the Tigris and Euphrates rivers. The war has devastated the economies of both countries.

In June 1982, Iraq declared a unilateral cease-fire, withdrew the last of its forces from Iran, and asked for peace. The Ayatollah refused. Instead, he called for the res-

ignation of Saddam Hussein (hoo SAYN), the leader of Iraq.

During the war, the United States stationed ships in the Persian Gulf to forestall any Iranian attack on the Saudi oil fields or the Strait of Hormuz. About 40 percent of Western oil imports flow through this strait. During the war, oil fields in both nations were bombed, and oil shipments to the rest of the world cut back. The two nations finally agreed to a truce in August 1988. In 1989 the Ayatollah Khomeini died.

Importance of the Middle East. The Middle East is important to the United States and other nations because of its vast petroleum reserves and strategic location. The Soviet Union exerts influence there through alliances with Syria, Iraq, and Yemen.

SECTION 2 *Study Skills*

Developing Vocabulary Define the following words: **1.** mediate. **2.** summit. **3.** unilateral. **4.** leftist. **5.** rightist.

Reviewing Main Ideas 1. How has the number of sovereign nations changed since World War II? **2.** What problems accompanied Iranian modernization under the Shah? **3.** What is the importance of the Middle East to the United States and the Soviet Union?

Understanding Chronology 1. Construct a time line showing five important events in Arab-Israeli relations. **2.** List significant dates and events in Iranian history from 1943 to 1982. **3.** How long were American embassy workers held hostage in Iran?

Understanding Cause and Effect 1. What was the purpose of Sadat's visit to Israel in 1977? **2.** What was the main agreement that came from the Camp David meeting in 1978? **3.** Why did Israel bomb Iraq in June 1981? **4.** List the factors that led to civil war in Lebanon. **5.** Why did Syria invade Lebanon in 1975? **6.** What caused the Iraq-Iran War?

Challenge What threat to world peace might the continued war between Iran and Iraq cause?

Acid Rain

Even when countries are friends, they have problems. The United States and Canada are friendly neighbors. They share the longest unpatrolled border in the world. Religious, political, and territorial disputes do not exist between them as in the Middle East. However, both face the environmental problem of acid rain.

The Problem

Anne LaBastille, who lives in the Adirondack Mountains of upstate New York along the Canadian and United States border, described the problem:

❝ My log cabin looks out over a lake that has grown increasingly clear [empty of life] in recent years . . . . Native trout are now scarce, as are loons, osprey, and otters. Bullfrogs are all but silent. As much as a third of the virgin red spruce around the lake have died . . . . My lake is now at least a hundred times more acidic than it was 53 years ago. ❞

The Causes of Dying Lakes. Acid rain begins with sulfur and nitrogen oxides contained in automobile exhaust and smoke from factories. The wind carries these substances into the atmosphere, where they come into contact with the water vapor that makes up clouds. Sunshine and water vapor convert the oxides into acids. The acidic water vapor falls to the ground as rain or snow, and damages the environment.

Effects on the Environment. Acid rain directly damages plants and harms animals. The effects of acid rain on people, however, are often indirect. When acid gets into bodies of water, it dissolves metals, such as discarded aluminum cans. These dissolved metals are in turn absorbed by the plant life in the water. When fish eat the plants they swallow these harmful substances and pass them on to people.

Another danger occurs when acid rain dissolves lead and copper plumbing carrying drinking water to homes. People drink the water and cook with it. In this way, dangerous metals enter the human body.

Just as acid dissolves metals, it also dissolves concrete and metal structures. Statues, buildings, and roads all succumb to damage. Acid rain is dissolving India's Taj Mahal, the Greek Acropolis, the Tower of London, and the Cologne Cathedral.

Weather and Acid Rain. To find a solution to this problem, scientists need to understand the relationship between weather and acid rain. Prevailing wind patterns in North America cause particular areas on the continent to suffer more damage from acid rain than others. In general, the winds in North America move weather patterns from west to east. Many of the oxides, which turn acidic, are produced in the Midwest. They fall to earth as acid rain in the United States and Canada. According to some studies, as much as 75 percent of the acid rain falling in Canada is created by oxides from the United States.

Acid Rain Agreement

In 1986, envoys of the United States and Canada began meeting to discuss the problem of acid rain. This issue may appear to be simply scientific. However, political concerns make a solution difficult. Money was one of the problems. The governments of both countries needed to decide whether money should be spent on research to learn

Inset, the Harz Mountains in Germany in 1980. Above, the same site five years later reflects acid rain's damaging effects on plant life.

more about the problem or allocated to prevent future acid rain.

Agreement on this point was hard to reach. The United States felt that more information was needed through research. Canada stated that the causes of acid rain were clear. The technology was available, and the time had come for preventative action. They cited the need for scrubbers on smokestacks to clean the smoke of harmful oxides. They also saw the need for emission control standards on automobiles.

Both Canada and the United States are under pressure from various lobbying groups that want their own interests considered. Automobile manufacturers and industrialists fear restrictions that increase their costs and thus hurt their products in the competitive marketplace. Environmentalists worry about the effects of acid rain on plant and animal life. Coal-producing states are afraid their industries will suffer.

Other concerns involve questions of responsibility for repairing the damages acid rain causes. Should damages be paid by the industry that caused the acid rain, the owner who suffered the loss, or the governments of either nation?

The acid rain problem shows once again how interdependent people are, even when political boundaries separate them. Some problems, such as acid rain, can be solved only by people working together.

STUDY SKILLS Understanding Geography

1. What is acid rain?
2. Name three necessary ingredients to make acid rain.
3. Create a diagram showing one route of the acid rain cycle.
4. Explain the damage caused by acid rain.
5. Describe three solutions to the acid rain problem. Explain why you feel one of these is best.
6. Since most acid rain damage is in southeastern Canada, discuss whether Canada should contribute more money for the acid rain research fund than the United States.

3 The Failures and Victories of Democracy

OBJECTIVE: *To understand the causes and consequences of the failure of democratic governments in some countries*

Failures of Democracy in Latin America

In the search for order in a world of more than 160 nations, numerous small wars break out between neighbors. Some governments become authoritarian and brutal, using torture against their political enemies.

This situation existed after World War II in Latin American countries that did not have stable governments. Two major causes contributed to political instability in Latin America: social inequality and economic underdevelopment.

VOCABULARY DEVELOPMENT

fluctuate (FLUHK choo WAYT) *verb:* to be constantly changing in an irregular way, as in fluctuating prices. From the Latin word, *fluctus,* meaning a wave, a flowing.

nationalize *verb:* to transfer ownership of land, resources, or private industry to the national government.

Afrikaner *noun:* a white South African of Dutch ancestry.

apartheid (uh PAHRT hayt) *noun:* the policy of strict racial segregation and discrimination against the native blacks as practiced in South Africa. An Afrikans word meaning apartness.

Bantustan (BAN too STAN) *noun:* any of several territories in South Africa set aside as reserves for native black people, supposedly with some system of self-government. From the African word, *Bantu,* and the Persian word, *stan,* meaning a place.

Social and Economic Problems. In most Latin American countries before World War II, only 5 percent of the population owned 70 to 90 percent of all the land. The wealthy 5 percent also controlled the major businesses not owned by foreigners. This minority, along with a growing middle class, strongly influenced the power structures of government, the military, and the church.

In addition to this social inequality, the economies of Latin American nations were underdeveloped. Often they depended on a single product whose price fluctuated on the international market.

The 1940s and 1950s Bring Change. After World War II, revolutionary leaders organized the poor and working classes. The revolutionaries took over governments in many Latin American countries. New governments in such countries as Chile, Bolivia, and Guatemala set up social services to provide food and medical care for people. They instituted land reform programs, dividing estates among landless peasants.

Latin American leaders worked to diversify and modernize their economies by industrializing. Often the first step toward economic growth was to nationalize, or take over, foreign-owned land and industries. New governments also concentrated on producing consumer goods instead of starting and developing basic industries, such as iron and steel.

Authoritarian Governments. Many times the results of these economic reforms were disappointing. Food production often fell, and money needed for modernization was spent on imported food or industrial products. Governments often printed more money and borrowed heavily. This caused huge national debts and runaway inflation.

Intervention in Latin America. In the early 1960s, the United States tried to end Fidel Castro's communist rule in Cuba (see page 693). The United States asked all American countries to cut off diplomatic relations with Cuba and to refuse to buy Cuban sugar. Sugar prices fell, damaging Cuba's economy. With massive military and economic aid from the Soviet Union, however, Castro remained in power.

Cuba and the United States intervened in other Latin American countries. During the 1960s, Castro trained Cuban guerrillas and sent them to Central America, Colombia, Venezuela, and Bolivia to encourage peasant revolutions. The United States sent military aid and advisers to Bolivia to counter Castro's influence. To combat communists in other Latin American nations, the United States used economic aid.

Revolutions in Central America. In the late 1970s, guerrilla warfare broke out in Nicaragua. A dictator, Anastasio Somoza (sah MOH sah), controlled the tiny nation. The rebels called themselves Sandinistas (sahn dah NEES tahs), after Augusto Sandino, a Nicaraguan rebel who opposed United States intervention in the 1920s. The Sandinistas overthrew Somoza in 1979. They set up a socialist government dedicated to land reform and social welfare.

In the mid-1980s, a new guerrilla movement, the Contras, opposed the Sandinistas. The Contras included soldiers who wanted to return the Somoza family to power, former Sandinistas unhappy with the lack of freedom in Nicaragua, and moderates fighting for a democratic government. The

Residents of Soyapango, El Salvador, wait to vote in the presidential runoff election on May 6, 1984. Salvadoran law requires citizens to vote.

United States government, afraid communism would spread throughout Latin America, aided the Contras. The Soviet Union supported the Sandinistas.

President Reagan was convinced that the Soviet Union and Cuba were expanding communism in Latin America. For the same reason, he also sent military aid and advisers to El Salvador. In both countries, thousands of civilians died in the fighting between the guerrillas and the government.

Democracy Fails in South Africa

In contrast to the rest of Africa, the Republic of South Africa is industrialized and ranks among the world's richest nations. The climate is moderate and the farmland fertile. Mineral resources, including gold, diamonds, platinum, manganese, and uranium, are plentiful.

Whites make up only 15 percent of the population. Nevertheless, the conservative Afrikaners, descendants of the original Dutch farmers, dominate the culture and government. They believe that God chose them for salvation.

Apartheid. After World War II, black nationalists in Africa worked for majority rule. To repress this movement, the white government of South Africa instituted apartheid (uh PAHRT hayt). This policy divides South Africa's people into four racial groups: whites, blacks, coloreds of mixed race, and Asians, mostly from India. These groups are rigidly separated.

Apartheid laws govern the jobs people may hold, their education, salaries, and voting. Black schools receive less government support. Black wages are low to maintain a supply of cheap labor, and blacks' movements are restricted. Blacks are not allowed to vote or hold elected offices. The Afrikaners believe that apartheid protects white persons so that the growing black population cannot dominate them.

Opposition to Apartheid. Many black nationalist leaders opposed apartheid and promoted strikes and demonstrations. In 1960, at the town of Sharpeville, police fired into a crowd of Africans who were protesting pass laws. As a result, 69 blacks were killed and 180 injured. The government then outlawed the African National Congress, the major black political party. Nelson Mandela (man DEHL luh), the leader of the party, was sentenced to life in prison.

Criticism from Great Britain and other Commonwealth members caused South Africa to leave the Commonwealth in 1961. In 1966, to lessen growing criticism, the government announced the creation of Bantustans, black states or homelands.

Bantustans. The government set aside less than 15 percent of South Africa's land for black states. In these black homelands, or Bantustans, blacks could govern themselves. Until 1986, blacks had to carry a pass indicating where they were legally allowed to live and travel. Racially segregated homelands, however, did not end the protests against apartheid.

Small Victories. To quiet growing criticism, South Africa allowed multiracial membership on sports teams in the 1980s. Blacks were also allowed to travel anywhere in the country in search of work, but could live only in townships and Bantustans.

Recently, the government allowed Asians to have their own 46-member parliament and coloreds a 92-seat parliament. The white parliament, however, can veto any decisions made by these bodies.

Protests continue almost daily in South Africa. Bishop Desmond Tutu, a black whose work for racial justice won him a Nobel Prize for Peace, pleaded for nonviolent protests. However, he no longer thinks violence can be avoided. "I still hope for peaceful change, but I think that because the government refuses to make meaningful reforms, more bloodshed is inevitable."

For his work in civil rights for blacks in South Africa, Bishop Desmond Tutu won a Nobel Prize for Peace.

The Organization of African Unity, as well as several industrialized countries, favor economic sanctions against South Africa. However, South Africa is a self-sufficient country that sells more to other countries than it buys. The economies of a number of black African nations, including Angola, Zambia, Zimbabwe, Mozambique, and Botswana, depend to some extent on South Africa. Sanctions would hurt these countries the most.

War in Namibia. Namibia, bordering on South Africa, was once the German colony of South West Africa. The League of Nations gave the Republic of South Africa a mandate to prepare the region for independence. However, South Africa annexed South West Africa in 1949. The United Nations renamed the area Namibia in 1968. Each year, the UN criticizes South Africa for its racist policies.

African nationalists struggled against the South African government in Namibia.

They formed the South West African People's Organization, SWAPO, in 1966, and worked to end South African domination. Namibia's African neighbors and the communists supported SWAPO. South Africa arrested SWAPO leaders. By 1972, however, demonstrations and armed skirmishes were common.

Finally, in 1988, South Africa agreed to a timetable that would make the last colony on the African continent into the independent nation of Namibia. SWAPO agreed to honor the cease-fire that would end the struggle of Namibians for independence.

Nelson and Winnie Mandela

FOCUS ON PEOPLE

To protect its privileged white government, South Africa has imprisoned many nationalist leaders. When Nelson Mandela was sent to prison in 1963, his wife, Winnie, continued to further his cause. After taking part in the 1976 Soweto uprising she was put under house arrest in a Bantustan near the town of Brandfort, about 250 miles from Johannesburg.

On September 26, 1936, Nomzamo Winifred Madikizela was born in a small village in the Republic of South Africa. Her family called her Winnie. She attended school, and at the age of 20 became South Africa's first black female social worker. About her education, she writes:

❝ At least during that time there was not yet a difference between white and black education. It was before the rubbish Bantu education was brought in in the early fifties. There was a common syllabus [outline of study] and we were doing academic subjects like Latin, English, chemistry, physics, and mathematics. There were strict standards . . . . The children who came after us . . . know nothing about the world and can't even speak English properly. ❞

Winnie met black nationalist leader Nelson Mandela, in 1956 when he was on trial for treason. The state was trying to prove that he, along with other members of the liberation movement, were part of a communist-inspired effort to overthrow the white government of South Africa.

Nelson and Winnie saw each other for only short periods because of Nelson's many duties as a black lawyer and leader. Nevertheless, two years later they were married. Winnie adopted Nelson's cause and became a black liberation leader. "I knew when I married him that I married the struggle, the liberation of my people."

Winnie was arrested for the first time in 1958. She had joined other women in a demonstration. As a consequence, she lost her job. Between 1958 and 1985, Winnie was arrested or detained more than a dozen times. Much of her life she spent either in jail or restricted to Orlando township. She was seldom able to keep a job.

"I lost so many jobs at the time—a furniture shop, a dry-cleaning shop, a shoe-repair shop—they were countless. I was hired on a Monday and fired on a Friday. The Security Police went to each and every employer to intimidate them and to prevent my employment.**"**

After her husband was sent to a maximum-security section of Robben Island prison off Cape Town, Winnie was allowed to send one letter to him and spend one-half hour with him every six months. Only personal and family matters, however, could be discussed.

In April 1982, Nelson Mandela was transferred to Pollsmoor Prison in Cape Town. He became ill with tuberculosis in 1988 and was transferred first to Tygerberg Hospital and later to a private nursing home outside Cape Town. The government then announced that Mandela would not be returned to prison but would be given suitable and secure living accommodations.

Nationalist leader Nelson Mandela before his imprisonment for treason. He has devoted his life to ending apartheid in South Africa.

In 1989 antiapartheid leaders forced Winnie Mandela out of the movement and asked blacks to distance themselves from her. Earlier she had publicly approved necklacing, the practice of igniting gasoline-filled tires which they had hung around the necks of blacks accused of collaborating with the government. She was also associated with a group called the Mandela United Football Club. These unofficial bodyguards gained a reputation for violence and were at the center of an investigation involving three murders.

Victories for Democracy

Democracy has not lived up to its promise in many of the countries of Africa and South and Central America. However, in the West, democratic governments have remained strong even though they have faced many problems.

Challenges for the United States. In the 1960s and 1970s, the United States weathered protest and change. The late 1960s were a time of student unrest and demonstrations against the Vietnam war.

The American system of government was also tested when scandals shook President Nixon's administration. Vice-President Spiro Agnew was accused of bribery, extortion, and tax evasion. In October 1973, Agnew resigned. President Nixon nominated a new vice-president, Representative Gerald R. Ford of Michigan. Ford was confirmed by a majority of both houses of Congress.

The Nixon administration then faced more serious accusations. During the 1972 presidential campaign, a guard had caught several burglars at the Democratic National Committee headquarters in the Watergate office complex in Washington, D.C. One of the defendants implicated Nixon's closest aides. Later investigation implicated Nixon.

At first, Nixon denied involvement and tried to cover up information. However, conversations in the White House incriminated the President. The House of Representatives held hearings and in July 1974 adopted three articles of impeachment. Before Nixon could be tried, he resigned, and Vice-President Gerald Ford was sworn in.

President Ford completed Nixon's term. In 1976 Jimmy Carter was elected president. During the Nixon, Ford, and Carter administrations, the United States suffered from a recession as well as from the highest inflation rate since World War II.

Rising prices helped conservative Republican Ronald Reagan defeat Carter in 1980. Reagan promised to reduce inflation and curb the size of the federal government. By the end of his second term, inflation had fallen to 4 percent. However, the federal government continued to spend more than it received in taxes, causing worldwide concern about the economic health of the United States.

President Reagan, relaxed, charming, and affable, remained popular. His popularity helped his vice-president, George Bush, win the 1988 presidential election.

Great Britain Faces Problems. Great Britain also faced numerous economic problems in the early 1970s. Slow economic growth, inflation, and unemployment troubled Britain. The Labor government imposed a freeze on wages and prices. This measure failed, however, and a series of strikes in 1972 further damaged the already weak economy.

Great Britain joined the European Economic Community in 1973. The British hoped that membership in the Common Market would stimulate the economy. However, unemployment, along with inflation, continued to rise.

In 1979, the British elected a majority of Conservative members to Parliament. The head of the party, Margaret Thatcher, became Britain's first female prime minister. To reduce inflation, Thatcher closed many inefficient mines and factories, denationalized major industries, and drastically cut government spending. Unemployment rose in the mid-1980s; however, by the late 1980s inflation had declined to 4 percent and unemployment had fallen sharply.

During the 1970s and 1980s, Great Britain also faced a continuing problem in Northern Ireland. Although self-governing, Northern Ireland is part of the United Kingdom. The Protestant majority controls the government and economy and discriminates against the Roman Catholic minority. The Catholics, led by the radical Irish Republican Army, IRA, want to leave the United Kingdom and join the Catholic Irish Republic. The Protestant majority of Northern Ireland is equally determined to remain linked to Great Britain.

Beginning in 1969, the IRA resorted more often to violence. British troops in Northern Ireland resisted, but bombings and murders continued to plague people in the divided country throughout the 1970s and 1980s.

French citizens stage a protest for school reforms in Paris during 1984.

Socialism in France. Charles de Gaulle retired from French politics in 1969. He died the following year. His successors continued to defend France's position in Europe. However, France, like Great Britain, suffered from labor unrest and inflation.

In 1981, the French elected a socialist, Francois Mitterrand, to the presidency. He nationalized much of French business. However, the economy worsened. In 1986, conservatives won a majority in the National Assembly and denationalized French companies. In the late 1980s, the economy improved as Socialists shared power with Conservatives.

Democracy in Other European Nations. In the late 1970s, the nations of Switzerland, Sweden, Denmark, West Germany, Norway, and Belgium also had strong democratic governments. The people of these countries all enjoyed a higher standard of living in the 1970s and 1980s than they had in earlier decades.

Italy, however, suffered from political problems. By 1981, the country had averaged slightly more than one new government every year since 1945. By contrast, dictators had ruled Spain and Portugal since before World War II. In the mid-1970s, when these leaders died, both countries restored democracy. In 1974, Greece replaced a military dictatorship with a constitutional government.

France, Italy, Spain, and Portugal all have legal communist parties. These parties, however, have grown increasingly independent of Moscow and emphasize their willingness to participate in politics in a democratic fashion.

Governments in Asia. Strong democratic traditions have grown in India, Japan, Australia, Malaysia, and New Zealand. Taiwan and Korea still have strong, central authoritative governments.

In the Philippines during the 1970s, Ferdinand Marcos remained a military dictator. In 1983, a leading political rival, Benigno Aquino (ah KEE noh) Jr., returned to the Philippines after three years of self-exile in the United States. As Aquino stepped off the plane, he was assassinated. Marcos appointed a commission to investigate the assassination. Marcos's opponents, however, blamed him for the killing.

The commission decided that government soldiers were the assassins. The sol-

Corazon Aquino campaigning in Manila in February 1984. Aquino became president after Marcos was charged with dishonestly winning the election.

diers were put on trial, but a government court found them not guilty. This verdict sparked demonstrations. In October, the United States urged Marcos to hold free and honest elections. When Marcos announced that an election would be held, opposition parties chose Corazon Aquino, the widow of Benigno Aquino, as their candidate.

In the 1986 elections, Marcos again won a majority of the votes; however, he was charged with massive voting fraud. Violent riots erupted, and the United States pressured Marcos to resign. He and his family moved to Hawaii. The new president, Corazon Aquino, promised land reform and a democratic government. However, she failed in negotiations with Communists, who held one-fifth of the country's villages, and the government remained unstable.

Democracy in Latin America. The 1980s witnessed a definite trend away from military regimes in Latin America. When the British defeated Argentina in the 1982 Falkland Islands war, the Argentine military

dictator lost popular support. In 1983, a new president moved to reduce the power of the military and place industries under civilian control.

Other nations of Latin America, such as Venezuela, Colombia, Costa Rica, and Brazil, moved toward elected governments and the protection of civil rights in the 1980s. Although a single political party continued to dominate Mexican politics, the country moved to protect individuals' civil rights.

Castro's hopes to spread Marxism failed as military governments overpowered guerrillas. He later sent revolutionaries to support communism in Africa but withdrew them for a time when the Soviet Union threatened to cut off aid. In the 1980s, Castro continued to support Marxist movements in Central America and in Africa.

SECTION 3 *Study Skills*

Developing Vocabulary 1. Why would a country nationalize its industries? **2.** What is the meaning of fluctuate? **3.** Where are Bantustans located?

Reviewing Main Ideas 1. Explain the causes of political instability in Latin America. **2.** What groups make up the Contras and the Sandinistas of Nicaragua? **3.** Explain South Africa's policy of apartheid. **4.** Why might economic sanctions against South Africa be ineffective or harmful to other African nations?

Understanding Chronology 1. How did the events of July 1974 help reaffirm confidence in the American government? **2.** List important dates and events in Nicaraguan history.

Understanding Cause and Effect 1. Explain several economic and political problems facing Latin America. **2.** What makes South Africa different from the rest of Africa? **3.** Explain Prime Minister Thatcher's attempts to reduce inflation in Great Britain.

Challenge Does there seem to be more or less hope for the development of democratic nations in the future? Explain.

CHAPTER 31 *Summary & Review*

Summarizing Main Ideas

Following the Cuban missile crisis in 1962, the United States and Soviet Union began working toward detente. In January 1979, the United States and China established diplomatic ties.

France withdrew its troops from Southeast Asia in 1954. The United States entered the conflict in the hopes of defeating communism in Vietnam. In January 1973, the United States withdrew its troops from Vietnam. In 1975, South Vietnam fell to the communists.

The Middle East continued to be plagued with problems. Terrorism, often led by the PLO, became a common occurence. Israel's occupation of Lebanon created international problems. The situation in Latin America and Africa became a struggle between the haves and have nots.

The SALT treaties, Helsinki Accords, and Camp David meeting brought nations closer to peace. As the 1980s advanced, there was hope for greater freedom in developing nations.

President Sadat, President Carter, and Prime Minister Begin shake hands. The three leaders met at Camp David, Maryland, in 1978 to work out a peace treaty between Egypt and Israel.

Questions for Critical Thinking

COMPREHENSION Interpreting Events

1. Why was President Nixon's move to have better relations with China such a great change in American foreign policy?
2. What was accomplished at Camp David in the fall of 1978?

ANALYSIS Identifying Trends

1. What communist satellite countries tried to gain independence in the 1960s? What were the results?
2. How much influence did protest movements have on American policy in Vietnam? Explain your answer.
3. What has been the impact of military dictators on Latin American countries?

APPLICATION Comparing Past and Present

1. Detente was strong in the late 1960s. What is the status of Soviet-American relations today?

2. What is the likelihood of the Soviet Union or the United States sending troops to an area they consider important?
3. Will the Middle East continue to be as important in the future as it has been? Explain.

SYNTHESIS Developing Writing Skills

Use the *Reader's Guide to Periodic Literature* to find current articles on one of the following:
1. Fall of Saigon – 1975
2. Nuclear Test Ban Treaty – 1963
3. Czechoslovakia – 1968
4. Boat People
5. Camp David Accords – 1979

EVALUATION Weighing Consequences

1. Explain the possible long-term results of the Non-Proliferation Treaty.
2. Explain the results that various Middle East wars have had on the area.
3. What have been the consequences of Ayatollah Khomeini's control of Iran?

CHALLENGE

Political unrest has often followed religious conflicts. How can such conflicts be avoided?

CHAPTER 32
The World in the Electronic Age

TIME

1970   1975

● **1971** American astronomers discover two galaxies adjacent to the earth's Milky Way

● **1974** A Soviet space probe lands on Mars

● **1975** United States Apollo an Soviet Soyuz 19 spacecraft lin up 140 miles above the earth

● **1976** United States space probe lands on Mars

PEOPLE

● **1969** United States astronauts Neil Armstrong and Buzz Aldrin, Jr. become the first humans to land on the moon

● **1971** Dr. Choh Hao Li synthesizes the hormone that controls human growth

● **1972** Richard Leakey and Glynn Isaac discover a 2.5 million-year-old human skull in Kenya

PLACE

● **1970** *United States;*[1] Scientists at the University of Wisconsin synthesize a complete gene

● **1974** *India;*[3] India becomes the sixth nation to explode a nuclear device

● **1972** *United States;*[1] United States government, along with other nations, restricts the use of DDT

● **1973** *Europe;*[2] Great Britain, Ireland, and Denmark formally join the Common Market

Linking Past to Present

On December 17, 1903, along a beach in Kitty Hawk, North Carolina, Orville and Wilbur Wright began the air age. For 12 seconds, they flew their heavier-than-air machine at speeds reaching 7 miles per hour.

Since that historic flight, technicians have improved on the Wright design and rapidly advanced the field of air travel. By 1962, the X-15 rocket plane had reached a speed of 1,500 miles per hour, soaring over 300,000 feet above the ground. Just 7 years later, the Apollo 11 spacecraft traveled through space at 25,000 miles per hour.

Both the Wright plane and the Apollo 11 spacecraft now hang in a museum. Each is obsolete, a victim of change. As you read, consider the many changes that will occur in your lifetime.

The Apollo 11 liftoff on July 16, 1969

1980   **1985**   **Present**

1977 Voyager I sends pictures of Jupiter to earth

1982 Cray computer performs 100 million arithmetical operations in a second

1985 Performers in Great Britain and the United States stage Live Aid concert to help starving people in Africa

1986 Nuclear reactor in the Soviet Union explodes spreading a cloud of radiation

1986 Seven American astronauts killed as rockets propelling space shuttle Challenger explode

1978 Explorer Thor Heyerdahl sails on reed boat from Iraq to the coast of Djibouti, Africa

1980 Martin Cline uses genetic engineering to treat a hereditary blood disease

1982 Dr. Michael Epstein identifies the first virus implicated in human cancer

1977 *United States;*[1] Scientists confirm testing of bomb that kills with radiation leaving buildings intact

1977 *Greece;*[4] Archaeologists discover the tomb of King Philip II of Macedon in northern Greece

1978 *Great Britain;*[5] First test tube baby, conceived outside the body of a woman, is born

1982 *United States;*[1] Over a ten-year period, the Whirlpool Corporation cuts the energy consumption of appliances by almost half

741

1 *The Global Economy*

OBJECTIVE: *To understand the causes and consequences of a global economy made up of interdependent national economic systems*

The Interdependent Economy

All nations interact with one another and are interdependent. Understanding contemporary history requires the study of the world as a whole instead of single nations, wars, or world leaders. For example, each nation manages its own economy. Through trade, national economies form an interdependent global marketplace.

Advantages of Trade. Each nation of the world has a unique mixture of natural, human, and capital resources. As a result of its different resources, each country specializes in supplying products in demand.

For example, Saudi Arabia has much more oil than it could possibly use. The hot, dry climate of Saudi Arabia, however, limits farm production. The United States grows much more wheat, corn, and other grains than its people can eat, but the United States has a limited supply of oil. Trade between Saudi Arabia and the United States, therefore, benefits both countries.

As a result of specialization, the economies of nations have become interdependent. Interdependence means that what happens in one part of the world affects what happens in other parts of the world. For example, wages in Taiwan are lower than those in the United States. As a result, shirts made in Taiwan are sold in the United States at a lower price than those made by American workers. Taiwan then uses some of the money earned in the United States to buy wheat and soybeans from American farmers. Therefore, while cheap clothing from Taiwan may hurt some American textile workers, it indirectly helps American farmers. The world economy is, of course, much more complex than this simple example.

Nations Compete in a Global Market. Nations compete with each other to sell their goods on the global market. Consumers benefit from such competition because they can choose from a wider variety and a larger range of prices. A consumer in the United States can find blouses from Taiwan competing with those from France, Italy, the United States, and other countries.

VOCABULARY DEVELOPMENT

contemporary (kuhn TEHM puh REHR ee) *adj.:* in recent times; modern. From the Latin prefix *com-*, meaning with, and word *tempus*, meaning time.

quota (KWOHT uh) *noun:* a certain amount or proportion that is allowed or admitted. From the Latin word, *quotare*, meaning to mark the number of.

sojourner (SOH juhrn uhr) *noun:* one who lives somewhere temporarily. From the Latin prefix *sub-*, meaning under, and word *diurnus*, meaning a day.

brain drain: a gradual lessening of the professional or intellectual resources of a country or region through emigration. Used in informal speech.

Automobiles made in Japan compete with those made in Germany, the United States, and Great Britain.

The Balance of Trade. The balance of trade is a measure of a country's performance on the global market. If a country sells more than it buys, the country has a positive, or favorable, balance of trade. If the country buys more than it sells, a negative balance of trade, or a trade deficit, results. For example, in 1984 the United States sold more than $5 billion worth of goods to Taiwan. Americans, however, bought over $14 billion worth of Taiwan's products. The United States trade deficit with Taiwan in 1984 was about $9 billion.

Governments sometimes try to protect their own industries and workers by raising tariffs on foreign goods. A tariff is a tax on an imported product (see page 487). The tariff raises the price of the product, dis-couraging consumers from buying it. Nations also protect their industries with quotas that restrict the amount of foreign imports. In recent years, the United States has limited the import of automobiles from Japan and textiles from Asia.

One country's use of tariffs and quotas, however, may lead other nations to set up their own restrictions. In general, trade restrictions reduce trade and harm countries as well as consumers.

Global Resources

The amount and kind of available resources influence a nation's economy. Natural, human, and capital resources produce the world's goods and services.

Natural Resources. All natural resources come from the earth. They include minerals that can be mined, land that can produce

Known Deposits of Minerals

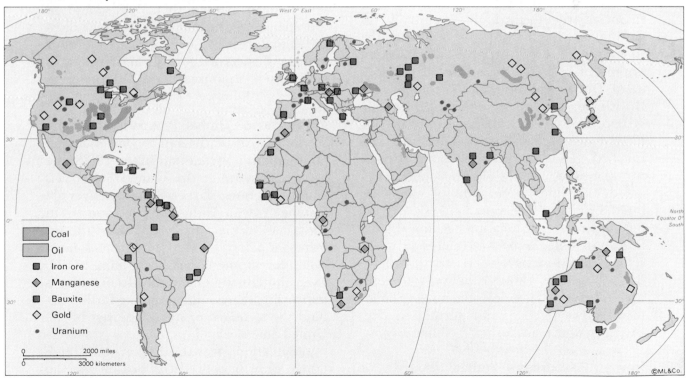

Map Skills **1.** List the mineral resources of the United States. **2.** In what hemisphere are most of the world's coal and oil deposits located?

food, and rivers that can generate power. Natural resources are raw materials from which goods are made.

Natural resources are unevenly distributed in the world. See the map, Known Deposits of Minerals, page 749. The Soviet Union and Canada are both rich in mineral resources. Their northern locations, however, limit the growing season and, therefore, their food production. Some countries depend largely on a single resource. Bangladesh, for example, produces most of the world's jute, a fiber used in the manufacture of rope.

Capital Resources. Capital resources include the money or property, such as tools, machines, and buildings, used to produce goods and services. For example, capital investments in factories, railroads, highways, telephone lines, and airports make trade within and between countries possible.

Unlike natural resources, capital resources are the results of human actions. The wealthy countries of Europe built their financial strength through a century of investing in capital resources. England, the first country to industrialize, illustrates an important sequence of events in development. During the Industrial Revolution, the British dug a canal system, built a railway system, and constructed a network of surfaced roads to transport raw materials and finished goods. Later, they built airports for planes. A late-developing country requires time and huge sums of money to build a modern transport network.

Only rarely can a nation become wealthy in a short time. Some Arab states did so by selling oil. Most developed countries have become wealthy through heavy, long-term investments in factories, machinery, buildings, railways, roads, air terminals, telephone systems, and other facilities.

Human Resources. Human resources, or people, are the third basic resource. A person's knowledge, skills, attitudes, and ability to work determine the person's value as a human resource. The age distribution of a population affects the quality of a nation's human resources, as do education and training. Workers in traditional agricultural economies learn tasks from family members. Industrialized or developed economies need workers who read, write, and have specialized skills. Education is a necessity.

The money spent on education often determines the quality of a nation's human resources. All but the poorest countries managed to send more than half their children to primary school in the 1980s. The United States leads the world in higher education with 58 percent of people aged 20 to 24 enrolled in postsecondary schools.

Sharing the World's Resources

Since the world's resources are not equally distributed, the quality of life differs greatly throughout the world. In the 1980s, television viewers in industrialized countries saw African people dying of starvation caused by drought. The televised news illustrated the great gap between rich and poor nations. Concerned British and American entertainers organized a Live Aid concert to help people who were starving in Africa.

Prospects for Global Prosperity. Despite economic growth, the gap between rich and poor nations is increasing. In the 1980s, the average income in the United States was almost 50 times larger than the average income in India. Industrial development in India has very gradually increased the income per person. In the United States, however, development has been more rapid. Even though the quality of life in India is improving, that country is falling farther behind the standard of living enjoyed in the United States.

Population growth that exceeds economic growth is the main reason for the growing gap between rich and poor nations. Since 1945, the earth's population has doubled. Most of the population increase occurred in the world's developing nations. See the map, Increase in World Population, 1981, page 752. Lower birthrates in poor nations would allow more food, clothing, and education for each child.

Some governments have tried to control population by limiting family size. Such policies, however, raise questions about basic human rights.

Mushrooming Cities. Population growth has contributed to an increase in the size and number of cities. The United Nations projects that in 35 years the number of urban areas containing more than 5 million people will increase from 34 to 93. Of those urban areas, 80 will be in the world's developing nations.

Large-scale urbanization is a recent development in world history. In the past, the size of cities depended on the ability of the surrounding land to produce food. After the Industrial Revolution, however, employment opportunities drew more people to cities. Expanding trade fed the expanding urban populations. This brought food to the cities from distant areas. See the map, Global Trade in Grains, page 754.

Rapid urbanization has created problems across the world, especially in the developing nations. Often, the rapid growth of cities has overwhelmed resources. Expanding cities often suffer from slums, pollution, and unemployment. Medical, educational, energy, and sanitation services become inadequate.

The Green Revolution. As population has increased, the world demand for grain has increased by about 30 million tons per year. To meet this demand, scientists developed new types of high-yield crops in the 1960s. Their work started the Green Revolution. The new plants yielded more food.

The new seeds, however, produced high yields only when combined with large amounts of fertilizer, pesticides, and water.

The population in India continues to increase every year, making it difficult to raise the country's low standard of living. Above is a street in Jaipur, India.

The impressive results of the Green Revolution are seen only where farmers can afford the added use of other resources. Poor climate and lack of funds severely limit the Green Revolution's impact in most of the developing nations.

Newly Industrialized Countries, NICs. Global trade stimulated industrialization in countries that previously lagged behind the developed nations. Several non-Western countries have moved toward stronger industrial economies.

Such countries as Taiwan, South Korea, Singapore, Mexico, China, and Brazil are producing more of the world's goods. They have hired technicians to set up, operate, and train workers to use new inventions. The success of these newly industrialized nations has shown the great economic growth potential of some of the underdeveloped countries.

Prospects for the Future. The developing nations seek a greater voice in world affairs. Some of these nations have used such organizations as the United Nations as forums to express their needs and concerns. Other nations have used their valuable resources as political weapons. The Arabs used their oil resources as a weapon in the 1970s.

The world's industrialized nations can help the less developed countries. Developed nations must share technological and educational skills to increase productivity in developing nations. Poor nations must also adopt policies to control their population growth and to produce more food.

Global Migrations

The migration of people from rural areas to cities within a nation has been an important part of modern history. Less obvious is the movement of large numbers of people from one country to another and from one continent to another. This also contributes to the interdependence of nations.

Workers Search for Employment. Many Turks work in Germany. Algerians have left their homes in Africa and moved to France in search of jobs. South Asians from India, Pakistan, and Sri Lanka can be found in Southeast Asia and Africa. Every year many thousands of Mexicans cross the border into the United States to find jobs. These people are able to find work because they are willing to work for lower wages. They are a part of the global migration of workers searching for employment.

Migrant workers are sojourners. They live and work in a host country for a few months or a few years. They then return to their own countries. Most migrant workers go from less developed countries to industrialized countries where they are willing to accept low-paying jobs.

Migrant workers often send much of their money home to their families. By earning money in a developed country and

Increase in World Population, 1981

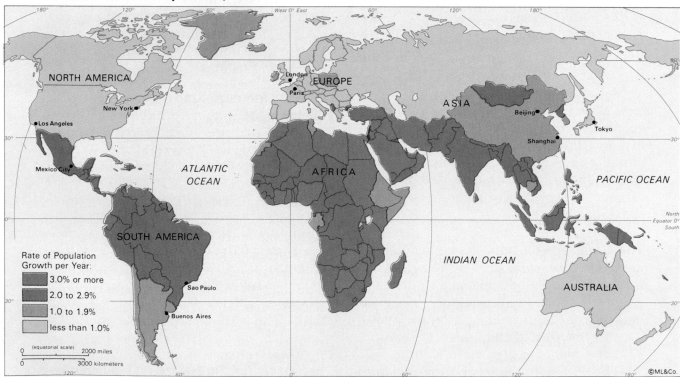

Map Skills 1. Which two continents have the highest population growth? **2.** Which continents have areas with both a high and low population growth?

sending it home to a poorer country, they help to redistribute wealth. They contribute to the economy of the host country with their labor and to their home country with currency. Often, they also bring new skills back to their homelands.

Controlled Labor Migration. Not all labor migration is voluntary. Some governments plan labor migration. South Korea, for example, organized construction companies to send Korean workers abroad for large-scale building projects. The mines of South Africa employ many workers from nearby countries. Such contracted labor exists because it benefits both countries. The host country acquires cheap or specialized labor, and the workers earn money not readily available at home.

Another form of organized labor migration is forced labor. The Soviet Union and the People's Republic of China have extensive systems of labor camps in remote regions of their countries. There, millions of people work for little or no wages. Most are prisoners sentenced to labor service. Using forced labor, China and the Soviet Union develop frontier areas where no one would choose to work.

Problems Created by Migrant Labor. Although migrant workers provide cheap labor for the host country, they also create problems. Migrants often do not know the language or share the culture of the host country. This leads to misunderstandings between migrants and citizens.

Some migrant workers enter a country illegally. Workers of the country resent them and believe the migrants are taking away jobs. Some migrants decide to stay in the host country and enjoy a higher standard of living. Then migrants add to the human resources of the host country at the expense of their homeland.

The Brain Drain. Another form of global labor migration involves skilled professionals. Many developing countries do not have

Every year thousands of Mexicans cross the border into the United States to find work. Pictured here, illegal immigrants from Mexico and a border patrol helicopter.

universities capable of training scientists and engineers at advanced levels. These countries often send students abroad to gain advanced training. In the early 1980s, Iran sent more than 60,000 students to study in the United States.

For several decades, many of the brightest graduates of universities in South Korea and Taiwan studied in the United States. They improved their English, adopted the American culture, and often stayed. This created a brain drain when as many as 90 percent of the students remained here.

The Migration of Refugees. Refugees leave home for many reasons. Indochinese emigrated to countries around the world when the communists took over their lands. More than a million Indians moved to Pakistan and Bangladesh during the 1950s. Ethiopians fled to the Sudan when their country suffered a famine. Palestinians have left Israel to settle in other Arab nations. People of Eastern Europe and Cuba have fled communist governments.

Some refugees hope to return to their homes in the future. Most, however, are ready to work and build new lives in their new countries. However, they are often il-

Global Trade in Grains

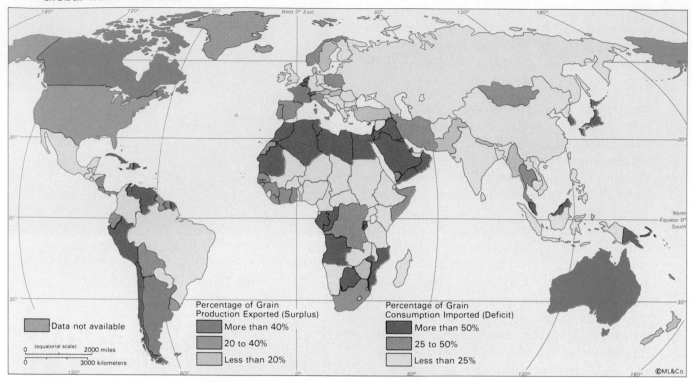

Data not available

Percentage of Grain Production Exported (Surplus)
- More than 40%
- 20 to 40%
- Less than 20%

Percentage of Grain Consumption Imported (Deficit)
- More than 50%
- 25 to 50%
- Less than 25%

(equatorial scale)
0   2000 miles
0   3000 kilometers

©ML&Co.

Map Skills **1.** What percent of the Soviet Union's grain is imported? **2.** What countries are leading exporters of grain? **3.** Why do countries import grain?

literate, sick, or unskilled. At times they are forced to move to poor countries that are already overcrowded.

Interdependence. Global trade benefits all nations. Through trade, nations obtain goods and services they cannot efficiently produce. Trade allows consumers a wider selection of goods and range of prices from which to choose. Trade enables developing countries to industrialize and add to the number of jobs available. Global trade and migrating labor forces expand nations' dependence on one another.

SECTION 1 *Study Skills*

Developing Vocabulary **1.** How does a brain drain affect a country? **2.** Explain the meaning of contemporary. **3.** Who is a sojourner? **4.** What is an immigration quota?

Reviewing Main Ideas **1.** What is a trade deficit? **2.** How has rapid urbanization affected developing nations? **3.** How can industrialized nations help Third World countries? **4.** Explain the benefits of global trade.

Understanding Cause and Effect **1.** What causes a negative balance of power? **2.** Explain the possible effects of tariffs and quotas on world trade. **3.** Why do developing countries continue to fall farther behind industrialized countries? **4.** Why do people from underdeveloped nations migrate to developed nations?

Understanding Geography **1.** Explain the three types of global resources. **2.** Name two countries that are rich in natural resources but do not have climates suitable for large amounts of food production. **3.** Explain the effects of the Green Revolution.

Challenge What are some possible ways developing nations might deal with the problem of brain drain?

People and the Environment

The North American culture realm was not the birthplace of the human race. Anthropologists believe that all the people in the world are descendants of the earliest human beings of East Africa. From East Africa, humans migrated to areas around the globe. Over many hundreds of years, as people migrated, they adapted physically to their new homes.

Adapting to the Environment

In East Africa, where the sun's rays are very strong, a dark complexion protects people from the harmful rays of the sun. In Scandinavia, where the sun's rays are much weaker, inhabitants need less protection from the sun. Instead, they need the sun's healthful rays which help people's bodies produce essential vitamins. In Scandinavia, therefore, a light complexion is an advantage. Over time, migrants to Scandinavia became light-complexioned.

People require many years for their bodies to adapt physically to their environments. Other adaptations, however, can be made quickly. For example, people adapted to cold climates by clothing themselves with animal skins.

People found ingenious ways to help them cope with their environment. The Eskimos, faced with harsh Arctic winters, made excellent use of snow. By compacting the snow into blocks, they constructed igloos that were both warm and durable.

Other Americans had their own methods for adapting to the environment. They used resources that were close at hand and plentiful. The Woodland Indians of the east coast used bark from birch trees to make trays, baskets, and buckets. They lived in wigwams, which had frameworks made of branches and covered with birch bark.

Many of the Plains Indians were farmers who raised crops of corn along the wide rivers that flowed across the grassy plains. They built earth lodges as their homes, because the plains had few trees. Thick sod formed the walls of these lodges. A mixture of earth and clay made roofs waterproof.

European explorers introduced horses into the Plains Indians' environment. The Plains Indians quickly learned ways to use horses in their environment. They discovered that such fast animals enabled them to hunt the buffalo more easily.

Buffalo hides were used to cover their tepees. These portable homes were ideal for those Indians who changed from farming to nomadic hunting. They also used buffalo hides for warm, comfortable clothing and for bedding to help them survive the cold plains nights.

People still adapt to the environment. Latin Americans adapt to the heat by taking a midday rest, a siesta. They return to work later in the day when it is cooler.

The government of the United States adopted daylight savings time as a wartime measure to conserve energy in 1918. Beginning in World War II, people resumed using daylight savings time in the summer. This North American adjustment to the sun extended daylight one hour into the workday. People set their clocks ahead in the spring and back in the fall to enjoy more daylight during their waking hours.

Changing the Environment

People cannot always adapt to their surroundings. When this occurs, people try to change their environment. Over a long period of time, early people learned that

Indians made their houses with available resources. These wigwams used by the Indians of Alberta, Canada, are similar to those of earlier American Indians.

planting crops was a more reliable method of getting food than hunting and gathering.

In the early days of farming, people prepared their fields by first cutting down the natural vegetation and then setting it on fire. They called this farming method slash-and-burn. Each year farmers continued to plant crops in the same field. After several years, weeds crowded out the crop. The farmer then moved to another field where he went through this same process again. In time, farmers learned to rotate crops and to control weeds by plowing. Later they learned to use fertilizers.

A trip through the United States farmlands of the Midwest and Plains states reveals how much farming has changed the environment. Fields of corn and soybeans cover mile after mile of land that was once heavily forested. Wheat extends over many miles of land that once was covered with prairie wildflowers.

People have changed the environment in other ways as well. For instance, where roads cannot easily be built over or around mountains, tunnels have been bored through the mountains. Where water transportation is best, canals have been dug to join rivers and lakes. Where cities have been built, average temperatures have risen.

People have filled in lakes to create more land. Land is hollowed out to form scenic lakes. Huge rivers are dammed to harness their energy and convert it to electrical power. In many ways, people have mastered their environment.

STUDY SKILLS Understanding Geography

1. Besides migration, identify two ways people can cope with their environment.
2. Explain one way people adapted to their environment.
3. Describe how people have changed their environment.
4. What are some of the consequences of changing or altering the environment in which we live?

2 *The Effects of Technology*

OBJECTIVE: *To understand the advantages and disadvantages of advanced technology*

A World of Technical Wonders

Change is a fact of history. For much of history, the rate of change was so slow that it went almost unnoticed. Improved technology accelerated change. The speed of technological change is one of the wonders of the present age.

Marriage of Science and Technology. Traditionally, individuals or small groups worked independently on scientific research. They usually concentrated on pure science rather than practical applications of their ideas and theories. They often shared their discoveries by publishing their findings. By the twentieth century, however, many scientists applied their knowledge to solve practical problems.

Facing the challenges of World War II, the United States and other nations brought research scientists and technicians together.

They cooperated to develop weapons and other materials. Under the code name the Manhattan Project, United States' scientists used nuclear fission to develop the atomic bomb. Nuclear fission was soon adapted for peacetime uses, such as generating electricity and making radioactive isotopes to diagnose medical problems.

Advances in Space. Following World War II, scientists made spectacular advances in space exploration. Progress depended on the development of rockets with enough power to escape the earth's gravity.

Scientists developed multistage rockets. As each stage consumed its fuel, the fuel container dropped from the assembly. The next stage then fired, propelling the lighter rocket forward faster. Rockets reaching speeds of over 18,125 miles per hour were able to escape the earth's gravitational pull.

VOCABULARY DEVELOPMENT

technician *noun*: one who is skilled in the practical application of new knowledge.

space probe *noun*: an instrumented, unmanned spacecraft for exploring to get information about environmental and physical properties. From the Latin word, *probare*, meaning to prove.

genetics (juh NEHT iks) *noun*: the branch of biology that deals with the way characteristics are transmitted from parent to offspring in plants and animals. From the Latin word, *genesis*, meaning birth.

synthetic (sihn THEHT ihk) *adj.*: made by a chemical process rather than by nature. From the Greek prefix *syn-*, meaning together, and word *tithenai*, meaning to place.

pollutant (puh LOOT uhnt) *noun*: a harmful chemical or waste material discharged into the water or the atmosphere. From the Latin word, *pollutus*, meaning to soil or pollute.

radioactive *adj.*: giving off radiant, or light ray, energy by the spontaneous breakup of atomic nuclei.

The space age began in 1957, when the Soviet Union launched a multistage rocket carrying a small aluminum globe. Called Sputnik 1, this satellite soon orbited the earth transmitting radio signals. In 1961, Soviet Flight Major Yuri Gagarin became the first human in space. A month later, Alan Shepard, Jr. became the first American to travel in space.

Throughout the 1960s, the United States and the Soviet Union continued their conquest of space. Finally, on July 20, 1969, United States astronauts Neil Armstrong and Buzz Aldrin, Jr. landed on the moon. An excited world audience viewed the historic moment on television. Stepping onto the moon's surface, Armstrong proclaimed: "That's one small step for a man, one giant leap for mankind." United States astronauts made five additional moon landings. On each, they gathered data to better understand the origin and nature of the moon.

Increased Knowledge of the Universe. Throughout the 1970s, both manned and unmanned vehicles were launched into space to collect data. As a result, scientists learned more about the universe, the solar system, and the earth. Soviet space probes first landed on the surface of Venus in 1967. A United States space probe landed on Mars in 1976. Millions of people on earth thrilled to the first photos of the red planet's surface transmitted on television.

Probes continued to examine planets throughout the 1970s. The probe Voyager I, launched in 1977, sent pictures of Jupiter and later helped to unravel the mysteries of Saturn's rings. Another probe, launched in 1980, flew by Uranus in 1986 and is scheduled to examine Neptune in 1989.

Routine Space Travel. In 1981, the reusable space shuttle Columbia made its first flight. Astronauts aboard the Columbia and

Apollo 11 astronauts Neil Armstrong and Buzz Aldrin, Jr., landed on the moon on July 20, 1969. Aldrin walks near the lunar module.

a second space shuttle, the Challenger, performed scientific and astronomical experiments. They also launched satellites and retrieved and repaired defective ones.

International cooperation has characterized recent space exploration. In the 1980s, scientists from Japan, the United States, and 12 other nations developed a series of 70 experiments to be performed in space. The United States and the Soviet Union also cooperated to develop a satellite system for locating downed aircraft or ships in distress on earth.

By the mid-1980s, Americans had begun to view space travel as routine. In 1986, however, tragedy struck the United States space program. Rockets propelling the shuttle Challenger with six astronauts plus a teacher aboard exploded in space killing all the occupants. This disaster reminded Americans that space technology continues to be complex and dangerous.

Advances in Medical Science.

Researchers have greatly advanced the field of medical science since 1945. Medical science has taken giant steps in controlling the outbreak of dangerous diseases.

Using the newly invented electron microscope to study viruses, scientists produced vaccines for use in disease control. In 1953, Jonas Salk developed a vaccine against polio. In 1954, scientists developed a measles vaccine. Other vaccines immunized individuals against diptheria, tetanus, whooping cough, polio, German measles, mumps, and smallpox.

Scientists have made significant progress in the area of genetics. In 1953, Francis Crick and James Watson made medical history by discovering the structure of DNA, the basic building block of cells. Using genetic engineering, scientists produced crops that were protein rich and disease resistant. Researchers also are developing new vaccines and artificial hormones, and modifying bacteria to change waste material into energy sources.

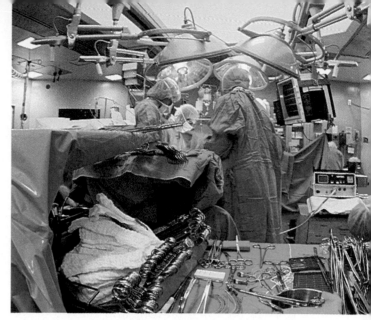

Medical researchers have made great advances during the past 35 years. These doctors are performing open heart surgery.

Advances in Surgery.

Since the first kidney transplant in 1952, medical researchers have made great strides in transplanting human organs. Heart surgery has also advanced. From first restarting a heart with electronic stimuli in 1952, medical science progressed to open heart surgery and the development and use of an artificial heart.

The development of fiber optics made possible microsurgery, another medical advance. Thin strands of glass or plastic transmit light and information. Using a flexible tube containing optical fibers and a camera, surgeons can view internal areas of the body on a television screen. This method causes only a minimum of discomfort to the patient. By connecting medical instruments to the tubing, a surgeon can also remove tumors, tissue, or bone chips through very small incisions.

In 1960, scientists produced the first laser beam, a highly amplified beam of light stimulated by radiation. Lasers are now used to destroy tumors, clear obstructions, and allow surgeons to perform almost bloodless operations. Because lasers have pinpoint accuracy, laser surgery does not affect surrounding tissue. Lasers have greatly revolutionized the scope of brain, spinal cord, and eye surgery.

Medical scientists, however, still struggle to find solutions to such problems as the effects of stress, high suicide rates, and neuroses. In addition, as diseases such as smallpox disappear, new ones, such as AIDS and Legionnaire's disease, appear.

The Electronic Revolution.
In the years following World War II, developments in computer technology and satellite communications ushered in a new era in human history, the Information Age.

In 1946, American scientists built ENIAC, the first electronic digital computer. ENIAC weighed 30 tons and filled a whole floor of a building. Early computers like ENIAC were so large that they filled several rooms and cost millions of dollars. The vacuum tubes processing electronic signals in these computers gave off large amounts of heat and often burned out. In 1947, scientists and technicians at Bell Telephone Laboratories developed the transistor to replace the unreliable vacuum tube.

Computer technology has transformed the flight industry. This is the radar control room at International Airport in Philadelphia, Pennsylvania.

Reliable transistors, however, at times broke off their circuit boards, causing malfunctions. To solve this problem, technicians and scientists developed the integrated circuit, called the computer chip, in 1959. Chips revolutionized the industry.

Produced on a small speck of silicon, a chip costs 30,000 times less than the first computer to make, yet performs 200 times as many functions. Each year scientists produce smaller and more powerful chips. Within the last 10 years, the number of calculations a single chip can perform has jumped from 50,000 to over 1 million.

Advances in TV Communications.
Computers also monitor and guide the flight of communications satellites. Using television signals bounced off these satellites, villages in India can view developments in Brazil as they happen. Individuals using satellite dish antennas can view any of 300 television channels from around the world.

Synthetic Materials.
Since 1945, many synthetic materials have been produced for industry and the home. Plastic, colored and molded, became an effective replacement for wood, metal, or glass. Synthetics improved medical instruments, clothes, and home furnishings.

Chemical technology has created new fertilizers and pesticides to greatly increase crop yields. As a result, in the United States 3 percent of the population produces enough food to feed the other 97 percent and have a surplus to export.

The Dark Side of Technology

Since the Industrial Revolution, people and factories have polluted the earth's air and water systems. As technology advanced, the amount and type of pollutants increased. Pollution currently endangers some plant and animal species. During the 1960s and 1970s, many people became aware of environmental concerns for the first time.

Radiation. Radioactive pollution is a global problem. In 1986, a cloud of radiation from the Soviet Union blew across parts of eastern Europe and Scandinavia. Dangerous radioactive material escaped into the atmosphere after an accident at a nuclear power plant at Chernobyl, near the Soviet city of Kiev.

Rainfall deposited the radioactive material on plants. Cows and other plant-eating animals were contaminated when they ate the plants. People were advised not to drink milk or eat meat and vegetables that might have picked up radiation.

Pesticides. To increase crop yields, farmers use chemicals to kill insects and rodents. These chemicals do not break down easily into less harmful elements but remain poisonous for long periods. Some insect populations have developed immunity to certain pesticides. The toxic remains of pesticides have washed into streams, killing millions of fish. Pesticide residues move through the food chain, affecting humans.

In 1953, people in the fishing village of Minamata, Japan, began to die from an unknown cause. In 1973, the government finally conducted a full investigation. Doctors traced the deaths to mercury poisoning from the fish people ate. Mercury, which industrial plants discharged into the water, was absorbed and accumulated in the fish tissues. As people ate the fish, mercury eventually killed them.

The Dangers of Reshaping the Earth. In an attempt to better their lives, people have significantly changed the environment. For example, the Egyptians built the Aswan High Dam across the Nile River to generate electric power, control flooding, and improve irrigation. The completed dam, however, has caused major problems.

The dam holds back much of the rich silt that fertilized the fields during the flood season each year. Farmers in Egypt must now use artificial fertilizers, more than farmers in any other country. In addition, the flow of the Nile's waters to the Mediterranean Sea held back the salty sea water. After the dam was built, less water flowed down to the Mediterranean. Salt water now enters the delta, making some of the once fertile land unfit for farming.

Pollution, as well as the search for minerals and other natural resources, has ruined formerly productive lands. In northern Africa, Arabia, and India, deserts are expanding at the rate of thousands of square miles each year because of overgrazing and poor irrigation. Safeguarding the world requires global cooperation.

The World Environment

FOCUS ON SOURCES

Most people believe that economic growth is good. Some critics, however, point out that the byproducts of growth are garbage and pollution. Popular song writers have written about the environmental effects of technology. Below is an excerpt from "Garbage," by Bill Steele.

❝ Mr. Thompson starts his Cadillac, winds it down the throughway track,
Leaving friends and neighbors in a hydrocarbon haze.
He's joined by lots of smaller cars, all sending gasses to the stars
There to form a seething cloud that hangs for 30 days.
And the sun licks down into it with an ultraviolet tongue,
Turns it into smog and then it settles in our lungs.
Oh, Garbage! Garbage! Garbage! Garbage!
We're filling up the sky with garbage.
What will we do when there's nothing left to breathe but garbage?
Garbage! Garbage! Garbage! Garbage!

• • •

Pollution and waste result from modern societies whose economic growth depends on increasing consumption.

In Mr. Thompson's factory, they're
    making plastic Christmas trees
Complete with silver tinsel and a
    geodesic stand.
The plastic's mixed in giant vats
    from some conglomeration
That's been piped from deep within the
    earth or strip mined from the land.
And if you ask them questions, they say,
    "Why don't you see?
It's absolutely needed for the economy!"
Oh, Garbage! Garbage! Garbage!
    Garbage!
Their stocks and their bonds—all
    garbage!
What will they do when their system
    goes to smash?
There's no value to their cash.
There's no money to be made,
But there's a world to be repaid.
Their kids will read in history books
'Bout financiers and other crooks,
And feudalism, and slavery
And nukes and all their knavery.
To history's dustbin they're consigned
Along with many other kinds of
    garbage. "

If humans are to survive and prosper, they must think about environmental dam-

age and the resources and living conditions needed to make life possible. The nations of the world must balance their technological creativity with a respect for humanity and the environment of the planet. ■

SECTION 2 *Study Skills*

Developing Vocabulary Define each of the following terms: **1.** space probe. **2.** pollutant. **3.** genetics. **4.** radioactive. **5.** synthetic.

Reviewing Main Ideas **1.** Explain the Manhattan Project. **2.** What is microsurgery? **3.** How are lasers used in medical treatment? **4.** How have advancements in communications given people a sense of world community?

Understanding Cause and Effect **1.** How has space travel led to cooperation between nations? **2.** How have synthetic materials affected everyday life? **3.** Explain the causes and effects of acid rain.

Understanding Chronology **1.** List significant dates in space travel. **2.** Construct a time line showing important breakthroughs in medical research.

Challenge What lessons can be learned by the accident at Chernobyl?

3 Culture and Values in the Electronic Age

OBJECTIVE: *To understand the causes and consequences of the influence of Western civilization throughout the world*

The Rise of a Global Culture

The Age of Imperialism coupled with the competition between the superpowers spread Western civilization throughout the world. Advances in communication and transportation since 1945 also increased the spread of Western civilization.

Television allows people to see events happening in all parts of the world. Telephone communication promotes contact with friends, relatives, and business associates in remote places. Jet travel has brought all parts of the earth within a few days' journey. As a result, other cultures and values influence people's lives.

The Spread of Western Civilization. In less-developed nations everywhere, people have been exposed to the culture and values of industrialized Western nations. Regional and local differences continue. However, the daily activities and living patterns of people throughout the world are far more similar today than before 1945.

VOCABULARY DEVELOPMENT

convergence (kuhn VER juhns) *noun*: a coming together, becoming similar. From the Latin prefix *com-*, meaning together, and word *vergere*, meaning to bend or turn.

lunar (LOO nuhr) *adj.*: measured by the moon's revolutions. From the Latin word, *luna*, meaning moon.

To gain current scientific and technological knowledge, students from around the world study in the Soviet Union and Western countries. While studying, they learn new attitudes, ideas, and beliefs. When they return to their homelands, they take back customs and values learned abroad. These new ideas dilute traditional culture and often result in value conflicts.

The lifestyles and institutions of the industrialized countries have influenced other nations in many ways. The name for this trend is convergence, the belief that cultures are becoming more and more alike due to Western influence. To retain traditional values, leaders of developing nations face a difficult task. They try to bring the benefits of modernization to their nations without destroying the legacy of the past.

Evidence of Convergence. Since the nineteenth century, non-Western nations have widely accepted some European customs. The Western calendar is used in most countries. Muslims and East Asians, however, still retain their traditional lunar calendars as well.

Western dress has become an international standard. Yet, other forms of dress have not disappeared. While people in India or Africa might wear a suit for business, they often change to more traditional dress at home and for social events.

The young people in non-Western nations are most open to Western cultural influences. Young people accept international styles faster than their parents. Through television, imports, and advertising, young people adopt Western lifestyles. Bluejeans have made their way from California to Senegal, Siberia, and Japan.

Young people around the world also enjoy Western rock music. Through records, sheet music, and personal appearances, the rock culture spread in the last two decades to remote areas of the globe.

A Shared World Culture

An English musical rock group, the Beatles, gained worldwide fame in the early 1960s. The four members of the group, Paul McCartney, John Lennon, George Harrison, and Ringo Starr, were all born in Liverpool, England, in the early 1940s. They came from working class families.

The Beatles arrive from England at Kennedy International Airport in 1964. The group performed in many cities across the United States that spring.

After the war, Liverpool, as well as the rest of Great Britain, suffered from high unemployment. Since unemployment was still high in the 1960s, many teenage rock 'n' roll bands performed in cellar clubs and dance halls around the city. Entertaining was a way teenagers could earn money.

In 1961, four musicians, John Lennon, Paul McCartney, George Harrison, and Pete Best played in a cellar club called the Cavern. After first calling the band Johnny and the Moon Dogs, John Lennon came up with the name that would become known worldwide. One of Lennon's heroes was Buddy Holly, a famous American rock 'n' roll star who died in a plane crash in the late 1950s. Holly's band had been called the Crickets. John, trying to dream up an insect name for his band, decided on the Beetles. Then he changed the spelling to Beatles. "When you said it," John explained, "people thought of crawly things; when you read it, it was beat music."

Dressed in leather jackets and playing cheap guitars, they often ignored their audience to talk among themselves, tune up, or eat snacks. However, when playing they had an almost magnetic appeal. Their music, raw and loud, differed from the softer sounds of British pop music. John and Paul wrote their own lyrics and music, which also set them apart from other struggling Liverpool groups.

Early in 1961, John, Paul, and George replaced Pete Best with a young drummer, Ringo Starr. The four remained together for the next 10 years. In November 1961, a young man, Brian Epstein, stopped in the Cavern. His parents owned a large department store, NEMS, where he managed the record department. Epstein had first heard of the Beatles when a customer requested a record, "My Bonnie," made by a group named the Beatles. Under Epstein's management, the group signed a record contract with EMI in 1962. With records of such songs as "Love Me Do," "Please Please Me," and "I Want to Hold Your Hand," the

Beatles became the most popular rock group in England. Teenaged girls fainted at the sight of them.

Capitol Records in the United States was the American branch of EMI. In 1963, *Time*, *Life*, and *Newsweek* magazines wrote stories about the hit English rock group. However, the American press believed that Beatlemania was purely a British brand of nuttiness. Someone at Capitol records, however, took a chance and released "I Want to Hold Your Hand," a song full of subtle shifts in rhythm.

Soon after, the Beatles were booked on the popular Ed Sullivan television show. Capitol decided to publicize the record with an advertising campaign. Capitol executives were photographed wearing Beatle wigs, and 5 million stickers reading "The Beatles Are Coming" were plastered across the United States.

The Beatles became an instant hit in the United States. Their music recaptured the freshness and excitement of the early days of rock 'n' roll. In addition, their openness and humor were engaging. When they stepped off the plane in the United States, a reporter asked:

" Will you sing something for us?"
"We need money first," Lennon replied.
"What's your message for American teenagers?"
"Our message," said McCartney, "is buy more Beatles' records. "

The Beatles' popularity spread, and they spent weeks on the road performing. During the spring of 1964, the Beatles appeared in 62 cities on 4 continents, and gave 110 performances. In Australia, a crowd of 300,000 fans lined the entire route from the airport to the hotel. Teenagers all over the world adopted their long hair and clothes styles. They not only won the hearts of teenagers but also were honored by Queen Elizabeth II, who made them members of the Order of the British Empire.

The Beatles also made two films that were popular with both fans and critics. *A Hard Day's Night* was released in 1964 and *Help!* in 1965. Both films played to audiences around the world. In 1971, however, the pressures of the musicians' public lives together and their growing outside interests led the group to split up. While together, the Beatles and their music helped to spread ideas and bring peoples of different cultures and backgrounds together. ■

Individualism and Human Rights

In the past century, non-Western societies have been widely exposed to the Western emphasis on individual freedom and civil rights. The United States constitution, as well as English common law, promises every person equal protection under the law.

The American notion of individualism, however, contradicts strong values in many societies. In other countries, the family or group is often more important than the individual. The freedom to pick and choose an occupation, a mate, or a place to live is not a universal freedom.

A World Political Order. As nations develop closer ties, the need for multinational cooperation increases. The major international organization is the United Nations. The UN has been a world forum for international opinion. The organization also makes industrialized countries aware of the economic and social needs in lesser developed countries. The UN has helped to channel aid to these countries.

Although it is more effective than was the League of Nations, the record of the United Nations peacekeeping force has been mixed. In 1946, the UN helped pressure the Soviet Union to leave Iran. A UN force has helped to maintain peace between India and Pakistan since 1947.

In 1950, the Soviet Union temporarily boycotted the UN. During this interval, the organization condemned North Korea for

The United Nations was established in 1945 to promote peace, international cooperation, and human rights. Shown here, a meeting of the UN Security Council.

invading South Korea. More important, the UN sent an international force to aid South Korea. The UN also sent several peacekeeping forces to the Middle East between 1956 and 1973. The troops, however, were only partially successful. A UN peacekeeping force helped to restore order in the Congo in 1960 and remained there for several years.

The United Nations has been less effective in preventing individual countries from violating the rights of others. In 1956, the premier of Hungary and the UN General Assembly demanded that Soviet forces withdraw from Hungary. The Soviets, however, refused to remove their troops. In 1982, the Israelis ignored United Nations forces when they invaded Lebanon. The United Nations continues to provide a meeting place where nations can discuss their differences.

The Value of Diversity in an Interdependent World

The convergence of cultures mainly affects people's buying habits. People around the world still find their greatest sense of security and commitment in their own cultures and beliefs. These traditional ideas continue to endure and thrive.

Resistance to Materialistic Values. Many nations resist the influence of Western civilization. Iran illustrates this opposition. When the people of Iran overthrew the shah, the Ayatollah Ruhollah Khomeini established an Islamic Republic. He issued strict laws to govern people's everyday life according to Islamic teaching. The Ayatollah and his followers rejected Western values and supported a return to pure Islamic ways. In other Muslim countries, parents worry when their children watch American movies and television programs that the parents consider immoral.

Asians and Africans do not want to imitate Westerners. At the same time, however, they do want to become modern, industrialized nations. Non-Western peoples are willing to adopt some Western customs. However, deciding what should be adopted and what rejected is a continuing challenge. Finding the solution to this problem will be a gradual and confusing task.

Capitalism and Socialism. A struggle for economic power continues between the two superpowers. The United States and its allies are mostly democracies; the Soviet Union and its allies are generally communist dictatorships. The Western nations have market economies, while the Soviet Union and Eastern bloc countries have planned socialist economies.

Both of these power blocs have tried to extend their power and influence to Asia, Africa, and Latin America. The Soviets have introduced Soviet weapons and military organization. American military advisers have spread American doctrine and weapons. Economic aid missions have done the same thing.

Americans and Russians may see their political and economic systems as competitors for the allegiance of Third World countries. Developing non-Western countries, however, sometimes see the American and Soviet models as similar. Both are European in origin and represent a great change from the traditional way of doing things.

The Persistence of Nationalism. After World War II, some Western leaders hoped that regional and international economic and political cooperation would lessen nationalistic rivalries. Despite the trend toward national independence and economic cooperation, however, some national or ethnic groups remain dissatisfied.

Nationalist movements in Eastern Europe and a number of the Soviet republics have disturbed the Soviet Union. Some French-speaking residents of the province of Quebec, Canada, continue to campaign for an independent state. The Basque minority in Spain also continues to work for an independent state. The Basques, as well as the Croatians and Serbs of Yugoslavia, at times resort to terrorism in their desire to obtain independence.

In Africa and the Middle East, nationalist feeling has led to border warfare between Morocco and Algeria, Kenya and Somalia, and other neighboring countries. Ethnic differences have also led to conflicts such as the civil wars in Nigeria, Sudan, and Angola. Nationalism among Arab nations continues to cause hostility.

Nationalism often stirs people to cooperation and great creative and technical effort. At the same time, nationalism divides people from one another and causes conflicts. In an age of interdependence, environmental problems, and atomic weapons, people can no longer afford the hostilities nationalism fosters.

The Persistence of Faith. Religion has been a part of human society throughout history. Religion is difficult to define. More than a set of beliefs, religion is an attitude, a search for meaning. Since the beginnings of history, religion has provided guidelines to help individuals order their lives.

Religion provides a group identity, a basis for social order, and the means to transmit a group's culture. For many people today, religion continues to provide order and security in a world of uncertainty. In a

In the Modern Age, religion continues to be important to many people. The pope, leader of the Roman Catholic Church, is pictured here.

Clockwise from the top left: a market in Manning, China; a city market in Abidjan, the capital of the Ivory Coast; a Yugoslavian market; an outdoor market in San'a Yemen.

world of competing ideas, the power of religion to influence human attitudes and actions remains as great as ever.

The Changing World. The challenges of the postwar world are many. The human accomplishments match the challenges. Since 1945, revolutionary developments in science, technology, communications, and economics have changed the nature of the world. Advances in science and technology opened new frontiers in medicine and space. Computers revolutionized communications. Businesses and governments expanded across the globe, creating a complex web of interrelationships. Events in other parts of the world increasingly affected nations and people. Population growth, rapid urbanization, industrialization, and increased use of resources caused problems. Yet, people throughout the world were developing a sense of interdependence.

SECTION 3 *Study Skills*

Developing Vocabulary Use each term in a sentence: **1.** convergence. **2.** lunar.

Reviewing Main Ideas 1. Name some Western customs widely accepted by non-Western nations. **2.** How does the American idea of individualism differ from the values of many other societies? **3.** Explain the political and economic differences between the United States and the Soviet Union. **4.** What does religion provide for people?

Understanding Cause and Effect 1. How does interaction among countries affect cultures and lifestyles? **2.** What made the Beatles so popular in the 1960s? **3.** What were some effects of the Ayatollah Khomeini's takeover of Iran? **4.** Explain the successes and failures of the United Nations peacekeeping forces.

Challenge Does religion influence life today in the same way it did in the Middle Ages? Explain.

CHAPTER 32 *Summary & Review*

Summarizing Main Ideas

Contemporary history is the history of an inter-acting community. As nations become interdependent, they compete and cooperate to maintain a balance of trade. The global community deals with problems of migration—both forced and voluntary.

Rapid technological advances have further increased the interaction among societies. Since World War II, the world has witnessed amazing advances in the fields of space exploration, medical science, electronics, and communications. Attempts to improve human life have been costly for the environment. A balance must be struck between technological advances and the preservation of the environment.

Since 1945, Western culture has spread throughout the world. One positive aspect of Western culture is its emphasis on individual freedom and civil rights. This idea has caused conflicts in many non-Western societies. Nations have resisted Western influence. Nationalism has had positive and negative effects.

The struggle for economic power continues between the United States and the Soviet Union. Each tries to extend its influence on developing nations. The UN serves as a forum for international opinions, channels aid to needy countries, and assumes the role of peacekeeper.

Questions for Critical Thinking

COMPREHENSION Interpreting Events

1. Why do people from developing nations migrate to industrialized nations?
2. How did the invention of the computer chip revolutionize the information industry?

ANALYSIS Identifying Trends

1. How does importing low-cost goods from Taiwan affect the American manufacturers and farmers?
2. How have the Americans and the Soviets tried to extend their influence into Africa, Asia, and Latin America?

"Trapped like rodentia!"

APPLICATION Comparing Past to Present

1. Explain how nations grow from an agricultural to an industrial economy.
2. Give examples of how computers affect everyday life.
3. Why are problems, such as water pollution, acid rain, and radiation contamination, now considered global rather than national?

EVALUATION Weighing Consequences

1. What are the consequences of rapid urbanization on developing nations?
2. What are some possible practical applications of genetic research?

CHALLENGE

1. How have space shuttle tragedies affected opinions on space research and travel?
2. What are some advantages and disadvantages involved in human organ transplants?

UNIT 8 *Review*

Critical Thinking for Today's World

ANALYSIS Understanding People

1. What changes did the Labor government make that affected the people of Great Britain after World War II?
2. Explain the condition of Europe's people which led to the formulation of the Marshall Plan.
3. What difficulties did Africans and Asians face in resisting European domination?
4. Explain Tom Mboya's plan for the economic and social development of African nations.
5. How have people like Winnie and Nelson Mandela tried to affect South Africa's policy of apartheid?
6. Why are human resources important to a nation's economy?
7. Give examples of forced and voluntary migration.
8. Why is the nationalist movement a recurring theme throughout history? Trace its development in the twentieth century.

ANALYSIS Recognizing Change Over Time

1. Explain the shift in political power in France when de Gaulle became president.
2. How did the nationalist movement in Africa and Asia change colonist's thoughts after World War II?
3. Explain the changes in China during Mao Zedong's rule.
4. Highlight the results of President Nixon's 1972 meeting with Mao Zedong.
5. What events triggered a change in America's involvement in Vietnam in 1973?
6. How has the Green Revolution changed farming?
7. Give five examples of how the development of synthetic material changed everyday life.

APPLICATION Solving Problems

1. How did governments try to combat the Great Depression?

2. What did the Soviets do to improve their economy?
3. How did the British and French try to solve the Suez Crisis? How successful were they?
4. How did Nehru propose to solve India's social and economic needs?
5. How can the effects of neocolonialism be minimized?
6. Why was the opening of embassies in Washington D.C. and Beijing important to United States–Chinese relations?
7. What measures have the governments of India and China taken to try to control population?

SYNTHESIS Developing Global Citizenship

1. How did the United States and Japan become allies after World War II?
2. How did colonial nationalism differ from European nationalism of the 1800s?
3. Why did the founding of the state of Israel cause conflict between the Jews and the Arabs?
4. Explain the United States concern over the domino theory.
5. What problems must be considered by a country with a large migrant labor force?
6. How does economic specialization lead to interdependence among nations?

EVALUATION Learning Lessons from the Past

1. Using Soviet reactions during the Berlin Airlift and the Cuban missile crisis as evidence, what conclusions might the United States draw about Soviet goals?
2. What was the goal of the United States in the Vietnam conflict? What is the goal of the Soviet Union in Afghanistan? Are the situations similar? Explain your answer.
3. Explain the relationship between the world economy and the United States economy.
4. What were the goals of European nations in forming the EEC? Which other nations could learn from this example?

The Interacting Global Community, 1945 – Present

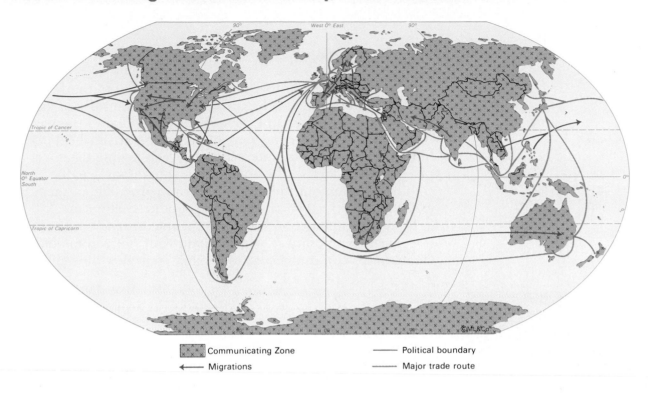

x Communicating Zone ————— Political boundary

◄——— Migrations ————— Major trade route

A Global Perspective

Twentieth century migrations have been largely from nonindustrialized nations to industrialized nations. The United States and western Europe have experienced the greatest influx of people. Central America and Africa have seen the greatest exodus. Communication zones grow larger as technology provides easier access to remote areas, and improved methods of communication and transportation speed up the movement of people, information, goods, and services.

Shifts in the centers of economic power have been slight. With the exceptions of Japan, Taiwan, and Korea, the industrialized nations remain concentrated in North America and Europe. LDCs are in South and Central America, and Central and South Africa. North African and Arabian nations, utilizing their oil resources, modernized dramatically in the 1960s and 1970s, but have not challenged the manufacturing output of the older industrial nations of Europe or North America.

COMPREHENSION Interpreting Maps

1. List any areas excluded from the communicating zone on this map.
2. Using the map on page 671, describe how the communicating zone has changed since 1850?
3. How have the political boundaries changed in western Africa since 1945?
4. To what country are some people from Central America migrating? How does this compare to migrations prior to 1945?

ANALYSIS Recognizing Global Trends

1. What are the similarities and differences between the trade routes on this map and those on page 179?
2. Describe the causes and consequences of the extent of today's communicating zone.
3. Write a statement describing the general pattern of migrations on this map.
4. What factors are changing the population on the West Coast of the United States? What factors contribute to this change?

Dear Reader,

This study of world history has encouraged you to think about a powerful idea—that world history is the story of an ever expanding interacting zone. You realize that in the past the expanding interacting zone has been the drive wheel of history. In the present, interaction between people takes place at many levels: in school, on the job, in our country, throughout the world. You can participate in the exchange of information, skills, and products. You can expand your interaction with other people to reach out to the global community or you can limit your horizon to your community. You can choose to expand your view of the world.

What if . . .?

I hope the idea of an expanding interacting zone stays with you. It can help you think beyond the limits of our time and place. What if a wider interacting zone exists in the universe?

As you read this, our Pioneer spacecraft explores that possibility. What message from earth would be an appropriate introduction? Certainly the names of current leaders or descriptions of political boundaries would be quite meaningless in a cosmic context. Instead, this message should tell any discoverer that humans on planet Earth can think beyond their own time and beyond their own solar system.

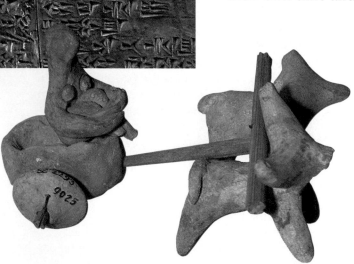

Today, as in the past, writing and transportation carry the ideas, skills, and products in the interacting zone.

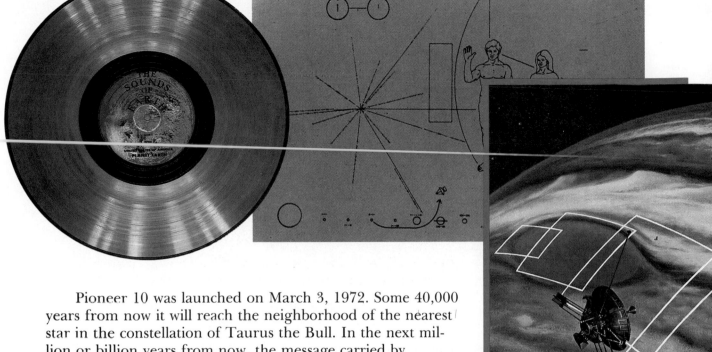

The Pioneer 10 message travels beyond the limits of our own time and solar system.

Pioneer 10 was launched on March 3, 1972. Some 40,000 years from now it will reach the neighborhood of the nearest star in the constellation of Taurus the Bull. In the next million or billion years from now, the message carried by Pioneer 10 may pass through a remote star's planetary system and encounter intelligent life. Then the message from earth may be found and deciphered.

This message, carried on a small plaque on Pioneer 10, has been called an intellectual cave painting. It contains information about people, time, and place. The plaque shows simple line drawings of a man and a woman. What could an extraterrestrial learn about humans based on the picture? Certainly physical characteristics, tool making capabilities, communication patterns, and human relationships could be inferred from this visual message.

The Pioneer 10 message also provides information that could help advanced civilizations beyond our solar system identify when and where the spacecraft originated. We do not know if an extraterrestrial would be able to understand this message. Just as we may not understand surviving messages or artifacts from past peoples, this message may not be found or deciphered. This message, as well as other signals sent across space, reaches beyond our own time and place. This human endeavor is another consequence of the great achievements in human history—tool-making, the creation of civilization, and the explorations of the Modern Age.

Keep thinking,

Ross E. Dunn

Ross E. Dunn

Reference Section

Atlas of Maps

Map Features

Legend

Most of the maps in this *Atlas* are *physical-political reference maps*. They show information about the Earth's surface in two ways—with color and with shading. The color areas show heights of the land (elevation) and depths of the water; the "Map Legend" tells how high or how deep in meters and feet. Some of the highest mountains and deepest ocean trenches are named and shown with a special symbol. Shading shows roughness (hills, mountains) on the Earth's surface; the highest areas are often (but not always) the roughest. Many physical features (capes, islands, mountains, etc.) are named on the maps. Some maps show ice features.

The maps in the *Atlas* also show political information about the Earth—boundaries of countries, names of countries and other political units, and names and locations of cities (the bigger the lettering, the larger the city's population). National capitals, and some state and province capitals, are shown with special symbols.

The map of the World does not show land elevations, water depths, or surface roughness, but it does name some physical features. The World map uses color to show the shape and area of each political unit; it is a *political* map.

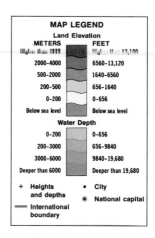

Scale

Every map is much smaller than the part of the Earth it shows. The *representative fraction* (or "RF") at the top corner of each map in this *Atlas* tells how much smaller the map is in this way: if the RF is 1:45,000,000, then *45 million* units of length (miles or kilometers) on the ground have been reduced to *one* unit on the map. The bigger the number on the right side of the RF, the more the part of the Earth shown on the map has been reduced.

Below each map in this *Atlas* is a Distance Scale. It is like a ruler and can be used to measure distances between places on the map in either kilometers or miles.

On all the maps in this *Atlas* there is also an Area Scale that shows how big a square covering 100,000 square kilometers (or 40,000 square miles) on the Earth would be. From this you can see whether the scale of one map is different from another.

1:45,000,000

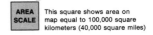

Direction

The grid of latitude and longitude lines on the map can be used to tell what direction one place is from another. North is toward the top of the map page, but exactly where it is depends on how much the lines of longitude (meridians) are curving. Because the meridians come together at the north and south poles, north and south are always found by following meridians. Similarly, east and west are determined by following the lines of latitude (parallels).

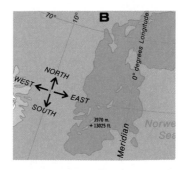

The World

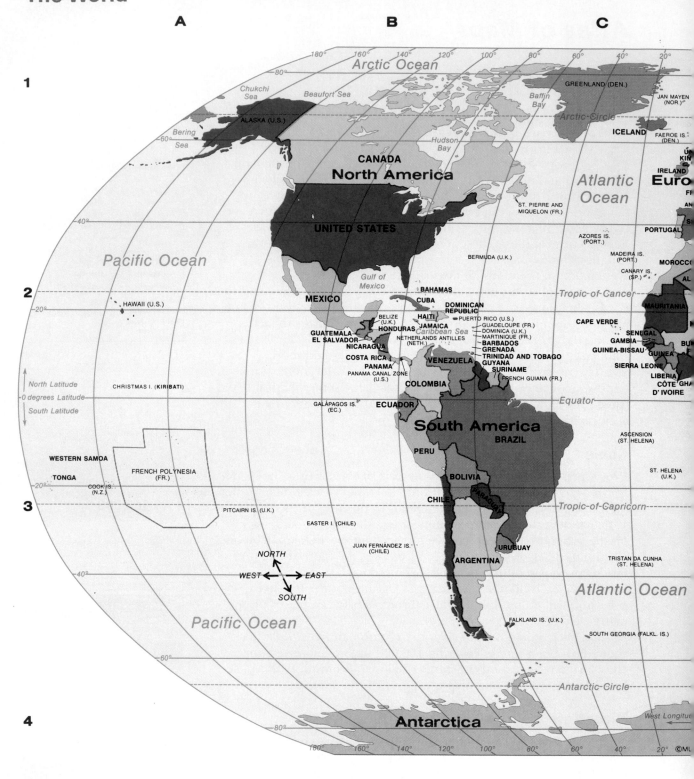

A   B   C

1

Arctic Ocean

Chukchi Sea

Beaufort Sea

GREENLAND (DEN.)

Baffin Bay

JAN MAYEN (NOR.)

Arctic Circle

ICELAND   FAEROE IS. (DEN.)

ALASKA (U.S.)

Bering Sea

UN. KIN.

IRELAND

CANADA

North America

Atlantic Ocean

Euro

Hudson Bay

ST. PIERRE AND MIQUELON (FR.)

Pacific Ocean

UNITED STATES

FF.

AN

PORTUGAL

BERMUDA (U.K.)

AZORES IS. (PORT.)

MADEIRA IS. (PORT.)

MOROCCO

CANARY IS. (SP.)

AL.

2   *Tropic of Cancer*

Gulf of Mexico

BAHAMAS

HAWAII (U.S.)

MEXICO

CUBA

DOMINICAN REPUBLIC

PUERTO RICO (U.S.)

MAURITANIA

BELIZE (U.K.)

HAITI

JAMAICA

GUADELOUPE (FR.)

DOMINICA (U.K.)

MARTINIQUE (FR.)

CAPE VERDE

GUATEMALA

HONDURAS

Caribbean Sea

NETHERLANDS ANTILLES (NETH.)

BARBADOS

SENEGAL

GAMBIA

EL SALVADOR

NICARAGUA

GRENADA

TRINIDAD AND TOBAGO

GUINEA-BISSAU

GUINEA

BU.

COSTA RICA

PANAMA

VENEZUELA

GUYANA

SURINAME

SIERRA LEONE

PANAMA CANAL ZONE (U.S.)

FRENCH GUIANA (FR.)

LIBERIA

CÔTE GHA D'IVOIRE

COLOMBIA

North Latitude

0 degrees Latitude

South Latitude

CHRISTMAS I. (KIRIBATI)

GALÁPAGOS IS. (EC.)

ECUADOR

Equator

ASCENSION (ST. HELENA)

South America

BRAZIL

PERU

WESTERN SAMOA

FRENCH POLYNESIA (FR.)

ST. HELENA (U.K.)

TONGA

BOLIVIA

COOK IS. (N.Z.)

CHILE

PARAGUAY

3   *Tropic of Capricorn*

PITCAIRN IS. (U.K.)

EASTER I. (CHILE)

URUGUAY

JUAN FERNÁNDEZ IS. (CHILE)

TRISTAN DA CUNHA (ST. HELENA)

NORTH

WEST ← → EAST

SOUTH

ARGENTINA

Atlantic Ocean

Pacific Ocean

FALKLAND IS. (U.K.)

SOUTH GEORGIA (FALKL. IS.)

Antarctic Circle

West Longitu

4

Antarctica

©ML

MAP LEGEND

CANADA   Country name (independent political unit)

GUAM (U.S.)   **Other political name**

AREA SCALE (AT EQUATOR)

This square shows area on map equal to 100,000 square kilometers (40,000 square miles)

1:110,000,000

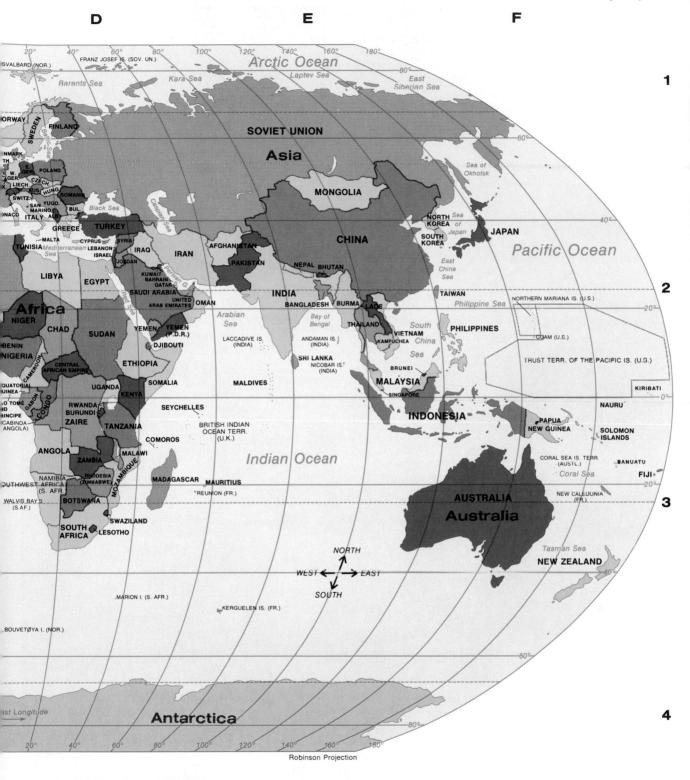

Robinson Projection

DISTANCE SCALE (AT EQUATOR)

0 Kilometers	2000		4000		6000		8000		10000		12000		14000		16000		18000
0 Miles		2000			4000			6000			8000				10000		

Europe

1:21,000,000

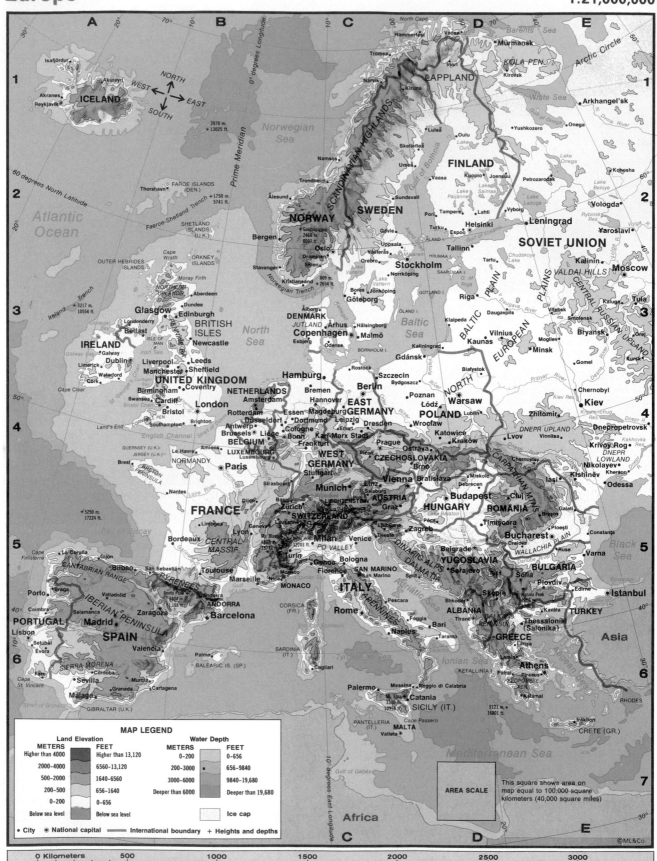

MAP LEGEND

Land Elevation

METERS	FEET
Higher than 4000	Higher than 13,120
2000-4000	6560-13,120
500-2000	1640-6560
200-500	656-1640
0-200	0-656
Below sea level	Below sea level

Water Depth

METERS	FEET
0-200	0-656
200-3000	656-9840
3000-6000	9840-19,680
Deeper than 6000	Deeper than 19,680
Ice cap	

• City   ⊚ National capital   ▬▬▬ International boundary   + Heights and depths

AREA SCALE

This square shows area on map equal to 100,000 square kilometers (40,000 square miles)

©ML&Co

0 Kilometers	500	1000	1500	2000	2500	3000
0 Miles	500	1000	1500	DISTANCE SCALE	2000	

778

Africa

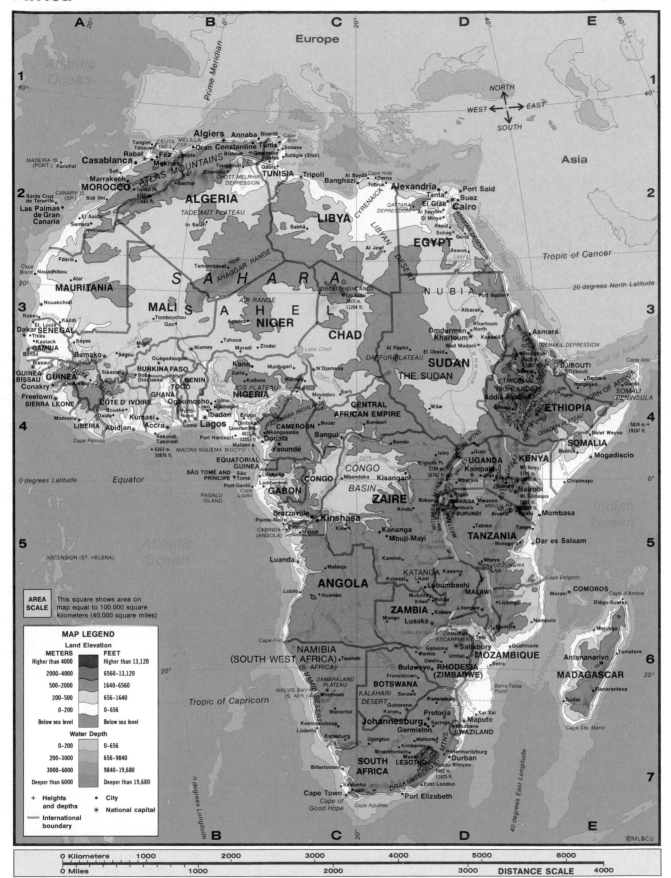

NORTH

WEST — EAST

SOUTH

AREA SCALE This square shows area on map equal to 100,000 square kilometers (40,000 square miles)

MAP LEGEND

Land Elevation

METERS	FEET
Higher than 4000	Higher than 13,120
2000–4000	6560–13,120
500–2000	1640–6560
200–500	656–1640
0–200	0–656
Below sea level	Below sea level

Water Depth

0–200	0–656
200–3000	656–9840
3000–6000	9840–19,680
Deeper than 6000	Deeper than 19,680

+ Heights and depths   • City

— International boundary   ◉ National capital

©ML&Co

0 Kilometers	1000	2000	3000	4000	5000	6000
0 Miles	1000	2000	3000		4000

DISTANCE SCALE

Asia and the Soviet Union

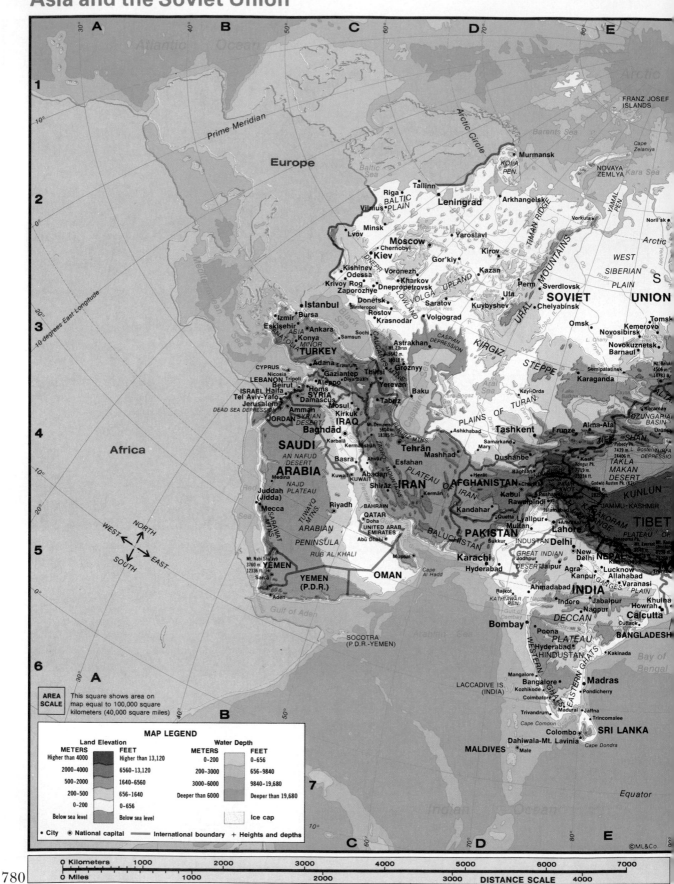

Map labels

Atlantic Ocean

Prime Meridian

Europe

FRANZ JOSEF ISLANDS

Arctic Circle

Barents Sea

Cape Zelaniya

NOVAYA ZEMLYA

Kara Sea

YAMAL PEN.

Murmansk

KOLA PEN.

Baltic Sea

Ladoga

Tallinn

Riga

BALTIC PLAIN

Vilnius

Leningrad

Arkhangelsk

TIMAN RIDGE

Vorkuta

Noril'sk

Arctic

Minsk

Lvov

Onega Res.

Yaroslavl

Moscow

Chernobyl

Kiev

Gor'kiy

Kirov

Kazan

Perm

Sverdlovsk

Kemerovo

Tomsk

WEST SIBERIAN PLAIN

Kishinev

Odessa

Voronezh

Kharkov

Kama

Uta

SOVIET

UNION

S

Krivoy Rog

Zaporozhye

Dnepropetrovsk

VOLGA UPLAND

Saratov

Kuybyshev

URAL MOUNTAINS

Chelyabinsk

Omsk

Novosibirsk

Istanbul

Bursa

Donetsk

Simferopol

Rostov

LOWLAND

Volgograd

CASPIAN DEPRESSION

KIRGIZ

Novokuznetsk

Barnaul

Izmir

Black Sea

Krasnodar

Sochi

Astrakhan

Mt. Elbrus 5642 m. 18510 ft.

STEPPE

Mt. Belukha 4506 m. 14783 ft.

Eskişehir

Ankara

Konya

ASIA MINOR

ANATOLIA

Samsun

CAUCASUS MTS.

Semipalatinsk

Karaganda

TURKEY

Adana

Erzurum

Groznyy

Tbilisi

Yerevan

Baku

Aral Sea

PLAINS OF TURAN

Kzyl-Orda

L. Zaysan

Lake Balkhash

Karamay

DZUNGARIA BASIN

Ürümqi

CYPRUS

Nicosia

Tripoli

LEBANON

Beirut

Aleppo

Gaziantep

Diyarbakir

Homs

Tabriz

Kara-Bogaz Gol Gulf

Ashkhabad

Samarkand

Mary

Tashkent

Frunze

Alma-Ata

TIEN SHAN

Pobedy Pk. 7439 m. Bostan 24406 ft. TURFA DEPRESSIO

ISRAEL Haifa

Tel Aviv-Yafo

Jerusalem

SYRIA

Damascus

Mosul

Kirkuk

SYRIAN DESERT

Mt. Demavend 5604 m. 18385 ft.

ELBURZ MTNS.

Dushanbe

Baghlan

Kashi

Kongur Pk. 7719 m. 25324 ft.

TAKLA MAKAN DESERT

KUNLUN

DEAD SEA DEPRESSION

Amman

JORDAN

Baghdad

Karbala

IRAQ

Kermanshah

Tehrān

Mashhad

Herāt

Godwin Austen Pk. (K2) 8611 m. 28250 ft.

KARAKORAM RANGE

JAMMU-KASHMIR

TIBET

SAUDI

AN NAFUD DESERT

Basra

Anva?

Esfahan

ZAGROS MOUNTAINS

PLATEAU

Baghlan

HINDU KUSH

Peshawar

Islamabad

PLATEAU OF

ARABIA

Medina

Kuwait

KUWAIT

Abadan

Shirāz

IRAN

Kerman

OF IRAN

Kabul

Rawalpindi

Lyallpur

Amritsar

Mt. Everest 8848 m. 29028 ft.

NAJD PLATEAU

Juddah (Jidda)

Mecca

TUWAYQ MTNS.

Riyadh

BAHRAIN

QATAR

Doha

UNITED ARAB EMIRATES

Kandahar

AFGHANISTAN

Quetta

BALUCHISTAN

Multan

PAKISTAN

Lahore

Delhi

New Delhi

NEPAL

SARAWAT MTNS.

ARABIAN PENINSULA

Abū Dhabi

Sukkur

INDUS RIVER

Jodhpur

GREAT INDIAN DESERT

Jaipur

Agra

Kanpur

Lucknow

Allahabad

Varanasi

Mt. Nabi Shu'ayb 3760 m. 12336 ft.

YEMEN

Sana

RUB AL KHALI

Muscat

OMAN

Cape Al Hadd

Karachi

Hyderabad

Ahmadabad

Rajkot

KATHIAWAR PEN.

Gulf of Cambay

INDIA

Indore

Jabalpur

GANGES PLAIN

Nagpur

Khulna

Howrah

Calcutta

Cuttack

YEMEN (P.D.R.)

Aden

Gulf of Aden

Bombay

Poona

Hyderabad

DECCAN PLATEAU

BANGLADESH

Kakinada

SOCOTRA (P.D.R.-YEMEN)

Arabian Sea

WESTERN GHATS

HINDUSTAN

EASTERN GHATS

Bay of Bengal

Africa

Red Sea

Mediterranean Sea

Mangalore

LACCADIVE IS. (INDIA)

Bangalore

Kozhikode

Coimbatore

Madras

Pondicherry

Trivandrum

Madurai

Jaffna

Trincomalee

Cape Comorin

Colombo

Dahiwala-Mt. Lavinia

SRI LANKA

Cape Dondra

MALDIVES

Male

Indian Ocean

Equator

©ML&Co.

Compass rose

NORTH

WEST — EAST

SOUTH

Area Scale box

AREA SCALE

This square shows area on map equal to 100,000 square kilometers (40,000 square miles)

Map Legend

MAP LEGEND

Land Elevation

METERS	FEET
Higher than 4000	Higher than 13,120
2000–4000	6560–13,120
500–2000	1640–6560
200–500	656–1640
0–200	0–656
Below sea level	Below sea level

Water Depth

METERS	FEET
0–200	0–656
200–3000	656–9840
3000–6000	9840–19,680
Deeper than 6000	Deeper than 19,680

Ice cap

• City   ◉ National capital   —— International boundary   + Heights and depths

Distance Scale

0 Kilometers	1000	2000	3000	4000	5000	6000	7000
0 Miles	1000	2000	3000	4000			

DISTANCE SCALE

1:46,000,000

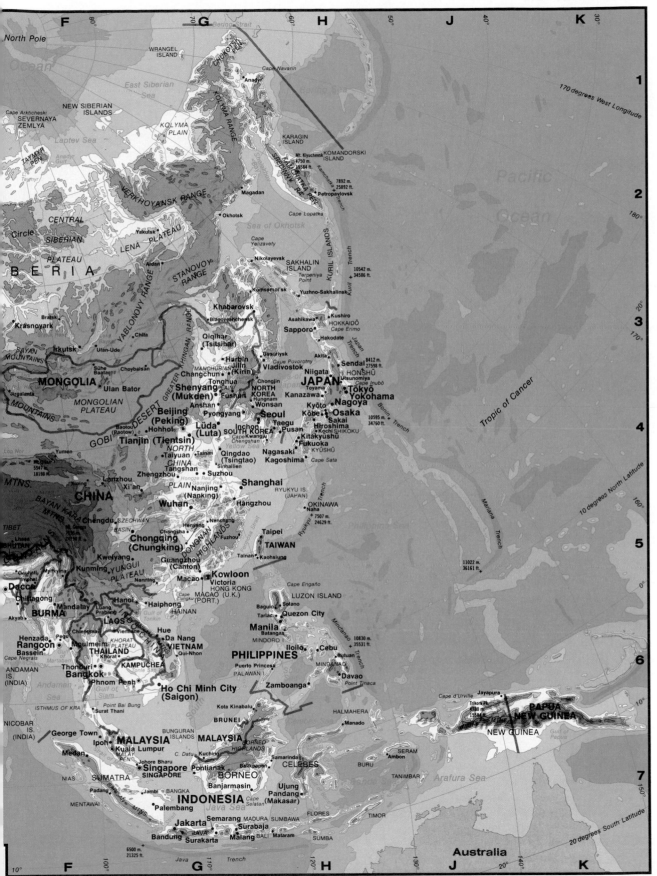

North Pole

Ocean

F 80° **G** 70° Bering Strait **H** 60° 50° **J** 40° **K** 30°

1

170 degrees West Longitude

WRANGEL
ISLAND

CHUKOTSK
PEN.

NEW SIBERIAN
ISLANDS

Cape Arktichecki
SEVERNAYA
ZEMLYA

Cape Navarin

Anadyr

East Siberian
Sea

KOLYMA
RANGE

KOLYMA
PLAIN

Laptev Sea

KARAGIN
ISLAND

TAYMYR
PEN.

Anadyr
Gulf

Taymyr

2

180°

KOMANDORSKI
ISLAND

Mt. Kiyuchevsk
4750 m.
15584 ft.

Magadan

KAMCHATKA PEN.

7892 m.
25892 ft.
Petropavlovsk

Kamchatka

CENTRAL

Circle

SIBERIAN

Okhotsk

Cape Lopatka

PLATEAU

VERKHOYANSK RANGE

Sea of Okhotsk

170°

B E R I A

LENA PLATEAU

Yakutsk

Aldan

STANOVOY
RANGE

Cape
Yelizavety

Nikolayevsk

KURIL ISLANDS

Kuril Trench

10542 m.
34586 ft.

20°

Bratsk

Krasnoyark

Chita

Irkutsk

Ulan-Ude

SAYAN
MOUNTAINS

Sühe
Baatar

Choybalsan

YABLONOW RANGE

Blagoveshchensk

Khabarovsk

Komsomol'sk

Terpeniya
Point

Yuzhno-Sakhalinsk

SAKHALIN
ISLAND

3

170°

Qiqihar
(Tsitsihar)

GREATER HINGAN RANGE

MANCHURIAN
PLAIN

Harbin

Jilin
(Kirin)

Changchun

Usuriysk

Vladivostok

Cape Povorotny

Kushiro

Asahikawa

Sapporo

HOKKAIDO
Cape Erimo

Hakodate

Akita

Japan Trench

Sendai

8412 m.
27598 ft.

MONGOLIA

Jirgalanta

MTS

Ulan Bator

MONGOLIAN
PLATEAU

Hohhot

GOBI DESERT

Baotou
(Paotow)

Shenyang
(Mukden)

Tonghua

Fushun

Anshan

Chongjin

NORTH
KOREA

Pyongyang

Hungnam

Wonsan

Niigata

Toyama

Utsunomiya

HONSHU

Kanazawa

JAPAN

Tokyo
Yokohama

Nagoya

Bonin
Trench

20°

Lüda
(Luta)

Beijing
(Peking)

Tianjin (Tientsin)

Seoul

Inchon

SOUTH KOREA

Chengshan

Taegu

Pusan

Kyoto

Kobe

Hiroshima

Kochi SHIKOKU

Osaka

Sakai

10595 m.
34760 ft.

Löa Nor

Yumen

NORTH

CHINA

Taiyuan

Tangshan

Qingdao
(Tsingtao)

Sinhailien

Tainan

Kwangju

Nagasaki

Kagoshima

KYUSHU

Cape Sata

4

Lanzhou

Xiping

CHINA

Xi'an

Zhengzhou

PLAIN

Hongze Res.

Suzhou

Nanjing
(Nanking)

Shanghai

RYUKYU IS.
(JAPAN)

10 degrees North Latitude

160°

5547 m.
18198 ft.

Wuhan

Hangzhou

OKINAWA
Naha

7507 m.
24629 ft.

Ryukyu Trench

Mariana Trench

Tropic of Cancer

MTNS.

TIBET

BAYAN KARA
MTNS

Chengdu

SZECHWAN
BASIN

Changsha

Henyang

Nanchang

Fuzhou

DONGNAN
HIGHLANDS

5

Lhasa

7556 m.
27790 ft.

Chongqing
(Chungking)

Kweiyang

Taipei

TAIWAN

Kaohsiung

Tainan

11022 m.
36161 ft.

0°

BHUTAN

Gauhati
Myitkyina

Kunming

YUNGUI
PLATEAU

Nanning

Guangzhou
(Canton)

Macao
MACAO (PORT.)

Kowloon
Victoria
HONG KONG
MACAO (U.K.)

Cape Engaño

LUZON ISLAND

Dacca

Imphal

Hanoi

Haiphong

HAINAN

Baguio

Solano

Chittagong

Mandalay

Luang
Prabang

Gulf of
Tonkin

Tarlac

Quezon City

BURMA

Akyab

LAOS

Hue

Da Nang

VIETNAM

Manila

Batangas

MINDORO I.

10830 m.
35531 ft.

Mindanao Trench

Henzada

Pegu

Moulmein

Chiengmai

Vientiane

KHORAT
PLATEAU

Qui-Nhon

Iloilo

Cebu

Butuan

6

Rangoon

Bassein

Cape Negrais

THAILAND

Khorat

PHILIPPINES

MINDANAO

Puerto Princesa

PALAWAN I.

Davao

ANDAMAN
IS.
(INDIA)

Thonburi

Bangkok

KAMPUCHEA

Phnom Penh

Gulf of
Siam

Ho Chi Minh City
(Saigon)

Zamboanga

Point Tinaca

Cape d'Urville

Jayapura

Trikora Pk.
4760 m.
15584 ft.

PAPUA
NEW GUINEA

ISTHMUS OF KRA

Point Bai Bung

Kota Kinabalu

HALMAHERA

Manado

NEW GUINEA

Gulf of
Papua

NICOBAR
IS.
(INDIA)

George Town

Ipoh

MALAYSIA

BRUNEI

MALAYSIA

BUNGURAN
ISLANDS

BORNEO
HIGHLANDS

SERAM

Ambon

10°

Medan

Kuala Lumpur

MALAY

Johore Bharu

Singapore
SINGAPORE

Pontianak

Kuching

C. Datu

Samarinda

BURU

CELEBES

TANIMBAR

150°

NIAS

SUMATRA

Padang

Jambi

BANGKA

BORNEO

Banjarmasin

Balikpapan

Ujung
Pandang
(Makasar)

7

MENTAWAI

Palembang

Java Sea

Cape
Selatan

FLORES

TIMOR

SUMBA

Arafura Sea

20 degrees South Latitude

6500 m.
21325 ft.

Jakarta

Bandung

Semarang

Surakarta

MADURA

Surabaja

Malang

JAVA

SUMBAWA

BALI

Mataram

INDONESIA

Australia

10° **F** 100° **G** 110° **H** 120° **J** 130° 140° **K** 150°

Java Trench

North America

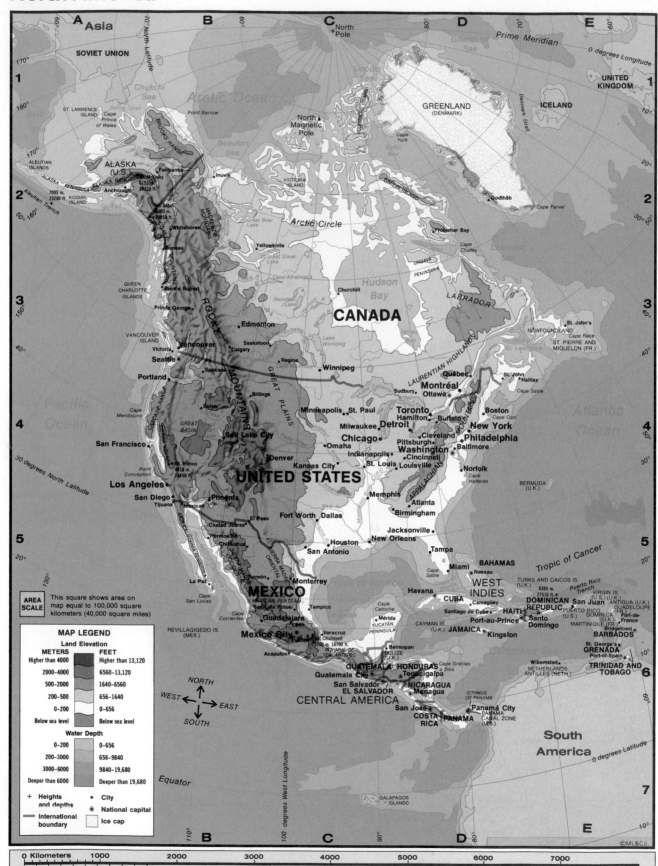

South America

1:35,000,000

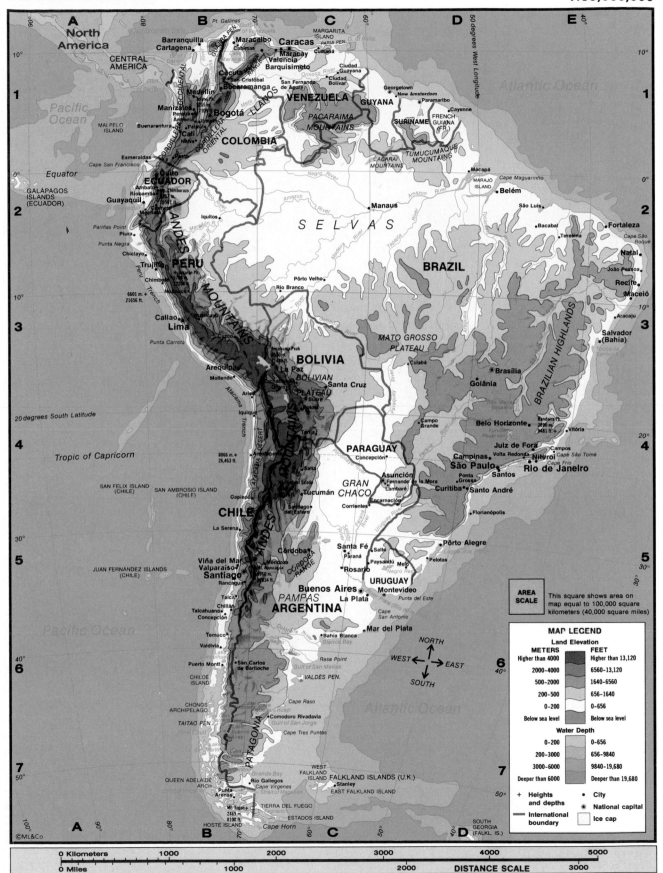

| | A | B | C | D | E |

North America

CENTRAL AMERICA

Pacific Ocean

Atlantic Ocean

VENEZUELA
COLOMBIA
GUYANA
SURINAME
FRENCH GUIANA (FR.)

Barranquilla
Cartagena
Maracaibo
Caracas
Maracay
Valencia
Barquisimeto
Cúcuta
Bucaramanga
Medellín
Manizales
Bogotá
Cali
Quito
ECUADOR
Guayaquil
Riobamba
Ambato

PACARAIMA MOUNTAINS

Georgetown
New Amsterdam
Paramaribo
Cayenne

ACARAI MOUNTAINS
TUMUCUMAQUE MOUNTAINS

Macapá
MARAJÓ ISLAND
Belém
São Luís

Equator

GALÁPAGOS ISLANDS (ECUADOR)

MALPELO ISLAND

Cape San Francisco
Esmeraldas

Buenaventura

LLANOS

Orinoco River
Negro River

Amazon River

Manaus

S E L V A S

BRAZIL

PERU
Iquitos
Piura
Chiclayo
Trujillo
Chimbote
Callao
Lima
Cuzco
Arequipa
Mollendo

Pariñas Point
Punta Negra

ANDES MOUNTAINS

Pôrto Velho
Rio Branco

MATO GROSSO PLATEAU

Cuiabá
Brasília
Goiânia

Bacabal
Teresina
Fortaleza
Natal
João Pessoa
Recife
Maceió
Aracaju
Salvador (Bahía)

BRAZILIAN HIGHLANDS

BOLIVIA
La Paz
Santa Cruz
Sucre
Potosí

BOLIVIAN PLATEAU

ATACAMA DESERT

Arica
Iquique
Antofagasta

Tropic of Capricorn

SAN FELIX ISLAND (CHILE)
SAN AMBROSIO ISLAND (CHILE)

JUAN FERNÁNDEZ ISLANDS (CHILE)

PARAGUAY
Asunción
Concepción
GRAN CHACO
Corrientes
Encarnación

Campo Grande
Belo Horizonte
Vitória
Juiz de Fora
Campos
Campinas
São Paulo
Santos
Niterói
Rio de Janeiro
Curitiba
Santo André
Florianópolis

Salta
Tucumán
Santiago del Estero
Córdoba
CÓRDOBA RANGE
Mendoza
Santa Fé
Paraná
Rosario

Pôrto Alegre
Pelotas

URUGUAY
Montevideo
Salto
Paysandú
Melo

CHILE
La Serena
Viña del Mar
Valparaíso
Santiago
Rancagua
Talca
Chillán
Talcahuano
Concepción

ARGENTINA
PAMPAS
Buenos Aires
La Plata
Mar del Plata
Bahía Blanca

Temuco
Valdivia
Puerto Montt
San Carlos de Bariloche

CHILOÉ ISLAND

CHONOS ARCHIPELAGO

TAITAO PEN.

PATAGONIA

Comodoro Rivadavia

QUEEN ADELAIDE ARCH.
Río Gallegos
Punta Arenas
TIERRA DEL FUEGO
HOSTE ISLAND
Cape Horn

WEST FALKLAND ISLAND
EAST FALKLAND ISLAND
FALKLAND ISLANDS (U.K.)
Stanley

ESTADOS ISLAND

SOUTH GEORGIA (FALKL. IS.)

AREA SCALE

This square shows area on map equal to 100,000 square kilometers (40,000 square miles)

NORTH
WEST — EAST
SOUTH

MAP LEGEND

Land Elevation

METERS	FEET
Higher than 4000	Higher than 13,120
2000–4000	6560–13,120
500–2000	1640–6560
200–500	656–1640
0–200	0–656
Below sea level	Below sea level

Water Depth

0–200	0–656
200–3000	656–9840
3000–6000	9840–19,680
Deeper than 6000	Deeper than 19,680

+ Heights and depths   • City
— International boundary   ⊙ National capital
   Ice cap

©ML&Co

| 0 Kilometers | 1000 | 2000 | 3000 | 4000 | 5000 |
| 0 Miles | | 1000 | 2000 | **DISTANCE SCALE** | 3000 |

Australia

1:32,000,000

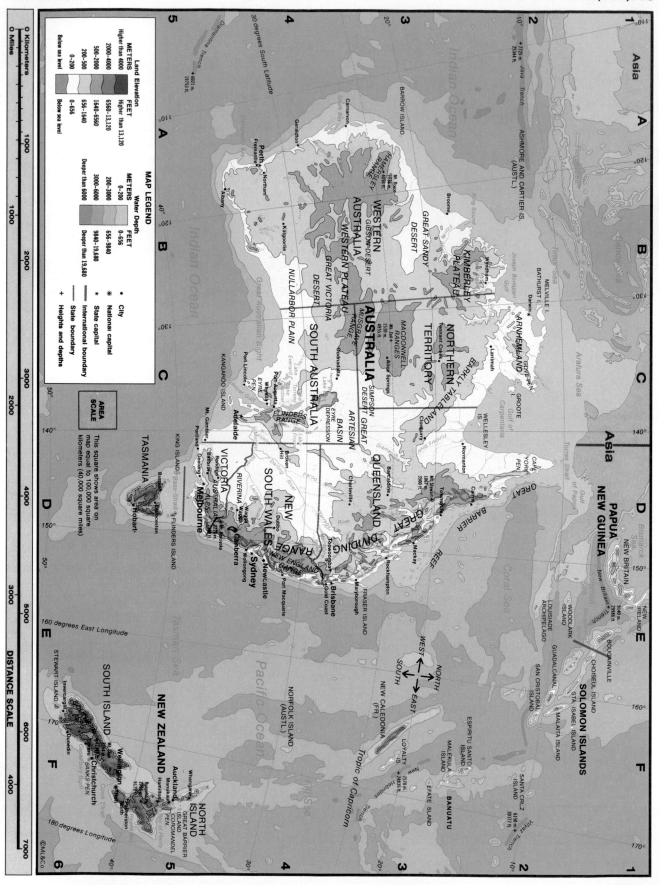

Glossary

A

abacus (AB uh kus) *noun:* a frame holding beads that slide back and forth, used to solve arithmetic problems. From the Greek word, *abax*, meaning counting board.

abdicate (AB duh KAYT) *verb:* to renounce, give up, such as a throne or authority. From the Latin word, *abdicare*, meaning to deny.

aborigines (AHB uh RIHJ uh NEES) *noun:* first inhabitants, usually applied to the original peoples of Australia. From the Latin prefix *ab-*, meaning from and the word *origine*, meaning the beginning.

absolute monarch: person whose power to govern is not limited.

acupuncture *noun:* a Chinese practice of puncturing the body with needles at specific locations to relieve pain and cure disease.

A.D. *abbreviation:* the years after the birth of Christ. From the Latin words, *anno Domini*, meaning in the year of the Lord.

Afrikaner *noun:* a South African of Dutch ancestry.

age (ayj) *noun:* a period of time characterized by a central feature, such as the age of dinosaurs.

agrarian (uh GREHR ee uhn) *adj.:* **1.** relating to land; **2.** in general, referring to agriculture or farmers. From the Latin word, *ager*, meaning a field or the country.

agricultural revolution: the far-reaching changes in human life resulting from the beginnings of farming. The consequences of the agricultural revolution include the creation of early civilizations.

alchemist (AL kuh mihst) *noun:* a person in the Middle Ages who tried to combine magic and chemistry. Many alchemists tried to turn a base metal, such as iron, into gold.

alienate (AYL yuhn AYT) *verb:* to change from a friendly to an unfriendly relationship.

Allies: in World War I, the nations that fought against the Central Powers, especially Great Britain, France, Russia, and the United States; in World War II, the nations that fought against the Axis, especially Great Britain, the Soviet Union, and the United States.

ally (AL eye) *noun:* a nation associated with another by treaty or alliance. In ancient Rome, a conquered country with some self-government. From the Latin word, *aligare*, meaning to bind to.

alms (ahmz) *noun:* money or gifts to the poor.

Amerindian (AM uh RIHND ee uhn) *noun:* an American Indian.

amnesty (AM nihs tee) *noun:* a general pardon for past offenses against a government.

amphibious (am FIHB ee uhs) *adj.:* for a military operation in which troops are moved from ships to the shore.

anatomical (AN uh TAHM ih kuhl) *adj.:* having to do with the structure of the body.

annex (AN ehks) *verb:* to add or incorporate within a political area. From the Latin prefix *ad-*, meaning to and the word *nectere*, meaning to bind.

anthropologist (an thruh PAHL uh juhst) *noun:* one who examines physical and cultural characteristics of people, their homes and customs, and their social relationships.

apartheid (uh PAHRT hayt) *noun:* the policy of strict racial segregation and discrimination against the native blacks as practiced in South Africa. An Afrikans word meaning apartness.

appease (uh PEEZ) *verb:* to quiet by giving in to the demands of. From the Latin prefix *a-*, meaning to and the word *pax*, meaning peace.

aqueduct (AK wuh duhkt) *noun:* a bridgelike structure for transporting water from a distant source.

arable (AIR uh buhl) *adj.:* land that can be farmed.

arbitrary (AHR buh TRER ee) *adj.:* not fixed by rules; based on one's preference.

archaeology (ahr kee AHL uh jee) *noun:* the scientific study of the life and activities of ancient peoples by excavation of past cities and relics.

archipelago (AHR kuh PEHL uh goh) *noun:* a group of many islands. From the Greek words *archi*, meaning chief and *pelagos*, meaning sea (originally the Aegean Sea).

archon (AHR kahn) *noun:* highest elected officials in ancient Greece; appointed officials and made laws. From the Greek word, *archon*, meaning leader.

arid (AR rihd) *adj.:* lacking water for things to grow. Excessively dry climate that supports farming only where rivers or underground water sources can be used for irrigation.

aristocracy (AR is TAHK ruh sih) *noun:* **1.** government by the best individuals or by a small privileged class; **2.** government by the upper class, usually a hereditary nobility. From the Greek words *aristos*, meaning best and *kratia*, meaning rule by.

armada (ahr MAH duh) *noun:* a fleet of warships such as that which Spain sent against England in 1588.

armistice (AHR muh stihs) *noun:* an agreement to temporarily stop fighting before signing a peace treaty. From the Latin words *arma*, meaning arms and *stitium*, meaning stand still.

armor plate *noun:* a heavy metal protective cover.

arsenal *noun:* **1.** a building where weapons are manufactured or stored; **2.** a collection of weapons.

artillery (ahr TIHL uhr ee) *noun:* large guns, such as cannons. From the Latin word, *ars*, meaning skill, art.

artisans (AHR tih zuhns) *noun:* people skilled in producing a particular product.

asceticism (uh SEHT uh siz uhm) *noun:* the practice of self-denial to develop personal and spiritual discipline. From the Greek word, *askcin*, meaning to train the body.

ascetics (uh SEHT ihks) *noun:* persons who live lives of self-denial and contemplation for religious purposes. From the Greek word, *askein*, meaning to train the body.

Asia Minor *noun:* a peninsula of western Asia, between the Black Sea and the Mediterranean Sea; present-day Turkey.

assimilate *verb:* to take over and make part of an existing cultural tradition.

astrolabe (AS truh LAYB) *noun:* an instrument used to find the altitude of a star; the sextant replaced it. From the Greek words *astron*, meaning a star and *lambanein*, meaning to take.

atrocity (uh TRAHS uh tee) *noun:* extreme cruelty or brutality, a horrifying act.

attrition (uh TRIHSH uhn) *noun:* a gradual weakening or wearing to the point of exhaustion, a reduction in numbers. From the Latin word, *atterere*, meaning to wear or to rub away.

autocratic (AW tuh KRAT ihk) *adj.:* having absolute power. From the Greek words *autos*, meaning self and *kratos*, meaning power.

autonomy (aw TAHN uh mee) *noun:* the right or power of self-government. From the Greek words *autos*, meaning self and *nomos*, meaning law.

Axis *noun:* the countries united against the Allies in World War II, originally Germany and Italy; later also Japan.

B

balance of power: a fairly even distribution of military and economic power among nations so that no nation will become too strong or too dangerous.

bankrupt (BANGK ruhpt) *adj.:* legally declared unable to pay debts.

Bantustan (BAN too STAN) *noun:* any of several territories in South Africa set aside as reserves for native black people, supposedly with some self-government. From the African word *Bantu*, and the Persian word *stan*, meaning a place.

barbarian (bar BER ee uhn) *noun:* one of a group whose culture is regarded as inferior or savage. From the Latin word, *barbaricus*, meaning foreign.

barricade (BAIR uh KAYD) *noun:* a barrier or obstruction, an obstacle. From the Italian word, *barricare*, meaning to fortify.

barter *verb:* to trade by exchanging goods or services without using money.

bazaar (buh ZAHR) *noun:* a marketplace selling many kinds of goods, a street of shops.

B.C. *abbreviation:* the years before the birth of Christ; literally before Christ.

Beijing (bay jihng) *noun:* city in northeastern China; until recently, Peking in English.

beneficence (buh NEHF uh suhns) *noun:* kindness or generosity. From the Latin words *bene*, meaning well or good and *facere*, meaning to do.

bloc *noun:* a group of nations acting together in support of one another; alliance.

bodhisattvas (bod duh SAHT wuhz) *noun:* in Buddhist belief, souls who wait to enter nirvana in order to save others.

Boer (bawr) *noun:* a South African whose ancestors were Dutch colonists.

bourgeoisie (BOOR zhwah ZEE) *noun:* the social class between the aristocracy or very wealthy, and the proletariat or working class; middle class. From the Latin word, *burgus*, meaning castle.

boycott *verb:* to refuse to buy, sell, or use something. From Captain C. C. Boycott, a land agent in Ireland in the 1880s.

brain drain: a gradual lessening of the professional or intellectual resources of a country or region through emigration. Used in informal speech.

breadbasket: a region that supplies much grain.

breech-loading *adj.:* loading at the breech, or back part, of a gun instead of at the muzzle, or front.

buffer zone: a neutral zone separating two potentially rival countries.

bunker *noun:* an underground steel or concrete fortification containing weapons.

bureaucracy (byoo RAH kruh see) *noun:* **1.** a group of officials who administer a government or other institution strictly according to established rules; **2.** governmental officialism or inflexible routine; **3.** a complex structure of administrative bureaus. From the French words *bureau*, meaning writing table or desk and *cratie*, meaning power.

Byzantium (buh ZAN shee uhm) *noun:* a city, overlooking the straits between the Black and Mediterranean seas, founded by the Greeks in 600 B.C. In 324 B.C., Byzantium was renamed Constantinople and became the capital of the Eastern Roman Empire, later called the Byzantine Empire. The Turks conquered Constantinople in 1453 and later renamed it Istanbul.

C

cabinet *noun:* a group of official advisers to a nation's ruler. Members head the major branches of government.

caliph (KAYL ihf) *noun:* the head of a Muslim religious community. From the Arabic word, *khalifa,* meaning successor.

calligraphy (kuh LIHG ruh fee) *noun:* handwriting, especially as an art. From the Greek words *kallos,* meaning beauty and *graphein,* meaning to write.

calorie (KAL uh ree) *noun:* the amount of heat needed to raise the temperature of one gram of water one degree centigrade, a unit used for measuring the energy produced by food. From the Latin word, *calor,* meaning heat.

canal locks *noun plu.:* enclosed parts of artificial waterways equipped with gates so that water levels can be changed to move boats from one level to another.

capillary (KAP uh LEHR ee) *noun:* a small blood vessel that connects arteries and veins. From the Latin word, *capillus,* meaning hair.

capital goods: items that are used to produce other goods such as tools, fertilizers, farm animals, and machinery.

capitalism (KAP uh tuhl ihz uhm) *noun:* an economic system in which individuals rather than the government own and operate businesses for profit.

caravansary (KAIR uh VAN suh ree) *noun:* a kind of inn where caravans stop. From the Persian words *kārwān,* meaning caravan and *sarāi,* meaning inn.

Caribbean (KAIR uh BEE uhn) **Sea** *noun:* part of the Atlantic Ocean, bounded by the West Indies, Central America, and the north coast of South America. From the Carib Indians, who once lived there.

cartel (KAHR TEHL) *noun:* an association of businesses that try to establish a monopoly by controlling a commodity's price, production, and sale. From the Latin word, *carta,* meaning a card, a paper.

caste system (KAST SIHS tehm): **1.** the social system of India based on exclusive social classes; **2.** the system of hereditary Hindu social classes, each traditionally forbidden to socialize with the others. From the Latin word, *castus,* originally meaning separated.

cataract (KAHT uh RAKT) *noun:* **1.** a large waterfall; **2.** steep rapids in a river. From the Greek word, *katarassein,* meaning to dash down.

causeway *noun:* a raised road or highway.

cavalry (KAV uh ree) *noun:* combat troops mounted on horses.

censor (SEHN suhr) *verb:* to remove information that might be useful to an enemy. From the Latin word, *censere,* meaning to judge.

Central Powers: in World War I, the nations that opposed the Allies: Germany, Austria-Hungary, and later Bulgaria and Turkey.

century (SEHN chuhr ee) *noun:* usually means 100; in the army of ancient Rome, 100 men. From the Latin word, *centuria,* meaning one hundred.

chancellor (CHAN suh luhr) *noun:* the prime minister of certain countries. From the Latin word, *cancellarius,* meaning secretary.

charter *noun:* a written grant of specified rights from a ruler, government, or business.

chattel (CHAT uhl) *noun:* personal property such as furniture, a car, livestock, or [Archaic] a slave. From the Old French word, *chatel,* meaning cattle.

chinampas (chuh NAM puhz) *noun:* farmland created by people in shallow lakes.

chivalry *noun:* a code of behavior knights were supposed to follow. From the French word, *cheval,* meaning horse.

chronology (kruh NAHL uh jee) *noun:* the arrangement of events in the order in which they occurred. From the Greek word, *chronikos,* meaning time.

citadel *noun:* a fortress that commands a city; a stronghold.

city-state *noun:* an independent state made up of a city and the surrounding territory.

civil disobedience: non-violent protest of a government policy or law by refusing to comply with it.

civil service system: method for selecting government employees that emphasizes hiring qualified workers through testing.

civilization (SIV uh luh ZAY shun) *noun:* a society characterized by specialization of labor, organized leadership, a system of writing, common beliefs, and the existence of cities. From the Latin word, *civitas,* meaning city.

clan (klan) *noun:* **1.** a number of households that believe they are all descended from the same ancestor, have the same family name, and follow the same chieftain; **2.** a division within a tribe.

cocoyam (KOH koh yam) *noun:* a yam grown in cacao (cocoa) groves.

collective farm: a large farm formed by consolidating many small farms into a single unit and supervised by the government.

collective responsibility system: each person is held responsible for the conduct of everyone in the group.

colony *noun:* an area where a foreign power gained complete control over a region and its inhabitants.

Columbian exchange: the exchange of plants and animals between the Old World and New World following Columbus's trips.

commerce *noun:* the buying and selling of goods, especially on a large scale; trade. From the Latin prefix *com-,* meaning together and the word *merx,* meaning merchandise.

commercial economy: a system of producing, distributing, and consuming goods on a large scale.

commissioning (kuh MIHSH uhn ing) *verb:* giving permission to; authorizing. From the Latin word, *commissio,* meaning delegating business.

commodity (kuh MAHD uh tee) *noun:* anything bought and sold. From the Latin word, *commodus*, meaning suitable.

common law: the law of a country or state based on custom, usage, and the decisions of a law court.

commonwealth *noun:* an association of self-governing states that hold a common allegiance, as to the British crown; a nation or other political unit.

commune (KAHM yoon) *noun:* a local body for self-government in towns during the Middle Ages. From the Latin word, *communis*, meaning common.

communism *noun:* an economic system based on community or government ownership of all property; characterized by a classless society and equal distribution of goods, envisioned by Marx as being achieved through revolution.

compensation (KAHM puhn SAY shun) *noun:* payment to make amends for a loss, such as from injury or unemployment. From the Latin word, *compensatus*, meaning to weigh one thing against another.

compromise (KAHM pruh MYZ) *noun:* a settlement in which both sides make concessions, yield some demands. From the Latin prefix *com-*, meaning together and the word *promittere*, meaning promise.

comrade (KAHM rad) *noun:* used as a form of address in the Communist party; a friend. From the Spanish word, *camarada*, meaning chamber mate, earlier—a Greek word, *kamara*, meaning high chamber.

concession (kuhn SEHSH uhn) *noun:* something granted, as a right or privilege. From the Latin prefix *com-*, meaning with and the word *cedere*, meaning to grant.

confederation (kuhn FEHD uh RAY shuhn) *noun:* a league or alliance of independent nations or states whose main purpose usually is limited to common defense or foreign relations.

confines (KAHN fynz) *noun:* boundary, border. From the Latin prefix *com-*, meaning with and the word *finis*, meaning end, limit.

confiscate (KAHN fuh SKAYT) *verb:* to seize private property; appropriate. From the Latin word, *confiscare*, meaning to lay up in a chest.

conspirator (kuhn SPIHR uh tuhr) *noun:* a person who takes part in a conspiracy, a secret planning of a harmful act. From the Latin prefix *com-*, meaning together and the word *spirare*, meaning to breathe.

consul *noun:* one of three highest officials of the French republic from 1799 to 1804.

consumer goods: goods that satisfy people's needs.

contemplative (KAHN tuhm PLAYT ihv) *adj.:* thoughtful, meditative. From the Latin word, *contemplatis*, meaning to gaze attentively, to observe.

contemporary (kuhn TEHM puh REHR ee) *adj.:* in recent times; modern. From the Latin prefix *com-*, meaning with and the word *tempus*, meaning time.

contiguous (kuhn TIHG yoo wuhs) *adj.:* touching along all or most of one side. From the Latin word, *contigere*, meaning to touch upon.

convergence (kuhn VER juhns) *noun:* a coming together, becoming similar. From the Latin prefix *com-*, meaning together and the word *vergere*, meaning to bend or turn.

corporation (KAWR puh RAY shuhn) *noun:* an association of employers and employees. From the Latin word, *corporare*, meaning to make into a body.

corpuscle (KAWR puhs uhl) *noun:* a cell that is capable of free movement in a fluid such as blood or lymph. From the Latin word, *corpus*, meaning body.

Cossack (KAHS ahk) *noun:* a member of a people of southern Russia, famous for fighting on horseback.

count (kownt) *noun:* a member of the nobility in European countries.

coup (koo) *noun:* a sudden, forcible overthrow of a government. A French word meaning a sudden blow or stroke.

Court of the Star Chamber: a special English court appointed by King Henry VII in order to seize the estates and fortunes of nobles. Trials were held in secret and without juries.

Crimea (kry MEE uh) *noun:* a peninsula in southwest Russia extending into the Black Sea.

cultural imperialism: the policy and practice of seeking to dominate the affairs and customs of a given people at a given time, especially those in underdeveloped areas or weaker countries.

culture (KUHL chuhr) *noun:* all the tools, skills, customs, arts, and ideas of a particular group of people in a certain period of time; a way of life.

cuneiform (kyoo NEE uh fawrm) *noun:* the Mesopotamian writing system, consisting of a system of wedge-shaped marks in soft clay made with the tip of a sharpened reed. From the Latin word, *cuneus*, meaning a wedge shape.

D

Dao (dow) *noun:* Chinese philosophy that emphasizes conformity to nature; until recently, translated into English as Tao.

Dark Ages: the years between A.D. 500 and 1000 when trade, urban centers, and literacy declined in Europe as a result of Germanic invasions. These years are called the Early Middle Ages.

decimation (DEHS uh MAY shuhn) *noun:* the practice of killing every tenth person as punishment; destroying a large part of the population. From the Latin word, *decimus*, meaning tenth.

decree (dih KREE) *noun:* an official order of a government, church, or court. From the prefix *de-*, meaning from and *cernere*, meaning to judge.

deduction *noun:* a process of reasoning from a generalization to specific information.

deductive reasoning: reasoning from a general to a specific conclusion.

default (dih FAWLT) *noun:* a circumstance in which an individual or country fails to pay money due. From the Latin prefix *de-*, meaning away and the word *fallere*, meaning to fail.

deficit (DEHF uh siht) *noun:* an excess of losses over profits, or expenditures over income. From the Latin word, *deficere*, meaning to lack or to fail.

deist (DEE ihst) *noun:* one who believes in the existence of a God because it is reasonable to do so. From the Latin word, *deus*, meaning God.

delegate (DEHL uh giht) *noun:* a person chosen to speak for others at a meeting or convention; a representative. From the Latin word, *delegare*, meaning to send from one place.

deliberative body: a group which thinks about and discusses issues and reaches decisions carefully.

delta (DEHL tuh) *noun:* a triangular piece of land formed by deposits of silt at a river's mouth. From the Greek word, *delta*, the fourth letter of their alphabet, which is a triangle when written.

democracy (dih MAHK ruh see) *noun:* government in which the people hold power either directly or through elected representatives; rule by the people. From the Greek words *demos*, meaning people and *kratia*, meaning to rule.

depict (dih PIHKT) *verb:* to picture, show, represent in a drawing. From the Latin word, *depingere*, meaning to paint.

depression (dih PREHSH uhn) *noun:* a period of declining business activity, high unemployment, and falling prices and wages.

detente (day TAHNT) *noun:* a lessening of tension between nations as through a treaty or trade agreement. A French word meaning to relax. From the Latin prefix *de-*, meaning from and the word *tedere*, meaning to stretch out.

dialects *noun:* regional varieties of a language differing distinctively from the standard language.

diplomacy (dih PLOH muh see) *noun:* the conduct of business between nations, such as making treaties.

dirigible (DIHR uh juh buhl) *noun:* a balloon-like airship filled with gas that is lighter than air. From the Latin word *dirigere*, meaning to direct and the English suffix *-ible*, meaning able.

displaced person: someone forced to leave home and country, usually because of war.

dissection *noun:* anything separated into pieces for scientific examination; analysis part by part.

diverse (dy VUHRS) *adj.:* different, varied. From the Latin word, *divertere*, meaning to turn aside.

divine right kings: kings who believed their right to rule came directly from God.

domestic (duh MEHS tihk) *adj.:* made or produced in the home country; native. From the Latin word, *domus*, meaning home.

domesticate (duh MEHS tuh kayt) *verb:* to adapt a plant or animal for human use.

domino theory: the theory that a certain result follows a certain cause the way a row of upright dominoes falls if the first one is pushed.

draftee *noun:* a person chosen for required service in the armed forces.

dromedary (DRAHM uh dair ih) *noun:* a swift, one-humped camel of Arabia. From the Greek word, *dromos*, meaning running.

Druids (DROO ihds) *noun:* Celtic religious leaders. From the Indo-European word, *dru-wid*, meaning oak-wise.

dynasty (DY nuhs tee) *noun:* a family of rulers who pass power to their children or a relative over many years. From the Greek word, *dynasteia*, meaning lordship or rule.

E

Eastern (EEST uhrn) **Hemisphere** (HEM us sfihr): the half of the globe that lies to the east of the Atlantic Ocean; consists of Eurasia, Africa, and Australia, their surrounding islands, and most of the Pacific Ocean.

economist (ih KAHN un mihst) *noun:* a specialist in economics, the science that deals with production, distribution, and consumption. From the Greek, *oikonomia*, meaning management of a household.

economy *noun:* the structure of economic life, how the people of a country produce, distribute, and use goods and services.

elite (ih LEET) *noun:* the group regarded as the best, most distinguished, or most powerful. From the French word, *eslire*, meaning to choose.

elliptical (ih LIHP tih kuhl) *adj.:* less than a perfect circle. From the Greek word, *elleipein*, meaning to fall short.

embargo (ihm BAHR goh) *noun:* a prohibiting of trade in a particular commodity. From the Latin prefix *in-*, meaning on and the word *barra*, meaning bar.

embassy (EHM buh see) *noun:* the official residence and office of an ambassador to a foreign country. From the Prussian word, *ambaissa*, meaning mission, task.

emigrate (EHM uh GRAYT) *verb:* to leave one's homeland and settle in another country. From the Latin prefix *ex-*, meaning out and the word *migrare*, meaning to move.

empire (EM pyr) *noun:* a usually large state governing peoples of several different languages or nationalities. From the Latin word, *imperare*, meaning to command.

enclosure *noun:* something that shuts in all around. From the Latin prefix *en-*, meaning in and the word *claudere*, meaning to close.

entente (ahn TAHNT) *noun:* a French word meaning an understanding or agreement between two or more governments.

entrepreneur (AHN truh pruh NYOOR) *noun:* a business manager or organizer who assumes the risk of forming a business for the sake of profit. From the French word, *entreprendre*, meaning to undertake.

envoy (EHN voy) *noun:* an agent sent by a ruler or a government on a diplomatic mission; a messenger.

epic poem: a long narrative poem, in a dignified style, about the deeds of a legendary hero.

epidemic (EHP uh DEHM ihk) *adj.:* spreading rapidly among the people; widespread. From the Greek prefix *epi-*, meaning among and the word *demos*, meaning people.

equal field system: government granted land reverts to the government at that person's death, the system prevents the formation of large estates.

escalate (EHS kuh LAYT) *verb:* to expand from a local conflict into a general, especially nuclear, war. From the Latin word, *scalare*, meaning to climb.

espionage (EHS pee uh NAHZH) *noun:* the act of spying; a government's use of spies to learn another country's military secrets. From the Italian word, *spia*, meaning spy.

essay (EHS ay) *noun:* a short, analytical literary composition written from a personal point of view.

ethical (EHTH ih kuhl) **monotheism** (MAHN uh thee ihz uhm): the belief in only one God, and in right conduct based on God-given laws.

ethnic (ETH nihk) *adj.:* designating the basic divisions of people as distinguished by such things as customs, characteristics, language, and common history. From the Greek word, *ethnos*, meaning people or nations.

etiquette (EHT ih kuht) *noun:* behavior established by custom as acceptable in social relations. From the French word, *etiquette*, literally, ticket.

evacuate (ih VAK yoo WAYT) *verb:* to remove people from a place for their protection; to withdraw. From the Latin word, *vacuus*, meaning empty.

evolution (EHV uh LOO shuhn) *noun:* the theory that all species of plants and animals developed from earlier forms. From the Latin prefix *e-*, meaning out or forth and the word *volvere*, meaning to roll.

exchequer (ihks CHECK uhr) *noun:* a treasury.

exile (EHG zyl) *noun:* a person who is forced to live away from his or her country, one who is banished. From the Latin word, *exilium*, meaning banished or sent out to wander aimlessly.

exotic (igh ZAHT ihk) *adj.:* foreign and unfamiliar rather than native. From the Greek word, *exotikos*, meaning outside.

exploit (ihk SPLOYT) *verb:* to use productively; to take advantage of or use unjustly. From the Latin word, *explicare*, meaning to unfold.

extinct *adj.:* no longer in existence or use.

F

facilitate (fuh SIHL uh TAYT) *verb:* to make easy or easier.

faction *noun:* a group of people in an organization working against other groups or the main body.

factors of production: in economics, land, labor, and capital; the resources needed to produce goods and services.

fallow (FAL oh) *noun:* land left uncultivated, or not seeded, for one or more growing seasons, to allow farmers to plow under the weeds and increase subsequent productivity.

famine (FAM uhn) *noun:* a serious shortage of food. From the Latin word, *fames*, meaning hunger.

fascism (FASH ihz uhm) *noun:* a system of government characterized by one-party dictatorship, extreme nationalism, militarism, racism, and suppression of opposition. The term comes from *fasces*, a bundle of rods tied around an ax and used by Roman magistrates as a symbol of authority.

federation *noun:* a union of nations, states or organizations.

feudalism (FYOOD uhl ihz uhm) *noun:* an economic, political, and social system, in which vassals received the use of land in exchange for services to the overlord. Serfs farmed the land. The feudal system developed in Europe about A.D. 900. Similar feudal systems existed in China during the second and third centuries B.C., and in Japan between the ninth and nineteenth centuries A.D.

fibula (FIHB yoo luh) *noun:* in ancient Greece or Rome, a buckle or clasp used to fasten flowing robes. From the Latin word, *figuere*, meaning to fasten or fix.

fief (feef) *noun:* land granted by a lord to another noble in exchange for service.

Fifth Column: any group of people who give aid to the enemy from within their own country. The term was coined in 1936 during the Spanish Civil War. General Mola, who was besieging Madrid, Spain, had four columns on the outside and boasted of a fifth column within.

Flemish (FLEHM ihsh) *adj.:* of the people of Flanders. In the Middle Ages, Flanders was a country on the North Sea. Today the area is a part of France, Belgium, and the Netherlands.

fluctuate (FLUHK choo WAYT) *verb:* to be constantly changing in an irregular way, as in fluctuating prices. From the Latin word, *fluctus*, meaning a wave, a flowing.

flying buttress (BUHT rihs) : a projecting structure, usually of stone or brick, built against a wall to support or reinforce it.

fortress cities: cities strengthened against attack by a fort or surrounding walls. From the Latin word, *fortis*, meaning strong.

frankincense (FRANG kuhn SEHNS) *noun:* a gum resin from various Arabian and northeast African trees. It is often burned as incense.

fresco (FREHS koh) *noun:* the art or technique of painting with watercolors on wet plaster. From the Old High German word, *frisc*, meaning fresh.

friar (FRY uhr) *noun:* a member of a religious order in which no one held any personal or community property but lived mostly on alms.

G

Gaul (gawl) *noun:* ancient region in western Europe, consisting of an area that now is mainly France and Belgium.

genealogy (JEE nee AHL uh jee) *noun:* an account of the descent of a person, family, or group from an ancestor.

genetics (juh NEHT iks) *noun:* the branch of biology that deals with the way characteristics are transmitted from parent to offspring in plants and animals. From the Latin word, *genesis*, meaning birth.

genocide (JEHN uh SYD) *noun:* the systematic killing of a whole ethnic group. From the Greek word, *genos*, meaning race (of people).

geocentric (JEE oh SEHN trihk) *adj.:* considering Earth the center of the universe. From the Greek words *ge*, meaning earth and *kentron*, meaning center.

geography (jee AH gruh fee) *noun:* the study of the earth's landforms, climates, resources, and life forms. From the Greek words *geo*, meaning earth and *graphia*, meaning to write.

glacier (GLAY zhur) *noun:* a large sheet of ice, often hundreds of feet high, that spreads across the land.

gluten (GLOOT uhn) *noun:* a gray, sticky protein, found in grains, that gives dough its elastic property. From the Latin word, *gluten*, meaning glue.

glyph (glihf) *noun:* a carved symbol; a hieroglyph. From the Greek word, *glyphein*, meaning carve.

grappling hook: an iron bar with claws at one end for grasping and holding things.

guerrilla (guh RIHL uh) *noun:* a member of a force of fighters, usually volunteers, who operate in small groups and usually make hit-and-run attacks against the enemy. From the Spanish word, *guerrilla*, meaning war.

guild (gihld) *noun:* a union of men in the same craft or trade, formed to uphold standards and protect the members. From the Old English word, *gyld*, meaning association (of paying members).

H

hajj (haj) *noun:* the pilgrimage to Mecca that every Muslim is expected to take at least once.

harem *noun:* a secluded part of the house where the women of a Muslim household live. From the Arab word, *harem*, meaning sanctuary.

heliocentric (HEE lee oh SEHN trihk) *adj.:* considering the sun the center of the universe. From the Greek words, *helios*, meaning sun and *kentron*, meaning center.

Hellenic culture: the achievements and way of life of the Greeks between 700 and 400 B.C. From the Greek word, *hellene*, meaning Greek.

Hellenistic culture: the blending of Hellenic culture with the cultures of Egypt and Asia.

hemisphere (HEM uh sfihr) *noun:* A view of half of the globe. From the Greek word, *hemisphairion*, meaning half of a sphere.

hemophilia (HEE muh FIHL ee uh) *noun:* a hereditary condition in which blood does not clot. It occurs only in males but is transmitted by females.

heretic (HAIR uh tihk) *noun:* a church member who holds beliefs opposed to church dogma. From the Greek word, *hairetikos*, meaning able to choose.

hieroglyphics (HY uhr uh GLIHF ihks) *noun:* ancient Egyptian writings. From the Greek words *hieros*, meaning *sacred* and *glyphein*, meaning to carve.

holocaust: the systematic destruction of Jews by the Nazis before and during World War II.

homage (HAHM ihj) *noun:* a public vow of allegience by a vassal to his lord.

homespun *noun:* cloth made of yarn spun at home.

hominid (HAHM uh nihd) *noun:* any of the family of recent humans, their immediate ancestors, and related forms.

horde *noun:* a wandering tribe or group.

Huang He (hwahng hee) *noun:* river in northern China where civilization developed; until recently, translated in English as Huang Ho.

humanism *noun:* the secular, cultural, intellectual movement started by the study of Greek and Roman literature.

hypnotize (HIHP nuh TYZ) *verb:* to put someone into a state of altered consciousnous. In this state the subconscious mind can respond to suggestion. From the Greek word, *hypnos*, meaning sleep.

I

Ice Age (IYS AYJ: the most recent period, 70,000 to 12,000 years ago, in which the average temperature dropped 15 to 20 degrees *fahrenheit,* and during which glaciers extended over all of present-day Canada and northern Europe.

idol (EYE duhl) *noun:* an image, or other object, worshipped as a god.

imperator (ihm puh RAYT uhr) *noun:* a Roman title of honor used by military and political leaders. From the Latin word, *imperativus*, meaning commanding.

imperialism (ihm PIHR ee uhl ihz uhm) *noun:* the policy of attempting to dominate the political, economic, or cultural life of another country or region. From the Latin word, *imperare*, meaning to command.

implement *verb:* to put into effect. From the Latin word, *implere*, meaning to fill up.

impulse *noun:* a momentary surge of electric current in one direction. From the Latin prefix *in-*, meaning in and the word *pellere*, meaning to drive.

incentive (ihn SEHN tihv) *noun:* something that encourages one to take action.

indemnity (ihn DEHM nuht ee) *noun:* compensation for some loss or damage; repayment. From the Latin prefix *in-*, meaning not and the word *damnum*, meaning damage.

indentured (ihn DEHN chuhrd) **servant:** one who is bound by contract to work for another for a given length of time.

Indo-European peoples: people who once lived in the grasslands north of the Black and Caspian seas and migrated in successive waves into Europe, India, and southwest Asia.

inductive reasoning: reasoning from particular facts or individual cases to a general conclusion.

indulgence (ihn DUHL juhns) *noun:* a favor or privilege in the Roman Catholic church, a means of pardoning sinners from part of the penalty for their sins. For example, a person could contribute money to a specific cause rather than go on a pilgrimage. The practice was sometimes abused as a means of raising money.

infamy (IHN fuh mee) *noun:* great wickedness, disgrace. From the Latin word, *infamis*, meaning not famous, or having a bad reputation.

infantry *noun:* soldiers who fight on foot.

inflation (ihn FLAY shuhn) *noun:* a general rise in prices. From the Latin word, *inflare*, meaning to blow into.

innovation (IN uh VAY shuhn) *noun:* something new, a change in the way of doing things.

intervene (IHN tuhr VEEN) *verb:* to come between so as to change or modify. From the Latin prefix *inter-*, meaning between and the word *venire*, meaning to come.

intimidate (ihn TIHM uh dayt) *verb:* to influence or force by fear; to frighten.

intrude (ihn TROOD) *verb:* to force oneself upon others without being asked or welcomed. From the Latin word, *intrudere*, meaing to thrust or push.

intuition (IHN too WIHSH uhn) *noun:* the ability to perceive or know things without conscious reasoning. From the Latin prefix *in-*, meaning in and the word *tueri*, meaning to look at.

inure (ihn YOOR) *verb:* to accustom someone to something difficult or undesirable.

invest (ihn VEHST) *verb:* to put money into something for the purpose of obtaining income or profit.

irrigate *verb:* to supply arid land with water by means of ditches or channels. From the Latin word, *irrigare*, meaning to bring water.

isthmus (IHS muhs) *noun:* a narrow strip of land connecting two larger sections of land.

J

Jiang Jieshi (JYANG ky SHEHK): Pinyin spelling, formerly Chiang Kai-shek.

joust *noun:* a competition in which two knights on horseback galloped at each other with lances lowered, each seeking to unseat the other. From the Latin word, *juxtare*, meaing to approach.

jurisdiction (JUR ihs DIHK shuhn) *noun:* authority, legal power. From the Latin words *juris*, meaning law and *dicere*, meaning to say or speak.

K

kaiser (KY zuhr) *noun:* title used by the rulers of Germany, 1871–1918.

karma (KAHR muh) *noun:* **1.** in the Indian religion, the combined effects of a person's actions that transfer to the next life; **2.** fate or destiny.

khipus *noun:* pieces of string whose colors and patterns of knots recorded statistics and past events.

kibbutz (kih BOOTS) *noun:* an Israeli collective farm.

kinship *noun:* being related to; sharing common ancestors.

koine (koy NAY) *noun:* the Greek language the common people spoke during the Hellenistic period. From the Greek word, *koinos*, meaning common.

Kong Qiu (kung chyoo): Chinese philosopher also known as Confucius; until recently, translated into English as K'ung Ch'iu.

kowtow (KOU TOU) *verb:* to kneel and touch the ground with the forehead to show respect. In Chinese, kowtow means a knock on the head.

L

lacquerwork *noun:* wood covered with a clear or colored coating that dries to a glossy finish.

laissez faire (LEHS ay FAIR): the practice of letting owners of industry and business set working conditions without government control or regulation. French word meaning let people do as they please.

laity *noun:* the people who practice a religious faith, as distinct from the clergy.

lamented (luh MEHN tihd) *verb:* expressed sorrow; regretted. From the Latin word, *lamentum,* meaning mourning.

Laozi (low dzuh) : founder of Chinese Daoist philosophy; until recently, translated as Lao Tzu.

lathe (layth) *noun:* a machine that shapes a piece of metal or wood by holding and turning it rapidly against the edge of a cutting tool. From the Middle English word, *lath,* meaning supporting stand.

latifundia (LAT uh FUHN dee uh) *noun:* In Ancient Rome, a large farming estate worked by slaves and tenants. From the Latin words *latus,* meaning broad and *fundus,* meaning estate.

lay investiture: the authority of a lay person, such as a king, to grant religious offices to clergy.

leach *verb:* to dissolve out, to remove nutrients.

leftist *noun:* politically favor socialism, reform, or revolution to improve the life of the people.

legacy (LEHG uh see) *noun:* anything handed down from, as from an ancestor. From the Latin word, *lex,* meaning law.

liberalism *noun:* a political philosophy based on the establishment and protection of individual rights.

limited monarchy: a government ruled by one person, in which the power is limited in some way. In England, Parliament limited the monarchy.

literacy (LIHT uhr uh see) *noun:* ability to read and write. From the Latin, *littera,* meaning letter.

lord *noun:* the owner of a feudal estate.

lunar (LOO nuhr) *adj.:* measured by the moon's revolutions. From the Latin, *luna,* meaning moon.

M

madrasas (muh DRAH suhs) *noun:* Muslim colleges.

malnutrition (MAL noo TRIHSH uhn) *noun:* poor health resulting from a lack of proper food. From the Latin words *malus,* meaning bad and *nutrire,* meaning to nourish.

mammal (MAM uhl) *noun:* an animal that is a warm-blooded vertebrate, usually hairy, that feeds its young with milk secreted by mammary glands. From the Latin word, *mamma,* meaning breast.

mandate *noun:* a commission from the League of Nations to a country to administer a certain region.

manor *noun:* the agricultural estate over which a feudal lord held authority.

mansas *noun:* early kings of west Africa.

Mao Zedong (mou zuh DONG) : Pinyin spelling, formerly Mao Tse-tung.

marathon (MAR uh thahn) *noun:* a footrace of 26 miles and 385 yards, run over an open course, especially as an event of the Olympic Games. After the legend of the Greek runner who ran from Marathon to Athens to tell of the Greek victory over the Persians (490 B.C.).

marsupial (mahr SOO pee uhl) *noun:* an animal with a pouch for carrying its young—for example, a kangaroo. From the Greek word, *marsypos,* meaning a pouch or bag.

martial law: temporary rule by military authorities over the civilian population as in time of war or civil disturbances.

martyrdom (MAHR tuhr duhm) *noun:* self-sacrifice or suffering for one's beliefs. From the Greek word, *martyr,* meaning a witness.

mechanize (MEHK uh NYZ) *verb:* to do or operate by machine instead of by hand.

mediate (MEE dee AYT) *verb:* to provide friendly or diplomatic intervention, usually by invitation, for settling differences between persons or nations.

mercantilism (MUR kuhn tihl ihzm) *noun:* the doctrine that the economic interests of a nation can be strengthened by tariffs, increased foreign trade, monopolies, and by a balance of exports over imports. From the Latin word, *mercari.* meaning to trade or buy.

mercenaries *noun:* professional soldiers hired to serve in a foreign army, sometimes called soldiers of fortune. From the Latin, *merces,* meaning pay.

mesa (MAY suh) *noun:* a high, flat hill rising above surrounding land. From the Latin word, *mensa,* meaning table.

Messiah (meh SY uh) *noun:* the expected king of the Hebrews, who would renew national strength and restore past glory. From the Hebrew word, *mashiah,* meaning annointed.

metate (may TAH tay) *noun:* a stone with a flat or concave surface used with a smaller stone called mano to grind corn into flour.

microbiology (MY kroh by AHL uh jee) *noun:* the branch of biology that deals with microorganisms.

microorganism (MY kroh AWR guh nihz uhm) *noun:* any organism which cannot be seen without magnification.

Middle America: area of land that includes the southern half of Mexico, the Yucatan Peninsula, and the Central American land bridge.

Middle East: a large region that includes Egypt, the Arabian Peninsula, Syria, and the Iranian Plateau.

Middle Stone Age (mihdl stohn ayj): the time period from about 10,000 B.C. to about 8,000 B.C., also called the Mesolithic Age.

military aristocracy: rule by a small group of individuals who control their own personal armies.

military dictatorship: a state in which a member of the armed forces has the absolute power to run the government.

military draft: the choosing and taking of individuals for required service in a country's armed forces.

missi dominici: Charlemagne's agents, or spies; messengers of the lord.

mobilize (MOH buh LYZ) *verb:* to bring into readiness for active participation. From the Latin word, *mobilis,* meaning movable.

moldboard *noun:* a piece of wood or iron attached to the side of a plow so as to turn the soil over. Moldboard plows opened more land to farming.

monastery (MAHN uh STUR ee) *noun:* a place of residence for a group of people, especially monks, who have taken religious vows. From the Greek word, *monazein,* meaning to live alone.

monk (muhnk) *noun:* a man who joins a religious order living away from the world and with religious vows of obedience, chastity, and poverty.

Monophysite (muh NAHF uh SYT) **Christian:** Christian who believes in the single divine nature of Christ, a view commonly held by members of the Coptic Church. From the Greek words *monos,* meaning single and *physis,* meaning nature.

monopoly (muh NAHP uh lee) *noun:* the exclusive control of a given market that virtually eliminates competition. From the Greek words *monos,* meaning single and *polein,* meaning to sell.

monsoon (mahn SOON) *noun:* a seasonal wind of the Indian Ocean and south Asia. It blows from the southwest from April to October, and from the northeast the rest of the year.

mosque (mahsk) *noun:* a Muslim house of worship.

mutiny (MYOOT uhn ee) *noun:* revolt; forcible resistance to authority, especially by soldiers or sailors.

myrrh (mur) *noun:* a sweet-smelling but bitter-tasting gum resin from certain plants of Arabia and east Africa, used in making perfume and as incense.

N

national state: in the 1500s, large territories that a ruler had consolidated under one government.

nationalize *verb:* to transfer ownership of resources or private industry to the national government.

negotiate (nih GOH shee AYT) *verb:* to confer, discuss, or bargain with a view to reaching an argeement. From the Latin word, *negotiari,* meaning to carry on business.

neocolonialism: the survival or revival of domination by a foreign power, of a region that has achieved independence.

New Stone Age (noo stohn ayj) : the time period from about 8000 B.C. to 4000 B.C., also called the Neolithic Age.

Nicaea (nih SEE uh) *noun:* ancient city in Asia Minor.

nirvana (nihr VAHN nuh) *noun:* in Buddhism, the state of freedom from all desire and individual consciousness and from the cycle of rebirth.

nonaligned: not cooperating closely, as in nations.

nuclear (NOO klee uhr) *adj.:* operated by the use of atomic energy.

nuclear reactor: a device for starting and maintaining a controlled nuclear chain reaction to produce energy.

nullify (NUHL uh FY) *verb:* to cancel. From the Latin words *nullus,* meaning none and *facare,* meaning to make.

nutrient (NOO tree uhnt) *noun:* a nourishing substance that aids growth.

O

obliterate ((uh BLIHT uh rayt)) *verb:* to wipe out, remove all traces of. From the Latin words, *ob litteras scribere,* meaning to erase.

obsolete (AHB suh LEET) *adj.:* no longer usable; out-of-date. From the Latin word, *obsolescere,* meaning to go out of use.

odious (OH dee uhs) *adj.:* hateful, disgusting. From the Latin word, *odium,* meaning hateful, disgusting.

Old Stone Age (ohld stohn ayj) : the time period from human beginnings to about 10,000 B.C., also called the Paleolithic Age from Greek words meaning ancient stone.

oracle (AWR uh kuhl) *noun:* **1.** the place where gods were consulted; **2.** the response of a medium or priest. From the Latin, *oraculum,* meaning to speak.

Orient (AWR ee uhnt) *noun:* Asia, especially the Far East, including China, Japan, and Korea. Sometimes the term includes the countries of Southeast Asia and the Malay Archipelago.

Orthodox (AWR thuh dahks) **Christianity:** the official religion of the Byzantine Empire.

P

pandemic (pan DEHM ihk) *adj.:* occurring over a wide geographic area and affecting an exceptionally large proportion of the population, as a pandemic outbreak of a disease. From the Greek word, *pandemos,* meaning of all the people.

parasite (PAIR uh syt) *noun:* organism that lives on others without making any return. From the Greek prefix *para-,* meaning beside, and the Greek word *sitos,* meaning food.

pastoral (PAS tuh ruhl) *adj.:* a rural or nomadic way of life based on the herding of domesticated animals. From the Latin word, *pastor,* meaning a shepherd.

patent *verb:* to obtain from the government the exclusive right to produce, use, and sell a product or invention.

paterfamilias (PAH tehr fah MIH lih ahs) *noun:* Latin word meaning father of the family.

peaceful coexistence: living together without conflict despite differences, as in political systems or among nations.

Peloponnesus (PEHL uh puh NEE suhs) *noun:* the southern tip of the Balkan Peninsula.

penicillin (PEHN uh SIHL ihn) *noun:* any of a group of bacteria-destroying compounds obtained from certain molds.

pension (PEHN shuhn) *noun:* a regular payment, not a fee, a sponsoring person or government gives someone, such as an artist. From the Latin word, *pendere*, meaning to pay.

peremptorily (puh REHMP tuh ruh lee) *adv.:* in a final or decisive manner.

perishable (PAIR ihsh uh buhl) *adj.:* liable to spoil, as some foods. From the Latin word, *perire*, meaning to go through.

perspective *noun:* the technique of making scenes, painted on a flat surface, appear to be three dimensional.

petition (puh TIHSH uhn) *noun:* a written request to someone in authority, often signed by a number of people. From the Latin, *petere*, meaning to ask.

phalanx (FAY lanks) *noun:* an ancient military formation of infantry in close and deep ranks with shields joined and overlapping. From the Greek word, *phalanx*, meaning line of battle.

pharaoh (FER oh) *noun:* the title of the rulers of ancient Egypt. From the Egyptian word, *pr-'o*, meaning great house.

philanthropy (fih LAN thruh pee) *noun:* a desire to help humanity through charitable gifts.

philhellene *noun:* an admirer of Greek culture. From the Greek words *phil*, meaning love of and *Hellene*, meaning Greek.

philosophe (fee law ZAWF) *noun:* the French word for philosopher.

philosopher (fih LAHS uh fuhr) *noun:* a person who investigates the basic principles of being, knowledge, or human conduct. From the Greek words *philos*, meaning loving and *sophos*, meaning wise.

phonetic (fuh NEHT ihk) **alphabet:** having a separate symbol for every speech sound.

physical (FIH zih kuhl) **environment** (ehn VY ruhn muhnt): all the conditions, including the climate, soil, and resources, that influence living things.

pig iron *noun:* crude iron as it comes from a blast furnace; called pig iron because of its shape.

plebiscite (PLEHB uh SYT) *noun:* a direct ballot on a political issue to determine the will of the voting people. From the Latin words *plebis*, meaning common people and *sciscere*, meaning vote for.

pogrom (poh GRAHM) *noun:* an organized massacre of helpless people. From the Russian words *po*, meaning of and *grom*, meaning thunder.

pollutant (puh LOOT uhnt) *noun:* a harmful chemical or waste material discharged into the water or the atmosphere. From the Latin word, *pollutus*, meaning to soil or pollute.

polytheism (PAHL ih thee ihz uhm) *noun:* belief in, or worship of, many gods. From the Greek words *poly*, meaning many and *theism*, meaning belief in a god or gods.

potential (puh TEHN shul) *noun:* all that a person is capable of being or becoming.

predator (PREHD uh tuhr) *noun:* an animal that lives by capturing and feeding on other animals.

predestination (pree DEHS tuh NAY shuhn) *noun:* in theology, the doctrine that one's fate, or destiny in life, has been preordained by God. From the Latin prefix *prae*, meaning before and the word *destinare*, meaning to fasten down, to secure.

premier (PREE mee uhr) *noun:* the prime minister of any of certain countries.

prescience (PREE shee uhns) *noun:* knowledge of an event before it happens. From the Latin word, *praescire*, meaning to know beforehand.

primary source: an eyewitness account.

prime minister: the head of a government.

primogeniture (PRY muh JEHN ih chuhr) *noun:* the right of the first child to inherit the family's property. From the Latin words *primus*, meaning first and *geniture*, meaning born.

procurator (PRAHK yuh RAYT uhr) *noun:* Roman official in charge of collecting revenue in a province.

professional diplomat: a person whose career involves the conduct of relations between nations.

proletariat (PROH luh TAIR ee uht) *noun:* the class of people whose status is the lowest in a society. From the Latin, *proletarius*, meaning of the lowest class.

prophets (PRAHF ihts) *noun:* religious leaders believed to speak for a god. From the Greek word, *prophetes*, meaning interpreter of a god's will.

protectorate (pruh TEHK tuhr iht) *noun:* a country that retains its own government but whose policies are guided by an imperial power.

Protestant (PRAHT ihs tuhnt) *adj.:* a member of any of the Christian churches that resulted from the Reformation; one who protests, or testifies for, the truth as he or she sees it. From the Latin prefix *pro-* meaning for and the word *testari*, meaning to testify or affirm.

provisional (pruh VIHZH uhn uhl) *adj.:* temporary; for the time being. From the Latin prefix *pro-*, meaning before and *videre*, meaning to see.

publicani (PUHB lih kuhn ee) *noun:* in ancient Rome, collectors of public taxes.

pueblos (PWEHB lohz) *noun:* communal dwellings with flat roofs, resembling apartment houses, and made of stone or adobe.

purge *verb:* to rid of individuals thought to be disloyal or undesirable. From the Latin word, *purgare*, meaning to cleanse.

pyre (pyhur) *noun:* a woodpile for burning a dead body as a funeral rite.

Q

Qin (chin) *noun:* Chinese dynasty founded in 221 B.C., until recently, translated into English as Ch'in.

quadrant (KWAHD ruhnt) *noun:* an instrument for measuring altitude in navigation and astronomy.

queue (kyoo) *noun:* a braid of hair hanging from the back of the head; a pigtail.

quota (KWOHT uh) *noun:* a certain amount or proportion that is allowed or admitted.

R

radioactive *adj.:* giving off radiant, or light ray, energy by the spontaneous breakup of atomic nuclei.

raja (RAH juh) *noun:* **1.** an Indian prince or chief; **2.** a title of nobility among the Hindus.

ratify (RAT uh FY) *verb:* to give official approval to.

ravage (RAV ihj) *verb:* to destroy violently, usually in a series of attacks over a period of time.

raw material: material still in its original state before processing or manufacturing.

reactionary (ree AK shuh NER ee) *adj.:* resisting change and prefering to return to a previous political or social system; ultraconservative.

realpolitik (ray AHL POH lih TEEK) *noun:* a German word meaning politics based on practical self-interest rather than on ideals.

reconnaissance (rih KAHN uh suhns) *noun:* observation and examination in order to learn something, especially for military purposes.

redeem (ri DEEM) *verb:* to buy back. From the Latin prefix *re-*, meaning back and the word *emere*, meaning to buy.

refine (rih FYN) *verb:* to free from impurities. From the French word, *raffiner*, meaning to purify.

Reformation *noun:* the sixteenth century religious movement to reform the Christian church.

refugee (REHF yoo JEE) *noun:* a person who flees his home to seek refuge elsewhere, as in time of war, natural disaster, or persecution. From the Latin word, *refugere*, meaning to retreat.

regent (REE jehnt) *noun:* a person appointed to rule a country when the king is absent, too young, or otherwise unable to rule.

Reich (ryk) *noun:* Germany as an empire or state; the German nation.

reincarnate (REE ihn KAHR nayt) *verb:* to be born again in a new earthly body.

Renaissance (REHN uh SAHNS) *noun:* the great European revival of interest in literature, art, and learning, stimulated by humanism during the fourteenth through sixteenth centuries.

reparation (REHP uh RAY shuhn) *noun:* a making of amends by paying debts such as by a nation defeated in war. From the Latin word, *reparare*, meaning to repair.

republic (rih PUB lihk) *noun:* a state or nation in which political power comes from all the citizens entitled to vote; that power is exercised by the elected representatives. From the Latin words *res*, meaning interest and *publica*, meaning public.

rhetoric (REHT uhr ihk) *noun:* the skill of using words effectively in writing or public speaking. From the Greek word, *rhetor*, meaning orator.

rightist *noun:* a person who politically favors the established order, traditional attitudes, national interests, and the security of private wealth.

ritual (RIHCH oo wuhl) *noun:* the observance of set forms or rites, as in public worship.

S

sacrament (SAK ruh muhnt) *noun:* in Christianity, rites to make humans pure and morally strong. Protestants generally recognize baptism and Holy Communion. Roman Catholic and Eastern Orthodox churches recognize seven sacraments.

samurai (SAM uh RY) *noun:* a member of the aristocratic military class in feudal Japan.

sanction (SANGK shuhn) *noun:* a penalty for breaking a law. From the Latin word, *sanctus*, meaning holy.

sans (sanz) *prep.:* without. Adopted into English directly from the French.

satellite nation: a nation that is dependent on a larger, more powerful state.

satrap (SAY trap) *noun:* the governor of a satrapy.

satrapy (SAY truh pee) *noun:* a province of ancient Persia.

savanna *noun:* grasslands holding scattered trees.

scale armor: a thin layer of metal made of small scales or plates used to protect the body.

schism (SIHZ uhm) *noun:* a split in an organized group, especially a church, as a result of a difference of opinion.

secede (sih SEED) *verb:* to withdraw formally from membership in a group or organization. From the Latin word, *secedere*, meaning to be apart.

seclusion *noun:* being apart from others; isolation, privacy. From the Latin prefix *se-*, meaning apart, the word *claudere*, meaning to close, and the suffix *-io*, meaning the condition of being.

sect (sehkt) *noun:* a religious denomination.

secular (SEHK yuh luhr) *noun:* worldly rather than religious. From the Latin word, *saecularis*, meaning worldly or heathen.

sedan (sih DAN) **chair:** a covered chair mounted on poles and carried by two people.

seismograph (SYZ muh graf) *noun:* a device that detects the occurrence of earthquakes and measures their severity.

separatist *noun:* one who withdraws from a larger group.

sepoy (SEE poy) *noun:* formerly, a native of India serving in the British army. From the Hindu and Persian word, *sipah,* meaning army.

serf *noun:* in feudal times, a person bound to the lord's land and sold with the land.

sheik (sheek) *noun:* the chief of an Arab tribe, family, or village. From the Arabian word, *shakha,* meaning to grow old.

Shinto (SHIHN toh) *noun:* religion of Japan whose followers worship many gods which represent the forces of nature.

siege (seej) *noun:* the surrounding of a fortified place, such as a big city, by an opposing armed force, preventing people and supplies from entering or leaving. From the Latin, *obsidere,* meaning to besiege.

silt (sihlt) *noun:* soil carried by flowing water such as rivers and deposited elsewhere.

Slavophile (SLAH vuh FYL) *noun:* a person who admires the Slavs and their customs.

socialism *noun:* an economic system in which all members of a community, often through its government, own means of production; everyone shares the work and products.

society (suh SY uh tee) *noun:* a group of people who share the same culture. From the Latin word, *socius,* meaning companion.

sojourner (SOH juhrn uhr) *noun:* one who lives somewhere temporarily. From the Latin prefix *sub-,* meaning under and *diurnus,* meaning a day.

sophist (SAHF uhst) *noun:* in ancient Greece, any of a group of teachers. From the Greek word, *sophistes,* meaning wise person.

soviet (SOH vee iht) *noun:* any of the various governing councils in a socialist system.

space probe: an instrumented, unmanned spacecraft for exploring to get information about environmental and physical properties. From the Latin word, *probare,* meaning to prove.

specimen (SPEHS uh muhn) *noun:* one individual of a class or group used as a sample or example. From the Latin word, *specere,* meaning to see.

sphere of influence: a region where an imperial power claims exclusive economic and political rights that are recognized by other nations.

stagnant (STAG nuhnt) *adj.:* not moving; inactive, such as stagnant water. From the Latin word, *stagnum,* meaning standing water, pond, or swamp.

stalemate (STAYL mayt) *verb:* to bring to a standstill or deadlock.

standing army: a permanent army of paid soldiers.

stelae (STEE lee) *noun plu.:* upright slabs or stone pillars containing an inscription or carved design.

steppes (stehps) *noun:* dry grasslands of central Eurasia, called prairie in North America and pampas in Argentina. From the Russian word, *step,* meaning lowland.

stereotype (STAIR ee uh TYP) *noun:* a fixed idea about a person or group, held by a number of people, without allowing for critical judgment.

Stone Age (stohn ayj): time during which people made most of their tools from stone.

subsistence farm: a farm that provides a family with the minimum amount of food and shelter needed to survive.

suffrage (SUHF rihj) *noun:* voting rights. From the Latin word, *suffragium,* meaning supporting vote.

sultan *noun:* a Muslim ruler; king.

summit *noun:* a conference of the heads of governments. From the Latin, *summus,* meaning highest.

Sunni (SOON ee) *noun:* the major Islamic sect.

superficial (soo puhr FIHSH uhl) *adj.:* apparent; seeming on the surface. From the Latin prefix *super-,* meaning above and *facies,* meaning face.

surplus (SUR pluhs) *noun:* an amount that remains after needs have been satisfied. From the Old French word *sur,* meaning above and the Latin word *plus,* meaning more.

suttee (suh TEE) *noun:* an Indian practice requiring a widow to throw herself on her husband's funeral pyre.

syllogistic premise (SIHL uh JIHS tihk PREHM ihs): a form of argument consisting of two statements assumed to be true and a conclusion drawn from them. For example: the two statements, teenagers go to school, and he is a teenager, lead to the conclusion, therefore he goes to school.

synthetic (sihn THEHT ihk) *adj.:* made by a chemical process rather than by nature. From the Greek prefix *syn-,* meaning together and the word *tithenai,* meaning to place.

synthetic fibers: threads produced by chemical synthesis rather than from materials that can be found in nature.

T

tapestry (TAP ihs tree) *noun:* a heavy cloth with decorative designs used as a wall hanging.

tariff (TAIR ihf) *noun:* a tax that a government places on goods imported into the country. From the Arabian word, *arafa,* meaning to inform.

technician *noun:* one who is skilled in the practical application of new knowledge.

technology *noun:* the body of knowledge available to a civilization that is of use in making tools, and extracting or collecting needed materials.

tenant farmer: a person who farms land owned by someone else and pays rent in the form of cash or a share of the crops.

tenement *noun:* an apartment that is run-down and overcrowded. From the Latin word, *tenere,* meaning to hold.

terra cotta (TEHR uh KAHT uh) *noun:* a hard, brown-red, glazed and unglazed fired clay used in making statues, vases, and other objects of art.

terrain (tuh RAYN) *noun:* ground or earth with its topographical features. From the Latin word, *terra,* meaning earth.

theologian (THEE uh LOH juhn) *noun:* a specialist in the study of religious faith and practice.

theory *noun:* an educated guess about how something might have been or might be done. From the Greek, *theoria,* meaning to look at or contemplate.

third world: the underdeveloped countries of the world, especially those in Africa and Asia.

topography (tuh PAHG ruh fee) *noun:* the surface features of a region, including rivers, lakes, and such man-made features as roads and bridges.

totalitarian (toh TAL uh TAIR ee uhn) *adj.:* characteristic of a government in which one political party maintains complete control and bans all other political parties.

trajectory (truh JEHK tuh ree) *noun:* the path of a moving particle or body curved by gravitational force. From the Latin word, *trajectus,* meaning to throw across.

treason (TREE zuhn) *noun:* betrayal of one's country, as in aiding the enemy. From the Latin prefix *trans-,* meaning over and *dare,* meaning to give.

treatise (TREET ihs) *noun:* a formal book or article on a subject.

trencher *noun:* a platter on which to serve food; in the Middle Ages, stale bread used as a plate.

tribe (tryb) *noun:* a group whose members believe they are descended from a common ancestor.

tributary (TRIHB yoo TAIR ee) *noun:* a stream or river flowing into a larger one.

tribute system: a system whereby one ruler or state regularly pays money or goods to another stronger ruler or state.

typhoon (ty FOON) *noun:* a violent, destructive storm originating in waters off the Asian coast.

tyrants (TY ruhnts) *noun:* absolute rulers without legal authority. From the Greek word, *tyros,* meaning master.

U

ultimatum (UHL tuh MAYT uhm) *noun:* a final offer or demand by one of the parties engaged in a conflict. From the Latin word, *ultimare,* meaning to end.

unambiguously (uhn am BIHG yoo wuhs lee) *adj.:* clearly, without having more than one meaning or interpretation. From the Latin word, *ambigere,* meaning to wander.

unilateral (YOO nuh LAT uhr uhl) *adj.:* of or affecting one side only. From the Latin words *unus,* meaning one and *lateralis,* meaning side.

universal (YOO nuh VUHR sil) *adj.:* including all, or a major part, as all people. From the Latin word, *universus,* meaning all together.

Utopia (yoo TOH pee uh) *noun:* an imaginary island with a perfect social and political system, described in a book by Thomas More. Today the word has come to mean any perfect place or situation. From the Greek word, *topos,* meaning no place.

V

vassal (VAS uhl) *noun:* **1.** a person who received land from an overlord in return for pledging loyalty, fighting for the lord, and performing other duties; **2.** a subordinate subject, servant, or slave. From the Latin word, *vassalus,* meaning manservant.

vassal state: a state owing tribute to, and recognizing the authority of, another more powerful state.

veneration (VEHN uhr AY shuhn) *noun:* reverence, deep respect. From the Latin, *venus,* meaning love.

veto *verb:* to forbid an action. From the Latin word, *veto,* meaning I forbid.

vocation (voh KAY shuhn) *noun:* the career toward which one feels called. From the Latin word, *vocare,* meaning to call.

vouchsafe (vowch SAYF) *verb:* to graciously grant.

W

warlord *noun:* a military commander using force to govern a limited area.

welfare state: a state in which the citizen's welfare—employment, medical care, retirement funds—is considered to be the government's responsibility.

Western (WEHST uhrn) **Hemisphere** (HEM us sfihr): the half of the globe chiefly to the west of the Atlantic Ocean; consists of North and South America, their surrounding islands, and the Atlantic Ocean.

X

Xiung-nu (shy uhng noo) *noun:* barbarian nomads living on the northern borders of China; until recently, *Hsiung-nu.*

Z

Zhou (joh) *noun:* pastoralists of Asia who lived on the northwest border of Shang China, until recently translated into English as Chow.

ziggurat (ZIHG oo raht) *noun:* a temple built of sun-dried bricks in the form of a terraced pyramid, in which each story is smaller than the one below it; a public building characteristic of Mesopotamian cities. From the Assyrian word, *zigguratu,* meaning height or pinnacle.

zone of communication: an area throughout which people exchange goods, ideas, and customs.

Index

When a word is defined in the Vocabulary Development section of the text, the page number of the definition is underlined. The letter *m*, *c*, *p*, or *g* preceding a page reference indicates a map, chart, picture, or graph. Page numbers for material found in Geography in History features appear in bold type.

A

A.D., 12, 13
Aachen (AH kuhn), 269
abacus, 285, 289
Abbas I, 430–432
Abbasid (AB uh sihd) **caliphate**, 252-257, *m* 253, 281
Abbasid Empire, 325
Abd al-Krim, 628
Abd al-Rahman
   (uhb DUL ra MAHN), 257
aborigines (AHB uh RIHJ uh NEES), 127
Abram, 68, *m* 69
absolute monarch, 394, in France, 479-480
Abu Bakr (uh BOO BAHK ehr), 235
Academy of Science, 473
acid rain, 735–736
Acropolis, 92
acupuncture, 285, 289
Adenauer (AD uhn ow ehr), **Konrad**, 678, 689
Aegean (ee JEE uhn) **Civilizations**, 58–59, *m* 58, 60 *Aeneid* (Virgil), 164
Aeschylus, (EHS kuh luhs), 105
Afghanistan (af GAN uh STAN), 172, **203**, 280, *m* 730, Soviet invasion, 727, *p* 727, 728
Africa, 10, 11, *m* 15, *m* 215, *p* 215, *p* 216, *m* 354, *c* 590, *m* 701, *p* 768. *See also countries in,* agriculture, **590**, 628, archeological discoveries, 217, arts, 355, cities, 311, colonial independence, *c* 717, commerce and trade, 309–310, 352–354, *m* 354, 356, 362, 638, deserts, 214, *m* 215, early settlement, 15, 16, *m* 354, economy, **590**, 627–628, 740, European imperialism, 500,

581–584, 624, 627, 703, first humans, 15, geography, 214, *m* 215, language, 217, migrations, 214–218, Muslim influence, 309–311, population in north Africa, *c* 204, post World War I, 624, 627–628, *p* 627, problems of new nations, 706–707, rain forest, 214, resistance movements, 583–584, slave trade, *p* 254, 458–464, *p* 459, *p* 461, *p* 462, *p* 463, Sub-Saharan, 125–126, 215–216, 253, **589–590**, World War II, **650–651**, *p* 651, *m* 656, 659
Afrika Korps, 655, 659
Africanus, Leo, 353
Afrikaner, 737, 739
Agamemnon, King, 60
Agnew, Spiro, 742
agricultural revolution, 18, 21–22, 366–367
agriculture, advances, 294, 366, 476–477, *c* 476, 760, in Africa, **590**, 628, foundations of civilization, 27, in China, 109, 170, 212, 213, 258, 287, domestication of plants, 21–22, early cultures, *m* 21, *m* 29, *m* 47, *m* 87, equal field system, 212, Green Revolution, 751, in India, 200, irrigation, **176**, in Japan, 262, in Middle Ages, 294, *p* 295, *p* 347, in Middle America, 78–79, 222–223, in Middle East, **203**, in monsoon areas, 313, in New World, 446–448, in prehistoric times, 19, *m* 21, in Rome, **121**, 159, slash-and-burn, 222, **756**, in Soviet Union, 685, in Spain, 257, in the United States, 460, 684, use of slave system, 460, and vegetation, **175–176**
Aguilar (ah gwee LAHR), **Geronimo de**, 385–386
Ahriman (AH rih muhn), 99
Ahura Mazda (AH hoo ruh MAHZ duh), 99, 100
airplanes, *p* 416, in World War I, 605, in World War II, 654–655, Wright brothers, 747
Aix-la-Chapelle, 269
Akbar the Great, 436–438, *p* 437
Akkadian language, 46, *p* 56
Alaska purchase, 580
Albania, communism, 722,

German invasion, 648, Soviet control, 679, 728
Aldrin, Buzz, Jr., 758
Alexander II, 577
Alexander III, 578
Alexander the Great, 136–140, *p* 137, *p* 139, *m* 140, 152, 171, **504**, accomplishments, 137
Alexandria, 138, 236, Hellenistic, 143–144, *p* 143, *p* 153, trade, 171–172
Algeria, 203, 220, *m* 220, *p* 716, French rule, 524, 678, *p* 678, independence, *m* 701, 702, revolution, 702
Alhambra, 342
al-Jabr (al-Khwarizmi), 255
Alliances, 1980s, *m* 687
All-India Muslim League, 628
All Quiet on the Western Front (Remarque), 614–615
alphabet. *See also Language; Writing,* Cyrillic, 267, Etruscan, 119, Phoenician, 57–58, Phonetic, 302, Roman, 163
Alps, 10, 121
Al-Qahira (al KAH hee RAW), 282
Alsace, 573, 582, 595, 597
Altai Mountains, 122
Amalfi, 314
Amazon River, **389**
American Revolution, 507
Amerindian(s), 357–362, *m* 360. *See also Aztecs; Incas; Mayans; Middle America; Olmecs,* adaptation to environment, **755**, domestication of animals, 446, Spanish treatment, 453, 454
Amur (ah MOO uhr) **River**, 501
Anasazi, *m* 360, 361, *p* 362
Anatolia (AN uh TOH lee uh), 51. *See also Turkey*
Anatomical Treatise on the Motion of the Heart and Blood in Animals (Harvey), 415
Andalusia (AN duh LOO zhuh), 257
Andes Mountains, **11, 389, 433**
Angkor Wat, 307
Angles, *m* 192, 193
Anglican Church, 409
Angola, 583, economy, 740, independence, 707
Annals (Tacitus), 164
Antarctica, **10, 11**
Anthony of Alexandria, 198
anthropologist, 18, 19

Captions: Art for Section Titles

UNIT 1

CHAPTER 1, Sections:
1 Made from a sea fossil, this flint hand axe was a beautiful, all-purpose tool for early humans. **2** The pattern etched into this ivory mammoth suggests that some 30,000 years ago early humans had meaningful symbols. **3** An ancient Pan-shan type Chinese vase.

CHAPTER 2, Sections:
1 A bronze sculpture of some genii, which Muslims believed were good or bad demons, was found in the Zagros Mountains in present-day Iran. **2** A bull's head from the ancient Mesopotamian city of Ur. **3** This clay model of a woman in a cart was made by an artisan in ancient India.

CHAPTER 3, Sections:
1 A muscular Hittite god illustrates the Hittites' desire to conquer. **2** A king's image is carved in this Kassite boundary marker. **3** An elephant was carved as a drinking cup for a Shang king.

CHAPTER 4, Sections:
1 This Assyrian mask of a woman once decorated a piece of furniture. **2** A jade hawk with outspread wings, carved in China about 770 B.C. **3** An Olmec wrestler illustrates one profession in the Olmec culture of Middle America.

UNIT 2

CHAPTER 5, Sections:
1 An Ancient Greek discus thrower, from the fifth century B.C. **2** An enameled brick frieze showing the Archers of Darius I, 522–486 B.C. **3** A Greek infantryman slays his Persian enemy on this vase from the fifth century B.C. **4** A Buddha head from Gandara, Pakistan.

CHAPTER 6, Sections:
1 A gold daric, or small Persian coin, from 400 B.C. **2** A dancing horseman fashioned in silver and covered with a thin layer of gold, found in Russia, from about A.D. 600. **3** A painting done by aborigines on the bark of a tree.

CHAPTER 7, Sections:
1 Alexander the Great shown on a mosaic in the fourth century B.C. **2** A third-century B.C. gold coin shows Arsinöe II, the sister and second wife of Ptolemy II Philadelphos of Egypt. **3** An Indian statue of a Bodhisattva in Greek robes, from the second century A.D.

CHAPTER 8, Sections:
1 A portrait of a third-century Roman family done in gold leaf on glass. **2** Detail from a statue of Caesar Augustus. **3** *Horse and Swallow*, a bronze sculpture, represents the art of the Han Dynasty, second century A.D. **4** A Han Dynasty pottery boat made for burial with the dead.

UNIT 3

CHAPTER 9, Sections:
1 A Germanic medallion from A.D. 600 glorifies war. **2** Sassanid Shapur I defeats Roman Emperor Valerian in A.D.

260. **3** A Visigothic cross from Spain. **4** The Mahabodhi Temple in Bodh Gaya, Bihar, India.

CHAPTER 10, Sections:
1 A Chinese bronze statuette of a barbarian from the north. **2** A life-sized Nok clay portrait from ancient Nigeria. **3** A Mayan hacha, or two-sided carved stone head, from A.D. 550–800.

CHAPTER 11, Sections:
1 A fourteenth-century miniature of the Archangel calling Muhammad. **2** A glazed ceramic of a horseman from Rakka, Syria. **3** Ornamental inscriptions from an early Islamic text.

CHAPTER 12, Sections:
1 This serving bowl features a human figure, a popular image with tenth-century Iraqi potters. **2** A lady on horseback wearing Iranian clothing is shown on this piece of polychrome-glazed pottery, from the Tang Dynasty. **3** Charlemagne's face was an important symbol of Christianity, from the fourteenth century.

UNIT 4

CHAPTER 13, Sections:
1 Legendary Iranian King Bahrām Gūr is depicted on this thirteenth-century clay bowl. **2** A Chinese family uses water-pumping devices to irrigate their rice. **3** King Geirraudr, pictured on a set of twelfth-century chess pieces.

CHAPTER 14, Sections:
1 This scene from a fourth-century scroll shows a Song ship. **2** Al-Idrisi, a Morrocan geographer, constructed this map of the world in 1154. **3** A sturdy, twelfth-century European ship shown in a fifteenth-century manuscript.

CHAPTER 15, Sections:
1 The speed and fierceness of Mongol archers is evident in this Han Period decoration. **2** A modern portrait shows Kublai Khan, the Mongol conquerer who reunited northern and southern China. **3** This stained-glass window from the Chartres Cathedral shows blacksmiths at work.

CHAPTER 16, Sections:
1 *Death and the Lady* is from fifteenth-century Flanders. **2** *Portrait of a Youth*, by Florentine master painter Filippino Lippi. **3** Delicate modeling characterizes this fifteenth-century African bronze head. **4** An Aztec wooden mask overlaid with a turquoise mosaic.

UNIT 5

CHAPTER 17, Sections:
1 A fifteenth-century Ming ship used in trading. **2** An early three-masted Portuguese ship decorates this Moorish bowl. **3** A fifteenth-century engraved copper globe shows the then-known world.

CHAPTER 18, Sections:
1 The Tudor coat of arms incorporated important political symbols. **2** Raphael titled this oil painting from 1515 *The Madonna of the Chair*. **3** A drawing from 1497 predicts the

end of the Christian church. **4** One of Galileo's original telescopes is displayed in a museum in Florence.

CHAPTER 19, Sections:
1 A fifteenth-century Ottoman sultan, Murad II. **2** Persia's Ardebil Carpet, woven in 1539, is one of the world's largest rugs. **3** A jeweled jade sword handle made in India during the eighteenth century.

CHAPTER 20, Sections:
1 Gold of the Mixtec Indians from the Monte Alban site at Oaxaca, Mexico. **2** The back of a 400-year-old banner shows an armored, mounted horseman. **3** A bronze head of a woman from sixteenth-century Benin.

UNIT 6

CHAPTER 21, Sections:
1 Seventeenth-century Polish astronomer Johannes Hevelius and his wife, Catherina, study the heavens. **2** Italian artist Gian Lorenzo Bernini's bronze bust of Louis XIV. **3** Use of gold and silver coins was widespread during the eighteenth century.

CHAPTER 22, Sections:
1 A seventeenth-century engraving of the British East India Company headquarters in London. **2** A colonial cartoon supporting the use of prayer and action to gain independence. **3** A pewter medallion made in France in 1793 illustrates the choice between liberty and death.

CHAPTER 23, Sections:
1 J. L. Bezard depicts the attack on the Louvre, a former palace and a symbol of French government, on July 29, 1830. **2** A diagram of George Stephenson's locomotive, the *Rocket*, from 1829. **3** A medal awarded for a U.S. industrial exhibit.

CHAPTER 24, Sections:
1 A medal commemorating Indian troop victories in Egypt in 1801. **2** A fan from 1784 showing the ship *Empress of China*. **3** Muslims at a mosque in northern Nigeria.

UNIT 7

CHAPTER 25, Sections:
1 A French Revolutionary Provisional Government five-lire coin from 1848. **2** A Hebrew language poster shows immigrants arriving in the United States. **3** The Rhodes Colossus,

a 120-foot-tall statue of Apollo, was one of the Seven Wonders of the Ancient World.

CHAPTER 26, Sections:
1 The cover of *Leslie's* from August 3, 1918, depicts the strength of the Allies. **2** A poster urges Americans to buy bonds to help the war effort. **3** A 1926 poster of Lenin commemorating the anniversary of the Russian Revolution of 1905. **4** A gravestone from the World War I Cemetary in France.

CHAPTER 27, Sections:
1 A French cartoon from 1914 ridicules the German army. **2** A wooden sculpture depicts the colonial perception of Queen Victoria. **3** A man standing in the White Angel breadline in San Francisco, 1933.

CHAPTER 28, Sections:
1 A World War I poster urges Americans to buy Liberty Bonds. **2** The German Junker JU87 dive bomber, called the Stuka, was a fast and incredibly accurate bomber. **3** Americans raise the flag over Iwo Jima in February 1945. **4** The United Nations symbol.

UNIT 8

CHAPTER 29, Sections:
1 Residents of Dresden, Germany, search through the ruins of their city after an Allied bombing on March 16, 1946. **2** Freedom fighters in Prague, 1968. **3** A Pershing II missile.

CHAPTER 30, Sections:
1 A poster promoting unity in Nigeria. **2** Samora Machel is inaugurated as president of the independent country of Mozambique in 1975. **3** A Peace Corps worker aids a woman and children in a third world country.

CHAPTER 31, Sections:
1 Vietnam veteran Joseph C. Fornelli used shell casings in his sculpture *Dressed to Kill*. **2** Israeli soldiers under attack by Egyptian and Syrian troops in 1973. **3** The seal of the Organization of American States, an association of 25 Latin-American countries and the United States.

CHAPTER 32, Sections:
1 The Telstar, a communications satellite launched into orbit in 1962. **2** The construction of an Anglo-French Concorde. **3** An Arabian phone booth.

Art for Focus Features

Focus on People
Mask by Pierre Matisse, 1950, a drawing with brush and India Ink.

Focus on Society
(linked hands) "Civilization is a method of living, an attitude of equal respect for all men." by George Giusti, 1955, Container Corporation of America commissioned Giusti to interpret this Jane Addams quotation.

Focus on Sources
The initial "S" from a fifteenth-century illuminated manuscript *Moralia of Pope Gregory the Great*.

Focus on Geography
Super Bowl 1985 by Alain Jacquet. See back cover and caption on page iv.

Text Acknowledgments

UNIT 1

CHAPTER 1 6, Excerpted from *We Seven,* by the Astronauts Themselves: M. Scott Carpenter and others. New York: Simon and Schuster, 1962; **14,** Excerpted from *The Restless Earth,* by Nigel Calder. New York: The Viking Press, 1972; **20,** Excerpted from "New Ways of Looking for the Past" by Jamie James. *Discover* Magazine, September, 1985.

CHAPTER 2 35–36, Adapted from *Babylonian and Assyrian Laws, Contracts, and Letters* edited by C. H. W. Johns. New York: Charles Scribner's Sons, 1904; **39,** Excerpted from "Admonition of Ipu-wer" translated by John Wilson in *The Ancient and Near East* edited by James B. Pritchard. New Jersey: Princeton University Press, 1955.

CHAPTER 4 68, Excerpted from *The Seven Wonders of the Ancient World* by Robert Silverberg. New York: Crowell-Collier Press, 1970; **73–74,** Excerpted from *Ramayana* by William Buck. Berkeley: University of California Press, 1976.

UNIT 2

CHAPTER 5 99, Excerpted from *Flames over Persepolis* by Mortimer Wheeler. New York: Reynal & Company, Inc., in association with William Morrow & Company, Inc., 1968.

CHAPTER 6 131–132, The Overlook Press: For excerpts from *Triumph of the Nomads* by Geoffrey Blainey; copyright © 1976 by Geoffrey Blainey, published by The Overlook Press, Lewis Hollow Road, Woodstock, N.Y. 12498.

CHAPTER 7 149–150, Excerpted from *Classical Accounts of India* edited by Dr. R. C. Majumdar, translated by A. L. Mukhopad. Hyay, Calcutta, 1960.

CHAPTER 8 165, Excerpted from "To the Emperor Trojan," and "Trojan to Pliny," in *Letters of Marcus Tullius Cicero,* translated by E. S. Shuckburgh and *Letters of Gaius Plinius Caecilius Secundus* translated by William Melmoth, revised by F.C.T. Bosanquet in the Harvard Classics, edited by Charles W. Eliot. New York: P. F. Collier & Son Corporation, 1937.

UNIT 3

CHAPTER 9 185–187, Excerpted from "Germany and its Tribes," in *The Complete Works of Tacitus* translated by Alfred John Church and William Jackson Brodribb, edited by Moses Hadas, The Modern Library Collection; **197,** Excerpted from "Of the Manner in which the Persecutors Died" by Lucius Caelius Lactantius Firminius, in *The Ante-Nicene Fathers; Translations of the Fathers Down to A.D. 325,* edited by Alexander Roberts, James Donaldson, and A. Cleveland Coxe. New York: Charles Scribner's Sons, 1899. 1st series, VII.

CHAPTER 10 210, Excerpted from *Ancient China* by Edward H. Schafer and The Editors of Time-Life Books. New York: Time, Inc., 1967; **211,** Excerpted from "Buddhism," by Fa Hsien in *A History of Chinese Literature* by Herbert A. Giles. New York: Frederick Unger Publishing Co., 1967; **224–225,** Excerpted from *The Mysterious Maya* by George E. and Gene S. Stuart. Washington, D.C.: National Geographic Society, 1977.

CHAPTER 11 243, "Daylight," prayer from *The Koran* translated by N. J. Dawood. New York: Penguin Books, 1974; **244–245,** Excerpted from *The Koran* translated by N. J. Dawood. New York: Penguin Books, 1974.

UNIT 4

CHAPTER 12 255, Excerpted from *Avicenna on Theology* by Arthur J. Arberry, Wisdom of the East series. London: John Murray, Ltd., 1951; **259,** Excerpted from *A Short History of the Chinese People* by L. Carrington Goodrich, Torch Series. New York: Harper & Row Publishers; **270,** Excerpted from Ermentarius of Noirmoutier, in *A History of the Vikings* by Gwyn Jones. New York: Oxford University Press, 1984.

CHAPTER 13 284, Verses 11, 12, 21, 23, 32 from *Rubáiyát of Omar Khayyam* in English verse by Edward Fitzgerald. New York: Thomas Y. Crowell Company, 1964; **287,** Excerpted from Wu Yung in *Commerce and Society in Sung China* by Yoshinobu Shiba, translated by Mark Elvin. Ann Arbor: University of Michigan Chinese Center, 1970; **288,** Excerpted from "Science in China's Past" by Nathan Sivin, in *Science in Contemporary China,* edited by Leo A. Orleans. California: Stanford University Press, 1980; **294,** Excerpted from "Anglo-Saxon Chronicle," in *English Historical Documents,* Vol. II. New York: Oxford University Press, 1981.

CHAPTER 14 303, Excerpted from *A Short History of the Chinese People* by L. Carrington Goodrich, Torch Series. New York: Harper & Row Publishers; **304–305,** Excerpted from *The Tale of Genji* by Murasake Shikibu. New York: Alfred A. Knopf, 1978; **311,** Excerpted from *The East African Coast* by Freeman-Grenville, G.S.P. United Kingdom: R. Collings; **315–316,** Excerpted from "Chronicle of the Slavs" by Helmhold, in *The Expansion of Europe: The First Phase* by Muldoon. Philadelphia: University of Pennsylvania Press, 1977; **318,** Excerpted from "Benjamin Tudela" in *Early Travels in Palestine* edited by Thomas Wright. New York: AMS Pr., Inc., 1848.

CHAPTER 15 324, Excerpted from Matthew Paris in *The Mongol World Empire* by J.A. Boyle. England: Variorum, 1980; **325,** Excerpted from Hamd-Allah Mustawfi in *The Geographical Part of the Nuzhat al-Qulub;* **327,** Excerpted from *The Empire of the Steppes* by Rene Grousset, translated by Naomi Walford. New Brunswick, N. J.: Rutgers University Press, 1970; **329,** Excerpted from *Jewish Travelers* by Elkin Adler, Hermon, 1966; **334,** Excerpted from Marco Polo's "Description of the World" in *Silks, Spices, and Empire* by Owen and Eleanor Lattimore. New York: Delacorte Press, 1968; **335,** Excerpted from *Medieval Europe: A Short History,* 2nd. edition, by W. Hollister. New York: Random House, 1982.

CHAPTER 16 341, Excerpted from *The Muqaddimah* by Ibn Khaldun, translated by F. Rosenthal. New Jersey: Princeton University Press, 1969; **354,** Excerpted from Ibn Battuta, in *Ibn Battuta in Black Africa* by Said Hamdun and Noel King; **358–359,** Excerpted from Hernan Cortés letter of 1520, in *Teotihuacán* by Karl E. Meyer and the Editors of the Newsweek Book Division. New York: Newsweek, 1973.

UNIT 5

CHAPTER 17 375–376, Excerpted from *European Expansion and the Counter-Example of Asia, 1300–1600* edited by Joseph R. Levenson. New Jersey: Prentice-Hall, Inc., 1967; **382–383,** Excerpted from "Christopher Columbus Reports his Impressions of America" [A letter to Gabriel Sanchez, Treasurer of King Ferdinand of Spain] in *A Treasury of the World's Great Letters: From Ancient Days to Our Own Time* edited by M.

Lincoln Schuster. New York: Simon and Schuster, 1940; **385,** Excerpted from Hernan Cortés letter to Charles V in *Teotihuacán* by Karl E. Meyer and the Editors of the Newsweek Book Division. New York: Newsweek, 1973.

CHAPTER 18 404, Excerpted from "Of Cruelty and Clemency, and Whether it is Better to be Loved than Feared" from *The Prince* by Niccolo Machiavelli. Reprinted in *Like It Was. Like It Is: People and Issues in the Western World,* edited by Knox Mellon, Jr. and Miriam U. Chrisman, Glenview, Ill.: Scott Foresman and Co., 1972; **406,** Excerpted from *Great Voices of the Reformation* by Harry Emerson Fosdick. New York: Random House, 1952.

CHAPTER 19 422, Excerpted from the writings of Ashikpashazade in *Istanbul and the Civilization of the Ottoman Empire* by Bernard Lewis. Norman: University of Oklahoma Press, 1963; **425–426,** Excerpted from *The Life and Letters of Ogier de Busbecg* by Charles Thornton Forster and F.H. Blackburne Daniell. London: C. Kegan, Paul & Co., 1881; **427–428,** Excerpted from *Atlas of the Islamic World Since 1500* by Francis Robinson, Cultural Atlas Series. New York: Facts on File, Inc., 1982; **430,** Excerpted from "The Schism in the Muslim World," pages 41–42; **435, 436,** Excerpted from *Memoirs* by Babur, translated by Leyden and Erskine, London, 1826; **439,** Excerpted from *A New History of India* by Stanley Wolpert. New York: Oxford University Press, 1982.

CHAPTER 20 445–448, Excerpted from *The Columbian Exchange: Biographical and Cultural Consequences of 1492* by Alfred W. Crosby, Jr. Westport, Connecticut: Greenwood Publishing Co., 1972; **454,** Excerpted from *Bartholomew de Las Casas: His Life, His Apostate, and His Writings* by Francis A. MacNutt. New York: G.P. Putnam's Sons, 1909; **458–459,** Excerpted from *History of African Civilization* by E. Jefferson Murphy. New York: Dell Pub. Co., Inc., 1974; **462–464,** Excerpted from "Olaudah Equiano of the Niger Ibo" by G. I. Jones, in *Africa Remembered: Narratives by West Africans from the Era of the Slave Trade* by Philip D. Curtin. Madison, Wis.: University of Wisconsin Press, 1967.

UNIT 6

CHAPTER 21 472, Excerpted from Roger Bacon in *Machina Ex Deo: Essays in the Dynamism of Western Culture* by Lynn White, Jr. Cambridge: The MIT Press, 1968; **485,** Excerpted from *The Human Adventure, Readings in World History,* V.I., selected and edited by Sydney Eisen and Maurice Filler, (General Editor, Lewis Paul Todd). New York: Harcourt, Brace & World, Inc., 1964; **489,** Excerpted from *Summa Theologica* by St. Thomas Aquinas. New York: Benziger Brothers, Inc., 1947, Volume 11.

CHAPTER 22 501, Excerpted from Francisco Pizarro in *The Living Past* by Ivar Lissner, translated from the German by J. Maxwell Brownjohn. New York: G.P. Putnam's Sons, 1957; **506 (all),** Excerpted from Baron de Montesquieu, Voltaire, and Marquis de Condorcet in *Panorama of the Past: Readings in World History* edited by Louis L. Snyder, et. al. Boston: Houghton Mifflin Company, 1966, Vol. 2; **507,** Excerpted from *The Social Contract* by Jean Jacques Rousseau, translated and adapted by Edwin Fenton. Geneva: Marc-Michel Bousquet, 1766; **511,** Excerpted from Emmanuel Siéyès in *The French Revolution,* Book 3, edited by Graham Bearman. London: Heinemann Educational Books, Ltd., 1977; **512,** Excerpted from "The Declaration of the Rights of Man and of the Citizen" in *Translations and Reprints from the Original Sources of European History.* Philadelphia: University of Pennsylvania Press, 1897, Vol. I, No. 5; **513,** Excerpted from Napoleon Bonaparte in *Mind of Napoleon* edited by J. Christopher Herold. New York: Columbia University Press, 1955.

CHAPTER 23 531–532, Excerpted from *Record of a Girlhood,* 3rd rev. ed. by Frances Ann Kemble. London: Richard Bentley and Son, 1879; **534,** Excerpted from *Reports on the Diseases in London,* 1801 by Dr. R. Willan; **534–535,** "William Cooper" adapted from the testimony of William Cooper, Sadler Commission, 1832; **535,** "Patience Kershaw" excerpted from *European Civilization: Basic Historical Documents* by Paul L. Hughes and Robert F. Fries. New Jersey: Littlefield, Adams & Co., 1972.

CHAPTER 24 550–551, Excerpted from *China's Response to the West* edited by Ssu-yü Teng and John K. Fairbank. Cambridge: Harvard University Press, 1961.

UNIT 7

CHAPTER 25 577–578, Excerpted from *A Source Book for Russian History from Early Time to 1917,* V. 3, *Alexander II to the February Revolution* by George Vernadsky, Senior Editor. New Haven and London: Yale University Press, 1972.

CHAPTER 26 602, Excerpted from "Lloyd George Calls for Volunteers" in *A Treasury of the World's Great Speeches* edited by Houston Peterson. New York: Simon and Schuster, 1965; **614–615,** Excerpted from *All Quiet on the Western Front* by Erich Maria Remarque. New York: Little, Brown and Company, 1928, 1929; copyright renewed 1957, 1958 by Erich Maria Remarque.

CHAPTER 27 622, Excerpted from *The Treaty of Versailles and After.* Washington, D.C.: United States Government Printing Office, 1947; **640,** Excerpted from *FDR's Last Year* by Jim Bishop. New York: William Morrow & Co., Inc., 1974.

CHAPTER 28 654 (both), Excerpted from *Churchill: The Life Triumphant: The Historical Record of Ninety Years.* American Heritage Publishing Co., Inc., 1965; **662,** Excerpted from *Through Japanese Eyes,* Vol. I: *The Past, The Road from Isolation* by Richard H. Minear, General Editor, Leon E. Clark. New York: A Cite Book, 1974–1981; **665–666,** "At Terezin" and "The Butterfly" from *. . . I Never Saw another Butterfly . . .* Children's Drawings and Poems from Terezin Concentration Camp 1942–1944. New York: Shocken Books, 1978.

UNIT 8

CHAPTER 29 685–686, Excerpted from *Beyond the Cold War* by Frederick L. Schuman. Baton Rouge: Louisiana State University Press, 1967; **686,** Excerpted from "The Sinews of Peace" in *A Treasury of the World's Great Speeches* edited by Houston Peterson. New York: Simon and Schuster, 1965; **691 (all),** Time Magazine, March 16, 1953, pages 30, 34, 35.

CHAPTER 30 710, Excerpted from *My Life* by Golda Meir. New York: G.P. Putnam's Sons, 1975; **716,** Excerpted from *The Challenge of Nationhood* by Tom Mboya. New York: Praeger Publishers, 1970.

CHAPTER 31 725–726, Excerpted from *The Refused: The Agony of the Indochina Refugees* by Barry Wain. New York: Simon and Schuster, 1981; **740, 741,** Excerpted from *Part of My Soul Went with Him* by Winnie Mandela. Edited by Anne Benjamin and adapted by Mary Benson. New York: W. W. Norton & Company, 1985.

CHAPTER 32 761–762, Excerpted from "Garbage" by Bill Steele. Copyright © 1969, © assigned 1978 to Whitfield Music, Inc.; **765,** Excerpted from *The Boys from Liverpool: John, Paul, George, Ringo* by Nicholas Schaffner. New York: Metheun, Inc., 1980.

Picture Acknowledgments

214, National Museum, Lagos © Dirk Bakker; 215, (upper left) George Hulton / Photo Researchers; 215, (upper right) Ian Berry/Magnum Photos; 215, (lower right) Robert Frerck / Odyssey Productions; 216, Photograph from the Library of Peter Johnson; 218, Eric Lessing / Magnum Photos; 221, *Ceremonial Hacha*, sandstone, red pigment traces, late classic Maya, The Art Institute of Chicago, Ada Turnbull Hertle Fund; 222, © Loren McIntyre; 225, (inset) The Art Museum, Princeton University, © 1985 Justin Kerr; 225, From *Art of the Maya* by Henri Stierlin, Rizzoli Publishers.

CHAPTER 11 229, Mehmet Biber / Photo Researchers; 230, The Granger Collection, New York; 233, The Granger Collection, New York; 235, National Museum of Damascus, photograph Scala / Art Resource; 236, Photograph The British Library; 238, Biblioteca Nacional, Madrid, photograph Arxiu Mas; 240, 243, Chester Beatty Library and Gallery of Oriental Art; 242, Eric Lessing / Magnum Photos; 244, Bibliothèque Nationale, Paris; 247, Free Library of Philadelphia, photograph Joseph Martin / Scala / Art Resource; 248, (left) Bibliothèque Nationale, Paris; 248 (right) and x, Shostal Associates.

CHAPTER 12 251, Richard Greenhill © Sinbad Voyage; 252, The Freer Gallery of Art, Smithsonian Institution; 254, Bibliothèque Nationale, Paris; 255, The Bettmann Archive; 256, *Water Clock,* 1354, from an illustrated manuscript of the "Automata," Museum of Fine Arts, Boston, Francis Bartlett Donation of 1912 and Picture Fund; 258, Nelson-Atkins Gallery © Wan-Go H.C. Weng; 259, Palace Museum, Peking © Wan-Go H.C. Weng; 261, National Palace Museum, Taipei © Wan-Go H.C. Weng; 263, Shostal Associates; 266, © Ann Munchow; 269, The Arsenal Library, photograph Scala / Art Resource; 270, Manuscript 736, folio 9 verso from the Pierpoint Morgan Library; 271, The Dean and Chapter of Durham Cathedral; 272, The Granger Collection, New York; 273, Alphonse Normandia in *Signature* Magazine, Aug. 30, 1984.

UNIT 4 276–277, The Bridgeman Art Library.

CHAPTER 13 279, © 1986 Art Brown; 280, *Iranian Bowl,* late 12th century, The Metropolitan Museum of Art, Rogers Fund and Gift of the Schiff Foundation, 1957; 281, Edinburgh University Library; 283, Courtesy of the British Library; 285, © Wan-Go H.C. Weng; 287, Palace Museum, Peking © Wan-Go H.C. Weng; 289, National Palace Museum, Taipei © Wan-Go H.C. Weng; 292, © Lee Boltin; 293, Musée de l'Evêche, Bayeux, photograph Giraudon / Art Resource; 295, Courtesy of the British Library; 297 and xi, Bibliothèque Nationale, Paris; 299, From *The Wall Street Journal,* permission, Cartoon Features Syndicate.

CHAPTER 14 301, © Alain McKenzie, Paris; 302, The Freer Gallery of Art, Smithsonian Institution; 304, Walter A. Compton Collection, photograph *American Heritage;* 305, (detail) Isabella Stewart Gardner Museum, photograph Art Resource; 306, Imperial Household Agency, Tokyo; 308, Ms. Pococke 375, folios 3v-4r, Bodleian Library; 309, (left) Bibliothèque Nationale, Paris; 309, (right) Shostal Associates; 311, Bibliothèque Nationale, Paris; 314, Courtesy of the British Library; 315, Ms. Bodley 264 f. 218r, Bodleian Library; 318, The Granger Collection, New York; 319, Marc and Evelyn Bernheim/ Woodfin Camp.

CHAPTER 15 321, Camera Press, London; 322, From *Ghenghis Khan* by Peter Brent, Weidenfeld & Nicolson, Publishers, London; 323, Bibliothèque Nationale, Paris; 324, Historical Pictures Service, Chicago; 326, National Palace Museum, Taipei © Wan-Go H.C. Weng; 327, National Palace Museum, Taipei © Wan-Go H. C. Weng; 332, (left) New

Delhi National Museum, photograph Borromeo / Art Resource; 332, (right) Steve McCurry/Magnum Photos; 333, Chartres Cathedral, photograph Art Resource; 335, Bibliothèque Nationale, Paris, photograph Giraudon / Art Resource; 337, Drawing by Dana Fradon © 1984 The *New Yorker* Magazine, Inc.

CHAPTER 16 339, Courtesy of the British Library; 340, Courtesy of the British Library; 342, Courtesy of the British Library; 346, *Portrait of a Youth,* c. 1485, Fillippino Lippi, National Gallery of Art, Washington, D.C., Andrew W. Mellon Collection; 347, Musée Condé, Chantilly, photograph Giraudon / Art Resource; 350–351, Public Palace, Siena, photograph Scala / Art Resource; 352, Dirk Bakker / Wunmonije Compound, Ife Museum of Ife Antiquities, Nigeria; 353, Courtesy of the British Library; 355, Axum Cathedral, photograph Marc and Evelyn Bernheim / Woodfin Camp; 356, George Gerster / Photo Researchers; 357, © Lee Boltin; 359 and xi, National Palace, Mexico City, photograph Robert Frerck / Odyssey Productions; 361, (left) Shostal Associates; 361, (inset) *Ceremonial Knife*—gold with turquoise inlays, repoussé, Peru, Tumi, Chimu Culture, The Art Institute of Chicago, Ada Turnbull Hertle Fund; 362, (left) George Gerster / Photo Researchers; 362, (right) Farrell Grehan / Photo Researchers; 363, The Granger Collection, New York; 364, Cartoon by Fritz Wilkinson, courtesy of Cathy Wilkinson Barash.

Another Letter from the Author, Turning Points of History 366, (left and inset) © Marc Riboud/ Magnum Photos; 366, (below) © W. Cambell/Sygma; 366, (right and inset) © Joseph Mettis/ Science Source/ Photo Researchers; 367, The Institute of Archaeology, Chinese Academy of Sciences, Beijing; 368, (above) © Donald Smetze/ CLICK/ Chicago; 368, (upper left) Erich Lessing/ Magnum Photos; 368, (upper right) © Robert Frerck/ Odyssey Productions; 369, (lower left) Ms. New Coll. 361/2, Warden and Fellows of New College, Oxford, and Bodleian Library; 369, (lower right) Shostal Associates; 369 (below) NASA/ Science Source/ Photo Researchers.

UNIT 5 370–371, Asian Art Museum of San Francisco, The Avery Brundage Collection.

CHAPTER 17 373, The Bettmann Archive; 374, © Wan-Go H.C. Weng; 375, *The Tribute Giraffe with Attendant,* Philadelphia Museum of Art, Gift of John T. Dorrance; 378, By courtesy of the Board of Trustees of the Victoria and Albert Museum; 381, (above) The Granger Collection, New York; 381, (right) Pegli Naval Museum, photograph Scala / Art Resource; 381, (below) Musée Condé, Chantilly, photograph Giraudon / Art Resource; 383, *First Landing of Christopher Columbus,* Frederick Kemmelmeyer, National Gallery of Art, Washington, D.C., Gift of Edgar William and Bernice Chrysler Garbisch; 385 and xii, Rare Books and Manuscripts, The New York Public Library, Astor, Lenox and Tilden Foundations; 386, Biblioteca Nacionale, Madrid, photograph The Bridgeman Art Library; 387, Archivo Oronoz, Madrid; 388, The Granger Collection, New York.

CHAPTER 18 393, The Granger Collection, New York; 394, By courtesy of the Board of Trustees of the Victoria and Albert Museum; 395, Historical Pictures Service, Chicago; 397, Royal Chapel, Granada, photograph Archivo Oronoz, Madrid; 400, Pitti Palace, Florence, photograph Giraudon / Art Resource; 401, Turin, photograph Scala / Art Resource; 403, (left) Courtesy of Kurt E. Schon, Ltd. from the collection of Mr. and Mrs. E. Hal Dickson, Mr. and Mrs. James R. Duncan, and Mr. and Mrs. Frank W. Rose of San Angelo, Texas; 403, (right) The Granger Collection, New York; 405,

Courtesy of the British Library; **407,** *Martin Luther and the Wittenberg Reformers,* (detail), c. 1543 Lucas Cranach the Younger, Toledo Museum of Art, Gift of Edward Drummond Libbey; **410,** Musée Cantonal des Beaux Arts, Lausanne, Switzerland; **412,** Eames Photo; **413,** The Granger Collection, New York; **415,** Museo Zoologico de "La Specola," Florence; **416,** (left) Photo Bulloz / The Institute of France; **416,** (right) Larry Mulvehill / Photo Researchers; **418,** (left) Catherine Ursillo / Photo Researchers; **418,** (right) F. Roiter / Image Bank.

CHAPTER 19 421, Sonia Halliday Photographs, Buckinghamshire, England; **422,** Sonia Halliday Photographs, Buckinghamshire, England; **423,** *Bayazid in Combat Against the Byzantines* (detail), late 16th century, Worcester Art Museum, Worcester, Massachusetts; **425,** Courtesy of the British Library; **427,** © Leo Hilber, Fribourg, Switzerland; **429,** By courtesy of the Board of Trustees of the Victoria and Albert Museum; **431,** Museum for Islamic Art, Berlin; **433,** Shostal Associates; **435,** By courtesy of the Trustees of the Victoria and Albert Museum; **437,** *Akbar Visited by Jahangir and Shah Jahan,* 1605–27, Balchand, The Metropolitan Museum of Art, Gift of Alexander Smith Cochran, 1913; **438,** By courtesy of the Freer Gallery of Art, Smithsonian Institution, Washington, D.C.; **439,** Shostal Associates; **441,** Drawing by Chas. Addams © 1985 The *New Yorker* Magazine, Inc.

CHAPTER 20 443, Kunsthistorische Museum, Vienna; **444,** Robert Frerck / Odyssey Productions; **446,** Nicolas Sanchez-Albornoz, *The Population of Latin America;* **446,** The Granger Collection, New York; **448,** Royal Palace Library, Madrid, photograph Archivo Oronoz, Madrid; **450 and xii,** Wide World Photos; **451,** Archivo Oronoz, Madrid; **453,** Photograph The Hispanic Society of America, New York; **454,** William L. Clements Library, University of Michigan; **456,** © Bradley Smith; **457,** © Bradley Smith; **458,** National Museum of Lagos © Dirk Bakker; **459,** The New York Public Library; **461,** The Granger Collection, New York; **462,** Historical Pictures Service, Chicago; **463,** National Maritime Museum, Greenwich, London; **465,** "The Far Side" cartoon panel by Gary Larson is reprinted by permission of Chronicle Features, San Francisco.

UNIT 6 468–469, Elton Collection, Ironbridge Gorge Museum Trust.

CHAPTER 21 471, Jeff Smith / Image Bank; **472,** By permission of Houghton Library, Harvard University; **473,** By permission of Harvard College Library; **475,** (above) National Trust, Petworth House, photograph The Bridgeman Art Library; **475,** (below) Ms. New Coll. 361/2, Warden and Fellows of New College, Oxford and Bodleian Library; **477,** Walker Art Gallery, Liverpool; **478,** By permission of the Houghton Library, Harvard University; **479,** *Louis XIV,* after Gian Lorenzo Bernini, National Gallery of Art, Washington, D.C., Samuel H. Kress Collection; **482,** Royal Holloway College, Egham, photograph The Bridgeman Art Library; **484,** National Portrait Gallery, London; **486,** (detail) Musée du Louvre, Paris, photograph Josse / Art Resource; **488,** Musée du Louvre, Paris, photograph Josse / Art Resource; **491,** The Guildhall Library, London, photograph The Bridgeman Art Library; **492,** The Granger Collection, New York; **495,** "The Far Side" cartoon by Gary Larson is reprinted by permission of Chronicle Features, San Francisco.

CHAPTER 22 497, National Palace, Mexico City, photograph Andrew Rakoczy / Art Resource; **498,** The Granger Collection, New York; **499,** (detail) Victoria & Albert Museum, photograph The Bridgeman Art Library / Art Resource;

500, The Granger Collection, New York; **504,** From the book *Images of Earth* by Peter Francis and Pat Jones, George Philip & Son, Ltd.; **506,** (left, upper right and lower right) The Granger Collection, New York; **507,** The Granger Collection, New York; **507,** (inset) Museum of Art and History, Geneva, photograph Giraudon / Art Resource; **508 and xiii,** Kirby Collection of Historical Paintings, Lafayette College, Easton, PA; **510,** The Granger Collection, New York; **512,** Carnavalet, Paris, photograph Giraudon / Art Resource; **514,** Mt. St. Bernard Pass, photograph Scala / Art Resource; **516,** © Bradley Smith.

CHAPTER 23 519, The Granger Collection, New York; **520,** The Granger Collection, New York; **522,** Hotel de Ville, Versailles Chateau, photograph Giraudon / Art Resource; **525,** Marvin E. Newman / The Image Bank; **526,** Harald Sund / The Image Bank; **527,** The Granger Collection, New York; **528,** The Granger Collection, New York; **531,** The Granger Collection, New York; **533,** Nawrocki Stock Photo; **535,** The Mansell Collection; **537,** (below) The Granger Collection, New York; **537,** (inset) The Mansell Collection.

CHAPTER 24 541, Werner Forman Archive; **542,** North Wind Archives; **543,** Hazem Palace, Damascus, photograph Giraudon / Art Resource; **544,** Robert Frerck / Odyssey Productions; **547,** The Granger Collection, New York; **548,** Historical Society of Pennsylvania, Philadelphia; **549,** Photograph Childs Gallery, Boston and New York; **551,** The Granger Collection, New York; **552,** © Bradley Smith; **554,** Marc and Evelyn Bernheim / Woodfin Camp; **555,** Robert Frerck / Odyssey Productions; **557,** Historical Pictures Service, Chicago.

UNIT 7 564–565, © Eli Reed / Magnum Photos.

CHAPTER 25 567, H. Armstrong Roberts, Inc.; **568,** Nawrocki Stock Photo; **570,** (left) The Bettmann Archive; **570,** (right) Museo del Risorgimento, Milan, photograph Scala / Art Resource; **573,** The Granger Collection, New York; **575,** The Bettmann Archive; **576,** The Granger Collection, New York; **578,** The Bettmann Archive; **579,** The Bettmann Archive; **580,** The Bettmann Archive; **581,** Historical Pictures Service, Chicago; **582,** (left) Neg. No. 322202, Photo by Boltin, Courtesy Department Library Services, American Museum of Natural History; **582,** (right) Culver Pictures; **585,** © Bradley Smith; **587,** Collection of Chaoying Fang © Wan-Go H.C. Weng; **588,** Historical Pictures Service, Chicago; **590,** From *Science* Magazine, Jan. 25, 1985.

CHAPTER 26 593, Trustees of the Imperial War Museum; **594,** Nawrocki Stock Photo; **595,** North Wind Archives; **598,** (left) AP / Wide World Photos; **598,** (right) Copyright © 1914 by The *New York Times* Company, reprinted by permission; **600,** Dr. A.C. Twomey / Photo Researchers; **601,** © Lee Boltin; **604 and xiv,** Trustees of the Imperial War Museum; **606,** The Bettmann Archive; **607,** The Granger Collection, New York; **608,** Brown Brothers; **610,** The New York Public Library, Astor, Lenox and Tilden Foundations; **612,** The Bettmann Archive; **613,** The Bettmann Archive; **614,** U.S. Army Center of Military History, Washington D.C.; **616,** Canadian War Museum, Canadian Museum of Civilization, National Museums of Canada.

CHAPTER 27 619, *Allies Day, May 1917,* Childe Hassam, National Gallery of Art, Washington, D.C., gift of Ethelyn McKinney in memory of her brother, Glenn Ford McKinney; **620,** (detail) The Bettmann Archive; **623,** National Portrait Gallery, London; **625,** Historical Pictures Service, Chicago; **626,** The Horniman Museum, London; **627,** Historical Pictures Service, Chicago; **629,** The Bettmann Archive; **631,** (left) © Bradley Smith; **631,** (right) © J. P. Laffont / Sygma; **634,** George Gerster / Photo Researchers; **635,** (detail) The Oakland Museum; **636,** The Bettman Archive; **637,** The Bettmann Archive; **639,** F.D.R. Library, by permission of Wide World Photos; **641,** Copyright © 1932 by *The New York Times* Company, reprinted by permission.

CHAPTER 28 643, The Prado, Madrid, photograph Giraudon / Art Resource with permission of S.P.A.D.E.M./Paris, V.A.G.A., New York, 1986; **644,** The Bettmann Archive; **645,** Historical Pictures Service, Chicago; **646,** (left) AP / Wide World Photos; **646,** (right) Culver Pictures; **648,** Historical Pictures Service, Chicago; **651,** (left) Culver Pictures; **651,** (right) Shostal Associates; **652,** SEF / Art Resource; **653,** © Karsh, Ottawa, photograph Woodfin Camp & Associates; **655,** Harris & Ewing / Photo Trends; **657,** Photograph The United States Naval Institute; **658,** UPI / Bettmann; **662,** Culver Pictures; **663,** United Nations; **664,** The Bettmann Archive; **665,** Brown Brothers; **669,** By permission of Bill Mauldin and Wil-Jo Associates, Inc.

UNIT 8   672–673, © Michel Tcherevkoff.

CHAPTER 29 675, UPI / Bettmann; **676,** UPI / Bettmann; **677,** UPI / Bettmann; **678,** © Roger Coral / Magnum Photos; **680,** Historical Pictures Service, Chicago; **681,** Henri Cartier-Bresson/Magnum Photos; **684,** P.P. / Magnum Photos; **685,** P.P. / Magnum Photos; **689,** © Randy Taylor / Sygma; **690,** AP / Wide World Photos; **692,** AP / Wide World Photos; **693,** Leonard Freed / Magnum Photos; **694,** AP / Wide World Photos; **695,** From the *Indianapolis Star,* Oct. 14, 1960, cartoon by Charles Weaver, photograph Culver Pictures.

CHAPTER 30 697, © J. P. Laffont / Sygma; **698,** Bruno Barbey / Magnum Photos; **699,** Henri Cartier-Bresson / Magnum Photos; **700,** Ian Berry / Magnum Photos; **702,** © Robert Capa / Magnum Photos; **705,** Karl Kummels / Shostal Associates; **706,** © Jean-Paul Paireault / Magnum Photos; **707,** AP / Wide World Photos; **709,** © Richard Melloul / Sygma; **711,** © Marilyn Silverstone / Magnum Photos; **712,** AP / Wide World Photos; **713,** AP / Wide World Photos; **714,** © M. Franck / Magnum Photos; **716,** Shostal Associates.

CHAPTER 31 719, © 1980 Robert Azzi/Woodfin Camp; **720,** Joseph C. Fornelli, photograph The Vietnam Veterans Arts Group; **721,** Associated Press; **723,** (left) Cleveland R. Wright, photograph The Vietnam Veterans Arts Group;

723, (right: AP / Wide World Photos; **724,** Kenneth Willhite, photograph The Vietnam Veterans Arts Group; **725,** and **xv,** © Laffont / Sygma; **727,** © Dennis Brack / Blackstar; **728,** © Michel Philippot / Sygma; **729,** © Leonard Freed / Magnum Photos; **731,** © J. Guichard / Sygma; **733,** (left) © Alan Dejean / Sygma; **733,** (right) AP / Wide World Photos; **736,** (above and inset) © Regis Bossu / Sygma; **737,** Museum of Modern Art, Latin America, photograph The Organization of American States; **738,** Wide World Photos; **740,** © W. Campbell / Sygma; **741,** Associated Press; **743,** © Richard Kalvar / Magnum Photos; **744,** © A. Tannenbaum / Sygma; **745,** AP / Wide World Photos.

CHAPTER 32 747 and **xv,** NASA / Science Source/ Photo Researchers; **748,** Shostal Associates; **751,** © 1982 Robert Frerck / Woodfin Camp; **753,** © Alex Webb / Magnum Photos; **756,** Shostal Associates; **757,** The Granger Collection, New York; **758,** NASA; **759,** Shostal Associates; **760,** © Joseph Mettis / Science Source / Photo Researchers; **762,** © 1980 Tom McCarthy / The Image Bank; **763,** © 1983 Robert Azzi / Woodfin Camp; **764,** AP / Wide World Photos; **766,** Shostal Associates; **767,** © Giansanti / Sygma; **768** (above left) and **v,** Don Klumpp / The Image Bank; **768,** (below left) Shostal Associates; **768,** (center) © Paul Slaughter / The Image Bank; **768,** (right) Robert Frerck / Odyssey Productions; **769,** "The Far Side" cartoon by Gary Larson is reprinted by permission of Chronicle Features, San Francisco.

A Postscript from the Author, New Beginnings 772, (upper left) United Nations Photographs and Exhibits; **772,** (above) Karachi Museum, photograph Scala/Art Resource; **772,** (lower right) H. Armstrong Roberts, Inc.; **773,** (upper left, upper right and above) NASA.

ALL CHAPTERS—Focus Feature Logos Focus on People (Mask), © 1986 SPADEM, Paris/VAGA, New York. **Focus on Society** (Linked Hands), National Museum of American Art, Smithsonian Institution, Gift of Container Corporation of America. **Focus on Sources** (The Initial "S"), Austrian National Library, Vienna. **Focus on Geography** (Globe), Daniel Varenne Gallery, Geneva. Photograph Michael Tropea.

McDougal, Littell and Company has made every effort to locate the copyright holders for the images used in this book and to make full acknowledgment for their use.

Illustrations

William Cigliano, 17; Candace Haught, 121, 147; Troy Thomas, 219, 313, 345.

Sources for charts on pages 204, 249, 291, 345, 390, 494, 590, and 683 include: *1987 Britannica Book of the Year,* Encyclopaedia Britannica, Inc., Chicago, 1987; *The 1987 Information Please Almanac,* Houghton Mifflin Company, Boston, 1987; *The World Almanac & Book of Facts 1987,* Newspaper Enterprise Association, Inc., N.Y., 1987; *The World Book Encyclopedia,* vol. 16, World Book, Inc., Chicago, 1987.